MACROECONOMIC PRINCIPLES

Cost of Holding Money

The cost of holding money (its opportunity cost) is measured by the alternative interest yield obtainable by holding some other asset.

Deposit Expansion Multiplier

The reciprocal of the required reserve ratio, assuming no leakages into currency and no excess reserves, is the deposit expansion multiplier.

$$\text{Deposit expansion multiplier} = \frac{1}{\text{required reserve ratio}}$$

Policy Irrelevance Proposition

Under the assumption of rational expectations on the part of decision makers in the economy, anticipated monetary policy cannot alter either the rate of unemployment or the level of real GDP. Regardless of the nature of the anticipated policy, the unemployment rate will equal the natural rate, and real GDP will be determined solely by the economy's long-run aggregate supply curve.

Modern Economic Growth (MEG)

This theory of economic growth characterizes growth by increases in per capita output accompanied by increases in population and driven by the application of science to the problems of economic production.

Natural Rate of Unemployment

The natural rate of unemployment is the rate of unemployment that exists when workers and employers correctly anticipate the rate of inflation.

Definition of Money Supply

M1 = currency + checkable accounts + traveler's checks

M2 = M1 +
1. savings and small-denomination time deposits at all depository institutions
2. overnight repurchase agreements at commercial banks
3. overnight Eurodollars issued to U.S. residents by foreign branches of U.S. banks worldwide
4. balances in money market mutual funds
5. money market deposit accounts (MMDAs)

Equation of Exchange

$$M_s V = PQ$$

where M_s = actual money balances held by the nonbanking public

V = income velocity of money, or the number of times, on average, each monetary unit is spent on final goods and services

P = price level, or price index

Q = real national output

Relationship Between Imports and Exports

In the long run, imports are paid for by exports.

Therefore,

any restriction of imports ultimately reduces exports.

Total Teaching/Learning Package for
economics today, eighth edition
ROGER LeROY MILLER

Economics Today
Combined Micro and Macro in hardback edition.

Economics Today: The Macro View
Macroeconomics in a paperback edition.

Economics Today: The Micro View
Microeconomics in a paperback edition.

Supplements for Instructors

Printed Material
Test Banks 1, 2, and 3
Instructor's Resource Binder
 • The Instructor's Manual
 • Reproducible Homework
   Assignments
 • Additional Supplemental
   Reproducible Materials

Instructor's Course Planning
 Guide and Media Handbook
Economics Today Newsletter
LOTS: Lecture Outline and
 Transparency System
Transparency Masters

Software and Multimedia
TestMaster
Computerized Instructor's
 Manual
Lecture Prep®

Full-Color Acetates and Acetate
 Overlays
QuizMaster

Videocassettes and Videodisc
HarperCollins *Economics Today* Videos
HarperCollins Economics Videodisc

Supplements for Students

Printed Materials
Extended-Coverage Topics
Your Economic Life: The Practical
 Applications of Economics

Reproducible Homework
 Assignments
Student Learning Guide

Software
ET8 Computer-Assisted Instruction
Economics Tutor (DOS/Windows)
Micro Tutorial

Graphing Tutorial
Macro Simulation

economics today

The HarperCollins Series in Economics

economics today

eighth edition

**ROGER
LeROY
MILLER**
University of Texas
at Arlington

HarperCollins*CollegePublishers*

To Clyde and Jane

For all the years past, and all those to come

Photo Credits

Page 3, Freeman, PhotoEdit; p. 17, © 1991, Merrifield, Photo Researchers; p. 50, © 1988, Nettis, Stock, Boston; p. 78, © 1991, Pickerell, Stock, Boston; p. 96, © Fujifotos/The Image Works; p. 121, Hires, Gamma Liaison; p. 143, Milacron, PhotoEdit; p. 167, © Daemmrich/The Image Works; p. 189, Duclos, Gamma Liaison; p. 209, © Richards, PhotoEdit; p. 235, © Okoniewski/ The Image Works; p. 255, © 1988, Braise, The Stock Market; p. 276, © Brenner, PhotoEdit; p. 297, © Young-Wolf, PhotoEdit; p. 319, © Freeman, PhotoEdit; p. 346, Markel, Gamma Liaison; p. 373, © Sohm/The Image Works; p. 399, © Borden, PhotoEdit; p. 417, © Ginn, The Picture Cube; p. 444, © Riley, Stock, Boston; p. 470, Oddie, PhotoEdit; p. 491, © Daemmrich/ The Image Works; p. 518, © Freeman, PhotoEdit; p. 544, © Alper, Stock, Boston; p. 566, © Schiller/ The Image Works; p. 590, © Merlino/The Image Works; p. 611, © Ginn, The Picture Cube; p. 637, © Pickerell/The Image Works; p. 665, © Curran, The Picture Cube; p. 686, © Palmer, The Picture Cube; p. 707, © Coletti, The Picture Cube; p. 736, © Davis, PhotoEdit; p. 757, © Antman/The Image Works; p. 779, © Mangino/The Image Works; p. 805, © Franken, Stock, Boston.

Executive Editor: John Greenman
Development Editor: Joan-Marie Cannon
Project Editor: Diane Williams
Design Supervisor: Jill Yutkowitz
Text and Cover Design: Edward Smith Design, Inc.
Photo Researcher: Mira Schachne
Production Manager/Administrator: Kewal Sharma/Jeffrey Taub
Compositor: York Graphic Services, Inc.
Printer and Binder: R. R. Donnelley & Sons Company
Cover Printer: The Lehigh Press, Inc.

Economics Today, Eighth Edition

Copyright © 1994 by HarperCollins College Publishers

Library of Congress Cataloging-in-Publication Data

Miller, Roger LeRoy.
    Economics today / Roger LeRoy Miller.—8th ed.
      p. cm.
    Includes index.
    ISBN 0-06-501465-0
    1. Economics. 2. Microeconomics. 3. Macroeconomics. I. Title.
HB171.5.M642 1994
330—dc20   93-8233
                                        CIP

94 95 96 9 8 7 6 5 4 3 2

contents in brief

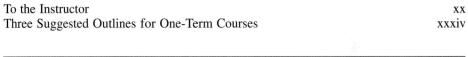

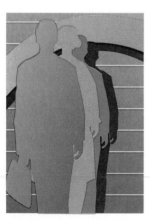

part 6   market structure, resource allocation, and public choice   489

part 7 productive factors, poverty, and the environment 635

to the instructor

As economists in the teaching profession, we could not have asked for more coverage of economic topics in the media over the last several years. Virtually every day there is a major story with economic implications about an issue or problem somewhere in the world. A cursory glance at newspapers 40 years ago would be instructive, for then there was little discussion of economic problems in other countries, problems with changing economic systems elsewhere, the money supply and the Federal Reserve, interest rates, and the like. We have truly reached the age of economics.

Economics Today, Eighth Edition, reflects the reality of today's globally interrelated economy. It offers your students a fresh, current outlook on the world around them while at the same time it presents them with a solid theoretical foundation of economics as a science.

THE USE OF EXAMPLES—BOTH INTERNATIONAL AND DOMESTIC

It is possible not only to excite students by examples, but also to teach them by using examples. Those of us who teach in economics find it immensely exciting. I have attempted to transfer that sense of excitement to your students by including numerous current international and domestic examples. In the chapters in this book you will find 65 international examples and 77 other examples. Here is just a *partial* listing.

Some Sample International Examples
- Capitalists Take to the Street in Moscow (Chapter 4)
- Inflation Rates, Hyperinflation, and Foreign Exchange (Chapter 7)
- Japanese Policymakers Ignore Potential Crowding-Out Effects (Chapter 12)
- Measuring the Kuwaiti Money Supply After the Persian Gulf War (Chapter 14)
- Are We Really So Bad Off? (Chapter 31)

Some Sample Domestic Examples
- The Dramatic Decrease in the Price of Computers (Chapter 3)
- Abrupt Shifts in Supply and Demand: The Case of Hurricane Andrew (Chapter 4)
- The End of the Do-It-Yourself Era (Chapter 23)
- Airline Passengers Just Love Those Price Wars (Chapter 25)
- Regulating Hazardous Waste: Superfund (Chapter 32)

AN EMPHASIS ON CRITICAL THINKING

All examples are interspersed throughout the text and so labeled by an icon and a specific name. But these examples would have little meaning if they did not serve further to help your students think critically. Consequently, I have added to the end of each example a question titled *For Critical Analysis.* You will find suggested answers to these critical-thinking questions in your *Instructor's Resource Binder.*

ISSUES AND APPLICATIONS—YET MORE EXAMPLES

It has been a tradition in all editions of *Economics Today* to present at the end of each chapter *Issues and Applications.* The 35 *Issues and Applications* are all *new.* The format is designed to encourage your students to apply economic concepts and to think critically about how they have applied those concepts. To this end, each *Issue and Application* has the following format:

- A list of *Concepts Applied* at the beginning
- Two to three critical-thinking questions titled *For Critical Analysis.* You will find suggested answers to these critical-thinking questions in the *Instructor's Resource Binder*

The titles of the new *Issues and Applications* for the eighth edition are found in the complete table of contents at the beginning of this preface.

REORGANIZING TO REFLECT CHANGING REALITY

It is a cliché to say that the world is changing, but certainly the world of comparative economic systems has changed more rapidly in the past few years than it had in the previous 45. To reflect the converging of economic systems toward more decentralization, I have placed my chapter on converging economic systems at the end of the introductory unit as Chapter 6. In that chapter I examine market capitalism in terms of the **three Ps**— prices, profits, and private property.

Also, the United States is certainly much more a part of the global economy than ever before. Consequently, I have fully integrated international coverage throughout the entire book, rather than keeping it restricted to the last unit on global economics. There are international examples in virtually every chapter.

PEDAGOGY WITH A PURPOSE

You and your students will notice how carefully the pedagogy in each chapter fits together as a whole. My purpose continues to be to guide your students in their study of our science with a positive, yet nonoffensive approach. The result is what I believe to be state-of-the-art motivational, conceptual, and review pedagogy.

A CHAPTER-OPENING ISSUE

Each chapter starts with a short motivating section in which students are presented with a real-world problem. They are told that they will examine this problem at the end of the chapter. These chapter-opening paragraphs relate directly to the *Issue and Application* presented at the end of each chapter.

PREVIEW POINTS AND COMPLETELY SELF-CONTAINED ANSWERS

Each chapter also begins with four preview questions. The student is given a notion of what he or she is about to learn. Perhaps more important, students can self-test at the end of the chapter by comparing their ideas of the answers to these questions with the actual answers given in paragraph form. These, therefore, serve as a self-contained, self-study module in each chapter.

MARGIN DEFINITIONS

Vocabulary remains a stumbling block in our discipline. To ease the burden, every important economic term is **boldfaced** when it is first introduced and then explained in the text. The term is defined again in the margin definition directly opposite where it first occurs. Finally, the definition of all boldfaced terms can be found in a full *Glossary* at the back of the text.

POINT-BY-POINT END-OF-CHAPTER SUMMARY

To reinforce the key concepts presented in each chapter, a point-by-point chapter summary (with an average of 10 key points) is given. These also serve as a review and learning check system.

PROBLEMS

Many students respond well to hands-on learning experiences. That's what they get when they work the problems at the end of every chapter. There are more problems in the eighth edition than in any previous edition of *Economics Today*. Instructors can assign even-numbered problems as homework, for only the answers to odd-numbered problems are found at the back of the book. These serve as an immediate reinforcement to students. (Step-by-step answers to all chapter-ending problems are found in the *Instructor's Resource Binder*.)

COMPUTER-AIDED INSTRUCTION

At the end of every chapter there is a preview of the computer-aided instruction that students can find on the free software titled *Economics Today Problem Diskette ET8* (see student software below).

MASTERING MACRO AND MICRO

The organization and presentation of macro- and microeconomics has been designed to be streamlined, functional, thought-provoking, and thoroughly contemporary. To these ends, your students will find an emphasis on international examples along with the application of the most modern economic theory.

THE GENERAL INTRODUCTION

Part 1 serves as the general introduction to methodology and analysis. Key aspects of Part 1 are:

- The distinction between substitution options in consumption and variety (Chapter 1)
- The relationship among scarcity, self-interest, and specialization (Chapter 2)
- The necessity of correcting for inflation and quality differences when discussing demand and supply (Chapter 3)
- Price flexibility, adjustment speed, and posted-offer pricing (Chapter 4)
- The principle of rival consumption and the theory of public goods (Chapter 5)

MACROECONOMICS FOR TODAY

All of the materials in the macroeconomic section of the text have been thoroughly revised. Your students will find both modern and understandable theories of how the macro economy works.

- The distinction between anticipated and unanticipated inflation and the repricing, or menu, cost of inflation (Chapter 7)
- The difference between GDP and GNP (Chapter 8)
- A simplified distinction between direct effects and indirect effects that create the downward slope of the aggregate demand curve, plus the open-economy effect (Chapter 9)

- A discussion of long- and short-run aggregate supply, including shifts in *SRAS* only (Chapter 9)
- Modern fiscal policy analysis using *AD-AS* curves with a discussion of offsets to fiscal policy, including indirect crowding out, the new classical economics and the Ricardian equivalence theorem, direct crowding out, and the open-economy effect (Chapter 12)
- An entire chapter on deficit spending and the public debt, including potential methods of reducing the deficit and the meaning of the deficit in an open economy (Chapter 13)
- Deposit insurance, adverse selection, moral hazard, and asymmetric information (Chapter 15)
- Direct and indirect effects of monetary policy shown with *AD-AS* curves (Chapter 16)
- Open-economy transmission of monetary policy (Chapter 16)
- Rational expectations and the new classical model (Chapter 17)
- Rational contracting theory, real business cycle theory, and the new Keynesian economics (Chapter 17)

MICROECONOMICS FOR TODAY

Although microeconomics has not experienced as many changes as has macroeconomics in the last few years, there are many theoretical improvements that have been made. Your students will find these throughout the pages in this section of the text as well as an easy-to-follow flow of material.

- The relationship between tax burdens and price elasticity (Chapter 20)
- Asymmetric information, adverse selection, moral hazard, the principle-agent problem and incentive compatible contracts (Chapter 21)
- Minimum efficient scale of operation (Chapter 22)
- Asymmetric information and the lemons problem (Chapter 23)
- Asymmetry of information problem and the quality-assuring price, with discussion of specific investments (Chapter 23)
- Monopoly rent seeking (Chapter 24)
- Strategic competition, strategic dependence, game theory, and entry-deterrence strategies (Chapter 25)
- Contestable markets, deregulation, and reregulation (Chapter 26)
- The medium voter theorem, distributional coalitions, and rational ignorance (Chapter 27)
- Labor market signaling (Chapter 28)
- Reasons for the decline in unions' importance (Chapter 29)
- The distinction between economic rents and transfer earnings (Chapter 30)
- Profits as a reward for bearing uninsurable risks (Chapter 30)
- New theories about poverty and the health care crisis (Chapter 31)
- The market for pollution rights, offset policies, recycling, and precycling (Chapter 32)

OPEN-ECONOMY ECONOMICS FOR TODAY

The world is getting smaller and the theory of open-economy economics is becoming more important. These chapters are completely updated and contain many exciting new elements of international trade theory.

- Intraindustry international trade, economies of scale, and differentiated products (Chapter 33)
- Protecting the nation's national economic security (Chapter 33)

- Bilateral trade, regional trade agreements, and the North American Free Trade Agreement (NAFTA) (Chapter 33)
- The relationship between the current account and capital account (Chapter 34)
- The dirty-float and managed exchange rates (Chapter 34)
- Property rights and economic development (Chapter 35)
- Modern economic growth (MEG) theory (Chapter 35)

A WORLD MAP FOR STUDENT REFERENCE

We all live in an open-economy world and this is a special focus of the eighth edition of *Economics Today*. Most of the world's economies are converging to a more market-oriented system; this too is a focus of *Economics Today*. Many of the issues and applications as well as the almost 70 international examples found throughout the text refer to areas in the globe with which students may have little familiarity. The map found on pages xviii and xix can be used by students in conjunction with all international examples and issues and applications. Be warned, however, that the four categories used are suggestions only. Many economic systems are in a transitional phase and by the time students read this text might properly be classified otherwise than is labeled here.

LIST OF EXAMPLES

INTERNATIONAL EXAMPLES

Filling an Emotional Void in Japan

Military Spending Versus Development Programs

Trading with Mexico

Buying Up Russian Goods

Keeping the Business at Home

Political Change, Change in Expectations

Bargaining at Home and Abroad

Capitalists Take to the Street in Moscow

The Black Market for Swatch Watches

Trying to End Legal Chaos in the Commonwealth of Independent States

Wiping Out Demerit Goods at Their Source

Russia's High Taxes Discourage Investment

Taxes Paid in the United States Relative to the Rest of the World

A Real Estate Boom in Moscow

The Business of the Party Is Business

The Cost of Breaking the Law in China

Even Capitalist Countries Go In for Privatization: The Case of Italy

Unemployment in Other Countries

Repressed Inflation in Germany and Japan

Inflation Rates, Hyperinflation, and Foreign Exchange

Anticipated Inflation and Nominal Interest Rates in Foreign Countries

Changes in the Accounting System: The Case of the French Franc

GDP and Costa Rica's Forestry Production

The Way the United Nations Treats Investment

The Effects of the Recession in the European Community

Is There a Worldwide Shortage of Saving?

The Japanese Policymakers Ignore Potential Crowding-Out Effects

How Does the United States Stack Up Against the Rest of the World?

Ukrainian Coupon Money Drives Out the Ruble

Can a Nation Use Different Monies for Different Functions?

The Birth of the Eurodollar Market

Measuring the Kuwaiti Money Supply After the Persian Gulf War

How the U.S Banking Structure Compares to the Rest of the World

A Roman Empire Bank Run

Declaring Large-Denomination Rubles Worthless

Money Supply Growth Rates and Inflation in Latin America

Hyperinflation in Modern Russia

European Monetary and Fiscal Coordination

International Price Flexibility

Rates of Saving in Various Countries

Forced Saving in Singapore

High-priced Restaurant Meals in Foreign Lands

Increasing Canadian Taxes on Cigarettes

Who Owns All Those Stocks?

Bursting the South Sea Bubble

Former Anticapitalist Countries and Their Booming Stock Markets

The Beer Industry Goes International

Diamonds Are Forever

Price Discrimination with Japanese Computer Chips
Farmers Go Cold Turkey in New Zealand
The National Labor Supply Curve and Immigration
The Strength of Unions in Western Europe and Japan
Economic Rents and OPEC
Riba (Interest) Rates in Islam
Income Inequality in the Rest of the World
Are We Really So Bad Off?
U.S. Poverty Programs Compared to Those in Other
  Countries
Poverty Pays in Ireland
Paying for the Lack of Incentives in Eastern Europe
The Trade-offs Between Energy and Birds
A Case History of Tariffs: Rubber Thread Imports
Big MacCurrency
Nutrition and Well-being in England over Time
Industrialized Poverty
Unexpected Results of Foreign Aid

DOMESTIC EXAMPLES

Are Economics Students Rational?
Getting Directions
Companies Substitute for High Airfares
Scarce Time and TV Commercials
How Wild Animals Choose Risk
The Opportunity Cost of Going to College
The Real-Life Problems of Downsizing the Military
Changing Age Distribution in the Population
The Dramatic Decrease in the Price of Computers
Abrupt Shifts in Supply and Demand: The Case of
  Hurricane Andrew
Restaurant Pricing
Is There a Shortage of Nurses?
The Effects of Import Quotas on Sugar
The Flat-Tax Proposal
An Alternative to Income Taxes: A Consumption Tax
The Treasury Department Study on Ending Double Taxation
Unemployment and the Underground Economy
How Reliable Is the CPI?
Correcting GDP for Price-Level Changes, 1982–1993
The Persian Gulf War
Massive Technological Change: The Computer Industry
The Entry of Women into the Labor Force
The Development of Pawnshops
The Price Level During the Great Depression
Changes in Investment and the Great Depression
The End of the Cold War
The Effect of Tax Cuts on Tax Revenues
Our History of Incorrect Fiscal Policy Timing
A Balanced-Budget Amendment
The Savings and Loan Crisis

The Phillips Curve Then and Now
How to Retire a Millionaire
The "Freshman 15": Gaining Weight While Living in
  the Dorm
Newspaper Vending Machines Versus Candy Vending
  Machines
Why Diamonds Are More Expensive than Water
The Price Elasticity of Minivans
Is the Demand for Crack Completely Inelastic?
Estimated Price Elasticities of Demand
Elasticity and Gasoline Taxes
Can You Get Rich in the Stock Market?
The Death of Small Airlines and the Minimum Efficient
  Scale of Operation
The Lemons Problem
The End of the Do-It-Yourself Era
The Meaning of Competition in the Digital Age
Monopoly Profits from Gambling
The Case of the Instant Camera
Coke's Effective Advertising Campaign
The Prisoners' Dilemma
Airline Passengers Just Love Those Price Wars
High Switching Costs in the University World
Is the Postal Service a Natural Monopoly?
Regulation in a Milk Market
Are the Airlines a True Contestable Market?
Price Fixing on College Campuses
Getting a Milking from the Milk Lobby
The Food Stamp Program
Superathletes' Marginal Revenue Product
Are Paralegals a Substitute for Lawyers?
The Effects of Minimum Wage Laws
Does a College Education Increase Labor Productivity?
The Shifting Demand for Dentists
Automation and the Telephone Workers' Union
Monopsony in the College Sports
Monopsony in Professional Sports
Giving the Fans a Fair Deal
Economic Rents and Past Presidents
Mobility Among Income Groups
The Persistent Inequality of Income Between the Races
Saving for College and AFDC Don't Go Together
Government Payment for Medical Services and Gam-
  man's Law
The High Cost of Pollution Clean-up
Regulating Hazardous Waste: Superfund
Fish as Common Property
The Tennessee Valley Authority Buys Pollution Credits
Competition or Dumping?
Higher-priced Peanut Butter, Thanks to Quotas
Is the United States' Current Account Deficit a Serious
  Problem?

THE REMAINDER OF THE TEACHING/ LEARNING PACKAGE

As you will discover, *Economics Today,* Eighth Edition, has the most comprehensive, usable, and effective teaching/learning package ever developed for a principles of economics text.

PRINTED MATERIALS FOR THE STUDENT

Extended-Coverage Topics.   This free 224-page booklet does just what the title suggests—it allows you to assign extended-coverage topics for each chapter in the text. The topics included are the following:

Chapter 1: Is Economics a Science?

Chapter 2: Comparative Advantage

Chapter 3: Reservation Demand and Reservation Supply; Stable and Unstable Equilibria

Chapter 4: Consumers' and Producers' Surplus

Chapter 5: Public Goods

Chapter 6: Consequences of Different Ownership Forms

Chapter 7: Disposable Workers

Chapter 8: Biases in the Consumer Price Index

Chapter 9: Oil, War, and Recession

Chapter 10: The Permanent-Income Hypothesis

Chapter 11: An Expanded Circular Flow of Income and Expenditures; Are There Different Government Spending Multipliers?

Chapter 12: Presidents, Promises, and Taxes; Keynesian Fiscal Policy

Chapter 13: State and Local Finance

Chapter 14: Why We Use Money: The Economics of Barter

Chapter 15: A History of Depository Institution Regulation in the United States

Chapter 16: Is the Fed Spinning Its Wheels?

Chapter 17: New Keynesian Theory: The Insider-Outsider Approach and the Input-Output Table Approach

Chapter 18: Some Early Models of Economic Growth

Chapter 19: The Economics of Time

Chapter 20: Elasticity and Slope

Chapter 21: Reading the Financial Pages

Chapter 22: Cost Minimization: The Isoquant-Isocost Approach

Chapter 23: Pricing Alternatives in the Immediate Run: The Competing Conceptions of Economic Analysis

Chapter 24: The Measurement of Monopoly Losses

Chapter 25: Game Theory

Chapter 26: Exclusive Dealing and Requirements Contract; Resale Price Maintenance Agreements

Chapter 27: The Paradox of Voting

Chapter 28: Resource Demand and Supply

Chapter 29: Bilateral Monopoly Situation: The Demand for Baseball Players

Chapter 30: Present Value and the Rule of 72

Chapter 31: The Process of Wage and Income Equalization

Chapter 32: The Coase Theorem

Chapter 33: Free Trade

Chapter 34: Exchange Rate Determination

Chapter 35: Population Economics and Robert Malthus

At the end of each chapter in this booklet you will find the following:

- **Extending the analysis:** This section presents two to four questions that suggest ways in which your students can extend the analysis just presented.
- **References:** These references present materials that are of a more advanced nature on which the extended-coverage topics have been based.

You can order *Extended-Coverage Topics* to accompany *Economics Today,* Eighth Edition, to be shrink-wrapped with all new copies of the text.

For the most part, the topics that I have chosen (along with my colleague, Daniel K. Benjamin) are those that represent slightly more advanced aspects of the topics within each chapter or extensions of the analysis that you normally teach.

Reproducible Homework Assignments.   (See printed materials for instructors.)

Your Economic Life: The Practical Applications of Economics.   New copies of *Economics Today,* Eighth Edition, are all shrink-wrapped with a copy of a booklet that I wrote for students titled *Your Economic Life: The Practical Applications of Economics.* My goal was to give students a motivating essay on the value of studying economics that they could keep and use later on. It shows them the application of economic analysis to everyday living, whether it be understanding economic references they read or hear or deciding whether to buy or to rent a house. There is also information on how to choose a career and what a career in economics entails.

Student Learning Guide.   Co-authored by Robert Pulsinelli of Western Kentucky University and myself, the *Student Learning Guide,* Eighth Edition, may be ordered in three versions, one each for *Economics Today, Economics Today: The Micro View,* and *Economics Today: The Macro View.* It contains the following items for each text chapter: a set of learning objectives, an overview of chapter contents and main points, a list of key terms, a pretest, 15 true–false questions, 15 multiple-choice questions, about 5 problems and essay questions, an issue, and 5 homework problems. Answers to all of the short-answer questions are given at the back of the study guide; answers to all the long-answer problems are provided in the *Instructor's Resource Binder.*

Students appreciate finding the answers to short questions at the end of each chapter. Also, instructors can assign the additional issues and applications that are included in the *Student Learning Guide* when desired. Finally, in this edition, there are special sections on taking class notes, outlining, summarizing, studying, and taking examinations.

COMPUTER SOFTWARE FOR THE STUDENT

This edition of *Economics Today* contains a large number of separate computerized teaching devices. Instructors now have a choice.

ET8 Computer-Assisted Instruction. This software has been developed by Professor Daniel K. Benjamin of Clemson University. There is one computer-assisted problem for each chapter. Students will find augmented discussions of key points within each chapter, expanded explanations, and motivational sound effects. *Computer-Assisted Instruction* problems are found on two separate diskettes for MS-DOS and for the Macintosh family of computers, all free to adopters.

Graphing Tutorial. This *Graphing Tutorial* developed by Bill Compton and me takes students step-by-step through the process of learning how to understand and manipulate graphs. The diskette is free to adopters.

The *Economics Tutor.* *Economics Tutor* (ET) is a Windows-compatible DOS tutorial program that differs from other computer tutorial programs in three important respects. First, *Economics Tutor* employs true graphical user interface (GUI) that may be driven by either mouse or keyboard. Second, *ET* goes beyond the conventional "textbook on a screen" approach by involving the student in a fully interactive way. Finally, the program's architecture recognizes that students who enjoy what they are doing are likely to do more of it, so *Economics Tutor* brings the "feel" of computer games into a college-level economics tutorial program for the first time.

Macro Simulation. A macro model called *Macro,* free to adopters, is presented in this diskette with all of the necessary actual data. Students are allowed to pick courses of action by the Federal Reserve or the Congress and to find out what then will happen to the economy. Experimentation of this kind stimulates interest in macroeconomics and economics in general.

Micro Tutorial. A selected number of important but sometimes difficult concepts are presented in the numerous lessons in this micro-tutorial diskette. Topics included are supply and demand, elasticity, marginal cost/marginal revenue, perfect competition, monopoly, and oligopoly. Free to adopters.

PRINTED MATERIALS FOR INSTRUCTORS

Test Banks 1, 2, and 3. A total of nearly 7,500 multiple-choice questions is now available in three separate test banks.

Test Bank 1 has been revised by Lynda M. Rush of California State Polytechnic University–Pomona. *Test Bank 2* has been revised by Clark G. Ross of Davidson College. *Test Bank 3,* a totally new test bank, has been developed by John Lunn of Hope College. These test banks include questions at all levels. Approximately one-third of the questions are definitional, involving recognition and memorization. Approximately one-third of the questions are conceptual, and the remaining third deal with applications.

Instructor's Resource Binder. The *Instructor's Resource Binder* contains the following:

- *Instructor's Manual*
- Reproducible homework assignments with answers
- Additional reproducible supplementary information

The Instructor's Manual.   This manual was prepared by Andrew J. Dane of Angelo State University. For each chapter, the instructor is provided with a chapter overview; lecture notes; sections titled "For Those Who Wish to Stress Theory"; answers to the questions that appear at the end of each *Issues and Applications* section; further questions for class discussion or essay tests; a list of selected references, films, and videos; and full answers to all problems and essay questions in the *Student Learning Guide.* Throughout the *Instructor's Resource Binder* you will find one-page biographies, suitable for copying, on key economists including:

- Adam Smith
- Joan Robinson
- John Keynes

Reproducible Homework Assignments.   Many of you using *Economics Today* have asked me to prepare homework assignments that can be passed out prior to lecturing on each chapter. I have worked with Steven Lile of Western Kentucky University to do just that. He has prepared approximately ten questions for each chapter, many of which use graphs. There is also a separate answers section that you will find in the *Instructor's Resource Binder.* These homework assignments can be copied from the sheets included in your *Instructor's Resource Binder* in order to pass them out to your students prior to each lecture. You can easily grade them using the suggested answers that we have developed.

Additional Supplemental Reproducible Materials.   If you decide to have additional materials to pass out in class, we have provided data articles and so on that you can easily reproduce them to pass out to your students.

Instructor's Course Planning Guide and Media Handbook.   This pocket-sized reference guide keys every chapter's teaching and learning aids to the text. Additionally, films and videos that are appropriate to each chapter are listed and annotated.

Economics Today **Newsletter.**   Each semester, I prepare a newsletter that instructors may obtain in quantity for use in class. At a minimum, each newsletter will cover one new macroeconomics issue or application or one new microeconomics issue or application. There will also be teaching hints and any important new empirical data or theoretical augmentations of information already in the text.

SOFTWARE AND MULTIMEDIA FOR INSTRUCTORS

TestMaster.   The HarperCollins TestMaster program is a computerized test generator that lets you construct tests by choosing questions from item banks that were prepared specifically for your textbook and course. The test construction process involves the use of a simple TestMaster Form that you fill in on the computer to choose questions for your test. If desired, test questions can be viewed on the screen, and test questions can be edited, saved, and printed. In addition, you can add questions to any test or item bank, or even create your own item banks of test questions, which may include graphics.

Program Features.   The TestMaster program offers the following features that are useful in test construction:

- Tests and item banks can include five types of questions: multiple-choice, true–false, matching, short answer (any kind, including fill-in and completion), and essay.
- A supplementary page attached to each item bank question can contain its topic, objective, skill, difficulty, and other user-added information.
- Test questions can be chosen in a variety of ways including manual selection, random selection, choose while viewing, and choose by searching.
- Questions chosen for a test can be viewed and edited without affecting the original versions of the questions in the item bank.
- Test size is limited only by the memory size of the computer and the length of questions you choose.
- Test questions can be printed in the exact order you specify or grouped and sorted automatically by the program.
- Test questions can be imported to or exported from the TestMaster program and your own word-processing software.
- Printer files can be created or modified to take advantage of the capabilities of your printer.

Package Components.   Each TestMaster package consists of:

- the TestMaster Program and the TestMaster Utilities
- one or more TestMaster Item Bank disks, and
- a TestMaster User's Guide

QuizMaster.   *QuizMaster-TM* is a new program for IBM and Macintosh computers that coordinates with the TestMaster test generator program. QuizMaster allows students to take timed or untimed tests created with TestMaster at the computer. Upon completing a test, a student can see his or her test score and view or print a diagnostic report that lists the topics or objectives that have been mastered or that need to be restudied. When QuizMaster is installed on a network, student scores are saved on disk and instructors can use the QuizMaster Utility program to view records and print reports for individual students, class sections, and entire courses.

Computerized *Instructor's Manual.*   A computerized version of the *Instructor's Manual* is available on disk in ASCII format and can be coded for any IBM PC or compatible or Macintosh. It can also be modified to your specifications so you can customize your lectures and use of the manual.

Lecture Prep®.   For those instructors who use the HarperCollins economics videodisc, Lecture Prep® allows you to customize the use of the videodisc during class presentation. The Lecture Prep® permits the instructor to pick and choose the order of the still frames and the motion videos from any part of the videodisc. Also, the motion videos can be edited by the instructor in any fashion desired. The Lecture Prep® also has a fully automated mode with programmable time segments.

TRANSPARENCIES AND ACETATES

LOTS: Lecture Outline and Transparency System.   This is a new teaching tool prepared by Andrew Dane of Angelo State University. Issued in a loose-leaf, large-print format, it consists of nearly 500 sheets of topic outlines, illustrations, and key tables from the text, problem solutions, and schematic diagrams for presenting economics concepts in lectures or to use as masters for projecting as overhead transparencies. This unusual new kind of support for instructors also assists students in their note taking for fuller comprehension of the subject.

Full-Color Acetates and Acetate Overlays. In addition to all of the transparencies that can be made from the LOTS (see above), approximately 100 of the most important graphs have been reproduced in full-color transparencies with expanded type for easy reading in large classrooms. Because all of the graph lines are color-keyed consistently, use of these acetates will greatly aid the student in understanding key graphic materials.

An additional ten key graphs are presented in acetate overlay form. As you present the theoretical materials to your students for these graphs, you can overlay additional curves in sequence. Such overlays greatly aid in presenting graphic materials.

Transparency Masters. For every graph in the text that has not been made into a full-color acetate, there is a transparency master that you can photocopy into a transparency acetate for use for overhead projection during classroom presentation of the materials.

VIDEOS

Many adopters have asked us to prepare short videos on different topics relating to the economic theory. We have done so for this edition of *Economics Today*. You will find the HarperCollins *Economics Today* Videos Library provides many "lecture starters." These videos, conceptualized by James D. Mason, cover both micro- and macroeconomic topics. They are accompanied by teaching notes.

USING TECHNOLOGY TO TEACH—A VIDEODISC

Anybody who has ever tried to find a particular spot on a videocassette knows what the word frustration means. A laser videodisc does not suffer from this maddening problem, however. With a hand-held remote controller, you can search to exactly the right spot on the videodisc for a particular lecture presentation. The HarperCollins Economics Videodisc is broken up into 40 chapters. Within each chapter there is a wide variety of full-motion videos with narration, numerous graphs, and a series of innovative animations that take your students step-by-step through some of the mechanics of micro and macro theory. You can obtain more information about the videodisc from your HarperCollins sales representative.

FOR USERS OF THE SEVENTH EDITION

First of all, I want to thank you for continuing to support my work. I would also like to let you know the specific changes to *Economics Today* for the eighth edition.

- All Issues and Applications are new.
- There are 77 new examples, so labeled with critical analysis questions at the end of each, suggested answers to which are found in the *Instructor's Resource Binder.*
- There are 65 new international examples with critical analysis questions, the answers to which are suggested in the *Instructor's Resource Binder.*
- There has been a slight reorganization in which I have moved the last chapter on converging economic systems to the end of Part 1. You will also notice some change in presentation of the material in the first two chapters.

- The macroeconomics section of the book has had changes listed on page xxii.
- The microeconomics section of the book has had the following changes listed on page xxiii.
- There are approximately 35 percent more problems at the end of the chapters.
- New supplements with the Eighth Edition:
  1. *Extended-Coverage Topics* (free student paperback)
  2. Reproducible homework problems
  3. New videos
  4. A new videodisc
  5. A third test bank
  6. A new computerized testing system
  7. *Economics Tutor* software
  8. Lecture Prep® software
  9 QuizMaster
- Changes to existing supplements:
  1. The *Instructor's Resource Binder* now contains suggested answers to all "Critical Analysis" questions.
  2. The *Instructor's Resource Binder* now contains reproducible profiles on important economists.
  3. The *Instructor's Manual* now contains reproducible additional lecture supplements for your students.
  4. The *ET8 Computer-Assisted Instruction* software now has one problem for each chapter.
  5. *Test Bank 1* and *Test Bank 2* have been completely revised.

ACKNOWLEDGMENTS

For many years now, I have had the good fortune of receiving numerous comments and criticisms from users of *Economics Today.* All of you who have continued to support my work will see the results of your comments in the eighth edition. Specifically, I would like to thank the following reviewers who went above the call of duty to help me improve the manuscript:

Fatima Antar, Manchester Community College

Leonard Atencio, Fort Lewis College

Scott Bloom, North Dakota State University

Fenton L. Broadhead, Ricks College

Maureen Burton, California State Polytechnic University

Conrad Caligaris, Northeastern University

Thomas H. Cate, Northern Kentucky University

Carol Cies, Rose State College

Eleanor Craig, University of Delaware

Joanna Cruse, Miami Dade Community College South

Andrew Dane, Angelo State University

Edward Dennis, Franklin Pierce College

William Dougherty, Carroll Community College

Zaki Eusufzai, Loyola Marymount University

John L. Ewing-Smith, Burlington County College

Arthur Friedburg, Mohawk Valley Community College

Sanford B. Helman, Middlesex Community College

Benjamin Hitchner, Glassboro State College

Nancy Howe-Ford, Hudson Valley Community College

Jack Inch, Oakland Community College

Devajyoti Kataky, Jefferson Community College

Margaret Landman, Bridgewater State College

Stephen Lile, Western Kentucky University

Bruce McClung, Southwest Texas State University

Warren T. Matthews, Texas A&I University

Thomas Molloy, Muskegon Community College

Margaret Moore, Franklin University

Renee Prim, Central Piedmont Community College

Robert Pulsinelli, Western Kentucky University

Ray C. Roberts, Furman University

John Roufagalas, Radford University

Robert Sexton, Pepperdine University

Alden Smith, Anne Arundel Community College

Steve Smith, Rose State College

William Stine, Clarion University

Osman Suliman, Grambling State University

Rebecca Summary, Southeast Missouri State University

Richard Trieff, Des Moines Area Community College

George Troxler, Manatee Community College

Lee Van Scyoc, University of Wisconsin, Oshkosh

Roy Van Til, University of Maine

Paul Young, Dodge City Community College

Those who reviewed previous editions and provided earlier valuable inputs:

Esmond Adams
John R. Aidem
M. C. Alderfer
Leslie J. Anderson
Fatma W. Antar
Aliakbar Ataiifar
Glen W. Atkinson
Thomas R. Atkinson
James Q. Aylesworth
Charlie Ballard
Maurice B. Ballabon
G. Jeffrey Barbour
Daniel Barszcz
Robin L. Bartlett
Robert Becker
Charles Beem
Glen Beeson
Charles Berry
M. L. Bodnar
Mary Bone
Karl Bonnhi
Thomas W. Bonsor
John M. Booth
Wesley F. Booth
Thomas Borcherding
Tom Boston
Barry Boyer
Maryanna Boynton
Ronald Brandolini
Elba Brown
William Brown
Ralph T. Byrns
Conrad P. Caligaris
Dancy R. Carr
Doris Cash
Richard Chapman
Gary Clayton

Warren L. Coats
Ed Coen
Pat Conroy
James Cox
Stephen R. Cox
John P. Cullity
Thomas Curtis
Mahmoud Davoudi
Carol Dimamro
Barry Duman
Diane Dumont
Floyd Durham
G. B. Duwaji
Robert P. Edwards
Alan E. Ellis
Mike Ellis
Frank Emerson
Frank Fato
Grant Ferguson
David Fletcher
James Foley
John Foreman
Ralph G. Fowler
Arthur Friedberg
Peter Frost
E. Gabriel
Steve Gardner
Peter C. Garlick
Joe Garwood
Otis Gilley
Frank Glesber
Jack Goddard
Allen C. Goodman
Nicholas Grunt
William Gunther
Demos Hadjiyanis
Martin D. Haney

Ray Harvey
E. L. Hazlett
John Hensel
Robert Herman
Gus W. Herring
Charles Hill
Morton Hirsch
James Horner
Christopher Inya
Tomotaka Ishimine
E. E. Jarvis
Parvis Jenab
S. D. Jevremovic
J. Paul Jewell
Fredrick Johnson
David Jones
Lamar B. Jones
Paul A. Joray
Daniel A. Joseph
Craig Justice
Septimus Kai Kai
Timothy R. Keely
Ziad Keilany
Norman F. Keiser
E. D. Key
M. Barbara Killen
Bruce Kimzey
Philip King
Terrence Kinal
E. R. Kittrell
David Klingman
Charles Knapp
Jerry Knarr
Michael Kupilik
Larry Landrum
Keith Langford
Anthony T. Lee

George Lieu
Lawrence W. Lovick
Robert McAuliffe
Howard J. McBride
John McDowell
E. S. McKuskey
John L. Madden
Glen Marston
John M. Martin
Paul J. Mascotti
James D. Mason
Paul M. Mason
Tom Mathew
Warren Matthews
John McDowell
G. Hartley Mellish
Mike Melvin
Herbert C. Milikien
Joel C. Millonzi
Glenn Milner
William E. Morgan
Stephen Morrell
Irving Morrissett
James W. Moser
Martin F. Murray
Jerome Neadly
James E. Needham
Claron Nelson
Douglas Nettleton
Gerald T. O'Boyle
Lucian T. Orlowski
Diane S. Osborne
Jan Palmer
Gerald Parker
Martin M. Perline
Timothy Perri
Jerry Petr

Maurice Pfannesteil
James Phillips
Raymond J. Phillips
I. James Pickl
Dennis Placone
William L. Polvent
Robert Pulsinelli
Kambriz Raffiee
John Rapp
Ron Reddall
Mitchell Redlo
Charles Reichhelu
Robert S. Rippey
Richard Romano
Duane Rosa
Richard Rosenberg
Larry Ross
Philip Rothman
Patricia Sanderson
Thomas N. Schaap
William A. Schaeffer
William Schaniel
David Schauer
A. C. Schlenker
Scott J. Schroeder
William Scott
Dan Segebarth
Augustus Shackelford
Richard Sherman Jr.
Liang-rong Shiau
David Shorow
Vishwa Shukla
R. J. Sidwell
David E. Sisk
Alden Smith
Howard F. Smith
Lynn A. Smith

William Doyle Smith
Lee Spector
George Spiva
Herbert F. Steeper
Allen D. Stone
J. M. Sullivan
Joseph L. Swaffar
Frank D. Taylor
Daniel Teferra
Robert P. Thomas
William T. Trulove
William N. Trumbull
Arianne K. Turner
John Vahaly
Jim VanBeek
Robert F. Wallace
Henry C. Wallich
Milledge Weathers
Robert G. Welch
Terence West
Wylie Whalthall
Everett E. White
Michael D. White
Raburn M. Williams
James Willis
George Wilson
Travis Wilson
Ken Woodward
Donald Yankovic
Alex Yguado
Shik Young
Mohammed Zaheer
Ed Zajicek
William J. Zimmer Jr.

This major revision required a team effort. I would like to thank all of the staff at HarperCollins that worked so hard at getting all of the elements together for this edition. I wish to thank the following people: my longtime editor, John Greenman, who continues to amaze me with his enthusiasm and new ideas; my developmental editor, Joan Cannon, who worked more than she needed to smooth out the manuscript; my project editor, Diane Williams, who broke the HarperCollins record for overtime; Julie Zasloff, who masterfully produced all of the printed supplements; my marketing manager, Kate Steinbacher, whose creative talents knew no bounds; my copyeditor (for the second time), Bruce Emmer, who knows more economics now than he probably wants to; and Dr. Willard W. Radell, who faithfully checked every single graph. I also wish to thank Marie-Christine Loiseau and Daniel K. Benjamin for their expert proofing services. Finally, I could never have completed this project without the expert assistance of Sue Jason of K & M Enterprises.

If you or your students have comments, please do not fail to write me. I always welcome knowledge of ways to improve this text.

R. L. M.

three suggested outlines for one-term courses

Macroeconomic Emphasis	Microeconomic Emphasis	Balanced Micro-Macro
1. The Nature of Economics	1. The Nature of Economics	1. The Nature of Economics
2. Scarcity and the World of Trade-offs	2. Scarcity and the World of Trade-offs	2. Scarcity and the World of Trade-offs
3. Demand and Supply	3. Demand and Supply	3. Demand and Supply
4. Extensions of Demand and Supply Analysis	4. Extensions of Demand and Supply Analysis	4. Extensions of Demand and Supply Analysis
5. The Public Sector	6. Converging Economic Systems	6. Converging Economic Systems
6. Converging Economic Systems	19. Consumer Choice (Optional)	20. Demand and Supply Elasticity
7. The Macroeconomy: Unemployment, Inflation, and Productivity	20. Demand and Supply Elasticity	22. The Firm: Cost and Output Determination
8. Measuring the Economy's Performance	21. The Financial Environment: The Stock Market and Global Capital Markets (Optional)	23. Perfect Competition
9. Introduction to Aggregate Demand and Aggregate Supply	22. The Firm: Cost and Output Determination	24. Monopoly
10. Desired Aggregate Demand	23. Perfect Competition	28. Resource Demand and Supply
11. Income and Employment Determination	24. Monopoly	29. Unions and Labor Market Monopoly Power
12. Fiscal Policy	25. Strategic Competition and Oligopoly	7. The Macroeconomy: Unemployment, Inflation, and Productivity
14. Money and the Banking System	26. Regulation and Antitrust Policy	9. Introduction to Aggregate Demand and Aggregate Supply
15. Money Creation and Deposit Insurance	27. Public Choice (Optional)	10. Desired Aggregate Demand
16. Monetary Policy	28. Resource Demand and Supply	11. Income and Employment Determination
18. Economic Growth	29. Unions and Labor Market Monopoly Power	12. Fiscal Policy
33. Comparative Advantage and the Open Economy	30. Rent, Interest, and Profits	14. Money and the Banking System
34. Exchange Rates and the Balance of Payments	31. Income, Poverty, and Health Care	15. Money Creation and Deposit Insurance
35. Development Economics	32. Environmental Economics	16. Monetary Policy

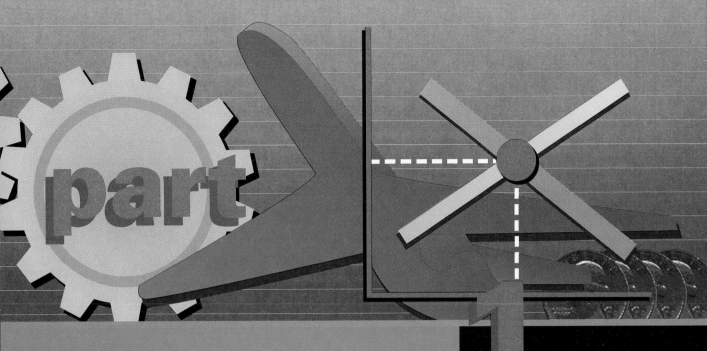

part

INTRODUCTION

THE NATURE OF ECONOMICS

Even the smallest city has one or more relatively well stocked video rental stores. If you cannot find the movie you want, you can get it through the mail from video rental outfits. Little more than a decade ago, the number of videos rented per week was zero. Movies on video were only for people in the TV and film industry because the machines needed to play them cost thousands of dollars. If we simply used the rate of growth of video rentals over the past few years to predict how many more videos will be rented per week in 10 years, the number is huge. Nevertheless, recent stories in the business and popular press present us with a different type of prediction, one of gloom and doom for the video rental industry. Some economists predict that in a decade there will be virtually *no* video rental stores. Understanding the fate of the video rental industry requires that you learn about the nature of economics.

After reading this chapter, you should be able to answer the following questions:

1. What is the difference between microeconomics and macroeconomics?
2. What role does rational self-interest play in economic analysis?
3. Why is the study of economics a science?
4. What is the difference between positive and normative economics?

INTRODUCTION

Your life as a student involves more than thinking about VCRs and videos. Essentially, a student's life is not different from anyone else's: Every life involves economic problems. You face an economic problem each time you sit down to study for this principles of economics course. The more you study, the greater your chance of getting a higher grade. But in doing so, you will also be sacrificing studying for other courses or watching a video or hanging out. If tuition is raised next year, you face an economic problem of whether to remain in school, work more during the summer, ask your parents for more money, or take out more loans. If you happen to be going to a state-supported institution, the decision to raise your tuition would have been made in the state capital. Also, many decisions made in Washington, D.C., affect you and your economic problems. If Congress implements higher federal income taxes, when you work you will take home less pay than you would otherwise. Finally, now more than ever before, what happens in the rest of the world can and will affect you as an individual. American businesses must fight aggressive competition from other countries. There is unmistakable evidence that to be globally competitive, American businesses need an increasingly well educated and skilled labor force. That's perhaps good news if you are going to finish some form of higher education, particularly in a technical area. But it might be bad news if you decide to drop out of school and try to find a job.

Economic problems can be looked at like layers of an onion: They affect you as an individual, as a resident of your city, as a resident of your state, as a citizen of the United States, and ultimately as a nation within an increasingly competitive global marketplace.

THE POWER OF ECONOMIC ANALYSIS

Just because you know that an economic problem exists everywhere and every time you make a decision is not enough. You also have to develop a framework that will allow you to analyze solutions to each economic problem—whether you are trying to decide how much to study, which courses to take, whether to finish school, or whether America should send troops abroad or raise tariffs. The framework that you will learn in this text is based on the *economic way of thinking*.

This framework gives you power—the power to reach informed conclusions about what is happening in the world. You can, of course, live your life without the power of economic analysis as part of your analytical framework. Indeed, most people do. But economists believe that economic analysis can help you make better decisions concerning your career, your education, financing your home, and other important areas. In the business world, the power of economic analysis can help you increase your competitive edge as an employee or as the owner of a business. Finally, just as taking a music, art, or literature appreciation class increases the pleasure you receive when you view paintings, listen to concerts, or read novels, taking an economics course will increase your understanding when watching the news on TV or reading the newspaper.

DEFINING ECONOMICS

Economics is part of the social sciences, which include sociology, psychology, and political science.

> **Economics is the study of how people make choices to satisfy their wants.**

Wants are defined as all the things that people would consume if they had unlimited incomes.

▶ **Economics**
The study of people's behavior as they make choices to satisfy their wants.

▶ **Wants**
What people would buy if their incomes were unlimited.

What does this definition of economics mean? It means that whenever an individual, a business, or a nation faces alternatives, a choice must be made, and economics helps you study how those choices are made. For example, somehow you have to choose how to spend your limited income. You have to choose how to spend your limited time. You may have to choose how much of your company's limited funds to spend on advertising and how much to spend on new-product research. In economics we examine situations in which individuals can choose how to do things, when to do things, and with whom to do them. Ultimately, the purpose of economics is to understand choices.

MICROECONOMICS VERSUS MACROECONOMICS

▶ **Microeconomics**
The study of decision making undertaken by individuals (or households) and by firms.

▶ **Macroeconomics**
The study of the behavior of the economy as a whole, including such economywide phenomena as changes in unemployment, the price level, and national income.

Economics is typically divided into two types of analysis: **microeconomics** and **macroeconomics.** Consider the definitions of the two terms:

> Microeconomics is the part of economic analysis that studies decision making undertaken by individuals (or households) and by firms. It is like looking through a microscope to focus on small parts of our economy.

> Macroeconomics is the part of economic analysis that studies the behavior of the economy taken as a whole. As such, it deals with economywide phenomena such as changes in unemployment, the general price level, and national income.

Microeconomic analysis, for example, is concerned with the effects of changes in the price of gasoline relative to that of other energy sources. It examines the effects of new taxes on a specific product or industry. If price controls were reinstituted in the United States, how individual firms and consumers would react to them would be in the realm of microeconomics. The raising of wages by an effective union strike would also be analyzed using the tools of microeconomics.

By contrast, questions relating to the rate of inflation, the amount of economywide unemployment, the growth in the output of goods and services in the nation, and numerous other economywide subjects all fall into the realm of macroeconomic analysis. In other words, macroeconomics deals with **aggregates,** or totals—such as total output in an economy.

▶ **Aggregates**
Total amounts or quantities; aggregate demand, for example, is total planned expenditures throughout a nation.

Be aware, however, of the blending of microeconomics and macroeconomics in modern economic theory. Modern economists are increasingly using microeconomic analysis—the study of decision making by individuals and by firms—as the basis of macroeconomic analysis. They do this because even though in macroeconomic analysis aggregates are being examined, those aggregates are made up of individuals and firms. Consider an example: Some economists believe that reducing income tax rates will lead to greater total output. Why? Because, using microeconomic analysis, they predict that individuals will respond to lower income tax rates by working longer, taking fewer vacations, and taking on second jobs and using the extra take-home pay to buy more goods and services.

THE ECONOMIC PERSON: RATIONAL SELF-INTEREST

Economists assume that individuals act *as if* motivated by self-interest and respond predictably to opportunities for gain. This central insight of economics was first articulated clearly by Adam Smith in 1776. Smith wrote in his most famous book, *An Inquiry into the Nature and Causes of the Wealth of Nations,* that "it is not from the benevolence of the butcher, the brewer, or the baker that we expect our dinner, but from their regard to their own interest." Otherwise stated, the typical person about whom economists make behavioral predictions is assumed to look out for his or her own self-interest in a rational manner. Because monetary benefits and costs of actions are often the most easily measured, economists most often make behavioral predictions concerning individuals' responses to ways to increase their wealth, measured in money terms. Two aspects of this matter should be explained more fully: (1) the rationality assumption and (2) what self-interest really means.

THE RATIONALITY ASSUMPTION

The **rationality assumption** of economics, simply stated, is as follows:

> We assume that individuals act *as though* they are rational.

▶ **Rationality assumption**
The assumption that people do not intentionally make decisions that would leave them worse off.

The distinction here is between what people may think—the realm of psychology and psychiatry and perhaps sociology—and what they do. Economics does *not* involve itself in analyzing individual or group thought processes. Economics looks at what people actually do in life with their limited resources. It does little good to criticize the rationality assumption by stating, "Nobody thinks that way" or "I never think that way" or "How unrealistic! That's as irrational as anyone can get!"

Consider how we try to figure out what a pool player will do with the cue stick and cue ball to try to hit the eight ball into the side pocket. We study physics to learn about angles of incidence and refraction and then predict what the pool player will do. In essence we are saying that we are predicting behavior *as though* the person actually understood the laws of physics. Some pool players may indeed understand those laws, but the majority do not. Does that mean that our assumption that the pool player understands such physical laws is unrealistic? Yes, most certainly. Useless? No, not at all, particularly if in using that assumption, we consistently predict behavior correctly with respect to where the pool player will hit the cue ball with the cue stick to make particular shots.

Another example concerns driving on the highway. When considering passing another car on a two-lane highway with oncoming traffic, you have to make very quick decisions. Implicitly you must estimate the speed of the car that you are going to pass, the speed of the oncoming cars, the distance between your car and the oncoming cars, and your car's potential rate of acceleration. If we were to apply a model to your behavior, we would use the laws of calculus. You and most other drivers in such a situation do not actually think of using the laws of calculus. But to predict your behavior, we would make the prediction *as if* you understood the laws of calculus.

⭐ EXAMPLE: Are Economics Students Rational?

If you did a survey in your economics class, not all of the students would agree with the statement "I am rational." In an attempt to show that the rationality assumption is accurate nonetheless, an increasing number of economists are doing research using the same kinds of experiments that are used in the physical sciences. One such researcher was David M. Grether, who ran some experiments with students at the University of California at Los Angeles in the early 1980s. His experiment involved separating economics students as volunteers into two groups—one group was paid the same amount no matter how well it performed, and the other group was paid less for poor performance and more for better performance. The sums involved were not large: $7 to each student in the first group no matter what performance; either $5 or $25 in the second group, depending on the level of performance. Performance was measured by how well students were able to pick gambles that had the greatest probability of winning. Students had to do some relatively complicated math calculations to make the best guess.

The results were consistent with the rationality assumption. One-third of the students in the group that was paid regardless of performance picked all of the gambles correctly. In the second group, for which better performance was distinctly rewarded, two-thirds of the students had no errors in making their calculations.

For Critical Analysis: Does this experiment prove *that students are rational? Why or why not?* ●

DEFINING SELF-INTEREST

Self-interest does not necessarily always mean increasing one's wealth measured in dollars and cents. We assume that individuals seek many goals, not just increased wealth measured in monetary terms. Thus the self-interest part of our economic-person assumption involves at a minimum goals relating to prestige, friendship, love, power, helping others, creating works of art, and many other matters. We can also think in terms of enlightened self-interest whereby individuals, in the pursuit of what makes them better off, also achieve the betterment of others around them. In brief, individuals are assumed to want the right to further their goals by making decisions about how things around them are used. A Mother Teresa will usually not turn down an additional contribution because accepting it allows her to control how that money is used—even if it is always for other people's benefit.

 INTERNATIONAL EXAMPLE: Filling an Emotional Void in Japan

The goals of love, friendship, and emotional fulfillment are all part of the economist's definition of "economic men and women." The Japan Efficiency Corporation in Tokyo has attempted to provide market alternatives to ways to fulfill these goals. This company actually rents families to the lonely. The company's success indicates that Japan's increasing material wealth has left some people there with an emotional void. The traditional extended family has broken down more and more, just as it has in the West. Not surprisingly, half of Japan Efficiency's clients are older couples. They rent younger couples with children for a day or a weekend. The family pretends that the elderly are the children's grandparents. The reverse works also. Couples in their twenties with young children rent older pairs as stand-ins for the children's grandparents, who may live too far away or may be too old or too frail to visit in person.

A filler for an emotional void doesn't come cheap in Tokyo. The Japan Efficiency Corporation recently charged a couple over $1,000 for a three-hour family visit by "grandmother."

For Critical Analysis: Can you think of similar market ways for filling "emotional voids" in the United States? ●

CONCEPTS IN BRIEF

- Economics is a social science that involves the study of how individuals choose among alternatives to satisfy their wants, where wants are what people would buy if their incomes were unlimited.
- Microeconomics, the study of the decision-making processes of individuals (or households) and firms, and macroeconomics, the study of the performance of the economy as a whole, are the two main branches into which the study of economics is divided.
- In economics, we assume that individuals act as though they were rational. This is called the rationality assumption: People are assumed never intentionally to make decisions that will leave them worse off.   **(Continued)**

- The assumption that individuals are primarily motivated by self-interest yields useful (and testable) predictions about human behavior.
- Self-interest is not confined to material well-being but rather involves any action that makes a person feel better off, such as having more friends, love, power, or affection or providing more help to others.

ECONOMICS AS A SCIENCE

Economics is a social science that makes use of the same kinds of methods used in other sciences, such as biology, physics, and chemistry. Similar to these other sciences, economics uses models, or theories. Economic **models,** or **theories,** are simplified representations of the real world that we use to help us understand, explain, and predict economic phenomena in the real world. There are, of course, differences between sciences. The social sciences—especially economics—make little use of laboratory methods in which changes in variables can be explained under controlled conditions. Rather, social scientists, and especially economists, usually have to examine what has already happened in the real world in order to test their models, or theories.

▶ **Models,** or **theories**
Simplified representations of the real world used as the basis for predictions or explanations.

For many centuries most people thought that the world was flat. Using this model, they predicted that a person who sailed to the edge of the world would fall off into space. Columbus, however, applied a different model. His model assumed that the world was round. He predicted that one could sail around the world without falling off because there was no edge. He tested his model by sailing continuously, way past the point where others said the edge was located. He did not fall off the edge; his evidence refuted the flat-earth model.

MODELS AND REALISM

At the outset it must be emphasized that no model in *any* science, and therefore no economic model, is complete in the sense that it captures *every* detail and interrelationship that exist. Indeed, a model, by definition, is an abstraction from reality. It is conceptually impossible to construct a perfectly complete realistic model. For example, in physics we cannot account for every molecule and its position and certainly not for every atom and subparticle. Not only is such a model impossibly expensive to build, but working with it would be impossibly complex. No model of the solar system, for example, could possibly take into account all aspects of the system.

The nature of scientific model building is such that the model should capture only the *essential* relationships that are sufficient to analyze the particular problem or answer the particular question with which we are concerned. *An economic model cannot be faulted as unrealistic simply because it does not represent every detail of the real world.* A map of a city that only shows major streets is not necessarily unrealistic if, in fact, all you need to know is how to pass through the city using major streets. As long as a model is realistic in terms of shedding light on the *central* issue at hand or forces at work, it may be useful.

A map is the quintessential model. It is always a simplified representation. It is always unrealistic. But it is also useful in making (refutable) predictions about the world. If the model—the map—predicts that when you take Campus Avenue to the north, you always run into the campus, that is a (refutable) prediction. If our goal is to explain observed behavior, the simplicity or complexity of the model we use is irrelevant. If a simple model can explain observed behavior in repeated settings just as well as a complex one, the simple model has some value and is probably easier to use.

ASSUMPTIONS

Every model, or theory, must be based on a set of assumptions. Assumptions define the set of circumstances in which our model is most likely to be applicable. When scientists predicted that sailing ships would fall off the edge of the earth, they used the *assumption* that the earth was flat. As we pointed out before, Columbus did not accept the implications of such a model. He assumed that the world was round. The real-world test of his own model refuted the flat-earth model. Indirectly, then, it was a test of the assumption of the flat-earth model.

⭐ EXAMPLE: Getting Directions

Assumptions are a shorthand for reality. Imagine showing up at your campus bookstore for the first time. You want to know where the magazines are displayed. You ask the store clerk where to go. The store clerk could offer the following detailed description of the path you should follow:

> Walk north past checkout counters three and four, then past the Cliff Notes section, and then to the stairs. Walk up the stairs. When you reach the top, go to the right past the bookcase that says "New Fiction," then the bookcase that says "Mysteries." Turn left and go past the bookcase marked "Art," then the bookcase marked "Fitness," and then on your left you will walk past an open cashier stand with an NCR automated cash register and inventory control system. Walk twenty-one feet past the sections for mysteries and poetry. Underneath the big sign that says "Magazines" hanging from the ceiling, you will find the magazines.

This is certainly a fairly complete description of reality, for the clerk hasn't used many simplifying assumptions. There is an alternative approach that the clerk could use:

> Go up the stairs. Then look for the big sign hanging from the ceiling that says "Magazines."

With this simple description, the clerk has told you all that you want to know. She has omitted all the details that are really not important. The models that you will be using in this text are more like the simplified description of how to find the magazine racks—they focus on what is important to the problem at hand; other details are omitted because they are not relevant to the present problem.

For Critical Analysis: In what way do small talk and gossip represent the use of simplifying assumptions? ●

The *Ceteris Paribus* Assumption: All Other Things Being Equal. Everything in the world seems to relate in some way to everything else in the world. It would be impossible to isolate the effects of changes in one variable on another variable if we always had to worry about the many other variables that might also enter the analysis. As with all sciences, economics uses the ***ceteris paribus* assumption.** *Ceteris paribus* means "other things constant, or equal."

▶ *Ceteris paribus* [KAY-ter-us PEAR-re-bus] **assumption** The assumption that nothing changes except the factors being studied.

Consider an example taken from economics. One of the most important determinants of how much of a particular good or service a family buys is how much more expensive that good or service is relative to other goods and services. We know that more factors influence decisions about making purchases than just relative prices. Some of them have to do with income, others with changes in taste, and yet others with custom and religious beliefs. What you will see throughout this text is that when the relationship between price and how much people purchase is examined, all other factors must be held constant, or equal.

DECIDING ON THE USEFULNESS OF A MODEL

We generally do not attempt to determine the usefulness, or "goodness," of a model merely by evaluating how realistic its assumptions are. Rather, we consider a model good if it yields usable predictions and implications for the real world. In other words, can we use the model to predict what will happen in the world around us? Does the model provide useful implications of how things happen in our world?

Once we have determined that the model does predict real-world phenomena, the scientific approach to the analysis of the world around us requires that we consider evidence. Evidence is used to test the usefulness of a model. This is why we call economics an **empirical** science, *empirical* meaning that evidence (data) is looked at to see whether we are right. Economists are often engaged in empirically testing their models.

▶ **Empirical**
Relying on real-world data in evaluating the usefulness of a model.

Consider two competing models for the way students act when doing complicated probability problems to choose the best gambles. (This was the experiment we described previously.) One model predicts that, based on the assumption of rational self-interest, students who are paid more for better performance will in fact perform better on average during the experiment. A competing model might be that students whose last names start with the letters *A* through *L* will do better than students with last names starting with *M* through *Z*, irrespective of how much they are paid. The model that consistently predicts more accurately would be the model that we would normally choose. In this example, the "alphabet" model did not work well: The first letter of the last name of the students who actually did the experiment at UCLA was irrelevant in predicting how well they would perform the mathematical calculations necessary to choose the correct gambles. The model based on rational self-interest is thus the more accurate model.

MODELS OF BEHAVIOR, NOT THOUGHT PROCESSES

Take special note of the fact that economists' models do not relate to the way people *think;* they relate to the way people *act,* to what they do in life with their limited resources. Models tend to generalize human behavior. Normally, the economist does not attempt to predict how people will think about a particular topic, such as a higher price of oil products, accelerated inflation, higher taxes, or the like. Rather, the task at hand is to predict how people will act, which may be quite different from what they say they will do (much to the consternation of poll takers and market researchers). The people involved in examining thought processes are psychologists and psychiatrists, not typically economists.

CONCEPTS IN BRIEF

- A model, or theory, uses assumptions and is by nature a simplification of the real world.
- The usefulness of a model can be evaluated by bringing empirical evidence to bear on its predictions.
- Models are not necessarily deficient simply because they are unrealistic and use simplified assumptions, for every model in every science requires simplification compared to the real world.
- Most of the models we use contain the *ceteris paribus* assumption, that all other things are held constant, or equal.
- Models in economics relate to behavior rather than to thought processes.

SUBSTITUTION OPTIONS

When you decide which classes to take each term, you have numerous options. Instead of French, you can take Spanish. Instead of world literature, you can take American literature. When you decide to go home for Christmas vacation, you may have options. You can take a train, a bus, a plane, or an automobile.

▶ **Substitution options**
Those alternatives that exist for any given activity for use of income or time. Virtually every aspect of one's life has a substitution option.

▶ **Consumption**
The use of goods and services for personal satisfaction.

▶ **Production**
Any activity that results in the conversion of natural resources, human resources, and other resources into goods and services that can be used in consumption.

You may decide that you want to climb to the top of Mount Everest. Options do exist. You can take the usual approach by beginning on the side of the mountain in Nepal. Some people start on the less difficult side in China. In essence, then, there are different ways to achieve virtually any objective. In economics we say that **substitution options** exist in virtually every aspect of how you spend your money, income, or time and how you can produce pieces of jewelry or food in your kitchen. The former activities are called **consumption,** and the latter, **production.**

SUBSTITUTION OPTIONS IN CONSUMPTION

Consumption substitution options clearly exist, but they are not the same thing as variety. When you think of the many different types of books that you can buy or the many different restaurants that you can dine at, you are thinking about the variety of *choices* before you. But to choose among your true substitution options, you must first establish an objective. Assume that you will receive the same level of satisfaction or happiness next week by either (1) going out to dinner once and renting three videos or (2) going out to dinner twice and renting one video. You truly have substitution options between eating out and renting videos without reducing your level of satisfaction or happiness during the week.

SUBSTITUTION OPTIONS IN PRODUCTION

Virtually every potential type of production has substitution options also. You may have several ways to obtain a given grade in your economics course. You can (1) study alone seven hours a week and expect to receive a B, or (2) you can study two hours a week with a private tutor whom you pay and expect to receive a B.

⭐ EXAMPLE: Companies Substitute for High Airfares

Recently, an executive of a small bank in Miami wanted to send an employee to its state headquarters in Orlando. The price of the round-trip airplane ticket was over $300. Sun Bank had a substitution option in production, which it used: It rented a car for the employee, who then drove to Orlando, stayed overnight in a hotel, and drove back. The total cost was less than the $300 that the round-trip ticket would have cost. When faced with high airfares, other companies are increasingly finding substitution options in production. One of them is the fax machine. A decent fax machine can now be bought for the cost of a trip from New York to just about anywhere in the United States. Another alternative for face-to-face conferences that might require air travel is a videoconference. The price of renting videoconferencing equipment has dropped dramatically in recent years. Large companies have even found it profitable to purchase their own equipment, which can now be had for less than a few thousand dollars. When the goal is a certain level of productive capacity, businesses will tend to substitute in favor of the options that cost less.

For Critical Analysis: Even though alternatives to face-to-face conferences between businesspersons exist, many still choose to travel, no matter what the price of airfare. Why? ●

THE UNIT OF ANALYSIS: THE INDIVIDUAL

Throughout this first chapter we have talked about individuals having to make choices. We talked about individuals desiring goods and seeking many goals. It would seem, therefore, that economists are fascinated with the individual rather than the public or society or any other unit of analysis. Many critics accuse economists of a value-laden judgment about the need to look at only the individual's desires and goals rather than those of society.

It is true that for *predictive* purposes, decisions that are made within a family, a government agency, a society, a business, or any other group of individuals are best analyzed under the assumption that the members of the group are pursuing their own *individual* interests—the individual economic person, pursuing rational self-interest, is at work. This is not a judgment in favor of individual values. Rather, the individual is used as the basic unit of analysis because this approach yields more accurate predictions.

Even in our increasingly competitive world, the unit of our economic analysis remains the individual. The decisions of governments at home and abroad are still the decisions that result from the preferences and actions of the individuals within those governments. If we wish to analyze what Japanese automakers might do because of a new U.S. restriction on Japanese cars coming in this country, we don't think of "the Japanese." Rather, we analyze how the individuals within Japanese management might react. We are always assuming that persons adapt to circumstances to achieve their objectives and goals. We start out with the simplifying assumption that behavior among individuals is sufficiently uniform everywhere in the world so that it can be successfully summarized using the assumptions of our economic models.

POSITIVE VERSUS NORMATIVE ECONOMICS

Economics is a social science that uses *positive analysis,* a scientific term that relates to the value-free nature of the inquiry. No subjective or moral judgments enter into the analysis. Positive analysis relates to statements such as "If A, then B." For example, if the price of gasoline goes up relative to all other prices, then the amount of it that people will buy will fall. That is a positive economic statement. It is a statement of *what is.* It is not a statement of anyone's value judgment or subjective feelings. For many problems analyzed in the hard sciences such as physics and chemistry, the analyses are considered to be virtually value-free. After all, how can someone's values enter into a theory of molecular behavior? But economists face a different problem. They deal with the behavior of individuals, not molecules. Thus it is more difficult to stick to what we consider to be value-free or **positive economics** without reference to our feelings.

When our values are interjected into the analysis, we enter the realm of **normative economics,** or normative analysis. A positive economic statement is "If the price of gas goes up, people will buy less." If we add to that analysis the statement "and therefore we should not allow the price to go up," we have entered the realm of normative economics; we have expressed a value judgment. In fact, any time you see the word *should,* you will know that values are entering into the discussion. Just remember that positive statements are concerned with what is, whereas normative statements are concerned with *what some person thinks should be.*

Each of us has a desire for different things. That means that we have different values. When we express a value judgment, we are simply saying what we prefer, like, or desire. Because individual values are quite diverse, we expect—and indeed observe—people expressing widely varying value judgments about how the world *ought* to be.

▶ **Positive economics**
Analysis that is strictly limited to making either purely descriptive statements or scientific predictions; for example, "If A, then B." A statement of *what is.*

▶ **Normative economics**
Analysis involving value judgments about economic policies; relates to whether things are good or bad. A statement of *what ought to be.*

A WARNING: RECOGNIZE NORMATIVE ANALYSIS

It is easy to define positive economics. It is quite another matter to catch all unlabeled normative statements in a textbook such as this one (or any other), even though an author goes over the manuscript many times before it is printed. Therefore, do not get the impression that a textbook author will be able to keep all personal values out of the book. They will slip through. In fact, the choice itself of which topics to include in an introductory textbook involves normative economics. There is no value-free, or objective, way to decide which topics to use in a textbook. The author's values ultimately make a difference when choices have to be made. But from your own standpoint, you might want to be able to recognize when you are engaging in normative as opposed to positive economic analysis. Reading this text should help equip you for that task.

CONCEPTS IN BRIEF

- Consumption activities involve options for which the same level of satisfaction (or happiness) can be obtained when choosing several alternative actions. Substitution options also exist for production.
- For the purposes of our analysis, the unit we choose to analyze is the individual, rather than one group or society as a whole.
- Positive economics is value-free and relates to statements that can be refuted, such as "If A, then B." Normative economics involves people's values and typically includes the word *should*.

CONTINUED ➡

Although video rentals have experienced phenomenal growth in the last ten years, changes in technology may, nonetheless, not only reduce the growth in demand for video rentals, but also may even eliminate it.

In the early 1980s, videocassette recorders became widely available to the general public. Since then, thousands of video rental companies have sprung up and rapidly expanded. (Blockbuster alone has over 3,000 stores throughout the United States.) Movies on video are a substitution option for you and virtually everybody else in America and much of the world. The substitution options involve renting videos, going to the movies, watching movies on commercial TV (with commercials), and watching movies on cable TV stations (without commercials and other interruptions).

NEW SUBSTITUTION OPTIONS   Technology, though, is quickly going to provide you and other consumers with at least one more viable and relatively cheap substitute option in consumption: pay-per-view TV. Pay-per-view television has actually been around since the late 1970s. But until the mid-1990s, relatively few American households could receive it, and programming was limited. Enter Time Warner's Quantum cable television system in the Queens section of New York City. Fifty-five of the 150 channels on the Quantum system deliver a choice of 17 movies around the clock, usually starting every half hour. The cost is less than $4 per view. The Time Warner Company believes that those 55 channels are a way of bringing a video store into your home.

TECHNOLOGY HAS HELPED   Time Warner can provide 150 channels by using a new technology called digital compression. This technology uses computerized techniques to squeeze 3 to 10 programs onto a single channel. The technology is supposed to be available nationwide by mid-1995. It is going to require the installation of new digital systems that cable carriers must install. And it is going to be costly, which means that the new cable installation process will carry over into the year 2000 and beyond.

OTHER OPTIONS MAY BE AVAILABLE   Technological breakthroughs may make even pay-per-view TV obsolete in the future. Movie consumers will conceivably be able to order any movie they want through the phone system of the future. The film will be sent via digital technology through the phone line or a satellite dish to their homes in less than a minute. The equipment at home will decompress the information and *voilà*—a movie to watch on demand. You will also be able to fast-forward, reverse, and pause, things you can't currently do on cable.

In the meantime, videocassettes may be replaced by $5\frac{1}{2}$-inch videodiscs that use laser technology to show a movie of superior quality sound and picture.

SUBSTITUTION OPTIONS WILL ALWAYS EXIST   As long as enough consumers have an objective of a certain amount of leisure-time activities, producers are going to try to develop substitution options to entice some consumers to spend their money in a different way than they currently do. At the beginning of this chapter, we asked how anybody could predict that video rentals will again be zero at the end of the following decade. The answer is now more obvious: As substitution options to video rentals become cheap enough and widespread enough, consumers may in fact no longer want to rent many videos.

FOR CRITICAL ANALYSIS

1. Prior to the mid-1970s, there were virtually no video rental stores. Video rental stores probably won't exist 10 or 20 years from now. What is the difference between the two situations?
2. Can you think of any disadvantages that the pay-per-view system of watching movies has compared to the alternative of renting videos?

CHAPTER SUMMARY

1. Economics as a social science is the study of how a society makes choices to satisfy wants. Wants are defined as what people would buy if their incomes were unlimited.

2. Economics is usually divided into microeconomic analysis, which is the study of individual decision making by households and firms, and macroeconomics, which is the study of nationwide phenomena, such as inflation and unemployment.

3. The rationality assumption is that individuals act as though they were rational and would never intentionally make decisions that would leave them worse off.

4. We use models, or theories, to explain and predict behavior. Models, or theories, are never completely realistic because by definition they are simplifications using assumptions that are not directly testable. The usefulness of a theory, or model, is determined not by the realism of its assumptions but by how well it predicts real-world phenomena.

5. An important simplifying assumption is that all other things are held equal, or constant. This is sometimes known as the *ceteris paribus* assumption.

6. No model in economics relates to individuals' thought processes; all models relate to what people do, not to what they think or say they will do.

7. Consumption involves how you spend your income and your time. There are substitution options in consumption. If eating two pizzas and renting one video gives you the same satisfaction as eating one pizza and renting two videos, those are two sets of substitution options in consumption from which you can choose. There are also substitution options in production.

8. We use the individual as a unit of analysis in economics because this approach yields more accurate predictions.

9. Much economic analysis involves positive economics; that is, it is value-free. Whenever statements embodying values are made, we enter the realm of normative economics, or what individuals and groups think should exist.

DISCUSSION OF PREVIEW POINTS

1. **What is the difference between microeconomics and macroeconomics?**

   Microeconomics is concerned with the choice-making processes of individuals, households, and firms, whereas macroeconomics focuses on the performance of the economy as a whole.

2. **What role does rational self-interest play in economic analysis?**

   Rational self-interest is the assumption that individuals behave in a reasonable (rational) way in making choices to further their interests. In other words, we assume that individuals' actions are motivated primarily by their self-interest, keeping in mind that self-interest can relate to monetary and nonmonetary objectives, such as love, prestige, and helping others.

3. **Why is the study of economics a science?**

   Economics is a science in that it uses models, or theories, that are simplified representations of the real world to analyze and make predictions about the real world. These predictions are then subjected to empirical tests in which real-world data are used to decide whether or not to reject the predictions.

4. **What is the difference between positive and normative economics?**

   Ideally, positive economics deals with *what is,* whereas normative economics deals with *what ought to be.* Positive economic statements are of the "if—then" variety; they are descriptive and predictive and are not related to what *should* happen. Normative economics, by contrast, is concerned with what ought to be and is intimately tied to value judgments.

PROBLEMS
(Answers to odd-numbered problems appear at the back of the book.)

1-1. Construct four separate models to predict the probability that a person will die within the next five years. Include only one determining factor in each of your models.

1-2. Does it matter whether all of a model's assumptions are "realistic"? Why or why not?

1-3. Give a refutable implication for each of the following models:
   a. The accident rate of drivers is inversely related to their age.
   b. The rate of inflation is directly related to the rate of change in the nation's money supply.
   c. The wages of professional basketball players are directly related to their high school grade point averages.
   d. The rate at which bank employees are promoted is inversely related to their frequency of absenteeism.

1-4. Is gambling an example of rational or irrational behavior? What is the difference between gambling and insurance?

1-5. Over the past 20 years, first-class mail rates have more than tripled, while prices of long-distance phone calls, televisions, and sound systems have decreased. Over a similar period, it has been reported that there has been a steady decline in the ability of high school graduates to communicate effectively in writing. Do you feel that this increase in the relative price of written communication (first-class mail rates) is related to the alleged decline in writing ability? If so, what do you feel is the direction of causation? Which is causing which?

1-6. If there is no way to test a theory with real-world data, can we determine if it is a good theory? Why is empirical evidence used to validate a theory?

1-7. Identify which of the following statements use positive economic analysis and which use normative economic analysis.
   a. The government should not regulate the banking system because recent problems have demonstrated that it does not know what it is doing.
   b. The elimination of barriers to the free movement of individuals across European borders has caused wages to become more equal in many industries.
   c. Paying members of Congress more provides them with less incentive to commit wrongful acts.
   d. We need more restrictions on companies that pollute because air pollution is destroying our way of life.

 ## COMPUTER-ASSISTED INSTRUCTION
(Complete problem and answer on disk.)

Key elements of the scientific way of thinking are illustrated by applying them to everyday situations.

SCARCITY AND THE WORLD OF TRADE-OFFS

No one will question that life is precious. When faced with the alternative of dying, most humans will spend virtually as much income as they can to stay alive. People who are not faced with the prospect of a premature death, in contrast, have many other things on their mind. They are interested in music, cars, houses, restaurant meals, and the environment. What happens when there is a clash between healthy people who are trying to protect the environment and the wishes of dying people whose cure is derived from an endangered species? The issues involved in medicine versus the environment are part of the general concepts of scarcity and trade-offs.

After reading this chapter, you should be able to answer the following questions:

1. Do affluent people face the problem of scarcity?

2. Fresh air and clean water may be consumed at no charge, but are they free of cost to society?

3. Why does the scarcity problem force individuals to consider opportunity costs?

4. Can a "free" college education ever be truly free?

INTRODUCTION

While you are reading this text, much of the world is in the process of transforming itself. We are, of course, referring to countries that haven't had the same kind of system that we are so used to in the United States—Russia and the surrounding republics, Poland, Romania, Bulgaria, and parts of China. Most of these countries were known for their low standard of living and the inability of their citizens to obtain many of the things they wanted, such as fresh meat and soap. Quite a few articles have been written on how these countries are changing. Journalists are fond of saying that these strides toward a system similar to the one that we have in the United States will "help them get rid of scarcity." If only that were true. Changing the way things are done doesn't change a basic fact of life: Everyone, everywhere, at every instant in time faces scarcity.

SCARCITY

Whenever individuals or communities cannot obtain everything they desire simultaneously, choices occur. Choices occur because of *scarcity*. **Scarcity** is the most basic concept in all of economics. Scarcity means that we do not and cannot have enough income or wealth to satisfy our *every* desire. Scarcity exists because human wants always exceed what can be produced with the limited resources and time that nature makes available.

> ▶ **Scarcity**
> A situation in which the ingredients for producing the things that people desire are insufficient to satisfy all wants.

WHAT SCARCITY IS NOT

Scarcity is not a shortage. After a hurricane hits and cuts off supplies to a community, TV newscasts often show people standing in line to get minimum amounts of cooking fuel and food. A news commentator might say that the line is caused by the scarcity of these products. But cooking fuel and food are always scarce—we cannot obtain all that we want at a zero price. Therefore, do not confuse the concept of scarcity, which is general and all-encompassing, with the concept of shortages as evidenced by people waiting in line to obtain a particular good.

Scarcity is not the same thing as poverty. Scarcity occurs among the poor and among the rich. Even the richest person on earth faces scarcity because available time is limited. Low income levels do not create more scarcity. High income levels do not create less scarcity.

Scarcity is a fact of life, like gravity. And just as physicists did not invent gravity, economists did not invent scarcity—it existed well before the first economist ever lived. It exists even when we are not using all of our resources.

⭐ EXAMPLE: Scarce Time and TV Commercials

How many times have you heard the comment that television commercials are better than the programs they are sponsoring? Such commercials are often so good that you can remember them days or weeks afterward, long after you have forgotten what the show itself was about. Some TV commercials are so good as to be called classics—everybody knows about them.

Why are such commercials so good while TV shows often aren't? The answer has to do with the relative scarcity of time. The series that is on, say, every day for 30 minutes means that about 27 of those minutes have to be filled with material. Producers, writers, and directors know that they have 27 minutes to develop a plot and introduce the characters. To be successful, a series has to keep people tuned in. But the creators of the series have a lot of time to do this, relatively speaking. Now what about the creators of TV commercials? They face a much more severe scarcity of time. To keep you tuned in, they have to grab your attention almost instantaneously. The choice of music, words, and video-motion sequences in the 30-second commercial are many times more critical than the same choices for the show that is going to last 27 minutes. It is not unusual, therefore, that jingles are often used, ones that last only a few seconds but are easily remembered.

The amount of money that is spent per 30 seconds for the TV commercial is dramatically more than for the TV series. A 27-minute episode of a series might cost $500,000 to $1 million. But one 30-second beer commercial can cost as much as $500,000. That commercial is used many times and, if it works, has a high payoff. Scarcity of time is what forces the creators of TV commercials to be much more creative than those who provide us with regular TV programming.

For Critical Analysis: Are all 30-second commercials of equally high quality? Explain your answer. ●

SCARCITY AND RESOURCES

The scarcity concept just discussed arises from the fact that resources are scarce. Scarce resources, or simply **resources,** for short, can be defined as the inputs used in the production of the things that we want. Production can be defined as virtually any activity that increases the value of things that exist and that we use. That means that production includes delivering things from one part of the country to another. It includes taking ice from an ice tray to put it in your soft-drink glass. When resources are used in production, they are called *factors of production.* Indeed, some economists use the terms *resources* and *factors of production* interchangeably. The total quantity of all resources that an economy has at any one time determines what that economy can produce. Factors of production can be classified in many ways. Here is one such classification:

1. **Land.** Land includes the gifts of nature, such as timber, water, fish, and minerals. Land is often called the natural resource, including the original fertility of land.
2. **Labor.** This is the human resource, which includes all productive contributions made by individuals who work, such as steelworkers, ballet dancers, and professional baseball players. Improvements to labor occur when a worker acquires new skills. When such improvements occur, we say that *human capital* has been improved.
3. **Capital.** Capital is the goods and services used to produce other goods and services. It includes machines, buildings, and tools. Capital can also consist of improvements to natural resources, such as irrigation ditches.

   References to capital, particularly in the financial press, are concerned with *financial capital*—the funds made available in the stock market for starting new businesses, for example. Whenever we are discussing resources and factors of production, we are *not* referring to financial capital.
4. **Entrepreneurship.** This fourth factor of production (actually a subdivision of labor) involves human resources that perform the functions of organizing, managing, and assembling the other factors of production to make business ventures. Entrepreneurship also encompasses taking risks that involve the possibility of losing large sums of wealth on new ventures. It includes new methods of doing common things and generally experimenting with any type of new thinking that could lead to making more money income. Without entrepreneurship, virtually no business organization could operate.

GOODS VERSUS ECONOMIC GOODS

Goods are defined as all things from which individuals derive satisfaction or happiness. Goods therefore include air to breathe and the beauty of a sunset as well as food, cars, and compact disc players.

▶ **Resources**
Inputs used to produce goods and services. (Also called *factors of production.*)

▶ **Land**
The natural resources that are available from nature. Land as a resource includes location, original fertility and mineral deposits, topography, climate, water, and vegetation.

▶ **Labor**
Productive contributions of humans who work, involving both mental and physical activities.

▶ **Capital**
All manufactured resources, including buildings, equipment, machines, and improvements to land that is used for production.

▶ **Entrepreneurship**
The factor of production involving human resources that perform the functions of raising capital, organizing, managing, assembling other factors of production, and making basic business policy decisions. The entrepreneur is a risk taker.

▶ **Goods**
Any things from which individuals derive satisfaction or happiness and are thus valued.

Economic goods are a subset of all goods—they are goods produced from scarce resources for which we must constantly make decisions about their best use. By definition, the desired quantity of an economic good exceeds the amount that is directly available from nature at a zero price.

Sometimes you will see references to economic goods and services. **Services** are tasks that are performed for someone else, such as laundry, cleaning, hospital care, restaurant meal preparation, car polishing, psychological counseling, and teaching. One way of looking at services is thinking of them as *intangible goods*.

▶ **Economic goods**
Any goods or services that are scarce.

▶ **Services**
Things purchased by consumers that do not have physical characteristics. Examples of services are actions provided by doctors, lawyers, dentists, repair personnel, housecleaners, educators, retailers, and wholesalers.

WANTS AND NEEDS

Wants are not the same as needs. Indeed, from the economist's point of view, the term *needs* is objectively undefinable. When someone says, "I need some new clothes," there is no way to know whether that person is stating a vague wish, a want, or an absolute necessity. If the individual making the statement were dying of exposure in a northern country during the winter, we might argue that indeed the person does need clothes—perhaps not new ones, but at least some articles of warm clothing. Typically, however, the term *need* is used very casually in most conversations. What people mean, usually, is that they want something that they do not currently have.

Humans have unlimited wants. Just imagine if every single material want that you might have were satisfied. You can have all of the clothes, cars, houses, compact discs, tickets to concerts, and so on that you want. Does that mean that nothing else could add to your total level of happiness? Probably not, because you might think of new goods and services that you could obtain, particularly as they came to market. You would also still be lacking in fulfilling all of your wants for compassion, friendship, love, affection, prestige, musical abilities, sports abilities, and so on.

In reality, every individual has competing wants but cannot satisfy all of them, given limited resources. This is the reality of scarcity. Each person must therefore make choices. Whenever a choice is made to do or buy something, something else that is also desired is not done or not purchased. In other words, in a world of scarcity, every want that ends up being satisfied causes one or more other wants to remain unsatisfied or to be forfeited.

CONCEPTS IN BRIEF

- Scarcity exists because human wants always exceed what can be produced with the limited resources and time that nature makes available.
- We use scarce resources, such as land, labor, capital, and entrepreneurship, to produce economic goods—goods that are desired but are not directly obtainable from nature to the extent demanded or desired at a zero price.
- Wants are unlimited; they include all material desires and all nonmaterial desires, such as love, affection, power, and prestige.
- The concept of need is difficult to define objectively for every person; consequently, we simply consider that every person's wants are unlimited. In a world of scarcity, satisfaction of one want necessarily means nonsatisfaction of one or more other wants.

SCARCITY, CHOICE, AND OPPORTUNITY COST

The natural fact of scarcity leads to the necessity of making choices. One of the most important results of this choice-making necessity is that every choice made (or not made, for that matter) means that some opportunity had to be sacrificed. Every choice involves giving up another opportunity to do or use something else.

Consider a practical example. Every choice you make to study one more hour of economics requires that you give up the opportunity to do at least one of the following activities: study more of another subject, listen to music, sleep, browse at a local store, read from a novel, and work out at the gym. You can add many more opportunities forgone if you choose to study economics one more hour.

Because there were so many alternatives from which to choose, how could you determine the value of what you gave up to engage in that extra hour of studying economics? First of all, no one else can tell you the answer because only you can *subjectively* put a value on the alternatives forgone. Only you know what is the value of another hour of sleep or of an hour looking for the latest CDs. That means that only you can determine the highest-valued, next-best alternative that you had to sacrifice in order to study economics one more hour. It is you who come up with the *subjective* estimate of the expected value of the next-best alternative.

> **▶ Opportunity cost**
> The highest-valued, next-best alternative that must be sacrificed to attain something or to satisfy a want.

The value of the next-best alternative is called its **opportunity cost.** The opportunity cost of any action is the value of what is given up—the next-highest-ranked alternative—because a choice was made. When you study one more hour, there may be many alternatives available for the use of that hour, but you can do only one thing in that hour—your next-highest-ranked alternative. What is important is the choice that you would have made if you hadn't studied one more hour. Your opportunity cost is the *next-highest-ranked* alternative, not *all* alternatives.

> In economics, cost is always a forgone opportunity.

One way to think about opportunity cost is to understand that when you choose to do something, you lose. What you lose is being able to engage in your next-highest-valued alternative. The cost of your choice is what you lose, which is by definition your next-highest-valued alternative. This is your opportunity cost.

⭐ EXAMPLE: How Wild Animals Choose Risk

During the rainy season in Africa, watering holes for zebras and other animals exist virtually everywhere. Many watering holes are relatively open; they are surrounded only by small bushes. When zebras drink at watering holes, they are exposed to their natural predator, lions. Lions will typically surround zebras that are watering (or eating) and try to attack them. But zebras can detect lions at a fairly long distance both by smell and movement.

When one or more lions show up at some distance from a watering hole during the rainy season, zebras will scatter quickly. They run to other watering holes. The actions of zebras start to change when the dry season begins because watering holes begin to disappear. When the dry season lasts longer than normal or turns into a drought, very few watering holes exist. Under those circumstances, zebras take an increasingly longer time before scattering in search of another watering hole. Consequently, lions have a much easier time catching prey for dinner. The zebras face an opportunity cost when they leave a watering hole that actually has water in it. If they run to another watering hole, it may be empty. Hence the longer the drought lasts, the longer the time they decide to remain at any given watering hole that still has water when lions approach. As the opportunity cost of running away rises, zebras in Africa choose to wait longer to run away.

For Critical Analysis: How might the behavior of lions during droughts differ from their behavior during the rainy season? ●

⭐ EXAMPLE: The Opportunity Cost of Going to College

What is the cost of going to college? The obvious costs are the costs of tuition, fees, and textbooks. The obvious costs of going to college do not include room and board because presumably these costs are incurred no matter what you do—go to work or go to school.

The biggest cost of going to college for most individuals is forgone income. That is to say, going to school usually means sacrificing a full-time salary. In the case of a typical 18-year-old, the opportunity cost of going to college may be $15,000 to $20,000 a year. The cost to Bono, lead singer of U2, might have been as high as $5 to $10 million a year! For the successful rock star, actor, or model, the old saw "Get all the education you can" certainly doesn't make much sense. The same can be said for athletes drafted by professional teams before they complete their college education.

Opportunity cost has something to do with one decision by members of rock groups. Ask yourself what the rock groups the Pixies, U2, Nirvana, and Public Enemy have in common. Other than earning high incomes, these groups all consist mainly of individuals who did not attend college between the ages of 18 and 25. You could argue that talented individuals can't stand to be placed in the confines of formal higher education. You could argue that talented and artistic individuals are different from everyone else and therefore don't need to go to college. Or you could use the power of economic analysis to realize that between the ages of 18 and 25, rock stars face a very high opportunity cost for going to college. That is to say, the alternative forgone—working as an entertainer—may yield spectacular incomes.

For Critical Analysis: *What is the opportunity cost of leaving college early for student athletes who join professional teams prior to graduation?* ●

THE WORLD OF TRADE-OFFS

Anytime you engage in any activity using any resource, even time, you are *trading off* the use of that resource for one or more alternative uses. The value of the trade-off is represented by the opportunity cost just discussed. The opportunity cost of studying economics has already been mentioned—it is the value of the next-best alternative. When you think of any alternative, you are thinking of trade-offs.

We are going to examine the trade-off between spending time studying two college subjects, economics and accounting. The more you study economics, it is assumed, the higher will be your expected grade. The more you study accounting, it is assumed, the higher will be your expected grade in that subject. The trade-off, then, is between spending one more hour reading this economics text, for example, and spending that hour reading your accounting text. One of the best ways to examine this trade-off is with a graph. Those of you who would like a refresher on graphic techniques should now study Appendix A at the end of this chapter before going on.

GRAPHIC ANALYSIS

In Figure 2-1 the expected grade in accounting is measured on the vertical axis of the graph. The expected grade in economics is measured on the horizontal axis. We simplify the world and assume that you have a maximum of 10 hours per week to spend studying these two subjects and that if you spend all 10 hours on economics, you will get an A in the course. You will, however, fail accounting. Conversely, if you spend all of your 10 hours studying accounting, you will get an A in that subject, but you will flunk economics. Here the trade-off is a special case: one-to-one. A one-to-one trade-off means that the

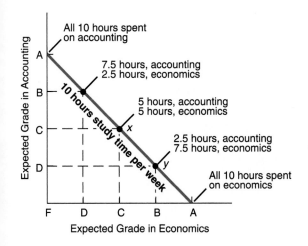

FIGURE 2-1
Production possibilities curve for grades in accounting and economics (trade-offs).
We assume that there are only 10 hours total time that can be spent per week on studying. If the student is at point *x*, equal time (5 hours a week) is spent on both courses and equal grades of C will be received. If a higher grade in economics is desired, the student may go to point *y*, thereby receiving a B in economics but a D in accounting. At point *y*, 2.5 hours are spent on accounting, 7.5 hours on economics.

opportunity cost of receiving one grade higher in economics (for example, improving from a C to a B) is one grade lower in accounting (falling from a C to a D).

THE PRODUCTION POSSIBILITIES CURVE (PPC)

The graph in Figure 2-1 illustrates the relationship between the possible results that can be produced in each of two activities, depending on how much time you choose to devote to each activity. This graph shows a representation of a **production possibilities curve (PPC).**

▶ **Production possibilities curve (PPC)**
A curve representing all possible combinations of total output that could be produced assuming (1) a fixed amount of productive resources of a given quality and (2) the efficient use of those resources.

Consider that you are producing a grade in economics when you study economics and a grade in accounting when you study accounting. Then the graph in Figure 2-1 can be related to the production possibilities that you face, given your background and ability in both activities. The line that goes from A on one axis to A on the other axis therefore becomes a production possibilities curve. It is defined as the maximum quantity of one good or service that can be produced, given that a specific quantity of another is produced. It is a curve that shows the possibilities available for increasing the output of one good or service by reducing the amount of another. In the example, your time for studying was limited to 10 hours per week. The two possible outputs were grades in accounting and grades in economics. The particular production possibilities curve presented in Figure 2-1 is a graphic representation of the opportunity cost of studying one more hour in one subject. It is a *straight-line production possibilities curve,* which is a special case. (The more general case will be discussed next.) If you decide to be at point *x* in Figure 2-1, 5 hours of study time will be spent on accounting and 5 hours will be spent on economics. The expected grade in each course will be a C. If you are more interested in getting a B in economics, you will go to point *y* on the production possibilities curve, spending only 2.5 hours on accounting but 7.5 hours on economics. Your expected grade in accounting will then drop from a C to a D.

Note that these trade-offs between expected grades in accounting and economics are the result of *holding constant* total study time as well as all other factors that might influence a student's ability to learn, such as computerized study aids. Quite clearly, if you wished to spend more total time studying, it would be possible to have higher grades in both economics and accounting. In that case, however, we would no longer be on the specific production possibilities curve illustrated in Figure 2-1. We would have to draw a new curve, farther to the right, to show the greater total study time and a different set of possible trade-offs.

CONCEPTS IN BRIEF

- Scarcity requires us to choose. When we choose, we lose the next-highest-valued alternative.
- Cost is always a forgone opportunity. To determine opportunity cost, we will look only at the highest-valued alternative.
- Another way to look at opportunity cost is the trade-off that occurs when one resource or activity is used rather than the next-best alternative resource or activity.
- A production possibilities curve (PPC) graphically shows the trade-off necessary when more of one output is obtained at the sacrifice of another. The PPC is a graphic representation of, among other things, opportunity cost.

THE CHOICES SOCIETY FACES

The straight-line production possibilities curve presented in Figure 2-1 can be generalized to demonstrate the related concepts of scarcity, choice, and trade-offs that our entire nation faces. The example we will use is the choice between the production of M-16 semiautomatic rifles and videodisc players. We assume for the moment that these are the only two goods that can be produced in the nation. Panel (a) of Figure 2-2 gives the various combinations of M-16s and videodisc players that are possible. If all resources are devoted to M-16 production, 10 billion per year can be produced. If all resources are devoted to videodisc production, 12 billion per year can be produced. In between are various possible combinations. These combinations are plotted as points *A, B, C, D, E, F,* and

FIGURE 2-2

Society's trade-off between M-16 rifles and videodisc players.

Both the production of M-16 semiautomatic rifles and the production of videodisc players are measured in billions of units per year. The various combinations are given in panel (a) and plotted in panel (b). Connecting the points *A–G* with a relatively smooth line gives the society's production possibilities curve for M-16 rifles and videodisc players. Point *R* lies outside the production possibilities curve and is therefore unattainable at the point in time for which the graph is drawn. Point *S* lies inside the production possibilities curve and therefore represents an inefficient use of available resources.

Panel (a)

COMBINATION	M-16 RIFLES (BILLIONS OF UNITS PER YEAR)	VIDEODISC PLAYERS (BILLIONS OF UNITS PER YEAR)
A	10.0	0
B	9.6	2
C	9.0	4
D	8.0	6
E	6.6	8
F	4.5	10
G	0	12

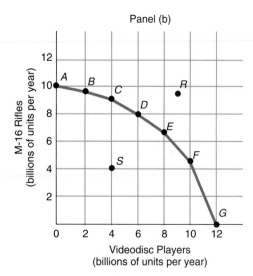

Panel (b)

G in panel (b) of Figure 2-2. If these points are connected with a smooth curve, the nation's production possibilities curve is shown, demonstrating the trade-off between the production of M-16 semiautomatic rifles and videodisc players. These trade-offs occur *on* the production possibilities curve.

Notice the major difference in the shape of the production possibilities curves in Figures 2-1 and 2-2. In Figure 2-1 there is a one-to-one trade-off between grades in economics and in accounting. In Figure 2-2 the trade-off between videodisc production and M-16 production is not constant, and therefore the production possibilities curve is a *bowed* line. To understand why the production possibilities curve for a society is typically bowed outward, you must understand the assumptions underlying the PPC.

ASSUMPTIONS UNDERLYING THE PRODUCTION POSSIBILITIES CURVE

When we draw the curve that is shown in Figure 2-2, we make the following assumptions:

1. That resources are fully employed
2. That we are looking at production over a specific time period, for example one year
3. That the resource inputs used to produce M-16 rifles or videodisc players are fixed over this one-year time period
4. That the labor force remains the same and that skill levels remain the same
5. That capital inputs remain the same
6. That technology does not change over this time period.

▶ **Technology**
Society's pool of applied knowledge concerning how goods and services can be produced.

Technology is defined as society's pool of applied knowledge concerning how goods and services can be produced by managers, workers, engineers, scientists, and craftspeople, using land and capital. You can think of technology as the formula (or recipe) used to combine factors of production. (When better formulas are developed, more production can be obtained from the same amount of resources.) The level of technology sets the limit on the amount and types of goods and services that we can derive from any given amount of resources. The production possibilities curve is drawn under the assumption that we use the best technology that we currently have available and that this technology doesn't change over the time period under study. When we draw a PPC, as in Figure 2-2, we assume that no invention that would reduce the cost of producing either good has occurred.

BEING OFF THE PRODUCTION POSSIBILITIES CURVE

Look again at panel (b) of Figure 2-2. Point *R* lies to the *outside* of the production possibilities curve. Point *R* is *impossible* to achieve during the time period assumed. By definition, the production possibilities curve indicates the *maximum* quantity of one good available given some quantity of the other.

It is possible, however, to be at point *S* in Figure 2-2. That point lies beneath the production possibilities curve. If the nation is at point *S*, it means that its resources are not being fully utilized. This occurs, for example, during periods of unemployment. Point *S* and all such points within the production possibilities curve are always attainable but usually not desirable.

EFFICIENCY

The production possibilities curve can be used to define the notion of efficiency. Whenever the economy is operating on the PPC, at points such as *A, B, C,* or *D,* we say that it is operating efficiently. Points such as *S* in Figure 2-2, which lie beneath the production possibilities curve, are said to represent situations that are not efficient.

Efficiency can mean many things to many people. Even within economics there are different types of efficiency. Here we are discussing efficiency in production, or productive efficiency. An economy is efficient whenever it is producing the maximum output with given technology and resources.

A simple commonsense definition of efficiency is getting the most out of what we have as an economy. Clearly, we are not getting the most that we have if we are at point *S* in panel (b) of Figure 2-2. We can move from point *S* to, say, point *C*, thereby increasing the total quantity of M-16s produced without any decrease in the total quantity of videodisc players produced. We can move from point *S* to point *E*, for example, and have both more M-16s and more videodisc players. Point *S* is called an **inefficient point,** which is defined as any point not lying on the production possibilities curve and is below it.

> ▶ **Efficiency**
> The situation in which a given output is produced at minimum cost. Alternatively, the case in which a given level of inputs is used to produce the maximum output possible.

> ▶ **Inefficient point**
> Any point that does not lie on the production possibilities curve (and is below it), at which resources are being used inefficiently.

THE LAW OF INCREASING COSTS

In the example in Figure 2-1, the trade-off between a grade in accounting and a grade in economics is one to one. The trade-off ratio was fixed. That is to say, the production possibilities curve was a straight line. The curve in Figure 2-2 is a more general case. It is bowed outward. The opportunity cost of obtaining more and more M-16s rises. That is to say, each additional M-16 costs society more in forgone alternatives in terms of producing videodisc players. We can see this more clearly in Figure 2-3. Each increment in M-16 output is the same, but look at what the nation has to give up in videodisc production when we go from the next-to-the-last M-16 produced to the last unit, which occurs when the entire economy is producing only M-16s. The opportunity cost is large relative to what an equivalent increase in M-16 production costs society when we start with none being produced at all.

Figure 2-3 is a graphic representation of the **law of increasing relative cost.** As society takes more and more resources and applies them to the production of any specific item, the opportunity cost increases for each additional unit produced. The reason that as a nation we face the law of increasing relative cost (which causes the production possibilities curve to bow outward) is that some resources are better suited for producing some goods than they are for other goods. Economic resources are not generally *perfectly* adaptable for alternative uses. Take an obvious example: the nation shifting from production of only wheat to progressive increments of production of oranges. The first increment of oranges will be grown in a suitable climate, such as in Florida or California. Eventually, though, we would find that we would have to give up a tremendous amount of wheat production in order to grow oranges in Minnesota. Some resources are simply better suited for orange production than other resources.

> ▶ **Law of increasing relative costs**
> The observation that the opportunity cost of additional units of a good generally increases as society attempts to produce more of that good. This causes the bowed-out shape of the production possibilities curve.

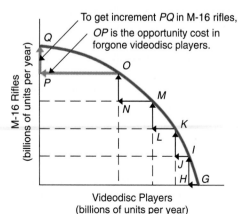

To get increment *PQ* in M-16 rifles, *OP* is the opportunity cost in forgone videodisc players.

M-16 Rifles (billions of units per year)

Videodisc Players (billions of units per year)

FIGURE 2-3
The law of increasing relative costs.
Consider equal increments in M-16 rifle production, as measured on the vertical axis in this diagram. All the vertical arrows—*HI, JK, LM, NO* and *PQ*—are of equal length. What is the cost to society of obtaining the first such increment in M-16 production? It is a reduction in videodisc player output, *GH*. This cost for each additional equal increment in M-16 production rises. Finally, to get the last increment in M-16 production, *PQ*, society must give up the entire distance *OP* in videodisc player production. The opportunity cost of each additional equal increase in M-16 production rises.

Consider being at point *G* in Figure 2-3. Here we are producing only videodisc players. War is declared. More M-16s are demanded. The nation desires to move from point *G* to point *I, K, M,* or *O* in Figure 2-3. But to do so requires more and more resources to shift from videodisc production to M-16 production. As this is done, fewer and fewer of those resources will be so easily adaptable to M-16 production. As more and more ill-suited resources are shifted into M-16 production, the opportunity cost in terms of videodisc player production given up for additional M-16 production will increase.

As a rule of thumb, *the more highly specialized the resources, the more bowed the production possibilities curve will be.* At the other extreme, if all resources are equally suitable for videodisc production or M-16 production, the curves in Figures 2-2 and 2-3 would simply approach the straight line shown in our first example in Figure 2-1.

Alternatively, in our first example of studying accounting and economics, a student with a greater aptitude for economics than accounting will find that his or her production possibilities curve in Figure 2-1 will be bowed outward.

⭐ EXAMPLE: The Real-Life Problems of Downsizing the Military

From the 1950s to the beginning of the 1990s, about half of America's defense spending was devoted to opposing the Soviet Union. When the Soviet Union "went out of business," the United States no longer needed bombers to avoid Soviet radar, nor did it need sophisticated hardware to hunt Soviet nuclear submarines. The downsizing of the American military might has meant a movement along the production possibilities curve from M-16s (military expenditures) to more videodiscs (all other expenditures). Theoretically, we can think of the movement after the Cold War from point *K* to point *I* in Figure 2-3. But the real world and our graphs aren't quite the same. In the real world it takes time to move from point *K* to point *I* in Figure 2-3. All the while, we are not really operating on the production possibilities curve.

Just consider that from 1985 to 1994, defense spending fell by more than one-fifth. By the year 2000 the defense budget will be considerably lower. This has a profound effect on businesses that sold most or all of their output to the military. The Pentagon's prime contractors—McDonnell Douglas, Northrop, Lockheed, General Dynamics, Rockwell, and Grumman—have taken the hardest hits; so too will General Motors (which owns Hughes Aircraft), General Electric (which builds submarines), and Boeing. Each of these large businesses is supported by small subcontractors, many of whom will also be hurt.

Some of the projects that have been abandoned or reduced involve the B-2 Stealth bomber, the Seawolf submarine, and the F-22 fighter jet. The Pentagon has also reduced its $40 billion annual research budget.

Some of the companies that make military hardware and do military research have adjusted and entered civilian markets. A small defense contractor, Harris Corporation, was able to outbid AT&T to obtain a $1.66 billion contract to build a new civilian air traffic control system. But the larger defense contractors have had a less easy time. It is hard to imagine that the big defense contractors such as General Dynamics could actually sell "civilian" submarines or tanks. And because they have gotten into new businesses with which they are not familiar, such as making buses, they have lost income. At any rate, it is still true that some resources are better used when making some products than others. What will probably happen is that these companies will simply shrink in size along with the U.S. military budget.

For Critical Analysis: What other countries are most likely facing similar downsizing problems with their military production facilities? What are some competing claims on resources currently used by defense contractors in the United States? ●

INTERNATIONAL EXAMPLE: Military Spending Versus Development Programs

Major problems of poverty and disease exist throughout the world. Developed nations such as the United States provide resources to the developing countries to improve their situation. The U.S. government, for example, provided over $400 million in 1993 for international family programs. In 1992 the Bush administration offered $150 million to fight deforestation in developing nations. But given that there are over 5.5 billion people on earth, such sums of money are relatively small. Indeed, expressed as a percentage of total yearly national income, the United States spends less than .25 percent on official development assistance programs. At the same time, in spite of the downsizing of the military, almost 5 percent of annual national income is devoted to defense.

Internationally, the trade-off between military spending and official development assistance is quite different across nations. Look at Figure 2-4. Here you see the percentage of annual national income for various members of the Organization for Economic Co-operation and Development (OECD). Norway, for example, devotes over 1 percent of its annual national income to official development assistance, compared to 3 percent on military spending. Norway has chosen to be at a different point on its military spending–development assistance production possibilities curve than we have chosen in the United States.

For Critical Analysis: Does the downsizing of the U.S. military necessarily mean that more of our resources will be spent on official development assistance? Why or why not? ●

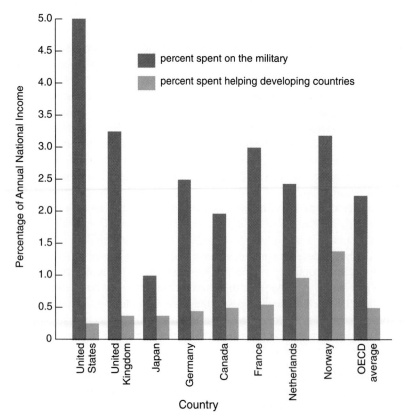

FIGURE 2-4
Military spending versus official development assistance.
This bar graph shows how much more money countries spend on the military than on helping developing nations. The percentage of annual national income going to the military is about five percent in the United States; less than .25 percent goes toward helping developing nations.

Source: U.S. Department of Commerce and United Nations. Data are estimates for 1992.

> **CONCEPTS IN BRIEF**
> ● Trade-offs are represented graphically by a production possibilities curve showing the maximum quantity of one good or service that can be produced, given a specific quantity of another, from a given set of resources over a specified period of time, for example one year.
> ● A PPC is drawn holding the quantity and quality of all resources fixed over the time period under study.
> ● Points outside the production possibilities curve are unattainable; points inside are attainable but represent an inefficient use or underuse of available resources.
> ● Because many resources are better suited for certain productive tasks than for others, society's production possibilities curve is bowed outward, following the law of increasing relative cost.

ECONOMIC GROWTH AND THE PRODUCTION POSSIBILITIES CURVE

Over any particular time period, a society cannot be outside the production possibilities curve. Over time, however, it is possible to have more of everything. This occurs through economic growth (why economic growth occurs will be discussed in a later chapter). Figure 2-5 shows the production possibilities curve for M-16 rifles and videodisc players shifting outward. The two additional curves shown represent new choices open to an economy that has experienced economic growth. Such economic growth occurs because of many things, including increases in the number of workers and productive investment in equipment, for example.

Scarcity still exists, however, no matter how much economic growth there is. At any point in time, we will always be on some production possibilities curve; thus we will always face trade-offs. The more we want of one thing, the less we will have of others.

If a nation experiences economic growth, the production possibilities curve between M-16 rifles and videodisc players will move outward, as is shown in Figure 2-5. This takes time and does not occur automatically. One reason it will occur involves the choice about how much to consume today.

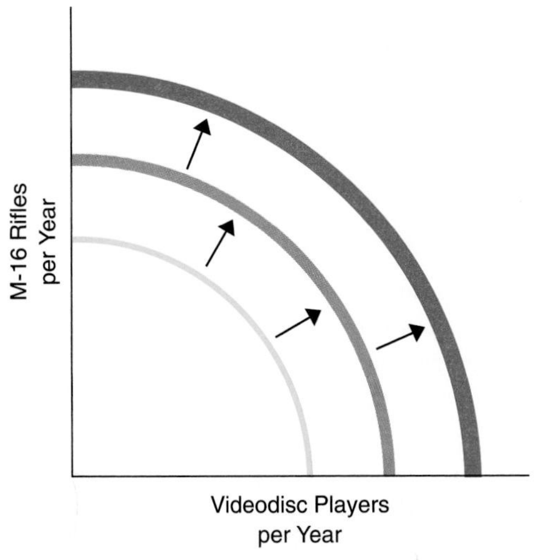

FIGURE 2-5
Economic growth allows for more of everything.
If the nation experiences economic growth, the production possibilities curve between M-16 rifles and videodisc players will move out, as is shown. This takes time, however, and it does not occur automatically. This means, therefore, that we can have more M-16s and more videodisc players only after a period of time during which we have experienced economic growth.

THE TRADE-OFF BETWEEN THE PRESENT AND THE FUTURE

The production possibilities curve and economic growth can be used to examine the trade-off between present consumption and future consumption. When we consume today, we are using up what we call consumption or consumer goods—food and clothes, for example. And we have already defined capital as the goods and services, such as machines and factories, used to make other goods and services.

WHY WE MAKE CAPITAL GOODS

Why would we be willing to use productive resources to make things—capital goods—that we cannot consume directly? For one thing, capital goods enable us to produce larger quantities of consumer goods or to produce them more inexpensively than we otherwise could. Before fish are "produced" for the market, equipment such as fishing boats, nets, and poles are produced first. Imagine how expensive it would be to obtain fish for market without using these capital goods. Catching fish with one's hands is not an easy task. The price per fish would be very high if capital goods weren't used.

FORGOING CURRENT CONSUMPTION

Whenever we use productive resources to make capital goods, we are implicitly forgoing current consumption. We are waiting for some time in the future to consume the fruits that will be reaped from the use of capital goods. In effect, when we forgo current consumption to invest in capital goods, we are engaging in an economic activity that is forward-looking—we do not get instant utility or satisfaction from our activity. Indeed, if we were to produce only consumer goods now and no capital goods, our capacity to produce consumer goods in the future would suffer. Here we see a trade-off situation.

THE TRADE-OFF BETWEEN CONSUMPTION GOODS AND CAPITAL GOODS

To have more consumer goods in the future, we must accept fewer consumer goods today. In other words, an *opportunity cost* is involved here. Every time we make a choice for more goods today, we incur an opportunity cost of fewer goods tomorrow, and every time we make a choice of more goods in the future, we incur an opportunity cost of fewer goods today. With the resources that we don't use to produce consumer goods for today, we invest in capital goods that will produce more consumer goods for us later. The trade-off is depicted in Figure 2-6. On the left in panel (a) you can see this trade-off depicted as a production possibilities curve between capital goods and consumption goods.

Assume that we are willing to give up $1 trillion worth of consumption today. We will be at point A in the left-hand diagram of panel (a). This will allow the economy to grow. We will have more future consumption because we invested in more capital goods today. In the right-hand diagram of panel (a) we see two goods represented, food and recreation. The production possibilities curve will move outward if we collectively decide to restrict consumption each year and invest in capital goods—that is, if we agree to be at point A.

In panel (b) we show the results of our willingness to forgo more current consumption. We move to point C, where we have many fewer consumer goods today but produce a lot more capital goods. This leads to more future growth in this simplified model, and thus the production possibilities curve in the right-hand side of panel (b) shifts outward more than it did in the right-hand side of panel (a).

In other words, the more we give up today, the more we can have tomorrow, provided, of course, that the capital goods are productive in future periods and that society desires the consumer goods produced by this additional capital.

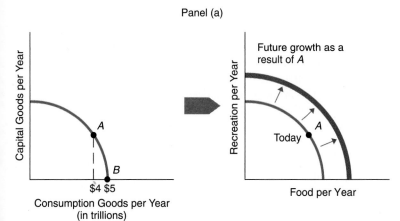

Panel (a)

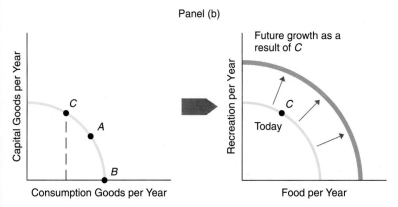

Panel (b)

FIGURE 2-6
Capital goods and growth.
In panel (a), the nation chooses to not consume $1 trillion, so it invests that amount of capital goods. In panel (b), it chooses even more capital goods. The PPC moves even more to the right in panel (b) as a result.

CONCEPTS IN BRIEF

- The use of capital requires using productive resources to produce capital goods that will later be used to produce consumer goods.
- A trade-off is involved between current consumption and capital goods, or, alternatively, between current consumption and future consumption, because the more we invest in capital goods today, the greater the amount of consumer goods we can produce in the future.

SPECIALIZATION AND GREATER PRODUCTIVITY

▶ **Specialization**
The division of productive activities among persons and regions so that no one individual or one area is totally self-sufficient. An individual may specialize, for example, in law or medicine. A nation may specialize in the production of coffee, computers, or cameras.

Specialization involves working at a relatively well defined, limited endeavor, such as accounting or teaching. Most individuals in fact do specialize. For example, you could, if you wanted to, change the oil in your car. Typically, though, you take your car to a garage and let the mechanic change the oil. You benefit by letting the garage mechanic specialize in changing the oil and in doing other repairs on your car. The specialist will get the job finished sooner than you could and has the proper equipment to make the job go more smoothly. Specialization usually leads to greater productivity, not only for each individual but also for the nation.

ABSOLUTE ADVANTAGE

Specialization occurs because different individuals and different nations have different skills. Sometimes it seems that some individuals are better at doing everything than anyone else. A president of a large company might be able to type better than any of the typists, file better than any of the file clerks, and wash windows better than any of the window washers. The president has an **absolute advantage** in all of these endeavors—he uses fewer labor hours for each task than anyone else in the company. The president does not, however, spend his time doing those other activities. Why not? Because he is being paid the most for undertaking the president's managerial duties. The president specializes in one particular task in spite of having an absolute advantage in all tasks. Indeed, absolute advantage is irrelevant; only comparative advantage matters.

COMPARATIVE ADVANTAGE

Comparative advantage is found by choosing the activity that has the lowest opportunity cost. You have a comparative advantage in one activity whenever you have the lowest opportunity cost of performing that activity. Comparative advantage is always a *relative* concept. You may be able to change the oil in your car; you might even be able to change it faster than the local mechanic. But if the opportunity cost you face by changing the oil exceeds the mechanic's opportunity cost, the specialist has a comparative advantage in changing the oil. The mechanic faces a lower opportunity cost for that activity.

You may be convinced that everybody can do everything better than you. In this extreme situation, do you still have a comparative advantage? The answer is yes. What you need to do to discover your comparative advantage is to find a job in which your *disadvantage* relative to others is the smallest. You do not have to be a mathematical genius to figure this out. The market tells you very clearly by offering you the highest income for the job for which you have the smallest disadvantage compared to others. Stated differently, to find your comparative advantage no matter how much better everybody else can do the jobs that you want to do, you simply find which job maximizes your income.

The coaches of sports teams are constantly faced with determining each player's comparative advantage. Babe Ruth was originally one of the best pitchers in professional baseball when he played for the Boston Red Sox. After he was traded to the New York Yankees, the owner and the coach decided to make him an outfielder, even though he was a better pitcher than anyone else on the team roster. They wanted "The Babe" to concentrate on his hitting. Good pitchers do not bring in as many fans as home-run kings. Babe Ruth's comparative advantage was clearly in hitting homers rather than practicing and developing his pitching game.

SCARCITY, SELF-INTEREST, AND SPECIALIZATION

In Chapter 1 you learned about the self-interest assumption. To repeat, for the purposes of our analyses we assume that individuals are rational in that they will do what is in their own self-interest. They will not consciously carry out actions that will make them worse off. In this chapter you learned that scarcity requires people to make choices. We assume that they make choices based on their self-interest. When they make these choices, they attempt to minimize their opportunity cost. In so doing, individuals choose their comparative advantage and end up specializing. Ultimately, when people specialize, they increase the money income they make and therefore are richer. When all individuals and businesses specialize simultaneously, the gains are seen in greater material well-being. With any given set of resources, specialization will result in higher output.

INTERNATIONAL EXAMPLE: Trading with Mexico

For several years there have been negotiations over a free trade treaty with Mexico. Advocates of such a treaty want virtually all restrictions on trade between the United States and Mexico to be eliminated. Currently, Mexico has a comparative advantage in such labor-intensive industries as tile making and clothing. This is because of the relatively low

▶ **Absolute advantage**
The ability to produce a good or service at an "absolutely" lower cost, usually measured in units of labor or resource input required to produce one unit of the good.

▶ **Comparative advantage**
The ability to produce a good or service at a lower opportunity cost.

cost of labor there: Mexican workers earn about one-tenth the average wage in the United States. We can therefore expect that as more restrictions are lifted on trade with Mexico, Mexico will export more labor-intensive products, such as clothes, that can be produced there at a lower price than in the United States.

In contrast, the United States has a comparative advantage in goods that require lots of technology or highly skilled labor. Compared to Mexico, we have a comparative advantage in machine tools and dies and computers. These are just the kind of goods that Mexican industries need to expand their own production. Consequently, freer trade with Mexico will see the United States exporting more goods, such as computers, to Mexico. The United States also has a comparative advantage in such services as marketing. Mexican firms, as they expand production, will demand more marketing services from the United States. In any event, it will take time to adjust.

For Critical Analysis: More free trade with Mexico will cause some groups in each country to be better off and some groups to be worse off. Which groups do you think will be made worse off in the United States? In Mexico? Explain your answer. ●

THE DIVISION OF LABOR

▶ **Division of labor**
The segregation of a resource into different specific tasks; for example, one automobile worker puts on bumpers, another doors, and so on.

In any firm that includes specialized human and nonhuman resources, there is a **division of labor** among those resources. The best-known example of all time comes from one of the earliest and perhaps one of the most famous economists, Adam Smith, who in *The Wealth of Nations* (1776) illustrated the benefits of a division of labor in the making of pins with this example:

> One man draws out the wire, another straightens it, a third cuts it, a fourth points it, a fifth grinds it at the top for receiving the head; to make the head requires two or three distinct operations; to put it on is a peculiar business, to whiten the pins is another; it is even a trade by itself to put them into the paper.

Making pins this way allowed 10 workers without very much skill to make almost 48,000 pins "of a middling size" in a day. One worker, toiling alone, could have made perhaps 20 pins a day; therefore, 10 workers could have produced 200. Division of labor allowed for an increase in the daily output of the pin factory from 200 to 48,000! (Smith did not attribute all of the gain to the division of labor according to talent but credited also the use of machinery and the fact that less time was spent shifting from task to task).

What we are discussing here involves a division of the resource called labor into different kinds of labor. The different kinds of labor are organized in such a way as to increase the amount of output possible from the fixed resources available. We can therefore talk about an organized division of labor within a firm leading to increased output.

CONCEPTS IN BRIEF

- With a given set of resources, specialization results in higher output; in other words, there are gains to specialization in terms of greater material well-being.
- Individuals and nations specialize in their comparative advantages in order to reap the gains of specialization.
- Comparative advantages are found by determining which activities have the lowest opportunity cost, that is, which activities yield the highest return for the time and resources used.
- A division of labor occurs when different workers are assigned different tasks. Together, the workers produce a desired product.

CONTINUED LIFE VERSUS THE ENVIRONMENT

Concepts Applied: Trade-offs, opportunity cost

The bark of the Pacific Yew tree *(Taxus brevifolia)* can be used to produce the cancer-fighting drug taxol, but the tree has to be cut down to do so. Recently, scientists have discovered how to make taxol from the Yew tree's needles, without cutting down the tree. And a synthetic version of taxol may be developed soon.

Every year more than 10,000 women are diagnosed with ovarian cancer. This cancer is often fatal, but some of these women are being saved. The cost of doing so is extremely high, according to concerned environmentalists. The relatively new cure for ovarian cancer is taxol. Taxol is found in the Pacific yew trees located in America's Northwest. There are about 13 million such trees. This may sound like a lot, but it isn't compared to the need to cut them down to yield taxol. It takes about 750,000 pounds of bark to make enough taxol to treat the 10,000 or so women who might otherwise die of ovarian cancer each year. That means that 150,000 trees have to be cut each year.

THE ENVIRONMENTAL TRADE-OFF Environmentalists are concerned. They, of course, do not want to be accused of being insensitive to death. Notwithstanding such concerns, they point out that yew trees grow in old-growth forests that have taken hundreds of years to develop. Logging of the yews in such areas could damage other trees as well as plants and animals there. Environmentalists contend that yew tree resources are finite. They also point out that taxol may be found to be effective in treating breast and lung cancer. If that is the case, the amount required by the medical profession could grow by 10 to 15 times, thereby further endangering the yew forest.

TECHNOLOGICAL ALTERNATIVES Biomedical companies are working on an alternative way to obtain taxol. Medi-Molecules, of Boulder, Colorado, thinks that it can extract taxol from the needles of the yew. There are also a few chemists who believe that eventually they can produce a synthetic taxol molecule. These alternatives may take years to develop. In the meantime, the public-policy decision is a clear trade-off: saving women who are dying from ovarian cancer or saving Pacific yew trees.

FOR CRITICAL ANALYSIS

1. What is the opportunity cost of saving yew trees? What is the opportunity cost of saving the lives of women suffering from ovarian cancer who could be treated with taxol?
2. Do all environmentalist attempts at saving plants and animals involve an opportunity cost? Why or why not?

CHAPTER SUMMARY

1. All societies at all times face the universal problem of scarcity because we cannot all obtain everything we want from nature without sacrifice. Thus scarcity and poverty are not synonymous. Even the richest persons face scarcity because they also have to make choices among alternatives.
2. The resources we use to produce desired goods and services can be classified into land, labor, capital, and entrepreneurship.

3. Goods are anything from which individuals derive satisfaction. Economic goods are those for which the desired quantity exceeds the amount that is directly available from nature at a zero price. The goods that we want are not necessarily those that we need. The term *need* is undefinable in economics, whereas humans have unlimited *wants,* which are defined as the goods and services on which we place a positive value.

4. We measure the cost of anything by what has to be given up in order to have it. This cost is called opportunity cost.

5. The trade-offs you face as an individual and we all face as a society can be represented graphically by a production possibilities curve (PPC) showing the maximum quantity of one good or service that can be produced, given a specific quantity of another, from a given set of resources over a specified period of time, usually one year.

6. Because resources are specialized, production possibilities curves bow outward. That means that each additional increment of one good can be obtained only by giving up more and more of the other goods. This is called the law of increasing relative cost.

7. It is impossible to be outside the production possibilities curve, but we can be inside it. When we are, we are in a situation of unemployment, inefficiently organized resources, or some combination of the two.

8. There is a trade-off between consumption goods and capital goods. The more resources we devote to capital goods, the more consumption goods we can normally have in the future (and less currently). This is because more capital goods allow the economy to grow, thereby moving the production possibilities curve outward.

9. One finds one's comparative advantage by looking at the activity that has the lowest opportunity cost. That is, one's comparative advantage lies in the activity that generates the highest income. Thus by specializing in one's comparative advantage, one is assured of reaping the gains of specialization.

DISCUSSION OF PREVIEW POINTS

1. **Do affluent people face the problem of scarcity?**
   Scarcity is a relative concept; scarcity exists because wants are great relative to the means of satisfying those wants (wealth or income). Thus even though affluent people have relatively and absolutely high levels of income or wealth, they nevertheless typically want more than they can have (in luxury goods, power, prestige, and so on).

2. **Fresh air and clean water may be consumed at no charge, but are they free of cost to society?**
   Air is free to individuals in the United States; specific individuals are not charged a price for the use of this good. Yet this good is not free to society. If a good were free to society, every person would be able to use all that he or she wanted to use; no one would have to sacrifice anything in order to use that good, and people would not have to compete for it. In the United States different groups compete for air and water. Environmentalists and concerned citizens compete with automobile drivers for clean air and with factories for clean water.

3. **Why does the scarcity problem force people to consider opportunity costs?**
   Individuals have limited incomes; as a consequence, an expenditure on an automobile necessarily precludes expenditures on other goods and services. The same is true for society, which also faces the scarcity problem; if society allocates specific resources to the production of a steel mill, those same resources cannot be allocated elsewhere. Because resources are limited, society is forced to decide how to allocate its available resources; scarcity means that the cost of allocating resources to produce specific goods is ultimately assessed in terms of other goods that are necessarily sacrificed. Because there are millions of ways in which the resources allocated to a steel mill might otherwise be allocated, one is forced to consider the *highest-valued* alternative. We define the opportunity cost of a good as its highest-valued alternative; the opportunity cost of the steel mill to society is the highest-valued output that those same resources could otherwise have produced.

4. **Can a "free" college education ever be truly free?**
   Suppose that you were given a college education without having to pay any fees whatsoever. You could say that you were receiving a free education. But someone is paying for your education because you are using scarce resources—buildings, professors' time, electricity for lighting, and so on. The opportunity cost of your education is certainly not zero, so in that sense it is not free. Furthermore, by going to college, you are giving up the ability to earn income during that time period. Therefore, there is an opportunity cost to your attending classes and studying. You can approximate that opportunity cost by estimating what your after-tax income would be if you were working instead of going to school.

PROBLEMS
(Answers to odd-numbered problems appear at the back of the book.)

2-1. The following sets of numbers represent hypothetical production possibilities for a nation in 1994. Plot these points on graph paper.

BUTTER	GUNS
4	0
3	1.6
2	2.4
1	2.8
0	3.0

Does the law of increasing relative costs seem to hold? Why? On the same graph, now plot and draw the production possibilities curve that will represent 10 percent economic growth.

2-2. Assume that a business has found that its most profitable output occurs when it produces $172 worth of output of a particular product. It can choose from three possible techniques, A, B, and C, that will produce the desired level of output. In the following table we see the amount of inputs these techniques use along with each input price.

PRICE OF INPUT (PER UNIT)	INPUT	PRODUCTION TECHNIQUES		
		A (UNITS)	B (UNITS)	C (UNITS)
$10	Land	7	4	1
2	Labor	6	7	18
15	Capital	2	6	3
8	Entrepreneurship	1	3	2

a. Which technique will the firm choose, and why?
b. What would the firm's maximum profit be?
c. If the price of labor increases to $4 per unit, which technique will be chosen, and why? What will happen to profits?

2-3. Answer the questions using the following information.

EMPLOYEE	DAILY WORK EFFORT	PRODUCTION
Ann Jones	4 hours	8 jackets
	4 hours	12 ties
Ned Lopez	4 hours	8 jackets
	4 hours	12 ties
Total daily output		16 jackets
		24 ties

a. Who has an absolute advantage in jacket production?
b. Who has a comparative advantage in tie production?
c. Will Jones and Lopez specialize?
d. If they specialize, what will total output equal?

2-4. Two countries, Workland and Playland, have similar populations and identical production possibilities curves. The production possibilities schedule is as follows:

POINT	CAPITAL GOODS	CONSUMPTION GOODS
A	0	20
B	1	19
C	2	17
D	3	14
E	4	10
F	5	5

Playland is located at point B of the PPC, and Workland is located at point E. Assume that this pattern continues into the future.

a. What is Workland's opportunity cost of capital goods in terms of consumption goods?
b. What is Playland's opportunity cost of capital goods in terms of consumption goods?
c. How would the PPCs of Workland and Playland be expected to compare to each other 50 years in the future?

2-5. Which of the following are part of the opportunity cost of going to a football game in town instead of watching it on TV at home? Explain why.
   a. The expense of lunch in a restaurant prior to the football game.
   b. The value of one hour of sleep lost because of a traffic jam after the game.
   c. The expense of a babysitter for your children if they are too young to go to a football game.

2-6. Assume that your economics and English exams are scheduled for the same day. How would you determine how much time you should spend studying for each exam? Does the grade you are currently receiving in each course affect your decision? Why or why not?

2-7. Some people argue that air is not an economic good. If you agree with this statement, explain why. If you disagree, explain why. (Hint: Is all air the same?)

COMPUTER-ASSISTED INSTRUCTION
(Complete problem and answer on disk.)

If you are given a production possibilities table, can you calculate the opportunity cost of successive units of one good in terms of forgone units of the other? By requiring specific calculations, the concept of opportunity cost is revealed.

appendix a

READING AND WORKING WITH GRAPHS

A picture is worth a thousand words, it has been said—and so is a graph! It is often easier to communicate an idea by using a picture than to read or listen to a lengthy description. A graph performs much the same function as a picture. A graph is a visual representation of the relationship between variables. In this appendix we'll stick to just two variables—an **independent variable,** which can change in value freely, and a **dependent variable,** which changes only as a result of changes in the value of the independent variable. For example, if nothing else is changing in your life, your weight depends on the amount of food you eat. Food is the independent variable and weight the dependent variable.

Before we present the "picture," that is, a graph, let's return to the "thousand words," that is, a table. A table is a list of numerical values showing the relationship between two (or more) variables. Any table can be converted into a graph, which is a visual representation of that list. Once you understand how a table can be converted to a graph, you will understand what graphs are and how to construct and use them.

Consider a practical example. A conservationist may try to convince you that driving at lower highway speeds will help you conserve gas. Table A-1 shows the relationship between speed—the independent variable—and the distance you can go on a gallon of gas at that speed—the dependent variable.

This table does show a pattern of sorts. As the data in the first column get larger in value, the data in the second column get smaller.

Now let's take a look at the different ways in which variables can be related.

DIRECT AND INVERSE RELATIONSHIPS

Two variables can be related in different ways, some simple, others more complex. For example, a person's weight and height are often related. If we measured the height and weight of thousands of people, we would surely find that taller people tend to weigh more than shorter people. That is, we would discover that there is a **direct relationship** between height and weight. By this we simply mean that an *increase* in one variable is usually associated with an *increase* in the related variable. This can easily be seen in panel (a) of Figure A-1.

Let's look at another simple way in which two variables can be related. Much evidence indicates that as the price of a specific commodity rises, the amount purchased decreases—there is an **inverse relationship** between the variable's price per unit and quantity purchased. A table listing the data for this relationship would indicate that for higher and higher prices, smaller and smaller quantities would be purchased. We see this relationship in panel (b) of Figure A-1.

Now for a slightly more complicated relationship between two variables: Beginning with the average person's first job, earnings increase each year up to a certain age; be-

▶ **Independent variable**
A variable whose value is determined independently of, or outside, the equation under study.

▶ **Dependent variable**
A variable whose value changes according to changes in the value of one or more independent variables.

TABLE A-1 **Gas consumption as a function of driving speed.**

MILES PER HOUR	MILES PER GALLON
45	25
50	24
55	23
60	21
65	19
70	16
75	13

▶ **Direct relationship**
A relationship between two variables that is positive, meaning that an increase in one is associated with an increase in the other and a decrease in one is associated with a decrease in the other.

▶ **Inverse relationship**
A relationship that is negative, meaning that an increase in one variable is associated with a decrease in the other and a decrease in one variable is associated with an increase in the other.

FIGURE A-1
Relationships.
The curve in panel (a) shows a simple direct relationship between the variables. The
curve in panel (b) shows a simple inverse relationship. The curve in panel (c) shows a
complex relationship that changes from direct to inverse.

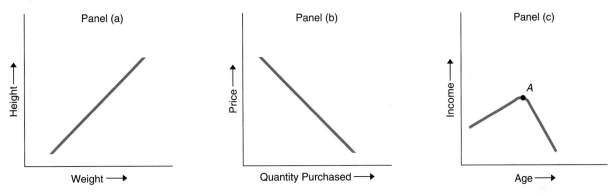

yond that age, however, earnings decline each year. This is not a surprising economic research finding. Most people are more energetic and productive in the early and middle
years of life. In this example the two variables—earnings and age—would yield a more
complex pattern. At earlier ages these variables are directly related—earnings increase as
age increases—and at later ages these variables are inversely related—earnings decline as
age increases. We have also implied the concept of *maximum*—there is an age at which
annual earnings are at a maximum over the lifetime of annual earnings. We see all this in
panel (c) of Figure A-1. The maximum annual earnings are labeled point A in panel (c).

GRAPHS AS RELATIONSHIPS

A graph of the type we are discussing is used to illustrate the relationship between two variables. Throughout this text we will be concerned with the relationship between two economic variables, as in panel (b) of Figure A-1, where we show the relationship between
the price of a good and its quantity purchased. Notice that the relationship is between only
two economic variables. But certainly, you might be saying now, other things besides price
influence how much of a particular good—such as compact discs or hamburgers—an individual chooses to buy during any given period of time. Of course, there are other influencing variables, but they are not explicitly shown on any graph that has only two variables, such as price and quantity purchased. In other words, the relationships shown on
our graphs, by their very nature, cannot include all the other relationships that are involved
in determining, for example, the quantity of a good purchased. We say, therefore, that
when we draw a graph showing the relationship between two economic variables, *we are
holding all other things constant*. The graph in panel (b) of Figure A-1 therefore holds constant, or fixed, people's income, tastes, and the like. This is sometimes referred to as the
ceteris paribus assumption; *ceteris paribus* in Latin means "other things equal." There is
a way to show the effect of changes in other things that are not explicitly depicted in a
two-dimensional graph. When some other determining variable changes, it will affect the
position of the line, or curve, representing the relationship between the two variables on
the curve. For example, consider again panel (b) of Figure A-1 showing the relationship
between price and quantity purchased. If income also affects quantity purchased, and there
is a change in income, the entire colored line will move when income does, in fact, change.
A more extensive discussion of this important concept is presented in Chapter 3.

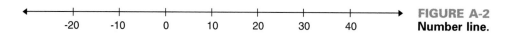

FIGURE A-2
Number line.

CONSTRUCTING A GRAPH

We shall now examine how to construct a graph to illustrate a relationship between two variables.

A NUMBER LINE

The first step is to become familiar with what is called a **number line.** One is shown in Figure A-2. There are three things that you should notice about it.

1. The points on the line divide the line into segments.
2. We have chosen the line segments so that they are equal.
3. The numbers associated with the points on the line increase in value from left to right; saying it the other way around, the numbers decrease in value from right to left. However you say it, what we're describing is formally called an *ordered set of points.*

On the number line we have shown the line segments, that is, the distance from 0 to 10 or the distance between 30 and 40. They all appear to be equal and, indeed, are equal to $\frac{1}{2}$ inch. When we use a distance to represent a quantity, such as barrels of oil, graphically, we are *scaling* the number line. In the example shown, the distance between 0 and 10 might represent 10 barrels of oil, or the distance from 0 to 40 might represent 40 barrels. Of course, the scale may differ on different number lines. For example, a distance of 1 inch could represent 10 units on one number line but 5,000 units on another.

Notice that on our number line, points to the left of 0 correspond to negative numbers and points to the right of 0 correspond to positive numbers.

Of course, we can construct a vertical number line. Consider the one in Figure A-3. As we move up this vertical number line, the numbers increase in value; conversely, as we descend, they decrease in value. Below 0 the numbers are negative, and above 0 the numbers are positive. And as on the horizontal number line, all the line segments are equal. This line is divided into segments such that the distance between -2 and -1 is the same as the distance between 0 and 1.

COMBINING THE VERTICAL AND HORIZONTAL NUMBER LINES

By drawing the horizontal and vertical lines on the same sheet of paper, we are able to express the relationships between variables graphically. We do this in Figure A-4.

We draw them (1) so that they intersect at each other's 0 point and (2) so that they are perpendicular to each other. The result is a set of coordinate axes, where each line is called an *axis.* When we have two axes, they span a plane.

For one number line you need only one number to specify any point on the line; equivalently, when you see a point on the line, you know that it represents one number or one value. With a coordinate value system you need two numbers to specify a single point in the plane; when you see a single point on a graph, you know that it represents two numbers or two values.

The basic things that you should know about a coordinate number system are that the vertical number line is referred to as the **y axis,** the horizontal number line is referred to as the **x axis,** and the point of intersection of the two lines is referred to as the **origin.**

Any point such as A in Figure A-4 represents two numbers—a value of x and a value of y. But we know more than that; we also know that point A represents a positive value of y because it is above the x axis, and we know that it represents a positive value of x because it is to the right of the y axis.

▶ **Number line**
A line that can be divided into segments of equal length, each associated with a number.

FIGURE A-3
Vertical number line.

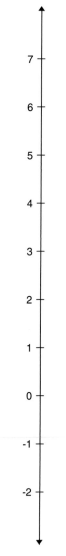

▶ **y axis**
The vertical axis in a graph.

▶ **x axis**
The horizontal axis in a graph.

▶ **Origin**
The intersection of the y axis and the x axis in a graph.

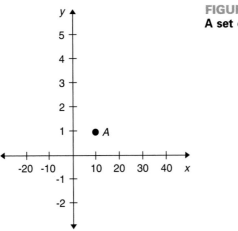

FIGURE A-4
A set of coordinate axes.

Point *A* represents a "paired observation" of the variables *x* and *y*; in particular, in Figure A-4, *A* represents an observation of the pair of values *x* = 10 and *y* = 1. Every point in the coordinate system corresponds to a paired observation of *x* and *y*, which can be simply written (*x*, *y*)—the *x* value is always specified first, then the *y* value. When we give the values associated with the position of point *A* in the coordinate number system, we are in effect giving the coordinates of that point. *A*'s coordinates are *x* = 10, *y* = 1.

Later in the text, instead of general variables *x* and *y*, we will be talking about pairs of related variables, such as prices of goods and quantities of goods purchased. Most of the variables that we deal with in economics have positive values because for the most part we are dealing with prices and quantities.

GRAPHING NUMBERS IN A TABLE

TABLE A-2   T-Shirts Purchased.

(1) PRICE OF T-SHIRTS	(2) NUMBER OF T-SHIRTS PURCHASED PER WEEK
$10	20
9	30
8	40
7	50
6	60
5	70

Consider Table A-2. Column 1 shows different prices for T-shirts, and column 2 gives the number of T-shirts purchased per week at these prices. Notice the pattern of these numbers. As the price of T-shirts falls, the number of T-shirts purchased per week increases. Therefore, an inverse relationship exists between these two variables, and as soon as we represent it on a graph, you will be able to see the relationship. We can graph this relationship using a coordinate number system—a vertical and horizontal number line for each of these two variables. Such a graph is shown in panel (b) of Figure A-5 (on p. 42).

In economics it is conventional to put dollar values on the *y* axis. We therefore construct a vertical number line for price and a horizontal number line, the *x* axis, for quantity of T-shirts purchased per week. The resulting coordinate system allows the plotting of each of the paired observation points; in panel (a) we repeat Table A-2, with a column added expressing these points in paired-data (*x*, *y*) form. For example, point *J* is the paired observation (30, 9). It indicates that when the price of a T-shirt is $9, 30 will be purchased per week.

If it were possible to sell parts of a T-shirt ($\frac{1}{2}$ or $\frac{1}{20}$ of a shirt), we would have observations at every possible price. That is, we would be able to connect our paired observations, represented as lettered points. Let's assume that we can make T-shirts perfectly divisible. We would then have a line that connects these points, as shown in the graph in Figure A-6 (on p. 42).

In short, we have now represented the data from the table in the form of a graph. Note that an inverse relationship between two variables shows up on a graph as a line or curve that slopes *downward* from left to right. (You might as well get used to the idea that economists call a straight line a "curve" even though it may not curve at all. Much of economists' data turn out to be curves, so they refer to everything represented graphically as curves, even straight lines.)

FIGURE A-5
Graphing the relationship between T-shirts purchased and price.

Panel (a)

PRICE	T-SHIRTS PURCHASED PER WEEK	POINT ON GRAPH	
$10	20	R	(20, 10)
9	30	J	(30, 9)
8	40	K	(40, 8)
7	50	L	(50, 7)
6	60	M	(60, 6)
5	70	N	(70, 5)

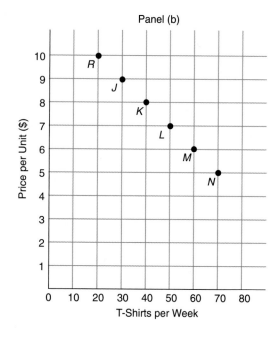

Panel (b)

THE SLOPE OF A LINE (A LINEAR CURVE)

An important property of a curve represented on a graph is its **slope.** Consider Figure A-7, which represents the quantities of shoes per week that a seller is willing to offer at different prices. Note that in panel (a) of Figure A-7, as in Figure A-5, we have expressed the coordinates of the points in parentheses in proper paired-data (x, y) form.

The slope of a line is defined as the change in the y values divided by the corresponding change in the x values as we move along the line. Let's move from point E to point D in

▶ **Slope**
The change in the y value divided by the corresponding change in the x value of a curve; the "incline" of the curve.

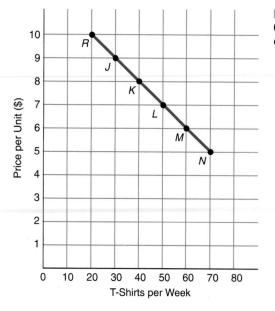

FIGURE A-6
Connecting the observation points.

FIGURE A-7
A positively sloped curve.

Panel (a)

PRICE PER PAIR	PAIRS OF SHOES OFFERED PER WEEK	POINT ON GRAPH
$100	400	A (400, 100)
80	320	B (320, 80)
60	240	C (240, 60)
40	160	D (160, 40)
20	80	E (80, 20)

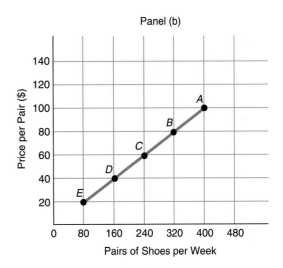

Panel (b)

panel (b) of Figure A-7. As we move, we note that the change in the *y* values, which is the change in price, is +$20, because we have moved from a price of $20 to a price of $40 per pair. As we move from *E* to *D*, the change in the *x* values is +80; the number of pairs of shoes willingly offered per week rises from 80 to 160 pairs. The slope calculated as a change in the *y* values divided by the change in the *x* values is therefore

$$\frac{20}{80} = \frac{1}{4}$$

It may be helpful for you to think of slope as a "rise" (movement in the vertical direction) over a "run" (movement in the horizontal direction). We show this abstractly in Figure A-8. The slope is measured by the amount of rise divided by the amount of run. In the example in Figure A-8, and of course in Figure A-7, the amount of rise is positive and so is the amount of run. That's because it's a direct relationship. We show an inverse relationship in Figure A-9 on page 44. The slope is still equal to the rise divided by the run, but in this case the rise is negative because the curve slopes downward. That means that the slope will have to be negative and that we are dealing with an inverse relationship.

Now let's calculate the slope for a different part of the curve in panel (b) of Figure A-7. We will find the slope as we move from point *B* to point *A*. Again, we note that the slope, or rise over run, from *B* to *A* equals

$$\frac{20}{80} = \frac{1}{4}$$

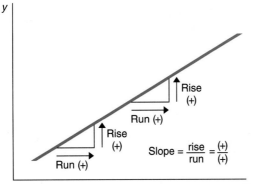

FIGURE A-8
Figuring positive slope.

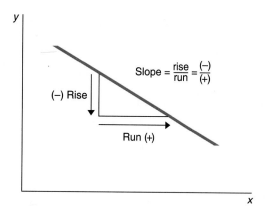

FIGURE A-9
Figuring negative slope.

A specific property of a straight line is that its slope is the same between any two points; in other words, the slope is constant at all points on a straight line in a graph.

We conclude that for our example in Figure A-7 the relationship between the price of a pair of shoes and the quantity of pairs of shoes willingly offered per week is *linear*, which simply means "in a straight line," and our calculations indicate a constant slope. Moreover, we calculate a direct relationship between these two variables, which turns out to be an upward-sloping (from left to right) curve, that is, a straight line. Upward-sloping curves have positive slopes—in this case, it is $+\frac{1}{4}$.

We know that an inverse relationship between two variables shows up as a downward-sloping curve—rise over run will be a negative slope because the "rise" is really a fall, as shown in Figure A-9. When we see a negative slope, we know that increases in one variable are associated with decreases in the other. Therefore, we say that downward-sloping curves have negative slopes. Can you verify that the slope of the graph representing the relationship between T-shirt prices and the quantity of T-shirts purchased per week in Figure A-6 is $-\frac{1}{10}$?

SLOPES OF NONLINEAR CURVES

The graph presented in Figure A-10 indicates a *nonlinear* ("not in a straight line") relationship between two variables, total yearly profits and output per year. Inspection of this graph indicates that at first, increases in output lead to increases in total profits; that is, total profits rise as output increases. But beyond some output level, further increases in output cause decreases in total profits.

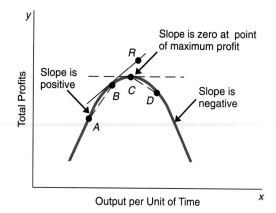

FIGURE A-10
The slope of a nonlinear curve.

Can you see how this curve rises at first, reaches a peak at point *C,* and then falls? This curve relating total annual profits to annual output levels appears mountain-shaped.

Considering that this curve is nonlinear (it is obviously not a straight line), should we expect a constant slope when we compute changes in *y* divided by corresponding changes in *x* in moving from one point to another? A quick inspection, even without specific numbers, should lead us to conclude that the slopes of lines joining different points in this curve, such as between *A* and *B, B* and *C,* or *C* and *D,* will *not* be the same. The curve slopes upward (in a positive direction) for some values and downward (in a negative direction) for other values. In fact, the slope of the line between any two points on this curve will be different from the slope of the line between any two other points. Each slope will be different as we move along the curve.

Instead of using a line between two points to discuss slope, mathematicians and economists prefer to discuss the slope *at a particular point.* The slope at a point on the curve, such as point *B* in the graph in Figure A-10, is the slope of a line *tangent* to that point. A tangent line is a straight line that touches a curve at only one point. For example, it might be helpful to think of the tangent at *B* as the straight line that just "kisses" the curve at point *B.*

To calculate the slope of a tangent line, you need to have some additional information besides the two values of the point of tangency. For example, in Figure A-10, if we knew that the point *R* also lay on the tangent line and we knew the two values of that point, we could calculate the slope of the tangent line. We could calculate rise over run between points *B* and *R,* and the result would be the slope of the line tangent to the one point *B* on the curve.

From now on we will refer to the slope of the line tangent to a curve at a point as the slope at that point.

MAXIMUM AND MINIMUM POINTS

Observe the two graphs in Figure A-11. In panel (a) point *W* is a point at the peak of the curve. The slope of the line tangent to point *W* is 0, because the rise for any run is zero. There is no change in the *y* value for any given change in the *x* value. At any value of *Q* less than Q_W, the curve is rising, and at any value of *Q* greater than Q_W, the curve is falling. Therefore, we refer to the peak point, *W,* as the *maximum* point.

On the graph in panel (b), the tangent line at point *B* also has a zero slope; that is, the slope at equal to zero. Inspection of this graph reveals that at values of *Q* greater than Q_B, the curve is rising; at any value of *Q* less than Q_B, the curve is falling. Point *B* is therefore referred to as the *minimum* point.

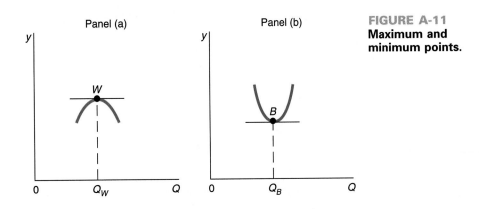

FIGURE A-11
Maximum and minimum points.

It is important for you to realize that there are many kinds of nonlinear curves. Some may not have a minimum point or a maximum point; some may have both; others may have several of either or both. Do not fear, as we don't stress these complicated nonlinear curves in this text.

You should be aware that direct relationships can be linear or nonlinear; and, of course, inverse relationships can be linear or nonlinear. Two examples are given in Figure A-12. In panel (a) we show a nonlinear inverse relationship between *y* and *x*. In panel (b) we show a nonlinear direct relationship between *y* and *x*.

GRAPHS AND THE REAL WORLD

So far we've talked about plotting relationships between two economic variables. Throughout much of this text, most of the graphs shown will be hypothetical, with reference, of course, to reasonable and logically based slopes. But economists do quite often examine actual (empirical) relationships between two economic variables to confirm theories about how the world works.[1] Consequently, economists gather one of two types of real-world data: **time-series data** and **cross-sectional data.** Time-series data involve obtaining information on the value of economic variables over time. For example, an economist collects information on average family income and average family expenditures each year over a 25-year period. These data are then plotted on a graph to show the relationship, over time, of family income and family expenditures. Alternatively, cross-sectional data are gathered at a point in time, using observations of different families with different incomes and their resulting expenditure levels. A graph of these data shows the relationship between family income and family expenditures at a point in time.

▶ **Time-series data**
Empirical observations about the value of one or more economic variables taken at different periods over time.

▶ **Cross-sectional data**
Empirical observations about one or more variables gathered at a particular point in time.

SCATTER DIAGRAMS

Of course, the economists who make these real-world measurements about economic variables do not usually get nice, neat curves like the ones in our hypothetical examples. Rather, economists typically obtain observations that are scattered "all over the place," and from these they try to derive relationships. Suppose that an economist has collected data on family income and expenditures as we have described. Using these data, the economist has plotted the observations on a graph, shown in panel (a) of Figure A-13. Such a graph is known, for obvious reasons, as a **scatter diagram.** Looking at this graph, it is easy to see that a pattern exists. The relationship isn't perfect, but it does seem clear that when income rises, expenditures rise, and when income falls, expenditures fall. There are techniques that can be used to "fit" a curve that best summarizes all the points in the scatter

▶ **Scatter diagram**
A graph showing the points that represent observations of the dependent and independent variables. These points are scattered throughout the *x-y* quadrant.

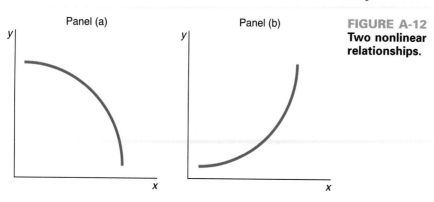

Panel (a)   Panel (b)

FIGURE A-12
Two nonlinear relationships.

---

[1]Actually, one never confirms a theory; one simply attempts to reject it by submitting it to real-world evidence.

diagram. Such a curve would be analogous to the nice, neat lines of the hypothetical graphs we have shown so far and the ones we will show throughout this text. It would not perfectly describe the *actual* relationship between the two economic variables (here, family income and expenditures), but it could come close. Of course, when economists fit lines to scatter diagrams, they have to report *how well* the lines fit, and there are statistics that do just that.

Now consider the scatter diagram in panel (b) of Figure A-13. Can a line be fitted to describe these observations? No. Any line would do just as well as any other, which means that no line will do. An economist who gets results such as these reports that no relationship appears to exist.

PLOTTING ACTUAL DATA

WHAT TO WATCH OUT FOR

Irrespective of the type of data collected, there are numerous pitfalls in the collection, interpretation, and use of such data in graphical analysis. In other words, it is easy to lie with graphs.

Improper Sampling Techniques and Bad Data.   Consider the information obtained on family income and expenditures at a point in time. Because it is impossible to collect data on all families in the United States, a sample must be taken. What if the sample is unrepresentative? Then the resulting plotted graphic relationship between family income and expenditures may not reflect the real underlying relationship. Also, the data could have been collected improperly—numbers transcribed incorrectly, some families left out, and so on. This means that the researcher must constantly be on the lookout for improper measurement before trusting the accuracy of the resulting graphic relationship.

Unrepresentative Beginning and Ending Points in Time-Series Data. Consider the time-series example just discussed. What if the time-series data on average family income and expenditures start during the Great Depression (1929–1933) and end during a deep recession? The resulting plotted relationship may not be indicative of the

FIGURE A-13
Scatter diagrams.
Panel (a) presents a scatter diagram of observations on family income and family expenditures. Panel (b) shows a random scatter pattern.

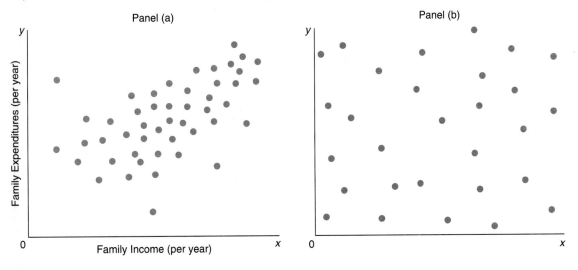

average relationship during most of the nation's history when we were not suffering from serious business slow-downs. The choice of years covered can therefore seriously bias a plotted graph.

Population Distortion.
The population in the United States has been increasing. Therefore, any graphs showing increases in crime, total alcohol consumption, sugar consumed, and the like are deceptive because they do not take population increases into account. Such data must be corrected and shown on a per capita basis to have any meaning.

Inflation Distortion.
Prices have risen for many, many years in the United States and elsewhere. Graphs plotting nominal, or current money, values over time can be distorted by not adjusting for inflation. A graph showing changes in nominal per capita disposable income from 1945 to the present, for example, would give the impression that per capita income has increased 11-fold. Correcting for the loss in purchasing power of the dollars earned—inflation—yields a more accurate view of improvements in living standards, with only a twofold increase in inflation-corrected per capita income.

Distorting the Slope Because of Scale.
It is possible to make the slope of a graph look just about any way you want by changing the scale on either axis. This is particularly true for time-series data. Compare panels (a) and (b) of Figure A-14. The slope appears dramatically different, even though the measurement of the Dow Jones Industrial Average is exactly the same. Simply by changing the scale on the vertical axis the slope

FIGURE A-14
The Dow Jones Industrial Average, 1980–1985.
Here we see that choosing the scale on the vertical axis can drastically change the appearance of the slope of the curve connecting data points on a particular variable. In panel (a) the vertical axis is measured in units one-half the size of those used on the vertical axis in panel (b). Not surprisingly, the increase in the Dow Jones average from 1980 to 1985 looks more dramatic in panel (b).

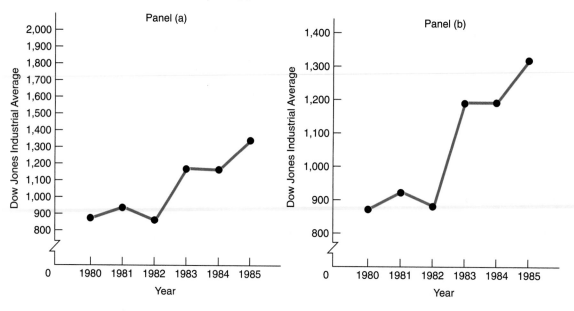

appeared to change. Be careful, then, in interpreting graphs appearing in newspapers and business magazines. Look at the scale on the axes. The smaller the range of values along the vertical axis, the greater any change in the variable under study will appear.

APPENDIX SUMMARY

1. Direct relationships involve a dependent variable changing in the same direction as the change in the independent variable.
2. Inverse relationships involve the dependent variable changing in the opposite direction of the change in the independent variable.
3. When we draw a graph showing the relationship between two economic variables, we are holding all other things constant (*ceteris paribus*).
4. We obtain a set of coordinates by putting vertical and horizontal number lines together. The vertical line is called the y axis; the horizontal line, the x axis.
5. The slope of any linear (straight line) curve is the change in the y values divided by the corresponding change in the x values as we move along the line. Otherwise stated, the slope is calculated as the amount of rise over the amount of run, where rise is movement

in the vertical direction and run is movement in the horizontal direction.
6. The slope of a nonlinear curve changes; it is positive when the curve is rising and negative when the curve is falling. At a maximum or minimum point, the slope of the nonlinear curve is zero.
7. Time-series data and cross-sectional data can be shown on scatter diagrams. Fitting a curve to these data is an attempt to infer the relationship between them.
8. Pitfalls to watch out for in graphs include (a) using improper data, (b) choosing unrepresentative beginning and ending dates for time-series data, (c) not correcting for population growth, (d) not taking account of inflation, and (e) altering the vertical scale to exaggerate apparent slope in a time-series descriptive graph.

PROBLEMS

(The answer to Problem A-1 appears at the back of the book.)

A-1. Complete the schedule and plot the following function:

$y = 3x$

y	x
	4
	3
	2
	1
	0
	−1
	−2
	−3
	−4

A-2. Complete the schedule and plot the following function:

$y = x^2$

y	x
	4
	3
	2
	1
	0
	−1
	−2
	−3
	−4

DEMAND AND SUPPLY

Until recently, virtually all college financial aid awards were given on the basis of need. Today an increasing percentage of financial awards are being used to entice the best students, regardless of their financial situation. Ten years ago acceptance letters to potential college entrants were always mailed out on April 15. Today most are mailed on April 1. Some colleges now actually pay to fly accepted students to campus. Such a practice was unheard of in the 1960s, 1970s, and most of the 1980s. To understand why some colleges are acting so differently today, you will need the tools of demand and supply analysis.

After reading this chapter, you should be able to answer the following questions:

1. Why does the law of demand indicate an inverse relationship between price and quantity demanded (other things being constant)?

2. How can we distinguish between a change in *demand* and a change in *quantity demanded*?

3. Why is there normally a direct relationship between price and quantity supplied (other things being equal)?

4. Why will the market clearing price be set at the intersection of the supply and demand curves rather than at a higher or lower price?

INTRODUCTION

One year consumers line up for hours to get meat and other staples in Moscow; the following year there are virtually no lines. One year an IBM-compatible computer has a street price of $2,000; six months later it has dropped to $1,000. In some cities apartment vacancy rates are such that any newcomer can easily find an apartment to rent; in other cities at the exact same time there are virtually no rentals to be had. Phenomena such as these occur year in and year out. They can be understood by using the economist's primary set of tools, *demand* and *supply*. Demand and supply are two ways of categorizing the influences on the price of goods that you buy and the quantities available. As such, demand and supply form the basis of virtually all economic analysis of the world around us.

As you will see throughout this text, the operation of the forces of demand and supply take place in **markets.** Goods and services are sold in markets for those goods and services, such as the automobile market, the health market, and the compact disc market. Workers offer their services in the labor market. Companies, or firms, buy workers' labor services in the labor market. Firms also buy other inputs in order to produce the goods and services that you buy as a consumer. Firms purchase machines, buildings, and land. These markets are in operation at all times. One of the most important activities in these markets is the setting of the prices of all of the inputs and outputs that are bought and sold in our complicated economy. To understand the determination of prices, you first need to look at the law of demand.

THE LAW OF DEMAND

Demand has a special meaning in economics. It relates to the prices that you are willing to pay, as well as a variety of other factors, for different quantities of a good or service. Specifically, the term *demand* in economics refers to the quantities that individuals, taken singly or as a group, will purchase at various possible prices for a good or service, other things being constant. We can therefore talk about the demand for microprocessor chips, French fries, compact disc players, children, and criminal activities.

Associated with the concept of demand is the **law of demand,** which can be stated as follows:

> **When the price of a good goes up, people buy less of it, other things being equal. When the price of a good goes down, people buy more of it, other things being equal.**

The law of demand tells us that the quantity demanded of any commodity is inversely related to its price, other things being equal. An inverse relationship is one in which one variable moves up in value when the other moves down. The law of demand states that a change in price causes a change in the quantity demanded in the *opposite* direction.

Notice that we tacked onto the end of the law of demand the statement "other things being equal." We referred to this in Chapter 1 and Appendix A as the *ceteris paribus* assumption. It means, for example, that when we predict that people will buy fewer videodisc players if their price goes up, we are holding constant the price of all other goods in the economy as well as people's incomes. Implicitly, therefore, if we are assuming that no other prices change when we examine the price behavior of videodisc players, we are looking at the *relative* price of videodisc players.

RELATIVE PRICES

The **relative price** of any good or service is its price compared to the prices of other goods or relative to an average of all other prices in the economy. The price that you and I pay in dollars and cents for any good or service at any point in time is called its **money price.**

Market
An abstract concept concerning all of the arrangements that individuals have for exchanging with one another. Thus we can speak of the labor market, the automobile market, and the credit market.

Demand
A schedule of how much of a good or service people will purchase at each different possible price during a specified time period, other things being constant.

Law of demand
There is a negative, or inverse, relationship between the price of any good or service and the quantity demanded, holding other factors constant.

Relative price
The price of a commodity expressed in terms of another commodity or the (weighted) average price of all other commodities.

Money price
The price that we observe today, expressed in today's dollars. Also called the *absolute, nominal,* or *current price.*

Consider an example that you might hear quite often around parents and grandparents. "When I bought my first new car, it cost only fifteen hundred dollars." The implication, of course, is that the price of cars today is outrageously high because the average new car might cost $16,000. But that is not an accurate comparison. What was the average price of the average house during that same year? Perhaps it was only $12,000. By comparison, then, given that houses today average about $125,000, the price of a new car today doesn't sound so far out of line, does it?

The point is that money prices during different time periods don't tell you much. You have to find out relative prices. Consider an example of the price of CDs versus cassettes from last year and this year. In Table 3-1 we show the money price of CDs and cassettes for two years during which they have both gone up. That means that we have to pay out in today's dollars and cents more for CDs and more for cassettes. If we look, though, at the relative prices of CDs and cassettes, we find that last year CDs were twice as expensive as cassettes, whereas this year they are only $1\frac{3}{4}$ times as expensive. Conversely, if we compare cassettes to CDs, last year they cost only half as much as CDs, but today they cost about 57 percent as much. In the one-year period, while both prices have gone up in money terms, the relative price of CDs has fallen (and, equivalently, the relative price of cassettes has risen). If the law of demand holds, then over this one-year period a larger quantity of CDs will be demanded and a smaller quantity of cassettes will be demanded, other things being equal.

 INTERNATIONAL EXAMPLE: Buying Up Russian Goods

As the former republics of the ex-Soviet Union went their separate ways, one of those ways involved choosing new national currencies. Ukraine, sharing a border with Russia, introduced a form of a new national currency at the beginning of 1992. The Soviet rubles that the Ukrainians were using were about to become virtually worthless in Ukraine. But they were still used as currency in the Russian republic. The realistic relative price of any goods that could be purchased using rubles held by Ukrainians suddenly dropped dramatically. The result was predictable: Ukrainians descended on Russian border towns such as Belgorod. Those Ukrainians bought everything in sight—meat, bread, vegetables, clothes, whatever. The peasants' markets in that city and other similarly situated cities on the Ukrainian-Russian border were cleared out in no time before prices could adjust upward.

For Critical Analysis: Why didn't the Russians at border towns simply refuse to sell goods to the Ukrainians? ●

TWO REASONS WHY WE OBSERVE THE LAW OF DEMAND

Two fundamental reasons explain why the quantity demanded of a good is inversely related to its price, other things being equal. One is the *substitution effect,* and the second is the *real-income effect.*

	MONEY PRICE		RELATIVE PRICE	
	PRICE LAST YEAR	PRICE THIS YEAR	PRICE LAST YEAR	PRICE THIS YEAR
CDs	$12	$14	$\frac{\$12}{\$6} = 2$	$\frac{\$14}{\$8} = 1.75$
Cassettes	$ 6	$ 8	$\frac{\$6}{\$12} = .5$	$\frac{\$8}{\$14} = .57$

TABLE 3-1 Money price versus relative price.
The money price of both compact discs (CDs) and cassettes has risen. But the relative price of CDs has fallen (or conversely, the relative price of cassettes has risen).

Substitution Effect.   We assume that people desire a variety of goods and pursue a variety of goals. That means that few, if any, goods are irreplaceable in meeting demand. We are generally able to substitute one product for another to satisfy demand. This is commonly called the **principle of substitution.**

> ▶ **Principle of substitution**
> The principle that consumers and producers shift away from goods and resources that become relatively higher priced in favor of goods and resources that are now relatively lower priced.

Let's assume now that there are several goods, not exactly the same, or perhaps even very different from one another, but all serving basically the same purpose. If the relative price of one particular good falls, we will most likely substitute in favor of the lower-priced good and against the other similar goods that we might have been purchasing. Conversely, if the price of that good rises relative to the price of the other similar goods, we will substitute in favor of them and not buy as much of the now higher-priced good.

Consider an example: The prices of tacos, hamburgers, and hot dogs are all about the same. Each of us buys a certain amount of each of these three substitutable fast foods. What if the price of tacos increases considerably, while the prices of hamburgers and hot dogs do not? What will we do? We will buy more hamburgers and hot dogs and fewer tacos, because tacos are relatively more expensive, while hot dogs and hamburgers are now relatively cheaper. In effect, we will be substituting hamburgers and hot dogs for tacos *because of* the relatively higher price of tacos. Thus you can see how the **substitution effect** affects the quantity demanded of a particular good.

> ▶ **Substitution effect**
> The tendency of people to substitute in favor of cheaper commodities and against more expensive commodities.

Real-Income Effect.   If the price of some item that you purchase goes down while your money income and all other prices stay the same, your ability to purchase goods in general goes up. That is to say that your effective **purchasing power** is increased, even though your money income has stayed the same. If you purchase 20 gallons of gas a week at $1.20 per gallon, your total outlay for gas is $24. If the price goes down by 50 percent, to 60 cents a gallon, you would have to spend only $12 a week to purchase the same number of gallons of gas. If your money income and the prices of other goods remain the same, it would be possible for you to continue purchasing 20 gallons of gas a week *and* to purchase more of other goods. You will feel richer and will indeed probably purchase more of a number of goods, including perhaps even more gasoline.

> ▶ **Purchasing power**
> The value of your money income in buying goods and services. If your money income stays the same but the price of one good that you are buying goes up, your effective purchasing power falls.

The converse will also be true. When the price of one good you are purchasing goes up, without any other prices changing and without your income changing, the purchasing power of your income will drop. You will have to reduce your purchases of either the now higher-priced good or other goods (or a combination).

In general, this **real-income effect** is usually quite small. After all, unless we consider broad categories, such as housing or food, a change in the price of one particular item that we purchase will have a relatively small effect on our total purchasing power (given a limited income). Thus we expect the substitution effect usually to be more important in causing us to purchase more of goods that have become cheaper and less of goods that have become more expensive.

> ▶ **Real-income effect**
> The change in people's purchasing power that occurs when, other things being constant, the price of one good that they purchase changes. When that price goes up, real income, or purchasing power, falls, and when that price goes down, real income, or purchasing power, increases.

CONCEPTS IN BRIEF

- The law of demand implies an inverse relationship between the quantity demanded of a good and its price, other things being equal.
- The law of demand holds when other things are held constant, such as income and the prices of all other goods and services.
- The law of demand holds because when the price of a good goes down, (1) we substitute in favor of it and (2) we are now richer and probably buy more of everything, including the now lower-priced good.

THE DEMAND SCHEDULE

Let's take a hypothetical demand situation to see how the inverse relationship between the price and the quantity demanded looks. We will consider the quantity of diskettes demanded *per year.* Without stating the *time dimension,* we could not make any sense out of this demand relationship, because the numbers would be different if we were talking about the quantity demanded per month or the quantity demanded per decade.

CONSTANT-QUALITY UNITS

Consider the prices and quantities demanded of diskettes given in panel (a) of Figure 3-1. We show the price per constant-quality unit. Notice the words *constant-quality.* We tack on this qualification to take care of the problem of varying qualities of diskettes when we wish to add up all the diskettes sold or that could be sold every year at different prices. There are different qualities of diskettes. Therefore, we have to pick some standard, say, a double-sided 3M DF-HD diskette, and then we compare all others with that standard. We don't actually have to worry about figuring how to complete such a task statistically. All we need is to be aware that we are conceptually correcting for differences in the qualities of diskettes purchased.

In panel (a) of Figure 3-1 we see that if the price were $1 per diskette, 50 of them would be bought each year by our representative individual, but if the price were $5 per diskette, only 10 diskettes would be bought each year. This reflects the law of demand. Panel (a) of Figure 3-1 is also called simply demand, or a *demand schedule,* because it gives a schedule of alternative quantities demanded per year at different possible prices.

THE DEMAND CURVE

Tables expressing relationships between two variables can be represented in graphic terms. To do this, we need only construct a graph that has the price per constant-quality diskette

FIGURE 3-1
The individual demand schedule and the individual demand curve.
In panel (a) we show combinations *A* through *E* of the quantities of diskettes demanded, measured in constant-quality units at prices ranging from $5 down to $1 per disk. In panel (b) we plot combinations *A* through *E* on a grid. The result is the individual demand curve for diskettes.

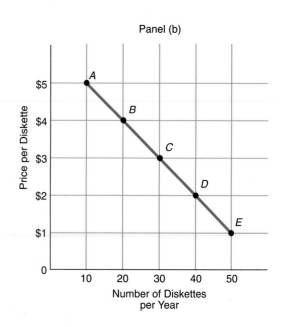

Panel (b)

Panel (a)

COMBINATION	PRICE PER CONSTANT-QUALITY DISKETTE	QUANTITY IN CONSTANT-QUALITY DISKETTES
A	$5	10
B	$4	20
C	$3	30
D	$2	40
E	$1	50

on the vertical axis and the quantity measured in constant-quality diskettes per year on the horizontal axis. All we have to do is take combinations *A, B, C, D,* and *E* from panel (a) of Figure 3-1 and plot those points in panel (b). Now we connect the points with a smooth line, and *voilà,* we have a **demand curve.**[1] It is downward-sloping (from left to right) to indicate the inverse relationship between the price of diskettes and the quantity demanded per year. Our presentation of demand schedules and curves applies equally well to all commodities, including toothpicks, hamburgers, textbooks, credit, and labor services. Remember, the demand curve is simply a graphical representation of the definition of demand.

▶ **Demand curve**
A graphic representation of the demand schedule. A negatively sloped line showing the inverse relationship between the price and the quantity demanded.

INDIVIDUAL VERSUS MARKET DEMAND CURVES

The demand schedule shown in panel (a) of Figure 3-1 and the resulting demand curve shown in panel (b) are both given for an individual. As we shall see, the determination of

FIGURE 3-2
The horizontal summation of two demand schedules.
Panel (a) shows how to sum the demand schedule for one buyer with that of another buyer. In column 2 is the quantity demanded by buyer 1, taken from panel (a) of Figure 3-1. Column 4 is the sum of columns 2 and 3. We plot the demand curve for buyer 1 in panel (b) and the demand curve for buyer 2 in panel (c). When we add those two demand curves horizontally, we get the market demand curve for two buyers, shown in panel (d).

Panel (a)

(1) PRICE PER DISKETTE	(2) BUYER 1 QUANTITY DEMANDED	(3) BUYER 2 QUANTITY DEMANDED	(4) TOTAL QUANTITY DEMANDED PER YEAR
$5	10	10	20
$4	20	20	40
$3	30	40	70
$2	40	50	90
$1	50	60	110

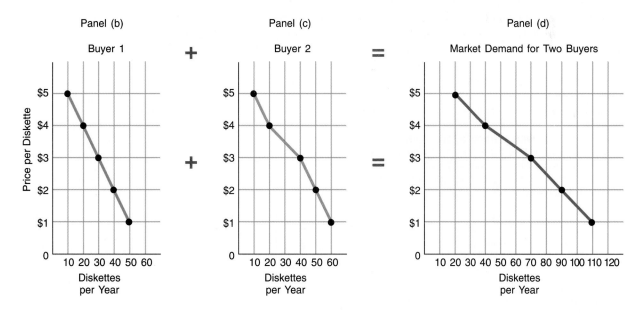

---

[1]Even though we call them curves, for the purposes of exposition we often draw straight lines. In many real-world situations, demand and supply "curves" will in fact be lines that do curve. In order to connect the points in panel (b) with a line, we assume that for all prices in between the ones shown, the quantities demanded will be found along that line.

price in the marketplace depends on, among other things, the **market demand** for a particular commodity. The way in which we measure a market demand schedule and derive a market demand curve for diskettes or any other commodity is by summing (at each price) the individual demand for all those in the market. Suppose that the market demand for diskettes consists of only two buyers: buyer 1, for whom we've already shown the demand schedule, and buyer 2, whose demand schedule is displayed in column 3 of panel (a) of Figure 3-2 on page 55. Column 1 shows the price, and column 2 shows the quantity demanded by buyer 1 at each price. These data are taken directly from Figure 3-1. In column 3 we show the demand by buyer 2. Column 4 shows the total quantity demanded at each price, which is obtained by simply adding columns 2 and 3. Graphically, in panel (d) of Figure 3-2 we add the demand curves of buyer 1 [panel (b)] and buyer 2 [panel (c)] to derive the market demand curve shown in the graph at the far right.

There are, of course, literally tens of millions of potential consumers of diskettes. We'll simply assume that the summation of all of the consumers in the market results in a demand schedule given in panel (a) of Figure 3-3 and a demand curve given in panel (b). The quantity demanded is now measured in billions of units per year. Remember, panel (b) in Figure 3-3 shows the market demand curve for the millions of users of diskettes. A "market" demand curve that we derived in Figure 3-2 was undertaken assuming that there were only two buyers in the entire market. That's why the "market" demand curve for two buyers in panel (d) of Figure 3-2 is not a smooth line, whereas the true market demand curve in panel (b) of Figure 3-3 is a smooth line with no kinks.

▶ **Market demand**
The demand of all consumers in the marketplace for a particular good or service. The summing at each price of the quantity demanded by each individual.

🌐 INTERNATIONAL EXAMPLE: Keeping the Business at Home

Shoppers around the world are sensitive to differences in prices for the same products. Those who live on the Canadian-American border are a case in point. For many years Canada has imposed high tariffs (taxes) on imported goods from America. Consequently, the same products in the United States have often been much cheaper. Price differentials have been dramatic, as much as 50 percent, on a broad range of items from beer to VCRs to cameras. It wasn't surprising that same-day trips to the United States registered at the U.S.-Canadian border went over 5 million in 1991, an increase of 25 percent in two years.

FIGURE 3-3
The market demand schedule for diskettes.
In panel (a) we add up the millions of existing demand schedules for diskettes. In panel (b) we plot the quantities from panel (a) on a grid; connecting them produces the market demand curve for diskettes.

Panel (a)

PRICE PER CONSTANT-QUALITY DISKETTE	TOTAL QUANTITY DEMANDED OF CONSTANT-QUALITY DISKETTES PER YEAR (BILLIONS)
$5	2
$4	4
$3	6
$2	8
$1	10

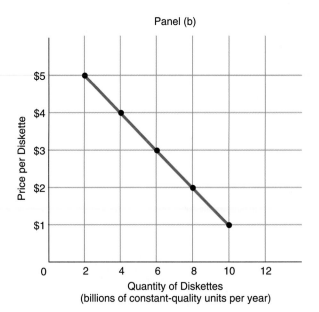

Panel (b)

Then the Canadian government took action. In 1992 it unilaterally reduced the taxes on imports of 25 popular goods. Canadian officials know that the demand curve by Canadian consumers for goods purchased in Canada slopes downward. Many Canadians now buy consumer electronics at home.

For Critical Analysis: *Why aren't prices of the same product dramatically different in different states within the United States?* ●

CONCEPTS IN BRIEF

- We measure the demand schedule in terms of constant-quality units.
- The market demand curve is derived by summing the quantity demanded by individuals at each price. Graphically, we add the individual demand curves horizontally to derive the total, or market, demand curve.

SHIFTS IN DEMAND

Assume that the federal government gives every student registered in a college, university, or technical school in the United States a personal computer that uses diskettes. The demand curve presented in panel (b) of Figure 3-3 would no longer be an accurate representation of total market demand for diskettes. What we have to do is shift the curve outward, or to the right, to represent the rise in demand. There will now be an increase in the quantity of diskettes demanded *at each and every possible price.* The demand curve shown in Figure 3-4 on page 58 will shift from D to D'. Take any price, say, $3 per diskette. Originally, before the federal government giveaway of personal computers, the amount demanded at $3 was 6 billion diskettes per year. After the government giveaway, however, the new amount demanded at $3 is 10 billion diskettes per year. What we have seen is a shift in the demand for diskettes.

The shift can also go in the opposite direction. What if colleges uniformly outlawed the use of personal computers by any of their students? Such a regulation would cause a shift inward—to the left—of the demand curve for diskettes. In Figure 3-4 the demand curve would shift to D''; the amount demanded would now be less at each and every possible price.

THE NONPRICE DETERMINANTS OF DEMAND

The demand curve in panel (b) of Figure 3-3 is drawn with other things held constant, including all of the other *nonprice* factors that determine how much will be bought. There are many such determinants. The major nonprice determinants are (1) income; (2) tastes and preferences; (3) the prices of related goods; (4) expectations regarding future prices, future incomes, and future product availability; and (5) population (market size). Let's look more closely at each one.

Income.   For most goods an increase in income will lead to an increase in demand. The phrase *increase in demand* always refers to a comparison between two different demand curves. Thus for most goods an increase in income will lead to a rightward shift in the position of the demand curve from, say, D to D' in Figure 3-4. You can avoid confusion about shifts in curves by always relating a rise in demand to a rightward shift in the demand curve and a fall in demand to a leftward shift in the demand curve. Goods for which the demand rises when income rises are called **normal goods.** Most goods are "normal" in this sense. For some goods demand *falls* as income rises. These are called **inferior goods.** Potatoes might be an example. (The terms *normal* and *inferior* are merely part of the economist's terminology; no value judgments are associated with them.)

▶ **Normal goods**
Goods for which demand rises as income rises. Most goods that we deal with are normal.

▶ **Inferior goods**
Goods for which demand falls as income rises.

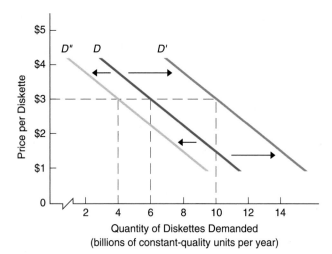

FIGURE 3-4
A shift in the demand curve.
If some factor other than price changes, the only way we can show its effect is by moving the entire demand curve, say, from D to D'. We have assumed in our example that the move was precipitated by the government's giving a free personal computer to every registered college student in America. That meant that at *all* prices, a larger amount of diskettes would be demanded than before. Curve D" represents reduced demand compared to curve D.

Remember, a shift to the left in the demand curve represents a fall in demand. A shift to the right in the demand curve represents a rise, or increase, in demand.

Tastes and Preferences.   A change in consumer tastes in favor of a good can shift its demand curve outward to the right. When Frisbees® became the rage, the demand curve for them shifted outward to the right; when the rage died out, the demand curve shifted inward to the left. Fashions depend to a large extent on people's tastes and preferences. Economists have little to say about the determination of tastes; that is, they don't have any "good" theories of taste determination or why people buy one brand of product rather than others. Advertisers, however, have various theories that they use to try to make consumers prefer their products over those of competitors.

Prices of Related Goods: Substitutes and Complements.   Demand schedules are always drawn with the prices of all other commodities held constant. That is to say, we assume that only the price of the good under study changes. For example, when we draw the demand curve for butter, we assume that the price of margarine is held constant. When we draw the demand curve for stereo speakers, we assume that the price of stereo amplifiers is held constant. When we refer to *related goods,* we are talking about goods for which demand is interdependent. If a change in the price of one good shifts the demand for another good, those two goods are related. There are two types of related goods: *substitutes* and *complements.* We can define and distinguish between substitutes and complements in terms of how the change in price of one commodity affects the demand for its related commodity.

Butter and margarine are **substitutes.** Let's assume that each originally costs $2 per pound. If the price of butter remains the same and the price of margarine falls from $2 per pound to $1 per pound, people will buy more margarine and less butter. The demand curve for butter will shift inward to the left. If, conversely, the price of margarine rises from $2 per pound to $3 per pound, people will buy more butter and less margarine. The demand curve for butter will shift outward to the right. In other words, an increase in the price of margarine will lead to an increase in the demand for butter, and an increase in the price of butter will lead to an increase in the demand for margarine. For substitutes, a price change in the substitute will cause a change in demand in the same direction.

▶ **Substitutes**
Two goods are substitutes when either one can be used for consumption—for example, coffee and tea. The more you buy of one, the less you buy of the other. For substitutes, the change in the price of one causes a shift in demand for the other in the same direction as the price change.

For **complements,** the situation is reversed. Consider stereo speakers and stereo amplifiers. We draw the demand curve for speakers with the price of amplifiers held constant. If the price per constant-quality unit of stereo amplifiers decreases from, say, $500 to $200, that will encourage more people to purchase component stereo systems. They will now buy more speakers, at any given price, than before. The demand curve for speakers will shift outward to the right. If, by contrast, the price of amplifiers increases from $200 to $500, fewer people will purchase component stereo systems. The demand curve for speakers will shift inward to the left. To summarize, a decrease in the price of amplifiers leads to an increase in the demand for speakers. An increase in the price of amplifiers leads to a decrease in the demand for speakers. Thus for complements, a price change in a product will cause a change in demand in the opposite direction.

Changes in Expectations.   Consumers' expectations regarding future prices, future incomes, and future availability may prompt them to buy more or less of a particular good without a change in its current money price. For example, consumers getting wind of a scheduled 100 percent price increase in diskettes next month may buy more of them today at today's prices. Today's demand curve for diskettes will shift from D to D' in Figure 3-4. The opposite would occur if there was a decrease in the price of diskettes scheduled for next month.

Expectations of a rise in income may cause consumers to want to purchase more of everything today at today's prices. Again, such a change in expectations of higher future income will cause a shift in the demand curve from D to D' in Figure 3-4.

Finally, expectations that goods will not be available at any price will induce consumers to stock up now, increasing current demand.

 INTERNATIONAL EXAMPLE: Political Change, Change in Expectations

After the fall of communism at the end of the 1980s, Serbs dominated the central government of the former Yugoslavia. The province of Bosnia-Herzegovina, like the provinces of Croatia, Slovenia, and Macedonia, declared its independence and was recognized by the United Nations. Nonetheless, the Serb-dominated government attempted to prevent the independence of that country. It continuously shelled Bosnian cities, major and minor. In reaction, the United Nations proposed an embargo on all shipments of goods in and out of the two remaining provinces of the former Yugoslavia. In anticipation of the lack of availability of many goods, the residents of many cities in Serbia and Montenegro, particularly in Belgrade, started stocking up on everything from toilet paper to gasoline. Their demand curve for virtually every consumer staple shifted outward to the right.

For Critical Analysis: Under what circumstances would the demand curve for consumer staples shift inward to the left in Belgrade?

Population.   Often an increase in the population in an economy (holding per capita income constant) shifts the market demand outward for most products. This is because an increase in population leads to an increase in the number of buyers in the market. Conversely, a reduction in the population will shift most market demand curves inward because of the reduction in the number of buyers in the market.

⭐ **EXAMPLE: Changing Age Distribution in the Population**

Changing population is certainly a determinant of the demand for many goods. So is the change in age distribution in the population for such goods as housing. The demand for housing jumps between ages 20 and 30. It is relatively nonexistent below the age of 20, and it starts declining after the age of 40 by about 1 percent a year. That means that if the age distribution in our population changes, so will the demand for housing. In 1960 about 13 percent of the U.S. population was between ages 20 and 30; in 1980 it had increased to 20 percent. Not surprisingly, the demand for housing did in fact increase more than the increase in population from 1960 to 1980. Currently, the age distribution is going in the opposite direction. We therefore predict a decline in the rate of growth of the demand for housing.

For Critical Analysis: What other goods or services may be facing declining demand because of the aging of the American population? Explain your answer. ●

CHANGES IN DEMAND VERSUS CHANGES IN QUANTITY DEMANDED

We have made repeated references to demand and to quantity demanded. More important, there is a difference between the *change in demand* and the *change in quantity demanded.*

Remember then that demand refers to a schedule of planned rates of purchase. Demand depends on a great many nonprice determinants. Whenever there is a change in a nonprice determinant, there will be a change in demand—a shift in the entire demand curve to the right or to the left.

Now remember that any quantity demanded is at a specific price, represented by a single point on a given demand curve. When price changes, quantity demanded changes according to the law of demand, and there will be a movement from one point to another along the same demand curve. Look at Figure 3-5. At a price of $3 per diskette, 6 billion diskettes per year are demanded. If the price falls to $1, quantity demanded increases to 10 billion per year. This movement occurs because the current market price for the product changes. In Figure 3-5 you can see the arrow moving down the given demand curve *D*.

Always try to remember that quantity demanded can only be changed along the *horizontal* axis of the price-quantity graph. This is because a quantity is a point along that axis referring to another point along the demand and curve. So whenever the word *quantity* appears in a discussion, always think of a point along the horizontal axis. As you change price, you move along the horizontal axis. Conversely, when you think of demand, do not think of the horizontal axis or a point along it. Think of the curve itself.

> A change or shift in demand causes the *entire* curve to move. The *only* way that the entire curve can move is if a variable other than the price of the good changes.

In economic analysis, we cannot emphasize too much the following distinction that must constantly be made:

> A change in price leads to a change in quantity demanded, for any given demand curve. This is a movement *on* the curve.

> A change in the other determinants of demand leads to a change in demand. This leads to a movement *of* the curve.

CONCEPTS IN BRIEF

● Demand curves are drawn with determinants other than the price of the good held constant. These other determinants are (1) income; (2) tastes; (3) prices of related goods; (4) expectations about future prices, future incomes, and future availability of goods; and (5) population (number of buyers in the market). If any one of these determinants changes, the demand schedule will shift to the right or to the left. **(Continued)**

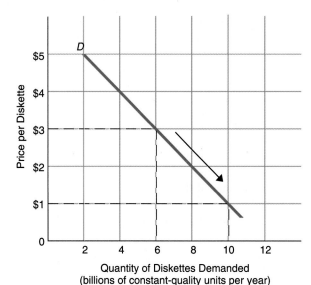

FIGURE 3-5
Movement along a given demand curve.
A change in price changes the quantity of a good demanded. This can be represented as movement along a given demand schedule. If, in our example, the price of diskettes falls from $3 to $1 apiece, the quantity demanded will increase from 6 billion to 10 billion units per year.

- A change in demand comes about only because of a change in the other determinants of demand. This change in demand shifts the demand curve to the left or to the right.
- A change in the quantity demanded comes about when there is a change in the price of the good. Such a change in quantity demanded involves a movement along a given demand curve.

SUPPLY AND THE SUPPLY SCHEDULE

The other side of the basic model in economics involves the quantities of goods and services that firms are prepared to *supply* to the market. The supply of any good or service is the amount that firms are prepared to sell under certain conditions during a specified time period. The relationship between price and quantity supplied, called **supply,** can be summarized as follows:

▷ **Supply**
A schedule showing the relationship between price and quantity supplied, other things being equal, for a specified period of time.

At higher prices, a larger quantity will generally be supplied than at lower prices, all other things held constant. At lower prices, a smaller quantity will generally be supplied than at higher prices, all other things held constant.

There is generally a direct relationship between quantity supplied and price. This is the opposite of the relationship we saw for demand. There, price and quantity demanded were inversely related. With supply, they are directly related. (Other direct relationships, for example, exist between caloric intake and body weight and between room temperature and the length of time a heater is left on.) For supply, as the price rises, the quantity supplied rises; as price falls, quantity supplied also falls. Producers are normally willing to produce and sell more of their product at a higher price than at a lower price, other things being constant. At $5 per diskette, 3M, Sony, Maxell, Fuji, and other manufacturers would almost certainly be willing to supply a larger quantity than at $1 per unit, assuming, of course, that no other prices in the economy had changed.

WHY A DIRECT, OR POSITIVE, RELATIONSHIP?

There are a number of intuitive reasons why there is normally a direct, or positive, relationship between price and quantity supplied. These involve suppliers' incentives for increasing production and the law of increasing relative costs, discussed in Chapter 2.

Incentives for Increasing Production. Consider a situation in which the only change in the marketplace is a price increase per diskette. If this occurs, diskette manufacturers will find it more rewarding monetarily than it was before to spend more of their time and resources producing diskettes than they used to. They may, for example, switch more of their production from videotape production to diskette production because the market price of diskettes has risen. The diskette maker may even find it now profitable to use more labor and machines in the production of diskettes because of their higher market price.

The Law of Increasing Costs. In Chapter 2 we explained why the production possibilities curve is bowed outward. The explanation basically involved the law of increasing costs—as society takes more and more resources and applies them to the production of any specific item, the opportunity cost for each additional unit produced increases. The law of increasing costs exists because resources are generally better suited for some activities than for others. Therefore, when we shift less well suited resources to a particular production activity, more and more units of it will have to be used to get the same increase in output as we expand production.

Now apply this analysis to diskette manufacturers wishing to increase the amount they supply. These manufacturers will eventually find that each additional output of diskette production will involve higher and higher costs. Hence, the only way that diskette makers would be induced to produce more and more diskettes would be because of the lure of a higher market price that these items could command. And, of course, only if the higher market price exceeds the rise in the cost of production will diskette manufacturers be willing to incur those higher costs. In a sense, then, it is because of the law of increasing costs that price has to go up in order to induce an increase in the quantity supplied.[2]

SUPPLY SCHEDULE

Just as we were able to construct a demand schedule, so we can construct a supply schedule, which is a table relating prices to the quantity supplied at each price. A supply schedule can also be referred to simply as *supply.* It is a set of planned production rates that depends on the price of the product. We show the individual supply schedule for a hypothetical producer in panel (a) of Figure 3-6. At $1 per diskette, for example, this producer will supply 20 million diskettes per year; at $5 this producer will supply 60 million diskettes per year.

SUPPLY CURVE

We can convert the supply schedule in panel (a) of Figure 3-6 into a **supply curve,** just as we earlier created a demand curve in Figure 3-1. All we do is take the price-quantity

▶ **Supply curve**
The graphic representation of the supply schedule; a line (curve) showing the supply schedule, which generally slopes upward (has a positive slope).

---

[2]Strictly speaking, the law of increasing costs can be used as an explanation for the generally positive relationship between quantity supplied and price only in the short run, when there is no possibility that improved production techniques resulting from the increased production will actually lower costs.

combinations from panel (a) of Figure 3-6 and plot them in panel (b). We have labeled these combinations *F* through *J*. Connecting these points, we obtain a curve. It is upward-sloping to show the normally direct relationship between price and quantity supplied. Again, we have to remember that we are talking about quantity supplied *per year*, measured in constant-quality units.

MARKET SUPPLY CURVE

Just as we had to sum the individual demand curves to get the market demand curve, we need to sum the individual producers' supply curves to get the market supply curve. Look at Figure 3-7 on page 64, where we horizontally sum two typical diskette manufacturers' supply curves. Supplier 1's data are taken from Figure 3-6; supplier 2 is added. The numbers are presented in panel (a). The graphic representation of supplier 1 is in panel (b), of supplier 2 in panel (c), and of the summation in panel (d). The result, then, is the supply curve for diskettes if only suppliers 1 and 2 were in the market. There are many more suppliers of diskettes, however. The total market supply schedule and total market demand curve for diskettes are represented in Figure 3-8 on page 65. The curve in panel (b) was obtained by adding all of the supply curves such as those shown in panels (b) and (c) of Figure 3-7. Notice the difference between the market supply curve with only two suppliers in Figure 3-7 and the one with a large number of suppliers—the entire true market—in panel (b) of Figure 3-8. There are no kinks in the true total market supply curve because there are so many suppliers.

Notice what happens when price changes. If the price is $3, the quantity supplied is 6 billion diskettes. If the price goes up to $4, the quantity supplied increases to 8 billion per year. If the price falls to $2, the quantity supplied decreases to 4 billion diskettes per year. Changes in quantity supplied are represented by movements along the supply curve in panel (b) of Figure 3-8.

FIGURE 3-6
The individual producer's supply schedule and supply curve for diskettes.
Panel (a) shows that at higher prices, a hypothetical supplier will be willing to provide a greater quantity of diskettes. We plot the various price-quantity combinations in panel (a) on the grid in panel (b). When we connect these points, we find the individual supply curve for diskettes. It is positively sloped.

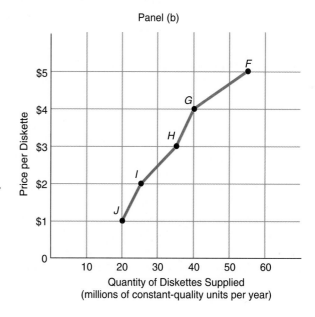

Panel (a)

COMBINATION	PRICE PER CONSTANT-QUALITY DISKETTE	QUANTITY OF DISKETTES SUPPLIED (MILLIONS OF CONSTANT-QUALITY UNITS PER YEAR)
F	$5	55
G	$4	40
H	$3	35
I	$2	25
J	$1	20

FIGURE 3-7
Horizontal summation of supply curves.
In panel (a) we show the data for two individual suppliers of diskettes. Adding how
much each is willing to supply at different prices, we come up with the total quantities
supplied in column 4. When we plot the values in columns 2 and 3 on grids in panels
(b) and (c) and add them horizontally, we obtain the combined supply curve for the two
suppliers in question, shown in panel (d).

Panel (a)

(1) PRICE PER DISKETTE	(2) SUPPLIER 1 QUANTITY SUPPLIED (MILLIONS)	(3) SUPPLIER 2 QUANTITY SUPPLIED (MILLIONS)	(4) = (2) +(3) TOTAL QUANTITY SUPPLIED PER YEAR (MILLIONS)
$5	55	35	90
$4	40	30	70
$3	35	20	55
$2	25	15	40
$1	20	10	30

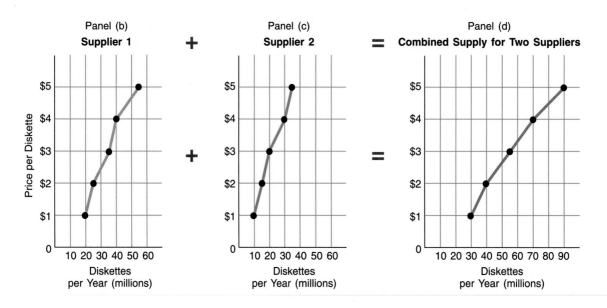

CONCEPTS IN BRIEF
● There is normally a direct, or positive, relationship between price and quantity of a good supplied, other things being constant.
● Because of the law of increasing costs, suppliers incur higher additional
  production costs when increasing output. Only if the market price they receive for their product goes up will they produce more.
● The supply curve normally shows a direct relationship between price and
  quantity supplied. The market supply curve is obtained by horizontally
  adding individual supply curves in the market.

FIGURE 3-8
The market supply schedule and the market supply curve for diskettes.
In panel (a) we show the summation of all the individual producers' supply schedules; in panel (b) we graph the resulting supply curve. It represents the market supply curve for diskettes and is upward-sloping.

Panel (a)

PRICE PER CONSTANT-QUALITY DISKETTE	QUANTITY OF DISKETTES SUPPLIED (BILLIONS OF CONSTANT-QUALITY UNITS PER YEAR)
$5	10
$4	8
$3	6
$2	4
$1	2

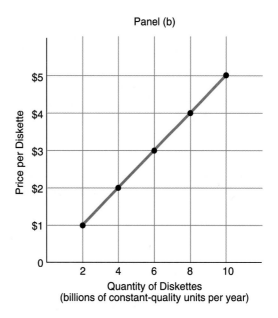

Panel (b)

SHIFTS IN SUPPLY

When we looked at demand, we found out that any change in anything relevant besides the price of the good or service caused the demand curve to shift inward or outward. The same is true for the supply curve. If something relevant changes besides the price of the product or service being supplied, we will see the entire supply curve shift.

Consider an example. A new method of putting magnetic material on diskettes has been invented. It reduces the cost of producing a diskette by 50 percent. In this situation, diskette producers will supply more product at *all* prices because their cost of so doing has fallen dramatically. Competition among diskette manufacturers to produce more at each and every price will shift the supply schedule of diskettes outward to the right from *S* to *S'* in Figure 3-9. At a price of $3, the quantity supplied was originally 6 billion diskettes

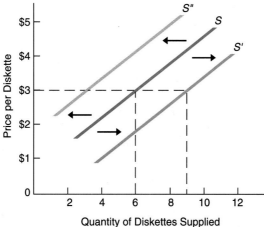

FIGURE 3-9
A shift in the supply schedule.
If the cost of producing diskettes were to fall dramatically, the supply schedule would shift rightward from *S* to *S'* such that at all prices a larger quantity would be forthcoming from suppliers. Conversely, if the cost of production rose, the supply curve would shift leftward to *S"*.

per year, but now the quantity supplied (after the reduction in the costs of production) at $3 a diskette will be 9 billion diskettes a year. (This is similar to what has happened to the supply curve of personal computers and fax machines in recent years as computer chip prices have fallen.)

Consider the opposite case. The cost of the magnetic material needed for making diskettes doubles. In this situation, the supply curve in Figure 3-9 will shift from S to S″, and at each and every price the quantity of diskettes supplied will fall due to the increase in the price of raw materials.

THE NONPRICE DETERMINANTS OF SUPPLY

When supply curves are drawn, only the price of the good in question changes, and it is assumed that other things remain constant. The other things assumed constant are (1) the costs of resources (inputs) used to produce the product, (2) technology and productivity, (3) taxes and subsidies, (4) producers' price expectations, and (5) the number of firms in the industry. These are the major nonprice determinants of supply. If *any* of them changes, there will be a shift in the supply curve.

Cost of Inputs Used to Produce the Product. If one or more input prices fall, the supply curve will shift outward to the right; that is, more will be supplied at each and every price. The opposite will be true if one or more inputs become more expensive. For example, when we draw the supply curve of new cars, we are holding the cost of steel (and other inputs) constant. When we draw the supply curve of blue jeans, we are holding the cost of cotton fixed.

 EXAMPLE: The Dramatic Decrease in the Price of Computers

At the beginning of this chapter we noted that the price of computers can drop relatively dramatically even in a six-month period. The cost of computers reflects the costs of its more expensive components, such as computer chips, hard-disk drives, and random-access memory (RAM). The price of chips of all kinds used in computers has dropped dramatically over the past 30 years. Figure 3-10 shows the cost per unit of speed for the average microprocessor chip. The unit here is millions of instructions per second (MIPS), but the real point is that however it is measured, computing power costs practically nothing compared to what it used to. One estimate shows that between 1960 and 1994, the real price of computing power in America shrank by a factor of over 6,000. Not surpris-

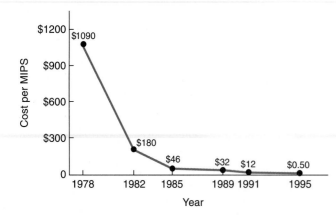

FIGURE 3-10
Evolution of the cost per unit of speed for microprocessor chips.
In less than two decades, the price per unit of speed (1 million instructions per second) has fallen from about $1,100 to 50 cents. Costs today are less than .04 percent of what they were in 1978.

ingly, private enterprises have increased their purchase of information-processing equipment dramatically. In 1970, for example, such equipment accounted for 11 percent of all equipment bought by private businesses. The estimate for 1995 is 54 percent. Clearly, the supply curve of computers has been shifting outward to the right virtually every year as the price of the key inputs—chips—has fallen dramatically.

For Critical Analysis: Has the dramatically decreased cost of computer chips had an impact on other products besides computers? If so, how and why? (Hint: What other products use computer chips?) ●

Technology and Productivity.   Supply curves are drawn by assuming a given technology, or "state of the art." When the types of production techniques available change, the supply curve will shift. For example, when a better production technique for diskettes becomes available, the supply curve will shift to the right. A larger quantity will be forthcoming at each and every price because the cost of production is lower.

Taxes and Subsidies.   Certain taxes, such as sales taxes, are effectively an addition to production costs and therefore reduce the supply. If the supply curve were S in Figure 3-9, a sales tax increase would shift it to S''. A **subsidy** would do the opposite; it would shift the curve to S'. Every producer would get a "gift" from the government of a few cents for each unit produced.

▶ **Subsidy**
A negative tax; a payment to a producer from the government, usually in the form of a cash grant.

Price Expectations.   A change in the expectation of a future relative price of a product can affect a producer's current willingness to supply, just as price expectations affect a consumer's current willingness to purchase. For example, diskette suppliers may withhold from the market part of their current supply if they anticipate higher prices in the future. The current amount supplied at each and every price will decrease.

Number of Firms in the Industry.   In the short run, when firms can only change the number of employees they use, we hold the number of firms in the industry constant. In the long run, the number of firms (or the size of some existing firms) may change. If the number of firms increases, the supply curve will shift outward to the right. If the number of firms decreases, it will shift inward to the left.

CHANGE IN QUANTITY SUPPLIED AND CHANGE IN SUPPLY

We cannot overstress the importance of distinguishing between a movement along the supply curve—which occurs only when the price changes for a given supply curve—and a shift in the supply curve—which occurs only with changes in other nonprice factors. A change in price always brings about a change in quantity supplied along a given supply curve. We move to a different coordinate on the existing supply curve. This is specifically called a *change in quantity supplied.* When price changes, quantity supplied changes, and there will be a movement from one point to another along the same supply curve.

Remember that quantity supplied can be changed along the horizontal axis of the price-quantity graph because the quantity is a point along that axis referring to another point along the supply curve. Whenever the word *quantity* appears in a discussion, you must think of a point along the horizontal axis. Then you realize that the way you will move along the horizontal axis is by changing price. Alternatively, when you see the word *supply*, think of the entire curve itself. Quantity supplied is represented by a single point on the supply curve; supply is the entire curve.

> **A change or shift in supply causes the *entire* curve to move. The *only* way the entire curve can move is if a variable other than the price of the good changes.**

Consequently,

> **A change in the price of a good or service leads to a change in the quantity of that good or service supplied, other things being constant.**

> **A change in the other determinants of supply leads to a change in supply.**

CONCEPTS IN BRIEF

- If the price changes, we *move along* a curve—there is a change in quantity demanded or supplied. If some other determinant changes, we *shift* a curve— there is a change in demand or supply.
- The supply curve is drawn with other things held constant. If other determinants of supply change, the supply curve will shift. The major other determinants are (1) input costs, (2) technology and productivity, (3) taxes and subsidies, (4) expectations of future relative prices, and (5) the number of firms in the industry.

PUTTING DEMAND AND SUPPLY TOGETHER

In the sections on supply and demand, we tried to confine each discussion only to supply or to demand. But you have probably already gotten the idea that we can't view the world just from the supply side or just from the demand side. There is an interaction between the two. In this section we will discuss how they interact and how that interaction determines the prices that prevail in our economy. In other words, understanding how demand and supply interact is essential to understanding how prices are determined in our economy and other economies in which the forces of supply and demand are allowed to work.

Let's first combine the demand and supply schedules, and then we will combine the curves.

DEMAND AND SUPPLY SCHEDULES COMBINED

Let's place panel (a) from Figure 3-3 (the market demand schedule) and panel (a) from Figure 3-8 (the market supply schedule) together in panel (a) of Figure 3-11. Column 1 shows the price; column 2, the quantity supplied per year at any given price; and column 3, the quantity demanded. Column 4 is merely the difference between columns 2 and 3, or the difference between the quantity supplied and the quantity demanded. In column 5 we label those differences as either an excess quantity supplied (surplus) or an excess quantity demanded (shortage). For example, at a price of $1, only 2 billion diskettes would be supplied, but the quantity demanded would be 10 billion. The difference would be -8 billion, which we label an excess quantity demanded (shortage). At the other end of the scale, a price of $5 per diskette would elicit 10 billion in quantity supplied, but quantity demanded would drop to 2 billion, leaving a difference of $+8$ billion units, which we call an excess quantity supplied (surplus).

FIGURE 3-11
Putting demand and supply together.
In panel (a) we see that at the price of $3, the quantity supplied and the quantity demanded are equal, resulting in neither an excess in the quantity demanded nor an excess in the quantity supplied. We call this price the equilibrium, or market clearing, price. In panel (b) the intersection of the supply and demand curves is at *E*, at a price of $3 per constant-quality diskette and a quantity of 6 billion per year. At point *E* there is neither an excess in the quantity demanded nor an excess in the quantity supplied. At a price of $1 the quantity supplied will be only 2 billion disks per year, but the quantity demanded will be 10 billion. The difference is excess quantity demanded at a price of $1. The price will rise, so we will move from point *A* up the supply curve to point *E*. At the other extreme, $5 elicits a quantity supplied of 10 billion but a quantity demanded of only 2 billion. The difference is excess quantity supplied at a price of $5. The price will fall, so we will move down the demand curve to the equilibrium price, $3 per diskette.

Panel (a)

(1) PRICE PER CONSTANT-QUALITY DISKETTE	(2) QUANTITY SUPPLIED (DISKETTES PER YEAR)	(3) QUANTITY DEMANDED (DISKETTES PER YEAR)	(4) DIFFERENCE (2) - (3) (DISKETTES PER YEAR)	(5) CONDITION
$5	10 billion	2 billion	8 billion	Excess quantity supplied (surplus)
$4	8 billion	4 billion	4 billion	Excess quantity supplied (surplus)
$3	6 billion	6 billion	0	Market clearing price–equilibrium (no surplus, no shortage)
$2	4 billion	8 billion	-4 billion	Excess quantity demanded (shortage)
$1	2 billion	10 billion	-8 billion	Excess quantity demanded (shortage)

Panel (b)

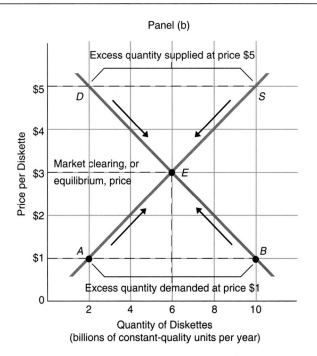

Quantity of Diskettes
(billions of constant-quality units per year)

Now, do you notice something special about a price of $3? At that price both the quantity supplied and the quantity demanded per year are 6 billion diskettes. The difference then is zero. There is neither an excess quantity demanded (shortage) nor an excess quantity supplied (surplus). Hence the price of $3 is very special. It is called the **market clearing price**—it clears the market of all excess supply or excess demand. There are no willing consumers who want to pay $3 per diskette but are turned away by sellers, and there are no willing suppliers who want to sell diskettes at $3 who cannot sell all they want at that price. Another term for the market clearing price is the **equilibrium price,** the price at which there is no tendency for change. Consumers are able to get all they want at that price, and suppliers are able to sell the amount that they want at that price.

▶ **Market clearing,** or **equilibrium, price**
The price that clears the market, at which quantity demanded equals quantity supplied; the price where the demand curve intersects the supply curve.

EQUILIBRIUM

We can define **equilibrium** in general as a point from which there tends to be no movement unless demand or supply changes. Any movement away from this point will set into motion certain forces that will cause movement back to it. Therefore, equilibrium is a stable point. Any point that is not at equilibrium is unstable and cannot be maintained.

▶ **Equilibrium**
A situation when quantity supplied equals quantity demanded at a particular price.

The equilibrium point occurs where the supply and demand curves intersect. The equilibrium price is given on the vertical axis directly to the left of where the supply and demand curves cross. The equilibrium quantity demanded and supplied is given on the horizontal axis directly underneath the intersection of the demand and supply curves. Equilibrium can change whenever there is a shock.

A shock to the supply-and-demand system can be represented by a shift in the supply curve, a shift in the demand curve, or a shift in both curves. Any shock to the system will result in a new set of supply-and-demand relationships and a new equilibrium; forces will come into play to move the system from the old price-quantity equilibrium (now a disequilibrium situation) to the new equilibrium, where the new demand and supply curves intersect.

Let's combine panel (b) in Figure 3-3 and panel (b) in Figure 3-8 as panel (b) in Figure 3-11 on page 69. The only difference now is that the horizontal axis measures both the quantity supplied and the quantity demanded per year. Everything else is the same. The demand curve is labeled *D*, the supply curve *S*. We have labeled the intersection of the supply curve with the demand curve as point *E*, for equilibrium. That corresponds to a market clearing price of $3, at which both the quantity supplied and the quantity demanded are 6 billion units per year. There is neither an excess quantity supplied nor an excess quantity demanded. Point *E*, the equilibrium point, always occurs at the intersection of the supply and demand curves. This is the price toward which the market price will automatically tend to gravitate.

🌐 **INTERNATIONAL EXAMPLE: Bargaining at Home and Abroad**

As an individual, normally you purchase things you want in the marketplace at the price at which they are offered. You usually deal with retail firms that use **posted-offer pricing** to price their goods and services. You don't bargain. Sometimes you do, though. For example, the "sticker price" of a new car is virtually never the price that you pay. You normally bargain with the dealer. The sticker price is the dealer's first offer. Then you make your counteroffer. The process is called **bargaining,** and it is a way of changing prices immediately. The bargaining requires time, information, and effort. You rarely go into a department store and bargain for a handbag, a pair of jeans, or a pair of shoes.

▶ **Posted-offer pricing**
A pricing technique in which retail firms post a specific offer and do not entertain the possibility of accepting a lower offer, nor do they attempt to raise prices above those posted either. This is a practice of posting prices before demand is actually known.

But if you go to most cities in Mexico, Peru, and a number of other countries, the opposite is true. People there often bargain for shoes or handbags in a department store. The question that you might ask is why the pricing process differs in Mexico and Peru from that in the United States. The main reason is that the opportunity cost of bargaining dif-

▶ **Bargaining**
The process of making counteroffers to a person's offer to sell a good or service at a particular price.

▶ **Time cost**
The value of the time necessary to complete an activity, including search costs, waiting time, transportation time, and time actually engaging in the activity.

fers. The average worker in many less developed countries receives a much lower wage rate than the average worker in the United States. Consequently, the **time cost** of bargaining is less for these workers. Consider some relative figures. Suppose that the per-person average annual income in Peru is a bit less than $2,000 and $20,000 in the United States. Assume that you can bargain over the price of a handbag and that through bargaining you save $10. If you make average earnings in the United States, you would save roughly .05 percent of your annual income. If you are the average worker in Peru, however, the same $10 represents .5 percent of your annual income—10 times more in relative importance. This also explains why you won't bargain over a handbag but you will do so over a $15,000 automobile or a $100,000 house. Successful bargaining for high-priced products makes a big difference in what you have left over to spend on other goods and services.

For Critical Analysis: Because Americans bargain less than people living in poorer countries, can it be said that the market clearing price in this country may take longer to reach? Explain. ●

SHORTAGES

The demand and supply curves depicted in Figure 3-11 represent a situation of equilibrium. But a non–market clearing, or disequilibrium, price will put into play forces that cause the price to change toward the market clearing price at which equilibrium will again be sustained. Look again at panel (b) in Figure 3-11. Suppose that instead of being at the market clearing price of $3 per diskette, for some reason the market price is $1 per diskette. At this price the quantity demanded exceeds the quantity supplied, the former being 10 billion diskettes per year and the latter, 2 billion per year. We have a situation of an excess quantity demanded at the price of $1. This is usually called a **shortage.** Consumers of diskettes would find that they could not buy all that they wished at $1 apiece. But forces will cause the price to rise: Competing consumers will bid up the price and/or suppliers will raise the price and increase output, whether explicitly or implicitly. (Remember, some buyers would pay $5 or more rather than do without diskettes. They do not want to be left out.) We would move from points *A* and *B* toward point *E*. The process would stop when the price again reached $3 per diskette.

▶ **Shortage**
A situation in which quantity demanded is greater than quantity supplied at a price below the market clearing price.

At this point, it is important to recall a distinction made in Chapter 2:

Shortages and scarcity are not the same thing.

A shortage is a situation in which the quantity demanded exceeds the quantity supplied at a price *below* the market clearing price. Our definition of scarcity was much more general and all-encompassing: a situation in which the resources available for producing output are insufficient to satisfy all wants. Any choice necessarily costs an opportunity, and the opportunity is lost. Hence we will always live in a world of scarcity because we must constantly make choices, but we do not necessarily have to live in a world of shortages.

SURPLUSES

Now let's repeat the experiment with the market price at $5 per diskette rather than at the market clearing price of $3. Clearly, the quantity supplied will exceed the quantity demanded at that price. The result will be an excess quantity supplied at $5 per unit. This excess quantity supplied is often called a **surplus.** Given *D* and *S*, however, there will be forces pushing the price back down toward $3 per diskette: Competing suppliers will attempt to reduce their inventories by cutting prices and reducing output, and/or consumers will offer to purchase more at lower prices. Suppliers will want to reduce inventories that

▶ **Surplus**
A situation in which quantity supplied is greater than quantity demanded at a price above the market clearing price.

will be above their optimal level; that is, there will be an excess over what each seller believes to be the most profitable stock of diskettes. After all, inventories are costly to hold. But consumers may find out about such excess inventories and see the possibility of obtaining increased quantities of diskettes at a decreased price. It behooves consumers to attempt to obtain a good at a lower price, and they will therefore try to do so. If the two forces of supply and demand are unrestricted, they will bring the price back to $3 per diskette.

Shortages and surpluses are resolved in unfettered markets—markets in which price changes are free to occur. The forces that resolve them are those of competition: In the case of shortages, consumers competing for a limited quantity supplied drive up the price; in the case of surpluses, sellers compete for the limited quantity demanded, thus driving prices down to equilibrium. The equilibrium price is the only stable price, and all (unrestricted) market prices tend to gravitate to it.

CONCEPTS IN BRIEF

- The market clearing price occurs at the intersection of the market demand curve and the market supply curve. It is also called the equilibrium price, the price from which there is no tendency to change unless there is a change in demand and/or supply.
- Whenever the price is greater than the equilibrium price, there is an excess quantity supplied (a surplus).
- Whenever the price is less than the equilibrium price, there is an excess quantity demanded (a shortage).

CHANGING SUPPLY AND DEMAND FOR GOOD STUDENTS

Concepts Applied: Demand and supply, shifts in demand and supply

Some of these college students received offers from many universities when they were seniors in high school. Shifts in the demand for students relative to the supply have changed college recruiting techniques recently.

The *New York Times* interviewed some students during the first week in April a few years ago. Many of the students were amazed at how much colleges and universities wanted them. Some were getting phone calls all the time. One prospective student, who had been accepted at Penn, Haverford, Cornell, and the University of Michigan, said that 10 alumni who were complete strangers to her family had visited her father in the hospital while he was recovering from surgery. One student got a letter from the associate dean of admissions at the University of Southern California in which he included his home phone number and asked the prospective student to call him anytime. When this student visited the campus in Los Angeles, the associate dean took him on a tour of Universal Studios and on a day trip to Mexico.

WHY ARE THEY BEING SO NICE TO ME?

Of course, good students in high school have always been courted by universities and colleges. But certainly a student with the same grades, same number of advanced placement courses, and same number of extracurricular activities is being treated much better now than that student would have been treated in the 1970s. The change has nothing to do with a new social consciousness on the part of college admissions officers. It has to do with a change in demand relative to supply. Even though a higher percentage of high school graduates is attending college today, the number of college-entry-aged Americans is lower than it used to be. The National Center for Educational Statistics points out that in 1977 some 3.15 million students graduated from college. That number was 2.58 million in 1990 and is projected to reach as low as 2.45 million in 1995. Clearly, the demand for a college education has decreased since the late 1970s.

A GRAPHIC ANALYSIS In Figure 3-12 you see the supply curve of college and university "slots." It has an upward slope to indicate that at high enough prices, colleges and universities can hire more faculty even in the short run and teach more students. There are two demand curves. One is labeled 1977, the other is labeled 1995. The D_{1995} is inward to the left of D_{1977}. In a smoothly functioning market, the price of a college education would fall from P_{1977} to P_{1995}. But it hasn't. In fact, actual prices for college education continued to rise every year.

Consequently, at any price above P_{1995}, say, P', there is an excess quantity supplied of college and university student slots.

FIGURE 3-12
A surplus of college slots.
Since 1977 the demand curve for college admissions has decreased from D_{1977} to D_{1995}. Because the price charged by colleges and universities has not dropped to its equilibrium level of P_{1995}, there is an excess quantity supplied (a surplus) at any price above that, such as at P'.

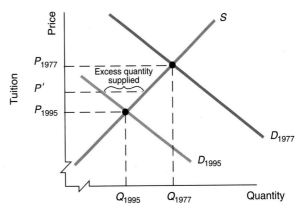

The new array of recruiting tools that colleges and universities are using is simply their answer to dealing with this surplus at price P'. Some colleges and universities have been unsuccessful and have been forced to go out of business. Others are downsizing their institutions. Of course, this analysis does not apply to every institution of higher learning. For example, recently there have been cutbacks in California's public institutions of higher learning. Consequently, the supply schedule of college slots in that state has probably shifted inward more than the demand.

FOR CRITICAL ANALYSIS

1. What do you think might prevent colleges and universities from simply lowering their tuition rates in order to attract more students?
2. Draw the supply and demand curves for an individual college or university. Show what aggressive recruiting tools are expected to do to those curves for that individual college or university.

CHAPTER SUMMARY

1. The law of demand says that at higher prices individuals will purchase less of a commodity and at lower prices they will purchase more, other things being equal.
2. Relative prices must be distinguished from absolute, or money, prices. During periods of rising prices, almost all prices go up, but some rise faster than others.
3. All reference to the laws of supply and demand refer to constant-quality units of a commodity. We must also specify a time period for our analysis.
4. The law of demand holds when there is a price change because of (a) the substitution effect and (b) the real-income effect.
5. The demand schedule shows the relationship between various possible prices and their respective quantities purchased per unit time period. Graphically, the demand schedule is a demand curve and is downward-sloping.
6. The other determinants of demand are (a) income, (b) taste and preferences, (c) the price of related goods, (d) expectations, and (e) the population, or market, size. Whenever any other determinant of demand changes, the demand curve shifts.

7. The supply curve is generally upward-sloping such that at higher prices, more will be forthcoming than at lower prices. At higher prices suppliers are willing to incur the increasing costs of higher rates of production.
8. The other determinants of supply are (a) technology and productivity, (b) taxes and subsidies, (c) price expectations, (d) input costs, and (e) entry and exit of firms.
9. A movement along a demand or supply curve is not the same thing as a shift in one of those curves. Whenever price changes, we move along the curve. A change in any other determinant of supply or demand shifts those curves.
10. Where the demand and supply curves intersect is the equilibrium point, or market clearing price, at which quantity demanded just equals quantity supplied. At that point the plans of buyers and sellers mesh exactly.
11. When the price of a good is greater than its market clearing price, an excess quantity is supplied at that price; it is called a surplus. When the price is below the market clearing price, an excess quantity is demanded at that price; it is called a shortage.

DISCUSSION OF PREVIEW POINTS

1. **The law of demand indicates that an inverse relationship exists between price and quantity demanded, other things being constant. Why?**
   Suppose that when the price of hamburgers was $1 per unit, John Smith purchased 10 hamburgers per week; he spent $10 per week on hamburgers. Let's further assume, for simplicity, that Smith spent *all* his weekly income of $100 per week. Now, if the price of hamburgers falls to 50 cents per unit, and all other things remain constant, what will happen? If Smith

makes exactly the same number of purchases he made the week before, he would now be spending the same amount on nonhamburgers and only $5 on hamburgers. In short, Smith has experienced an increase in his real income of $5; his $100 weekly income can buy everything he purchased last week and he still has $5 left over. We predict that he will spend some of this $5 on hamburgers.

2. **How can we distinguish between a change in demand and a change in quantity demanded, with a given demand curve?**

Use the accompanying graphs to aid you. Because demand is a curve, a change in demand is equivalent to a *shift* in the demand curve. Changes in demand result from changes in the other determinants of demand, such as income, tastes and preferences, expectations, prices of related goods, and population. A change in quantity demanded, given demand, is a movement along a demand curve and results only from a change in the price of the commodity in question.

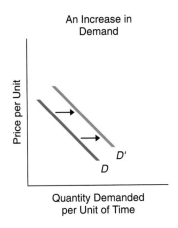

An Increase in
Demand

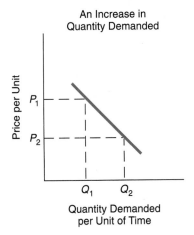

An Increase in
Quantity Demanded

3. **There is generally a direct relationship between price and quantity supplied, other things being constant. Why?**

Economists maintain that there generally is a direct relationship between price and quantity supplied. In general, businesses experience increasing *extra* costs as they expand output in the short run. This means that later units of output, which may be quite similar in physical attributes to earlier units of output, actually cost the firm more to produce. Consequently, firms often require a higher and higher price (as an incentive) in order to produce more in the short run; "incentive" effect maintains that higher prices, other things being constant, lead to increases in quantity supplied.

4. **Why will the market clearing (equilibrium) price be set at the intersection of supply and demand and not at a higher or lower price?**

Consider the accompanying graph. To demonstrate that the equilibrium price will be at P_e, we can eliminate all other prices as possibilities. Consider a price above P_e, $8 per unit. By inspection of the graph we can see that at that price the quantity supplied exceeds the quantity demanded for this product ($B > A$). Clearly, sellers are not maximizing total profits, and they therefore find it profitable to lower price and decrease output. In fact, this surplus situation exists at *all* prices above P_e. Sellers, competing for sales, will reduce prices if a surplus exists.

Consider a price of $4 per unit, where the quantity demanded exceeds the quantity supplied ($F > C$); a shortage of this commodity exists at a price of $4 per unit. Buyers will not be able to get all they want at that relatively low price. Because buyers are competing for this good, buyers who are willing to give up

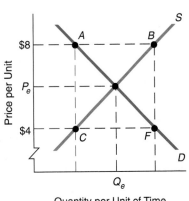

more of other goods in order to get this one will offer higher and higher prices. By doing so, they eliminate buyers who are not willing to give up more of other goods. An increase in price encourages sellers to produce and sell more. A shortage exists at *any* price below P_e, and therefore price will rise if it is below P_e.

At P_e the quantity supplied equals the quantity demanded, Q_e, and both buyers and sellers are able to realize their intentions. Because neither group has an incentive to change its behavior, equilibrium exists at P_e.

PROBLEMS
(Answers to the odd-numbered problems appear at the back of the book.)

3-1. Construct a demand curve and a supply curve for skateboards, based on the data provided in the following tables.

PRICE PER SKATEBOARD	QUANTITY DEMANDED PER YEAR
$75	3 million
$50	6 million
$35	9 million
$25	12 million
$15	15 million
$10	18 million

PRICE PER SKATEBOARD	QUANTITY SUPPLIED PER YEAR
$75	18 million
$50	15 million
$35	12 million
$25	9 million
$15	6 million
$10	3 million

What is the equilibrium price? What is the equilibrium quantity at that price?

3-2. "Drugs are obviously complementary to physicians' services." Is this statement always correct?

3-3. Five factors, other than price, that affect the demand for a good were discussed in this chapter. Place each of the following events in its proper category, and state how it would shift the demand curve in parentheses.

a. New information is disclosed that large doses of vitamin C prevent common colds. (Demand for vitamin C)

b. A drop in the price of tape recorders occurs. (Demand for stenographic services)

c. A fall in the price of pretzels occurs. (Demand for beer)

3-4. Examine the following table, and then answer the questions.

PRICE PER UNIT LAST YEAR		PRICE PER UNIT TODAY
Heating oil	$1.00	$2.00
Natural gas	$ .80	$3.20

What has happened to the absolute price of heating oil? Of natural gas? What has happened to the price of heating oil relative to the price of natural gas? What has happened to the relative price of heating oil? Will consumers, through time, change their relative purchases? If so, how?

3-5. Suppose that the demand for oranges remains constant but a frost occurs in Florida that could potentially destroy one-third of the orange crop. What will happen to the equilibrium price and quantity for Florida oranges?

3-6. What's wrong with the following assertion? "The demand has increased so much in response to our offering of a $500 rebate that our inventory of cars is now running very low."

3-7. Analyze the following statement: "Federal farm price supports can never achieve their goals because the above-equilibrium price floors that are established by Congress and the Department of

Agriculture invariably create surpluses (quantities supplied in excess of quantities demanded), which in turn drive the price right back down toward equilibrium."

3-8. Suppose that an island economy exists in which there is no money. Suppose further that every Sunday morning, at a certain location, hog farmers and cattle ranchers gather to exchange live pigs for cows. Is this a market, and if so, what do the supply and demand diagrams use as a price? Can you imagine any problems arising at the price at which cows and pigs are exchanged?

3-9. Here is a supply and demand schedule for rain in an Amazon jungle settlement where cloud seeding or other scientific techniques can be used to coax rainfall from the skies.

PRICE (CRUZEIROS PER YEARLY CENTIMETER OF RAIN)	QUANTITY SUPPLIED (CENTIMETERS OF RAIN)	QUANTITY DEMANDED (CENTIMETERS PER YEAR)
0	200	150
10	225	125
20	250	100
30	275	75
40	300	50
50	325	25
60	350	0
70	375	0
80	400	0

What are the equilibrium price and the equilibrium quantity? Explain.

COMPUTER-ASSISTED INSTRUCTION
(Complete problem and answer on disk.)

By examining the consequence of a specific price change, we examine the roles of the substitution effect and the income effect in producing the law of demand.

EXTENSIONS OF DEMAND AND SUPPLY ANALYSIS

A few years ago, more than 500,000 Californians who purchased their car insurance through the Automobile Club of Southern California received a rebate that averaged over $200 each. Over a quarter of a million Mercury General policyholders each received $172. In New Jersey at about the same time, auto insurance rates were cut on average by $222 per year. In an era of ever-increasing automobile insurance rates, such rebates don't seem to fit. After all, auto insurers are facing increasingly high liability awards assessed against their policyholders involved in accidents. Are auto insurers in California and New Jersey different? Understanding the answer to this question requires knowledge of government policies that affect supply and demand.

After reading this chapter, you should be able to answer the following questions:

1. Does an increase in demand always lead to a rise in price?
2. Can there ever be shortages in a market with no restrictions?
3. How are goods rationed?
4. When would you expect to encounter black markets?

INTRODUCTION

If you judged the world by the popular press, you would get the impression that shortages and surpluses are everywhere. You read about purported shortages of apartments in Berkeley and New York City. The lack of affordable housing is constantly in the news throughout the nation. Hospitals tell reporters that there is a shortage of skilled nurses. But even in your own life, you probably encounter situations in which you are certain that there is a surplus or a shortage, yet the price just isn't changing. After all, have you ever gone into an empty restaurant and had the owner offer to lower prices if you eat there? Probably not, even though there is a "surplus" of seats. Have you ever been unable to buy a popular item because it is out of stock—an apparent shortage? Probably so. What you will see in this chapter is that relatively straightforward extensions of the supply and demand analysis you learned in Chapter 3 can be used to explain such phenomena. The best place to start is with the process of exchange itself.

EXCHANGE AND MARKETS

▶ Voluntary exchange
An act of trading, done on a voluntary basis, in which both parties to the trade are subjectively better off after the exchange.

▶ Terms of exchange
The terms under which trading takes place. Usually the terms of exchange are equal to the price at which a good is traded.

▶ Transaction costs
All of the costs associated with exchanging, including the informational costs of finding out price and quality, service record, and durability of a product, plus the cost of contracting and enforcing that contract.

The price system features **voluntary exchange,** acts of trading between individuals that make both parties to the trade subjectively better off. The **terms of exchange**—the prices we pay for the desired items—are determined by the interaction of the forces underlying supply and demand. In our economy the majority of exchanges take place voluntarily in markets. A market encompasses the exchange arrangements of both buyers and sellers that underlie the forces of supply and demand. Indeed, one definition of market is a low-cost institution for facilitating exchange. A market in essence increases incomes by helping resources move to their highest-valued uses by means of prices. Prices are the providers of information. All individuals turn to markets because markets reduce the cost of exchanges, sometimes referred to as **transaction costs,** which are broadly defined as costs of negotiating and enforcing contracts as well as of acquiring and processing information about alternatives.

The most obvious markets are the highly organized ones such as the New York Stock Exchange and the American Stock Exchange. The latest information on the price of a listed stock can be obtained, as can information on how many shares have been bought and sold in the past several hours.

Generally, the less organized the market, the higher the transaction costs. Historically, the less costly it has become to disseminate information through technological improvements, the more transaction costs have fallen.

 INTERNATIONAL EXAMPLE: Capitalists Take to the Street in Moscow

For over 70 years, an explicit noncapitalist, nonmarket economic system existed in Russia. That does not mean that markets didn't exist, but those that did exist were illegal and underground. Many commentators maintained that the opening up of the Russian economy would do little to change the situation. Their explanation was that the entrepreneurial spirit had died out during the 74 years of communist rule. After all, buying and reselling for a profit was against the law and punishable as an economic crime with severe penalties, sometimes even death.

A few short years after independence came to the Russian republic, street markets had already become common in Moscow. In spite of the city authority's attempt to prevent the spread of such markets, there are well over 20,000 daily street market traders in that capital city. When they were banned from central squares and boulevards, they moved into designated areas, but spread out soon thereafter.

One of the biggest street markets has been on the sidewalk outside the former secret police (KGB) headquarters in the center of Moscow. On some days traders are lined up shoulder to shoulder for five city blocks. They sell American beer, British disposable syringes, French candy, Swiss chocolates, German hair dye, leather jackets made in Turkey, and sneakers made in China. These foreign goods have been swamping the so-called *tolkuchka,* a word that means "crush" and is now applied to the street markets. Individual Muscovites are flying to foreign countries to bring back their wares. For example, Igor Yavlinsky flies to Beijing every 10 days to buy sneakers at $1.50 a pair, which he then resells in Moscow for about $15.00.

For Critical Analysis: Are there any reasons why exchanges of certain goods and services can't take place in normal markets in the United States? Name those goods and services and explain why. (Hint: Think of legislation affecting the production and sale of certain goods and services.) ●

CHANGES IN DEMAND AND SUPPLY

It is in markets that we see the results of changes in demand and supply. In certain situations it is possible to predict what will happen to equilibrium price and equilibrium quantity when a change occurs in demand and/or supply. Specifically, whenever one curve is stable while the other curve shifts, we can tell what will happen to price and quantity. Consider the four possibilities in Figure 4-1. In panel (a) the supply curve remains stable but

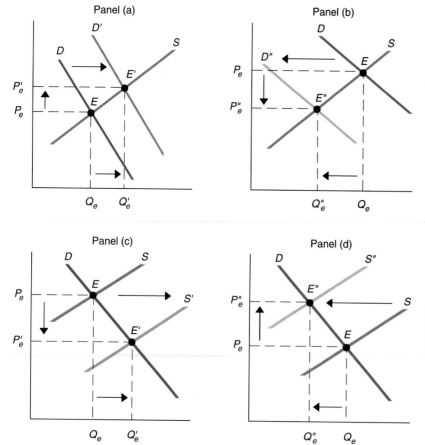

FIGURE 4-1

Shifts in demand and in supply: determinate results.

In panel (a) the supply curve is stable at S. The demand curve shifts out from D to D'. The equilibrium price and quantities rise from P_e, Q_e to P'_e, Q'_e, respectively. In panel (b) again the supply curve remains stable at S. The demand curve, however, shifts inward to the left, showing a decrease in demand from D to D''. Both equilibrium price and equilibrium quantity fall. In panel (c) the demand curve now remains stable at D. The supply curve shifts from S to S'. The equilibrium price falls from P_e to P'_e. The equilibrium quantity increases, however, from Q_e to Q'_e. In panel (d) the demand curve is stable at D. Supply decreases, as shown by a leftward shift of the supply curve from S to S''. The market clearing price increases from P_e to P''_e. The equilibrium quantity falls from Q_e to Q''_e.

demand increases from D to D'. Note that the result is both an increase in the market clearing price from P_e to P'_e and an increase in the equilibrium quantity from Q_e to Q'_e.

In panel (b) there is a decrease in demand from D to D''. This results in a decrease in both the relative price of the good and the equilibrium quantity. Panels (c) and (d) show the effects of a shift in the supply curve while the demand curve is stable. In panel (c) the supply curve has shifted rightward. The relative price of the product falls; the equilibrium quantity increases. In panel (d) supply has shifted leftward—there has been a supply decrease. The product's relative price increases; the equilibrium quantity decreases.

WHEN BOTH DEMAND AND SUPPLY SHIFT

The examples given in Figure 4-1 each showed a theoretically determinate outcome of a shift in either the demand curve holding the supply curve constant or the supply curve holding the demand curve constant. When both supply and demand curves change, the outcome is indeterminate for either equilibrium price or equilibrium quantity. Consider panel (a) of Figure 4-2. Both demand and supply rise, causing demand to shift from D to D' and supply from S to S'. The only thing that we can be certain of is that the equilibrium quantity will rise and be something greater than Q_e. The way we have drawn the diagram, demand has increased more than supply, so price has gone up from P_e to P'_e. But the converse could have been true, and the price could have fallen.

FIGURE 4-2
Shifts in supply and demand: indeterminate results.
Whenever both supply and demand change, we cannot predict the movement of *both* equilibrium price and quantity. When demand and supply both rise, as in panel (a), quantity will definitely increase from Q_e to Q'_e. We have shown price rising to P'_e because demand has increased more than supply. The converse could hold, however, and price would fall. In panel (b) both demand and supply have fallen. We know that equilibrium quantity will fall too. Price can go up or down, though. In panels (c) and (d) the shift in demand is opposite the shift in supply. We know what will happen to price but not equilibrium quantity.

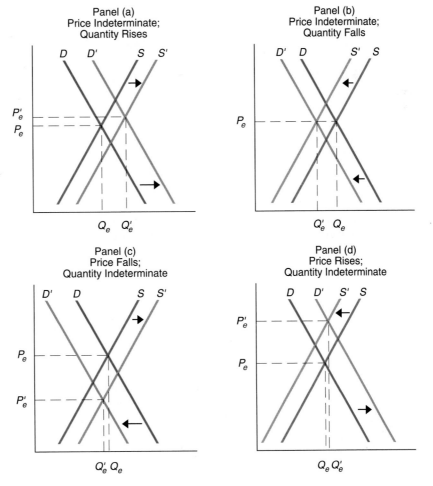

Consider the opposite situation, in which both the supply curve and the demand curve shift inward. The only thing we know for certain is that the equilibrium quantity will fall from Q_e to Q_e'. The equilibrium price stays the same at P_e, but it could easily have fallen. It would have been below P_e had the demand curve shifted inward more than the supply curve in panel (b).

Look at panel (c). Here demand fell and supply increased. We can say for sure that the equilibrium price would fall, but we are not certain what will happen to the equilibrium quantity. In this example we showed it decreasing from Q_e to Q_e'.

Finally, in panel (d) supply falls and demand rises. The only thing we can say for sure is that the equilibrium price will increase (here from P_e to P_e'). We have shown the equilibrium quantity increasing from Q_e to Q_e', but it could have decreased also. In every situation in which both supply and demand change, you should always create a graph to determine the resulting change in equilibrium price and quantity.

✪ EXAMPLE: Abrupt Shifts in Supply and Demand: The Case of Hurricane Andrew

On August 24, 1992, the most destructive hurricane in the history of the United States struck southern Florida. In its wake it left several hundred thousand Floridians homeless, close to another 100,000 without electricity, and at least an equal number without phone service. For many items, the demand curve shifted dramatically outward and the supply curve simultaneously shifted dramatically inward, as in panel (d) of Figure 4-2. For example, because so few people had electricity, the demand for ice skyrocketed. At the same time, many of the makers of ice had lost their businesses, and many that still existed did not have electricity. And even when ice was brought in, supermarkets did not have refrigeration. Immediately after Hurricane Andrew hit, bags of ice were selling for $10 each. Within a few days, though, entrepreneurs were selling ice out of semitrailers on the side of South Dixie Highway for $1.50 a bag. Chain saws were another item for which demand increased dramatically but supply in the immediate area had disappeared because businesses that sold chain saws were destroyed. Again, right after the storm, chain saws that normally sold for $150 were being peddled for at least twice that and sometimes more by enterprising north Florida residents who drove down to the south Florida disaster area. But within several weeks, chain saws were being advertised around the area of greatest destruction at only a slight premium over the prehurricane price.

Both the governor of Florida and the city councils in the affected area publicly opposed "price gouging." Several individuals were arrested for selling various items at "too high" a price. There was even a toll-free telephone number to report "price gougers."

For Critical Analysis: *If the price of building materials, construction workers' services, and so on were capped by government fiat in south Florida after the hurricane, how would this affect the speed of reconstruction in the long run and why?* ●

PRICE FLEXIBILITY AND ADJUSTMENT SPEED

We have used as an illustration for our analysis a market in which prices are quite flexible. Some markets are indeed like that. In others, however, price flexibility may take the form of indirect adjustments such as hidden payments or quality changes. For example, although the published price of bouquets of flowers may stay the same, the freshness of the flowers may change, meaning that the price per constant-quality unit changes. The published price of French bread might stay the same, but the quality could go up or down, thereby changing the price per constant-quality unit. There are many ways to change prices without actually changing the published price for a *nominal* unit of a product or service.

We must also consider the fact that markets do not get back into equilibrium immediately. There must be an adjustment time. A shock to the economy in the form of an oil embargo, a drought, or a long strike will not be absorbed overnight. This means that even in unfettered market situations, in which there are no restrictions on changes in price and quantities, temporary excess quantities supplied and excess quantities demanded may appear. Our analysis simply indicates what the market clearing price will ultimately be, given a demand curve and a supply curve. Nowhere in the analysis is there any indication of the speed with which a market will get to a new equilibrium if there has been a shock. The price may overshoot the equilibrium level. Remember this warning when we examine changes in demand and in supply due to changes in their nonprice determinants.

⭐ EXAMPLE: Restaurant Pricing

When you go to a restaurant, you typically do not see complete flexibility of prices in order to equate quantity demanded with quantity supplied on every day at all times. If you enter a restaurant when only a few people are dining, you might think to yourself that because there is an excess quantity of seats supplied at current prices, the price of this restaurant's meals should fall. But when you sit down to eat, the waiter will not bring you a menu that necessarily reflects a reduction in prices from the last time you were in when the place was filled with people.

Probably the last time you came when the restaurant was filled was a weekend night at 7 o'clock. When you go to the restaurant and it is not filled, it is usually either a weeknight or a very early or late hour. The menu remains the same, at least at first blush. Typically, though, restaurants will have "chalkboard" specials during the week that are a much better deal than regular menu prices. Sometimes the waiter may recite specials, or there may be actually a separate "early bird" menu that offers complete meals with some small variation from the regular full menu at a disproportionately lower price. You are then seeing the restaurant actually respond to the inward shift in the demand curve of restaurant meals during the week and at early hours.

Why doesn't a restaurant simply change the price on its menus to reflect changes in demand? Reprinting menus just because demand varies by day of the week, season of the year, or hour of the day can be costly. Now some restaurants do change their menus according to the season if they are in a resort town that has a high and a low season. Most others do not, however. The practice of keeping prices the same in spite of changing demand is called *posted-offer pricing* discussed in Chapter 3. (Sometimes it is called *menu pricing* even when applied to nonrestaurants.) It reflects the relatively high cost of changing prices whenever there is a temporary change in demand.

We would predict that as the cost of changing menus goes down, there would be less posted-offer pricing and more menu price changes. This is exactly what has occurred with the popularization of the laser printer. A growing number of restaurants actually print a new menu every day, which they then slip into a cardboard menu holder. The print job looks good, thanks to the quality of laser printing, and it is easy to do. Restaurants can then alter prices depending on the availability of ingredients as well as expected changes in demand.

For Critical Analysis: What are some other examples of goods and services whose price does not always fall when demand shifts inward at a regular time of the day, week, or year? (Hint: Think of services that you buy.) ●

⭐ EXAMPLE: Is There a Shortage of Nurses?

Off and on since the end of World War II there has been a "shortage" of professional nurses. Is it possible for a shortage to exist in the labor market (or in any market, for that matter) into which there is free entry? In the short run, specialized labor is relatively fixed in supply. Therefore, whenever there is an increase in demand for nurses, a shortage may temporarily exist.

There are a number of reasons why there has been an increase in the demand for nurses, not the least of which is the aging of the U.S. population. Older people use hospitals more and have chronic ailments that require more nursing. Moreover, as hospitals reduce the length of stay of patients, people who are discharged earlier than in previous years need more home care, usually provided by nurses. At the same time as demand has been rising, the supply of nurses has decreased somewhat. The age distribution of women between 18 and 24 has decreased in the past decade. Because this is the group from which nurses traditionally come, there have been fewer potential nurses. In addition, women have more alternatives in the labor market than they did years ago.

Putting demand and supply together in Figure 4-3, we can visualize what has happened in the market for nursing. The initial position is demand curve D and supply curve S with equilibrium at point E. The equilibrium wage is W_1 with an equilibrium quantity of Q_1. When the demand curve shifts outward to D' and the supply curve shifts to S', if the wage rate remains at W_1, there will be a shortage. Indeed, unfilled positions for registered nurses increased from 6.3 percent in 1986 to an estimated 13.1 percent in 1994. In response, hospitals are actually raising wage rates explicitly and implicitly. Furthermore, federal and state governments have increased the amount of financial assistance to nursing students. Hospitals themselves provide scholarships to students who contractually agree to work at their hospital after graduation. Since 1985, average wages for nurses have increased almost 50 percent. Where we are today is probably at wage rate W_2 in Figure 4-3. In the long run, when all adjustments have been made, the wage rate will increase to W_3 and the quantity demanded and supplied of nurses will be Q'_e.

For Critical Analysis: *What are some of the results of the short-run shortage of professional nurses?* ●

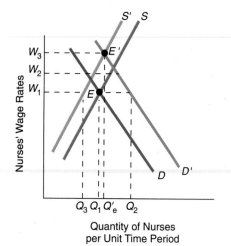

Nurses' Wage Rates

Quantity of Nurses
per Unit Time Period

FIGURE 4-3
The market for nurses.
The initial equilibrium is at point *E,* yielding wage rate W_1 and equilibrium quantity Q_1. When the supply curve shifts inward to S' and the demand curve shifts outward to D', long-run equilibrium will be at wage rate W_3 and equilibrium quantity Q'_e. In the interim, at wage rates of W_1 and W_2 there will be an excess quantity of nurses demanded, or a shortage.

CONCEPTS IN BRIEF

- The terms of exchange in a voluntary exchange are determined by the interaction of the forces underlying demand and supply. These forces take place in markets, which tend to minimize transaction costs.
- When the demand curve shifts outward or inward with a stable supply curve, equilibrium price and quantity increase or decrease. When the supply curve shifts outward or inward given a stable demand curve, equilibrium price moves in the opposite direction of equilibrium quantity.
- When both demand and supply shift, some of the results are indeterminate. Each case must be examined separately.
- When there is a shift in demand or supply, the new equilibrium price is not obtained instantaneously. Adjustment takes time.

THE RATIONING FUNCTION OF PRICES

A shortage creates a situation that forces price to rise toward a market clearing, or equilibrium, level. A surplus brings into play forces that cause price to fall toward its market clearing level. The synchronization of decisions by buyers and sellers that creates a situation of equilibrium is called the *rationing function of prices.* Prices are indicators of relative scarcity. An equilibrium price clears the market. The plans of buyers and sellers, given the price, are not frustrated.[1] It is the free interaction of buyers and sellers that sets the price that eventually clears the market. Price, in effect, rations a commodity to demanders who are willing and able to pay the highest price. Whenever the rationing function of prices is frustrated by government-enforced price ceilings that set prices below the market clearing level, a prolonged shortage situation is not allowed to be corrected by the upward adjustment of the price.

There are other ways to ration goods. *First-come, first-served* is one method. *Political power* is another. *Physical force* is yet another. Cultural, religious, and physical differences have been and are used as rationing devices throughout the world.

Consider first-come, first-served as a rationing device. In countries that do not allow prices to reflect true relative scarcity, first-come, first-served has become a way of life. Whoever is willing to wait in line the longest obtains meat that is being sold at less than the market clearing price. All who wait in line are paying a higher *total* price than the money price paid for the meat. Personal time has an opportunity cost. To calculate the total price of the meat, we must add up the money price plus the opportunity cost of the time spent waiting.

RATIONING BY WAITING

Rationing by waiting also occurs in situations in which entrepreneurs are free to change prices to equate quantity demanded with quantity supplied but choose not to do so. In other words, even in the United States we see many goods being allocated by *queuing up*

---

[1]There is a difference between frustration and unhappiness. You may be unhappy because you can't buy a Rolls Royce, but if you had sufficient income, you would not be frustrated in your attempt to purchase one at the current market price. By contrast, you would be frustrated if you went to your local supermarket and could get only two cans of your favorite soft drink when you had wanted to purchase a dozen and had the necessary income.

(waiting in line). The most obvious conclusion seems to be that the price in the market is being held below equilibrium by some noncompetitive force. That is not true, however.

The reason is that queuing may also arise when the demand characteristics of a market are subject to large or unpredictable fluctuations, and the additional costs to firms (and ultimately to consumers) of holding sufficient inventories or providing sufficient excess capacity to cover these peak demands are greater than the costs to consumers of waiting for the good. This is the usual case of waiting in line to purchase a fast-food lunch or to purchase a movie ticket a few minutes before the next show.

CONCEPTS IN BRIEF

- Prices in a market economy perform a rationing function because they reflect relative scarcity. The market is allowed to clear. Other ways to ration goods include first-come, first-served; political power; and physical force.
- Even when businesspeople can change prices, some rationing by waiting will occur. Such queuing arises when there are large unexpected changes in demand coupled with high costs of satisfying those changes in the short run.

THE POLICY OF GOVERNMENT-IMPOSED PRICE CONTROLS

The rationing function of prices is often not allowed to operate when governments impose price controls. **Price controls** typically involve setting a **price ceiling**—the maximum price that can be allowed in an exchange. The world has had a long history of price ceilings applied to some goods, wages, rents, and interest rates, among other things. Occasionally a government will set a **price floor**—a minimum price below which a good or service cannot be sold. These have most often been applied to wages and agricultural products. Let's consider price controls in terms of price ceilings.

Price controls
Government-mandated minimum or maximum prices that can be charged for goods and services.

Price ceiling
A legal maximum price that can be charged for a particular good or service.

Price floor
A legal minimum price below which a good or service cannot be sold. Legal minimum wages are an example.

PRICE CEILINGS AND BLACK MARKETS

As long as a price ceiling is below the market clearing price, imposing a price ceiling creates a shortage, as can be seen in Figure 4-4. At any price below the market clearing, or equilibrium, price of P_e, there will always be a larger quantity demanded than quantity supplied. This was discussed initially in Chapter 3. Normally, whenever a shortage exists, there is a tendency for price and output to rise to equilibrium levels. This is exactly what we pointed out when discussing shortages in the labor market. But with a price ceiling, this tendency cannot be fully realized because everyone is forbidden to trade at the equilibrium price.

The result is fewer exchanges and **nonprice rationing devices.** In Figure 4-4, at an equilibrium price of P_e, the equilibrium quantity demanded and supplied (or traded) is Q_e. But at the price ceiling of P_1, the equilibrium quantity traded is only Q_s. What happens if there is a shortage? The most obvious nonprice rationing device to help clear the market is queuing, or long lines, which we have already discussed.

Nonprice rationing devices
All methods used to ration scarce goods that are price-controlled. Whenever the price system is not allowed to work, nonprice rationing devices will evolve to ration the affected goods and services.

Typically, an effective price ceiling leads to a **black market.** A black market is a market in which the price-controlled good is sold at an illegally high price through various methods. For example, if the price of gasoline is controlled at lower than the market clearing price, a gas station attendant may take a cash payment on the side in order to fill up a driver's car. If the price of beef is controlled at below its market clearing price, the butcher may give special service to a customer who offers the butcher great seats at an upcoming football game. Indeed, the number of ways in which the true implicit price of a price-controlled good or service can be increased is infinite, limited only by the imagination. (Black markets also occur when goods are made illegal.)

Black market
A market in which goods are traded at prices above their legal maximum prices.

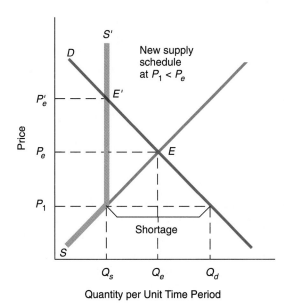

FIGURE 4-4
Black markets.
The demand curve is D. The supply curve is S. The equilibrium price is P_e. The government, however, steps in and imposes a maximum price of P_1. At that lower price, the quantity demanded will be Q_d, but the quantity supplied will only be Q_s. There is a shortage, and black markets develop. The implicit full price rises to P_e' because that is where the new supply curve, S', intersects the demand curve at E'. Black-market transactions include any number of devices, such as under-the-counter payments to retailers.

 INTERNATIONAL EXAMPLE: The Black Market for Swatch Watches

Swatch watches are generally not expensive. They are made in Switzerland and exported throughout the world, particularly to England and the United States. The manufacturer may sell as many Swatches as it wants at whatever price it wants to the dealers. Nevertheless, there is a black market in Swatch watches. If you are able to buy the Chrono, the Automatic, or the Scuba at a dealer in London, you will pay about £45 (about $70). If you then immediately take that watch to Italy, you can sell it on the black market for the equivalent of more than $400. Not surprisingly, when a shipment arrives in London, the jewelers on Oxford Street have no trouble selling out their stock almost immediately. Indeed, they limit sales of these popular models to one per customer. Some dealers force customers to buy a second, less fashionable model for every Chrono, Automatic, or Scuba model of Swatch watch that they buy.

Why would the Swatch company allow this black market to exist? Each Swatch model is sold at a fixed price throughout the world. Considering that Swatch knows that the black market exists, why doesn't it simply raise its fixed price? And why doesn't Swatch increase its production of these very popular models for which a black market exists? It would appear that Swatch would make more money by either raising prices or expanding supply.

Nobel laureate Gary Becker of the University of Chicago has come up with an explanation for the existence of black markets in unrestricted situations. He argues that some goods are demanded partly because others demand them too. These are "in" goods. The existence of the black market is proof positive to some consumers that the goods are "in" and therefore highly desirable, almost irrespective of actual quality. This analysis can be applied to "in" restaurants. These are restaurants that constantly form lines and for which such lines could be eliminated by simply raising prices. But prices are kept low on purpose in order to create a sense that the restaurant is truly "in."

For Critical Analysis: If "in" pricing can work with Swatch watches, why don't we see it with a large number of other products for which there would then exist black markets? ●

CONCEPTS IN BRIEF
- Government policy can impose price controls in the form of price ceilings and price floors. Price ceilings have been imposed for thousands of years in different countries.
- An effective price ceiling is one that sets the legal price below the market clearing price and is enforced. Effective price ceilings lead to nonprice rationing devices and black markets.

THE POLICY OF CONTROLLING RENTS

Santa Monica and Berkeley, California; New York City; and 200 other American cities and towns have some kind of rent control. **Rent control** is the system whereby the local government tells building owners how much they can charge their tenants in rent. In the United States, rent controls date back to at least World War II. The objective of rent control is to keep rents below levels that would be observed in a freely competitive market.

▶ **Rent control**
The placement of price ceilings on rents in particular municipalities.

THE FUNCTIONS OF RENTAL PRICES

In any housing market, rental prices serve three functions: (1) to promote the efficient maintenance of existing housing and stimulate the construction of new housing, (2) to allocate existing scarce housing among competing claimants, and (3) to ration the use of existing housing by current demanders.

Rent Controls and Construction.   Rent controls have discouraged the construction of new rental units. Rents are the most important long-term determinant of profitability, and rent controls have artificially depressed them. Consider some examples. In a recent year in Dallas, Texas, with a 16 percent rental vacancy rate but no rent control laws, 11,000 new rental housing units were built. In the same year in San Francisco, California, only 2,000 units were built. The major difference? San Francisco has only a 1.6 percent vacancy rate but stringent rent control laws. In New York City, except for government-subsidized construction, the only rental units being built are luxury units, which are exempt from controls. In Santa Monica, California, new apartments are not being constructed at all. New office rental space and commercial developments are, however. They are exempt from rent controls.

Effects on the Existing Supply of Housing.   When rental rates are held below equilibrium levels, property owners cannot recover the cost of maintenance, repairs, and capital improvements through higher rents. Hence they curtail these activities. In the extreme situation, taxes, utilities, and the expenses of basic repairs exceed rental receipts. The result is abandoned buildings. Numerous buildings have been abandoned in New York City. Some owners have resorted to arson, hoping to collect the insurance on their empty buildings before the city claims them for back taxes.

In Santa Monica the result is bizarre contrasts: run-down rental units sit next to homes costing more than $500,000, and abandoned apartment buildings share the block with luxury car dealerships.

Rationing the Current Use of Housing.   Rent controls also affect the current use of housing because they restrict tenant mobility. Consider the family whose children have gone off to college. That family might want to live in a smaller apartment. But in a rent-controlled environment, there can be a substantial cost to giving up a rent-controlled unit. In New York City, for example, rents can be adjusted only when a tenant leaves. That means that a move from a long-occupied rent-controlled apartment to a smaller apartment can involve a hefty rent hike. This has become known in New York as "housing gridlock."

ATTEMPTS AT EVADING RENT CONTROLS

The distortions produced by rent controls lead to efforts by both landlords and tenants to evade the rules. This leads to the growth of expensive government bureaucracies whose job it is to make sure that rent controls aren't evaded. In New York City landlords have an incentive to make life unpleasant for tenants or to evict them on the slightest pretense. This may be the only way the landlord can raise the rent. The city has responded by making evictions extremely costly for landlords. Eviction requires a tedious and expensive judicial proceeding. Tenants, for their part, routinely try to sublet all or part of their rent-controlled apartments at fees substantially above the rent they pay to the owner. Both the city and the landlords try to prohibit subletting and typically end up in the city's housing courts—an entire judicial system developed to deal with disputes involving rent-controlled apartments. The overflow and appeals from the city's housing courts is now clogging the rest of New York's judicial system. In Santa Monica there is a similar rent control board. Its budget grew 500 percent in less than a decade. The landlords pay for it through a special annual assessment of over $150 per rental unit per year.

WHO GAINS AND WHO LOSES FROM RENT CONTROLS?

The big losers from rent controls are clearly landlords. But there is another group of losers—low-income individuals, especially single mothers, trying to find their first apartment. Some observers now believe that rent controls have worsened the problem of homeless people in such cities as New York.

Typically, landlords of rent-controlled apartments often charge "key money" before a new tenant is allowed to move in. This is a large up-front cash payment, usually illegal but demanded nonetheless. This is just one aspect of the black market in rent-controlled apartments. Poor individuals cannot afford a hefty key-money payment, nor can they assure the landlord that their rent will be on time or even paid each month. Because controlled rents are usually below market clearing levels, there is little incentive for apartment owners to take any risk on low-income-earning individuals as tenants. This is particularly true when a prospective tenant's chief source of income is a welfare check. Indeed, a large percentage of the litigants in the New York housing courts is made up of welfare mothers who have missed their rent payments due to emergency expenses or delayed welfare checks. Often their appeals end in evictions and a new home in a temporary public shelter—or on the streets.

Who, then, gains from rent controls? Two studies of the New York City rent control situation provided an answer. Harvard's Joint Center for Housing Studies reported that for the city as a whole, rent controls benefit the average tenant in a rent-controlled apartment to the tune of $44 a month. In the borough of Manhattan, where the most expensive apartments are, however, this benefit is $160 a month. In the city's four other boroughs, the benefits tend to be negligible or nonexistent. Researcher Casandra Chronesmoor of the Competitive Enterprise Institute estimated that 42 percent of all rent-regulated apartments in New York City are occupied by households with incomes greater than $20,000. Fourteen percent have incomes above $40,000, and 6 percent have incomes above $50,000. These studies essentially reach the same conclusion about rent control, at least in New York City: Rent controls do not, contrary to their intent, appear to benefit the lowest income classes. At best, then, they represent a transfer of wealth from landlords to the middle-class people who are lucky enough to live in rent-controlled apartments at the time the legislation is passed.

CONCEPTS IN BRIEF

- Rental prices perform three functions: (1) allocating existing scarce housing among competing claimants, (2) promoting efficient maintenance of existing houses and stimulating new housing construction, and (3) rationing the use of existing houses by current demanders.
- Effective rent controls reduce or alter the three functions of rental prices. Construction of new rental units is discouraged. Rent controls decrease the amount of maintenance on existing ones and also lead to "housing gridlock."
- There are numerous ways to evade rent controls; key money is one.

QUANTITY RESTRICTIONS

Governments can impose quantity restrictions on a market. The most obvious restriction is an outright ban on the ownership or trading of a good. It is presently illegal to buy and sell human organs. It is also currently illegal to buy and sell certain psychoactive drugs such as cocaine, heroin, and marijuana. In some states it is illegal to start a new hospital without obtaining a license for a particular number of beds to be offered to patients. This licensing requirement effectively limits the quantity of hospital beds in some states. From 1933 to 1973 it was illegal for U.S. citizens to own gold except for manufacturing, medicinal, or jewelry purposes.

Some of the most common quantity restrictions exist in the area of international trade. The U.S. government, as well as many foreign governments, imposes import quotas on a variety of goods. An **import quota** is a supply restriction that prohibits the importation of more than a specified quantity of a particular good in a one-year period. In the United States there have been import quotas on tobacco, sugar, and immigrant labor. For many years there were import quotas on oil coming into the United States. There are also "voluntary" import quotas on certain goods. Japanese automakers have agreed since 1973 "voluntarily" to restrict the amount of Japanese cars they send to the United States.

To see the effects of this type of quantity restriction, let's look at the sugar import quota program in the United States.

▶ **Import quota**
A physical supply restriction on imports of a particular good, such as sugar. Foreign exporters are unable to sell in the United States more than the quantity specified in the import quota.

⭐ EXAMPLE: The Effects of Import Quotas on Sugar

The domestic price of sugar in the United States is approximately twice the world price. Low-cost imports of sugar (at the world price) are restricted by the government, which sets sugar import quotas annually. Sugar consumption in the United States is about 16 billion pounds annually, but annual domestic production is only 15.5 billion pounds. The remaining .5 billion pounds are imported. Without the import quotas, the domestic price of sugar would immediately fall to the world price, and the annual quantity of sugar demanded would increase to about 18 billion pounds. At least an additional 2 billion pounds would have to be imported.

The major beneficiaries of import quota restrictions on sugar are sugarbeet and sugarcane growers. Sugar import quotas create a transfer of about $100 per year per American family of four. Each family of four is thereby annually transferring $400 to each of the 11,400 sugarbeet and sugarcane growers in this country. The business users of sugar, however, have not stood by idly while the price of sugar has increased. They have searched for and found sugar substitutes. The most often used substitute is high-fructose corn syrup. Use of that substitute 20 years ago was less than 1 billion pounds per year; today it exceeds 16 billion pounds.

For Critical Analysis: What do you think the motivation is behind the quotas on imported sugar? ●

CONCEPTS IN BRIEF

● Quantity restrictions are imposed by governments. The most extreme involves an outright ban on ownership or trading of a good, such as the trade in human organs or certain psychoactive drugs, such as cocaine and heroin.

● Another type of quantity restriction is a quota, which has been applied to imports of goods as diverse as sugar, tobacco, immigrant labor, and foreign-produced oil.

● The beneficiaries of quotas are the importers who get the quota rights and the domestic producers of the restricted good.

CONTINUED →

CAPPING AUTOMOBILE INSURANCE RATES
Concepts Applied: Supply-and-demand price controls, price ceilings

Automobile insurance rates in California have been relatively high, prompting the passage of legislation that attempted to cap and even to reduce auto insurance premiums.

A few years ago, consumer advocates in California got an initiative on the ballot, Proposition 103, that would require insurance premiums to be reduced by 20 percent from their November 1987 levels. Rates were to be frozen until November 1989. At that time insurers were to apply "good driver" rates that were 20 percent lower than any other rates. About 80 percent of California drivers would qualify for these discounts. Proposition 103 passed in spite of the fact that its opponents—insurance companies—outspent its supporters by a factor of 32 to 1. A nationwide poll showed that 9 out of 10 voters would support measures like Proposition 103 in their own state. In New Jersey, Governor Jim Florio supported similar legislation to reduce auto insurance rates in that state. Consumer groups have pushed for similar proposals in at least 15 more states in the 1990s.

CAN SUPPLY AND DEMAND BE WRONG?
Can legislation change the laws of supply and demand? After all, there are numerous auto insurance companies in competition. The prices of automobile insurance in California and New Jersey (as well as elsewhere) presumably reflect supply and demand.

Certainly, all of the auto insurance consumers in California who received the cash rebates mentioned at the beginning of this chapter are convinced that legislating lower rates can work to their benefit. It took over $3\frac{1}{2}$ years

from the time Proposition 103 was passed for the rebates to be paid, but many were paid.

APPLYING SUPPLY AND DEMAND ANALYSIS The proponents of Proposition 103 claimed that insurance premiums in California could be slashed by an estimated $4 billion to $6 billion per year. Such a statement does not coincide with current use of the tools of supply and demand analysis. There are thousands of insurance companies in the United States; it is difficult to believe that the insurance premiums charged to Californians are truly monopoly rates. In a competitive market, the *price per constant-quality unit* of any good or service is obtained when the quantity demanded equals the quantity supplied. Whenever a *price control,* in this case a legislative reduction in insurance prices, is imposed, the quantity demanded will increase and the quantity of insurance coverage supplied will decrease. The difference is commonly known as a *shortage,* or an *excess quantity demanded,* at the controlled price.

Faced with price controls, insurance companies will attempt to reduce their insurance coverage. Proposition 103 anticipated this problem and prohibits insurance companies from both canceling policies or refusing to write new ones. That will either force insurers to go out of business or, for the larger companies, simply to leave the state. The California State Insurance Commission estimated initially that 75 to 100 insurers would be forced into insolvency or to leave the state under the new rates mandated by Proposition 103. This has already occurred for a number of small companies in California. In New Jersey a major auto insurer, Allstate, gave notice in 1991 that it was pulling out of the state altogether because overregulation was causing increased losses. In New Jersey the law says that if a company offers insurance on houses, it must also offer auto insurance. So New Jersey insurers could not simply abandon their auto insurance line of business. Allstate has had a very profitable home insurance business, but its auto insurance line has been unprofitable. It lost $450 million in the 1970s and 1980s and $72 million in 1990 alone.

We haven't heard the last of legislative attempts to defy the laws of supply and demand. Auto insurance rates will be the subject of legislative maneuvering for years to come.

FOR CRITICAL ANALYSIS

1. Which groups of automobile owners might benefit most from legislated decreases in automobile insurance? Which groups might be hurt the most? Explain.

2. What is there to prevent citizens in California from passing additional propositions that mandate lower prices for a wide variety of other goods and services?

CHAPTER SUMMARY

1. Exchanges take place in markets. The terms of exchange—prices—are registered in markets that tend to minimize transactions cost.

2. With a stable supply curve, a rise in demand leads to an increase in equilibrium price and quantity; a decrease in demand leads to a reduction in equilibrium price and quantity. With a stable demand curve, a rise in supply leads to a decrease in equilibrium price and an increase in equilibrium quantity; a fall in supply leads to an increase in equilibrium price and a decrease in equilibrium quantity.

3. When both demand and supply shift at the same time, indeterminate results occur. We must know the direction and degree of each shift in order to predict the change in equilibrium price and quantity.

4. When there is a shift in demand or supply, it takes time for markets to adjust to the new equilibrium. During that time there will be temporary shortages or surpluses.

5. In a market system, prices perform a rationing function—they ration scarce goods and services. Other ways of rationing include first-come, first-served; political power; and physical force.

6. Government-imposed price controls can take the form of price ceilings and price floors. Effective price ceilings—ones that are set below the market clearing price and enforced—create nonprice rationing devices and black markets.

7. Rent controls interfere with many of the functions of rental prices. For example, effective rent controls discourage the construction of new rental units. They also encourage "housing gridlock."

8. Landlords lose during effective rent controls. Other losers are typically low-income individuals, especially single mothers, trying to find their first apartment.

9. Government quantity restrictions can range from outright bans on ownership and trading of goods and services to mandatory import quotas to "voluntary" import quotas on certain goods. The beneficiaries of import quotas are those who obtain the rights to import and those who produce restricted goods domestically.

DISCUSSION OF PREVIEW POINTS

1. **Does an increase in demand always lead to a rise in price?**

   Yes, provided that the supply curve doesn't shift also. If the supply is stable, every rise in demand will cause a shift outward to the right in the demand curve. The new equilibrium price will be higher than the old equilibrium price. If, however, the supply curve shifts at the same time, you have to know in which direction and by how much. If the supply curve shifts outward, indicating a rise in supply, the equilibrium price can rise if the shift is not as great as in demand. If the increase in supply is greater than in demand, the price can actually fall. We can be sure, though, that if demand increases and supply decreases, the equilibrium price will rise. This can be seen in the diagram in the next column.

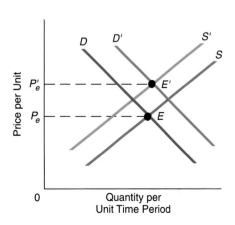

2. Can there ever be shortages in a market with no restrictions?

Yes, there can, because adjustment is never instantaneous. It takes time for the forces of supply and demand to work. In all our diagrams we draw new equilibrium points where a new supply curve meets a new demand curve. That doesn't mean that in the marketplace buyers and sellers will react immediately to a change in supply or demand. Information is not perfect. Moreover, people are often slow to adapt to higher or lower prices. Suppliers may require months or years to respond to an increase in the demand for their product. Consumers take time to respond to new information about changing relative prices.

3. How are goods rationed?

In a pure price system, prices ration goods. Prices are the indicators of relative scarcity. Prices change so that quantity demanded equals quantity supplied. In the absence of a price system, an alternative way to ration goods is first-come, first-served. In many systems, po-

litical power is another method. In certain cultures, physical force is a way to ration goods. Cultural, religious, and physical differences among individuals can be used as rationing devices. The fact is that given a world of scarcity, there has to be some method to ration goods. The price system is only one alternative.

4. When would you expect to encounter black markets?

Black markets occur in two separate situations. The first occurs whenever a good or service is made illegal by legislation. There are black markets in illegal goods and services in the United States for prostitution, gambling, and drugs. Second, there are black markets whenever a price ceiling (one type of price control) is imposed on any good or service. The price ceiling has to be below the market clearing price and enforced for a black market to exist, however. Price ceilings on rents in cities in the United States have created black markets for rental units.

PROBLEMS

(Answers to odd-numbered problems appear at the back of the book.)

4-1. This is a graph of the supply and demand for oranges.

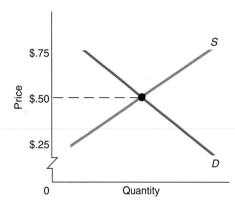

Explain the effect on this graph of each of the following events.

a. It is discovered that oranges can cure acne.

b. A new machine is developed that will automatically pick oranges.

c. The government declares a price floor of 25 cents.

d. The government declares a price floor of 75 cents.

e. The price of grapefruits increases.

f. Income decreases.

4-2. What might be the long-run results of price controls that maintained a good's money price below its equilibrium price? Above its equilibrium price?

4-3. Here are a demand schedule and a supply schedule for scientific hand calculators.

PRICE	QUANTITY DEMANDED	QUANTITY SUPPLIED
$10	100,000	0
$20	60,000	0
$30	20,000	0
$40	0	0
$50	0	100,000
$60	0	300,000
$70	0	500,000

What are the equilibrium price and the equilibrium quantity? Explain.

4-4. This is a graph of the supply and demand for raisins.

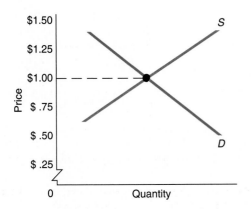

The following series of events occurs. Explain the result of the occurrence of each event.

a. An advertising campaign for California raisins is successful.

b. A fungus wipes out half the grape crop (used to make raisins) in California.

c. The price of bran flakes (a complement) increases.

d. The price of dried cranberries (a substitute) increases.

e. The government declares a price floor of 75 cents.

f. The government imposes and enforces a price ceiling of 75 cents.

g. Income increases (assume that raisins are an inferior good.)

*4-5. Suppose that the demand curve for cantaloupes is

$$P = 100 - .02Q_d$$

and the supply curve for cantaloupes is

$$P = .06Q_s$$

where P is the price per pound (in cents) and Q is the amount supplied or demanded in pounds.

a. What is the equilibrium quantity of cantaloupes for the market?

b. What is the equilibrium price per pound of cantaloupes produced?

c. Suppose that the government declares a price support (minimum price) of 80 cents per pound on cantaloupes. Will a shortage or a surplus result?

d. How large will the resulting shortage or surplus be?

*4-6. You have designed a new and improved financial calculator. You estimate the supply and demand curves for your product to be as follows:

$$P = 60 + .04Q_s$$

$$P = 100 - .01Q_d$$

a. Find the equilibrium quantity of the new calculators that you will produce.

b. Find the equilibrium price of these new calculators.

c. Suppose that the government imposes a maximum price of $100 on your new calculator. Will a shortage or a surplus result? If so, how large will it be?

d. Now suppose that the government lowers the price control to $90. Is there a shortage or a surplus at this new price? If so, how large is it?

4-7. Rent control is a price ceiling. There are also legislated price floors. Assume that the equilibrium price for oranges is 10 cents each. Draw the supply and demand diagram to show the effect of a government-imposed price floor, or minimum price, of 15 cents per orange. Be sure to label any shortages or surpluses that result. Then show the effect of a price floor of 5 cents per orange.

COMPUTER-ASSISTED INSTRUCTION
(Complete problem and answer on disk.)

A set of price ceiling and price floor situations is presented. You are asked to predict different outcomes for each situation in both the short and the long run.

---

*Asterisked problems are optional; algebra is required.

THE PUBLIC SECTOR

Government sometimes steps in and dictates what rents can be charged and how much sugar can be imported. In many industrialized countries, the government does much more. Japan, for example, has the Ministry of International Trade and Industry (MITI). MITI has a hand in betting on some winning industries and then creating them by providing low-interest loans, tax breaks, protection from foreign competitors, and numerous other favors. Some observers now believe that America needs its own form of MITI, its own *industrial policy*. Whether the United States should have an industrial policy is just one part of the study of the public sector.

After reading this chapter, you should be able to answer the following questions:

1. What problems will you encounter if you refuse to pay a portion of your income tax because you oppose national defense spending?

2. Why is it that the proportional intensity of desire can be expressed in the marketplace but not in the political process?

3. In what ways do regressive, proportional, and progressive tax structures differ?

4. Who pays the corporate income tax?

INTRODUCTION

Imagine a world without government. Living without government-imposed laws might mean that every individual would be responsible for his or her own behavior. There wouldn't be any government taxes on goods you buy, property you own, or income you earn. Of course, without any form of revenue, there would also be no state and federal highways, public libraries, or state colleges, nor any government programs such as unemployment benefits, medical treatment for veterans, or welfare payments. Certainly, some services that are provided by government today could be provided voluntarily. Prior to government welfare programs, local communities and individuals did, in fact, offer work and shelter at community "poor farms." Some services, such as park maintenance, might be taken over by private corporations. But the reality is that government is a major part of our economy, and one that is growing. Understanding economics requires understanding the nature and economic size of government. What are the economic and political functions of government today, and how does the government pay for itself?

THE ECONOMIC FUNCTIONS OF GOVERNMENT

The government provides many economic functions that affect the way in which exchange is carried out in the economy. In contrast, the political functions of government have to do with deciding how income should be redistributed among households and selecting which goods and services have special merits and should therefore be treated differently. The economic and political functions of government can and do overlap.

Let's look at five of the most important economic functions of government.

PROVIDING A LEGAL SYSTEM

The courts and the police may not at first seem like economic functions of government (although judges and police personnel must be paid). Their activities nonetheless have important consequences on economic activities within any country. You and I enter into contracts constantly, whether they be oral or written, expressed or implied. When we believe that we have been wronged, we seek redress of our grievances within our legal institutions. Moreover, consider the legal system that is necessary for the smooth functioning of our system. Our system has defined quite explicitly the legal status of businesses, the rights of private ownership, and a method for the enforcement of contracts. All relationships among consumers and businesses are governed by the legal rules of the game. We might consider the government in its judicial function, then, as the referee when there are disputes in the economic arena.

Basically, government can provide a legal structure that encourages or discourages economic activities. In the United States our legal structure tends most of the time to allow the *unorganized* majority to compete effectively in most markets. Conversely, the legal structure in many developing countries tends to protect the rights of the organized minority, thereby decreasing both incentives for the unorganized majority and protection of their rights.

🌐 INTERNATIONAL EXAMPLE: Trying to End Legal Chaos in the Commonwealth of Independent States

A good example of how important a legal system is for an economy to function can be seen throughout the Commonwealth of Independent States (CIS), the confederation of 12 of the original 15 republics of the former Soviet Union. These countries have not had free markets for 70 years prior to this decade. Now their governments have been passing laws almost without much care in order to encourage an increasingly free exchange economy.

One major problem is that some new laws conflict with the old laws still on the books. Many of these new laws don't contain any details and are therefore impossible to enforce; they are simply a set of slogans. For countries such as those in the CIS that want foreign investment, their changing and confusing legal structure only increases uncertainty. This increased uncertainty reduces the supply of foreign investment. After all, Western businesspersons are accustomed to relatively clear "rules of the game," particularly when it comes to standardized transactions.

American lawyers and industry are trying to help. The Russian Petroleum Legislation Project is a joint venture of the University of Houston Law Center and the Russian republic. Half of the project is being financed by big oil companies in the United States. The goal is to draft Russian law and legally to gain access to underground resources, such as oil.

One Russian lawyer, Alexander Minakov, said in 1992 that only 10 to 15 percent of the legal structure was in place. But even when the legal structure is established, lawmakers must then persuade bureaucrats, businesspersons, and even just plain citizens that the new economic laws haven't been made to be broken.

For Critical Analysis: *Why would members of the Commonwealth of Independent States necessarily have to change the legal structure from what it was under the Soviet Union?* ●

PROMOTING COMPETITION

Many people believe that the only way to attain economic efficiency is through competition. One of the roles of government is to serve as the protector of a competitive economic system. Congress and the various state governments have passed **antitrust legislation.** Such legislation makes illegal certain (but not all) economic activities that might, in legal terms, restrain trade—that is, prevent free competition among actual and potential rival firms in the marketplace. The avowed aim of antitrust legislation is to reduce the power of **monopolies**—firms that have great control over the price of the goods they sell. A large number of antitrust laws have been passed that prohibit specific anticompetitive business behavior. Both the Antitrust Division of the Department of Justice and the Federal Trade Commission attempt to enforce these antitrust laws. Various state judicial agencies also expend efforts at maintaining competition.

▶ **Antitrust legislation**
Laws that restrict the formation of monopolies and regulate certain anticompetitive business practices.

▶ **Monopoly**
A firm that has great control over the price of a good. In the extreme case, a monopoly is the only seller of a good or service.

CORRECTING FOR SPILLOVERS, OR EXTERNALITIES

Our discussions in the first four chapters of this text were all couched in terms of markets. Supply and demand work themselves out in particular markets—the wheat market, the labor market, and so on. Unless supply and demand reflect *all* the benefits and *all* the costs to producing and consuming a product, the prices that result from the interaction of supply and demand may not be "right." Then we say that a **market failure** has occurred. One such market failure involves pollution.

Consider a hypothetical world in which there is no government regulation against pollution. You are living in a town that has clean air. A steel mill moves in. It has paid for the inputs for producing the steel: land, labor, capital, and entrepreneurship. The price it charges for the steel reflects, in this example, only the costs that the steel mill incurred. In the course of production, however, the mill gets one part of an input—smoke dispersal—at no charge by simply allowing the wind to disperse the smoke it produces as a by-product. It is the people in the community who pay that cost in the form of dirtier clothes, dirtier cars and houses, and more respiratory illnesses. The effect is similar to what would happen if the steel mill could take coal or oil or workers' services free. There has been a **spillover** effect, or an **externality.** Actually, there has been a spillover, or external, cost.

▶ **Market failure**
A situation in which the operation of supply and demand fails to produce a solution that truly reflects all of the costs and benefits that go into producing and consuming a good or service.

▶ **Spillover,** or **externality**
A situation in which a benefit or a cost associated with an economic activity affects third parties.

Some of the costs associated with the production of the steel have "spilled over" onto **third parties,** parties other than the buyer and the seller of the steel. A negative spillover is called a negative externality because there are costs that you and your neighbors pay—dirtier clothes, cars, and houses, respiratory problems—even though your group is external to (not a direct participant in) the market transaction between the steel mill and the buyers of steel.

How the Government Corrects Externalities.

The government can in theory correct externality situations in a variety of ways in all cases that warrant such action. In the case of negative externalities, at least two avenues are open to the government: special taxes and legislative regulation or prohibition.

1. **Special taxes through legislation.** In our example of the steel mill, the externality problem originates from the fact that the air as a waste disposal place is costless to the firm but not to society. The government could make the steel mill pay a tax for dumping its pollutants into the air. The government could attempt to tax the steel mill commensurate with the cost to third parties from smoke in the air. This, in effect, would be a pollution tax or **effluent fee.** The ultimate effect would be to raise the price to consumers, ideally making the price equal to the full cost of production to society.
2. **Regulation.** To correct a negative externality arising from steel production, the government could specify a maximum allowable rate of pollution. This action would require that the steel mill install pollution abatement equipment within its facilities, that it reduce its rate of output, or some combination of the two. Note that the government's job would not be that simple, for it still would have to determine the level and then actually measure the pollution output from steel production in order to enforce such regulation.

What can the government do when the production of one good spills *benefits* over to third parties? It has several policy options: (1) financing the production of the good or producing the good itself, (2) special subsidies (negative taxes), and (3) regulation.

1. **Government financing and production.** If the positive externalities seem extremely large, the government has the option of financing the desired additional production facilities so that the "right" amount of the good will be produced. Consider inoculations against communicable diseases. The government could—and often does—finance campaigns to inoculate the population. It could (and does) even produce and operate centers for inoculation in which such inoculations would be free.
2. **Special subsidies.** A subsidy is a negative tax; it is a payment made either to a business or to a consumer when the business produces or the consumer buys a good or a service. In the case of inoculations against communicable diseases, the government could subsidize everyone who obtains an inoculation by reimbursing those inoculated directly or by making payments to private firms that provide inoculations. If you are attending a state university, taxpayers are helping to pay the cost of providing your education; you are being subsidized as much as 80 percent of the total cost. Subsidies reduce the net price to consumers, thereby causing a larger quantity to be demanded.
3. **Regulation.** In some cases involving positive externalities, the government can require by law that a certain action be undertaken by individuals in the society. For example, regulations require that all school-age children be inoculated before entering public and private schools. Some people believe that a public-school education itself generates positive externalities. We have regulations—laws—that require all school-age children to be enrolled in a public or private school.

▶ **Third parties**
Parties who are external to negotiations and activities between buyers and sellers. For example, if you agree to buy a car with no brakes and then run me over, I am a third party to the deal struck between you and the seller of the car, and my suffering is the negative externality.

▶ **Effluent fee**
A charge to a polluter that gives the right to discharge into the air or water a certain amount of pollution. Also called a *pollution tax.*

> ## CONCEPTS IN BRIEF
> - Negative spillovers, or negative externalities, lead to an overallocation of resources to the specific economic activity. Two possible ways of correcting these spillovers are taxation and regulation.
> - Positive spillovers, or positive externalities, result in an underallocation of resources to the specific activity. Three possible government corrections are financing the production of the activity, subsidizing private firms or consumers to engage in the activity, and regulation.

PROVIDING PUBLIC GOODS

The goods used in our examples up to this point have been **private goods.** When I eat a cheeseburger, you cannot eat the same one. So you and I are rivals for that cheeseburger, just as much as rivals for the title of world champion. When I use a videodisc player, you cannot use the same player. When I use the services of an electronic serviceperson, that person cannot work at the same time for you. That is the distinguishing feature of private goods—their use is exclusive to the people who purchase or rent them. The **principle of rival consumption** applies to all private goods by definition. Rival consumption is easy to understand. With private goods, either you use them or I use them.

There is an entire class of goods that are not private goods. These are called **public goods.** The principle of rival consumption does not apply to them. That is, they can be consumed *jointly* by many individuals simultaneously. National defense, police protection, and the legal system, for example, are public goods. If you partake of them, you do not necessarily take away from anyone else's share of those goods.

Characteristics of Public Goods.
Several distinguishing characteristics of public goods set them apart from all other goods.[1]

1. **Public goods are usually indivisible.** You can't buy or sell $5 worth of our ability to annihilate the world with bombs. Public goods cannot be produced or sold very easily in small units.
2. **Public goods can be used by more and more people at no additional cost.** Once money has been spent on national defense, the defense protection you receive does not reduce the amount of protection bestowed on anyone else. The opportunity cost of your receiving national defense once it is in place is zero.
3. **Additional users of public goods do not deprive others of any of the services of the goods.** If you turn on your television set, your neighbors don't get weaker reception because of your action.
4. **It is difficult to design a collection system for a public good on the basis of how much individuals use it.** It is nearly impossible to determine how much any person uses or values national defense. No one can be denied the benefits of national defense for failing to pay for that public good. This is often called the **exclusion principle.**

Free Riders.
This last point leads us to the **free-rider problem,** a situation in which some individuals believe that *others* will take on the burden of paying for public goods

> **Private goods**
> Goods that can be consumed by only one individual at a time. Private goods are subject to the principle of rival consumption.
>
> **Principle of rival consumption**
> Individuals are rivals in consuming private goods because one person's consumption reduces the amount available for others to consume.
>
> **Public goods**
> Goods to which the principle of rival consumption does not apply; they can be jointly consumed by many individuals simultaneously at no additional cost and with no reduction in the quality or quantity of the good.
>
> **Exclusion principle**
> The principle that no one can be excluded from the benefits of a public good, even if that person hasn't paid for it.
>
> **Free-rider problem**
> A problem associated with public goods when individuals presume that others will pay for the public goods so that, individually, they can escape paying for their portion without causing a reduction in production.

---

[1] Sometimes the distinction is made between pure public goods, which have all the characteristics we have described here, and quasi- or near-public goods, which do not. The major feature of near-public goods is that they are jointly consumed, even though nonpaying customers can be, and often are, excluded—for example, movies, football games, and concerts.

such as national defense. The free riders will argue that they receive no value from such government services as national defense and therefore really should not pay for it. Suppose that citizens were taxed directly in proportion to how much they tell an interviewer that they value national defense. Some people will probably tell interviewers that they are unwilling to pay for national defense because they don't want any of it—it is of no value to them. Many of us may end up being free riders when we assume that others will pay for the desired public good. We may all want to be free riders if we believe that someone else will provide the commodity in question that we actually value.

ENSURING ECONOMYWIDE STABILITY

The government attempts to stabilize the economy by smoothing out the ups and downs in overall business activity. Our economy seems to be plagued with the problems of unemployment and rising prices. The government, especially the federal government, has taken on the task of attempting to solve these problems to stabilize the economy. The notion that the federal government should undertake actions to stabilize business activity is a relatively new idea in the United States, encouraged by high unemployment rates during the Great Depression of the 1930s and subsequent theories about possible ways in which government could reduce umemployment. In 1946, the government passed the Employment Act, a landmark law concerning government responsibility for economic performance. It established three goals for government accountability: full employment, price stability, and economic growth. These goals have provided the justification for many government economic programs during the post–World War II period.

CONCEPTS IN BRIEF

- Public goods can be consumed jointly. The principle of rival consumption does not apply as it does with private goods.
- Public goods have the following characteristics: (1) they are indivisible; (2) once they are produced, there is no opportunity cost when additional consumers use them; (3) your use of a public good does not deprive others of its simultaneous use; and (4) consumers cannot conveniently be charged on the basis of use.
- The economic activities of government include (1) providing a judicial system, (2) promoting competition, (3) correcting spillovers, (4) producing public goods, and (5) ensuring economywide stabilization.

THE POLITICAL FUNCTIONS OF GOVERNMENT

At least two areas of government are in the realm of political, or normative, functions rather than that of the economic ones discussed in the first part of this chapter. These two areas are (1) the regulation and/or provision of merit and demerit goods, and (2) income redistribution.

MERIT AND DEMERIT GOODS

▶ **Merit good**
A good that has been deemed socially desirable via the political process. Museums are an example.

Certain goods are considered to have special merit. A **merit good** is defined as any good that the political process has deemed socially desirable. (Note that nothing inherent in any particular good makes it a merit good. It is a matter of who chooses.) Some examples of merit goods in our society are museums, ballets, plays, and concerts. In these areas the government's role is the provision of merit goods to the people in society who would not otherwise purchase them at market clearing prices or who would not purchase an amount of them judged to be sufficient. This provision may take the form of government production and distribution of merit goods. It can also take the form of reimbursement for payment on merit goods or subsidies to producers and/or consumers for part of the cost of merit goods. Governments do indeed subsidize such merit goods as concerts, ballets, museums, and plays. In most cases, such merit goods would rarely be so numerous without subsidization.

Demerit goods are the opposite of merit goods. They are goods that, through the political process, are deemed socially undesirable. Heroin, cigarettes, gambling, and cocaine are examples. The government exercises its role in the area of demerit goods by taxing, regulating, or prohibiting their manufacture, sale, and use. Governments justify the relatively high taxes on alcohol and tobacco by declaring them demerit goods. The best-known example of governmental exercise of power in this area is the prohibition against certain psychoactives—drugs that alter the psyche. Most psychoactives (except nicotine, caffeine, and alcohol) are either expressly prohibited, as is the case for heroin, cocaine, and opium, or heavily regulated, as in the case of prescription drugs.

▶ **Demerit good**
A good that has been deemed socially undesirable via the political process. Heroin is an example.

 INTERNATIONAL EXAMPLE: **Wiping Out Demerit Goods at Their Source**

The U.S. government has extended its attempt to prevent Americans from consuming certain demerit goods to the very source of those goods. It maintains an active program helping certain Latin American countries reduce the supply of the raw materials for cocaine. This program involves coca bush eradication in Bolivia and Peru. The U.S. military, the Central Intelligence Agency, and the State Department all have programs aimed at stopping the production as well as the refining of cocaine and its shipment to the United States. America's foreign policy has often turned on the drug question. For example, the United States put strong pressure on Turkey in the 1970s and 1980s to stop its production of opium poppy plants, the source of heroin. The annual federal government payments for drug eradication programs in Latin America are estimated to be $400 million in 1994.

In spite of what administration officials have been saying, economists have used simple supply and demand models to predict the continuing failure of such programs. First of all, the supply of the necessary ingredient to grow coca bushes is almost unlimited. Coca bushes, opium poppies, and marijuana plants can grow virtually anywhere on the globe between the Tropic of Cancer and the Tropic of Capricorn. This is a 2,500-mile wide band skirting Central and South America, Africa, India, Southeast Asia, northern Australia, and southern Florida. Consider South America alone, where the U.S. Department of Agriculture has estimated that more than 2.5 million square miles are suitable for growing coca. Less than 1,000 square miles are currently used for that purpose, or less than .04 percent. Therefore, efforts by the U.S. military (the invasion of Panama), State Department, and CIA will have little effect on the total supply of the raw source of cocaine. Evidence on the streets of America confirms the economists' predictions. The price of cocaine (corrected for inflation and improved quality) is no more than 20 percent of what it was in the 1960s. So much for eradicating cocaine at the source.

One effect of stepped-up government efforts at eliminating coca bushes in Bolivia, Peru, and Colombia is that the natives there are increasingly shifting to growing opium poppy, which is reaching our shores in the form of heroin. The economics is straightforward. A kilogram of processed heroin yields profits 10 to 15 times higher than a kilogram of processed cocaine.

For Critical Analysis: Are there alternative ways for the U.S. government to restrict the production of currently illegal psychoactives? ●

INCOME REDISTRIBUTION

Another relatively recent political function of government has been the explicit redistribution of income. This redistribution uses two systems: the progressive income tax (described later in this chapter) and **transfer payments.** Transfer payments are payments made to individuals for which no services or goods are concurrently rendered. The three key money transfer payments in our system are welfare, Social Security, and unemployment insurance benefits; there are others. Income redistribution also includes a large amount of income **transfers in kind,** as opposed to money transfers. Some income transfers in kind are food stamps, Medicare and Medicaid, government health care services, and low-cost public housing.

The government has also engaged in other activities as a form of redistribution of income. For example, the provision of public education is at least in part an attempt to redistribute income by making sure that the very poor have access to education.

> ▶ **Transfer payments**
> Money payments made by governments to individuals for which no services or goods are concurrently rendered. Examples are welfare, Social Security, and unemployment insurance benefits.

> ▶ **Transfers in kind**
> Payments that are in the form of actual goods and services, such as food stamps, low-cost public housing, and medical care, and for which no goods or services are rendered concurrently.

CONCEPTS IN BRIEF

- Political, or normative, activities of the government include the provision and regulation of merit and demerit goods and income redistribution.
- Merit and demerit goods do not have any inherent characteristics that qualify them as such; rather, collectively, through the political process, we make judgments about which goods and services are "good" for society and which are "bad."
- Income redistribution can be carried out by a system of progressive taxation, coupled with transfer payments, which can be made in money or in kind, such as food stamps and Medicare.

COLLECTIVE DECISION MAKING: THE THEORY OF PUBLIC CHOICE

The public sector has a vast influence on the American economy. Yet the economic model used until now has applied only to the behavior of the private sector—firms and households. Such a model does not adequately explain the behavior of the public sector. We shall attempt to do so now.

Governments consist of individuals. No government actually thinks and acts; rather, government actions are the result of decision making by individuals in their roles as elected representatives, appointed officials, and salaried bureaucrats. Therefore, to understand how government works, we must examine the incentives for the people in government as well as those who would like to be in government—avowed candidates or would-be candidates for elective or appointed positions—and special-interest lobbyists attempting to get government to do something. At issue is the analysis of **collective decision making.** Collective decision making involves the actions of voters, politicians, political parties, special-interest groups, and many other groups and individuals. The analysis of collective decision making is usually called the **theory of public choice.** It has been given this name because it involves hypotheses about how choices are made in the public sector, as opposed to the private sector. At the basis of public-choice theory is the assumption that individuals will act within the political process to maximize their *individual* (not collective) well-being. In that sense the theory is similar to our analysis of the market economy, in which we also assume that individuals are motivated by self-interest.

To understand public-choice theory, it is necessary to point out other similarities between the private market sector and the public, or government, sector; then we will look at the differences.

> ▶ **Collective decision making**
> How voters, politicians, and other interested parties act and how these actions influence nonmarket decisions.

> ▶ **Theory of public choice**
> The study of collective decision making.

SIMILARITIES IN MARKET AND PUBLIC-SECTOR DECISION MAKING

In addition to the similar assumption of self-interest being the motivating force in both sectors, there are other similarities.

Scarcity.   At any given moment, the amount of resources is fixed. This means that for the private and the public sectors combined, there is a scarcity constraint. Everything that is spent by all levels of government, plus everything that is spent by the private sector, must add up to the total income available at any point in time. Hence every government action has an opportunity cost, just as in the market sector.

Competition.   Although we typically think of competition as a private market phenomenon, it is also present in collective action. Given the scarcity constraint government also faces, bureaucrats, appointed officials, and elected representatives will always be in competition for available government funds. Furthermore, the individuals within any government agency or institution will act as individuals do in the private sector: They will try to obtain higher wages, better working conditions, and higher job-level classifications. They will compete and act in their own, not society's, interest.

Similarity of Individuals.   Contrary to popular belief, there are not two types of individuals—those who work in the private sector and those who work in the public sector; rather, on average, the individuals working in similar types of positions can be considered similar. The difference, as we shall see, is that the individuals in government face a different **incentive structure** than those in the private sector. That is to say, the costs and benefits of being efficient or inefficient, for example, differ when one goes from the private to the public sector.

> ▶ **Incentive structure**
> The system of rewards and punishments individuals face with respect to their own actions.

One approach to predicting government bureaucratic behavior is to ask what incentives bureaucrats face. Take the United States Postal Service as an example. The bureaucrats running that government corporation are human beings with IQs not dissimilar to those possessed by workers in similar positions at Microsoft or American Airlines. Yet the U.S. Postal Service certainly does not function like either of these companies. At least in part, the difference can be explained in terms of the incentives provided for managers in the two types of institutions. When the bureaucratic managers and workers at Microsoft make incorrect decisions, work slowly, produce shoddy products, and are generally "inefficient," the profitability of the company declines. The owners—millions of shareholders—express their displeasure by selling some of their shares of company stock. The market value, as tracked on the stock exchange, falls. But what about the U.S. Postal Service? Every time a manager, a worker, or a bureaucrat in the U.S. Postal Service gives shoddy service, there is no straightforward mechanism by which the owners of the U.S. Postal Service—the taxpayers—can express their dissatisfaction. In spite of the appellation "government corporation," taxpayers as shareholders do not really own shares of stock in the U.S. Postal Service that they can sell.

The key, then, to understanding purported inefficiency in the government bureaucracy is not found in an examination of people and personalities but rather in an examination of incentives and institutional arrangements.

DIFFERENCES BETWEEN MARKET AND COLLECTIVE DECISION MAKING

There are probably more dissimilarities between the market sector and the public sector than there are similarities.

Government Goods at Zero Price.

▶ **Government, or political, goods**
Goods (and services) provided by the public sector; they can be either private or public goods.

The majority of goods that governments produce are furnished to the ultimate consumers without direct money charge. **Government, or political, goods** can be either private goods or public goods, as defined in this chapter. In any event, the fact that they are furnished to the ultimate consumer free of charge does *not* mean that the cost to society of those goods is zero. It only means that the price *charged* is zero. The full opportunity cost to society is the value of the resources used in the production of goods produced and provided by the government.

For example, none of us pays directly for each unit of consumption of defense or police protection. Rather, we pay for all these things indirectly through the taxes that support our governments—federal, state, and local. This special feature of government can be looked at in a different way. There is no longer a one-to-one relationship between the consumption of a government, or politically provided, good and the payment for that good. Consumers who pay taxes collectively pay for every government, or politically provided, good, but the individual consumer may not be able to see the relationship between the taxes that he or she pays and the consumption of a government-provided good. Indeed, most taxpayers will find that their tax bill is the same whether or not they consume, or even like, government-provided goods.

Use of Force.

All governments are able to engage in the legal use of force in their regulation of economic affairs. For example, governments can exercise the use of *expropriation,* which means that if you refuse to pay your taxes, your bank account and other assets may be seized by the Internal Revenue Service. In fact, you have no choice in the matter of paying taxes to governments. Collectively, we decide the total size of government through the political process, but individually we cannot determine how much service we purchase just for ourselves during any one year.

Voting Versus Spending.

In the private market sector, a dollar voting system is in effect. This dollar voting system is not equivalent to the voting system in the public sector. There are, at minimum, three differences:

▶ **Majority rule**
A collective decision-making system in which group decisions are made on the basis of 50.1 percent of the vote. In other words, whatever more than 50 percent of the population votes for, the entire population has to take.

▶ **Proportional rule**
A decision-making system in which actions are based on the proportion of the "votes" cast and are in proportion to them. In a market system, if 10 percent of the dollar votes are cast for blue cars, 10 percent of the output will be blue cars.

1. In a political system, one person gets one vote, whereas in the market system, one dollar equals one vote.
2. The political system is run by **majority rule,** whereas the market system is run by **proportional rule.**
3. Dollars can indicate intensity of want, whereas because of the all-or-nothing nature of political voting, a vote cannot.

Ultimately, the main distinction between political votes and dollar votes here is that political outcomes may differ from economic outcomes. Remember that economic efficiency is a situation in which, given the prevailing distribution of income, consumers get the economic goods they want. There is no corresponding situation using political voting. Thus we can never assume that a political voting process will lead to the same decisions that a dollar voting process will lead to in the marketplace.

Indeed, consider the dilemma every voter faces. Usually a voter is not asked to decide on a single issue (although this happens); rather, a voter is asked to choose among candidates who present a large number of issues and state a position on each of them. Just consider the average U.S. senator who has to vote on several thousand different issues during a six-year term. When you vote for that senator, you are voting for a person who must make thousands of decisions during the next six years.

CONCEPTS IN BRIEF

- The theory of public choice analyzes how collective decision making is carried out in the public sector.
- The market sector and the public sector have the following similarities: (1) Both sectors face scarcity, (2) both feature competition, and (3) individuals are similar in both sectors.
- The difference between market and collective decision making involves the following: (1) Many government, or political, goods are provided at zero price (there is no user charge system); (2) collective action may involve the use of force; and (3) political voting is not the same as dollar voting.
- Government bureaucrats can be viewed as economic agents who face different incentives than their counterparts in the private sector.

PAYING FOR THE PUBLIC SECTOR

Jean-Baptiste Colbert, the seventeenth-century French finance minister, said the art of taxation was in "plucking the goose so as to obtain the largest amount of feathers with the least possible amount of hissing." In the United States, governments have designed a variety of methods of plucking the private-sector goose. To analyze any tax system, we must first understand the distinction between marginal tax rates and average tax rates.

MARGINAL AND AVERAGE TAX RATES

If somebody says, "I pay 28 percent in taxes," you cannot really tell what that person means unless you know if he or she is referring to average taxes paid or the tax rate on the last dollars earned. The latter concept has to do with the **marginal tax rate.**[2]

The marginal tax rate is expressed as follows:

$$\text{Marginal tax rate} = \frac{\text{change in taxes due}}{\text{change in taxable income}}$$

> **Marginal tax rate**
> The change in the tax payment divided by the change in income, or the percentage of additional dollars that must be paid in taxes. The marginal tax rate is applied to the highest tax bracket of taxable income reached.

It is important to understand that the marginal tax rate applies only to the income in the highest **tax bracket** reached, where a tax bracket is defined as a specified level of taxable income to which a specific and unique marginal tax rate is applied.

The marginal tax rate is not the same thing as the **average tax rate,** which is defined as

$$\text{Average tax rate} = \frac{\text{total taxes due}}{\text{total taxable income}}$$

> **Tax bracket**
> A specified interval of income to which a specific and unique marginal tax rate is applied.

> **Average tax rate**
> The total tax payment divided by total income. It is the proportion of total income paid in taxes.

TAXATION SYSTEMS

No matter how governments raise revenues—from income taxes, sales taxes, and other taxes—all of those taxes can fit into one of three types of taxation systems—proportional, progressive, and regressive, expressing a relationship between the percentage tax, or tax rate, paid and income. To determine whether a tax system is progressive, regressive, or proportional, we simply ask the question, What is the relationship between the average tax rate and the marginal tax rate?

---

[2]The word *marginal* means "incremental" (or "decremental") here.

▶ **Proportional taxation**
A tax system in which as the individual's income goes up, the tax bill goes up in exactly the same proportion. Also called a *flat-rate tax*.

Proportional Taxation.   **Proportional taxation** means that as an individual's income goes up, his or her taxes rise in exactly the same proportion. In terms of marginal versus average tax rates, in a proportional taxation system, the marginal tax rate is always equal to the average tax rate. You can see this in the top part of Table 5-1. The marginal tax is 20 percent applied to each tax bracket, and the average tax rate turns out to be 20 percent also.

TABLE 5-1   Three different types of taxing systems.
In a proportional tax system, no matter what an individual's taxable income level, the marginal tax rate and the average tax rate remain the same. In a progressive system, as the individual's taxable income goes up—in our example, from $10,000 to $20,000 to $30,000—a higher and higher marginal tax rate is applied. The average tax rate therefore increases. Finally, in a regressive system, a lower and lower marginal tax rate is applied, and the average tax rate is seen to decrease—in our example, from 30 percent to 20 percent.

Hypothetical Individuals: Individual A, $10,000 of taxable income; individual B, $20,000 of taxable income; individual C, $30,000 of taxable income.

A Proportional System: The proportional tax rate is 20 percent, applied to all taxable income.

	MARGINAL TAX RATE AND TAXES PAID	AVERAGE TAX RATE
Individual A	.20 × $10,000 = $2,000	$\frac{\$2,000}{\$10,000} = 20\%$
Individual B	.20 × $20,000 = $4,000	$\frac{\$4,000}{\$20,000} = 20\%$
Individual C	.20 × $30,000 = $6,000	$\frac{\$6,000}{\$30,000} = 20\%$

A Progressive System: Marginal tax rates in three tax brackets are as follows: 10 percent on first $10,000, 20 percent on second $10,000, 30 percent on third $10,000.

	MARGINAL TAX RATE AND TAXES PAID		AVERAGE TAX RATE
Individual A	.10 × $10,000 = $1,000		$\frac{\$1,000}{\$10,000} = 10\%$
Individual B	.10 × $10,000 = $1,000 .20 × $10,000 = $2,000 Total $3,000		$\frac{\$3,000}{\$20,000} = 15\%$
Individual C	.10 × $10,000 = $1,000 .20 × $10,000 = $2,000 .30 × $10,000 = $3,000 Total $6,000		$\frac{\$6,000}{\$30,000} = 20\%$

A Regressive System: Marginal tax rates in three tax brackets: 30 percent on the first $10,000, 20 percent on the second $10,000, 10 percent on the third $10,000.

	MARGINAL TAX RATE AND TAXES PAID		AVERAGE TAX RATE
Individual A	.30 × $10,000 = $3,000		$\frac{\$3,000}{\$10,000} = 30\%$
Individual B	.30 × $10,000 = $3,000 .20 × $10,000 = $2,000 Total $5,000		$\frac{\$5,000}{\$20,000} = 25\%$
Individual C	.30 × $10,000 = $3,000 .20 × $10,000 = $2,000 .10 × $10,000 = $1,000 Total $6,000		$\frac{\$6,000}{\$30,000} = 20\%$

A proportional tax system is also called a *flat-rate tax*. Taxpayers at all income levels end up paying the same *percentage* of their income in taxes. If the proportional tax rate were 20 percent, an individual with an income of $10,000 would pay $2,000 in taxes, while an individual making $100,000 would pay $20,000, the identical 20 percent rate being levied on both.

⭐ EXAMPLE: The Flat-Tax Proposal

During the 1992 presidential primary campaign, a strictly proportional tax system, deemed a flat-tax proposal, was presented by one of the Democratic candidates, ex-governor of California Jerry Brown. Actually, he proposed a 13 percent flat tax on personal income and another 13 percent tax on the value added that corporations generate when they produce things, called a **value-added tax (VAT).** He argued that such a system could be used in place of the current one, which includes personal income taxes, corporate income taxes, employee taxes, and many others. Under the Brown flat-tax plan, there would only be three deductions from personal income before the 13 percent flat tax was applied: mortgage interest, rent, and charitable contributions. Brown's flat-tax idea isn't new. After all, America's income tax subsequent to the passage of the Sixteenth Amendment in 1913 was basically a flat 1 percent on most taxpayers. The flat tax was later proposed in the 1950s and again in the late 1970s.

> ▶ **Value-added tax (VAT)**
> A tax assessed on the value added by a firm. The value added by a firm is the value of the products that firm sells minus the value of the materials (goods) that it bought and used to produce those products. The tax is usually imposed as a percentage of this difference. It is heavily used in Europe.

Many people argue against a flat tax because they are worried that it would not help the government in its political role as redistributor of income from the rich to the poor. Others believe that it would not generate enough government revenues.

Proponents of the flat tax argue that it would simplify the U.S. tax code immensely and reduce the number of hours that Americans spend filling out their tax forms. Professor Joel Slemrod of the University of Michigan Business School has estimated that the average household spends almost 30 hours a year preparing tax returns. Furthermore, supporters of the flat tax argue that the economy would grow faster because this lower tax rate would encourage businesses to invest more and workers to work more.

For Critical Analysis: Which professions would suffer from less work if a flat tax were passed? ●

Progressive Taxation.   Under **progressive taxation,** as a person's taxable income increases, the percentage of income paid in taxes increases. In terms of marginal versus average tax rates, in a progressive system, the marginal tax rate is above the average tax rate. This can be seen in the middle of Table 5-1. The first $10,000 in taxable income is taxed at 10 percent, the next $10,000 at 20 percent, and the third $10,000 at 30 percent. The average tax rate is less than the marginal tax rate in a progressive tax system. In contrast, in a proportional tax system, the marginal tax rate is constant and always the same as the average tax rate.

> ▶ **Progressive taxation**
> A tax system in which as income increases, a higher percentage of the additional income is taxed. The marginal tax rate exceeds the average tax rate as income rises.

🌐 INTERNATIONAL EXAMPLE: Russia's High Taxes Discourage Investment

There are several problems with high marginal tax rates. They decrease the incentives for people to work and to save. They encourage individuals to illegally avoid paying taxes. And for developing countries, they discourage foreign investment. Russia found this out (after it became independent) when it imposed what turned out to be an extremely progressive system. The highest personal tax rate in Russia, 60 percent, kicks in at an annual income of about $3,000. There are also a value-added tax of 28 percent, import and export taxes, and a variety of business taxes. In the first eight months of 1992 alone, 20 amendments were made to the tax code. Law-abiding entrepreneurs ended up paying 80 percent of their income to the government. Not surprisingly, Western governments and businesses have repeatedly warned Russia that such a tax system would only increase the time it took the country to attract foreign capital and to develop.

For Critical Analysis: Why would a relatively poor country such as Russia believe that it is necessary to have such high marginal tax rates? ●

▶ **Regressive taxation**
A tax system in which as more dollars are earned, the percentage of tax paid on them falls. The marginal tax rate is less than the average tax rate as income rises.

Regressive Taxation. With **regressive taxation,** a smaller percentage of taxable income is taken in taxes as taxable income increases. The marginal rate is *below* the average rate. In the bottom part of Table 5-1 you see a regressive tax system demonstrated. As income increases, the marginal tax rate falls, and so does the average tax rate. The U.S. Social Security tax is regressive. Once the legislative maximum taxable wage base is reached, no further Social Security taxes are paid. Consider a simplified hypothetical example: Every dollar up to $50,000 is taxed at 10 percent. After $50,000 there is no Social Security tax. Someone making $100,000 still pays only $5,000 in Social Security taxes. That person's average Social Security tax is 5 percent. The person making $50,000, by contrast, pays in 10 percent. The person making $1 million faces an average Social Security tax rate of only .5 percent in our simplified example.

CONCEPTS IN BRIEF

- Marginal tax rates are applied to marginal tax brackets, defined as spreads of income over which the tax rate is constant.
- Tax systems can be proportional, progressive, or regressive, depending on whether the marginal tax rate is the same as, greater than, or less than the average tax rate as income rises.

THE MOST IMPORTANT FEDERAL TAXES

The federal government imposes income taxes on both individuals and corporations and collects Social Security taxes and a variety of other taxes.

THE FEDERAL PERSONAL INCOME TAX

The most important tax in the U.S. economy is the federal personal income tax, which accounts for about 44 percent of all federal revenues. All American citizens, resident aliens, and most others who earn income in the United States are required to pay federal income taxes on all taxable income. The rates that are paid rise up to a specified amount, depending on marital status, and then fall, as can be seen in Table 5-2. Marginal income tax rates at the federal level have varied from as low as 1 percent after the passage of the Sixteenth Amendment to as high as 91 percent (which was reduced in 1964). There

TABLE 5-2 Federal marginal income tax rates.
These rates were proposed for 1994 in the summer of 1993. The highest rate includes a 10 percent surcharge on taxable income above $250,000.
Source: Treasury Department.

SINGLE PERSONS		MARRIED COUPLES	
MARGINAL TAX BRACKET	MARGINAL TAX RATE	MARGINAL TAX BRACKET	MARGINAL TAX RATE
$0–$22,100	15%	$0–$36,900	15%
$22,101–$53,500	28%	$36,901–$89,150	28%
$53,501–$115,500	31%	$89,151–$140,000	31%
$115,501–$250,000	36%	$140,001–$250,000	36%
$250,001 and up	39.6%	$250,001 and up	39.6%

were 14 separate tax brackets prior to the Tax Reform Act of 1986, which reduced the number to three. Advocates of a more progressive income tax system in the United States argue that such a system (1) redistributes income from the rich to the poor, (2) taxes people according to their ability to pay, and (3) taxes people according to the benefits they receive from government. Although there is much controversy over the redistributional nature of our progressive tax system, there is no strong evidence that in fact the tax system has never done much income redistribution in this country. Currently about 85 percent of all Americans, rich or poor, pay roughly the same proportion of their income in federal income taxes.

⭐ EXAMPLE: An Alternative to Income Taxes: A Consumption Tax

Currently, the federal tax code requires that everyone pay taxes on income whether they save or consume that income. People who believe that we should encourage more saving have proposed that our current income tax system be replaced by a **consumption tax.** The concept of such a tax is relatively straightforward: Taxpayers would pay taxes only on what they consume out of income, not what they earn. One way to determine such consumption in any year is simply to subtract what is saved from what is earned. The difference is consumption, and that is the base to which a consumption tax would apply. In essence, this provides an unlimited deduction for saving. The idea was first brought forward by the Treasury Department in its *Blueprints for Tax Reform,* published in 1977. Congress thought about a consumption tax in the 1986 tax reform debate. More recently, the consumption tax has been endorsed by Strengthening of America, a national commission headed by Senators Sam Nunn and Pete Domenici. Most advocates of a consumption tax argue in favor of exempting the first $15,000 of consumption. The consumption tax could be a flat rate or a progressive system. It could conceivably raise as much in revenues as the current tax system.

Even though there appears to be growing interest in switching to a consumption tax, any overhaul of the current federal income tax system faces tremendous political barriers. Moreover, questions about how to define saving are not easily answered. Is the purchase of a house consumption or saving? What about the elderly, who save very little?

For Critical Analysis: Which sectors of the economy would favor a switch from an income tax to a consumption tax and why? ●

> ▶ **Consumption tax**
> A tax system in which taxes are paid only on the income that individuals actually spend, not on what they earn. What is not spent would be untaxed saving.

THE TREATMENT OF CAPITAL GAINS

The difference between the buying and selling price of an asset, such as a share of stock or a plot of land, is called a **capital gain** if it is a profit and a **capital loss** if it is not. As of the middle of 1993 capital gains were taxed at ordinary income marginal tax rates.

Capital gains are not always real. If you pay $100,000 for a house in one year and sell it for 50 percent more 10 years later, your capital gain is $50,000. But what if, during those 10 years, there had been inflation such that average prices had also gone up by 50 percent? Your *real* capital gain would be zero. But you still have to pay taxes on that $50,000. To counter this problem, many economists have argued that capital gains should be indexed to the rate of inflation. This is exactly what is done with the marginal tax brackets in the federal income tax code. Tax brackets for the purposes of calculating marginal tax rates each year are expanded at the rate of inflation, or the rate at which the average of all prices is rising. So if the rate of inflation is 10 percent, each tax bracket is moved up by 10 percent. The same concept could be applied to capital gains. Some employees at the Treasury Department argued in favor of this, but it was not enacted.

> ▶ **Capital gain**
> The positive difference between the purchase price and the sale price of an asset. If a share of stock is bought for $5 and then sold for $15, the capital gain is $10.

> ▶ **Capital loss**
> The negative difference between the purchase price and the sale price of an asset.

THE CORPORATE INCOME TAX

Corporate income taxes account for about 11 percent of all federal taxes collected and almost 8 percent of all state and local taxes collected. Corporations are generally taxed on the difference between their total revenues or receipts and their expenses. The corporate income tax structure is given in Table 5-3.

Double Taxation.

Because individual stockholders must pay taxes on the dividends they receive, paid out of *after-tax* profits by the corporation, corporate profits are taxed twice. If you receive $1,000 in dividends, you have to declare them as income, and you must pay taxes at your marginal tax rate. Before the corporation was able to pay you those dividends, it had to pay taxes on all its profits, including any that it put back into the company or did not distribute in the form of dividends. Eventually the new investment made possible by those **retained earnings**—profits not given out to stockholders—along with borrowed funds will be reflected in the increased value of the stock in that company. When you sell your stock in that company, you will have to pay taxes on the difference between what you paid for the stock and what you sold it for. In both cases dividends and retained earnings (corporate profits) are taxed twice.

▶ **Retained earnings**
Earnings that a corporation saves, or retains, for investment in other productive activities; earnings that are not distributed to stockholders.

 EXAMPLE: The Treasury Department Study on Ending Double Taxation

In 1992 a long-awaited 268-page Treasury Department study was released. The authors argued that the United States should stop taxing corporate profits twice. They argued that tax laws should be changed to exempt dividends from the recipients' taxable income. The report is the fourth in 20 years issued by the Treasury Department on the double taxation of corporate profits. The Treasury report pointed out that under the current system of double taxation, corporations have an incentive to rely on debt, called bonds, rather than selling more shares of stock. The reason is that interest payments on bonds are deductible from taxable income, but dividends paid to shareholders are not. There is also an increased incentive for companies to retain earnings and to invest in noncorporate forms of businesses. All in all, these distortions raise the cost of capital for corporate investment.

For Critical Analysis: Explain why under the current system of double taxation of corporate profits, corporations tend to favor obtaining funds by selling debt (bonds) over selling stock. ●

Who Really Pays the Corporate Income Tax?

Corporations can exist only as long as consumers buy their products, employees make their goods, stockholders (owners) buy their shares, and bondholders buy their bonds. Corporations per se do not do anything. We must ask, then, who really pays the tax on corporate income. This is a question of **tax incidence.** (The question of tax incidence applies to all taxes, including sales taxes and Social Security taxes.) There remains considerable debate about the incidence

▶ **Tax incidence**
The distribution of tax burdens among various groups in society.

TABLE 5-3 Corporate income tax schedule.
The rates were in effect through the beginning of 1993.
Source: Internal Revenue Service.

CORPORATE TAXABLE INCOME	CORPORATE TAX RATE
$0–$50,000	15%
$50,001–$75,000	25%
$75,001–$99,999	34%
$100,000+	34% plus 5% of the taxable income in excess of $100,000 or $11,750, whichever is less.

of corporate taxation. Some economists say that corporations pass their tax burdens on to consumers by charging higher prices. Other economists believe that it is the stockholders who bear most of the tax. Still others believe that employees pay at least part of the tax by receiving lower wages than they would otherwise. Because the debate is not yet settled, we will not hazard a guess here as to what the correct conclusion should be. Suffice it to say that you should be cautious when you advocate increasing corporation income taxes. You may be the one who ultimately ends up paying the increase, at least in part, if you own shares in a corporation, buy its products, or work for it.

CONCEPTS IN BRIEF

- Because corporations must first pay an income tax on most earnings, when shareholders pay personal income tax on dividends received (or realized capital gains), they are double-taxed.
- The corporate income tax is paid by one or more of the following groups: stockholder-owners, consumers of corporate-produced products, and employees in corporations.

SOCIAL SECURITY AND UNEMPLOYMENT TAXES

An increasing percentage of federal tax receipts is accounted for each year by taxes (other than income taxes) levied on payrolls. These taxes are for Social Security, retirement, survivors' disability, and old-age medical benefits (Medicare). As of mid-1993 the Social Security tax was imposed on earnings up to $57,600 at a rate of 6.2 percent on employers and 6.2 percent on employees. That is, the employer matches your "contribution" to Social Security. (The employer's contribution is really paid, at least in part, in the form of a reduced wage rate paid to employees.) A Medicare tax was imposed on earnings up to $135,000 at a combined rate of 2.9 percent. These taxes and the base on which they are levied will rise in the next decade. Social Security taxes came into existence when the Federal Insurance Contributions Act (FICA) was passed in 1935.

There is also a federal unemployment tax, which obviously has something to do with unemployment insurance. This tax rate is less than 1 percent on the first $7,000 of annual wages of each employee. Only the employer makes the tax payment. This tax covers the costs of the unemployment insurance system and the costs of employment services. In addition to this federal tax, some states with an unemployment system impose an additional tax of up to about 3 percent, depending on the past record of the particular employer. An employer who lays off workers frequently will have a slightly higher state unemployment tax rate than an employer who never lays off workers.

It has been argued that Social Security is a system in which current workers subsidize already retired workers. It is also argued that the system is not an insurance system because Social Security benefits are legislated by Congress; they are not part of the original Federal Insurance Contributions Act. Therefore, future generations may decide that they do not want to give large Social Security benefits to retired workers. Even if workers had paid large amounts into Social Security, they could conceivably be denied the benefits of a large Social Security retirement income.

SPENDING, GOVERNMENT SIZE, AND TAX RECEIPTS

The size of the public sector can be measured in many different ways. One way is to count the number of public employees. Another way is to look at total government expenditures. But there are two distinct types of government expenditures: resource-using ex-

FIGURE 5-1
Rising government purchases.
Here we show government purchases of goods and services at all levels—federal, state, and local—expressed as a percentage of total national output (gross domestic product). In other words, this graph shows resource-using government expenditures in the U.S. economy expressed as a percentage of GDP. The biggest jumps occurred during World War I and World War II; although government spending fell dramatically after World War II, it did not return to previous peacetime levels.

Sources: Economic Report of the President, 1993; Economic Indicators, various issues. 1994 is an estimate.

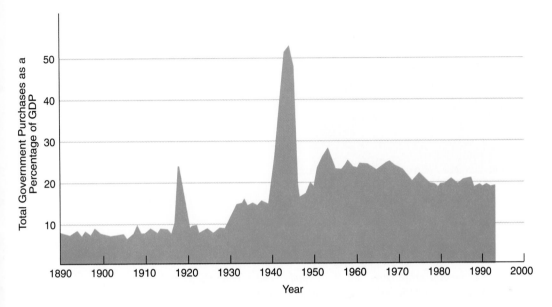

▶ **Resource-using government expenditures**
Expenditures by the government that involve the use of land, labor, capital, or entrepreneurship; to be contrasted with pure transfers, in which the government taxes one group and pays some of those taxes to another without demanding any concurrent services in return.

penditures and transfer payments. We have already discussed transfer payments such as welfare and Social Security. **Resource-using government expenditures** are the purchase by governments—federal, state, and local—of goods and services that divert economic resources from the private sector, thereby making them no longer available for private use. Figure 5-1 shows resource-using government expenditures expressed as a percentage of total national output, or gross domestic product (GDP). These government purchases account for more than 20 percent of total national output. Those expenditures make up 65 percent of total government spending. When we add transfer payments, as in Figure 5-2 on the next page, we see that total government spending accounts for about 40 percent of U.S. GDP.

 INTERNATIONAL EXAMPLE: Taxes Paid in the United States Relative to the Rest of the World

It is instructive to compare the average person's tax burden in America to that in other countries. An article in *Business Week* titled "High Taxes Are Not What's Ailing the U.S. Economy" presented the figures shown in Figure 5-3 (on the next page). But another group of economists and statisticians reexamined the data taken from the Organization for Economic Cooperation and Development. In the high-tax countries surveyed—Sweden, France, Germany, Italy, Great Britain, and Canada—90 percent or more of medical costs are paid for by the government out of tax revenues. In the United States about 45 percent of medical costs are covered by the government through Medicaid and Medicare. The

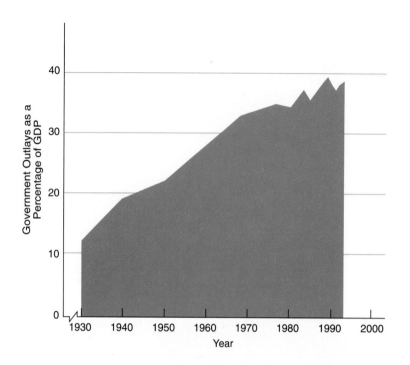

FIGURE 5-2
**Government outlays
(including transfers) as
a percentage of gross
domestic product.**
Taking account of all government outlays, including
transfer payments, shows
an increasing trend for
government outlays as a
percentage of GDP.

*Sources: Facts and Figures on
Government Finance,* 20th and
21st eds. (New York Tax Foundation, 1979, 1981); *Economic Report of the President, 1993; Economic Indicators,* various issues.

remainder is paid for by private-sector employers and individuals. The private sector's
medical bill equals about 7.5 percent of U.S. gross domestic product. If this amount is
added to total federal, state, and local tax receipts, the United States would place right after France in total tax revenues as a percentage of GDP, ahead of Germany, Italy, Great
Britain, Canada, and Japan.

*For Critical Analysis: How would you describe the economic differences in an eco-
nomic system with high tax rates as compared to an economy with low tax rates?* ●

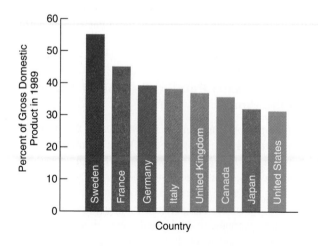

FIGURE 5-3
**The average person's
tax burden around the
world.**
The average American's
tax burden does not seem
unduly harsh when com-
pared to the rest of the
industrialized world.

*Source: Organization for Eco-
nomic Cooperation and Development; Business Week,* February
10, 1992, p. 20.

FIGURE 5-4
Sources of government tax receipts.

Source: U.S. Department of Commerce, Bureau of Economic Analysis.

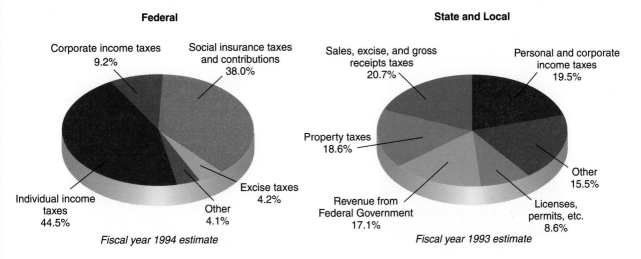

Federal

Corporate income taxes
9.2%

Social insurance taxes
and contributions
38.0%

Individual income
taxes
44.5%

Other
4.1%

Excise taxes
4.2%

Fiscal year 1994 estimate

State and Local

Sales, excise, and gross
receipts taxes
20.7%

Personal and corporate
income taxes
19.5%

Property taxes
18.6%

Other
15.5%

Revenue from
Federal Government
17.1%

Licenses,
permits, etc.
8.6%

Fiscal year 1993 estimate

GOVERNMENT RECEIPTS

The main revenue raiser for all levels of government is taxes. We show in the two pie diagrams in Figure 5-4 the percentage of receipts from various taxes obtained by the federal government and by state and local governments.

The Federal Government. The largest source of receipts for the federal government is the individual income tax. It accounts for 44.5 percent of all federal revenues. After that come social insurance taxes and contributions (Social Security), which account for 38 percent of total revenues. Next come corporate income taxes and then a number of other items, such as taxes on imported goods and excise taxes on such things as gasoline and alcoholic beverages.

State and Local Governments. As can be seen in Figure 5-4, there is quite a bit of difference between the origin of receipts for state and local governments and for the federal government. Personal and corporate income taxes account for only 19.5 percent of total state and local revenues. There are even a number of states that collect no personal income tax. The largest source of state and local receipts is from property taxes (used by local government), sales taxes (used mainly by state governments), and corporate income taxes.

Comparing Federal with State and Local Spending. A typical federal government budget is given in Figure 5-5. The largest three categories are defense, income security, and Social Security, which together constitute 54 percent of the total federal budget.

The makeup of state and local expenditures is quite different. Education is the biggest category, accounting for over 34 percent of all expenditures.

FIGURE 5-5 :
Federal government spending compared to state and local spending.
The federal government's spending habits are quite different from those of the states
and cities. On the left you can see that the categories of most importance in the federal budget are defense, income security, and Social Security, which make up almost 60
percent. The most important category at the state and local level is education, which
makes up 34.3 percent.
Sources: Budget of the United States Government; Government Finances.

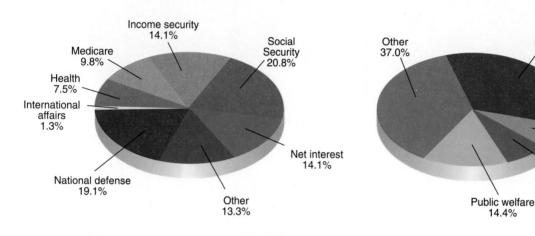

Federal Spending	State and Local Spending

CONCEPTS IN BRIEF

● Resource-using government expenditures—expenditures on goods and services—have leveled off at around 20 percent of GDP. Total government outlays including transfers, however, have continued to grow since World War
II and now account for about 40 percent of GDP.

● Government spending at the federal level is different from that at the state
and local levels. At the federal level, defense, income security, and Social
Security account for almost 60 percent of the federal budget.

DOES THE UNITED STATES NEED AN INDUSTRIAL POLICY?

Concepts Applied: Role of the public sector; incentives

Virtually all VCRs are produced in Asia, as at this JVC assembly plant in Japan. Some economists and policymakers argue that the United States should follow the Japanese industrial policy model.

Who, in economic terms, will "own" the twenty-first century—America, Japan, or Europe? According to many commentators, including economist Lester Thurow of the Massachusetts Institute of Technology, a united Europe will most likely have "the honor of having the 21st century named for it." Who is going to come in second place? Maybe not the United States—unless, according to a growing number of observers, America adopts an industrial policy similar to that which has been used in Japan and elsewhere.

THE JAPANESE MODEL At the beginning of the 1980s, the Japanese had a per capita income of about half that in America. Today it is arguably in the range of American per capita income, and it is growing faster than in either the United States or Europe. Japan's *industrial policy* has consisted of the influencing of the economic system in two important areas, finance and investment. The Ministry of Finance encourages private banks to increase or decrease lending to specific industries. Typically, the Ministry of Finance targets industries selected by another important part of Japan's industrial policy, the Ministry of International Trade and Industry (MITI). MITI is empowered to intervene in the market process by providing export insurance to individual firms' export projects. Thus it induces firms to take greater risks in the export sector. MITI can also designate special regions as industrial parks and provide a social infrastructure for such parks. Whenever MITI determines that growth in an industry should be promoted, it acts to coordinate research efforts by firms in the industry. It also protects firms from foreign competition by putting up trade barriers in the form of supply restrictions on goods sent from abroad and tariffs (taxes) on imports.

CRITICS OF THE JAPANESE MODEL The critics of Japanese industrial policy point out that MITI has not been infallible. In the 1960s it decided that two automobile companies were sufficient for the entire export market. MITI pressured Honda Motor Company and others to abandon the industry. (Fortunately for Japanese automakers, they ignored MITI's recommendations.) MITI tried to establish a petrochemical industry, an effort that ended up in total failure. The same is true for the billions of yen it spent on an electric car and on a nuclear-powered glass furnace for steelmaking.

Economists also point to the model of public choice discussed in this chapter. How can government bureaucrats be expected to allocate capital better than private entrepreneurs? Won't any American government's attempts to promote a few particular industries simply fall prey to special-interest group legislation in Congress?

THE NEW INDUSTRIAL POLICY A number of books have appeared in the 1990s promoting the idea that we need an American form of industrial policy that would combine some of the policies of both Europe and Japan. The European Community is particularly important to us, according to some observers, because it represents over 350 million consumers whose production base eventually will be integrated like that in the United States. Here are some of the suggestions that Thurow of MIT, Robert Reich, secretary of labor, and Robert Kuttner, syndicated columnist and coeditor of *American Prospect,* believe will make us globally competitive in the twenty-first century.

- Force cooperative research between government and the private sector in the form of national laboratories.
- Loosen antitrust rules pertaining to groups of firms that wish to coordinate activities in order to be globally competitive.

- Increase government investment to promote technical progress in state-of-the-art production technology.
- Increase hard bargaining with our trading partners to ensure equal access to foreign markets and fair rules of the game.
- Increase government spending on our infrastructure—roads, harbors, bridges, and especially communications in the form of fiber-optic cables and high-speed digital switching equipment.

IN THE FINAL ANALYSIS Many economists will remain leery of any new industrial policy that involves government sponsorship of technologies. The reason is that individuals, companies, and industries that have new ideas will move into the political arena to compete for taxpayer subsidies. Members of Congress will become advocates of their states' pet projects. Officials who run the government-sponsored technologies will undoubtedly shy away from ventures that take a long time to pay off.

One good example is the Synfuels Corporation, a government entity started in 1980 to develop synthetic fuels to replace oil. Oil prices fell and the Synfuels Corporation died without fanfare in 1986 at a total cost to taxpayers of $2.9 billion. In Japan, private industry supplies about 75 percent of research and development funds. It is not the government that is fueling R&D in Japan.

FOR CRITICAL ANALYSIS
1. Government in the United States accounts for at least one-third of all economic activity. Under what circumstances would an increase in the size of government be warranted because of problems with our global competitiveness? Elaborate.
2. World oil prices dropped in the late 1980s and caused the Synfuels project to be abandoned by the U.S. government. Can you think of an argument in favor of maintaining that project in spite of lower world oil prices?

CHAPTER SUMMARY

1. Government provides a legal system in which the rights of private ownership, the enforcement of contracts, and the legal status of businesses are provided. In other words, government sets the legal rules of the game and enforces them.
2. To ensure competition, government passes and enforces antitrust legislation and provides for regulation of certain sectors of the economy.
3. Government can correct external costs by taxation and/or legislation and prohibition. It can correct external benefits by subsidies, financing and/or production of a good or service, and regulation.
4. Public goods, once produced, can be consumed jointly by additional individuals at zero opportunity cost.
5. If users of public goods know that they will be taxed on the basis of their expressed valuation of those public goods, their expressed valuation will be low. They expect to get a free ride.
6. Merit goods (chosen as such, collectively, through the political process) may not be purchased at all or not in sufficient quantities at market clearing prices. Therefore, government subsidizes or provides such merit goods at a subsidized or zero price to specified classes of consumers.
7. When it is collectively decided that something is a demerit good, government taxes, regulates, or prohibits the manufacture, sale, and use of that good.
8. Decision making in the market sector shares certain similarities with decision making in the public sector, including the facts that both sectors face scarcity, competition exists in both sectors, and individuals can be treated similarly in both sectors for analytical purposes.
9. Differences between market and collective decision making include the following: Many government goods are provided at zero price (without a user charge), collective decision making may involve the legal use of force, and dollar voting is not the same as political voting.
10. Resource-using government expenditures—expenditures on goods and services—have leveled off at around 20 percent of GDP. Total government outlays including transfers, however, have continued to grow since World War II and now account for about 40 percent of GDP.
11. Government spending at the federal level is different from that at the state and local levels. Defense, income security, and Social Security account for almost 60 percent of the federal budget.

DISCUSSION OF PREVIEW POINTS

1. **What problems will you encounter (besides going to jail) if you refuse to pay a portion of your income tax because you oppose national defense spending?**

   You must share in national defense collectively with the rest of the country. Unlike private goods, national defense is a public good and must be consumed collectively. You receive national defense benefits whether you choose to or not; the exclusion principle does not work for public goods, such as national defense. The government could make the exclusion principle work better by deporting you to foreign shores if you don't wish to pay for national defense. This is typically not done. If you were allowed to forgo taxes allocated to national defense, the IRS would be swamped with similar requests. Everyone would have an incentive to claim no benefits from national defense (whether true or not) because it must be consumed collectively.

2. **Why is it that the proportional intensity of desire can be expressed in the marketplace but not in the political process?**

   We are free to indicate the intensity of our wants in the marketplace; for example, T-shirt enthusiasts are allowed to spend greater percentages of their income on T-shirts. Thus dollar votes are allocated by consumers in a manner that indicates their proportional intensity of wants for goods and services. By contrast, when the political process requires a one-person, one-vote situation, intensity of wants is not measured; the voting procedure is of an all-or-nothing nature. For example, consider the decision as to whether a park

   should be created in a given scenic area. By a system of dollar votes people can indicate the intensity of their desires; park lovers will spend higher percentages of their incomes on the park than nonlovers of parks will. Conversely, in a political decision each person would have the same weight in the decision. It is possible for a park to be unprofitable because people value the land more highly in another use; the market solution is no park. In contrast, a one-person, one-vote situation may indicate that a park is wanted; in theory the political process could decide in favor of a park while the marketplace would decide against it.

3. **In what ways do regressive, proportional, and progressive tax structures differ?**

   Under a regressive tax structure, the average tax rate (the percentage of income paid in taxes) falls as income rises. The marginal tax rate is below the average tax rate. Proportional tax structures are those in which the average tax rate remains constant as income rises; the marginal tax rate equals the average tax rate. Under a progressive tax structure, the average tax rate rises as income rises; the marginal tax rate is above the average tax rate.

4. **Who pays the corporate income tax?**

   Ultimately, only people can be taxed. As a consequence, corporate taxes are ultimately paid by people: corporate owners (in the form of reduced dividends and less stock appreciation for stockholders), consumers of corporate products (in the form of higher prices for goods), and/or employees working for corporations (in the form of lower wages).

PROBLEMS
(Answers to odd-numbered problems appear at the back of the book.)

5-1. Consider the following system of taxation, which has been labeled *degressive*. The first $5,000 of income is not taxed. After that, all income is assessed at 20 percent (a proportional system). What is the marginal tax rate on $3,000 of taxable income? $10,000? $100,000? What is the average tax rate on $3,000? $10,000? $100,000? What is the maximum average tax rate?

5-2. You are offered two possible bonds to buy as part of your investing program. One is a corporate bond yielding 9 percent. The other is a tax-exempt municipal bond yielding only 6 percent. Assuming that you are certain you will be paid your interest and principal on these two bonds, what marginal tax bracket must you be in to decide in favor of the tax-exempt bond?

5-3. Consider the following tax structure:

INCOME BRACKET	MARGINAL TAX RATE
$0–$1,500	0%
$1,501–$2,000	14%
$2,001–$3,000	20%

Mr. Smith has an income of $2,500 per annum. Calculate his tax bill for the year. What is his average tax rate? His highest marginal tax rate?

5-4. In 1990 Social Security tax payments on wages were 7.65 percent of wages, on wages up to $51,300. No *further* Social Security payments were made on earnings above this figure. Calculate the *average* Social Security tax rate for annual wages of (a) $4,000, (b) $51,300, (c) $56,000, (d) $100,000. Is the Social Security system a progressive, proportional, or regressive tax structure?

5-5. Briefly, what factors could be included as part of the requirements for a "good" tax structure?

5-6. We have used national defense as an example of a public good. Alaska and Hawaii are part of the United States. Is our example still valid? If not, why not?

5-7. Is local police protection a public good? Explain.

5-8. TV signals have characteristics of public goods, yet TV stations and commercial networks are private businesses. Analyze this situation.

5-9. Assume that you live in a relatively small suburban neighborhood called Parkwood. The Parkwood Homeowners' Association collects money from homeowners to pay for upkeep of the surrounding stone wall, lighting at the entrances to Parkwood, and mowing the lawn around the perimeter of the area. Each year you are asked to donate $50. No one forces you to do it. There are 100 homeowners in Parkwood.
   a. What percentage of the total yearly revenue of the homeowners' association will you account for?

   b. At what level of participation will the absence of your $50 contribution make a difference?
   c. If you do not contribute your $50, are you really receiving a totally free ride?

5-10. Assume that a textile firm has created a negative externality by polluting a nearby stream with the wastes associated with production. Assume further that the government can measure the external costs to the community with accuracy and charges the firm for its pollution, based on the social cost of pollution per unit of textile output. Show how such a charge will lead to a higher selling price for textiles and a reduction in the equilibrium quantity of textiles.

5-11. Label two columns on your paper "Private Goods" and "Public Goods." List each of the following under the heading that describes it better.
   a. Sandwich
   b. Public television
   c. Cable television
   d. National defense
   e. Shirt
   f. Elementary education
   g. College education
   h. Health clinic flu shots
   i. Opera
   j. Museum
   k. Automobile

5-12. One source of complaints about government bureaucracy is the burden of red tape involved in all decisions and activities. Yet this practice survives in the face of hostility. What is the economic function of red tape in government enterprises? Why do we see less of it in private profit-making firms?

COMPUTER-ASSISTED INSTRUCTION
(Complete problem and answer on disk.)

The decisions made by people in the government (bureaucrats) and people in the private sector often differ because of the different constraints they face. We show the impact of this on innovation in the ethical drug industry.

6

CONVERGING ECONOMIC SYSTEMS

A new word was coined in the 1990s—*ecocide,* the systematic destruction of our ecology. Pollution has been viewed as the undesirable by-product of a freely functioning economic system that doesn't force polluters to do anything about the negative externalities they cause. One of the suggested ways to "internalize" pollution externalities was through the creation of a centrally planned economy. The former Union of Soviet Socialist Republics (USSR) was often singled out as a place where central planning could help the environment. Today historians, economists, and political scientists are continuing with their autopsy on the former USSR. All agree on one thing: Communist rulers encouraged a 74-year assault on nature; they committed ecocide. What central planners did or did not do with respect to the environment in the Soviet Union is part of the study of alternative economic systems.

After reading this chapter, you should be able to answer the following questions:

1. Why does the scarcity problem force all societies to answer the questions *what, how,* and *for whom?*

2. How can economies be classified?

3. What are the characteristics of a command socialist economy?

4. What are some problems that command socialist economies face?

INTRODUCTION

The day McDonald's opened in Beijing, 40,000 customers went through its doors, setting a one-day sales record for any McDonald's restaurant in the world. The previous record holders were the two McDonald's outlets on the Chinese border city of Shenchen, not far from Hong Kong. The Beijing McDonald's has 700 seats and 29 cash registers and boasts 1,000 employees selected from 22,000 applicants. Just a few years earlier, the biggest McDonald's in the world was in Moscow. It still serves 22,000 customers a day.

Does the existence of McDonald's in countries such as Russia and China mean that their economies are the same as in the United States and Western Europe? To answer this question adequately, we must first look at the definition of an economic system, the three questions that all economic systems must answer, and the polar extremes of systems that have existed in the world. We will then examine how all countries' economic systems seem to be converging and the differences that still exist across countries such as China, Poland, Hungary, Russia, North Korea, and India. No one chapter in an economics textbook can do justice to the myriad differences that exist among economic systems. The goal in this chapter is nonetheless to give you the flavor of the differences that do exist and to indicate which will remain in the future despite convergence of the various systems.

ECONOMIC SYSTEMS

The fundamental economic problem in any society, regardless of place and point in history, is to provide a set of rules for channeling competition and resolving conflict among individuals who can't satisfy their every want, given the constraint of scarcity. The rules that each **economic system** provides are embedded in a framework of formal institutions, such as laws, and informal institutions, such as customs. The institutions in any economic system are created by humans and hence can be changed by humans.

Among the spectrum of economic systems, three are most important.

1. **Capitalism.** Under **capitalism,** individuals hold government-protected private **property rights** to all goods, including those used in production and their own labor.
2. **Socialism.** Under **socialism,** individuals typically have exclusive rights to **consumption goods,** or **consumer goods,** such as stereos and books, which they can buy and sell, but restricted rights to income-producing goods, such as machinery and often to their own labor. Typically in socialist systems, the rights to income-producing goods are assigned and enforced by government employees.
3. **Communism. Communism** used to be thought to provide greater motivation of workers to contribute to community service and the public sector rather than to work out of self-interest. In pure communism, we would see the absence of economic class distinctions. In practice, nations that were called communist had centrally planned (command) economies in which the state also extended its control to the choice of jobs for all workers.

Another way of defining economic systems is to classify them according to whether they are market systems or command systems. A **market system** is one in which decision making is decentralized. A **command system** is one in which decision making is centralized.

All the principles of economics that you have learned in Chapters 1 through 5 apply to all economic systems. No matter what the system, the fundamental economic problem of scarcity must be solved. Every economy faces opportunity costs in making decisions.

▶ **Economic system**
The institutional means through which resources are used to satisfy human wants.

▶ **Capitalism**
An economic system in which individuals own productive resources; these individuals can use the resources in whatever manner they choose, subject to common protective legal restrictions.

▶ **Property rights**
The rights of an owner to use and to exchange property.

▶ **Socialism**
An economic system in which the state owns the major share of productive resources except labor. Socialism also usually involves the redistribution of income.

▶ **Consumption goods,** or **consumer goods**
Goods bought by households to use up, thereby providing satisfaction. Examples are food, clothing, and movies.

▶ **Communism**
In its purest form, an economic system in which the state has disappeared and in which individuals contribute to the economy according to their productivity and are given income according to their needs.

▶ **Market system**
A system in which individuals own the factors of production and decide individually how to use them; a system with decentralized economic decision making.

▶ **Command system**
A system in which the government controls the factors of production and makes all decisions about their use and about the distribution of income.

THREE BASIC ECONOMIC QUESTIONS

In every nation, no matter what the form of government, what the type of economic system, who is running the government, or how poor or rich it is, three basic economic questions must be answered. They concern the problem of **resource allocation,** which is simply how resources shall be allocated. As such, resource allocation answers the three basic economic questions of *what, how,* and *for whom* goods and services will be produced.

▶ **Resource allocation**
The assignment of resources to specific uses by determining what will be produced, how it will be produced, and for whom it will be produced.

1. **What and how much will be produced?** Literally billions of different things could be produced with society's scarce resources. Some mechanism must exist that causes some things to be produced and others to remain as either inventors' pipe dreams or individuals' unfulfilled desires.

2. **How will it be produced?** There are many ways to produce a desired item. It is possible to use more labor and less capital or vice versa. It is possible to use more unskilled labor and fewer units of skilled labor. Somehow, in some way, a decision must be made as to the particular mix of inputs, the way they should be organized, and how they are brought together at a particular place.

3. **For whom will it be produced?** Once a commodity is produced, who should get it? In a market economy, individuals and businesses purchase commodities with money income. The question then is what mechanism there is to distribute income, which then determines how commodities are distributed throughout the economy.

THE PRICE SYSTEM AND HOW IT ANSWERS THE THREE ECONOMIC QUESTIONS

▶ **Price system**
An economic system in which (relative) prices are constantly changing to reflect changes in supply and demand for different commodities. The prices of those commodities are signals to everyone within the system about what is relatively scarce and what is relatively abundant.

A **price system** (or market system) is an economic system in which (relative) prices are constantly changing to reflect changes in supply and demand for different commodities. In addition, the prices of those commodities are the signals to everyone within the system as to what is relatively scarce and what is relatively abundant. Indeed, it is the *signaling* aspect of the price system that provides the information to buyers and sellers about what should be bought and what should be produced. The price system, which is characteristic of a market economy, is only one possible way to organize society. Others were briefly explained earlier in this chapter.

WHAT AND HOW MUCH SHOULD BE PRODUCED?

In a price system the interaction of demand and supply for each good determines what and how much to produce. Note, however, that if the highest price that consumers are willing to pay is less than the lowest cost at which a good can be produced, output will be zero. That doesn't mean that the price system has failed. Today consumers do not purchase their own private space shuttles. The demand is not high enough in relation to the supply to create a market. But it may be someday.

HOW SHOULD IT BE PRODUCED?

▶ **Least-cost combination**
The level of input use that produces a given level of output at minimum cost.

The question of how output will be produced in a price system relates to the efficient use of scarce inputs. Consider the possibility of using only two types of resources, capital and labor. A firm may have the options given in Table 6-1 (page 124). It can use various combinations of labor and capital to produce the same amount of output. Two hypothetical combinations are given in the table. How, then, is it decided which combination should be used? In the price system the **least-cost combination** (technique B in our example) will in fact be chosen because it maximizes profits. To be sure, different production techniques will have to be used, depending on which combination is selected. We are

INPUTS	INPUT UNIT PRICE	A PRODUCTION TECHNIQUE A (INPUT UNITS)	COST	B PRODUCTION TECHNIQUE B (INPUT UNITS)	COST
Labor	$10	5	$50	4	$40
Capital	$ 8	4	$32	5	$40
Total cost of 100 units of product X			$82		$80

TABLE 6-1 Production costs for 100 units of product X.
Technique A or B can be used to produce the same output. Obviously, B will be used because its total cost is less than A's. Using production technique B will generate a $2 savings for every 100 units produced.

virtually guaranteed that the least-cost production technique will be chosen because if any other technique were chosen, firms would be sacrificing potential profit.

Moreover, in a price system, competition will in effect *force* firms to use least-cost production techniques. Any firm that fails to employ the least costly technique will find that other firms can undercut its price. In other words, other firms that choose the least-cost production technique will be able to offer the product at a lower price and still make a profit. This lower price will induce consumers to shift purchases from the higher-priced firm to the lower-priced firm. Inefficient firms will be forced out of business.

FOR WHOM WILL IT BE PRODUCED?

This last question that every economic system must answer involves who gets what. In a market system, the choice about what is purchased is made by individuals, but that choice is determined by ability to pay. Who gets what is determined by the distribution of money income.

Determination of Money Income.   In a price system, a consumer's ability to pay for consumer products is based on the size of that consumer's money income. That in turn depends on the quantities, qualities, and types of the various human and nonhuman resources that the individual owns and supplies to the marketplace. It also depends on the prices, or payments, for those resources. When you are selling your human resources as labor services, your money income is based on the wages you can earn in the labor market. If you own nonhuman resources—capital and land, for example—the level of interest and rents that you are paid for your capital and land will clearly influence the size of your money income and thus your ability to buy consumer products.

Which Consumers Get What?   In a price system, the distribution of finished products to consumers is based on consumers' ability and willingness to pay the market price for the product. If the market price of compact discs is $9, consumers who are able and willing to pay that price will get those CDs. All others won't.

Here we are talking about the *rationing* function of market prices in a price system. Rather than have a central political figure or agency decide which consumers will get which goods, those consumers who are willing and able to pay the market price obtain the goods. That is to say, relative prices ration the available resources, goods, and services at any point in time among those who place the highest value on those items. If scarcity didn't exist, we would not need any system to ration available resources, goods, and services. All of us could have all of everything that we wanted without taking away from what anyone else obtained.

CONCEPTS IN BRIEF

- Any economic system must answer three questions: (1) *What* will be produced? (2) *How* will it be produced? (3) *For whom* will it be produced?
- In a price system, supply and demand determine the prices at which exchanges shall take place.
- In a price system, firms choose the least-cost combination use of inputs to produce any given output. Competition forces firms to do so.
- In a price system, who gets what is determined by consumers' money income and choices about how to use that money income.

TWO EXTREME ECONOMIC SYSTEMS: MARKET CAPITALISM AND COMMAND SOCIALISM

Market capitalism is what we in America know best, for that is the economic system under which we live. Much of what you have studied to this point in the book is consistent with market capitalism. In contrast, relatively few countries today have systems that even approach pure command socialism, which requires strict centralized planning. But it is instructive to compare these two extremes nonetheless.

MARKET CAPITALISM IN THEORY

In its purest theoretical form, market capitalism, or pure capitalism, has the following attributes:

1. Private property rights exist, are legal, and are upheld by the judicial system.
2. Prices are allowed to seek their own level as determined by the forces of supply and demand. In this sense, pure capitalism is a price system.
3. Resources, including human labor, are free to move in and out of industries and geographic locations. The movement of resources follows the lure of profits—higher expected profits create an incentive for more resources to go where those profits might occur.
4. Risk takers are rewarded by higher profits, but those whose risks turn out to be bad business decisions suffer the consequences directly in terms of reduced wealth.
5. Decisions about what and how much should be produced, how it should be produced, and for whom it should be produced are left to the market. In a pure market capitalist system, all decisions are decentralized and made by individuals in a process of *spontaneous coordination* throughout the economy.

> One way to remember the attributes of market capitalism is by thinking of the three *P*s: prices, profits, and private property.

The role of government is limited to provision of certain public goods, such as defense, police protection, and a legal framework within which property rights and contracts are enforced.

To be sure, these tenets of a purely capitalist system do not fit 100 percent the reality in the United States or in any other country in the world today or in the past. In the United States, our economic system is more of a mixed one that includes primarily capitalist elements but also a strong dose of elements of command socialism.

INTERNATIONAL EXAMPLE: A Real Estate Boom in Moscow

There is no better place to observe the three *P*s—profits, prices, and private property—in action than in the city that switched from state ownership and control without the three *P*s to a housing market with the three *P*s. That city is Moscow. Even as tanks were rolling into Red Square during the attempted *coup d'état* by hard-line Communists in 1991, an auction of city apartments was being held. The city government, through its Housing Initiative, had authorized the more or less unrestricted buying and selling of Moscow's housing stock. Within a year, Moscow became one of the hottest real estate markets in the world. Some apartments that were purchased for around $350 jumped in value to over $15,000. Six months after the auctions began, one three-bedroom apartment went for over $100,000. Commercial rents have gone even higher—some are more than double the rate per square foot in New York. McDonald's Corporation—owner of one of the biggest McDonald's in the world in Red Square—reinvested its profits in a new 12-story downtown office building.

But with private property and changing prices set by supply and demand come the possibility of negative profits too. No doubt by the time you read this, some wild real estate speculators will have gone broke. The move to capitalism does not guarantee profits.

For Critical Analysis: Explain why it is possible for commercial rents in Moscow to be more expensive than they are in New York. ●

COMMAND SOCIALISM IN THEORY

The name **command socialism** gives you an idea of the basic tenets of the system. Remember, though, that there is much disagreement among socialist theoreticians about what constitutes theoretically pure socialism. In any event, the following characteristics are usually associated with it:

▶ **Command socialism**
An economic system in which there is virtually no private property and the state owns virtually all the factors of production. Decisions about what and how much, by whom, and for whom are decided by command from a central authority.

1. Most of the major factors of production are owned by the state. Private property rights are strictly limited to small tools that an individual needs for an occupation. Land, factories, and major machinery are never privately owned.
2. Most prices are set by the state rather than by the forces of supply and demand.
3. The movement of resources, including labor, is strictly controlled. Resources typically move only when dictated by a centralized planning authority.
4. Economic decisions about what and how much, how, and for whom are all made by the state through its central planning agencies and other administrative units.
5. Little individual risk taking is allowed; rather, risk taking in the form of new ventures is undertaken by the state. All citizens benefit from successful risk taking, and all citizens pay for unsuccessful risk taking, but not directly through immediate reductions in individual income and wealth.
6. Taxation is often used to redistribute income.

In summary, in a pure command socialist system, private property in production equipment and resources basically does not exist, and economic decisions are made by a centralized authority.

Few examples of pure command socialism exist today. China used to be considered one, but it has much more decentralized planning today than ever before and, as we will see, it even has a growing market economic sector. North Korea probably has the most extensive centrally controlled command social system today. (Cuba has also had one under the Castro dictatorship.)

THE QUESTIONS OF PLANNING

Do not get the impression that the main distinction between a centralized command economy and a decentralized market economy has to do with the degree of planning. All economies are planned in one way or another. The United States has a highly planned economy. The difference between economic planning in the United States and in command economies is who does the planning. The United States has a decentralized planned economy, with planning undertaken by firms, individuals, and elected representatives. These plans take the form of budgets and detailed projects. Companies and state, city, and county governments in the United States that don't plan well often experience financial difficulties. In the private sector in the United States, all the plans are built around relative prices, which in a market economy communicate scarcity and priorities. In effect, the market system coordinates the plan.

Planning is unavoidable, no matter what the economic system. Whereas in market economies private individuals and businesses do the planning on their own behalf, in command socialist systems central planners undertake the planning on behalf of everyone in their community. The signals given to central planners in command economies have proved to be weak, inaccurate, or nonexistent. The result has been low rates of growth, low standards of living, and, as we pointed out at the beginning of this chapter, environmental destruction on a sometimes massive scale.

CONVERGING TO THE THREE *P*s: MIXED ECONOMIES

▶ **Mixed economy**
An economic system in which decisions about how resources should be used are made partly by the private sector and partly by the government, or the public sector.

Aspects of a command economy permeate all economic systems to some extent, including that of the United States. In the post–World War II era, economists developed the concept of a **mixed economy.** They believed that a combination of command socialism and market capitalism would be the ultimate convergence of diverse economic systems. Truly centralized command economies have almost all failed, though. Despite the rosy predictions of the modelers of centralized command economies, the real world has proved that ignoring the three *P*s—prices, profits, and private property—results in less than desirable consequences for the average citizen. This has been the case in the former Soviet Union and its Eastern European satellites, in Cuba under Castro, North Korea under Kim Il Sung, in India, and elsewhere. In a nutshell, formerly planned economies, in which the state owned virtually everything, are gradually selling off state enterprises and establishing private property rights. Profits are no longer illegal, and prices are being determined more and more by market supply and demand conditions rather than by government edict. We might surmise that all mixed economies will come to resemble what we already have in the United States: market capitalism with government regulation but relatively small government ownership of resources.

CONCEPTS IN BRIEF

- Pure capitalism can be defined by the three *P*s: prices, profits, and private property.
- Under socialism, governments own major productive resources.
- Under command socialism, individuals can only enter certain endeavors and cannot, for example, set up their own factories.
- Under command socialism, planning is centralized rather than decentralized. The rewards for producing are usually set by the state rather than by the market.
- In a purely capitalist system, planning is done by individual firms and by elected representatives rather than by central planners.

CHINA: PAST, PRESENT, AND FUTURE

Since the demise of the centrally planned economies of the Soviet Union and most Eastern European countries, the People's Republic of China remains the largest nation on earth that has some form of command socialism. As you will see, though, a growing geographic area of China has an economic system much closer to that of Hong Kong, Taiwan, and the United States.

UNDERSTANDING CHINA'S PAST

After the Communists emerged victorious in China's civil war following World War II, they instituted an economic system based on so-called five-year plans. In 1953 the first five-year plan was implemented. It was not a success. Starting in the mid-1950s, the Chinese debated economic reform strategies. In 1958 economic reforms consisted mainly of enlarged decision-making powers of *local* governments rather than of the central government. Such powers were applied to raw materials allocation and investment. The national planning system was transformed into a regional planning system.

The 1958 reforms did not transform the Chinese economy because it was still a command economy. Capitalism's three *P*s—prices, profits, and private property—were not yet part of the Chinese economic landscape. Economic chaos ensued, causing the Chinese government to *recentralize* rather than decentralize. (Local governments still retained some power.)

The 1978 Reform.   In 1978 came a new attempt at decentralization and the stimulation of individual initiatives. Local authorities and local government-enterprise production units were given more decision-making power, and reforms were implemented in agriculture and in the foreign economic sector. The state purchase prices of agricultural products were increased. Land leases of up to 15 years were provided for peasants. Urban and rural cooperatives and private enterprises were encouraged to grow rapidly.

In agriculture, the commune system implemented in the 1950s was replaced by what is known as the responsibility, or contract, system. Each peasant household became responsible for its own plot of land. Whatever was produced in excess of the minimum obligation to the state remained the property of the household. Peasants were encouraged to enrich themselves further by engaging in a variety of economic activities. The result was impressive. From 1979 to 1984 there was an increase from virtually zero to 3.4 million jobs in the urban and rural private sector. Farm productivity increased dramatically.

The state-owned industrial sector, however, has not had such impressive economic growth. This is because in that sector, price reforms were not carried out—many prices are still administered by local governments and bear little resemblance to scarcity values.

The 1984 Reforms.   In 1984 the decision-making power of state-owned enterprises was expanded. These businesses are now allowed to set production according to market demand after they fulfill state production quotas. They are allowed to sell part of their output to whomever they choose at prices they choose and to lease or sell idle assets and to make administrative personnel changes.

The result of the 1980s economic restructuring has been dramatic. The size of the state-run sector dropped from almost 70 percent of industrial production to less than 50 percent by most estimates in 1994. This decline in state-run industrial enterprises occurred even while the Communist Party leader, Jiang Zemin, stated that state-run enterprises are the "backbone of the socialist economy." Certainly, not everyone agrees with the changes in China. Jan Qiaowen, a journal editor in Shanghai, called the debts of state-run enterprises a "cancer on the economy." Part of the problem is that China has no legal framework to enforce loan repayments from state-run enterprises. The central government has a difficult, if not impossible, task in collecting bad loans owed it by inefficiently run, virtually bankrupt, state-owned industrial companies.

The problem with state-run factories is that many managers have little incentive to maximize the equivalent of profits. Rather, they attempt to maximize incomes and benefits for their workers. For them, workers constitute a political constituency that is increasingly much more important than the politicians running the show at the national level. To avoid increased scrutiny by national government regulators, many state-run Chinese businesses incur hidden losses. One Chinese newspaper, the *People's Daily,* reported an investigation into the accounts of 257 enterprises. It found that more than 200 of them had hidden losses that were twice the size of losses officially reported.

 **INTERNATIONAL EXAMPLE: The Business of the Party Is Business**

While much of the rhetoric of the Chinese Communist Party is consistent with its anti-capitalist origins, the actions of party bosses, at least in Beijing, seem more like business as usual in a capitalist economy. According to reporter Nicholas Kristof of the *New York Times,* increasingly the business of the Communist Party is business. He reports that the government's intelligence agency is currently running a bakery, the statistics bureau is charging $25 per answered question, and the army is operating one of the capital's best hotels. The Chinese Women's Federation, an organization designed to promote communism and women's rights, also operates a hotel in the Guangzhou. The Central Party School for a while operated a fruit stand in Beijing. It also made a nice profit selling bootlegged copies of a video of a confidential speech in which a high-ranking party leader made fun of other leaders who were trying to stop capitalism's spread. The Ministry of Public Security has two stores in which it sells walkie-talkies, handcuffs, electric cattle prods, and bulletproof vests.

For Critical Analysis: Why is the fact that Communist Party members in China are engaging in business activities newsworthy? ●

THE FUTURE OF CHINA IS NOW, AND IT'S CALLED GUANGDONG

Perhaps the most dramatic example of converging economic systems can be found in the Guangdong province of China (see Figure 6-1 on the next page). This formerly full-tilt command socialist region of the country has been moving steadily toward unfettered decentralized capitalism since Communist Party Secretary Deng Xiaoping let go of many controls there in 1979. Since then the economy has grown faster every year than any other place in the world. This region has been likened to Asia's so-called Four Tigers—South Korea, Taiwan, Hong Kong, and Singapore. While leaders of Guangdong contend that they will match the Four Tigers' living standards and industrial output by the year 2010, a foreigner dropped into Shenzhen (a city not far from Hong Kong) would have difficulty in thinking it will take that long. This city is in a special economic zone. It has its own McDonald's, volatile stock and property markets, business executives with portable phones and pagers, and advertisements for Levi's, Seven-Up, and Head and Shoulders shampoo. This city's population has grown from 50,000 in 1980 to almost 2 million today. When the $1 billion six-lane superhighway between Guangdong province and Hong Kong is completed, the resemblance between those two areas will be complete.

FIGURE 6-1
People's Republic of China—Guangdong Province.

The results of switching from command socialism to the three *P*s of market capitalism have been touted in the Western press for years now. The Pearl River Delta area where this is happening contains about 16 million people, less than 1.5 percent of the 1.1 billion Chinese. Yet the area accounts for over 5 percent of the entire country's industrial output and over 10 percent of its exports.

THE CONTINUED CLASH BETWEEN THE OLD AND THE NEW

The success of the Pearl River Delta regions' "experiment" in capitalism does not mean that China's leadership is ready to turn the whole nation into a free market. Political power is not so easily given up. Moreover, some of the major requirements for a well-functioning

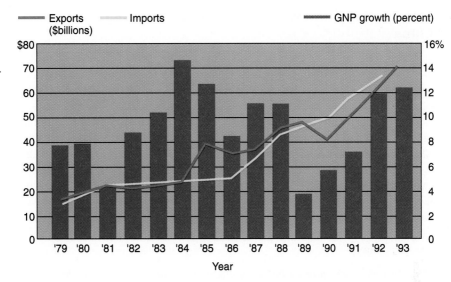

FIGURE 6-2
China's economic growth.
This bar chart shows different annual rates of economic growth in China since it instituted economic reforms in 1979.

Source: Forbes, September 28, 1992, p. 43. 1993 data are estimates.

market system are not quite in place. In 1991 when 2,661 delegates of the National People's Congress met in Beijing's Great Hall of the People, they heard Chinese Premier Ling Peing call for a renewed emphasis on central planning. He said that they had to "resist and oppose bourgeois liberalization." He called for the revitalization of the 10,000 state-run enterprises, which to him "are important pillars of China's modernization program."

What is actually happening in China, however, does not correspond to the verbal statements of China's old-guard political leadership. The nation is slowly but surely moving toward a market economy. China announced in the summer of 1992 that it would abolish state-controlled pricing of raw materials within five years as part of its market-style reforms. The government in Beijing had already begun phasing out artificially low prices for oil, electricity, coal, iron, steel, telecommunications, and transportation services. At the same time that the government announced this move toward market prices, it also approved a major expansion of private stockholdings in 3,200 state industries.

THE RESULT OF CHINA'S ECONOMIC REFORMS

True economic reform started in China in 1979. Since then, the giant nation's annual rate of economic growth (the increase in total national output per year) has averaged between 9 and 10 percent. This is one of the highest rates of increase in the world. You can see how much the economy grew in the various years through 1993 in Figure 6-2. China is predicted to have a higher national income than Japan by the year 2005.

China's trade with the rest of the world—exports and imports—has also increased, from $30 billion in 1979 to more than $150 billion in 1993. China has virtually no foreign debt, and foreign investment is pouring in. In 1992, foreigners invested about $14 billion, and that figure probably tripled in the next two years.

Most of China's growth has been in its nonstate sector, which includes private enterprises, foreign-invested businesses, and joint-venture firms. It also includes entrepreneurial village and township companies. Party officials estimated in 1992 that by the year 2000, the state-run sector of manufacturing would account for only 25 percent of business volume, down from 50 percent today. The government's share of national output continues to fall in the mid-1990s. Consequently, China watchers predict that the nation's rapid economic growth will continue.

INTERNATIONAL EXAMPLE: The Cost of Breaking the Law in China

There is no better example of the problems with China's complicated and ever-changing legal system than the one involving Joseph B. Collins, Jr., a fashion designer from Atlanta. His passport was seized because he was being sued by a Shanghai hotel. Ugene Wang, another American citizen, had his passport taken away in 1990. "I am a hostage here," he said. He is awaiting the resolution of a trade dispute between his California-based company, Richmark Corporation, and Beijing Everbright Industrial Company. Beijing Everbright claims that Richmark Corporation owes it more than $600,000. Wang claims that the money owed was part of a fraudulent scheme by a Beijing Everbright executive to void a contract and that Richmark really doesn't owe anything. Although no Chinese law explicitly allows Chinese judges to confiscate passports, they have done so on numerous occasions. Chinese judges have more power than American judges. The lack of specific legal guidelines regarding trade disputes has discouraged many foreigners from doing business in China.

For Critical Analysis: Do foreign businesspersons who have dealings in the United States face problems similar to those of the two businessmen mentioned here? Explain. ●

CONCEPTS IN BRIEF

● The People's Republic of China followed a Soviet-style command socialist system after China's civil war. Since 1958 there have been a series of reforms, all of which have attempted in one way or another to give more decision-making power to local levels of the economy.

● In China the percentage of state-run industrial production is now 50 percent and will likely fall to 25 percent by the year 2000. Most growth is in the nonstate sector, which is expected to grow dramatically during this period.

MOVEMENT TOWARD THE MARKET IN RUSSIA

Although China is the largest country with any pretense of centralized planning, the Soviet Union is where centralized planning got its start. That system lasted for 74 years in the Soviet Union and over 40 years in its satellite nations of Eastern Europe. In the Soviet Union from the Revolution in 1917 until dissolution in 1991, it consisted of five-year plans, central planning commissions, and hundreds of other types of commissions from the Ministry of Prices to the Ministry of Tourism.

Russia and the other republics with former centrally planned economies are now all moving, more or less, toward market capitalism. They are moving at different speeds, and their success varies greatly. You will read more about proposals for helping these developing countries later in this text; here we will talk about one of the most important aspects of their transitions: privatization.

PRIVATIZATION

Privatization simply means the change from state ownership of businesses, land, and buildings to private ownership. These private owners can be individuals, partnerships, or domestic or foreign corporations. Sometimes workers buy the companies in which they work. This occurred at the Ust Ilimsk Lumber plant in central Siberia. Foreign companies have purchased a large number of formerly state-owned companies. Volkswagen, for example, bought the state-owned autoworks before Czechoslovakia split in two in 1993.

▶ **Privatization**
The sale or transfer of state-owned property and businesses to the private sector, in part or in whole.

FIGURE 6-3
The trend in farming privatization in Russia.

Source: Foreign Agricultural Service of the U.S.D.A. in Moscow.

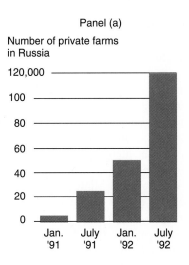

Panel (a)

Number of private farms in Russia

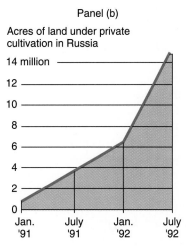

Panel (b)

Acres of land under private cultivation in Russia

Workers can be disrupted when state assets are sold off. Any private individual entity that purchases a state enterprise will almost, by definition, want to make it profitable. This may require ending inefficient practices that are labor-intensive. The result has often been long-time unemployed workers.

In any event, the trend toward privatization in Russia, by far the largest of the 15 former Soviet republics, is moving along relatively unabated. According to *The Economist,* by the beginning of 1993, fully 50 percent of all shops had been sold by the state in Moscow, 30 percent of all restaurants, and 40 percent of other services. In St. Petersburg (formerly Leningrad), the percentages run a bit higher. In Russia's third largest city, Nizhny Novgorod, almost 90 percent of restaurants have been sold to private individuals. Figure 6-3 shows the trend in privatization of farms in Russia.

 INTERNATIONAL EXAMPLE: Even Capitalist Countries Go in for Privatization: The Case of Italy

Modern Italy has always been classified as basically a market capitalist system. But for more than 60 years, a state company started by Mussolini has been Europe's all-encompassing enterprise, employing more than 400,000 people. What do they do? They run cafés, work in banks, pave highways, and build missiles. The name of the company is Instituto per la Ricostruzione Industriale (IRI)—the Institute for Industrial Reconstruction. IRI is one of the most obvious parts of the Italian state sector, which accounts for over 40 percent of the economy. Like the U.S. government, the Italian government has been running deficits—spending more than it has been receiving—for years. As a partial cure, the current crop of politicians is now asking the Italian treasury to sell off at least $5 billion of state assets every year for three to five years. What we will be observing is Italian privatization of public government companies. One subsidiary of IRI, Finmeccanica, a big engineering and technology group, has already sold 40 percent of its shares to private investors.

Not everyone believes that privatization in this form will have much effect on how these companies are run. One Italian stock market analyst, Angelo Di Cresce, stated, "There is no interest in these privatizations when the state will still have control." He is saying that even when state companies sell off *part* of their ownership to private hands, the state still owns the majority and will still make all the decisions.

For Critical Analysis: Does privatization of state-run firms in capitalist countries differ in any way from the process used in former command economies such as Poland? Explain. ●

DOES THE TRANSITION TO A MARKET SYSTEM HAVE TO BE PAINFUL?

Myriad advisers from the West have descended on formerly planned economies to help in their transition to market economies. All have one goal: to make the transition as painless as possible. The reality is that such an abrupt change in economic systems cannot come about without many people incurring costs, albeit temporary ones. By necessity, the elimination of controls on prices will cause some prices to rise. People purchasing higher-priced goods subsequently will be worse off, at least in the short run. When an economy with virtually zero unemployment converts to one in which unemployment is permitted to exist, those workers who become unemployed will be worse off.

It is therefore impossible for these nations to undergo a smooth and painless transition. China has a better chance of doing so because it appears that market capitalism, started in Guangdong province in 1978, will simply spread throughout the rest of the country. This will occur over a long period of time. In contrast, the economic systems in Eastern Europe and the former Soviet republics have to move more rapidly because of the total collapse of their former command economic systems. Consider the disruption in the Russian economy as an example of how painful a transition is. Industrial production in 1992 dropped to 75 percent of the preceding year's, poverty was up, and purchasing power was down. When it comes to changing the entire organization of an economy, there never has been and never will be any way to do the job without a lot of casualties.

CHANGES IN OTHER PARTS OF THE WORLD

The economic world is changing virtually everywhere. This overview will give you the flavor of some of these changes.

NORTH KOREA

This country has had a true centrally planned command system for over 40 years. It has been ruled by a virtual dictator, Kim Il Sung, who will pass the mantle to his son. Orthodox communism has brought this country to a level of poverty similar to that of the republics of the former Soviet Union. North Korea, having lost its markets in Eastern Europe when those Communist regimes fell, has not been able to replace them. Its per capita production of goods and services is about one-sixth that in South Korea. Industrial production differences between these two countries are even greater: With only twice the population, South Korea produces 60 times more cars and televisions and 10 times more textiles than its neighbor to the north.

There is a small but growing movement toward attracting foreign capital to North Korea. The government has developed a small northeastern free trade zone next to the Russian frontier. It has convinced the South Korean industrial group Daewoo to build several light industrial plants.

North Korea remains the most tightly controlled noncapitalist country in the world and may be the only one left after the probable fall of Castro in Cuba.

ISRAEL

Although it is thought of as a capitalist country, Israel is highly socialized. The central government directly controls about two-thirds of the country's gross domestic product and heavily regulates the rest. About 12 percent of the economy is devoted to defense, somewhat higher than the percentage so devoted in the United States at the height of the Cold War.

The Israeli government consistently runs in the red. One of the reasons it can do so is that the United States provides $4 billion a year in aid, or about 8 percent of Israel's total annual national economic activity. Consequently, even though some Israelis have argued for a diminished role of the state in the economy, there are few political forces that will cause this to happen. Some observers find it ironic that many former Soviets, so recently liberated from a heavily centralized economy, are moving to Israel, where they are encountering another one. There seems little chance that government domination of Israel's economy will diminish soon.

SWEDEN

▶ **Welfare state**
A society in which the government is responsible for providing "cradle to grave" social services for all citizens, including prenatal care, daycare, health care, schooling, and retirement.

Sweden has been labeled a **welfare state**—a blend of capitalism and socialism. It combines private ownership of the means of production and competitive allocation of resources with an egalitarian approach to the welfare of its citizens. The so-called Swedish model was highly successful in transforming what was an underdeveloped country in 1870 into a modern nation with one of the highest per capita incomes in the world a century later.

Currently about 60 percent of annual economic activity is accounted for by government expenditures. As recently as 1960 this figure was little more than 30 percent. Tax levels in Sweden at that time were about equal to those in the United States but have since risen to more than 20 percentage points higher. The Swedish government passed an employment security bill in the 1970s that almost guarantees lifelong employment. It also passed a law requiring labor union participation in company decision making. Full employment has existed for a number of years as the government took over many large industries and firms, such as steelworks. The government sector's share of employment was 20 percent in 1970 but today is close to 35 percent.

Changes in the Swedish model of combining capitalism with welfare socialism are now in the works. In the 1990s the government started to cut taxes and eliminate some public jobs. It also eased business regulation and approved foreign ownership of certain companies. It has ended the government monopoly in both taxis and airlines. According to the Swedish minister of education and science, Per Unckel, the Swedish government's plan for privatization is extensive. It is currently developing a plan to sell 30 government industries, utilities, and services to the private sector. It plans to end the government's monopoly in electric utilities, telecommunications, railroads, and postal services.

As with the transition from extreme command socialism to market capitalism in the former Soviet Union, there have been costs associated with the Swedish transition. Unemployment reached a postwar high in 1992, and some classes of workers are experiencing a reduction in their standard of living.

LATIN AMERICA

Many of the nations in Latin America—especially Mexico, Venezuela, Chile, Brazil, and Argentina—have experienced high rates of growth since the mid-1980s. Though virtually all Latin American countries have economic systems that operate under market capitalism, most have had large government sectors. Since 1985 many government enterprises have been privatized. Mexico is a good example. In 1989 it made a wholesale move to free markets. The government started to sell off its vast holdings of companies and at the same time reduced the size of the government bureaucracy. Private companies in Mexico are building toll roads and phone systems. Other countries in Latin America are trying to follow the Mexican model, but because of multiparty infighting, they are not having an easy time (Mexico has had a one-party system for many years). Nonetheless, Chile has privatized its airlines, phones, utilities, and pension funds. The Argentinean government has sold off state-run oil fields, waterworks, petrochemical plants, and even army housing.

CONVERGING ECONOMIC SYSTEMS AND THE POWER OF ECONOMICS

Many of the consequences of the changes in economic systems throughout the world can be analyzed using the economic analysis that you have already learned in this text. The supply and demand model will take you a long way in predicting what will happen when property is privatized, markets are freed, and the lure of profits becomes legal. Just remind yourself that the differences across countries are less related to cultures, religions, creeds, and ethnic characteristics and more related to different **incentive structures** and how they are changing. The model that you can use most successfully always asks the question, How will people react to a changed incentive structure?

> ▶ **Incentive structure**
> The motivational rewards and costs that individuals face in any given situation. Each economic system has its own incentive structure. The incentive structure is different under a system of private property than under a system of government-owned property, for example.

CONCEPTS IN BRIEF

- The Russian economy is moving toward privatization in restaurants, shops, and farmland.
- Abrupt transition from a command economy to a decentralized market economy has caused reductions in industrial production and in living standards in Russia.
- Other countries that are still centrally planned include North Korea and Cuba. Many somewhat socialized countries, such as Israel and Sweden, are privatizing state-owned assets.
- The way to analyze the consequences of changing economic systems is to look at what has happened to the incentive structures.

ECOCIDE, CENTRALLY PLANNED

Concepts Applied: Command socialism, theory of public choice, incentives, trade-offs

Smog, as seen in this town in the Czech Republic, is common throughout the former Soviet Union and Eastern Europe. Some contend that under central planning, the incentives were such that "ecocide" occurred.

Malnutrition has existed in Russia and Ukraine for several years. Many observers have argued that the newly independent states simply don't have the infrastructure—roads, trucks, railways—to deliver their food from the farms that can produce it. These observers are not wrong, but they are missing a singularly important point: There has been so much ecological damage in the former Soviet Union that much of it is an agricultural wasteland. Murray Feshbach and Alfred Friendly, Jr., authors of *Ecocide in the USSR,* estimate that 30 percent of all food in the new republics is so badly contaminated that it should not be eaten and that over 40 percent of baby food is contaminated by pesticides. This striking situation is the result of inordinate pesticide use. Even after DDT was banned in the Soviet Union (as in the United States), officials simply called it by another name and used it anyway. As many as 25 million acres of arable land are contaminated with it. In short, these researchers point out that much of the land has been treated so badly that it is reverting to desert. Desert is spreading by 100,000 acres a year just in southern Russia alone, where since 1954 the size of the desert has increased from 30,000 acres to 2 million acres.

THE REST OF THE ECOLOGICAL DAMAGE

There are three other ecological disasters that occurred in the Soviet Union under centralized planning.

1. **Deforestation.** Inefficient harvesting methods have created massive deforestation and topsoil erosion. In Siberia alone, 5 million acres of forests are disappearing each year. Noxious sulfur oxide from the Tyunmen oil fields in the northern wilderness of Siberia has ruined more than 1,500 square miles of timber, an area $1\frac{1}{2}$ times the size of Rhode Island.

2. **Water pollution.** Industrial waste and untreated sewage have turned thousands of lakes, rivers, and seas into toxic wastelands. Some 3,000 factories dump 10 billion cubic yards of contaminated waste into the Volga River every year. When other sewage is added, that single river alone receives 2.5 cubic miles of waste every year.

3. **Air pollution.** Every day, 70 million out of 190 million Russians living in 100 major cities breathe air that is polluted at more than five times the recommended maximum level.

CENTRAL PLANNING IN THEORY AND IN REALITY

As we mentioned at the beginning of this chapter, central planning was supposed to be able to take care of negative externalities in a way that decentralized market capitalism could not. In principle, the Soviet state apparatus could have taken account of the well-being of all citizens and prevented the ecocide that occurred. Why, then, did the centrally planned system end up creating more pollution than exists in most decentralized market economies? The answer lies in an examination of the incentives facing the individual managers of the various sources of pollution in centrally planned economies. These managers were rewarded in whatever way—sometimes higher pay, sometimes more fringe benefits, sometimes a *dacha* (vacation house) in the country—according to output. In the eyes of a central planner in Moscow, the output of the steel factory along the Volga River had nothing to do with sulfur dioxide in the air and effluents in the water, only the cold-rolled steel ready for shipment. In no centrally planned economy anywhere in the world was there an incentive for decision makers to protect the environment. Note that these decision makers were all acting rationally. They were not simply individuals who did not "care about the environment." Also, even those who might have wished to speak out did not have the luxury of a free press in which to do so.

CAN THE ECOCIDE BE REVERSED?   With enough resources, the ecocide in the former Soviet Union can be reversed. Has it started? Not really. This is because of the trade-off between a cleaner environment and less output, at least in the immediate future. Many industrial plants along the Volga River, for example, are beyond salvation in terms of turning them into less polluting industrial enterprises. They have to be shut down and replaced. But to do so would mean a loss of jobs and a loss of output to the economy. For the moment, jobs and output are more important than a cleaner environment. Consequently, we can expect the degradation of the former Soviet Union's environment to continue for some years to come. In any event, historically, pollution output has increased during the early stages of any country's development; only when that country has become relatively well off has pollution abated.

FOR CRITICAL ANALYSIS

1. Why would analysts of centrally planned economies believe that negative externalities would not have been a problem?
2. What can the richer countries in the West do to help clean up the environmental mess in the former Soviet Union?
3. Given what you now know about the decision-making process with respect to industrial production in the Soviet Union, should you be worried about how they engineered and constructed their nuclear power facilities?

CHAPTER SUMMARY

1. The price system answers the resource allocation and distribution questions relating to (a) what and how much will be produced, (b) how it will be produced, and (c) for whom it will be produced. The question of what to produce is answered by the value people place on a good—the highest price they are willing to pay for it. How goods are produced is determined by competition, which inevitably results in least-cost production techniques. Finally, goods and services are distributed to the individuals who are willing and able to pay for them. This answers the question about for whom goods are produced.

2. Pure capitalism can be defined by the three Ps: prices, profits, and private property.

3. The key attributes of socialism are as follows: The government owns the major productive resources. The rewards for producing are usually set by the state rather than the market. Individuals can enter only certain endeavors and cannot, for example, set up their own factories.

4. The People's Republic of China followed a Soviet-style command socialist system after China's civil war. Since 1958 there have been a series of reforms, all of which have attempted in one way or another to give more decision-making power to local levels of the economy.

5. A growing percentage of China's industrial output is accounted for by nonstate enterprises. It is estimated that by the year 2000 state enterprises will account for only 25 percent of industrial output. Part of China, particularly in the area near Hong Kong, is starting to follow the three Ps of market capitalism, but this trend is being resisted by the old guard.

6. There has been an even more rapid movement toward the price system in the republics of the former Soviet Union, especially in the largest, Russia. Privatization, though getting off to a slow start, is proceeding in farming, retailing, and in industrial production. The transition to a market system has led to increased unemployment and other problems in Russia.

7. Many other areas are tending toward market capitalism, and a growing percentage of state-run enterprises are being sold to the private sector. North Korea is resisting this trend but is nevertheless setting up free trade zønes next to the Russian border. Sweden has started to privatize, as have Italy and many countries in Latin America.

8. According to economic analysts, differences across countries relate less to culture, religion, and ethnic characteristics than to different incentive structures.

DISCUSSION OF PREVIEW POINTS

1. **Why does the scarcity problem force all societies to answer the questions *what, how,* and *for whom?***
   Scarcity exists for a society because people want more than their resources will allow them to have. Society must decide *what* to produce because of scarcity. But, if wants are severely restricted and resources are relatively superabundant, the question of *what* to produce is trivial—society simply produces *everything* that everyone wants. Superabundant resources relative to restricted wants also make the question of *how* to produce trivial. If scarcity doesn't exist, superabundant resources can be combined in *any* manner; waste and efficiency have no meaning without scarcity. Similarly, *for whom* is meaningless without scarcity; *all* people can consume *all* they want.

2. **How can economies be classified?**
   All societies must answer the three fundamental economic problems: what, how, and for whom? One way to classify economies is according to the manner in which they answer these questions. In particular, we can classify them according to the degree to which *individuals* are allowed to make these decisions. Under pure command socialism, practically all economic decisions are made by a central authority; under pure capitalism, practically all economic decisions are made by private individuals pursuing their own economic self-interest.

3. **What are the characteristics of a command socialist economy?**
   A main characteristic of a command socialist economy is government control over the (large-scale) means of production; as a practical matter, private ownership of small-scale enterprises is usually permitted. Another major characteristic of command socialist economies is central planning; most resources are allocated according to a centrally directed economic plan. Finally, command socialist economies are usually characterized (at least in theory) by wide-scale redistribution-of-income programs. Redistribution is carried on by a system of taxing high-income earners and transferring income to low-income earners.

4. **What are some problems that command socialist economies face?**
   Economic planning was hailed as the wave of the future. Rational planning was supposed to be economically superior to the anarchy of the marketplace; under planning, goods are produced for "use," not for profit. However, planning, to date, has not been conspicuously successful; living standards in planned economies have been lower than in other economies, and economic growth rates have been generally lower. A major problem of planning is that enormous administrative problems exist; in the former Soviet Union, hundreds of millions of planning decisions had to be made to keep over 200,000 industrial enterprises running on schedule.

PROBLEMS
(Answers to odd-numbered problems appear at the back of the book.)

6-1. Suppose that you are an economic planner and you have been told by your country's political leaders that they want to increase automobile production by 10 percent over last year. What other industries will be affected by this decision?

6-2. Proponents of centralized planning argue that it is superior to capitalism as a method of organizing production and promoting economic growth. Does the actual performance of countries that have tried centralized planning support this view?

6-3. A business has found that its most profitable output occurs when it produces $172 worth of output of a particular product. It can choose from three possible techniques, A, B, and C, that will produce the desired level of output. In the table on the next page we see the amount of inputs these techniques use along with each input price.
   a. Which technique will the firm choose, and why?
   b. What would the firm's maximum profit be?
   c. If the price of labor increases to $4 per unit, which technique will be chosen, and why? What will happen to profits?

PRICE OF INPUT (PER UNIT)	INPUT	PRODUCTION TECHNIQUES		
		A (UNITS)	B (UNITS)	C (UNITS)
$10	Land	7	4	1
$ 2	Labor	6	7	18
$15	Capital	2	6	3
$ 8	Entrepreneurship	1	3	2

6-4. Answer the questions on the basis of the accompanying graph.

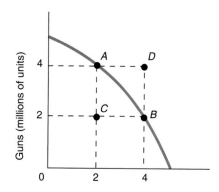

Butter (millions of barrels)

a. A switch to a decentralized, more market-oriented economy might do what to the production possibilities curve, and why?
b. What point on the graph represents an economy with unemployment?

6-5. The table gives the production costs for 100 units of product X.

INPUT	INPUT UNIT PRICE	TECHNIQUE		
		A	B	C
Labor	$10	6	5	4
Capital	$ 8	5	6	7

a. In a market system, which techniques will be used to produce 100 units of product X?
b. If the market price of a unit of X is $1, which technique will lead to the greatest profit?
c. The output of X is still $1, but the price of labor and capital change so that labor is $8 and capital is $10. Which production technique will be used?
d. Using the information in (c) above, what is the potential profit of producing 100 units of X?

6-6. The table gives the production costs for one unit of product Y.

INPUT	INPUT UNIT PRICE	TECHNIQUE		
		A	B	C
Labor	$10	1	3	2
Capital	$ 5	2	2	4
Land	$ 4	3	1	1

a. If the market price of a unit of product Y is $50, which technique generates the greatest potential profit?
b. If input unit prices change so that labor is $10, capital is $10, and land is $10, which technique will be chosen?
c. Assuming that the unit cost of each input is $10 and the price of a unit of Y is $50, which technique generates the greatest profit?

COMPUTER-ASSISTED INSTRUCTION
(Complete problem and answer on disk.)

The role of prices in communicating information and allocating goods and services are illustrated by examining the ongoing transformation of the economies of Russia and China.

INTRODUCTION TO MACROECONOMICS

part

2

THE MACROECONOMY: UNEMPLOYMENT, INFLATION, AND PRODUCTIVITY

The more the average worker is able to produce in output each year, the more each worker on average gets paid. Ultimately, our nation's average standard of living depends on how productive the average worker is in America—how much output he or she can produce for each hour worked. Today who in fact are the most productive workers in the world, and if they aren't Americans, should we be worried? The answer to these questions forms part of a larger study of the macroeconomy, which includes the topics of unemployment and inflation as well as productivity.

After reading this chapter, you should be able to answer the following questions:

1. Why is frictional unemployment not necessarily harmful?

2. Does it matter whether inflation is anticipated or not?

3. Who is hurt by inflation?

4. How do we measure productivity?

INTRODUCTION

In Chapter 1 we made the distinction between microeconomics and macroeconomics. Macroeconomics is the study of the performance and structure of the national economy. Macroeconomics also encompasses the study of the policies that governments use to try to change national economic performance. In this chapter you will read about three major macroeconomic policy (and problem) areas: (1) the problem of people out of work (unemployment), (2) the problem of rising prices (inflation), and (3) the problem of slow growth in the amount that the average worker can produce (productivity). Of course, macroeconomics encompasses other subject areas, such as the growing federal budget deficit, our economic relations with other nations, and the causes of fluctuations between periods of prosperity and difficult times. In the chapters that follow, you will be exposed to these subjects and many more. Right now let's examine one of the problems that faces all countries—unemployment.

UNEMPLOYMENT

Unemployment creates a cost to the entire economy in terms of loss of output. One researcher estimated that at the beginning of the 1990s when unemployment was about 7 percent and factories were running at 80 percent of their capacity, the amount of output that the economy lost due to idle resources was almost 4 percent of the total production throughout the United States. (In other words, we were somewhere inside the production possibilities curve that we talked about in Chapter 2.) That was the equivalent of almost $250 billion of schools, houses, restaurant meals, cars, and movies that *could have been* produced. It is no wonder the policymakers closely watch the unemployment figures published by the Department of Labor's Bureau of Labor Statistics (BLS).

On a more personal level, the state of being unemployed often results in hardship and failed opportunities as well as a lack of self-respect. Psychological researchers believe that being fired creates at least as much stress as the death of a close friend. The numbers that we present about unemployment can never fully convey its true cost to this or any other nation.

▶ **Unemployment**
The total number of adults (aged 16 years or older) who are willing and able to work and who are actively looking for work but have not found a job.

HISTORICAL UNEMPLOYMENT RATES

The unemployment rate, defined as a proportion of the measured **labor force** that is unemployed, reached a low of 1.2 percent of the labor force at the end of World War II after having exceeded 25 percent during the Great Depression in the 1930s. The rate of unemployment is measured by dividing the total number of unemployed persons by the total number of persons in the civilian labor force. You can see in Figure 7-1 what happened to unemployment in the United States over the past century. The highest level ever was reached in the Great Depression, but unemployment was also very high during the Panic of 1893.

▶ **Labor force**
Individuals aged 16 years or older who either have jobs or are looking and available for jobs; the number of employed plus the number of unemployed.

🌐 INTERNATIONAL EXAMPLE: **Unemployment in Other Countries**

Figure 7-2 shows U.S. unemployment compared to that in other industrialized nations. U.S. unemployment rates have typically been lower than those in Europe. Japan has even lower rates. We should be careful in making comparisons, however, because each country's government has its own definition of who is classified as unemployed and its own techniques to measure unemployment rates. Each country also provides for its unemployed citizens in different ways. Some foreign countries provide more extensive unemployment benefits and for longer periods of time than the United States. These benefits serve as incentives to remain out of work. Unemployed adults in France are even given a special

FIGURE 7-1

A century of unemployment.
Unemployment reached lows during World Wars I and II of less than 2 percent and highs during the Great Depression of more than 25 percent.

Source: U.S. Department of Labor, Bureau of Labor Statistics.

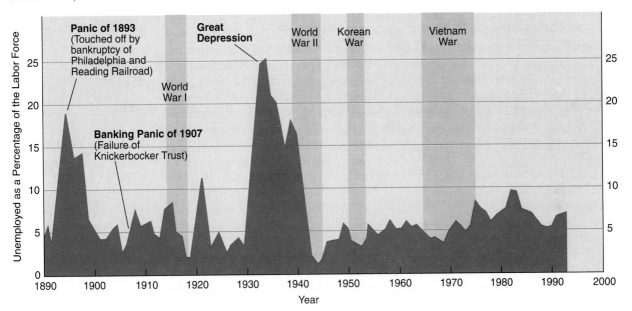

FIGURE 7-2
Recent U.S. unemployment compared to that of other industrialized nations.

When we compare the unemployment rate in the United States to that of other industrialized nations since 1980, we find that although it is relatively high historically, it is lower than throughout Europe. Only Japan has a consistently lower rate of unemployment than the United States.

Source: U.S. Department of Labor, Bureau of Labor Statistics; Organization for Economic Cooperation and Development.

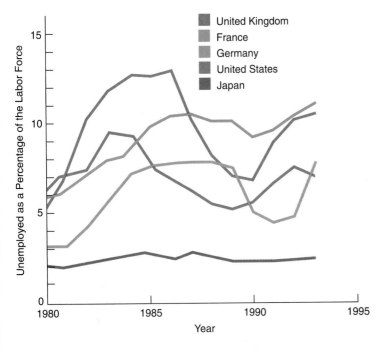

lower rate at the movies! Therefore, the differences in unemployment rates can be partly due to government policies with respect to the unemployed.

For Critical Analysis: *Explain in what way better and longer unemployment benefits can affect the unemployment rate in other nations.* ●

ESTIMATING UNEMPLOYMENT AND ITS RATE

Consider Table 7-1 from a recent issue of the monthly BLS publication *Employment and Earnings.* We start with the total population in the United States and subtract from that all inmates of institutions such as jails, mental hospitals, and nursing homes and persons under 16 years of age. We thus arrive at the total noninstitutionalized adult population, estimated at 194.3 million. From that number we subtract people not in the labor force, which includes those in the noninstitutionalized population who are engaged in own-home housework, are in school, or are unable to work because of mental or physical illness, and those who are voluntarily idle, retired, too old to work, and so on. The estimate of those not in the labor force was 65.5 million people. We have now derived the total labor force of 128.8 million, from which we subtract 1.5 million resident armed services personnel, yielding an estimated total civilian labor force of 127.3 million. From the total civilian labor force we subtract the employed—all people who (during the week in which the survey was taken) did any work at all as paid employees in their own business, profession, or on their own farm or who worked 15 hours or more as unpaid employees in a business operated by a member of the family. The employed category also includes individuals who could not work because of bad weather, illness, vacation, or strikes or were taking time off to look for another job.

As the table indicates, 127.3 million people were estimated to be in the employed category in that month. Subtracting the employed from the total civilian labor force gives the unemployed, estimated at 8.9 million people. The unemployed category includes everybody who didn't work during the survey week but who made a bona fide effort to find a job within the previous four weeks. The unemployed also include people who were not working but were waiting to be called back to a job from which they had been laid off and those who were waiting to report to a job within 30 days.

On the basis of these figures, we can now calculate the unemployment rate, which is defined as the number of unemployed divided by the total civilian labor force. The civilian unemployment rate was therefore $8.9 \div 127.3 = 6.99$ percent.

255.5 million − 61.2 million = 194.3 million	Noninstitutionalized adults
− 65.5 million	Not in labor force
= 128.8 million	Total labor force
− 1.5 million	Resident armed services
= 127.3 million	Total civilian labor force
− 118.4 million	Employed
= 8.9 million	Unemployed

TABLE 7-1
Determining unemployment.

Unemployment Criteria.   According to the Bureau of Labor Statistics, an individual is considered unemployed in any of four circumstances:

1. If the person is a **job loser** whose employment was involuntarily terminated or who was laid off (varies between 40 and 60 percent of the unemployed)
2. If the person is a **reentrant,** having worked a full-time job before but having been out of the labor force (varies from 20 to 30 percent of the unemployed)

▶ **Job loser**
An individual in the labor force who was employed and whose employment was involuntarily terminated or who was laid off.

▶ **Reentrant**
An individual who used to work full time but left the labor force and has now reentered it looking for a job.

▶ **Job leaver**
An individual in the labor force who voluntarily quits.

▶ **New entrant**
An individual who has never held a full-time job lasting two weeks or longer but is now in the labor force.

3. If the person is a **job leaver** who voluntarily ended employment (varies between less than 10 to around 15 percent of the unemployed)
4. If the person is a **new entrant** who has never worked a full-time job for two weeks or longer (varies from 10 to 13 percent of the unemployed)

Job losers typically constitute the largest category of the unemployed. Reentrants are the next most significant category. Job leavers and new entrants account for the rest. The point to remember is that usually only about half of unemployed individuals have actually been dismissed.

⭐ EXAMPLE: Unemployment and the Underground Economy

When the government sets out to measure the size of the labor force or the number of unemployed, its statisticians obviously cannot interview every single worker or potential worker. Survey data must be used. Although the survey technique is extensive—consisting of almost 60,000 households in almost 2,000 counties and cities in all 50 states and the District of Columbia—it is imperfect. One of the main reasons, argue some economists, is because of the **underground economy.** The underground economy consists of individuals who work for cash payments without paying any taxes. It also consists of individuals who engage in illegal activities such as prostitution, gambling, and drug trafficking.

▶ **Underground economy**
The part of the economy that does not pay taxes and so is not directly measured by government statisticians. Also called the *subterranean* or *unreported economy.*

Some who are officially unemployed and are receiving unemployment benefits do nonetheless work "off the books." Although they are counted as unemployed by the BLS, they really are employed. The same analysis holds for anyone who works and does not report income earned. The question, of course, is, How big is the underground economy? If it is small, the official unemployment statistics may still be adequate to give a sense of the state of the national economy. Various researchers have come up with different estimates of the size of the underground economy. Professor Peter Guttman believes that it is at least 10 percent of the size of the national economy. Other researchers have come up with estimates ranging from 5 to 15 percent. In dollars and cents that may mean that the underground economy represents between $300 billion and $900 billion a year. How many members of the true labor force work in this economy and their effect on the true unemployment rate is anyone's guess.

For Critical Analysis: What changes in national legislation would reduce the size of the underground economy? ●

Duration of Unemployment.   If you are out of a job for a week, your situation is much less serious than if you are out of a job for 14 weeks. An increase in the duration of unemployment can increase the unemployment rate because workers stay unemployed longer, thereby creating a greater number of them at any given time. The most recent information on duration of unemployment paints the following picture: 36.5 percent of those who become unemployed find a new job within one month, 28.1 percent find a job within two months, and only 21.5 percent are still unemployed after six months. The average duration of unemployment for all unemployed has been 3.8 months over the past decade.

When overall business activity goes into a downturn, the duration of unemployment tends to rise, thereby causing much of the increase in the estimated unemployment rate. In a sense, then, it is the increase in the duration of unemployment during a downturn in national economic activity that generates the bad news that concerns policymakers in Washington, D.C. Furthermore, the 21.5 percent who stay unemployed longer than six months are the ones who create the pressure on Congress to "do something." What Congress does typically is extend and supplement unemployment benefits.

The Discouraged-Worker Phenomenon.   Critics of the published unemployment rate calculated by the federal government believe that there exist numerous **discouraged workers** and "hidden unemployed." Though there is no exact definition or way to measure discouraged workers, the Department of Labor defines them as people who have dropped out of the labor force and are no longer looking for a job because they believe that the job market has little to offer them. To what extent do we want to include in the measured labor force individuals who voluntarily choose not to look for work or those who take but two minutes a day to scan the want ads and then decide that there are no jobs?

Some economists argue that people who work part time but are willing to work full time should be classified as "semihidden" unemployed. Estimates range as high as 6 million workers at any one time. To offset this factor, though, there is *overemployment.* An individual working 50 or 60 hours a week is still counted as only one full-time worker.

Labor Force Participation.   The way in which we define unemployment and members of the labor force will affect what is known as the **labor force participation rate.** It is defined as the proportion of working-age individuals who are employed or seeking employment. If there are discouraged, or hidden, unemployed within any particular group, the labor force participation rate for that particular group will drop.

▶ **Discouraged workers**
Individuals who have stopped looking for a job because they are convinced that they will not find a suitable one. Typically, they become convinced after unsuccessfully searching for a job.

▶ **Labor force participation rate**
The percentage of noninstitutionalized working-age individuals who are employed or seeking employment.

FIGURE 7-3
Labor force participation rates by sex.
The combined labor force participation rate has increased slightly in recent years. However, over the same period, the male participation rate has fallen, and the female rate has risen.
Source: U.S. Department of Labor, Bureau of Labor Statistics.

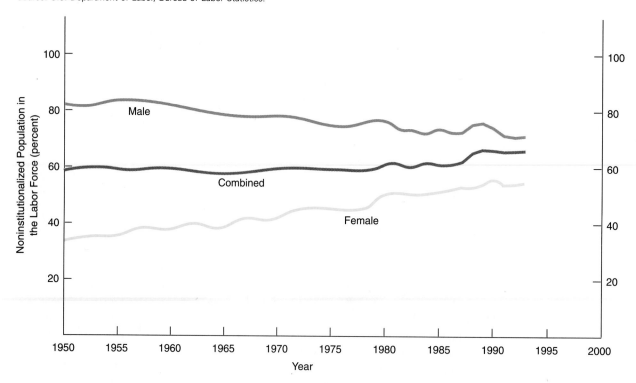

Figure 7-3 on the previous page shows the labor force participation rate by sex. While male participation rates have been falling steadily since the end of World War II, until recently female labor force participation rates have been rising. Since the mid-1960s, there has been a slight trend upward in the combined labor force participation rate, leading to the occasional phenomenon of concurrent increases in both unemployment *and* employment.

RECENT TRENDS IN EMPLOYMENT AND LABOR FORCE PARTICIPATION

Even though the population in America continues to grow, much of the growth in employment in recent years has been in health and social services. Growth in the labor force has almost stopped. If the labor force had continued to grow at the same rate that it had from 1960 to 1990, the recession of 1990–1991 would have shown higher unemployment.

Several factors have contributed to this "no growth" labor force. First, the labor force participation rate by youths has been dropping. Second, women's labor force participation rate has leveled off for the first time since World War II. Finally, more workers are taking early retirement. There has also been a major restructuring of the labor force. During the 1990–1991 recession, there was essentially no growth in employment after the trough of the recession, which was in July 1990. This was the first recession during which there was massive elimination of white-collar jobs rather than the usual blue-collar (factory worker) layoffs.

CONCEPTS IN BRIEF

- Unemployment is usually measured as the total number of adults who are willing and able to work and are actively looking for a job but have not found one.
- Historically, unemployment rates have been as low as 1.2 percent during World War II and as high as 25 percent during the Great Depression.
- The Bureau of Labor Statistics includes in its measure of the unemployed people who are job losers, reentrants, job leavers, and new entrants to the labor force.
- The duration of unemployment affects the unemployment rate. The number of unemployed workers can remain the same, but if the duration of unemployment increases, the measured unemployment rate will go up.
- Critics of the published unemployment figures contend that they underestimate unemployment because of discouraged workers, workers who are working part time who would like to work full time, and hidden unemployment.
- Labor force participation rates overall have remained relatively stable, but male participation has fallen while female participation has increased.

THE MAJOR TYPES OF UNEMPLOYMENT

Unemployment has been categorized into four basic types: frictional, cyclical, seasonal, and structural.

Frictional Unemployment.   Of the almost 130 million Americans in the labor force, more than 12 million will have either changed jobs or taken new jobs during the year; about 1 in 20 workers will have quit, been laid off (told that they will be rehired later), or been permanently fired every single month; another 6 percent will have gone to new jobs or returned to old ones. In the process, more than 20 million persons will have reported themselves unemployed at one time or another. What we call **frictional unemployment** is the continuous flow of individuals from job to job and in and out of employment. There will always be some frictional unemployment as resources are redirected in the market because transaction costs are never zero. To eliminate frictional unemployment, we would have to prevent workers from leaving their present jobs until they had already lined up other jobs at which they would start working immediately and we would have to guarantee first-time job seekers a job *before* they started looking.

Cyclical Unemployment.   **Cyclical unemployment** is related to business fluctuations. It is defined as unemployment associated with changes in business conditions—primarily recessions and depressions. The way to lessen cyclical unemployment would be to reduce the intensity, duration, and frequency of ups and downs of business activity. Economic policymakers attempt, through their policies, to reduce cyclical unemployment by keeping business activity on an even keel.

Seasonal Unemployment.   **Seasonal unemployment** comes and goes with seasons of the year in which the demand for particular jobs rises and falls. In northern states, construction workers can often work only during the warmer months; they are seasonally unemployed during the winter. Summer resort workers can usually get jobs in resorts only during the summer season. They, too, become seasonally unemployed during the winter; the opposite is true for ski resort workers.

Structural Unemployment.   Structural changes in our economy cause some workers to become unemployed permanently or for very long periods of time because they cannot find jobs that use their particular skills. They simply can't find *any* job that they can do. Such **structural unemployment** has often been associated with **technological unemployment**—unemployment resulting from the increased use of laborsaving machines.

Unlike cyclical unemployment, structural unemployment is not caused by general business fluctuations, although business fluctuations may affect it. And unlike frictional unemployment, structural unemployment is not related to the movement of workers from low-paying to high-paying jobs. Structural unemployment results when the consuming public no longer wants to buy an individual's services in that location.

FULL EMPLOYMENT

Does full employment mean that everybody has a job? Certainly not, for not everyone is looking for a job—full-time students and full-time homemakers, for example, are not. Is it possible for everyone to be looking for a job to always find one? No, because transaction costs in the labor market are not zero. Transaction costs include any activity whose goal is to enter into, carry out, or terminate contracts. In the labor market, these costs involve time spent looking for a job, being interviewed, negotiating the pay, and so on.

We will always have some frictional unemployment as individuals move in and out of the labor force, seek higher-paying jobs, and move to different parts of the country. **Full employment** is therefore a vague concept implying some sort of balance or equilibrium

▶ **Frictional unemployment**
Unemployment associated with costly job market information. Because workers do not know about all job vacancies that may be suitable, they must search for appropriate job offers. This takes time, and so they remain temporarily ("frictionally") unemployed.

▶ **Cyclical unemployment**
Unemployment resulting from business recessions that occur when aggregate (total) demand is insufficient to create full employment.

▶ **Seasonal unemployment**
Unemployment resulting from the seasonal pattern of work in specific industries, usually due to seasonal fluctuations in demand or to changing weather conditions, rendering certain work difficult, if not impossible, as in the agriculture, construction, and tourist industries.

▶ **Structural unemployment**
Unemployment resulting from fundamental changes in the structure of the economy. Structural unemployment occurs, for example, when the demand for a product falls drastically so that workers specializing in the production of that product find themselves out of work.

▶ **Technological unemployment**
Unemployment caused by technological changes that reduce labor demands for specific tasks.

▶ **Full employment**
As presented by the Council of Economic Advisers, an arbitrary level of unemployment that corresponds to "normal" friction in the labor market. In 1986, the council declared that 6.5 percent unemployment was full employment.

in an ever-shifting labor market. Of course, this general notion of full employment must somehow be put into numbers so that economists and others can determine whether the economy has reached the full employment point. In 1986, the President's Council of Economic Advisers, which generates the *Economic Report of the President* each year (published in February), estimated that full employment in 1986 was at 6.5 percent unemployed. Using this definition, the economy was running at more than full employment from 1987 through the first few months of 1991! In the most recent *Economic Report of the President,* there is no use of the term *full employment* or any explanation of how it is measured.

CONCEPTS IN BRIEF

- There are many types of unemployment; the four basic ones are frictional, cyclical, seasonal, and structural. Total unemployment is the sum of these.
- Frictional unemployment occurs because of transaction costs in the labor market. For example, workers do not have all the information necessary about vacancies, nor do employers know about all of the qualified workers to fill those vacancies.
- Structural unemployment occurs when the demand for a commodity permanently decreases, so that workers find that the jobs that they are used to doing are no longer available.
- The level of frictional unemployment is used in part to determine our (somewhat arbitrary) definition of full employment.

INFLATION

▶ Inflation
The situation in which the average of all prices of goods and services in an economy is rising.

▶ Deflation
The situation in which the average of all prices of goods and services in an economy is falling.

During the middle of World War II, you could buy bread for 8 to 10 cents a loaf and have milk delivered fresh to your door for about 25 cents a half gallon. The average price of a new car was less than $700, and the average house cost less than $3,000. Today bread, milk, cars, and houses all cost more—a lot more. Prices in the mid-1990s are roughly 10 times what they were in 1940. Clearly, this country has experienced quite a bit of **inflation** since then. We define inflation as an upward movement in the average level of prices. The opposite of inflation is **deflation,** defined as a downward movement in the average level of prices. Notice that these definitions depend on the *average* level of prices. That means that even during a period of inflation, some prices can still be falling if enough other prices are rising at a fast enough rate. The price of computers and computer-related equipment has dropped dramatically since the 1960s even though there has been general inflation.

To discuss what has happened to inflation in this and other countries, we have to know how to measure it.

INFLATION AND THE PURCHASING POWER OF MONEY

▶ Purchasing power
The value of your money income in buying goods and services. If your money income stays the same but the price of one good that you are buying goes up, your effective purchasing power falls.

A rose may be a rose may be a rose, but a dollar is not always a dollar. The value of a dollar does not stay constant when there is inflation. The value of money is usually talked about in terms of the **purchasing power** of money. A dollar's purchasing power is the real goods and services that it can buy. Consequently, another way of defining inflation is as a decline in the purchasing power of money. The faster the rate of inflation, the greater the drop in the purchasing power of money.

🌐 INTERNATIONAL EXAMPLE: Repressed Inflation in Germany and Japan

During World War II, virtually every major country experienced inflation. Most governments responded by freezing prices at low levels. You read about the effects of price ceilings in Chapter 4. Effectively enforced price ceilings result in shortages (excess quantities demanded) at the artificially low prices. In both Germany and Japan, city dwellers were consequently unable to find enough food to feed their families in the 1940s. The phenomenon of city dwellers trekking to the countryside to strike black-market deals with farmers became common. They would pay, in one way or another, higher than the price-controlled price for food. Jerome B. Cohen has estimated that almost a million persons trekked from Tokyo to the countryside to buy food on any given weekend toward the end of World War II. Although no such data are available for Germany, we do have circumstantial evidence that the phenomenon was just as impressive: When price controls were abolished in 1948, railroad passenger traffic in and out of German cities immediately dropped by 60 percent.

For Critical Analysis: What would be a more accurate way to measure the true cost of goods in Germany and Japan during World War II? (Hint: Think about opportunity cost.) ●

MEASURING THE RATE OF INFLATION

How do we come up with a measure of the rate of inflation? This is indeed a thorny problem for government statisticians. It is easy to determine how much the price of an individual commodity has risen: If last year a light bulb cost 50 cents and this year it costs 75 cents, there has been a 50 percent rise in the price of that light bulb over a one-year period. We can express the change in the individual light bulb price in one of several ways: The price has gone up 25 cents; the price is one and a half (1.5) times as high; the price has risen by 50 percent. An *index number* of this price rise is simply the second way (1.5) multiplied by 100, meaning that the index number would be 150. We multiply by 100 to eliminate decimals because it is easier to think in terms of percentage changes using integers. This is the standard convention adopted for convenience in dealing with index numbers or price levels.

Computing a Price Index.

The measurement problem becomes more complicated when it involves a large number of goods, some of whose prices have risen faster than others and some that have even fallen. What we have to do is pick a representative bundle, a so-called market basket, of goods and compare the cost of that market basket of goods over time. When we do this, we obtain a **price index,** which is defined as the cost of a market basket of goods today, expressed as a percentage of the cost of that identical market basket of goods in some starting year, known as the **base year.**

$$\text{Price index} = \frac{\text{cost today of market basket}}{\text{cost of market basket in base year}} \times 100$$

▶ **Price index**
The cost of today's market basket of goods expressed as a percentage of the cost of the same market basket during a base year.

▶ **Base year**
The year that is chosen as the point of reference for comparison of prices in other years.

In the base year the price index will always be 100, because the year in the numerator and in the denominator of the above fraction is the same; therefore, the fraction equals 1, and when we multiply it by 100, we get 100. A simple numerical example is given in Table 7-2. In the table there are only two goods in the market basket—corn and microcomputers. The *quantities* in the basket remain the same between the base year, 1986, and the current year, 1995; only the *prices* change. Such a *fixed-quantity* price index is the easiest to compute because the statistician need only look at prices of goods and services sold every year rather than actually observing how much of these goods and services consumers actually purchase each year.

TABLE 7-2 Calculating a price index for a two-good market basket.
In this simplified example, there are only two goods—corn and micro-computers. The quantities and base-year prices are given in columns 2 and 3. The cost of the 1986 market basket, calculated in column 4, comes to $1,400. The 1995 prices are given in column 5. The cost of the market basket in 1995, calculated in column 6, is $1,700. The price index for 1995 compared with 1986 is 121.43.

(1) COMMODITY	(2) MARKET BASKET QUANTITY	(3) 1986 PRICE PER UNIT	(4) COST OF MARKET BASKET IN 1986	(5) 1995 PRICE PER UNIT	(6) COST OF MARKET BASKET AT 1995 PRICES
Corn	100 bushels	$4	$400	$8	$800
Microcomputers	2	$500	$1,000	$450	$900
Totals			$1,400		$1,700

$$\text{Price index} = \frac{\text{cost of market basket in 1995}}{\text{cost of market basket in base year 1986}} \times 100 = \frac{\$1,700}{\$1,400} \times 100 = 121.43$$

▶ **Consumer Price Index (CPI)**
A statistical measure of a weighted average of prices of a specified set of goods and services purchased by wage earners in urban areas.

▶ **Producer Price Index (PPI)**
A statistical measure of a weighted average of prices of commodities that firms purchase from other firms.

▶ **GDP deflator**
A price index measuring the changes in prices of *all* goods and services produced by the economy.

Real-World Price Indexes.   Government statisticians calculate a number of price indexes. The most often quoted are the **Consumer Price Index (CPI),** the **Producer Price Index (PPI),** and the **GDP deflator.** The changes in the CPI attempt to measure changes in the level of prices with respect to goods and services purchased by wage earners. The CPI measures changes in the prices only of goods and services that families purchase for consumption, which account for about 65 percent of total output. The remaining 35 percent goes to business investment, government services, and the goods and services that we buy from and sell to foreigners. Changes in the PPI attempt to show what has happened to the price level for commodities that firms purchase from other firms. Finally, changes in the GDP deflator attempt to show changes in the level of prices of all goods and services produced in the economy. The most general indicator of inflation is the GDP deflator because it measures the changes in the prices of everything produced by the economy.

The CPI.   The Bureau of Labor Statistics (BLS) has the task of identifying a market basket of goods and services of the typical consumer. It did a survey in 1982–1984 and came up with its estimates. For example, out of every consumer dollar spent, almost 17 cents was spent on food and almost 4 cents on transportation. Entertainment got a little more than 10 cents and clothing 6 cents. The largest item was housing, taking about 16 cents of every consumer dollar.

⭐ **EXAMPLE: How Reliable Is the CPI?**

The CPI is a fixed-quantity price index, meaning that each month the BLS samples only prices rather than relative quantities purchased by consumers. Data are collected for about 95,000 items. The problem in using such a survey technique to measure changes in the price level starts with basic economics—the demand curve. When goods and services go up in relative price, consumers substitute in favor of other, relatively less expensive items. When relative prices go down, the opposite occurs. An important way that consumers deal with inflation is by buying less of products that become "too expensive." If McIntosh apples go up in price, some consumers will switch to Golden Delicious.

There is another problem with simply getting survey data on prices: The BLS obtains only *list* prices. When times are tough, in periods of recession, more consumers will haggle for lower prices or better deals, such as a free warranty, free installation, or a later payment. Finally, the BLS is unable to take account of *quality* changes as they occur. A VCR one year may cost $250 and the next year cost the same. But what if in the second year it is sold with a universal remote control unit that can also operate other electronic equipment? Clearly the price per constant quality unit of that VCR has fallen.

FIGURE 7-4

Inflationary periods in U.S. history.
Since the Civil War there have been numerous periods of inflation in the United States. Here we show them as reflected by changes in the Consumer Price Index. Since World War II the periods of inflation have not been followed by periods of deflation. That is to say, since World War II, even during peacetime, the price index has continued to rise. The dark gray areas represent wartime.

Source: U.S. Department of Labor, Bureau of Labor Statistics.

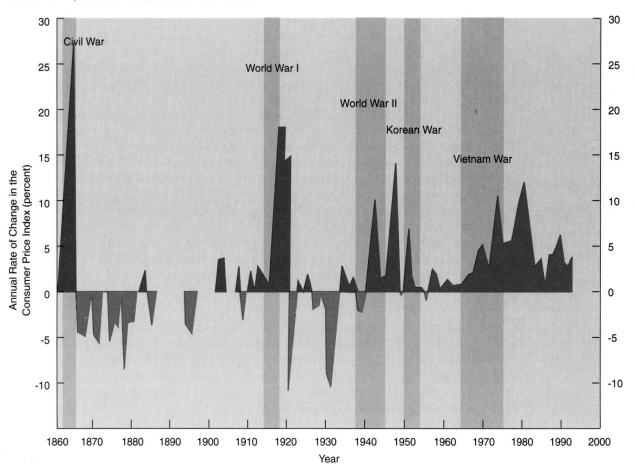

For Critical Analysis: Would there be problems similar to the ones discussed in this example during periods of deflation? Why or why not? ●

The PPI. Actually there are a number of Producer Price Indexes, including one for food materials, another for intermediate goods (goods used in the production of other goods), and one for finished goods. Most of the producer prices included are in mining, manufacturing, and agriculture. The PPIs can be considered general-purpose indexes for non-retail markets.

Although in the long run the various PPIs and the CPI generally show the same rate of inflation, such is not the case in the short run. Most often the PPIs increase before the CPI because it takes time for producer price increases to show up in the prices that consumers pay for final products. Often changes in the PPIs are watched closely as a hint that inflation is going to increase or decrease.

The GDP Deflator.   The broadest price index reported in the United States is the GDP deflator, where GDP stands for gross domestic product, or total national output. Unlike the CPI and the PPIs, the GDP deflator is not based on a fixed market basket of goods and services. The basket is allowed to change with people's consumption and investment patterns. In this sense, the changes in the GDP deflator reflect both price changes and the public's market responses to those price changes. Why? Because new expenditure patterns are allowed to show up in the GDP deflator as people respond to changing prices.

Historical Changes in the CPI.   The Consumer Price Index has shown a fairly

dramatic trend upward since about World War II. Figure 7-4 on the previous page shows the annual rate of change in the Consumer Price Index since 1860. Prior to World War II there were numerous periods of deflation along with periods of inflation. Persistent year-in and year-out inflation seems to be a post–World War II phenomenon, at least in this country. As far back as before the American Revolution, prices used to rise during war periods but then would fall back to more normal levels afterward. This occurred after the Revolutionary War, the War of 1812, the Civil War, and World War I. Consequently, the overall price level in 1940 wasn't much different from 150 years earlier.

⊕ INTERNATIONAL EXAMPLE: Inflation Rates, Hyperinflation, and Foreign Exchange

Inflation rates vary dramatically across countries. Table 7-3 shows some sample inflation rates for different countries. Notice Nicaragua in 1988. Its inflation rate was 10,205 percent per year! That means that a television set costing 100 pesos at the beginning of the year cost almost 10,350 pesos at the end. Newspapers double in price overnight. This phenomenon is what we call **hyperinflation,** an extreme form of inflation when average prices rise very rapidly.

▶ **Hyperinflation**
Extremely rapid rise of the average of all prices in an economy.

▶ **Foreign exchange rate**
The rate of exchange between one country's currency and another country's currency. When the foreign exchange rate for the dollar falls, a dollar purchases less of other currencies.

When countries have distinctly different rates of inflation, the rate of exchange between currencies will fluctuate accordingly. This is called the **foreign exchange rate,** defined as the rate at which one currency exchanges for another currency. A country that experiences a relatively rapid rate of inflation compared to others will see the value of its domestic currency fall with respect to foreign currencies. A good example is Israel, whose price-level increase for 1955-1993 was about 8 times greater than that in the United States. Consequently, in 1955 a dollar bought about a third of a shekel, but in 1993 a dollar could buy 2.69 shekels. The value of Israel's currency with respect to the dollar dropped.

For Critical Analysis: The rate of inflation in the United States has been consistently higher than the rate of inflation in Japan and Germany. What do you think would have happened to the foreign exchange rate between the dollar and the currencies of Japan and Germany, and why? ●

TABLE 7-3 Rates of inflation in other countries.
These are all annual percentage rates of change in the consumer price indexes.

NATION	1988	1989	1990	1991
Yugoslavia	194.1	1239.9	583.1	117.4
Argentina	343.0	4923.0	2314.0	171.7
Brazil	682.3	1287.0	2937.8	440.8
Peru	667.0	3398.7	7481.7	409.5
Israel	28.7	22.3	7.6	17.1
Nicaragua	10,205	—	—	—

> **CONCEPTS IN BRIEF**
> ● Once we pick a market basket of goods, we can construct a price index that compares the cost of that market basket today with the cost of the same market basket in a base year.
> ● The Consumer Price Index (CPI) is the most often used price index in the United States. The Producer Price Index (PPI) is the second most mentioned.
> ● The GDP deflator measures what is happening to the average price level of *all* final goods and services in our economy.

ANTICIPATED VERSUS UNANTICIPATED INFLATION

Before examining who is hurt by inflation and what the effects of inflation are in general, we have to distinguish between anticipated and unanticipated inflation. We will see that the effects on individuals and the economy are vastly different, depending on which type of inflation exists.

Unanticipated inflation is inflation that comes as a surprise to individuals in the economy. For example, if the inflation rate in a particular year turns out to be 10 percent when on average people thought it was going to be 5 percent, there will have been unanticipated inflation—inflation greater than anticipated.

Anticipated inflation is that rate of inflation that the majority of individuals believe will occur. If the rate of inflation this year turns out to be 10 percent, and that's about what most people thought it was going to be, we are in a situation of fully anticipated inflation.

Many of the problems caused by inflation are caused by the fact that it is unanticipated, for when it is anticipated, many people are able to protect themselves from its ravages. With the distinction in mind between anticipated and unanticipated inflation, we can easily see the relationship between inflation and interest rates.

> ▶ **Unanticipated inflation**
> Inflation at a rate that comes as a surprise; unanticipated inflation can be either higher or lower than the rate anticipated.

> ▶ **Anticipated inflation**
> The inflation rate that we believe will occur; when it does, we are in a situation of fully anticipated inflation.

INFLATION AND INTEREST RATES

Let's start in a hypothetical world in which there is no inflation and anticipated inflation is zero. In that world you may be able to borrow money—to buy a house or a car, for example—at a **nominal rate of interest** of, say, 10 percent. If you borrow the money to purchase a house or a car and your anticipation of inflation turns out to be accurate, neither you nor the lender will have been fooled. The dollars you pay back in the years to come will be just as valuable in terms of purchasing power as the dollars that you borrowed.

What you are usually interested in when you borrow money is the **real rate of interest** that you will have to pay. The real rate of interest is defined as the nominal rate of interest minus the anticipated rate of inflation. If you are able to borrow money at 10 percent and you anticipated an inflation rate of 10 percent, your real rate of interest would be zero—lucky you, particularly if the actual rate of inflation turned out to be 10 percent. In effect, we can say that the nominal rate of interest is equal to the real rate of interest plus an *inflationary premium* to take account of anticipated inflation. That inflationary premium covers depreciation in the purchasing power of the dollars repaid by borrowers.[1] Consider the purchase of a home. In 1982, mortgage rates for the purchase of new homes were around 15 percent. By 1993, they had fallen to around 8 percent. Why would any-

> ▶ **Nominal rate of interest**
> The rate of interest expressed in contracts today, in terms of today's dollars. The rate of interest that you have to pay for credit or that you obtain from your savings.

> ▶ **Real rate of interest**
> The nominal rate of interest minus the anticipated rate of inflation.

[1] Whenever there are relatively high rates of anticipated inflation, we must add an additional factor to the inflationary premium—the product of the real rate of interest times the anticipated rate of inflation. Usually this last term is omitted because the anticipated rate of inflation is not high enough to make much of a difference.

one have paid 15 percent in 1982 to borrow money to buy a home? Well, home prices in much of the country had been rising for several years at 25 percent per year, so at 15 percent, mortgage rates seemed like a good deal. By the mid-1990s, home prices in most places were either falling or at best stable.

There is fairly strong evidence that inflation rates and nominal interest rates move in parallel fashion. Periods of rapid inflation create periods of high interest rates. In the early 1970s, when the inflation rate was between 4 and 5 percent, average interest rates were around 8 percent. At the beginning of the 1980s, when the inflation rate was near 9 percent, interest rates had risen to between 12 and 14 percent. By the early 1990s, when the inflation rate was about 3 percent, nominal interest rates had again fallen to between 4 and 8 percent.

 INTERNATIONAL EXAMPLE: Anticipated Inflation and Nominal Interest Rates in Foreign Countries

Is the relationship between anticipated inflation and nominal interest rates a worldwide phenomenon? The answer seems to be yes, at least for industrialized countries. In Figure 7-5 you can see that nominal interest rates and anticipated inflation in nine foreign industrialized countries moved pretty much together. When anticipated inflation rises, so do nominal interest rates.

FIGURE 7-5
The relationship between nominal interest rates and the expected rate of inflation in industrialized countries.
This graph shows the relationship between the average nominal rate of interest in Germany, France, Japan, Great Britain, Sweden, and Italy. Anticipated inflation is also charted. Interest rates appear to rise and fall with anticipated rates of inflation in these industrialized countries.

Sources: Federal Reserve; International Monetary Fund.

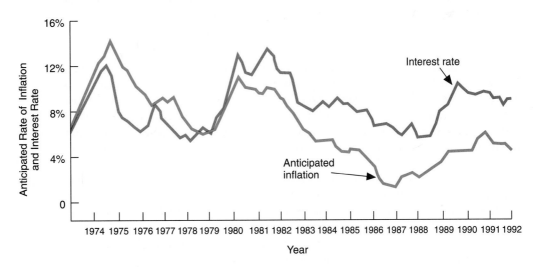

For Critical Analysis: What would happen to nominal interest rates during a period of anticipated deflation? ●

DOES INFLATION NECESSARILY HURT EVERYONE?
Most people think that inflation is bad. After all, inflation means higher prices, and when we have to pay higher prices, are we not necessarily worse off? But inflation affects different people differently. It also affects different people differently depending on whether it is anticipated or unanticipated.

Unanticipated Positive Inflation: Creditor Losses, Debtor Gains.
Creditors lose and debtors gain with unanticipated positive inflation. In most situations unanticipated inflation can cause borrowers to benefit. Why? Because they would not initially be charged a nominal interest rate that covered the rate of inflation that actually occurred. Why? Because the lender did not anticipate inflation correctly. The point to understand is that creditors lose and debtors gain whenever inflation rates are underestimated for the life of a loan. In the past several decades there have apparently been periods in which there was considerable unanticipated (higher than anticipated) inflation—the late 1960s, early 1970s, and late 1970s. During those years creditors lost and debtors gained.

It is possible, of course, for the rate of inflation to be overestimated. When inflation is lower than anticipated, creditors gain and debtors lose. Some economists argue that the abrupt drop in the rate of inflation in 1982, for example, created just such a situation. Obviously, whenever inflation is correctly anticipated by both creditors and debtors, neither creditors nor debtors lose or gain.

Protecting Against Inflation.
Banks attempt to protect themselves against inflation by raising nominal interest rates to reflect anticipated inflation. Adjustable-rate mortgages in fact do just that: The interest rate varies according to what happens to interest rates in the economy. Workers can protect themselves by **cost-of-living adjustments (COLAs),** which are automatic increases in wage rates to take account of increases in the price level.

> ▶ **Cost-of-living adjustments (COLAs)**
> Clauses in contracts that allow for increases in specified nominal values to take account of changes in the cost of living or the Consumer Price Index.

To the extent that you hold non-interest-bearing cash, you will lose because of inflation. If you have $100 put in a mattress and the inflation rate is 10 percent for the year, you will have lost 10 percent of the purchasing power of that $100. If you have your cash in a non-interest-bearing checking account, you will suffer the same fate. Individuals attempt to reduce the cost of holding cash by putting available cash into interest-bearing accounts, a wide variety of which often pay nominal rates of interest that reflect anticipated inflation.

The Resource Cost of Inflation.
Some economists believe that the main cost of unanticipated inflation is the opportunity cost of resources used to protect against inflation and the distortions introduced as firms attempt to plan for the long run. Individuals have to spend time and resources to figure out ways to cover themselves in case inflation is different from what it has been in the past. That may mean spending a longer time working out more complicated contracts for employment, for purchases of goods in the future, and for purchases of raw materials.

Inflation requires the changing of price lists. This is called the **repricing, or menu, cost of inflation.** The higher the rate of inflation, the higher the repricing cost of inflation. Imagine the repricing cost of inflation in Brazil with its rapid inflation compared to that in the United States, where the average inflation rate has rarely reached double digits.

> ▶ **Repricing,** or **menu, cost of inflation**
> The cost associated with recalculating prices and printing new price lists when there is inflation.

Another major problem with inflation is that usually it does not proceed perfectly evenly. Consequently, the rate of inflation is not exactly what people anticipate. When this is so, the purchasing power of money changes in unanticipated ways. Because money is what we use as the measuring rod of the value of transactions we undertake, we have a more difficult time figuring out what we have really paid for things. As a result, resources tend to be misallocated in such situations because people have not really valued them accurately.

Think of any period during which you have to pay a higher price for something that was cheaper before. You are annoyed. But every time you pay a higher price, that represents the receipt of higher income for someone else. Therefore, it is impossible for all of us to be worse off because of rising prices. There are numerous costs to inflation, but they aren't the ones commonly associated with inflation. One way to think of inflation is that it is simply a *change in the accounting system.* One year the price of fast-food hamburgers averages $1; 10 years later the price of fast-food hamburgers averages $2. Clearly, $1 doesn't mean the same thing 10 years later. If we changed the name of our unit of accounting each year so that one year we paid $1 for fast-food hamburgers and 10 years later we paid, say, 1 peso, this lesson would be driven home.

🌐 INTERNATIONAL EXAMPLE: Changes in the Accounting System: The Case of the French Franc

In 1959 the French government decided on a monetary reform. New currency was issued, and during the transition period, all prices were specified in either *nouveaux francs* (new francs) or *anciens francs* (old francs). One *nouveau franc* equaled 100 *anciens francs.* In essence, everybody simply dropped two zeros when expressing values in terms of the newly defined francs. *Monetary reform* meant no change in the real value of anybody's wealth or salaries or in the real cost of any goods or services. The French government could have just as easily changed the name of its currency and the effect would have been the same. So-called monetary reforms have occurred in Argentina, Ukraine, and Peru in recent years. Argentina did in fact change the name of its currency from a peso to an austral in 1985. (In April 1991, they went to the "new" peso.) Argentinians were no better or worse off because of this so-called monetary reform. The name given to a nation's currency does not determine its purchasing power.

For Critical Analysis: *If so-called monetary reform really does not change anything, why have so many countries throughout history done exactly what the French government did in 1959?* ●

CONCEPTS IN BRIEF

- Whenever inflation is greater than anticipated, creditors lose and debtors gain.
- Whenever the rate of inflation is less than anticipated, creditors gain and debtors lose.
- Holders of cash lose during periods of inflation because the purchasing power of their cash depreciates at the rate of inflation.
- Households and businesses spend resources in attempting to protect themselves against unanticipated inflation, thus imposing a resource cost on the economy whenever there is unanticipated inflation.

▶ **Business fluctuations**
The ups and downs in overall business activity, as evidenced by changes in national income, employment, and the price level.

▶ **Expansion**
A business fluctuation in which overall business activity is rising at a more rapid rate than previously or at a more rapid rate than the overall historical trend for the nation.

▶ **Contraction**
A business fluctuation during which the pace of national economic activity is slowing down.

CHANGING INFLATION AND UNEMPLOYMENT: BUSINESS FLUCTUATIONS

Some years unemployment goes up, some years it goes down. Some years there is a lot of inflation, other years there isn't. We have fluctuations in all aspects of our macroeconomy. The ups and downs in economywide economic activity are sometimes called **business fluctuations.** When business fluctuations are positive, they are called **expansions**—speedups in the pace of national economic activity. The opposite of an expansion is a **contraction,** which is a slowdown in the pace of national economic activity. The top of an expansion is usually called its *peak,* and the bottom of a contraction is usually called its *trough.* Business fluctuations used to be called *business cycles,* but that term no longer seems appropriate because *cycle* implies predetermined or automatic recurrence, and we certainly haven't had automatic recurrent fluctuations in general business and economic activity. What we have had are contractions and expansions that vary greatly in length. For example, nine post–World War II expansions averaged 48 months, but three of those exceeded 55 months, and two lasted less than 25 months.

If the contractionary phase of business fluctuations become severe enough, we call it a **recession.** An extremely severe recession is called a **depression.** Typically, at the beginning of a recession interest rates rise, and as the recession gets worse they fall. At the same time, people's income starts to fall and the duration of unemployment increases, so that the unemployment rate increases. In times of expansion, the opposite occurs.

In Figure 7-6 you see that typical business fluctuations occur around a growth trend in overall national business activity shown as straight upward-sloping line. Starting out at a peak, the economy goes into a contraction (recession). Then an expansion starts that moves up to its peak, higher than the last one, and the sequence starts over again.

The official dating of business recessions is done by the National Bureau of Economic Research in New York City; Cambridge, Massachusetts; and Palo Alto, California.

▶ **Recession**
A period of time during which the rate of growth of business activity is consistently less than its long-term trend, or is negative.

▶ **Depression**
An extremely severe recession.

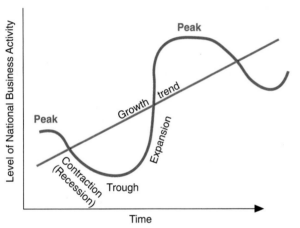

FIGURE 7-6
The typical course of business fluctuations.

CONCEPTS IN BRIEF

- The ups and downs in economywide business activity are called business fluctuations.
- Business fluctuations consist of expansions and contractions in overall business activity.
- When a contraction has reached its lowest point, this is called the trough. When an expansion has reached its highest point, this is called a peak.
- A recession is a downturn in business activity for some length of time. Official dating of business recessions is done by the National Bureau of Economic Research.

PRODUCTIVITY

One of the most serious problems the United States faces is the lack of improvement in labor productivity. **Labor productivity** is normally measured by dividing the value of total domestic output (gross domestic product) by the number of workers. Labor productivity increases whenever average output produced per worker during a specified time period increases.

▶ **Labor productivity**
Total domestic output (GDP) divided by the number of workers (output per worker).

WHY IMPROVEMENTS IN LABOR PRODUCTIVITY ARE IMPORTANT

Improvements in labor productivity ultimately increase wages and salaries. Wages and salaries constitute about 75 percent of all income in the United States. Consequently, labor productivity is the major determinant of this (and all other) nations' living standards. If labor productivity improves because of an advance in technology, the rate of output increases without the need for additional labor. The dollar value of all goods increases as a result, which implies that consumers ultimately receive more income.

Entrepreneurs have a profit incentive to increase labor productivity. They do so by providing their workers with better equipment and creating more efficient ways for their workers to use that equipment. Entrepreneurs also have an incentive to discover new products that are more highly valued relative to their cost of production.

Some of the largest increases in productivity occur because of major technological advancements. The steam engine and the internal combustion engine are two examples. The advances in the computer industry have been nothing short of phenomenal. Advances in technology depend in part on businesses making sustained investment in new technology and new products. A major issue in today's economy is whether businesses are doing this and what incentives are being provided by the government to companies to encourage investment. Another issue is whether labor productivity in the United States has fallen behind other countries. We will look at this more closely in the *Issues and Applications* discussion at the end of this chapter.

There have also been dramatic increases in productivity in our agricultural sector. Because of the increased use of chemicals, the yields per acre are many times greater than they were 100 years ago, and consequently, many fewer Americans now engage in farming, yet agricultural output is the highest it has ever been.

HISTORICAL GROWTH IN LABOR PRODUCTIVITY

Labor productivity is measured by the amount of private business sector output per labor hour worked. From 1889 to 1937, the rate of growth was 1.9 percent per year. It was at 3 percent per year until 1973. Since then it has been slightly less than 1 percent per year. We see the historical record in Figure 7-7.

FIGURE 7-7
U.S. labor productivity, 1889–1989.
The American worker produced in 1989 about four times as much as did his or her 1889 counterpart.

Source: Economic Report of the President, February 1992, p. 91.

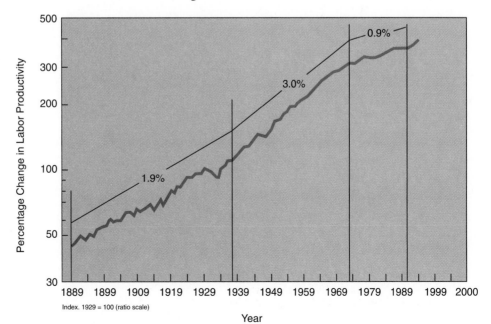

Index. 1929 = 100 (ratio scale)

CONCEPTS IN BRIEF

- Productivity is defined as total domestic output (gross domestic product) divided by the number of workers.
- Improvement in labor productivity normally determine increases in wages and salaries and therefore increases in living standards.
- The largest increases in productivity occur because of major technological advances.
- Historically, labor productivity has been slower since about 1973 than earlier in the century.

SHOULD WE BE WORRIED ABOUT DECLINING U.S. LABOR PRODUCTIVITY?
Concepts Applied: Labor productivity, service sector

This hydraulic robot is capable of increasing labor productivity. Improvements in labor productivity can occur through increased automation, but the question remains whether they are occurring rapidly enough in the United States.

You just learned that a rise in a nation's standard of living depends in large part on improvements in labor productivity. Therefore, if America's labor productivity growth is less than that in other nations, eventually the U.S. standard of living will fall behind that of other nations. Table 7-4 shows U.S. labor productivity compared to some developed and developing countries. The table shows that growth in labor productivity in the United States averaged about 2 percent a year from 1950 to 1990, lower than all other countries except Chile and

Peru. In contrast, labor productivity growth in Japan has averaged over 6 percent per year. The conclusion that many economists draw from this is that the Japanese are quickly catching up with the U.S. standard of living and in fact may pass it relatively soon. Indeed, in 1950 the average American enjoyed a 200 percent better standard of living than the average Japanese, but that advantage had fallen to an estimated 25 percent in 1994.

PRODUCTIVITY IN THE SERVICE SECTOR
It is much more difficult to improve labor productivity in the *service sector*—the part of the economy involved in providing the services of doctors, lawyers, accountants, repair persons, piano teachers, educators, dry cleaners, housekeepers, and the like—because relatively less capital equipment is used in this sector. Hence technological improvements do not have as great an effect on productivity as they do in manufacturing. Therefore, when the service sector of an economy grows more than the other sectors, it is more difficult to improve labor productivity.

The service sector has grown in the United States, but it has grown in other countries as well. In fact, in the past, service-sector growth in all other industrialized nations has been higher than that in the United States. This means that their level of growth has already factored in service-sector growth, so in the future it will be easier for them to improve labor productivity.

TABLE 7-4 Growth in labor productivity in selected developing and developed countries, 1950–1990 (percent per year)

| | DEVELOPING COUNTRIES | | | | DEVELOPED COUNTRIES | | | |
YEARS	EGYPT	MEXICO	CHILE	PERU	JAPAN	WEST GERMANY	UNITED KINGDOM	UNITED STATES
1950–1990	3.29	2.20	1.19	1.44	6.09	3.61	2.22	1.88
1950–1973	2.45	3.06	1.77	2.79	8.30	4.92	2.60	2.17
1973–1983	7.01	1.74	−.90	−1.13	2.56	1.66	1.17	.85
1983–1988	.08	−1.14	2.71	.63	3.53	2.52	3.49	3.50
1973–1990	4.61	.94	.38	−.27	2.71	1.84	1.80	1.11

Sources: Robert Summers and Alan Heston, "The Penn World Tables (Mark 5): An Expanded Set of International Comparisons, 1950–1988," *Quarterly Journal of Economics,* (May 1991), pp. 327–368; and Council of Economic Advisers.

WE BENEFIT FROM LABOR PRODUCTIVITY IMPROVEMENTS ELSEWHERE Although it is true that more rapid labor productivity growth in other countries means that their standard of living will ultimately increase faster than that in the United States, this country will nonetheless still benefit from improvements in foreign labor productivity. Consumers in America can, after all, buy more goods from other countries more cheaply when productivity growth increases abroad. The average U.S. consumer has certainly benefited from the dramatic labor productivity growth in the low-cost, high-quality electronics industry in Japan. The moral is that productivity growth, whether it be at home or abroad, is good, not bad, for all economies.

FOR CRITICAL ANALYSIS

1. Even if it is true that other countries, such as Japan, will overtake U.S. living standards, why should the average American be concerned?
2. What are some of the ways in which you can experience improvements in your own labor productivity?

CHAPTER SUMMARY

1. The United States has a history of ups (expansions) and downs (contractions) in its national business activity. This economy has been plagued with periods of relatively high unemployment and inflation.

2. Unemployment in the United States is of four types: frictional, seasonal, structural, and cyclical. It is difficult to discern what part of total unemployment is of any one type.

3. Frictional unemployment is caused by the temporary inability of workers to match their skills and talents with available jobs. Frictional unemployment might be eliminated if we passed a law that required employers never to fire workers and employees never to quit a job until they could go immediately to a new one.

4. Structural unemployment occurs when the demand for a particular skill falls off abruptly. Structural unemployment is often associated with technological unemployment—that is, it occurs when machines put men and women out of work.

5. Inflation occurs when the average of all prices of goods and services is rising; deflation occurs when the average of all prices is falling. During periods of inflation, the purchasing power of money falls (by definition).

6. The most commonly used measures of changes in general prices are the Consumer Price Index (CPI), the Producer Price Index (PPI), and the GDP deflator.

7. The nominal rate of interest includes the anticipated rate of inflation. Therefore, when anticipated inflation increases, market rates of interest will rise.

8. Whenever the actual rate of inflation turns out to exceed the expected rate of inflation, creditors lose and debtors gain because the latter are able to repay debts in cheaper dollars. Of course, if everybody anticipates rising prices, interest rates will rise to take account of this future expected reduction in the purchasing power of the dollar.

9. Workers protect themselves against inflation by having cost-of-living adjustment (COLA) clauses in their employment contracts.

10. Labor productivity is normally measured by dividing total domestic product by the number of workers.

11. Improvements in labor productivity are important because they are the basis of increases in wages and salaries and hence in living standards.

12. Some of the largest increases in productivity have occurred because of major technological advances such as the steam engine and the internal combustion engine. By historical standards, labor productivity growth in the United States has been relatively slow since 1973.

DISCUSSION OF PREVIEW POINTS

1. Why is frictional unemployment not necessarily harmful?

Because imperfect information exists in the real world, at any given time some people seeking jobs won't be matched with job vacancies. Given imperfect information, frictional unemployment indicates that the economy is reacting to changes in tastes; frictional unemployment may result from one industry expanding while another is contracting. Moreover, frictional unemployment occurs when people climb up the occupational ladder. Thus frictional unemployment is not really harmful to society (or to the individuals involved), and hence the overall unemployment percentage may be a misleading statistic.

2. Does it matter whether inflation is anticipated or not?

Whether inflation is anticipated or not is important to households and firms. When everyone fully and correctly anticipates the rate of future inflation, all contracts will take account of the declining purchasing power of the dollar. Debtors will not be able to gain at the expense of creditors, and employers will not be able to fool employees into agreeing to accept wage increases that do not have an inflationary factor built in. Only when inflation is not anticipated can it have unexpected negative effects on households and firms.

3. Who is hurt by inflation?

In periods of inflation, fixed-income groups are obviously hurt; however, because most retired people collect Social Security payments (which have increased

more rapidly than the price level for the past quarter century), this point is easily overstressed. In periods of unanticipated inflation (or when the rate of inflation is more than that anticipated), creditors are hurt at the expense of borrowers, who gain. Also, people locked into long-term contracts to receive fixed nominal-money amounts (laborers, bondholders and other moneylenders, pensioners) are hurt if the rate of inflation is greater than they had anticipated. People who hold cash are also hurt by inflation; as prices rise, a given amount of cash can buy less.

4. How do we measure productivity?

Productivity is often measured by looking at labor productivity. Consequently, the value of a nation's annual domestic output (usually called gross domestic product, or GDP) is divided by the number of workers who were working that year. The result is the amount of output per worker. It is also possible to measure productivity by dividing annual output by the entire population. Then we come up with a measure of output per capita.

PROBLEMS

(Answers to the odd-numbered problems appear at the back of the book.)

7-1. Assume that your taxable income is $30,000 per year. Assume further that you are in the 15 percent tax bracket applied to all income from $0 to $30,000. If your taxable income increases to $30,001 per year, you will move into the 28 percent tax bracket. Your boss gives you a raise equal to 4 percent. How much better off are you?

7-2. Assume that you are receiving unemployment benefits of $100 a week. You are offered a job that will pay you $150 a week before taxes. Assume further that you would have to pay 7 percent Social Security taxes plus federal income taxes equal to 15 percent of your salary. What is the opportunity cost of remaining unemployed—that is, how much will it cost you to refuse the job offer?

7-3. Assume that the labor force consists of 100 people and that every month five people become unemployed and five others who were unemployed find jobs.
   a. What is the frictional unemployment rate?
   b. What is the average duration of unemployment?
   Now assume that the only type of unemployment in this economy is frictional.
   c. What is the unemployment rate?
   Suppose that a system of unemployment compen-

sation is instituted, and the average duration of unemployment rises to two months.
   d. What will the unemployment rate for this economy be now?
   e. Does a higher unemployment rate necessarily mean that the economy is sicker or that laborers are worse off?

7-4. Study the following table for a few minutes, and then answer the questions below it.

YEAR	PPI
1982	100.0
1984	103.7
1987	105.4
1991	121.7
1992	124.1

   a. What is the base year for the PPI?
   b. What happened to the price level between 1982 and 1992?
   c. By how much did prices rise from 1984 to 1987?
   d. If the intermediate goods cost $100 in 1982, what did they cost in 1992?

7-5. a. Suppose the nominal interest rate is currently 12 percent. If the inflation rate is zero, what is the real interest rate?

     b. The inflation rate rises to 13 percent while the nominal interest rate remains at 12 percent. Does it make sense to lend money under these circumstances?

7-6. An economic slump occurs and two things happen:

     a. Many people stop looking for jobs because they know that the probability of finding a job is low.

     b. Many people who become laid off start doing such work at home as growing food and painting and repairing their houses and autos.

     Which of these events implies that the official unemployment rate overstates unemployment, and which implies the opposite?

7-7. Columns 1 and 2 in the table show the relationship between employment and the price level in the economy.

(1) EMPLOYMENT (MILLIONS OF WORKERS)	(2) PRICE LEVEL ($)	(3) UNEMPLOYMENT RATE (%)	(4) RATE OF INFLATION (%)
90	1.00	___	___
91	1.08	___	___
92	1.17	___	___
93	1.28	___	___
94	1.42	___	___
95	1.59	___	___
96	1.81	___	___
97	2.10	___	___

     a. Assume that full employment in the economy occurs when 100 million workers are employed. Compute and enter in column 3 the unemployment rate at each level of employment. (Hint: Divide the number of workers unemployed by the number that would be employed at full employment.)

     b. At each unemployment rate (except 10 percent), compute and enter in column 4 the rate of inflation by dividing the increase in the price level by the price level.

7-8. Suppose that a country has a labor force of 100 people. In January, Miller, Pulsinelli, and Hooper are unemployed; in February those three find jobs but Stevenson, Conn, and Romano become unemployed. Suppose further that every month the previous three that were unemployed find jobs and three different people become unemployed.

     a. What is this country's unemployment rate?

     b. What is its frictional unemployment rate?

     c. What is the average duration of unemployment?

COMPUTER-ASSISTED INSTRUCTION
(Complete problem and answer on disk.)

In this problem a consumer spends all of her income on pizza, jeans, and wine. Through time the price of each of these goods changes, and the consumer changes the quantities that she buys. The problem requires you to make step-by-step calculations to derive a Consumer Price Index for specific price-quantity values in specific years.

MEASURING THE ECONOMY'S PERFORMANCE

Someone who works around the house preparing meals, doing minor repairs, or washing the dishes does not normally get paid. Of course, if the homemaker becomes ill or is injured and the same work has to be purchased from others, the price tag can get pretty high. Nevertheless, when government statisticians count up their estimate of annual national economic activity, they ignore un-remunerated work in the home. Representative Barbara-Rose Collins of Michigan thinks this is wrong and has introduced a bill that would require the government to place a value on "unwaged work." Should the government comply? The issue of the value of homemakers' work is part of the larger study of how we measure national economic activity.

After reading this chapter, you should be able to answer the following questions:

1. What is gross domestic product (GDP), and what does it measure?

2. Why are only *final* goods and services evaluated in deriving GDP?

3. Why must depreciation and indirect taxes be added to national income at factor cost in order to derive GDP via the income approach?

4. How does correcting GDP for changes in price level and population improve the usefulness of GDP estimates?

INTRODUCTION

Most people like to know where they stand financially at the end of some period, whether it be a week, a month, or a year. How much did you make? How much did you pay in taxes? How much did you save? This information is useful to show not only how well you did financially but also what your goals can reasonably be for the following period. The national economy is no different. Macro policymakers want to know how well the economy is doing in order to set goals for the next period. Consequently, there has to be a way to estimate the level and changes in overall national activity. That is the purpose for what has become known as **national income accounting,** the main focus of this chapter.

Before we delve into that subject, we need first to look at the flow of income within every economy, for it is the flow of goods and services from businesses to consumers and payments from consumers to businesses that constitutes economic activity.

THE SIMPLE CIRCULAR FLOW

The concept of a circular **flow** of income (ignoring taxes) involves two principles:

1. In every economic exchange, the seller receives exactly the same amount that the buyer spends.
2. Goods and services flow in one direction and money payments flow in the other.

In the simple economy shown in Figure 8-1, there are only businesses and households. It is assumed that businesses sell their *entire* output *immediately* to households and that households spend their *entire* income *immediately* on consumer products. Households receive their income by selling the use of whatever factors of production they own, such as labor services.

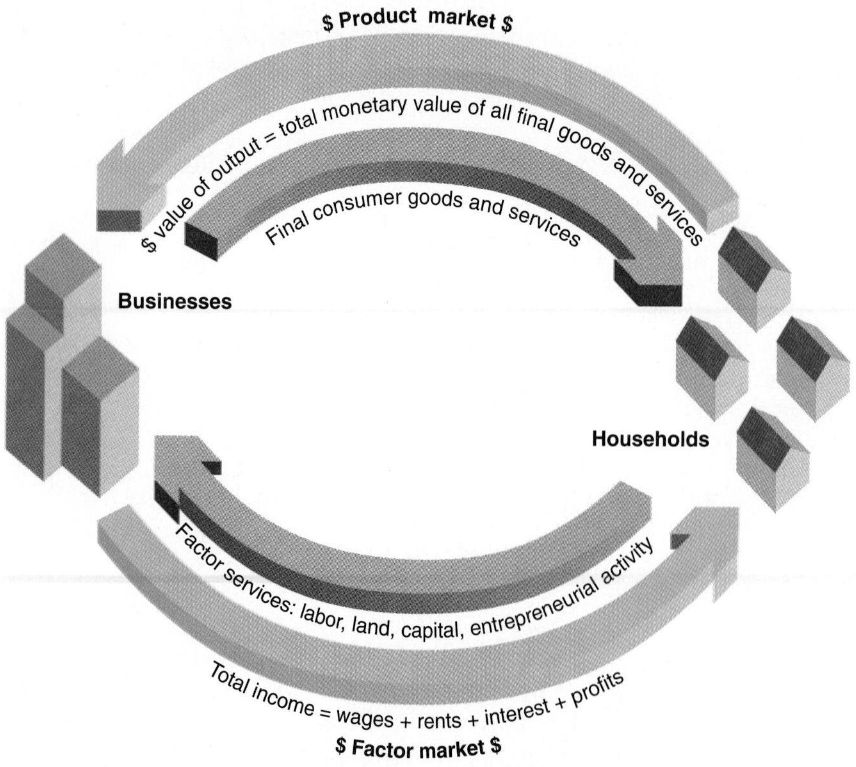

▸ **National income accounting**
A measurement system used to estimate national income and its components. This is one approach to measuring an economy's aggregate performance.

▸ **Flow**
Any activity that occurs over time. For example, income is a flow that occurs per week, per month, or per year. Consumption is also a flow, as is production.

$ Product market $

$ value of output = total monetary value of all final goods and services

Final consumer goods and services

Businesses

Households

Factor services: labor, land, capital, entrepreneurial activity

Total income = wages + rents + interest + profits

$ Factor market $

FIGURE 8-1
The circular flow of income and product.
Businesses provide final goods and services to households (upper clockwise loop), who in turn pay for them with money (upper counterclockwise loop). Money flows in a counterclockwise direction and can be thought of as a circular flow. The dollar value of output is identical to total income because profits are defined as being equal to total business receipts minus business outlays for wages, rents, and interest.

PROFITS EXPLAINED

We have indicated in Figure 8-1 that profit is a cost of production. You might be under the impression that profits are not part of the cost of producing goods and services; but profits are indeed a part of this cost because entrepreneurs must be rewarded for providing their services or they won't provide them. Their reward, if any, is profit. The reward—the profit—is included in the cost of the factors of production. If there were no expectations of profit, entrepreneurs would not incur the risk associated with the organization of productive activities. That is why we consider profits a cost of doing business.

TOTAL INCOME OR TOTAL OUTPUT

▶ **Total income**
The yearly amount earned by the nation's resources (factors of production). Total income therefore includes wages, rent, interest payments, and profits that are received, respectively, by workers, landowners, capital owners, and entrepreneurs.

▶ **Final goods and services**
Goods and services that are at their final stage of production and will not be transformed into yet other goods or services. For example, wheat is not a final good because it is used to make bread, which is a final good.

The lower arrow that goes from businesses to households in Figure 8-1 is labeled "Total income." What would be a good definition of **total income?** If you answered "the total of all individuals' income," you would be right. But all income is actually a payment for something, whether it be wages paid for labor services, rent paid for the use of land, interest paid for the use of capital, or profits paid to entrepreneurs. It is the amount paid to the resource suppliers. Therefore, total income is also defined as the annual *cost* of producing the entire output of **final goods and services.**

The upper arrow going from households to businesses represents the dollar value of output in the economy. This is equal to the total monetary value of all final goods and services for this simple economy. In essence, it represents the total business receipts from the sale of all final goods and services produced by businesses and consumed by households. Business receipts are the opposite side of household expenditures. When households purchase goods and services with money, that money becomes a *business receipt.* Every transaction, therefore, simultaneously involves an expenditure as well as a receipt.

Product Markets.   Transactions in which households buy goods take place in the product markets—that's where households are the buyers and businesses are the sellers of consumer goods. *Product market* transactions are represented in the upper loops in Figure 8-1. Note that consumer goods and services flow to household demanders, while money flows in the opposite direction to business suppliers.

Factor Markets.   *Factor market* transactions are represented by the lower loops in Figure 8-1. In the factor market, households are the sellers; they sell resources such as labor, land, capital, and entrepreneurial ability. Businesses are the buyers in factor markets; business expenditures represent receipts or, more simply, income for households. Also, in the lower loops of Figure 8-1, factor services flow from households to businesses, while the money paid for these services flows in the opposite direction from businesses to households.

Observe also the circular flow of money (counterclockwise) from households to businesses and back again from businesses to households; it is an endless circular flow.

WHY THE DOLLAR VALUE OF TOTAL OUTPUT MUST EQUAL TOTAL INCOME

The dollar value of total output produced in an economy in one year is equal to the total monetary value of all final goods and services produced in that economy. Total income represents the income received by households in payment for the production of these goods and services. Why must total income be identical to the dollar value of total output? The reason is simple accounting and the way economists define profit. Profit is considered a cost of production. It is defined as what is *left over* from total business receipts after all other costs—wages, rents, interest—have been paid. If the dollar value of total output is $1,000 and the total of wages, rent, and interest for producing that output is $900, profit is $100. Profit is always the *residual* item that makes total income equal to the dollar value of total output.

CONCEPTS IN BRIEF

- In a circular flow model of income and output, households sell factor services to businesses that pay for those factor services. The receipt of payments is total income. Businesses sell goods and services to households that pay for them.
- The dollar value of total output is equal to the total monetary value of all final goods and services produced.
- The dollar value of final output must always equal total income.

NATIONAL INCOME ACCOUNTING

We have already mentioned that policymakers need information about the state of the national economy. Historical statistical records on the performance of the national economy aid economists in testing their theories about how the economy really works. National income accounting is therefore important. Let's start with the most commonly presented statistic on the national economy.

GROSS DOMESTIC PRODUCT

Gross domestic product (GDP) represents the total market value of the nation's annual final product, or output, produced per year by factors of production located within national borders. We therefore formally define GDP as the total market value of all final goods and services produced in an economy during a year. We are referring here to a flow of production. A nation produces at a certain rate, just as you receive income at a certain rate. Your income flow might be at a rate of $5,000 per year or $50,000 per year. Suppose you are told that someone earns $500. Would you consider this a good salary? There is no way to answer that question unless you know whether the person is earning $500 per month or per week or per day. Thus you have to specify a time period for all flows. Income received is a flow. You must contrast this with, for example, your total accumulated savings, which are a **stock** measured at a point in time, not across time. Implicit in just about everything we deal with in this chapter is a time period—usually one year. All the measures of domestic product and income are specified as rates measured in dollars per year.

▶ **Gross domestic product (GDP)**
The total market value of all final goods and services produced by factors of production located within a nation's borders.

▶ **Stock**
The quantity of something, measured at a given point in time—for example, an inventory of goods or a bank account. Stocks are defined independently of time, although they are assessed at a point in time.

IT WASN'T ALWAYS GDP

Some of you may remember, or even still read about, gross national product, or GNP. A few years ago, government statisticians decided to change from reporting gross national product to reporting gross domestic product to be more consistent with the way annual national activity is estimated in other countries. GNP measures the value of output of final goods and services provided by factors of production owned by a nation's residents, even when the production takes place *outside* national borders. GDP measures the value of output of final goods and services produced *within* the nation's borders. The difference between GDP and GNP is small in the United States—less than 1 percent in any given year.

STRESS ON FINAL OUTPUT

▶ **Intermediate goods**
Goods used up entirely in the production of final goods.

▶ **Value added**
The dollar value of an industry's sales minus the value of intermediate goods (for example, raw materials and parts) used in production.

GDP does not count **intermediate goods** (goods used up entirely in the production of final goods) because to do so would be to count them twice. For example, even though grain that a farmer produces may be that farmer's final product, it is not the final product for the nation. It is sold to make bread. Bread is the final product.

We can use a numerical example to clarify this point further. Our example will involve determining the value added at each stage of production. **Value added** is the amount of dollar value contributed to a product at each stage of its production. In Table 8-1 we see the difference between total value of all sales and value added in the production of a donut. We also see that the sum of the values added is equal to the sale price to the final consumer. It is the 15 cents that is used to measure GDP, not the 32 cents. If we used the 32 cents, we would be double-counting from stages 2 through 5, for we would include the total value of all of the intermediate sales that took place prior to the donut's being sold to its final consumer. Such double counting would grossly exaggerate GDP if it were done for all goods and services sold.

EXCLUSION FROM GDP OF PURELY FINANCIAL TRANSACTIONS, USED GOODS, AND TRANSFER PAYMENTS

Remember that GDP is the measure of the value of all final goods and services produced in one year. Many more transactions occur that have nothing to do with final goods and services produced. There are financial transactions, transfers of the ownership of used goods, as well as other transactions that should not and do not get included in our measure of GDP.

TABLE 8-1 Sales value and value added at each stage of donut production.

(1) STAGE OF PRODUCTION	(2) DOLLAR VALUE OF SALES	(3) VALUE ADDED
Stage 1: Fertilizer and seed	$.01	$.01
Stage 2: Growing	.02	.01
Stage 3: Milling	.04	.02
Stage 4: Baking	.10	.06
Stage 5: Retailing	.15	.05
Total dollar value of all sales	$.32	Total value added $.15

Stage 1: A farmer purchases a penny's worth of fertilizer and seed, which are used as factors of production in growing wheat.

Stage 2: The farmer grows the wheat, harvests it, and sells it to a miller for 2¢. Thus we see that the farmer has added 1¢ worth of value. That 1¢ represents income paid in the form of rent, wages, interest, and profit to the farmer.

Stage 3: The miller purchases the wheat for 2¢ and adds 2¢ as the value added, that is, there is 2¢ for the miller as income to be paid as rent, wages, interest, and profit. The miller sells the ground wheat flour to a donut-baking company.

Stage 4: The donut-baking company buys the flour for 4¢ and adds 6¢ as the value added. It then sells the donut to the final retailer.

Step 5: The donut retailer sells fresh hot donuts at 15¢ apiece, thus creating an additional value of 5¢.

We see that the total value of sales resulting from the production of one donut was 32¢, but the total value added was 15¢, which is exactly equal to the retail price. The total value added is equal to the sum of all income payments, including rent, wages, interest, and profit.

Financial Transactions.   There are three general categories of purely financial transactions: (1) the buying and selling of securities, (2) government transfer payments, and (3) private transfer payments.

1. **Buying and selling securities.** When you purchase a share of existing stock in Microsoft Corporation, someone else has sold it to you. In essence, there was merely a *transfer* of ownership rights. You paid $100 in cash to obtain the stock certificate. Someone else, through the brokerage system, received the $100 and gave up the stock certificate. No producing activity was consummated at that time. Hence the $100 transaction is not included when we measure gross domestic product. The dollar value of the activities of brokers who helped you transfer the shares in Microsoft are included in GDP, however, because they constitute a service, an end in itself.
2. **Government transfer payments.** Transfer payments are payments for which no productive services are concurrently provided in exchange. The most obvious government transfer payments are Social Security benefits, veterans' payments, and unemployment compensation. The recipients make no contribution to current production in return for such transfer payments (although they may have made contributions in the past to receive them). Government transfer payments are not included in GDP.
3. **Private transfer payments.** Are you receiving money from your parents in order to live at school? Has a wealthy relative ever given you a gift of money? If so, you have been the recipient of a private transfer payment. This is merely a transfer of funds from one individual to another. As such, it does not constitute productive activity and is not included in gross domestic product.

Transfer of Used Goods.   If I sell you my two-year-old stereo, no current production is involved. I transfer to you the ownership of a sound system that was produced several years ago; in exchange, you transfer to me $550. The original purchase price of the stereo was included in GDP in the year I purchased it. To include it again when I sell it to you would be counting the value of the stereo a second time. (The value added by firms that sell used goods *is* counted, of course, and is an important part of our economy.)

Other Excluded Transactions.   Many other transactions are not included in GDP. Some are excluded for practical reasons, some for political reasons. The other excluded transactions are these:

1. Household production—home cleaning, child care, and other tasks performed by homemakers within their own households and for which they are not paid through the marketplace
2. Legal underground transactions—those that are legal but not reported and hence not taxed
3. Illegal underground activities—these include prostitution, illegal gambling, and the sale of illicit drugs

 **INTERNATIONAL EXAMPLE: GDP and Costa Rica's Forestry Production**

Many developing countries depend on natural resources for much of their national income and employment. When a forest is cut down in Costa Rica, the output is sold, and if we look only at GDP figures, the country appears to be growing richer. But what if the trees are not replaced so that their removal results in flooding, soil erosion, and loss of fuel and food gathered by the indigenous population? Robert Repetoo of the World Resources Institute in Washington, D.C., has recalculated GDP in Costa Rica to reflect the impact of resource depletion. His figures show that within the forestry sector itself, net forestry product—after resource depletion is calculated—was actually strongly negative through most of the 1980s. Repetoo argues that such statistics are important because they educate developing countries and show them that their natural wealth is not limitless. He wants the United Nations to take into account the depletion of natural resources when calculating each nation's GDP. He points out that currently a benefit from commercial forests is recorded in national income accounts only when the trees are cut down.

Peter Bartelmus in the United Nation's statistics department has already developed a set of guidelines for "satellite" GDP accounts. These guidelines show how to adjust GDP for the depletion of natural resources and for deterioration of the environment, such as increases in air pollution and loss of wildlife. The problem, of course, is how to place a dollar value on the extinction of a species or the contamination of a river.

For Critical Analysis: In the United States, there are actually more trees in our forests than there were 50 years ago. Does this mean that we should be adding to our GDP figures for this increase in forests? Should we be concerned about our depletion of petroleum reserves? ●

CONCEPTS IN BRIEF

- GDP is the total market value of final goods and services produced in an economy during a one-year period by factors of production within the nation's borders. It represents the flow of production over a one-year period.
- To avoid double counting, we look only at final goods and services produced or, alternatively, at value added.
- In measuring GDP, we must exclude (1) purely financial transactions, such as the buying and selling of securities, government transfer payments, and private transfer payments; and (2) the transfer of used goods.
- Many other transactions are excluded from GDP, among them household services rendered by homemakers in their own households, underground economy transactions, and illegal economic activities.

TWO MAIN METHODS OF MEASURING GDP

If the definition of GDP is the total value of all final goods and services produced during a year, then to measure GDP we could add up the prices times the quantities of everything produced. But this would involve a monumental, if not impossible, task for government statisticians.

The circular flow diagram presented in Figure 8-1 gives us a shortcut method for calculating GDP. We can look at the *flow of expenditures,* which consists of government purchases of goods and services, consumption, investment, and net expenditures in the foreign sector (net exports). This is called the **expenditure approach** to measuring GDP. We could also use the *flow of income,* looking at the income received by everybody producing goods and services. This is called the **income approach.**

▶ **Expenditure approach**
A way of computing national income by adding up the dollar value at current market prices of all final goods and services.

▶ **Income approach**
A way of measuring national income by adding up all components of national income, including wages, interest, rent, and profits.

DERIVING GDP BY THE EXPENDITURE APPROACH

To derive GDP using the expenditure approach, we must look at each of the separate components of expenditures and then add them together. These components are consumption expenditures, government expenditures, investment, and net exports.

Consumption Expenditures. How do we spend our income? As households or as individuals, we spend our income through consumption expenditure (C), which falls into three categories: **durable consumer goods, nondurable consumer goods,** and **services.** Durable goods are *arbitrarily* defined as items that last more than three years; they include automobiles, furniture, and household appliances. Nondurable goods are all the rest, such as food and gasoline. Services are just what the name suggests: medical care, education, and so on.

Housing expenditures constitute a major proportion of anybody's annual expenditures. Rental payments on apartments are automatically included in consumption expenditure estimates. People who own their homes, however, do not make rental payments. Consequently, government statisticians estimate what is called the *implicit rental value* of owner-occupied homes. It is equal to the amount of rent you would have to pay if you did not own the home but were renting it from someone else.

Government Expenditures. In addition to personal consumption expenditures, there are government purchases of goods and services (G). The government buys goods and services from private firms and pays wages and salaries to government employees. Generally, we value goods and services at the prices at which they are sold. But many government goods and services are not sold in the market. Therefore, we cannot use their market value when computing GDP. The value of these goods is considered equal to their *cost*. For example, the value of a newly built road is considered equal to its construction cost and is included in the GDP for the year it was built.

Gross Private Domestic Investment. We now turn our attention to **gross private domestic investment** (I) undertaken by businesses. When economists refer to investment, they are referring to additions to productive capacity. **Investment** may be thought of as an activity that uses resources today in such a way that they allow for greater production in the future and hence greater consumption in the future. When a business buys new equipment or puts up a new factory, it is investing; it is increasing its capacity to produce in the future.

The layperson's notion of investment often relates to the purchase of stocks and bonds. For our purposes such transactions simply represent the *transfer of ownership* of assets called stocks and bonds. Thus you must keep in mind the fact that in economics investment refers *only* to additions to productive capacity, not to transfers of assets.

The Components of Investment. In our analysis we will consider the basic components of investment. We have already mentioned the first one, which involves a firm's buying equipment or putting up a new factory. These are called **producer durables,** or **capital goods.** A producer durable, or a capital good, is simply a good that is purchased not to be consumed in its current form, but to be used to make other goods and services. The purchase of equipment and factories—capital goods—is called **fixed investment.**

The other type of investment has to do with the change in inventories of raw materials and finished goods. Firms do not immediately sell off all their products to consumers. Some of this final product is usually held in inventory waiting to be sold. Firms hold inventories to meet future expected orders for their products. When a firm increases its in-

▶ **Durable consumer goods**
Goods used by consumers that have a life span of more than three years, that is, goods that endure and can give utility over a long period of time.

▶ **Nondurable consumer goods**
Goods used by consumers that are used up within three years.

▶ **Services**
Things purchased by consumers that do not have physical characteristics. Examples of services are those purchased from doctors, lawyers, dentists, repair personnel, housecleaners, educators, retailers, and wholesalers.

▶ **Gross private domestic investment**
The creation of capital goods, such as factories and machines, that can yield production and hence consumption in the future. Also included in this definition are changes in business inventories and repairs made to machines or buildings.

▶ **Investment**
Any use of today's resources to expand tomorrow's production or consumption.

▶ **Producer durables,** or **capital goods**
Durable goods having an expected service life of more than three years that are used by businesses to produce other goods and services.

▶ **Fixed investment**
Purchases by businesses of newly produced producer durables, or capital goods, such as production machinery and office equipment.

▶ **Inventory investment**
Changes in the stocks of finished goods and goods in process, as well as changes in the raw materials that businesses keep on hand. Whenever inventories are decreasing, inventory investment is negative; whenever they are increasing, inventory investment is positive.

ventories of finished products, it is engaging in **inventory investment.** Inventories consist of all finished goods on hand, goods in process, and raw materials.

The reason that we can think of a change in inventories as being a type of investment is that an increase in such inventories provides for future increased consumption possibilities. When inventory investment is zero, the firm is neither adding to nor subtracting from the total stock of goods or raw materials on hand. Thus if the firm keeps the same amount of inventories throughout the year, inventory *investment* has been zero.

In estimating gross private domestic investment, government statisticians also add consumer expenditures on new residential structures because new housing represents an addition to our future productive capacity in the sense that a new house can generate housing services in the future.

 INTERNATIONAL EXAMPLE: The Way the United Nations Treats Investment

The United Nations has recently designed a system of national accounts (SNA) that contains a major difference in the way it treats government expenditures: It classifies them as either investment or consumption. (In the United States all government expenditures statistically are considered current consumption—there is no investment component.) Consequently, when a government pays for the construction of a new road system, that is designated a fixed investment under the SNA because it will not be consumed in the same year that it is built. When a government spends on welfare payments that, of course, is considered consumption.

If the U.S. national accounts were changed to conform to the United Nations methodology, the reported level of investment (I) would rise and the government (G) component of GDP would fall because some of government spending is on capital. But GDP itself would not be affected. As you will see in later chapters, investment represents an important policy area in the United States because Americans are worried that this country is not engaged in enough capital formation and consequently will suffer in the future. But much of the difference in the reported levels of investment across countries is due to different national income accounting practices. Because the United States considers all of its government expenditures to be consumption, the money that is really being invested in new roads, buildings, and the like is not reflected in the national income accounting system as investment.

For Critical Analysis: Would you include military spending on rockets and planes as investment for national income accounting purposes? Does your answer depend on the fact that the Cold War is over? ●

Net Exports (Foreign Expenditures).   To get an accurate representation of gross domestic product, we must include the foreign sector. As Americans, we purchase foreign goods called *imports*. The goods that foreigners purchase from us are our *exports*. To get an idea of the *net* expenditures from the foreign sector, we subtract the value of imports from the value of exports to get net exports (X) for a year:

$$\text{Net exports } (X) \equiv \text{total exports} - \text{total imports}$$

This is an identity; that's why we use the $\equiv$ sign.

MATHEMATICAL REPRESENTATION FOR GDP USING THE EXPENDITURE APPROACH

We have just defined the components of GDP using the expenditure approach. When we add them all together, we get a definition for GDP, which is as follows:

$$GDP \equiv C + I + G + X$$

where

$$C = \text{consumption expenditures}$$
$$I = \text{investment expenditures}$$
$$G = \text{government expenditures}$$
$$X = \text{net exports}$$

The Historical Picture.   To get an idea of the relationship among *C, G, I,* and *X,* look at Figure 8-2, which shows gross domestic product, personal consumption expenditures, government purchases, and gross private domestic investment plus net exports from 1929 to 1993. When we sum up the expenditures of the household, government, business, and foreign sectors, we get GDP.

FIGURE 8-2

GDP and its components.

Here we see a display of gross domestic product, personal consumption expenditures, government purchases, and gross private domestic investment plus net exports for the years 1929–1993. As can be seen, during the Great Depression of the 1930s, gross private domestic investment *plus* net exports was negative because we were investing very little at that time.

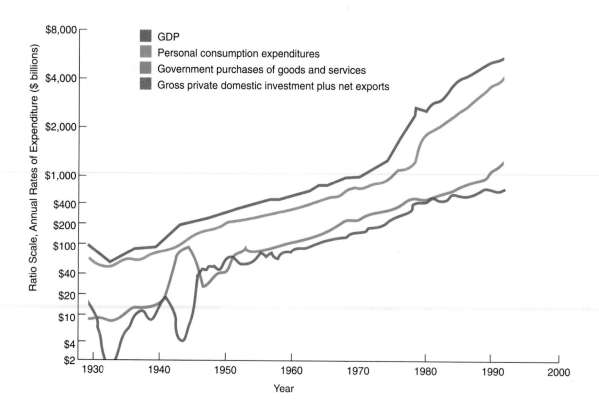

Depreciation and Net Domestic Product.   We have used the terms *gross domestic product* and *gross private domestic investment* without really indicating what *gross* means. The dictionary defines it as "without deductions," as opposed to *net*. Deductions for what? you might ask. The deductions are for something we call **depreciation.** In the course of a year, machines and structures wear out or are used up in the production of domestic product. For example, houses deteriorate as they are used, and machines need repairs or they will fall apart and stop working. Most capital, or durable, goods therefore depreciate. An estimate of this is subtracted from gross domestic product to arrive at a figure called **net domestic product (NDP),** which we define as follows:

$$\text{NDP} \equiv \text{GDP} - \text{depreciation}$$

> **Depreciation**
> Reduction in the value of capital goods over a one-year period due to physical wear and tear and also to obsolescence; also called *capital consumption allowance.*

> **Net domestic product (NDP)**
> GDP minus depreciation.

> **Capital consumption allowance**
> Another name for depreciation, the amount that businesses would have to save in order to take care of the deterioration of machines and other equipment.

Depreciation is also called **capital consumption allowance** because it is the amount of the capital stock that has been consumed over a one-year period. Because we know that

$$\text{GDP} \equiv C + I + G + X$$

we know that the formula for NDP is

$$\text{NDP} \equiv C + I + G + X - \text{depreciation}$$

Alternatively, because net $I \equiv I -$ depreciation,

$$\text{NDP} \equiv C + \text{net } I + G + X$$

> **Net investment**
> Gross private domestic investment minus an estimate of the wear and tear on the existing capital stock. Net investment therefore measures the change in capital stock over a one-year period.

Net investment measures *changes* in our capital stock over time and is positive nearly every year. Because depreciation does not vary greatly from year to year as a percentage of GDP, we get a similar picture of what is happening to our national economy by looking at either NDP or GDP data.

CONCEPTS IN BRIEF

- The expenditure approach to measuring GDP requires that we add up consumption expenditures, government purchases, gross private investment, and net exports.
- Consumption expenditures include consumer durables, consumer nondurables, and services.
- We value government expenditures at their cost because we do not usually have market prices at which to value government goods and services.
- Gross private domestic investment *excludes* transfers of asset ownership. It includes only additions to the productive capacity of a nation plus repairs on existing capital goods plus changes in business inventories.
- To obtain net domestic product (NDP), we subtract from GDP the year's depreciation of the existing capital stock.

DERIVING GDP BY THE INCOME APPROACH

If you go back to the circular flow diagram in Figure 8-1, you see that product markets are at the top of the diagram and factor markets are at the bottom. We can calculate the value of the circular flow of income and product by looking at expenditures—which we just did—or by looking at total factor payments. Factor payments are called income. We calculate **gross domestic income (GDI),** which we will see is identical to gross domestic product (GDP). Using the income approach, we have four categories of payments to individuals:

> **Gross domestic income (GDI)**
> The sum of all income paid to the four factors of production, i.e., the sum of wages, interest, rent, and profits.

1. **Wages.** The most important category is, of course, wages, including salaries and other forms of labor income, such as income in kind and incentive payments. We also count Social Security taxes (both the employees' and the employers' contributions).
2. **Interest.** Here interest payments do not equal the *sum* of all payments for the use of funds in a year. Instead, interest is expressed in *net* rather than in gross terms. The interest component of total income is only net interest received by households plus net interest paid to us by foreigners. Net interest received by households is the difference between the interest they receive (from savings accounts, certificates of deposit, etc.) and the interest they pay (to banks for mortgages, credit cards, etc.). Interest as a component of GDP does not include payment of interest on U.S. government bonds.
3. **Rent.** Rent is all income earned by individuals for the use of their real (nonmonetary) assets, such as farms, houses, and stores. As stated previously, we have to include here the implicit rental value of owner-occupied houses. Also included in this category are royalties received from copyrights, patents, and assets such as oil wells.
4. **Profits.** Our last category includes total gross corporate profits plus so-called *proprietors' income*. Proprietors' income is income earned from the operation of unincorporated businesses, which include sole proprietorships, partnerships, and producers' cooperatives. It is unincorporated business profit.

All of the payments listed are *actual* factor payments made to owners of the factors of production. When we add them together, though, we do not yet have gross domestic income. We have to take account of two other components: **indirect business taxes,** such as sales and business property taxes, and depreciation, which we have already discussed.

> **Indirect business taxes**
> All business taxes except the tax on corporate profits. Indirect business taxes include sales and business property taxes.

Indirect Business Taxes.   Indirect taxes are the (nonincome) taxes paid by consumers when they buy goods and services. When you buy a book, you pay for the price of the book plus any state and local sales tax. The business is actually acting as the government's agent in collecting the sales tax, which it in turn passes on to the government. Such taxes therefore represent a business expense and are included in gross domestic income.

Depreciation.   Just as we had to deduct depreciation to get from GDP to NDP, so we must *add* depreciation to go from net domestic income to gross domestic income. Depreciation can be thought of as the portion of the current year's GDP that is used to replace physical capital consumed in the process of production. Because somebody has paid for the replacement, depreciation must be added as a component of gross domestic income.

The last two components of GDP—indirect business taxes and depreciation—are called **nonincome expense items.**

> **Nonincome expense items**
> The total of indirect business taxes and depreciation.

Figure 8-3 shows a comparison between gross domestic product and gross domestic income for 1993. Whether you decide to use the expenditure point of view or the income point of view, you will come out with the same number. There are sometimes statistical discrepancies, but they are usually relatively small.

CONCEPTS IN BRIEF

- To derive GDP using the income approach, we add up all factor payments, including wages, interest, rent, and profits.
- To get an accurate estimate of GDP with this method, we must also add indirect business taxes and depreciation to those total factor payments.

FIGURE 8-3
Gross domestic product and gross domestic income, 1993 (in billions of 1993 dollars per year).
By using the two different methods of computing the output of the economy, we come up with gross domestic product and gross domestic income, which are by definition equal. One approach focuses on expenditures, or the flow of product; the other approach concentrates on income, or the flow of costs.

Source: U.S. Department of Commerce. First quarter preliminary data annualized.

Expenditure Approach

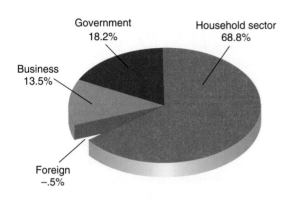

Income Approach

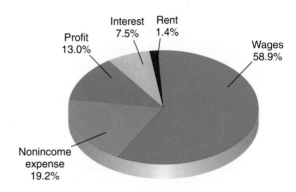

EXPENDITURE POINT OF VIEW—PRODUCT FLOW		INCOME POINT OF VIEW—COST FLOW	
EXPENDITURES BY DIFFERENT SECTORS:		DOMESTIC INCOME (AT FACTOR COST):	
Household sector		*Wages*	
Personal consumption expenses	$4,237.2	All wages, salaries, and supplemental employee compensation	$3,630.3
Government sector		*Rent*	
Purchase of goods and services	1,118.2	All rental income of individuals plus implicit rent on owner-occupied dwellings	88.7
Business sector		*Interest*	
Gross private domestic investment (including depreciation)	836.4	Net interest paid by business	459.8
Foreign sector		*Profit*	
Net exports of goods and services	-33.1	Proprietorial income	431.2
		Corporate profits before taxes deducted	390.6
		Nonincome expense items	
		Indirect business taxes and other adjustments	562.3
		Depreciation	621.7
		Statistical discrepancy	-25.8
Gross domestic product	$6,158.8	Gross domestic income	$6,158.8

OTHER COMPONENTS OF NATIONAL INCOME ACCOUNTING

Gross domestic income or product does not really tell how much income people have access to for spending purposes. To get to those kinds of data, we must make some adjustments, which we now do.

NATIONAL INCOME (NI)

We know that net domestic product (NDP) represents the total market value of goods and services available for both consumption, used in a broader sense here to mean "resource exhaustion," and net additions to the economy's stock of capital. NDP does not, however, represent the income available to individuals within that economy because it includes indirect business taxes, such as sales taxes. We therefore deduct these indirect business taxes from NDP to arrive at the figure for all factor income of resource owners. The result is what we define as **national income (NI)**—income *earned* by the factors of production.

PERSONAL INCOME (PI)

National income does not actually represent what is available to individuals to spend because some people obtain income for which they have provided no concurrent good or service and others earn income but do not receive it. In the former category are mainly recipients of transfer payments from the government, such as Social Security, welfare, and food stamps. These payments represent shifts of funds within the economy by way of the government, where no good or service is concurrently rendered in exchange. For the other category, income earned but not received, the most obvious examples are corporate retained earnings that are plowed back into businesses, contributions to social insurance, and corporate income taxes. When transfer payments are added and when income earned but not received is subtracted, we end up with **personal income (PI)**—income *received* by the factors of production prior to the payment of personal income taxes.

DISPOSABLE PERSONAL INCOME (DPI)

Everybody knows that you do not get to take home all your salary. To get **disposable personal income (DPI),** subtract all personal income taxes from personal income. This is the income that individuals have left for consumption and saving.

DERIVING THE COMPONENTS OF GDP

Table 8-2 takes you through the steps necessary to derive the various components of GDP. It shows how you go from gross domestic product to net domestic product to national income to personal income and then to disposable personal income. On the endpapers of your book, you can see the historical record for GDP, NDP, NI, PI, and DPI for selected years since 1929.

We have completed our rundown of the different ways that GDP can be computed and of the different variants of national income and product. What we have not yet even touched on is the difference between national income measured in this year's dollars and national income representing real goods and services.

▶ **National income (NI)**
The total of all factor payments to resource owners. It can be obtained by subtracting indirect business taxes from NDP.

▶ **Personal income (PI)**
The amount of income that households actually receive before they pay personal income taxes.

▶ **Disposable personal income (DPI)**
Personal income after personal income taxes have been paid.

	BILLIONS OF DOLLARS
Gross domestic product (GDP)	6,158.8
Minus depreciation	−621.7
results in	
Net domestic product (NDP)	5,537.1
Minus indirect business taxes and other adjustments	−562.3
results in	
National income (NI)	4,974.8
Minus corporate taxes, Social Security contributions, corporate retained earnings	−827.5
Plus government and business transfer payments	+1,089.4
results in	
Personal income (PI)	5,236.7
Minus personal income tax and nontax payments	−656.4
results in	
Disposable personal income (DPI)	4,580.3

TABLE 8-2 Going from GDP to disposable income, 1993.

Source: U.S. Department of Commerce.

> ## CONCEPTS IN BRIEF
> - To obtain national income, we subtract indirect business taxes from net domestic product. National income gives us a measure of all factor payments to resource owners.
> - To obtain personal income, we must add government transfer payments, such as Social Security benefits and food stamps. We must subtract income earned but not received by factor owners, such as corporate retained earnings, Social Security contributions, and corporate income taxes.
> - To obtain disposable personal income, we subtract all personal income taxes from personal income. Disposable personal income is income that individuals actually have for consumption or saving.

DISTINGUISHING BETWEEN NOMINAL AND REAL VALUES

▶ Nominal values
The values of variables such as GDP and investment expressed in current dollars, also called *money values;* measurement in terms of the actual market prices at which goods are sold.

▶ Real values
Measurement of economic values after adjustments have been made for changes in the average of prices between years.

So far we have shown how to measure *nominal* income and product. When we say "nominal," we are referring to income and product expressed in the current "face value" of today's dollar. Given the existence of inflation or deflation in the economy, we must also be able to distinguish between the **nominal values** that we will be looking at and the **real values** underlying them. Real income involves our command over goods and services—purchasing power—and therefore depends on money income and a set of prices. Thus real income refers to nominal income corrected for changes in the weighted average of all prices. In other words, we must make an adjustment for changes in the price level. Consider an example. Nominal income *per person* in 1960 was only about $2,800 per year. In 1993 nominal income per person was close to $24,000. Were people really that bad off in 1960? No, for nominal income in 1960 is expressed in 1960 prices, not in the prices of today. In today's dollars the per-person income of 1960 would be closer to $9,500, or about 40 percent of today's income per person. This is a meaningful comparison between income in 1960 and income today. The uncorrected 1960 data show per-person income to be only 11.7 percent of today's income. Next we will show how we can translate nominal measures of income into real measures by using an appropriate price index, such as the CPI or the GDP deflator discussed in Chapter 7.

CORRECTING GDP FOR PRICE CHANGES

▶ Constant dollars
Dollars expressed in terms of real purchasing power using a particular year as the base or standard of comparison, in contrast to current dollars.

If a compact disc (CD) costs $15 this year, 10 CDs will have a market value of $150. If next year they cost $20 each, the same 10 CDs will have a market value of $200. In this case there is no increase in the total quantity of CDs, but the market value will have increased by one-third. Apply this to every single good and service produced and sold in the United States and you realize that changes in GDP, measured in *current* dollars, may not be a very useful indication of economic activity. If we are really interested in variations in the *real* output of the economy we must correct GDP (and just about everything else we look at) for changes in the average of overall prices from year to year. Basically, we need to generate an index that approximates the changes in average prices and then divide that estimate into the value of output in current dollars to adjust the value of output to what is called **constant dollars**. This price-corrected GDP is called *real GDP.*

⭐ EXAMPLE: Correcting GDP for Price Level Changes, 1982–1993

Let's take a numerical example to see how we can adjust GDP for changes in prices. We must pick an appropriate price index in order to adjust for these price level changes. We mentioned the Consumer Price Index, the Producer Price Index, and the GDP deflator in Chapter 7. Let's use the GDP deflator to adjust our figures. In Table 8-3 we have recorded 12 years of GDP figures. Nominal GDP figures are shown in column 2. The price level index (GDP deflator) is in column 3, with base year of 1987 when the GDP deflator equals 100. Column 4 shows real (inflation-adjusted) GDP in 1987 dollars.

The step-by-step derivation of real (constant-dollar) GDP is as follows: The base year is 1987, so the price index must equal 100. In 1987 nominal GDP was $4,539.9 billion, and so too was real GDP expressed in 1987 dollars. In 1988, the price level increased to 103.9. Thus to correct 1988's nominal GDP for inflation, we divide the price index, 103.9, into the nominal GDP figure of $4,900.4 billion and then multiply it by 100. The result is $4,716.5 billion, which is 1988 GDP expressed in terms of the purchasing power of dollars in 1987. What about a situation when the price level is lower than in 1987? Look at 1982. Here the price index shown in column 3 is only 83.8. That means that in 1982, the average of all prices was about 84 percent of prices in 1987. To obtain 1982 GDP expressed in terms of 1987 purchasing power, we divide nominal GDP, $3,149.6 billion, by 83.8 and then multiply by 100. The result is a larger number—$3,758.5 billion. Column 4 in Table 8-3 is a better measure of how the economy has performed than column 2, which shows nominal GDP changes.

For Critical Analysis: A few years ago, the base year for the GDP deflator was 1982, and before that it was 1967. What does a change in the base year for the price level index affect? ●

PLOTTING NOMINAL AND REAL GDP
Nominal GDP and real GDP from 1970 to 1993 are plotted in Figure 8-4. Notice that there is quite a big gap between the two GDP figures, reflecting the amount of inflation that has occurred. Note, further, that the choice of a base year is arbitrary. We have chosen 1987 as the base year in our example. This happens to be the base year currently used by the government.

TABLE 8-3 Correcting GDP for price changes. To correct GDP for price changes, we first have to pick a price level index (the GDP deflator) with a specific year as its base. In our example, the base level is 1987 prices; the price level index for that year is 100% = 1.00. To obtain 1987 constant-dollar GDP, we divide the price level index into nominal GDP. In other words, we divide column 3 into column 2 (and multiply by 100). This gives us column 4, which is a measure of real GDP expressed in 1987 purchasing power.

(1) YEAR	(2) NOMINAL GDP (BILLIONS OF DOLLARS PER YEAR)	(3) PRICE LEVEL INDEX (BASE YEAR 1987 = 100)	(4) = [(2) ÷ (3)] ×100 REAL GDP (BILLIONS OF DOLLARS PER YEAR IN CONSTANT 1987 DOLLARS)
1982	3,149.6	83.8	3,758.5
1983	3,405.0	87.2	3,904.8
1984	3,777.2	91.0	4,150.8
1985	4,038.7	94.4	4,278.3
1986	4,268.6	96.9	4,405.2
1987	4,539.9	100.0	4,539.9
1988	4,900.4	103.9	4,716.5
1989	5,250.8	108.5	4,839.4
1990	5,222.2	113.2	4,613.3
1991	5,677.5	117.8	4,819.6
1992	5,967.1	121.2	4,923.3
1993	6,158.8	122.9	5,011.2

Source: U.S. Department of Commerce, Bureau of Economic Analysis.

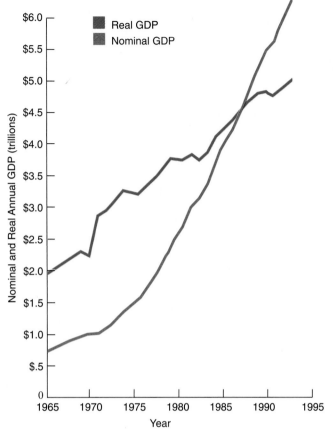

FIGURE 8-4
Nominal and real GDP, 1970–1993.
Here we plot both nominal and real GDP. Real GDP is expressed in the purchasing power of 1987 dollars. The gap between the two represents price-level changes.

Source: U.S. Department of Commerce.

PER CAPITA GDP

Even looking at changes in real gross domestic product may be deceiving, particularly if the population size has changed significantly. If real GDP over a 10-year period went up 100 percent, you might jump to the conclusion that the material well-being of the economy had increased by that amount. But what if during the same period population increased by 200 percent? Then what would you say? Certainly, the amount of GDP per person, or *per capita GDP,* would have fallen, even though total deflated (or real) GDP had risen. What we must do to account not only for price changes but also for population changes is first deflate GDP and then divide by the total population, doing this for each year. If we were to look at certain less developed countries, we would find that in many cases, even though real GDP has risen over the past several decades, real GDP per capita has remained constant or fallen because the population has grown just as rapidly or more quickly.

The difficulties of using GDP as an indicator of social well-being do not end here. In fact, there has been a running battle over the use of GDP statistics because, according to its critics, such numbers do not capture the true overall well-being of a nation. How do we take account of changes in leisure time? How do our national income accounts recognize increased traffic congestion, air pollution in our cities, crime in the streets, and so on? And a major amount of work in the United States isn't even counted in GDP. That work is called housework, the subject of this chapter's *Issues and Applications.*

CONCEPTS IN BRIEF

- To correct nominal GDP for price changes, we first use a base year for our price index and assign it the number 100 percent (or 1). Then we construct an index based on how a weighted average of the price level has changed relative to that base year. For example, if in the next year a weighted average of the price level indicates that prices have increased by 10 percent, we would assign it the number 110 (or 1.10). We then divide each year's price index, so constructed, into its respective nominal GDP figure (and divide by 100).
- We can further divide the population into real GDP to obtain per capita real GDP.

SHOULD UNPAID HOUSEWORK BE INCLUDED IN GDP?

Concepts Applied: National income accounting, social valuation

When they calcuate GDP, government statisticians include for the most part only the value of services that were explicitly paid for in the marketplace. Many services, such as home repairs, have a value but are not included in official estimates of GDP.

If you are a typical American, during much of your life you will do work around the house for which you are not paid. That work could consist of gardening, caring for children, or repairing a leaky faucet. In spite of the increasing participation of women in the labor force, it is still true that the bulk of unremunerated (unpaid for) housework is carried out by women. An increasing number of critics of national income accounting argue that housework should be included in the calculation of GDP. Representative Barbara-Rose Collins of Michigan argues that doing so would raise the status of women. Economist Carole Clark contends that if we had been counting women's unremunerated labor for the past three decades, during which time women began entering the labor force, "policymakers would have foreseen and prevented the current child-care and elder-care crisis."

WHAT THE GOVERNMENT ALREADY DOES

Government statisticians cannot simply reply that they do not value unremunerated work. Currently, they already place a value on food grown by farmers that is consumed by farmers' families rather than sent to market for sale. They also make an attempt at estimating the implicit rental value of owner-occupied housing. Conceivably, then, these same statisticians could come up with an estimate of the value of unremunerated housework.

MEASUREMENT PROBLEMS
When a homemaker is killed in an auto accident, that person's family can often sue for the value of the services that were lost. Attorneys (who rely on economists) are often asked to make an attempt to estimate this value to present to the court. They add up the cost of purchasing babysitting, cooking, housecleaning, and tutoring services. The number turns out to be quite large, often in excess of $30,000 a year. Of course one of the problems in measuring the value of unremunerated housework in such a way is that we could often purchase the services of a full-time live-in housekeeper for less money than if we paid for the services of the various components of housekeeping. And what about quality? Some homemakers serve fabulous gourmet meals; others simply warm up canned and frozen foods. Should they be valued equally? Another problem lies in knowing when to stop counting. A person can hire a valet to help him or her get dressed in the morning. Should we therefore count the time spent in getting dressed as part of unpaid work? Both men and women perform services around the house virtually every day of the year. Should all of those unremunerated services be included in a "new" measure of GDP? If they were, measured GDP would be increased dramatically.

SATELLITE GDP
In spite of the problems just mentioned, the Decade for Women World Conference in Nairobi passed a resolution in 1984 that calls for all nations to measure and include in GDP the unpaid contributions of women. If this were done, United Nations economists believe that an additional $4 trillion in annual worldwide income would be calculated. In reality, no country has begun counting unremunerated work in GDP. France and Norway have nonetheless created "satellite" GDP estimates that do include it. Australia, Canada, and Germany have begun studying a similar procedure.

A TAXING MATTER
Critics of the idea of including unpaid remuneration, particularly for women, claim that it would be empty symbolism. They also point out a much more important problem: the possibility that the federal government would then want to tax unremunerated work in order to raise more revenues.

FOR CRITICAL ANALYSIS

1. If more and more homemakers leave the home to enter the labor force, replacing their domestic services with machines and hired help, will our estimate of GDP change? If so, in what way? If not, why not?

2. Should illicit drug trafficking, non-government-sponsored gambling, and prostitution also be included in GDP? Why or why not?

CHAPTER SUMMARY

1. Households provide labor services, land, capital, and entrepreneurship, for which they are paid wages, rent, interest, and profits. Profits are considered a factor cost—they are the reward for entrepreneurship or risk taking. Profits are a residual payment.

2. In the simplest representation of our economy, there are only households and businesses. The circular flow goes from households to factor markets to businesses and from businesses to product markets to households.

3. National income accounting is the method by which economists attempt to measure statistically the variables with which they are concerned in their study of macroeconomics.

4. One of the concepts most often used in national income accounting is gross domestic product, which is defined as the total market value of all *final* goods and services produced annually by domestic factors of production. The stress on *final* is important to avoid the double counting of intermediate goods used in the production of other goods.

5. We can compute GDP using the expenditure approach or the income approach. In the former we merely add up the dollar value of all final goods and services; in the latter we add up the payments generated in producing all those goods and services, or wages, interest, rent, and profits, plus indirect business taxes and depreciation.

6. It is difficult to measure the market value of government expenditures because generally government-provided goods are not sold at a market clearing price. We therefore value government expenditures at their cost for inclusion in our measure of GDP.

7. Investment does not occur when there is merely a transfer of assets among individuals; rather, it occurs only when new productive capacity is generated, such as when a machine is built.

8. Part of our capital stock is worn out or becomes obsolete every year. To take account of the expenditures made merely to replace such capital equipment, we subtract depreciation from GDP to yield net domestic product.

9. To correct for price changes, we deflate GDP with a price index to come up with real GDP. To take account of rising population, we then correct for population and come up with real GDP per capita.

DISCUSSION OF PREVIEW POINTS

1. **What is gross domestic product (GDP), and what does it measure?**

Gross domestic product is defined as the market value of all final goods and services produced during one year by domestic factors of production. Because GDP is measured per unit of time, it is a flow concept. Economists try to estimate GDP in order to evaluate the productive performance of an economy during the year; economists also use GDP estimates to aid them in judging overall economic well-being.

2. **Why are only *final* goods and services evaluated in deriving GDP?**

Because GDP estimates are an attempt to evaluate an economy's performance and to generalize about group well-being, we must be careful to evaluate only final goods and services; otherwise GDP would be exaggerated. For example, because an automobile uses plastic, steel, coke, rubber, coal, and other products in its manufacture, to count each of these *and* the value of an automobile would be double counting. Thus to count coal *and* the automobile when it is sold is to count coal twice and hence to exaggerate the economy's performance and the group's economic well-being. Coal in this instance would not be a final good; it would be an intermediate good.

3. Why must depreciation and indirect business taxes be added to national income at factor cost in order to derive GDP via the income approach?

The expenditure approach to GDP counts expenditures on all final goods and services; in particular, expenditures on *all* investment goods amount to gross investment. The income approach to GDP estimation, by contrast, sums the wages, interest, rent, and profit receipts of income earners. Because depreciation is not a wage, rent, interest, or profit, the expenditure approach would yield a higher number. In order to compare correctly, we must add depreciation to national income at factor cost to calculate GDP via the income approach. Similarly, indirect business taxes (excise, sales, and property taxes) are automatically reflected in the expenditure approach, whereas indirect business taxes are not wages, interest, rent, or profit receipts to factors of production.

4. How does correcting GDP for changes in price level and population improve the usefulness of GDP estimates?

When the price level is rising (during periods of inflation), GDP estimates would overstate true productive activity and group economic well-being. Similarly, when the general price level is falling (during periods of deflation), GDP estimates would understate productive activity and group economic well-being. If population is rising more rapidly than real output, real GDP estimates would rise, but living standards might well be falling. Dividing by population corrects for such cases. Real per capita GDP is a better clue to productive activity and overall economic well-being than nominal GDP.

PROBLEMS

(Answers to the odd-numbered problems appear at the back of the book.)

8-1. The following are a year's data for a hypothetical economy.

	BILLIONS OF DOLLARS
Consumption	400
Government spending	350
Gross private domestic investment	150
Exports	150
Imports	100
Depreciation	50
Indirect business taxes	25

a. Based on the data, what is the value of GDP? NDP? NI?

b. Suppose that in the next year exports increase to $175 billion, imports increase to $200 billion, and consumption falls to $350 billion. What will GDP be in that year?

c. If the value of depreciation (capital consumption allowance) should ever exceed that of gross private domestic investment, how would this affect the future productivity of the nation?

8-2. Look at Table 8-3 on page 182, which explains how to correct GDP for price level changes.

Column 4 of that table gives real GDP in terms of 1987 constant dollars. Change the base year to 1982. Recalculate the price level index and then recalculate real GDP—that is, express column 4 in terms of 1982 dollars instead of 1987 dollars.

8-3. Study the following table; then answer the questions.

STAGE OF PRODUCTION	SALES RECEIPTS	INTERMEDIATE COSTS	VALUE ADDED
Coal	$2	$0	$2
Steel	5	2	3
Manufactured autos	8	5	3
Sold autos	9	8	1

a. What is the intermediate good for steel production? How much did it cost?

b. What is the value added resulting from auto manufacturing?

c. If automobiles are the only final goods produced in this economy, what would GDP via the expenditures approach be equal to?

d. If automobiles are the only final goods produced in this economy, what would GDP via the income approach be equal to?

8-4. At the top of a piece of paper, write the headings "Productive Activity" and "Nonproductive Activity." List the following under one of these two headings by determining which would go into our measure of GDP.

a. Mr. X sells his used car to Mr. Y.

b. Joe's used car lot sells a car to Mr. Z and receives a $50 profit for doing so.

c. Merrill Lynch receives a brokerage commision for selling stocks.

d. Mr. Arianas buys 100 shares of AT&T stock.

e. Mrs. Romano cooks and keeps house for her family.

f. Mr. Gonzalez mows his own lawn.

g. Mr. Gonzalez mows lawns for a living.

h. Mr. Smith receives a welfare payment.

i. Mr. Johnson sends his daughter $500 for a semester of studies at College U.

8-5. What happens to the official measure of GDP in each of the following situations?

a. A man marries his housekeeper, who then quits working for wages.

b. A drug addict marries her supplier.

c. Homemakers perform the same jobs but switch houses and charge each other for their services.

8-6. Construct a value-added table for various stages in the production and sale of bread.

8-7. Consider the following table for an economy that produces only four goods.

GOOD	1987 PRICE	1987 QUANTITY	1994 PRICE	1994 QUANTITY
Pizza	$ 4	10	$ 8	12
Cola	12	20	36	15
T-shirts	6	5	10	15
Business equipment	25	10	30	12

Assuming a 1987 base year:

a. What is nominal GDP for 1987 and 1994?

b. What is real GDP for 1987? For 1994?

8-8. Examine the following figures for a hypothetical year.

	BILLIONS OF DOLLARS
Consumption	400
Net exports	−20
Transfer payments	20
Gross investment	100
Social Security contributions	10
Government purchases	120
Net investment	50
Dividends	20
Indirect business taxes	10
Corporate income taxes	30
Personal income taxes	60
Undistributed corporate profits	20

Calculate GDP, NDP, NI, PI, and DI.

COMPUTER-ASSISTED INSTRUCTION
(Complete problem and answer on disk.)

Coal is transformed into steel, steel is turned into a manufactured auto, and a manufactured auto is sold to final buyers. You are required to calculate value added at various stages; in the process it is revealed that the expenditure approach and the income approach to national income accounting yield identical estimates of GDP.

AGGREGATE DEMAND AND AGGREGATE SUPPLY

The shift from a centralized command socialist economy to a decentralized capitalist economy is not easy. Such shifts have created decreases in the living standards of a large number of peoples living in the former Soviet Union and its satellite countries in Eastern Europe. Per capita income appeared to fall by 20 percent in Russia from 1991 to 1993, for example. Proponents of the shift to a market economy, however, contend that in the long run, living standards in these nations will increase dramatically. In the meantime, most of these countries have experienced high rates of inflation, high rates of unemployment, and lower living standards. Will the change from communism to capitalism lead to a better life in the future? Without actually making a prediction, we can use the tools of aggregate demand and supply to analyze the possibilities.

After reading this chapter, you should be able to answer the following questions:

1. Why does the aggregate demand curve slope downward?

2. Why does the short-run aggregate supply curve slope upward?

3. Why is the long-run aggregate supply curve vertical?

4. How can we show improvements in technology using aggregate demand and aggregate supply analysis?

INTRODUCTION

During the month of March 1933 some 12.8 million members of the labor force were unemployed, yielding an unemployment rate of 25.2 percent. During March 1989 the unemployment rate hovered at 5.2 percent. And in March 1993 unemployment had increased to 7.0 percent. The phenomenon of unemployment encompasses more than just the definition you encountered in Chapter 7. Why was the unemployment rate 25.2 percent in 1933 and then 5.2 percent in 1989, only to rise again to 7.0 percent in 1993? During those same years the estimated rate of inflation was a *negative* 5.1 percent (deflation), 4.6 percent, and 3.6 percent, respectively. In Chapter 7 you also learned how government statisticians estimate rates of inflation, but so far there has been no explanation of why rates of inflation differ from one period to another.

Ultimately, questions about what causes changes in the rates of unemployment and inflation are tied to what causes changes in overall economic activity. One measure of that activity that you have learned about is gross domestic product. But *nominal* GDP can mushroom if there is enough inflation, without any increases in *real* output.

In this chapter we are going to develop a way to answer two related questions: What will the level of GDP be, that is, the total level of spending in the economy over a year? And how will any given total level of spending be broken down into its elements, prices and quantities? In Chapters 3 and 4 you saw how demand and supply determined equilibrium prices and quantities for individual goods. In this chapter you will see how analogous (but not identical) concepts work for the total economy too.

SPENDING AND TOTAL EXPENDITURES

As explained in Chapters 7 and 8, nominal GDP is the dollar value of total expenditures on domestically produced final goods and services. Because all expenditures are made by individuals, firms, or governments, the total value of these expenditures must be what each of these market participants decides it shall be. The decisions of individuals, managers of firms, and government officials determine the annual dollar value of total expenditures. You can certainly see this in your role as an individual. You decide what the total value of your expenditures will be in a year. You decide how much you want to spend and how much you want to save. Thus if we want to know what determines the total value of nominal GDP, the answer would be clear: the spending decisions of individuals like you, firms, and local, state, and national governments. In an open economy, we must also include foreign individuals, firms, and governments (foreigners, for short) that decide to spend their money income in the United States.

Simply stating that the dollar value of total expenditures in this country depends on what individuals, firms, governments, and foreigners decide to do really doesn't tell us much, though. Two important issues remain:

1. What determines the total amount that individuals, firms, governments, and foreigners want to spend?
2. What determines whether this spending will result in more goods and services (quantities) or in higher prices (inflation)?

The way we will answer these questions in this chapter is by developing the concepts of *aggregate demand* and *aggregate supply*. **Aggregate demand** is the sum total of all planned expenditures in the economy. **Aggregate supply** is the sum of all planned production in the economy. Given these definitions, we can now proceed to construct an aggregate demand curve and an aggregate supply curve.

▶ **Aggregate demand**
The sum of all planned expenditures for the entire economy.

▶ **Aggregate supply**
The sum of all planned production for the entire economy.

THE AGGREGATE DEMAND CURVE

▶ **Aggregate demand curve**
A curve showing planned purchase rates for all goods and services in the economy at various price levels.

The **aggregate demand curve,** *AD,* gives the various quantities of all final commodities demanded at various price levels.

AGGREGATE DEMAND CURVE

The aggregate demand curve gives the total amount of *real* domestic income that will be purchased at each price level. Real domestic income consists of the output of final goods and services in the economy—everything produced for final use by either businesses or households. This includes stereos, socks, shoes, medical and legal services, videodisc players, and millions of other goods and services that people buy each year. A graphic representation of the aggregate demand curve is seen in Figure 9-1. On the horizontal axis is measured real gross domestic output, or real GDP. For our measure of the price level, we use the GDP price deflator on the vertical axis. The aggregate demand curve is labeled *AD.* If the GDP deflator is 100, aggregate quantity demanded is $6 trillion per year (point *A*). At price level 120 it is $5 trillion per year (point *B*). At price level 130 it is $4 trillion per year (point *C*). The higher the price level, the lower will be the total real output demanded by the economy, everything else remaining constant, as shown by the upward-sloping arrow along *AD* in Figure 9-1. The lower the price level, the higher will be the total real output demanded by the economy, everything else staying constant.

Let's take the year 1992. Looking at U.S. Department of Commerce statistics will reveal the following information:

- Nominal GDP was $5,951.4 billion.
- The price level as measured by GDP deflator was 120.9 (base year 1987, when the index equals 100.)
- Real GDP (output) was $4,922.6 billion in 1987 dollars.

What can we say about 1992? Given the dollar cost of buying goods and services and all of the other factors that go into spending decisions by individuals, firms, governments, and foreigners, the total amount of real domestic output demanded by firms, individuals, governments, and foreigners was $4,922.6 billion in 1992 (in terms of 1987 dollars).

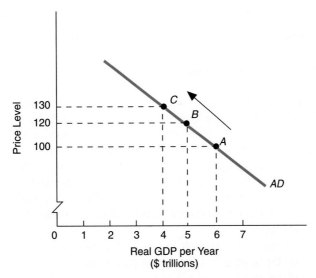

FIGURE 9-1
The aggregate demand curve.
Because of the real-balance, interest rate, and open-economy effects, the aggregate demand curve, *AD,* slopes downward. If the price level is 100, we will be at point *A* with $6 trillion of real GDP demanded per year. As the price level increases to 120 and 130, we will move up the aggregate demand curve to points *B* and *C.*

WHAT HAPPENS WHEN THE PRICE LEVEL RISES?

What if the price level in our economy rose to 160 tomorrow? What would happen to the amount of real goods and services that individuals, firms, governments, and foreigners wish to purchase in the United States? When we asked that question about individual commodities in Chapter 3, the answer was obvious: The quantity demanded would fall if the price went up. Now we are talking about the *price level*—the average price of *all* goods and services in the economy. The answer is still that the total quantities of real goods and services demanded would fall, but the reasons are different. Remember that in Chapter 3, when the price of one good or service went up, the consumer would substitute other goods and services. For the entire economy, when the price level goes up, the consumer doesn't simply substitute one good for another. For now we are dealing with the demand for all goods and services in the entire nation. There are *economywide* reasons that cause the aggregate demand curve to slope downward. They involve at least three distinct forces: the *real-balance effect,* the *interest rate effect,* and the *open-economy effect.*

The Direct Effect: The Real-Balance Effect.

A rise in the price level will have a direct effect on spending. Individuals, firms, governments, and foreigners carry out transactions using money. Money in this context consists of currency and coins that you have in your pocket right now. Because people use money to purchase goods and services, the amount of money that people have influences the amount of goods and services they want to buy. For example, if you found a $10 bill on the sidewalk, the amount of money you had would rise. This would likely have a *direct* effect on the amount of spending in which you would engage. Given your greater level of money balances—currency in this case—you would almost surely increase your spending on goods and services. Similarly, if while on a trip downtown you had your pocket picked, there would be a direct effect on your desired spending. For example, if your wallet had $30 in it when it was stolen, the reduction in your cash balances—in this case currency—would no doubt cause you to reduce your planned expenditures. You would ultimately buy fewer goods and services. This response is sometimes called the **real-balance effect** (or wealth effect) because it relates to the real value of your cash balances. While your nominal cash balances may remain the same, any change in the price level will cause a change in the real value of those cash balances—hence the real-balance effect on the quantity of aggregate goods and services demanded.

> ▌ **Real-balance effect**
> The change in the real value of money balances when the price level changes, all other things held constant. Also called the *wealth effect.*

The Indirect Effect: The Interest Rate Effect.

There is a more subtle, but equally important, *indirect* effect on your desire to spend. As we said before, when the price level goes up, the real value of your money balances declines. You end up with too few real money balances relative to other things that you own. After all, we all own a bit of everything—clothes, money balances, bicycles, cars, compact disc players, and perhaps houses and stocks and bonds. If, because of the price level increase, you find out that you have too few real money balances, you might actually go out to borrow to replenish them. When there are more people going in the front door of lending institutions to borrow money than there are people coming in the back door, as it were, to lend the money, the price of borrowing is going to go up. The price you pay to borrow money is the interest rate you have to pay. Because more people want to borrow now to replenish their real cash balances, interest rates will rise, and this is where the indirect effect—the **interest rate effect**—on total spending comes in.

But higher interest rates make it more costly for people to buy houses and cars. Higher interest rates also make it more costly for firms to install new equipment and to erect new office buildings. Whether we are talking about individuals or firms, the indirect effect of

> ▌ **Interest rate effect**
> The effect on desired spending caused by a change in the price level, said effect that works through resulting changes in the rate of interest. An indirect effect on desired demand due to a change in the price level.

a rise in the price level will cause a higher level of interest rates, which in turn reduces the amount of goods and services that people are willing to purchase when the price level rises. Therefore, an increase in the price level will tend to reduce the quantity of aggregate goods and services demanded. (The opposite occurs if the price level declines.)

The Open-Economy Effect: The Substitution of Foreign Goods. Remember from Chapter 8 that GDP also consists of net exports—the difference between exports and imports. In an open economy, we buy imports from other countries and ultimately pay for them through the foreign exchange market. The same is true for foreigners who purchase our goods (exports). Given any set of exchange rates between the U.S. dollar and other currencies, an increase in the price level in the United States makes American goods more expensive relative to foreign goods. Foreigners have downward-sloping demand curves for American goods. When the relative price of American goods goes up, foreigners buy fewer American goods and more of their own. In America, the cheaper-priced foreign goods now result in Americans wanting to buy more foreign goods rather than American goods. The result is a fall in exports and a rise in imports when the domestic price level rises. That means that a price level increase tends to reduce net exports, thereby reducing the amount of real goods and services purchased in the United States. This is known as the **open-economy effect.**

▶ **Open-economy effect**
The effect on desired spending caused by a change in the price level, said effect that works through resulting changes in the relative price of imports and exports and in their relative quantities demanded.

WHAT HAPPENS WHEN THE PRICE LEVEL FALLS?

What about the reverse? Suppose now that the GDP deflator falls to 100 from an initial level of 120. Once again we have three effects on desired purchases of goods and services; the difference is that now people want to buy more.

The Direct Effect. The decline in the price level *raises* the real value of money balances held by people. This increase in their real wealth induces them to go out to buy more goods and services.

The Indirect Effect. The price level–induced rise in real money balances means that people find themselves with "too many" money balances compared to their other assets such as cars, stereos, TVs, clothes, houses, stocks, and bonds. They therefore want to convert some of these "excess" money balances into other assets. One way they can do this is by lending money to others. If they have outstanding balances on their credit cards, they may pay them off. In both cases the number of people going in the back door of lending institutions willing to lend money has now increased relative to the number of people coming in the front door wanting to borrow money. There is a downward pressure on interest rates. The fall in interest rates lowers the cost of buying such things as cars and houses as well as new equipment and buildings. The interest rate decrease induces individuals to buy more of these things, thereby increasing the desired expenditure level of goods and services in the nation.

The Open-Economy Effect. If we hold the exchange rate constant, a fall in the price level in the United States makes domestic goods less expensive relative to foreign goods. Americans will want to "buy American." At the same time, foreigners will also want to buy American. Imports decline, exports rise, and thus net exports increase. Desired real GDP will go up.

On all three counts, a reduction in the price level induces people to buy more output. The lower the price level, the greater the quantity of output of goods and services demanded. The aggregate demand curve, *AD,* shows the quantity of aggregate output that will be demanded at alternative price levels. It is downward-sloping, as is the demand curve for individual goods. The higher the price level, the lower the quantity of aggregate output demanded, and vice versa.

AGGREGATE DEMAND IS NOT THE SAME AS *INDIVIDUAL* DEMAND

Even though the aggregate demand curve, *AD,* in Figure 9-1 looks quite similar to the individual demand curve, *D,* to which you were introduced in Chapters 3 and 4, it is not the same. When we derive the aggregate demand curve, we are looking at the entire economic system. The total income of the economy is not given as it is when we draw the individual demand curve, *D.* The aggregate demand curve, *AD,* differs from an individual demand curve, *D,* because we are looking at the *entire* circular flow of income and product when we construct *AD.*

SHIFTS IN THE AGGREGATE DEMAND CURVE

In Chapter 3 you learned that any time a nonprice determinant of demand changed, the demand curve shifted inward to the left or outward to the right. The same analysis holds for the aggregate demand curve, except we are now talking about the non-price-level determinants of aggregate demand. So when we ask the question, "What determines the position of the aggregate demand curve?" the fundamental proposition is as follows:

> **Any non-price-level change that increases aggregate spending (on domestic goods) shifts *AD* to the right. Any non-price-level change that decreases aggregate spending (on domestic goods) shifts *AD* to the left.**

The list of potential determinants of the position of the aggregate demand curve is virtually without limit. Some of the most obvious non-price-level determinants of aggregate demand are government spending, taxes, population, and expected future profits. Take changes in population, for example. If population increases, the aggregate demand curve will shift outward to the right. If population decreases, the aggregate demand curve will shift inward to the left, holding all other things constant, of course.

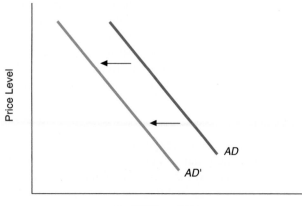

Real GDP per Year

FIGURE 9-2
Aggregate demand curve shift.
Any non-price-level determinant that causes a decrease in total desired aggregate spending will shift the aggregate demand curve from *AD* to *AD'.*

INTERNATIONAL EXAMPLE: The Effects of the Recession in the European Community

The European Community (EC) became a relatively unified single trading block on December 31, 1992. It represents about 360 million consumers in the 12 countries: France, Greece, Germany, Great Britain, Portugal, the Netherlands, Belgium, Spain, Italy, Denmark, Ireland, and Luxembourg. Consumers in those countries buy some American goods, including jeans, California wines, batteries, Hollywood-made movies, and computer software. A recession in the EC would therefore have an effect on aggregate spending in the United States on domestically produced goods. The way we show this is by shifting the aggregate demand curve, *AD*, in to the left. Look at Figure 9-2. There you see the aggregate demand curve shifting from *AD* to *AD'*. *AD* shifts because a non-price-level determinant of aggregate demand has changed. In this particular international example, the non-price determinant was foreigners' income.

For Critical Analysis: It used to be said that when the United States sneezes, Europe gets a cold. The European Community consists of over 360 million consumers. Do you think it is now true that when the EC sneezes, the United States will get a cold? Why or why not? Also, can you show the effect of a bumper agricultural crop in the EC on the U.S. aggregate demand curve? ●

CONCEPTS IN BRIEF

- Aggregate demand is the sum total of all planned expenditures in the economy, and aggregate supply is the sum of all planned production in the economy.
- The aggregate demand curve shows the various quantities of all commodities demanded at various price levels; it is downward-sloping.
- There are three reasons why the aggregate demand curve is downward-sloping: the direct effect, the indirect effect, and the open-economy effect.
- The direct effect, sometimes called the real-balance effect, occurs because price level changes alter the real value of cash balances, thereby directly causing people to desire to spend more or less, depending on whether the price level decreases or increases.
- The indirect, or interest rate, effect is caused via interest rate changes that mimic price level changes. At higher interest rates, people desire to buy fewer houses and cars, and vice versa.
- The open-economy effect occurs because of the substitution toward foreign goods when the domestic price level increases and a shift away from foreign goods when the domestic price level decreases.
- Any non-price-level change that increases aggregate spending on domestic goods shifts the aggregate demand curve to the right.
- Any non-price-level change that decreases aggregate spending on domestic goods shifts the aggregate demand curve to the left.

THE AGGREGATE SUPPLY CURVE

The aggregate demand curve tells us how much output will be demanded given the price level. It also indicates the level to which the price level will gravitate for any *given* total output. Knowing the position and shape of the aggregate demand curve does not tell us anything about how the *total* dollar value of spending will ultimately be divided between output—real goods and services—and prices. To determine this and the equilibrium level of real GDP, we must introduce supply conditions.

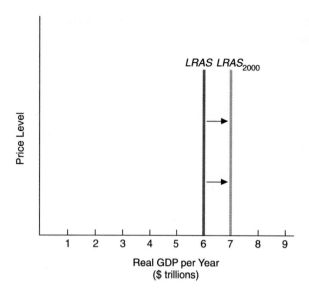

FIGURE 9-3
The long-run aggregate supply curve and shifts in it.
The long-run aggregate supply curve is initially a vertical line at *LRAS* at $6 trillion of real GDP per year. As our endowments increase, the *LRAS* moves outward to *LRAS*$_{2000}$.

When we talk about aggregate supply, we have to distinguish between the long run, when all adjustments to changes in the price level can be made, and the short run, when all adjustments to changes in the price level cannot be made. Therefore, we must derive two different aggregate supply curves.

LONG-RUN AGGREGATE SUPPLY CURVE

Put yourself in a world in which nothing has been changing, year in and year out. The price level has not changed. Technology has not changed. The prices of inputs that firms must purchase have not changed. Labor productivity has not changed. This is a world that is fully adjusted and in which people have all the information they ever are going to get about that world. The **long-run aggregate supply curve,** *LRAS*, in this world is some amount of output of real goods and services, say, $6 trillion of real GDP. We can show long-run aggregate supply simply by a vertical line at $6 trillion of real GDP. This is what you see in Figure 9-3. That curve, labeled *LRAS*, is a vertical line determined by tastes, technology, and the **endowments** of resources that exist in our economy. It is the full-information and full-adjustment level of real output of goods and services. It is the level of real output that will continue being produced year after year, forever, if nothing changes.

To understand why the long-run aggregate supply curve is vertical, think about the long run. The price level has no effect on real output (real GDP per year) because higher output prices will be accompanied by comparable changes in input prices and suppliers will therefore have no incentive to increase or decrease output. Remember that in the long run, everybody has full information and there is full adjustment to price level changes.

What If Non–Price-Level Variables Change?   Clearly, as the years go by, things do change. Population increases, we discover more resources, and we improve technology. That means that over time, at least in a growing economy such as ours, *LRAS* will shift outward to the right in Figure 9-3. We have drawn *LRAS* for the year 2000 to the right of our original *LRAS* of $6 trillion of real GDP. The number we attached to *LRAS*$_{2000}$ is $7 trillion of real GDP, but that is only a guess. The point is that it is to the right of today's LRAS.

▶ **Long-run aggregate supply curve**
A vertical line representing real output of goods and services based on full information and after full adjustment has occurred.

▶ **Endowments**
The various resources in an economy, including both physical resources and such human resources as ingenuity and management skills.

Aggregate Demand and Long-Run Output. Because *LRAS* depends on technology and endowments, aggregate demand in the long run has no bearing on the level of output of real goods and services. Draw any *AD* curve on $LRAS_{2000}$ in Figure 9-3 and you will see that the only thing that changes will be the price level. In the long run, the output of real goods and services is supply-side determined. Only shifts in *LRAS* will change long-run levels of output of real goods and services.

SHORT-RUN AGGREGATE SUPPLY CURVE

▶ **Short-run aggregate supply curve**
The relationship between aggregate supply and the price level in the short run; normally positively sloped.

The **short-run aggregate supply curve,** *SRAS,* represents the relationship between the price level and the real output of goods and services in the economy *without* full adjustment and full information. Just as we drew the supply curve for an individual good or service in Chapter 3 holding everything constant except the price of the good or service, we will do the same here. The short-run aggregate supply curve will be drawn under the assumption that all determinants of aggregate supply other than the price level will be held constant. Most notably, we hold constant the prices of the inputs used in the production of real goods and services. Now, what does this mean? It means that when we hold the prices of the factors of production constant in the short run, as the price level rises, it becomes profitable for all firms to expand production. Otherwise stated, changes in the price level in the short run can affect real output because some production costs might be relatively fixed. Therefore, an increase in the price level increases expected profits.

Why Can Output Be Expanded in the Short Run? In the short run, if the price level rises, output can be expanded (even beyond the economist's notion of the normal capacity of a firm). That is to say, the overall economy can temporarily produce beyond its normal limits or capacity, for a variety of reasons:

1. In the short run, most labor contracts implicitly or explicitly call for flexibility in hours of work at the given wage rate. Therefore, firms can use existing workers more intensively in a variety of ways: They can get them to work harder. They can get them to work more hours per day. And they can get them to work more days per week. Workers can also be switched from *uncounted* production, such as maintenance, to *counted* production, which generates counted output. The distinction between counted and uncounted is simply what is measured in the marketplace, particularly by government statisticians and accountants. If a worker cleans a machine, there is no change in measured output. But if that worker is put on the production line and helps increase the number of units produced each day, measured output will go up. That worker's production has then been counted.
2. Existing capital equipment can be used more intensively. Machines can be worked more hours per day. Some can be made to work at a faster speed. Maintenance can be delayed.
3. Finally, and just as important, if wage rates are held constant, a higher price level means that profits go up, which induces firms to hire more workers. The duration of unemployment falls, and thus the unemployment rate falls. And people who were previously not in the labor force (homemakers and younger or older workers) can be induced to enter.

When Capacity Is Reached. Even if firms want to continue increasing production because the price level has risen, they cannot do this forever. That means that when we hold input prices constant, the extra output that will be forthcoming for reasons 1 through 3 (listed above) must eventually come to an end. Individual workers get tired. Workers are more willing to work one extra weekend than they are eight extra weekends

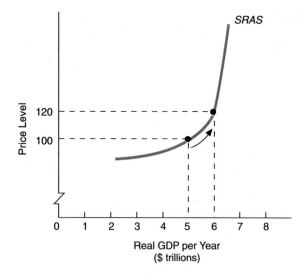

FIGURE 9-4
The short-run aggregate supply curve.
The short-run aggregate supply curve, *SRAS*, slopes upward because with fixed input prices, at a higher price level firms make more profits and desire more output. They use workers and capital more intensively. At price level 100, $5 trillion of real GDP per year is supplied. If the price level rises to 120, $6 trillion of real GDP per year will be supplied.

in a row. Machines cannot go forever without maintenance. Finally, as all firms are hiring more workers from the pool of unemployed, it gets harder (more costly) to find workers at the existing level of wages.

What does all this mean? Simply that the short-run aggregate supply curve at some point must get steeper and steeper.

Graphing the Short-Run Aggregate Supply Curve. Look at Figure 9-4. There you see the short-run aggregate supply curve, *SRAS*. As we have drawn it, after a real GDP of $6 trillion, it starts to become steeper and steeper, and by the time it reaches $7 trillion, it is very steep indeed.[1] If the price index, as represented by the GDP deflator, is 100, the economy will supply $5 trillion per year real GDP in Figure 9-4. If the GDP deflator increases to 120, the economy will move up the *SRAS* to $6 trillion dollars of real GDP per year.

The Difference Between Aggregate and Individual Supply. Although the aggregate supply curve tends to look like the supply curve for an individual commodity, they are not exactly the same. A commodity supply curve reflects a change in the price of an *individual* commodity, whereas the aggregate supply curve shows the effects of changes in the price *level* for the entire economy.

SHIFTS IN THE AGGREGATE SUPPLY CURVE

Just as there were non–price-level factors that could cause a shift in the aggregate demand curve, there are non–price-level factors that can cause a shift in the aggregate supply curve. The analysis here is not quite so simple as the analysis for the non–price-level determi-

---

[1]If there is a maximum short-run amount of output, at some point the *SRAS* becomes vertical. However, there is always some way to squeeze a little bit more out of an economic system, so the *SRAS* does not necessarily have to become vertical, just extremely steep.

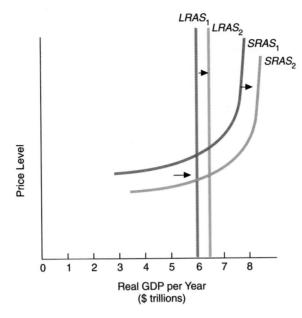

FIGURE 9-5
**Shifts in both short-
and long-run
aggregate supply.**
Initially, the two supply
curves are $SRAS_1$ and
$LRAS_1$. Now consider a
big oil find in Ten-
nessee in an area
where no one thought
oil existed. This shifts
$LRAS_1$ to $LRAS_2$ at
$6.5 trillion of real
GDP. $SRAS_1$ also shifts
outward horizontally
to $SRAS_2$.

nants for aggregate demand, for here we are dealing with both the short run and the long run—*SRAS* and *LRAS*. Still, anything other than the price level that affects supply will shift aggregate supply curves.

SHIFTS IN BOTH SHORT- AND LONG-RUN AGGREGATE SUPPLY

There is a core class of events that causes a shift in both the short-run aggregate supply curve and the long-run aggregate supply curve. These include any change in our endowments of the factors of production.[2] Any change in land, labor, or capital will shift *SRAS* and *LRAS*. Furthermore, any change in the level of our technology or knowledge will also shift *SRAS* and *LRAS*. Look at Figure 9-5. Initially, the two curves are $SRAS_1$ and $LRAS_1$. Now consider a big oil discovery in Tennessee in an area where no one thought oil existed. This shifts $LRAS_1$ to $LRAS_2$ at $6.5 trillion of real GDP. $SRAS_1$ also shifts outward horizontally to $SRAS_2$.

SHIFTS IN *SRAS* Only

Some events, particularly those that are short-lived, will temporarily shift *SRAS* but not *LRAS*. One of the most obvious is a temporary shift in input prices, particularly those caused by external events that are not expected to last forever. Consider the possibility of an announced 90-day embargo of oil from the Middle East to the United States. Oil is an important input in many production activities. The 90-day oil embargo will cause at least

---

[2]There is a complication here. A big enough increase in natural resources not only shifts aggregate supply outward, but also affects aggregate demand. Aggregate demand is a function of people's wealth, among other things. A big oil discovery in America will make enough people richer that desired total spending will increase. For the sake of simplicity, we ignore this complication.

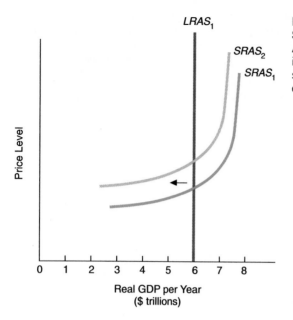

FIGURE 9-6
Shifts in *SRAS* only.
A temporary increase in an input price will shift the short-run aggregate supply curve from $SRAS_1$ to $SRAS_2$.

a temporary increase in the price of this input. You can see what happens in Figure 9-6. *LRAS* remains fixed, but $SRAS_1$ shifts to $SRAS_2$ to take account of the increase in input prices—the higher price of oil. This is because the rise in costs at each level of real GDP per year requires a higher price level to cover those costs plus a profit.

CONCEPTS IN BRIEF

- The long-run aggregate supply curve, *LRAS*, is a vertical line determined by technology and endowments of natural resources in an economy. It is the full-information and full-adjustment level of real output of goods and services. In the long run, the price level has no effect on real GDP per year.
- If population increases, more resources are discovered, or technology improves, *LRAS* will shift outward to the right.
- The short-run aggregate supply curve, *SRAS*, shows the relationship between the price level and the real output of goods and services in the economy without full adjustment or full information. It is upward-sloping.
- Output can be expanded in the short run because firms can use existing workers and capital equipment more intensively. Also, in the short run, when input prices are fixed, a higher price level means higher profits, which induces firms to hire more workers.
- Any change in land, labor, or capital will shift both *SRAS* and *LRAS*. A temporary shift in input prices, however, will shift only *SRAS*.

EQUILIBRIUM

As you discovered in Chapter 3, equilibrium occurs where demand and supply curves intersect. It is a little more complicated here because we have two types of aggregate supply curves, long-run and short-run. Let's look first at short-run equilibrium, which can be almost anywhere. It occurs at the intersection of aggregate demand, *AD*, and short-run aggregate supply, *SRAS*, as shown in Figure 9-7. The equilibrium price level is 120 and the equilibrium annual level of real GDP is $6 trillion. If the price level increased to 140,

FIGURE 9-7
Equilibrium.
Equilibrium will occur where the aggregate demand curve intersects the short-run aggregate supply curve and the long-run aggregate supply curve. In this diagram it is at price level 120 and a real GDP of $6 trillion per year.

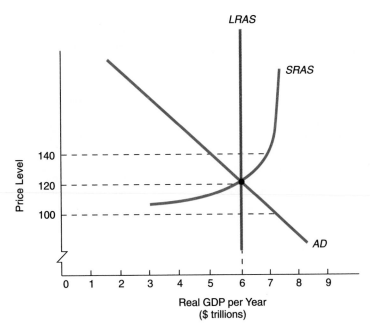

there would be an excess quantity of real goods and services supplied in the entire economy, and the price level would tend to fall. If the price level were 100, aggregate quantity demanded would be greater than aggregate quantity supplied, and buyers would bid up prices so that the price level would move toward 120.

In Figure 9-7 you see that we have drawn the long-run aggregate supply curve, *LRAS*, so that there is full equilibrium in both the short run and the long run at price level 120. At price level 120 this economy can operate forever at $6 trillion without the price level changing.

In the short run, it is possible for us to be on *SRAS* to the right and above the intersection with *AD* and *LRAS*. Why? Because more can be squeezed out of the economy in the short run than would occur in the long-run, full-information, full-adjustment situation. Although a real GDP in this economy greater than $6 trillion per year is possible, it is not consistent with long-run aggregate supply. Firms would be operating beyond long-run desired capacity, and inputs would be working too long and too hard for too little money. Input prices would begin to rise. When this happens, we can no longer stay with the same *SRAS*, because it was drawn with input prices held constant.

If the economy finds itself on *SRAS* below and to the left of the intersection of *AD* and *LRAS*, the opposite will occur. Firms are operating well below long-run capacity, and there are too many unemployed inputs. Input prices will begin to fall. We can no longer stay with the same *SRAS* because it was drawn with constant input prices. *SRAS* will shift down.

CONSEQUENCES OF CHANGES IN AGGREGATE SUPPLY AND DEMAND

▶ **Aggregate demand shock**
Any shock that causes the aggregate demand curve to shift inward or outward.

▶ **Aggregate supply shock**
Any shock that causes the aggregate supply curve to shift inward or outward.

We now have a basic model of the entire economy. We can trace the movement of the equilibrium price level and the equilibrium real GDP when there are shocks to the economy. Whenever there is a shift in our economy's curves, the equilibrium price level or real GDP level (or both) may change. These shifts are called **aggregate demand shocks** on the demand side and **aggregate supply shocks** on the supply side, and we shall focus chiefly on *unanticipated* shifts.

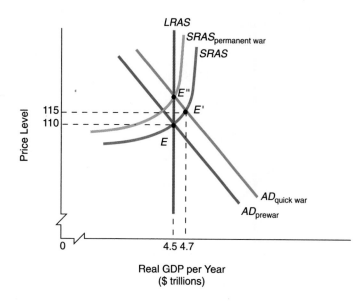

FIGURE 9-8
Effects of war on equilibrium.
A quick temporary war will shift aggregate demand to $AD_{\text{quick war}}$. Equilibrium will move E to E'. If the war becomes permanent, though, $SRAS$ eventuallly will move to $SRAS_{\text{permanent war}}$, and equilibrium will be E''—a higher price level at the same real GDP per year as before the permanent war.

⭐ EXAMPLE: The Persian Gulf War

To show what happens to the equilibrium price level and the equilibrium real GDP level with an aggregate demand shock, consider a quick war, such as the one that occurred in the Persian Gulf from August 1990 through early 1991. Look at Figure 9-8. There you see the equilibrium price level of 110 and the equilibrium real GDP of $4.5 trillion at the long-run aggregate supply curve. (This is not historically accurate, because the American economy was already in a recession at that time.) The quick war shifts aggregate demand from AD_{prewar} to $AD_{\text{quick war}}$. Equilibrium moves from E to E'. The price level moves from 110 to 115. The short-run equilibrium real GDP moves to $4.7 trillion per year. Clearly, if the war were to continue for very long, the $SRAS$ curve would shift up vertically, and the equilibrium level of real GDP would fall at the higher price level. But if it is a quick war, which the Persian Gulf War was, $AD_{\text{quick war}}$ will shift back down to AD_{prewar}. The price level will fall, and the equilibrium level of real GDP will drop back down to its original level.

Several points are worth mentioning with this example. The first is that government spending for the short war caused AD to shift outward to the right. In actuality, our allies paid us for most of our expenses in the war; this clearly increased the level of national spending. Second, the quick war clearly pushed us above long-run aggregate supply—above the level at which the economy would work permanently year in and year out with full information and full adjustment. Third, if the war were to become permanent, the economy would simply experience a higher price level with no change in long-run aggregate supply and therefore no change in the long-run equilibrium level of real GDP per year. If there is a permanent war, $SRAS$ would simply move to $SRAS_{\text{permanent war}}$. Finally, the example illustrates the difference between an unanticipated transitory shock and a permanent one. If the war is quick and unanticipated, it can temporarily cause the equilibrium level of real GDP to rise. If it becomes anticipated, the only thing that happens in this model is that the price level will increase.

For Critical Analysis: In spite of the Persian Gulf War, the American economy did not pull out of its recession for many months thereafter. Does this mean that our analysis is flawed? Why or why not? ●

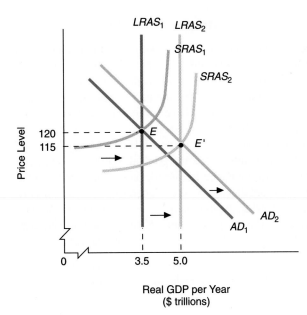

FIGURE 9-9
Changes in the long-run aggregate supply curve. Massive technological changes in the computer world have shifted long-run aggregate supply from $LRAS_1$ to $LRAS_2$. Short-run aggregate supply has also shifted from $SRAS_1$ to $SRAS_2$. Aggregate demand has increased from AD_1 to AD_2. Equilibrium moves from E to E', with the price level falling somewhat and real GDP per year increasing from $3.5 trillion to $5 trillion per year.

CHANGES IN THE LONG-RUN AGGREGATE SUPPLY CURVE

Anything that changes our endowments of land, labor, and capital or alters our technology or knowledge will shift the long-run aggregate supply curve. By looking at two examples, we can demonstrate what happens in a nation when this occurs.

⭐ EXAMPLE: Massive Technological Change: The Computer Industry

We already pointed out in Chapter 3 what has occurred to the cost of computing power in the United States. It has dropped from over $1,000 per unit[3] to an anticipated 50 cents per unit or less in 1995. The effect of this increase in technology can be modeled using our aggregate demand–aggregate supply curve analysis. Look at Figure 9-9. There you see the long-run aggregate supply curve before computers, $LRAS_1$. The aggregate demand curve is AD_1. The equilibrium price level is 120. The equilibrium level of real GDP was $3.5 trillion per year. Over a 30-year period, $LRAS$ shifts out to $LRAS_2$. In the long run, the economy can operate at $5 trillion of real GDP per year. This change, in part due to the computer revolution, was not unanticipated; in fact, it is a permanent feature of our landscape now. Computing power is an important input into the cost of doing business these days. Because its price has fallen, the short-run aggregate supply curve has shifted from $SRAS_1$ to $SRAS_2$. Population has grown in the meantime, and so have wealth and a variety of other factors. So AD shifts from AD_1 to AD_2. Final equilibrium is at $5 trillion of real GDP at a price level of 115, or slightly lower than what it was before the computer revolution. This analysis is done holding all other things constant. In reality, all things were not constant, and the price level actually rose over this time period. But it would have risen even higher were it not for the tremendous reduction in computing costs.

For Critical Analysis: *What would have happened to the price level had the aggregate demand curve not shifted outward to the right?* ●

---

[3]Unit = millions of instructions per second (MIPS).

⭐ EXAMPLE: The Entry of Women into the Labor Force

Just prior to World War II, the labor force participation rate of women in the United States was around 30 percent. In 1960 it was 36.5 percent; today it is over 55 percent. This constitutes a dramatic change in the labor force over the past half century. Clearly, the long-run aggregate supply curve cannot remain constant with such an increase in our endowment of labor. The same diagram that was used for massive technological change in the computer industry can be used to show the effects of the massive entry of women into the labor force. The increase in female labor participation shifts $LRAS_1$ to $LRAS_2$ in Figure 9-9. Over this period, because this is a fully anticipated and gradual change, the short-run aggregate supply curve cannot remain constant either. In essence, labor costs are less than they would have been otherwise with a smaller labor force. Therefore, $SRAS_1$ shifts to $SRAS_2$. At the same time, because of growing population and wealth, aggregate demand shifts from AD_1 to AD_2. The price level drops slightly from 120 to 115, and the equilibrium level of real GDP rises from $3.5 trillion per year to $5.0 trillion per year.

For Critical Analysis: In Chapter 7 you read that the labor force has grown relatively slowly or not at all in the 1990s. Show this using aggregate demand and aggregate supply analysis. ●

CONCEPTS IN BRIEF

- Equilibrium occurs at the intersection of the aggregate demand curve, AD, the short-run aggregate supply curve, $SRAS$, and the long-run aggregate supply curve, $LRAS$.
- Unanticipated shifts in aggregate demand are called aggregate demand shocks.
- Unanticipated shifts in aggregate supply are called aggregate supply shocks.

WILL THE CHANGE FROM COMMUNISM TO CAPITALISM MAKE MUCH DIFFERENCE IN LIVING STANDARDS?

Concepts Applied: Long-run aggregate supply, short-run aggregate supply, aggregate demand

This makeshift market for fruits and vegetables in St. Petersburg (formerly Leningrad) is just the start of the movement from communism to capitalism.

After the fall of communism in the Soviet Union and Eastern Europe, most of those countries suffered from increased poverty, lower per capita real income, high inflation rates, and assorted other economic disasters. For example, in Russia, the largest of the ex-Soviet republics, per capita real income was estimated to have

fallen by 20 percent from 1991 to 1992. The rate of inflation was at times over 2,000 percent. Although standards of living have improved in these former communist countries recently, the situation is not yet stable and in most cases not as good as it was under the best years of communism.

GRAPHING THE SITUATION   We graph the situation in Poland in Figure 9-10. Prior to the demise of communism, we assume that the price level is at 100 and that long-run aggregate supply, $LRAS_1$, is at \$500 billion of real GDP per year. Short-run aggregate supply is $SRAS_1$, and aggregate demand is AD_1. Equilibrium is at E. After communism's demise, a number of things happened. Unemployment shot up. Factories closed. Trade with the rest of the world almost stopped. Foreign investment dried up. As a result:

1. $LRAS$ shifted inward to \$400 billion of real GDP per year, to $LRAS_2$.

2. $SRAS$ shifted to $SRAS_2$ because everything cost more, particularly all of the tools and supplies that had to be bought from other countries.

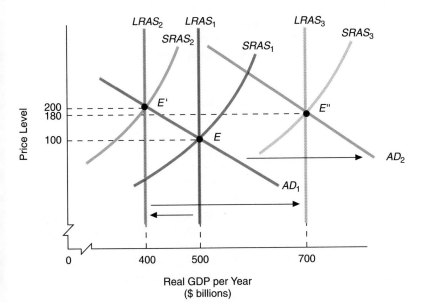

FIGURE 9-10

The shift from communism to capitalism in Poland.
Initial equilibrium is at E with $LRAS_1$ and AD_1. During the transition to capitalism, long-run aggregate supply shifts to $LRAS_2$ and short-run aggregate supply shifts to $SRAS_2$. Equilibrium moves to E' at a reduced real GDP per year at a higher price level. It is hoped that eventually equilibrium will be at E'' with increased real GDP per year and a lower price level.

3. There was inflation, as shown by an increase in the price level to 200, and real GDP fell. Clearly, living standards dropped for many people in Poland.

4. Equilibrium moved to E'.

AFTER CAPITALISM HAS BECOME ESTABLISHED

The growth of capitalism in Poland leads to an increase in its domestic capital stock. Foreigners also bring capital from abroad to add to Poland's capital stock. The labor force gets more training. Long-run aggregate supply shifts to $LRAS_3$. As wealth increases, the final equilibrium, E'', shows an increase in aggregate demand because of increased wealth and perhaps immigration of workers from neighboring poorer countries. So AD_1 shifts to AD_2. As input costs start to fall, the short-run aggregate supply eventually shifts to $SRAS_3$. Long-run equilibrium is at a price level of 150 and a real GDP of $700 billion per year.

THE COSTS DURING TRANSITION Certainly, Poland is nowhere near its final long-run equilibrium at E'' in Figure 9-10. But it and all of the other countries that are facing the costs of transition to capitalism do believe that there is a better life on the horizon. Countries that used to have command economies are finding transition periods difficult, as evidenced by skyrocketing prices, high unemployment, and low productivity.

Data from Poland do seem to indicate that our analysis is correct. Industrial production dropped almost 40 percent in 1990 and 1991 but increased 3 percent in 1992 and an estimated 5 percent in 1993. Gross domestic product fell in 1990 and was still below its 1989 level in 1991 but surpassed that level in 1992 and 1993.

FOR CRITICAL ANALYSIS

1. What are the forces that will cause $LRAS_2$ to move outward to $LRAS_3$? In other words, why do we believe that the long-run aggregate supply curve for Poland will eventually exceed the long-run aggregate supply curve that existed under command socialism?

2. Who should bear the costs of transition from command socialism to capitalism, and why?

CHAPTER SUMMARY

1. Aggregate demand is the sum total of all planned expenditures on final goods and services, and aggregate supply is the sum total of all planned production.

2. The aggregate demand curve gives the various quantities of all commodities demanded at various price levels. It slopes upward because of the real-balance effect, the interest rate effect, and the open-economy effect.

3. Aggregate demand is not the same thing as individual demand because individual demand curves are drawn holding income, among other things, constant. The aggregate demand curve reflects the entire circular flow of income and product.

4. Any non–price-level change that increases aggregate spending on domestic goods shifts the aggregate demand curve to the right. Any non–price-level change that decreases aggregate spending on domestic goods shifts the aggregate demand curve to the left.

5. There are two aggregate supply curves. The long-run aggregate supply curve is a vertical line the location of which depends on tastes, technology, and endowments of natural resources; it assumes full information and full adjustment. The short-run aggregate supply curve is drawn without full information and full adjustment and slopes upward, but it is not vertical.

6. Output can be expanded in the short run because firms can work both capital and labor more intensively and because firms with fixed input prices experience higher profits as the price level increases and therefore desire to hire more workers. The closer to capacity the economy is running, the steeper the short-run aggregate supply curve becomes.

7. There are events that shift both the long-run and short-run aggregate curves simultaneously. These include any change in the endowments of factors of production (land, labor, or capital). A temporary change in the input price, by contrast, shifts only the short-run aggregate supply curve.

8. Equilibrium occurs at the intersection of aggregate demand, short-run aggregate supply, and long-run aggregate supply.

9. The economy may experience shifts in aggregate demand and supply, called aggregate demand shocks and aggregate supply shocks. The results of such shocks on the equilibrium level of real output depend on the time period under study and other factors.

DISCUSSION OF PREVIEW POINTS

1. Why does the aggregate demand curve slope downward?

There are three reasons for believing that the quantity demanded for real output rises as the price level falls, and vice versa. A decrease in the price level leads to higher *real* money balances, all other things held constant. This increased real wealth causes a direct effect on consumers' spending decisions. There is an indirect effect via interest rates, which move with price level changes. As the price level falls, the interest rate will fall, and consumers will want to spend more on houses and cars. Finally, in an open economy, if the price level falls, Americans will want to spend more on domestic goods, and foreigners will want to buy more of our goods.

2. Why does the short-run aggregate supply curve slope upward?

As the price level increases, firms presumably face fixed input prices in the short run. Their profits go up, and they have an incentive to increase real output. They do so by working their labor force and their capital equipment more intensively, thereby generating more output.

3. Why is the long-run aggregate supply curve vertical?

The definition of the long-run aggregate supply curve is the amount of real output of goods and services that will be produced in the long run with full information and full adjustment. With full information and full adjustment, changes in the price level do not affect real output. Real output is solely a function of tastes, technology, and endowments of land, labor, and capital. Hence the long-run aggregate supply curve is a vertical line.

4. How can we show improvements in technology using aggregate demand and aggregate supply analysis?

Improvements in technology shift both the long-run aggregate supply curve and the short-run aggregate supply curve outward. Essentially, you can show this using aggregate supply and aggregate demand analysis by drawing the curves that are shown in Figure 9-5.

PROBLEMS

(Answers to the odd-numbered problems appear at the back of the book.)

9-1. Given the curves in the graph below, discuss why the equilibrium price level will be at P_e and not at P_1 or P_2.

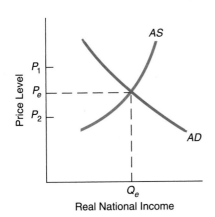

9-2. In the discussion of why the *AD* curve slopes downward from left to right, notice that nothing was said about what happens to the quantity demanded for real output when the price level rises and causes wealth to fall for people in businesses who own mortgages on houses and buildings. Why not? (Hint: What is the *net* effect to the whole economy when the price level rises and causes a wealth loss to lenders who get paid back in fixed nominal dollars?)

9-3. Distinguish between short-run and long-run supply curves.

9-4. How is aggregate demand affected when the price level in *other* economies decreases? What happens to aggregate demand when the price level in *this* economy falls?

9-5.   Suppose that aggregate supply decreases while aggregate demand is held constant.
   a. What happens to the price level?
   b. What happens to national output?

*9-6.   The aggregate demand and aggregate supply schedules are given by $P = \$5 - .002Q_d$ and $P = \$2 + .003Q_s$, respectively. What are the equilibrium values for Q and P?

---

*Asterisked problems are optional; algebra is required.

COMPUTER-ASSISTED INSTRUCTION
(Complete problem and answer on disk.)

When the price level falls, what happens to (1) mortgage owners and (2) holders of $1,000 bills? The differential impact of a lower price level on these two groups helps explain the real-balance effect. That effect can in turn help explain a negatively sloped aggregate demand curve.

10

DESIRED AGGREGATE DEMAND

For any given year in your life, you earn some amount of income. You have two choices during the year concerning that income: You can spend it or save it. A trade-off exists: The more you save today, the more you will have tomorrow. In the past few years, the trade-off that Americans collectively have made seems to be in favor of more spending and less saving. A major policy issue involves the question of whether the saving rate is too low in the United States. That issue is part of the larger picture dealing with desired aggregate demand.

After reading this chapter, you should be able to answer the following questions:

1. Why do Keynesian economists believe that the short-run aggregate supply curve is horizontal?

2. Why is real GDP said to be demand-determined when the short-run aggregate supply curve is horizontal?

3. How are saving, consumption, and income related in a closed private economy?

4. What are the determinants of investment?

INTRODUCTION

During your working life, you may experience one or more periods of unemployment. You might be permanently fired, be temporarily laid off and then rehired at some later date, or quit. The number of people who are unemployed for whatever reason varies over time. Our economy can experience periods of recession and even depression. Just as medical researchers would like to discover what causes cancer, economists have attempted to model the causes of fluctuations in employment, output, and prices. In Chapter 9 you were exposed to the aggregate demand and aggregate supply model of our macroeconomy. In particular, you looked at the macroeconomy in terms of aggregate supply and aggregate demand, which related equilibrium aggregate output to different price levels. In this chapter we go into the reasons why individuals and businesses desire to spend different amounts of money income at different times in the business cycle. We want eventually to come up with a model that helps explain what causes an individual or a business to consume, save, or invest.

THE CLASSICAL MODEL

The classical model, which traces its origins to the 1770s, was the first systematic attempt to explain the determinants of the price level and the national levels of output, income, employment, consumption, saving, and investment. The term *classical model* was coined by John Maynard Keynes, a Cambridge University economist, who used the term to refer to the way in which earlier economists had analyzed economic aggregates. Classical economists—Adam Smith, J. B. Say, David Ricardo, John Stuart Mill, Thomas Malthus, and others—wrote from the 1770s to the 1870s. They assumed, among other things, that all wages and prices were flexible and that competitive markets existed throughout the economy. Starting in the 1870s, so-called neoclassical economists, including Alfred Marshall, introduced a mathematical approach that allowed them to refine earlier economists' models.

SAY'S LAW

Every time you produce something for which you receive income, you generate the income necessary to make expenditures on other goods and services. That means that an economy producing $7 trillion of GDP (final goods and services) simultaneously produces the income with which these goods and services can be supplied. As an accounting identity, *actual* aggregate income always equals *actual* aggregate expenditures. Classical economists took this accounting identity one step further by arguing that total national supply creates its own demand. They asserted what has become known as **Say's law:**

> Supply creates its own demand; hence *desired* expenditures will equal *actual* expenditures.

▶ **Say's law**
A dictum of J.B. Say that supply creates its own demand; producing goods and services generates the means and the willingness to purchase other goods and services.

What does Say's law really mean? It states that the very process of producing specific goods (supply) is proof that other goods are desired (demand). People produce more goods than they want for their own use only if they seek to trade them for other goods. Someone offers to supply something only because he or she has a demand for something else. The implication of this, according to Say, is that no general glut, or overproduction, is possible in a market economy. From this reasoning, it seems to follow that full employment of labor and other resources would be the normal state of affairs in such an economy.

Underlying Say's law is the premise that wants are unlimited and, further, that the primary goal of economic activity is consumption for oneself or one's family, either in the present or in the future. If a more or less self-sufficient family wants to increase its consumption, it can do so by producing more and trading off its surplus of one good in order to get more of another good.

All this seems reasonable enough in a simple barter economy in which households produce most of the goods they need and trade for the rest. This is shown in Figure 10-1, where there is a simple circular flow. But what about a more sophisticated economy in which people work for others and there is no barter but rather the use of money? Can these complications create the possibility of unemployment? And does the fact that laborers receive money income, some of which can be saved, lead to unemployment? No, said the classical economists to these two questions. They based their reasoning on a number of key assumptions.

ASSUMPTIONS OF THE CLASSICAL MODEL

The classical model makes four major assumptions:

1. **Pure competition exists.** No single buyer or seller of a commodity or an input can affect its price.
2. **Wages and prices are flexible.** The assumption of pure competition leads to the notion that prices, wages, interest rates, and the like are free to move to whatever level supply and demand dictate (in the long run). Although no *individual* buyer can set a price, the community of buyers or sellers can cause prices to rise or to fall to an equilibrium level.
3. **People are motivated by self-interest.** Businesses want to maximize their profits, and households want to maximize their economic well-being.
4. **People cannot be fooled by money illusion.** Buyers and sellers react to changes in relative prices. That is to say, they do not suffer from **money illusion.** For example, a worker will not be fooled into thinking that he or she is better off by a doubling of wages if the price level has also doubled during the same time period.

> **Money illusion**
> Reacting to changes in money prices rather than relative prices. If a worker whose wages double when the price level also doubles thinks he or she is better off, the worker is suffering from money illusion.

THE PROBLEM WITH SAVING

When some income is saved, it is not reflected in product demand. It is a type of *leakage* in the circular flow of income and output because saving is a withdrawal of funds from the income stream. Consumption expenditures can fall short of total output now. In such a situation, it does not appear that supply necessarily creates its own demand.

FIGURE 10-1

Say's law and the circular flow.
Here we show the circular flow of income and output. The very act of supplying a certain level of goods and services necessarily equals the level of goods and services demanded, in Say's simplified world.

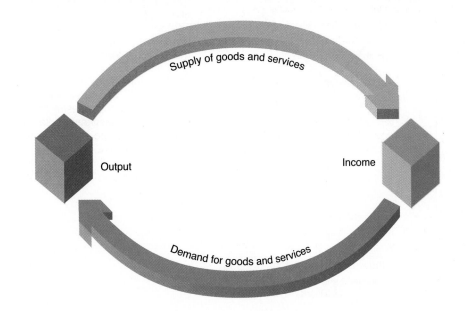

The classical economists did not believe that the complicating factor of saving in the circular flow of income and output model was a problem. They contended that each dollar saved would be invested by businesses so that the leakage of saving would be matched by the injection of business investment. *Investment* here refers only to additions to the nation's capital stock. The classical economists believed that businesses as a group would intend to invest as much as households wanted to save. Equilibrium between the saving plans of consumers and the investment plans of businesses comes about, in the classical economists' world, through the working of the credit market. In the credit market, the *price* of credit is the interest rate. At equilibrium, the price of credit—the interest rate—is such that the quantity of credit demanded equals the quantity of credit supplied. Planned investment just equals planned saving, for saving represents the supply of credit and investment represents the demand for credit.

The Interest Rate: Equating Desired Saving and Investment. In Figure 10-2 the vertical axis measures the rate of interest in percentage terms; on the horizontal axis are the quantities of desired saving and desired investment per unit time period. The desired saving curve is really a supply curve of saving. It shows how much individuals and businesses wish to save at various interest rates. People wish to save more at higher interest rates than at lower interest rates.

Investment, primarily desired by businesses, responds in a predictable way. The higher the rate of interest, the more expensive it is to invest, and the lower the level of desired investment. The desired investment curve slopes downward, like all demand curves. In this simplified model, the equilibrium rate of interest is 10 percent, and the equilibrium quantity of saving and investment is $700 billion per year.

 EXAMPLE: The Development of Pawnshops

When we talk about the interest rate, we assume that it is determined by the intersection of the supply of (credit) saving with the demand for credit (investment). Working within

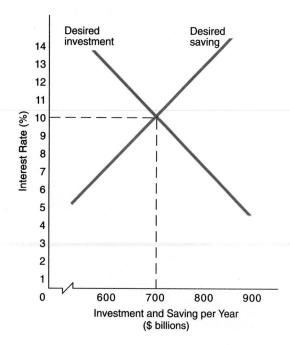

FIGURE 10-2
Equating desired saving and investment in the classical model.
The demand curve for investment is labeled "Desired investment." The supply of resources used for investment occurs when individuals do not consume but save instead. The desired saving curve is shown as an upward-sloping supply curve of saving. The equilibrating force here is, of course, the interest rate. At higher interest rates, people desire to save more. But at higher interest rates, businesses demand less investment because it is more expensive to invest. In this model, at an interest rate of 10 percent, the quantity of investment desired just equals the quantity of saving desired (supply), which is $700 billion per year.

the overall economy are many separate markets, all of which affect the market rate of interest. One such institution is the pawnshop: it extends very small loans (in the range of $50 to $75) with very short maturities. People leave their personal property, such as jewelry or musical instruments, and ultimately pay rates of interest that are very high, anywhere from 30 to 240 percent per year! Pawnshops have been around for hundreds of years. One of the most famous frequenter of pawnshops was the nineteenth-century Russian author Fyodor Dostoyevsky who wrote *Crime and Punishment* and *The Brothers Karamazov,* among other works. He got his ideas for many of his down-and-out characters from visiting these places.

The pawnshop industry has been in decline in most parts of the world. In Great Britain in 1900 there were 3,000 pawnshops; in the 1990s there are fewer than 150. In the United States, however, the pawnshop business actually grew during the same time period, from under 2,000 to more than 7,000 today. Pawnshops in this country currently make about 40 million loans a year with an aggregate dollar amount over $1 billion. Most of these pawnshops are in the Southeast and Rocky Mountain areas. One of the reasons for the growth of pawnshops is that many states have relaxed their restrictions (called *usury laws*) on the maximum interest rates that can be charged. Pawnshops in these states can now legally charge the high rates needed to stay in business. Furthermore, the percentage of U.S. citizens classified as low-income has risen in recent decades. These individuals cannot get loans from mainstream financial institutions, such as banks and savings and loan associations, and so must turn to alternatives, one of which is the pawnshop.

For Critical Analysis: Because pawnshops charge very high rates of interest, some legislators have attempted to outlaw them. Who would be affected by such restrictions, and in what ways? ●

Unemployment.   If the world is as modeled by the classical economists, only voluntary unemployment exists. That is to say, labor is just like any other good or service. If an excess quantity is supplied at a particular wage level, the wage level is too high. By accepting lower wages, unemployed workers will quickly be put back to work. We show equilibrium in the labor market in Figure 10-3.

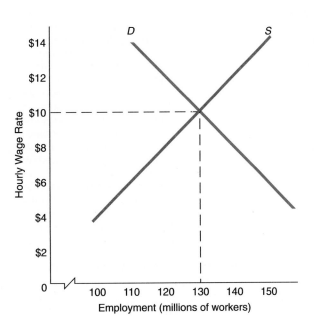

FIGURE 10-3
Equilibrium in the labor market.
The demand for labor is downward-sloping; at higher wage rates, firms will employ fewer workers. The supply of labor is upward-sloping; at higher wage rates, more workers will work longer and more people will be willing to work. The equilibrium wage rate is $10 with an equilibrium employment per year of 130 million workers.

CLASSICAL THEORY, VERTICAL AGGREGATE SUPPLY, AND THE PRICE LEVEL

In the classical mold of reasoning, long-term involuntary unemployment is impossible. Say's law, coupled with flexible interest rates, prices, and wages, would always tend to keep workers fully employed so that the aggregate supply curve, as shown in Figure 10-4, is vertical at Q_0. We have labeled the supply curve *LRAS*, consistent with the long-run aggregate supply curve introduced in Chapter 9. It was defined there as the quantity of output that would be produced in an economy with full information and full adjustment of wages and prices year in and year out. In the classical model, this happens to be the *only* aggregate supply curve that exists in equilibrium. Everything adjusts so fast that we are essentially always quickly moving toward *LRAS*. Furthermore, because the labor market is working well, Q_0 is always at, or soon to be at, **full employment.** Here full employment is defined as the amount of employment that would exist year in and year out if all adults in the economy, particularly those in the labor market, fully anticipated any inflation or deflation that was occurring. Full employment does not mean zero unemployment because there is always some frictional unemployment (discussed in Chapter 7), even in the classical world. Full employment exists in the sense that the number of jobs and the number of workers are equated at the going wage rate.

In this model, any change in aggregate demand will soon cause a change in the price level. Consider starting at E, at price level 100. If the aggregate demand shifts to AD', at price level 100, output would increase to Q_1. But that is greater than the full-employment level of output of real GDP, Q_0. The economy will attempt to get to point A, but because this is beyond full employment, prices will rise, and the economy will find itself back on the vertical *LRAS* at point E' at a higher price level, 110. The price level will increase at output rates in excess of the full-employment level of output because employers will end up bidding up wages for now relatively scarce workers. In addition, factories will be bidding up the price of other inputs at this greater-than-full-employment rate of output.

A decrease in aggregate demand can be shown similarly (but is not drawn in). A reduction in the price level quickly ensues, where the new *AD* intersects the vertical *LRAS*.

▶ **Full employment**
The amount of employment that would exist year in and year out if everybody in the economy fully anticipated any inflation or deflation that was occurring.

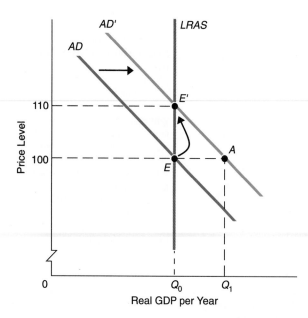

FIGURE 10-4
Classical theory and increases in aggregate demand.
The classical theorists believed that Say's law, flexible interest rates, prices, and wages would always lead to full employment at Q_0 such that the aggregate supply curve, *LRAS*, was vertical. With aggregate demand, *AD*, the price level is 100. An increase in aggregate demand shifts *AD* to *AD'*. At price level 100, the quantity of real GDP per year demanded is A on AD', or Q_1. But this is greater than at full employment. Prices rise, and the economy eventually moves from E to E' at the higher price level of 110.

The level of real GDP per year clearly does not depend on any changes in aggregate demand. Hence we say that in the classical model, the equilibrium level of real GDP per year is completely *supply-determined*. Changes in aggregate demand change only the price level, not the output of real goods and services.

CONCEPTS IN BRIEF

- Say's law states that supply creates its own demand. In a barter economy, the very fact that households produce more goods than they can use is proof that other goods are desired because people produce more goods than they wish to consume only when they want to trade them for other goods. Hence there can be no glut, or overproduction.
- The assumptions of the classical model are (1) pure competition, (2) wage and price flexibility in the long run, (3) self-interest motivation throughout the economy, and (4) no money illusion, defined as a change in individual behavior in response to changes in nominal rather than real values.
- Saving in the classical model represents a leakage. Classical economists believed that it would be offset by the injection of investment and that planned saving and planned investment would be equated in the credit market via the process of changes in the interest rate, which is simply the price of credit. Saving represents the supply of credit, and investment represents the demand for credit.
- In the classical model, Say's law, coupled with flexible interest rates, prices, and wages, creates a long-run aggregate supply curve that is vertical at the full-employment rate of output. Any shift in aggregate demand soon leads to a corresponding change in the price level without changing the full-employment level of output.

KEYNESIAN ECONOMICS AND THE KEYNESIAN SHORT-RUN AGGREGATE SUPPLY CURVE

The classical economists' world was one of fully utilized resources.[1] There would be no unused capacity and no unemployment. However, post–World War I Europe entered a period of long-term economic decline that could not be explained with the classical model. A British economist, John Maynard Keynes, developed an explanation that has since become known as the Keynesian model, which presented an explanation of the Great Depression in the 1930s. Keynes argued that if we are in a world in which there are large amounts of excess capacity and unemployment, a positive aggregate demand shock will not raise prices and a negative aggregate demand shock will not cause firms to lower prices. This situation is depicted in Figure 10-5 on the next page. The short-run aggregate supply curve is labeled as the horizontal line *SRAS*. If we start out in equilibrium with aggregate demand at AD_1, the equilibrium level of real GDP per year will be Q_1 and the equilibrium price level will be P_0. If there is an aggregate demand shock such that the aggregate demand curve shifts outward to the right to AD_2, the equilibrium price level will not change; only the equilibrium level of real GDP per year will increase, to Q_2.

---

[1]Full utilization of resources in the classical model was a long-run proposition. The classical economists recognized and understood "industrial crises." What could not be explained by classical economics was a *prolonged* period of underutilized resources such as the Great Depression of the 1930s.

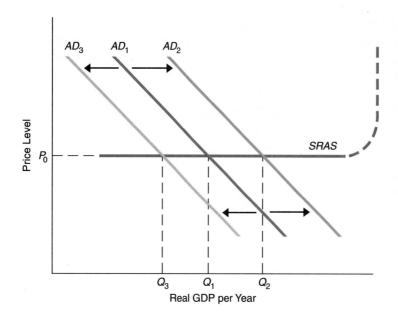

FIGURE 10-5
Demand-determined income equilibrium.
If we assume that prices will not fall when aggregate demand falls and that there is excess capacity so that prices will not rise when aggregate demand increases, the short-run aggregate supply curve is simply a horizontal line at the given price level, P_0, represented by *SRAS*. An aggregate demand shock that increases aggregate demand to AD_2 will increase the equilibrium level of real national income per year to Q_2. An aggregate demand shock that decreases aggregate demand to AD_3 will decrease the equilibrium level of real national income to Q_3. The equilibrium price level will not change.

Conversely, if there is an aggregate demand shock that shifts the aggregate demand curve to AD_3, the equilibrium price level will again remain at P_0, but the equilibrium level of real GDP per year will fall to Q_3.

In such a situation, the equilibrium level of real GDP per year is completely *demand-determined*. Thus to construct a model of income and employment determination, all we need do is understand the determinants of desired aggregate demand. We will first examine what determines both the rate of planned *consumption* expenditures and the rate of planned *investment* expenditures. Later we will examine the remaining components of desired aggregate demand—expenditures by government and net expenditures from the foreign sector, the difference between what we sell to foreigners and what we buy from foreigners, or the difference between exports and imports, called *net exports* and designated by the letter X.

The horizontal short-run aggregate supply curve represented in Figure 10-5 has often been called the **Keynesian short-run aggregate supply curve.** It is so named because Keynes hypothesized that many prices, especially the price of labor (wages), are "sticky downward." According to Keynes, the existence of unions, minimum wage laws, and long-term contracts between workers in and outside of unionized environments are real-world factors that can explain the downward inflexibility of *nominal* wage rates. Such "stickiness" of wages makes *involuntary* unemployment of labor a distinct possibility. The classical assumption of everlasting full employment no longer holds.

Further, even in situations of excess capacity and large amounts of unemployment, we will not necessarily see the price level falling; rather, all we will see is continuing unemployment and a reduction in the equilibrium level of real GDP per year. Thus general economywide equilibrium can occur and endure even if there is excess capacity. Keynes and his followers argued that capitalism was therefore not necessarily a self-regulating system sustaining full employment. At the time, Keynes was attacking the classical view of the world, which argued that markets would all eventually be in equilibrium—prices and wages would adjust—so that full employment would never be far away.

For the next few pages we will simplify our analysis and use the Keynesian short-run aggregate supply curve as given in Figure 10-5. To discover how the equilibrium level of real GDP per year is determined, all we need do is examine the elements of desired ag-

▶ **Keynesian short-run aggregate supply curve**
The horizontal portion of the aggregate supply curve in which there is unemployment and unused capacity in the economy.

gregate expenditures. Also, for the time being we will not be concerned with the problem of inflation, because by definition, along the Keynesian short-run aggregate supply curve, inflation is impossible. Finally, given that the price level is assumed to be unchanging, all of the variables with which we will be dealing will be expressed in real terms. After all, with no change in the price level, any change in the magnitude of an economic variable, such as income, will be equivalent to a real change in terms of purchasing power. Hence we will be examining Keynes's income-expenditure model of real GDP determination in a world of inflexible prices.

SOME OTHER SIMPLIFYING ASSUMPTIONS

To simplify the income determination model that follows, a number of assumptions are made:

1. Businesses pay no indirect taxes (for example, sales taxes).
2. Businesses distribute all of their profits to shareholders.
3. There is no depreciation (capital consumption allowance), so gross private domestic investment equals net investment.
4. The economy is closed—that is, there is no foreign trade.

Given all these simplifying assumptions, real disposable income will be equal to real national income minus taxes.[2]

CONCEPTS IN BRIEF

- If we assume that we are operating on a horizontal short-run aggregate supply curve, the equilibrium level of real GDP per year is completely demand-determined.
- The horizontal short-run aggregate supply curve has been called the Keynesian short-run aggregate supply curve because Keynes believed that many prices, especially wages, would not be reduced even when aggregate demand decreased.

DEFINITIONS AND RELATIONSHIPS REVISITED

▶ **Consumption**
Spending on new goods and services out of a household's current income. Whatever is not consumed is saved. Consumption includes such things as buying food and going to a concert.

▶ **Saving**
The act of not consuming all of one's current income. Whatever is not consumed out of spendable income is, by definition, saved. *Saving* is an action measured over time (a flow), whereas *savings* are an accumulation resulting from the act of saving in the past (a stock).

▶ **Consumption goods**
Goods bought by households to use up, such as food, clothing, and movies.

As we said earlier, you can do only two things with a dollar of income (in the absence of taxes): consume it or save it. If you consume it, it is gone forever. If you save the entire dollar, however, you will be able to consume it (and perhaps more if it earns interest) at some future time. That is the distinction between **consumption** and **saving.** Consumption is the act of using income for the purchase of consumption goods. **Consumption goods** are goods purchased by households for immediate satisfaction. Consumption goods are such things as food, clothing, and movies. By definition, whatever you do not consume you save and can consume at some time in the future.

STOCKS AND FLOWS: THE DIFFERENCE BETWEEN SAVING AND SAVINGS

It is important to distinguish between *saving* and *savings*. *Saving* is an action that occurs at a particular rate—for example, $10 a week or $520 a year. This rate is a flow. It is

---

[2]Strictly speaking, we are referring here to net taxes, that is, the difference between taxes paid and transfer payments received. If taxes are $1 trillion but individuals receive transfer payments—Social Security, unemployment benefits, and so forth—of $300 billion, net taxes are equal to $700 billion.

expressed per unit of time, usually a year. Implicitly, then, when we talk about saving, we talk about a *flow* or rate of saving. *Savings*, by contrast, is a *stock* concept, measured at a certain point or instant in time. Your current saving*s* are the result of past saving. You may presently have saving*s* of $2,000 that are the result of four years' saving at a rate of $500 per year. Consumption, being related to saving, is also a flow concept. You consume from after-tax income at a certain rate per week, per month, or per year.

RELATING INCOME TO SAVING AND CONSUMPTION

Obviously, $1 of take-home income can be either consumed or not consumed. Realizing this, we can see the relationship among saving, consumption, and disposable income:

$$\text{Consumption} + \text{saving} \equiv \text{disposable income}$$

This is called an *accounting identity*. It has to hold true at every moment in time. From it we can derive the definition of saving:

$$\text{Saving} \equiv \text{disposable income} - \text{consumption}$$

INVESTMENT

Investment is also a flow concept. *Investment* as used here differs from the common use of the term, as we have already pointed out. In common vocabulary it's used in relation to the stock market or to real estate. In our analysis investment is defined as expenditures by firms on new machines and buildings—**capital goods**—that are expected to yield a future stream of income. This we have already called *fixed investment*. We also included changes in business inventories in our definition. This we have already called *inventory investment*.

> ▶ **Investment**
> The spending by businesses on things such as machines and buildings, which can be used to produce goods and services in the future. The investment part of total income is the portion that will be used in the process of producing goods in the future.

> ▶ **Capital goods**
> Producer goods; nonconsumable goods that firms use to make other goods.

CONCEPTS IN BRIEF

- *Saving* is a flow, something that occurs over time. *Savings* are a stock. They are the accumulation due to saving.
- Saving equals disposable income minus consumption.
- Investment is also a flow. It includes expenditures on new machines, buildings, and equipment and changes in business inventories.

DETERMINANTS OF PLANNED CONSUMPTION AND PLANNED SAVING

In the classical model, the supply of saving was determined by the rate of interest: The higher the rate of interest, the more people wanted to save and therefore the less people wanted to consume. According to Keynes, the interest rate is not the primary determinant of an individual's saving and consumption decisions.

> **Keynes argued that saving and consumption depend primarily on an individual's real current income.**

The relationship between planned consumption expenditures of households and their current level of real income has been called the **consumption function**. It shows how much all households plan to consume per year at each level of real disposable income per year. Using for the moment only columns 1, 2, and 3 of Table 10-1, we will present a consumption function for a hypothetical household.

> ▶ **Consumption function**
> The relationship between amount consumed and disposable income. A consumption function tells us how much people plan to consume at various levels of disposable income.

TABLE 10-1 **A hypothetical case of real consumption and saving schedules.**
Column 1 presents real disposable income from zero up to $20,000 per year; column 2 indicates planned consumption per year; column 3 presents planned saving per year. At levels of disposable income below $10,000, planned saving is negative. In column 4 we see the average propensity to consume, which is merely planned consumption divided by disposable income. Column 5 lists average propensity to save, which is planned saving divided by disposable income. Column 6 is the marginal propensity to consume, which shows the proportion of additional income that will be consumed. Finally, column 7 shows the proportion of additional income that will be saved, or the marginal propensity to save.

COMBINA-TION	(1) REAL DISPOSABLE INCOME PER YEAR (Y_d)	(2) PLANNED REAL CON-SUMPTION PER YEAR (C)	(3) PLANNED REAL SAVING PER YEAR $(S \equiv Y_d - C)$ (1) − (2)	(4) AVERAGE PROPENSITY TO CONSUME $(APC \equiv C/Y_d)$ (2) ÷ (1)	(5) AVERAGE PROPENSITY TO SAVE $(APS \equiv S/Y_d)$ (3) ÷ (1)	(6) MARGINAL PROPENSITY TO CONSUME $(MPC \equiv C/\Delta Y_d)$	(7) MARGINAL PROPENSITY TO SAVE $(MPS \equiv S/\Delta Y_d)$
A	$ 0	$2,000	$−2,000	—	—	—	—
B	2,000	3,600	−1,600	1.8	−.8	.8	.2
C	4,000	5,200	−1,200	1.3	−.3	.8	.2
D	6,000	6,800	− 800	1.133	−.133	.8	.2
E	8,000	8,400	− 400	1.05	−.05	.8	.2
F	10,000	10,000	0	1.0	.0	.8	.2
G	12,000	11,600	400	.967	.033	.8	.2
H	14,000	13,200	800	.943	.057	.8	.2
I	16,000	14,800	1,200	.925	.075	.8	.2
J	18,000	16,400	1,600	.911	.089	.8	.2
K	20,000	18,000	2,000	.9	.1	.8	.2

We see from Table 10-1 that as real disposable income goes up, planned consumption rises also, but by a smaller amount, as Keynes suggested. Planned saving also increases with disposable income. Notice, however, that below an income of $10,000, the planned saving of this hypothetical family is actually negative. The further that income drops below that level, the more the family engages in **dissaving,** either by going into debt or by using up some of its existing wealth.

▶ **Dissaving**
Negative saving; a situation in which spending exceeds income. Dissaving can occur when a household is able to borrow or use up existing owned assets.

INTERNATIONAL EXAMPLE: **Is There a Worldwide Shortage of Saving?**

An international financial institution called the International Monetary Fund (IMF) has issued dire predictions about the worldwide shortage of funds available for productive investment. The IMF has argued in favor of industrial nations' drastically cutting military spending and curtailing the subsidies they give to businesses engaged in international trade. According to the IMF, if these actions are not taken, the world economy will suffer. There is evidence that the average annual saving rate across countries has fallen rather consistently. Studies performed by IMF staff economists show that the average annual saving rate for virtually all industrialized countries in the world has dropped somewhat from the period 1960 to 1974 to the period 1980 to 1992. These individual decreases are shown in Table 10-2 on page 220.

There are several reasons why rates of saving have dropped worldwide. In some nations, such as the United States and the United Kingdom, governmental social security programs require taxes on the incomes of their citizens, leaving less to count as saving. In many countries, social insurance programs, particularly for old age, have improved, thereby improving the ability of citizens to guard against uncertainty and reducing the desire for precautionary saving. Finally, it is possible that high government borrowing to finance deficits may reduce saving.

COUNTRY	REDUCTION IN ANNUAL AVERAGE SAVING RATES FROM 1960–1974 TO 1980–1992 (%)
Australia	15.9
Austria	14.3
Belgium	25.9
Canada	6.4
Denmark	25.4
Finland	13.5
France	21.1
Germany	17.4
Greece	18.5
Ireland	14.7
Italy	15.6
Japan	13.9
Netherlands	21.1
New Zealand	7.0
Sweden	25.9
United Kingdom	40.5
United States	50.0

TABLE 10-2 **The decline in annual average saving rates in selected industrialized countries.**

Source: Adapted from Roger LeRoy Miller and David D. VanHoose, *Modern Money and Banking.* Third Edition. (New York: McGraw-Hill, 1993), p. 78.

There is hope, though, that saving rates may start to climb now that worldwide military spending as a percentage of world income has fallen from its peak in 1982–1983, when it represented 5.3 percent of worldwide income. It is now down to below 5 percent and may fall even further. Also, a few researchers claim that the rate of saving depends on whether citizens believe in the possibility of nuclear war. Their theory is that the greater the possibility of nuclear war, the less people want to save. Since the Berlin Wall came down in 1989, the threat of a worldwide nuclear holocaust has steadily diminished. And since 1989, saving rates have increased somewhat in many nations. Does this change reflect the reduced threat of nuclear war since the breakup of the communist bloc? This is a question that enterprising researchers will consider in future years.

For Critical Analysis: Why should it matter whether a nation decides to save more or less during any given time period? ●

GRAPHING THE NUMBERS

When we constructed demand and supply curves in Chapter 3, we merely plotted the points from a table showing price-quantity pairs onto a diagram whose axes were labeled "Price" and "Quantity." We will graph the consumption and saving relationships presented in Table 10-1 in the same manner. In the upper part of Figure 10-6, the vertical axis measures the level of planned real consumption per year, and the horizontal axis measures the level of real disposable income per year. In the lower part of the figure, the horizontal axis is again real disposable income per year, but now the vertical axis is planned real saving per year. All of these are on a dollars-per-year basis, which emphasizes the point that we are measuring flows, not stocks.

As you can see, we have taken the income-consumption and income-saving combinations *A* through *K* and plotted them. In the upper part of Figure 10-6, the result is called the consumption function. In the lower part, the result is called the saving function. The saving function is the *complement* of the consumption function in the mathematical sense

FIGURE 10-6
The consumption and saving functions.
If we plot the combinations of real disposable income and planned consumption from columns 1 and 2 in Table 10-1, we get the consumption function. At every point on the 45-degree line, a vertical line drawn to the income axis is the same distance from the origin as a horizontal line drawn to the consumption axis. Where the consumption function crosses the 45-degree line at *F*, we know that consumption equals real disposable income and there is zero saving. The vertical distance between the 45-degree line and the consumption function measures the rate of saving or dissaving at any given income level. If we plot the relationship between column 1, real disposable income, and column 3, planned real saving, from Table 10-1, we arrive at the saving function shown in the lower part of this diagram. It is the complement of the consumption function presented above it.

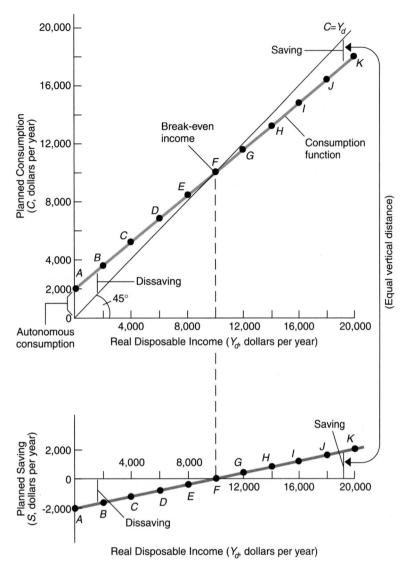

of the word. Why? Because consumption plus saving always equals disposable income. What is not consumed is, by definition, saved. The difference between actual disposable income and the planned level of consumption per year *must* be the planned level of saving per year.

How can we find the rate of saving or dissaving in the upper part of Figure 10-6? We draw a line that is equidistant from both the horizontal and the vertical axes. This line is 45 degrees from either axis and is often called the *45-degree reference line*. At every point on the 45-degree reference line, a vertical line drawn to the income axis is the same distance from the origin as a horizontal line drawn to the consumption axis. Thus at point *F*, where the consumption function intersects the 45-degree line, real disposable income equals planned consumption. Point *F* is sometimes called the *break-even income point* because there is neither positive nor negative saving. This can be seen in the lower part of Figure 10-6 as well. The planned annual rate of saving at a real disposable income level of $10,000 is indeed zero.

DISSAVING AND AUTONOMOUS CONSUMPTION

To the left of point *F* in either part of Figure 10-6, this hypothetical family engages in dissaving, either by going into debt or by consuming existing assets, including savings. The amount of saving or dissaving in the upper part of the figure can be found by measuring the vertical distance between the 45-degree line and the consumption function. This simply tells us that if our hypothetical family starts above $10,000 of real disposable income per year and then temporarily finds its real disposable income below $10,000, it will not cut back its consumption by the full amount of the reduction. It will instead go into debt or consume existing assets in some way to compensate for part of the loss.

Now look at the point on the diagram where real disposable income is zero but planned consumption per year is $2,000. This amount of planned consumption, which does not depend at all on actual disposable income, is called **autonomous consumption.** The autonomous consumption of $2,000 is *independent* of the level of disposable income. That means that no matter how low the level of income of our hypothetical family falls, that family will always attempt to consume at least $2,000 per year. (We are, of course, assuming here that the family's real disposable income does not equal zero year in and year out. There is certainly a limit to how long our hypothetical family could finance autonomous consumption without any income.) That $2,000 of yearly consumption is determined by things other than the level of income. We don't need to specify what determines autonomous consumption; we merely state that it exists and that in our example it is $2,000 per year. Just remember that the word *autonomous* means "existing independently." In our model, autonomous consumption exists independently of the hypothetical family's level of real disposable income. (Later we will review some of the non-real-disposable-income determinants of consumption.) There are many possible types of autonomous expenditures. Hypothetically, we can consider that investment is autonomous—independent of income. We can assume that government expenditures are autonomous. We will do just that at various times in our discussions to simplify our analysis of income determination.

▶ **Autonomous consumption**
The part of consumption that is independent of (does not depend on) the level of disposable income. Changes in autonomous consumption shift the consumption function.

AVERAGE PROPENSITY TO CONSUME AND TO SAVE

Let's now go back to Table 10-1, and this time let's look at columns 4 and 5: **average propensity to consume (APC)** and **average propensity to save (APS).** They are defined as follows:

$$APC \equiv \frac{\text{consumption}}{\text{real disposable income}}$$

$$APS \equiv \frac{\text{saving}}{\text{real disposable income}}$$

▶ **Average propensity to consume (APC)**
Consumption divided by disposable income; for any given level of income, the proportion of total disposable income that is consumed.

▶ **Average propensity to save (APS)**
Saving divided by disposable income; the proportion of total disposable income that is saved.

Notice that for this hypothetical family, the average propensity to consume decreases as real disposable income increases. This decrease simply means that the fraction of the family's real disposable income going to saving rises as income rises. The same fact can be found in column 5. The average propensity to save, which at first is negative, finally hits zero at an income level of $10,000 and then becomes positive. In this example, it reaches a value of 0.1 at income level $20,000. This means that the household saves 10 percent of a $20,000 income.

It's quite easy for you to figure out your own average propensity to consume or to save. Just divide your total real disposable income for the year into what you consumed and what you saved. The result will be your personal APC and APS, respectively, at your current level of income. This gives the proportions of total income that are consumed and saved.

MARGINAL PROPENSITY TO CONSUME AND TO SAVE

▶ **Marginal propensity to consume (MPC)**
The ratio of the change in consumption to the change in disposable income. A marginal propensity to consume of .8 tells us that an additional $100 in take-home pay will lead to an additional $80 consumed.

▶ **Marginal propensity to save (MPS)**
The ratio of the change in saving to the change in disposable income. A marginal propensity to save of .2 indicates that out of an additional $100 in take-home pay, $20 will be saved. Whatever is not saved is consumed. The marginal propensity to save plus the marginal propensity to consume must always equal 1, by definition.

Now we go to the last two columns in Table 10-1: **marginal propensity to consume (MPC)** and **marginal propensity to save (MPS).** We have already used the term *marginal.* It refers to a small incremental or decremental change. The marginal propensity to consume, then, is defined as

$$\text{MPC} \equiv \frac{\text{change in consumption}}{\text{change in real disposable income}}$$

The marginal propensity to save is defined similarly as

$$\text{MPS} \equiv \frac{\text{change in saving}}{\text{change in real disposable income}}$$

What do MPC and MPS tell you? They tell you what percentage of an increase or decrease in income will go toward consumption and saving, respectively. The emphasis here is on the word *change.* The marginal propensity to consume indicates how much you will change your planned rate of consumption if there is a change in your real disposable income. If your marginal propensity to consume is .8, that does not mean that you consume 80 percent of *all* disposable income. The percentage of your real disposable income that you consume is given by the average propensity to consume, or APC, which is not, at most income levels, equal to .8. An MPC of .8 means that you will consume 80 percent of any *increase* in your disposable income. In general, we assume that the marginal propensity to consume is between zero and one. We assume that individuals increase their planned consumption by more than zero and less than 100 percent of any increase in real disposable income that they receive.

Consider a simple example in which we show the difference between the average propensity to consume and the marginal propensity to consume. Assume that your consumption behavior is exactly the same as our hypothetical family's behavior depicted in Table 10-1. You have an annual real disposable income of $18,000. Your planned consumption rate, then, from column 2 of Table 10-1 is $16,400. So your average propensity to consume is $16,400 ÷ $18,000 = .911. Now suppose that at the end of the year your boss gives you an after-tax bonus of $2,000. What would you do with that additional $2,000 in real disposable income? According to the table, you would consume $1,600 of it and save $400. In that case, your *marginal* propensity to consume would be $1,600 ÷ $2,000 = .8, and your marginal propensity to save would be $400 ÷ $2,000 = .2. What would happen to your *average* propensity to consume? To find out, we add $1,600 to $16,400 of planned consumption, which gives us a new consumption rate of $18,000. The average propensity to consume is then $18,000 divided by the new higher salary of $20,000. Your APC drops from .911 to .9. By contrast, your MPC remains in our simplified example .8 all the time. Look at column 6 in Table 10-1. The MPC is .8 at every level of income. (Therefore, the MPS is always equal to .2 at every level of income.) Underlying the constancy of MPC is the assumption that the amount that you are willing to consume out of additional income will remain the same in percentage terms no matter what level of real disposable income is your starting point.

SOME RELATIONSHIPS

Consumption plus saving must equal income. Both your total real disposable income and the change in total real disposable income are either consumed or saved. The proportions of either measure must equal 1, or 100 percent. This allows us to make the following statements:

$$\text{APC} + \text{APS} = 1 \text{ (i.e., 100 percent of total income)}$$

$$\text{MPC} + \text{MPS} = 1 \text{ (i.e., 100 percent of the change in income)}$$

The average propensities as well as the marginal propensities to consume and save must total 1, or 100 percent. Check the two statements by adding the figures in columns 4 and 5 for each level of real disposable income in Table 10-1. Do the same for columns 6 and 7.

CAUSES OF SHIFTS IN THE CONSUMPTION FUNCTION

A change in any other relevant economic variable besides real disposable income will cause the consumption function to shift. There is a virtually unlimited number of such nonincome determinants of the position of the consumption function. When population increases or decreases, for example, the consumption function will shift up or down, respectively. Changes in expectations can also shift the consumption function. If the average household believes that the rate of inflation is going to fall dramatically in the years to come, the current consumption function will probably shift down: Planned consumption would be less at every level of real disposable income than before this change in expectations. Real household **wealth** is also a determinant of the position of the consumption function. An increase in real wealth of the average household will cause the consumption function to shift upward. A decrease in real wealth will cause it to shift downward.

▶ **Wealth**
The stock of assets owned by a person, household, firm or nation. For a household, wealth can consist of a house, cars, computers, bank accounts, and cash.

CONCEPTS IN BRIEF

- The consumption function shows the relationship between planned rates of consumption and real disposable income per year. The saving function is the complement of the consumption function because saving plus consumption must equal real disposable income.
- The average propensity to consume (APC) is equal to consumption divided by real disposable income.
- The average propensity to save (APS) is equal to saving divided by real disposable income.
- The marginal propensity to consume (MPC) is equal to the change in planned consumption divided by the change in real disposable income.
- The marginal propensity to save (MPS) is equal to the change in planned saving divided by the change in real disposable income.
- APC + APS = 1.
- MPC + MPS = 1.
- Any change in real disposable income will cause the planned rate of consumption to change; this is represented by a movement along the consumption function.
- Any change in a non-income determinant of consumption will shift the consumption function.

DETERMINANTS OF INVESTMENT

Investment, you will remember, is defined as expenditures on new buildings and equipment and changes in business inventories. Real gross private domestic investment in the United States has been extremely volatile over the years relative to real consumption. If we were to look at net private domestic investment (investment after depreciation has been deducted), we would see that in the depths of the Great Depression and at the peak of the World War II effort, the figure was negative. In other words, we were eating away at our capital stock—we weren't even maintaining it by completely replacing depreciated equipment.

If we compare real investment expenditures historically with real consumption expenditures, we find that the latter are relatively less variable over time than the former. Why is this so? The answer is that the real investment decisions of business people are based on highly variable, subjective estimates of how the economic future looks. We just discussed the role of expectations in determining the position of the consumption function. Expectations play an even greater role in determining the position of the investment function. This could account for much of the instability of investment over time.

THE PLANNED INVESTMENT FUNCTION

Consider that at all times businesses perceive an array of investment opportunities. These investment opportunities have rates of return ranging from zero to very high, with the number (or dollar value) of all such projects inversely related to the rate of return. Because a project is profitable only if its rate of return exceeds the opportunity cost of the investment—the rate of interest—it follows that as the interest rate falls, planned investment spending increases, and vice versa. Even if firms use retained earnings (corporate savings) to finance an investment, the higher the market rate of interest, the greater the *opportunity cost* of using those retained earnings. Thus it does not matter in our analysis whether the firm must seek financing from external sources or can obtain such financing by using retained earnings. Just consider that as the interest rate falls, more investment opportunities will be profitable, and planned investment will be higher.

It should be no surprise, therefore, that the investment function is represented as an inverse relationship between the rate of interest and the quantity of planned investment. A hypothetical investment schedule is given in panel (a) of Figure 10-7 and plotted in panel (b). We see from this schedule that if, for example, the rate of interest is 13 percent, the

FIGURE 10-7
Planned investment.
In the hypothetical planned investment schedule in panel (a), the rate of planned investment is asserted to be inversely related to the rate of interest. If we plot the data pairs from panel (a), we obtain the investment function *I* in panel (b). It is negatively sloped.

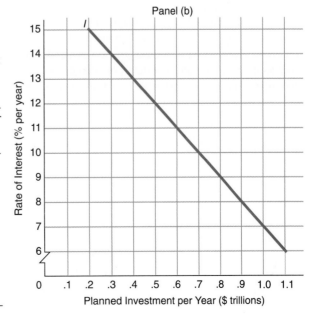

Panel (a)

RATE OF INTEREST (% PER YEAR)	PLANNED INVESTMENT PER YEAR ($ TRILLIONS)
15	.2
14	.3
13	.4
12	.5
11	.6
10	.7
9	.8
8	.9
7	1.0
6	1.1

dollar value of planned investment will be $400 billion per year. Notice, by the way, that planned investment is also given on a per-year basis, showing that it represents a flow, not a stock. (The stock counterpart of investment is the stock of capital in the economy measured in dollars at a point in time.)

WHAT CAUSES THE INVESTMENT FUNCTION TO SHIFT?

Because planned investment is assumed to be a function of the rate of interest, any non–interest rate variable that changes can have the potential of shifting the investment function. Expectations of business people is one of those variables. If higher future sales are expected, more machines and bigger plants will be planned for the future. More investment will be undertaken because of the expectation of higher future profits. In this case the investment schedule, *I*, would shift outward to the right, meaning that more investment would be desired at all rates of interest. Any change in productive technology can potentially shift the investment function. A positive change in productive technology would stimulate demand for additional capital goods and shift the investment schedule, *I*, outward to the right. Changes in business taxes can also shift the investment schedule. If they increase, we predict a shift in the planned investment function leftward.

CONCEPTS IN BRIEF

- The planned investment schedule shows the relationship between investment and the rate of interest; it slopes downward.
- The non–interest rate determinants of planned investment are expectations, innovation and technological changes, and business taxes.
- Any change in the non–interest rate determinants of planned investment will cause the planned investment function to shift so that at each and every rate of interest a different amount of planned investment will obtain.

MORE ON DESIRED AGGREGATE DEMAND: GOVERNMENT AND THE FOREIGN SECTOR

We know from our study of national income accounting in Chapter 8 that gross domestic product consists not only of consumption and investment but also of government purchases of goods and services and net exports. In the following chapters we will add these two important elements of desired aggregate demand. We will discover that changes in government spending are an important potential policy tool. Also, you will find out why the continuing excess of imports over exports—negative net exports—is of concern to the nation.

IS SAVING TOO LOW IN THE UNITED STATES?

Concepts Applied: Saving, marginal propensity to save, average propensity to save

By definition, consumption means not saving. Policy makers are concerned that the saving rate in the United States is too low.

For more than two decades concern has been growing about the declining rate of saving in America. Look at Figure 10-8. You can see that the rate of personal saving has been steadily falling. Both the average and the marginal propensity to save by U.S. households has been dropping for a quarter century. One of the first reasons given for this slump in saving has to do with the baby boom generation.

ARE THE BABY BOOMERS AT FAULT?
The baby boom generation was born right after World War II

and caused a bulge in the demographics of the U.S. population. Baby boomers, now approaching middle age, are high-spending, low-saving individuals who have swelled the work force. Baby boomer households do save less than older working households. However, the differences in their marginal and average propensities to save are not sufficient enough to be the cause of the quarter-century slump in personal saving rates. Saving rates declined among nearly all age groups in the 1980s.

ARE TAXES THE CULPRIT?
In the United States, interest earned from savings is taxed. Any decision about how to divide income between present consumption and saving for future consumption will depend on the *after-tax* rate of return from saving. The higher the tax rate, the lower the after-tax rate of return. The lower the after-tax rate of return from saving, the more people are likely to substitute present consumption for future consumption and the less likely they are to save.

Although it is true that there would necessarily have to be more saving if the return from saving had a lower tax applied to it, marginal tax rates in the United States have actually fallen, particularly during the 1980s, when personal saving rates nonetheless continued to drop. We could certainly stimulate saving if we did not tax the returns from savings, but taxes cannot be an explanation of why saving rates have fallen in the United States.

FIGURE 10-8

The steady decline in saving rates in the United States, 1981–1992.

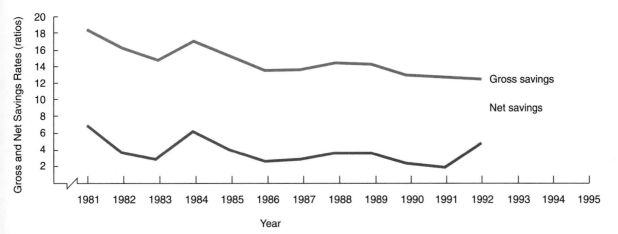

IS A LOWER SAVING RATE BAD?   Saving always involves a trade-off between present consumption and future consumption. To consume more in the future, society must save more now—and convert those saved funds into capital expansion. If households in America have simply changed their desired trade-off between present and future consumption and are therefore saving less, the nation is not necessarily worse off because of the lower rate of saving. This lower rate of saving might simply reflect the community's preference for present versus future consumption. People may be inclined to save less now, relative to what they saved in the past, because they are not as willing to wait to consume in the future.

FOR CRITICAL ANALYSIS

1. Assume that lower-income groups have lower marginal and average propensities to save. In the 1980s the most affluent households made big relative income gains. What should have happened to the nation's rate of saving, and why?
2. How is saving related to investment?

CHAPTER SUMMARY

1. The classical model was developed in the 1770s by such economists as Adam Smith, David Ricardo, John Stuart Mill, and Thomas Malthus. It attempted to explain the determinants of the price level and national income and employment.

2. Say's law holds that supply creates its own demand. A more complete classical model assumes (1) pure competition, (2) wage and price flexibility, (3) self-interest motivation throughout the population, and (4) no money illusion. With the introduction of saving, the classical economists believed, the market economy would still reach full employment of resources because planned saving would be met by planned investment. Saving is the supply of credit, and investment is the demand for credit. The interest rate in the credit market was assumed to be flexible, like all other prices, so equilibrium would always prevail, and therefore planned saving would always equal planned investment.

3. Whenever we are operating on a horizontal short-run aggregate supply curve, the equilibrium level of real GDP is completely demand-determined by the position of the aggregate demand curve. The Keynesian short-run aggregate supply curve is typically given as horizontal because Keynes assumed that wages and prices would not be reduced even if aggregate demand decreased substantially.

4. A consumption function, in its simplest form, shows that current real consumption is directly related to current real disposable income. The complement of a consumption function is a saving function. A saving function shows the relationship between current real saving and current real disposable income.

5. The marginal propensity to consume shows how much additional income is devoted to consumption. The marginal propensity to save is the difference between 1 and the marginal propensity to consume. Otherwise stated, the marginal propensity to save plus the marginal propensity to consume must equal 1.

6. We must be careful to distinguish between average and marginal propensities. The average propensity to consume is the amount of total real consumption divided by total real disposable income. The average propensity to save is the total amount of real saving divided by total real disposable income. The marginal propensities relate to changes in consumption and saving resulting from changes in income.

7. Some non-income determinants of planned consumption are wealth, expectations, and population.

8. Investment is made by the business sector of the economy. Investment is the spending by businesses on such things as new machines and buildings that can be used later in the production of goods and services. Investment is the use of resources to provide for future production.

9. There are numerous determinants of investment, including the rate of interest, changes in expectations, innovation and technology, and business taxes.

DISCUSSION OF PREVIEW POINTS

1. **Why do Keynesian economists believe that the short-run aggregate supply curve is horizontal?**
   In the horizontal range of the *SRAS* curve, changes in real GDP (output) occur without changes in the price level. This purely quantity response (no price response) to changes in *AD* reflects Keynes's assumption that during a depression or very deep recession, businesses have so much excess capacity that *increases* in *AD* will elicit only an increase in output; businesses that try to increase prices in such a situation discover that they lose sales to competitors. Similarly, a reduction in *AD* will lead only to a reduction in output; businesses won't reduce prices. Keynes assumed that in modern economies the existence of unions, minimum wage laws, and welfare policies that support the unemployed imply that wages are "sticky downward"—wages aren't likely to fall even during periods of significant unemployment. Businesses have a certain control over prices and, confronting wages that are sticky, prefer to reduce output instead of price.

2. **Why is real GDP said to be demand-determined when the short-run aggregate supply curve is horizontal?**
   When the *SRAS* curve is horizontal, real GDP will change only in response to a change in *AD*. If *AD* increases, real GDP rises; if *AD* decreases, real GDP falls. Therefore, real GDP merely responds to changes in *AD,* which is therefore the primary mover in the economy. According to Keynes, businesses are prepared to produce *any* output level; the output level that they do produce is the most profitable one, and that depends on *AD*. This theory says that if you want to predict what real GDP and national employment will be in the future, discover what is happening to *AD* now.

3. **How are saving, consumption, and income related in a closed private economy?**
   In a closed private economy, the community (or any individual) can dispose of income in only two ways: by consuming or by saving. We define consumption as household allocation of income for the purpose of using up goods and services that render economic satisfaction. Saving represents nonconsumption of income; by definition, the part of income that is not consumed is saved. Income, consumption, and saving are all measured per unit of time; hence all are flow concepts. Thus $Y \equiv C + S$ and $Y - C \equiv S$. If we divide both sides of the identity $Y \equiv C + S$ by Y, we get $Y/Y \equiv 1 \equiv C/Y + S/Y$. Because income can only be consumed or saved, if we add the percentage of income that is consumed (the APC, or C/Y) to the percentage of income that is saved (the APS, or S/Y), they must sum to 100 percent, which is the number 1. Similarly, a *change* in income can only lead to a change in consumption or a change in saving (or both). Thus if we add the percentage of a change in income that is consumed (the MPC, or a change in consumption divided by a change in income) to the percentage of a change in income that is saved (the MPS, or the change in saving divided by a change in income), they must sum to 100 percent, or 1. Thus APC + APS $\equiv$ 1 and MPC + MPS $\equiv$ 1 in a closed private economy, according to the definition of saving.

4. **What are the determinants of investment?**
   It is generally agreed that investment is inversely related to interest rates, other things being constant. Because interest payments have to be paid out of profits, fewer investment projects are profitable at higher interest rates than at lower interest rates. Stated differently, given profit expectations, lower and lower interest rates are required to induce businesses to make more and more investment expenditures. The non–interest rate determinants of investment expenditures are (a) the cost of capital relative to output prices, (b) future profit expectations, (c) innovations and technology, and (d) business taxes. If we define the relationship between interest rates and investment expenditures as the planned investment function, changes in all four determinants listed will lead to shifts in the planned investment function.

PROBLEMS
(Answers to the odd-numbered problems appear at the back of the book.)

10-1. Complete the table below.
   a. Plot the consumption and saving schedules on graph paper.
   b. Determine the marginal propensity to consume and the marginal propensity to save.
   c. Determine the average propensity to consume and the average propensity to save for each level of income.

DISPOSABLE INCOME	CONSUMPTION	SAVING
$ 500	$510	$_____
600	600	_____
700	690	_____
800	780	_____
900	870	_____
1,000	960	_____

10-2. Answer the questions based on the table below.

DISPOSABLE INCOME ($ BILLIONS)	CONSUMPTION ($ BILLIONS)
0	20
100	110
200	200
300	290
400	380
500	470

   *a. If the linear function $C = a + bY$ describes this consumption relationship:
      (i) What is the value of a?
      (ii) What is the significance of a?
      (iii) What is the value of b?
      (iv) What is the significance of b?
   b. If disposable income in this model increased to $800 billion, what would we expect C to be?

10-3. Consider the following table; then answer the questions.

ANNUAL CONSUMPTION	ANNUAL INCOME
$ 5	$ 0
80	100
155	200

   a. What is the APC at annual income level $100? At $200?
   b. What happens to the APC as annual income rises?
   c. What is the MPC as annual income goes from $0 to $100? From $100 to $200?
   d. What happens to the MPC as income rises?
   e. What number is the APC approaching?
   *f. What is the equation for the consumption function in this table?
   *g. Of what significance is a positive y intercept in this equation?

10-4. Make a list of determinants, other than income, that might affect your personal MPC.

10-5. List each of the following under the heading "Stock" or "Flow."
   a. The Chens have $100 of savings in the bank.
   b. Smith earns $200 per week.
   c. General Electric owns 2,000 autos.
   d. Inventories rise at 400 units per year.
   e. Lopez consumes $80 per week out of income.
   f. The equilibrium quantity is 1,000 per day.
   g. The corporation spends $1 billion per year on investments.

10-6. The rate of return on an investment on new machinery is 9 percent.
   a. If the market interest rate is 9.5 percent, will the investment be carried out?
   b. If the interest rate is 8 percent, will the machinery be purchased?
   c. If the interest rate is 9 percent, will the machinery be purchased?

---

*Asterisked problems are optional; algebra is required.

10-7. Are firms or industries and the economy generally able to carry out investments as much as they would like to in a given period of time?

10-8. The accompanying table below is a consumption schedule for a closed private economy. (All figures in the table are in trillions of dollars.)
   a. Compute the value of S at each Y_d.
   b. When Y_d is $2 trillion, what is the APC? When Y_d is $2.5 trillion, what is the APS?
   c. What is the MPC?
   d. What is the MPS?

Y_d	C	S
$2.00	$1.80	$_____
2.10	1.88	_____
2.20	1.96	_____
2.30	2.04	_____
2.40	2.12	_____
2.50	2.20	_____
2.60	2.28	_____

10-9. If the consumption function is $C = \$20 + 0.7Y_d$, determine the following:
   *a. The level of C for $Y_d = \$50, \$150$, and $250
   *b. The level of S for $Y_d = \$50, \$150$, and $250
   *c. The APC at each level of Y_d in part (a)

10-10. In the basic Keynesian model, suppose that MPC = .8.
   a. If income increased from $80 billion to $100 billion, consumption would be expected to increase by how much?
   b. By how much would saving be expected to increase?
   c. Is the sum of your two answers equal to the change in income?

10-11. Suppose that consumption equals $500 billion and total income equals $650 billion.
   a. If the marginal propensity to consume is equal to .8, what must saving be equal to?
   b. What does the MPS equal?
   c. At the income level of $650 billion, what does the APC come to?

COMPUTER-ASSISTED INSTRUCTION
(Complete problem and answer on disk.)

Consumption spending is the single most important component of desired aggregate demand. This computer session examines the determinants of consumption spending and saving, as well as the link between the marginal and average propensities to consume.

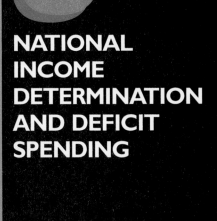

NATIONAL INCOME DETERMINATION AND DEFICIT SPENDING

3

INCOME AND EMPLOYMENT DETERMINATION

If you are between the ages of 18 and 25 and attending college, your surviving grandparents have more assets than any generation in our nation's history. Normally, then, you would think that because consumption depends on wealth, they should be spending as if they are rich. It turns out that they are not spending that way. One of the reasons has to do with future taxes that they—and you—are going to have to pay. We are all poorer than we might think. In examining the underpinnings of the relationship between consumption and wealth, you will see how income and employment are determined in our economy.

After reading this chapter, you should be able to answer the following questions:

1. What does the total planned expenditures curve indicate?

2. How do we interpret the 45-degree reference line?

3. What is the concept of the multiplier, how does it work, and what is its main determinant?

4. What might cause shifts in the total planned expenditures curve?

INTRODUCTION

Why is the equilibrium level of real GDP per year what it is? One way to answer this question would be to use the simplified assumptions normally associated with a Keynesian model of income determination. The most important assumption was given at the beginning of Chapter 10: The short-run aggregate supply curve is horizontal at the existing price level. Therefore, the implication is that the equilibrium level of real GDP per year is determined by demand only. We do not have to worry about either supply constraints or changes in the price level (at least not initially). This simplified Keynesian model helps us understand how macroeconomic thought has developed in the past several decades.

EXAMPLE: The Price Level During the Great Depression

A pretty good example of a horizontal short-run aggregate supply curve can be seen by examining data from the Great Depression during the 1930s. Look at Figure 11-1, where you see real GDP in billions of 1987 dollars on the horizontal axis and the price level index on the vertical axis. From the end of the trough of the Great Depression in 1934 to just prior to World War II in 1940, real GDP increased without much rise in the price level. During this period the economy experienced neither supply constraints nor any dramatic changes in the price level. The most simplified Keynesian model in which prices do not change is essentially an immediate post-Depression model that fits the data very well during this period.

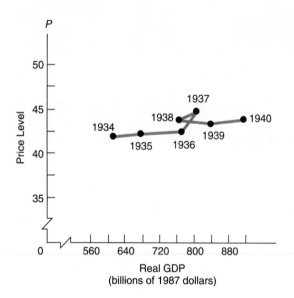

FIGURE 11-1
Real GDP and the price level, 1934–1940.
In a depressed economy it is possible that increased aggregate spending can increase output without raising prices. This is what John Maynard Keynes believed, and the data seemed to show this during the United States recovery from the Great Depression. In such circumstances the level of real output is demand-determined.

For Critical Analysis: *During the Great Depression there were massive amounts of unemployed resources relative to most other times in U.S. history. Would you have expected the price level to act differently than is shown in Figure 11-1? Explain.* ●

CONSUMPTION AS A FUNCTION OF REAL NATIONAL INCOME

We are interested in determining the equilibrium level of real national income per year. But when we examined the consumption function in Chapter 10, it related planned consumption expenditures to the level of real disposable income per year. We have already shown where adjustments must be made to GDP in order to get real disposable income (see Table 8-2 in Chapter 8). Real disposable income turns out to be less than real national income because net taxes (taxes minus government transfer payments) are usually about 11 to 18 percent of national income. A representative average in the 1990s is about 15 percent, so disposable income, on average, has in recent years been around 85 percent of national income.

If we are willing to assume that real disposable income, Y_d, is the same proportion of real national income every year, we can relatively easily substitute real national income for real disposable income in the consumption function.

We can now plot any consumption function on a diagram in which the horizontal axis is no longer real disposable income but rather real national income, as in Figure 11-2. Notice that there is an autonomous part of consumption that is so labeled. The change between this graph and the graphs in Chapter 10 is the change in the horizontal axis from real disposable income to real national income per year. For the rest of this chapter, assume that this calculation has been made, and the result is that the MPC out of real national income equals .8, suggesting that 20 percent of changes in real national income are either saved or paid in taxes: in other words, of an additional $100 earned, an additional $80 will be consumed.

THE 45-DEGREE REFERENCE LINE

▶ 45-degree reference line
The line along which planned real expenditures equal real national income per year; a line that bisects the total planned expenditures/real national income quadrant.

Like the graphs in Chapter 10, Figure 11-2 shows a 45-degree reference line. Remember that a 45-degree line bisects the quadrant into two equal spaces. Thus along the **45-degree reference line,** planned consumption expenditures, C, equal real national income per year, Y. One can see, then, that at any point where the consumption function intersects the 45-degree reference line, planned consumption expenditures will be exactly equal to real national income per year, or $C = Y$. Note that in this graph, because we are looking only at planned consumption on the vertical axis, the 45-degree reference line is where planned consumption, C, is always equal to real national income per year, Y. Later, when we add investment, government spending, and net exports to the graph, the 45-degree reference line with respect to *all* planned expenditures will be labeled as such on the vertical axis.

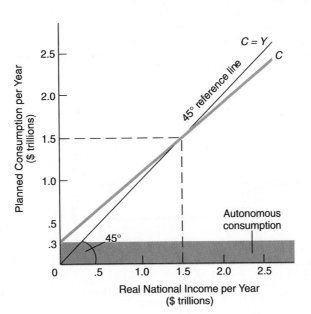

FIGURE 11-2
Consumption as a function of real national income.
This consumption function shows the rate of planned expenditures for each level of real national income per year. There is an autonomous factor in the consumption function. Along the 45-degree reference line, planned consumption expenditures per year, C, are identical to real national income per year, Y. The consumption curve intersects the 45-degree reference line at a value of $1.5 trillion per year.

In any event, looking only at consumption yields an equality between consumption and real national income at $1.5 trillion per year. That is where the consumption curve, C, intersects the 45-degree reference line. At that income level all income is consumed.

ADDING THE INVESTMENT FUNCTION

Another component of private aggregate demand is investment spending *(I)*. In Chapter 10 we showed the planned investment function, which related investment to the rate of interest. We show this again in panel (a) of Figure 11-3. Here we show that the equilibrium rate of interest is established where the demand for saving—investment, *I*—intersects the supply of saving, *S*. The equilibrium rate of interest is 10 percent, and the equilibrium rate of investment is $700 billion per year.

In the simplified Keynesian model in this chapter, we will assume that the $700 billion of real investment per year is *autonomous* with respect to real national income—that is, it is independent of real national income. In other words, given that we have a determinant investment level of $700 billion at a 10 percent rate of interest, we can treat this level of investment as constant, regardless of the level of national income. This is shown in panel (b) of Figure 11-3. The vertical distance of investment spending is $700 billion. Businesses plan on investing a particular amount—$700 billion per year—and will do so no matter what the level of real national income.

How do we add this amount of investment spending to our consumption function? We simply add a line above the C line that we drew in Figure 11-2 that is higher by the vertical distance equal to $700 billion of autonomous investment spending. This is shown by the arrow in panel (c) of Figure 11-3. Our new line, now labeled $C + I$, is called the *consumption plus investment line*. If we ignore government expenditures and net exports, the $C + I$ curve represents total planned expenditures for the economy as they relate to different levels of real national income per year. Because the 45-degree reference line shows

FIGURE 11-3
Combining consumption and investment.
In panel (a) we show the determination of real investment demanded in trillions of dollars per year. It occurs where the investment schedule intersects the supply schedule at an interest rate of 10 percent and is equal to $700 billion per year. In panel (b) investment is a constant $700 billion per year. When we add this amount to the consumption line, we obtain in panel (c) the $C + I$ line, which is vertically higher than the C line by exactly $700 billion. Real national income is equal to $C + I$ at $5 trillion per year where the total planned expenditure function $(C + I)$ is equal to actual real national income, for this is where the $C + I$ line intersects the 45-degree reference line on which $C + I$ is equal to Y at every point.

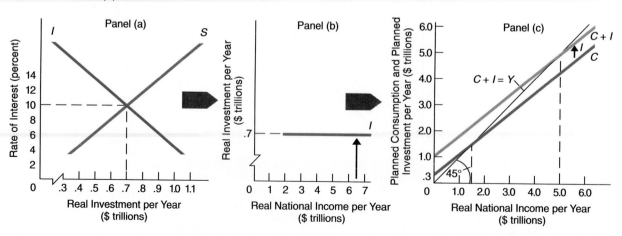

all the points whose planned expenditures (now $C + I$) equal real national income, we label it $C + I = Y$. Equilibrium Y equals $5 trillion per year.

CONCEPTS IN BRIEF

- On all graphs relating planned expenditures to real national income, we will use a 45-degree reference line, along which planned expenditures will be identically equal to real national income per year.
- We assume that the consumption function has an autonomous part that is independent of the level of real national income per year. It is labeled "autonomous consumption."
- For simplicity, we assume that investment is autonomous with respect to real national income and therefore unrelated to the level of real national income per year.

SAVING AND INVESTMENT: PLANNED VERSUS ACTUAL

Figure 11-4 shows the planned investment curve as a horizontal line at $700 billion per year. Investment is completely autonomous in this simplified model—it does not depend on the level of income.

The planned saving curve is represented by S. Because in our model whatever is not consumed is by definition saved, the planned saving schedule is the complement of the planned consumption schedule, represented by the C line in Figure 11-2. For better exposition, we look at only a small part of the saving and investment schedules—real national incomes between $4 and $6 trillion per year.

Why does equilibrium have to occur at the intersection of the planned saving and planned investment schedules? If we are at E in Figure 11-4, planned saving equals planned investment. All anticipations are validated by reality. There is no tendency for businesses to alter the rate of production or the level of employment because they are neither increasing nor decreasing their inventories in an unplanned way.

FIGURE 11-4
Planned and actual rates of saving and investment.
Only at the equilibrium level of real national income of $5 trillion per year will planned saving equal actual saving, planned investment equal actual investment, and hence planned saving equal planned investment.

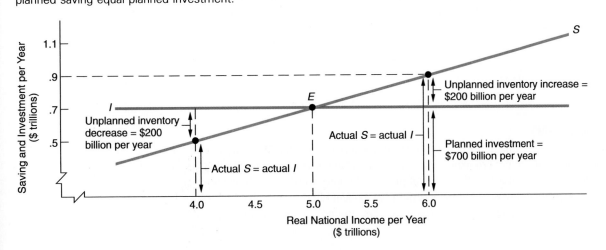

However, if we are producing at a real national income level of $6 trillion instead of $5 trillion, planned investment, as usual, is $700 billion per year, but it is exceeded by planned saving, which is $900 billion per year. This means that consumers will purchase less of total output than businesses had anticipated. Unplanned business inventories will now rise at the rate of $200 billion per year, bringing actual investment into line with actual saving because the $200 billion increase in inventories is included in actual investment. But this rate of output cannot continue for long. Businesses will respond to this unplanned increase in inventories by cutting back production and employment, and we will move toward a lower level of real national income.

Conversely, if the real national income is $4 trillion per year, planned investment continues annually at $700 billion; but at that output rate, planned saving is only $500 billion. This means that households and businesses are purchasing more of real national income than businesses had planned. Businesses will find that they must draw down their inventories below the planned level by $200 billion (business inventories will fall now at the unplanned rate of $200 billion per year), bringing actual investment into equality with actual saving because the $200 billion decline in inventories is included in actual investment (thereby decreasing it). But this situation cannot last forever either. In their attempt to increase inventories to the desired previous level, businesses will increase output and employment, and real national income will rise toward its equilibrium value of $5 trillion per year. Figure 11-4 demonstrates the necessary equality between actual saving and actual investment. Inventories adjust so that saving and investment, after the fact, are *always* equal in this simplified model, which ignores government and foreign transactions. (Remember also that changes in inventories count as part of investment.)

Every time the saving rate planned by households differs from the investment rate planned by businesses, there will be a shrinkage or an expansion in the circular flow of income and output (introduced in Chapter 8) in the form of unplanned inventory changes. Real national income and employment will change until unplanned inventory changes are again zero, that is, until we have attained the equilibrium level of real national income.

CONCEPTS IN BRIEF

- The equilibrium level of real national income can be found where planned saving equals planned investment.
- Whenever planned saving exceeds planned investment, there will be unplanned inventory accumulation, and national income will fall as producers reduce output.
- Whenever planned saving is less than planned investment, there will be unplanned inventory depletion, and national income will rise as producers increase output.

KEYNESIAN EQUILIBRIUM WITH GOVERNMENT AND THE FOREIGN SECTOR ADDED

GOVERNMENT

We have to add government spending to our macroeconomic model. We assume that the level of resource-using government purchases of goods and services, *not* including transfer payments, is determined by the political process. In other words, *G* will be considered autonomous, just like investment (and a certain component of consumption). In the United States resource-using government expenditures are around 25 percent of real national

TABLE 11-1 **The determination of equilibrium real national income with net exports (in trillions of dollars).**

(1) REAL NATIONAL INCOME	(2) TAXES	(3) REAL DISPOSABLE INCOME	(4) PLANNED CONSUMPTION	(5) PLANNED SAVING	(6) PLANNED INVESTMENT	(7) GOVERNMENT SPENDING	(8) NET EXPORTS (EXPORTS − IMPORTS)	(9) TOTAL PLANNED EXPENDITURES (4) + (6) + (7) + (8)	(10) UNPLANNED INVENTORY CHANGES	(11) DIRECTION OF CHANGE IN REAL NATIONAL INCOME
2.0	1.0	1.0	1.1	−.1	.7	1.0	.1	2.9	−.9	Increase
2.5	1.0	1.5	1.5	0	.7	1.0	.1	3.3	−.8	Increase
3.0	1.0	2.0	1.9	.1	.7	1.0	.1	3.7	−.7	Increase
4.0	1.0	3.0	2.7	.3	.7	1.0	.1	4.5	−.5	Increase
5.0	1.0	4.0	3.5	.5	.7	1.0	.1	5.3	−.3	Increase
6.0	1.0	5.0	4.3	.7	.7	1.0	.1	6.1	−.1	Increase
6.5	1.0	5.5	4.7	.8	.7	1.0	.1	6.5	0	Neither (equilibrium)
7.0	1.0	6.5	5.1	.9	.7	1.0	.1	6.9	+.1	Decrease
8.0	1.0	7.0	5.9	1.1	.7	1.0	.1	7.7	+.3	Decrease

▶ **Lump-sum tax**
A tax that does not depend on income or the circumstances of the taxpayer. An example is a $1,000 tax that every family must pay, irrespective of its economic situation.

income. The other side of the coin, of course, is that there are taxes, which are used to pay for much of government spending. We will simplify our model greatly in this chapter by assuming that there is a constant **lump-sum tax** of $1 trillion a year to finance $1 trillion of government spending. This lump-sum tax will reduce disposable income and consumption by the same amount. We show this in Table 11-1, where we give the numbers for a complete model.

THE FOREIGN SECTOR

Not a week goes by without a commentary in major newspapers and news magazines about the problem of our foreign trade deficit. For many years we have been buying merchandise from foreigners—imports—whose value exceeds what we have been selling them—exports. The difference between exports and imports is *net exports,* which we label X in our graphs. The level of exports depends on international economic conditions, especially in the countries that buy our products. Imports depend on economic conditions here at home. For simplicity, let us assume that exports exceed imports (net exports, X, is positive) and furthermore that the level of net exports is autonomous—independent of national income. Assume a level of X of $100 billion per year. In Table 11-1 net exports is shown in column 8 as $100 billion per year.

DETERMINING THE EQUILIBRIUM LEVEL OF REAL NATIONAL INCOME PER YEAR

We are now in a position to determine the equilibrium level of real national income per year under the continuing assumptions that the short-run aggregate supply curve is horizontal; that investment, government, and the foreign sector are autonomous; and that planned consumption expenditures are determined by the level of real national income. As can be seen in Table 11-1, total planned expenditures of $6.5 trillion per year equal real national income of $6.5 trillion per year, and this is where we reach equilibrium.

Equilibrium always occurs when total planned expenditures equal total production (given that any amount of production in this model in the short run can occur without a change in the price level).

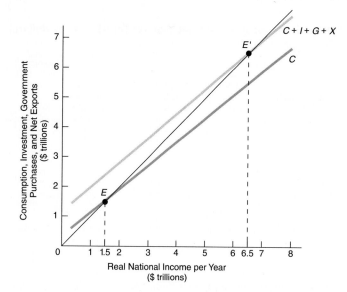

FIGURE 11-5
The equilibrium level of real national income.
The consumption function is shown as *C*. When we add autonomous investment, government, and net exports, we obtain $C + I + G + X$. We move from *E* to *E'*. The equilibrium level of real national income is $6.5 trillion per year.

Now look at Figure 11-5, which shows the equilibrium level of real national income. There are two curves, one showing the consumption function, which is the exact duplicate of the one shown in Figure 11-2, and the other is the $C + I + G + X$ curve, which intersects the 45-degree reference line (representing equilibrium) at $6.5 trillion per year.

Whenever total planned expenditures differ from real national income, there are unplanned inventory changes. When total planned expenditures are greater than real national income, inventory levels drop in an unplanned manner. To get them back up, firms seek to expand their production, which increases real national income. Real national income rises toward its equilibrium level. Whenever total planned expenditures are less than real national income, the opposite occurs. There are unplanned inventory increases, causing firms to cut back on their production. The result is a drop in real national income toward the equilibrium level.

CONCEPTS IN BRIEF

- When we add autonomous investment, *I*, and autonomous government spending, *G*, to the consumption function, we obtain the $C + I + G$ curve, which represents total planned expenditures for a closed economy.
- In an open economy, we add the foreign sector, which consists of exports minus imports, or net exports. Total planned expenditures are represented by the $C + I + G + X$ curve.
- The equilibrium level of real national income can be found by locating the intersection of the total planned expenditures curve with the 45-degree reference line. At that level of real national income per year, planned consumption plus planned investment plus government expenditures plus net exports will equal real national income.
- Whenever total planned expenditures exceed real national income, there will be unplanned decreases in inventories; the size of the circular flow of income will increase, and a higher level of equilibrium real national income will prevail.
- Whenever planned expenditures are less than real national income, there will be unplanned increases in inventories; the size of the circular flow will shrink, and a lower equilibrium level of real national income will prevail.

THE MULTIPLIER

Look again at panel (c) in Figure 11-3 on page 238. Assume for the moment that the only expenditures included in real national income are consumption expenditures. Where would the equilibrium level of income be in this case? It would be where the consumption function *(C)* intersects the 45-degree reference line, which is at $1.5 trillion per year. Now we add the autonomous amount of planned investment, or $700 billion, and then determine what the new equilibrium level of income will be. It turns out to be $5 trillion per year. Adding $700 billion per year of investment spending increased the equilibrium level of income by *five* times that amount, or by $3.5 trillion per year.

What is operating here is the multiplier effect of changes in autonomous spending. The **multiplier** is the number by which a permanent change in autonomous investment or autonomous consumption is multiplied to get the change in the equilibrium level of real national income. Any permanent increases in autonomous investment or in any autonomous component of consumption will cause a more than proportional increase in real national income. Any permanent decreases in autonomous spending will cause a more than proportional decrease in the equilibrium level of real national income per year. To understand why this multiple expansion (or contraction) in the equilibrium level of real national income occurs, let's look at a simple numerical example.

We'll use the same figures we used for the marginal propensity to consume and to save. MPC will equal .8, or $\frac{4}{5}$, and MPS will equal .2, or $\frac{1}{5}$. Now let's run an experiment and say that businesses decide to increase planned investment permanently by $100 billion a year. We see in Table 11-2 that during what we'll call the first round in column 1, investment is increased by $100 billion; this also means an increase in real national income of $100 billion, because the spending by one group represents income for another, shown in column 2. Column 3 gives the resultant increase in consumption by households that received this additional $100 billion in real income. This is found by multiplying the MPC by the increase in real income. Because the MPC equals .8, consumption expenditures during the first round will increase by $80 billion.

▶ **Multiplier**
The ratio of the change in the equilibrium level of real national income to the change in autonomous expenditures; the number by which a change in autonomous investment or autonomous consumption, for example, is multiplied to get the change in the equilibrium level of real national income.

TABLE 11-2 **The multiplier effect of a permanent $100 billion per year increase in *I*—the multiplier process.**
We trace the effects of a permanent $100 billion increase in autonomous investment spending on the equilibrium level of real national income. If we assume a marginal propensity to consume of .8, such an increase will eventually elicit a $500 billion increase in the equilibrium level of real national income per year.

ASSUMPTION: MPC = .8, OR $\frac{4}{5}$			
(1) ROUND	(2) ANNUAL INCREASE IN REAL NATIONAL INCOME ($ billions per year)	(3) ANNUAL INCREASE IN PLANNED CONSUMPTION ($ billions per year)	(4) ANNUAL INCREASE IN PLANNED SAVING ($ billions per year)
1 ($100 billion per year increase in *I*)	100.00	80.000	20.000
2	80.00	64.000	16.000
3	64.00	51.200	12.800
4	51.20	40.960	10.240
5	40.96	32.768	8.192
.	.	.	.
.	.	.	.
.	.	.	.
All later rounds	163.84	131.072	32.768
Totals (*C* + *I'* + *G*)	500.00	400.000	100.000

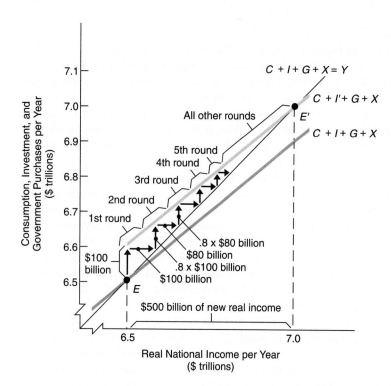

FIGURE 11-6
Graphing the multiplier.
We can translate Table 11-2 into graphic form by looking at each successive round of additional spending induced by an autonomous increase in planned investment of $100 billion. The total planned expenditures curve shifts from $C + I + G + X$, with its associated equilibrium level of real national income of $6.5 trillion, to a new curve labeled $C + I' + G + X$. The new equilibrium level of real national income is $7 trillion. Equilibrium is again established.

But that's not the end of the story. This additional household consumption is also spending, and it will provide $80 billion of additional real income for other individuals. Thus during the second round, we see an increase in real income of $80 billion. Now, out of this increased real income, what will be the resultant increase in consumption expenditures? It will be .8 times $80 billion, or $64 billion. We continue these induced expenditure rounds *ad infinitum* and find that because of an initial increase in autonomous investment expenditures of $100 billion, the equilibrium level of real national income has increased by $500 billion. A permanent $100 billion increase in autonomous investment spending has induced an additional $400 billion increase in consumption spending, for a total increase in real national income of $500 billion. In other words, the equilibrium level of real national income has changed by an amount equal to five times the change in investment.

THE MULTIPLIER IN GRAPHIC FORM

We can see the multiplier effect more clearly if we look at Figure 11-6, in which we see only a small section of the graphs that we have been using in this chapter. We start with an equilibrium level of real national income of $6.5 trillion per year. This equilibrium occurs with total planned expenditures represented by $C + I + G + X$. The $C + I + G + X$ curve intersects the 45-degree reference line at $6.5 trillion per year. Now we increase investment, I, by $100 billion. This increase in investment shifts the entire $C + I + G + X$ curve vertically to $C + I' + G + X$. The vertical shift represents that $100 billion increase in autonomous investment. With the higher level of planned expenditures per year, we are no longer in equilibrium at E. Inventories are falling. Production will increase. Eventually, planned production will catch up with total planned expenditures. The new equilibrium level of real national income is established at E' at the intersection of the new $C + I' + G + X$ curve and the 45-degree reference line, along which $C + I + G + X = Y$ (total planned expenditures equal real national income). The new equilibrium level of real national income is $7.0 trillion per year. Thus the increase in equilibrium real national income is equal to five times the permanent increase in planned investment spending.

There's an easier way to find the multiplier than by drawing a graph, however.

THE MULTIPLIER FORMULA

It turns out that the autonomous spending multiplier is equal to the reciprocal of the marginal propensity to save. In our example, the MPC was $\frac{4}{5}$; therefore, because MPC + MPS = 1, the MPS was equal to $\frac{1}{5}$. The reciprocal is 5. That was our multiplier. A $100 billion increase in planned investment led to a $500 billion increase in the equilibrium level of real income. Our multiplier will always be the following:

$$\text{Multiplier} \equiv \frac{1}{1 - \text{MPC}} \equiv \frac{1}{\text{MPS}}$$

You can always figure out the multiplier if you know either the MPC or the MPS. Let's take some examples. If MPS = $\frac{1}{4}$,

$$\text{Multiplier} = \frac{1}{\frac{1}{4}} = 4$$

Repeating again that MPC + MPS = 1, then MPS = 1 − MPC. Hence we can always figure out the multiplier if we are given the marginal propensity to consume. In this example, if the marginal propensity to consume were given as $\frac{3}{4}$, the multiplier would equal

$$\text{Multiplier} = \frac{1}{1 - \frac{3}{4}} = \frac{1}{\frac{1}{4}} = 4$$

By taking a few numerical examples, you can demonstrate to yourself an important property of the multiplier:

> The smaller the marginal propensity to save, the larger the multiplier.

Otherwise stated:

> The larger the marginal propensity to consume, the larger the multiplier.

Prove this to yourself by computing the multiplier when the marginal propensities to save equals $\frac{3}{4}$, $\frac{1}{2}$, and $\frac{1}{4}$. What happens to the multiplier as the MPS gets smaller?

When you have the multiplier, the following formula will then give you the change in the equilibrium level of real national income due to a permanent change in autonomous spending:

> Multiplier × change in autonomous spending = change in equilibrium level of real national income

The multiplier, as we have mentioned, works for a permanent increase or permanent decrease in autonomous spending. In our earlier example, if the autonomous component of consumption had fallen by $100 billion, the reduction in the equilibrium level of real national income would have been $500 billion per year.

THE SIGNIFICANCE OF THE MULTIPLIER

Depending on the size of the multiplier, it is possible that a relatively small change in planned investment or planned consumption can trigger a much larger change in the equilibrium level of real national income per year. In essence, the multiplier magnifies the fluctuations in the equilibrium level of real national income initiated by changes in autonomous spending.

As was just stated, the larger the marginal propensity to consume, the larger the multiplier. If the marginal propensity to consume is $\frac{1}{2}$, the multiplier is 2. In that case a $1 billion decrease in (autonomous) investment will elicit a $2 billion decrease in the equilibrium level of real national income per year. Conversely, if the marginal propensity to consume is $\frac{9}{10}$, the multiplier will be 10. That same $1 billion decrease in planned investment expenditures with a multiplier of 10 will lead to a $10 billion decrease in the equilibrium level of real national income per year.

⭐ EXAMPLE: Changes in Investment and the Great Depression

Changes in autonomous spending lead to shifts in the total expenditures $(C + I + G + X)$ curve and, as you have seen, cause a multiplier effect on the equilibrium level of real GDP per year. A classic example apparently occurred during the Great Depression. Indeed, some economists believe that it was an autonomous downward shift in the investment function that provoked the Great Depression. Look at panel (a) of Figure 11-7. There you see the net investment in the United States from 1929 to 1941 (expressed in 1987 dollars). Clearly, during business contractions, decision makers in the business world can and do decide to postpone long-range investment plans for buildings and equipment. This causes the business recovery to be weak unless those business plans are revised. If you examine real GDP in panel (b) of Figure 11-7, you see that the contraction that started in 1929 reached its trough in 1933. The expansion was relatively weak for the following four years, and then there was another contraction from 1937 to 1938. Some researchers argue that even though the 1937–1938 contraction was more severe than the initial one that started in 1929, it was short-lived because long-range investment plans were revised upward in 1938.

For Critical Analysis: Relatively speaking, how healthy was the national economy in 1941? (Hint: Look at panel (b) in Figure 11-7.) ●

FIGURE 11-7

Net private domestic investment and real GDP during the Great Depression.
In panel (a) you see how net private investment expressed in billions of 1987 dollars became negative starting in 1931 and stayed negative for several years. It became positive in 1936 and 1937, only to become negative again in 1938. Look at panel (b). There you see how changes in GDP seem to mirror changes in net private domestic investment.
Source: U.S. Bureau of the Census.

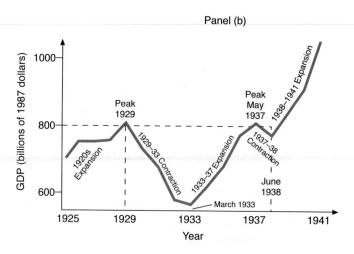

Panel (a)

YEAR	NET PRIVATE DOMESTIC INVESTMENT (BILLIONS OF 1987 DOLLARS)
1929	$ 70.52
1930	20.08
1931	-22.06
1932	-68.37
1933	-65.79
1934	-35.69
1935	-5.03
1936	15.09
1937	44.46
1938	-7.83
1939	19.91
1940	54.87
1941	88.36

CONCEPTS IN BRIEF

- Any change in autonomous spending shifts the expenditure curve and causes a multiplier effect on the equilibrium level of real national income per year.
- The multiplier is equal to the reciprocal of the marginal propensity to save.
- The smaller the marginal propensity to save, the greater the multiplier. Otherwise stated, the greater the marginal propensity to consume, the greater the multiplier.

EXPANSIONARY AND CONTRACTIONARY GAPS

We have presented in simplified form a theory of income determination. Now consider the possibility of the equilibrium level of real national income per year being greater than the full-employment level of real national income per year. In panel (a) of Figure 11-8 we

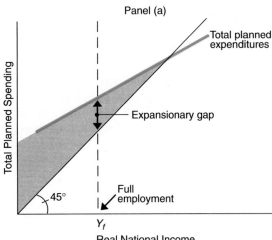

FIGURE 11-8
Expansionary and contractionary gaps.
In panel (a), at the full-employment level of real national income per year, Y_f, total planned expenditures exceed real national income per year. There is therefore an expansionary gap. In panel (b) total planned expenditures fall short of real national income at the full-employment level or real national income. Thus there is a contractionary gap.

see that this has occurred. Full employment is given as Y_f per year, but the intersection of the total planned expenditures curve with the 45-degree reference line is at a higher level of real national income per year. There therefore exists at the full-employment level of national income an **expansionary gap.** An expansionary gap exists whenever the equilibrium level of real national income exceeds the full-employment level (prices are assumed constant). Clearly, an expansionary gap means that there will be pressure on the price level and that we would have to abandon our assumption of a fixed price level.

It is also possible for the equilibrium level of real national income per year to be less than the full-employment level. When this occurs, we talk in terms of a **contractionary gap.** We show an output gap in panel (b) of Figure 11-8. There the intersection of the total planned expenditures curve with the 45-degree reference line is at a level of real national income that is below the full-employment level.

THE RELATIONSHIP BETWEEN EMPLOYMENT AND OUTPUT

We have just talked about the full-employment level of real national income. It turns out that in any economy at any given time, there is a fairly well defined relationship between the level of employment and real national income. You can see a hypothetical relationship between input (number of employees) and output (rate of real national income per year) in Table 11-3. In that table we have highlighted the row that has 130 million workers per year as the labor input. That is our hypothetical level of full employment, and it is related to a rate of real national income of $6 trillion per year. If this were the exact relationship in our economy today, the full-employment level of real national income would be $6 trillion per year, and that is the number that would appear on the horizontal axis in Figure 11-8 at the point labeled Y_f.

▶ **Expansionary gap**
Gap that exists whenever the equilibrium level of real national income exceeds the full-employment level of real national income; the positive difference between total desired spending and the full-employment level of real national income.

▶ **Contractionary gap**
Gap that exists whenever the equilibrium level of real national output is less than the full-employment level; the negative difference between total desired expenditures and the full-employment level of real national income.

TABLE 11-3   Relationship between real national income and labor.

REAL NATIONAL INCOME PER YEAR ($ TRILLIONS)	LABOR INPUT PER YEAR (MILLIONS OF WORKERS)
2	60
3	70
4	95
5	110
6	130
7	145
8	170

INCOME DETERMINATION USING AGGREGATE DEMAND—AGGREGATE SUPPLY ANALYSIS: RELAXING THE ASSUMPTION OF A FIXED PRICE LEVEL

In the aggregate demand–aggregate supply analysis presented in Chapter 9, the price level was not fixed. In the simplified Keynesian model that you have just learned, the price level was constant. The underlying assumption of the simplified Keynesian model is that

FIGURE 11-9
Income determination with flexible prices.
In panel (a) the price level index is fixed at 120. An increase in aggregate demand from AD_1 to AD_2 moves the equilibrium level of real national income from $5 trillion per year to $6 trillion per year. In panel (b) *SRAS* is upward-sloping. The same shift in aggregate demand yields an equilibrium level of real national income of only $5.5 trillion per year and a higher price level index at 130.

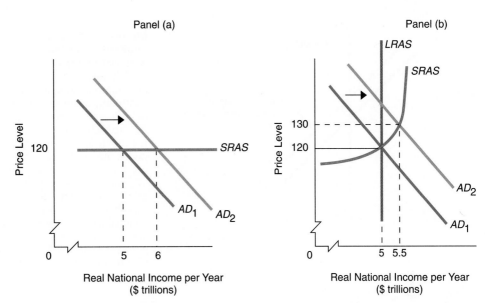

Panel (a)

Panel (b)

the relevant range of the short-run aggregate supply schedule *(SRAS)* is horizontal, as depicted in panel (a) of Figure 11-9. There you see short-run aggregate supply is fixed at price level 120. If aggregate demand is AD_1, the equilibrium level of real national income is at $5 trillion per year. If aggregate demand increases to AD_2, the equilibrium level of real national income increases to $6 trillion per year. Compare this situation with the standard upward-sloping short-run aggregate supply curve presented in Chapter 9. In panel (b) of Figure 11-9, *SRAS* is upward-sloping, with its slope becoming steeper and steeper after it crosses long-run aggregate supply, *LRAS*. Recall that *LRAS* is the level of real national income that the economy would produce year in and year out with full information and full adjustment. It is sometimes called the full-employment level of real national income because presumably full employment (with only frictional unemployment) occurs when there is full information and full adjustment possible in the economy. If aggregate demand is AD_1, the equilibrium level of real national income in panel (b) is also $5 trillion per year, also at a price level of 120. A similar increase in aggregate demand to AD_2 as occurred in panel (a) produces a different equilibrium, however. Equilibrium real national income increases to $5.5 trillion per year, which is less than in panel (a) because part of the increase in *nominal* national income has occurred through an increase in the price level to 130.

THE MULTIPLIER WHEN THE PRICE LEVEL CAN CHANGE

Clearly, the multiplier effect on the equilibrium overall level of *real* national income will not be as great if part of the increase in *nominal* national income occurs because of increases in the price level. We show this in Figure 11-10 on the next page. The intersection of AD_1 and *SRAS* is at a price level of 120 with equilibrium real national income of $5 trillion per year. An increase in autonomous spending shifts the aggregate demand curve outward to the right to AD_2. If price level remained at 120, the equilibrium level of real GDP would increase to $5.5 trillion per year because, for the $100 billion increase in autonomous spending, the multiplier would be 5, as it was in Figure 11-9 and Table 11-2. But the price level does not stay fixed because ordinarily *SRAS* is positively sloped. In this diagram the new equilibrium level of real national income is hypothetically $5.3 trillion of real national income per year. Instead of the multiplier being 5, the multiplier with respect to the

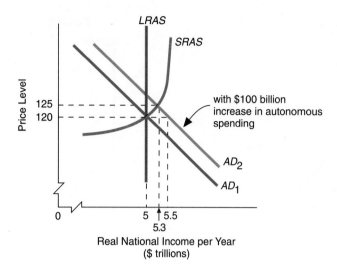

FIGURE 11-10
Multiplier effect on equilibrium of real national income.
A $100 billion increase in autonomous spending (investment, government, or net exports), which moves AD_1 to AD_2, will yield a full multiplier effect only if prices are constant. If the price index increases from 120 to 125, the multiplier effect is less, and the equilibrium level of real national income goes up only to, say, $5.3 trillion per year instead of $5.5 trillion per year.

equilibrium changes in the output of real goods and services—real national income—is only 3. The multiplier is smaller because part of the additional income is used to pay higher prices; not all is spent on increased output, as is the case when the price level is fixed.

If the economy is at an equilibrium level of real national income that is greater than *LRAS*, the implications for the multiplier are even more severe. Look again at Figure 11-10. The *SRAS* curve starts to slope upward more dramatically after $5 trillion of real national income per year. Therefore, any increase in aggregate demand will lead to a proportionally greater increase in the price level and a smaller increase in the equilibrium level of real national income per year. The multiplier effect of any increase in autonomous spending will be relatively small because most of the changes will be in the price level. Moreover, any increase in the equilibrium level of real national income will tend to be temporary because the economy is temporarily above *LRAS*—the strain on its productive capacity will raise prices.

CONCEPTS IN BRIEF

- An expansionary gap exists when total planned expenditures exceed real national income at the full-employment level of real national income. A contractionary gap exists when total planned expenditures are less than the full-employment level of real national income.
- Because output requires inputs, there is a relationship between the number of employees and the rate of real national income per year.
- When the fixed price level assumption is dropped, the *SRAS* slopes upward. Consequently, any increase in *AD* will have less than a full multiplier effect on the equilibrium rate of real national income per year.

THE NEW INHERITORS
Concepts Applied: Consumption, wealth, saving

The wealth—here in the form of an estate with a nice swimming pool—that has been acquired by people born during the first 20 years after World War II will in the next 25 years be inherited by their children. This represents the largest intergenerational transfer of wealth in U.S. history.

The largest intergenerational transfer of wealth in U.S. history is under way. The baby boomers—people born during the 20 years following World War II—are reaching middle age, and many of their parents are entering their seventies. According to economist Robert Avery of Cornell University, the boomers' parents—people aged 60 and over—have accumulated a net worth of $6.8 trillion. All of it has to go somewhere, and most of it is likely to end up in the pockets and bank accounts of their children and perhaps eventually their grandchildren.

As shown in Table 11-4, the wealth has already started to trickle down, and when it reaches its maximum flood during the first decade of the twenty-first century, it is likely to amount to 6.5 percent of gross domestic product each year. About one-third of this vast wealth is now in the form of the homes in which the boomers' parents are living; another one-third is in financial instruments, such as corporate stocks and corporate and government bonds. Where did all this wealth come from, and where is it all going?

SAVING AND WEALTH   Today's elderly grew up during the Great Depression (1929–1933), when real GDP was falling year after year and the unemployment rate hit 25 percent. Many of them came away from the experience with a fear of growing old in poverty, and so they saved diligently for their retirement. Then, during the 1960s and 1970s, Social Security benefits began a sharp rise in real terms and were supplemented by Medicare, which covers many of the medical expenses of the elderly.

The saving behavior of today's senior citizens was enhanced by the economic expansion of the 1980s. The houses in which they had raised their children more than doubled in value, even as the Dow Jones Industrial Average tripled, pushing the value of their corporate stock holdings to record levels. By the beginning of the 1990s, many retirees literally had more money than they knew what to do with. You learned in Chapter 10 that one of the nonincome determinants of the position of the consumption function is wealth. You would think that this increased wealth that your grandparents have would cause their consumption functions to shift up. But that has not happened.

Meanwhile, the baby boomers now face the prospect of putting their own children through college and then somehow financing their own retirement. There is no doubt that many of the boomers have their eyes on the bounty that is headed their way. Given the magnitude of the money that will be changing hands, some analysts think the passing of one generation will spark a wave of conspicuous consumption by the new inheritors. Other observers are more cautious, noting, "There's many a slip 'twixt the will and the wallet."

DEATH AND TAXES   Indeed, health care costs are likely to chew up a substantial portion of the seniors' wealth before it ever gets passed on to their children. Although Medicare covers the basics of health care for the elderly, the rapidly rising cost of high-tech medical care

TABLE 11-4   The coming inheritance.

	TOTAL ESTATES	
YEARS	IN TRILLIONS OF 1992 DOLLARS	AS A PERCENTAGE OF GDP
1987–1991	1.02	4.3
1992–1996	1.45	5.3
1997–2001	1.95	6.3
2002–2006	2.26	6.5
2007–2011	2.34	6.1

is often covered only in part. Moreover, the cost of staying in a nursing home now averages between $25,000 and $30,000 per year. More than 30 percent of elderly Americans currently require such care, and many experts expect the number to rise as life expectancies grow.

Then, too, the government has its eye on all that cash. The Congressional Budget Office has already estimated that it would take only minor revisions to the inheritance laws to generate $1 billion a year in new revenue for the federal government. With revenue estimates in hand, can new tax bills be far behind?

Perhaps the biggest reason that the new inheritors are unlikely to binge with their apparent wealth is the prospect of *future* taxes. The net federal debt is now over $3.5 trillion and rising at a rate of more than $300 billion per year. Moreover, in an effort to keep down the apparent cost of federal spending, Congress has increasingly been moving big-ticket items "off-budget"—where they won't show up in the official debt numbers but will

ultimately have to be paid for out of higher taxes. Finally, the big increases in Social Security benefits that helped fund the retirement of today's seniors will ultimately produce higher payroll taxes down the road. All in all, then, the huge intergenerational transfer that has started taking place might be just enough to pay for the higher taxes that the baby boomers will face as they enter their golden years—which may be the whole reason their parents set it aside for them in the first place.

FOR CRITICAL ANALYSIS

1. If you knew that your children were going to face enormous tax bills in the future, do you think you would try to put money aside to help them pay those bills?
2. The baby boomers developed a reputation for spending first and waiting until later to ask whether they could afford it. Do you think this behavior had any link to the fact that their parents were accumulating substantial amounts of wealth?

CHAPTER SUMMARY

1. If we assume that there are large amounts of excess capacity and labor unemployment, we can use the horizontal portion of the short-run aggregate supply curve. Therefore, prices are assumed to be constant, and nominal values are equivalent to real values.

2. When we add the consumption function, autonomous investment, autonomous government spending, and the autonomous net exports function, we obtain the $C + I + G + X$ curve, which gives us total planned expenditures per year.

3. The equilibrium level of real national income occurs where the $C + I + G + X$ curve intersects the 45-degree reference line, or where total planned expenditures exactly equal real national income (total production).

4. When total planned expenditures exceed real national income, inventories will be drawn down more rapidly than planned. As a result, firms will expand production and, in the process, hire more workers, thus leading to an increase in output and employment. The opposite occurs when total planned expenditures are less than real national income.

5. Planned saving and planned investment must be equal at the equilibrium rate of real national income (ignoring government and foreign transactions). Whenever the actual level of real national income exceeds the

equilibrium level, an unplanned inventory increase will trigger production cuts and layoffs. Whenever actual real national income is less than the equilibrium level of real national income, an unplanned inventory decrease will cause increased production and employment.

6. A key aspect of simplified Keynesian analysis is that a change in investment will result in a multiple change in equilibrium income. The size of the multiplier effect of a change in autonomous investment is positively related to the marginal propensity to consume. The higher the marginal propensity to consume, the greater the autonomous investment multiplier. We find the autonomous investment multiplier by first finding the marginal propensity to save (1 minus the marginal propensity to consume), expressed as a fraction, and taking the inverse of that fraction. A marginal propensity to consume of .8 means that the marginal propensity to save is .2 or $\frac{1}{5}$. The inverse of $\frac{1}{5}$ is 5; thus the investment multiplier is 5.

7. Whenever the equilibrium level of real national income exceeds the full-employment level (with fixed prices), an expansionary gap exists. Whenever the equilibrium level of real national income is less than the full-employment level, a contractionary gap exists.

8. It is possible to find the equilibrium level of employment associated with the equilibrium level of real national income by deriving a production relationship between real national income and employment at each level of real national income.

9. If we relax the assumption of a fixed price level, we are then operating on the upward-sloping portion of the short-run aggregate supply curve. Hence an increase in aggregate demand will lead to some increase in the price level. This increase in the price level will have an offsetting effect on equilibrium total planned expenditures because of wealth, interest rate, and foreign goods substitution effects. Under such circumstances, any increase in aggregate demand will lead to both an increase in the price level and an increase in output.

DISCUSSION OF PREVIEW POINTS

1. **What does the total planned expenditures curve indicate?**

   The total planned expenditures curve indicates what the community intends to spend at every level of real national income. In a closed (omitting international transactions), private (omitting government transactions) economy, the total planned expenditures curve equals the value of consumption expenditures plus the value of investment expenditures at every level of real national income.

2. **How do we interpret the 45-degree reference line?**

   Because the 45-degree reference line bisects the total planned expenditures/real national income quadrant, total planned expenditures *exactly* equal real national income at all points on this line. Hence equilibrium is possible at any point on the 45-degree reference line.

3. **What is the concept of the multiplier, how does it work, and what is its main determinant?**

   The multiplier concept says, simply, that a $1 shift in the total planned expenditures curve will cause the equilibrium level of national income to change by more than $1. In particular, a $1 increase (shift upward) in the total planned expenditures curve will cause the equilibrium level of national income to rise by more than $1; a $1 decrease (shift downward) in the total planned expenditures curve will cause the equilibrium level of national income to fall by more than $1. In a closed, private economy, changes (shifts) in the total planned expenditures curve are caused by changes (shifts) in autonomous consumption and autonomous investment.

   Let's take an example. Suppose that we start from an equilibrium position and then autonomous net investment rises by $1 due to an increase in the output and sale of one machine priced at $1. The people who produced this machine receive an extra $1 in income (above last year's income). Thus income already rises by $1 in the first round. The people who produced the machine will spend some of the increase in their income and save some of it. Because one person's expenditure is another's income, income will rise again. Thus if the MPC is $\frac{3}{4}$, the group that produced the machine (and received a $1 increase in income) will spend 75 cents on goods and services and will save 25 cents. The 75 cents spent becomes income for the people who produced the 75 cents' worth of consumer goods. Note that after two rounds, national income has already increased by $1.75 ($1 + $.75); we already have a multiplier effect. Moreover, there is no reason why this process should stop here; the people who just received an increase in income of 75 cents will spend some and save some. The amount they spend becomes income for others. Thus the multiplier effect exists because increases in income lead to increases in consumption expenditures, which in turn lead to further income increases. Because one person's expenditure is another's income, it follows that the higher the MPC, the more the equilibrium level of income will change for given changes in autonomous expenditures.

4. **What might cause shifts in the total planned expenditures curve?**

   In our model total planned expenditures equal consumption *(C)*, investment *(I)*, government purchases of goods and services *(G)*, and net exports *(X)*. For simplicity we have made the last three components of total planned expenditures autonomous, that is, independent of the level of real disposable income. Consumption also has an autonomous component. Therefore, any change in the non-income determinants of consumption—for example, changes in expectations—will shift the $C + I + G + X$ curve. Furthermore, because *I, G,* and *X* are all considered autonomous, any change in those functions will also shift the $C + I + G + X$ curve.

PROBLEMS

(Answers to the odd-numbered problems appear at the back of the book.)

REAL NATIONAL INCOME	CONSUMPTION EXPENDITURES	SAVING	INVESTMENT	APC	APS	MPC	MPS
$1,000	$1,100	$_____	$100	_____	_____	_____	_____
2,000	2,000	_____	_____	_____	_____	_____	_____
3,000	_____	_____	_____	_____	_____	_____	_____
4,000	_____	_____	_____	_____	_____	_____	_____
5,000	_____	_____	_____	_____	_____	_____	_____
6,000	_____	_____	_____	_____	_____	_____	_____

11-1. The information in the table above applies to a hypothetical economy. Assume that the marginal propensity to consume is constant at all levels of income. Further assume that investment is autonomous.
  a. Draw a graph of the consumption function. Then add the investment function, giving you $C + I$.
  b. Right under the first graph, draw in the saving and investment curves. Does the $C + I$ curve intersect the 45-degree line in the upper graph at the same level of real national income as where saving equals investment in the lower graph? (If not, redraw your graphs.)
  c. What is the multiplier effect from the inclusion of investment?
  d. What is the numerical value of the multiplier?
  e. What is the equilibrium level of real national income and output without investment? With investment?
  f. What will happen to income if autonomous investment increased by $100?
  g. What will the equilibrium level of real national income be if autonomous consumption increases by $100?

11-2. Assume a closed, private economy.
  a. If the MPC = 0, what is the multiplier?
  b. What is the multiplier if the MPC = $\frac{1}{2}$? If the MPC = $\frac{3}{4}$? If the MPC = $\frac{9}{10}$? If the MPC = 1?
  c. What happens to the multiplier as the MPC rises?
  d. In what range does the multiplier fall?

11-3. Consider a closed, private economy in which $C = \$30 + \frac{3}{4}Y$ and $I = \$25$. What will the equilibrium level of real national income (Y) be equal to in this economy? (Hint: In equilibrium, real national income must equal total planned expenditures, or $Y = C + I$.)

11-4. Use the model in Problem 11-3.
  a. What is the multiplier?
  b. What will the new equilibrium level of real national income be if investment increases by $5?

11-5. Using the model in Problem 11-3, calculate the new equilibrium level of real national income if the consumption function becomes $C = \$35 + \frac{3}{4}Y$ (the consumption function shifts upward by $5).

11-6. Define a contractionary gap and an expansionary gap.

11-7. When prices are flexible, why is there an offsetting movement on the level of aggregate output following an initial upward shift in the $C + I$ curve?

*11-8. If the consumption function is $C = \$20 + 0.8Y$ and the level of investment is $I = \$10$, determine the levels of consumption expenditures for $Y = \$50$, $\$150$, and $\$250$. Determine the level of Y that makes saving, S = investment, I.

11-9. Calculate the multiplier for the following cases:
  a. MPC = .9   c. MPS = .15
  b. MPS = .3   d. $C = \$100 + .65Y$

11-10. Other things being constant, if the MPS = .1 and investment spending falls by $100 million, what will be the change in national income? What is the value of the multiplier for this economy?

 COMPUTER-ASSISTED INSTRUCTION (Complete problem and answers on disk.)

A blend of numerical and graphical exercises is used to examine the basics of income determination, emphasizing the central role of the multiplier.

*Asterisked problems are optional; algebra is required.

FISCAL POLICY

When you work, you normally get paid on a regular basis. Your employer is required in almost all instances to withhold federal income taxes. The employer then remits them to the federal government on your behalf. As an individual you have some flexibility about how much withholding your employer takes out from every paycheck, but not much. There are specific Internal Revenue Service rules that are fairly strictly enforced. You typically have to "keep current" with your federal tax liabilities as you earn income. Would your behavior change if the federal government told you that you could now have your employer withhold fewer federal taxes? This is exactly what happened during the 1990–1991 recession. How would a rational person react to such a change in federal government taxing policy? You will learn about this issue in your study of fiscal policy.

After reading this chapter, you should be able to answer the following questions:

1. What is fiscal policy?

2. What is automatic fiscal policy? How does it lend stability to an economy?

3. How does the crowding-out effect offset expansionary fiscal policy?

4. What types of time lags exist between the need for fiscal stimulus and the time when such stimulus actually affects the national economy?

INTRODUCTION

When people talk about the "good old days," they might be referring to the period in U.S. history prior to the passage of the Sixteenth Amendment in 1913 because for most of that period there was absolutely no federal income tax. Also, federal government spending programs (and even those of the states) were not very impressive. Federal government spending averaged less than 8 percent of GDP each year until the 1930s. Similar statistics today tell a different story: In any one year, federal government expenditures on goods and services, transfer payments, and everything else total about one-fourth of GDP and are rising. Federal taxes collected average about 19 percent of GDP per year and are also rising. Today, clearly, federal government tax and spending policies can have significant effects on our national economy. Indeed, deliberate changes in federal government spending and taxing policies can and have altered the equilibrium level of nominal GDP and real GDP. How and when government can change nominal and real GDP are the focus of this chapter.

FISCAL POLICY

Deliberate, discretionary change in government expenditures and/or taxes in order to achieve certain national economic goals is the realm of **fiscal policy.** Some national goals are high employment (low unemployment), price stability, economic growth, and improvement in the nation's international payments balance. Fiscal policy can be thought of as a deliberate attempt to cause the economy to move to full employment and price stability more quickly than it otherwise might.

▶ **Fiscal policy**
The discretionary changing of government expenditures and/or taxes in order to achieve national economic goals, such as high employment with price stability.

FISCAL POLICY MADE EASY

When There Is a Contractionary Gap. The government, along with firms, individuals, and foreigners, is one of the spending agents in the economy. When the government decides to spend more, all other things held constant, the dollar value of total spending must rise. Look at panel (a) of Figure 12-1. We start off at equilibrium with AD_1 intersecting $SRAS$ at $5.5 trillion of real GDP per year. There is contractionary gap of

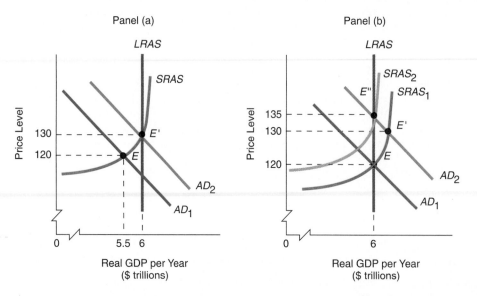

Panel (a)

Panel (b)

FIGURE 12-1
Expansionary fiscal policy: two scenarios.
If there is a contractionary gap and equilibrium is at E in panel (a), fiscal policy can presumably increase aggregate demand to AD_2. The new equilibrium is at E' at higher real GDP per year and a higher price level. If, though, we are already on $LRAS$ as in panel (b), expansionary fiscal policy will simply lead to a temporary equilibrium at E' and a final equilibrium at E'', again at $LRAS$ of $6 trillion of real GDP per year but at a higher price level of 135.

$500 billion per year of real GDP—the difference between *LRAS* (the economy's long-run potential) and the equilibrium level of real GDP per year. When the government decides to spend more, the aggregate demand curve shifts to the right to AD_2. Here we assume that the government knows exactly how much more to spend so that AD_2 intersects *SRAS* at $6 trillion, or at *LRAS*. Because of the upward-sloping *SRAS*, the price level has risen from 120 to 130. Real GDP has gone to $6 trillion per year. (Nominal GDP has gone up by even more because it consists of the price level index times real GDP. Here the GDP deflator has gone up by $10 \div 120 = 8.33$ percent.[1])

When the Economy Is Operating on Its *LRAS*.   Suppose that the economy is operating on *LRAS*, as in panel (b) of Figure 12-1. An increase in government spending shifts the aggregate demand curve from AD_1 to AD_2. Both prices and real output of goods and services begin to rise to the intersection of E'. But this rate of real GDP per year is untenable in the long run because it exceeds *LRAS*. In the long run, expectations of input owners—workers, owners of capital and raw materials, and so on—are revised. The short-run aggregate supply curve shifts from $SRAS_1$ to $SRAS_2$ because of higher prices and higher resource costs (see Chapter 9). Real GDP returns to the *LRAS* level of $6 trillion per year. The full impact of the increased government expenditures is on the price level only, which increases to 135.

Reductions in Government Spending.   The entire process shown in Figure 12-1 can be reversed. Government can reduce spending, thereby shifting the aggregate demand curve inward. You should be able to show how this affects the equilibrium level of the price index and the real output of goods and services (real GDP) on similar diagrams.

CHANGES IN TAXES

The spending decisions of firms, individuals, and foreigners depend on the taxes levied on them. Individuals in their role as consumers look to their disposable (after-tax) income when determining their desired rate of consumption. Firms look at their after-tax profits when deciding on the level of investment to undertake. Foreigners look at the tax-inclusive cost of goods when deciding whether to buy in the United States or elsewhere. Therefore, holding all other things constant, a rise in taxes causes a reduction in aggregate demand for one of three reasons: (1) It reduces consumption, (2) it reduces investment, or (3) it reduces net exports. What actually happens depends, of course, on whom the taxes are levied.

When the Current Equilibrium Is Greater than *LRAS*.   Assume that aggregate demand is AD_1 in panel (a) of Figure 12-2 on the next page. It intersects *SRAS* at *E*, which is at greater than *LRAS*. In this situation an increase in taxes shifts the aggregate demand curve inward to the left. For argument's sake, assume that it intersects *SRAS* at E', or exactly where *LRAS* intersects AD_2. In this situation the equilibrium level of real GDP falls from $6.5 trillion per year to $6 trillion per year. The price level index falls from 120 to 100.

If the Economy Is at Both Short-Run and Long-Run Equilibrium.   Assume that the economy is already in short-run and long-run equilibrium as shown in panel

---

[1]Percent change in price index $= \dfrac{\text{change in price index}}{\text{price index}} = \dfrac{130 - 120}{120} = 8.33$ percent

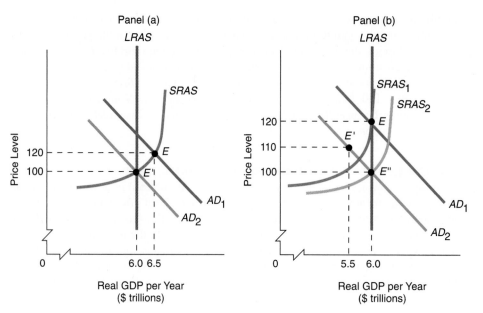

FIGURE 12-2
Contractionary fiscal policy: two scenarios.
In panel (a) the economy is initially at *E*, which exceeds *LRAS*. Contractionary fiscal policy can move aggregate demand to AD_2 so the new equilibrium is at *E'* at a lower price level and at *LRAS*. In panel (b) similar contractionary fiscal policy initially moves equilibrium from *E* to *E'*, but then it goes to *E"* at *LRAS*. The only long-run effect is to lower the price level to 100.

(b) of Figure 12-2. The aggregate demand curve, AD_1, intersects both *LRAS* and *SRAS* at $6 trillion of real GDP per year. If aggregate demand decreases to AD_2, a new temporary equilibrium will occur at *E'* with the price level at 110 and real equilibrium GDP at $5.5 trillion per year. That means that in the short run, prices and the real output of goods and services fall. Input suppliers revise their expectations downward. The short-run aggregate supply curve shifts to $SRAS_2$. The real level of equilibrium GDP returns to the *LRAS* level of $6 trillion per year. The full *long-run* impact of fiscal policy in this situation is solely on the price level, which falls to 100.

Effects of a Reduction in Taxes. The effects of a reduction in taxes are exactly the reverse of the effects of an increase in taxes. Figure 12-1 and the accompanying discussion of the effects of an increase in government expenditures provide the full analysis.

CONCEPTS IN BRIEF

- Fiscal policy is defined as the discretionary change in government expenditures and/or taxes in order to achieve such national goals as high employment or reduced inflation.
- If there is a contractionary gap and the economy is operating at less than long-run average supply (*LRAS*), an increase in government spending can shift the aggregate demand curve to the right and perhaps lead to a higher equilibrium level of real GDP per year. If the economy is already operating on *LRAS*, in contrast, expansionary fiscal policy in the long run simply leads to a higher price level.
- Changes in taxes can have similar affects on the equilibrium rate of real GDP and the price level. A decrease in taxes can lead to an increase in real GDP, but if the economy is already operating on its *LRAS*, eventually such decreases in taxes will lead only to increases in the price level.

POSSIBLE OFFSETS TO FISCAL POLICY

Fiscal policy does not operate in a vacuum. Important questions have to be answered: If government expenditures increase, how are they paid for? If taxes are increased, what does the government do with the taxes? What will happen if individuals worry about increases in *future* taxes because there is more government spending today with no increased taxes? All of these questions involve *offsets* to the effects of fiscal policy. We will look at each of them and others in detail.

INDIRECT CROWDING OUT

Let's take the first example of fiscal policy in this chapter, an increase in government expenditures. If government expenditures rise and taxes are held constant, something has to give. Our government does not simply take goods and services when it wants them. It has to pay for them. When it pays for them and does not simultaneously collect the same amount in taxes, it must borrow. That means that an increase in government spending without raising taxes creates additional government borrowing from the private sector (or from foreigners).

The Interest Rate Effect.
Holding everything else constant, if the government attempts to borrow more from the private sector to pay for its increased budget deficit, it is not going to have an easy time selling its bonds. If the bond market is in equilibrium, when the government tries to sell more bonds, it is going to have to offer a better deal in order to get rid of them. A better deal means offering a higher interest rate. This is the interest rate effect of expansionary fiscal policy financed by borrowing from the public. In this sense, when the federal government finances increased spending by additional borrowing, it may push interest rates up. When interest rates go up, it is more expensive for firms to finance new construction, equipment, and inventories. It is also more expensive for individuals to finance their cars and homes. Thus a rise in government spending, holding taxes constant (in short, deficit spending), tends to crowd out private spending, dampening the positive effect of increased government spending on aggregate demand. This is called the **crowding-out effect.** In the extreme case, the crowding out may be complete, with the increased government spending having no net effect on aggregate demand. The final result is simply more government spending and less private investment and consumption. Figure 12-3 shows how the crowding-out effect occurs.

▶ **Crowding-out effect**
The tendency of expansionary fiscal policy to cause a decrease in planned investment or planned consumption in the private sector; this decrease normally results from the rise in interest rates.

FIGURE 12-3
The crowding-out effect.

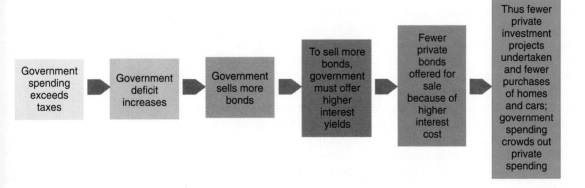

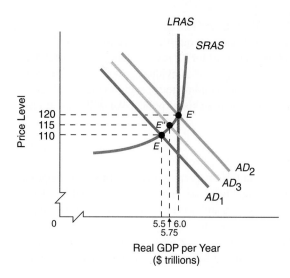

FIGURE 12-4
The crowding-out effect.
Expansionary fiscal policy that causes deficit financing initially shifts AD_1 to AD_2. Equilibrium initially moves toward E'. But because of crowding out, the aggregate demand curve shifts inward to AD_3, and the new equilibrium is at E''.

The Firm's Investment Decision. To understand the interest rate effect better, consider a firm that is contemplating borrowing $100,000 to expand its business. Suppose that the interest rate is 9 percent. The interest payments on the debt will be 9 percent times $100,000, or $9,000 per year ($750 per month). A rise in the interest rate to 12 percent will push the payments to 12 percent of $100,000, or $12,000 per year ($1,000 per month). The extra $250 per month will discourage some firms from making the investment. Consumers face similar decisions when they purchase houses and cars. An increase in the interest rate causes their monthly payments to go up, thereby discouraging some of them from purchasing cars and houses.

Graphical Analysis. You see in Figure 12-4 that the initial equilibrium, E, is below *LRAS*. But suppose that government expansionary fiscal policy in the form of increased government spending (without increasing taxes) shifts aggregate demand from AD_1 to AD_2. In the absence of the crowding-out effect, the real output of goods and services would increase to $6 trillion per year, and the price level would rise to 120 (point E'). With the crowding-out effect, however, as investment and consumption decline, partly offsetting the rise in government spending, AD shifts inward to the left to AD_3. The new equilibrium is now at E'', with real GDP of $5.75 trillion per year at a price level of 115.

INTERNATIONAL EXAMPLE: Japanese Policymakers Ignore Potential Crowding-Out Effects

The Japanese economy experienced a relatively severe recession that started before the 1990–1991 recession in the United States and lasted longer. Japanese policymakers sought numerous ways to pull the Japanese economy out of its recession. Many of its governmental leaders argued in favor of traditional fiscal policy stimuli—cutting taxes and especially increasing government spending on roads, bridges, and other infrastructure. The Japanese stock market jumped abruptly in the summer of 1992 when the government "leaked" a story about an $80 billion fiscal stimulus package that was going to be passed. Apparently, investors in the stock market were convinced that increased government spending and lower taxes—leading to bigger deficits—would not have any crowding-out effect. Again in April, 1993, the Japanese government announced a $116 billion fiscal stimulus plan. The stock market again took off, in spite of the fact that the previous stimulus plan had not succeeded.

Apparently, President Bill Clinton, during his campaign in 1992, also wished to ignore any crowding-out effects of fiscal policy. He and his campaign advisers argued vigorously for a multi-billion-dollar fiscal stimulus package that would be aimed at improving America's infrastructure—roads, railroads, and the like.

For Critical Analysis: Why might government deficit spending on the infrastructure lead to an increase in the equilibrium level of real GDP and employment? ●

WHEN PEOPLE PLAN FOR THE FUTURE—THE NEW CLASSICAL ECONOMICS

Economists have implicitly assumed that people look at changes in taxes or changes in government spending only in the present. What if people actually think about the size of future tax payments? Does this have an effect on how they react to an increase in government spending with no tax increases? Some economists, who call themselves the *new classical economists,* believe that the answer is yes. What if people's horizons extend beyond this year? Don't we then have to take into account the effects of today's government policies on the future?

Consider an example. The government increases spending without increasing taxes today. That means that the government budget deficit increases. When the government borrows more, it has to pay more in interest and principal payments, but more of such payments in the future constitute increased government spending. Eventually, the government will have to raise taxes to pay for these additional payments. If people understand this, they will want to prepare for increased taxes in the future. The way to prepare is to save more today. Increased government spending without an increase in taxes, according to the new classical economists, will not have a necessarily large impact on aggregate demand. In terms of Figure 12-4, the aggregate demand curve will shift inward from AD_2 to AD_3. In the extreme case, if consumers fully compensate for a higher tax liability in the future by saving more, the aggregate demand curve shifts all the way back to AD_1 in Figure 12-4. This is the case of individuals fully discounting their increased tax liabilities. The result is that an increased budget deficit created entirely by a current tax cut has literally no effect on the economy. This is known as the **Ricardian equivalence theorem,** after the nineteenth-century economist David Ricardo, who first developed the argument publicly.

▶ **Ricardian equivalence theorem**
The proposition that an increase in the government budget deficit has no effect on aggregate demand.

DIRECT CROWDING OUT

Government has a distinct comparative advantage over the private sector in certain activities such as diplomacy and national defense. Otherwise stated, certain resource-using activities in which the government engages are pure monopolies that do not compete with the private sector. In contrast, some of what government does competes directly with the private sector, such as education. When government competes with the private sector, **direct expenditure offsets** to fiscal policy may occur. For example, if the government starts providing free milk to students who are already purchasing milk, there is a direct expenditure offset. Households spend less directly on milk, but government spends more.

▶ **Direct expenditure offsets**
Actions on the part of the private sector in spending money that offset government fiscal policy actions. Any increase in government spending in an area that competes with the private sector will have some direct expenditure offset.

The normal way to analyze the impact of an increase in government spending on aggregate demand is implicitly to assume that government spending is *not* a substitute for private spending. This is clearly the case for an ICBM missile. Whenever government spending is a substitute for private spending, however, a rise in government spending causes a direct reduction in private spending to offset it.

The Extreme Case.   In the extreme case, the direct expenditure offset is dollar for dollar, so we merely end up with a relabeling of spending from private to public. Assume that you have decided to spend $100 on groceries. Upon your arrival at the checkout counter, you are met by a U.S. Department of Agriculture official. She announces that she will pay for your groceries—but only the ones in the cart. Here increased government spending is $100. You leave the store in bliss. But just as you are deciding how to spend the $100, an Internal Revenue Service agent meets you. He announces that as a result of the current budgetary crisis, your taxes are going to rise by $100. You have to pay right now. Increases in taxes have now been $100. We have a balanced-budget increase in government spending. Under the assumption of a complete direct expenditure offset, there would be no change in total spending. We simply end up with higher government spending, which directly crowds out exactly the same amount of consumption. Aggregate demand and GDP are unchanged.

The Less Extreme Case.   Much government spending has a private-sector substitute. When government expenditures increase, there is a tendency for private spending to decline somewhat, thereby mitigating the upward impact on total aggregate demand. To the extent that there are some direct expenditure offsets to expansionary fiscal policy, predicted changes in aggregate demand will be lessened. Consequently, real output and the price level will be less affected.

 EXAMPLE: The End of the Cold War

For all intents and purposes, the Cold War has been over for several years. The big, bad Soviet Union with which America had to compete internationally is no longer. The Cold War entailed military spending that did not clearly have any direct expenditure offset to private spending. Military spending is the best example of government spending that is truly different from private expenditures. Changes in military expenditures are the most likely government expenditures to have real effects on the national economy whenever they go up or down.

The so-called peace dividend that may occur because of the ending of the Cold War is not insignificant. It has been estimated as high as $1 trillion during the 1990s. Considered as fiscal policy, the way we spend the possible peace dividend is important because of the possibility of direct expenditure offsets. If the peace dividend is spent on higher education, the expansionary effect on equilibrium GDP may not be as great as anticipated. Why? Because many individuals privately purchase higher education. The greater the amount of education paid for by the federal government, the less some households will spend themselves. Consequently, the predicted change in the equilibrium level of real GDP may be less than otherwise.

For Critical Analysis: In what other areas of spending are there possible direct expenditure offsets? Is there any type of government spending other than military that has no private-sector counterpart and hence would have no direct expenditure offset? If so, what is it? ●

THE OPEN-ECONOMY EFFECT

The last offset to fiscal policy that we will discuss involves the open economy-effect. It is a variant of the crowding-out effect, but one that now works its way through changes in net exports. If government spending is increased without a rise in taxes or if taxes are decreased without a reduction in government spending, the federal government must borrow more. As we pointed out, the government has to offer more attractive interest rates, so overall interest rates go up. When interest rates go up in the United States, foreigners demand more securities such as U.S. government bonds. When they do this, they have to pay for the bonds with dollars. After all, the typical Japanese stock and bond firm cannot buy more U.S. government bonds without getting its hands on more U.S. dollars. This increases the demand for dollars at the same time that it increases the supply of yen. The value of the yen falls relative to the value of the dollar in international transactions. When this occurs, Japanese-made goods become cheaper in America. American-made goods in Japan become more expensive. Americans want to buy more Japanese goods and the Japanese want to buy fewer American goods. This causes a reduction in net exports (X) and cuts into any increase in aggregate demand. In sum, to the extent that federal deficit spending reduces net exports, the effect of expansionary fiscal policy will be less.

THE SUPPLY-SIDE EFFECTS OF CHANGES IN TAXES

We have talked about changing taxes and changing government spending, the traditional tools of fiscal policy. We have not really talked about the possibility of changing marginal tax rates. Recall from Chapter 5 that the marginal tax rate is the rate applied to the last bracket of taxable income. In our federal tax system, rising marginal tax rates are applied to rising income. In that sense, the United States has a progressive federal individual income tax system. Expansionary fiscal policy might involve reducing marginal tax rates. Advocates of such changes argue that (1) lower tax rates will lead to an increase in productivity because individuals will work harder and longer, save more, and invest more; and (2) increased productivity will lead to more economic growth, which will lead to higher real GDP. The government, by applying lower marginal tax rates, will not necessarily lose tax revenues. For the lower marginal tax rates will be applied to a growing tax base because of economic growth—after all, tax revenues are the product of a tax rate times a tax base. People who support this notion are called supply-side economists. **Supply-side economics** involves changing the tax structure to create incentives to increased productivity.

> ▶ **Supply-side economics**
> Attempts at creating incentives for individuals and firms to increase productivity, thereby causing the aggregate supply curve to shift.

Effect of Changes in Tax Rates on Labor.   Consider the supply-side effects of taxes on labor. A change in tax rates has both a substitution and real-income effect (discussed in Chapter 3). An increase in tax rates reduces the opportunity cost of leisure, thereby inducing individuals (at least on the margin) to reduce their work effort and to consume more leisure. This is the substitution effect. But an increase in tax rates will also reduce spendable income and have a real-income effect, thereby shifting the demand for leisure curve inward to the left. Here a reduction in real spendable income shifts the demand curve for all goods and services, including leisure, inward to the left. The outcome of these two effects—substitution and income—depends on which of them is stronger. Supply-side economists argue that in the 1970s and 1980s the substitution effect dominated to the extent that increases in marginal tax rates caused workers to work less and decreases caused workers to work more.

Supply-Side Economics and the Laffer Curve.   When supply-side economics became a popular theory during the presidential campaign of 1980, the effects on government tax revenues of changes in tax *rates* were at issue. Notice the emphasis on rates. Supply-side economics deals only with changes in marginal tax rates. The underlying assumption is that individuals, in their capacities as workers, savers, and investors, will respond to changes on the margin. The higher the marginal tax rate, the greater the incentive to avoid paying taxes, either through legal tax avoidance, illegal tax evasion, or less work, saving, and investment. This simple proposition dates back perhaps several thousand years. It was reborn as the **Laffer curve,** named after Arthur Laffer, an economist at the University of Southern California. Basically, the Laffer curve shows that people do

> ▶ **Laffer curve**
> A graphical representation of the relationship between tax rates and total tax revenues raised by taxation.

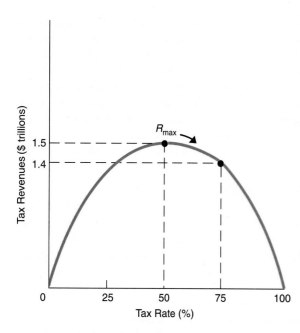

FIGURE 12-5
The Laffer curve.
The Laffer curve represents the relationship between tax *rates* and tax *revenues* collected. On the vertical axis are tax revenues, R, measured in trillions of dollars per year. On the horizontal axis are tax rates from 0 to 100 percent. The maximum revenues collected, R_{max}, are equal to $1.5 trillion per year. They can be generated by a tax rate of 50 percent. If the tax rate is 75 percent, however, only $1.4 trillion of tax revenues is generated per year. A reduction from 75 to 50 percent will cause tax revenues collected to increase rather than decrease.

respond to incentives. If this is the case, there is indeed a relationship between marginal tax rates and total tax revenues collected by the government. The curve suggests that marginal tax rates can reach a point at which people reduce their work effort, spend more time seeking ways to reduce tax liabilities, and engage in more nonreported (nontaxed) exchanges. After some point and after some time, an increase in tax rates actually reduces total tax revenues. Look at Figure 12-5. We measure tax rates on the horizontal axis and tax revenues, R, on the vertical axis. A tax rate of 18 percent is the maximum rate that the government can impose before the relationship between tax rates and revenues becomes negative. For example, at a tax rate of 25 percent, revenues will have dropped from an R_{max} of $1.5 trillion to $1 trillion.

EXAMPLE: **The Effects of Tax Cuts on Tax Revenues**

According to the Laffer curve, if tax *rates* are high enough, it may be possible to increase tax *revenues* by lowering those rates. Although many skeptics scoffed when this idea was first proposed, its validity had already been demonstrated some 70 years ago. Between 1922 and 1925, income tax rates were cut sharply, particularly at the upper end. Top marginal tax rates, for example, were slashed from 73 percent to 58 percent. For individuals making less than $50,000 per year, the lower tax rates reduced their share of total taxes paid by 51 percent. For people earning more than $50,000 per year, just the reverse happened: As predicted by the Laffer curve, their share of taxes paid went *up* by 80 percent.

More recent history provides additional evidence on the predictive power of the Laffer curve. In 1964 and again in a series of steps over the period 1981–1988, marginal income tax rates were cut sharply. In 1964, for example, the top rate was cut from 91 percent to 70 percent; during the 1980s this top rate was further reduced to 33 percent. Table 12-1 summarizes the impact of these tax cuts. For the vast majority of individuals, those in the bottom 95 percent of the income distribution, the lower tax rates also reduced their tax burdens— by 9.5 percent in the first period and by 6.1 percent in the second. For the very wealthiest individuals—those in the top 5 percent of the income distribution—lower tax rates actually *increased* their tax obligation. The 1964 tax cut caused the tax obligations of the very rich to rise by 7.7 percent; during the 1980s the tax bite for the wealthy soared 44 percent.

TABLE 12-1 **The effects of tax cuts on tax revenues: percentage change in tax revenues, by income category.**

	TIME PERIOD	
INCOME CATEGORY	1963–1965	1981–1988
Top 5%	+7.7	+44.0
Bottom 95%	−9.5	−6.1

Source: U.S. Department of Treasury, Internal Revenue Service.

For Critical Analysis: *A recent government proposal to increase taxes on "the rich" concluded that tax revenues would rise by $100 billion over four years. How does the Laffer curve analysis affect such projections?* ●

CONCEPTS IN BRIEF

- Indirect crowding out occurs because of an interest effect in which the government, in order to finance its deficit spending, causes interest rates to rise, thereby crowding out private investment and spending, particularly on cars and houses. This is called the crowding-out effect.
- Graphically, the crowding-out effect can be shown as first an outward shift in the aggregate demand curve and then an inward shift in that curve as interest rates rise and private investment is crowded out.
- Many new classical economists believe in the Ricardian equivalence theorem, which argues that an increase in the government budget deficit has no effect on aggregate demand because individuals correctly perceive their increased future taxes and therefore save more today to pay for them.
- Direct crowding out occurs when government spending competes with the private sector and is increased. Direct expenditure offsets to fiscal policy may occur.
- There is an open-economy effect that offsets fiscal policy. Like the crowding-out effect, it occurs because the government's increased deficit causes interest rates to rise. This encourages foreigners to invest more in American securities. When they do so, they demand more dollars, thereby increasing the international value of the dollar. American-made goods become more expensive abroad, so America exports fewer goods and imports more.
- Changes in marginal tax rates may cause supply-side effects if a reduction in marginal tax rates induces enough additional work, saving, and investing. Government tax receipts can actually increase. This is called supply-side economics.

DISCRETIONARY FISCAL POLICY IN PRACTICE

We can discuss fiscal policy in a relatively precise way. We draw graphs with aggregate demand and supply curves to show what we are doing. We could even in principle estimate the offsets that were just discussed. However, even if we were able to measure all of these offsets exactly, would-be fiscal policymakers still face problems: the political process of fiscal policy and the various time lags involved in conducting fiscal policy.

THE POLITICAL PROCESS OF FISCAL POLICY

It is important to realize that no single governmental body designs and implements fiscal policy. The president, with the aid of the director of the Office of Management and

Budget (OMB), the secretary of the Treasury, and the Council of Economic Advisers, designs but only *recommends* the desired mix of taxes and government expenditures. It is Congress, with the aid of many committees (the House Ways and Means Committee, the Senate Finance Committee, and the Senate Budget Committee, to name a few), that *enacts* fiscal policy. The president has veto power over congressional fiscal policy. Thus an inherent organizational problem exists from the very beginning: The power to enact fiscal policy does not rest with one institution. Disagreement as to proper fiscal policy might—and usually does—emerge among members of Congress or between Congress and the president. Although the procedure required for an ultimate solution is clearly spelled out in the U.S. Constitution, in practice it is often a tedious and time-consuming process. During the process, numerous hearings are called and many expert witnesses testify. They usually disagree.

Choosing the Fiscal Policy Mix.   Suppose that it is agreed that fiscal policy is desirable. What is the proper mix of taxes and government expenditures? Let's say that policymakers decide that a change in taxes is desirable. At least eight options are available:

1. Permanent change in personal income taxes
2. Permanent change in corporate income taxes
3. Temporary change in personal income taxes
4. Temporary change in corporate income taxes
5. Change in employment subsidies
6. Change in investment tax credit
7. Change in depreciation allowance on investment expenditures
8. Change in specific consumption tax, such as on oil

Note that all of these are tax changes, but their effects on individual groups will be different, and special-interest groups will be lobbying powerful politicians to protect their interests.

Alternatively, assume that policymakers decide that a change in government expenditures is desirable. There are disadvantages to these changes. Political wrangling will arise over the amount, type, and geographic location of the expenditure change ("spend more in my district or state, less in someone else's"). Furthermore, if the expenditure is to be made on a capital goods project, such as a highway, a dam, or a public transportation system, the problem of timing arises. If started during a recession, should or could such a project be abandoned or delayed if inflation emerges before the project is finished? Are delays or reversals politically feasible, even if they are economically sensible?

TIME LAGS

Policymakers must be concerned with various time lags. Quite apart from the fact that it is difficult to measure economic variables, it takes time to collect and assimilate such data. Thus policymakers must be concerned with the **recognition time lag**, the period of months that may elapse before economic problems can be identified.[2]

After an economic problem is recognized, a solution must be formulated; thus there will be an **action time lag**, the period between the recognition of a problem and the implementation of policy to solve it. For fiscal policy the action time lag is particularly long. It must be approved by Congress, and much political wrangling and infighting

▶ **Recognition time lag**
The time required to gather information about the current state of the economy.

▶ **Action time lag**
The time required between recognizing an economic problem and putting policy into effect. The action time lag is short for monetary policy but quite long for fiscal policy, which requires congressional approval.

---

[2]Final annual data for GDP, after various revisions, are not forthcoming for at least nine months after the year's end.

accompany congressional fiscal policy decision making. It is not at all unusual for the action time lag to last a year or two. Then it takes time to put the policy into effect. After Congress enacts a fiscal policy as legislation, it takes time to decide, for example, who gets the new federal construction contract, and so on.

Effect time lag
The time that elapses between the onset of policy and the results of that policy.

Finally, there is the **effect time lag**; after fiscal policy is enacted, it takes time for it to affect the economy. Multiplier effects take more time to work through the economy than it takes an economist to shift a curve on a chalkboard.

Because the various fiscal policy time lags are long, a policy designed to combat a recession might not produce results until the economy is experiencing inflation, in which case the fiscal policy would worsen the situation. Or a fiscal policy designed to eliminate inflation might not produce effects until the economy is in a recession; in that case, too, fiscal policy would make the economic problem worse rather than better.

Furthermore, because fiscal policy time lags tend to be *variable* (anywhere from one to three years), policymakers have a difficult time fine-tuning the economy. Clearly, fiscal policy is more an art than a science.

EXAMPLE: Our History of Incorrect Fiscal Policy Timing

A cursory examination of fiscal-policy responses to recessions shows a startling fact: Virtually all of the fiscal policy actions were enacted well after the end of the recessions. Here are some examples. A recession began in November 1948, but it was not until July 11, 1949, that President Truman advanced an 11-point program to combat it. Congress enacted only one proposal, called the Advanced Planning for Public Works Act, which was signed in October 1949—just as the recession ended. During the recession from August 1957 to April 1958, fiscal policy actions were signed into law in the same month as the end of the recession and for several months thereafter. They included the Emergency Highway Act and Rivers and Harbors Public Works Act.

There was a recession from December 1969 to November 1970. The only major fiscal policy legislation that addressed it was passed on August 5, 1971—more than a year after the end of the recession. (It was the Public Works Impact Program which targeted public works spending to areas with high unemployment.) During the very serious recession that lasted from July 1981 to November 1982, no fiscal policy legislation was instituted until January 6, 1983, with the passage of the Surface Transportation Assistance Act. A few months later, on March 24, 1983, the Emergency Jobs Appropriations Act was passed, with its effects being felt well after the recession ended. No major fiscal policy actions occurred during the recession at the beginning of the 1990s even though Bill Clinton campaigned on a promise to make an investment tax credit into law. After he had been elected in November 1992 and after the economy was clearly out of the recession—unemployment had been dropping for five straight months—congressional tax writers announced that any tax credits adopted in 1993 would be retroactive to December 4, 1992. (As of the summer of 1993, no such policy had become law, though.)

The fact is that no matter how appropriate fiscal policy may be in principle, Congress never seems to act in time. Fiscal policy normally ends up being destabilizing rather than stabilizing.

For Critical Analysis: *What prevents Congress from enacting counterrecessionary fiscal policy in time?* ●

AUTOMATIC STABILIZERS

Not all changes in taxes (or in tax rates) or in government spending (including government transfers) constitute discretionary fiscal policy. There are several types of automatic

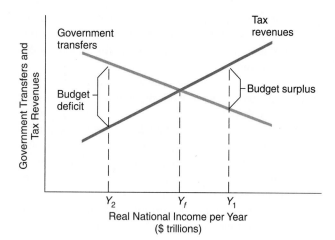

FIGURE 12-6
Automatic stabilizers.
Here we assume that as real national income rises, tax revenues rise and government transfers fall, other things remaining constant. Thus as the economy expands from Y_f to Y_1, a budget surplus automatically arises; as the economy contracts from Y_f to Y_2, a budget deficit automatically arises. Such automatic changes tend to drive the economy back toward its full-employment output level.

(or nondiscretionary) fiscal policies. Such policies do not require new legislation on the part of Congress. Specific automatic fiscal policies include the progressive federal income tax system itself and the government transfer system; the latter includes unemployment compensation.

Thus when national income rises during an expansionary period, the government receives more money in taxes and reduces its expenditures on such transfers as welfare and unemployment compensation. That is, during such periods more people will be employed and tax revenues will rise; moreover, fewer people will be eligible for welfare and unemployment compensation. Or when national income falls during a contractionary period, tax revenues fall and government spending on transfers in the form of welfare and unemployment compensation rises. Simply put, with a contractionary gap, unemployment rises, which leads to an increase in unemployment compensation benefits and a reduction in tax payments by the people so affected.

Note that such automatic changes in tax receipts and government expenditures may act as shock absorbers. When the economy is affected so as to cause it to depart from its full-employment levels, automatic fiscal policy tends to move the economy back toward its full-employment levels.[3] For this reason such changes are referred to as **automatic**, or **built-in, stabilizers**; the economy is moved automatically toward its full-employment levels by changes in government spending on transfers and by changes in tax receipts. Figure 12-6 depicts automatic stabilizers.

▶ **Automatic, or built-in, stabilizers**
Special provisions of the tax law that cause changes in the economy without the action of Congress and the president. Examples are the progressive income tax system and unemployment compensation.

CONCEPTS IN BRIEF

- No one government body designs and implements fiscal policy. The result is a mixture of inputs from the president, the rest of the executive branch, and Congress.
- There are many time lags that reduce the effectiveness of fiscal policy. These include the recognition time lag, the action time lag, and the effect time lag.
- Two automatic, or built-in, stabilizers are the progressive income tax and unemployment compensation.
- Built-in stabilizers tend to automatically moderate changes in disposable income resulting from changes in overall business activity.

---

[3]The economic mechanisms that drive the economy back to its full-employment levels include changes in the price level, wage rates, and interest rates. To these we now add automatic fiscal policy.

WHAT DO WE REALLY KNOW ABOUT FISCAL POLICY?

There are two ways of looking at fiscal policy, one that involves normal times and the other that involves abnormal times.

FISCAL POLICY DURING NORMAL TIMES

During normal times (without "excessive" unemployment, inflation, or problems in the national economy), we know more or less the following: Given the time lag between the recognition of the need to increase aggregate demand and the impact of any expansionary fiscal policy, and given the very modest size of any fiscal policy action that Congress actually will take, discretionary fiscal policy is probably not very effective. Congress ends up doing too little too late to help in a minor recession. To the extent the fiscal policy does anything during normal times, it probably does so by way of automatic stabilizers rather than by way of discretionary policy.

FISCAL POLICY DURING ABNORMAL TIMES

During abnormal times, fiscal policy can be important. Consider some classic examples: the Great Depression and war periods.

The Great Depression.   When there is a substantial catastrophic drop in real GDP, as there was during the Great Depression, fiscal policy probably can do something to stimulate aggregate demand. Because so many people are cash-constrained, government spending is a good way during such periods to get cash into their hands. Nonetheless, during the Great Depression, although there was a lot of talk about expansionary fiscal policy, when federal, state, and local government spending was totaled on a national basis, there was in fact very little stimulation by government in the form of aggressive expansionary fiscal policy. Indeed, all government budgets taken together were actually in surplus at various times during the Great Depression.

Wartime.   Wars are in fact reserved for governments. War expenditures are not good substitutes for private expenditures—they have little or no direct expenditure offsets. Consequently, war spending as part of expansionary fiscal policy usually has noteworthy effects, such as occurred while we were waging World War II, during which real GDP increased dramatically.

WHAT IF THE RICARDIAN EQUIVALENCE THEOREM IS CORRECT?

There is a growing, albeit not yet conclusive, body of evidence that the world is importantly Ricardian. People do in fact worry about future tax liabilities. Expansionary government spending without raising current taxes therefore may not necessarily have much of an effect on aggregate demand. The final word is not yet in and is unlikely to be available soon. Just keep in mind that the Ricardian equivalence theorem may be at work, thereby reducing the effectiveness of discretionary fiscal policy.

A 1990s FISCAL POLICY EXPERIMENT: REDUCING WITHHOLDING

Concepts Applied: Fiscal policy, Ricardian equivalence theorem

Normally anyone who earns income must fill out and submit an income tax return by April 15th. For salaried workers, if insufficient taxes were withheld during the year, unpaid taxes must be paid by April 15th, otherwise penalties and interest may be assessed by the IRS.

In 1992, during the recovery from the 1990–1991 recession, the federal government decided to "put some steam back into the economy." The administration reduced the amount of taxes withheld while keeping tax rates (and thus tax liabilities) constant. Put another way, current tax payments were reduced, but total tax liabilities remained unchanged. Therefore, future tax payments (liabilities) had to be higher.

WHAT THE NEW CLASSICAL ECONOMISTS PREDICTED
The new classical economists argue that people responded to lower tax payments by saving a larger proportion of their "after-tax income." They predicted that the impact of those "lower" taxes would be no increase in total spending and so no rise in aggregate demand, the price level, or real GDP. Although not all the evidence is in, the fact that the recovery from the 1990–1991 recession was so slow and mild lends credibility to the new classical economists' predictions.

In effect, then, the Bush administration experiment in the early 1990s gave more evidence that the Ricardian equivalence theorem cannot be taken lightly.

FURTHER ANECDOTAL EVIDENCE
Some anecdotal evidence also suggests that people were not persuaded to increase spending because of the temporary change in withholding rules in 1991. In the academic world, many university employees were sent letters from the payroll office that basically said: "The Bush administration has reduced required withholding, but your tax liabilities have not changed. Would you like us to fix things so that the impact of this nonsense is zero?" "Fixing things" simply meant actually withholding more than required by law.

The moral of the story is that to the extent that people recognize and respond to the future implications of today's actions, a change in government spending implicitly means an exactly corresponding change in taxes in the same direction.

FOR CRITICAL ANALYSIS
1. Why might government officials believe that reducing withholding payments would help the economy out of a recession?
2. Some people ask their employers to withhold more than required by law from each paycheck. These people like to have a federal tax refund every year. What is the cost of engaging in such behavior?

CHAPTER SUMMARY

1. Fiscal policy involves deliberate discretionary changes in government expenditures and personal income taxes. Typically, policymakers argue in favor of fiscal policy during a contractionary gap.
2. Increased government spending when there is a contractionary gap can lead to a shift outward in the aggregate demand curve such that the equilibrium level of real GDP per year increases. If, however, the economy is already operating on its long-run aggregate supply curve *(LRAS)*, the increase in aggregate demand will simply lead in the long run to a rise in the price level, all other things held constant.

3. Individuals respond to changes in after-tax profits, after-tax (disposable) income, and the tax-inclusive cost of foreign goods. Consequently, changes in taxes will change aggregate demand by changing consumption, investment, or net exports.

4. A decrease in taxes can lead to an increase in aggregate demand and in the equilibrium level of real GDP per year, provided that the economy is not already on its long-run aggregate supply curve. If it is, such tax decreases will simply lead to a higher price level.

5. There are numerous possible offsets to any fiscal policy. Indirect crowding out occurs when increased deficit spending requires the government to borrow more and probably drive interest rates up. Increased interest rates cause private firms to undertake fewer investments. This is called the crowding-out effect.

6. The new classical economists believe in the Ricardian equivalence theorem, a proposition stating that an increase in the government budget deficit has no effect on aggregate demand because individuals properly discount increased future tax liabilities and therefore increase saving when the government engages in new deficit spending.

7. Direct crowding out occurs when the government competes with the private sector and then increases spending in those areas. There is a direct expenditure offset. This occurs, for example, when the government increases direct payments for school lunches that students' parents have been paying for anyway.

8. There is a possible open-economy effect offsetting fiscal policy. Deficit spending that leads to increased interest rates causes foreigners to invest more in America. To do so, they demand more dollars, thereby increasing the international price of our currency. Our goods become more expensive to foreigners, they buy less, and therefore there is a reduction in net exports that offsets the fiscal policy stimulus.

9. If marginal tax rates are lowered, individuals and firms may react by increasing work, saving, and investing. People who believe this favor supply-side economics, which involves changing our tax structure to create incentives to increase productivity.

10. The political process of fiscal policy is much less well-defined than our economic analysis. No one government body designs and implements fiscal policy. Moreover, there are wide varieties of fiscal policy mixes, including permanent and temporary changes in tax rates, subsidies, and other areas.

11. Time lags, including the recognition time lag, the action time lag, and the effect time lag, tend to reduce the effectiveness of fiscal policy.

12. Automatic stabilizers include personal and corporate income taxes and unemployment insurance. Automatic stabilizers automatically counter ups and downs in fiscal activity.

13. After numerous decades of experimenting with fiscal policy, we know fairly well that Congress tends to end up doing too little too late to help out in minor recessions. Fiscal policy may be effective during abnormal times, such as depression and war periods, however.

DISCUSSION OF PREVIEW POINTS

1. What is fiscal policy?

Fiscal policy refers to the changing of governmental expenditures and/or taxes in order to eliminate expansionary and contractionary gaps. Proponents of fiscal policy make the value judgment that price stability and full employment are worthwhile goals. Proponents also assume that our knowledge of positive economics is sufficient to achieve these normative goals.

2. What is automatic fiscal policy, and how does it lend stability to an economy?

With discretionary fiscal policy, government spending and taxing policies are consciously applied to stabilize an economy. Automatic fiscal policy, by contrast, does not require conscious policy or congressional legislation; automatic fiscal policy results from institu-

tional characteristics in the economy. Thus a progressive tax structure and an unemployment compensation system (which are already in force) automatically change taxes and government outlays as national income changes. In particular, as national income falls in a recession, government outlays for unemployment automatically increase, and tax revenues fall as lower incomes push people into lower marginal tax brackets. These automatic stabilizers counteract a declining national income. Similarly, in an inflationary period, tax revenues automatically rise (as people are forced into higher marginal tax brackets), and unemployment compensation outlays fall. Thus inflation is automatically counteracted by higher tax revenues and decreased government outlays. Because income increases or decreases are automatically countered (somewhat) by a progressive tax system and an unemployment compensation program, we say that automatic fiscal policy lends stability to the U.S. economy.

3. How does the crowding-out effect tend to offset expansionary fiscal policy?

When the government spends more without increasing taxes or taxes less without reducing spending, it increases the government budget deficit. When the government attempts to sell more bonds to finance the increased deficit, it may end up increasing interest rates. Higher interest rates tend to force private businesses to reduce investment projects and also cause consumers to reduce their purchases of houses and cars. Therefore, expansionary fiscal policy tends to crowd out private investment and spending.

4. What types of time lags exist between the need for fiscal stimulus and the time when such stimulus actually affects the national economy?

There are three time lag effects involved here: the recognition time lag, the action time lag, and the effect time lag. There is a lag between the start of a recession and the availability of relevant data—the recognition time lag. There is a lag between the recognition of a need for a fiscal policy and putting one in motion—the action time lag. Then there is a lag between policy implementation and tangible results—the effect time lag.

PROBLEMS

(Answers to the odd-numbered problems appear at the back of the book.)

12-1.   What is *discretionary fiscal policy?* What are *automatic stabilizers?* Give examples of each.

12-2.   Answer the following questions based on the accompanying graph.

   a. What two points indicate zero tax revenues? How can this situation exist?

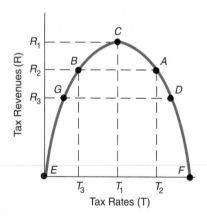

   b. What two points indicate tax revenues equal to R_2?

   c. If the economy is at point A (tax rate T_2 yielding tax revenues R_2), what will happen to tax revenues if the tax rate falls below T_2?

   d. If the economy is at point B (tax rate below T_3 yielding tax revenues R_3), what will happen to total tax revenues if the tax rate falls below T_3?

   e. What point indicates the highest tax rate above which further tax rate increases will yield lower tax revenues?

12-3.   Given the existence of automatic stabilizers, a recession is expected to generate a budget deficit and an expansion is expected to generate a budget surplus. If the generation of such budget deficits or surpluses is to be countercyclical, what assumptions must be made about how consumers react to such budget deficits or surpluses?

12-4.   How do economists distinguish between budget deficits or surpluses that occur automatically and those that are the result of discretionary policy?

COMPUTER-ASSISTED INSTRUCTION

(Complete problem and answer on disk.)

Key elements of successful—and unsuccessful—fiscal policy are illustrated in a series of exercises that examine the implications of changes in both taxes and government expenditures.

- - - - - - - - - - - - - - -

FISCAL POLICY:
A KEYNESIAN PERSPECTIVE

The Keynesian approach to fiscal policy differs in three ways from that presented in Chapter 12. First, it emphasizes the underpinnings of the components of aggregate demand. Second, it assumes that government expenditures are not substitutes for private expenditures and that current taxes are the only taxes taken into account by consumers and firms. Third, the Keynesian approach focuses on the short run and so assumes that as a first approximation, the price level is constant.

CHANGES IN GOVERNMENT SPENDING

Figure B-1 measures real national income along the horizontal axis and total planned expenditures (aggregate demand) along the vertical axis. The components of aggregate demand are consumption (C), investment (I), government spending (G), and net exports (X). The height of the schedule labeled $C + I + G + X$ shows total planned expenditures (aggregate demand) as a function of income. This schedule slopes upward because consumption depends positively on income. Everywhere along the 45-degree reference line, planned spending equals income. At the point Y^*, where the $C + I + G + X$ line intersects the 45-degree line, planned spending is consistent with income. At any income less than Y^*, spending exceeds income, and so income and thus spending will tend to rise. At any level of income greater than Y^*, planned spending is less than income, and so income and thus spending will tend to decline. Given the determinants of C, I, G, and X, total spending (aggregate demand) will be Y^*.

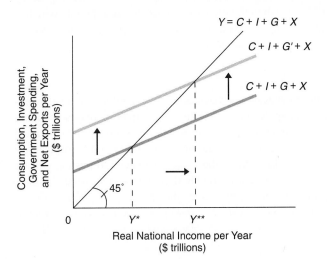

FIGURE B-1

The impact of higher government spending on aggregate demand.

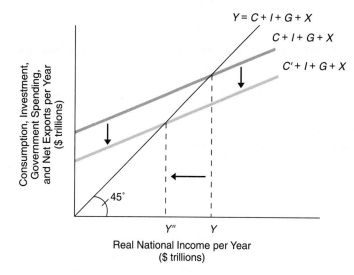

FIGURE B-2
The impact of higher taxes on aggregate demand.

The Keynesian approach assumes that changes in government spending cause no direct offsets in either consumption or investment spending because G is not a substitute for C, I, or X. Hence a rise in government spending from G to G' causes the $C + I + G + X$ line to shift upward by the full amount of the rise in government spending, yielding the line $C + I + G' + X$. The rise in government spending causes income to rise, which in turn causes consumption spending to rise, which further increases income. Ultimately, aggregate demand rises to Y^{**}, where spending again equals income. A key conclusion of the Keynesian analysis is that total spending rises by *more* than the original rise in government spending because consumption spending depends positively on income.

CHANGES IN TAXES

According to the Keynesian approach, changes in current taxes affect aggregate demand by changing the amount of disposable (after-tax) income available to consumers. A rise in taxes reduces disposable income and thus reduces consumption; conversely, a tax cut raises disposable income and thus causes a rise in consumption spending. The effects of a tax increase are shown in Figure B-2. Higher taxes cause consumption spending to decline from C to C', causing total spending to shift down to $C' + I + G + X$. In general, the decline in consumption will be less than the increase in taxes because people will also reduce their saving to help pay the higher taxes. Thus, although aggregate demand declines to Y'', the decline is *smaller* than the tax increase.

THE BALANCED-BUDGET MULTIPLIER

One interesting implication of the Keynesian approach concerns the impact of a balanced-budget change in government spending. Suppose that the government increases spending by $1 billion and pays for it by raising current taxes by $1 billion. Such a policy is called a *balanced-budget increase in spending.* Because the higher spending tends to push aggregate demand *up* by *more* than $1 billion while the higher taxes tend to push aggregate demand *down* by *less* than $1 billion, a most remarkable thing happens. A balanced-budget increase in G causes total spending to rise by *exactly* the amount of the rise in G—in this case, $1 billion. We say that the *balanced-budget multiplier* is equal to 1. Similarly, a balanced-budget reduction in spending will cause total spending to fall by exactly the amount of the spending cut.

THE FIXED-PRICE LEVEL ASSUMPTION

The final key feature of the Keynesian approach is that it typically assumes that as a first approximation, the price level is fixed. Recall that nominal income equals the price level multiplied by real output. If the price level is fixed, an increase in government spending that causes nominal income to rise will show up exclusively as a rise in *real* output. This will in turn be accompanied by a decline in the unemployment rate because the additional output can be produced only if additional factors of production, such as labor, are utilized.

Thus, according to this traditional Keynesian analysis, not only does a rise in government spending yield an even greater rise in aggregate demand, but the rise in aggregate demand also causes a one-for-one rise in real income and a corresponding reduction in the unemployment rate. This is why traditional Keynesian policy analysts place so much emphasis on fiscal policy as a tool for ending recessions.

OUR NATIONAL DEBT:
$3,869,498,783,578.

YOUR *Family share* $51,565.

THE NATIONAL DEBT CLOCK

NATIONAL DEBT INCREASE PER SECOND 13,000.

13

DEFICIT SPENDING AND THE PUBLIC DEBT

Your generation and every other living generation have two things in common: You can expect to be eligible to receive benefits from the federal government throughout your life, mostly in the form of Social Security and Medicare benefits. You can also expect to pay the government throughout your life in the form of taxes. When a comparison is made between your generation and your parents', the older generation definitely comes out ahead—on average they will have received more than they had to pay for. What about your generation? What about the generations to come? The answers to these questions have to do with deficit spending and the public debt.

After reading this chapter, you should be able to answer the following questions:

1. By what methods can the U.S. federal government obtain purchasing power?

2. What are some suggested ways to reduce the federal government deficit?

3. What is the difference between the gross public debt and the net public debt?

4. What is the burden of the public debt?

INTRODUCTION

America is awash in debt. Private household debt as a percentage of GDP exceeds 70 percent. Private corporate debt as a percentage of GDP is over 35 percent. And the government—federal, state, and local—is taking an ever bigger share of total debt in the economy. Look at Figure 13-1. There you see that government's debt as a percentage of total debt grew rapidly in the first half of the 1980s, leveled out, and then started its climb upward again at the beginning of this decade. Should we be worried about the rising share of total debt accounted for by government? To answer this question you first have to realize that government borrowing is only one of the ways in which the government can control our resources. Let's examine the various ways in which government can finance its expenditures.

HOW THE GOVERNMENT OBTAINS ITS SHARE OF TOTAL OUTPUT

Government controls over a third of total output in this economy. Considering that we do not live in a dictatorship in which the government simply confiscates private resources, it is important to find out what methods the government uses to obtain its share of total national output. This is the question of government finance. The government finances its outlays in three ways: taxing, borrowing, and creating money.

TAXING

The use of taxes is the most obvious form of government finance. In the United States it accounts for the major share of the way our government is financed at the federal level and for the most part the way it has to be financed by law at the state and local levels. When taxes do not cover all government outlays, borrowing must occur.

BORROWING FROM THE PRIVATE SECTOR

When government spending exceeds government receipts obtained through taxation, a deficit is created. This deficit—the excess of expenditures over tax receipts—must be financed by issuing government bonds whereby the government borrows from the private sector. When the government borrows, the private sector transfers purchasing power to the government (and the national, or public, debt increases).

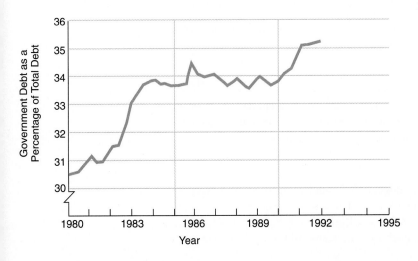

FIGURE 13-1
Government's share of total debt, 1980–1992.
Government's share of total debt increased from a little over 30 percent in 1980 to about 35.5 percent in 1992.

CREATING MONEY

A third way for government to be financed, not used in the United States to the same extent as in certain developing countries, is creating money. The federal government (but not state and local governments) has the power to create new money. Most people think of government money creation as occurring via the printing press. In actuality, the government prints a very small percentage of the money that is created each year in the United States. The rest is created by the banking system, a topic to which we turn in Chapters 14, 15, and 16.

Perhaps the easiest way to understand this method of government finance is to think in terms of the government creating money to purchase output from the private sector. The process is actually somewhat more complicated, but the effects are the same—more command over resources for the public sector and less for the private sector.

FEDERAL DEFICIT SPENDING

The last time the U.S. federal government spent less money than it collected was in 1969. In fact, federal deficit spending has become a way of government life. Panel (a) of Figure 13-2 is impressive because it shows that the annual federal budget deficit has been getting larger on average for over two decades. But the graph in panel (a) of Figure 13-2 is not quite relevant because for one thing it does not take account of inflation. In panel (b) of Figure 13-2 you see the annual federal budget deficit expressed as a percentage of GDP. It reached its peak in 1948 at over 25 percent. Today it is running at about 5 percent of GDP.

 INTERNATIONAL EXAMPLE: How Does the United States Stack Up Against the Rest of the World?

Figure 13-3 shows the annual deficit for the United States expressed as a percentage of GDP for 1992. For comparison we have shown the relevant percentage for nine other countries. So how does the United States stack up against other industrialized countries? We have a smaller annual federal budget deficit (expressed as a percentage of GDP) than Canada and Italy, but we have a considerably larger one than China, France, Japan, and Mexico (these last two were actually in surplus). The important point that this international information gives is that virtually all industrialized countries have recently depended in part on borrowing from the private sector to finance increases in government expenditures. The interesting question is why modern governments have chosen deficit financing over increased taxation for their financing.

For Critical Analysis: In the long run, is it possible for any government in the world to spend more than it receives forever? Why or why not? ●

SUGGESTIONS FOR REDUCING THE DEFICIT

There have been many suggestions about how to reduce the government deficit. They include increasing taxes, reducing federal government expenditures, changing the accounting system, and passing a balanced-budget amendment. Let's examine these.

INCREASING TAXES

From an arithmetic point of view, a federal budget deficit can be wiped out by simply increasing the amount of taxes collected. Let's see what this would require. The data for 1993 are instructive. The Office of Management and Budget estimated the 1993 federal budget deficit at $343.7 billion. This is as much as Americans paid in total income taxes

FIGURE 13-2

Two ways to view the Federal budget deficit.

In panel (a), you see the deficit in *absolute* terms. In panel (b), you can see it expressed as a percentage of GDP.

Source: U.S. Bureau of the Census.

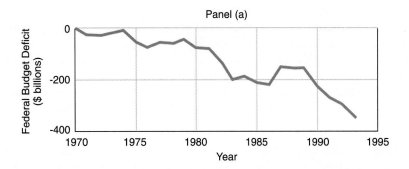

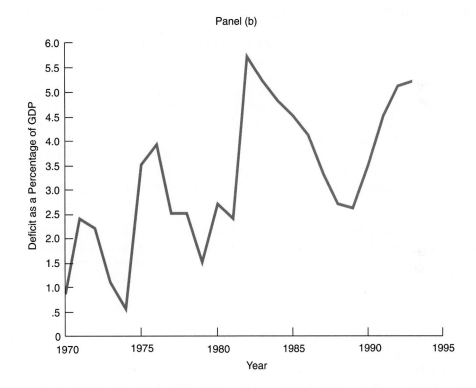

FIGURE 13-3

The relative importance of government deficits around the world, 1992.

These data show the ratio of the government deficit to GDP for 10 countries. The U.S. performance, relatively speaking, does not look too bad. Japan and Mexico show a surplus.

Sources: Economic Report of the President, February 1993; Organization for Economic Cooperation and Development.

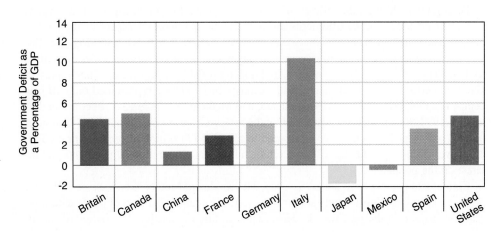

to the federal government in all of 1988. That deficit in 1993 shows that for the year, the federal government spent $1,350 more than it had in tax revenues for every person in the country. To eliminate the deficit by raising taxes, we need $300 more in taxes *every month* from *every worker* in America just to balance the budget. In 1993, Americans paid about $500 billion in personal income taxes. Every taxpayer would have to pay 80 percent more in income taxes to balance the budget. Needless to say, reality is such that we will never see a simple tax increase that will wipe out the annual federal budget deficit.

Tax the Rich.   Some people suggest that the way to eliminate the deficit is to raise taxes on the rich. Currently, over 70 percent of all federal income taxes are already being paid by the top 20 percent of families. The entire bottom 60 percent of families (those earning below $45,000 per year) pay only slightly more than 11 percent of federal income taxes. Families earning below $30,000 pay less than 3 percent of federal income taxes. Currently, families whose income are in the top 5 percent pay about 45 percent of all federal income taxes paid. The richest 1 percent pay about 25 percent of all income taxes paid. What does it mean to tax the rich more? If you talk about taxing "millionaires," you are referring to those who pay taxes on more than $1 million income per year. There are only around 57,000 of them. Even if you doubled the taxes they paid, the reduction in the deficit would be relatively trivial. Changing marginal tax rates at the upper end will show similarly unimpressive results. An increase in the top marginal tax rate from 31 percent to 36 percent will raise, at best, only about $18 billion in additional taxes (assuming that people do not figure out a way to avoid the higher tax rate). This $18 billion per year in extra tax revenues represent only 5 percent of the estimated 1993 federal budget deficit.

The Historical Reality.   The data do not support the notion that tax increases can reduce deficits. Though it is possible arithmetically, politically just the opposite has occurred. Since World War II, for every dollar increase in taxes legislated, federal government spending has increased $1.59. It is not surprising, then, that few politicians really believe that raising taxes will eliminate the deficit.

REDUCING EXPENDITURES, PARTICULARLY ON ENTITLEMENTS

Reducing expenditures is another way to reduce the federal budget deficit. Look at Figure 13-4, which shows spending on the military as a percentage of GDP. There you see that the military budget will be shrinking in real terms at least through 1997.

During the Cold War, the military budget was the most important aspect of the federal budget; it no longer is. **Entitlements** are now the most important aspect of the federal budget. These include payments for Social Security, welfare, Medicare, and Medicaid. Entitlements are legislated federal government payments; anybody who qualifies is entitled to them. They are consequently often called noncontrollable expenditures. They represent about 50 percent of the total federal budget today. In 1960 they represented only 10 percent. Let's look at Social Security, Medicaid, and Medicare in Table 13-1. In constant dollars, in 1993 Social Security, Medicaid, and Medicare represented about $484 billion of federal government expenditures, compared to almost $374 billion of other domestic federal government expenditures. (These exclude military and international payments and interest on the public debt.)

Entitlement payments on Social Security, Medicaid, and Medicare now exceed all other domestic spending. Entitlements are growing faster than any other part of the federal government budget. In the past two decades, real spending on entitlements (adjusted for in-

▶ **Entitlements**
Guaranteed benefits under a government program such as Social Security or unemployment compensation.

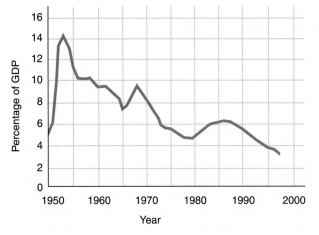

FIGURE 13-4
Defense outlays as a percentage of GDP, 1950–1997 (projected).

Source: Office of Management and Budget.

flation) grew between 6 and 7 percent a year, while the economy grew by less than 3 percent per year. Social Security payments are growing in real terms at about 6 percent a year, but Medicare and Medicaid are growing at double-digit rates.

Entitlement programs are believed to be necessary. Interest on the public debt must be paid, but just about every other federal expenditure that is labeled necessary can be changed by Congress. The federal deficit is not expected to drop in the near future because of the elimination of entitlement programs. It is difficult to cut government benefits once they are established.

 EXAMPLE: A Balanced-Budget Amendment

Some people believe that the way to eliminate federal budget deficits is to have a constitutional convention draft a balanced-budget amendment to the U.S. Constitution. Two-thirds of the state legislatures must petition Congress for a convention to be called. The required number of legislative petitions have not yet been filed. Alternatively, Congress can pass a balanced-budget amendment and submit it to the states for ratification. Such an amendment failed to obtain the required two-thirds vote of Congress in 1986, 1990, and 1992. The balanced-budget amendment most commonly proposed includes the following provisions:

1. Each year the president must present a balanced budget to Congress—it must show that revenues match expenditures.
2. Congress then works on the budget to its satisfaction. A budget that has a deficit can be approved only by 60 percent of the members of the Senate and of the House, on a roll-call vote, name by name.
3. The balanced-budget requirement can be waived if a declaration of war is in effect or there is a national emergency.

TABLE 13-1 Federal domestic spending (billions of 1992 dollars).

YEAR	SOCIAL SECURITY, MEDICARE, AND MEDICAID	ALL OTHER DOMESTIC PROGRAMS
1953	17.93	87.82
1963	74.01	136.52
1973	183.65	255.63
1983	325.29	340.95
1993	484.45	373.60

4. Bills for any new taxes or increase in the national debt must be approved by a 60 percent vote of the members of both houses on a roll-call vote.

Critics of the annual balanced-budget amendment concept argue that even if it were passed, Congress would simply figure out ways to put excessive spending "off budget." In 1985 Congress passed the Gramm-Rudman-Hollings Deficit Reduction Act in an effort to require that Congress reduce the size of its budget deficits. The deficit was required to drop from $171.9 billion in 1986 to zero in 1991. After the first two years of failure to comply with the target deficit reductions, Congress passed a revised act requiring that the 1988 deficit be $144 billion and that it drop to zero by 1993. The first three years of the Revised Deficit Reduction Act saw Congress again fail to meet deficit reductions. In 1990 another revised set of Gramm-Rudman targets was proposed, allowing for a 1991 deficit of over $200 billion, excluding the cost of the savings and loan bailout. In fact, the true deficit in 1991 turned out to be closer to $270 billion and almost $300 billion in 1992.

Some observers believe that Congress's inability to comply with its own law indicates that our governing body can no longer be fiscally responsible. In reality, the prospect of ever balancing the budget is dim. Apparently giving up, Congress in 1990 passed a deficit reduction act that rendered the Gramm-Rudman Act ineffective.

For Critical Analysis: Why should Americans care whether or not the federal budget is balanced? ●

FEDERAL BUDGET DEFICITS IN AN OPEN ECONOMY

Many economists, and most noneconomists, believe that the U.S. trade deficit (a situation in which the value of a nation's imports of goods and services exceeds the value of its exports) is just as serious a problem as its government budget deficit. The U.S. trade deficit went from a surplus of $32 billion in 1980 to a deficit of $119.9 billion in 1987; in 1993 the U.S. trade deficit was an estimated $80 billion.

By virtue of such trade deficits, foreigners have accumulated U.S. dollars and purchased U.S. assets (real estate, corporate stocks, bonds, and so on). If this country continues to incur huge trade deficits, foreigners will continue to purchase assets here. This could eventually present problems. For one, what if foreign investors suddenly decide to sell such assets or take their money out of our country? Another concern is with foreigners gaining political power along with their accumulation of U.S. assets. Here we concentrate on the linkage between federal budget deficits and trade deficits.

WHAT THE EVIDENCE SAYS

Figure 13-5 shows U.S. international trade deficits and surpluses compared to federal budget deficits and surpluses. The year 1983 appears to be a watershed year, for that is when imports exceeded exports on an annual basis for the first time in the United States. Concurrently, the federal budget fiscal deficit moved progressively into new territory.

On the basis of the evidence presented in Figure 13-5, it appears that there is a close relationship between the trade and fiscal deficits: Larger trade deficits follow shortly after larger fiscal deficits.

FIGURE 13-5
America's twin deficits.
The United States exported more than it imported until 1983. Then it started running large trade deficits, as shown in this diagram. The federal budget has been in deficit for many years, starting in earnest in the late 1960s. The question is, has the federal budget deficit created the trade deficit?

Source: Economic Indicators.

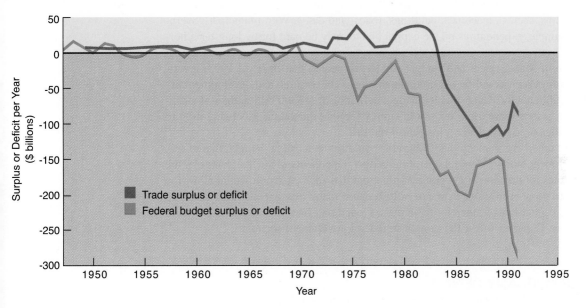

WHY THE TWO DEFICITS ARE RELATED

Intuitively, there is a reason why we would expect federal budget deficits to lead to trade deficits. You might call this the unpleasant arithmetic of trade and federal budget deficits.

Assume that the federal government runs a budget deficit. Assume further that domestic consumption and domestic investment haven't decreased relative to GDP. Where, then, does the money come from to finance the federal government deficit? Part of it must come from abroad. That is to say, dollar holders abroad are buying our newly created federal government–issued bonds. If that's the case, dollar holders abroad have fewer dollars to spend on our goods, our exports. Hence when we run large federal government deficits, we should expect to see foreign dollar holders spending more on U.S. government securities (bonds) and less on U.S.-produced goods and services (exports).

The reason that foreign dollar holders are induced to buy U.S. government securities is that domestic U.S. interest rates will normally rise, all other things held constant, whenever there is an increase in government deficits financed by increased borrowing.

HAS THE DEFICIT BEEN MEASURED CORRECTLY?

Part of the problem, according to some economists, is that we are measuring the deficit incorrectly. One such economist is Robert Eisner of Northwestern University, who claims that we need to change the government accounting system to come up with a better measure of the deficit.

CAPITAL BUDGETING THEORY

The federal government has only one budget to guide its spending and taxing each fiscal year. It does not distinguish between current spending for upkeep on the White House, for example, and spending for a new park that's going to last for many years to come. By contrast, businesses, as well as state and local governments, have two budgets. One, called the *operating budget,* includes expenditures for current operations, such as salaries and interest payments. The other is called a *capital budget,* which includes expenditures on investment items, such as machines, buildings, roads, and dams. With municipal governments, for example, expenditures on the capital budget may be paid for by long-term borrowing.

The Office of Management and Budget (OMB) estimated that in fiscal 1993, investment-type outlays such as military equipment and loans for research and development exceeded $285 billion. Given an estimated budget deficit of over $300 billion then, if a capital budgeting system were used, we would simply see that the deficit was being used to finance activities or assets yielding long-term returns.

Eisner and others recommend that Congress should set up a capital budget, thereby removing investment outlays from its operating budget. Opponents of such a change in the accounting rules for the federal government point out that such an action would allow the government to grow even faster than currently because many new expenditures could be placed in the capital budget, thereby reducing the operating budget deficit and reducing the pressure on Congress to cut the growth in federal government spending.

PICK A DEFICIT, ANY DEFICIT

Even using standard accounting techniques, the federal budget deficit that is "officially" announced can vary dramatically depending on what is included or is not included. The OMB comes up each year with its predictions about the federal budget deficit. The Congressional Budget Office has its own set of deficit calculations. The two budget agencies produce a minimum of eight deficit estimates for each fiscal year. They call them *the baseline* deficit, *the policy* deficit, *the on-budget* deficit, and the deficit *that includes the bailout to save failing savings and loan associations.* There is also a deficit that includes the Social Security surplus plus the cost of the savings and loan bailout. Rather than going into the details to explain each of these deficits, the point to understand is that no one number gives a complete picture of how much the government is spending over and above what it is receiving.

LIABILITIES THAT AREN'T SHOWING UP

Even the highest figures shown for the federal budget deficit do not include liabilities that the federal government is incurring each year. In particular, the federal government has increasingly become liable for civilian and military employee pension plans. These are as much an obligation as a formal bond contract that is sold to finance the federal budget deficit. One estimate by economist Henning Bohn of the Wharton School shows that the federal government is liable for over $1.2 trillion for just the pension obligations for government employees. The federal government is also incurring liabilities for private pension plans, savings and loan and bank deposits, and shareholders' brokerage accounts. No one has an accurate estimate of these liabilities, but they could amount to several trillions of dollars.

CONCEPTS IN BRIEF

- The federal government can obtain control over purchasing power by taxing, borrowing from the private sector, and creating money.
- Federal deficit spending reached its peak right after World War II. In recent years it has been running at about 5 percent of GDP.
- Suggested ways to reduce the deficit are to increase taxes, particularly on the rich, and to reduce expenditures, particularly on entitlements, defined as legally owed benefits under a government program such as Social Security or Medicare.
- Some people argue that the federal budget deficit is measured incorrectly because it lumps together spending on capital and spending on consumption. It is therefore argued that there should be an operating budget and a capital budget.
- Some observers see a close correlation between foreign trade deficits and federal budget deficits.
- There are many deficits measured and announced by various government offices. Also, there are many liabilities that are not shown, such as future pension obligations.

THE PUBLIC DEBT

▶ **Federal public,** or **national, debt**
The total value of all outstanding federal government securities.

▶ **Gross public debt**
All federal government debt irrespective of who owns it.

▶ **Net public debt**
Gross public debt minus all government interagency borrowing.

Every time the federal government runs a deficit, it must borrow from the private sector and from foreigners, thereby increasing its debt. This debt has been called the **federal public,** or **national, debt.** When we look at all federal public debt, it is typically called the **gross public debt.** When we subtract from the gross public debt the portion that is held by government agencies (what the federal government owes to itself), we arrive at the **net public debt.** The net public debt normally increases whenever the federal government runs a budget deficit, that is, whenever total government outlays are greater than total government revenues. Look at column 3 in Table 13-2 on the next page. The total net public debt has been growing continuously for many years. Expressed in terms of per capita figures, however, it has not grown so rapidly. (We should also take account of inflation.) Perhaps a better way to look at the U.S. national debt is to examine it as a percentage of GDP, which we do in Figure 13-6 on page 287. We see that it fell steadily until the early 1970s, leveled off for a few years, and then started rising again. The same seems to be true for many of the industrialized nations. France, Japan, Italy, and Canada all saw rising national debt–to–GDP ratios starting at the same time.

ANNUAL INTEREST PAYMENTS ON THE NATIONAL DEBT

Consider the size of interest payments on the public debt as shown in column 5 of Table 13-2. Around 1975 those interest payments started rising dramatically. Expressed as a percentage of GDP, today they are more than twice what they were a half century ago. The true size of the government deficit each year has not fallen as planned. Therefore, it is possible that interest payments expressed as a percentage of national income will rise, as is apparent in column 6 in Table 13-2. As long as the government borrows from Americans, the interest payments will be made to Americans. In other words, we owe the debt to ourselves; some people are taxed so government can pay interest to others (or the same

TABLE 13-2 The federal deficit, our public debt, and the interest we pay on it.
Net public debt in column 3 is defined as total federal debt excluding all loans between federal government agencies.
Per capita net public debt is obtained by dividing population into the net public debt.
Source: U.S. Department of the Treasury and Office of Management and Budget. Data for 1993 are estimates.

(1) YEAR	(2) FEDERAL BUDGET DEFICIT (BILLIONS OF CURRENT DOLLARS)	(3) NET PUBLIC DEBT (BILLIONS OF CURRENT DOLLARS)	(4) PER CAPITA NET PUBLIC DEBT (CURRENT DOLLARS)	(5) NET INTEREST COSTS (BILLIONS OF CURRENT DOLLARS)	(6) NET INTEREST AS A PERCENTAGE OF GDP
1940	3.9	42.7	323.2	0.9	0.90
1945	53.9	235.2	1,681.2	3.1	1.45
1950	3.1	219.0	1,438.0	4.8	1.68
1955	3.0	226.6	1,365.9	4.9	1.23
1960	0.31	237.2	1,312.7	6.9	1.37
1965	1.6	261.6	1,346.4	8.6	1.26
1970	2.8	284.9	1,389.1	14.4	1.47
1975	45.1	396.9	1,837.5	23.3	1.52
1980	73.8	709.3	3,140.5	52.5	1.92
1981	78.9	804.7	3,501.7	68.7	2.25
1982	127.9	929.3	4,003.9	85.0	2.68
1983	207.8	1,141.8	4,875.3	89.8	2.63
1984	185.3	1,312.6	5,538.4	111.1	2.94
1985	212.3	1,499.4	6,322.9	129.4	3.22
1986	221.2	1,736.2	7,357.2	136.0	3.21
1987	149.7	1,888.1	7,867.8	138.6	3.06
1988	155.1	2,050.2	8,473.6	151.7	3.23
1989	152.5	2,189.3	8,941.3	169.1	3.23
1990	221.4	2,410.4	9,641.6	175.6	3.23
1991	269.5	2,687.4	10,664.2	173.0	3.22
1992	290.2	2,998.6	11,759.2	177.9	3.21
1993	327.3	3,309.7	12,828.1	202.8	3.32

people). But we have seen a rising share of the public debt owned by foreigners, as shown in Figure 13-7, reaching its peak in 1978 at 22 percent. Foreigners still own around 17 percent of the U.S. public debt. So we don't just owe it to ourselves.

THE BURDEN OF THE PUBLIC DEBT

From 1984 to 1994 the net public debt of the United States almost tripled, to over $3.5 trillion. The public debt is the sum total of all the outstanding debt owed by the Treasury to its individual and institutional lenders. Whenever the federal government is in deficit, the public debt rises; for example, in fiscal 1993 the federal government deficit was about $350 billion, so the public debt increased by that amount in that fiscal year. Thus because of the large deficits incurred by the federal government during the 1980s and 1990s, the public debt rose dramatically—at least in nominal values. We shall now analyze whether federal deficits, and the accompanying increase in the public debt that they generate, impose a burden on future generations or are irrelevant.

As you read the remainder of this chapter, try to keep two things in mind. First, given the level of government expenditures, the main alternative to the deficit is higher taxes; therefore, the costs of a deficit should be compared to the costs of higher taxes, not to zero. Second, it is important to distinguish between the effects of deficits when full employment exists and when substantial unemployment exists.

FIGURE 13-6

Net U.S. public debt as a percentage of national output.

During World War II the net public debt grew dramatically. It fell until the 1970s, then started rising again.

Source: U.S. Department of the Treasury.

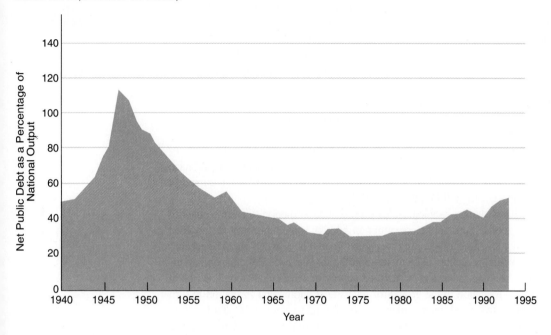

FIGURE 13-7

U.S. public debt held by foreigners.

Here we show the percentage of U.S. public debt owned by non-Americans. It peaked in the late 1970s at more than 20 percent.

Source: Federal Reserve Board of Governors.

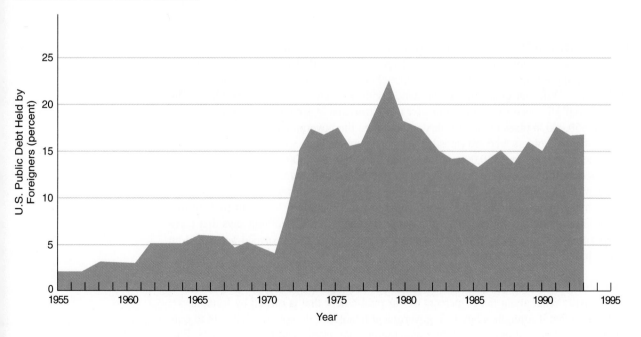

FEDERAL BUDGET DEFICITS: A BURDEN ON FUTURE GENERATIONS?

Assume that the federal government decides to increase government expenditures on final goods and services by $100 billion and that it can finance such expenditures either by raising taxes by $100 billion or by selling $100 billion of bonds. Many economists maintain that the second option, deficit spending, would lead to a higher level of national consumption and a lower level of national saving than the first option.

The reason this is so, say these economists, is that if people are taxed, they will have to forgo private consumption now as they substitute government goods for private goods. Suppose that taxes are not raised, but instead the public buys bonds to finance the $100 billion in government expenditures. The community's disposable income is the same, and it has increased its assets by $100 billion in the form of bonds. The community will either (1) fail to realize that its liabilities (in the form of future taxes due to an increased public debt that must eventually be paid) have *also* increased by $100 billion or (2) believe that it can consume the governmentally provided goods and simultaneously purchase the same quantity of privately provided consumer goods because the bill for the currently governmentally provided goods will be paid by *future* taxpayers.

If full employment exists, then as people raise their present consumption (the same quantity of private consumption goods, more public consumption goods), something must be crowded out. In a closed economy, investment (spending on capital goods) is crowded out. The mechanism by which this crowding out occurs is an increase in the interest rate: Deficit spending increases the total demand for credit but leaves the total supply of credit unaltered. The rise in interest rates that cause a reduction in the growth of investment and capital formation in turn slows the growth of productivity and improvement in the community's living standard.

The foregoing analysis suggests that deficit spending can impose a burden on future generations in two ways. First, unless income grows dramatically, future generations will have to be taxed at a higher rate to retire the higher public debt resulting from the present generation's increased consumption of government-provided goods. Second, the increased level of consumption by the present generation crowds out investment and reduces the growth of capital goods; this leaves future generations with a smaller capital stock and thereby reduces their wealth.

Paying Off the Public Debt in the Future.   Suppose that after 50 years of running deficits, the public debt becomes so large that each adult person's tax liability is $50,000. Suppose further that the government chooses (or is forced) to pay off the debt at that time. Will that generation be burdened with our generation's overspending? The debt is, after all, owed (mostly) to ourselves. It's true that every adult will have to come up with $50,000 in taxes to pay off the debt; but then the government will use that money to pay off bondholders who are (mostly) the same people. Thus *some* people will be burdened because they owe $50,000 and they own less than $50,000 in government bonds. But others will receive more than $50,000 for the bonds they own. As a generation or a community, they will pay and receive about the same amount of money.

Of course, there could be a burden on some low-income adults who will find it difficult or impossible to obtain $50,000 to pay the tax liability. Still, nothing says that taxes to pay off the debt must be assessed equally; it seems likely that a special tax would be levied, based on ability to pay.

Our Debt to Foreigners.   We have been assuming that most of the debt is owed to ourselves. What about the 17 percent of our public debt that is owned by foreigners?

It is true that if foreigners buy U.S. government bonds, we do not owe that debt to ourselves, and a potential burden on future generations may result. But not necessarily. Foreigners will buy our government's debt if the inflation-adjusted, risk-adjusted, after-tax rate of return on such bonds exceeds what the investors can earn in their own country or some other country. If they buy U.S. bonds voluntarily, they perceive a benefit to doing so.

It is important to realize that not all government expenditures can be viewed as consumption; government expenditures on such things as highways, bridges, dams, research and development, and education might properly be perceived as investments. If the rate of return on such investments exceeds the interest rate paid to foreign investors, both foreigners and future Americans will be economically better off. What really matters is on what the government spends its money. If government expenditures financed by foreigners are made on wasteful projects, a burden may well be placed on future generations.

We can use the same reasoning to examine the problem of current investment and capital creation being crowded out by current deficits. If deficits lead to slower growth rates, future generations will be poorer. But if the government expenditures are really investments, and if the rate of return on such public investments exceeds the interest rate paid on the bonds, both present and future generations will be economically richer.

The Effect of Unemployment.   If the economy is operating at a level substantially below full-employment real GDP, crowding out need not take place. In such a situation an expansionary fiscal policy via deficit spending can increase current consumption (of governmentally provided goods) without crowding out investment. Indeed, if some government spending is in the form of high-yielding public investments, both present and future generations can be economically richer; no trade-off would exist between present and future consumption.

ARE DEFICITS RELEVANT?

Much of the analysis to this point has assumed that deficit spending increases the demand for credit, while the supply of credit remains constant. Hence the interest rate rises and investment is crowded out. But what if the community realizes that an increase in the public debt also represents an increase in its future tax liabilities—the Ricardian equivalence theorem? Further, what if people wish not to burden their own children with an increased public debt? Because the deficit has increased, they would increase their current saving in order to enable their children to meet future debt obligations. In fact, because their taxes do not rise, their disposable income is higher, and they can save by purchasing the new government bonds. In the process, interest rates will not rise. Deficit spending may not lead to crowding out. Let's see how this works.

Crowding Out Not Inevitable.   The analysis just given is not as farfetched as it seems. Many people plan to (and do) bestow wealth on their heirs. To illustrate the point, assume that parents intend to leave $200,000 to their heirs and that they have saved sufficiently to achieve that goal. Then suppose that the government engages in deficit spending so that their heirs' future tax liabilities rise by $20,000. Realizing that they no longer have achieved their goal, they might increase the amount they save now so as to cover their heirs' future $20,000 tax liability.

If both the supply of credit (saving) and the demand for credit rise, there is no theoretical reason for believing that the interest rate will rise. If that is so, crowding out won't occur; the growth of investment and capital production won't be retarded, and future generations need not have lower living standards.

CONCEPTS IN BRIEF

- The cost of a deficit must be compared to the cost of higher taxes.
- To the extent that federal budget deficits create less saving and therefore less investment, future generations may be burdened by inheriting less wealth. The lower saving and investment, the lower the productivity of the American economy.
- To the extent that the existence of the federal deficit encourages foreigners to purchase American assets, there is a potential problem that we no longer owe the public debt to ourselves. To the extent that the capital invested by foreigners in the United States has been productively used, however, future generations will be no worse off and in fact may be better off by the fact that foreigners have invested in this country.
- If all taxpayers perfectly anticipate increased future tax liabilities due to higher deficits, saving will increase to cover those tax liabilities. Future productivity will therefore not be affected, nor will interest rates rise; there will be no crowding-out effect.

GENERATIONAL ACCOUNTING
Concept Applied: Burden of public debt

Part of the reason our national debt is so great and still growing is that the current "oldest" generation is receiving a wide variety of benefits, including Medicare, Medicaid, and Social Security. Future "oldest" generations will not be so lucky—they will receive a relatively smaller, or even negative, transfer from the then current "younger" generation.

Everybody likes getting something for nothing. It is wonderful to receive benefits from the federal government, but it is not so wonderful to have to pay for them. Today the oldest generation of Americans is receiving a wide variety of benefits in the form of Medicare, Medicaid, and Social Security benefits. Most recipients have paid for these benefits in differing amounts during their working lives. Virtually none, however, has contributed anywhere near the amount currently being received. In essence, the oldest generation has gotten a great deal. Currently, a 65-year-old male will receive approximately $32,000 more than he contributed. A 70-year-old

male will get $43,000 more, and an 80-year-old male will get $54,000 to $60,000 more. That sounds like a good deal for the oldest generation, but what about other generations?

NO JOY FOR 40-YEAR-OLDS If you look at the baby-boom generation, according to Boston University economics professor Lawrence J. Kotlikoff, its members do not have much about which to be happy. A 40-year-old male will pay about $175,000 more in taxes than he will receive in benefits. A 40-year-old female will pay almost $80,000 more in taxes than she will receive in benefits. (The difference is due to the fact that females live longer and therefore receive more federal government benefits.)

THE NEXT GENERATION How about the next generation? According to Kotlikoff's generational accounting system, the next generation is going to fare even worse. Today's male college students may pay more than $220,000 more in taxes than they receive in benefits

The generation after that will be even worse off. Its members' lifetime net tax burden will be more than 20 percent larger than that of their predecessors.

FOR CRITICAL ANALYSIS
1. Is there anything you can do to avoid the reality of generational accounting with respect to federal government taxes and benefits?
2. How could the federal government change the generational accounting arithmetic just presented?

CHAPTER SUMMARY

1. The government can finance its spending by taxing, borrowing from the private sector, and creating money.
2. Whenever government expenditures exceed government revenues, a budget deficit occurs. Federal deficit spending reached its peak right after World War II. In recent years it has been running at about 5 percent of GDP.
3. Suggested ways to reduce the deficit are to increase taxes, particularly on the rich, and to reduce expendi-

tures, particularly on entitlements, defined as legally owed benefits under a government program such as Social Security or Medicare.
4. Some people argue that the federal budget deficit is measured incorrectly because it lumps together spending on capital and spending on consumption. It is therefore argued that there should be an operating budget and a capital budget.
5. The federal government will not go bankrupt just because the public debt is rising, for it has its taxing

authority to cover interest payments on the debt, which is constantly rolled over.

6. Government use of resources today must be paid for by people living today, because there is a trade-off between private use of resources and government use of resources in any one year.

7. To the extent that the existence of the federal deficit encourages foreigners to purchase American assets, there is a potential problem that we no longer owe the public debt to ourselves. To the extent that the capital invested by foreigners in the United States has been productively used, however, future generations will be no worse off and in fact may be better off by the fact that foreigners have invested in this country.

8. If all taxpayers perfectly anticipate increased future tax liabilities due to higher deficits, saving will increase to cover those tax liabilities. Future productivity will therefore not be affected, nor will interest rates rise; there will be no crowding-out effect.

DISCUSSION OF PREVIEW POINTS

1. By what methods can the U.S. federal government obtain purchasing power?

In the United States the federal government is able to obtain purchasing power by selling bonds, taxing, or creating money. State and local governments can also obtain purchasing power by selling bonds and by taxing, but only the federal government has the power to create money in the United States. Perhaps surprisingly, regardless of how government expenditures are financed, most of the burden of government expenditures falls on the present generation; the effects of government money creation and bond sales are similar to the effects of taxation. All of the methods of financing government expenditures require the present generation to consume fewer consumer goods now in order to get more government, or publicly provided, goods. Taxation does so in an obvious way; government bond sales compete with private industry bond sales, thereby contracting the private sector.

2. What are some suggested ways to reduce the federal government deficit?

The two most obvious ways to reduce the federal budget deficit are increasing taxes and reducing expenditures. Historically, though, for every dollar increase in federal taxes there has been $1.59 increase in federal government spending. Reductions in federal spending face political problems because of the difficulty of reducing entitlements.

3. What is the difference between the gross public debt and the net public debt?

The gross public debt, which is often erroneously reported as the "national debt" in newspapers, is all federal government debt irrespective of who owns it. The net public debt eliminates all government interagency borrowing. The net public debt is the only relevant figure to examine when examining the absolute size of the national debt.

4. What is the burden of the public debt?

If federal spending that increases the public debt crowds out private investment, future generations will be burdened with a lower capital stock and lower incomes. If the Ricardian equivalence theorem holds—if people in fact increase saving today to pay for higher tax liabilities in the future when there is deficit spending—crowding out is not inevitable, and this burden may not be as great as presumed.

PROBLEMS

(Answers to the odd-numbered problems appear at the back of the book.)

13-1. In 1995 government spending is $7 trillion and taxes collected are $6.7 trillion. What is the federal budget deficit in that year?

13-2. Look at the accompanying table showing federal budget spending and federal budget receipts. Calculate the federal budget deficit as a percentage of GDP for each year.

YEAR	FEDERAL BUDGET RECEIPTS ($ BILLIONS)	FEDERAL BUDGET SPENDING ($ BILLIONS)	GDP ($ TRILLIONS)
1988	972.3	1,109.0	4,900.4
1989	1,059.3	1,181.6	5,250.8
1990	1,107.4	1,273.6	5,522.2
1991	1,122.2	1,332.7	5,677.5

13-3.   It may be argued that the effects of a higher public debt are the same as the effects of higher taxes. Why?

13-4.   To reduce the size of the deficit (and reduce the growth in the net public debt), a politician suggests that "we should tax the rich." The politician makes a simple arithmetic calculation in which he applies the increased tax rate to the total income reported by "the rich" in a previous year. He says that this is how many revenues the government could receive from the increased taxes on "the rich." What is the major fallacy in such calculations?

13-5.   Proponents of capital budgeting theory argue that whenever the government invests in capital expenditures, such as on roads and dams, such government spending should be put in a separate budget called the capital budget. In doing so, the federal government's budget deficit would thereby be reduced by the amount of government capital spending. Would such a change in measuring the government deficit change anything? Explain.

What is the relationship between the gross public debt and the net public debt? What is the relationship between the annual federal government budget deficit and the net public debt?

COMPUTER-ASSISTED INSTRUCTION
(Complete problem and answer on disk.)

A series of conceptual and numerical exercises illustrates the links among taxation, government spending, and the size of the public debt.

part

4

MONEY, MONETARY POLICY, AND ECONOMIC GROWTH

MONEY AND THE BANKING SYSTEM

There has been a tremendous amount of inflation in the United States, particularly since World War II. Indeed, the purchasing power of the dollar is only 17 percent of what it was in 1950. Prior to World War II, during World War II, and up until the late 1960s, large-denomination bills were routinely used. There were $500, $1,000, and even $10,000 bills. In spite of the tremendous reduction in purchasing power, not only are we unable to find even larger-denomination bills, but today the largest one you can legally use is $100. Some government officials propose making the maximum bill size $20. Clearly, government officials in charge of our currency have an ulterior motive. Studying about currency is only one part of understanding about our money supply and the banking system.

After reading this chapter, you should be able to answer the following questions:

1. What is money?

2. What backs the U.S. dollar?

3. What are the functions of the Federal Reserve System?

4. Who is involved in the process of financial intermediation?

INTRODUCTION

Money makes the world go round, or so the saying goes. As far back as 300 B.C., Aristotle claimed that everything had to "be accessed in money, for this enables men [and women] always to exchange their services, and so makes society possible." Money is indeed a part of our everyday existence. We have to be careful, though, when we talk about money because it means two different things. Most of the time when people say "I wish I had more money," they mean that they want more income. Thus, the normal use of the term *money* implies the ability to purchase goods and services. In this chapter, in contrast, you will use the term **money** to mean anything that people generally accept in exchange for goods and services. Most people think of money as the paper bills and coins they carry. But as you will see in this chapter, the concept of money is normally more inclusive. Table 14-1 provides a small list of the types of money that have been used throughout the history of civilization. The best way to understand money is to examine its functions.

▶ **Money**
Any medium that is universally accepted in an economy both by sellers of goods and services as payment for those goods and services and by creditors as payment for debts.

THE FUNCTIONS OF MONEY

Money traditionally serves four functions. The one that most people are familiar with is money's function as a *medium of exchange.* Money also serves as a *unit of accounting,* a *store of value* or *purchasing power,* and a *standard of deferred payment.* Anything that serves these four functions is money. Anything that could serve these four functions could be considered money.

MONEY AS A MEDIUM OF EXCHANGE

When we say that money serves as a **medium of exchange,** what we mean is that sellers will accept it as payment in market transactions. Without some generally accepted medium of exchange, we would have to resort to **barter.** In fact, before money was used, transactions took place by means of barter. Barter is simply a direct exchange—no intermediary good called money is used. In a barter economy, the shoemaker who wants to obtain a dozen water glasses must seek out a glassmaker who at exactly the same time is interested in obtaining a pair of shoes. For this to occur, there has to be a *double coincidence of wants.* If there isn't, the shoemaker must go through several trades in order to obtain the desired dozen glasses—perhaps first trading shoes for jewelry, then jewelry for some pots and pans, and then the pots and pans for the desired glasses.

▶ **Medium of exchange**
Any asset that sellers will accept as payment.

▶ **Barter**
The direct exchange of goods and services for other goods and services without the use of money.

Money facilitates exchange by reducing the transaction costs associated with means-of-payment uncertainty, that is, with regard to goods that the partners in any exchange are willing to accept. The existence of money means that individuals no longer have to hold

Iron	Red woodpecker scalps	Playing cards
Copper	Feathers	Leather
Brass	Glass	Gold
Wine	Polished beads (wampum)	Silver
Corn	Rum	Knives
Salt	Molasses	Pots
Horses	Tobacco	Boats
Sheep	Agricultural implements	Pitch
Goats	Round stones with centers	Rice
Tortoise shells	removed	Cows
Porpoise teeth	Crystal salt bars	Paper
Whale teeth	Snail shells	Cigarettes
Boar tusk		

TABLE 14-1   Types of money.
This is a partial list of things that have been used as money. American Indians used wampum, which was beads made from shells. Fijians have used whales' teeth. The early colonists in North America used tobacco. And cigarettes were used in prisoner-of-war camps during World War II and in post–World War II Germany.

Source: Roger LeRoy Miller and David D. VanHoose, *Modern Money and Banking,* 3d ed. (New York: McGraw-Hill, 1993), p. 13.

a diverse collection of goods as an exchange inventory. As a medium of exchange, money allows individuals to specialize in any area in which they have a comparative advantage and to receive money payments for their labor. Money payments can then be exchanged for the fruits of other people's labor. The use of money as a medium of exchange permits more specialization and the inherent economic efficiencies that come with it. Money is even more important when used for large amounts of trade. Money would not be as important in self-sufficient communities as it is in modern commercial economies.

 INTERNATIONAL EXAMPLE: Ukrainian Coupon Money Drives Out the Ruble

The ruble was the official currency in all 15 former Soviet republics for over 70 years. When Ukraine became independent a few years ago, it still used Russian rubles. Because times were tough, the Ukrainian government did not want non-Ukrainians to be able to buy that republic's limited supplies of food. Therefore, the government printed up ration coupons that were given out only to Ukrainian citizens. Until January 1992, citizens still had to pay for food with Russian rubles, but they also had to provide the official coupons. When Russia was unable to supply enough ruble notes to Ukraine, however, things changed. The coupons became money. The de facto Ukrainian money—ration coupons—started to be used as currency alongside the Russian ruble, which slowly began to disappear as a medium of exchange. Even though the ration coupons did not have a national seal or a serial number, they were used as money. As one observer stated, "It looks odd, but it pays wages and buys chickens." In the beginning, counterfeiting was a serious problem because the first coupons were printed like sheets of stamps. Only later did the Ukrainian government start printing coupon bills in a more intricate and more difficult-to-counterfeit manner.

For Critical Analysis: Why would the Ukrainians care who brought their food, as long as the purchasers paid the market clearing price? ●

MONEY AS A UNIT OF ACCOUNTING

▶ **Unit of accounting**
A measure by which prices are expressed; the common denominator of the price system; a central property of money.

A **unit of accounting** is a way of placing a specific price on economic goods and services. Thus as a unit of accounting, the monetary unit is used to measure the value of goods and services *relative to* other goods and services. It is the common denominator, or measure. The dollar, for example, is the monetary unit in the United States. It is the yardstick that allows individuals easily to compare the relative value of goods and services. Accountants at the U.S. Department of Commerce use dollar prices to measure national income and domestic product, a business uses dollar prices to calculate profits and losses, and a typical household budgets regular expenses using dollar prices as its unit of accounting.

Another way of describing money as a unit of accounting is to say that it serves as a standard of value that allows economic transactors to compare the relative worth of various goods and services.

MONEY AS A STORE OF VALUE

▶ **Store of value**
The ability of an item to hold value over time; a necessary property of money.

To see how money serves as a **store of value** or purchasing power, consider this example. A fisherman comes into port after several days of fishing. At the going price of fish that day, he has $1,000 worth of fish. Those fish are not a good store of value, because if the fisherman keeps them too long, they will rot. If he attempts to exchange them with other tradespeople, some of the fish may rot before he can exchange the entire catch for the goods and services that he desires. But if the fisherman sells the entire catch for money, he can store the value of his catch in the money that he receives. (Of course, he can freeze the fish, but that is costly; it's also not a very precise way to store the value of *fresh* fish.)

MONEY AS A STANDARD OF DEFERRED PAYMENT

The fourth function of the monetary unit is as a **standard of deferred payment.** This function involves the use of money both as a medium of exchange and as a unit of accounting. Debts are typically stated in terms of a unit of accounting; they are paid with a monetary medium of exchange. That is to say, a debt is specified in a dollar amount and paid in currency (or by check). A corporate bond, for example, has a face value—the dollar value stated on it, which is to be paid upon maturity. The periodic interest payments on that corporate bond are specified and paid in dollars, and when the bond comes due (at maturity), the corporation pays the face value to the holder of the bond in dollars.

Not all countries, or the firms and individuals in those countries, will specify that debts owed must be paid in their own national monetary unit. For example, individuals, private corporations, and governments in other countries incur debts in terms of the U.S. dollar, even though the dollar is neither the medium of exchange nor the monetary unit in those countries. Also, contracts for some debts specify repayment in gold rather than in a nation's currency.

> ▶ **Standard of deferred payment**
> A property of an asset that makes it desirable for use as a means of settling debts maturing in the future; an essential property of money.

LIQUIDITY

Money is an asset—something of value—that accounts for part of personal wealth. Wealth in the form of money can be exchanged later for some other asset. Although it is not the only form of wealth that can be exchanged for goods and services, it is the one most widely and readily accepted. This attribute of money is called **liquidity.** We say that an asset is liquid when it can easily be acquired or disposed of without high transaction costs and with relative certainty as to its value. Money is by definition the most liquid asset there is. Just compare it, for example, with a share of stock listed on the New York Stock Exchange. To buy or sell that stock, you must call a stockbroker, who will place the buy or sell order for you. This must be done during normal business hours. You have to pay a commission to the broker. Moreover, there is a distinct probability that you will get more or less for the stock than you originally paid for it. This is not the case with money. Money can be easily converted to other asset forms. Therefore, most individuals hold at least a part of their wealth in the form of the most liquid of assets, money.

When we hold money, however, we pay a price for this advantage of liquidity. That price is the interest yield that could have been obtained had the asset been held in another form—for example, in the form of stocks and bonds.

> ▶ **Liquidity**
> The degree to which an asset can be acquired or disposed of without much danger of any intervening loss in *nominal* value and with small transaction costs. Money is the most liquid asset.

The cost of holding money (its opportunity cost) is measured by the alternative interest yield obtainable by holding some other asset.

🌐 INTERNATIONAL EXAMPLE: Can a Nation Use Different Monies for Different Functions?

In the United States the U.S. dollar serves all of the functions of money just listed. In some countries different monetary units have been used for different functions of money. Consider the example of Israel in the early 1980s. Inflation was rampant then, so managers of grocery stores and other retail outlets decided to save the expense of changing prices regularly. They therefore began listing their prices in terms of U.S. dollars. At various places throughout their stores, they would list the latest dollar-shekel foreign exchange rate. Israeli shoppers with hand calculators would make the conversions themselves. The shekel continued to function as the medium of exchange, but the unit of accounting became the dollar.

Bolivia also experienced inflation on an even greater scale in the 1980s and 1990s. Sometimes prices rose at annual rates of over 38,000 percent (compared to only 300 percent in Israel in a typical year in the early 1980s). The Bolivian government continued to collect taxes in pesos and pay government employees in pesos. Private firms, however, began to pay their employees in U.S. dollars. An increasing number of stores began pricing their goods in dollars. People started using dollars not only as a medium of exchange but as a store of purchasing power and a unit of accounting as well. But pesos continued to circulate.

For Critical Analysis: The inflation rate in Bolivia dropped to below 25 percent per year in the early 1990s. Would the monetary chaos that existed in previous years necessarily come to an end? Why or why not? (Hint: How difficult is it to deal with 25 percent per year increases in prices?) ●

MONETARY STANDARDS, OR WHAT BACKS MONEY

▶ **Transactions accounts**
Checking account balances in commercial banks and other types of financial institutions, such as credit unions and mutual savings banks; any accounts in financial institutions on which you can easily write checks without many restrictions.

▶ **Fiduciary monetary system**
A system in which currency is issued by the government, and its value is based uniquely on the public's faith that the currency represents command over goods and services.

Today in the United States, all of us accept coins, paper currency, and balances in **transactions accounts** (checking accounts with banks and other financial institutions) in exchange for items sold, including labor services. The question remains, why are we willing to accept as payment something that has no intrinsic value? After all, you could not sell checks to anybody for use as a raw material. The reason is that in this country the payments arise from a **fiduciary monetary system.** This means that the value of the payments rests on the public's confidence that such payments can be exchanged for goods and services. *Fiduciary* comes from the Latin *fiducia,* which means "trust" or "confidence." In our fiduciary monetary system, money, in the form of currency or transactions accounts, is not convertible to a fixed quantity of gold, silver, or some other precious commodity. The paper money that people hold cannot be exchanged for a specified quantity of some specified commodity. The bills are just pieces of paper. Coins have a value stamped on them that is normally greater than the market value of the metal in them. Nevertheless, currency and transactions accounts are money because of their acceptability and predictability of value.

ACCEPTABILITY

Transactions accounts and currency are money because they are accepted in exchange for goods and services. They are accepted because people have confidence that they can later be exchanged for other goods and services. This confidence is based on the knowledge that such exchanges have occurred in the past without problems. Even during a period of relatively rapid inflation, we would still be inclined to accept money in exchange for goods and services because it is so useful. Barter is a very costly, time-consuming alternative.

Realize always that money is socially defined. Acceptability is not something that you can necessarily predict. For example, the U.S. government tried, at least on two occasions, to circulate types of money that were socially unacceptable. How many Susan B. Anthony dollars or $2 bills have you seen lately? The answer is probably none. Susan B. Anthony dollars looked too much like quarters, so people rejected them as a medium of exchange. And no one wanted to make room for $2 bills in their register tills or billfolds.

PREDICTABILITY OF VALUE

The purchasing power of the dollar (its value) varies inversely with the price level. The more rapid the rate of increase of some price level index, such as the Consumer Price Index, the more rapid the decrease in the value, or purchasing power, of a dollar. Money still retains its usefulness even if its value—its purchasing power—is declining year in and year out, as in periods of inflation, because it still retains the characteristic of predictability of value. If you believe that the inflation rate is going to be around 10 percent next year, you know that any dollar you receive a year from now will have a purchasing power equal to 10 percent less than that same dollar this year. Thus you will not necessarily refuse to use money or accept it in exchange simply just because you know that its value will decline by the rate of inflation next year.

GRESHAM'S LAW: BAD MONEY DRIVES OUT GOOD MONEY

Sir Thomas Gresham (1519–1579) was the financial adviser to Queen Elizabeth I. It is believed that he coined the phrase "Bad money drives good money out of circulation."

To understand **Gresham's law,** as it is called, we need a definition of *bad money.* We can define it by using the dime as an example. Dimes minted after 1965 had a metal content value of less than 10 cents, whereas those minted before 1965 had a metal content value greater than 10 cents. The dimes minted after 1965 were "bad" money; the dimes minted before 1965 were "good" money. The terms *bad* and *good* refer only to the *nonmonetary* value of money. Given a choice, at a fixed "price," people prefer to own good money rather than bad money. Holding good money makes the owner richer because the good money is worth more than its face value. In the case of pre- and post-1965-minted dimes, the "bad" money—post-1965 dimes—has driven out the "good" money—pre-1965 dimes—in that the post-1965 dimes are now circulating, while the pre-1965 dimes are being hoarded or sold for their silver content. If you look at your coins over a period of several days, you will find pennies and nickels with pre-1965 dates but no higher-denomination coins with those dates. The reason is that higher-denomination coins contained some silver before 1965. As the price of silver rose, coins containing silver disappeared. People either hoarded them or melted them. The "bad" money now circulates instead of "good" silver-content money.

Only when there is a government-fixed exchange rate between two kinds of money can bad money drive out good money. In the case of dimes minted before and after 1965, the fixed exchange rate under law was one for one. Had there not been a fixed exchange rate, sellers could have expressed the prices of goods in two different ways; in terms of old dimes or in terms of new dimes. Consider the purchase of $1 worth of goods after 1965. A merchant might have expressed the price of the product as 10 post-1965 dimes or 7 pre-1965 dimes. If this had been the case, the two dimes could have coexisted in circulation.

> ▸ **Gresham's law**
> Bad money drives out good money; whenever currency that is depreciated, mutilated, or debased is circulated at a fixed rate along with money of higher value, the latter—good money—will disappear from circulation, with only the bad remaining.

CONCEPTS IN BRIEF

- Money is defined by its functions, which are (1) a medium of exchange, (2) a unit of accounting or standard of value, (3) a store of value or purchasing power, and (4) a standard of deferred payment.
- Because money is widely accepted in exchange for goods and services, it is a highly liquid asset. It can be disposed of without high transaction costs and with relative certainty as to its value.
- The United States has a fiduciary monetary system because our money is not convertible into a fixed quantity of a commodity such as gold or silver.
- Money is accepted in exchange for goods and services because people have confidence that it can later be exchanged for other goods and services.
- Another reason that we continue to accept money is that it has a predictable value.
- Whenever there is a fixed exchange rate between money that is debased, mutilated, or depreciated—"bad" money—and "good" money, the good money will disappear from circulation. This is called Gresham's law.

DEFINING THE U.S. MONEY SUPPLY

▶ **Money supply**
The amount of money in circulation. There are numerous ways of defining the money supply.

Money is important. Changes in the total **money supply** and changes in the rate at which the money supply increases or decreases affect important economic variables, such as the rate of inflation, interest rates, employment, and the equilibrium level of real national income. Although there is widespread agreement among economists that money is indeed important, they have never agreed on how to define or measure it. There are two approaches to defining and measuring money: the **transactions approach,** which stresses the role of money as a medium of exchange, and the **liquidity approach,** which stresses the role of money as a temporary store of value.

▶ **Transactions approach**
A method of measuring the money supply by looking at money as a medium of exchange.

▶ **Liquidity approach**
A method of measuring the money supply by looking at money as a temporary store of value.

THE TRANSACTIONS APPROACH TO MEASURING MONEY: M1

Using the transactions approach to measuring money, the money supply consists of the following:

1. Currency
2. Checkable deposits
3. Traveler's checks

The official designation of the money supply, including currency, checkable deposits, and traveler's checks, is **M1.** The various elements of M1 for a typical year are presented on the left side of Table 14-2.

▶ **M1**
The total value of currency plus checkable deposits (demand deposits in commercial banks and other checking-type accounts in thrift institutions), as well as traveler's checks not issued by banks.

Currency.   Currency includes coins minted by the U.S. Treasury and paper currency, usually in the form of Federal Reserve notes, issued by the Federal Reserve banks (to be discussed shortly). Both on a per capita basis and as a percentage of the money supply, however defined, currency has increased in significance in the United States. One of the major reasons for the increased use of currency in the U.S. economy is the growing number of illegal transactions, especially with respect to illegal drugs.

Checkable Deposits.   Most major transactions are done with checks today. The convenience and safety of using checks has made checking accounts the most important

TABLE 14-2   **Composition of the M1 and M2 U.S. money supply, 1993.**

Sources: Federal Reserve; *Economic Indicators*, March 1993.

M1		M2	
COMPONENT	AMOUNT ($ BILLIONS)	COMPONENT	AMOUNT ($ BILLIONS)
Currency and coins	296.9	M1	1,032.8
Checkable deposits	728.0	Savings deposits including money market deposit accounts (MMDAs)	1,182.4
Traveler's checks	7.9	Small time deposits (less than $100,000) at all depository institutions	855.2
Total	1,032.8	Overnight repurchase agreements at commercial banks and overnight Eurodollars	73.2
		Money market mutual fund shares	536.2
		Total	3,476.1[a]

[a]M2 is not equal to the sum of its components for a technical reason. See any H.6 Series Federal Reserve statistical release for an explanation.

component of the money supply. For example, in 1993 it is estimated that currency transactions accounted for less than .5 percent of the dollar amount of all transactions. The majority of the rest involved checks. Checks are a way of transferring the ownership of deposits in financial institutions. They are normally acceptable as a medium of exchange. The financial institutions that offer **checkable deposits** are numerous and include virtually all **thrift institutions**—mutual savings banks, savings and loans associations (S&Ls), and credit unions. Regular banks, called commercial banks, used to be the only financial institutions that could offer checkable deposits.

Traveler's Checks.

Traveler's checks are paid for by the purchaser at the time of transfer. The total quantity of traveler's checks outstanding issued by institutions other than banks is part of the M1 money supply.[1] American Express, Citibank, Cook's, and other institutions issue traveler's checks.

WHAT ABOUT CREDIT CARDS?

Even though a large percentage of transactions are accomplished by using a plastic credit card, we do not consider the credit card itself money. Remember the functions of money. A credit card is not a unit of accounting, a store of value, or a standard of deferred payment. The use of your credit card is really a loan to you by the issuer of the card, be it a bank, a retail store, a gas company, or American Express. The proceeds of the loan are paid to the business that sold you something. You must pay back the loan to the issuer of the credit card, either when you get your statement or with interest throughout the year if you don't pay off your balance. Basically, credit card "money" represents a future claim on money that you will have later. It is not a store of value. Credit cards *defer* rather than complete transactions that ultimately involve the use of money.

A relative newcomer, the *debit card,* automatically withdraws money from a checkable account. When you use your debit card to purchase something, you are giving an instruction to your bank to transfer money directly from your bank account to the store's bank account. If the store in which you are shopping has a direct electronic link to the bank, that transfer may be made instantaneously. Use of a debit card does not create a loan. Debit card "money" is similar to checkable deposit money.

THE LIQUIDITY APPROACH TO MEASURING MONEY: M2

The liquidity approach to defining and measuring the U.S. money supply involves taking into account not only the most liquid assets that people use as money, which are already included in the definition of M1, but also other assets that are highly liquid—that is, that can be converted into money quickly without loss of nominal dollar value and without much cost. Any (non-M1) assets that come under this definition have been called **near monies.** Thus the liquidity approach to the definition of the money supply will include M1 plus near monies. Also consider that the liquidity approach views money as a temporary store of value and thus includes all of M1 plus all near monies. Table 14-2 on the previous page shows the components of **M2**—money as a temporary store of value. We examine each of these components in turn.

▶ **Checkable deposits**
Any deposits in a thrift institution or a commercial bank on which a check may be written.

▶ **Thrift institutions**
Financial institutions that receive most of their funds from the savings of the public; they include credit unions, mutual savings banks, and savings and loan associations.

▶ **Traveler's checks**
Financial instruments purchased from a bank or a nonbanking organization and signed during purchase that can be used as cash upon a second signature by the purchaser.

▶ **Near monies**
Assets that are almost money. They have a high degree of liquidity; they can be easily converted into money without loss in value. Time deposits and short-term U.S. government securities are examples.

▶ **M2**
M1 plus (1) savings and small-denomination time deposits at all depository institutions, (2) overnight repurchase agreements at commercial banks, (3) overnight Eurodollars held by U.S. residents other than banks at Caribbean branches of member banks, (4) balances in money market mutual funds, and (5) money market deposit accounts (MMDAs).

---

[1]Banks place the funds that are to be used to redeem traveler's checks in a special deposit account, and they are therefore already counted as checkable accounts. Nonbank issuers, however, do not place these funds in checkable accounts. Improvements in data collection made it possible to estimate the total amount of nonbank traveler's checks; since June 1981 they have been included in M1.

▶ Savings deposits
Interest-earning funds that can be withdrawn at any time without payment of a penalty.

▶ Depository institutions
Financial institutions that accept deposits from savers and lend those deposits out at interest.

Savings Deposits.   **Savings deposits** in all **depository institutions** (such as commercial banks, mutual savings banks, savings and loan associations, and credit unions) are part of the M2 money supply. A savings deposit is distinguishable from a time deposit because savings funds may be withdrawn without payment of a penalty. Funds are fully protected against loss in their nominal value. There are two types of savings deposits, statement and passbook.

1. **Statement savings deposit.** A statement savings deposit is similar to a checking account because the owner (depositor) receives a monthly statement or record of the deposits and withdrawals and the interest earned during the month. Deposits and withdrawals from a statement savings account can be made by mail.
2. **Passbook savings account.** A passbook savings account requires that the owner present a physical passbook each time he or she makes a deposit or a withdrawal. Deposits and withdrawals are recorded in the passbook.

▶ Time deposit
A deposit in a financial institution that requires a notice of intent to withdraw or must be left for an agreed period. Withdrawal of funds prior to the end of the agreed period results in a penalty.

Time Deposits.   A basic distinction has always been made between a checkable deposit, which is a checking account, and a **time deposit,** which theoretically requires notice of withdrawal and on which the financial institution pays the depositor interest. The name indicates that there is an agreed period during which the funds must be left in the financial institution. If they are withdrawn prior to the end of that period, a penalty may be applied. Recently the distinction between checkable and time deposits has been blurred, but it is still used in the official definition of the money supply.

▶ Certificate of deposit (CD)
A time deposit with a fixed maturity date offered by banks and other financial institutions.

Small-Denomination Time Deposits.   Time deposits include savings certificates and small **certificates of deposit (CDs).** To be included in the M2 definition of the money supply, such time deposits must be less than $100,000—hence the name *small-denomination time deposits.* The owner of a savings certificate is given a receipt indicating the amount deposited, the interest rate to be paid, and the maturity date. A CD is an actual certificate that indicates the date of issue, its maturity date, and other relevant contractual matters.

A variety of small-denomination time deposits are available from depository institutions, ranging in maturities from one month to 10 years.

▶ Money market deposit accounts (MMDAs)
Accounts issued by banks yielding a market rate of interest with a minimum balance requirement and a limit on transactions. They have no minimum maturity.

Money Market Deposit Accounts (MMDAs).   Since 1982, banks and thrift institutions have offered **money market deposit accounts (MMDAs),** which usually require a minimum balance and set limits on the number of monthly transactions (deposits and withdrawals by check).

▶ Repurchase agreement (REPO, or RP)
An agreement made by a bank to sell Treasury or federal agency securities to its customers, coupled with an agreement to repurchase them at a price that includes accumulated interest.

Overnight Repurchase Agreements at Commercial Banks (REPOs, or RPs).   A **repurchase agreement (REPO, or RP)** is made by a bank to sell Treasury or federal agency securities to its customers coupled with an agreement to repurchase them at a price that includes accumulated interest. REPOs fill a gap in that depository institutions are not yet allowed to offer to businesses interest-bearing commercial checking accounts. Therefore, REPOs can be thought of as a financial innovation that bypasses regulation because businesses can park their excess cash in REPOs instead of leaving it in non-interest-bearing commercial checking accounts.

▶ Eurodollar deposits
Deposits denominated in U.S. dollars but held in banks outside the United States, often in overseas branches of U.S. banks.

Overnight Eurodollars.   **Eurodollar deposits** are dollar-denominated deposits in foreign commercial banks and in foreign branches of U.S. banks. The phrase *dollar-*

denominated simply means that although the deposit might be held at a Caribbean commercial bank, its value is stated in terms of U.S. dollars rather than in terms of the local currency. The term *Eurodollar* is inaccurate because banks outside continental Europe participate in the so-called Eurodollar market and also because banks in some countries issue deposits denominated in German marks, Swiss francs, British sterling, and Dutch guilders.

INTERNATIONAL EXAMPLE: The Birth of the Eurodollar Market

The Eurodollar market was started, ironically, by the former Soviet Union in the early 1950s. The Cold War was raging, and the Soviets were worried about how the United States government might treat its assets held in dollar balances in U.S. banks. The Soviets were worried that the U.S. government might someday freeze these assets, so they moved them to Europe. Rather than convert them into marks, francs, and pounds, the Soviets asked European financial institutions to keep them in dollar-denominated accounts. In this way, the Soviets could continue to conduct their international transactions in U.S. dollars. When the Soviets and the European banks worked out the system of dollar-denominated accounts held by foreigners, the Eurodollar market was born.

For Critical Analysis: Why didn't the Soviets simply set up accounts in other countries' local currencies? ●

Money Market Mutual Fund Balances.   Many individuals keep part of their assets in the form of shares in **money market mutual funds.** These mutual funds invest only in short-term credit instruments. The majority of these money market funds allow check-writing privileges, provided that the size of the check exceeds some minimum.

> ▶ **Money market mutual funds**
> Funds of investment companies that obtain funds from the public that are held in common and used to acquire short-maturity credit instruments, such as certificates of deposit and securities sold by the U.S. government.

M2 and Other Money Supply Definitions.   When all these assets are added together, the result is M2. The composition of M2 is given on the right side of Table 14-1.

Economists and researchers have come up with even broader definitions of money than M2.[2] More assets are simply added to the definition. Just remember that there is no one best definition of the money supply. For different purposes, different definitions are appropriate. For example, if we wish to know which definition of the money supply is most controllable by the government, it is probably M1. If we want to use a definition that seems to correlate best with economic activity on an economywide basis, M2 is probably better.

INTERNATIONAL EXAMPLE: Measuring the Kuwaiti Money Supply After the Persian Gulf War

From August 1990 to February 1991, the Iraqi army occupied Kuwait. During that time the government of Iraq declared the Kuwaiti dinar worthless. Iraq tried to force Kuwait to use the Iraqi dinar. During the occupation, before the liberation by U.S. and coalition forces, many Kuwaiti citizens buried their holdings of Kuwaiti dinars in their backyards or behind their businesses. At the same time, some Kuwaitis were using Saudi Arabian

---

[2]They include M3, which is equal to M2 plus large-denomination time deposits and REPOs (in amounts over $100,000) issued by commercial banks and thrift institutions, Eurodollars held by U.S. residents and foreign branches of U.S. banks worldwide and all banking offices in the United Kingdom and Canada, and the balances in both taxable and tax-exempt institution-only money market mutual funds. An even broader definition is called L, for liquidity. It is defined as M3 plus nonbank public holdings of U.S. savings bonds, short-term Treasury securities, commercial paper, and bankers' acceptances.

riyals, and others were using U.S. dollars. After liberation in March 1991, the Kuwaiti government and its people tried to get the economy back to normal. One of the most pressing problems was to decide what constituted money—Kuwaiti dinars, Iraqi dinars, U.S. dollars, and Saudi riyals were all circulating. The people in the country clearly could not decide on their medium of exchange, so it was very difficult to measure the money supply using the transactions approach. The government also had to decide how much of Kuwaiti dinar–denominated accounts to restore to Kuwaiti citizens. One estimate was that it would take the equivalent of $20 billion to bail out the Kuwaiti monetary system, not to mention the thousands of person-years necessary for accountants to sort out the assets and liabilities.

For Critical Analysis: What interest did the Kuwaiti government have in restoring Kuwaiti dinar–denominated accounts to their pre-invasion balances, regardless of what had subsequently been deposited or withdrawn? ●

THE U.S. BANKING STRUCTURE

The United States' banking system consists of a **central bank** called the Federal Reserve System, or **the Fed.** In addition there are a large number of commercial banks, which are privately owned, profit-seeking institutions, and thrift institutions (savings and loan associations, mutual savings banks, and credit unions).

FINANCIAL INTERMEDIARIES: SOURCES AND USES OF FUNDS

The financial institutions in our banking system are all in the same business—transferring funds from savers to investors. This process has become known as **financial intermediation,** and its participants are called **financial intermediaries.** The process of financial intermediation is illustrated in Figure 14-1.

Each financial intermediary in the U.S. system has its own primary source of funds, which are called **liabilities.** When you deposit $100 in your checking account in the bank, the bank creates a liability—it owes you $100—in exchange for the funds deposited. A commercial bank gets its funds from checking and savings accounts; an insurance company gets its funds from insurance policy premiums.

▶ **Central bank**
A banker's bank, usually an official institution that also serves as a country's treasury's bank. Central banks normally regulate commercial banks.

▶ **The Fed**
The Federal Reserve System; the central bank of the United States.

▶ **Financial intermediation**
The process by which financial institutions accept savings from households and lend the savings to businesses, households, and government.

▶ **Financial intermediaries**
Institutions that transfer funds between ultimate lenders (savers) and ultimate borrowers.

▶ **Liabilities**
Amounts owed; the legal claims against a business or household by nonowners.

FIGURE 14-1
The process of financial intermediation.
The process of financial intermediation is depicted here. Note that ultimate lenders and ultimate borrowers are the same economic units—households, businesses, and governments—but not necessarily the same individuals. Whereas individual households can be net lenders or borrowers, households as an economic unit are net lenders. Specific businesses or governments similarly can be net lenders or borrowers; as economic units, both are net borrowers.

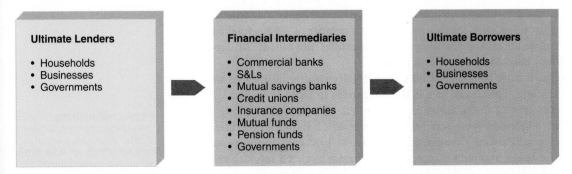

FINANCIAL INTERMEDIARY	ASSETS	LIABILITIES
Commercial banks	Car loans and other consumer debt, business loans, government securities, home mortgages	Checkable accounts, saving deposits, various other time deposits, money market deposit accounts
Savings and loan associations	Home mortgages, some consumer and business debt	Savings and loan shares, checkable accounts, various time deposits, money market deposit accounts
Mutual savings banks	Home mortgages, some consumer and business debt	Checkable accounts, savings accounts, various time deposits, money market deposit accounts
Credit unions	Consumer debt, long-term mortgage loans	Credit union shares, checkable accounts
Insurance companies	Mortgages, stocks, bonds, real estate	Insurance contracts, annuities, pension plans
Pension and retirement funds	Stocks, bonds, mortgages, time deposits	Pension plans
Money market mutual funds	Short-term credit instruments such as large-bank CDs, Treasury bills, and high-grade commercial paper	Fund shares with limited checking privileges

TABLE 14-3 **Financial intermediaries and their assets and liabilities.**

Each financial intermediary normally has a different primary use of its funds (or its **assets**). For example, a credit union usually makes small consumer loans, whereas a mutual savings bank makes mainly home mortgage loans. Table 14-3 lists the assets and liabilities of financial intermediaries.

▶ **Assets**
Amounts owned; all items to which a business or household holds legal claim.

INTERNATIONAL EXAMPLE: How the U.S. Banking Structure Compares to the Rest of the World

Foreigners arriving in the United States are often overwhelmed by the number and kinds of financial institutions that exist. The structure of the banking industry in the United States is quite different from that of other industrialized nations. America is the only country that does not have a true national banking system in which a relatively small number of banks have a large number of branches throughout the country. The reason is that the United States banking system is governed by both federal and state regulations. Until recently, interstate banking has been prohibited by such regulations. As a result the United States has approximately 12 times the number of commercial banks that other industrial countries have. Japan has only about 1 percent of the number of commercial banks that we do. (Note that we are talking about separate legal entities, not offices. All Japanese financial institutions have numerous branch offices.)

Because we have more banks, our banks are generally smaller institutions than those in the rest of the world. This can be seen in the comparison in Table 14-4. And U.S. banks may become even smaller in the future as banks in the European Community (EC) increasingly offer complete banking services throughout all 12 European countries. In addition, the EC Second Banking Coordination Directive of 1988 calls for **universal banking**—the right for banks to offer a complete line of banking-related services and to own shares of stock in companies. To date, American banks are not allowed to engage in uni-

▶ **Universal banking**
The right of commercial banks to offer a complete line of banking-related services. Under such a system, banks can underwrite securities.

TABLE 14-4   **The Top Twenty Banks.**

RANK[a]	NAME	NATION	ASSETS	PROFITS	EMPLOYEES
1	Dai-Ichi Kangyo Bank	Japan	435,718.4[b]	1,012.2[b]	18,466
2	Sumitomo Bank	Japan	407,105.5	1,287.1	16,479
3	Fuji Bank	Japan	403,725.3	1,075.6	15,377
4	Mitsubishi Bank	Japan	392,208.9	995.7	14,026
5	Sanwa Bank	Japan	387,452.2	1,134.5	13,604
6	Crédit Agricole	France	304,706.1	862.5	74,451
7	Banque Nationale De Paris	France	291,394.6	296.8	59,772
8	Crédit Lyonnais	France	286,859.8	680.8	68,486
9	Industrial Bank of Japan	Japan	285,158.8	592.5	5,067
10	Deutsche Bank	Germany	267,308.1	633.9	68,552
11	Barclays Bank	Britain	260,129.6	1,051.4	116,500
12	Tokai Bank	Japan	246,017.3	349.0	11,754
13	National Westminster Bank	Britain	233,541.3	662.2	112,600
14	ABN Amro Holding	Netherlands	232,831.9	727.4	59,634
15	Bank of Tokyo	Japan	228,443.0	550.2	17,081
16	Mitsubishi Trust & Banking	Japan	226,291.2	477.1	6,513
17	Norinchukin Bank	Japan	224,034.7	245.4	3,094
18	Mitsui Bank	Japan	221,297.5	502.6	10,565
19	Société Générale	France	219,662.9	491.8	45,776
20	Citicorp	U.S.	216,986.0	458.0	95,000

[a]Ranking by assets, in $ millions.

[b] in millions

Source: Fortune Magazine, August 26, 1992.

versal banking. That means that unless U.S. banks are allowed to become larger and more diversified, European banks will grow at an even more rapid rate in the future, leaving U.S. banks behind, at least with respect to size.

For Critical Analysis: Do you think that competitive forces from Europe and elsewhere will cause the U.S. banking structure to change? If so, in what ways? ●

CONCEPTS IN BRIEF

- The money supply can be defined in a variety of ways, depending on whether we use the transactions approach or the liquidity approach.
- Using the transactions approach, the money supply consists of currency, checkable deposits, and traveler's checks. This is called M1.
- Checkable deposits are any deposits in financial institutions on which the deposit owner can write checks.
- Credit cards are not part of the money supply, for they simply defer transactions that ultimately involve the use of money.
- Using the liquidity approach for measuring money, to M1 we add savings deposits, time deposits, small-denomination time deposits (certificates of deposits), money market deposit accounts, overnight REPOs, overnight Eurodollars, and money market mutual fund balances. This total is called M2.
- Financial intermediaries transfer funds from ultimate lenders (savers) to ultimate borrowers. This process of financial intermediation is undertaken by commercial banks, savings and loans, mutual savings banks, credit unions, insurance companies, mutual funds, pension funds, and the government.
- Each financial intermediary has a relatively distinct set of liabilities and a distinct set of assets. For example, an insurance company has liabilities of insurance contracts and pension plans and assets of mortgages, stocks, bonds, and real estate.

THE FEDERAL RESERVE SYSTEM

The Federal Reserve System is the most important regulatory agency in our monetary system and is usually considered the monetary authority. Our central bank was established by the Federal Reserve Act, signed on December 23, 1913, by President Woodrow Wilson. The act was the outgrowth of recommendations from the National Monetary Commission, which had been authorized by the Aldridge-Vreeland Act of 1908. Basically, the commission had attempted to find a way to counter the periodic financial panics that had occurred in our country. The Federal Reserve System was set up to aid and supervise banks and also to provide banking services for the U.S. Treasury.

ORGANIZATION OF THE FEDERAL RESERVE SYSTEM

Figure 14-2 shows how the Federal Reserve is organized. It is run by the Board of Governors, composed of seven salaried, full-time members appointed by the nation's president with the approval of the Senate. The 12 Federal Reserve banks have a total of 25 branches. The boundaries of the 12 federal reserve districts and the cities in which a Federal Reserve bank is located are shown in Figure 14-3 on page 312. The very important Federal Open Market Committee (FOMC) determines monetary policy actions for the Fed. This committee is composed of the members of the Board of Governors, the president of the New York Federal Reserve Bank, and representatives of four other reserve banks, rotated periodically. The FOMC determines the future growth of the money supply and other important variables.

DEPOSITORY INSTITUTIONS

The banks and other depository institutions—all financial institutions that accept deposits—that make up our monetary system consist of approximately 12,000 commercial banks, 2,100 savings and loan associations, 12,000 credit unions, and 500 mutual savings banks. No one financial institution dominates the marketplace. For example, the largest bank holds only 6 percent of total banking system deposits. All depository institutions, including member and nonmember commercial banks, as well as savings and loan associations, credit unions, and mutual savings banks, may purchase services from the Federal Reserve System on an equal basis. Also, almost all depository institutions are required to keep a certain percentage of their deposits in reserve at the Federal Reserve district banks or as vault cash. This percentage depends on the bank's volume of business.

FUNCTIONS OF THE FEDERAL RESERVE SYSTEM

Here we will lay out in detail what the Federal Reserve does in this country.

1. **Supplies the economy with fiduciary currency.** The Federal Reserve banks must supply the economy with paper currency called Federal Reserve notes. For example, at Christmastime, when there is an abnormally large number of currency transactions, more paper currency is desired. Commercial banks find this out as deposit holders withdraw large amounts of cash from their accounts. Commercial banks then turn to the Federal Reserve banks to replenish vault cash. Hence the Federal Reserve banks must have on hand a sufficient amount of cash to accommodate the demands for paper currency at different times of the year. Note that even though all Federal Reserve notes are printed at the Bureau of Printing and Engraving in Washington, D.C., each note is assigned a code indicating from which of the 12 Federal Reserve banks it "originated."

2. **Provides a system for check collection and clearing.** The Federal Reserve System has established a clearing mechanism for checks. Consider an example. Suppose that John Smith in Chicago writes a check to Jill Jones, who lives in San Francisco. When

FIGURE 14–2

Organization of the Federal Reserve System.
The 12 regional Federal Reserve banks are headed by 12 separate presidents. The main authority of the Fed resides with the Board of Governors of the Federal Reserve System, whose seven members are appointed for 14-year terms by the president and confirmed by the Senate. Open-market operations are carried out through the Federal Open Market Committee (FOMC), consisting of the seven members of the Board of Governors plus five presidents of the regional banks (always including the president of the New York bank, with the others rotating).

Source: Board of Governors of the Federal Reserve System, *The Federal Reserve System: Purposes and Functions,* 7th ed. (Washington, D.C., 1984), p. 5.

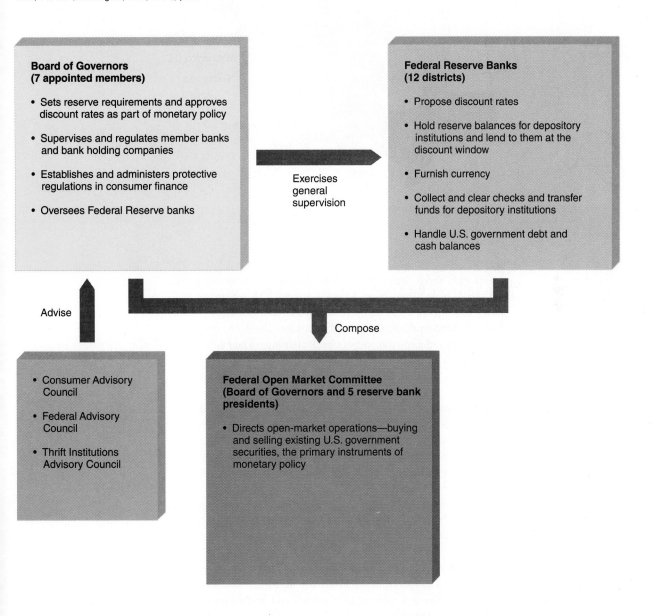

Jill receives the check in the mail, she deposits it at her commercial bank. Her bank then deposits the check in the Federal Reserve Bank of San Francisco. In turn, the Federal Reserve Bank of San Francisco sends the check to the Federal Reserve Bank of

FIGURE 14-3

The Federal Reserve System.

The Federal Reserve System is divided into 12 districts, each served by one of the Federal Reserve banks, located in the cities indicated. The Board of Governors meets in Washington, D.C.

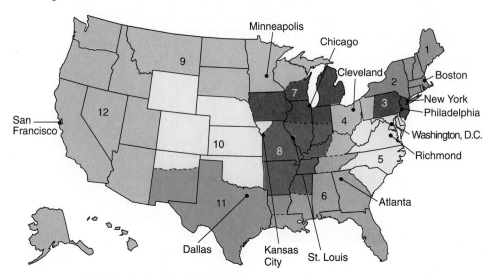

Chicago. The Chicago Fed then sends the check to John Smith's commercial bank. There the amount of the check is deducted from John's account. The schematic diagram in Figure 14-4 shows how this is done. All member banks and depository institutions in a particular Federal Reserve district can send deposited checks to one location—their district bank—thereby reducing the cost of check clearing. (The Fed's check collection and clearing operations compete with private clearinghouses. Since the Fed began charging for these services, some of this business has shifted back to the private sector.)

3. **Holds depository institutions' reserves.** The 12 Federal Reserve banks hold the reserves (other than vault cash) of depository institutions. As you will see in Chapter 15, depository institutions are required by law to keep a certain percentage of their deposits in reserves. Even if they weren't required to do so by law, they would still wish to keep some reserves. Depository institutions act just like other businesses. A firm would not try to operate with a zero balance in its checking account, would it? It would keep a positive balance on hand from which it could draw for expected and unexpected transactions. So, too, would a depository institution desire to have reserves in its banker's bank (the Federal Reserve) on which it could draw funds needed for expected and unexpected transactions.

4. **Acts as the government's fiscal agent.** The Federal Reserve is the banker and fiscal agent for the federal government. The government, as we are all aware, collects large sums of money through taxation. The government also spends and distributes equally large sums. Consequently, the U.S. Treasury has a checking account with the Federal Reserve. Thus the Fed acts as the government's banker, along with commercial banks that hold government deposits. The Fed also helps the government collect certain tax revenues and aids in the purchase and sale of government securities.

FIGURE 14-4
How a check clears.

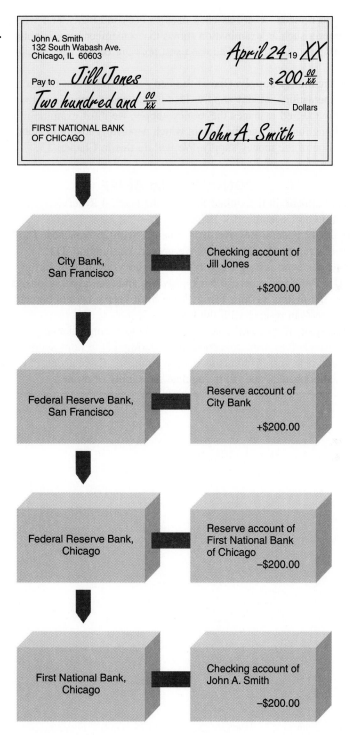

John A. Smith
132 South Wabash Ave.
Chicago, IL 60603

April 24 19 *XX*

Pay to _____*Jill Jones*_____ $ *200.⁰⁰/ₓₓ*

Two hundred and ⁰⁰/ₓₓ ——————— Dollars

FIRST NATIONAL BANK
OF CHICAGO

John A. Smith

City Bank,
San Francisco

Checking account of
Jill Jones

+$200.00

Federal Reserve Bank,
San Francisco

Reserve account of
City Bank

+$200.00

Federal Reserve Bank,
Chicago

Reserve account of
First National Bank
of Chicago

–$200.00

First National Bank,
Chicago

Checking account of
John A. Smith

–$200.00

5. **Supervises member banks.** The Fed (along with the comptroller of the currency and the Federal Deposit Insurance Corporation) is the supervisor and regulator of depository institutions. (All banks are regulated by some agency. No bank, savings and loan association, or credit union in the United States is unregulated.) The Fed will periodically and without warning examine member commercial banks to see what kinds of

loans have been made, what has been used to back the loans, and who has received them. Whenever such an examination shows that a member bank is not conforming to current banking standards, the Fed can exert pressure on the bank to alter its banking practices.

6. **Regulates the money supply.** One of the Fed's most important functions is its ability to regulate the nation's money supply. That is perhaps its most important task. To understand how the Fed manages the money supply, we must examine more closely its reserve-holding function and the way in which depository institutions aid in expansion and contraction of the money supply. We will do this in Chapter 15.

CONCEPTS IN BRIEF

- The central bank in the United States is the Federal Reserve System, which was set up on December 13, 1913.
- There are 12 Federal Reserve district banks, with 25 branches. The Federal Reserve is run by the Board of Governors in Washington, D.C.
- The Fed has control over virtually all depository institutions in the United States, including commercial banks, savings and loan associations, credit unions, and mutual savings banks. Most must keep a certain percentage of their deposits in reserve with the Fed.
- The functions of the Federal Reserve are (1) to supply fiduciary currency, (2) to provide for check collection and clearing, (3) to hold depository-institution reserves, (4) to act as the government's fiscal agent, (5) to supervise member banks, and (6) to regulate the supply of money.

MONEY LAUNDERING, AMERICAN STYLE
Concepts Applied: Price level, currency, banking transactions

Monetary transactions occur at the rate of billions per day. It is increasingly difficult to trace the origins of money that might be illegally laundered.

In most countries, when the price level rises, so do the denominations of their monetary currencies. Just the reverse of this has been happening in the United States. Even though the U.S. price level is roughly four times higher than it was 30 years ago, Americans are required to use smaller, not larger, bills. Until 1969, $500 and $1,000 bills circulated routinely, and it was even possible to obtain $10,000 bills. Now the largest bill in circulation is the $100, and some officials have proposed that nothing larger than a $20 be permitted.

Although these developments sound strange, they have a simple explanation: Drug dealers like cash. It's readily transportable, and unlike checks and money orders, it leaves no paper trail. A million dollars in $100 bills, for example, weighs only 22 pounds and will fit into a stylish, inconspicuous briefcase. And if the drug dealers could get their hands on larger denominations, they could even dispense with the briefcase.

DRUGS AND BANKS Currency-denomination limitations are not the only way the federal government is using the financial system to wage its war on drugs. Current law requires that most financial institution transactions involving more than $10,000 in cash must be reported to the federal government. Although the law was originally developed to prevent people from evading taxes on cash income, it is now being used in an effort to trace cash from supposed drug deals. The notion is that drug

dealers won't want to leave their cash in briefcases forever but will eventually want to get it into financial institutions, where it is safe and can earn interest. Requiring that financial institutions report large cash withdrawals and deposits thus gives the federal government a means of identifying potential drug dealers.

About $350 billion spread across more than 20 million separate transactions is now reported each year to the U.S. Department of the Treasury. This sounds like an enormous sum until you realize that $200 *trillion* changes hands in the United States every year—an amount nearly 40 times GDP and 600 times the size of the banking transactions covered by the currency-reporting requirements. Most of this money actually changes hands by means of wire transfers, which are electronic messages flashed from the memory of one bank's computer to another's. Using a wire transfer, it takes less than three seconds, at a cost of 40 cents, to move a million dollars across the country or around the globe. A drug trafficker can launder money through many bank accounts so easily that it becomes almost impossible for an outside observer (or a government auditor) to figure out where the money started or who really owns it now.

THE COLOR OF MONEY The legal authorities are aware of and frustrated by facts such as these. Over the past few years they have proposed a variety of plans that purportedly would help them prevent traffickers from hiding their ill-gotten gains. Among the proposals that would affect the banking system are the following:

- *Every* wire transfer—all $200 trillion worth of them—would have to be reported to the U.S. Treasury.
- Banks would be required to refuse deposits from individuals declared by the government to be "known or suspected" drug dealers and would also have to report any existing deposits owned by these persons.
- To make sure that none of the "little fish" escape the net, the limit for currency transactions that must be reported by banks would be lowered from $10,000 to $1,000.

Although the high costs and administrative burdens of proposals such as these make it unlikely that they will be adopted in the near future, Treasury officials have not given up looking for ways to ferret out the drug dealers. One plan, for example, would be covertly to print up new versions (in different colors and sizes) of the $50 and $100 bills favored by drug traffickers. Then the legal tender status of the old bills would be nullified on only 10 days' notice. Presumably, anyone trying to exchange more than a briefcase full of old bills for new would be immediately identified as a drug dealer.

FOR CRITICAL ANALYSIS

1. Do you think that the increased use of computers has made it easier or more difficult for the government to monitor the transactions in which people engage?

2. If banks were required to report all cash transactions over $1,000, how would this likely affect the structure of the banking industry? Would banks have an incentive to become larger or smaller?

CHAPTER SUMMARY

1. The functions of money are (a) a medium of exchange, (b) a unit of accounting (standard of value), (c) a store of value or purchasing power, and (d) a standard of deferred payment.

2. We have a fiduciary monetary system in the United States because our money, whether in the form of currency or checkable accounts, is not convertible into a fixed quantity of a commodity, such as gold or silver.

3. Our money is exchangeable for goods and services because it has acceptability: People have confidence that whatever money they receive can be exchanged for other goods and services later. Our money also has a predictable value.

4. Gresham's law states that bad money drives out good money; in other words, whenever currency that is depreciated or debased circulates at a fixed rate alongside money of higher value, the latter (good money) will disappear from circulation.

5. There are numerous ways to define the U.S. money supply. One method is called the transactions approach, which stresses the role of money as a medium of exchange. The other method is the liquidity ap-

proach, which stresses the role of money as a temporary store of value.

6. The transactions approach generates the M1 definition of money, which includes (a) currency, (b) checkable deposits, and (c) traveler's checks.

7. The liquidity approach generates the M2 definition of money, which includes M1 plus such near monies as savings deposits, overnight repurchase agreements, money market mutual fund balances, money market deposit accounts, and overnight Eurodollars.

8. Our central bank is the Federal Reserve System, which consists of 12 district banks with 25 branches. The governing body of the Federal Reserve System is the Board of Governors. The group that makes monetary policy decisions is the Federal Open Market Committee.

9. The basic functions of the Federal Reserve System are (a) supplying the economy with fiduciary currency, (b) providing a system of check collection and clearing, (c) holding depository institutions' reserves, (d) acting as the government's fiscal agent, (e) supervising member banks, and (f) regulating the money supply.

DISCUSSION OF PREVIEW POINTS

1. What is money?
Money is defined by its functions. Thus money is whatever is generally accepted for use as a medium of exchange, a unit of accounting, a store of value or purchasing power, and a standard of deferred payment. In various places in the world, throughout history, different items have performed these functions: wampum, gold, silver, cows, boulders, paper, diamonds, salt, cigarettes, and many others.

2. What backs the U.S. dollar?
Students usually think that the U.S. dollar is "backed"

by gold, but alas (some experts say fortunately), this is not the case. The United States is presently on a fiduciary monetary standard, and as such the U.S. dollar is backed only by faith—the public's confidence that it can be exchanged for goods and services. This confidence comes from the fact that other people will accept the dollar in transactions because our government has declared it legal tender and because, despite inflation, it still retains the characteristic of predictability of value.

3. What are the functions of the Federal Reserve System?

The Fed's most important function is to regulate the U.S. money supply, a topic covered in the next several chapters. The Fed also holds depository institutions' reserves, acts as the U.S. government's fiscal agent, supervises member banks, clears checks, and supplies fiduciary currency to the public.

4. Who is involved in the process of financial intermediation?

Financial intermediation involves the transfer of funds from *savers* to *investors*. The ultimate lenders are the savers—households, businesses, and governments, including the federal government and state and local governments. The ultimate borrowers are also households, businesses, and governments—the same economic units but not necessarily the same individuals. Between ultimate lenders and ultimate borrowers are financial intermediaries, including commercial banks, savings and loans, mutual savings banks, credit unions, insurance companies, mutual funds, pension funds, and governments.

PROBLEMS

(Answers to the odd-numbered problems appear at the back of the book.)

14-1. Consider each type of asset in terms of its potential use as a medium of exchange, a unit of accounting, and a store of value or purchasing power. Indicate which use is most appropriately associated with each asset.
   a. a painting by Renoir
   b. a 90-day U.S. Treasury bill
   c. a time deposit account in a savings and loan association in Reno, Nevada
   d. one share of IBM stock
   e. a $50 Federal Reserve note
   f. a MasterCard credit card
   g. a checkable account in a mutual savings bank in New England
   h. a lifetime pass to the Los Angeles Dodgers' home baseball games

14-2. The value of a dollar bill is the reciprocal of the price index. In 1983 the CPI had a value of 1; hence the value of a dollar in 1983 equaled $1. If the price index now is 2, what is the value of the dollar in 1983 prices? If the price index is 2.5?

14-3. What are the components of M2?

14-4. How have technological changes altered the form of money?

14-5. Elsa Lee can make several uses of her money. Indicate for each case whether her money is being used as a medium of exchange (E), a store of value (V), a unit of accounting (A), or a standard of deferred payment (P).
   a. Lee has accumulated $600 in her checking account at a depository institution.
   b. Lee decides to use this $600 to purchase a new washing machine and goes shopping to compare the prices being charged by different dealers for the machine she wishes to buy.
   c. Lee finds that the lowest price at which she can purchase the machine she wants is $498.50. She has the dealer deliver the machine and agrees to pay the dealer in 30 days.
   d. Thirty days later Lee sends the dealer a check drawn on her checking account to pay for the washer.

14-6. A hypothetical country is on a bimetal standard of copper and tin, meaning that the government sets official prices for both copper and tin. The official price for copper is "too high," meaning that tin will sell for a higher price on unofficial world markets than the government's official price for tin.
   a. According to Gresham's law, which metal would circulate as currency?
   b. Which metal would be held by the public for other nonmonetary purposes?
   c. How could the government make the other metal circulate as currency?

14-7. Consider a barter economy in which 10 goods and services are produced and exchanged. How many exchange rates exist in that economy, which does not use money?

14-8. Use the data in the table to compute M1.

COMPONENTS	AMOUNT ($ BILLIONS)
Currency outside of the Treasury, Federal Reserve banks, and vaults of depository institutions	193.2
Checkable accounts other than those owned by depository institutions, the U.S. government, foreign banks, and foreign institutions	541.9
Large time deposits, short-term REPOs, liabilities, and overnight Eurodollars	743.4
Nonbank public holdings of U.S. savings bonds	643.0
Traveler's checks	8.1

14-9. Cash and currency account for nearly 98 percent of the total number of all payments in the United States, but wire transfers account for over 82 percent of the dollar value of all payments in the United States. How can both situations be true simultaneously?

COMPUTER-ASSISTED INSTRUCTION
(Complete problem and answer on disk.)

The key conceptual and institutional features of our monetary and banking systems are illuminated with the aid of real-world questions.

MONEY CREATION AND DEPOSIT INSURANCE

During the Great Depression hundreds of thousands of American families with deposits in banks throughout the country lost these deposits as thousands of banks failed. To prevent a recurrence of that misfortune, the federal government created the Federal Deposit Insurance Corporation. For half a century small savers never lost a penny due to depository institution failure. In the 1990s, however, some unfortunate savers have lost part of their savings when the bank or savings and loan in which they had placed their money failed. An important question is, How safe is our money? Learning the answer to that question involves understanding how money is created in America and how deposits are insured.

   After reading this chapter, you should be able to answer the following questions:

1. What is a fractional reserve banking system?

2. What happens to the total money supply when a person deposits in one depository institution a check drawn on another depository institution?

3. What happens to the overall money supply when a person who sells a U.S. government security to the Federal Reserve places the proceeds in a depository institution?

4. How does the existence of deposit insurance affect a financial institution's choice of risky versus nonrisky assets?

INTRODUCTION

If you were to attend a luncheon of local bankers and ask the question, "Do you as bankers create money?" you would get a uniformly negative response. Bankers are certain that they do not create money. Indeed, no individual bank can create money. But along with the Federal Reserve System, depository institutions do create money; they do determine the total deposits outstanding. In this chapter we will examine the **money,** or **deposit, multiplier process.** We will also take a look at federal deposit insurance and its role in provoking the crisis in the savings and loan industry.

How fast the money supply grows or does not grow is important because no matter what model of the economy is used, theories link the money supply growth rate to economic growth or to business fluctuations. There is in fact a long-standing relationship between changes in the money supply and changes in nominal GDP. Some economists use this historical evidence to argue that money is an important determinant of the level of economic activity in the economy.

Another key economic variable in our economy is the price level. At least one theory attributes changes in the rate of inflation to changes in the growth rate of money in circulation. Figure 15-1 shows the relationship between the rate of growth of the money supply and the rate of inflation. There seems to be a loose, albeit consistent, direct relationship between changes in the money supply and changes in the rate of inflation. Increases in the money supply growth rate seem to lead to increases in the inflation rate, after a time lag.

▶ **Money, or deposit, multiplier process**
The process by which an injection of new money into the banking system leads to a multiple expansion in the total money supply.

A FRACTIONAL RESERVE BANKING SYSTEM

Predecessors to modern-day banks were goldsmiths and moneylenders. These individuals had the strongest vaults. Other people who had gold (and other valuables) but no means of protection began to ask goldsmiths and moneylenders to hold their valuables for safekeeping. The goldsmiths and moneylenders charged a fee for this safekeeping service. It turned out that only a fraction of the total amount of gold and other valuables left with these guardians was ever withdrawn over any time period. That is to say, only a small fraction of clients would ask for their deposits at any one time. Thus to meet the requests of these clients, the vault owners needed to keep only a relatively small fraction of the total deposits in reserve.

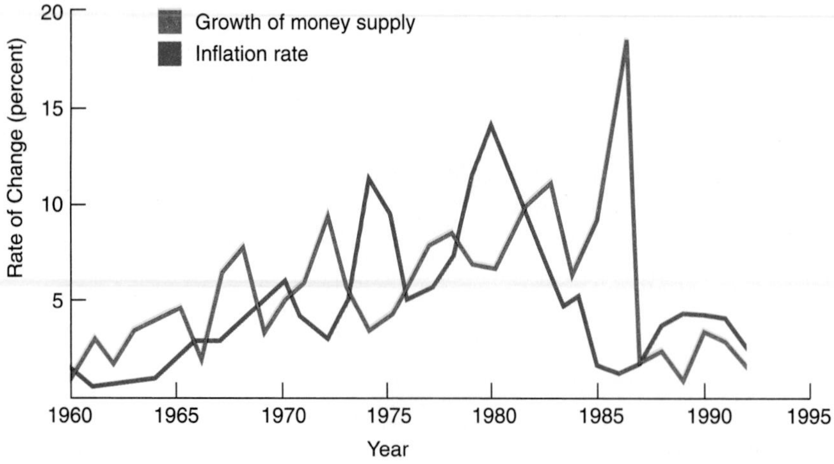

FIGURE 15-1
Money supply growth versus the inflation rate.
These times-series curves indicate a loose correspondence between money supply growth and the inflation rate. Actually, closer inspection reveals a direct relationship between changes in the growth rate of money and changes in the inflation rate *in a later period.* Increases in the rate of growth of money seem to lead to subsequent increases in the inflation rate; decreases in the rate of money growth seem to lead to subsequent reductions in the inflation rate.

Sources: Economic Report of the President, 1993; Federal Reserve Bulletin.

Now, if you were a vault owner and knew that only a certain percentage of deposits would be requested in any one time period, you could lend the remainder out at interest and make income in addition to the fee for the use of your vault. This is how banks grew up—as part of a **fractional reserve banking system.** In other words, in such a system, reserves on hand to meet net withdrawal demands by depositors are some fraction less than 100 percent of total deposits. Today in the United States, the ratio of reserves to deposits is less than 100 percent. The reserves of depository institutions are not kept in gold but rather in the form of deposits in reserve with Federal Reserve district banks and in vault cash.

> **Fractional reserve banking system**
> A system of banking in which member banks keep only a fraction of their deposits in reserve.

RESERVES

Depository institutions are required to maintain a specified percentage of their customer deposits as **reserves.** Different types of depository institutions are required to hold different percentages of reserves. Also, within one type of depository institution, the larger the institution, the larger the reserve requirements. On checkable accounts, most depository institutions have to keep 10 percent as reserves.

> **Reserves**
> In the U.S. Federal Reserve System, deposits held by district Federal Reserve banks for depository institutions, plus depository institutions' vault cash.

Take a hypothetical example. If the required level of reserves is 10 percent and the bank[1] has $1 billion in customer checkable deposits, it must hold at least $100 million as reserves. These can be either deposits with the district Federal Reserve bank or vault cash. There are three distinguishable types of reserves: legal, required, and excess.

> **Legal reserves**
> Reserves that depository institutions are allowed by law to claim as reserves—for example, deposits held at district Federal Reserve banks and vault cash.

1. **Legal reserves.** For depository institutions, **legal reserves** constitute anything that the law permits them to claim as reserves. Today that consists only of deposits held at the district Federal Reserve bank plus vault cash. Government securities, for example, are not legal reserves, even though the owners and managers of the depository institutions may consider them such because they can easily be turned into cash, should the need arise, to meet unusually large net withdrawals by customers.

> **Required reserve ratio**
> The percentage of total deposits that the Fed requires depository institutions to hold in the form of vault cash or on deposit with the Fed.

2. **Required reserves. Required reserves** are the *minimum* amount of legal reserves—vault cash plus deposits at the Fed—that a depository institution must have to back its checkable deposits. They are expressed as a ratio of required reserves to total checkable deposits (banks need hold no reserves on noncheckable deposits). The **required reserve ratio** is currently 10 percent.

> **Required reserves**
> The value of reserves that a depository institution must hold in the form of vault cash or on deposit with the Fed.

> **Excess reserves**
> The difference between legal reserves and required reserves.

3. **Excess reserves.** Depository institutions often hold reserves in excess of what is required by law. This difference between actual (legal) reserves and required reserves is called **excess reserves.** (Excess reserves can be negative, but they rarely are. Negative excess reserves indicate that depository institutions do not have sufficient reserves to meet their required reserves. When this happens, they borrow from other depository institutions or from a Federal Reserve bank, sell assets such as securities, or call in loans.) Excess reserves are an important determinant of the rate of growth of the money supply, for as we shall see, it is only to the extent that depository institutions have excess reserves that they can make loans. Because reserves produce no income, profit-seeking financial institutions have an incentive to minimize excess reserves. They use them either to purchase income-producing securities or to make loans with which they earn income through interest payments received. In equation form, we can define excess reserves in this way:

$$\text{Excess reserves} = \text{legal reserves} - \text{required reserves}$$

---

[1]The term *bank* will be used interchangeably with the term *depository institution* in this chapter because distinctions among financial institutions are becoming less and less meaningful.

In the analysis that follows, we examine the relationship between the level of reserves and the size of the money supply. This analysis implies that factors influencing the level of the reserves of the banking system as a whole will ultimately affect the level of the money supply, other things held constant. We show first that when someone deposits in one depository institution a check that is written on another depository institution, the two depository institutions involved are individually affected, but the overall money supply does not change. Then we show that when someone deposits in a depository institution a check that is written on the Fed, a multiple expansion in the money supply results.

CONCEPTS IN BRIEF

- Ours is a fractional reserve banking system in which depository institutions must hold only a percentage of their deposits as reserves, either on deposit with the district Federal Reserve bank or as vault cash.
- Required reserves are usually expressed as a ratio, in percentage terms, of legal reserves to total deposits.

THE RELATIONSHIP BETWEEN RESERVES AND TOTAL DEPOSITS IN DEPOSITORY INSTITUTIONS

To show the relationship between reserves and depository institution deposits, we first analyze a single bank (existing alongside many others). A single bank is able to make loans to its customers only to the extent that it has reserves above the level legally required to cover the new deposits. When an individual bank has no excess reserves, it cannot make loans.

HOW A SINGLE BANK REACTS TO AN INCREASE IN RESERVES

To examine the **balance sheet** of a single bank after its reserves are increased, the following assumptions are made:

▶ **Balance sheet**
A statement of the assets and liabilities of any business entity, including financial institutions and the Federal Reserve System. Assets are what is owned; liabilities are what is owed.

1. The required reserve ratio is 10 percent for all checkable deposits; that is, the federal government requires that an amount equal to 10 percent of all checkable deposits be held in reserve in a district Federal Reserve bank or in vault cash.
2. Checkable deposits are the bank's only liabilities; reserves at the district Federal Reserve bank and loans are the bank's only assets. Loans are promises made by customers to repay some amount in the future; that is, they are IOUs and as such are assets to the bank.
3. There is such a ready loan demand that the bank has no trouble lending additional money.
4. Every time a loan is made to an individual (consumer or business), all the proceeds from the loan are put into a checkable account; no cash (currency or coins) is withdrawn.
5. Depository institutions seek to keep their excess reserves at a zero level because reserves at the district Federal Reserve bank do not earn interest. All depository institutions are currently at zero excess reserves. Depository institutions will wish to convert excess reserves into interest-bearing loans.

Look at the simplified initial position of the bank in Balance Sheet 15-1. Liabilities consist of $1 million in checkable deposits. Assets consist of $100,000 in reserves, which you can see are required reserves in the form of vault cash or in the depository institution's reserve account at the district Federal Reserve branch, and $900,000 in loans to customers. Total assets of $1 million equal total liabilities of $1 million. With a 10 percent reserve requirement and $1 million in checkable deposits, the bank has the actual required

BALANCE SHEET 15-1 Bank 1.

ASSETS			LIABILITIES	
Total reserves		$100,000	Checkable deposits	$1,000,000
Required reserves	$100,000			
Excess reserves	0			
Loans		900,000		
Total		$1,000,000	Total	$1,000,000

▶ **Net worth**
The difference between assets and liabilities.

reserves of $100,000 and no excess reserves. The simplifying assumption here is that assets equal liabilities and that the bank has a zero **net worth.** A depository institution rarely has a net worth of more than a small percentage of its total assets.

Assume that a *new* depositor writes a $100,000 check drawn on another depository institution and deposits it in Bank 1. Checkable deposits in Bank 1 therefore immediately increase by $100,000, bringing the total to $1.1 million. Once the check clears, total reserves of Bank 1 increase to $200,000. A $1.1 million total in checkable deposits means that required reserves will have to be 10 percent of $1.1 million, or $110,000. Bank 1 now has excess reserves equal to $200,000 minus $110,000, or $90,000. This is shown in Balance Sheet 15-2.

BALANCE SHEET 15-2 Bank 1.

ASSETS			LIABILITIES	
Total reserves		$200,000	Checkable deposits	$1,100,000
Required reserves	$110,000			
Excess reserves	90,000			
Loans		900,000		
Total		$1,100,000	Total	$1,100,000

Look at excess reserves in Balance Sheet 15-2. Excess reserves were zero before the $100,000 deposit, and now they are $90,000—that's $90,000 worth of assets not earning any income. By assumption, Bank 1 will now lend out this entire $90,000 in excess reserves in order to obtain interest income. Loans will increase to $990,000. The borrowers who receive the new loans will not leave them on deposit in Bank 1. After all, they borrow money to spend it. As they spend it by writing checks written on other banks,

BALANCE SHEET 15-3 **Bank 1.**

ASSETS			LIABILITIES	
Total reserves		$110,000	Checkable deposits	$1,100,000
Required reserves	$110,000			
Excess reserves	0			
Loans		990,000		
Total		$1,100,000	Total	$1,100,000

actual reserves will eventually fall to $110,000 (as required), and excess reserves will again become zero, as indicated in Balance Sheet 15-3.

In this example, a person came in and deposited an additional $100,000 check drawn on another bank. That $100,000 became part of the reserves of Bank 1. Because that deposit immediately created excess reserves in Bank 1, further loans were possible for Bank 1. The excess reserves were lent out to earn interest. A bank will not lend more than its excess reserves because, by law, it must hold a certain amount of required reserves.

Effect on the Money Supply. A look at the balance sheets for Bank 1 might give the impression that the money supply increased because of the new customer's $100,000 deposit. Remember, though, that the deposit was a check written on *another* bank. Therefore, the other bank suffered a *decline* in its checkable deposits and its reserves. While total assets and liabilities in Bank 1 have increased by $100,000, they have *decreased* in the other bank by $100,000. The *total* amount of money and credit in the economy is unaffected by the transfer of funds from one depository institution to another.

Each individual depository institution can create loans (and deposits) only to the extent that it has excess reserves. In our example, Bank 1 had $90,000 of excess reserves after the deposit of the $100,000. Conversely, the bank on which the check was written found that its excess reserves were now a *negative* $90,000 (assuming that it had zero excess reserves previously). That bank now has fewer reserves than required by law; it has deficit reserves.[2] It will have to call in loans in order to make actual reserves meet required reserves. The amount of checkable deposits will therefore decline.

The thing to remember is that new reserves are not created when checks written on one bank are deposited in another bank. The Federal Reserve System can, however, create new reserves; that is the subject of the next section.

THE FED'S DIRECT EFFECT ON THE OVERALL LEVEL OF RESERVES

Now we shall examine the Fed's direct effect on the level of reserves. An explanation of how a change in the level of reserves causes a multiple change in the total money supply follows. Consider the Federal Open Market Committee (FOMC), whose decisions essentially determine the level of reserves in the monetary system.

---

[2]If Bank 2 held zero excess reserves, it held $1 in required reserves for every $10 in checkable deposit liabilities. If a $1 loss in checkable deposit liabilities led to a 10-cent reduction in total reserves, Bank 2 would still have zero excess reserves. A $1 reduction in checkable deposit liabilities, however, leads to a $1 loss in total reserves; therefore, Bank 2 will experience a 90-cent net reduction for every $1 it loses in checkable deposit liabilities.

FEDERAL OPEN MARKET COMMITTEE

▶ **Open market operations**
The buying and selling of existing U.S. government securities (such as bonds) in the open private market by the Federal Reserve System.

Open market operations are the buying and selling of *existing* U.S. government securities in the open market (the private secondary U.S. securities market) by the FOMC in order to change the money supply. If the FOMC decides that the Fed should buy or sell bonds, it instructs the New York Federal Reserve Bank trading desk to do so.[3]

A SAMPLE TRANSACTION

Assume that the trading desk at the New York Fed has received an order from the FOMC to purchase $100,000 worth of U.S. government securities.[4]

The Fed pays for these securities by writing a check on itself for $100,000. This check is given to the bond dealer in exchange for the $100,000 worth of bonds. The bond dealer deposits the $100,000 check in its transactions account at a bank, which then sends the $100,000 check back to the Federal Reserve. When the Fed receives the check, it adds $100,000 to the reserve account of the bank that sent it the check. The Fed has created $100,000 of reserves. The Fed can create reserves because it has the ability to "write up" (add to) the reserve accounts of depository institutions whenever it buys U.S. securities. When the Fed buys a U.S. government security in the open market, it initially expands total reserves and the money supply by the amount of the purchase.

Using Balance Sheets.   Consider the balance sheets of the Fed and of the depository institution, such as a typical bank, receiving the check. Balance Sheet 15-4 shows the results for the Fed after the bond purchase and for the bank after the bond dealer deposits the $100,000 check.[5] The Fed's balance sheet (which here reflects only *changes*) shows that after the purchase, the Fed's assets have increased by $100,000 in the form of U.S. government securities. Liabilities have also increased by $100,000 in the form of an increase in the reserve account of the bank. The balance sheet for the bank shows an increase in assets of $100,000 in the form of reserves with its district Federal Reserve bank. The bank also has an increase in its liabilities in the form of $100,000 in the checkable account of the bond dealer; this is an immediate $100,000 increase in the money supply.

BALANCE SHEET 15-4   **Balance sheets for the Fed and the bank when a U.S. government security is purchased by the Fed, showing changes in assets and liabilities.**

THE FED		BANK	
ASSETS	LIABILITIES	ASSETS	LIABILITIES
+ $100,000 U.S. government securities	+ $100,000 depository institution's reserves	+ $100,000 reserves	+ $100,000 checkable deposit owned by bond dealer

---

[3]Actually, the Fed usually deals in Treasury bills that have a maturity date of one year or less.

[4]In practice, the trading desk is never given a specific dollar amount to purchase or to sell. The account manager uses personal discretion in determining what amount should be purchased or sold in order to satisfy the FOMC's latest directive. For expositional purposes, assume nonetheless that the account manager is directed to make a specific transaction.

[5]Strictly speaking, the balance sheets that we are showing should be called the *consolidated balance sheets* for the 12 Federal Reserve district banks. We will simply refer to them as the Fed, however.

SALE OF A $100,000 U.S. GOVERNMENT SECURITY BY THE FED

The process is reversed when the account manager at the New York Fed trading desk sells a U.S. government security from the Fed's portfolio. When the individual or institution buying the security from the Fed writes a check for $100,000, the Fed reduces the reserves of the bank on which the check was written. The $100,000 sale of the U.S. government security leads to a reduction in reserves in the banking system.

Using Balance Sheets Again. Balance Sheet 15-5 shows the results for the sale of a U.S. government security by the Fed. The Fed's balance sheet is on the left. When the $100,000 check goes to the Fed, the Fed reduces by $100,000 the reserve account of the bank on which the check is written. The Fed's assets are also reduced by $100,000 because it no longer owns the U.S. government security. The bank's liabilities are reduced by $100,000 when that amount is deducted from the account of the bond purchaser, and the money supply is thereby reduced by that amount. The bank's assets are also reduced by $100,000 because the Fed has reduced its reserves by that amount.

BALANCE SHEET 15-5 **Balance sheets after the Fed has sold $100,000 of U.S. government securities, showing changes only.**

THE FED		BANK	
ASSETS	LIABILITIES	ASSETS	LIABILITIES
− $100,000 reduction in U.S. government securities	− $100,000 depository institution's reserves	− $100,000 reserves	− $100,000 checkable deposit balances

CONCEPTS IN BRIEF

● If a check is written on one depository institution and deposited in another, there is no change in total deposits or in the total money supply. No new reserves have been created.

● The Federal Reserve, through its Federal Open Market Committee (FOMC), can directly increase depository institutions' reserves by purchasing U.S. government securities in the open market; it can decrease depository institutions' reserves by selling U.S. government securities in the open market.

MONEY (DEPOSIT) EXPANSION BY THE BANKING SYSTEM

Consider now the entire banking system. For practical purposes we can look at all depository institutions taken as a whole. To understand how money is created, we must understand how depository institutions respond to Fed actions that increase reserves in the entire system.

FED PURCHASES OF U.S. GOVERNMENT SECURITIES

Assume that the Fed purchases a $100,000 U.S. government security from a bond dealer. The bond dealer deposits the $100,000 check in Bank 1 (which started out in the position depicted in Balance Sheet 15-1). The check, however, is not written on another depository institution; rather, it is written on the Fed itself.

Look at the balance sheet for Bank 1 shown in Balance Sheet 15-6. It is the same as Balance Sheet 15-2. Reserves have been increased by $100,000 to $200,000, and checkable deposits have also been increased by $100,000. Because required reserves on $1.1 million of checkable deposits are only $110,000, there is $90,000 in excess reserves.

BALANCE SHEET 15-6   Bank 1.

ASSETS			LIABILITIES	
Total reserves		$200,000	Checkable deposits	$1,100,000
Required reserves	$110,000			
Excess reserves	90,000			
Loans		900,000		
Total		$1,100,000	Total	$1,100,000

Effect on the Money Supply.   The major difference between this example and the one given previously is that here the money supply has increased by $100,000 immediately. Why? Because checkable deposits held by the public—the bond dealers are members of the public—are part of the money supply, and no other bank has lost reserves. Thus the purchase of a $100,000 U.S. government security by the Federal Reserve from the public (a bond dealer or a bank) increases the money supply immediately by $100,000.

Not the End of the Process.   The process of money creation does not stop here. Look again at Balance Sheet 15-6. Bank 1 has excess reserves of $90,000. No other depository institution (or combination of depository institutions) has negative excess reserves of $90,000 as a result of the Fed's bond purchase. (Remember, the Fed simply created the money to pay for the bond purchase.)

Bank 1 will not wish to hold non-interest-bearing excess reserves. It will expand its loans by creating deposits equal to $90,000. This is shown in Balance Sheet 15-7. Which is exactly like Balance Sheet 15-3, but there has been no corresponding reduction in loans at any other depository institution. The money supply thus rises by an additional $90,000.

BALANCE SHEET 15-7   Bank 1.

ASSETS			LIABILITIES	
Total reserves		$110,000	Checkable deposits	$1,100,000
Required reserves	$110,000			
Excess reserves	0			
Loans		990,000		
Total		$1,100,000	Total	$1,100,000

The individuals who have received the $90,000 of new loans will spend (write checks on) these funds, which will then be deposited in other banks. To make this example simple, assume that the $90,000 in excess reserves was lent to a single firm for the purpose of buying a Burger King franchise. After the firm buys the franchise, Burger King deposits the $90,000 check in its account at Bank 2. For the sake of simplicity, ignore the previous assets and liabilities in Bank 2 and concentrate only on the balance sheet *changes* resulting from this new deposit, as shown in Balance Sheet 15-8. A plus sign indicates that the entry has increased, and a minus sign indicates that the entry has decreased. For the depository institution, Bank 2, the $90,000 deposit, after the check has been sent to the Fed, becomes an increase in reserves (assets) as well as an increase in checkable deposits (liabilities). Because the reserve requirement is 10 percent, or $9,000, Bank 2 will have excess reserves of $81,000. But, of course, excess reserves are not income-producing, so Bank 2 will reduce them to zero by making loans of $81,000 (which will earn interest income) by creating deposits for borrowers equal to $81,000. The money supply, because it includes checkable deposits, thus rises by another $81,000. This is shown in Balance Sheet 15-9.

BALANCE SHEET 15-8   Bank 2 (changes only).

ASSETS		LIABILITIES	
Total reserves	+$90,000	Checkable deposits	+$90,000
Required reserves $9,000			
Excess reserves +81,000			
Total	+$90,000	Total	+$90,000

BALANCE SHEET 15-9   Bank 2 (changes only).

ASSETS		LIABILITIES	
Total reserves	$9,000	Checkable deposits	$90,000
Required reserves $9,000			
Excess reserves 0			
Loans	+81,000		
Total	$90,000	Total	$90,000

Remember that in this example the original $100,000 deposit was a check issued by a Federal Reserve bank to the bond dealer. That $100,000 constituted an immediate increase in the money supply of $100,000 when deposited in the bond dealer's account. The deposit creation process (in addition to the original $100,000) occurs because of the fractional reserve banking system, coupled with the desire of depository institutions to maintain a minimum level of excess reserves (given sufficient loan demand).

Continuation of the Deposit Creation Process.   Assume that another company has received an $81,000 loan from Bank 2 because it wants to buy into an oil-drilling firm. This oil-drilling firm has an account at Bank 3. Look at Bank 3's simplified account in Balance Sheet 15-10, where, again, only changes in the assets and liabilities are shown. When the firm borrowing from Bank 2 pays the $81,000 to the oil-drilling firm's manager, the manager deposits the check in Bank 3. Total reserves of Bank 3 go up by that amount when the check is sent to the Fed.

BALANCE SHEET 15-10   **Bank 3 (changes only).**

ASSETS			LIABILITIES	
Total reserves		+$81,000	New checkable deposits	+$81,000
Required reserves	$8,100			
Excess reserves	+72,900			
Total		+$81,000	Total	+$81,000

Because the reserve requirement is 10 percent, required reserves rise by $8,100, and excess reserves are therefore $72,900. Bank 3 will also want to lend those non-interest-earning assets (excess reserves). When it does, loans (in the form of created checkable deposits) will increase by $72,900. Total reserves will fall to $8,100, and excess reserves become zero as the oil-drilling firm's manager writes checks on the new deposit. The money supply has thereby increased by another $72,900, as indicated in Balance Sheet 15-11.

BALANCE SHEET 15-11   **Bank 3 (changes only).**

ASSETS			LIABILITIES	
Total reserves		$8,100	Checkable deposits	$81,000
Required reserves	$8,100			
Excess reserves	0			
Loans		+72,900		
Total		$81,000	Total	$81,000

Progression to Other Banks.   This process continues to Banks 4, 5, 6, and so forth. Each bank obtains smaller and smaller increases in deposits because 10 percent of each deposit must be held in reserve; therefore, each succeeding depository institution makes correspondingly smaller loans. Table 15-1 on p. 330 shows the new deposits, possible loans, and required reserves for the remaining depository institutions in the system.

Effect on Total Deposits.   In this simple example, deposits increased initially by the $100,000 that the Fed paid the bond dealer in exchange for a bond. They were further increased by a $90,000 deposit in Bank 2, and they were again increased by an $81,000 deposit in Bank 3. Eventually, total deposits will increase by $1 million, as shown in Table 15-1 on the next page.

INCREASE IN OVERALL RESERVES

Even with fractional reserve banking, if there are zero excess reserves, deposits cannot expand unless overall reserves are increased. The original new deposit in Bank 1, in our example, was in the form of a check written on a Federal Reserve district bank. It therefore represented new reserves to the banking system. Had that check been written on Bank 3, for example, nothing would have happened to the total amount of checkable deposits; there would have been no change in the total money supply. To repeat: Checks written on banks within the system represent assets and liabilities that simply cancel each other out. Only when excess reserves exist or are created by the Federal Reserve System can the money supply increase.

BANK	NEW DEPOSITS (NEW RESERVES)	NEW REQUIRED RESERVES	MAXIMUM NEW LOANS PLUS INVESTMENTS (EXCESS RESERVES)
1	$100,000 (from Fed)	$10,000	$90,000
2	90,000	9,000	81,000
3	81,000	8,100	72,900
4	72,900	7,290	65,610
.	.	.	.
.	.	.	.
.	.	.	.
All other banks	656,100	65,610	590,490
Totals	$1,000,000	$100,000	$900,000

TABLE 15-1
Maximum money creation with 10 percent required reserves.
This table shows the maximum new loans plus investments that banks can make given the Fed's deposit of a $100,000 check in Bank 1. The required reserve ratio is 10 percent. We assume that all excess reserves in each bank are used for new loans or investments.

In our example, the depository institutions use their excess reserves to make loans. It is not important how they put the money back into the system. If they bought certificates of deposit or any other security, the analysis would be the same because whoever they bought those securities from would receive a check from the purchasing depository institution. The recipient of the check would then deposit it into his or her own depository institution. The deposit expansion process would be the same as we have already outlined.

CONCEPTS IN BRIEF

● When reserves are increased by the Fed through a purchase of U.S. government securities, the result is a multiple expansion of deposits and therefore of the supply of money.
● When the Fed reduces reserves by selling U.S. government securities, the result is a multiple contraction of deposits and therefore of the money supply.

THE DEPOSIT EXPANSION MULTIPLIER

In the example just given, a $100,000 increase in excess reserves generated by the Fed's purchase of a security yielded a $1 million increase in total deposits; deposits increased by a multiple of 10 times the initial $100,000 increase in overall reserves. Conversely, a $100,000 decrease in excess reserves generated by the Fed's sale of a security will yield a $1 million decrease in total deposits; they will decrease by a multiple of 10 times the initial $100,000 decrease in overall reserves. We can now make a generalization about the extent to which total deposits will increase when the banking system's reserves are either increased or decreased. If we assume that no excess reserves are kept and that all loan proceeds are deposited in depository institutions in the system, the following equation applies:

$$\text{Deposit expansion multiplier} = \frac{1}{\text{required reserve ratio}}$$

▶ **Deposit expansion multiplier**
The reciprocal of the required reserve ratio, assuming no leakages into currency and no excess reserves. It is equal to 1 ÷ required reserve ratio.

The **deposit expansion multiplier** gives the maximum potential change in total deposits due to a change in reserves. The actual change in the money supply—currency plus checkable account balances—will be equal to the following:

$$\begin{array}{c}\text{Actual change}\\ \text{in money supply}\end{array} = \begin{array}{c}\text{actual deposit}\\ \text{expansion multiplier}\end{array} \times \begin{array}{c}\text{change in}\\ \text{excess reserves}\end{array}$$

Now we examine why there is a difference between the potential deposit expansion multiplier—1/required reserve ratio—and the actual multiplier.

FORCES THAT REDUCE THE DEPOSIT EXPANSION MULTIPLIER

We made a number of simplifying assumptions to come up with the deposit expansion multiplier. In the real world, the expansion (or contraction) multiplier is considerably smaller. Several factors account for this.

Leakages. The entire loan (check) from one bank is not always deposited in another bank. At least two leakages can occur:

1. **Currency drains.** When deposits increase, the public may want to hold more currency. Currency that is kept in a person's wallet or handbag or stashed in a safe deposit box or hidden underneath a mattress remains outside the banking system and cannot be held by banks as reserves from which to make loans. The greater the amount of cash leakage, the smaller the actual deposit expansion multiplier.
2. **Excess reserves.** Depository institutions may wish to maintain excess reserves. Depository institutions do not, in fact, always keep excess reserves at zero. To the extent that they want to keep positive excess reserves, the deposit expansion multiplier will be smaller. A bank receiving $1 million in new deposits might, in our example with the 10 percent required reserve, keep more than $100,000 as reserves. The greater the excess reserves, the smaller the actual deposit expansion multiplier. Empirically, the currency drain is more significant than the effect of excess reserves.

REAL-WORLD MONEY MULTIPLIERS

The required reserve ratio determines the maximum potential deposit multiplier because the reciprocal of the required reserve ratio tells us what that is. The maximum is never attained for the money supply as a whole because of currency drains and excess reserves. Also, each definition of the money supply, M1 or M2, will yield different results for money multipliers. For several decades the M1 multiplier has varied between 2.5 and 3.5. The M2 multiplier, however, has shown a trend upward, ranging from 6.5 at the beginning of the 1960s to over 12 at the beginning of the 1990s.

Ways in Which the Federal Reserve Changes the Money Supply. As we have just seen, the Fed can change the money supply by directly changing reserves available to the banking system. It does this by engaging in open market operations. To repeat, a sale of a U.S. government security by the Fed results in a decrease in reserves and leads to a multiple contraction in the money supply. The purchase of a U.S. government security by the Fed results in an increase of reserves and leads to a multiple expansion in the money supply.

The Fed changes the money supply in two other ways, both of which will have multiplier effects similar to those outlined earlier in this chapter.

Borrowed Reserves and the Discount Rate.

If a depository institution wants to increase its loans but has no excess reserves, it can borrow reserves. One place it can borrow reserves is from the Fed itself. The depository institution goes to the Federal Reserve and asks for a loan of a certain amount of reserves. The Fed charges these institutions for any reserves that it lends them. The interest rate that the Fed charges used to be called the *rediscount rate* but now is called the **discount rate.** In most other English-speaking countries, it is called the *bank rate.* When newspapers report that the Fed has increased the discount rate from 5 to 6 percent, you know that the Fed has increased its charge for lending reserves to depository institutions. Borrowing from the Fed increases reserves and thereby enhances the ability of the depository institution to engage in deposit creation, thus increasing the money supply.

▶ **Discount rate**
The interest rate that the Federal Reserve charges for reserves that it lends to depository institutions. It is sometimes referred to as the rediscount rate or, in Canada and England, as the bank rate.

The Federal Reserve System makes changes in the discount rate not necessarily to encourage or discourage depository institutions from borrowing from the Fed but rather as a signal to the banking system and financial markets that there has been a change in the Fed's monetary policy. We discuss monetary policy in more detail in Chapter 16.

Depository institutions actually do not often go to the Fed to borrow reserves because the Fed will not lend them all they want. In addition, the Fed can always refuse to lend reserves even when the depository institutions need the reserves to make their reserve accounts meet legal requirements. There are, however, alternative sources for the banks to tap when they want to expand their reserves or when they need reserves to meet a requirement. The primary source is the **federal funds market.** The federal funds market is an interbank market in reserves, with one bank borrowing the excess reserves of another. The generic term *federal funds market* refers to the borrowing or lending (purchase or sale) of reserve funds repaid within the same 24-hour period.

▶ **Federal funds market**
A private market (made up mostly of banks) in which banks can borrow reserves from other banks that want to lend them. Federal funds are usually lent for overnight use.

Reserve Requirement Changes.

Another method by which the Fed can alter the money supply is by changing reserve requirements. Earlier we assumed that reserve requirements were given. Actually, these requirements are set by the Fed within limits established by Congress. Also, from the very beginning the Fed has set different reserve requirements for different types of banks. Initially they depended on the location of the bank, whether it was in a central reserve city, a reserve city, or the country. Higher reserve requirements were imposed on central reserve city banks and reserve city banks. In 1972 the Fed changed its policy so that reserve requirements are set according to the net amount of checkable deposits in a given bank. The Fed reserve requirements were initially imposed only on member banks, but now they are imposed on all depository institutions.

What would a change in reserve requirements from 10 to 20 percent do (if there were no excess reserves)? We already discovered that the maximum deposit expansion multiplier was the reciprocal of the required reserve ratio. If reserve requirements are 10 percent, the maximum deposit expansion multiplier would be the reciprocal of $\frac{1}{10}$, or 10 (assuming no leakages). If, for some reason, the Fed decided to increase reserve requirements to 20 percent, the maximum deposit expansion multiplier would equal the reciprocal of $\frac{1}{5}$, or 5. The maximum deposit expansion multiplier is therefore inversely related to the required reserve ratio. If the Fed decides to increase reserve requirements, there will be a decrease in the maximum deposit expansion multiplier. With any given level of legal reserves already in existence, the money supply will therefore contract.

Notice the difference between this method and the first method the Federal Reserve has for changing the total money supply in circulation. When the Fed makes open market purchases or sales of bonds, it directly alters reserves. When the Fed alters reserve *requirements,* however, it does not change reserves as we have defined them. Rather, it changes the maximum deposit expansion multiplier and the level of excess reserves. When the Fed changes the maximum deposit expansion multiplier without any offsetting change in reserves, a change in total deposits will result.

Open market operations allow the Federal Reserve to control the money supply much more precisely than changes in reserve requirements do, and they also allow the Fed to reverse itself quickly. In contrast, a small change in reserve requirements can result in a very large change in the money supply. That is why the Federal Reserve does not change reserve requirements very often.

CONCEPTS IN BRIEF

- The maximum deposit expansion multiplier is equal to the reciprocal of the required reserve ratio.
- The actual multiplier is much less than the maximum deposit expansion multiplier because of currency drains and excess reserves voluntarily held by banks.
- The Fed changes the money supply in three ways: (1) It can change reserves and hence the money supply through open market operations in which it buys and sells existing U.S. government securities. Open market operations are the primary form of monetary policy. (2) It can encourage changes in reserves by changing the discount rate. (3) It can change deposits by changing reserve requirements.

DEPOSIT INSURANCE AND FLAWED BANK REGULATION

▶ **Federal Deposit Insurance Corporation (FDIC)**
A government agency that insures the deposits held in member banks; all members of the Fed and other banks that qualify can join.

When businesses fail, they create hardships for creditors, owners, workers, and customers. But when a depository institution fails, an even greater hardship results because many individuals and businesses depend on the safety and security of banks. Figure 15-2 on the next page indicates that during the 1920s an average of about 600 banks failed each year. In the 1930s, during the Great Depression, that average soared to 2,000 failures each year. In 1933, at the height of such bank failures, the **Federal Deposit Insurance Corporation (FDIC)** was founded to insure the funds of depositors and remove the reason for ruinous runs on banks. In 1934 the Federal Savings and Loan Insurance Corporation (FSLIC) was installed to insure deposits in savings and loan associations and mutual savings banks. In 1971 the National Credit Union Share Insurance Fund (NCUSIF) was created to insure deposits in credit unions. In 1989 the FSLIC was dissolved. Deposits remained protected by the newly created Savings Association Insurance Fund (SAIF).

As can be seen in Figure 15-2, a tremendous drop in bank failure rates occurred after the passage of the early federal legislation. The long period from 1935 until the 1980s was relatively quiet: From World War II to 1984, fewer than nine banks failed per year. From 1985 until the beginning of 1993, however, 1,065 commercial banks failed—an annual average of nearly 163 bank failures per year, almost 12 times the average for the preceding years! We will examine the reasons shortly. But first we need to understand the way deposit insurance works.

FIGURE 15-2

Commercial bank closings, 1921–1993.

During the Great Depression, a tremendous number of commercial banks were closed. Federal deposit insurance was created in 1933. Thereafter, bank closures were few until around 1982. Since then, 100 or more commercial banks have closed each year.

Source: Federal Deposit Insurance Corporation.

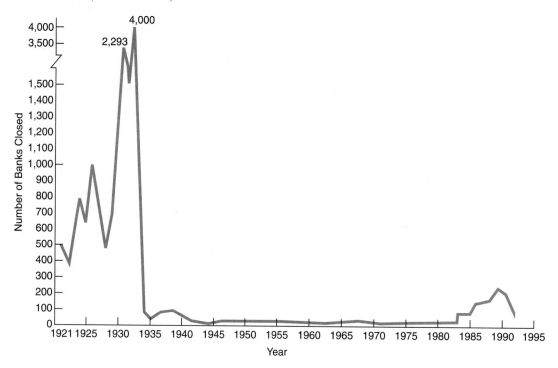

HOW DEPOSIT INSURANCE WORKS

The FDIC, FSLIC, and NCUSIF were established to mitigate the primary cause of bank failures, the simultaneous rush of depositors to convert their demand deposits or saving deposits into currency (**bank runs**).

Consider the following scenario. A bank begins to look shaky; its assets may not seem sufficient to cover its liabilities. If the bank has no deposit insurance, depositors in this bank (and any banks associated with it) will all want to withdraw their money from the bank at the same time. Their concern is that this shaky bank will not have enough money to return their deposits to them in the form of currency. Indeed, this is what happens in a bank failure when insurance doesn't exist. Just as with the failure of a regular business, the creditors of the bank may not all get paid, or if they do, they will get paid less than 100 percent of what they are owed. Depositors are creditors of a bank because their deposits are liabilities of the bank. In a fractional reserve banking system, banks do not have 100 percent of their depositors' money in the form of vault cash. All depositors cannot simultaneously withdraw all their money. It is therefore necessary to assure depositors that they can have their deposits converted into cash when they wish, no matter how serious the financial situation of the bank.

The FDIC (and later the FSLIC, NCUSIF, and SAIF) provided this assurance. By insuring deposits, the FDIC bolstered depositors' trust in the banking system and provided depositors with the incentive to leave their deposits with the bank, even in the face of widespread talk of bank failures. In 1933 it was sufficient for the FDIC to cover each account up to $2,500. The current maximum is $100,000.

▶ **Bank runs**
Attempts by many of a bank's depositors to convert checkable and time deposits into currency out of fear for the bank's solvency.

INTERNATIONAL EXAMPLE: A Roman Empire Bank Run

Bank runs were not confined to the United States during the Great Depression. In A.D. 33 there was a massive bank panic in the Roman Empire. It started with the loss of three spice ships in a Red Sea hurricane. They were owned by the firm of Seuthes and Son. The rumor spread in Rome that the firm was near bankruptcy. Another important firm, Malchus and Company of Tyre, started to go under because of a strike by its Phoenician workers and because of fraud committed by a trusted manager. Citizens of Rome meanwhile learned that the Roman banking firm of Quintus Maximus and Lucius Vibo had loaned significant sums of money to both jeopardized firms. Depositors started a run on this bank. This run spilled over to a larger banking firm owned by the Pettius Brothers because that bank had extensive dealings with the bank of Maximus and Vibo. But the Pettius Brothers' bank happened to be temporarily strapped for cash because it held many securities issued by Belgium, whose citizens had recently revolted.

Maximus and Vibo closed its doors; Pettius Brothers suspended operations on exactly the same day. To make matters worse, the Roman Senate had just passed a law requiring one-third of each senator's capital to be invested in Italian land. These wealthy senators needed to reduce their own deposit balances at their banks in Rome in order to buy land. Finally, word arrived from Corinth and Carthage of bank failures in those towns. A true bank panic hit the streets of Rome. Ultimately, every banking house in Rome closed its doors.

The panic ended when the emperor, Tiberius, ordered the distribution of a large sum of Roman currency from the imperial treasury to reliable banks, which were to lend the funds to needy debtors with no interest to be collected for three years.

For Critical Analysis: *Could a similar bank panic end up closing all the banks in America today? Why or why not?* ●

MAJOR FLAWS IN THE DEPOSIT INSURANCE SYSTEM

The U.S. deposit-insuring agencies have serious design flaws. First, the price of deposit insurance to individual depository institutions was until recently relatively low; the depository institutions are subsidized by the depository insurers. Second, the insurance premium is the same percentage of total deposits for all depository institutions, regardless of the riskiness of the institution's portfolio. Also until recently, all deposit-insuring agencies charged a depository institution about .25 percent of the institution's total (not just insured) deposits.[6] For example, federally insured commercial banks pay a flat fee for the FDIC guarantee of the first $100,000 of each deposit account in the bank. The flaw in this pricing structure is that an individual depository institution's premium is set without regard to its probability of failure, the riskiness of its portfolio, or the estimated cost to the insurer should the institution fail.

Finally, another flaw is that the *deposit* rather than the *depositor* is insured. Consequently, huge certificate of deposits are "brokered" into $100,000 segments to get guaranteed 100 percent insurance coverage. A system that was initially meant to protect the small saver has been used to protect the very wealthy and businesses.

INCENTIVES TO INCREASED RISK TAKING

The net result of these flaws in the deposit insurance scheme is that bank managers have an incentive to invest in more assets of higher yield, and therefore higher risk, than they

---

[6]Because the gross premium is a flat rate on all deposits, not just insured deposits, this amounts to a subsidy from larger to smaller insured banks. This is because larger banks have more uninsured deposits; that is, for deposits in excess of $100,000, the amounts above $100,000 are, in principle, uninsured.

would if there were no deposit insurance. Thus the premium rate is artificially low, permitting institution managers to obtain deposits at less than market price (because depositors will accept a lower interest payment on insured deposits); and even if the institution's portfolio becomes riskier, its insurance premium does not rise. Consequently, depository institution managers can increase their net interest margin by using lower-cost insured deposits to purchase higher-yield, higher-risk assets. The gains to risk taking accrue to the managers and stockholders of the depository institutions; the losses go to the deposit insurer (and, as we will see, ultimately to taxpayers).

To combat the inherent flaws in the financial institution industry and in the deposit insurance system, a vast regulatory apparatus was installed. The FDIC was given regulatory powers to offset the risk-taking temptations to depository institution managers; these powers included the ability to require higher capital requirements, regulation, examination, supervision, and enforcement. In the early 1990s, yet higher capital requirements were imposed. But the basic flaws in the system remain.

The financial industry has been organized so as to protect firms in the industry from the rigors of competition; market discipline on the behavior of financial institutions was replaced by regulatory discipline. In many respects the system worked well until 1982. No small saver had lost a penny of insured money since federal deposit insurance was established. (Today a few smaller banks are allowed to fail and some of their bigger depositers don't get all of their deposits back.) Furthermore, there have been no true bank runs on federally insured institutions. Nevertheless, in recent years the number of depository institution closures and insolvencies increased to record post–Depression highs. The situation seems to be improving, though, in the mid-1990s.

DEPOSIT INSURANCE, ADVERSE SELECTION, AND MORAL HAZARD

When financial transactions take place, one party often does not have all the knowledge needed about the other party to make correct decisions. The inequality of information between the two parties is called **asymmetric information.** For example, borrowers generally know more about the returns and risks associated with the investment projects they intend to undertake than with the borrowed funds lenders do.

▶ **Asymmetric information**
Imbalance and inequality of information about the parties to a transaction.

Adverse Selection. **Adverse selection** arises when there is asymmetric information before a transaction takes place. In financial markets it often occurs because individuals and firms that are worse credit risks than they appear to be are the ones most willing to borrow at any given interest rate. This willingness makes them likely to be selected by lenders, yet their inferior ability to repay (relative to the interest rate being charged) means that loans to them more often yield adverse outcomes for lenders (default). The potential risks of adverse selection make lenders less likely to lend to anyone and more inclined to charge higher interest rates when they do lend.

Adverse selection is also often a problem when insurance is involved because people or firms that are relatively poor risks are sometimes able to disguise that fact from insurers. It is instructive to examine the way this works with the deposit insurance provided by the FDIC. Deposit insurance shields depositors from the potential adverse effects of risky decisions and so makes depositors willing to accept riskier investment strategies by their banks. Clearly, this encourages high-flying, risk-loving entrepreneurs to become managers of banks. Moreover, because depositors have so little incentive to monitor the activities of insured banks, it is also likely that the insurance actually encourages outright crooks—embezzlers and con artists—to enter the industry. The consequences for the FDIC—and often for the taxpayer—are larger losses.

▶ **Adverse selection**
A problem created by asymmetric information prior to a transaction. Individuals who are the most undesirable from the other party's point of view end up being the ones who are most likely to want to engage in a particular financial transaction, such as borrowing.

▶ **Moral hazard**
A situation in which, after a transaction has taken place, one of the parties to the transaction has an incentive to engage in behavior that will be undesirable from the other party's point of view.

Moral Hazard.   **Moral hazard** arises as the result of information asymmetry after a transaction has occurred. In financial markets lenders face the hazard that borrowers may engage in activities that are contrary to the lender's well-being and thus might be said to be immoral from the lender's perspective. For example, because lenders do not share in the profits of business ventures, they generally want borrowers to agree to invest prudently. Yet once the loan has been made, borrower-investors have an incentive to invest in high-risk, high-return projects because they are able to keep all of the extra profits if the projects succeed. Such behavior subjects the lender to greater hazards than are being compensated for under the terms of the loan agreement.

Moral hazard is also an important phenomenon in the presence of insurance contracts, such as the deposit insurance provided by the FDIC. Insured depositors know that they will not suffer losses if their bank fails. Hence they have little incentive to monitor their bank's investment activities or to punish their bank by withdrawing their funds if the bank assumes too much risk. Thus insured banks have incentives to take on more risks than they otherwise would—and with those risks come higher losses for the FDIC and for taxpayers.

⭐ EXAMPLE: The Savings and Loan Crisis

A couple of years ago Congress committed you and everybody else in America to about $1,500 in future tax liabilities. The Thrift Bailout Act of 1989, officially known as the Financial Institutions Reform, Recovery and Enforcement Act (FIRREA), was passed to salvage the savings and loan industry, which was quickly spiraling into disaster. By the end of 1985, some 130 thrifts had become insolvent—unable to pay their bills on an ongoing basis. In 1986 the number jumped to 255, and in 1987 it increased to 351.

What was occurring at that time was a perfect example of the perverse incentives that occur when deposit insurance exists. Depository institution managers undertake riskier actions than they otherwise would because of the existence of deposit insurance. Moreover, because of the existence of deposit insurance, depositors in savings and loan associations and other depository institutions have little incentive to check out the financial dealings and stability of those institutions. After all, deposits are guaranteed by an agency of the federal government, so why worry? Hence there is little incentive for households and firms to monitor depository institutions or even to diversify their deposits across institutions.

From a savings and loans manager's point of view, as long as deposit insurance protected their depositors, managers could feel confident to "go for the gold." One result was the increased amount of high-risk, high-yielding assets purchased by many savings and loans associations. The most extreme example was fraudulent activities conducted by managers of savings and loan associations in the 1980s. Many managers crossed the line from participating in risky ventures to committing outright fraud. Estimates of the extent of fraudulent activities in failed savings and loans during the 1980s have ranged from 3 percent to 50 percent of all failures. In the two-year period ending September 30, 1990, the Justice Department convicted and, in most cases, sentenced 331 S&L felons. The average sentence was $3\frac{1}{2}$ years, although Woody S. Lemons, former chairman of Vernon Savings and Loan in Dallas, Texas, was sentenced to 30 years. The people convicted had caused billions of dollars of direct losses to the savings and loan associations that they controlled. Some of those convicted were simple low-level loan officers who took small bribes to approve shaky, often worthless loans that would normally not be repaid. At the other end of the spectrum, one savings and loans associations head, Miami Centrust's David Paul, allegedly used $30 million of his institution's money to buy himself such luxuries as Old Masters paintings and silver-plated lobster tongs.

The Thrift Bailout Act did a number of things, almost none of which changed the incentive structure facing the managers of savings and loan associations or any other depository institutions today. One of the things the law did was dissolve the FSLIC and create in its place the Savings Association Insurance Fund (SAIF) under the control of the FDIC. The separate Bank Insurance Fund (BIF) was created for commercial banks. In addition, the Resolution Trust Corporation (RTC) was created with the purpose of taking over 400 to 500 insolvent savings associations with assets in excess of $300 billion. The RTC is supposed to find buyers for the sick institutions and liquidate those for which there are no buyers. The schedule for closing sick S&Ls appears to be grossly inadequate. At the time of the bill's passage some 264 thrifts were already in government hands.

For Critical Analysis: *Critics of the savings and loan disaster argue in favor of abolishing government-sponsored deposit insurance. How would this change the incentive structure facing depository institutions?* ●

CONCEPTS IN BRIEF

- Federal deposit insurance was created in 1933 when the Federal Deposit Insurance Corporation (FDIC) was founded. In 1934 the Federal Savings and Loan Insurance Corporation (FSLIC) was founded to insure deposits in savings and loan associations and mutual savings banks.
- In 1989 the FSLIC was dissolved. Deposits remain protected by the Savings Association Insurance Fund (SAIF).
- Deposit insurance was designed to prevent bank runs in which individual demand deposit and saving deposit holders attempt to turn their deposits into currency. Since the advent of federal deposit insurance there have been no true bank runs at federally insured banks.
- The two major flaws in the deposit insurance system have been the relatively low price for the insurance and the flat rate charged. In particular, the flat rate does not take account of the riskiness of the depository institution's portfolio. This encourages depository institution managers to take greater risks.

HOW SAFE IS YOUR MONEY?
Concepts Applied: Deposit insurance, moral hazard

No person with a deposit less than $100,000 in an F.D.I.C.-insured depository institution has ever lost a penny. But what about those who have more than $100,000 in deposits?

Between 1929 and 1933 one-third of all banks in the United States disappeared. Although some of these banks merged with other institutions, most of them failed outright, taking with them 10 percent of all bank deposits. In today's terms, the losses suffered by depositors were the equivalent of nearly $90 billion. It is no exaggeration to say that the savings of tens of thousands of Americans were wiped out by these bank failures.

UNLIMITED DEPOSIT INSURANCE? The Federal Deposit Insurance Corporation (FDIC) was founded in 1933 to insure bank deposits and thereby prevent a tragedy like this from ever happening again. In the 60 years since, the legal limit on the maximum deposit insured by the FDIC has risen to $100,000. As a practical matter, however, the FDIC has until recently effectively insured sums far larger than the legal maximum.

The FDIC has extended insurance coverage beyond the statutory limit of $100,000 in two ways. First, it has permitted individuals to have multiple deposits within the same bank and spread across different banks. Each of these deposits is insured up to $100,000 because the limit on FDIC insurance has been per account owned by a separate legal entity, not per depositor. Second, in cases in which banks have failed, the FDIC has routinely paid off the losses suffered by all depositors and all accounts, even when the size of individual accounts have exceeded the

$100,000 statutory limit. Thus despite the limitations set by law, the FDIC has historically provided unlimited insurance on all accounts.

ARE INSURANCE LIMITS COMING? This policy of the FDIC has meant that depositors have had little incentive to monitor the solvency or soundness of the banks in which they have deposited their money. Although FDIC regulations and inspections have limited irresponsible bank behavior to some extent, the virtual absence of depositor oversight has sharply reduced incentives for prudent behavior on the part of bank managers. The consequences have been both predictable and costly.

During the late 1980s and early 1990s, bank failures rose sharply, as a result of poor investment decisions by the banks, combined with the recession of 1990–1991. FDIC payoffs on the depositor losses caused by more than 1,000 bank failures have cost the agency tens of billions of dollars. Even a 150 percent increase in the insurance premiums charged member banks has not brought the FDIC back into the black, and so it has sought means of limiting its losses. Since December 19, 1992, federal regulators have had to close banks that fall short of tough new capital requirements or do not have a detailed plan to meet them. That means that more sick banks will be likely to fail. Furthermore, and perhaps even more important, the FDIC announced that it will no longer necessarily pay on deposits over $100,000. There is also talk that the agency will seek to limit individuals' ability to insure multiple $100,000 accounts in different depository institutions, thereby returning the insurance program to what it was originally envisioned to be—insurance for the typical small banking customer.

IS $100,000 RELEVANT? If the FDIC proceeds with its efforts to limit insurance to $100,000 per depositor, this will return to large depositors the incentive for monitoring the behavior of banks. That, in turn, is likely to put substantial pressure on banks to lend and invest more prudently. Even though less than 10 percent of all accounts currently have more than $100,000 in them, these accounts contain about 80 percent of all bank deposit dollars. Uninsured depositors cannot afford imprudent behavior by banks, and banks cannot afford to lose their big customers.

All of this might seem academic because few individuals have bank accounts greater than $100,000, and hence it would appear, few people need worry about the future course of FDIC policy. In fact, however, many college graduates go on to found or play crucial roles in small businesses, firms that have two characteristics that make FDIC policy a key issue. First, these companies often have bank accounts well in excess of $100,000, simply to meet the routine needs of paying their workers and their suppliers. Second, these firms are typically small enough that the loss of all or a major part of their deposit funds due to a bank failure would drive them out of business and their employees into unemployment.

The moral of this story is that even if you personally don't have more than $100,000 in a bank account, there is a good chance that your future may ride on some firm or individual that does. So the next time you see a headline about the FDIC, you may at least want to read enough

to answer the question, How safe is my money? Prior to the 1990s, virtually all deposits over $100,000 were fully repaid by federal regulators when depository institutions failed. In 1991 some 17 percent of depositors in 124 failed banks did not get all of their money bank. In 1992 the number had risen to over 45 percent.

FOR CRITICAL ANALYSIS

1. Suppose that you went to Las Vegas to gamble. Would your behavior there be different if you were gambling with someone else's money rather than your own? How does this relate to the way banks behave in the presence of deposit insurance?
2. Until recently, the FDIC charged banks an insurance premium that was unrelated to the banks' riskiness. Do privately owned insurance companies charge automobile drivers the same premiums regardless of their driving record? Can you suggest an explanation for why private companies behave differently from a federal agency such as the FDIC?

CHAPTER SUMMARY

1. All depository institutions are required to maintain reserves, which consist of deposits in district Federal Reserve banks plus vault cash. The Federal Reserve requires that certain reserve ratios be maintained, depending on the size of the bank and the types of deposits it has.
2. When depository institutions have more reserves than are required, they are said to have excess reserves.
3. The Federal Reserve can control the money supply through open market operations—by buying and selling U.S. government securities.
4. When the Fed buys a bond, it pays for the bond by writing a check on itself. This constitutes additional reserves to the banking system. The result will be an increase in the money supply that is a multiple of the value of the bond purchased by the Fed. If the Fed sells a bond, it reduces reserves in the banking system. The result will be a decrease in the money supply that is a multiple of the value of the bond sold by the Fed.
5. Single depository institutions that have no excess reserves cannot alter the money supply.
6. The banking system as a whole can change the money supply pursuant to a change in reserves brought about by a Federal Reserve purchase or sale of government bonds.
7. The maximum deposit expansion multiplier is equal to the reciprocal of the required reserve ratio.
8. The actual money multiplier will be less than the maximum deposit expansion multiplier because of leakages—currency drains and excess reserve holdings of some banks.
9. The Federal Deposit Insurance Corporation was created in 1933 to insure commercial bank deposits. Because of the existence of federal deposit insurance, the probability of a run on the banking system, even if a significant number of depository institutions were to fail, is quite small.
10. Two major flaws in the deposit insurance system have been the relatively low price for the insurance and the flat-rate charge irrespective of risk. Moral hazard under the current federal deposit insurance system has led to overly risky and fraudulent behavior on the part of numerous depository institution managers. The result has been the savings and loan crisis.

DISCUSSION OF PREVIEW POINTS

1. What is a fractional reserve banking system?

A fractional reserve banking system is one in which the reserves kept by the depository institutions are only a fraction of total deposits owned by the public. In general, depository institutions accept funds from the public and offer their depositors interest and/or other services. In turn the depository institutions lend out some of these deposits and earn interest. Because at any given time new deposits are coming in while people are drawing down on old deposits, prudent banking does not require a 100 percent reserve-deposit ratio. Because U.S. depository institutions keep less than 100 percent of their total deposits in the form of reserves, we refer to our banking structure as a *fractional* reserve system.

2. What happens to the total money supply when a person deposits in one depository institution a check drawn on another depository institution?

Nothing; the total money supply is unaffected. A transfer of checks from one depository institution to another does not generate any excess reserves in the banking system; hence there will be no overall deposit (and therefore money) creation. Suppose that Calvin Wong deposits in Bank A a $1,000 check that he received for services rendered to Linda Romano, who deals with Bank B. Wong deposits a $1,000 check in Bank A, drawn on Bank B. Note that Bank A experiences an increase in total deposits and reserves and can increase its lending. However, just the opposite happens to Bank B: It experiences a reduction in deposits and reserves and must curtail its lending. There will be no net change in excess reserves; hence no net change in deposit creation and therefore no net change in the money supply occurs.

3. What happens to the overall money supply when a person who sells a U.S. government security to the Federal Reserve places the proceeds in a depository institution?

Assume that Wong now sells a $1,000 bond to the Fed and in exchange receives a check for $1,000, which he deposits in Bank A. Wong has received a $1,000 checkable deposit (which is money) in exchange for a $1,000 bond (which is not money); the money supply has just increased by $1,000. Furthermore, Bank A has now increased its reserves by $1,000, $900 of which is excess reserves (assuming a 10 percent required reserve ratio). We stress that this increase in excess reserves for Bank A is *not* offset elsewhere in the banking institution; hence a net increase in excess reserves has occurred. Bank A may well lend all $900 (create $900 in checkable deposits for borrowers), thereby increasing the overall money supply by another $900, the total change so far is $1,900. There is no need for the process to end here, because the people who borrowed $900 from Bank A will now spend this $900 on goods or services provided by people who may well deal with Bank B—which receives $900 in deposits and reserves and now has $720 in excess reserves that *it* can lend. And so the process of deposit and money creation continues.

4. How does the existence of deposit insurance affect a financial institution's choice of risky versus non-risky assets?

The best way to answer this question is with an analogy. Assume that you are given $1 million to gamble in Las Vegas. In situation 1 you share equally with your benefactor in losses and in gains. In situation 2 your benefactor lets you share in the gains (at a reduced percentage) but incurs all losses. Will your behavior be any different in situation 1 than in situation 2 while you are in Las Vegas? The answer is, of course, yes. In situation 1 you will be much more careful—you will choose games of chance that offer less risk but lower potential payoffs. In situation 2 you might as well try to break the bank. At the roulette wheel, rather than going for odd or even or red or black, you might as well bet your benefactor's money on single numbers or groups of numbers or even zero or double zero because if you hit it, you stand to gain a lot, but if you don't, you stand to lose nothing. Situation 2 is analogous to that of today's managers in depository institution and loan industry. When times get tough and business is bad, they have had a tendency to "go for broke." They bought risky but high-yielding assets, such as dubious real estate loans, loans at high interest rates to Third World countries, and oil development loans. For those whose bets didn't pay off, the federal government has bailed out all the depositors. The few whose bets did pay off look like heroes.

PROBLEMS

(Answers to the odd-numbered problems appear at the back of the book.)

15-1. Bank 1 has received a deposit of $1 million. Assuming that the banks retain no excess reserves, answer the following questions.
a. The reserve requirement is 25 percent. Fill in the blanks in the table below. What is the deposit multiplier?
b. Now the reserve requirement is 5 percent. Fill in the blanks in a similar table. What is the deposit multiplier?

MULTIPLE DEPOSIT CREATION			
ROUND	DEPOSITS	RESERVES	LOANS
Bank 1	$1,000,000	$	$
Bank 2			
Bank 3			
Bank 4			
Bank 5			
All other banks			
Totals			

15-2. Arrange the following items on the proper side of a bank's balance sheet below.
a. Checkable deposits
b. Vault cash
c. Time deposits
d. Deposits with district Federal Reserve bank
e. Loans to private businesses
f. Loans to households
g. Holdings of U.S. government, state, and municipal bonds
h. Bank buildings and fixtures
i. Borrowings from other banks

ASSETS	LIABILITIES

15-3. If the required reserve ratio is 10 percent, what will be the maximum change in the money supply in each of the following situations?

a. Theola Smith deposits in Bank 2 a check drawn on Bank 3.
b. Smith buys a $5,000 U.S. government bond from the Fed by drawing down on her checking account.
c. Smith sells a $10,000 U.S. government bond to the Fed and deposits the $10,000 in Bank 3.
d. Smith finds $1,000 in coins and paper currency buried in her backyard and deposits it in her checking account.
e. Smith writes a $1,000 check on her own account and takes $1,000 in currency and buries it in her backyard.

15-4. The Fed purchases a $1 million government security from Sandro Mondrone, who deposits it in Bank 1. Use balance sheets to show the immediate effects of this transaction on the Fed and on Bank 1.

15-5. Continuing the example from Problem 15-4:
a. Indicate Bank 1's position more precisely if required reserves equal 5 percent of checkable deposits.
b. By how much can Bank 1 increase its lending?

15-6. Assume a required reserve ratio of 8 percent. A check for $60,000 is drawn on an account in Bank B and deposited in a checkable deposit in Bank A.
a. How much have the excess reserves of Bank A increased?
b. How much in the form of new loans is Bank A now able to extend to borrowers?
c. By how much have reserves of Bank B decreased?
d. By how much have excess reserves of Bank B decreased?
e. The money supply has increased by how much?

15-7. Assume that the required reserve ratio is 15 percent and that the Fed sells $3 million worth of government securities to a customer who pays with a check drawn on the Second National Bank.
a. The excess reserves of the Second National Bank have changed by how much?
b. By how much has the money supply changed?

c. What is the maximum change in the money supply that can result from this sale?

15-8.   Examine the following balance sheet of B Bank.

B BANK			
ASSETS		**LIABILITIES**	
Total reserves	$ 50	Checkable deposits	$200
Loans	100	Capital stock	200
U.S. government securities	50		
Property	200		

Assume that the required reserve ratio is 10 percent.

a. Calculate the excess reserves of B Bank.

b. How much money can B Bank lend out?

c. If B Bank lends the money in part (b), what are the new values for total reserves? For checkable deposits? For loans?

d. What is the maximum expansion of the money supply if B Bank lends the amount suggested in part (b)?

15-9.   Assume a 5 percent required reserve ratio, zero excess reserves, no currency leakage, and a ready loan demand. The Fed buys a $1 million treasury bill from a depository institution.

a. What is the maximum money multiplier?

b. By how much will total deposits rise?

15-10.   The year is A.D. 2310. Residents of an earth colony on Titan, the largest moon of the planet Saturn, use checkable deposits at financial institutions as the only form of money. Depository institutions on Titan wish to hold 10 percent of deposits as excess reserves at all times. There are no other deposits in the banking system. If the banking system on Titan has $300 million in total reserves and the total quantity of money is $1.5 billion, what is the required reserve ratio set by the Titan colony's central bank?

COMPUTER-ASSISTED INSTRUCTION
(Complete problem and answer on disk.)

What happens to the money supply (and to the value of bank deposits) when the Fed purchases a $100,000 government security on the open market? Step-by-step calculations using balance sheets show how bank deposits (money) rise with each transaction. In the process the mechanics of the bank deposit and money supply expansion process are revealed.

appendix c

DERIVATION OF THE DEPOSIT EXPANSION MULTIPLIER

In the example given in Chapter 15, a $100,000 increase in excess reserves generated by the Fed's purchase of a security yielded a $1 million increase in the money supply; the money supply increased by a multiple of 10 of the initial $100,000 increase in overall reserves. The relationship between the *maximum* increase in demand deposits and the change in reserves can be derived mathematically. Again assume that there are only demand deposits in the system, that the required reserve ratio is the same for all depository institutions, and that banks hold zero excess reserves. Consider the following equation:

$$R = r_r \times D \qquad (C-1)$$

where

$$R = \text{total reserves}$$
$$r_r = \text{required reserve ratio}$$
$$D = \text{demand deposits}$$

In other words, total reserves in the system equal the required reserve ratio times total demand deposits.

Now divide each side of Equation C-1 by the required reserve ratio, r_r.

$$\frac{R}{r_r} = \frac{r_r \times D}{r_r} \qquad (C-2)$$

The right side of this equation can be simplified by eliminating r_r, so that

$$\frac{R}{r_r} = D \qquad (C-3)$$

and

$$\frac{R \times 1}{r_r} = D \qquad (C-4)$$

Now multiply the left and right sides of this equation by a small change, which we denote by Δ, so that

$$\frac{\Delta R \times 1}{r_r} = \Delta D \qquad (C-5)$$

Equation C-5 shows that a change in reserves that produces excess reserves will increase demand deposits by the factor $1/r_r$ times the change in reserves; $1/r_r$ is the deposit expansion multiplier.[1] Consider the example used earlier. The Fed increased reserves by $100,000 and the required reserve ratio was 10 percent. Putting those values into Equation C-5 yields

$$\frac{\$100,000 \times 1}{.1} = \$100,000 \times 10 = \$1,000,000 \tag{C-6}$$

In this example, the deposit expansion multiplier was 10: $1/.1 = 10$.

The deposit expansion multiplier given in Equation C-5 can also be used for deposit contraction. If the Fed sells a $100,000 Treasury bill, reserves in the system are reduced by $100,000. Given a required reserve ratio of 10 percent, demand deposits (and hence the money supply) will decrease by $1 million.

This formula gives the maximum that the money supply will change for a specific change in reserves, or the maximum deposit multiplier. It is a formula for a very simplified world in which all depository institutions have the same required reserve ratio, all deposits are demand deposits, the public wants neither more nor less currency on hand, and banks always hold zero excess reserves. In reality, the reserve ratio for checkable deposits is different from that for time deposits. Also, when the community wants to hold more or less currency, the deposit expansion multiplier changes.

---

[1]The deposit expansion process can be expressed as the sum of a geometric series. In particular, $1 + b + b^2 + \cdots + b^{n-1} + \cdots = 1/(1 - b)$, if $0 < b < 1$. In our example, $b = .9$, which represents the percentage of a change in deposits that can be used to create new deposits; $r_r = 1 - b = .1$, which equals the required reserve ratio. Thus $1 + .9 + (.9)^2 + \cdots + (.9)^{n-1} + \cdots = 1/.1 = 10$. Thus $\Delta D = \Delta R(1 + b + b^2 + b^{n-1} + \cdots) = \Delta R \times 1/r_r$.

MONETARY POLICY

When you vote for a presidential candidate, your vote may be influenced by the state of the economy, among other things. In fact, economic researchers have discovered that the amount of growth in real gross domestic product (GDP) and unemployment in the six months prior to a presidential election can often determine its outcome. This research has led to a theory of a political business cycle. Is there in fact a relationship between the presidential election years, the actions of the Federal Reserve, and the success or failure of incumbents? This question is part of the broader study of monetary policy.

After reading this chapter, you should be able to answer the following questions:

1. What is the demand for money curve, and how is it related to the interest rate?

2. Why is the price of existing bonds inversely related to the interest rate?

3. How do the supply of and demand for money determine the interest rate?

4. What is a monetarist?

INTRODUCTION

Chapter 15 was concerned with the supply of money and how the Fed can change it. This chapter deals with monetary policy—the Fed's changing of the supply of money (or the rate at which it grows) in order to achieve national economic goals. When you were introduced to aggregate demand in Chapter 9, you discovered that the position of the aggregate demand curve is determined by the willingness of firms, individuals, governments, and foreigners to purchase domestically produced goods and services. Monetary policy works in a variety of ways to change this willingness, both directly and indirectly.

Think about monetary policy in an intuitive way: An increase in the money supply adds to the amount of money that firms and individuals have on hand and so increases the amount that they wish to spend. The result is an increase in aggregate demand. Conversely, a decrease in the money supply reduces the amount of money that people have on hand to spend and so decreases aggregate demand.

WHAT'S SO SPECIAL ABOUT MONEY?

By definition, monetary policy has to do, in the main, with money. But what is so special about money? Money is the product of a "social contract" in which we all agree to do two things:

1. Express all prices in terms of a common unit of account, which in the United States we call the dollar
2. Use a specific medium of exchange for every market transaction

These two features of money distinguish it from all other things in the economy. As a practical matter, money is involved on one side of every nonbarter transaction in the economy—the trillions of them that occur every year. What this means is that something that changes the amount of money in circulation will have some effect on many transactions and thus upon elements of GDP. If something affects the number of snowmobiles in existence, only the snowmobile market will probably be altered. But something that affects the amount of money in existence is going to affect *all* markets.

HOLDING MONEY

All of us engage in a flow of transactions. We buy and sell things all of our lives. But because we use money—dollars—as our medium of exchange, all *flows* of nonbarter transactions involve a *stock* of money. We can restate this as follows:

> To use money, one must hold money.

Given that everybody must hold money, we can now talk about the *demand* to hold it. People do not demand to hold money just to look at pictures of past presidents. They hold it to be able to use it to buy goods and services.

THE DEMAND FOR MONEY: WHAT PEOPLE WISH TO HOLD

People have a certain motivation that causes them to want to hold money balances. Individuals and firms could try to have zero non-interest-bearing money balances. But life is inconvenient without a ready supply of money balances. There is a demand for money by the public, motivated by several factors.

The Transactions Demand. The main reason why people hold money is that money can be used to purchase goods and services. People are paid at specific intervals (once a week, once a month, and so on), but they wish to make purchases more or less continuously. To free themselves from making expenditures on goods and services only on payday, people find it beneficial to hold money. The benefit they receive is convenience: they willingly forgo interest earnings in order to avoid the inconvenience and expense of cashing in such nonmoney assets as bonds every time they wish to make a purchase.

Thus people hold money to make regular, *expected* expenditures under the **transactions demand.** As national income rises, the community will want to hold more money. Suppose that national income rises due exclusively to price-level increases. If people are making the same volume of physical purchases but the goods and services cost more due to higher prices, people will want to hold more money.

There is a cost to holding money, though. For any given level of transactions, if the opportunity cost of holding non-interest-bearing money balances rises, people are going to want to hold less of them. The opportunity cost of holding money is the interest that could have been earned had that asset—money balances—been changed into some other form, such as small certificates of deposit. Thus when interest rates are high, individuals and firms attempt to reduce the amount of money balances they hold for transactions purposes. That way they have more money funds that they can place into interest-earning assets.

The Precautionary Demand.   The transactions demand involves money held to make *expected* expenditures; people hold money for the **precautionary demand** to make *unexpected* purchases or to meet emergencies. It is not unreasonable to maintain that as the price level or real national income rises, people will want to hold more money. In effect, when people hold money for the precautionary demand, they incur a cost in forgone interest earnings that is offset by the benefit that the security provides. Nonetheless, the higher the rate of interest, the less money balances people wish to hold because of their precautionary demand for them.

The Asset Demand.   Remember that one of the functions of money is a store of value. People can hold money balances as a store of value, or they can hold bonds or stocks or other interest-earning assets. The desire to hold money as a store of value leads to the **asset demand** for money. The reason that people choose to hold money as an asset as opposed to other assets is because of its liquidity and lack of risk. Moreover, if deflation is expected, holding money balances makes sense.

The disadvantage of holding money balances as an asset, of course, is the interest earnings forgone. Each individual or business decides how much money to hold as an asset by looking at the opportunity cost of holding money. The higher the interest rate—which is our proxy for the opportunity cost of holding money—the fewer money balances people will want to hold as assets. The lower the interest rate offered on alternative assets, the more money balances people will want to hold as assets.

THE DEMAND FOR MONEY CURVE

One common determinant of the transactions demand, the precautionary demand, and the asset demand is the opportunity cost of holding money. If we assume that the interest rate represents the cost of holding money balances, we can graph the relationship between the interest rate and the quantity of money demanded. In Figure 16-1 the demand for money curve shows a familiar downward slope. The horizontal axis measures the quantity of money demand, and the vertical axis is the interest rate. In this sense the interest rate is the price of holding money. At a higher price, a lower quantity of money is demanded, and vice versa.

▶ **Transactions demand**
Holding money as a medium of exchange to make payments. The level varies directly with nominal national income.

▶ **Precautionary demand**
Holding money to meet unplanned expenditures and emergencies.

▶ **Asset demand**
Holding money as a store of value instead of other assets such as certificates of deposit, corporate bonds, and stocks.

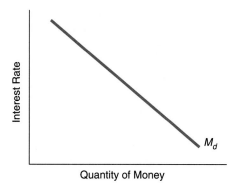

FIGURE 16-1
The demand for money curve.
If we use the interest rate as a proxy for the opportunity cost of holding money balances, the demand for money curve, M_d, is downward-sloping, similar to other demand curves.

CONCEPTS IN BRIEF

● To use money, people must hold money. Therefore, they have a demand for money balances.
● The determinants of the demand for money balances are the transactions demand, the precautionary demand, and the asset demand.
● Because holding money carries with it an opportunity cost—the interest income forgone—the demand for money curve showing the relationship between money balances and the interest rate slopes downward.

EFFECTS OF AN INCREASE IN THE MONEY SUPPLY

To understand how monetary policy works in its simplest form, we are going to run an experiment in which you increase the money supply in a very direct way. Assume that you have hundreds of millions of dollars of cash that you load into a helicopter. You will go around the country, dropping the money out of the window. People pick it up and put it in their billfolds. Some deposit the money in their checking accounts. The first thing that happens is that they have too much money—not in the sense that they want to burn it or throw it away but rather, that they have too much money relative to other things that they own. There are a variety of ways to dispose of this "new'" money.

DIRECT EFFECT

The simplest thing that people can do when they have excess money balances is to go out and spend it on goods and services. Here we have a direct impact on aggregate demand. Aggregate demand rises because with an increase in the money supply at any given price level, people now want to purchase more output of real goods and services.

INDIRECT EFFECT

Not everybody will necessarily spend their new found money on real output. Some people may wish to deposit some or all of this excess cash in banks. The recipient banks now discover that they have higher reserves than they need to hold. As you learned in Chapter 15, one thing that banks can do to get interest-earning assets is to lend out the excess reserves. But banks cannot induce people to borrow more money than they were borrowing before unless the banks lower the interest rate that they charge on loans. This lower interest rate encourages people to take those loans. Businesses will therefore engage in new investment with the money loaned. Individuals will engage in more consumption.

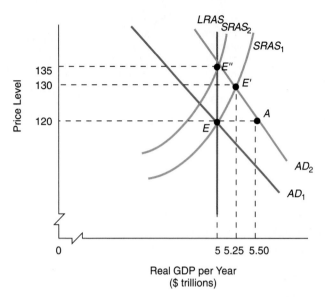

FIGURE 16-2
The direct and indirect effects of expansionary monetary policy.
If we start with equilibrium at E, an increase in the money supply will cause the aggregate demand curve to shift to AD_2. There is an excess quantity of real goods and services demanded. The price level increases so that we move to E' at an output rate of $5.25 trillion per year and a price level of 130. But input owners revise their expectations, and $SRAS_1$ shifts to $SRAS_2$. The new equilibrium is E'' at the long-run aggregate supply of $5 trillion of real GDP per year and a price level of 135.

Either way, the increased loans have created a rise in aggregate demand. More people will be involved in more spending, even those who did not pick up any of the money that was originally dropped out of your helicopter.

GRAPHING THE EFFECTS OF AN EXPANSIONARY MONETARY POLICY

We have now established the existence of both the direct and indirect effects on aggregate demand when there is an expansion in the money supply. Look at Figure 16-2. We start out in long-run and short-run equilibrium with long-run aggregate supply at $LRAS$, short-run aggregate supply at $SRAS_1$, and aggregate demand at AD_1. All three intersect at $5 trillion of real GDP at a price level of 120, at point E. Because of the direct and indirect effects of the increase in the money supply, aggregate demand shifts outward to the right to AD_2. At price level 120, there is an excess demand for real goods and services equal to the horizontal distance between E and A. This horizontal distance, here shown as $500 billion, is the increase in the money supply. The excess demand for goods and services must be matched, dollar for dollar, by the corresponding excess supply of money. It is this excess supply of money that has caused the aggregate demand curve to shift outward to AD_2.

In the short run, something has to give. Here the excess demand for real output induces a move to point E'. The price level rises to 130 at an output rate of $5.25 trillion per year. In the long run, though, expectations are revised, and input prices are revised accordingly. Therefore, the short-run aggregate supply curve, $SRAS_1$, begins to shift upward vertically to $SRAS_2$. Long-run equilibrium occurs at E'', and the ultimate effect is a rise in the price level.

CONCEPTS IN BRIEF

- The direct effect of an increase in the money supply is through people desiring to spend more on real goods and services when they have excess money balances.
- The indirect effect of an increase in the money supply works through a lowering of the interest rates, thereby encouraging businesses to make new investments with the money loaned to them. Individuals will also engage in more consumption (on consumer durables) because of lower interest rates.

MONETARY POLICY IN THE REAL WORLD

Of course, monetary policy does not consist of dropping dollar bills from a helicopter. Nonetheless, it is true that the Fed seeks to alter consumption, investment, and aggregate demand as a whole by altering the rate of growth of the money supply. The Fed uses three tools as part of its policymaking action:

1. Open market operations
2. Discount rate changes
3. Reserve requirement changes

OPEN MARKET OPERATIONS

The Fed changes the amount of reserves in the system by its purchases and sales of government bonds issued by the U.S. Treasury. To understand how the Fed does so, you must first start out in an equilibrium in which everybody, including the holders of bonds, is satisfied with the current situation. There is some equilibrium level of interest rate (and bond prices) outstanding. Now if the Fed wants to conduct open market operations, it must somehow induce individuals, businesses, and foreigners to hold more or fewer U.S. Treasury bonds. The inducement must be in the form of making people better off. So if the Fed wants to buy bonds, it is going to have to offer to buy them at a higher price than exists in the marketplace. If the Fed wants to sell bonds, it is going to have to offer them at a lower price than exists in the marketplace. Thus an open market operation must cause a change in the price of bonds.

Graphing the Sale of Bonds. The Fed sells some of the bonds in its portfolio. This is shown in panel (a) of Figure 16-3. Notice that the supply of bonds is shown here as a vertical line with respect to price. The demand for bonds is downward-sloping. If the Fed offers more bonds for sale, it shifts the supply curve from S_1 to S_2. It cannot induce people to buy the extra bonds at the original price of P_1, so it must lower the price to P_2.

The Fed's Purchase of Bonds. The converse occurs when the Fed purchases bonds. In panel (b) of Figure 16-3, the original supply curve is S_1. The new supply curve will end up being S_3 because of the Fed's purchases of bonds. You can view this purchase

FIGURE 16-3
Determining the price of bonds.
In panel (a) the Fed offers more bonds for sale. The price drops from P_1 to P_2. In panel (b) the Fed purchases bonds. This is the equivalent of a reduction in the supply of bonds available for private investors to hold. The price of bonds must rise from P_1 to P_3 to clear the market.

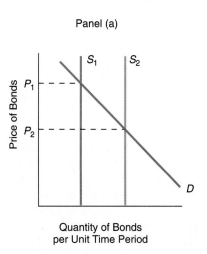

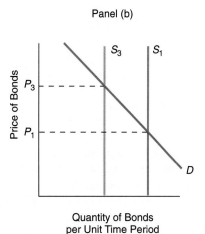

of bonds as a reduction in the stock of bonds available for private investors to hold. To get people to give up these bonds, the Fed must offer them a more attractive price. The price will rise from P_1 to P_3.

Relationship Between the Price of Existing Bonds and the Rate of Interest.

There is an inverse relationship between the price of existing bonds and the rate of interest. Suppose that you already own some bonds. Bonds by definition have a fixed coupon payment, paid per time period, usually every year. Let's say that you have a $1,000 bond that promises to pay you $100 a year forever. That means that your interest yield is $100 divided by $1,000, which is equal to 10 percent a year. Now the Fed comes into the marketplace and wants to purchase bonds. The only way it can do so is by increasing the price of bonds. It is willing to pay more than the current market price. You now find that you can sell the existing bond that you have for $2,000. It still pays $100 a year as before, but what has happened to the effective interest yield on that bond received by the *buyer* of the bond? It has fallen, for it is now $100 per year ÷ $2,000 = 5 percent per year.

The important point to be understood is this:

> The market price of existing bonds (and all fixed-income assets) is inversely related to the rate of interest prevailing in the economy.

To drive this point home, look at another example taken from the other side of the picture. Assume that the average yield on bonds is 5 percent. You decide to purchase a bond. A local corporation agrees to sell you a bond that will pay you $50 a year forever. What is the price you are willing to pay for it? $1,000. Why? Because $50 ÷ $1,000 = 5 percent. You purchase the bond. The next year something happens in the economy. For whatever reason, you can go out and obtain bonds that have effective yields of 10 percent. That is to say, the prevailing interest rate in the economy is now 10 percent. What has happened to the market price of the existing bond that you own, the one you purchased the year before? It will have fallen. If you try to sell it for $1,000, you will discover that no investors will buy it from you. Why should they when they can obtain $50 a year from someone else by paying only $500? Indeed, unless you offer your bond for sale at a price of $500, no buyers will be forthcoming. Hence an increase in the prevailing interest rate in the economy has caused the market value of your existing bond to fall. Once again, existing bond prices are inversely related to the prevailing interest rate in the economy.

Contractionary Monetary Policy: Effects on Aggregate Demand, the Price Level, and Real GDP.

Consider contractionary monetary policy by the Fed. When the Fed engages in contractionary monetary policy, it increases its sales of U.S. government bonds. Remember that to do so, it must lower bond prices. But lowering the price of bonds is the same thing as raising the interest rate on existing bonds. In any event, let's assume that the Fed sells bonds exclusively to banks. (This is not quite accurate because it actually deals with a small number of bond dealers.) The banks that purchase the bonds from the Fed do so with reserves. This puts banks too close to not being able to meet their reserve requirements. They replenish their reserves by reducing their lending. The way they ration available money among potential borrowers is by raising the rate of interest they charge on loans. Some borrowers, deeming the new rate too high, will eliminate themselves from the market. The interest rate in the economy will have already gone up a bit anyway because of the initial sale of bonds to the banks. Consequently, some borrowers who otherwise would have borrowed in order to spend no longer will do so at the higher rate of interest. The aggregate demand curve shifts from AD_1 to AD_2 in

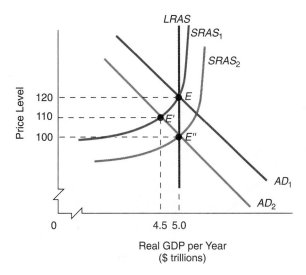

FIGURE 16-4
Contractionary monetary policy via open market sales.
If we start out in long-run and short-run equilibrium at point *E*, contractionary monetary policy by open-market sales will shift aggregate demand to AD_2. The new short-run equilibrium will be at *E'*. This is at a lower price level, however. Input owners will revise their expectations, and $SRAS_1$ will shift to $SRAS_2$. The new long-run equilibrium will be at *E''*.

Figure 16-4. If we started off in equilibrium, we would have been at point *E* with price level of 120 and real GDP of $5 trillion per year. AD_1, $SRAS_1$, and *LRAS* all intersect at point *E*. Now that the Fed has sold bonds, the aggregate demand curve shifts to AD_2. In the short run, we move along $SRAS_1$ to point *E'*, at which the price level has dropped to 110 and real GDP has decreased to $4.5 trillion per year.

In the long run, in a fully adjusting economy, expectations adjust and so do factor (input) prices. All of the shock is absorbed in a lower price level as $SRAS_1$ moves to $SRAS_2$. The new equilibrium is at *E''*, again at $5 trillion real GDP per year but at a lower price level of 100.

Expansionary Monetary Policy: Effect of a Purchase of Bonds. The Fed engages in expansionary monetary policy by purchasing bonds. Remember that for the Fed to purchase bonds, it has to raise the price it pays for bonds. That means that the interest rate on existing bonds will go down. In any event, the Fed buys the bonds from banks, which now have more reserves. Flush with excess reserves, the banks seek ways to lend them out. To induce customers to borrow more, the banks will cut interest rates even further. People who thought they were not going to be able to afford a new car, house, or whatever now find themselves able to do so. Their spending rises. The aggregate demand curve shifts outward to the right from AD_1 to AD_2 in Figure 16-5 on the next page. If we started out at equilibrium at point *E* where *LRAS* and $SRAS_1$ intersect *AD* at $5 trillion of real GDP per year, we now move to point *E'*. In the short run, equilibrium real GDP per year increases to $5.5 trillion a year, and the price level rises from 120 to 125. In the long run, ultimately, expectations and input prices change, so that $SRAS_1$ shifts up to $SRAS_2$. The new equilibrium is on $LRAS_1$ at *E''*. The price level has increased to 135. Ultimately, all of the increase in aggregate demand is translated into a higher price level, given that we started in long- and short-run equilibrium.

CHANGES IN THE DISCOUNT RATE

Originally, the most important tool in the Fed's monetary policy kit was changes in the discount rate, discussed in Chapter 15. The Fed used the discount rate so much in the beginning to carry out monetary policy because it had no power over reserve requirements. More

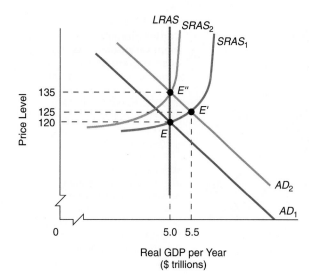

FIGURE 16-5
Expansionary monetary policy via open-market purchases.
If we start out with equilibrium at E, expansionary monetary policy by open-market purchases will shift aggregate demand to AD_2, and the new short-run equilibrium will be at E'. At the higher price level, though, input owners will change their expectations, and $SRAS_1$ will shift to $SRAS_2$. The new long-run equilibrium will be at E", at price level 135 and $5 trillion of real GDP per year.

important, its initial portfolio of government bonds was practically nonexistent. Therefore, it did not have much to play with in terms of open market operations. Over time, particularly since World War II, the discount rate as a tool of monetary policy has been used less frequently as the Fed increasingly relies on open market operations.

Increasing the Discount Rate. Recall that the discount rate is the interest rate the Fed charges depository institutions when they borrow reserves directly from the Fed. An increase in the discount rate increases the cost of funds. This forces banks to raise their interest rates. Therefore, some borrowers who would have borrowed to spend no longer do so. The aggregate demand curve shifts from AD_1 to AD_2 in Figure 16-4, just as it did with contractionary open market operations (the sale of bonds). In the short run, both the equilibrium level of real GDP per year and the price level fall. In the long run, as expectations adjust and so do factor (input) prices, all of the shock is absorbed in a lower price level. Real output returns to its long-run equilibrium level.

Decreasing the Discount Rate. A reduction in the discount rate lowers depository institutions' cost of funds. It enables them to lower the rates they charge their customers for borrowing. People who thought they were not able to afford to purchase consumer durables, for example, now find themselves able to do so. The aggregate demand curve shifts out as shown in Figure 16-5, just as it did with expansionary open market operations (the purchase of bonds). In the short run, real output may increase without too much increase in the price index (unless the SRAS is virtually vertical in the relevant range). Ultimately, though, all of the increase in demand is translated into a higher price level with output returning to its long-run equilibrium.

CHANGES IN RESERVE REQUIREMENTS

Although the Fed rarely uses changes in reserve requirements as a form of monetary policy, most recently it did so in 1992, when it decreased reserve requirements on checkable deposits to 10 percent. In any event, here is how changes in reserve requirements affect the economy.

An Increase in the Required Reserve Ratio. If the Fed increases reserve requirements, this makes it harder for banks to meet their reserve requirements. They attempt to replenish their reserves by reducing their lending. They induce potential borrowers not to borrow so much by raising the interest rates they charge on the loans they offer. Therefore, some borrowers who would have borrowed to purchase goods and service will no longer do so. The aggregate demand curve shifts from AD_1 to AD_2 in Figure 16-4. In the short run, both the price index and real GDP fall. In the long run, as expectations adjust and so do input prices, all of the shock is absorbed in a lower price level.

A Decrease in the Required Reserve Ratio. When the Fed decreases reserve requirements, as it did in 1992, some depository institutions attempt to lend their excess reserves out. To induce customers to borrow more, depository institutions cut interest rates. Individuals and firms that thought they would be unable to make new purchases now find themselves able to do so, and their spending increases. The aggregate demand curve shifts from AD_1 to AD_2 in Figure 16-5. In the short run, output increases and the price index does not rise by much. In the long run, changes in expectations and input costs cause the short-run aggregate supply curve to shift so that the increase in aggregate demand is simply translated into a higher price level.

CONCEPTS IN BRIEF

- Monetary policy consists of open market operations, discount rate changes, and reserve requirement changes.
- When the Fed sells bonds, it must offer them at a lower price. When the Fed buys bonds, it must pay a higher price.
- There is an inverse relationship between the prevailing rate of interest in the economy and the market price of existing bonds.
- If we start out in long-run and short-run equilibrium, contractionary monetary policy first leads to a decrease in aggregate demand, resulting in a reduction in real GDP and in the price level. Eventually, though, the short-run aggregate supply curve shifts downward, and the new equilibrium is at *LRAS* but at an even lower price level.
- Expansionary monetary policy works the opposite way if we are starting out in both long-run and short-run equilibrium. The end result is simply a higher price level rather than a change in the equilibrium level of real GDP per year.

OPEN-ECONOMY TRANSMISSION OF MONETARY POLICY

So far we have discussed monetary policy in a closed economy. When we move to an open economy in which there are international trade and the international purchase and sale of all assets including dollars and other currencies, monetary policy becomes more arduous. Consider first the effect on exports of any type of monetary policy.

THE NET-EXPORT EFFECT

When we examined fiscal policy, we pointed out that deficit financing can lead to higher interest rates in the United States. Higher interest rates do something in the foreign sector—they attract foreign financial investment. More people want to purchase U.S.

government securities, for example. But to purchase U.S. assets, people first have to obtain U.S. dollars. This means that the demand for dollars goes up in foreign exchange markets. The international price of the dollar therefore rises. This is called an *appreciation* of the dollar, and it tends to reduce net exports because it makes our exports more expensive in terms of foreign currency and imports cheaper in terms of dollars. Thus foreigners demand fewer of our goods and we demand more of theirs. Thus expansionary fiscal policy that creates deficit spending financed by U.S. government borrowing can lead to a reduction in exports.

But what about expansionary monetary policy? If expansionary monetary policy reduces U.S. interest rates, there will be a positive net-export effect because foreigners will want fewer U.S. financial instruments, demanding fewer dollars and thereby causing the international price of the dollar to fall. This makes our exports cheaper for the rest of the world, which then demands a larger quantity of our exports. It also means that foreign goods are more expensive in the United States, so we therefore demand fewer imports. We come up with two conclusions:

1. Expansionary fiscal policy may cause international flows of financial capital (responding to interest rate increases) to offset its effectiveness to some extent. The net-export effect is in the opposite direction of fiscal policy.
2. Expansionary monetary policy may cause interest rates to fall. Such a fall will be strengthened by international flows of financial capital. The net-export effect of expansionary monetary policy will be positive.

TIGHT MONETARY POLICY

Now assume that the economy is experiencing inflation and the Federal Reserve wants to tighten monetary policy. In so doing, it may cause interest rates to rise. Rising interest rates will cause financial capital to flow into the United States. The demand for dollars will increase, and their international price will go up. Foreign goods will now look cheaper to Americans, and imports will rise. Foreigners will not want our exports as much, and exports will fall. The result will be a deterioration in our international trade balance. In this case, tight monetary policy may conflict with the goal of improving our international balance of trade.

GLOBALIZATION OF INTERNATIONAL MONEY MARKETS

On a broader level, the Fed's ability to control the rate of growth of the money supply may be hampered as U.S. money markets become less isolated. With the push of a computer button, millions or even billions of dollars can change hands halfway around the world. In the world dollar market, the Fed finds an increasing number of dollars coming from *private* institutions. If the Fed reduces the growth of the money supply, individuals and firms in the United States can increasingly obtain dollars from other sources. People in the United States who want more liquidity can obtain their dollars from foreigners or can even obtain foreign currencies and convert them into dollars in the world dollar market. Indeed, it is possible that as world markets become increasingly integrated, U.S. residents may someday conduct transactions in *foreign* currencies.

The globalization of money markets may not be a serious problem for the Fed now, but it could become one at some time in the future. The Fed would be unable to reach its money stock growth rate targets, and it might not be able to reach its interest rate targets either.

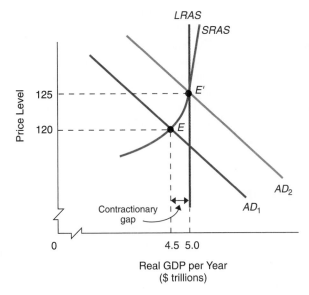

FIGURE 16-6
Expansionary monetary policy with underutilized resources.
If we start out with equilibrium at *E*, expansionary monetary policy will shift AD_1 to AD_2. The new equilibrium will be at *E′*. *SRAS* will not shift.

MONETARY POLICY DURING PERIODS OF UNDERUTILIZED RESOURCES

If the national economy is operating at an equilibrium output level that is below that given by the long-run aggregate supply curve, monetary policy (like fiscal policy) can generate increases in the equilibrium level of real GDP per year that remain in the long run. In Figure 16-6 you see initial aggregate demand as AD_1. It intersects *SRAS* at *E*, real GDP per year of $4.5 trillion and a price level 120. There is a contractionary gap of $500 billion. That is the difference between *LRAS* and the current equilibrium. The Fed can engage in expansionary monetary policy, the direct and indirect effects of which will cause AD_1 to shift to AD_2. The new equilibrium is at *E′*, at an output rate of $5 trillion of real GDP per year and a price level of 125.

CONCEPTS IN BRIEF
- Monetary policy in an open economy has repercussions for net exports.
- If expansionary monetary policy reduces U.S. interest rates, there is a positive net-export effect because foreigners will demand fewer U.S. financial instruments, thereby demanding fewer dollars and hence causing the international price of the dollar to fall. This makes our exports cheaper for the rest of the world. Thus the net-export effect of expansionary monetary policy may be positive.
- Expansionary monetary policy during periods of underutilized resources can cause the equilibrium level of real GDP to increase up to that rate of real output consistent with the vertical long-run aggregate supply curve.

MONETARY POLICY AND INFLATION

Most theories of inflation relate to the short run. The price index in the short run can fluctuate because of events such as oil price shocks, labor union strikes, or discoveries of large amounts of new natural resources. In the long run, however, empirical studies show a relatively stable relationship between excessive growth in the money supply and inflation.

Simple supply and demand can explain why the price level rises when the money supply is increased. Suppose that a major oil discovery is made, and the supply of oil increases dramatically relative to the demand for oil. The relative price of oil will fall; now it will take more units of oil to exchange for specific quantities of nonoil products. Similarly, if the supply of money rises relative to the demand for money, it will take more units of money to purchase specific quantities of goods and services. That is merely another way of stating that the price level has increased or that the purchasing power of money has fallen. In fact, the classical economists referred to inflation as a situation in which more money is chasing the same quantity of goods and services.

THE EQUATION OF EXCHANGE AND THE QUANTITY THEORY

A simple way to show the relationship between changes in the quantity of money in circulation and the price level is through the **equation of exchange,** developed by Irving Fisher of Yale University:

$$M_s V \equiv PQ$$

where

M_s = then the actual money balances held by the nonbanking public

V = income velocity of money, or the number of times, on average, each monetary unit is spent on final goods and services

P = price level or price index

Q = real national output (real GDP)

▶ **Equation of exchange**
The number of monetary units times the number of times each unit is spent on final goods and services is identical to the price level times output (or nominal national income).

▶ **Income velocity of money**
The number of times per year a dollar is spent on final goods and services; equal to GDP divided by the money supply.

Consider a numerical example involving a one-commodity economy. Assume that in this economy the total money supply, M_s, is $100; the quantity of output, Q, is 50 units of a good; and the average price, P, of this output is $10 per unit. Using the equation of exchange,

$$M_s V = PQ$$
$$\$100V = \$10 \times 50$$
$$\$100V = \$500$$
$$V = 5$$

Thus each dollar is spent an average of five times a year.

The Equation of Exchange as an Identity.

The equation of exchange must always be true—it is an *accounting identity.* The equation of exchange states that the total amount of money spent on final output, $M_s V$, is equal to the total amount of money *received* for final output, PQ. Thus a given flow of money can be seen from either the buyers' side or the producers' side. The value of goods purchased is equal to the value of goods sold.

If Q represents real national output and P is the price level, PQ equals the value of national output, or *nominal* national income. Thus

$$M_s V \equiv PQ \equiv Y$$

The Quantity Theory of Money and Prices. If we now make some assumptions about different variables in the equation of exchange, we come up with the simplified theory of why prices change, called the **crude quantity theory of money and prices.** If you assume that the velocity of money, V, is constant and that real national output, Q, is basically stable, the simple equation of exchange tells you that a proportionate change in the money supply can lead only to a proportionate change in the price level. Continue with our numerical example. Q is 50 units of the good. V equals 5. If the money supply increases to 200, the only thing that can happen is that the price index, P, has to go up from 10 to 20. Otherwise the equation is no longer in balance.

> ▶ **Crude quantity theory of money**
> The belief that changes in the money supply lead to proportional changes in the price level.

 INTERNATIONAL EXAMPLE: Declaring Large-Denomination Rubles Worthless

The ex-Soviet Union in one sense provided an experiment in the quantity theory of money and prices. In early 1991 the government declared all 50- and 100-ruble currency notes worthless. Citizens only had three days to convert these large notes into smaller-denomination notes. Many citizens found that deadline impossible to meet. The intended total reduction in large-denomination ruble notes amounted to 26 billion rubles, or nearly a 20 percent reduction in nominal money balances supplied by the government. Look at the equation of exchange on page 358. If velocity, V, is constant and if real GDP, Q, is relatively stable, a 20 percent reduction in the money supply, M, has to lead to a 20 percent reduction in the price level, P. Did this happen? The answer is no. The reason is that income velocity of money, V, increased. As a result, aggregate demand did not fall significantly following the reduction in the nominal money supply. In effect, the only thing that really happened was that large amounts of wealth that Soviet citizens held as money were "expropriated" by the elimination of large-denomination ruble notes that many citizens had saved for years.

For Critical Analysis: Some policymakers in the United States have argued in favor of eliminating $100 bills in order to make large cash transactions undertaken by drug dealers more difficult. Could the ex-Soviet Union's experiment be duplicated in the United States? Why or why not? ●

Empirical Verification. There is considerable evidence of the empirical validity of the relationship between excessive monetary growth and high rates of inflation. Look back at Figure 15-1 on page 320. There you see the loose correspondence between the money supply growth and the rate of inflation in the United States from 1960 to the present. The relationship is even more apparent when you look at countries in Latin America.

 INTERNATIONAL EXAMPLE: Money Supply Growth Rates and Inflation in Latin America

Latin America has been known as a place where inflation is sometimes in the hundreds of percent per month. Argentina, for example, experienced periods of hyperinflation. Is there a relationship between increases in the quantity of money in circulation and the rate of inflation? The answer seems to be yes in Latin America, judging from Figure 16-7 on the next page. Although the correlation is not perfect, you can see that there is a fairly obvious direct relationship between money supply growth rates, expressed as a percentage rate of growth per year, and the average annual rate of inflation, also expressed as a percentage rate of growth of the price index per year. When news articles in the popular press talk about the money printing presses "not being able to keep up with inflation," the direction of causation is dead wrong. High rates of inflation in Latin America and elsewhere have not been the cause of excessive printing of money but rather the effect.

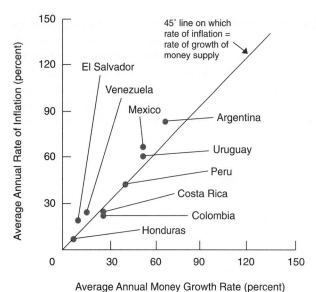

FIGURE 16-7
Money and inflation in Latin America.
There is a loose but obvious relationship between rates of inflation and rates of monetary growth in Latin America.

Source: International Monetary Fund, *International Financial Statistics, 1993.*

For Critical Analysis: Do you think it is possible that in countries such as Argentina and Peru that have experienced rapid rates of inflation, government officials are unaware of the relationship between monetary growth and those high inflation rates? ●

 INTERNATIONAL EXAMPLE: Hyperinflation in Modern Russia

Since the breakup of the Soviet Union, Russia has experienced near hyperinflation. People visiting that country in the early 1990s claimed that the inflation rate was running about 1 percent per day. Estimates for 1992 were around 1,000 to 2,000 percent for that year. Accurate statistics have not been available, but all signs indicate that near hyperinflation occurred. Again, the incorrect comment in the popular press was that there was a shortage of rubles in the streets of Moscow.

Prior to the dissolution of the Soviet Union, there was relatively little inflation in that part of the world. The economy was centrally planned and controlled. Government expenditures were normally matched by government revenues. But during the period of transition, the chain of command and control virtually disintegrated. The government has had a difficult time collecting any tax revenues through normal sources. Although there is a complicated and fairly progressive tax rate schedule in Russia, there are literally thousands of ways, legal and illegal, to avoid those taxes. But the government continues to engage in numerous expenditures. When the government spends and doesn't pay for it with tax revenues collected, it has only two choices: deficit financing or printing money. Deficit financing is almost out of the question for the moment in Russia. No one has enough confidence in the new government to purchase its bonds. Consequently, the government is paying for its expenditures by using the equivalent of the ruble printing presses. Although the relationship between small changes in the rate of growth of the money supply and inflation may not be clear-cut, when there are massive increases in the rate of growth of the money supply, inflation is certain to follow. The inflation in post-USSR Russia can be blamed on the government's inability to carry out fiscal policy in any reasonable manner. That government just did not have the ability to tax the population effectively or to sell bonds.

For Critical Analysis: How is rapid inflation the equivalent to a tax on people's holdings of money balances? (Hint: What happens to the purchasing power of your money balances when there is inflation?) ●

CONCEPTS IN BRIEF

- The equation of exchange states that the expenditures by some people will equal income receipts by others, or $M_sV = PQ$ (money supply times velocity equals nominal national income).
- Viewed as an accounting identity, the equation of exchange is always correct, because the amount of money spent on final output must equal the total amount of money received for final output.
- The crude quantity theory of money and prices states that a change in the money supply will bring about a proportional change in the price level.

MONETARY POLICY IN ACTION: THE TRANSMISSION MECHANISM

At the start of this chapter, we talked about the direct and indirect effects of monetary policy. The direct effect is simply that an increase in the money supply causes people to have excess money balances. To get rid of these excess money balances, they increase their expenditures. The indirect effect occurs because some people have decided to purchase interest-bearing assets with their excess money balances. This causes the price of such assets—bonds—to go up. Because of the inverse relationship between the price of existing bonds and the interest rate, the interest rate in the economy falls. This lower interest rate induces people and businesses to spend more than they would otherwise have spent.

THE KEYNESIAN TRANSMISSION MECHANISM

One school of economists believes that the indirect effect of monetary policy is the more important. This group, typically called Keynesian because of its belief in John Maynard Keynes's work, asserts that the main effect of monetary policy occurs through changes in the interest rate. The Keynesian money transmission mechanism is shown in Figure 16-8. There you see that the money supply changes the interest rate, which in turn changes the desired rate of investment. This transmission mechanism can be seen more explicitly in Figure 16-9 on the next page. In panel (a) you see that an increase in the money supply reduces the interest rate. This reduction in the interest rate causes desired investment expenditures to increase from I_1 to I_2 in panel (b). This increase in investment shifts out aggregate demand from AD_1 to AD_2 in panel (c).

▶ **Monetarists**
Macroeconomists who believes that inflation is always caused by excessive monetary growth and that changes in the money supply directly affect aggregate demand.

The Monetarists' View of Money Supply Changes. **Monetarists**, economists who believe in a modern quantity theory of money and prices, contend that monetary policy works its way more directly into the economy. They believe that changes in the money supply lead to changes in nominal GDP in the same direction. An increase in

FIGURE 16-8
The Keynesian money transmission mechanism.

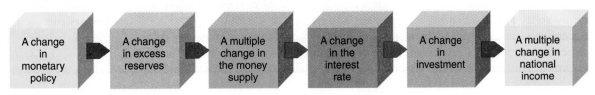

A change in monetary policy → A change in excess reserves → A multiple change in the money supply → A change in the interest rate → A change in investment → A multiple change in national income

FIGURE 16-9
Adding monetary policy to the Keynesian model.
In panel (a) we show a demand for money function, M_d. It slopes downward to show that at lower rates of interest, a larger quantity of money will be demanded. The money supply is given initially as M_s, so that the equilibrium rate of interest will be r_1. At this rate of interest, we see from the planned investment schedule given in panel (b) that the quantity of planned investment demanded per year will be I_1. After the shift in M_s', in panel (c) the increase in investment shifts the aggregate demand curve from AD_1 to AD_2. Equilibrium moves from E to E', at $5 trillion real GDP per year.

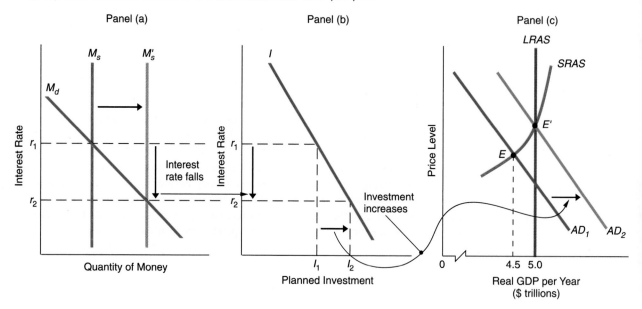

the money supply because of expansionary open market operations (purchases of bonds) by the Fed leads the public to have larger money holdings than desired. This excess quantity of money demanded induces the public to buy more of everything, especially more durable goods such as cars, stereos, and houses. If the economy is starting out at its long-run equilibrium rate of output, there can only be a short-run increase in real GDP. Ultimately, though, the public cannot buy more of everything; it simply bids up prices so that the price level rises.

Monetarists' Criticism of Monetary Policy.
The monetarists' belief that monetary policy works directly through changes in desired spending does not mean that they consider such policy an appropriate government stabilization tool. According to the monetarists, although monetary policy can affect real GDP (and employment) in the short run, the length of time required before money supply changes take effect is so long and variable that such policy is difficult to conduct. For example, an expansionary monetary policy to counteract a contractionary gap (see Chapter 11) may not take effect for a year and a half, by which time inflation may be a problem. At that point the expansionary monetary policy will end up making the then current inflation worse. Monetarists therefore see monetary policy as a *destabilizing* force in the economy.

According to the monetarists, therefore, policymakers should follow a **monetary rule:** Increase the money supply *smoothly* at a rate consistent with the economy's long-run average growth rate. *Smoothly* is an important word here. Increasing the money supply at

▶ **Monetary rule**
A monetary policy that incorporates a rule specifying the annual rate of growth of some monetary aggregate.

20 percent per year half the time and decreasing it at 17 percent per year the other half of the time would average out to about a 3 percent increase, but the results would be disastrous, say the monetarists. Instead of permitting the Fed to use its discretion in setting monetary policy, monetarists would force it to follow a rule such as this: "Increase the money supply smoothly at 3.5 percent per year."

A POLICY DEBATE: DISCRETION VERSUS RULES

Monetarists and others who believe in a monetary rule are part of a group of economists and politicians who believe in nonactivism. They argue against activism by the Federal Reserve (and by Congress) with respect to fiscal and monetary policy. An opposing group argues in favor of activism. They offer several criticisms of a monetary rule.

CRITICISMS OF A MONETARY RULE

Critics of the monetary rule point out that the Fed may not be able to increase the money supply exactly at the desired rate. Even though monetarists believe that the Fed can pinpoint money supply growth by controlling the monetary base, critics of the monetary rule point out that from 1979 to 1982 Fed policy was apparently to control the rate of growth of the money supply, yet it was unable to obtain its targets.

Such criticisms must be taken seriously, but not too seriously. Certainly the Federal Reserve can create a computer program that allows it to take into account all aspects of what determines the rate of growth of the money supply. In so doing, it can generate computerized directions on how much or how little to inject new reserves into the economy over time.

THE INTERRELATIONSHIP BETWEEN MONETARY AND FISCAL POLICY

▶ **Debt monetization**
The process by which deficit financing induces the Federal Reserve simultaneously to purchase government securities. That open market operation monetizes part of the public debt.

People who argue in favor of a monetary rule point out that for it to work, active fiscal policy must also be eliminated. Thus a monetary discipline rule and federal fiscal discipline rule are interrelated. Remember that government purchases of goods and services plus government transfers (total government outlays) can be financed by taxation, borrowing, and money creation. But whenever the government borrows, this means that either future taxes must rise or **debt monetization** must occur. That is to say, the Fed can simply accommodate this increased borrowing by the Treasury by purchasing U.S. government securities through its open market operations. Ultimately, debt monetization may cause inflation. In this sense monetary policy simply becomes a fiscal instrument. A monetary rule will no longer be possible.

In any event, while it may be possible academically to discuss combining a monetary rule with the elimination of active fiscal policy, the real world, at least in the United States, is not so simple. After all, monetary policy is carried out by the independent Federal Reserve. Fiscal policy, however defined, is carried out mainly by the Congress. (The president can at times influence the Congress, however.) No matter how much the chairman of the Board of Governors of the Federal Reserve System implores Congress to eschew fiscal policy, Congress does not have to listen. For example, if the Fed follows a monetary rule, the Congress can simultaneously increase spending much more than taxes, thereby increasing the federal budget deficit. What is the Fed to do in such a situation? Should it simply let the U.S. Treasury sell more bonds, thereby crowding out private investment? Or should the Fed in fact "help out" the profligate Congress by at least partial debt monetization?

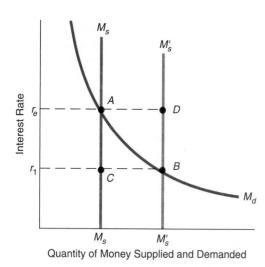

FIGURE 16-10
Choosing a monetary policy target.
The Fed, in the short run, can select an interest rate or a money supply target, but not both. It cannot, for example, choose r_e and M'_s; if it selects r_e, it must accept M_s; if it selects M'_s, it must allow the interest rate to fall to r_1. The Fed can obtain point A or B. It cannot get to point C or D. It must therefore chose one target or another.

Quantity of Money Supplied and Demanded

FED TARGET CHOICE: INTEREST RATES OR MONEY SUPPLY?

Money supply and interest rate targets cannot be pursued simultaneously. Interest rate targets force the Fed to abandon control over the money supply; money stock growth targets force the Fed to allow interest rates to fluctuate.

Figure 16-10 shows the relationship between the total demand for money and supply of money. Note that in the short run (in the sense that nominal national income is fixed), the demand for money is constant; short-run money supply changes leave the demand for money curve unaltered. In the longer run, however, as the changed money supply causes nominal national income to change, the money demand curve will shift. In the short run, the Fed can choose either a particular interest rate (r_e or r_1) or a particular money supply (N_s or M'_s).

If the Fed wants interest rate r_e, it must select money supply M_s; if it desires a lower interest rate in the short run, it must increase the money supply. Thus by targeting an interest rate, the Fed must relinquish control of the money supply. Conversely, if the Fed wants to target the money supply at, say, M'_s, it must allow the interest rate to fall to r_1.

Consider now the case in which the Fed wants to maintain the present level of interest rates. If actual market interest rates in the future rise above the present (desired) rates, the Fed will be continuously forced to increase the money supply. This will only temporarily lower interest rates. The increased money stock will induce inflation, and inflationary premiums will be included in nominal interest rates. To pursue its low-interest-rate policy, the Fed must *again* increase the money stock. Note that to maintain an interest rate target (stable interest rates), the Fed must abandon an independent money stock target. Complementary reasoning indicates that by setting growth rate targets at M_s or M'_s, the Fed must allow short-run fluctuations in interest rates when the economy experiences a contraction or an expansion.

But which should the Fed target, interest rates or monetary aggregates? (And which interest rate or which money stock?) It is generally agreed that the answer depends on the source of instability in the economy. If the source of instability is variations in private or public spending, monetary aggregate (money supply) targets should be set and pursued. However, if the source of instability is an unstable demand for (or perhaps supply of) money, interest rate targets are preferred.

COORDINATION OF MONETARY AND FISCAL POLICY: PRO AND CON

Both monetary and fiscal policy can affect aggregate economic variables. In principle, fiscal and monetary policymaking could *jointly* achieve target levels of both real GDP and the rate of interest. The result would be **monetary and fiscal policy coordination.**

▶ **Monetary and fiscal policy coordination**
Cooperation between central bank authorities (the Fed) and the U.S. Treasury and Congress to attain specific national policy goals, such as reduced inflation or less unemployment.

Should monetary and fiscal policymakers coordinate their actions? Like many questions in economics this one is difficult to answer. Coordination of policymaking can potentially improve on noncoordinated policymaking if coordination means agreeable cooperation. If both the Federal Reserve and the rest of the federal government share the same goals and if those goals are truly what is best for the economy, theoretically society could gain from policy coordination.

However, realize that monetary and fiscal policymakers may wish to achieve different goals. For instance, the Fed might seek greater financial-market stability, while the president and Congress might desire greater real income stability. It is likely that different combinations of real income and interest rates would be consistent with these differing policy goals. This would generate tensions between the policymakers.

Indeed, it is arguable that such tensions might be desirable. An overemphasis by the president and Congress on achieving stability around a high level of real income might produce financial instability if the Fed were to coordinate its monetary policymaking with fiscal policy actions. In contrast, an overemphasis on financial stability on the part of the Fed might cause significant instability of real income if the president and Congress were to coordinate fiscal policies with the Fed's monetary policies. For this reason, noncoordinated policymaking might be the best compromise between potentially competing objectives. Coordinated policies might be undesirable.

Some economists argue that another reason that policy coordination might not be a good idea is that coordinated monetary and fiscal policy efforts to expand real national income could place upward pressure on the level of prices in the economy—that is, greater monetary and fiscal coordination could have inflationary consequences.

🌐 INTERNATIONAL EXAMPLE: European Monetary and Fiscal Coordination

In 1958 six Western European nations formed the *European Economic Community* (EEC), an institutional structure intended to promote various forms of economic cooperation. Since that time the organization has simplified its name to the European Community (EC) and added six members. On December 31, 1992, EC members dropped many restrictions on trade across the borders of their nations. Additionally, in 1978 a group of nations within the EC formed the *European Monetary System* (EMS). The EMS tries to coordinate monetary policies within the member group of nations. The consistent goal of this subgroup of nations within the EC has been to induce all EC members to join the EMS. Another, more controversial goal has been to turn the EMS, ultimately, into a single monetary policy making authority that has been termed the "EuroFed." Many proponents of this plan have argued that if it is to be successful, there must be greater harmonization of fiscal policymaking within the EC. In short, proponents of a EuroFed claim that monetary and fiscal policy coordination would be desirable not only within individual European nations but also between these nations. A debate on this issue has been ongoing since the formation of the EMS.

In light of our discussion of the issues involved in coordinating monetary and fiscal policies within a single nation like the United States, it should not be too surprising that the European debate has not yet reached a conclusion. Obviously, the interests of policymakers within a single nation may differ, and perhaps for legitimate reasons. In Europe the added problem is that national interests may differ, making coordination of policy-making potentially attractive for some nations but potentially unattractive for others.

There is a historical precedent for optimism on the part of proponents of European monetary coordination: the history of monetary policy in the United States. Through the late eighteenth century and much of the nineteenth century, individual states tried to conduct their own banking and monetary policies, often placing state interests above the interests of the United States. As we saw earlier, Congress ultimately established a single federal monetary authority, the Federal Reserve System. It effectively coordinates monetary policy for all the states within the United States. In principle, European governments could duplicate this institutional change.

In contrast, the United States also offers another historical precedent that may dampen the hopes of the promoters of European policy coordination. It is apparent that the divided aims of monetary and fiscal policymakers have made close monetary-fiscal coordination in the United States at best a fleeting achievement and at worst a nonexistent ideal. *A fortiori,* the national interests that divide European nations would complicate European monetary-fiscal coordination whether or not Europe ever forms a EuroFed. This is likely to be an issue in Europe for some time to come.

For Critical Analysis: What might be required for effective monetary-fiscal coordination throughout the European Community on a regular basis? ●

CONCEPTS IN BRIEF

- In the Keynesian model, monetary transmission operates through a change in the interest rates, which changes investment, causing a multiple change in the equilibrium level of national income.
- Monetarists believe that changes in the money supply lead to changes in nominal GDP in the same direction. The effect is direct, however, because individuals have excess money balances that they spend on cars, stereos, houses, and other things.
- Monetarists, among others, argue in favor of a monetary rule—an increase in the money supply smoothly at a rate consistent with the economy's long-run average growth rate. Monetarists do not believe in discretionary monetary (or fiscal) policy.
- If expansionary fiscal policy creates increased federal deficits and if the Fed increases its purchases of U.S. Treasury securities, this is in effect debt monetization.
- The Fed can choose to stabilize interest rates or to change the money supply, but not both.
- Some economists argue that monetary and fiscal policymakers should coordinate their actions. Others argue that such coordination will inevitably lead to upward pressure on the price level.

POLITICAL BUSINESS CYCLE: TRUTH OR FICTION?

Concepts Applied: Monetary policy, time lags, ineffectiveness

Some argue that presidents, such as Bill Clinton, can generate a political business cycle to ensure their reelection.

Do politicians influence monetary and fiscal policy in order to win elections? If they do, we have a theory of a political business cycle. It rests on two premises: (1) The electorate dislikes inflation and unemployment. (2) The electorate is myopic (shortsighted). Consequently, an incumbent president following the political business cycle should pursue restrictive monetary and fiscal policy early in the administration. The short-run effect of such restrictive monetary and fiscal policy is to raise the unemployment rate, but it will also help reduce the rate of inflation. About 18 months before the next presidential election, the president should then switch to expansionary monetary and fiscal policy. On election day, in the best of all possible worlds, the economy will be experiencing a low unemployment rate as a result of the short-run effects of the expansionary monetary and fiscal policies. It will also be experiencing less inflation because the economy will still be in a favorable position brought about by the previous restrictive monetary and fiscal policies. The full inflationary consequences of the expansionary policies that had started 18 months before the election will not be felt until after the election.

THE EMPIRICAL EVIDENCE The evidence about a political business cycle does not guarantee its validity. Nonetheless, the presidential elections of 1956, 1964, 1972, and 1984 all had the basic pattern of unemploy-

ment and inflation predicted by the political business cycle, and the incumbents—Eisenhower, Johnson, Nixon, and Reagan, respectively—won by landslides. The elections of 1960, 1968, 1976, and 1980 did not have the political business cycle pattern and, as predicted, the White House changed hands in 1960 and 1968, and Ford and Carter lost. Also, the election in 1988 resulted in a major victory by Republican candidate, George Bush, who benefited from low unemployment, slowing but still healthy economic growth, and moderate inflation inherited from the Reagan years. Bush's loss in the 1992 election appears to contradict the political business cycle. Although the economy had been in a recession that started in 1990, the rate of growth of real GDP had been rising for several quarters and the unemployment level had been falling slightly for four months prior to the election. Clinton was nonetheless effectively able to campaign on Bush's "dismal" economic record. It was only after the election that government statistics were released showing improvement in the rate of growth of real GDP.

THE BEHAVIOR OF THE FEDERAL RESERVE

If the political business cycle is correct, one important line of inquiry concerns the possibility that Federal Reserve behavior might be influenced by political aims. Indeed, in the past two decades there has been considerable economic research investigating whether or not the Fed brings about temporary increases in the nominal money supply as part of a political business cycle. It does this presumably to achieve short-run output and employment gains immediately before the election of incumbent presidents. There is in fact some evidence that certain Federal Reserve chairmen, such as Arthur Burns during the presidency of Richard Nixon, may have pursued such politically motivated policies.

DOES THE POLITICAL BUSINESS CYCLE EXPLAIN SUSTAINED INFLATION? If Federal Reserve policymaking is somewhat motivated by political considerations, the political business cycle theory may offer at least a partial explanation for the twentieth-century tendency for most democratic republics to experience sustained inflation. The terms of politicians in most democratic republics range from two to six years in length. The political business cycle theory therefore implies that every two to six years there should be an incentive for central banks to increase the nominal money supply to achieve short-run economic gains. However, there is no political incentive to reduce the nominal supply of money after elections; the politicians and central banks permit their economies to revert, on their own, to natural levels of employment and output. Therefore, the nominal money supply in these countries would, according to the political business cycle theory, tend only to grow over time, bringing about sustained inflationary trends in these economies. Hence this theory can potentially explain the existence of inflation and the absence of deflation in much of the industrialized world.

FOR CRITICAL ANALYSIS

1. What kind of legislation could Congress pass that would make the political business cycle impossible?
2. If the public is made aware of the political business cycle, can expansionary monetary and fiscal policy still have a short-run impact on real output and employment? Why or why not?

CHAPTER SUMMARY

1. The determinants of the demand for money balances are the transactions demand, the precautionary demand, and the asset demand.

2. Because holding money carries an opportunity cost—the interest income forgone—the demand for money curve showing the relationship between money balances and the interest rate slopes downward.

3. The direct effect of an increase in the money supply is through people desiring to spend more on real goods and services when they have excess money balances. The indirect effect of an increase in the money supply works through a lowering of the interest rates, thereby encouraging businesses to make new investments with the money loaned to them. Individuals will also engage in more consumption because of lower interest rates.

4. When the Fed sells bonds, it must offer them at a lower price. When the Fed buys bonds, it must pay a higher price. There is an inverse relationship between the prevailing rate of interest in the economy and the market price of existing bonds.

5. If we start out in long-run and short-run equilibrium, contractionary monetary policy first leads to a decrease in aggregate demand, resulting in a reduction in real GDP and in the price level. Eventually, though, the short-run aggregate supply curve shifts downward, and the new equilibrium is at *LRAS* but at an even lower price level. Expansionary monetary policy works the opposite way if we are starting out in both long-run and short-run equilibrium. The end result is simply a higher price level rather than a change in the equilibrium level of real GDP per year.

6. If expansionary monetary policy reduces U.S. interest rates, there is a positive net-export effect because foreigners will demand fewer U.S. financial instruments, thereby demanding fewer dollars and hence causing the international price of the dollar to fall. This makes our exports cheaper for the rest of the world. Thus the net-export effect of expansionary monetary policy may be positive.

7. Expansionary monetary policy during periods of underutilized resources can cause the equilibrium level of real GDP to increase up to that rate of real output consistent with the vertical long-run aggregate supply curve.

8. The equation of exchange states that the expenditures by some people will equal income receipts by others: $M_s V = PQ$ (money supply times velocity equals nominal national income). Viewed as an accounting identity, the equation of exchange is always correct because the amount of money spent on final output must equal the total amount of money received for final output.

9. The crude quantity theory of money and prices states that a change in the money supply will bring about a proportional change in the price level.

10. In the Keynesian model, monetary transmission operates through a change in the interest rates, which changes investment, causing a multiple change in national income.

11. Monetarists believe that changes in the money supply lead to changes in nominal GDP in the same direction. The effect is direct because individuals have excess money balances that they spend on cars, stereos, houses, and other things. Monetarists, among others, argue in favor of a monetary rule—an increase in the money supply smoothly at a rate consistent with the economy's long-run average growth rate. Monetarists do not believe in discretionary monetary (or fiscal) policy.

DISCUSSION OF PREVIEW POINTS

1. What is the demand for money curve, and how is it related to the interest rate?

Three types of demands—transactions, precautionary, and asset—motivate people to hold money, and each type provides benefits to money holders. Because people get paid at discrete intervals but want to make expenditures more or less continuously, they find it convenient to hold a stock of money (transactions demand); the benefit they receive is *convenience*. People also desire a pool of readily available purchasing power in order to meet emergencies (precautionary demand); the benefit is a measure of security. Finally, money is an asset; it is a means of storing value or wealth. At certain times money becomes a superior form of wealth—superior to other asset forms (bonds, stocks, real estate, and the like) that are risky. Asset demand money holders receive the benefit of *liquidity*. However, there is an opportunity cost to holding money (especially the narrow form of money, M1). The opportunity cost is forgone interest. The demand for money curve shows an inverse relationship between the interest rate and desired money holdings. As the interest rate falls, the opportunity cost of holding money falls concomitantly; people are more and more disposed to avail themselves of the benefits of holding money as the cost of doing so falls.

2. Why is the price of existing bonds inversely related to the interest rate?

Suppose that you know nothing about some faraway planet except that a bond (or an investment project) there yields $100 per year forever. Can you determine whether that bond or investment project will have a high price; that is, will it be "valuable"? No, you can't; you would have to know what the interest rate was on that planet. If interest rates are very, very low, say, one-thousandth of 1 percent, that bond or investment would be very valuable indeed. This is because the interest rate summarizes the opportunity cost for investment projects or bonds; if interest rates are very low, a given amount of money can earn very little annually, but if interest rates are very high, a given amount of money can earn a great deal annually. Thus $100 per year looks good (high) or bad (low) depending on whether prevailing interest rates are low or high, respectively. The nature of a bond is such that it yields a given and known stream of revenues (nominal dollar amounts) over time. This given revenue stream will be priced relatively high if interest rates are relatively low and will command a low price if interest rates are high. In

short, an inverse relationship exists between the price (market value) of an existing bond and the prevailing economywide interest rate.

3. How do the supply of and demand for money determine the interest rate?

The accompanying graph depicts the total supply and demand for money in an economy. To demonstrate that given these supply and demand for money schedules, the equilibrium interest rate will eventually be established at i_e, we must rule out all other possible interest rates. Thus let i_2 represent any interest rates below i_e. At i_2 the group wants to hold more money than is actually available ($M_d = 300 > M_s = 200$), and a shortage of liquidity exists. People become more liquid (hold more cash) by selling bonds (converting bonds, which are nonmoney, into money). As many people try to become more liquid, they attempt to sell many bonds. This forces bond prices down and interest rates up. These same conditions exist at all interest rates below i_e. Similarly, at all interest rates above i_e (i_1 in particular), $M_s > M_d$, and the group will be holding more money than it wants to hold to meet the three money-holding demands. Hence many people will buy bonds (to rid themselves of the opportunity cost of holding money), forcing bond prices up—and interest rates down toward i_e. At i_e, $M_d = M_s = 200$, and the group is voluntarily holding the available money supply.

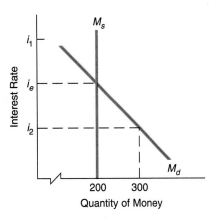

4. What is a monetarist?

Monetarists are economists who maintain that changes in the money supply are the *primary* influence on the levels of employment, output, and prices. They maintain that there is little theoretical or empirical evidence to indicate the effectiveness of fiscal policy. Moreover, they maintain that monetary policy is not desirable either. This is because the time lag between changes in the money supply and changes in these macroeconomic variables is too long and imprecise and that control of the money supply is not independent of politics. Consequently, present-day monetarists suggest that the government get out of the stabilization business; governments should use neither fiscal nor monetary policy. Instead, they maintain, governments should only raise taxes and make expenditures for pressing social matters (national defense, welfare, and so on), and monetary authorities should be commanded to increase the money supply at some constant and predetermined rate.

PROBLEMS
(Answers to the odd-numbered problems appear at the back of the book.)

16-1. Assume that the following conditions exist:
   a. All banks are fully loaned up—there are no excess reserves, and desired excess reserves are always zero.
   b. The money multiplier is 3.
   c. The planned investment schedule is such that at 10 percent, investment is $200 billion; at 9 percent, investment is $225 billion.
   d. The investment multiplier is 3.
   e. The initial equilibrium level of national income is $2 trillion.
   f. The equilibrium rate of interest is 10 percent.
   Now the Fed engages in expansionary monetary policy. It buys $1 billion worth of bonds, which increases the money supply, which in turn lowers the market rate of interest by 1 percent. Indicate by how much the money supply increased, and then trace out the numerical consequences of the associated reduction in interest rates on all the other variables mentioned.

16-2. The equation that indicates the value (price) right now of a nonmaturing bond (called a consol) is

$V = R/i$, where V is the present value, R is the annual net income generated from the bond, and i is the going interest rate.
   a. Assume that a bond promises the holder $1,000 per year forever. If the interest rate is 10 percent, what is the bond worth now?
   b. Continuing part (a), what happens to the value of the bond if interest rates rise to 20 percent? What if they fall to 5 percent?
   c. Suppose there were an indestructible machine that was expected to generate $2,000 per year in revenues but costs $1,000 per year to maintain—forever. How would that machine be priced relative to the bond described in part (a)?

16-3. Show in the form of a chart the processes by which the Fed can reduce inflationary pressures by raising the discount rate.

16-4. Assume that $M = $300 billion, $P = $1.72, and $Q = 900$ billion units. What is the income velocity of money?

16-5. Briefly outline the Keynesian transmission mechanism.

COMPUTER-ASSISTED INSTRUCTION
(Complete problem and answer on disk.)

The basic comparative statics implications of changes in monetary policy are demonstrated with extensive use of graphics. An additional series of questions illustrates the operation of the basic tools of the Federal Reserve System.

-- -- -- -- -- -- -- -- -- --

MONETARY POLICY:
A KEYNESIAN PERSPECTIVE

According to the traditional Keynesian approach to monetary policy, changes in the money supply can affect the level of aggregate demand only through their effect on interest rates. Moreover, interest rate changes act on aggregate demand solely by changing the level of investment spending. Finally, the traditional Keynesian approach argues that there exist plausible circumstances under which monetary policy may have little or no effects on aggregate demand.

Figure D-1 measures real national income along the horizontal axis and total planned expenditures (aggregate demand) along the vertical axis. The components of aggregate demand are consumption (C), investment (I), government spending (G), and net exports (X). The height of the schedule labeled $C + I + G + X$ shows total planned expenditures (aggregate demand) as a function of income. This schedule slopes upward because consumption depends positively on income. Everywhere along the line labeled "$Y = C + I + G + X$," planned spending equals income. At point Y^*, where the $C + I + G + X$ line intersects the 45-degree reference line, planned spending is consistent with income. At any income less than Y^*, spending exceeds income, so income and thus spending will tend to rise. At any level of income greater than Y^*, planned spending is less than income, so income and thus spending will tend to decline. Given the determinants of C, I, G, and X, total spending (aggregate demand) will be Y^*.

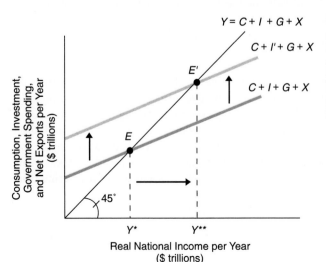

FIGURE D-1
An increase in the money supply.
An increase in the money supply increases income by lowering interest rates and thus increasing investment from I to I'.

INCREASING THE MONEY SUPPLY

According to the Keynesian approach, an increase in the money supply pushes interest rates down. This reduces the cost of borrowing and thus induces firms to increase the level of investment spending from I to I'. As a result, the $C + I + G + X$ line shifts upward in Figure D-1 by the full amount of the rise in investment spending, yielding the line $C + I' + G + X$. The rise in investment spending causes income to rise, which in turn causes consumption spending to rise, which further increases income. Ultimately, aggregate demand rises to Y^{**}, where spending again equals income. A key conclusion of the Keynesian analysis is that total spending rises by *more* than the original rise in investment spending because consumption spending depends positively on income.

DECREASING THE MONEY SUPPLY

Not surprisingly, contractionary monetary policy works in exactly the reverse manner. A reduction in the money supply pushes interest rates up, which increases the cost of borrowing. Firms respond by reducing their investment spending, and this starts income downward. Consumers react to the lower income by scaling back on their consumption spending, which further depresses income. Thus the ultimate decline in income is larger than the initial drop in investment spending. Indeed, because the change in income is a multiple of the change in investment, Keynesians note that changes in investment spending (similar to changes in government spending) have a *multiplier* effect on the economy.

ARGUMENTS AGAINST MONETARY POLICY

It might be thought that this multiplier effect would make monetary policy a potent tool in the Keynesian arsenal, particularly when it comes to getting the economy out of a recession. In fact, however, many traditional Keynesians argue that monetary policy is likely to be relatively ineffective as a recession fighter. According to their line of reasoning, although monetary policy has the potential to reduce interest rates, changes in the money supply have little actual impact on interest rates. Instead, during recessions, people try to build up as many liquid assets as they can, to protect themselves from risks of unemployment and other losses of income. Thus when the monetary authorities increase the money supply, individuals are willing to allow most of it to accumulate in their bank accounts. This desire for liquidity thus prevents interest rates from falling very much, which in turn means that there will be virtually no change in investment spending and thus little change in aggregate demand.

THE LIQUIDITY TRAP

In the limiting case, people may be willing to hold *all* of the extra money at current interest rates, so that rates do not decline at all. This circumstance is known as a *liquidity trap*. It prevents monetary policy from having any potency in raising the economy out of recession because in the traditional Keynesian view, monetary policy can have no impact on aggregate demand unless it changes interest rates. Although it is unlikely that a complete liquidity trap has ever been observed, the mere fact that it is possible makes many traditional Keynesians reluctant to rely on monetary policy as a means of recovering from recessions.

NEW DIRECTIONS IN MACRO POLICY ANALYSIS

There was a time when a college degree seemed to be a guarantee of an exciting job at a high wage. In contrast, today's students often worry whether there will be any job at any wage. And for those who find employment, it is often only after many weeks or months of diligent searching. There are serious questions that every college graduate must ask: Should I go into the labor market immediately after graduation, and if so, what is the minimum annual salary that I should accept for employment? If I do not want to go into the labor force, should I take a low-paying or unremunerated internship, join the Peace Corps, or go to graduate school? To answer such questions, it is helpful to understand a theory of job search, which is only one part of an analysis of the new directions in macro policy thinking.

After reading this chapter, you should be able to answer the following questions:

1. What does the rational expectations hypothesis say about people's forecasting errors?

2. How do the new classical economists view economic policy?

3. What does the real business cycle theory have to say about the causes of recession?

4. How does new Keynesian economics explain the stickiness of wages and prices?

INTRODUCTION

Each year thousands of individuals graduate from college and begin work at a full-time job. If you are an undergraduate, when you graduate the transition may be smooth and painless or it may be arduous and time-consuming. You might pick up your degree one week and your first paycheck the next. Or you might remain unemployed for many weeks or months after graduation. Despite the possible variety of job market experiences that you might face as a college graduate, the one thing that you and every other person searching for a job learns is that information about job opportunities is a scarce good. Because this is true, individuals must *search* for information about job opportunities. Moreover, they are sometimes surprised by what they learn in the job market and thus take a job far sooner than they expected or search for a job far longer than they had hoped.

This process is mirrored every day throughout the economy as millions of people actively search for information about job opportunities. Many of them—perhaps 5 to 10 percent of the labor force—are recorded as unemployed. But all of them are responding to the scarcity of information by investing their time, money, and shoe leather in looking not just for jobs but for jobs that are better than the ones they already know about.

Ordinarily, this process takes place without much fanfare. But when the economy is in a recession, the process of job search and the accompanying unemployment are often in the headlines and sometimes are factors in determining who will occupy the White House. Clearly, the success or failure of an individual in searching for job information plays a key role in determining that person's well-being and happiness. And because millions of people are similarly engaged at any point in time, their combined successes and failures can be critical in determining the overall health of the economy. Given the importance of the job search process, it is essential that we develop an understanding of how the process works and what can happen to make it go wrong. Along the way, we will journey to the very frontiers of macro policy analysis.

JOB SEARCH AND UNEMPLOYMENT

When you graduate from college, you will think in terms of finding a job. But of course, you are not looking for just any job; you are looking for the *best* job. Finding a job is typically a simple but unrewarding matter. Fast-food restaurants, car washes, janitorial and lawn services, and numerous other employers are almost always hiring people, even when the economy is in a recession. If you are like most people, however, whether entering the labor force initially or moving between jobs in mid-career, it is extremely unlikely that the first job you stumble on will be the right job for you. But if you don't simply take the first job you find, two questions arise: First, how should you decide which job to accept? Second, how long is it likely to take to find that job? Not surprisingly, the answers to both questions can be framed in terms of costs and benefits. But to answer these questions, we need to develop an explicit model, called a *job search model.*

THE JOB SEARCH MODEL

To keep things as simple as possible, we will assume that jobs differ only in the salaries they offer. Clearly, there are many other characteristics of jobs that are important, but by focusing solely on salary, the analysis will be much easier. We also assume that once the job seeker has found a given job offer, the employer is willing to hold the offer open until the job seeker has decided whether or not to accept the offer. Finally, we assume that the job search takes place while the searcher is unemployed. Although some people do

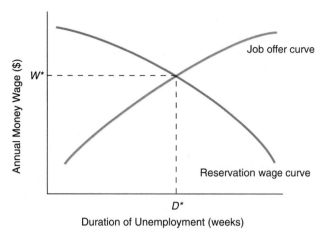

FIGURE 17-1
Optimal duration of unemployment.
The intersection of the job offer curve and the reservation wage curve determines the optimal duration of unemployment, D^*.

move directly from one job to another without any intervening unemployment, people are often jobless for some period of time between jobs, particularly when changing employers.

Job Offer Curve.   With these assumptions in mind, imagine the process of accumulating information about jobs. As you call, write, or visit each potential employer, you find out whether or not there are job openings and what the available jobs pay. You keep track of this information, and at the end of each day you write down the highest salary you have been offered thus far. If we were to plot these best offers as a function of the time you have been searching, you would have something like the **job offer curve** in Figure 17-1. This curve shows, for any given duration of search, the highest-paying job offer received thus far. There are two key features of the job curve. First, as the duration of search increases, the highest salary offered rises: The curve is positively sloped. Second, as the period of search gets longer, the offers improve by smaller and smaller increments: The curve gets flatter moving from left to right.

> **Job offer curve**
> The curve showing over time the highest-paying job offers obtainable by a job searcher. As the duration of unemployment increases, the expected wage offers also increase.

Reservation Wage Curve.   Presumably, when you start the job search process, you have some notion, correct or not, of what you are worth. The minimum wage or salary at which you would accept a job offer is called your **reservation wage.** If we were to plot your reservation wage as a function of the length of time spent searching for a job, we would have your **reservation wage curve.** As shown in Figure 17-1, it is downward-sloping: The longer the duration of search, the lower will be the wage at which an individual would accept employment. There are several reasons why this reservation wage curve is likely to be downward-sloping for you, just as it is for other individuals:

> **Reservation wage**
> The lowest wage that an unemployed worker will accept in a job offer.

> **Reservation wage curve**
> A downward-sloping curve showing the relationship between the reservation wage and the duration of unemployment.

1. Many people support themselves out of their savings as they search for new jobs; as the duration of search increases, there is an increasing chance that they will be forced to take jobs simply to avoid financial ruin.

2. Most people don't spend every spare minute between jobs searching for their next job. Instead, while they are unemployed, they also spend more time with their families, do repairs around the house, engage in community service work, and possibly even catch up on their favorite leisure activities. As the duration of unemployment increases the marginal value to them of these activities declines, thereby reducing the lowest wage at which they would accept employment.

3. As the period of unemployment lengthens, someone looking for work faces the prospect that his or her job skills will deteriorate from lack of use. Just to protect the market value of their skills, individuals are likely to become less demanding, and thus willing to accept a lower wage as the duration of search increases.

Optimal Duration of Unemployment.   Like most things in life, searching for a job involves trade-offs—there are costs and benefits. The job offer curve shows the best you can do if you stop searching and accept a job in hand. The reservation wage curve shows the best you can do if you remain unemployed and continue to look for a job. Eventually the two curves cross, as shown in Figure 17-1, at point D^*. We say that D^* is the optimal (or best) duration of unemployment, once both the costs and benefits of being unemployed have been taken into account.

Let's consider for a moment why D^* is superior to unemployment durations that are either longer or shorter. Suppose that you search for a period shorter than D^*. The height of the reservation wage curve is the benefit—as judged by you—of continuing to search. The height of the job offer curve is the benefit of taking a job (ending your search). For search durations less than D^*, the benefit of search (the height of the reservation wage) exceeds the benefit of taking a job, so it pays to continue searching. Conversely, if we consider durations greater than D^*, we have the reverse circumstances: The benefits of the last unit of search are less than the benefits of being in a job; thus search time should be reduced.

It is true that if you were to search for a year rather than a month, there is perhaps a small chance that you would discover a job that paid more than any other for a person of your qualifications and experience; but there is also a very large chance that you would go bankrupt before you found that job. As the old saying goes, "A bird in the hand is worth two in the bush," and so you sensibly cut short your job search well before finding the job that might pay more than all other jobs.

VOLUNTARY UNEMPLOYMENT

It is important to recognize that while you or anyone else is engaged in this type of job search, the accompanying unemployment is *voluntary,* in the sense that D^* is chosen as the amount of unemployment that is best under the circumstances. Note also that even though jobs are being turned down up to duration D^*, this is quite rational, for the expected benefits of turning them down exceed the expected costs. Although it may seem strange to think in terms of an optimal duration of unemployment, an example may help you understand. Hardly anybody actually enjoys studying. Nevertheless, given the benefits and costs of studying, it makes sense to think in terms of there being an optimal amount of study time. Life would be better if you could get straight As without studying, but for most people that simply isn't possible; so instead of accepting the disastrous consequences of not studying at all, you willingly choose to study an amount that for you is the best (optimal) amount, given the circumstances you face. Similarly, unemployment is not pleasant, but there is an optimal duration for each person out of a job.

Different people will have different optimal durations of unemployment, depending on their savings, the rate at which their job skills deteriorate while unemployed, and other factors. The overall economywide duration of unemployment will be an average of individual durations. What we want to do next is to see how changes in the national economy affect the individual's decisions about unemployment, which in turn affect the overall unemployment rate for the economy as a whole.

CONCEPTS IN BRIEF

- The longer an individual searches for job information, the higher will be the best wage offer that person receives. The schedule depicting the best offer received as a function of duration of search is called the job offer curve.
- The lowest wage at which an unemployed individual will accept a job is called that person's reservation wage; as the duration of unemployment rises, the person's reservation wage declines. The schedule depicting the relationship between the reservation wage and the duration of unemployment is called the reservation wage curve.
- The optimal duration of unemployment occurs where the individual's job offer and reservation wage curves intersect.
- Much of the unemployment that we observe is voluntary in the sense that job searchers are choosing that unemployment; under the existing circumstances, these individuals would be made worse off if they were forced to search longer or were prevented from searching as long.

THE NATURAL RATE OF UNEMPLOYMENT

The type of unemployment we have been discussing is sometimes called *search unemployment* or *frictional unemployment.* It has been given these names because individuals are searching for the best job opportunities in the presence of "frictions" (costs of information). Except when the economy is in a recession or a depression, most unemployment is of this type.

Note that we did not say that search unemployment was the sole form of unemployment during normal times. There is also *structural unemployment,* caused by a variety of "rigidities" throughout the economy. Structural unemployment results from factors such as these:

1. Union activity that sets wages above the equilibrium level and also restricts the mobility of labor
2. Government-imposed licensing arrangements that restrict entry into specific occupations or professions
3. Government-imposed minimum wage laws and other laws that require all workers to be paid union wage rates on government contract jobs
4. Welfare and unemployment insurance benefits that reduce incentives to work

In each case, these factors reduce individuals' abilities or incentives to choose employment rather than unemployment.

Frictional and structural unemployment both exist even when the economy is in long-run equilibrium—they are a natural consequence of costly information and the existence of rigidities such as those noted above. If we add up these two types of unemployment and divide by the labor force, we can calculate the **natural rate of unemployment.** It is simply the unemployment rate that exists in long-run equilibrium. Just as output tends to return to the level implied by the long-run aggregate supply curve, the unemployment rate tends to return to the natural rate of unemployment.

▶ **Natural rate of unemployment**
That rate of measured unemployment that is estimated to prevail in long-run macroeconomic equilibrium with no money illusion, when employees and employers both correctly anticipate the rate of inflation.

DEPARTURES FROM THE NATURAL RATE OF UNEMPLOYMENT

Even though the unemployment rate has a strong tendency to stay at and return to the natural rate, it is possible for fiscal and monetary policy to move the actual unemployment

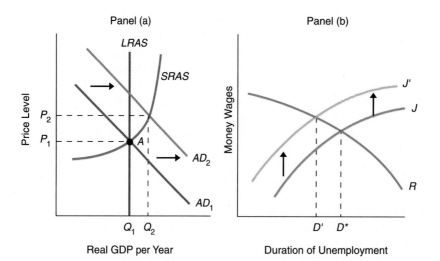

FIGURE 17-2
The impact of a rise in aggregate demand on unemployment.
A rise in aggregate demand shifts the job offer curve upward and thus reduces the duration and amount of unemployment.

rate away from the natural rate, at least in the short run. Deviations of the actual unemployment rate from the natural rate are called **cyclical unemployment,** because they are observed over the course of the national business fluctuations. During recessions, the overall unemployment rate exceeds the natural rate; cyclical unemployment is positive. During periods of economic booms, the overall unemployment rate can go below the natural rate; at such times, the cyclical unemployment rate is in essence negative.

▶ **Cyclical unemployment**
Unemployment resulting from business recessions that occur when aggregate (total) demand is insufficient to create full employment.

To see how departures from the natural rate of unemployment can occur, let's consider two examples. Referring to panel (a) of Figure 17-2, we begin in equilibrium at point A, with the associated price level P_1 and real GDP per year of level Q_1. Panel (b) of Figure 17-2 illustrates the associated search by individuals for information about job opportunities, with D^* reflecting the actual duration of search undertaken by a representative individual. Thus D^* is the average duration of search, given that the economy is in long-run equilibrium at a point such as A.

The Impact of Expansionary Policy.

Now imagine that the government decides to use fiscal or monetary policy to stimulate the economy. Further suppose, for reasons that will soon become clear, that this policy surprises decision makers throughout the economy in the sense that they did not anticipate that the policy would occur. The aggregate demand curve shifts from AD_1 to AD_2 in panel (a) of Figure 17-2, so both the price level and real GDP rise to P_2 and Q_2. In the labor market, individuals would find that conditions had improved markedly relative to what they expected. Firms seeking to expand output will want to hire more workers. To accomplish this, they will recruit more actively and possibly even offer higher nominal wages, so that individuals in the labor market will find more job openings and higher nominal wages at those jobs. From the perspective of the individual, the job offer curve, J, shifts upward, as from J to J' in panel (b) of Figure 17-2. As a result, individuals accept jobs sooner (the duration of search falls from D^* to D'), and the unemployment rate falls. Matching up both sides of the picture, we see that this unexpected, or surprise, increase in aggregate demand simultaneously causes the price level to rise to P_2 [in panel (a)] and the unemployment rate to fall.

The Consequences of Contractionary Policy.

Instead of expansionary policy, the government could have decided to engage in contractionary (or deflationary) policy. As shown in Figure 17-3, the sequence of events would have been in the opposite direction of those in Figure 17-2. Again, beginning from an initial equilibrium A in panel

FIGURE 17-3
The impact of a decline in aggregate demand on unemployment.
A decline in aggregate demand shifts the job offer curve downward and thus increases the duration and amount of unemployment.

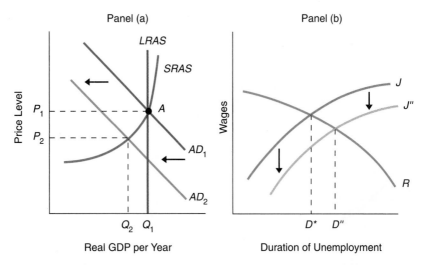

Panel (a)   Panel (b)

(a), an unanticipated reduction in aggregate demand puts downward pressure on both prices and real GDP; the price level falls to P_2, and real GDP declines to Q_2. Fewer firms will be hiring, and those that are hiring will be inclined to offer lower wages. Individuals looking for jobs will find that the job offer curve has shifted downward to J'' in panel (b). As a result, individuals remain unemployed longer (the duration of search rises from D^* to D''), and so the unemployment rate rises. Matching up both sides of the picture, we see that this unexpected decrease in demand simultaneously causes the price level to fall and the unemployment rate to rise.

THE PHILLIPS CURVE

Let's recap what we have just observed. An *unexpected* increase in aggregate demand causes the price level to rise and the unemployment rate to fall. Conversely, an *unexpected* decrease in aggregate demand causes the price level to fall and the unemployment rate to rise. Moreover, although not shown explicitly in either diagram, two additional points are true:

1. The greater the increase in aggregate demand, the greater will be the amount of inflation that results, and the lower will be the unemployment rate.
2. The greater the decrease in aggregate demand, the greater will be the deflation that results, and the higher will be the unemployment rate.

The Negative Relationship Between Inflation and Unemployment.
Figure 17-4 on the next page summarizes these findings. The inflation rate (*not* the price level) is measured along the vertical axis, and the unemployment rate is measured along the horizontal axis. Point E shows an initial starting point, with the unemployment rate at the natural rate, U^*. Note that as a matter of convenience, we are starting from an equilibrium in which the price level is stable (the inflation rate is zero). Unexpected increases in aggregate demand cause the price level to rise—the inflation rate becomes positive—and cause the unemployment rate to fall. Thus the economy moves up to the left from E to E'. Conversely, unexpected decreases in aggregate demand cause the price level to fall and the unemployment rate to rise above the natural rate—the economy moves from point E to the point E''. If we look at both increases and decreases in aggregate demand, we see that high inflation rates tend to be associated with low unemployment rates (as at E') and that low (or negative) inflation rates tend to be accompanied by high unemployment rates (as at E'').

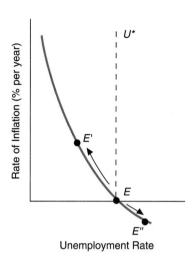

FIGURE 17-4
The Phillips curve.
Unanticipated changes in aggregate demand produce a negative relationship between the inflation rate and unemployment. U^* is the natural rate of unemployment.

Is There a Trade-off?   The apparent negative relation between the inflation rate and the unemployment rate shown in Figure 17-4 has come to be called the **Phillips curve,** after A. W. Phillips, who discovered that a similar relationship existed historically in Great Britain. Although Phillips presented his findings only as an empirical regularity, economists quickly came to view the relationship as representing a *trade-off* between inflation and unemployment. In particular, policymakers believed they could *choose* alternative combinations of unemployment and inflation. Thus it seemed that a government that disliked unemployment could select a point like E' in Figure 17-4, with a positive inflation rate but a relatively low unemployment rate. Conversely, a government that feared inflation could choose a stable price level at E, but only at the expense of a higher associated unemployment rate. Indeed, the Phillips curve seemed to suggest that it was possible for policymakers to fine-tune the economy by selecting the policies that would produce the exact mix of unemployment and inflation that suited current government objectives. As it turned out, matters are not this simple.

THE IMPORTANCE OF EXPECTATIONS

The reduction in unemployment that takes place as the economy moves from E to E' in Figure 17-4 occurs because the wage offers encountered by unemployed workers are unexpectedly high. As far as the workers are concerned, these higher *nominal* wages appear, at least initially, to be increases in *real* wages; it is this fact that induces them to reduce their duration of search. This is a sensible way for the workers to view the world if aggregate demand fluctuates up and down at random, with no systematic or predictable variation one way or another. But if policymakers attempt to exploit the apparent trade-off in the Phillips curve, aggregate demand will no longer move up and down in an unpredictable way.

The Effects of an Unanticipated Policy.   Consider Figure 17-5, for example. If the Federal Reserve attempts to reduce the unemployment rate to U_1, it must increase the money supply enough to produce an inflation rate of π_1. If this is a one-shot affair in which the money supply is first increased and then held constant, the inflation rate will temporarily rise to π_1 and the unemployment rate will temporarily fall to U_1; but as soon as the money supply stops growing, the inflation rate will return to zero and unemployment will return to U^*, its natural rate. Thus a one-shot increase in the money supply will move the economy from point E to point E', and the economy will move of its own accord back to E.

▶ **Phillips curve**
A curve showing the relationship between unemployment and changes in wages or prices. It was long thought to reflect a trade-off between unemployment and inflation.

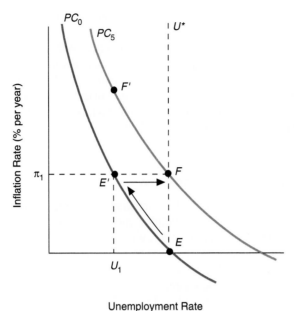

FIGURE 17-5
**A shift in the Phillips
curve.**
When there is a change in
the expected inflation
rate, the Phillips curve
(*PC*) shifts to incorporate
the new expectations.
PC$_0$ shows expectations
of zero inflation; *PC*$_5$ reflects an expected infla-
tion rate of 5 percent.

If the authorities wish to prevent the unemployment rate from returning to U^*, it appears that they must keep the money supply growing fast enough to keep the inflation rate up at π_1. But if they do this, all of the economic participants in the economy—workers and job seekers included—will come to *expect* that inflation rate to continue. This in turn will change their expectations about wages. For example, suppose that $\pi_1 = 5$ percent per year. When the expected inflation rate was zero, a 5 percent rise in nominal wages meant a 5 percent expected rise in real wages, and this was sufficient to induce some individuals to take jobs rather than remain unemployed. It was this perception of a rise in real wages that reduced search duration and caused the unemployment rate to drop from U^* to U_1. But if the expected inflation rate becomes 5 percent, a 5 percent rise in nominal wages means *no* rise in *real* wages. Once workers come to expect the higher inflation rate, the rising nominal wages will no longer be sufficient to entice them out of unemployment. As a result, as the *expected* inflation rate moves up from 0 percent to 5 percent, the unemployment rate will move up also.

The Role of Expected Inflation.   In terms of Figure 17-5, as authorities initially increase aggregate demand, the economy moves from point E to point E'. If the authorities continue the stimulus in an effort to keep the unemployment rate down, workers' expectations will adjust, causing the unemployment rate to rise. In this second stage, the economy moves from E' to point F: The unemployment rate returns to the natural rate, U^*, but the inflation rate is now π_1, instead of zero. Once the adjustment of expectations has taken place, any further changes in policy will have to take place along a curve such as PC_5. This new schedule is also a Phillips curve, differing from the first, PC_0, in that the actual inflation rate consistent with any given unemployment rate is higher because the expected inflation rate is higher.

Not surprisingly, when economic policymakers found that economic participants engaged in such adjustment behavior, they were both surprised and dismayed. If decision makers can adjust their expectations to conform with fiscal and monetary policies, then policymakers cannot choose a permanently lower unemployment rate of U_1, even if they are willing to tolerate an inflation rate of π_1. Instead, the policymakers would end up with an unchanged unemployment rate in the long run, at the expense of a permanently higher inflation rate.

Initially, however, there did seem to be a small consolation, for it appeared that in the short run—before expectations adjusted—the unemployment rate could be *temporarily* reduced from U^* to U_1, even though eventually it would return to the natural rate. If an important national election were approaching, it might be possible to stimulate the economy long enough to get the unemployment rate low enough to assure reelection. However, policymakers came to learn that not even this was likely to be a sure thing.

⭐ EXAMPLE: The Phillips Curve Then and Now

In separate 1968 articles, Milton Friedman and E. S. Phelps published pioneering studies suggesting that the apparent trade-off suggested by the Phillips curve could not be exploited by policymakers. Friedman and Phelps both argued that any attempt to reduce unemployment by inflating the economy would soon be thwarted by economic participants incorporating the new higher inflation rate into their expectations. The Friedman-Phelps research thus implies that for any given unemployment rate, *any* inflation rate is possible, depending on the actions of policymakers. As reflected in Figure 17-6, Friedman and Phelps were to prove remarkably accurate.

In panel (a) we plot the inflation and unemployment rates for the United States during the 1950s and 1960s. We have also drawn a line showing the negative relationship between them for that period. Policymakers of the time noticed this negative relationship and attempted to exploit it by stimulating aggregate demand. This caused inflation to rise and, it would appear, induced economic participants to revise their forecasts accordingly. In panel (b) we include the data on inflation and unemployment for the ensuing years. Clearly the negative relationship is gone: Once policymakers attempted to exploit the Phillips curve, the apparent trade-off disappeared.

For Critical Analysis: Do the data shown in panel (b) of Figure 17-6 support or refute the arguments presented by supporters of a monetary rule discussed in Chapter 16? ●

CONCEPTS IN BRIEF

- The natural rate of unemployment is the rate that exists in long-run equilibrium, when workers' expectations are consistent with actual conditions.
- Departures from the natural rate of unemployment can occur when individuals are surprised by unanticipated changes in fiscal or monetary policy; an unexpected rise in aggregate demand will reduce unemployment below the natural rate, whereas an unanticipated decrease in aggregate demand will push unemployment above the natural rate.
- The Phillips curve exhibits a negative relationship between the inflation rate and the unemployment rate that can be observed when there are *unanticipated* changes in aggregate demand.
- It was originally believed that the Phillips curve represented a trade-off between inflation and unemployment. In fact, no useful trade-off exists because workers' expectations adjust to any systematic attempts to reduce unemployment below the natural rate.

FIGURE 17-6
**The disappearing
Phillips curve.**
Until about 1970, there
seemed to be a trade-off
between inflation and un-
employment, as shown in
panel (a). The relationship
disappears once we add
the data for the years
since then, in panel (b).

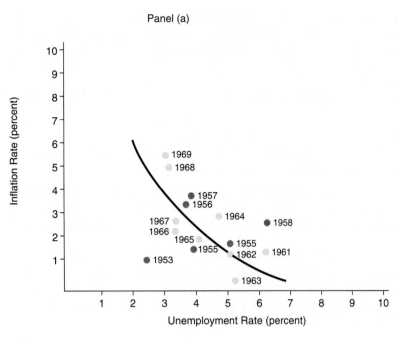

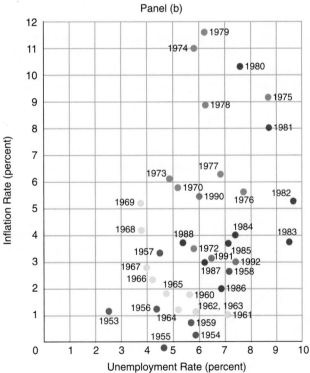

RATIONAL EXPECTATIONS AND THE NEW CLASSICAL MODEL

You already know that economists assume that economic participants act as *though* they were rational and calculating. We think of firms that rationally maximize profits when they choose today's rate of output and consumers who rationally maximize utility when they choose how much of what goods to consume today. One of the pivotal features of current macro policy research is the assumption that rationality also applies to the way that economic participants think about the future as well as the present. In particular, there is widespread agreement among many leading macro researchers that the **rational expectations hypothesis** extends our understanding of the behavior of the macroeconomy. There are two key elements to this hypothesis:

1. Individuals base their forecasts (or expectations) about the future values of economic variables on all available past and current information.
2. These expectations incorporate individuals' understanding about how the economy operates, including the operation of monetary and fiscal policy.

In essence, the rational expectations hypothesis assumes that Abraham Lincoln was correct when he stated, "It is true that you may fool all the people some of the time; you can even fool some of the people all of the time; but you can't fool all of the people all of the time."

If we further assume that there is pure competition in all markets and that all prices and wages are flexible, we obtain the **new classical model** (referred to in Chapter 12 when discussing the Ricardian equivalence theorem). To see how rational expectations operate within the context of this model, let's take a simple example of the economy's response to a change in monetary policy.

> ▶ **Rational expectations hypothesis**
> A theory stating that people combine the effects of past policy changes on important economic variables with their own judgment about the future effects of current and future policy changes.

> ▶ **New classical model**
> A modern version of the classical model in which wages and prices are flexible and there is pure competition in all markets. Furthermore, the rational expectations hypothesis is assumed to be working.

THE NEW CLASSICAL MODEL

Consider Figure 17-7, which shows the long-run aggregate supply curve (*LRAS*) for the economy, as well as the initial aggregate demand curve (*AD*$_1$) and the short-run aggregate supply curve (*SRAS*$_1$). The money supply is initially given by $M = M'$, and the price level and real GDP are shown by P_1 and Q_1, respectively. Thus, point *A* represents the initial equilibrium.

Suppose now that the money supply is increased to M'', thereby causing the aggregate demand curve to shift outward to *AD*$_2$. Given the location of the short-run aggregate supply curve, this increase in aggregate demand will cause output and the price level to rise to Q_2 and P_2, respectively. The new short-run equilibrium is at *B*. Because output is *above*

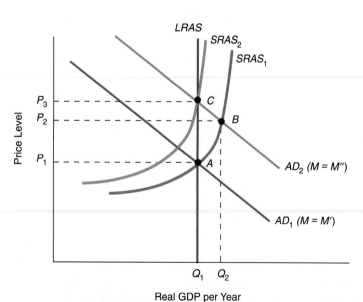

FIGURE 17-7
The response to an unanticipated rise in aggregate demand.
Unanticipated changes in aggregate demand have real effects. In this case, the rise in demand causes real output to rise from Q_1 to Q_2.

the long-run equilibrium level of Q_1, unemployment must be below long-run levels (the natural rate), and so workers will soon respond to the higher price level by demanding higher nominal wages. This will cause the short-run aggregate supply curve to shift upward vertically, moving the economy to the new long-run equilibrium at C. The price level thus continues its rise to P_3, even as real GDP declines back down to Q_1 (and unemployment returns to the natural rate). So, as we have seen before, even though an increase in the money supply can raise output and lower unemployment in the short run, it has no effect on either variable in the long run.

The Response to Anticipated Policy.   Now let's look at this disturbance with the perspective given by the rational expectations hypothesis, as it is embedded in the new classical model. Suppose that workers (and other input owners) know ahead of time that this increase in the money supply is about to take place. Assume also that they know when it is going to occur and understand that its ultimate effect will be to push the price level from P_1 to P_3. Will workers wait until after the price level has increased to insist that their nominal wages go up? The rational expectations hypothesis says that they will not. Instead, they will go to employers and insist on nominal wages that move upward in step with the higher prices. From the workers' perspective, this is the only way to protect their real wages from declining due to the anticipated increase in the money supply.

The Policy Irrelevance Proposition.   As long as economic participants behave in this manner, when we draw the *SRAS* curve, we must be explicit about the nature of their expectations. This we have done in Figure 17-8. In the initial equilibrium, the short-run aggregate supply curve is labeled to show that the expected money supply (M_e) and the actual money supply (M') are equal ($M_e = M'$). Similarly, when the money supply changes in a way that is anticipated by economic participants, the aggregate supply curve shifts to reflect this expected change in the money supply. The new short-run aggregate

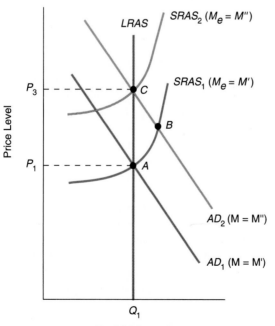

FIGURE 17-8
The effects of an anticipated rise in aggregate demand.
When policy is fully anticipated, a rise in the money supply causes a rise in the price level from P_1 to P_3, with no change in real output.

supply curve is labeled ($M_e = M''$) to reveal this. According to the rational expectations hypothesis, the short-run aggregate supply will shift upward *simultaneously* with the rise in aggregate demand. As a result, the economy will move directly from point A to point C in Figure 17-8 without passing through B: The *only* response to the rise in the money supply is a rise in the price level from P_1 to P_3; neither output nor unemployment changes at all. This conclusion—that fully anticipated monetary policy is irrelevant in determining the levels of real variables—is called the **policy irrelevance proposition:**

> Under the assumption of rational expectations on the part of decision makers in the economy, anticipated monetary policy cannot alter either the rate of unemployment or the level of real GDP. Regardless of the nature of the anticipated policy, the unemployment rate will equal the natural rate, and real GDP will be determined solely by the economy's long-run aggregate supply curve.

▶ **Policy irrelevance proposition**
The new classical conclusion that policy actions have no real effects in the short run if the policy actions were anticipated and none in the long run even if the policy actions were unanticipated.

What Must People Know?   There are two important matters to keep in mind when considering this proposition. First, our discussion has assumed that economic participants know in advance exactly what the change in monetary policy is going to be and precisely when it is going to occur. In fact, the Federal Reserve does not announce exactly what the future course of monetary policy (down to the last dollar) is going to be. Instead, the Fed tries to keep most of its plans secret, announcing only in general terms what policy actions are intended for the future. It is tempting to conclude that because the Fed's intended policies are not freely available, they are not available at all. But such a conclusion would be wrong. Economic participants have great incentives to learn how to predict the future behavior of the monetary authorities, just as businesses try to forecast consumer behavior and college students do their best to forecast what their next economics exam will look like. Even if the economic participants are not perfect at forecasting the course of policy, they are likely to come a lot closer than they would in total ignorance. The policy irrelevance proposition really assumes only that *people don't persistently make the same mistakes in forecasting the future.*

What Happens If People Don't Know Everything?   This brings us to our second point. Once we accept the fact that people are not perfect in their ability to predict the future, the possibility emerges that some policy actions will have systematic effects that look much like the movements A to B to C in Figure 17-7. For example, just as other economic participants sometimes make mistakes, it is likely that the Federal Reserve sometimes makes mistakes—meaning that the money supply may change in ways that even the Fed does not predict. And even if the Fed always accomplished every policy action it intended, there is no guarantee that other economic participants will fully forecast those actions. What happens if the Fed makes a mistake or if firms and workers misjudge the future course of policy? Matters will look much as they do in panel (a) of Figure 17-9, which shows the effects of an unanticipated increase in the money supply. Economic participants expect the money supply to be M_0, but the actual money supply turns out to be M_1. Because $M_1 > M_0$, aggregate demand shifts relative to aggregate supply. The result is a rise in real output (real GDP) in the short run from Q_1 to Q_2; corresponding to this rise in real output will be an increase in employment and hence a fall in the unemployment rate. So even under the rational expectations hypothesis, monetary policy *can* have an effect on real variables in the short run, but only if the policy is unsystematic and therefore unanticipated.

FIGURE 17-9
The effects of an unanticipated rise in aggregate demand.
Even with rational expectations, an unanticipated change in demand can affect output in the short-run.

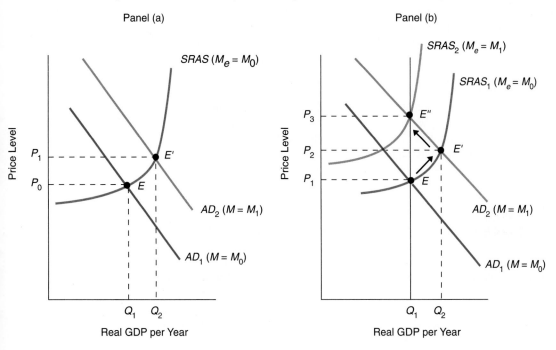

In the long run, even this short-run effect on real variables will disappear. This is because people will figure out that the Fed either accidentally increased the money supply or intentionally increased it in a way that somehow fooled individuals. Either way, people's expectations will soon be revised so that the short-run aggregate supply curve will shift upward far enough that real input prices return to their long-run equilibrium levels. As shown in panel (b) of Figure 17-9, real GDP will return to long-run levels, meaning that so too will the employment and unemployment rates.

THE POLICY DILEMMA

Perhaps the most striking and disturbing feature of the new classical model is that it seems to suggest that only mistakes can have real effects. If the Federal Reserve always does what it intends to do and if other economic participants always correctly anticipate the Fed's actions, monetary policy will affect only the price level and nominal input prices. It appears that only if the Fed makes a mistake in executing monetary policy or people err in anticipating that policy will changes in the money supply cause fluctuations in real output and employment. If this reasoning is correct, the Fed is effectively precluded from using monetary policy in any rational way to lower the unemployment rate or to raise the level of real GDP. This is because fully anticipated changes in the money supply will lead to exactly offsetting changes in prices and hence no real effects. Many economists were disturbed at the prospect that if the economy happened to enter a recessionary period, policymakers would be powerless to push GDP and unemployment back to long-run levels. As a result, they asked the question, In light of the rational expectations hypothesis, is it *ever* possible for systematic policy to have real effects on the economy? The answer has led to even more developments in the way we think about macroeconomics.

CONCEPTS IN BRIEF

- The rational expectations hypothesis assumes that individuals' forecasts include all available information, including an understanding of government policy and its effects on the economy.
- The new classical economics assumes that the rational expectations hypothesis is valid and also that there is pure competition and that all prices and wages are flexible.
- The policy irrelevance proposition says that under the assumptions of the new classical model, fully anticipated monetary policy cannot alter either the rate of unemployment or the level of real GDP.
- The new classical model implies that policies can alter real economic variables only if the policies are unsystematic and therefore unanticipated.

THE FRONTIERS OF MACROECONOMICS

National business fluctuations have been in existence for as long as we have data recording the state of the economy. Moreover, for at least two centuries, economists have sought to understand the nature and causes of these ups and downs in the economy. It is little surprise, then, that many economists were dissatisfied with the new classical model in its pure form. After all, the model says that fluctuations in real variables are the result of mistakes on the part of either policymakers or other economic participants. Moreover, the new classical model implies that once those mistakes have occurred, no rational, calculating policy can be employed to offset them. Was the Great Depression just one big mistake? Isn't it ever possible to improve the state of the economy with reasoned, judicious economic policy? Is there a systematic explanation for the existence of national business fluctuations? The search for answers to questions such as these is taking place today on the frontiers of macroeconomics.

RATIONAL CONTRACTING

The simplest objection to the core of the new classical economics is based on a remarkably obvious fact: The new classical model assumes that all prices and wages are perfectly flexible, as they would be if all goods and services were sold at auction each day. Taken to its logical extreme, the new classical model assumes that when college students show up for class each day, the tuition to be paid for that day's lecture is determined in an auction held just before the start of class. Similarly, when the professor shows up for class, the model implicitly assumes that her wage for the day is also determined on the spot.

The Importance of Contracts.   Such assumptions are clearly at odds with reality for many goods and services. Although some prices are in fact determined on a day-to-day basis (or a minute-by-minute basis, in the case of the stock market), most prices are not. Nominal prices and wages are often determined by *contracts,* either explicitly or implicitly. One obvious class of examples is found in union wage agreements, which specify nominal wages at from one to three years at a time. Similarly, many users of raw materials, including coal and oil, often sign contracts that specify nominal prices for extended periods of time, permitting purchasers to order and use as much of the raw materials as they see fit. Research that has focused on the importance of such contracts is called **rational contracting theory.**

▶ **Rational contracting theory**
A set of hypotheses that deals with the nominal wage that workers and firms would choose to set in a contractual agreement. The main requirement of this theory is that the chosen wage must be consistent with the rational behavior of workers and firms, that is, one based on their rational expectations of what economic conditions will be during the wage contract period.

FIGURE 17-10
The importance of contracts.
When preexisting contracts are important, monetary policy can have real effects even when expectations are rational.

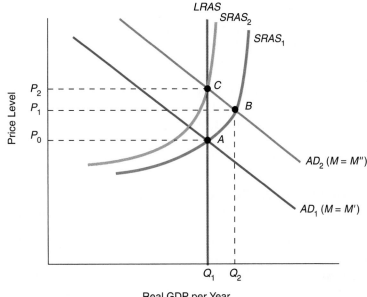

There are a variety of reasons why firms and individuals might wish to enter into contracts such as these. For example, there is a transaction costs motive, which focuses on the fact that it would be very costly for market participants to adjust their behavior continuously to the fluctuating prices of an auction market setting. In addition, there is a risk-aversion motive for contracts, particularly as they apply to consumers and workers. By specifying ahead of time what prices or wages will be, individuals are able to make their future consumption plans without facing the uncertainty of fluctuating prices.

The Policy Implications of Contracting.   If a substantial amount of economic activity is covered by contracts, then even if expectations are rational, it is possible for systematic policy actions to have real consequences on the economy. All that is required is that the policies differ from those that were expected at the time the contracts were entered into. This conclusion is illustrated with the aid of Figure 17-10, which shows the long-run aggregate supply curve ($LRAS$) for the economy, as well as the initial aggregate demand curve (AD_1) and the short-run aggregate supply curve ($SRAS_1$). The money supply is initially given by $M = M'$, and the price level and real GDP are shown by P_1 and Q_1, respectively. Thus point A represents the initial equilibrium.

Suppose now that the money supply is increased to M'', thereby causing the aggregate demand curve to shift outward to AD_2. As long as some nominal prices and wages are contractually fixed before the increase in the money supply, the short-run aggregate supply curve will be upward sloping, as shown by $SRAS_1$. Given the existence of contracts, this increase in aggregate demand will cause output and the price level to rise to Q_2 and P_2, respectively. The new short-run equilibrium is at B. Because real output is above the long-run equilibrium level of Q_1, unemployment must be below long-run equilibrium levels, and so contracts will be rewritten as they expire, to reflect the higher price level. This causes the short-run aggregate supply curve to shift upward vertically, eventually moving the economy to the new long-run equilibrium at C. The presence of contracts can thus make it possible for current policy to have real effects in the short run, although as in the new classical model, these effects eventually disappear in the long run as the contracts are rewritten.

REAL BUSINESS CYCLES

Although rational contracting theory at first appeared to be a significant improvement on new classical theory, important objections soon emerged. According to contracting theory, monetary policy has real effects because it differs from what was expected at the time the contracts were signed. But if there is a significant change in policy after a contract is signed, there would appear to be a large incentive for the parties to recontract to reflect the change in policy. (Just this sort of behavior emerged during the disinflation of the early 1980s in the United States.) Yet if recontracting is both possible and not too difficult, then although contracting theory is interesting from a theoretical perspective, its empirical relevance may be minor.

The Distinction Between Real and Monetary Shocks.   Given this apparent flaw in contracting theory, some researchers returned to the assumption of fully flexible prices and began to look elsewhere for explanations of what they observed. Their research differed importantly from new classical theory in that they sought to determine whether real, as opposed to purely monetary, forces might help explain aggregate economic fluctuations. An important stimulus for the development of **real business cycle theory,** as it has come to be known, was the 1970s. During that decade, world economies were staggered by two major disruptions to the supply of oil. The first occurred in 1973, the second in 1979. In both episodes, members of the Organization of Petroleum Exporting Countries (OPEC) reduced the amount of oil they were willing to supply and raised the price at which they offered it for sale. Each time, the price level rose sharply in the United States, and real GDP declined. Thus each episode produced a period of "stagflation"—real economic stagnation combined with high inflation. Figure 17-11 illustrates the pattern of events.

We begin at point *A* with the economy in both short- and long-run equilibrium, with the associated supply curves, $SRAS_1$ and $LRAS_1$. Initially, the level of real GDP is Q_1, and

▶ **Real business cycle theory**
An extension and modification of the theories of the new classical economists of the 1970s and 1980s, in which money is neutral and only real, supply-side factors matter in influencing labor employment and real output.

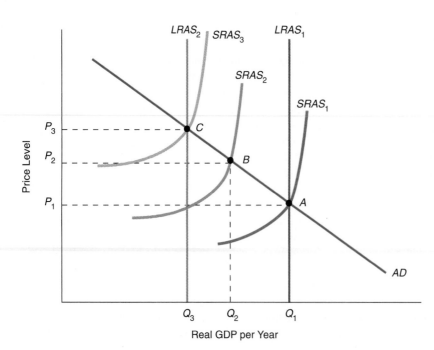

FIGURE 17-11
The effects of a reduction in the supply of resources.
A reduction in the supply of resource such as oil causes a reduction in aggregate supply, a rise in the price level, and a fall in output.

the price level is P_1. Because the economy is in long-run equilibrium, the unemployment rate must be at the natural rate.

A reduction in the supply of oil, as occurred in 1973 and 1979, causes the *SRAS* curve to shift to the left to $SRAS_2$ because fewer goods will be available for sale due to the reduced supplies. If the reduction in oil supplies is (or is believed to be) permanent, the *LRAS* shifts to the left also. This assumption is reflected in Figure 17-11, where $LRAS_2$ shows the new long-run aggregate supply curve associated with the lowered output of oil.

In the short run, two adjustments begin to occur simultaneously. First, the prices of oil and petroleum-based products begin to rise, so that the overall price level rises to P_2. Second, the higher costs of production occasioned by the rise in oil prices induce firms to cut back production, so total output falls to Q_2 in the short run. The new short-run equilibrium occurs at B, with a higher price level (P_2) and a lower level of real GDP (Q_2).

Impact on the Labor Market.

If we were to focus on the labor market while this adjustment from A to B was taking place, we would find two developments occurring. The rise in the price level pushes the real wage rate downward, even as the scaled-back production plans of firms induce them to reduce the amount of labor inputs they are using. So not only does the real wage rate fall, but the level of employment declines as well. On both counts, workers are made worse off due to the reduction in the supply of oil.

Now this is not the full story, because owners of nonoil inputs (such as labor) who are willing to put up with reduced real payments in the short run simply will not tolerate them in the long run. Thus, for example, some workers who were willing to continue working at lower wages in the short run will eventually decide to retire, switch from full-time work to part-time employment, or drop out of the labor force altogether. In effect, there is a reduction in the supply of nonoil inputs, reflected in an upward shift in the *SRAS* from $SRAS_2$ to $SRAS_3$. This puts additional upward pressure on the price level and exerts a downward force on real GDP. The final long-run equilibrium thus occurs at point C, with the price level at P_3 and real GDP at Q_3.

Generalizing the Theory.

Naturally, the focus of real business cycle theory goes well beyond the simple "oil shock" that we have discussed here, for it encompasses all types of real disturbances, including technological changes and shifts in the composition of the labor force. Moreover, a complete treatment of real shocks to the economy is typically much more complex than we have allowed for in our discussion. For example, an oil shock such as is shown in Figure 17-11 would likely also have effects on the real wealth of Americans, causing a reduction in aggregate demand as well as aggregate supply. Nevertheless, our simple example still manages to capture the flavor of the theory.

It is clear that real business cycle theory has improved our understanding of the economy's behavior, but there is also agreement among economists that it alone is incapable of explaining all of the facets of business cycles that we observe. For example, it is difficult to imagine a real disturbance that could possibly account for the Great Depression in this country, when real income fell more than 30 percent and the unemployment rate rose to 25 percent. Moreover, real business cycle theory continues to assume that prices are perfectly flexible and so fails to explain a great deal of the apparent rigidity of prices throughout the economy.

INTERNATIONAL EXAMPLE: International Price Flexibility

Estimates have recently been made of the degree of price flexibility across several countries. Although there are many ways to measure price rigidity, one important way is to determine whether the price level is slow to change over time. Table 17-1 on the next page

TABLE 17-1   Measures of inertia in the price level for five nations.
As this table indicates, among these nations, the United States shows the greatest price inertia, and Japan shows the least. The other nations fall in between the United States and Japan. Although this measure of price inertia is surely not perfect, it does suggest that for the United States any assumption of perfect price flexibility needs to be scrutinized carefully.

COUNTRY	TIME PERIOD	ESTIMATED PRICE INERTIA VALUE
United States	1954–1987	0.87
United Kingdom	1960–1986	0.57
France	1960–1986	0.55
Germany	1960–1986	0.73
Japan	1960–1986	0.15

Source: Robert J. Gordon, "What is New Keynesian Economics?" *Journal of Economic Literature,* 28 (September 1990).

displays estimates for five key nations of the degree to which the inflation rate in a given year depends on the inflation rate in the previous year. A value of 1 for this measure would indicate that the inflation rate depends completely on last year's inflation rate, which would imply full **price inertia,** the tendency for inflation to resist change. By contrast, a value of 0 for this measure indicates that the inflation rate in any one year is wholly independent of past inflation, so no price inertia is present.

For Critical Analysis: *Why do you think the United States displays relatively little price flexibility?* ●

NEW KEYNESIAN ECONOMICS

Although the new classical and real business cycle theories both embody pure competition and flexible prices, a body of research called the **new Keynesian economics** drops both of these assumptions. This research also emphasizes the possibility that optimal performance by an economy may require activist intervention by the relevant fiscal and monetary authorities. There is a variety of approaches that attempt to capture the essentials of this thinking.

Menu Cost Theory.   If prices do not respond to demand changes, two conditions must be true: Someone must be consciously deciding not to change prices, and that decision must be in the decision maker's self-interest. One combination of facts that is consistent with this scenario is the **menu cost theory,** which supposes that much of the economy is characterized by imperfect competition and that it is costly for firms to change their prices in response to changes in demand. The costs associated with changing prices are called *menu costs,* and they include the costs of renegotiating contracts, printing price lists (such as menus), and informing customers of price changes. Although most economists agree that such costs exist, there is considerably less agreement on whether they are sufficient to explain the extent of price rigidity that is observed.

Efficiency Wage Theory.   An alternative approach within the new Keynesian framework is called the **efficiency wage theory.** It proposes that worker productivity actually *depends* on the wages that workers are paid, rather than being independent of wages, as is assumed in other theories. According to this theory, higher real wages encourage

▶ **Price inertia**
A tendency for the level of prices to resist change with the passage of time.

▶ **New Keynesian economics**
Economic models based on the idea that "demand creates its own supply" as a result of various possible government fiscal and monetary coordination failures.

▶ **Menu cost theory**
A hypothesis that it is costly for firms to change prices in response to demand changes because of the cost of negotiating contracts, printing price lists, and so on.

▶ **Efficiency wage theory**
The hypothesis that the productivity of workers depends on the level of the real wage rate.

workers to work harder, improve their efficiency, increase morale, and raise their loyalty to the firm. Across the board, then, higher wages tend to increase workers' productivity, which in turn discourages firms from cutting real wages because of the damaging effect that such an action would have on productivity and profitability. Under highly competitive conditions, there will generally be an optimal wage—called the *efficiency wage*—that the firm should continue paying, even in the face of large fluctuations in the demand for its output.

There are significant, valid elements in the efficiency wage theory, but its importance in understanding national business fluctuations remains uncertain. For example, although the theory explains rigid real wages, it does not explain rigid prices. Moreover, the theory ignores the fact that firms can (and apparently do) rely on a host of incentives other than wages to encourage their workers to be loyal, efficient, and productive.

DIRECTIONS FOR FUTURE RESEARCH

Although many advances have been made in macroeconomics over the past quarter century, the debate over macro policy is far from over. There remain two broad schools of thought today, just as there were a generation ago. The various Keynesian approaches—traditional, modern, and new—argue that the economy is, if not inherently unstable, fragile to say the least. Moreover, the economy is presumably racked with various market imperfections and rigidities that result in economic outcomes that are far from optimal. As a result, proponents of this set of views argue that there is a need for active policy involvement in the economy and that the economy must be carefully watched and regulated by monetary and fiscal authorities.

This view is in sharp contrast to the classical branch of macroeconomics—whether traditional, new, or modern. Proponents of this school of thought see the economy as a mechanism that is inherently self-regulating and remarkably stable. Moreover, it is said, although truly perfect competition and price flexibility may not be literally true, actual competition and price flexibility are close enough to the ideal as to be the best we can possibly achieve. And finally, this group would argue, past policy decisions by monetary and fiscal authorities have more often than not *destabilized* rather than stabilized the economy. As a result, intervention by the authorities is likely to result in slim benefits and substantial costs, suggesting that it should be undertaken rarely and only with great circumspection.

Although further research will likely evolve in ways that attempt to resolve these fundamental differences in world views, it is much less clear how the theoretical and empirical advances will tip the scales of the debate. What is clear, however, is that for the foreseeable future the development of macro policy is likely to be an exciting and dynamic field.

A COMPARISON OF MACROECONOMIC MODELS

Although it is impossible to compare accurately and completely every single detail of the various macroeconomic approaches we have examined, it is useful to summarize and contrast some of their key aspects. Table 17-2 presents features of our four key models: (1) traditional classical, (2) traditional Keynesian, (3) new (modern) classical, and (4) new (modern) Keynesian. Realize when examining the table that we are painting with a broad brush.

TABLE 17-2 **A comparison of macroeconomic models.**

ISSUE	MACROECONOMIC MODEL			
	TRADITIONAL CLASSICAL	TRADITIONAL KEYNESIAN	NEW CLASSICAL	NEW KEYNESIAN
Stability of capitalism	Yes	No	Yes	Yes, but can be enhanced by policy
Price-wage flexibility	Yes	No	Yes	Yes, but imperfect
Belief in natural rate of employment hypothesis	Yes	No	Yes	Yes
Factors sensitive to interest rate	Saving, consumption, investment	Demand for money	Saving, consumption, investment	Saving, consumption, investment
View of the velocity of money	Stable	Unstable	No consensus	No consensus
Effect of changes in money supply on economy	Changes aggregate demand	Changes interest rates, which change investment and real output	No effect on real variables if anticipated	Changes aggregate demand
Effects of fiscal policy on the economy	Not applicable	Multiplier changes in aggregate demand and output	Generally ineffective[a]	Changes aggregate demand
Causes of inflation	Excess money growth	Excess real aggregate demand	Excess money growth	Excess money growth
Stabilization policy	Unnecessary	Fiscal policy necessary and effective; monetary policy ineffective	Too difficult to conduct	Both fiscal and monetary policy may be useful

[a] Some fiscal policies affect relative prices (interest rates) and so many have real effects on economy.

CONCEPTS IN BRIEF

- Rational contracting theory demonstrates that even with rational expectations, monetary and fiscal policy can have real effects on the economy. All that is required is that some nominal magnitudes (such as prices and wages) be fixed by contracts and that the policies differ from those that were expected at the time the contracts were entered into.
- Real business cycle theory shows that even if all prices and wages are perfectly flexible, real shocks to the economy (such as technological change and changes in the supplies of factors of production) can cause national business fluctuations.
- The new Keynesian economics explains why various features of the economy, such as menu costs and wage rates that affect productivity, make it possible for monetary shocks to cause real effects.
- Although there remain significant differences between the classical and Keynesian branches of macroeconomics, the rivalry between them is an important source of innovation that helps improve our understanding of the economy.

HIDDEN UNEMPLOYMENT AND THE DURATION OF SEARCH

Concepts Applied: Unemployment, duration of search, job offer curve, reservation wage curve

Many of these graduates of Santa Monica City College have to make decisions about which job offers to accept. If they do not have good information about the job market, the duration of their searches may not be optimal.

Even a college degree is no guarantee of a job—at least not when the economy is in a recession. That's the message that the college classes of 1990–1992 learned, just as the classes of 1980–1982 had learned before them. It's true that college graduates fare far better than the average worker when it comes to getting and keeping a job, for their unemployment rate is less than half the national average. Nevertheless, when employers stop hiring, they stop hiring across the board, and that includes even bright-eyed, freshly minted baccalaureates.

HIDDEN UNEMPLOYMENT According to economic theory—see panel (b) of Figure 17-3—the job offer curve shifts downward during a recession. This leads to lower wages and, because the reservation wage curve does not immediately shift down, also increases the duration of search for jobs and increases the unemployment rate. Although these developments occur in the market for graduating seniors, they are often difficult to measure. For example, when most people are out of work, they show up in the unemployment statistics, and the duration of their job search can be readily measured. By contrast, college seniors typically begin searching for their jobs while still in school and thus are not officially unemployed. During recessions, many seniors start looking for work during the fall semester of their last year rather than

waiting until the spring; but because they are full-time students, and thus not considered unemployed, there is no place in the official statistics to record their longer job search duration.

It is also difficult to examine the impact of recession on the wages paid to graduating seniors and on their overall unemployment rate. If you are like most seniors, you will go directly from graduation ceremony to a paying job. Nevertheless, some seniors opt for graduate school, others choose low-paying internships, and some select unpaid volunteer activities. When the economy turns sour, recent graduates turn to these other options in droves rather than languish jobless in the labor market. During the recession of 1990–1991 and the recovery during 1992, for example, applications to graduate schools soared as much as 75 percent in some disciplines. Inquiries to the Peace Corps jumped to 800 per day, more than triple their normal level of 250. And for students who couldn't afford graduate tuition or didn't want to endure the year-long wait for a Peace Corps slot, even unpaid internships were more attractive than vacant places on their résumés. Although individuals pursuing these paths don't get counted among the unemployed, they would be counted as *employed* if the economy were in better condition. Moreover, although their earnings are much lower than they would be in a regular job, there is no official record of anybody having taken a cut in wages.

DURATION OF SEARCH: A PROXY Despite the many options open to seniors, there is little doubt that hitting the job market during a recession is a scary prospect. You will probably land your first real job after interviewing as a senior with the corporate recruiters who visit campuses across the nation each year. But during a recession, fewer of these recruiters show up, and even when they do come, they're hiring fewer people. At campuses from Yale to the University of California, the number of college recruiters dropped by as much as 20 percent during the last recession. Companies like San Francisco–based Wells Fargo Bank cut their hiring of new graduates by up to 40 percent. Even giants like American Telephone and Telegraph skimped on college recruiting. In 1988, for example, AT&T visited 300 campuses and hired 2,000 graduates. In 1992 it visited half as many campuses and hired half as many graduates.

FIGURE 17-12
Changes in the number of college graduates that companies plan to hire.
Years begin September 1. Change is expressed as a percentage change from the previous year.
Source: Collegiate Employment Research Institute, Michigan State University.

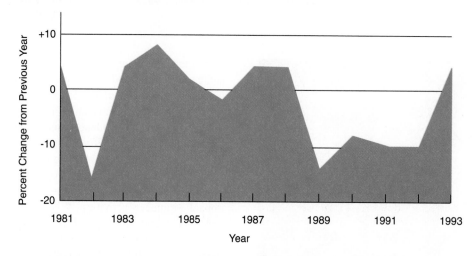

Indeed, the activities of college recruiters provide perhaps the best overall measure of just what the job market is like for each year's graduating class. Every year these recruiters are surveyed as to their hiring intentions, and their responses are generally an accurate index of what actually took place. Figure 17-12 uses these recruiting data to track year-to-year changes in the job market fortunes of college graduates. It shows the percentage change from the previous year in the number of college graduates that companies planned to hire. Thus, for example, hirings were up 3 percent in 1980, but then plunged 16 percent in 1981. Following a sharp rebound in 1983 and 1984, the job market for graduates was fairly stable until the bottom fell out in 1989—and stayed out for the next three years. Overall, the recession of the early 1990s cut recruiting for new graduates by over 30 percent—more than double the cuts suffered during the recession of the early 1980s. Figure 17-12 thus leaves no doubt that even though college seniors may not show up in the official unemployment statistics, they are not immune to the effects of recessions.

FOR CRITICAL ANALYSIS

1. Based on what you know about recessions, would you expect college seniors who graduate during a recession to concentrate their job search activities in consumer goods industries or investment goods industries?

2. When people decide on their majors, do you think they take into account how easy or difficult it will be to find jobs at graduation? Do you think they take into account the wages and working conditions of the jobs they are likely to obtain?

CHAPTER SUMMARY

1. The schedule showing the best wage offer received as a function of duration of search is the job offer curve. The lowest wage at which an individual will accept a job is called that person's reservation wage; the schedule showing the relationship between the reservation wage and unemployment duration is the reservation wage curve. The optimal duration of unemployment occurs where the individual's job offer curve and reservation wage curve intersect.

2. Much of the unemployment we observe is voluntary, in the sense that job searchers are choosing to be unemployed; under the existing circumstances, these individuals would be made worse off if they were forced to search longer or prevented from searching as long.

3. The natural rate of unemployment is the rate that exists in long-run equilibrium, when workers' expectations are consistent with actual conditions. Departures from the natural rate of unemployment can occur when

individuals are surprised by unanticipated changes in fiscal or monetary policy.

4. The Phillips curve shows a negative relationship between the inflation rate and the unemployment rate that can be observed when there are unanticipated changes in aggregate demand. It was originally believed that the Phillips curve represented a trade-off between inflation and unemployment. In fact no useful trade-off exists because workers' expectations adjust to systematic attempts to reduce the unemployment rate below the natural rate.

5. The rational expectations hypothesis assumes that individuals' forecasts incorporate all available information, including an understanding of government policy and its effects on the economy. The new classical economics assumes that the rational expectation hypothesis is valid and also that there is pure competition and that all prices and wages are flexible.

6. The policy irrelevance proposition says that under the assumptions of the new classical model, anticipated monetary policy cannot alter either the rate of unemployment or the level of real GDP. Thus according to the new classical model, policies can alter real economic variables only if the policies are unsystematic and therefore unanticipated.

7. Rational contracting theory demonstrates that even with rational expectations, monetary and fiscal policy can have real effects on the economy. All that is required is that some nominal magnitudes (such as prices and wages) be fixed by contracts and that the policies differ from those that were expected at the time the contracts were entered into.

8. Real business cycle theory shows that even if all prices and wages are perfectly flexible, real shocks to the economy (such as technological change and changes in the supplies of factors of production) can cause national business fluctuations.

9. The new Keynesian economics explains why various features of the economy, such as menu costs and wage rates that affect productivity, make it possible for monetary shocks to cause real effects.

DISCUSSION OF PREVIEW POINTS

1. What does the rational expectations hypothesis say about people's forecasting errors?

The simplest version of the rational expectations hypothesis simply says that people do not persistently make the same mistakes in forecasting the future. More generally, the hypothesis says that (a) individuals base their forecasts about the future values of economic variables on the basis of all available past and current information and (b) these forecasts incorporate individuals' understanding about how the economy operates, including the operation of monetary and fiscal policy. As a result, people's forecasting errors are completely unpredictable over time and thus cannot be used by policymakers in formulating policy.

2. How do the new classical economists view economic policy?

The new classical economists assume that the rational expectations hypothesis is valid and also that there is pure competition and that all prices and wages are flexible. As a result, they argue, anticipated monetary policy cannot alter either the rate of unemployment or the level of real GDP. Regardless of the nature of the anticipated policy, the unemployment rate will equal the natural rate, and real GDP will be determined solely by the economy's long-run aggregate supply curve. This conclusion is called the policy irrelevance theorem.

3. What does the real business cycle theory say about the causes of recession?

Real business cycle theory shows that even if all prices and wages are perfectly flexible, real shocks to the economy (such as technological change and changes in the supplies of factors of production) can cause national business fluctuations. One example of such real shocks is the type of oil shock that hit the United States economy during the 1970s.

4. How does the new Keynesian economics explain the stickiness of wages and prices?

Generally, a combination of factors is cited, including the existence of contracts, menu costs, and efficiency wages. The key point is that there are a variety of rational reasons that economic participants have for entering into agreements that fix either nominal or real relative prices (including wages). Given the existence of such agreements, as well as the existence of costs of changing prices of all types, monetary policy can have real effects on the economy by changing aggregate demand.

PROBLEMS

(Answers to the odd-numbered problems appear at the back of the book.)

17-1. Answer the following questions based on the accompanying graph.

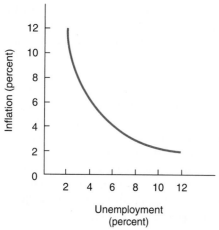

a. If we regard this curve as showing a trade-off between inflation and unemployment, how much unemployment will it "cost" to reduce inflation to 2 percent per year?
b. What might cause this curve to shift upward?
c. Why do economists argue that there is generally no useable trade-off between unemployment and inflation?

17-2. The natural rate of unemployment is a function of a variety of factors, including wage and price rigidities and interferences with labor mobility. Give some examples of such rigidities and interferences.

17-3. How does the existence of contracts, menu costs, and efficiency wages affect the amount of discretion available to policymakers?

17-4. Explain how the average duration of unemployment may be different for a given rate of unemployment.

17-5. What effect does the average duration of unemployment have on the rate of unemployment if we hold constant the variables you used to explain Problem 17-4?

17-6. What is meant by an optimal duration of unemployment? What may affect such an optimal duration of unemployment?

17-7. If both employers and workers incorrectly perceive the rate of inflation to the same extent, would the Phillips curve still be expected to be negatively sloped?

17-8. Unemployment is arbitrarily defined. What differences do different definitions have with respect to policy?

COMPUTER-ASSISTED INSTRUCTION
(Complete problem and answer on disk.)

This session focuses on changes in the unemployment rate to illustrate the views of the new classical economists, the real business cycle theorists, and the new Keynesian economists.

ECONOMIC GROWTH

Some observers of today's economic scene believe that you and everyone else who is getting some form of higher education will be able to compete in tomorrow's increasingly competitive marketplace. In particular, if you become a skilled worker who can solve problems and broker transactions—in engineering, investment banking, consulting, and the like—the future looks promising. Less skilled factory workers and people in the service trades do not have such a bright future. Only skilled Americans may be able to compete in the ever increasing global marketplace; the less skilled may not. Can America as a nation remain globally competitive? The issue of global competitiveness is part of the bigger question of how an economy can grow over time.

After reading this chapter, you should be able to answer the following questions:

1. What does economic growth measure?

2. What is the rule of 72?

3. What are some of the ways in which you can experience economic growth for yourself or for your family?

4. What are the determinants of economic growth?

INTRODUCTION

Though there is some dispute about whether America is still the richest country on earth, there was no doubt about where we stood in the nineteenth century. Indeed, America had already passed England in per capita living standards by the early 1800s. Nonetheless, life was not great by today's standards. Researcher Edgar W. Martin estimated that in 1860 only 2 percent of American families had indoor toilets and cold running water. No homes had electricity; almost none had gas. Bathtubs and hot running water were virtually unheard of, even in cities. Martin estimated that a city of 60,000 had fewer than 20 bathtubs.

Food was relatively abundant, but because of the lack of refrigeration and the limited means to transport goods, there was not much variety. A one-pot stew was the main meal of the day. The stew was eaten in a house that had few or no glass windows and little lighting. Basically, then, the high living standards of people in America today is a relatively recent phenomenon, particularly if you look back at the hundreds of years during which it has been inhabited. If you examine the history of civilization, current living standards for most Americans today have existed for a tiny percentage of the time that civilization has existed.

The way we got from there to here has been through economic growth.

DEFINING ECONOMIC GROWTH

Most people have a general idea of what economic growth means. When a nation grows economically, its citizens must be better off in at least some ways, usually in terms of their material well-being. Typically, though, we do not measure the well-being of any nation solely in terms of its total output of real goods and services or in terms of real GDP without making some adjustments. After all, India has a GDP about three times as large as Switzerland. The population in India, though, is about 125 times greater than that in Switzerland. Consequently, India is a relatively poor country and Switzerland is a relatively rich country. That means that to measure how much a country is growing in terms of annual increases in real GDP, we have to adjust for population growth. Our formal definition of economic growth becomes this: **Economic growth** is present when there are increases in per capita real GDP; it is measured by the rate of change in per capita real GDP.

▶ **Economic growth**
Increases in per capita real GDP measured by its rate of change.

PROBLEMS IN DEFINITION

Our definition of economic growth says nothing about the *distribution* of output and income. A nation might grow very rapidly in terms of increases in per capita real output, while at the same time its poor people remain poor or become even poorer. Therefore, in assessing the economic growth record of any nation, we must be careful to pinpoint which income groups have benefited the most from such growth.

Accounting for Changes in Leisure Time.
Real standards of living can go up without any positive economic growth. This can occur if individuals are, on average, enjoying more leisure by working fewer hours but producing as much as they did before. For example, if per capita real GDP in the United States remained at $20,000 a year for a decade, we could not automatically jump to the conclusion that Americans were, on average, no better off. What if, during that same 10-year period, average hours worked fell from 37 per week to 33 per week? That would mean that during the 10 years under study, individuals in the labor force were earning four hours more leisure a week. Actually, nothing so extreme has occurred in this country, but something similar has. Average hours worked per week fell steadily until the 1960s, at which time they leveled off. That means

TABLE 18-1 Costs and benefits of economic growth.

BENEFITS	COSTS
Reduction in illiteracy	Environmental pollution
Reduction in poverty	Breakdown of the family
Improved health	Isolation, alienation, and clinical depression
Longer lives	Urban congestion
Political stability	

that during much of the history of this country, the increase in real per capita GDP *understated* the actual economic growth that we were experiencing because we were enjoying more and more leisure as things progressed.

IS ECONOMIC GROWTH BAD?

Some commentators on our current economic situation believe that the definition of economic growth ignores its negative effects. Some psychologists even contend that we are made worse off because of economic growth. They say that the more we grow, the more "needs" are created so that we feel worse off as we become richer. Our expectations are rising faster than reality, so we presumably always suffer from a sense of disappointment. Clearly, the measurement of economic growth cannot take into account the spiritual and cultural aspects of the good life. As with all activities, there are costs and benefits. You can see some of those listed in Table 18-1.

Increased Pollution.   Some people argue that an undesired side effect of economic growth is increased pollution. Pollution levels seem overwhelming in such major cities in the world as Mexico City, Tokyo, Los Angeles, and Madrid. Antigrowth proponents argue that such pollution is evidence that growth is not all good. Worldwide evidence suggests that in the early stages of development, economic growth does indeed lead to more pollution. But at the later stages of development, pollution actually declines. There appears to be a critical point in a country's economic development after which it starts devoting an increasing percentage of a higher real GDP to cleaning up the environment.

Increased Sociological and Psychological Problems.   Antigrowth proponents point out that clinical studies show that there is more clinical depression than ever before. They argue that economic growth has created an environment that leads to more depression, isolation, and alienation. Changing technologies reportedly create new sources of insecurities for workers and add anxiety. After all, new technologies may make workers' skills obsolete. Growth critics also point out that there seems to be a breakdown in the traditional family in today's richer nations.

Urban Congestion.   There is no doubt that poor rural areas have little urban congestion. Major cities in both developing and developed countries—Mexico City, Tokyo, New York, Paris, London—all suffer from obvious urban congestion. Antigrowth proponents argue that such urban congestion can only get worse as nations get richer.

In any event, any measure of economic growth that we use will be imperfect. Nonetheless, the measures that we do have allow us to make comparisons across countries and over time and, if used judiciously, can enable us to gain important insights. GDP, used so often, is not always an accurate measure of economic well-being, but it is a serviceable measure of productive activity.

COUNTRY	AVERAGE ANNUAL RATE OF GROWTH OF INCOME PER CAPITA, 1970–1992(%)	DOUBLING TIME (YEARS)
Switzerland	1.9	38
Sweden	2.0	36
United Kingdom	2.2	33
Germany	2.5	29
Netherlands	2.5	29
United States	2.9	25
Italy	2.9	25
France	3.0	24
Spain	3.4	21
Canada	3.5	21
Japan	4.7	15
Turkey	5.1	14
China	5.9	12

TABLE 18-2 Per capita growth rates in various countries.

Sources: World Bank; International Monetary Fund.

THE IMPORTANCE OF GROWTH RATES

Look at the growth rates in real per capita income for selected countries listed in Table 18-2. The differences between the growth rates of different countries are not large; they generally vary by only 1 to 3 percentage points. You might want to know why such small differences in growth rates are important. What does it matter, you could say, if we grew at 3 percent or at 4 percent per year?

It matters a lot—not for next year or the year after but for the more distant future. The power of compound interest is impressive. Let's see what happens with three different annual rates of growth: 3 percent, 4 percent, and 5 percent. We start with $1 trillion per year, which is approximately equal to the gross domestic product of the United States in 1971. We then compound this $1 trillion, or allow it to grow, into the future at these three different growth rates. The difference is huge. In 50 years, $1 trillion per year becomes $4.38 trillion per year if compounded at 3 percent per year. Just one percentage point more in the growth rate, 4 percent, results in a real GDP of $7.11 trillion per year in 50 years, almost double the previous amount. Two percentage points difference in the growth rate—5 percent per year—results in a real GDP of $11.5 trillion per year in 50 years, or nearly three times as much. Obviously, there is a great difference in the results of economic growth for very small differences in annual growth rates. That is why nations are concerned if the growth rate falls even a little in absolute percentage terms.

COMPOUND INTEREST

When we talk about growth rates, we are basically talking about compound interest. In Table 18-3 we show how $1 compounded annually grows at different interest rates. We see in the 3 percent column that $1 in 50 years grows to $4.38. We merely multiplied $1 trillion times 4.38 to get the growth figure in our earlier example. In the 5 percent column, $1 grows to $11.50 after 50 years. Again, we multiplied 11.50 times $1 trillion to get the growth figure for 5 percent in the preceding example.

DOUBLING TIMES AND THE RULE OF 72

You will notice in the right-hand column of Table 18-2 the column headed "Doubling time," which gives the number of years that it takes for real income per capita to double in the listed countries. One of the easiest ways to approximate doubling time is to use the **rule of 72.** You simply divide the annual percentage rate of growth of real per capita

▶ **Rule of 72**
A simple rule that allows you to find the approximate time it takes any quantity to double, given its annual growth rate. To find doubling time, divide the annual percentage rate of growth (times 100) into 72.

TABLE 18-3 One dollar compounded annually at different interest rates.
Here we show the value of a dollar at the end of a specified period during which it has been compounded annually at a specified interest rate. For example, if you took $1 today and invested it at 5 percent per year, it would yield $1.05 at the end of one year. At the end of 10 years, it would equal $1.63, and at the end of 50 years, it would equal $11.50.

NUMBER OF YEARS	INTEREST RATE						
	3%	4%	5%	6%	8%	10%	20%
1	1.03	1.04	1.05	1.06	1.08	1.10	1.20
2	1.06	1.08	1.10	1.12	1.17	1.21	1.44
3	1.09	1.12	1.16	1.19	1.26	1.33	1.73
4	1.13	1.17	1.22	1.26	1.36	1.46	2.07
5	1.16	1.22	1.28	1.34	1.47	1.61	2.49
6	1.19	1.27	1.34	1.41	1.59	1.77	2.99
7	1.23	1.32	1.41	1.50	1.71	1.94	3.58
8	1.27	1.37	1.48	1.59	1.85	2.14	4.30
9	1.30	1.42	1.55	1.68	2.00	2.35	5.16
10	1.34	1.48	1.63	1.79	2.16	2.59	6.19
20	1.81	2.19	2.65	3.20	4.66	6.72	38.30
30	2.43	3.24	4.32	5.74	10.00	17.40	237.00
40	3.26	4.80	7.04	10.30	21.70	45.30	1,470.00
50	4.38	7.11	11.50	18.40	46.90	117.00	9,100.00

output (multiplied by 100) into the number 72. For example, if real per capita annual growth is 2 percent, the doubling time is found by dividing .02 × 100, or 2, into 72, which is equal to 36 years; at a 2 percent annual growth rate, $1 will grow to $2 in 36 years.

Notice in Table 18-2 that both Japan and Turkey have doubling times that are almost twice as fast as that of the United States. Turkey's base, however, is so low that even if it continues to grow so rapidly, it will take many years to catch up with other countries.

⭐ EXAMPLE: How to Retire a Millionaire

At last count, there were almost a million Americans who could be classified as million-aires—individuals who have at least $1 million in net worth. (Remember that net worth is defined as the difference between what you own and what you owe.) Due to inflation, the term *millionaire* doesn't have quite the same connotation that it did 50 years ago. Nonetheless, most individuals wouldn't mind retiring with a net worth of at least $1 million. To do so does not require the astuteness of a Wall Street wizard. Rather, you can obtain this financial goal with a relatively modest endowment early in your life, provided that you get a steady decent compounded rate of return. For example, assume that at age 20 a rich relative dies and leaves you $30,000. If you can obtain an 8 percent rate of return for the next 40 years, you can see from Table 18-3 that $1 will grow to $21.70. Thus at age 60 you would have $30,000 × 21.7 = $651,000. You can also see in the next row that by age 70, from the value given your $30,000 compounded at 8 percent per year would give you $1,407,000. Therefore, somewhere between ages 60 and 70, you can retire with $1 million in net worth. The two requirements are that you start out with $30,000 at age 20 and that you obtain an 8 percent rate of return on this money. Neither is impossible, but the odds are admittedly not in your favor.

For Critical Analysis: What are some alternative ways to retire a millionaire? ●

GROWTH AND THE PRODUCTION POSSIBILITIES CURVE

We can graphically show economic growth by using the production possibilities curve presented in Chapter 2. Figure 18-1 shows the production possibilities curve for 1995. On the horizontal axis is measured the annual output of agricultural goods, and on the

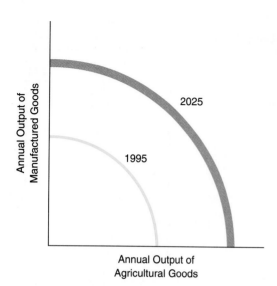

FIGURE 18-1
Economic growth.
If there is growth between 1995 and 2025, the production possibilities curve for the entire economy will shift outward from the line labeled 1995 to the heavier curve labeled 2025. The distance that it shifts represents an increase in the productive capacity of the nation.

vertical axis, manufactured goods. If there is economic growth between 1995 and 2025, the production possibilities curve will shift outward to the heavy line. The distance that it shifts represents the amount of economic growth—that is, the increase in the productive capacity of the nation.

USING AGGREGATE SUPPLY AND AGGREGATE DEMAND TO SHOW ECONOMIC GROWTH

We can demonstrate the effects of economic growth analytically in terms of aggregate supply and aggregate demand. Look at Figure 18-2. We start in equilibrium with *AD* and *SRAS* intersecting at the long-run aggregate supply curve, *LRAS*, at a price level of 100. Real GDP per year is $6 trillion. Economic growth occurs due to labor force expansion,

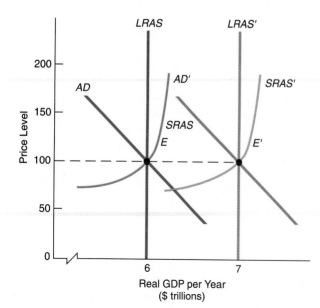

FIGURE 18-2
Economic growth, aggregate demand, and aggregate supply.
Economic growth can be shown using short-run and long-run aggregate demand and supply curves. Aggregate demand, *AD*, intersects short-run aggregate supply, *SRAS*, at *E*, $6 trillion of real GDP per year at a price level of 100. This GDP is consistent with the natural rate of unemployment. The long-run aggregate supply curve is vertical at $6 trillion and is labeled *LRAS*. With economic growth, *LRAS* moves outward to $7 trillion per year. Short-run aggregate supply shifts to *SRAS'*, and aggregate demand increases to *AD'*. New equilibrium is at *E'*, still at a price level of 100. There is no inflation.

capital investments and other occurrences. The result is a rightward shift in the long-run aggregate supply curve to *LRAS'*. As the long-run productive capacity of the nation grows, the economy doesn't stay on its short-run aggregate supply curve, *SRAS*. Rather, *SRAS* shifts along with shifts in aggregate demand due to population increases. It is thus possible for us to achieve real GDP of $7 trillion without any increase in the price level. The short-run aggregate supply curve moves outward to *SRAS'* and intersects *AD'* at *E'*, where the new long-run aggregate supply curve, *LRAS'*, has moved.

In the world just hypothesized, aggregate demand shifts outward so that at the same price level, 100, it intersects the new short-run aggregate supply curve, *SRAS'*, at the rate of real GDP that is consistent with the natural rate of unemployment (on *LRAS'*). Firms sell all the output produced at the new level without changing prices. In some situations, however, inflation may accompany growth.

SHOWING GROWTH WITH INFLATION

Now instead of aggregate demand shifting outward at exactly the same rate as long-run aggregate supply, it shifts outward faster. This can be seen in Figure 18-3. Long-run aggregate supply has moved to $7 trillion of real GDP per year, but the intersection of *AD"* with *SRAS'* is now at *E"*, which is to the right and above the previous intersection of *E'* shown in Figure 18-2. The equilibrium price level rises from 100 to 120. Aggregate demand has grown more rapidly than is consistent with the increase in potential output, $7 trillion per year, shown by long-run aggregate supply curve *LRAS'*. The short-run aggregate supply curve will have to rise because of rising input prices. It moves to *SRAS"*. It now intersects the new aggregate demand curve, *AD"*, at *E'''*. Prices have risen even further to 140. Now real GDP is consistent with the rate that can be produced on the long-run aggregate supply curve.

FIGURE 18-3
Growth with inflation.
In this graph the aggregate demand curve shifts outward faster than the short-run aggregate supply curve so that the new equilibrium moves from *E* to *E"*. But *E"* is consistent with real GDP of $7.5 trillion per year. This exceeds the level that is consistent with *LRAS*, $7 trillion per year. Prices will continue to rise and shift the short-run aggregate supply curve upward (because it is a function of input prices) so that the final equilibrium is at *E'''*. Here the new short-run aggregate demand curve, *SRAS"*, intersects the new aggregate curve, *AD"*, at $7 trillion per year on the new vertical long-run aggregate demand curve, *LRAS'*.

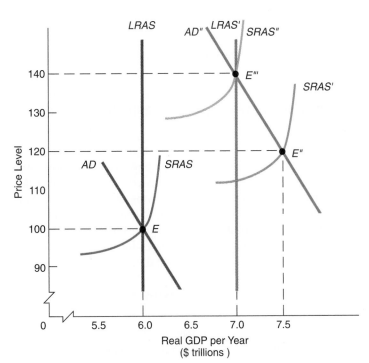

CONCEPTS IN BRIEF

- Economic growth can be defined as the increase in real per capita output measured by its annual rate of change.
- The benefits of economic growth are reductions in illiteracy, poverty, and illness and increases in life spans and political stability. The costs of economic growth include environmental pollution, alienation, and urban congestion.
- Small percentage-point differences in growth rates lead to large differences in real GDP over time. These differences can be seen by examining a compound-interest table such as the one in Table 18-3.
- To estimate the time it takes real GDP or per capita real GDP to double at any annual growth rate, we can use the rule of 72: We divide the annual percentage rate of growth (times 100) into 72.
- Growth can be shown by an outward movement in the long-run aggregate supply curve, *LRAS*, which is a vertical line at the rate of real GDP consistent with the natural rate of unemployment.
- Growth can occur with or without inflation, depending on how fast the short-run aggregate supply curve, *SRAS*, shifts outward relative to the shift outward in aggregate demand and in the long-run vertical aggregate supply curve.

THE FUNDAMENTAL DETERMINANTS OF THE RATE OF ECONOMIC GROWTH

Economic growth does not occur in a vacuum. It is not some predetermined fate of a nation. Rather, economic growth depends on certain fundamental factors. Some of the most important factors that affect the rate of economic growth and hence long-term living standards are the rate of saving, the rate of population growth, and the rate of productivity growth. Knowledge and property rights are also important.

THE RATE OF SAVING

A basic proposition in economics is that if you want more tomorrow, you have to take less today.

> To have more consumption in the future, you have to consume less today and save the difference between your consumption and your income.

On a national basis, this implies that higher saving rates eventually mean higher living standards in the long run, all other things held constant. You have read about this issue in other chapters in this book. There has been a growing concern in America that this country is not saving enough, which means that our rate of saving may be too low. Saving is important for economic growth because without saving we cannot have investment. This has to do with an accounting identity. If all income is consumed each year, there is nothing left over for saving, which could be used by businesses for investment. If there is no investment in our capital stock, there could be little hope of much economic growth.

INTERNATIONAL EXAMPLE: Rates of Saving in Various Countries

Economists have argued for decades that any nation that devotes a relatively high proportion of its income to savings will ultimately also have a relatively high level of income.

FIGURE 18-4
The relationship between rate of saving and per capita real GDP.
This diagram shows the combination of per capita real GDP and the rate of saving expressed as the average percentage of annual real GDP for many nations over the period 1960–1985. Centrally planned economies and major oil-producing countries are not shown.

Source: After Robert Summers and Alan Heston, "A New Set of International Comparisons of Real Product and Price Level," *Review of Income and Wealth (March 1988).*

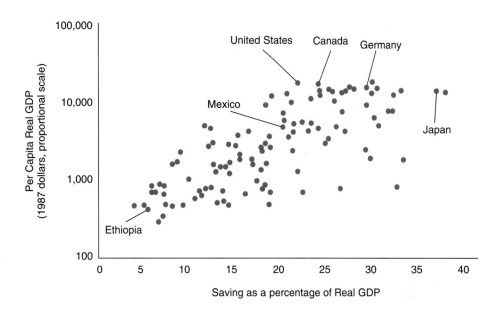

This economic growth proposition is supported by a consistent body of data of saving rates in various countries. In Figure 18-4 you see a scatter diagram showing the relationship between per capita real GDP and the percentage rate of saving. There seems to be a well-established correlation between higher levels of per capita real GDP and higher rates of savings.

For Critical Analysis: How can we expect relatively poor countries, such as Ethiopia, to save more? (Hint: Does the rate of saving depend on income?) ●

 INTERNATIONAL EXAMPLE: Forced Saving in Singapore

If we invest our savings in productive assets, this enhances the capital stock and thus makes future income larger. So the general argument is that a higher saving rate stimulates more rapid growth in income. In their quest for economic growth, some governments have embraced such reasoning by forcing their citizens to save.

▶ Forced saving
Nonconsumption forced by the government through such techniques as requiring payments into a pension plan.

Singapore provides the best-known example of **forced saving**—the use of tax policy and government regulations to compel individuals to save much of their income rather than consume it. This Asian city-state has a tax system that harshly penalizes consumption, as well as tight controls that compel individuals and firms to set aside current income for future retirement benefits. The government has also directed that the huge savings produced by these policies be put into capital investment programs. Between 1970 and 1990, gross investment in Singapore averaged nearly 40 percent of GDP (compared to about 15 percent in the United States). Not surprisingly, with such rapid capital accumulation, Singapore has been a world leader in economic growth, with real per capita GDP growing at 6 percent per year—triple the rate experienced in the United States.

Before concluding that forced saving is the path to prosperity, it is wise to look also at Hong Kong. This nation is remarkably similar to Singapore in most important dimensions, including the fact that over the past 35 years, it too has experienced real growth of 6 percent a year. Yet Hong Kong differs in one important way from Singapore: It permits private individuals to consume and invest as they wish, resulting in gross investment equal to about 20 percent of GDP—high by U.S. standards but still puny compared to Singapore.

Moreover, although Hong Kong and Singapore have virtually identical levels of per capita income, per capita *consumption* in Hong Kong is about 40 percent higher than in Singapore. The additional saving and investment that has been forced by government edict in Singapore have bought the citizenry no extra increase in well-being. The net rate of return on the extra investment has been zero—which beats the *negative* rates of return earned behind the Iron Curtain during the last years of Communist rule but is still not enough to generate additional growth. So the conclusion seems to be that although it is possible to save too little, it is also possible to save too much, especially when the saving is forced.

For Critical Analysis: *What are some of the ways that the U.S. government could force Americans to save more?* ●

THE RATE OF POPULATION GROWTH

Labor is obviously an important factor of production. Therefore, it is not surprising that an increase in the population growth rate implies that more workers are entering the labor force than before. This may lead to increases in real GDP for the entire economy, but not necessarily economic growth as we have defined it. If there is not enough new physical investment for the additional entrants into the labor force, increased population growth will actually lower living standards. When the work force is growing extremely rapidly, a large part of the current output of real goods and services has to be devoted just to providing capital for these new workers. Not surprisingly, many theories of development economics, a subject you will look at in the last chapter, involve policies to reduce population growth. Not all nations want this to occur, however. The governments of European countries, Canada, and Japan are worried about declining birthrates. They are worried that their labor force will shrink too much.

GROWTH IN PRODUCTIVITY: HUMAN CAPITAL AND TECHNOLOGICAL CHANGE

For any given rate of saving and investment (given population growth), living standards can rise only through increases in worker productivity. By definition, when productivity growth occurs, it is possible to obtain more output from the same amount of inputs as before. Productivity growth results in outward shifts in the production possibilities curve. It results in the *LRAS* moving outward to the right. The ability of a nation to create and sustain productivity growth depends on the scientific capabilities of the population, the quality and size of the nation's educational and training system, and the percentage of income that goes into basic research and development each year. Productivity growth does not just occur in the industrial sector of developed nations. In all nations, productivity growth has affected the agricultural sector through the use of pesticides, higher-yielding hybrid seeds, and improved irrigation techniques.

Growth in Human Capital.   A major determinant in productivity growth is the quality and size of the nation's educational and training system. This is because the better the educational and training system, the more improvements to **human capital** occur. Human capital can be defined as the skills, training, and health acquired through on-the-job training and education. All other things held constant, the greater the human capital for a given labor supply, the greater its productivity. Not surprisingly, one of the major differences between developed nations and developing nations is the difference in the rate of improvement to human capital.

▶ **Human capital**
The endowment of abilities to produce that exists in each human being. It can be increased through formal education, on-the-job training, and improved health and psychological well-being.

Technological Improvement.   People who study economic growth in the United States often argue that technological advances are responsible for as much as one-third of the nation's economic growth since 1929. This is not surprising when you realize how technological improvements are defined: They include new production techniques, new managerial techniques, and new forms of business organizations. Moreover, technological improvements are closely linked to investment in new buildings and equipment; when a new process to convert petroleum into plastic is developed, investments in new machines that use this process must be made.

Over the past century, the list of technological improvements has been impressive and almost endless. That list includes the assembly-line technique, conveyer belts, containerized shipping, air transport, genetically engineered food, computer chips, and computers.

Continuing Improvements in Productivity.   A *one-time* improvement in productivity will not keep an economy growing or living standards increasing. For there to be a continuing improvement in living standards, productivity must grow on a continuing basis. In the United States and in many developed countries, productivity growth has been continuous for at least 100 years. In the long run it is primarily through productivity improvement that living standards will rise. After all, the saving rate can rise only so far, and the population growth rate can fall only so much.

THE IMPORTANCE OF KNOWLEDGE

Economist Paul Romer has added at least one important factor that determines the rate of economic growth. He contends that production and manufacturing knowledge is just as important as the other determinants just mentioned—perhaps even more so. He considers knowledge a factor of production that, like capital, has to be paid for by forgoing current consumption. Economies must therefore invest in knowledge just as they invest in machines. Because past investment in capital may make it more profitable to acquire more knowledge, there exists the possibility of an investment–knowledge cycle in which investment spurs knowledge and knowledge spurs investment. A once-and-for-all increase in a country's rate of investment may permanently raise that country's growth rate. According to traditional theory, a once-and-for-all increase in the rate of saving and therefore in the rate of investment simply leads to a new steady-state standard of living but not one that continues to increase.

From Romer's theoretical ideas come some suggestions for policy changes. He argues that to promote growth, the appropriate copyright protection should be established. But because some innovations are costly to develop and may have wide-ranging benefits, he argues that government should give the process a nudge. Specifically, he believes that companies should be allowed to act collectively to raise research and training monies through a voluntary tax on themselves and then decide among themselves how to allocate those funds.

THE IMPORTANCE OF PROPERTY RIGHTS
AND ENTREPRENEURSHIP

If you were in a country where bank accounts and businesses were periodically expropriated by the government, how willing would you be to leave your money in a savings account or to invest in a business? Certainly you would be less willing than if such things never occurred. In general, the more certain private property rights are, the more capital accumulation there will be. People will be willing to invest their savings in endeavors that will increase their wealth in future years. They have property rights in their wealth that are sanctioned and enforced by the government. In fact, some economic historians have attempted to show that it was the development of well-defined private-property rights that allowed Western Europe to increase its growth rate after many centuries of stagnation. The ability and certainty with which they can reap the gains from investing also determine the extent to which business owners in other countries will invest capital in underdeveloped countries. The threat of nationalization that hangs over some Latin American nations probably prevents the massive amount of foreign investment that might be necessary to allow these nations to become more developed.

The property rights, or legal structure, in a nation are closely tied to the degree with which individuals use their own entrepreneurial skills. In Chapter 2 we identified entrepreneurship as the fourth factor of production. Entrepreneurs are the risk takers who seek out new ways to do things and create new products. To the extent that entrepreneurs are allowed to capture the rewards from their entrepreneurial activities, they will seek to engage in those activities. In countries where such rewards cannot be captured because of a lack of property rights (or a property rights structure in which the well-established minority has succeeded in passing laws to exclude the unestablished majority), there will be less entrepreneurship. Typically, this results in fewer investments and a lower rate of growth.

CONCEPTS IN BRIEF

- To have more consumption in the future, we must consume less today and save the difference.
- Population growth can under some circumstances increase economic growth, provided that there is enough new physical investment for the additional entrants in the labor force.
- Improvements in human capital and technological change can both lead to increased productivity and growth.
- A one-time improvement will not increase living standards continuously.
- Knowledge of production and manufacturing techniques may be just as important as the other determinants of economic growth; so too may be the existence of well-defined property rights and entrepreneurship.

CAN AMERICA REMAIN GLOBALLY COMPETITIVE?

Concepts Applied: Global competitiveness, infrastructure, investment

Advances in the development, production, and use of micro-computers may allow the United States to remain globally competitive in a number of critical industries.

The 1990s are being hailed as the decade of American decline. Just a couple of years ago, the Third Decade Council of the American Film Institute held a private conference on the following subject: Was Hollywood, like the American automobile industry, about to lose its superiority over the world's entertainment industry? Would foreign rivals take away Hollywood's business? In industry after industry, similar questions are being asked. Books are being written about the subject, conferences being held, and plans made to stop the decline of America in the world marketplace.

Some researchers even believe that the new international economy is causing skilled workers quietly to secede from the majority. So believes Secretary of Labor Robert Reich, who thinks that this quietly seceding part of America is going to neglect public investment and not finance needed social programs for the less fortunate majority.

TO COMPETE, YOU HAVE TO BE EDUCATED

Reich and others contend that the government must spend more on training and education. Those who are part of the unskilled majority must be given a chance, according to some, to bring up their skills to the level necessary to compete in a new international economy. Still others argue for massive government investments in the infrastructure. President Bill Clinton argued for doing so during his election campaign.

IMPROVEMENTS IN AN ECONOMY'S INFRASTRUCTURE

Each economy's *infrastructure* consists of its roads, communication systems, financial system, and educational and training institutions. It has been argued that one way to improve economic growth in any nation is to improve its infrastructure. Indeed, some people argue that many developing countries cannot increase their rates of growth because they lack the infrastructure that is so obvious in the most developed countries.

We must separate the part of the infrastructure that will take care of itself from the rest. For example, our communication systems are for the most part privately owned and have been expanding by leaps and bounds without government subsidization or government production of equipment. The same is true of our financial system. We cannot talk about our transportation networks, however, without recognizing that a large part is publicly owned. Many people believe that the state of deterioration of our publicly owned transportation network will eventually lead to a deterioration of our infrastructure and hence lower economic growth. Our education and training network is also a mixture of private and public institutions. People who favor growth believe that we need to invest more of the nation's public resources in improving our education and training network.

INTERNATIONAL COMPETITION AND U.S. INVESTMENT

Currently, American firms are investing less than 10 percent of GDP. In Japan the figure is closer to 20 percent; in Germany, 14 percent. American companies are also investing less than their Japanese and German counterparts in basic research and development and in employee training. Most American chief executives think more about the short term than the long term. The opposite appears to be true in both Japan and the European Community. One reason why American firms are more shortsighted is that they are owned by a wide variety of groups—individuals, pension plans, companies, and the like. In contrast, in both Japan and Germany the dominant owners are banks and other institutions or families that hold their stock for long periods of time. These owners have a greater interest in the long term than the diversified group of owners of corporations in America.

411

Can America compete internationally? To answer that question, we must first ask what the true situation is today. The truth is, the United States is not the loser people sometimes take it for. Professor Edward N. Wolff of New York University found that the United States was more efficient in the early 1990s than both Japan and Germany in all areas except fire insurance and real estate. Within the manufacturing sector, Japan was more efficient than the United States in chemicals and plastics; car and plane production; steel, aluminum, and copper; and electronic equipment. But in every other aspect of manufacturing, the United States still remains the most efficient producer in the world. On average, output per worker in the United States is 45 percent higher than in either Germany or Japan.

That is the current situation, but it does not tell us what the future looks like. The future, of course, will depend on what actually happens in the Pacific Rim (particularly in Japan) and in United Europe. The rate of productivity growth has in fact fallen somewhat in both Japan and the EC. There is less evidence now that these parts of the world will surpass American standards of living in the near future. That does not mean that certain parts of the American economy will not get battered in the meantime. A more open international economy means more competition in areas in which we cannot yet compete effectively.

So the answer to the opening question is yes, we can effectively compete internationally, but perhaps not in every industry that currently exists.

FOR CRITICAL ANALYSIS
1. Why should we care whether America can be globally competitive?
2. What skills might be most useful in an increasingly internationalized marketplace?

CHAPTER SUMMARY

1. We define economic growth as an increase in an economy's per capita real GDP. Economic growth can therefore be measured by the rate of change in per capita real GDP.
2. Small changes in rates of growth lead to large differences in GDP over time because of compounding. To find the time that it takes for any quantity to double, we divide the annual percentage rate of growth (times 100) into 72. This is known as the rule of 72.
3. Growth can be shown by an outward movement in the long-run aggregate supply curve, *LRAS*, which is a vertical line at the rate of real national income consistent with the natural rate of unemployment.
4. Growth can occur with or without inflation, depending on how fast the short-run aggregate supply curve, *SRAS*, shifts outward relative to the shift outward in aggregate demand and in the long-run vertical aggregate supply curve.

5. Population growth can under some circumstances increase economic growth, provided that there is enough new physical investment for the additional entrants in the labor force.
6. Improvements in human capital and technological change can both lead to increased productivity and growth. A one-time improvement will not increase living standards continuously.
7. Knowledge of production and manufacturing techniques may be just as important as the other determinants of economic growth; so too may be the existence of well-defined property rights and entrepreneurship.
8. Increased certainty about property rights may lead to more capital accumulation and higher rates of economic growth in nations in which property rights are uncertain.

DISCUSSION OF PREVIEW POINTS

1. What does economic growth measure?
   Many people try to make inferences about changes in economic well-being from a nation's economic growth rate; presumably, higher growth rates imply more

rapid increases in living standards. Others have argued that increased income inequality may accompany rapid economic growth, as a relatively small percentage of the population may benefit from economic growth while the majority experiences little economic improvement. Critics also point out that rapid economic growth is not necessarily consistent with increases in the spiritual, cultural, and environmental quality of life. However, because per capita increases in real GDP do not measure the increased leisure that usually accompanies economic growth, this measure may *understate* economic well-being. Economic growth is therefore a rather crude measure of changes in a nation's well-being and is perhaps a better indicator of its productive activity.

2. What is the rule of 72?
The rule of 72 is simply a rule of thumb for estimating doubling times for things growing at some constant rate per year. For example, if a country's economy is growing at a rate of 3 percent per year, its per capita real GDP will double in approximately 24 years. This result was obtained by dividing the annual percentage growth rate (3 percent) into 72: 72 divided by 3 is 24; hence at 3 percent the initial amount will double in 24 years. Similarly, at a 4 percent economic growth rate, per capita real GDP will double in approximately 18 years. Note that small differences in growth rates account for large differences in output over the long run.

3. What are some of the ways in which you can experience economic growth, either for yourself or for your family?
You can experience economic growth only if you are

willing to sacrifice something. When you continue to go to school, you are sacrificing your current ability to earn and consume income. But in exchange for that sacrifice, you are developing skills and talents that will allow you to have a higher income in the future. You are investing in yourself (human capital) by sacrificing current consumption now.

If you wish to accumulate much wealth during your lifetime, you must be willing to sacrifice current consumption. You do this by not consuming all of your income—that is, by saving part of it. The more you save, the more you can accumulate. In particular, if you invest your accumulated savings in wise savings outlets, you will be rewarded by a compounded rate of growth, so that in the future you will have accumulated larger amounts of wealth.

4. What are the determinants of economic growth?
One obvious determinant of economic growth is the quantity and quality of a nation's natural resources—although this determinant can easily be exaggerated. Thus many slowly developing nations have bountiful natural resources, while some rapidly developing areas have very few. The quality and quantity of labor and capital are also important determinants of economic growth, as is a nation's rate of technological progress. A decidedly underrated determinant of economic growth is the industriousness and willingness of people to be productive—which is surely related to personal incentives related to property rights.

PROBLEMS
(Answers to the odd-numbered problems appear at the back of the book.)

18-1. Using the rule of 72, calculate the approximate doubling times for (a) real GDP in an economy growing at 4, 5, 6, and 7 percent per year; (b) a $1,000 savings account balance that earns $5\frac{3}{4}$ percent per year.

18-2. Why might an economy be operating inside its production possibilities curve?

18-3. The graph shows the production possibilities frontier for an economy. Which of the labeled points would be associated with the highest feasible growth rate for this economy?

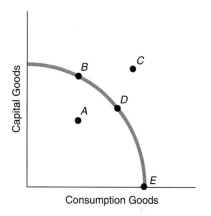

18-4. Consider the following table, which describes growth rate data for four countries between 1985 and 1994.

a. Which country has the largest rate of output growth per capita?

b. Which country has the smallest rate of output growth per capita?

| | Annual Growth Rate (%) | | | |
COUNTRY	J	K	L	M
Nominal GDP	20	15	10	5
Price level	5	3	6	2
Population	5	8	2	1

18-5. In 1993, median family income in the United States was about $36,000. Over the 120 or so years prior to 1993, real income in the United States grew at a rate of about 3 percent per year. Use these two facts, together with the rule of 72, to compute the approximate value of family income in 1873.

COMPUTER-ASSISTED INSTRUCTION
(Complete problem and answer on disk.)

Here the links among global integration, markets, and economic growth are explored.

INTRODUCTION TO MICROECONOMICS

CONSUMER CHOICE

The largest proportion of the average American's leisure time is spent watching television. Some studies show that the average adult looks at television about five hours per day. There was a time long ago when the average TV viewer actually watched entire shows on a regular basis. Switching channels was a relatively infrequent activity. Today switching channels seems to be a national pastime. What happened between then and now to cause us to become a nation of channel switchers during all those hours that we watch television? To delve into this issue, you must understand more about the determinants of consumer choice.

After reading this chapter, you should be able to answer the following questions:

1. What is the law of diminishing marginal utility?
2. How does a consumer maximize total utility?
3. What happens to consumer optimum when price changes?
4. How can the law of diminishing marginal utility account for the law of demand?

INTRODUCTION

When we first discussed the law of demand, we gave several reasons why the quantity demanded increased when the price of a commodity went down. As the price of a good falls, individuals will substitute some of that good for other things. Furthermore, when the price of one good in a consumer's budget decreases, with all other prices constant, that person's buying power becomes greater. A person not only feels richer but actually is richer. With a constant money income, when the price of one good falls, a person clearly has more real spending, or purchasing, power.

Because the law of demand is important, its derivation is useful because it allows us to arrange the relevant variables, such as price, income, and taste, in such a way as to understand the real world better and even perhaps generate predictions about it. One way of deriving the law of demand involves an analysis of the logic of consumer choice in a world of limited resources. In this chapter, therefore, we discuss utility analysis.

UTILITY THEORY

When you buy something, you buy it because of the satisfaction you expect to receive from having and using it. For everything that you like to have, the more you have of it, the higher the level of satisfaction you receive. Another term that can be used for satisfaction is **utility,** or want-satisfying power. This property is common to all goods that are desired. The concept of utility is purely subjective, however. There is no way that you or I can measure the amount of utility that a consumer might be able to obtain from a particular good, for utility does not mean "useful" or "utilitarian" or "practical." For this reason there can be no accurate scientific assessment of the utility that someone might receive by consuming a frozen dinner or a movie relative to the utility that another person might receive from that same good. Nevertheless, we can infer whether a person receives more utility from consuming one good versus another by that person's behavior. For example, if an individual buys more coffee than tea (when both tea and coffee are priced equally), we are able to say that the individual receives more utility from consuming coffee than from consuming tea.

▶ **Utility**
The want-satisfying power of a good or service.

The utility that individuals receive from consuming a good depends on their tastes and preferences. These tastes and preferences are assumed to be given and stable for a given individual. An individual's tastes determine how much utility that individual derives from consuming a good, and this in turn determines how that individual allocates his or her income. People spend a greater proportion of their incomes on goods they like. But we cannot explain why tastes are different between individuals. For example, we cannot explain why some people like yogurt but others do not.

We can analyze in terms of utility the way consumers decide what to buy, just as physicists have analyzed some of their problems in terms of what they call force. No physicist has ever seen a unit of force, and no economist has ever seen a unit of utility. In both cases, however, these concepts have proved useful for analysis.

Throughout this chapter we will be discussing **utility analysis.** This is the analysis of consumer decision making based on utility maximization.

▶ **Utility analysis**
The analysis of consumer decision making based on utility maximization.

UTILITY AND UTILS

Economists once believed that utility could be measured. They therefore first developed utility theory in terms of units of measurable utility, to which they applied the term **util.** For the moment, we will also assume that we can measure satisfaction using this representative unit called the *util.* Our assumption will allow us to quantify the way we ex-

▶ **Util**
A representative unit by which utility is measured.

TABLE 19-1 Total and marginal utility of watching videos.
If we were able to assign specific values to the utility derived from watching videos each week, we could obtain a marginal utility schedule similar in pattern to the one shown here. In column 1 is the number of videos watched per week; in column 2, the total utility derived from each quantity; and in column 3, the marginal utility derived from each additional quantity, which is defined as the change in total utility due to a change of one unit of watching videos per week.

(1) NUMBER OF VIDEOS WATCHED PER WEEK	(2) TOTAL UTILITY (UTILS PER WEEK)	(3) MARGINAL UTILITY (UTILS PER WEEK)
0	0	
		10
1	10	
		6
2	16	
		3
3	19	
		1
4	20	
		0
5	20	
		−2
6	18	

amine consumer behavior.[1] Thus the first chocolate bar that you eat might yield you 4 utils of satisfaction; the first peanut cluster, 6 utils; and so on. Today no one really believes that we can actually measure utils, but the ideas forthcoming from such analysis will prove useful in our understanding of the way in which consumers choose among alternatives.

TOTAL AND MARGINAL UTILITY

Consider the satisfaction, or utility, that you receive each time that you rent and watch a video on your VCR. To make the example straightforward, let's say that there are hundreds of videos to choose from each year and that each of them is of the same quality. Let's say that you normally rent one video per week. You could, of course, rent two, or three, or four per week. Presumably, each time you rent another video per week, you will get additional satisfaction, or utility. The question, though, that we must ask is, given that you are already renting one per week, will the next one give you the same amount of additional utility?

That additional, or incremental, utility is called **marginal utility,** where *marginal,* as before, means "incremental" or "additional." (Marginal changes also refer to decreases, in which cases we talk about *decremental* changes.) The concept of marginality is important in economics because we make decisions at the margin. At any particular point, we compare additional (marginal) benefits with additional (marginal) costs.

▶ **Marginal utility**
The change in total utility due to a one-unit change in the quantity of a good consumed.

APPLYING MARGINAL ANALYSIS TO UTILITY

The specific example presented in Table 19-1 will clarify the distinction between total utility and marginal utility. The table shows the total utility and the marginal utility of watching videos each week. Marginal utility is the difference between total utility derived

---

[1]What follows is typically called *cardinal utility analysis* by economists. It requires cardinal measurement. Numbers such as 1, 2, and 3 are cardinals. We know that 2 is exactly twice as many as 1 and that 3 is exactly 3 times as many as 1. You will see in Appendix E at the end of this chapter a type of consumer behavior analysis that requires only *ordinal* measurement of utility, meaning ranked or ordered. *First, second,* and *third* are ordinal numbers; nothing can be said about their exact size relationships. We can only talk about their importance relative to each other. Temperature, for example, is an ordinal ranking. One hundred degrees Celsius is not twice as warm as 50 degrees Celsius. All we can say is that 100 degrees Celsius is warmer than 50 degrees Celsius.

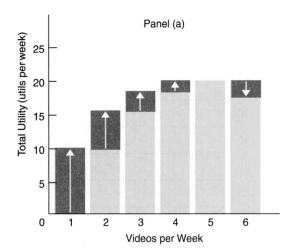

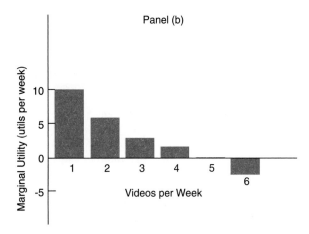

FIGURE 19-1
Total and marginal utility in discrete units.
In panel (a) the colored bars indicate a total utility for each rate of viewing of videos per week. The red portion of each bar indicates a marginal utility for each video watched per week. When we transfer the red portions to panel (b), we have a diagram of discrete marginal utility.

from one level of consumption and total utility derived from another level of consumption. A simple formula for marginal utility is this:

$$\text{Marginal utility} = \frac{\text{Change in total utility}}{\text{Change in number of units consumed}}$$

In our example, when a person has already watched two videos in one week and then watches another, total utility increases from 16 utils to 19. Therefore, the marginal utility (of watching one more video after already having watched two in one week) is equal to 3 utils.

GRAPHIC ANALYSIS

We can transfer the information in Table 19-1 onto a graph, as we do in panels (a) and (b) of Figure 19-1. Total utility, which is represented in column 2 of Table 19-1, is transferred in blocks (represented by bars) to panel (a) of Figure 19-1.

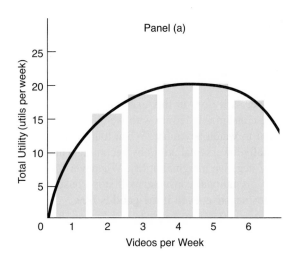

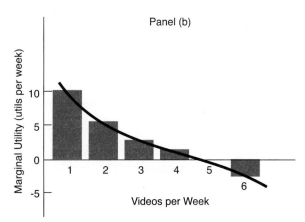

FIGURE 19-2
Total and marginal utility.
If we take the total utility units from column 2 in Table 19-1, we obtain bars like those presented in panel (a) of Figure 19-1. If we connect the tops of those bars with a smooth line, we come up with a total utility curve that peaks somewhere between four and five videos per week and then slowly declines, as shown in panel (a) here. Marginal utility is represented by the increment in total utility, shown as the red blocks in panel (b) of Figure 19-1. When these blocks are connected by a smooth line as in panel (b) here, we obtain the marginal utility curve.

Total utility continues to rise until four videos are watched per week. This measure of utility remains at 20 utils through the fifth video, and at the sixth video per week it falls to 18 utils; we assume that at some quantity consumed per unit time period, boredom sets in. If we connect the tops of the total utility blocks with a smooth line, we come up with a representation of the total utility curve associated with watching videos during a one-week period. This is shown in panel (a) of Figure 19-2. Note that the total utility curve rises, reaches a peak, and then falls.

MARGINAL UTILITY

If you look carefully at both panels (a) and (b) of Figure 19-1, the notion of marginal utility becomes very clear. In economics, the term *marginal* always refers to a change in the total. The marginal utility of watching three videos a week as opposed to two videos a week is the increment in total utility and is equal to 3 utils per day. Marginal utility is represented by the red portion of the bars in panel (a) of Figure 19-1. We can transfer these red portions down to panel (b) of Figure 19-1 and come up with a graphic representation of marginal utility. When we connect the tops of these marginal utility rectangles in panel (b) of Figure 19-2, we get a smoothly sloping marginal utility curve. Notice that that curve hits zero when more than four videos are watched per week. At zero marginal utility, the consumer has watched all the videos that he or she wants to and doesn't want to watch any more. The last video watched at zero marginal utility gives the consumer no additional satisfaction, or utility.

When marginal utility becomes negative, as it does in this example after more than four videos are watched, it means that the consumer is fed up with watching videos and would require some form of compensation to watch any more. When marginal utility is negative, an additional unit consumed actually lowers total utility by becoming a nuisance. Rarely does a consumer face a situation of negative marginal utility. Whenever this point is reached, goods become in effect "bads." A rational consumer will stop consuming at the point at which marginal utility becomes negative, even if the good is free.

CONCEPTS IN BRIEF

- Utility is defined as want-satisfying power; it is a power common to all desired goods and services.
- We arbitrarily measure utility in units called utils.
- It is important to distinguish between total utility and marginal utility. Total utility is the total satisfaction derived from the consumption of a given quantity of a good. Marginal utility is the *change* in total utility due to a one-unit change in the consumption of the good.

DIMINISHING MARGINAL UTILITY

Notice that in panel (b) of Figure 19-2, marginal utility is continuously declining. This property has been named the principle of **diminishing marginal utility.** There is no way that we can prove diminishing marginal utility; nonetheless, economists and others have for years believed strongly in the notion. Diminishing marginal utility has even been called a law. This supposed law concerns a psychological, or subjective, utility that you receive as you consume more and more of a particular good. Stated formally, the law is as follows:

> As an individual consumes more of a particular commodity, the total level of utility, or satisfaction, derived from that consumption usually increases. At some point, however, the *rate* at which it increases diminishes as more is consumed.

▶ **Diminishing marginal utility**
The principle that as more of any good or service is consumed, its extra benefit declines. Otherwise stated, there are smaller and smaller increases in total utility from the consumption of a good or service as more is consumed during a given time period.

Take a hungry individual at a dinner table. The first serving is greatly appreciated, and the individual derives a substantial amount of utility from it. The second serving does not have quite as much impact as the first one, and the third serving is likely to be even less satisfying. This individual experiences diminishing marginal utility of food until he or she stops eating, and this is true for most people. All-you-can-eat restaurants count on this fact; a second helping of ribs may provide some marginal utility, but the third helping would have only a little or even negative marginal utility. The fall in the marginal utility of other goods is even more dramatic.

⭐ EXAMPLE: The "Freshman 15": Gaining Weight While Living in the Dorm

Many dormitory contracts include a meal plan. Such meal plans allow students to take one or all of their meals at the dormitory cafeteria or another designated cafeteria on campus. Studies have shown that students who sign up for full-meal dorm contracts end up gaining weight relative to those who purchase their meals separately or who live in apartments. Economics helps predict this result. Those who eat in cafeterias on a full-meal plan at a college or university are in essence facing an all-you-can-eat restaurant every day. These students can therefore take as many helpings as they want until their marginal utility reaches zero. Students who purchase their food separately will eat only until the marginal utility of food reaches some nonzero point because they have to pay for their food each time. Students not on full-meal-plan contracts consequently eat less, on average, than students on full-meal contracts.

For Critical Analysis: *How do school cafeterias serving students on full-meal plans attempt to limit the total quantity of food served at each sitting?* ●

⭐ EXAMPLE: Newspaper Vending Machines Versus Candy Vending Machines

Have you ever noticed that newspaper vending machines virtually everywhere in the United States allow you to put in the correct change, lift up the door, and take as many newspapers as you want? Contrast this type of vending machine with candy machines. They are completely locked at all times. You must designate the candy that you wish normally by using some type of keypad. The candy then drops down to a place from which you reach to retrieve it, but from which you cannot grab any other candy. The difference between these two types of vending machines relates to diminishing marginal utility. Newspaper companies dispense newspapers from coin-operated boxes that allow dishonest people to take more copies than they pay for. What would a dishonest person do with more than one copy of a newspaper, however? The marginal utility of a second newspaper is normally zero. The benefit of storing excessive newspapers is usually nil because yesterday's news has no value. But the same analysis does not hold for candy. The marginal utility of a second candy bar is certainly less than the first, but it is normally not zero. Moreover, one can store candy for relatively long periods of time at relatively low cost. Consequently, food vending machine companies have to worry about dishonest users of their machines and must make their machines much more theftproof than newspaper companies do.

For Critical Analysis: *Can you think of a circumstance under which a substantial number of newspaper purchasers might be inclined to take more than one newspaper out of a vending machine?* ●

OPTIMIZING CONSUMPTION CHOICES

Every consumer has a limited income. Choices must be made. When a consumer has made all of his or her choices about what to buy and in what quantities, and when the total level of satisfaction, or utility, from that set of choices is as great as it can be, we say that the consumer has *optimized*. When the consumer has attained an optimum consumption set of goods and services, we say that he or she has reached **consumer optimum.**[2]

Consider a simple two-good example. The consumer has to choose between spending income on the rental of videos and on purchasing deluxe hamburgers at $3 each. Let's say that the last dollar spent on hamburgers yields 3 utils of utility, but the last dollar spent on video rentals yields 10 utils. Wouldn't this consumer increase total utility if some

▶ **Consumer optimum**
A choice of a set of goods and services that maximizes the level of satisfaction for each consumer, subject to limited income.

---

[2]Optimization typically refers to individual decision-making processes. When we deal with many individuals interacting in the marketplace, we talk in terms of an equilibrium in the marketplace. Generally speaking, equilibrium is a property of markets rather than of individual decision making.

TABLE 19-2 Total and marginal utility from consuming videos and hamburgers on an income of $26.

(1) VIDEOS PER PERIOD	(2) TOTAL UTILITY OF VIDEOS PER PERIOD (UTILS)	(3) MARGINAL UTILITY (UTILS) MU_v	(4) MARGINAL UTILITY PER DOLLAR SPENT (MU_v/P_v) (PRICE = $5)	(5) HAMBURGERS PER PERIOD	(6) TOTAL UTILITY OF HAMBURGERS (UTILS)	(7) MARGINAL UTILITY (UTILS) MU_h	(8) MARGINAL UTILITY PER DOLLAR SPENT (MU_h/P_h) (PRICE = $3)
0	0.0	—	—	0	0	—	—
1	50.0	50.0	10.0	1	25	25	8.3
2	95.0	45.0	9.0	2	46	22	7.3
3	135.0	40.0	8.0	3	64	18	6.0
4	171.5	36.5	7.3	4	79	15	5.0
5	200.0	30.0	6.0	5	88	9	3.0

dollars were taken away from hamburger consumption and allocated to video rentals? The answer is yes. Given diminishing marginal utility, more dollars spent on video rentals will reduce marginal utility per last dollar spent, whereas fewer dollars spent on hamburger consumption will increase marginal utility per last dollar spent. The optimum—where total utility is maximized—might occur when the satisfaction per last dollar spent on both hamburgers and video rentals per week is equal for the two goods. Thus the amount of goods consumed depends on the prices of the goods and the income of the consumers.

Table 19-2 presents information on utility derived from consuming various quantities of videos and hamburgers. Columns 4 and 8 show the marginal utility per dollar spent on videos and hamburgers, respectively. If the prices of both goods are zero, individuals will consume each as long as their respective marginal utility is positive (at least five units of each and probably much more). It is also true that a consumer with infinite income will continue consuming goods until the marginal utility of each is equal to zero. When the price is zero or the consumer's income is infinite, there is no effective constraint on consumption.

As mentioned, consumer optimum is attained when the marginal utility of the last dollar spent on each good yields the same utility and income is completely exhausted. The individual's income is $26. From columns 4 and 8 of Table 19-2, maximum equal marginal utilities occur at the consumption level of four videos and two hamburgers (the marginal utility per dollar spent equals 7.3). Notice that the marginal utility per dollar spent for both goods is also (approximately) equal at the consumption level of three videos and one hamburger, but here total income is not completely exhausted. Likewise, the marginal utility per dollar spent is also equal at five videos and three hamburgers, but here the expenditures necessary for that level of consumption exceed the individual's income.

Table 19-3 shows the steps taken to arrive at consumer optimum. The first video would yield a marginal utility per dollar of 10, while the first hamburger would yield a marginal utility of only 8.3 per dollar. Because it yields the higher marginal utility per dollar, the video is purchased. This leaves $21 of income. The second video yields a higher marginal utility per dollar (9 versus 8.3 for hamburgers), so it is also purchased, leaving an unspent income of $16. At the third purchase, the first hamburger now yields a higher marginal utility per dollar than the next video (8.3 versus 8), so the first hamburger is purchased. This leaves income of $13 to spend. The process continues until all income is exhausted and the marginal utility per dollar spent is equal for both goods.

TABLE 19-3 Steps to consumer optimum.
In each purchase situation described here, the consumer always purchases the good with the higher relative marginal utility per dollar spent (MU/P). For example, at the time of the third purchase, the marginal utility per last dollar spent on videos is 8, but it is 8.3 for hamburgers, and $16 of income remains, so that the next purchase will be a hamburger. Here $P_v = \$5$ and $P_h = \$3$.

	CHOICES					
	VIDEOS		HAMBURGERS			
PURCHASE	UNIT	(MU_v/P_v)	UNIT	(MU_h/P_h)	BUYING DECISION	REMAINING INCOME
1	First	10.0	First	8.3	First video	$26 – $5 = $21
2	Second	9.0	First	8.3	Second video	$21 – $5 = $16
3	Third	8.0	First	8.3	First hamburger	$16 – $3 = $13
4	Third	8.0	Second	7.3	Third video	$13 – $5 = $8
5	Fourth	7.3	Second	7.3	Fourth video and second hamburger	$ 8 – $5 = $3 $ 3 – $3 = $0

To restate, consumer optimum requires the following:

> A consumer's money income should be allocated so that the last dollar spent on each good purchased yields the same amount of marginal utility.

A LITTLE ALGEBRA

We can state the rule of consumer optimum in algebraic terms by examining the ratio of marginal utilities and prices of individual products. This is sometimes called the *rule of equal marginal utilities per dollar spent* on a basket of goods. The rule simply states that a consumer maximizes personal satisfaction when allocating money income in such a way that the last dollars spent on good *a*, good *b*, good *c*, and so on, yield equal amounts of marginal utility. Marginal utility (*MU*) from good *a* is indicated by *MU* of good *a*. For good *b*, it is *MU* of good *b*. Our algebraic formulation of this rule, therefore, becomes

$$\frac{MU \text{ of good } a}{\text{price of good } a} = \frac{MU \text{ of good } b}{\text{price of good } b} = \cdots = \frac{MU \text{ of good } z}{\text{price of good } z}$$

The letters $a, b, \ldots, z$ indicate the various goods and services that the consumer might purchase.

We know, then, that the marginal utility of good *a* divided by the price of good *a* must equal the marginal utility of any other good divided by its price in order for the consumer to maximize her or his utility. Note, though, that the application of the rule of equal marginal utility per dollar spent is not an explicit or conscious act on the part of consumers. Rather, this is a model of consumer optimum.

HOW A PRICE CHANGE AFFECTS CONSUMER OPTIMUM

Consumption decisions are summarized in the law of demand, which states that the amount purchased is inversely related to price. We can now see why by using the law of diminishing marginal utility.

Purchase decisions are made such that the value of the marginal utility of the last unit purchased and consumed is just equal to the price that had to be paid, that is, the oppor-

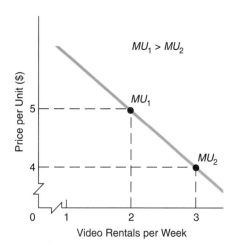

$MU_1 > MU_2$

MU_1

MU_2

Price per Unit ($)

5

4

0   1   2   3

Video Rentals per Week

FIGURE 19-3
Video rental prices and marginal utility.
The rate of video rentals per week will increase as long as the marginal utility per last video rental per week exceeds the cost of that rental. Therefore, a reduction in price from $5 to $4 per video rental will allow consumers to increase consumption until marginal utility falls from MU_1 to MU_2 (because of the law of diminishing marginal utility).

tunity cost for that last unit. Here the opportunity cost is the sacrifice of utility of another product. No consumer will, when optimizing, buy 10 units of a good per unit time period when the subjective valuation placed on the tenth unit is less than the price of the tenth unit.

If we start out at consumer optimum and then observe a price decrease, we can predict that consumers will respond to the price decrease by consuming more. Why? Because before the price change, the marginal utility of the last unit was about equal to the price paid for the last unit. Now, with a lower price, it is possible to consume more than before and still not have the marginal utility be less than the price, because the price has fallen. If the law of diminishing marginal utility holds, the purchase and consumption of additional units will cause marginal utility to fall. Eventually it will fall to the point at which it is equal to the price of the final good consumed. The limit to this increase in consumption is given by the law of diminishing marginal utility. At some point the marginal utility of an additional unit will be less than what the person would have to give up (price) for that additional unit, and the person will stop buying.

A hypothetical demand curve for video rentals per week for a typical consumer is presented in Figure 19-3. At a rental price of $5 per video, the marginal utility of the last video rented per week is MU_1. At a rental price of $4 per video per week, the marginal utility is represented by MU_2. Because of the law of diminishing marginal utility—with the consumption of more videos, the marginal utility of the last unit of these additional videos is lower—MU_2 must be less than MU_1. What has happened is that at a lower price, the number of video rentals per week increased from two to three; marginal utility must have fallen. At a higher consumption rate, the marginal utility falls to meet the lower price for video rentals per week.

THE SUBSTITUTION EFFECT

What is happening as the price of video rental falls is that consumers are substituting the now relatively cheaper video rentals for other goods and services, such as restaurant meals and live concerts. We call this the substitution effect of a change in price of a good because it occurs when consumers substitute relatively cheaper goods for relatively more expensive ones.

THE INCOME EFFECT

There is another reason that a reduction in price will cause an increase in the quantity demanded (or an increase in price will cause a reduction in the quantity demanded). It has to do with the ability of individuals to purchase more or fewer goods and services when there is a price change in one of the goods and services now being consumed. A fall in the price of any one item being purchased during a week increases the purchasing power of any given amount of money income. A fall in the price of any good being consumed results in an increase in real income—the amount of goods and services that one is able to purchase. Given this increase in real income, most individuals will tend to buy more of most goods and services that they are now consuming. This increase in quantity demanded due to a price reduction, which causes an increase in real income, is called the income effect of a change in price. In an affluent society, the substitution effect is more important than the income effect for just about all the goods that a typical consumer might purchase. Only when a single item constitutes a major portion of the consumer's budget does the income effect become significant.

 INTERNATIONAL EXAMPLE: **High-priced Restaurant Meals in Foreign Lands**

Assume that you and your family have decided to visit friends who live in London, Paris, Rome, or Tokyo. You will be visiting them for a 10-day period. You and your family make the trip, stay the 10 days, visit with your friends, engage in tourist activities, and eat in restaurants. After you return home, you can calculate the average cost of restaurant meals. You will find that on average you ended up spending considerably more per person per restaurant meal than during the rest of the year back in the United States. Now your first thought may be that it is because the cost of living is higher in those other cities just mentioned. But actually, even if we assume that the cost of living is exactly the same as where you are currently living, you will normally still end up spending more per restaurant meal when you travel abroad than when you stay at home. The reason is that the price of high-quality (expensive) restaurant meals relative to lower-quality (lower-cost) restaurant meals is different when you take an expensive trip abroad than when you decide to go out to dinner in your hometown.

Assume that a high-quality meal in both your hometown and the foreign city you visit costs $50 per person and a lower-quality meal costs $25 per person. In both places the relative price of high- versus low-quality restaurant meals is 2:1. But what is the *total* cost of eating these restaurant meals? Doesn't it also include the cost of transportation? The cost of getting to London, Paris, Rome, or Tokyo is a lot more than getting into your car and driving to a restaurant across town. Let's say that it costs $10 to drive to that restaurant in town versus $500 to ship yourself to London, Paris, Rome, or Tokyo. Now let's look at the relative prices of a high-quality and a low-quality restaurant meal. In your town the relative price is ($50 + $10) ÷ ($25 + $10) = 1.71. In the foreign city, however, the equation is different: ($500 + $50) ÷ ($500 + $25) = 1.05. What has happened here is that the *relative* price of high- versus low-quality restaurant meals has dropped significantly when you travel abroad and include your total travel costs.

For Critical Analysis: Can you use the same analysis to explain why New Yorkers purchase a relatively higher proportion of high-quality California oranges relative to low-quality California oranges than do fruit customers in California? ●

THE DEMAND CURVE REVISITED

Linking the "law" of diminishing marginal utility and the rule of equal marginal utilities per dollar gives us a negative relationship between the quantity demanded of a good or service and its price. As the relative price of video rental goes up, for example, the quantity demanded will fall; and as the relative price of video rental goes down, the quantity demanded will rise. Figure 19-3 shows this demand curve for video rentals. As the price of video rental falls, the consumer can maximize total utility only by renting more videos, and vice versa. In other words, the relationship between price and quantity desired is simply a downward-sloping demand curve. Note, though, that this downward-sloping demand curve (the law of demand) is derived under the assumption of constant tastes and incomes. You must remember that we are keeping these important determining variables constant when we simply look at the relationship between price and quantity demanded.

 EXAMPLE: Why Diamonds Are More Expensive than Water

Even though water is essential to life and diamonds are not, water is cheap and diamonds are dear. The economist Adam Smith in 1776 called this the "diamond-water paradox." The paradox is easily understood when we make the distinction between total utility and marginal utility. The total utility of water greatly exceeds the total utility derived from diamonds. What determines the price, though, is what happens on the margin. We have relatively few diamonds, so the marginal utility of the last diamond consumed is high. The opposite is true for water. Total utility does not determine what people are willing to pay for a particular commodity; marginal utility does. Look at the situation graphically in Figure 19-4. We show the demand curve for diamonds, labeled $D_{diamonds}$. The demand curve for water is labeled D_{water}. We plot quantity in terms of kilograms per unit time period on the horizontal axis. On the vertical axis we plot price in dollars per kilogram. We use kilograms as our common unit of measurement for water and for diamonds. We could just as well have used gallons, acre-feet, or liters.

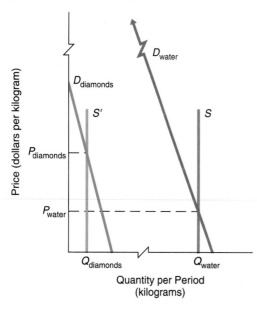

FIGURE 19-4
The diamond-water paradox.
We pick kilograms as a common unit of measurement for both water and diamonds. To demonstrate that the demand for water is immense, we have put a break in the demand curve, D_{water}. We have also put a break indication on the vertical axis to show that it goes much higher than indicated in this graph. Although the demand for water is much greater than the demand for diamonds, the marginal valuation of water is given by the marginal value placed on the last unit of water consumed. To find that, we must know the supply of water, which is given as S. At that supply, the price of water is P_{water}. But the supply for diamonds is given by S'. At that supply, the price of diamonds is $P_{diamonds}$. The total valuation that consumers place on water is tremendous relative to the total valuation consumers place on diamonds. What is important for price determination, however, is the marginal valuation, or the marginal utility received.

Notice that we have drawn the demand curve for water with a break in it to illustrate that the demand for water is many, many times the demand for diamonds. We draw the supply curve of water as S at a quantity of Q_{water}. The supply curve for diamonds is given as S' at quantity $Q_{diamonds}$. At the intersection of the supply curve of water with the demand curve of water, the price per kilogram is P_{water}. The intersection of the supply curve of diamonds with the demand curve of diamonds is at $P_{diamonds}$. Notice that $P_{diamonds}$ exceeds P_{water}. Diamonds sell at a higher price than water.

For Critical Analysis: Would the analysis just presented apply to other necessities such as food and if so, why? ●

CONCEPTS IN BRIEF

- The law of diminishing marginal utility tells us that each successive marginal unit of a good consumed adds less extra utility.
- Each consumer with a limited income must make a choice about the basket of commodities to purchase; economic theory assumes that the consumer chooses the basket of commodities that yields optimum consumption.
- The consumer maximizes total utility by equating the marginal utility of the last dollar spent on one good with the marginal utility per last dollar spent on all other goods. That is the state of consumer optimum.
- To remain in consumer optimum, a price decrease requires an increase in consumption; a price increase requires a decrease in consumption.
- Each change in price has a substitution effect and an income effect. When price falls, the consumer substitutes in favor of the relatively cheaper good. When price falls, the consumer's real purchasing power increases, causing the consumer to purchase more of most goods. The opposite would occur when price increases.
- Assuming that the law of diminishing marginal utility holds, the demand curve must slope downward.

CONTINUED ➔

CHANNEL SWITCHING: THE NATIONAL PASTIME
Concept Applied: Diminishing marginal utility

The advent of numerous channels linked to a remote, infrared channel-switching device has launched a nation of "channel surfers." Analytically, how long will a "channel surfer" watch one particular channel?

Television, viewed in the larger scope of things, is relatively young. An early prototype was patented in Germany in 1884. The development of an electron tube and electronic scanning methods made the marketing of television signals practicable in 1945. After World War II, black-and-white television sets started showing up in households throughout America. Today 99.9 percent of all households are estimated to have at least one television set, and many have two or more. Not only do Americans have more television sets to watch, but they have more channels, too, and they tend to switch channels frequently—far more frequently then they did in the 1940s or even in the 1970s. According to the Cable Television Administration and Marketing Society, anywhere from 20 to 30 percent of TV viewers consistently engage in channel switching. That is to say, they never watch any one program for more than a couple of minutes. Does this mean that Americans today are somehow different from those who watched television after World War II? The answer is probably not.

DIMINISHING MARGINAL UTILITY   You have learned in this chapter that after a certain point, the more any activity is engaged in, the lower the marginal utility of that activity. Most people can be presumed to experience diminishing marginal utility with just about anything they consume, including TV shows. That means that the first few minutes of a particular TV show will yield more utility per minute than the minutes viewed thereafter. The lower the marginal utility of any particular TV program, the more incentive the TV viewer has to do one of two things: turn the TV off or switch to another program. There are two relatively recent changes in the history of television that have increased TV viewers' desire to switch channels.

THE ADVENT OF THE REMOTE CONTROL
In 1980, the percentage of households with television sets with remote controls was extremely small. They were expensive and required a cord on which people could trip. A mere 15 years later, it is estimated that over 90 percent of U.S. households have remote controls, and virtually no television sets are sold without them. The relative cost of being a channel switcher has dropped dramatically since television became the staple in America's leisure diet. Prior to the advent of the remote control, not even an individual with incredibly rapidly diminishing marginal utility for TV programs would have imagined getting up every 120 seconds to change the channel *mechanically*.

MORE NUMEROUS ALTERNATIVES
The other factor that has increased the amount of channel switching in America is the advent of cable and satellite-dish TV. In the early days there were the networks—ABC, NBC, and CBS—and a few independent stations in the big cities. That was it. Today the average person with cable has 37 channels from which to choose. Some have many more, and thanks to new transmission technologies, the number should increase dramatically in the next decade. At any rate, the potential channel switcher now has an increased likelihood of finding another show that is preferred to the one he or she is currently watching. This offers an additional inducement to switch channels with the remote control unit.

FOR CRITICAL ANALYSIS
1. How do you think the proliferation of remote controls and the number of cable channels have affected the way commercials are produced? Why?
2. How do you think the proliferation of the TV remote control and the number of channels have affected the TV coverage of political speeches?

CHAPTER SUMMARY

1. As an individual consumes more of a particular commodity, the total level of utility, or satisfaction, derived from that consumption increases. However, the *rate* at which it increases diminishes as more is consumed. This is known as the law of diminishing marginal utility.

2. An individual reaches consumer optimum when the marginal utility per last dollar spent on each commodity consumed is equal to the marginal utility per dollar spent on every other good.

3. When the price of a particular commodity goes up, to get back into an optimum position, the consumer must reduce consumption of the now relatively more expensive commodity. As this consumer moves back up the marginal utility curve, marginal utility increases. A change in price has both a substitution effect and an income effect. As the price goes down, for example, the consumer substitutes in favor of the cheaper good, and also as the price goes down, real purchasing power increases, causing a general increase in consumer purchases of most goods and services.

4. It is possible to derive a downward-sloping demand curve by using the principle of diminishing marginal utility.

DISCUSSION OF PREVIEW POINTS

1. **What is the law of diminishing marginal utility?**
   The law of diminishing marginal utility states that as an individual consumes more and more units of a commodity per unit of time, eventually the extra benefit derived from consuming successive units will fall. Thus the fourth hamburger consumed in an eight-hour period yields less satisfaction than the third, and the third less than the second. The law is quite general and holds for almost any commodity; it is difficult to think of an exception to this "law."

2. **How does a consumer maximize total utility?**
   This question deals with the maximization of utility derived not from the consumption of one commodity but from the consumption of all commodities that the individual wants, subject to an income constraint. The rule is that maximization of total utility requires that the last dollar spent on each commodity consumed by the individual have the same marginal utility. Stated differently, the consumer should purchase goods and services up to the point where the consumer's marginal utilities per dollar (marginal utility divided by price) for all commodities are equated and all income is spent (or saved for future spending). For example, assume that Frank Romano is about to spend all of his income but discovers that the marginal utility per dollar's worth for bread will be 10 utils and the marginal utility per dollar's worth of milk will be 30 utils. This means that the last dollar he is going to spend on bread will increase his total utility by 10, whereas the last dollar he is going to spend on milk will increase his total utility by 30. By spending one dollar more on milk and one dollar less on bread, he raises his total utility by about 20 utils, while his total dollar expenditures remain constant. This reallocation causes the marginal utility per dollar's worth of milk to fall and the marginal utility per dollar's worth of bread to rise. To maximize total utility, Romano will continue to buy more or less of each commodity until the marginal utilities per dollar's worth of all goods he consumes are equated.

3. **What happens to consumer optimum when price changes?**
   Assume that in point 2, Frank Romano has reached an optimum: The marginal utilities per dollar's worth for all the goods he purchases are equated. Assume that the last dollar spent on each of the commodities he purchases increases his total utility by 20 utils. Now suppose that the price of bread falls—all other prices remaining constant. Because the price of bread has fallen, the last dollar spent on bread now has a higher marginal utility. This is true because at a lower price for bread, a $1 bill can purchase a greater quantity of bread. This means that marginal utility per dollar's worth for bread now *exceeds* 20 utils, whereas the marginal utility per dollar's worth of each of the other goods he purchases still equals 20 utils. In short, Romano is no longer optimizing; his old pattern of expenditures does not maximize his total utility. Romano can now increase his total utility by purchasing more bread. Note that a reduction in the price of bread (other things held constant) led to Romano's purchasing more bread per unit of time.

4. How can the law of diminishing marginal utility account for the law of demand?

When a consumer is optimizing, total utility is maximized. An increase in expenditures on any specific commodity will necessarily lead to a reduction in expenditure on another commodity and a reduction in overall total utility. Why? Because of the law of diminishing marginal utility. For example, suppose that Frank Romano is maximizing his overall total utility and that the marginal utility per dollar's worth of each commodity he purchases is 20 utils. Suppose that he experiments and spends another dollar on bread—and

therefore spends one dollar less on milk. His total utility must fall because he will receive less than 20 utils for the next dollar's worth of bread, and he loses 20 utils by spending a dollar less on milk. Thus, on net balance, he loses utility. We can see intuitively, then, that because Romano gets less and less additional benefit from consuming more and more bread (or any other commodity), the price of bread (or any other commodity) *must fall* before he will voluntarily purchase more of it. In short, diminishing marginal utility helps explain the law of demand.

PROBLEMS

(Answers to the odd-numbered problems appear at the back of the book.)

19-1. Suppose that you are standing in the checkout line of a grocery store. You have 5 pounds of oranges and three ears of corn. A pound of oranges costs 30 cents; so does an ear of corn. You have $2.40 to spend. You are satisfied that you have reached the highest level of satisfaction, or total utility. Your sister comes along and tries to convince you that you have to put some of the corn back and replace it with oranges. From what you know about utility analysis, how would you explain this disagreement?

If the price is $2? How do we calculate marginal utility per dollar's worth of specific commodities?

19-4. A fall in the price of one good leads to more of that good being consumed, other things remaining constant. How might this increase in consumption be broken down?

19-5. Consider the table below. Following the optimizing rule, how much of each good will be consumed?

19-6. If total utility is increasing as more is consumed, what is happening to marginal utility?

QUANTITY OF GOOD A	MARGINAL UTILITY OF GOOD A	PRICE OF GOOD A	QUANTITY OF GOOD B	MARGINAL UTILITY OF GOOD B	PRICE OF GOOD B
100	15	$4.51	9	7	$1.69
101	12	4.51	10	5	1.69
102	8	4.51	11	3	1.69
103	6	4.51	12	2	1.69

19-2. To increase marginal utility, the consumer must decrease consumption (other things being constant). This sounds paradoxical. Why is it a correct statement nonetheless?

19-3. Assume that Alice Warfield's marginal utility is 100 utils for the last hamburger she consumed. If the price of hamburgers is $1 apiece, what is Warfield's marginal utility per dollar's worth of hamburger? What is her marginal utility per dollar's worth if the price is 50 cents per hamburger?

19-7. Yesterday you were consuming four eggs and two strips of bacon. Today you are consuming three eggs and three strips of bacon. Your tastes did not change overnight. What might have caused this change? Are you better or worse off?

19-8. The marginal utility of X is five times the marginal utility of Y, but the price of X is only four times the price of Y. How can this disequilibrium be remedied?

19-9. Look at the following table:

QUANTITY OF X CONSUMED	TOTAL UTILITY (UTILS)
0	0
1	20
2	50
3	70
4	80

a. What is the marginal utility of consuming the first unit of X?
b. What is the marginal utility of consuming the fourth unit of X?
c. When does marginal utility start to diminish?

COMPUTER-ASSISTED INSTRUCTION
(Complete problem and answer on disk.)

The consumer is optimizing when $MU_a/P_a = MU_b/P_b = \cdots = MU_z/P_z$. What does it mean if $MU_a/P_a > MU_b/P_b$? If $MU_a/P_a < MU_b/P_b$? How is a consumer likely to react to such inequalities? Why will the consumer's total utility increase on buying more or less of each good if an inequality exists? Specific calculations shed light on these questions.

MORE ADVANCED CONSUMER CHOICE THEORY

It is certainly possible to analyze consumer choice verbally, as we did for the most part in Chapter 19. The theory of diminishing marginal utility can be fairly well accepted on intuitive grounds and by introspection. If we want to be more formal and perhaps more elegant in our theorizing, however, we can translate our discussion into graphic analysis with what we called indifference curves and the budget constraint. Here we discuss these terms and their relationship and demonstrate consumer equilibrium in geometric form.

ON BEING INDIFFERENT

What does it mean to be indifferent? It usually means that you don't care one way or the other about something—you are equally disposed to either of two alternatives. With this interpretation in mind, we will turn to two choices, video rentals and restaurant meals. In panel (a) of Figure E-1 we show several combinations of video rentals and restaurant meals per week that a representative consumer considers equally satisfactory. That is to say, for each combination, A, B, C, and D, this consumer will have exactly the same level of total utility.

FIGURE E-1

Combinations that yield equal levels of satisfaction.
The combinations A, B, C, and D represent combinations of video rentals and restaurant meals per week that give an equal level of satisfaction to this consumer. In other words, the consumer is indifferent among these four combinations.

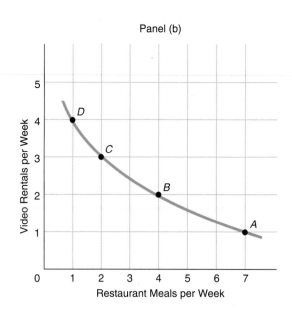

Panel (b)

Panel (a)

COMBINATION	VIDEO RENTALS PER WEEK	RESTAURANT MEALS PER WEEK
A	1	7
B	2	4
C	3	2
D	4	1

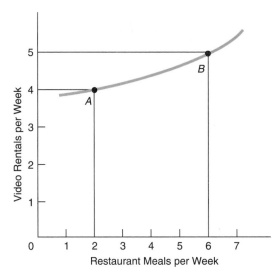

FIGURE E-2
Indifference curves cannot slope up.
Point *B* represents a consumption of more video rentals per week and more restaurant meals per week than point *A*. *B* is always preferred to *A*. Therefore, *A* and *B* cannot be on the same indifference curve, which is positively sloped, because an indifference curve shows *equally preferred* combinations of the two goods.

The simple numerical example that we have used happens to concern video rentals and restaurant meals per week. This example is used to illustrate general features of indifference curves and related analytical tools that are necessary for deriving the demand curve. Obviously, we could have used any two commodities. Just remember that we are using a *specific* example to illustrate a *general* analysis.

We can plot these combinations graphically in panel (b) of Figure E-1, with restaurant meals per week on the horizontal axis and video rentals per week on the vertical axis. These are our consumer's indifference combinations—the consumer finds each combination as acceptable as the others. When we connect these combinations with a smooth curve, we obtain what is called the consumer's **indifference curve.** Along the indifference curve, every combination of the two goods in question yields the same level of satisfaction. Every point along the indifference curve is equally desirable to the consumer. For example, four video rentals per week and one restaurant meal per week will give our representative consumer exactly the same total satisfaction as two video rentals per week and four restaurant meals per week.

▶ **Indifference curve**
A curve composed of a set of consumption alternatives, each of which yields the same total amount of satisfaction.

PROPERTIES OF INDIFFERENCE CURVES

Indifference curves have special properties relating to their slope and shape.

Downward Slope.   The indifference curve shown in panel (b) of Figure E-1 slopes downward; that is, it has a negative slope. Now consider Figure E-2. Here we show two points, *A* and *B*. Point *A* represents four video rentals per week and two restaurant meals per week. Point *B* represents five video rentals per week and six restaurant meals per week. Clearly, *B* is always preferred to *A* because *B* represents more of everything. If *B* is always preferred to *A*, it is impossible for points *A* and *B* to be on the same indifference curve because the definition of the indifference curve is a set of combinations of two goods that are equally preferred.

Curvature.   The indifference curve that we have drawn in panel (b) of Figure E-1 is special. Notice that it is curved. Why didn't we just draw a straight line, as we have usually done for a demand curve? To find out why we don't posit straight-line indifference curves, consider the implications. We show such a straight-line indifference curve in

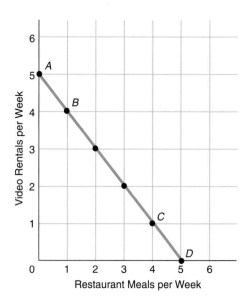

FIGURE E-3
The implications of a straight-line indifference curve.
If the indifference curve is a straight line, the consumer will be willing to give up the same number of video rentals (one for one in this simple example) to get one more restaurant meal per week, whether the consumer has no restaurant meals or a lot of restaurant meals per week. For example, the consumer at point *A* has five video rentals and no restaurant meals per week. He or she is willing to give up one video rental in order to get one restaurant meal per week. At point *C*, however, the consumer has only one video rental and four restaurant meals per week. Because of the straight-line indifference curve, this consumer is willing to give up the last video rental in order to get one more restaurant meal per week, even though he or she already has four.

Figure E-3. Start at point *A*. The consumer has no restaurant meals and five video rentals per week. Now the consumer wishes to go to point *B*. He or she is willing to give up only one video rental in order to get one restaurant meal. Now let's assume that the consumer is at point *C*, consuming one video rental and four restaurant meals per week. If the consumer wants to go to point *D*, he or she is again willing to give up one video rental in order to get one more restaurant meal per week.

In other words, no matter how many videos the consumer rents, he or she is willing to give up one video rental to get one restaurant meal per week—which does not seem plausible. Doesn't it make sense to hypothesize that the more videos the consumer rents per week, the less he or she will value an *additional* video rental? Presumably, when the consumer has five video rentals and no restaurant meals per week, he or she should be willing to give up more than one video rental in order to get one restaurant meal. Therefore, a straight-line indifference curve as shown in Figure E-3 no longer seems possible.

In mathematical jargon, an indifference curve is convex with respect to the origin. One reason for this is the law of diminishing marginal utility, which we discussed in Chapter 19.[1] As the individual consumes more of a particular item, the marginal utility of consuming one additional unit of that item falls, or, conversely, as the person consumes less of it, that good will have a higher marginal utility.

We can measure the marginal utility of something by the quantity of a substitute good that would leave the consumer indifferent. Let's look at this in panel (a) of Figure E-1. Starting with combination *A*, the consumer has one video rental but seven restaurant meals per week. To remain indifferent, the consumer would have be willing to give up three restaurant meals to obtain one more video rental (as shown in combination *B*). However, to go from combination *C* to combination *D*, notice that the consumer would have to be willing to give up only one restaurant meal for an additional video rental per week. The quantity of the substitute considered acceptable changes as the relative scarcity of the original item changes.

Diminishing marginal utility exists throughout this set of choices, and consequently the indifference curve in Figure E-1 (b) will be convex when viewed from the origin. If it were a straight line, marginal utility would be not diminishing but constant; if it were curved the other way (concave with respect to the origin), marginal utility would be increasing.

---

[1]Actually, it can be shown that only diminishing marginal rates of substitution are required.

TABLE E-1 Calculating the marginal rate of substitution.
As we move from combination A to combination B, we are still on the same indifference curve. To stay on that curve, the number of restaurant meals decreases by three and the number of video rentals increases by one. The marginal rate of substitution is 1 to 3. A one-unit increase in video rentals requires a reduction in three restaurant meals to leave the consumer's total utility unaltered.

(1) COMBINATION	(2) RESTAURANT MEALS PER WEEK	(3) VIDEO RENTALS PER WEEK	(4) MARGINAL RATE OF SUBSTITUTION OF RESTAURANT MEALS FOR VIDEO RENTALS
A	7	1	
			1:3
B	4	2	
			1:2
C	2	3	
			1:1
D	1	4	

THE MARGINAL RATE OF SUBSTITUTION

We have discussed marginal utility in terms of the marginal rate of substitution between restaurant meals and video rentals per week. We can more formally define the consumer's marginal rate of substitution (MRS) as follows:

> MRS is equal to the change in the quantity of one good that just offsets a one-unit change in the consumption of another good, such that total satisfaction remains constant.

We can see numerically what happens to the marginal rate of substitution in our example if we rearrange panel (a) of Figure E-1 into Table E-1. Here we show restaurant meals in the second column and video rentals in the third. Now we ask the question, What change in the consumption of restaurant meals per week will just compensate for a one-unit change in the consumption of video rentals per week and leave the consumer's total utility constant? The movement from A to B reduces restaurant meal consumption by three. Here the marginal rate of substitution is 1:3—a one-unit increase in video rentals requires a reduction in three restaurant meals to leave the consumer's total utility unaltered. Thus the consumer values the first video rental as the equivalent of three restaurant meals. We do this for the rest of the table and find that as video rental consumption increases, the marginal rate of substitution goes from 1:3 to 1:1. The marginal rate of substitution of restaurant meals for video rentals per week rises as the consumer obtains more video rentals. That is, the consumer values successive units of video rentals less and less in terms of restaurant meals. The first video rental is valued at three restaurant meals; the last (fourth) video rental is valued at only one restaurant meal. The fact that the marginal rate of substitution falls is sometimes called the *law of substitution*.

In geometric language, the slope of the consumer's indifference curve (actually, the negative of the slope) measures the consumer's marginal rate of substitution. Notice that this marginal rate of substitution is purely subjective or psychological.

THE INDIFFERENCE MAP

Let's now consider the possibility of having both more video rentals *and* more restaurant meals per week. When we do this, we can no longer stay on the same indifference curve that we drew in Figure E-1. That indifference curve was drawn for equally satisfying combinations of video rentals and restaurant meals per week. If the individual can now attain more of both, a new indifference curve will have to be drawn, above and to the right of the one shown in panel (b) of Figure E-1. Alternatively, if the individual faces the

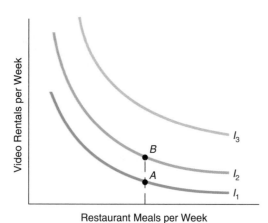

FIGURE E-4
A set of indifference curves.
An infinite number of indifference curves can be drawn. We show three possible ones. Realize that a higher indifference curve represents the possibility of higher rates of consumption of both goods. Hence a higher indifference curve is preferred to a lower one because more is preferred to less. Look at points A and B. Point B represents more video rentals than point A; therefore, indifference curve I_2 has to be preferred over I_1 because the number of restaurant meals per week is the same at points A and B.

possibility of having less of both video rentals and restaurant meals per week, an indifference curve will have to be drawn below and to the left of the one in panel (b) of Figure E-1. We can map out a whole set of indifference curves corresponding to these possibilities.

Figure E-4 shows three possible indifference curves. Indifference curves that are higher than others necessarily imply that for every given quantity of one good, more of the other good can be obtained on a higher indifference curve. Looked at another way, if one goes from curve I_1 to I_2, it is possible to consume the same number of restaurant meals *and* be able to rent more videos per week. This is shown as a movement from point A to point B in Figure E-4. We could do it the other way. When we move from a lower to a higher indifference curve, it is possible to rent the same number of videos *and* to consume more restaurant meals per week. Thus the higher a consumer is on the indifference map, the greater that consumer's total level of satisfaction—assuming, of course, that the consumer does not become satiated.

THE BUDGET CONSTRAINT

Our problem here is to find out how to maximize consumer satisfaction. To do so, we must consult not only our *preferences*—given by indifference curves—but also our *market opportunities*—given by our available income and prices, called our **budget constraint.** We might want more of everything, but for any given budget constraint we have to make choices, or trade-offs, among possible goods. Everyone has a budget constraint; that is, everyone faces a limited consumption potential. How do we show this graphically? We must find the prices of the goods in question and determine the maximum consumption of each allowed by our budget. For example, let's assume that videos rent for $10 apiece and restaurant meals cost $20. Let's also assume that our representative consumer has a total budget of $60 per week. What is the maximum number of videos the consumer can rent? Obviously, six. And the maximum number of restaurant meals per week he or she can consume? Three. So now, as shown in Figure E-5, we have two points on our budget line, which is sometimes called the *consumption possibilities curve.* These anchor points of the budget line are obtained by dividing money income by the price of each product. The first point is at *b* on the vertical axis; the second at *b'* on the horizontal axis. The budget line is linear because prices do not change.

Any combination along line *bb'* is possible; in fact, any combination in the colored area is possible. We will assume, however, that the individual consumer completely uses up the available budget, and we will consider as possible only those points along *bb'*.

▶ **Budget constraint**
All of the possible combinations of goods that can be purchased (at fixed prices) with a specific budget.

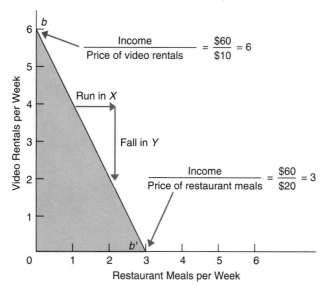

The budget constraint.
The line *bb'* represents this individual's budget constraint. Assuming that video rentals cost $10 each, restaurant meals cost $20 each, and the individual has a budget of $60 per week, a maximum of six video rentals or three restaurant meals can be bought each week. These two extreme points are connected to form the budget constraint. All combinations within the colored area and on the budget constraint line are feasible.

SLOPE OF THE BUDGET CONSTRAINT

The budget constraint is a line that slopes downward from left to right. The slope of that line has a special meaning. Look carefully at the budget line in Figure E-5. Remember from our discussion of graphs in Appendix A that we measure a negative slope by the ratio of the fall in *Y* over the run in *X*. In this case *Y* is video rentals per week and *X* is restaurant meals per week. In Figure E-5, the fall in *Y* is −2 video rentals per week (a drop from 4 to 2) for a run in *X* of one restaurant meal per week (an increase from 1 to 2); therefore, the slope of the budget constraint is −2/1, or −2. This slope of the budget constraint represents the rate of exchange between video rentals and restaurant meals; it is the realistic rate of exchange, given their prices.

Now we are ready to determine how the consumer achieves the optimum consumption rate.

CONSUMER OPTIMUM REVISITED

Consumers will try to attain the highest level of total utility possible, given their budget constraints. How can this be shown graphically? We draw a set of indifference curves similar to those in Figure E-4, and we bring in reality—the budget constraint, *bb'*. Both are drawn in Figure E-6 on the next page. Because a higher level of total satisfaction is represented by a higher indifference curve, we know that the consumer will strive to be on the highest indifference curve possible. However, the consumer cannot get to indifference curve I_3 because the budget will be exhausted before any combination of video rentals and restaurant meals represented on indifference curve I_3 is attained. This consumer can maximize total utility, subject to the budget constraint, only by being at point *E* on indifference curve I_2 because here the consumer's income is just being exhausted. Mathematically, point *E* is called the tangency point of the curve I_2 to the straight line *bb'*.

Consumer optimum is achieved when the marginal rate of substitution (which is subjective) is just equal to the feasible, or realistic, rate of exchange between video rentals and restaurant meals. This realistic rate is the ratio of the two prices of the goods involved. It is represented by the absolute value of the slope of the budget constraint. At point *E*,

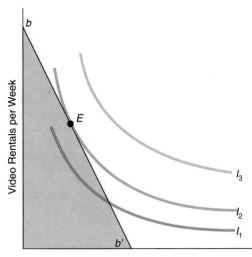

FIGURE E-6
Consumer optimum.
A consumer reaches an optimum when he or she ends up on the highest indifference curve possible, given a limited budget. This occurs at the tangency between an indifference curve and the budget constraint. In this diagram the tangency is at *E*.

the point of tangency between indifference curve I_2 and budget constraint bb', the rate at which the consumer wishes to substitute video rentals for restaurant meals (the numerical value of slope of the indifference curve) is just equal to the rate at which the consumer *can* substitute video rentals for restaurant meals (the slope of the budget line).

EFFECTS OF CHANGES IN INCOME

A change in income will shift the budget constraint bb' in Figure E-6. Consider only increases in income and no changes in price. The budget constraint will shift outward. Each new budget line will be parallel to the original one because we are not allowing a change in the relative prices of video rentals and restaurant meals. We would now like to find out how an individual consumer responds to successive increases in income when nominal and relative prices remain constant. We do this in Figure E-7. We start out with an in-

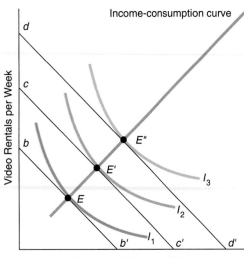

FIGURE E-7
Income-consumption curve.
We start off with income sufficient to yield budget constraint bb'. The highest attainable indifference curve is I_1, which is just tangent to bb' at E. Next we increase income. The budget line moves outward to cc', which is parallel to bb'. The new highest indifference curve is I_2, which is just tangent to cc' at E'. We increase income again, which is represented by a shift in the budget line to dd'. The new tangency point of the highest indifference curve, I_3, with dd', is at point E''. When we connect these three points, we obtain the income-consumption curve.

come that is represented by a budget line bb'. Consumer optimum is at point E, where the consumer attains the highest indifference curve I_1, given the budget constraint bb'. Now we let income increase. This is shown by a shift outward in the budget line to cc'. The consumer attains a new optimum at point E'. That is where a higher indifference curve, I_2, is reached. Again, the consumer's income is increased so that the new budget line is dd'. The new optimum now moves to E''. This is where indifference curve I_3 is reached. If we connect the three consumer optimum points, E, E', and E'', we have what is called an income-consumption curve. The **income-consumption curve** shows the optimum consumption points that would occur if income for that consumer were increased continuously, holding the prices of video rentals and restaurant meals constant.

▶ **Income-consumption curve**
The set of optimum consumption points that would occur if income were increased, nominal and relative prices remaining constant.

THE PRICE-CONSUMPTION CURVE

In Figure E-8 we hold money income and the price of video rentals constant while we lower the price of restaurant meals. As we keep lowering the price of restaurant meals, the quantity of meals that could be purchased if all income were spent on restaurant meals increases; thus the extreme points for the budget constraint keep moving outward to the right as the price of restaurant meals falls. In other words, the budget line rotates outward from bb' to bb'' and bb'''. Each time the price of restaurant meals falls, a new budget line is formed. There has to be a new optimum point. We find it by locating on each new budget line the highest attainable indifference curve. This is shown at points E, E', and E''. We see that as price decreases for restaurant meals, the consumer purchases more restaurant meals per week. We call the line connecting points E, E', and E'' the **price-consumption curve.** It connects the tangency points of the budget constraints and indifference curves, thus showing the amounts of two goods that a consumer will buy when money income and the price of one commodity are held constant while the price of the remaining good changes.

▶ **Price-consumption curve**
The set of consumer optimum combinations of two goods that the consumer would choose as the relative price of the goods changes, while money income remains constant.

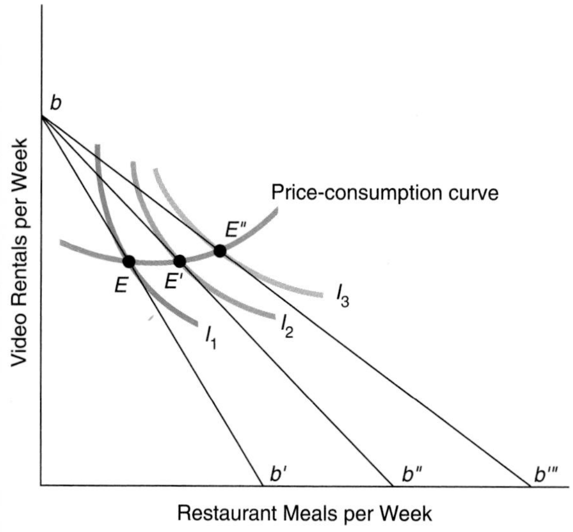

FIGURE E-8
Price-consumption curve.
As we lower the price of restaurant meals, income measured in terms of restaurant meals per week increases. We show this by rotating the budget constraint from bb' to bb'' and finally to bb'''. We then find the highest indifference curve that is attainable for each successive budget constraint. For budget constraint bb', the highest indifference curve is I_1, which is tangent to bb' at point E. We do this for the next two budget constraints. When we connect the optimum points, E, E', and E'', we derive the price-consumption curve, which shows the combinations of the two commodities that a consumer will purchase when money income and the price of one commodity remain constant while the other commodity's price changes.

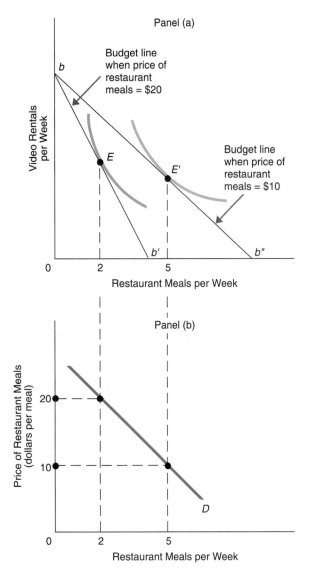

FIGURE E-9
Deriving the demand curve.
In panel (a) we show the effects of a decrease in the price of restaurant meals from $20 to $10. At $20, the highest indifference curve touches the budget line *bb'* at point *E*. The quantity of restaurant meals consumed is two. We transfer this combination—price, $20; quantity demanded, 2—down to panel (b). Next we decrease the price of restaurant meals to $10. This generates a new budget line, or constraint, which is *bb"*. Consumer optimum is now at *E'*. The optimum quantity of restaurant meals demanded at a price of $10 is five. We transfer this point—price, $10; quantity demanded, 5—down to panel (b). When we connect these two points, we have a demand curve, *D*, for restaurant meals.

DERIVING THE DEMAND CURVE

We are now in a position to derive the demand curve using indifference curve analysis. In panel (a) of Figure E-9 we show what happens when the price of restaurant meals decreases, holding both the price of video rentals and income constant. If the price of restaurant meals decreases, the budget line rotates from *bb'* to *bb"*. The two optimum points are given by the tangency at the highest indifference curve that just touches those two budget lines. This is at *E* and *E'*. But those two points give us two price-quantity pairs. At point *E* the price of restaurant meals is $20; the quantity demanded is 2. Thus we have one point that we can transfer to panel (b) of Figure E-9. At point *E'* we have another price-quantity pair. The price has fallen to $10. The quantity demanded has increased to 5. We therefore transfer this other point to panel (b). When we connect these two points (and all the others in between), we derive the demand curve for restaurant meals; it slopes downward.

APPENDIX SUMMARY

1. Along an indifference curve, the consumer experiences equal levels of satisfaction. That is to say, along any indifference curve, every combination of the two goods in question yields exactly the same level of satisfaction.
2. Indifference curves usually slope downward and are usually convex to the origin.
3. To measure the marginal rate of substitution, we find out how much of one good has to be given up in order to allow the consumer to consume one more unit of the other good while still remaining on the same indifference curve. The marginal rate of substitution falls as one moves down an indifference curve.
4. Indifference curves represent preferences. A budget constraint represents opportunities—how much can be purchased with a given level of income. Consumer optimum is obtained when the highest indifference curve is just tangent to the budget constraint line; at that point the consumer reaches the highest feasible indifference curve.
5. When income increases, the budget constraint shifts outward to the right, parallel to the previous budget constraint line.
6. As income increases, the consumer optimum moves up to higher and higher indifference curves. When we connect those points with a line, we derive the income-consumption curve.
7. As the price of one good decreases, the budget line rotates. When we connect the tangency points of the highest indifference curves to these new budget lines, we derive the price-consumption curve.

PROBLEMS

(Answers to the odd-numbered problems appear at the back of the book.)

E-1. Suppose that a consumer prefers A to B and B to C but insists that she also prefers C to A. Explain the logical problem here.

E-2. Suppose that you are indifferent among the following three combinations of food (f) and drink (d): 1f and 10d, 2f and 7d, 3f and 2d. Calculate the marginal rate of substitution (MRS) in consumption between the two goods. Does the substitution of the third f imply a greater sacrifice of d than the second did?

E-3. Construct a budget line from the following information: nominal income of $100 per week, price of beef, P_b, $2 per pound; price of shelter, P_s, $20 per week; all income is spent on beef and/or shelter. Suppose that your money income remains constant, the price of beef doubles to $4 per pound, and the price of housing falls to $10 per week. Draw the new budget line. Are you now better off or worse off? What do you need to know before deciding?

E-4. Given the following three combinations of goods, $A = 3x + 4y$, $B = 4x + 6y$, and $C = 5x + 4y$, answer the following questions:
   a. Is any one bundle preferred to the other two?
   b. Could a consumer possibly find B and C to be equally acceptable? How about A and C?

E-5. Calculate the marginal rate of substitution of burritos for yogurt for the following consumer's indifference schedule:

YOGURT PINTS PER WEEK	BURRITOS PER WEEK
10	1
6	2
3	3
1	4

E-6. Assume that you are consuming only yogurt (Y) and gymnasium exercise (G). Each serving of yogurt costs $4, and each visit to the gym costs $8. Given your food and exercise budget, you consume 15 servings of yogurt and five visits to the gym each week. One day the price of yogurt falls to $3 per serving and the price of gym visits increases to $10. Now you buy 20 servings of yogurt and four gym visits per week.
   a. Draw the old and new budget constraints, and show the two equilibrium bundles of yogurt servings and visits to the gym.
   b. What is your weekly budget for food and exercise?

E-7. Explain why each of the following statements is or is not consistent with our assumptions about consumer preferences.
   a. I can't decide whether to go abroad this summer or to stay at home.
   b. That is mine. You cannot have it. There is nothing you can do to make me change my mind.
   c. I love hot pretzels with mustard at football games. If I had my way, I would never stop eating them.

20

DEMAND AND SUPPLY ELASTICITY

"He's rich; he can afford it." How many times have you heard those words? The rich are different from everyone else because they do indeed have more money income and more wealth. But does that mean that the rich do not respond to relatively small changes in price? One way to find out is to examine what happened to the market for new luxury boats, furs, and jewelry when the federal government applied a 10 percent luxury tax a few years ago. Did the rich simply ignore this small increase in the price of luxury goods? Answering this question forms part of the larger study of elasticity, a concept that permits us to measure how sales and output respond to changes in price.

After reading this chapter, you should be able to answer the following questions:

1. How is total revenue related to price elasticity of demand?

2. What are the determinants of price elasticity of demand?

3. What is income elasticity of demand?

4. What is price elasticity of supply?

INTRODUCTION

The law of demand is straightforward: The higher the price of a commodity, the less will be purchased, and vice versa (all other things held constant). Why is it, then, that the leaders of the Organization of Petroleum Exporting Countries (OPEC) always seem to be trying to do whatever they can to raise the price of petroleum? Don't higher prices mean lower quantities demanded? The answer is, of course, yes. Those oil ministers who attend OPEC meetings know that higher world oil prices do in fact mean a lower quantity demanded, but not *that* much lower. In contrast, the supermarket manager who finds herself with too many very ripe strawberries does the opposite—she tells her staff to lower the price on fresh strawberries by 50 percent.

The typical firm is not in existence to maximize the number of items sold. Both of our examples—OPEC and the supermarket—involve organizations that want to maximize *profits,* even though they seem to be acting differently. To understand that, you have to look at consumers' *responsiveness* to any price change. We already know the direction, for it is always opposite that of the price change. What we do not know necessarily is how much consumers will respond to any given price change. Consumers' responsiveness to any given percentage price change is not the same for all goods. Clearly it is different for oil than for fresh strawberries. Managers in private firms as well as decision makers within governments must have an idea of how responsive people in the real world will be to changes in price. Economists have a special name for price responsiveness—*elasticity.* Elasticity is the subject of this chapter.

PRICE ELASTICITY

To begin to understand what elasticity is all about, just keep in mind that it means "responsiveness" or "stretchiness." Here we are concerned with the price elasticity of demand and the price elasticity of supply. We wish to know the extent to which a change in the price of, for example, petroleum products will cause the quantity demanded and the quantity supplied to change, other things held constant. Let's restrict our discussion at first to the demand side.

PRICE ELASTICITY OF DEMAND

▶ **Price elasticity of demand (E_p)**
The responsiveness of the quantity demanded of a commodity to changes in its price. The price elasticity of demand is defined as the percentage change in quantity demanded divided by the percentage change in price.

We will formally define the **price elasticity of demand,** which we will label E_p, as follows:

$$E_p = \frac{\text{percentage change in quantity demanded}}{\text{percentage change in price}}$$

What will price elasticity of demand tell us? It will tell us the relative amount by which the quantity demanded will change in response to a change in the price of a particular good.

Consider an example in which a 10 percent rise in the price of oil leads to a reduction in quantity demanded of only 1 percent. Putting these numbers into the formula, we find that the price elasticity of demand for oil in this case equals the percentage change in quantity demanded divided by the percentage change in price, or

$$E_p = \frac{-1\%}{+10\%} = -.1$$

An elasticity of $-.1$ means that a 1 percent *increase* in the price would lead to a mere .1 percent *decrease* in the quantity demanded. If you were now told, in contrast, that the price elasticity of demand for oil was -1, you would know that a 1 percent increase in the price of oil would lead to a 1 percent decrease in the quantity demanded.

Relative Quantities Only.   Notice that in our elasticity formula, we talk about *percentage* changes in quantity demanded divided by *percentage* changes in price. We are therefore not interested in the absolute changes, only in relative amounts. This means that it doesn't matter if we measure price changes in terms of cents, dollars, or hundreds of dollars. It also doesn't matter whether we measure quantity changes in ounces, grams, or pounds. The percentage change will be independent of the units chosen.

🌐 INTERNATIONAL EXAMPLE: Increasing Canadian Taxes on Cigarettes

Smoking is responsible for a variety of illnesses, including emphysema and lung cancer. The Canadian government decided to do something about this problem behavior. At the end of the 1980s it launched a two-pronged attack on smoking. The first prong involved banning virtually all advertising, even the printing of cigarette brand names on T-shirts. Smoking was prohibited in all public areas and work sites under federal jurisdiction and on all flights of Canadian airlines. Part two involved a steep increase in the price of cigarettes via an increase in the sales tax, both at the federal level and at the provincial level. The price of cigarettes went up by over 30 percent in a three-year period. By the start of 1992, a pack of cigarettes cost $5.50. This dramatic price increase brought about a reduction in the quantity demanded. As the price rose, per capita cigarette consumption dropped by 7 percent in 1989, an additional 6.5 percent in 1990, and 13 percent in 1991.

Data over a longer period of time confirm the responsiveness of cigarette consumers to price increases. From 1980 to 1993, the inflation-corrected price of cigarettes in Canada increased by 60 percent. Over that time span the estimated reduction in adult smoking was 43 percent. The approximate price elasticity of demand is therefore 43 percent ÷ 60 percent = .72. That means that in the long run, for every 10 percent increase in the relative price of cigarettes, the expected reduction in adult smoking will be about 7 percent. Canadian observers contend that among teenagers the price elasticity of demand for cigarette smoking is even greater.

For Critical Analysis: *What are the other possible reasons why cigarette consumption fell in Canada, besides the dramatic increase in the price of cigarettes?* ●

Always Negative.   The law of demand states that quantity demanded is *inversely* related to the relative price. In the example above, an increase in the price of cigarettes led to a decrease in the quantity demanded. We could have used an example of a decrease in the relative price of cigarettes, in which case the quantity demanded would increase by a certain percentage. The point is that price elasticity of demand will always be negative. By convention *we will ignore the minus sign in our discussion from this point on.*

Basically, the greater the *numerical* price elasticity of demand (disregarding sign), the greater the demand responsiveness to relative price changes—a small change in price has a great impact on quantity demanded. The smaller the *numerical* price elasticity of demand, the smaller the demand responsiveness to relative price changes—a large change in price has little effect on quantity demanded.

CONCEPTS IN BRIEF

- Elasticity is a measure of the price responsiveness of the quantity demanded and quantity supplied.
- The price elasticity of demand is equal to the percentage change in quantity demanded divided by the percentage change in price.
- The law of demand states that quantity demanded and price are inversely

related. Therefore, the price elasticity of demand is always negative, because an increase in price will lead to a decrease in quantity demanded and a decrease in price will lead to an increase in quantity demanded. By convention we ignore the negative sign in discussions of the price elasticity of demand.

● Price elasticity of demand is calculated in terms of relative percentage changes in quantity demanded and in price. Thus it is expressed as a unitless, dimensionless number.

CALCULATING ELASTICITY

To calculate the price elasticity of demand, we have to compute percentage changes in quantity demanded and in relative price. To obtain the percentage change in quantity demanded, we divide the change in the quantity demanded by the original quantity demanded:

$$\frac{\text{Change in quantity demanded}}{\text{Original quantity demanded}}$$

To find the percentage change in price, we divide the change in price by the original price:

$$\frac{\text{Change in price}}{\text{Original price}}$$

Because percentage change is based on the original value, it makes a difference where you start—whether you move from point A to point B or from point B to point A.

Let's take a set of hypothetical numbers to show how price elasticity of demand is calculated. Look at the demand curve in panel (a) of Figure 20-1 on the next page. It shows quantity demanded of oil in million of barrels per day at various hypothetical prices. It is downward-sloping because of the law of demand. The relevant numbers are shown in panel (b). Columns 1 and 3 are quantity demanded and price, respectively. Columns 2 and 4 show changes in quantity demanded corresponding to changes in price.

Let's start with a quantity at point A in panel (a) with one unit demanded at the price of $10 per unit and move down the demand curve to point B in panel (a). If we start at a price of $10 with one unit demanded, price falls to $9. Quantity demanded increases to two. The percentage change in quantity demanded is

$$\frac{2-1}{1} = \frac{1}{1} = 1 = 100\%$$

The percentage change in price is

$$\frac{\$10 - \$9}{\$10} = \frac{\$1}{\$10} = .1 = 10\%$$

Thus the elasticity of demand is equal to

$$\frac{100\%}{10\%} = 10$$

Now let's calculate the price elasticity of demand when we move up the demand curve in panel (a) of Figure 20-1 from point B to point A . We start at a price of $9 with two units demanded. The price goes up to $10 and one unit is demanded. The percentage change in quantity demanded is

$$\frac{2-1}{2} = \frac{1}{2} = .5 = 50\%$$

FIGURE 20-1
Numerical calculation of price elasticity of demand for oil.
In panel (a) the demand curve for oil is shown. The data that generated this demand
curve are presented in panel (b) in columns 1 and 2. The price elasticity of demand is
calculated with these data in the rest of panel (b).

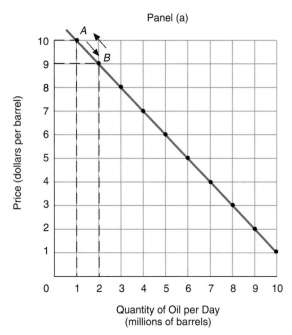

Panel (a)

Quantity of Oil per Day
(millions of barrels)

Panel (b)

(1) QUANTITY DEMANDED, Q (MILLIONS OF BARRELS PER DAY)	(2) CHANGE IN Q (MILLIONS OF BARRELS PER DAY)	(3) PRICE, P (DOLLARS PER BARREL)	(4) CHANGE IN P	(5) $\dfrac{Q_1 + Q_2}{2}$	(6) $\dfrac{P_1 + P_2}{2}$	(7) $E_P = \dfrac{\text{CHANGE IN } Q}{(Q_1 + Q_2)/2} \div \dfrac{\text{CHANGE IN } P}{(P_1 + P_2)/2}$
0		11				
	1		$1	.5	$10.5	1/.5 ÷ 1/10.5 = 21
1		10				
	1		1	1.5	9.5	1/1.5 ÷ 1/9.5 = 6.333
2		9				
	1		1	2.5	8.5	1/2.5 ÷ 1/8.5 = 3.4
3		8				
	1		1	3.5	7.5	1/3.5 ÷ 1/7.5 = 2.143
4		7				
	1		1	4.5	6.5	1/4.5 ÷ 1/6.5 = 1.444
5		6				
	1		1	5.5	5.5	1/5.5 ÷ 1/5.5 = 1
6		5				
	1		1	6.5	4.5	1/6.5 ÷ 1/4.5 = .692
7		4				
	1		1	7.5	3.5	1/7.5 ÷ 1/3.5 = .467
8		3				
	1		1	8.5	2.5	1/8.5 ÷ 1/2.5 = .294
9		2				
	1		1	9.5	1.5	1/9.5 ÷ 1/1.5 = .158
10		1				

The percentage change in price is now equal to

$$\frac{\$10 - \$9}{\$9} = \frac{\$1}{\$9} = .111 = 11.11\%$$

Thus the price elasticity of demand is now equal to

$$\frac{50\%}{11.11\%} = 4.5$$

Using Average Values.   For the same segment of the demand curve we get different values of price elasticity of demand because the original prices and quantities depend on whether we raise or lower the price. The *absolute* changes in price and quantity are the same size regardless of direction. But when we move down the demand curve, the *original* price is higher than when we move up the demand curve. When we move up the demand curve, the original quantity demanded is greater. Because a percentage change depends on the size of the original value, the percentages we calculate for price elasticity of demand will be affected by choosing a higher price and smaller quantity or a lower price and greater quantity. One way out of this difficulty is to take the average, or midpoint, between points *A* and *B* in panel (a) of Figure 20-1. That means we take the average of the two prices and the two quantities over the range we are considering and compare the change with these averages or midpoints, which have been computed. The formula for computing price elasticity of demand then becomes

$$E_p = \frac{\text{change in quantity}}{\text{sum of quantities/2}} \div \frac{\text{change in price}}{\text{sum of prices/2}}$$

We can rewrite this more simply if we do two things: (1) We can let Q_1 and Q_2 equal the two different quantities demanded before and after the price change and let P_1 and P_2 equal the two different prices. (2) Because we will be dividing a percentage by a percentage, we simply use the ratio, or the decimal form, of the percentages. Therefore,

$$E_p = \frac{\Delta Q}{(Q_1 + Q_2)/2} \div \frac{\Delta P}{(P_1 + P_2)/2}$$

Let's redo the example that showed a price elasticity of demand equal to 10 when moving from a \$10 to a \$9 price—when moving from point *A* to point *B* in panel (b) of Figure 20-1—but an elasticity of 4.5 when moving from \$9 to \$10. We insert our numbers in the average formula just given, so that in either case price elasticity of demand becomes

$$E_p = \frac{1/[(1 + 2)/2]}{1/[(9 + 10)/2]} = \frac{1/(3/2)}{1/(19/2)} = \frac{2/3}{2/19} = \frac{38}{6} = 6.33$$

Thus calculating the price elasticity of demand using the midpoint (or average) formula yields $E_p = 6.33$. This calculation is not affected by the direction of movement along the demand curve; that is, $E_p = 6.33$ whether we move up or down the demand curve over the range we have been considering.

Consider again the hypothetical data presented in panel (b) of Figure 20-1 for the quantities of oil demanded by U.S. consumers at various prices. Columns 5 and 6 give us the average quantities and the average prices. In column 7 a numerical example of price elasticity of demand is given. We see that the computation of elasticity ranges from 21 down to .158. What does that mean? Simply that at relatively high prices for oil, such as between $10 and $11 a barrel, the response to a 1 percent decrease in price will be a 21 percent increase in the quantity demanded. At the other extreme, at relatively low prices for oil—between $1 and $2 per barrel—the elasticity of .158 means that a 1 percent reduction in price will be followed by only .158 percent increase in the quantity demanded. Thus price elasticity of demand falls as price falls.

⭐ EXAMPLE: The Price Elasticity of Minivans

Automobile prices have been going up for years. Yet in certain subcategories of vehicles, intense competition, both domestic and foreign, has caused at least one company to cut prices on minivans. The Chrysler Corporation created the minivan market and dominated it during the 1980s. A few years ago it started to see its market share slip. In response, it reduced the price of its basic model minivan from $14,111 to $13,811. As expected, average sales of minivans per month did increase after the price reduction. At the higher price Chrysler was selling approximately 31,000 minivans per month. At the lower price it was selling 32,240 minivans per month. We can estimate the price elasticity of demand for minivans using the midpoint, or average, formula presented earlier (under the assumption, of course, that all other things are held constant):

$$
E_p = \frac{\Delta Q}{(Q_1 + Q_2/2)} \div \frac{\Delta P}{(P_1 + P_2/2)}
$$

$$
= \frac{32,240 - 31,000}{(31,100 + 32,240/2)} \div \frac{\$14,111 - \$13,811}{(\$13,811 + 14,111/2)}
$$

$$
= \frac{1240}{31,670} \div \frac{300}{13,961} = 1.8
$$

An elasticity of 1.8 means that a 1 percent decrease in price will lead to a 1.8 percent increase in quantity demanded.

For Critical Analysis: *Would the estimated price elasticity of Chrysler's minivans have been different if we had not used the average-values formula? How?* ●

PRICE ELASTICITY RANGES

We have names for the varying ranges of price elasticities, depending on whether a 1 percent change in price elicits more or less than a 1 percent change in the quantity demanded.

1. **Elastic demand.** We say that a good has an elastic demand whenever the price elasticity of demand is greater than 1. A 1 percent change in price causes a response greater than a 1 percent change in quantity demanded. Candidates for elastic demand sections of our demand schedule in panel (b) of Figure 20-1 are obviously an E_p of 1.444 and above. The most extreme elastic demand curve is called perfectly elastic; its price elasticity of demand is infinite, such that even the slightest increase in price will cause quantity demanded to fall to zero, so the elasticity of demand is infinite.
2. **Unit elasticity of demand.** In this situation, a 1 percent change in price causes a response of exactly a 1 percent change in the quantity demanded.
3. **Inelastic demand.** Here a 1 percent change in price causes a response of less than a 1 percent change in quantity demanded. An elasticity of .692 and below in the last four lines of panel (b) of Figure 20-1 represents a situation of inelastic demand. The most extreme form of an inelastic demand is one that is perfectly inelastic; no matter what

▶ **Elastic demand**
A demand relationship in which a given percentage change in price will result in a larger percentage change in quantity demanded. Total revenues and price are inversely related in the elastic portion of the demand curve.

▶ **Unit elasticity of demand**
A demand relationship in which the quantity demanded changes exactly in proportion to the change in price. Total revenue is invariant to price changes in the unit-elastic portion of the demand curve.

▶ **Inelastic demand**
A demand relationship in which a given change in price will result in a less than proportionate change in the quantity demanded. Total revenue and price are directly related in the inelastic region of the demand curve.

the price, the quantity demanded remains the same, so the price elasticity of demand is zero.

When we say that a commodity's demand is elastic, we are indicating that consumers are relatively responsive to changes in price. When we say that a commodity's demand is inelastic, we are indicating that its consumers are relatively unresponsive to price changes. When economists say that demand is inelastic, it does not mean that quantity demanded is totally unresponsive to price changes. Remember, the law of demand suggests that there will be some responsiveness in quantity demanded to a price change. The question is how much? That's what elasticity attempts to determine.

ELASTICITY AND TOTAL REVENUES

Suppose that you are in charge of the pricing decision for a cellular telephone service company; how would you know when it is best to raise or not to raise prices? The answer depends in part on the effect of your pricing decision on total revenues, or the total receipts of your company. (The rest of the equation is, of course, your cost structure, a subject we examine in Chapter 22.) It is commonly thought that the way to increase total receipts is to increase price per unit. But is this always the case? Is it possible that a rise in price per unit could lead to a decrease in total revenues? The answers to these questions depend on the price elasticity of demand.

Let's look at Figure 20-2 on the next page. In panel (a), column 1 shows the price of cellular telephone service in dollars per minute, and column 2 represents billions of minutes per year. In column 3 we multiply column 1 times column 2 to derive total revenue because total revenue is always equal to the number of units (quantity) sold times the price per unit, and in column 4 we calculate values of elasticity. Notice what happens to total revenues throughout the schedule. They rise steadily as the price rises from 10 cents to 50 cents per minute; but when the price rises further to 60 cents per minute, total revenues remain constant at $3. At prices per minute higher than 60 cents, total revenues actually fall as price increases. Indeed, if prices are above 60 cents per minute, total revenues can be increased only by *cutting* prices, not by raising them.

LABELING ELASTICITY

The relationship between price and quantity on the demand schedule is given in columns 1 and 2 of panel (a) in Figure 20-2. In panel (b) the demand curve, *D*, representing that schedule is drawn. In panel (c) the total revenue curve representing the data in column 3 is drawn. Notice first the level of these curves at small quantities. The demand curve is at a maximum height, but total revenue is zero, which makes sense according to this demand schedule—at that price and above, no units will be purchased, and therefore total revenue will be zero. As price is lowered, we travel down the demand curve, and total revenues increase up to a price of 60 cents per minute, remain constant from 60 cents to 50 cents per minute, and then fall at lower unit prices. Corresponding to those three sections, demand is price-elastic, unit-elastic, and price-inelastic. Hence we have three relationships among the three types of price elasticity and total revenues.

1. **Price-elastic demand.** A negative relationship exists between small changes in price and changes in total revenues. That is to say, if price is lowered, total revenues will rise when the firm faces demand that is price-elastic, and if it raises price, total revenues will fall. Consider another example. If the price of Diet Coke were raised by 25 percent and the price of all other soft drinks remained constant, the quantity demanded of Diet Coke would probably fall dramatically. The decrease in quantity demanded due

FIGURE 20-2
The relationship between price elasticity of demand and total revenues.
In panel (a) we show the elastic, unit-elastic, and inelastic sections of the demand schedule according to whether a reduction in price increases total revenues, causes them to remain constant, or causes them to decrease, respectively. In panel (b) we show graphically what happens to the demand curve. In panel (c) we show what happens to the total revenue curve.

Panel (a)

(1) PRICE, P (DOLLARS PER MINUTE)	(2) QUANTITY DEMANDED, D (BILLIONS OF MINUTES)	(3) TOTAL REVENUE ($ BILLIONS) = (1) X (2)	(4) ELASTICITY: $E_p =$ $\dfrac{\text{CHANGE IN } Q}{(Q_1 + Q_2)/2} \div \dfrac{\text{CHANGE IN } P}{(P_1 + P_2)/2}$
1.10	0	0	
			21
1.00	1	1.0	
			6.33
.90	2	1.8	
			3.4 — Elastic
.80	3	2.4	
			2.143
.70	4	2.8	
			1.144
.60	5	3.0	
			1 — Unit-elastic
.50	6	3.0	
			.692
.40	7	2.8	
			.467 — Inelastic
.30	8	2.4	
			.294
.20	9	1.8	
			.158
.10	10	1.0	

Panel (b)

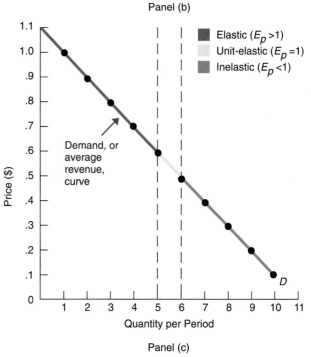

Panel (c)

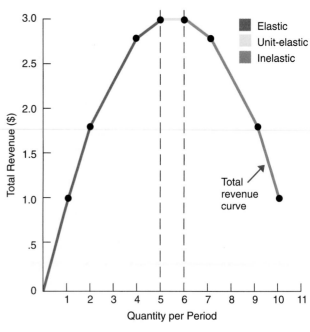

to the increase in the price of Diet Coke would lead in this example to a reduction in the total revenues of the Coca-Cola Company. Therefore, if demand is price-elastic, price and total revenues will move in *opposite* directions.

2. **Unit-price-elastic demand.** Small changes in price do not change total revenues. When the firm is facing demand that is unit-price-elastic, if it increases price, total revenues will not change; if it decreases price, total revenues will not change either.

3. **Price-inelastic demand**. A positive relationship exists between small changes in price and total revenues. When the firm is facing demand that is price-inelastic, if it raises price, total revenues will go up; if it lowers price, total revenues will fall. Consider another example. You have just invented a cure for the common cold that has been approved by the Food and Drug Administration for sale to the public. You are not sure what price you should charge, so you start out with a price of $1 per pill. You sell 20 million pills at that price over a year. The next year you decide to raise the price by 25 percent, to $1.25. The number of pills you sell drops to 18 million per year. The price increase of 25 percent has led to a 10 percent decrease in quantity demanded. Your total revenues, however, will rise to $22.5 million because of the price increase. We therefore conclude that if demand is price-inelastic, price and total revenues move in the *same* direction.

The elastic, unit-elastic, and inelastic areas of the demand curve are shown in Figure 20-2. For prices from $1.10 per minute of cellular phone time to 60 cents per minute, as price decreases, total revenues rise from zero to $3. Demand is price-elastic. When prices change from 60 cents to 50 cents, however, total revenues remain constant at $3; demand is unit-elastic. Finally, when price falls from 50 cents to 10 cents, total revenues decrease from $3 to $1; demand is price-inelastic. In panels (b) and (c) of Figure 20-2 we have labeled the sections of the demand curve accordingly, and we have also shown how total revenues first rise, then remain constant, and finally fall.

The relationship between price elasticity of demand and total revenues brings together some important microeconomic concepts. Total revenues, as we have noted, are the product of price per unit times number of units sold. The law of demand states that along a given demand curve, price and quantity changes will move in opposite directions: One increases as the other decreases. Consequently, what happens to the product of price times quantity depends on which of the opposing changes exerts a greater force on total revenues. But this is just what price elasticity of demand is designed to measure—responsiveness of quantity demanded to a change in price. The relationship between price elasticity of demand and total revenues (TR) is summarized in Table 20-1.

CHANGING PRICE ELASTICITY

We have seen in the example of the demand for oil that price elasticity changes as we move along the demand curve. Price elasticity is high when price is high and low when

TABLE 20-1 **The relationship between price elasticity of demand and total revenues.**

PRICE ELASTICITY OF DEMAND		PRICE CHANGE AS IT AFFECTS TOTAL REVENUES (TR)	
		PRICE DECREASE	PRICE INCREASE
Price-inelastic	$(E_p < 1)$	TR ↓	TR ↑
Unit-elastic	$(E_p = 1)$	No change in TR	No change in TR
Price-elastic	$(E_p > 1)$	TR ↑	TR ↓

price is low—look again at columns 3 and 7 in panel (b) of Figure 20-1. As a general rule, along any demand curve that is a straight line, price elasticity declines as we move down the curve. Consider the reason why. In our example in Figure 20-1, the change in price was always $1 and the change in the absolute quantity demanded was always 1 million barrels per day. These are absolute changes. What about percentage changes? At the upper end of the demand curve, a $1 price change is in percentage terms relatively small ($1/[($9 + $10)/2] = 10.5 percent), whereas the 1 million barrel change in quantity demanded is a large percentage change of the small quantity demanded (1/[(1 + 2)/2] = 66.7 percent).

Thus at the top of the demand curve, the elasticity formula will have a large numerator and a small denominator; therefore, price is relatively elastic (66.7 percent ÷ 10.5 percent = 6.33). At the lower end of the curve, the price elasticity formula will have a small numerator and a large denominator; thus the demand curve is relatively inelastic (10.5 percent ÷ 66.7 percent = .158). Elasticity will equal 1 at the midpoint of a straight-line demand curve. It is important not to confuse elasticity with slope. A straight-line demand curve, one that has constant slope, will nevertheless have a different price elasticity at every point, as you have seen in the elasticity calculations for Figure 20-2.

CONCEPTS IN BRIEF

- Price elasticity of demand is related to total revenues (and total consumer expenditures).
- When demand is *elastic,* the change in price elicits a change in total revenues (and total consumer expenditures) in the direction opposite that of the price change.
- When demand is *unit-elastic,* a change in price elicits no change in total revenues (or in total consumer expenditures).
- When demand is *inelastic,* a change in price elicits a change in total revenues (and in consumer expenditures) in the same direction as the price change.

EXTREME ELASTICITIES

There are two extremes in price elasticities of demand: One represents total unresponsiveness of quantity demanded to price changes, which is called **perfectly inelastic demand,** or zero elasticity; the other represents total responsiveness, which is called unlimited, infinite, or **perfectly elastic demand.**

We show perfect inelasticity in panel (a) of Figure 20-3. Notice that the quantity demanded per year is 8 million units, no matter what the price. Hence for any percentage price change, the quantity demanded will remain the same, and thus the change in the quantity demanded will be zero. Look at our formula for computing elasticity on page 449. If the change in the quantity demanded is zero, the numerator is also zero, and a nonzero number divided into zero results in an answer of zero too. Hence there is perfect inelasticity. At the opposite extreme is the situation depicted in panel (b) of Figure 20-3. Here we show that at a price of 30 cents, an unlimited quantity will be demanded. At a price that is only slightly above 30 cents, no quantity will be demanded. There is complete, or infinite, responsiveness here, and hence we call the demand schedule in panel (b) infinitely elastic.

▶ **Perfectly inelastic demand**
A demand that exhibits zero responsiveness to price changes; no matter what the price is, the quantity demanded remains the same.

▶ **Perfectly elastic demand**
A demand that has the characteristic that even the slightest increase in price will lead to zero quantity demanded.

FIGURE 20-3
Two extreme price elasticities.
In panel (a) we show complete price unresponsiveness. The demand curve is vertical at the quantity of 8 million units per year. This means that the price elasticity of demand is zero. In panel (b) we show complete price responsiveness. At a price of 30 cents in this example, consumers will demand an unlimited quantity of the particular good in question. This is a case of infinite price elasticity of demand.

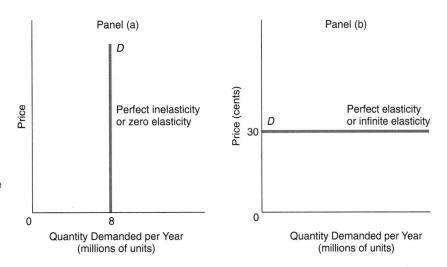

⭐ EXAMPLE: Is the Demand for Crack Completely Inelastic?

Some observers of the illicit drug scene contend that more enforcement of drug laws against crack use will have little effect. Their argument is straightforward: Addiction means an absolute need for a particular drug. In economic terminology, we are talking about perfectly inelastic demand. Suppose that the demand curve for a hypothetical individual crack user is d in Figure 20-4. The quantity demanded will be q_1 "regardless of price." No matter how expensive crack becomes, because of increased law enforcement against sellers and users, the same quantity will be demanded.

There is a hitch here. Figure 20-4 is a hypothetical individual demand curve for crack. Only if every individual who is *addicted* to crack has such a demand curve and *no budget constraint* will the market demand curve also be a vertical line. The market price elasticity of demand would in that case be zero—a completely inelastic demand curve.

Many researchers contend that users of hard drugs such as crack become psychologically and physiologically addicted so that jail sentences cease to be a deterrent. Because the quantity of crack demanded will be the same no matter what the implicit price charged, according to these researchers, they suggest that emphasis must be placed on therapeutic

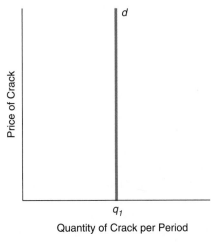

FIGURE 20-4
Hypothetical individual demand curve for crack.
If an individual is willing to pay "any price" for a given quantity of crack, that individual's demand curve is represented by vertical line d, at quantity q_1. The price elasticity of demand is equal to zero.

programs directed toward altering the addict's lifestyle (moving the addict's demand curve to the left) as opposed to raising the implicit price of the illegal drug.

But the *market* demand curve cannot ever be a vertical line over all price ranges similar to the one in Figure 20-4 because even severe addicts have a budget constraint. Though it may be true that throughout a relatively large price range, crack addicts will purchase about the same quantity of the drug, there exists for each one of them a price per unit that is so high that their consumption must fall because of their budget constraint (even if this budget constraint is dictated by how much they can steal). Therefore, the assumption of a vertical demand curve is erroneous.

On a more fundamental level, the entire discussion of the price elasticity of the demand for crack or any other addictive drug is often based on a confusion of averages with margins. The market demand curve for crack may be relatively inelastic, but there will be some users and potential users on the margin, deciding to use or not to use the drug or deciding to use less or more. For example, curious teenagers deciding whether to try the drug once or a few times more may have a relatively elastic demand for crack and for other addictive drugs. Thus the market demand curve for any drug will rarely exhibit zero price elasticity of demand over the entire range of possible prices.

For Critical Analysis: Can our analysis be applied to alcoholism? Why or why not? ●

CONCEPTS IN BRIEF

- As we move down a straight-line demand curve, the price elasticity of demand falls.
- There are two extreme elasticities: (1) When a demand curve is vertical, it has zero price elasticity of demand; it is completely inelastic. (2) When a demand curve is horizontal, it has completely elastic demand; its price elasticity of demand is infinite.

DETERMINANTS OF THE PRICE ELASTICITY OF DEMAND

We have learned how to calculate the price elasticity of demand. We know that theoretically, it ranges numerically from zero—completely inelastic—to infinity—completely elastic. What we would like to do now is come up with a list of the determinants of the price elasticity of demand. The price elasticity of demand for a particular commodity at any price depends, at a minimum, on the following:

1. The existence and similarity of substitutes
2. The percentage of a consumer's total budget devoted to purchases of that commodity
3. The length of time allowed for adjustment to changes in the price of the commodity.

EXISTENCE OF SUBSTITUTES

The closer the substitutes for a particular commodity and the more substitutes there are, the greater will be its price elasticity of demand. At the limit, if there is a perfect substitute, the price elasticity of the commodity will be infinity. Thus even the slightest increase in the commodity's price will cause an enormous reduction in the quantity demanded: quantity demanded will fall to zero. We are really talking about two goods that the consumer believes are exactly alike and equally desirable, like dollar bills whose only difference is serial numbers. When we talk about less extreme examples, we can only speak in terms of the number and the similarity of substitutes that are available. Thus we will find that the more narrowly we define a good, the closer and greater will be the number of substitutes available. For example, the demand for a Diet Coke may be highly elastic because consumers can switch to Diet Pepsi. The demand for diet drinks in general, however, is relatively more inelastic because there are fewer substitutes.

SHARE OF BUDGET

We know that the greater the percentage of a total budget spent on the commodity, the greater the person's price elasticity of demand for that commodity. The demand for pepper is thought to be very inelastic merely because individuals spend so little on it relative to their total budgets. In contrast, the demand for things such as transportation and housing is thought to be far more elastic because they occupy a large part of people's budgets—changes in their prices cannot be ignored so easily without sacrificing a lot of other alternative goods that could be purchased.

Consider a numerical example. A household earns $40,000 a year. It purchases $4 of pepper per year and $4,000 of transportation services. Now consider the spending power of this family when the price of pepper and the price of transportation both go up by 100 percent. If the household buys the same amount of pepper, it will now spend $8. It will thus have to reduce other expenditures by $4. This $4 represents only .01 percent of the entire household budget. By contrast, a doubling of transportation costs requires that the family spend $8,000, or $4,000 more on transportation, if it is to purchase the same quantity. That increased expenditure on transportation of $4,000 represents 10 percent of total expenditures that must be switched from other purchases. We would therefore predict that the household will react differently to the doubling of prices for pepper than it will for transportation. It will buy about the same amount of pepper but will spend significantly less on transportation.

TIME FOR ADJUSTMENT

When the price of a commodity changes and that price change persists, more people will learn about it. Further, consumers will be better able to revise their consumption patterns the longer the time period they have to do so. And in fact, the longer the time they do take, the less costly it will be for them to engage in this revision of consumption patterns. Consider a price decrease. The longer the price decrease persists, the greater will be the number of new uses that consumers will discover for the particular commodity, and the greater will be the number of new users of that particular commodity.

It is possible to make a very strong statement about the relationship between the price elasticity of demand and the time allowed for adjustment:

> The longer any price change persists, the greater the price elasticity of demand, other things held constant. Price elasticity of demand is greater in the long run than in the short run.

Let's take an example. Suppose that the price of electricity goes up 50 percent. How do you adjust in the short run? You can turn the lights off more often, you can stop using the stereo as much as you do, and so on. Otherwise it's very difficult to cut back on your consumption of electricity. In the long run, though, you can devise methods to reduce your consumption. Instead of using electric heaters, the next time you have a house built you will install gas heaters. Instead of using an electric stove, the next time you move you will have a gas stove installed. You will purchase fluorescent bulbs because they use less electricity. The longer you have to figure it out, the more ways you will find to cut

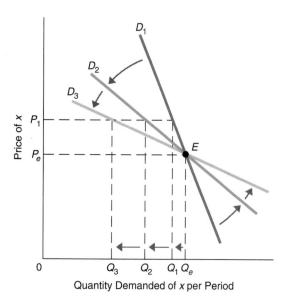

FIGURE 20-5
Short-run and long-run price elasticity of demand.
Consider an equilibrium situation in which the market price is P_e and the quantity demanded is Q_e. Then there is a price increase to P_1. In the short run, as evidenced by the demand curve D_1, we move from equilibrium quantity demanded, Q_e, to Q_1. After more time is allowed for adjustment, the demand curve rotates at original price P_e to D_2. Quantity demanded falls again, now to Q_2. After even more time is allowed for adjustment, the demand curve rotates at price P_e to D_3. At the higher price P_1, in the long run, the quantity demanded falls all the way to Q_3.

electricity consumption. We would expect, therefore, that the short-run demand curve for electricity would be relatively inelastic (in the price range around P_1), as demonstrated by D_1 in Figure 20-5. However, the long-run demand curve may exhibit much more elasticity (in the neighborhood of P_1), as demonstrated by D_3. Indeed, we can think of an entire family of demand curves such as those depicted in that figure. The short-run demand curve is for the period when there is no time for adjustment. As more time is allowed, the demand curve goes first to D_2 and then all the way to D_3. Thus in the neighborhood of P_1, elasticity differs for each of these curves. It is greater for the less steep curves (but remember, slope alone does not measure elasticity for the entire curve).

How to Define the Short Run and the Long Run.

We've mentioned the short run and the long run. Is the short run one week, two weeks, a month, two months? Is the long run three years, four years, five years? The answer is that there is no single answer. What we mean by the long run is the period of time necessary for consumers to make a relatively full adjustment to a given price change, all other things held constant. In the case of the demand for electricity, the long run will be however long it takes consumers to switch over to cheaper sources of heating, to buy houses that are more energy-efficient, to purchase manufactured appliances that are more energy-efficient, and so on. The long-run price elasticity of demand for electricity therefore relates to a period of at least several years. The short run—by default—is any period less than the long run.

⭐ EXAMPLE: Estimated Price Elasticities of Demand

In Table 20-2 we present demand elasticities for selected goods. None of them is zero, and the largest is 3.8—a far cry from infinity. Remember that even though we are leaving off the negative sign, there is an inverse relationship between price and quantity demanded, and the minus sign is understood. Also remember that these elasticities represent averages over given price ranges. Choosing different price ranges would yield different elasticity estimates for these goods.

Economists have consistently found that estimated price elasticities of demand are greater in the long run than in the short run, as seen in Table 20-2. There you see, for example, in the far right column that the long-run price elasticity of demand for tires and

TABLE 20-2 Demand elasticity for selected goods.
Here are estimated demand elasticities for selected goods. All of them are negative, although we omit the minus sign. We have given some estimates of the long-run price elasticities of demand. The long-run is associated with the time necessary for consumers to adjust fully to any given price change.

Sources: P. S. George and G. A. King, *Consumer Demand for Food Commodities in the United States with Projections for 1980* (Berkeley: University of California Press, 1971); Herbert Scarf and J. B. Shoven, *Applied Equilibrium Analysis* (New York: Cambridge University Press, 1984); Bruce Domazlicky and Peter Kerr, "Baseball Attendance and the Designated Hitter," *American Economist*, (1990).

CATEGORY	ESTIMATED ELASTICITY	
	SHORT RUN	LONG RUN
Food		
Lamb	2.65	
Potatoes	.3	
Peas, fresh	2.8	
Peas, canned	1.6	
Bread	.15	
Eggs	.32	
Nondurable goods		
Shoes	.9	
Newspapers and magazines	.4	
Tires and related items	.8	1.2
Services		
Auto repair and related services	1.4	2.4
Radio and television repair	.5	3.8
Travel and entertainment		
Legitimate theater and opera	.2	.31
Motion pictures	.87	3.7
Foreign travel by U.S. residents	.1	1.8
Major league baseball	.23	
Public transportation		
Taxicabs	.6	
Local public transportation	.6	1.2
Intercity bus	.2	2.2
Utility services		
Electricity	.1	1.8
Telephone	.25	
Miscellaneous		
Jewelry and watches	.4	.6

related items is 1.2, whereas the estimate for the short run is .8. Throughout the table you see that all estimates of long-run price elasticities of demand exceed their short-run counterparts.

For Critical Analysis: Explain the intuitive reasoning behind the difference between long-run and short-run price elasticity of demand. ●

CROSS ELASTICITY OF DEMAND

In Chapter 3 we discussed the effect of a change in the price of one good on the demand for a related good. We defined substitutes and complements in terms of whether a reduction in the price of one caused a decrease or an increase, respectively, in the demand for the other. If the price of butter is held constant, the amount of butter demanded (at any price) will certainly be influenced by the price of a close substitute such as margarine. If the price of stereo speakers is held constant, the quantity of stereo speakers demanded (at any price) will certainly be affected by changes in the price of stereo amplifiers

What we now need to do is come up with a numerical measure of the price responsiveness of demand to the prices of related goods. This is called the **cross elasticity of demand** (E_{xy}), which is defined as the percentage change in the quantity demanded for one good divided by the percentage change in the price of the related good. In equation form, the cross elasticity of demand for good x with good y is

▶ **Cross elasticity of demand (E_{xy})**
The percentage change in the quantity demanded of one good (holding its price constant) divided by the percentage change in the price of a related good.

$$E_{xy} = \frac{\text{change in quantity demanded of good } x}{\text{change in price of good } y}$$

Alternatively, the cross elasticity for demand for good *y* with good *x* would use the percentage change in the quantity demanded in good y as the numerator and the percentage change in the price of good x as the denominator.

When two goods are substitutes, the cross elasticity of demand will be positive. For example, when the price of margarine goes up, the quantity demanded of butter will rise too as consumers shift away from the now relatively more expensive margarine to butter. A producer of margarine would benefit from a numerical estimate of the cross elasticity of demand between butter and margarine. For example, if the price of butter went up by 10 percent and the margarine producer knew that the cross elasticity of demand was 1, the margarine producer could estimate that the quantity demanded for margarine would also go up by 10 percent at any given price. Plans for increasing margarine production could then be made.

When two related goods are complements, the cross elasticity of demand will be negative. When the price of stereo amplifiers goes up, the quantity of stereo speakers demanded will fall at any given price. This is because as prices of amplifiers increase, the quantity of amplifiers demanded will naturally decrease. Because amplifiers and stereo speakers are often used together, the quantity of speakers demanded is likely to fall. Any manufacturer of stereo speakers must take this into account in making production plans.

If goods are completely unrelated, their price cross elasticity of demand will be zero.

INCOME ELASTICITY OF DEMAND

In Chapter 3 we talked about the determinants of demand. One of those determinants was income. Briefly, we can apply our understanding of elasticity to the relationship between changes in income and changes in demand. We measure the responsiveness of quantity demanded to income changes by the **income elasticity of demand** (E_i):

$$E_i = \frac{\text{percentage change in quantity demanded}}{\text{percentage change in income}}$$

▶ **Income elasticity of demand (E_i)**
The percentage change in quantity demanded for any good, holding its price constant, divided by the percentage change in income; the responsiveness of the quantity demanded to changes in income, holding the good's relative price constant.

holding relative price constant.

Income elasticity of demand refers to a *horizontal shift* in the demand curve in response to changes in income, whereas price elasticity of demand refers to a movement *along* the curve in response to price changes. Thus income elasticity of demand is calculated at a given price, and price elasticity of demand is calculated at a given income.

A simple example will demonstrate how income elasticity of demand can be computed. Table 20-3 gives the relevant data. The product in question is compact discs. We assume that the price of compact discs remains constant relative to other prices. In period 1, six CDs per month are purchased. Income per month is $400. In period 2, monthly income increases to $600, and the quantity of CDs demanded per month is increased to eight. We can apply the following calculation:

$$E_i = \frac{(8-6)/6}{(600-400)/400} = \frac{1/3}{1/2} = \frac{2}{3} = .667$$

Hence measured income elasticity of demand for CDs for the individual represented in this example is .667. Note that this holds only for the move from six CDs to eight CDs purchased per month. If the situation were reversed, with income decreasing from $600 to $400 per month and CDs purchased dropping from eight to six CDs per month, the calculation becomes

$$E_i = \frac{(6-8)/8}{(400-600)/600} = \frac{-2/8}{-1/3} = \frac{-1/4}{-1/3} = \frac{3}{4} = .75$$

TABLE 20-3 How income affects quantity of CDs demanded.

PERIOD	QUANTITY OF COMPACT DISCS DEMANDED PER MONTH	INCOME PER MONTH
1	6	$400
2	8	600

In this case the measured income elasticity of demand is equal to .75.

In order to get the same income elasticity of demand over the same range of values regardless of direction of change (increase or decrease), we can use the same midpoint formula that we used in computing the price elasticity of demand. When doing so, we have:

$$E_i = \frac{\text{change in quantity}}{\text{sum of quantities}/2} \div \frac{\text{change in income}}{\text{sum of incomes}/2}$$

You have just been introduced to three types of elasticities. Two of them—the price elasticity of demand (E_p), and income elasticity (E_i)—are the two most important factors in influencing the quantity demanded for most goods. Reasonably accurate estimates of these can go a long way toward making accurate forecasts of demand for goods or services.

CONCEPTS IN BRIEF

● Some determinants of price elasticity of demand are (1) the number and similarity of substitutes, (2) the percentage of the total budget spent on the good in question, and (3) the length of time allowed for adjustment to a change in prices.

● Cross elasticity of demand measures one good's quantity responsiveness to another's price changes. For substitutes, it is positive; for complements, it is negative.

● Income elasticity of demand tells you by what percentage quantity demanded will change for a particular percentage change in income.

ELASTICITY OF SUPPLY

▶ **Price elasticity of supply (E_s)**
The responsiveness of the quantity supplied of a commodity to a change in its price; the percentage change in quantity supplied divided by the percentage change in price.

The **price elasticity of supply (E_s)** is defined similarly to the price elasticity of demand. Supply elasticities are generally positive; this is because at higher prices, larger quantities will generally be forthcoming from suppliers. The definition of the price elasticity of supply is as follows:

$$E_s = \frac{\text{percentage change in quantity supplied}}{\text{percentage change in price}}$$

Let's look at some hypothetical data to illustrate the price elasticity of supply for oil. In Table 20-4 on the next page, note that the price elasticity of supply remains constant and equal to 1 in this particular example. This is a special feature of any *straight-line* supply curve that passes through the origin (zero point), that is, whose intercept is zero.[1]

---

[1]If the straight-line supply curve intersects the vertical axis, price elasticity of supply is greater than 1 (elastic throughout); if a straight-line supply curve intersects the horizontal axis, its price elasticity of supply is less than 1 (inelastic throughout).

TABLE 20-4   Calculating the price elasticity of supply for oil.
We use hypothetical data to demonstrate how to calculate price elasticity of supply. We use the midpoint, or average, formula. Column 2 gives the change in quantity of oil supplied derived from column 1. Column 4 gives the change in price derived from column 3, Columns 5 and 6 give the average quantity and price values. Column 7 presents the price elasticity of supply, which is constant and equal to 1 because the curve intercepts the origin.

(1) QUANTITY SUPPLIED, Q (MILLIONS OF BARRELS PER DAY)	(2) CHANGE IN Q (MILLIONS OF BARRELS PER DAY)	(3) PRICE, P (DOLLARS PER BARREL)	(4) CHANGE IN P	(5) $\dfrac{Q_1 + Q_2}{2}$	(6) $\dfrac{P_1 + P_2}{2}$	(7) $E_s = \dfrac{\Delta Q}{(Q_1 + Q_2)/2} \div \dfrac{\Delta P}{(P_1 + P_2)/2}$
0		0				
	2		$10	1	$ 5	(2/1) ÷ (10/5) = 1
2		10				
	2		10	3	15	(2/3) ÷ (10/15) = 1
4		20				
	2		10	5	25	(2/5) ÷ (10/25) = 1
6		30				
	2		10	7	35	(2/7) ÷ (10/35) = 1
8		40				
	2		10	9	45	(2/9) ÷ (10/45) = 1
10		50				

CLASSIFYING SUPPLY ELASTICITIES

Just as with demand, there are different types of supply elasticities. They are similar in definition to the types of demand elasticities.

If a 1 percent increase in price elicits a greater than 1 percent increase in the quantity supplied, we say that at the particular price in question on the supply schedule, *supply is elastic*. The most extreme elastic supply is called **perfectly elastic supply**—the slightest reduction in price will cause quantity supplied to fall to zero.

If, conversely, a 1 percent increase in price elicits a less than 1 percent increase in the quantity supplied, we refer to that as an *inelastic supply situation*. The most extreme inelastic supply is called **perfectly inelastic supply**—no matter what the price, the quantity supplied remains the same.

If the percentage change in the quantity supplied is just equal to the percentage change in the price, we talk about *unit elasticity of supply*.

We show in Figure 20-6 two supply schedules, *S* and *S'*. You can tell at a glance, without reading the labels, which one is infinitely elastic and which one is perfectly inelastic. As you might expect, most supply schedules exhibit elasticities that are somewhere between zero and infinity.

▶ **Perfectly elastic supply**
A supply characterized by a reduction in quantity supplied to zero when there is the slightest decrease in price.

▶ **Perfectly inelastic supply**
A supply for which quantity supplied remains constant, no matter what happens to price.

PRICE ELASTICITY OF SUPPLY AND LENGTH OF TIME FOR ADJUSTMENT

We pointed out earlier that the longer the time period allowed for adjustment, the greater will be the price elasticity of demand. It turns out that the same proposition applies to supply. The longer the time for adjustment, the more price-elastic is the supply curve. Consider why this is true:

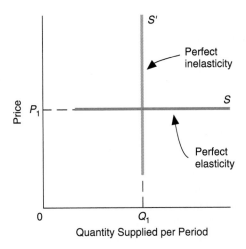

FIGURE 20-6
The extremes in supply curves.
Here we have drawn two extremes of supply schedules: S is a perfectly elastic supply curve; S' is a perfectly inelastic one. In the former, an unlimited quantity will be supplied at price P_1. In the latter, no matter what the price, the quantity supplied will be Q_1. An example of S' might be the supply curve for fresh fish on the morning the boats come in.

1. The longer the time allowed for adjustment, the more firms are able to figure out ways to increase (or decrease) production in an industry.
2. The longer the time allowed for adjustment, the more resources can flow into (or out of) an industry through expansion (or contraction) of existing firms.

We therefore talk about short-run and long-run price elasticities of supply. The short run is defined as the time period during which full adjustment has not yet taken place. The long run is the time period during which firms have been able to adjust relatively fully to the change in price.

Consider an example: an increase in the price of housing. In the very short run, when there is no time allowed for adjustment, the amount of housing offered for rent or for sale is relatively inelastic. However, as more time is allowed for adjustment, current owners of the housing stock can find ways to increase the amount of housing they will offer for rent from given buildings. The owner of a large house can decide, for example, to have two children move into one room so that a "new" extra bedroom can be rented out. This can also be done by the owner of a large house who decides to move into an apartment and

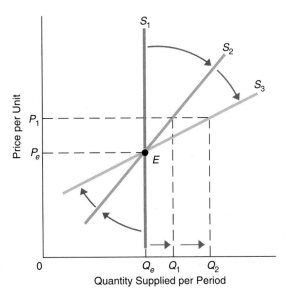

FIGURE 20-7
Short-run and long-run price elasticity of supply.
Consider a situation in which the price is P_e and the quantity supplied is Q_e. In the short run we hypothesize a vertical supply curve, S_1. With the price increase to P_1, therefore, there will be no change in the short run in quantity supplied; it will remain at Q_e. Given some time for adjustment, the supply curve will rotate at price P_e to S_2. The new quantity supplied will increase to Q_1. The long-run supply curve is shown by S_3. The quantity supplied again increases to Q_2.

rent each floor of the house to a separate family. Thus the quantity of housing supplied will increase. With more time, landlords will find it profitable to build new rental units.

We can show a whole set of supply curves similar to the ones we generated for demand. In Figure 20-7 on the previous page, when nothing can be done in the short run, the supply curve is vertical, S_1. As more time is allowed for adjustment, the supply curve rotates to S_2 and then to S_3, becoming more elastic as it rotates.

⭐ EXAMPLE: Elasticity and Gasoline Taxes

Governments often levy taxes on commodities such as gasoline, tobacco products, and alcohol. In some cases the objective of the tax is simply to raise revenues; in others it serves to discourage the consumption of commodities that are considered harmful. Whatever the reasons might be, taxes do have economic effects on buyers and sellers of a commodity. Generally, the sellers of a taxed good will attempt to pass some or all of the tax on to consumers if they can. The degree to which taxes are shifted onto buyers and sellers depends on the relative elasticities of demand and supply.

Figure 20-8 illustrates this point. D and S_1 represent the demand and supply curves for gasoline before the tax. The initial equilibrium price is $1.00, and the initial quantity is 2.5 billion gallons per day. The imposition of a $1.00 tax per gallon shifts the supply curve upward by $1.00, the amount of the tax; for sellers to continue to supply 2.5 billion gallons of gasoline per day, they require $1.00 per gallon for themselves plus $1.00 tax, but that doesn't occur. The new equilibrium price is at $1.60, where the new supply curve, S_2, intersects the original demand curve. At the price of $1.60, sellers send the $1.00 tax to the government and keep only 60 cents for themselves. The difference between $1.00 (the original equilibrium price) and $1.60 (the new equilibrium price) shows the amount of the tax burden that falls on buyers. The difference between $1.00 and 60 cents, or 40 cents, shows the amount of the tax burden that falls on sellers.

In this example, 60 percent of the tax burden was passed on to buyers, leaving 40 percent to be borne by the sellers. In this case the buyers' burden is greater than the sellers' burden because the demand curve is less elastic than the supply curve.

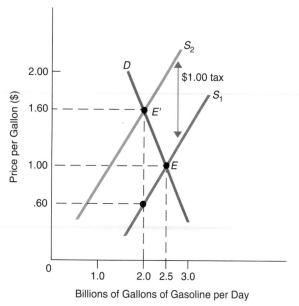

FIGURE 20-8
The effect of a $1 tax on gas.
A $1 tax per gallon of gas will shift S_1 up by $1. Given D, equilibrium will go from E to E'. The new equilibrium will be $1.60 with 2 billion gallons sold. Buyers will pay 60 cents, suppliers 40 cents of the $1 tax per gallon.

The more inelastic the demand curve, the greater the tax burden on the buyer; the more inelastic the supply curve, the greater the tax burden on the seller.

For Critical Analysis: If the demand curve were perfectly inelastic, what percentage of the tax burden would fall on buyers and what percentage on sellers? If the supply curve were perfectly elastic, what percentage of the tax burden would fall on suppliers and what percentage on sellers? If the demand curve were perfectly elastic or if the supply curve were perfectly inelastic, what proportion of the tax burden would fall on buyers and what proportion on sellers? (Hint: Draw the graphs of these extreme cases to help you.) ●

CONCEPTS IN BRIEF

- Price elasticity of supply is calculated by dividing the percentage change in quantity supplied by the percentage change in price.
- Usually, price elasticities of supply are positive—higher prices yield larger quantities supplied.
- Long-run supply curves are more elastic then short-run supply curves because the longer the time allowed, the more resources can flow into or out of an industry when price changes.
- Any unit tax on a commodity will be shared in part by consumers and in part by suppliers.

CONTINUED ➞

IS THE DEMAND FOR LUXURY GOODS INELASTIC?

Concepts Applied: Price elasticity of demand, cross elasticity of demand

The purchase of both yachts and planes was affected by the 1991 luxury tax. If the quantity demanded of such "luxury" items declined, what would that mean about the price elasticity of demand for them?

As we said in the opening of this chapter, the rich are different because they have more money income per year and more wealth. It is impossible to predict, though, how the rich will react to an increase in the price of anything that they buy simply by assuming that "they can afford it." This point was driven home after Congress passed a so-called luxury tax at the beginning of the 1990s.

ONLY 10 PERCENT As part of an attempt to reduce the federal budget deficit, Congress passed a variety of tax changes in 1990 that took effect in 1991. Always hungry for new revenue sources and politically sensitive to populist ideas, part of the new tax package included a 10 percent tax on part of the purchase price of new boats, jewelry, furs, cars, and aircraft. Here is how it worked. Effective January 21, 1991, the 10 percent luxury tax was applied to the purchase price above the following cutoff points:

$10,000 for furs
$10,000 for jewelry
$30,000 for autos
$100,000 for boats
$250,000 for airplanes

Consider the additional tax a person would have to pay on a brand-new $400,000 boat. The 10 percent tax would apply to $300,000 of the price; that comes to $30,000. Because of the luxury tax, the purchaser of the new yacht would pay more—$430,000 instead of $400,000, or an increase of 7.5 percent—than he or she would have paid in the absence of the luxury tax.

THE SEARCH FOR SUBSTITUTES AND THE CROSS ELASTICITY OF DEMAND The rich may be rich, but they also think in terms of limited incomes and getting the best deal for their money. Consequently, as soon as the luxury tax was imposed, they started searching for substitutes for new boats. Relatively recently used boats turned out to be close substitutes for new boats. Because the luxury tax did not apply to used boats, they became relatively less expensive. Although no full-fledged studies have been done on the cross elasticity of demand (E_{xy}) between new and used luxury yachts, a good guess might be around the range of 2.5. That means that a 7.5 percent increase in new $400,000 luxury yachts would yield an increase in quantity demanded of used boats at the same price of 18.75 percent. The price elasticity of demand (E_p) for expensive yachts has also been estimated in the same approximate range (but with an implicit negative sign, of course). That means that the 7.5 percent increase in new boat prices should have caused about a similar reduction (18.75 percent) in the quantity of new boats demanded.

In sum, the results of the luxury boat tax included reduced sales of new boats, increased purchases of existing (used) boats, substitution of other types of luxuries for boats, and reduced employment (layoffs) of workers in the new-boat industry.

WHAT ACTUALLY HAPPENED Economic policies do not always work the way policymakers predict. In trying to raise additional revenues by levying a luxury tax, Congress actually ended up acquiring very few additional revenues. Because the luxury tax applied to new goods, but not to used goods, sales in the new and used goods markets for so-called luxury items have moved in opposite directions. The antique jewelry market boomed in 1991, with some pieces going for twice their pre-sale estimates. The opposite occurred in the new jewelry market for expensive pieces. Further, the sales of new large sailboats dropped by 30 percent in 1991 and by 45 percent for larger boats. Sales of the used versions of each held up as individuals switched to avoid the luxury tax. With respect to expensive cars, in the first five months of 1991, overall auto sales dropped by 15 percent, but sales of Jaguars (for which the tax could account to as much as $3,360 per car) were off by 55 percent. So too were the sales of Rolls Royces.

FOR CRITICAL ANALYSIS

1. Federal government staffers estimating the impact of the new tax revenues to be derived from the luxury tax apparently multiplied current sales of affected luxury items by the proposed tax. They came up with expected new tax revenues for the federal government. What was wrong with their analysis?

2. Is it possible to raise taxes and yet receive less in tax revenues than with lower taxes? Explain your answer.

CHAPTER SUMMARY

1. Price elasticity of demand is a measure of the percentage change in quantity demanded relative to the percentage change in price, given income, the prices of other goods, and time. Because of the law of demand, price elasticity of demand is always negative.

2. We classify demand as *elastic* if a 1 percent change in price leads to a more than 1 percent change in quantity demanded, *unit-elastic* if it leads to exactly a 1 percent change in quantity demanded, and *inelastic* if it leads to less than a 1 percent change in quantity demanded.

3. When facing a perfectly elastic demand, the slightest increase in price leads to zero quantity demanded; when facing a perfectly inelastic demand, no matter what the price, the quantity demanded remains unchanged. Perfect inelasticity means absolutely no price responsiveness.

4. Price elasticity of demand falls as we move down a straight-line demand curve. It goes from infinity to zero. Elasticity and slope are not equivalent because the slope of a straight-line curve is always constant, whereas elasticity changes as we move along a linear curve. A vertical demand curve is perfectly inelastic; a horizontal demand curve is perfectly elastic.

5. Price elasticity of demand depends on (a) the existence and similarity of substitutes, (b) the percentage of total budget accounted for by the commodity, and (c) the length of time allowed for adjustment.

6. Cross elasticity of demand measures the responsiveness of one product, either a substitute or a complement, to changes in the price of another product. When the cross elasticity of demand is negative, the two commodities under study are complements; when the cross elasticity of demand is positive, they are substitutes.

7. Income elasticity of demand is given by the percentage change in quantity demanded divided by the percentage change in income, given relative price.

8. Price elasticity of supply is given by the percentage change in quantity supplied divided by the percentage change in price. The greater the time allowed for adjustment, the greater the price elasticity of supply.

DISCUSSION OF PREVIEW POINTS

1. How is total revenue related to price elasticity of demand?

Total revenue is defined as price times quantity demanded; because price changes lead to changes in quantity demanded, total revenue and elasticity are intimately related. If, over the price range in question, demand is inelastic, this means that buyers are not responsive to price changes. Intuitively, then, we know that if price rises and quantity demanded doesn't fall by much, total revenue will rise. Conversely, if price falls and quantity demanded rises only slightly, total revenue will fall. If, over the price range in question, demand is elastic, buyers will be quite responsive to price changes. We can tell intuitively that if price rises and quantity demanded falls greatly, total revenue will fall. Similarly, if price falls and quantity demanded rises greatly, total revenue will rise. Finally, if we are in the range of unit elasticity, given percentage changes in price will lead to equal percentage changes in quantity. Thus for small price changes, total revenue remains unaffected in the unit-elasticity range.

2. What are the determinants of price elasticity of demand?

Three major determinants of price elasticity of demand are (a) the existence and similarity of substitutes, (b) the percentage of the total budget that the commodity represents, and (c) the length of time buyers have to react to price changes. Clearly, the more substitutes and the better they are, the greater will be the price elasticity of demand. Thus price elasticity of demand rises as we consider the commodities "fruit," then "oranges," then "Sunkist oranges"; more and better substitutes exist for a specific brand of oranges than for the fruit group. Also, when a commodity takes up a small percentage of the consumer budget (other things being constant), we expect price elasticity of demand to be relatively lower, compared with items important to a budget. Presumably, buyers will have a greater incentive to shop around and seek substitutes for high-cost items than for low-cost items. Finally, for a given percentage change in price, quantity responsiveness (and therefore elasticity) will increase with the time period allowed for adjustment. With the passage of time, buyers are better able to find and use substitutes.

3. What is income elasticity of demand?

Income elasticity of demand refers to the responsiveness of buyers to income changes, given relative price. Technically, income elasticity of demand is defined as the percentage change in quantity demanded divided by the percentage change in income. The resulting measure is referred to as being income-elastic, unit-elastic, or income-inelastic, depending on whether or not it is greater than, equal to, or less than 1.

4. What is price elasticity of supply?

Price elasticity of supply refers to the responsiveness of sellers to changes in price. Technically, price elasticity of supply is defined as the percentage change in quantity supplied divided by the percentage change in price. The resulting measure can be greater than, equal to, or less than the number 1—referred to as elastic, unit-elastic, and inelastic price elasticity of supply, respectively. The longer the period of adjustment time, the greater the quantity responsiveness (and hence the price elasticity of supply) of sellers to given price changes.

PROBLEMS

(Answers to the odd-numbered problems appear at the back of the book.)

20-1. Use the following hypothetical demand schedule for tea to answer the questions.

QUANTITY DEMANDED PER WEEK (OUNCES)	PRICE PER OUNCE	ELASTICITY
1,000	$ 5	_____
800	10	_____
600	15	_____
400	20	_____
200	25	_____

a. Using the demand schedule, determine the elasticity of demand for each price change. (Example: When price changes from $5 to $10, quantity demanded changes from 1,000 to 800 ounces, so the elasticity of demand, using average values, is $\frac{1}{3}$, or .33.)

b. The data given in the demand schedule would plot as a straight-line demand curve. Why is demand more elastic the higher the price?

20-2. Calculate the price elasticity of demand for the product in the table below using average values for the prices and quantities in your formula. Over the price range in question, is this demand schedule price-inelastic, unit-elastic, or price-elastic? Is total revenue greater at the lower price or the higher price?

PRICE PER UNIT	QUANTITY DEMANDED
$4	22
6	18

20-3. Calculate the income elasticity of demand for the product in the accompanying table, using average values for incomes and quantities.

QUANTITY OF VCR'S PER YEAR	PER CAPITA ANNUAL GROUP INCOME
1,000	$15,000
2,000	20,000

a. Is the demand for this product income-elastic or income-inelastic?
b. Would you consider this commodity a luxury or a necessity?

20-4. Can any demand curve possibly be perfectly inelastic ($E_p = 0$) regardless of price? Explain.

20-5. A new mobile-home park charges nothing whatsoever for water used by its inhabitants. Consumption is 100,000 gallons per month. The decision is then made to charge according to how much each mobile-home owner uses, at a rate of $10 per 1,000 gallons. Consumption declines to 50,000 gallons per month. What is the difficulty here in accurately estimating the price elasticity of water for these residents?

20-6. Which of the following cross elasticities of demand would you expect to be positive and which to be negative?
a. Tennis balls and tennis racquets
b. Tennis balls and golf balls
c. Dental services and toothpaste
d. Dental services and candy
e. Liquor and ice cubes
f. Liquor and cocaine

20-7. Suppose that the price of salt per pound rises from 15 cents to 17 cents. The quantity demanded decreases from 525 pounds to 475 pounds per month, and the quantity supplied increases from 525 pounds to 600 pounds per month. (Use averages in calculating elasticities.)
a. Calculate the price elasticity of demand (E_p) for salt.
b. Is the demand for salt price-elastic or price-inelastic?
c. Calculate the elasticity of supply (E_s) for salt.
d. Is the supply for salt price-elastic or price-inelastic?

20-8. Suppose that an automobile dealer cuts his car prices by 15 percent. He then finds that his car sales have increased by 10 percent.
a. What can you say about the price elasticity of demand for cars?
b. What will happen to the dealer's total revenue?

20-9. For any given relative price, would you think that the demand for canal transportation was more or less elastic in 1840 than in 1880? How about the demand for Pony Express messengers before and after the transcontinental telegraph? The demand for rail transportation before and after the Model T Ford? The demand for transatlantic cable-laying equipment before and after communications satellites? The demand for slide rules before and after introduction of the pocket-sized calculator? Why?

COMPUTER-ASSISTED INSTRUCTION
(Complete problem and answer on disk.)

Given a (linear) demand schedule, can you demonstrate that the price elasticity of demand falls as price falls? This problem requires specific calculations of the price elasticity of demand at various prices.

21

THE FINANCIAL ENVIRONMENT: THE STOCK MARKET AND GLOBAL CAPITAL MARKETS

Centuries ago, London was the financial center of the world. Then, as America became the leading industrial nation, New York became a powerhouse. After World War II, Tokyo added itself to this list of established financial centers. These centers have always been thought of as geographic locations. After all, the New York Stock Exchange is in New York and the Nikkei Stock Exchange is in Tokyo. But is it possible in this age of technology and communications electronics that world finance is being freed from geographic constraints? Your understanding of this question will be easier after you study the firm's financial environment.

After reading this chapter, you should be able to answer the following questions:

1. What are the main organizational forms that firms take, and what are their advantages and disadvantages?

2. What are corporations' primary sources of financial capital?

3. Is there a world market for U.S. government securities?

4. What is one of the perils of global financial integration?

INTRODUCTION

Virtually everyone has heard of the stock market. It is a place where some people get rich and other people lose everything. While you and I may be interested in the stock market because it is one place we can put our savings, the stock market serves an underlying basic function: It allows companies to raise **financial capital** either to start a business or to expand. You've been introduced to the term *capital* as one of the four factors of production. In that context, capital consists of the goods that do not directly satisfy human wants but are used to make other goods. *Financial capital* is the money that is made available to purchase capital goods.

Different types of businesses are able to raise financial capital in different ways. Your first step in understanding the firm's financial environment is therefore to understand the way firms are organized.

▶ **Financial capital**
Money used to purchase capital goods such as buildings and equipment.

THE ORGANIZATION OF FIRMS

We all know that firms differ from one another. Some sell frozen yogurt, others make automobiles; some advertise, some do not; some have annual sales of a few thousand dollars, others have sales in the billions of dollars. The list of differences is probably endless. Yet for all of this diversity, the basic organization of *all* firms can be thought of in terms of a few simple structures, the most important of which are the proprietorship, the partnership, and the corporation.

PROPRIETORSHIPS

The most common form of business organization is the **proprietorship;** as shown in Table 21-1, about 70 percent of all firms in the United States are proprietorships. Each is owned by a single individual who makes the business decisions, receives all of the profits, and is legally responsible for all the debts of the firm. Although proprietorships are numerous, generally they are rather small businesses, with annual sales typically under $50,000. For this reason, even though there are more than 10 million proprietorships in the United States, they account for only about 6 percent of all business revenues.

▶ **Proprietorship**
A business owned by one individual who makes the business decisions, receives all of the profits, and is legally responsible for all the debts of the firm.

Advantages of Proprietorships.   Proprietorships offer several advantages as a form of business organization. First, they are *easy to form and to dissolve.* In the simplest case, all one must do to start a business is to start working; to dissolve the firm, one simply stops working. Even a more complicated proposition, such as starting a restaurant or a small retail shop, involves only meeting broadly defined health and zoning rules and the payment of a modest business license fee to the local government. To go out of business, one simply locks the front door. The second advantage of the proprietorship is that *all decision-making power resides with the sole proprietor.* The owner decides what and how much will be offered for sale, what the hours of operation will be, and who will perform what tasks. No partners, shareholders, or board of directors need be consulted. The third

TABLE 21-1   **Forms of business organization.**

TYPE OF FIRM	PERCENTAGE OF U.S. FIRMS	AVERAGE SIZE (ANNUAL SALES IN DOLLARS)	PERCENTAGE OF TOTAL BUSINESS REVENUES
Proprietorship	72.4	49,124	6.1
Partnership	8.7	280,532	4.2
Corporation	18.9	2,751,331	89.7

Source: U.S. Bureau of the Census, *Statistical Abstract of the United States, 1993,* Washington, D.C.: U.S. Government Printing Office.

advantage is that its *profit is taxed only once.* All profit is treated by law as the net income of the proprietor and as such is subject only to personal income taxation.

Disadvantages of Proprietorships.

The most important disadvantage of a proprietorship is that the proprietor faces **unlimited liability** *for the debts of the firm.* This means that the owner is personally responsible for all of the firm's debts. Thus the owner's personal assets—home, car, savings account, coin collection,—can be subject to seizure by the firm's creditors. The second disadvantage is that it has *limited ability to raise funds,* to expand the business or even simply to help it survive bad times. Because the success of a proprietorship depends so heavily on the good judgment and hard work of but one person—the owner—many lenders are reluctant to lend large sums to a proprietorship. Thus much of the financing of proprietorships often comes from the personal funds of the owner, which helps explain why proprietorships are usually small. The third disadvantage of proprietorships is that they normally *end with the death of the proprietor.* This, of course, creates added uncertainty for prospective lenders or employees, for a freak accident or sudden illness can turn a prosperous firm into a bittersweet memory.

▶ **Unlimited liability**
A legal concept whereby the personal assets of the owner of a firm may be used to pay off the firm's debts.

PARTNERSHIPS

The second important form of business organization is the **partnership.** As shown in Table 21-1, partnerships are far less numerous than proprietorships but tend to be significantly larger, with average sales about five times greater. A partnership differs from a proprietorship chiefly in that there are two or more co-owners, called partners. They share the responsibilities of operating the firm and its profits, and they are *each* legally responsible for *all* of the debts incurred by the firm. In this sense, a partnership may be viewed as a proprietorship with more than one owner. The partners may contribute equal or different amounts of financial capital to the firm, may have widely different operating responsibilities, and may share the profits in any way they see fit. Not surprisingly, partnerships share many of the advantages and disadvantages of proprietorships.

▶ **Partnership**
A business owned by two or more co-owners, or partners, who share the responsibilities and the profits of the firm and are individually liable for all of the debts of the partnership.

Advantages of Partnerships.

The first advantage of a partnership is that it is *easy to form.* In fact, it is almost as easy as forming a proprietorship, except that it requires two or more participants. Second, partnerships, like proprietorships, often help *reduce the costs of monitoring job performance.* This is particularly true when interpersonal skills are important for successful performance and in lines of business where, even after the fact, it is difficult to measure performance objectively. Thus attorneys and physicians often organize themselves as partnerships. Similarly, in professions such as these, a spectacular success may consist of a greatly reduced jail term for the client or greatly delayed death for the patient. In such circumstances, each partner has far more incentive to monitor his or her own work performance than he or she would as an employee, because the partner shares in the profits of the firm. A third advantage of the partnership is that it *permits more effective specialization* in occupations where, for legal or other reasons, the multiple talents required for success are unlikely to be uniform across individuals. Finally, partnerships share with proprietorships the advantage that the income of the partnership is treated as personal income and thus is subject only to personal taxation.

Disadvantages of Partnerships.

Not surprisingly, partnerships also have their disadvantages. First, the *partners each have unlimited liability.* Thus the personal assets of *each* partner are at risk due to debts incurred on behalf of the partnership by *any* of the partners. One partner's poor business judgment may impose substantial losses on all the other partners, a problem the sole proprietor need not worry about. Second, *decision making is generally more costly* in a partnership than in a proprietorship; there are more people involved in making decisions, and they may have differences of opinion that must be resolved before action is possible. Finally, *dissolution of the partnership is generally necessary* when a partner dies or voluntarily withdraws or when one or more partners wish to remove someone from the partnership. As with proprietorships, this creates potential uncertainty for creditors and employees.

CORPORATIONS

▶ **Corporation**
A legal entity that may conduct business in its own name just as an individual does; the owners of a corporation, called shareholders, own shares of the firm's profits and enjoy the protection of limited liability.

A **corporation** is a legal entity that may conduct business in its own name just as an individual does. The owners of a corporation are called *shareholders* because they own shares of the profits earned by the firm. By law, shareholders enjoy **limited liability,** which means that if the corporation incurs debts that it cannot pay, creditors have no recourse to the shareholders' personal property. As shown in Table 21-1, corporations are far less numerous than proprietorships, but because of their large size they are responsible for nearly 90 percent of all business revenues in the United States. Many, such as Microsoft, IBM, AT&T, and Exxon, are so large that their annual sales are measured in billions of dollars and their names are household words.

▶ **Limited liability**
A legal concept whereby the responsibility, or liability, of the owners of a corporation is limited to the value of the shares in the firm that they own.

Advantages of Corporations.   The fact that corporations conduct most of the nation's business suggests that the corporation offers significant advantages as a form of business organization. Perhaps the greatest of these is that the owners of a corporation (the shareholders) enjoy *limited liability.* The liability of shareholders is limited to the value of their shares. The second advantage arises because the law treats it as a legal entity in and of itself; thus the corporation *continues to exist* even if one or more owners of the corporation cease to be owners. A third advantage of the corporation stems from the first two: Corporations are well positioned for *raising large sums of financial capital.* People are able to buy ownership shares or lend money to the corporation knowing that their liability is limited to the amount of money they invest and confident that the corporation's existence does not depend on the life of any one of the firm's owners.

▶ **Dividends**
Portion of a corporation's profits paid to its owners (shareholders).

Disadvantages of Corporations.   The chief disadvantage of the corporation is the fact that corporate income is subject to *double taxation.* The profits of the corporation are subject first to corporate taxation. Then, if any of the after-tax profits are distributed to shareholders as **dividends,** such payments are treated as personal income to the shareholders and subject to personal taxation. The combined effect is that owners of corporations pay about twice as much in taxes on corporate income as they do on other forms of income.

A second disadvantage of the corporation is that corporations are potentially subject to problems associated with the *separation of ownership and control.* Specifically, it is commonplace for the owners (shareholders) of corporations to have little, if anything, to do with the actual management of the firm. Instead, these tasks are handled by professional managers who may have little or no ownership interest in the firm. The objective of the shareholders is presumably to maximize the value of their holdings. Unless their sole compensation is in the form of shares of stock in the corporation, however, the objective of the managers may differ from this. For example, managers may choose to have more luxurious offices than are needed for the efficient operation of the firm. If there are costs to the shareholders in preventing such behavior, the result may be that the market value of the firm is not maximized.

In principle, such problems could arise with a partnership or a proprietorship if the owner or partners hired a manager to take care of day-to-day operations. Nevertheless, the separation of ownership and control is widely regarded as a more important problem for corporations; their attractiveness as a means of raising financial capital from many investors makes them subject to higher costs of agreement among owners with respect to penalties for managers who fail to maximize the value of the firm.

HYBRIDS: LIMITED PARTNERSHIPS AND S CORPORATIONS

The law permits some small firms to organize themselves as one of two types of so-called *hybrid* firms: limited partnerships and S corporations (formerly called Subchapter S corporations), so named after the subchapter of the Internal Revenue Code that established the tax rules applicable to them.

A **limited partnership** is simply a firm in which *some* of the partners are granted limited liability. At least one of the partners, however, including any partner who participates in the operation and management of the firm, must be designated a *general partner*. The general partner faces unlimited liability: If the firm cannot meet its debts, the company's creditors can sue the general partner to collect money from his or her personal assets. The other partners, called *limited partners,* cannot be sued in this way; they enjoy limited liability, just as they would if the firm were a corporation. Limited partnerships are frequently used when a group of individuals wish to share in the potential profits of a venture but do not wish to bother themselves with managing it and do not want to expose their other assets to the risks of unlimited liability.

An **S corporation** is a firm that is exempt from most of the burden of the double taxation that is imposed on other corporations. Compared to the limited partnership, it has the advantage that *all* of the owners enjoy the protection of limited liability. However, it also has disadvantages. First, the number of owners is limited to 35. Second, in some states it is not exempt from all corporate taxation. Third, profits are taxed promptly as owner income rather than retained for possible future reinvestment in the firm. Finally, investors in an S corporation are limited in the extent to which they may use the firm's losses to reduce their tax liability on other income.

▶ **Limited partnership**
A firm in which some partners, called limited partners, are granted limited liability; at least one general partner, responsible for managing the partnership, must accept unlimited liability.

▶ **S corporation**
A type of corporation in which the owners are largely exempt from the double taxation of corporate income.

CONCEPTS IN BRIEF

- Proprietorships are the most common form of business organization, comprising 70 percent of all firms. Each is owned by a single individual who makes all business decisions, receives all the profits, and has unlimited liability for the firm's debts.
- Partnerships are much like proprietorships, except that two or more individuals, or partners, share the decisions and the profits of the firm. In addition, each partner has unlimited liability for the debts of the firms.
- Corporations are responsible for the largest share of business revenues. The owners, called shareholders, share in the firm's profits but normally have little responsibility for the firm's day-to-day operations. They enjoy limited liability for the debts of the firm.
- Limited partnerships and S corporations are variants, enabling smaller companies to enjoy the limited liability of corporations and yet keep many of the tax advantages of proprietorships and partnerships.

METHODS OF CORPORATE FINANCING

When the Dutch East India Company was founded in 1602, it raised financial capital by selling shares of its expected future profits to investors. The investors thus became the owners of the company, and their ownership shares eventually became known as "shares of stock," or simply *stocks.* The company also issued notes of indebtedness, which involved borrowing money in return for interest on the funds, plus eventual repayment of the principal amount borrowed. In modern parlance, these notes of indebtedness are called *bonds.* As the company prospered over time, some of its revenues were used to pay lenders the interest and principal owed them; of the profits that remained, some were paid to shareholders in the form of dividends, and some were retained by the company for reinvestment in further enterprises. The methods of financing used by the Dutch East India Company nearly four centuries ago—stocks, bonds, and reinvestment—remain the principal methods of financing for today's corporations.

▶ **Share of stock**
A legal claim to a share of a corporation's future profits; if it is *common stock,* it incorporates certain voting rights regarding major policy decisions of the corporation; if it is *preferred stock,* its owners are accorded preferential treatment in the payment of dividends.

A **share of stock** in a corporation is simply a legal claim to a share of the corporation's future profits. If there are 100,000 shares of stock in a company and you own 1,000 of them, you own the right to 1 percent of that company's future profits. If the stock you own is *common stock,* you also have the right to vote on major policy decisions affecting the company, such as the selection of the corporation's board of directors. Your 1,000 shares would entitle you to cast 1 percent of the votes on such issues. If the stock you own is *preferred stock,* you also own a share of the future profits of the corporation, but you do *not* have regular voting rights. You do, however, get something in return for giving up your voting rights: preferential treatment in the payment of dividends. Specifically, the owners of preferred stock generally must receive at least a certain amount of dividends in each period before the owners of common stock can receive *any* dividends.

▶ **Bond**
A legal claim against a firm usually entitling the owner of the bond to receive a fixed annual coupon payment, plus a lump-sum payment at the bond's maturity date; bonds are issued in return for funds lent to the firm.

A **bond** is a legal claim against a firm, entitling the owner of the bond to receive a fixed annual *coupon* payment, plus a lump-sum payment at the maturity date of the bond.[1] Bonds are issued in return for funds lent to the firm; the coupon payments represent interest on the amount borrowed by the firm, and the lump-sum payment at maturity of the bond generally equals the amount originally borrowed by the firm. Bonds are *not* claims to the future profits of the firm; legally, bondholders are to be paid whether the firm prospers or not. To help ensure this, bondholders generally must receive their coupon payments each year, and any principal that is due, before *any* shareholders can receive dividend payments.

▶ **Reinvestment**
Profits (or depreciation reserves) used to purchase new capital equipment.

Reinvestment takes place when the firm uses some of its profits to purchase new capital equipment rather than paying the money out as dividends to shareholders. Although sales of stock are an important source of financing for new firms, reinvestment and borrowing are the principal means of financing for existing firms. Indeed, reinvestment by established firms is such an important source of financing that it dominates the other two sources of corporate finance, amounting to roughly 75 percent of new financial capital for corporations in recent years. Also, small businesses, which are the source of much current growth, usually cannot rely on the stock market to raise investment funds.

🌐 INTERNATIONAL EXAMPLE: **Who Owns All Those Stocks?**

Contrary to popular belief, the ownership of shares of stock in the United States is not confined to the very rich. What has happened over the past half century is that individual investors do not directly own many of the shares of the stock either in New York or in

---

[1]Coupon payments on bonds get their name from the fact that bonds once had coupons attached to them when they were issued. Each year, the owner would clip a coupon off the bond and send it to the issuing firm in return for that year's interest on the bond.

FIGURE 21-1
Ownership of shares listed on the London Stock Exchange and the New York Stock Exchange.
Over 30 percent of the value of all shares listed on the London Stock Exchange and on the New York Stock Exchange are now owned by pension plans.

Sources: London Stock Exchange; New York Stock Exchange.

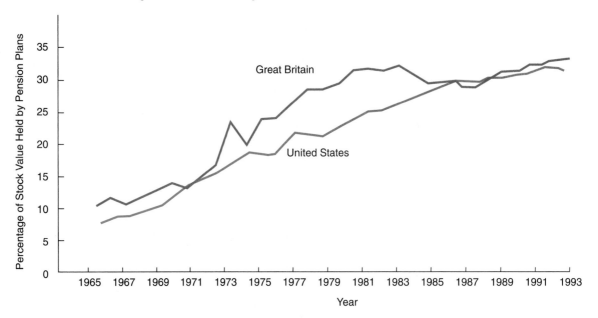

London. In 1950, for example, more than half the shares on the New York and London stock markets were owned by individuals. It is estimated that fewer than 20 percent are now owned by individuals in London and New York. The other 80 percent are owned by what are called institutional investors—pension funds and life insurance companies for the most part. Pension funds alone account for about 30 percent of the total value of shares listed on the London and New York stock exchanges. The trend is shown in Figure 21-1.

There are literally thousands of pension funds that invest money for company employees. That means that the majority of working Americans indirectly own the majority of shares of stock in corporate America and corporate Great Britain.

For Critical Analysis: What does the information just given tell you about a middle-income-earning individual who thinks that corporations should pay more taxes? ●

ASYMMETRIC INFORMATION: THE PERILS OF ADVERSE SELECTION AND MORAL HAZARD

When financial transactions take place, one party often does not know all that he or she needs to know about the other party in order to make correct decisions. The inequality of information between the two parties is called **asymmetric information.** If asymmetric information exists before a transaction takes place, we have a circumstance of **adverse selection.** In financial markets, adverse selection occurs because borrowers who are the worst credit risks (and thus likely to yield the most adverse outcomes) are the ones most likely to be selected by lenders to receive loans.

Consider two firms seeking to borrow funds by selling bonds. Suppose that one of the firms, the Dynamic Corporation, is pursuing a project with a small chance of yielding large profits and a large chance of bankruptcy. The other firm, the Reliable Company, in-

▶ **Asymmetric information**
Information possessed by one side of a transaction only. The side that has relatively more information will be at an advantage.

▶ **Adverse selection**
The circumstance that arises in financial markets when borrowers that are the worst credit risks are most likely to receive loans.

tends to invest in a project that is guaranteed to yield the competitive rate of return, thereby ensuring repayment of its debts. Because Dynamic knows the chance is high that it will go bankrupt and never have to pay its debts, it can offer a high interest rate on the bonds it issues. Unless prospective bond purchasers can distinguish perfectly between the two firms' projects, they will select the high-yielding bonds offered by Dynamic and refuse to buy the low-yielding bonds offered by Reliable. Firms like Reliable will be unable to get funding, yet lenders will lose money on firms like Dynamic. Adverse selection thus makes investors less likely to lend to anyone and more inclined to charge higher interest rates when they do lend.

> **Moral hazard**
> A problem that occurs because of asymmetric information *after* a transaction occurs. In financial markets, a person to whom money has been lent may indulge in more risky behavior, thereby increasing the probability of default on the debt.

Moral hazard occurs as a result of asymmetric information *after* a transaction occurs. To continue with our example of the Dynamic Corporation, once the firm has sold the bonds, it must choose among alternative strategies in executing its project. Lenders face the hazard that Dynamic may choose strategies contrary to the lenders' well-being and thus immoral from their perspective. Because bondholders are entitled to a fixed amount regardless of the firm's profits, Dynamic has an incentive to select strategies offering a small chance of high profits, thereby enabling the owners to keep the largest amount after paying bondholders. Such strategies are also the riskiest—ones that make it more likely that lenders will not be repaid—so the presence of moral hazard makes lenders less likely to lend to anyone and more inclined to charge higher interest rates when they do lend.

THE PRINCIPAL-AGENT PROBLEM

> **Principal-agent problem**
> The conflict of interest that occurs when agents—managers of firms—pursue their own objectives to the detriment of the goals of the firms' principals, or owners.

A type of moral hazard problem that occurs within firms is called the **principal-agent problem.** Stockholders who own a firm are referred to as *principals,* and the managers who operate the firm are called the *agents* of the owners. When the managers do not own all of a firm, we say that there is a **separation of ownership and control.** When such separation is present, if the stockholders have less information about the firm's opportunities and risks than the managers do, the managers may act in their own self-interests rather than in the interests of the stockholders.

> **Separation of ownership and control**
> A situation that exists in corporations in which the owners—shareholders—are not the people who control the operation of the corporation—the managers. The goals of these two groups often are different.

Consider, for example, the choice between two investment projects, one of which involves an enormous amount of work but also promises high profits, while the other requires little effort and promises small returns. Because the managers must do all the work while the stockholders receive all the profits, the managers' incentives are different from those of the stockholders. In this case the presence of moral hazard will induce the managers to choose the "good life," the easy but low-yielding project—an outcome that fails to maximize the economic value of the firm.

SOLVING PRINCIPAL-AGENT AND MORAL HAZARD PROBLEMS

> **Collateral**
> An asset pledged as security for the payment of a loan.

> **Incentive-compatible contract**
> A loan contract under which a significant amount of the borrower's assets are at risk, providing an incentive for the borrower to look after the lender's interests.

The dangers associated with asymmetric information are well known to participants in financial markets, and they regularly undertake vigorous steps to minimize its costly consequences. For example, research companies such as Standard & Poor's gather financial data and other information about corporations and sell the information to their subscribers. When even this is insufficient to eliminate the dangers of adverse selection, lenders often require that borrowers post **collateral**—assets that the borrower forfeits in the event that repayment of a debt is not made. A variant of this strategy, designed to reduce moral hazard problems, is called the **incentive-compatible contract:** Lenders make sure that borrowers have a large amount of their own assets at risk, so that the incentives of the borrower are compatible with the interests of the lender. Although measures such as these cannot eliminate the losses caused by asymmetric information, they reduce them below what would otherwise be the case.

CONCEPTS IN BRIEF

- When two parties to a transaction have different amounts of information, we call this asymmetric information. Whenever asymmetric information occurs before a transaction takes place, we call this adverse selection. Adverse selection causes borrowers who are the worst credit risks to be the ones most likely to receive loans.
- When asymmetric information occurs after a transaction, this is a situation of moral hazard. Lenders often face the hazard that borrowers will choose more risky actions after borrowers have taken out loans.
- The separation of ownership and control in today's large corporations can give rise to the principal-agent problem, whereby the agents (managers) may have interests that differ from those of the principals (shareholders).
- Several methods exist for solving the principal-agent and moral hazard problems. They include requiring lenders to post collateral and devising incentive-compatible contracts in which borrowers have a large amount of their own assets at risk.

THE MARKETS FOR STOCKS AND BONDS

Economists often refer to the market for wheat or the market for labor. For stocks and bonds there really are markets—centralized, physical locations where exchange takes place. By far the largest and most prestigious of these are the New York Stock Exchange (NYSE) and the New York Bond Exchange, both located in New York City. Numerous other stock and bond markets, or exchanges, are located throughout the United States and in various financial capitals of the world, such as London and Tokyo. Although the exact process by which exchanges are conducted in these markets varies slightly from one to another, the process used on the NYSE is representative of the principles involved.[2]

More than 2,000 stocks are traded on the NYSE, which is sometimes called the "Big Board." Leading brokerage firms—about 600 of them—own seats on the NYSE. These seats, which are actually rights to buy and sell stocks on the floor of the Big Board, are themselves regularly exchanged. In recent years their value has fluctuated between $350,000 and $1 million. These prices reflect the fact that ultimately stock trades on the NYSE are handled by the firms owning these seats, and the firms earn commissions on each trade. As trading volume rises, as it did during the 1980s, the value of the seats rises.

 INTERNATIONAL EXAMPLE: Bursting the South Sea Bubble

In England until 1757 there was no law against obtaining money under false pretenses. And that is just what a group of men did in 1710 when they founded the South Sea Company, an enterprise similar to our corporation for which shares of stock were sold and resold. To induce the public to purchase shares in the South Sea Company, its founders argued that the company would have a monopoly on trade with the South Seas, which at that time were considered the pearl of the Spanish possessions in South America.

The founders needed authorization from the British Parliament before they took money from the public. To convince Parliament to grant them authorization, they agreed that in exchange for their monopoly on trade with Spanish America, the South Sea Company

---

[2]A number of stocks and bonds are traded in so-called over-the-counter (OTC) markets, which, although not physically centralized, otherwise operate in much the same way as the NYSE and so are not treated separately in this text.

would take over a large part of Britain's national debt. The people who owned government bonds would exchange them for shares of stock in the South Sea Company.

The problem with this scheme was that the potential for profits was virtually zero. None of the directors of the South Sea Company had even been to the South Seas. Moreover, the king of Spain was making good money trading with his own New World colonies and was not about to share that trade willingly. In fact, only a few halfhearted attempts at actual trading by the South Sea Company took place. For the 10 years of its existence, it was basically a big financial scam. The South Sea Company would borrow money at a favorable interest rate. Then it would issue new shares of stock offering high dividends. The price of a single share of stock rose from 250 pounds sterling to 400, 600, and 800. As this occurred, owners of government bonds rushed to exchange them for shares of stock in the South Sea Company. By the summer of 1720, the stock hit 1,000 pounds. Then the bubble burst. The South Sea directors wanted to choke off competition from anyone else who wanted to take the public's cash. They got Parliament to pass a bill actually prohibiting the sale of stock in any company not authorized by Parliament. The act that was passed was called the Bubble Act.

By the fall of 1720, South Sea stock had dropped to 830 pounds, and within the next 30 days to 180. An angry speculator tried to kill one of the directors of the company, John Blunt. The stock collapsed to nothing, which led to the collapse of virtually all credit in England. No one wanted "paper" anymore. The real estate market collapsed, and bankruptcies were everywhere. The government finally fell.

For Critical Analysis: *What prevents schemes similar to that used by the South Sea Company from occurring in the United States today?* ●

⭐ EXAMPLE: Can You Get Rich in the Stock Market?

Virtually anytime anybody talks about the stock market, there is always a question about whether it is possible to get rich quickly by buying and selling stock. The answer, as you will see, is usually no.

At any point in time, there are tens of thousands, even millions of persons looking for any bit of information that will enable them to forecast correctly the future prices of stocks. Responding to any information that seems useful, these people try to buy low and sell high. The result is that all publicly available information that might be used to forecast stock prices gets taken into account by those with access to the information and the knowledge and ability to learn from it, leaving no forecastable profit opportunities. And because so many people are involved in this process, it occurs quite swiftly. Indeed, there is some evidence that *all* information entering the market is fully incorporated into stock prices within less than a minute of its arrival. One view of the stock market is that most public information you will obtain will prove to have little value.

The result of this process is that stock prices tend to follow a *random walk,* which is to say that the best forecast of tomorrow's price is today's price. This is called the **random walk theory.** Although large values of the random component of stock price changes are less likely than small values, nothing else about the magnitude or sign (positive or negative) of a stock price change can be predicted. Indeed, the random component of stock prices exhibits behavior much like what would occur if you rolled two dice and subtracted 7 from the resulting score. On average, the dice will show a total of 7, so after you subtract 7, the average result will be zero. It is true that rolling a 12 or a 2 (resulting in a net score of +5 or −5) is less likely than rolling an 8 or a 6 (yielding a net score of +1 or −1). Nevertheless, positive and negative net scores are equally likely, and the expected net score is zero.

▶ **Random walk theory**
The theory that successive prices are independent of each other in security markets. Because there are no predictable trends in prices, today's prices cannot be used to predict future prices.

Isn't there any way to "beat the market"? The answer is yes—but normally only if you have **inside information** that is not available to the public. Suppose that your best friend is in charge of new product development at the country's largest software firm, Microsoft Corporation. Your friend tells you that the company's smartest programmer has just come up with major new software that millions of computer users will want to buy. No one but your friend and the programmer—and now you—is aware of this. You could indeed make money using this information by purchasing shares of Microsoft and then selling them (at a higher price) as soon as the new product is publicly announced. There is one problem: Stock trading based on inside information such as this is normally illegal, punishable by substantial fines and even imprisonment. So unless you happen to have a stronger than average desire for a long vacation in a federal prison, you might be better off investing in Microsoft after the new program is publicly announced.

▶ **Inside information**
Information about what is happening in a corporation that is not available to the general public.

For Critical Analysis: *Do you agree that only inside information will give a potential investor an edge over other investors? What other circumstances do you feel might enable an investor to outperform the overall market in the long run?* ●

GLOBAL CAPITAL MARKETS

Financial institutions in the United States are tied to the rest of the world via their lending capacities. In addition, integration of all financial markets is increasing. Indeed, recent changes in world finance have been nothing short of remarkable. Distinctions among financial institutions and between financial institutions and nonfinancial institutions have blurred. As the legal barriers that have preserved such distinctions are dismantled, multinational corporations offering a wide array of financial services are becoming dominant worldwide.

GLOBALIZING FINANCIAL MARKETS

The globalization of financial markets is not entirely new. U.S. banks developed worldwide branch networks in the 1960s and 1970s for loans, check clearing, and foreign exchange (currency) trading. Also in the 1970s, firms dealing in U.S. securities (stocks and bonds) expanded their operations in London (on the Eurobond market) and then into other financial centers, including Tokyo. Similarly, foreign firms invaded U.S. shores: first the banks, then securities firms. The "big four" Japanese securities firms now have offices in New York and London.

Money and capital markets today are truly international. Markets for U.S. government securities, interbank lending and borrowing, foreign exchange trading, and common stocks are now trading continuously, in vast quantities, around the clock and around the world.

The World Market for U.S. Government Debt. Trading for U.S. government securities has been described as "the world's fastest growing 24-hour market." This market was made possible by (1) sophisticated communications and computer technology, (2) deregulation of financial markets in foreign countries to permit such trading, (3) U.S. legislation in 1984 to enable foreign investors to buy U.S. government securities tax-free, and (4) huge annual U.S. government budget deficits, which have poured a steady stream of tradable debt into the world markets.

In 1987 the Federal National Mortgage Association ("Fannie Mae," a U.S. quasi-governmental agency) created a worldwide market for some of its securities (bonds). In October of that year it sold a dollar-denominated bond issue in Tokyo. Just a month earlier Fannie Mae had announced a $1 billion medium-term note program aimed at European investors: It featured fixed-rate and variable-rate securities denominated in U.S. dollars and other currencies.

A Worldwide Stock Market.   William C. Freund, former chief economist of the New York Stock Exchange, has indicated that representatives of the stock exchanges around the world who were once very friendly (when their exchanges were isolated) have begun to "fight fiercely to entice company listings, attract international brokers and bankers to membership, and solicit orders from investors around the world."

The globalization of this market began when the Securities Act of 1975 banned fixed commission rates on U.S. stock exchanges and Congress passed legislation that opened exchanges to all financial institutions able to meet capital requirement rules. Stock exchanges in other countries feared that the United States would capture most of the international investment business, and they followed suit. In 1986 London made commission rates competitive and permitted foreigners to acquire British securities firms and to gain admission to the London exchange; Germany and France soon followed. In 1988 even Japan opened the door to limited foreign membership on the Tokyo exchange.

 INTERNATIONAL EXAMPLE: Former Anticapitalist Countries and Their Booming Stock Markets

For 74 years of Communist control in the Soviet Union and for over 40 years in its Eastern-bloc satellites, *profit* was a dirty word. All major businesses were owned "by the people" (that is, the state). In the 1990s all of that is indeed history. In Hungary, the government has essentially privatized most of that nation's businesses, transferring shares of ownership to the population at large. Czechoslovakia before its breakup also engaged in a mass-privatization effort. Shares in 1,500 state-owned companies valued at about $10 billion were offered to the public. Almost 9 million of that nation's 11 million adults purchased shares of stock in those formerly state-owned companies. The way they did this was quite unique: Each person wishing to participate paid about $40 for voucher booklets to buy stock. Each booklet had a value of 100 points to pay for shares. The government then offered shares of state-owned companies at the rate of three shares for 100 points. The scheme created millions of shareholders overnight. After several rounds of auctioning off the shares of stock, most of the 1,500 formerly state-owned companies are now in private hands. Only a few huge debt-ridden engineering companies were unable to sell shares of stock.

In the People's Republic of China, the opening of a small stock market in the town of Shenzhen in the summer of 1992 turned out a bit differently. Over a million people from all over China poured in to that town, swelling the population by 50 percent. They lined up for share applications. During a three-day period, would-be shareholders smashed windows and cars and attacked each other as well as the police. Finally, the Shenzhen Stock market—one of two authorized stock markets in all of China—had to be closed temporarily. By 1993 there were 70 companies listed on the two stock exchanges. Volume of sales had increased over 30 times since 1991. Foreigners are now even allowed to own shares in Chinese companies, including those that were wholly state-owned. The government had its first-ever stock issue for foreigners in December 1992 when it raised $11 million by selling shares in China's Southern Glass.

For Critical Analysis: *Why do you think the pace of privatization of state-owned companies has proceeded at such widely differing rates in different formerly communist and socialist countries?* ●

Other Globalized Markets.   Foreign exchange—the buying and selling of foreign currencies—became a 24-hour, worldwide market in the 1970s. Instruments tied to government bonds, foreign exchange, stock market indexes, and commodities (grains, metals, oil) are now traded increasingly in financial futures markets in all the world's major centers of commerce. Most financial firms are coming to the conclusion that to survive as a force in any one of the world's leading financial markets, a firm must have a significant presence in all of them. It is predicted that by the turn of the twenty-first century, between 30 and 50 financial institutions will be at the centers of world finance—New York, London, Tokyo, and Frankfurt—and they will be competing in all those markets to do business with the world's major corporations and portfolio managers. Today major corporate borrowers throughout the world can choose to borrow from a wide variety of lenders, also located throughout the world. Borrowing on the international capital markets was estimated at $600 billion for the year 1993 for the 24 leading industrialized nations, according to the Organization for Economic Cooperation and Development (OECD).

PERILS OF GLOBAL INTEGRATION: A WORLDWIDE STOCK MARKET CRASH

The U.S. stock market crash on October 24, 1929 (Black Thursday), signaled the beginning of the Great Depression. Other stock markets throughout the world followed, triggering a worldwide depression. Almost sixty years later, on Black Monday, October 19, 1987, the New York Stock Exchange crashed again—the Dow Jones Industrial Average fell 501 points, the largest one-day loss in U.S. history. In less than seven hours, more than $500 billion of corporate equity disappeared. The stock markets in Sydney, London, and Hong Kong soon followed suit. It took almost two years for the U.S. stock market to regain its previous level and longer elsewhere in the world.

The important lesson of the crash of 1987 was that a globalized financial market system holds perils as well as rewards. An electronic information system now lets everybody enjoy the benefits of panic equally. In Table 21-2 you can see that most other countries experienced even more severe drops in their stock market index than the United States did in the crash of 1987.

What happened was that U.S. speculators sold off stocks. Managers of investment portfolios looked worldwide to sell their shares, which they could not sell in the United States at attractive enough prices. Investment managers in other countries did the same. The U.S. crash led to stock sales in foreign markets, which caused their indexes to fall. In turn, foreigners sold on the U.S. market. Money market managers worldwide raised cash by selling shares in the 200 or so companies that are traded in significant volume around the world because those stocks are the most liquid. The globalization of financial markets, like most things economic, has turned out to have costs as well as benefits.

COUNTRY	PERCENT CHANGE (IN LOCAL CURRENCY)
Australia	−43.4
West Germany	−38.4
France	−34.7
Netherlands	−33.6
Switzerland	−30.5
Canada	−28.4
United States	−27.8
United Kingdom	−27.2
Japan	−19.8
Italy	−18.7

TABLE 21-2   1987's worldwide stock market collapse.
Percentage change in Morgan Stanley's index for 10 world stock markets between August 25,1987—the record high for the U.S. market at the time—and Wednesday, October 21, 1987.

Source: Morgan Stanley Capital International Perspective

CONCEPTS IN BRIEF

- Financial markets throughout the world have become increasingly integrated, leading to a global financial market. Interbank lending and borrowing, foreign exchange trading, and common stock sales now occur virtually 24 hours a day throughout the world.
- Many U.S. government or government-supported securities trade 24 hours a day.
- Because of global financial integration, the world is more susceptible to a worldwide stock market crash. For example, in 1987 a severe drop in stock prices in the United States was reflected around the world almost immediately.

THE MARKET FOR CORPORATE CONTROL

During the 1980s and early 1990s a host of normally reclusive financiers became regular subjects of prime-time newscasts and front-page headlines. Their names became household words simply because they were buying and selling things—companies, *big* companies. As time went on, the deals got bigger: $7.5 billion, $10.1 billion, $13.4 billion, even $25 billion.

Along the way, controversy erupted. Some observers argued that most of the buying and selling was little more than a shell game in which ownership of existing assets was simply rearranged to no productive purpose. These critics said that the financiers doing the rearranging made hundreds of millions of dollars, but only by selling stocks and bonds at inflated prices, typically at the expense of stockholders and the general public. Other observers maintained that the mergers and corporate buyouts were essential to maintaining the efficiency of the marketplace. When there are costs of obtaining agreement among thousands of widely dispersed stockholders, they argue, corporate management can operate firms so as to maximize their own wealth rather than the wealth of stockholders. Corporate financiers, or even other firms, can marshal the financial resources needed to gain control of such companies, replace the offending management, and so increase the efficiency of the acquired firms. Along the way, the stockholders in the acquired firms benefit from higher stock prices, and consumers and the general public benefit from enhanced efficiency. The rewards earned by the **corporate raiders** masterminding these deals is simply the payoff to improving resource allocation. Although not all of the evidence needed to settle this controversy is yet available, enough has been developed to help us understand the basic issues.

> ▶ **Corporate raiders**
> People or firms that specialize in seeking out corporations that are potential targets for takeovers.

BACKGROUND

An impressive series of takeovers and buyouts began with a bang in 1981 with du Pont's purchase of Conoco, the ninth largest oil company in the country. At the time, Conoco owned oil and gas reserves estimated to be worth about $160 for each share of outstanding stock, yet the market price of Conoco's stock was only $50. The enormous difference between the asset value of the company and the market value of its stock made Conoco a ripe takeover target: Anyone who could buy up enough stock to capture majority control could then sell the company's oil and gas reserves at a huge profit.

The first firm to try to take advantage of this opportunity was Seagram, a large Canadian liquor distiller. Apparently, Seagram intended to replace the top management of Conoco if it were successful in buying the firm. As a result, Conoco's board of directors went looking for a **white knight**—a buyer willing to execute a "friendly" takeover, in which Conoco's management team would be retained. The du Pont company, a major

> ▶ **White knight**
> A buyer of a firm that is willing to execute a "friendly" takeover, typically one that retains the management of the acquired firm.

producer of chemicals, was happy to oblige Conoco, offering $87.50 a share. Before the deal could be consummated, the nation's second biggest oil company, Mobil, made a **hostile takeover** offer of $90 a share.

The bidding war among Mobil, du Pont, and Seagram escalated until Mobil made a top offer of $120 per share—more than double the price at which Conoco stock had been trading when the battle began. Ultimately, however, du Pont won the bidding at a price lower than Mobil's offer because of its agreement to a friendly takeover.

Valued at $7.5 billion, du Pont's purchase of Conoco was at the time the most costly business acquisition in history—but not for long. In 1984 Texaco purchased the Getty Oil Company for $10.1 billion. Later that same year Chevron purchased Gulf Oil for $13.4 billion. In 1988, Kohlberg Kravis Roberts purchased the giant food and tobacco company RJR Nabisco for nearly $25 billion.

PREVENTING HOSTILE TAKEOVERS

One method used by firms to make a hostile takeover more costly has been the **golden parachute,** a guarantee to the top managers of a firm that if they are fired due to a takeover, they will receive multimillion-dollar severance payments. Another ploy is the **poison pill,** a maneuver that makes the target either unattractive or prohibitively expensive. For example, the target firm's management may quickly arrange the sale of a major asset known to be coveted by the acquiring firm. Management may also arrange matters so that if a corporate raider gets control of a certain percentage of the target firm's stock, other shareholders are allowed to purchase extra shares at a substantially reduced price. A third technique used by management to stave off corporate raiders has been **greenmail**—the payment of a large premium for the shares held by the raider in return for the raider's shares *and* an agreement that the raider will cease the takeover attempt.

ARE TAKEOVER BATTLES PRODUCTIVE?

Takeover opponents have argued that takeover battles absorb the energies and talents of individuals highly capable in financial manipulation rather than in productive and innovative activity and that the billions of dollars exchanged for the shares of target firms would be better spent on new productive capacity. Such arguments ignore three important points. First, takeover battles *are* productive, for they help reveal the correct prices for assets, facilitating their employment in their highest-value uses. Second, to the extent that small, widely dispersed shareholders face high costs of monitoring management, corporate raiders help ensure that complacent or incompetent management does not squander the value of the assets under its control. Third, the money that goes to purchase the stock of takeover targets does not simply disappear once the takeover is completed. Previous shareholders receive it and will presumably be looking for new ways to invest it. If the returns from newly produced physical assets exceed the returns from existing assets, that is where the money should—and will—be invested. If newly produced assets offer lower returns than existing assets, investors will (efficiently) refrain from purchasing them.

Lost in the foregoing arguments, however, are the human costs of corporate takeover battles. Often when one corporation is taken over by another, divisions are shut down or sold off. This leads to disruption in entire communities where these divisions might have been operating for many years.

JUNK BONDS

In recent years yet another factor has entered the takeover controversy—the so-called junk bonds used to finance some takeovers. **Junk bonds** are risky bonds, offering high coupon

▶ **Hostile takeover**
Purchase of a firm that is opposed by the target firm's current management, sometimes because it appears likely that the managers will lose their jobs if the takeover is successful.

▶ **Golden parachute**
A guarantee to the existing managers of a firm that if they are ousted as a result of a takeover, they will receive large severance payments.

▶ **Poison pill**
In general, any maneuver by the management of a target firm that makes the firm either unattractive to a potential raider or prohibitively expensive.

▶ **Greenmail**
Payment by a target firm of a substantial premium for shares held by a corporate raider in return for the raider's agreement to cease attempts at a takeover.

▶ **Junk bonds**
Risky bonds offering high coupon yields, sometimes issued by corporate raiders to finance takeovers.

payments, issued to finance acquisitions. In general, purchasers of junk bonds have the lowest priority of the issuing firm's creditors; the holders of these bonds are least likely to receive what is owed them. Virtually unknown before 1983, junk bonds were used to finance more than $30 billion worth of corporate takeovers in 1986, and comparable amounts were issued in each of the remaining years of the 1980s. At the beginning of the 1990s the use of junk bonds declined somewhat, but recently they are being used again.

THE BENEFITS OF A TAKEOVER
TO SHAREHOLDERS

One feature of the corporate takeover controversy that has been studied intensively is the impact of takeovers on shareholders. The evidence seems to favor the argument that takeovers generally benefit shareholders. Successful takeovers (those in which the raider acquires the target) increase the wealth of stockholders in the target companies. Estimates of the gains vary considerably from study to study, but the appreciation in the value of the stock of acquired companies typically ranges from 15 to 35 percent. There is also evidence that the value of the *acquiring* firm's shares increase too, although by amounts that are a good deal smaller. Thus stockholders on both sides of the deal often benefit from corporate takeovers, with the bulk of the gains going to shareholders of the target firms.

We now have enough experience with junk bonds to determine how the owners of these takeover securities will fare. Many issuers are making their promised coupon payments, although some have defaulted, even on bonds that are only a year or two old. Overall, the evidence so far suggests that default rates on junk bonds are fairly low initially—about 2.5 percent per year—but may rise as the bonds age.

Many of the huge junk bond issuings that went to finance the expansion of the information industry in the United States in the 1980s have proven to be spectacular successes. A total of $10 billion was raised to finance expansion activities by MCI, Tele-Communications, Inc. (TCI), McCaw Cellular, Turner Broadcasting, Warner Communications (now Time Warner), 20th Century Fox (now part of News Corp.), and Metro-Media Broadcasting. At the time of their expansion and financing by junk bonds, those companies had a market value of somewhere in the neighborhood of $10 billion. As of 1993, those companies had a market value of over $60 billion. Most of the shareholders and purchasers of junk bonds in the 1980s in at least those companies did quite well.

CONCEPTS IN BRIEF

- The decade of the 1980s witnessed an enormous expansion in the active market for corporate takeovers—the practice of firms or corporate financiers attempting to purchase control of existing corporations.
- Supporters of corporate takeovers argue that takeovers improve managerial effort to maximize the value of firms, enhance the wealth of shareholders, and improve the efficiency with which resources are allocated.
- Opponents of corporate takeovers argue that takeovers devote too many valuable resources to financial manipulation, distract management from managerial tasks, and may harm the interests of shareholders.
- The evidence to date indicates that successful takeovers increase the value of the shares of stock held by the owners of both the acquiring company and the target firm.
- Junk bonds, which are high-risk corporate bonds, have been an important means of financing many corporate takeovers.

HAVE WE SEEN THE END OF WORLD FINANCIAL CENTERS?

Concepts Applied: Stock markets, global financial integration

The New York Stock Exchange has always considered itself the center of the international financial world. Nonetheless, recent developments in telecommunications have caused New York as a financial center to lose market share compared to the entire world of finance.

It may be true that everybody has to be somewhere, but it no longer seems true that financial transactions have to take place in London, New York, and Tokyo. These "big three" centers have dominated international bank lending and securities trading for decades.

MAJOR CAPITAL CENTERS IN DECLINE

New York has steadily seen its market share in international financial transactions decline. After a severe stock market crash in 1992, Tokyo also saw its share in world financial dealings decline. London has been battered for years by other major cities in Europe, especially Frankfurt. London, in particular, will be under pressure in the coming decades as new creditor countries come on board in the international financial marketplace. The economic growth in Eastern Europe and in the former Soviet republics will undoubtedly lead to business being spread out over all of Europe, if not the world. As Southeast Asia becomes less dominated by the Japanese, a financial center could develop in Shanghai. And if the North American free trade zone actually works for Mexico, Mexico City could become a financial center in the Americas.

Some observers predict, however, that by the middle of the twenty-first century there may be no longer any financial centers in the traditional geographic sense.

GETTING RID OF THE INTERMEDIARIES

Financial intermediaries—banks, pension plans, and insurance companies—have always been around to serve the purpose of linking savers with borrowers. This intermediary activity is costly, though, to those involved. What we are about to see is the gradual elimination of at least some financial intermediaries in favor of direct dealings between savers and borrowers. Consider the following possibilities. Financial intermediaries located in city centers may be replaced by computer terminals that can be placed anywhere in the world. The over-the-counter securities markets in both the United States and the United Kingdom are already contemplating this move.

WALL STREET IS NOT ABOUT TO DISAPPEAR

Just because New York may not be a major financial center by the middle of the century does not mean that Wall Street is going to disappear. A lot of people in the financial world want to live and work in large cities "where the action is." There will always be a Fleet Street in London and a Wall Street in New York. The change may simply be one in which the amount of office space rented to those dealing uniquely in the financial marketplace will decline.

FOR CRITICAL ANALYSIS

1. What role has technology played in reducing the importance of geographic financial centers?
2. If financial intermediation is so costly, why does it continue to occur? In other words, why do savers and borrowers have to seek the services of financial intermediaries?

CHAPTER SUMMARY

1. Proprietorships are the most common form of business organization, comprising 70 percent of all firms. Each is owned by a single individual who makes all business decisions, receives all the profits, and has unlimited liability for the firm's debts.

2. Partnerships are much like proprietorships, except that two or more individuals, or partners, share the decisions and the profits of the firm; each partner has unlimited liability for the debts of the firm.

3. Corporations are responsible for the largest share of business revenues. The owners, called shareholders, share in the firm's profits but normally have little responsibility for the firm's day-to-day operations. Owners of corporations enjoy limited liability for the debts of the firm.

4. Limited partnerships and S corporations are variants of the three major types of firms, enabling smaller companies to enjoy the limited liability of corporations and many of the tax advantages of proprietorships and partnerships.

5. When two parties to a transaction have different amounts of information, we call this asymmetric information. Whenever asymmetric information occurs before a transaction takes place, we call this adverse selection. Adverse selection causes borrowers who are the worst credit risks to be the ones most likely to seek loans.

6. When asymmetric information occurs after a transaction, this is a situation of moral hazard. Lenders often face the hazard that borrowers will choose more risky actions after borrowers have taken out loans.

7. The separation of ownership and control in today's large corporation has led to the principal-agent problem, whereby the agents (managers) may have interests that differ from those of the principals (shareholders).

8. Several problems exist with corporations. For example, the agent—managers—may have interests that differ from the principals—shareholders. This is called the principal-agent problem.

9. Several methods exist for solving the principal-agent and moral hazard problems, including requiring lenders to post collateral and devising incentive compatible contracts in which borrowers have a large amount of their own assets at risk.

10. The decade of the 1980s witnessed an enormous expansion in the active market for corporate takeovers—firms or corporate financiers attempting to purchase control of existing corporations.

DISCUSSION OF PREVIEW POINTS

1. What are the main organizational forms that firms take, and what are their advantages and disadvantages?

The primary organizational forms businesses take are the proprietorship, the partnership, and the corporation. The proprietorship is owned by a single person, the proprietor, who makes the business decisions, is entitled to all the profits, and is subject to unlimited liability, that is, is personally responsible for all debts incurred by the firm. The partnership differs from the proprietorship chiefly in that there are two or more owners, called partners. They share the responsibility for decision making, share the firm's profits, and each have unlimited liability for the firm's debts. The net income, or profits, of both proprietorships and partnerships is subject only to personal income taxes. Both types of firms legally cease to exist when the proprietor or a partner gives up ownership or dies. The corporation differs from proprietorships and partnerships in three important dimensions. Owners of corporations enjoy limited liability; that is, their responsibility for the debts of the corporation is limited to the value of their ownership shares. In addition, the income from corporations is subject to double taxation—corporate taxation when income is earned by the corporation and personal taxation when after-tax profits are paid as dividends to the owners. Finally, corporations do not legally cease to exist due to a change of ownership or the death of an owner.

2. What are corporations' primary sources of financial capital?

The main sources of financial capital for corporations are stocks, bonds and reinvestment of profits. Stocks are ownership shares, promising a share of profits, sold to investors. Common stocks also embody voting rights regarding the major decisions of the firm; preferred stocks typically have no voting rights but enjoy preferred status in the payment of dividends. Bonds are notes of indebtedness, issued in return for the loan of money. They typically promise to pay interest in the form of annual coupon payments, plus repayment of the original principal amount upon maturity. Bondholders are generally promised payment of coupon payments and principal due prior to the payment of dividends to shareholders, and for this reason bonds are less risky than stocks. Reinvestment involves the purchase of assets by the firm, using retained profits or depreciation reserves it has set aside for this purpose. No new stocks or bonds are issued in the course of reinvestment, although its value is fully reflected in the price of existing shares of stock.

3. Is there a world market for U.S. government securities?

Trading in U.S. government securities is one of the fastest-growing 24-hour markets in the world. It includes sophisticated communications and computer technology. It has occurred not only because of that but also because of the deregulation of financial markets in foreign countries that permit such trading. Also,

in 1984 the United States allowed foreign investors to buy U.S. government securities tax-free. Both securities issued by the United States Treasury and those issued by the Federal National Mortgage Association, a U.S. quasi-governmental agency, are traded worldwide.

4. What is one of the perils of global financial integration?

Since financial markets are linked so tightly throughout the world, a problem in one country may have repercussions around the globe. This is exactly what happened when the U.S. stock market crashed in October 1987. Within hours of a dramatic drop in prices of stocks on the New York Stock Exchange, stock markets throughout the world also experienced dramatic drops. Indeed, the drops in most other countries were more severe than the one in the United States.

PROBLEMS
(Answers to the odd-numbered problems appear at the back of the book.)

21-1. Suppose that federal tax policy were changed to exempt the first $10,000 in dividends each year from personal taxation. How would this affect the choice of organizational form for businesses?

21-2. How would the change in corporate tax policy mentioned in Problem 21-2 affect the method of financing corporations use?

21-3.* Consider a firm that wishes to borrow $10,000 for one year. Suppose that there is a 20 percent chance that this firm will go out of business before the end of the year (repaying none of its debts) and

an 80 percent chance that it will survive and repay all of its debts. If potential lenders can earn 10 percent per year by lending to other firms that are certain to repay their debts, what rate of interest will the risky firm have to offer if it is to be able to borrow the $10,000?

21-4. Should the government guarantee junk bonds to make sure that the buyers of these bonds do not lose money? What would happen if the government did this?

 COMPUTER-ASSISTED INSTRUCTION
(Complete problem and answer on disk.)

Key determinants of the prices of shares of corporate stock are illustrated using numerical problems.

*Asterisked problems are optional; algebra is required.

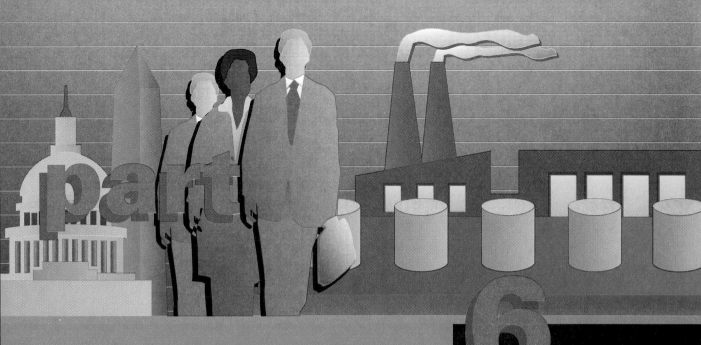

part
6

MARKET STRUCTURE, RESOURCE ALLOCATION, AND PUBLIC CHOICE

THE FIRM
COST AND OUTPUT DETERMINATION

In virtually every city in the United States, crime is a major concern. The crime rate has been hovering at record levels since the mid-1970s. The chance that a household will be victimized by a serious crime in any given year is more than 20 percent. Part of the increase in crime involves the spread of illegal drugs and the violence that accompanies them. We are witnessing record homicide rates, children being killed by stray bullets, drug-bust shootouts, and drive-by shootings. The vocabulary of today's violence includes automatic weapons—Uzi, AR-15, AK-47. As one solution to this increased violence, legislators have increased the penalties for dealing drugs, particularly when the dealers are so-called drug kingpins. Some observers argue, however, that increased penalties for drug dealing have actually caused violence to increase. The link involves drug dealers' reactions to increased costs, which form part of the study of cost and output determination for any business.

After reading this chapter, you should be able to answer the following questions:

1. How does the economist's definition of profit differ from the accountant's?

2. What distinguishes the long run from the short run?

3. How does the law of diminishing marginal returns account for an *eventually* increasing marginal cost curve for a firm in the short run?

4. Why is the short-run average total cost curve U-shaped?

INTRODUCTION

No consumer can get through life without making decisions about how to allocate his or her income among virtually unlimited available goods and services. Suppliers of those goods and services face perhaps more limited but nonetheless real choices. How much should the company produce each month? Should a new machine be bought that can replace 10 workers? Should more workers be hired, or should the existing workers be paid overtime? If supplies of aluminum are becoming tight, should the company try to make do with plastic? Virtually every decision that a producer makes has to do with the cost of those decisions. What you will learn about in this chapter is how producers can select the best combination of inputs for any given output that is desired.

Before we look at the firm's costs, we need to define a firm.

THE FIRM

We define a business, or **firm,** as follows:

> **A firm is an organization that brings together factors of production—labor, land, capital, and entrepreneurial skill—to produce a product or service that it hopes can be sold at a profit.**

A typical firm will have an organizational structure consisting of an entrepreneur, managers, and workers. The entrepreneur is the person who takes the risks, mainly of losing his or her personal wealth. In compensation, the entrepreneur will get any profits that are made. Recall from Chapter 2 that entrepreneurs take the initiative in combining land, labor, and capital to produce a good or a service. Entrepreneurs are the ones who innovate in the form of new production and new products. The entrepreneur also decides who to hire to manage the firm. Some economists maintain that the true quality of an entrepreneur becomes evident with his or her selection of managers. Managers, in turn, decide who should be hired and fired and how the business generally should be set up. The workers ultimately use the other inputs to produce the products or services that are being sold by the firm. Workers and managers are paid contractual wages. They receive a specified amount of income for a specified time period. Entrepreneurs are not paid contractual wages. They receive no reward specified in advance. Rather, they receive what is left over, if anything, after all expenses are paid. The entrepreneurs make profits if there are any, for profits accrue to those who are willing to take risks. (Because the entrepreneur gets only what is left over after all expenses are paid, he or she is often referred to as a *residual claimant.* The entrepreneur lays claim to the residual—whatever is left.)

PROFIT AND COSTS

Most people think of profit as the difference between the amount of revenues a business takes in and the amount it spends for wages, materials, and so on. In a bookkeeping sense, the following formula could be used:

$$\text{Accounting profits} = \text{total revenues} - \text{explicit costs}$$

where **explicit costs** are expenses that the business managers must take account of because they must actually be paid out by the firm. This definition of profit is known as **accounting profit.** It is appropriate when used by accountants to determine a firm's taxable income. Economists are more interested in how firm managers react not just to changes in explicit costs but also to changes in **implicit costs,** defined as expenses that business managers do not have to pay out of pocket but are costs to the firm nonetheless because they represent an opportunity cost. These are noncash costs—they do not involve any

▶ **Firm**
A business organization that employs resources to produce goods or services for profit. A firm normally owns and operates at least one plant in order to produce.

▶ **Explicit costs**
Costs that business managers must take account of because they must be paid; examples are wages, taxes, and rent.

▶ **Accounting profit**
Total revenues minus total explicit costs. Losses are negative profits.

▶ **Implicit costs**
Costs that business managers do not necessarily calculate, such as the opportunity cost of factors of production that are owned; examples are owner-provided capital and owner-provided labor.

direct cash outlay by the firm and must therefore be measured by the alternative cost principle. That is to say, they are measured by what the resources (land, capital) currently used in producing a particular good or service could earn in other uses. Economists therefore use the full opportunity cost of all resources as the figure to subtract from revenues to obtain a definition of profit. Another definition of implicit cost is therefore the opportunity cost of using factors that a producer does not buy or hire but already owns.

OPPORTUNITY COST OF CAPITAL

▶ **Normal rate of return (NROR)**
The amount that must be paid to an investor to induce investment in a business; also known as the *opportunity cost of capital.*

▶ **Opportunity cost of capital**
The normal rate of return. Economists consider this a cost of production, and it is included in our cost examples.

Firms enter or remain in an industry if they earn, at minimum, a **normal rate of return (NROR).** People will not invest their wealth in a business unless they obtain a positive normal, competitive, rate of return—that is, unless their invested wealth pays off. Any business wishing to attract capital must expect to pay at least the same rate of return on that capital as all other businesses (of similar risk) are willing to pay. Put another way, when a firm requires the use of a resource in producing a particular product, it must bid against alternative users of that resource. Thus the firm should offer a price that is at least as much as other users are offering to pay. For example, if individuals can invest their wealth in almost any publishing firm and get a rate of return of 10 percent per year, each firm in the publishing industry must *expect* to pay 10 percent as the normal rate of return to present and future investors. This 10 percent is a *cost to the firm*, the **opportunity cost of capital.** The opportunity cost of capital is the amount of income, or yield, that could have been earned by investing in the next-best alternative. Capital will not stay in firms or industries in which the expected rate of return falls below its opportunity cost, or what could be earned elsewhere. If a firm owns some capital equipment, it can either use it or lease it and earn a return. If the firm uses the equipment for production, part of the cost of using that equipment is the foregone revenue that the firm could have earned had it leased out that equipment.

OPPORTUNITY COST OF OWNER-PROVIDED LABOR

Single-owner proprietorships often grossly exaggerate their profit rates because they overlook the opportunity cost of the labor that the proprietor provides to the business. Here we are referring to the opportunity cost of labor. For example, you may know people who run small grocery stores. These people will sit down at the end of the year and figure out what their "profits" are. They will add up all their sales and subtract what they had to pay to other workers, what they had to pay to their suppliers, what they had to pay in taxes, and so on. The end result they will call "profit." They normally will not, however, have figured into their costs the salary that they could have made if they had worked for somebody else in a similar type of job. But by working for themselves, they become residual claimants—they receive what is left after all costs have been accounted for. However, part of the costs should include the salary the owner-operator could have received working for someone else.

Consider a simple example of a skilled auto mechanic working 14 hours a day at his own service station, six days a week. Compare this situation to how much he could earn as a trucking company mechanic 84 hours a week. This self-employed auto mechanic might have an opportunity cost of about $20 an hour. For his 84-hour week in his own service station, he is forfeiting $1,680. Unless his service station shows accounting profits of more than that per week, he is losing money in an economic sense.

Another way of looking at the opportunity cost of running a business is that opportunity cost consists of all explicit and implicit costs. Accountants are only able to take account of explicit costs. Therefore, accounting profit ends up being the residual after only explicit costs are subtracted from total revenues.

ACCOUNTING PROFITS VERSUS ECONOMIC PROFITS

You should have a good idea by now of the meaning of profits in economics. The term *profits* in economics means the income that entrepreneurs earn, over and above all costs including their own opportunity cost of time, plus the opportunity cost of the capital they have invested in their business. Profits can be regarded as total revenues minus total costs— which is how accountants think of them—but we must now include *all* costs. Our definition of **economic profits** will be the following:

$$\text{Economic profits} = \text{total revenues} - \text{total opportunity cost of all inputs used}$$

or

$$\text{Economic profits} = \text{total revenues} - (\text{explicit} + \text{implicit costs})$$

Remember that implicit costs include a normal rate of return to invested capital. We show this relationship in Figure 22-1.

▶ **Economic profits**
Total revenues minus total opportunity costs of all inputs used, or the total of all implicit and explicit costs.

THE GOAL OF THE FIRM: PROFIT MAXIMIZATION

When we examined the theory of consumer demand, utility (or satisfaction) maximization by the individual provided the basis for the analysis. In the theory of the firm and production, *profit maximization* is the underlying hypothesis of our predictive theory. The goal of the firm is to maximize economic profits, and the firm is expected to try to make the positive difference between total revenues and total costs as large as it can.

Our justification for assuming profit maximization by firms is similar to our belief in utility maximization by individuals. To obtain labor, capital, and other resources required to produce commodities, firms must first obtain financing from investors. In general,

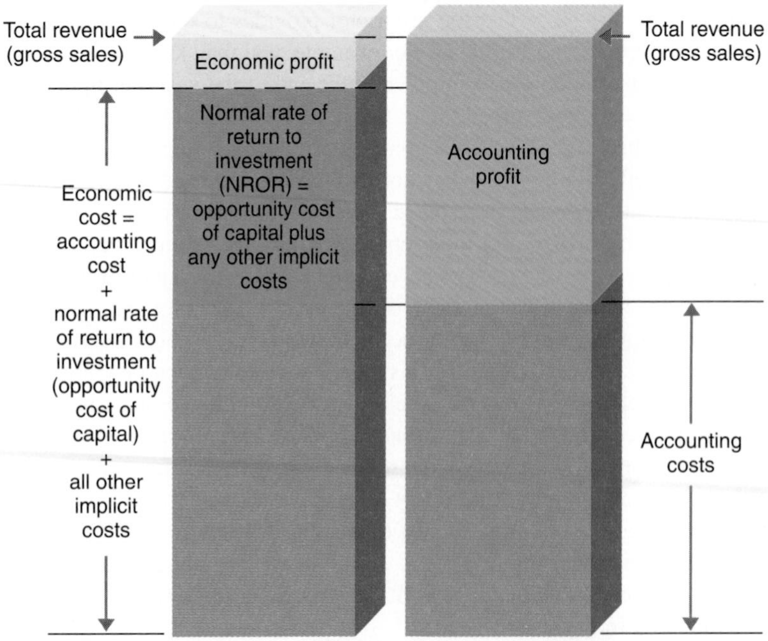

FIGURE 22-1
Simplified view of economic and accounting profit.
Here we see on the right side that total revenues are equal to accounting costs plus accounting profit. That is, accounting profit is the difference between total revenues and total explicit accounting costs. Conversely, we see in the left column that economic profit is equal to total revenues minus economic costs. Economic costs equal explicit accounting costs plus all implicit costs, including a normal rate of return on invested capital (NROR).

investors are indifferent about the details of how a firm uses the money they provide. They are most interested in the earnings on this money and the risk of obtaining lower returns or losing the money they have invested. Firms that can provide high returns and less risk will therefore have an advantage in obtaining the financing needed to continue or expand production. Over time we would expect a policy of profit maximization to become the dominant mode of behavior for firms that survive. This rationale applies only to for-profit firms operating in unregulated markets. Nonprofit charitable or education foundations and self-financed sole proprietorships face other constraints on their actions and maximize other goals.

CONCEPTS IN BRIEF

- Accounting profits differ from economic profits. Economic profits are defined as total revenues minus total costs, where costs include the full opportunity cost of all of the factors of production plus all other implicit costs.
- Single-owner proprietorships often fail to consider the opportunity cost of the labor services provided by the owner.
- The full opportunity cost of capital invested in a business is generally not included as a cost when accounting profits are calculated. Thus accounting profits often overstate economic profits.
- We assume throughout these chapters that the goal of the firm is to maximize economic profits.

SHORT RUN VERSUS LONG RUN

In Chapter 20 we discussed short-run and long-run price elasticities of supply and demand. For consumers, the long run meant the time period during which all adjustments to a change in price could be made, and anything shorter than that was considered the short run. For suppliers the long run was the time in which all adjustments could be made, and anything shorter than that was the short run.

Now that we are discussing firms only, we will maintain a similar distinction between the short and the long run, but we will be more specific. In the theory of the firm, the **short run** is defined as any time period that is so short that the firm cannot alter some inputs, such as its current **plant size.**[1] In other words, during the short run, a firm makes do with whatever big machines and factory size it already has, no matter how much more it wants to produce because of increased demand for its product. We consider the plant and heavy equipment, the size or amount of which cannot be varied in the short run, as fixed resources. In agriculture and in some other businesses, land may be a fixed resource.

There are, of course, variable resources that the firm can alter when it wants to change its rate of production. These are called *variable inputs* or *variable factors of production*. Typically, the variable inputs of a firm are its labor and its purchases of raw materials. Hence in the short run, in response to changes in demand, the firm can, by definition, vary only its variable inputs.

The **long run** can now be considered the period of time in which *all* inputs can be varied. Specifically, in the long run, the firm can alter its plant size. How long is the long run? That depends on each individual industry. For Wendy's or McDonald's, the long run

> ▶ **Short run**
> The time period when some inputs, such as plant size, cannot be changed.

> ▶ **Plant size**
> The physical size of the factories that a firm owns and operates to produce its output. Plant size can be defined by square footage, maximum physical capacity, and other physical measures.

> ▶ **Long run**
> The time period in which all factors of production can be varied.

---

[1]There can be many short runs but only one long run. For ease of analysis, in this section we simplify the case to one short run and talk about short-run costs.

may be four or five months, because that is the time it takes to add new franchises. For a steel company, the long run may be several years, because that's how long it takes to plan and build a new plant. An electric utility might need over a decade to build a new plant, for example.

Short run and *long run* in our discussion are in fact management planning terms that apply to decisions made by managers. The firm can operate only in the short run in the sense that decisions must be made and are made today. The same analysis applies to your own behavior. You may have many long-run plans about graduate school, vacations, and the like, but you always operate in the short run—you make decisions every day about what you do every day.

THE RELATIONSHIP BETWEEN OUTPUT AND INPUTS

A firm takes numerous inputs, combines them using a technological production process, and ends up with an output. There are, of course, a great many factors of production, or inputs. We classify production inputs into two broad categories (ignoring land)—labor and capital. The relationship between output and these two inputs is as follows:

Output per time period = some function of capital and labor inputs

In simple math, the production relationship can be written $Q = f(K, L)$, where Q = output per time period, K = capital, and L = labor.

We have used the word *production* but have not defined it. **Production** is any use of resources that transforms one commodity (a good or a service) into another. Production includes not only making things but also transporting them, retailing, repackaging them, and so on. Notice that if we know that production occurs, we do not necessarily know the value of the output. The production relationship tells nothing about the worth or value of the inputs or the outputs.

▶ **Production**
Any transformation of materials that makes them more valuable. The use of resources that transforms any good or service into a different good or service.

THE PRODUCTION FUNCTION: A NUMERICAL EXAMPLE

The relationship between maximum physical output and the quantity of capital and labor used in the production process is sometimes called a **production function.** The production function is a technological relationship between inputs and outputs. It depends on the available technology. Firms that are inefficient or wasteful in their use of capital and labor will obtain less output than the production function in theory will show. No firm can obtain more output than the production function shows, however. The production function specifies the maximum possible output that can be produced with a given amount of inputs. It also specifies the minimum amount of inputs necessary to produce a given level of output. As mentioned, the production function depends on the technology available to the firm. It follows that an improvement in technology that allows the firm to produce more output with the same amount of inputs (or the same output with fewer inputs) results in a new production function.

▶ **Production function**
The relationship between inputs and output. A production function is a technological, not an economic, relationship.

Look at panel (a) of Figure 22-2. It shows a production function relating total output in column 2 to the quantity of labor measured in worker-weeks in column 1. When there are zero worker-weeks of input, there is no output. When there are 5 worker-weeks of input (given the capital stock), there is a total output of 50 bushels per week. (Ignore for the moment the rest of that panel.) Panel (b) of Figure 22-2 shows this particular hypothetical production function graphically. Note again that it relates to the short run and that it is for an individual firm.

▶ **Law of diminishing (marginal) returns**
The observation that after some point, successive equal-sized increases in a variable factor of production, such as labor, added to fixed factors of production, will result in smaller increases in output.

Panel (b) shows a total physical product curve, or the maximum amount of physical output that is possible when we add successive equal-sized units of labor while holding all other inputs constant. The graph of the production function in panel (b) is not a straight line. In fact, it peaks at 7 worker-weeks and starts to go down. To understand why such a phenomenon occurs with an individual firm in the short run, we have to analyze in detail the **law of diminishing (marginal) returns.**

FIGURE 22-2
Diminishing returns, production function, and marginal product: a hypothetical case.
Marginal product is the addition to the total product that results when one additional worker is hired. Thus the marginal product of the fourth worker is eight bushels of wheat. With four workers 44 bushels are produced, but with three workers only 36 are produced; the difference is 8. In panel (b) we plot the numbers from columns 1 and 2 of panel (a). In panel (c) we plot the numbers from columns 1 and 4 of panel (a). When we go from 0 to 1, marginal product is 10. When we go from one worker to two workers, marginal product increases to 16. After two workers, marginal product declines, but it is still positive. Total product (output) reaches its peak at seven workers, so after seven workers marginal product is negative. When we move from seven to eight workers, marginal product becomes −1 bushel.

Panel (a)

(1) INPUT OF LABOR (NUMBER OF WORKER-WEEKS)	(2) TOTAL PRODUCT (OUTPUT IN BUSHELS OF WHEAT PER WEEK)	(3) AVERAGE PHYSICAL PRODUCT (TOTAL PRODUCT ÷ NUMBER OF WORKER-WEEKS, IN BUSHELS PER WEEK)	(4) MARGINAL PHYSICAL PRODUCT (OUTPUT IN BUSHELS OF WHEAT PER WEEK)
0	—	—	
			10
1	10	10.00	
			16
2	26	13.00	
			10
3	36	12.00	
			8
4	44	11.00	
			6
5	50	10.00	
			4
6	54	9.00	
			2
7	56	8.00	
			−1
8	55	6.88	
			−2
9	53	5.89	
			−3
10	50	5.00	
			−4
11	46	4.18	

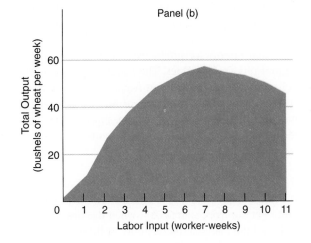

Panel (b)

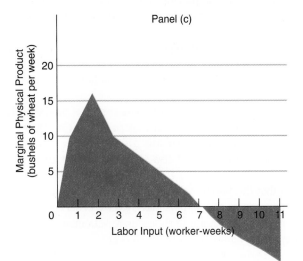

Panel (c)

DIMINISHING MARGINAL RETURNS

The concept of diminishing marginal returns applies to many situations. If you put on one seat belt over your lap, a certain amount of safety is obtained. If you add another seat belt over your shoulder, some additional safety is obtained, but less than when the first belt was secured. When you add a third seat belt over the other shoulder, the amount of *additional* safety obtained is even smaller.

The same analysis holds for firms in their use of productive inputs. When the returns from hiring more workers are diminishing, it does not necessarily mean that more workers won't be hired. In fact, workers will be hired until the returns, in terms of the *value* of the *extra* output produced, are equal to the additional wages that have to be paid for those workers to produce the extra output. Before we get into that decision-making process, let's demonstrate that diminishing returns can be represented graphically and can be used in our analysis of the firm.

MEASURING DIMINISHING RETURNS

How do we measure diminishing returns? First, we limit the analysis to only one variable factor of production (or input)—let's say the factor is labor. Every other factor of production, such as machines, must be held constant. Only in this way can we calculate the marginal returns from using more workers and know when we reach the point of diminishing marginal returns.

Marginal returns for productive inputs are sometimes specifically referred to as the **marginal physical product.** The marginal physical product of a worker, for example, is the change in total product that occurs when that worker joins an already existing production process. (The term *physical* here emphasizes the fact that we are measuring in terms of physical units of production, not in dollar terms.) It is also the *change* in total product that occurs when that worker quits or is laid off an already existing production process. The marginal productivity of labor therefore refers to the *change in output caused by a one-unit change in the labor input.*

The marginal productivity of labor may increase at the very beginning—that is, a firm starts with no workers, only machines. The firm then hires one worker, who finds it difficult to get the work started. But when the firm hires more workers, each is able to *specialize,* and the marginal productivity of those additional workers may actually be greater than it was with the previous few workers. Beyond some point, however, diminishing returns must set in as each worker has (on average) fewer machines with which to work (remember, all other inputs are fixed). In fact, eventually the firm will become so crowded that workers will start to get in the way of each other. At this point total production declines and marginal physical product becomes negative.

Using these ideas, we can define the law of diminishing returns as follows:

> **As successive equal increases in a variable factor of production are added to fixed factors of production, there will be a point beyond which the extra, or marginal, product that can be attributed to each additional unit of the variable factor of production will decline.**

Note that the law of diminishing returns is a statement about the *physical* relationships between inputs and outputs that we have observed in many firms. If the law of diminishing returns were not a fairly accurate statement about the world, what would stop firms from hiring additional workers forever?

▶ **Marginal physical product**
The physical output that is due to the addition of one more unit of a variable factor of production; the change in total product occurring when a variable input is increased and all other inputs are held constant.

AN EXAMPLE OF THE LAW OF DIMINISHING RETURNS

An example of the law of diminishing returns is found in agriculture. With a fixed amount of land, fertilizer, and tractors, the addition of more farm workers eventually yields decreasing increases in output. A hypothetical set of numbers illustrating the law of diminishing marginal returns is presented in panel (a) of Figure 22-2. The numbers are presented graphically in panel (c) of Figure 22-2. Marginal productivity (returns from adding more workers) first increases, then decreases, and finally becomes negative.

When one worker is hired, total output goes from 0 to 10. Thus marginal physical product is 10 bushels of wheat per week. When the second worker is hired, total product goes from 10 to 26 bushels of wheat per week. Marginal physical product therefore increases to 16 bushels of wheat per week. When a third worker is hired, total product again increases, from 26 to 36 bushels of wheat per week. This represents a marginal physical product of only 10 bushels of wheat per week. Therefore, the point of diminishing marginal returns occurs after two workers are hired.

Notice that after 7 worker-weeks, marginal physical product becomes negative. That means that the hiring of an eighth worker would create a situation that reduces total product. Sometimes this is called the *point of saturation*, indicating that given the amount of fixed inputs, there is no further positive use for more of the variable input. We have entered the region of negative marginal returns.

CONCEPTS IN BRIEF

- The technological relationship between output and input is called the production function. It relates output per time period to the several inputs, such as capital and labor.
- After some rate of output, the firm generally experiences diminishing marginal returns.
- The law of diminishing returns states that if all factors of production are held constant except one, equal increments in that one variable factor will eventually yield decreasing increments in output.

SHORT-RUN COSTS TO THE FIRM

You will see that costs are the extension of the production ideas just presented. Let's consider the costs the firm faces in the short run. To make this example simple, assume that there are only two factors of production, capital and labor. Our definition of the short run will be the time during which capital is fixed but labor is variable.

▶ **Total costs**
All the costs of a firm combined, including rent, payments to workers, interest on borrowed money, and all implicit costs.

In the short run, a firm incurs certain types of costs. We label all costs incurred **total costs.** Then we divide total costs into total fixed costs and total variable costs, which we will explain shortly. Therefore,

$$\text{Total costs (TC)} = \text{total fixed costs (TFC)} + \text{total variable costs (TVC)}$$

Remember that these total costs include both explicit and implicit costs, including the normal rate of return on investment.

After we have looked at the elements of total costs, we will find out how to compute average and marginal costs.

TOTAL FIXED COSTS

Let's look at an ongoing business such as Apple Computer. The decision makers in that corporate giant can look around and see big machines, thousands of parts, huge buildings, and a multitude of other components of plant and equipment that have already been bought and are in place. Apple has to take account of the wear and tear and technological obsolescence of this equipment, no matter how many computers it produces. The payments on the loans taken out to buy the equipment will all be exactly the same. The opportunity costs of any land that Apple owns will all be exactly the same. These costs are the same for Apple no matter how many computers it produces.

We also have to point out that the opportunity cost (or normal rate of return) of capital must be included along with other costs. Remember that we are dealing in the short run, during which capital is fixed. Thus if investors in Apple Computer have already put $100 million into a new factory addition, the opportunity cost of that capital invested is now, in essence, a *fixed cost*. Why? Because in the short run nothing can be done about that cost. The investment has already been made. This leads us to a very straight-forward definition of fixed costs: All costs that do not vary—that is, costs that do not depend on the rate of production—are called **fixed costs.**

Let's now take as an example the fixed costs incurred by an assembler of pocket calculators. This firm's total fixed costs will equal the cost of the rent on its equipment and the insurance it has to pay. We see in panel (a) of Figure 22-3 that total fixed costs per day are $10. In panel (b) these total fixed costs are represented by the horizontal line at $10 per day. They are invariant to changes in the output of calculators per day—no matter how many are produced, fixed costs will remain at $10 per day.

▶ **Fixed costs**
Costs that do not vary with output. Fixed costs include such things as rent on a building and the cost of machinery. These costs are fixed for a certain period of time; in the long run they are variable.

TOTAL VARIABLE COSTS

Total **variable costs** are costs whose magnitude varies with the rate of production. One obvious variable cost is wages. The more the firm produces, the more labor it has to hire; therefore, the more wages it has to pay. There are other variable costs, though. One is parts. In the assembly of calculators, for example, microchips must be bought. The more calculators that are made, the more chips must be bought. Part of the rate of depreciation (the rate of wear and tear) on machines that are used in the assembly process can also be considered a variable cost if depreciation depends partly on how long and how intensively the machines are used. Total variable costs are given in panel (a) of Figure 22-3 in column 3. These are translated into the total variable cost curve in panel (b). Notice that the total variable cost curve lies below the total cost curve by the vertical distance of $10. This vertical distance represents, of course, total fixed costs.

▶ **Variable costs**
Costs that vary with the rate of production. They include wages paid to workers and purchases of materials.

SHORT-RUN AVERAGE COST CURVES

In panel (b) of Figure 22-3 we see total costs, total variable costs, and total fixed costs. Now we want to look at average cost. The average cost concept is one in which we are measuring cost per unit of output. It is a matter of simple arithmetic to figure the averages of these three cost concepts. We can define them as follows:

$$\text{Average total costs (ATC)} = \frac{\text{total costs (TC)}}{\text{output } (Q)}$$

$$\text{Average variable costs (AVC)} = \frac{\text{total variable costs (TVC)}}{\text{output } (Q)}$$

$$\text{Average fixed costs (AFC)} = \frac{\text{total fixed costs (TFC)}}{\text{output } (Q)}$$

The arithmetic is done in columns 5, 6, and 7 in panel (a) of Figure 22-3. The numerical results are translated into a graphical format in panel (c). Because total costs (TC) equal variable costs (TVC) plus fixed costs (TFC), the difference between average total

FIGURE 22-3

Cost of production: an example.

In panel (a) the derivation of columns 4 through 9 are given in parentheses in each column heading. For example, column 6, average variable costs, is derived by dividing column 3, total variable costs, by column 1, total output per day. Note that marginal cost (MC) in panel (c) intersects average variable costs (AVC) at the latter's minimum point. Also, MC intersects average total cost (ATC) at that latter's minimum point. It is a little more difficult to see that MC equals AVC and ATC at their respective minimum points in panel (a) because we are using discrete one-unit changes. You can see, though, that the marginal cost of going from 4 units per day to 5 units per day is $2 and increases to $3 when we move to 6 units per day. Somewhere in the middle it equals AVC of $2.60, which is in fact the minimum average variable cost. The same analysis holds for ATC, which hits minimum at 7 units per day at $4.28 per unit. MC goes from $4 to $5 and just equals ATC somewhere in between.

Panel (a)

(1) TOTAL OUTPUT (Q/DAY)	(2) TOTAL FIXED COSTS (TFC)	(3) TOTAL VARIABLE COSTS (TVC)	(4) TOTAL COSTS (TC) (4) = (2) + (3)	(5) AVERAGE FIXED COSTS (AFC) (5) = (2) ÷ (1)	(6) AVERAGE VARIABLE COSTS (AVC) (6) = (3) ÷ (1)	(7) AVERAGE TOTAL COSTS (ATC) (7) = (4) ÷ (1)	(8) TOTAL COSTS (TC) (4)	(9) MARGINAL COST (MC) (9) = CHANGE IN (8) / CHANGE IN (1)
0	$10	$ 0	$10	—	—	—	$10	
1	10	5	15	$10.00	$5.00	$15.00	15	$5
2	10	8	18	5.00	4.00	9.00	18	3
3	10	10	20	3.33	3.33	6.67	20	2
4	10	11	21	2.50	2.75	5.25	21	1
5	10	13	23	2.00	2.60	4.60	23	2
6	10	16	26	1.67	2.67	4.33	26	3
7	10	20	30	1.43	2.86	4.28	30	4
8	10	25	35	1.25	3.13	4.38	35	5
9	10	31	41	1.11	3.44	4.56	41	6
10	10	38	48	1.00	3.80	4.80	48	7
11	10	46	56	.91	4.18	5.09	56	8

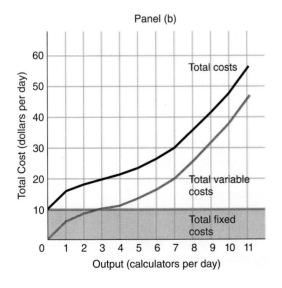

Panel (b)

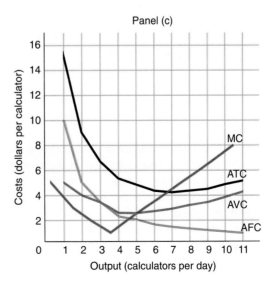

Panel (c)

costs (ATC) and average variable costs (AVC) will always be identical to average fixed costs (AFC). That means that average total costs and average variable costs move together as output expands.

Now let's see what we can observe about the three average cost curves in Figure 22-3.

Average Fixed Costs (AFC).

Average fixed costs continue to fall throughout the output range. In fact, if we were to continue the diagram farther to the right, we would find that average fixed costs would get closer and closer to the horizontal axis. That is because total fixed costs remain constant. As we divide this fixed number by a larger and larger number of units of output, the resulting AFC has to become smaller and smaller. In business, this is called "spreading the overhead."

▶ **Average fixed costs**
Total fixed costs divided by the number of units produced.

Average Variable Costs (AVC).

We assume a particular form of the curve for **average variable costs.** The form that it takes is U-shaped: First it falls; then it starts to rise. It is possible for the AVC curve to take other shapes in the long run.

▶ **Average variable costs**
Total variable costs divided by the number of units produced.

Average Total Costs (ATC).

This curve has a shape similar to that of the AVC curve. However, it falls even more dramatically in the beginning and rises more slowly after it has reached a minimum point. It falls and then rises because **average total costs** are the summation of the AFC curve and the AVC curve. Thus when AFC and AVC are both falling, ATC must fall too. At some point, however, AVC starts to increase while AFC continues to fall. Once the increase in the AVC curve outweighs the decrease in the AFC curve, the ATC curve will start to increase and will develop its familiar U shape.

▶ **Average total costs**
Total costs divided by the number of units produced; sometimes called *average per-unit total costs.*

MARGINAL COST

We have stated repeatedly that the basis of decisions is always on the margin—movement in economics is always determined at the margin. This dictum also holds true within the firm. Firms, according to the analysis we use to predict their behavior, are very interested in their **marginal costs.** Because the term *marginal* means "additional" or "incremental" (or "decremental," too) here, marginal costs refer to costs that result from a one-unit change in the production rate. For example, if the production of 10 calculators per day costs a firm $48 and the production of 11 calculators costs it $56 per day, the marginal cost of producing the eleventh calculator per day is $8.

▶ **Marginal costs**
The change in total costs due to a one-unit change of production rate.

Marginal costs can be measured by using the formula

$$\text{Marginal cost} = \frac{\text{change in total cost}}{\text{change in output}}$$

We show the marginal costs of calculator production per day in column 9 of panel (a) in Figure 22-3, where marginal cost is defined as the change in total cost divided by the change in output. In our particular example, we have changed output by one unit every time, so we can ignore variations in the denominator in that particular formula.

This marginal cost schedule is shown graphically in panel (c) of Figure 22-3. Just like average variable costs and average total costs, marginal costs first fall and then rise. The U-shape of the marginal cost curve is a result of increasing and then diminishing marginal returns. At lower levels of output, when there are increasing returns, the marginal cost curve declines. The reasoning is that as marginal physical product increases with each addition of output, the marginal cost of this last unit of output must fall. Conversely, when diminishing marginal returns set in, marginal physical product decreases (and eventually becomes negative); it follows that the marginal cost of the last unit must rise. These relationships are clearly reflected in the geometry of panels (b) and (c) of Figure 22-3.

In summary:

> As long as marginal physical product rises, marginal cost will fall, and when marginal physical product starts to fall (after reaching the point of diminishing marginal returns), marginal cost will begin to rise.

Let's now examine the relationship between marginal costs and average costs.

RELATIONSHIP BETWEEN AVERAGE AND MARGINAL COSTS

There is always a definite relationship between averages and marginals. Consider the example of 10 football players with an average weight of 200 pounds. An eleventh player is added. His weight is 250 pounds. That represents the marginal weight. What happens now to the average weight of the team? It must increase. Thus when the marginal player weighs more than the average, the average must increase. Likewise, if the marginal player weighs less than 200 pounds, the average weight will decrease.

There is a similar relationship between average variable costs and marginal costs. When marginal costs are less than average costs, the latter must fall. Conversely, when marginal costs are greater than average costs, the latter must rise. When you think about it, the relationship makes sense. The only way for average variable costs to fall is for the extra cost of the marginal unit produced to be less than the average variable cost of all the preceding units. For example, if the average variable cost for two units of production is $4.00 a unit, the only way for the average variable cost of three units to fall is for the variable costs attributable to the last unit—the marginal cost—to be less than the average of the past units. In this particular case, if average variable cost falls to $3.33 a unit, total variable cost for the three units would be three times $3.33, or almost exactly $10.00. Total variable cost for two units is two times $4.00, or $8.00. The marginal cost is therefore $10.00 minus $8.00, or $2.00, which is less than the average variable cost of $3.33.

A similar type of computation can be carried out for rising average variable costs. The only way for average variable costs to rise is for the average variable cost of additional units to be more than that for units already produced. But the incremental cost is the marginal cost. In this particular case, the marginal costs have to be higher than the average variable costs.

There is also a relationship between marginal costs and average total costs. Remember that average total cost is equal to total cost divided by the number of units produced. Remember also that marginal cost does not include any fixed costs. Fixed costs are, by definition, fixed and cannot influence marginal costs. Our example can therefore be repeated substituting the term *average total cost* for the term *average variable cost*.

These rising and falling relationships can be seen in Figure 22-3, where MC intersects AVC and ATC at their respective minimum points.

MINIMUM COST POINTS

At what rate of output of calculators per day does our representative firm experience the minimum average total costs? Column 7 in panel (a) of Figure 22-3 shows that the minimum average total cost is $4.28, which occurs at an output rate of seven calculators per day. We can also find this minimum cost by finding the point in panel (c) of Figure 22-3 at which the marginal cost curve intersects the average total cost curve. This should not be surprising. When marginal cost is below average total cost, average total cost falls. When marginal cost is above average total cost, average total cost rises. At the point where average total cost is neither falling nor rising, marginal cost must then be equal to average total cost. When we represent this graphically, the marginal cost curve will intersect the average total cost curve at the latter's minimum.

The same analysis applies to the intersection of the marginal cost curve and the average variable cost curve. When are average variable costs at a minimum? According to panel (a) of Figure 22-3, average variable costs are at a minimum of $2.60 at an output rate of five calculators per day. This is exactly where the marginal cost curve intersects the average variable cost curve in panel (c) of Figure 22-3.

CONCEPTS IN BRIEF

- The short run is the period of time during which the firm cannot alter its existing plant size; the long run is the time during which all inputs can be varied.
- Total costs equal total fixed costs plus total variable costs.
- Fixed costs are those that do not vary with the rate of production; variable costs are those that do vary with the rate of production.
- Average total costs equal total costs divided by output (ATC = TC/Q).
- Average variable costs equal total variable costs divided by output (AVC = TVC/Q).
- Average fixed costs equal total fixed costs divided by output (AFC = TFC/Q).
- Marginal cost equals the change in total cost divided by the change in output (MC = ΔTC/ΔQ).
- The marginal cost curve intersects the minimum point of the average total cost curve and the minimum point of the average variable cost curve.

THE RELATIONSHIP BETWEEN DIMINISHING MARGINAL RETURNS AND COST CURVES

There is a unique relationship between output and the shape of the various cost curves we have drawn. Let's consider specifically the relationship between marginal cost and the example of diminishing marginal physical returns in panel (a) of Figure 22-4. It turns out that if wage rates are constant, the shape of the marginal cost curve in panel (d) of Figure 22-4 is both a reflection and a consequence of the law of diminishing returns. Let's assume that each unit of labor can be purchased at a constant price. Further assume that labor is the only variable input. We see that as more workers are hired, marginal physical product first rises and then falls after the point at which diminishing returns are encountered. Thus the marginal cost of each extra unit of output will first fall as long as marginal physical product is rising, and then it will rise as long as marginal physical product is falling. Recall that marginal cost is defined as

$$MC = \frac{\text{Change in total cost}}{\text{Change in output}}$$

Because the price of labor is assumed to be constant, the change in total cost is simply the constant price of labor, W (we are increasing labor by only one unit). The change in

Panel (a)

(1) LABOR INPUT	(2) TOTAL PRODUCT (NUMBER OF PAIRS SOLD)	(3) AVERAGE PHYSICAL PRODUCT (PAIRS PER SALESPERSON) $(3) = (2) \div (1)$	(4) MARGINAL PHYSICAL PRODUCT	(5) AVERAGE VARIABLE COST $(5) = W$ $(\$100) \div (3)$	(6) MARGINAL COST $(6) = W$ $(\$100) \div (4)$
0	0	—	—	—	—
1	50	50	50	2.0	2.0
2	110	55	60	1.8	1.7
3	180	60	70	1.7	1.4
4	240	60	60	1.7	1.7
5	290	58	50	1.7	2.0
6	330	55	40	1.8	2.5
7	360	51	30	2.0	3.3

FIGURE 22-4

The relationship between physical output and costs. As the number of salespersons is increased, the total number of pairs of shoes sold rises, as shown in panels (a) and (b). In panel (c) marginal product (MP) first rises and then falls. Average product (AP) follows. The mirror image of panel (c) is shown in panel (d), in which MC and AVC first fall and then rise.

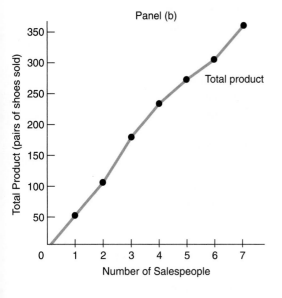

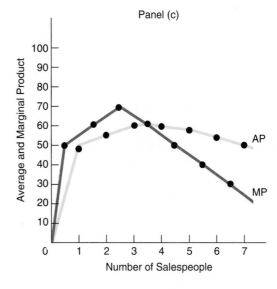

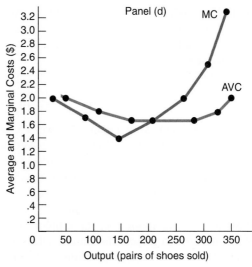

output is simply the marginal physical product (MPP) of the one-unit increase in labor. Therefore, we see that

$$\text{Marginal cost} = \frac{W}{\text{MPP}}$$

This means that initially, when there are increasing returns, marginal cost falls (we are dividing W by increasingly large numbers), and later, when diminishing returns sets in and marginal physical product is falling, marginal cost must increase (we are dividing W by smaller numbers). As marginal physical product increases, marginal cost decreases, and as marginal physical product decreases, marginal cost must increase. Thus when marginal physical product reaches its maximum, marginal cost necessarily reaches its minimum. To illustrate this, let's return to Figure 22-2 on p. 497 and consider specifically panel (a). Assume that a worker is paid $100 a week. When we go from zero labor input to one unit, output increases by 10 bushels of wheat. Each of those 10 bushels of wheat has a marginal cost of $10. Now the second unit of labor is hired, and it too costs $100 per week. Output increases by 16. Thus the marginal cost is $100 ÷ 16 = $6.25. We continue the experiment. We see that the next unit of labor yields only 10 additional bushels of wheat, so marginal cost starts to rise again back to $10. The following unit of labor increases marginal physical product by only 8, so marginal cost becomes $100 ÷ 8 = $12.50.

All of the foregoing can be restated in relatively straightforward terms:

> **Short-run firm cost curves are a reflection of the law of diminishing marginal returns. Given any constant price of the variable input, marginal costs decline as long as the marginal product of the variable resource is rising. At the point of diminishing marginal returns, the reverse occurs. Marginal costs will rise as the marginal product of the variable input declines.**

The result is a marginal cost curve that slopes down, hits a minimum, and then slopes up. The average total cost curves and average variable cost curve are of course affected. They will have their familiar U shape in the short run. Again, to see this, recall that

$$\text{AVC} = \frac{\text{total variable costs}}{\text{total output}}$$

As we move from zero labor input to one unit in panel (a) of Figure 22-2, output increases from zero to 10 bushels. The total variable costs are the price per worker, W ($100), times the number of workers (1). Because the average product of one worker (column 3) is 10, we can write the total product, 10, as the average product, 10, times the number of workers, 1. Thus we see that

$$\text{AVC} = \frac{100 \times 1}{10 \times 1} = \frac{100}{10} = \frac{W}{\text{AP}}$$

From column 3 in panel (a) of Figure 22-2 we see that the average product increases, reaches a maximum, and then declines. Because AVC = W/AP, average variable cost decreases as average product increases and increases as average product decreases. AVC reaches its minimum when average product reaches its maximum. Furthermore, because ATC = AVC + AFC, the average total cost curve inherits the relationship between the average variable cost and diminishing returns.

To illustrate, consider a shoe store that employs salespeople to sell shoes. Panel (a) of Figure 22-4 on page 505 presents in column 2 the total number of pairs of shoes sold as the number of salespeople increases. Notice that the total product first increases at an increasing rate and later increases at a decreasing rate. This is reflected in column 4, which shows that the marginal physical product increases at first and then falls. The average physical product too first rises and then falls. The marginal and average physical products are graphed in panel (c) of Figure 22-4. Our immediate interest here is the average variable and marginal costs. Because we can define average variable cost as $100/AP (assuming that the wage paid is constant at $100), as the average product rises from 50 to 55 to 60 pairs of shoes sold, the average variable cost falls from $2.00 to $1.80 to $1.70. Conversely, as average product falls from 60 to 50, average variable cost rises from $1.70 to $2.00. Likewise, because marginal cost can also be defined as W/MPP, we see that as marginal physical product rises from 50 to 70, marginal cost falls from $2.00 to $1.40. As marginal physical product falls to 30, marginal cost rises to $3.30. These relationships are also expressed in panels (b), (c), and (d) of Figure 22-4.

LONG-RUN COST CURVES

The long run is defined as a time period during which full adjustment can be made to any change in the economic environment. Thus in the long run, *all* factors of production are variable. Long-run curves are sometimes called planning curves, and the long run is sometimes called the **planning horizon.**

▶ **Planning horizon**
The long run, during which all inputs are variable.

We start out our analysis of long-run cost curves by considering a single firm contemplating the construction of a single plant. The firm has three alternative plant sizes from which to choose on the planning horizon. Each particular plant size generates its own short-run average total cost curve. Now that we are talking about the difference between long-run and short-run cost curves, we will label all short-run curves with an *S*; short-run average (total) costs will be labeled SAC, and all long-run average cost curves will be labeled LAC.

Panel (a) of Figure 22-5 shows three short-run average cost curves for three successively larger plants. Which is the optimal size to build? That depends on the anticipated

FIGURE 22-5
Preferable plant size and the long-run average cost curve.
If the anticipated permanent rate of output per unit time period is Q_1, the optimal plant to build would be the one corresponding to SAC$_1$ in panel (a) because average costs are lower. However, if the permanent rate of output increases to Q_2, it will be more profitable to have a plant size corresponding to SAC$_2$. Unit costs fall to C_3.

If we draw all the possible short-run average cost curves that correspond to different plant sizes and then draw the envelope (a curve tangent to each member of a set of curves) to these various curves, SAC$_1$—SAC$_8$, we obtain the long-run average cost curve, or the planning curve, as shown in panel (b).

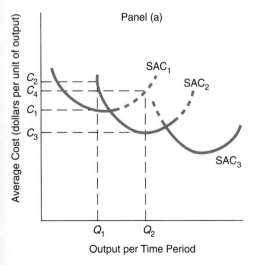

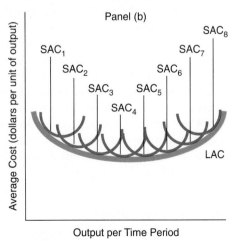

normal, sustained (permanent) rate of output per time period. Assume for a moment that the anticipated normal, sustained rate is Q_1. If a plant of size 1 is built, the average costs will be C_1. If a plant of size 2 is built, we see on SAC_2 that the average costs will be C_2, which is greater than C_1. Thus if the anticipated rate of output is Q_1, the appropriate plant size is the one from which SAC_1 was derived.

However, if the anticipated permanent rate of output per time period goes from Q_1 to Q_2 and a plant of size 1 had been decided on, average costs would be C_4. If a plant of size 2 had been decided on, average costs would be C_3, which are clearly less than C_4.

In choosing the appropriate plant size for a single-plant firm during the planning horizon, the firm will pick the size whose short-run average cost curve generates an average cost that is lowest for the expected rate of output.

LONG-RUN AVERAGE COST CURVE

If we make the further assumption that the entrepreneur faces an infinite number of choices of plant sizes in the long run, we can conceive of an infinite number of SAC curves similar to the three in panel (a) of Figure 22-5. We are not able, of course, to draw an infinite number; we have drawn quite a few, however, in panel (b) of Figure 22-5. We then draw the "envelope" to all these various short-run average cost curves. The resulting envelope is the **long-run average cost curve (LAC).** This long-run average cost curve is sometimes called the **planning curve,** for it represents the various average costs attainable at the planning stage of the firm's decision making. It represents the locus (path) of points giving the least unit cost of producing any given rate of output. Note that the LAC curve is *not* tangent to each individual SAC curve at the latter's minimum points. This is true only at the minimum point of the LAC curve. Then and only then are minimum long-run average costs equal to minimum short-run average costs.

WHY THE LONG-RUN AVERAGE COST CURVE IS U-SHAPED

Notice that the long-run average cost curve, LAC, in panel (b) of Figure 22-5 is U-shaped, similar to the U shape of the short-run average cost curve developed earlier in this chapter. The reason behind the U shape of the two curves is not the same, however. The short-run average cost curve is U-shaped because of the law of diminishing marginal returns. But the law cannot apply to the long run, because in the long run all factors of production are variable; there is no point of diminishing marginal returns because there is no fixed factor of production. Why, then, do we see the U shape in the long-run average cost curve? The reasoning has to do with economies of scale, constant economies of scale, and diseconomies of scale. When the firm is experiencing **economies of scale,** the long-run average cost curve slopes downward—an increase in scale and production leads to a fall in unit costs. When the firm is experiencing **constant economies of scale,** the long-run average cost curve is at its minimum point, such that an increase in scale and production does not change unit costs. When the firm is experiencing **diseconomies of scale,** the long-run average cost curve slopes upward—an increase in scale and production increases unit costs. These three sections of the long-run average cost curves are broken up into panels (a), (b), and (c) in Figure 22-6.

REASONS FOR ECONOMIES OF SCALE

We shall examine three of the many reasons why a firm might be expected to experience economies of scale: specialization, the dimensional factor, and improved productive equipment.

▶ **Long-run average cost curve (LAC)**
The locus of points representing the minimum unit cost of producing any given rate of output, given current technology and resource prices.

▶ **Planning curve**
The long-run average cost curve.

▶ **Economies of scale**
Decreases in long-run average costs resulting from increases in output.

▶ **Constant economies of scale**
No change in long-run average costs when output increases.

▶ **Diseconomies of scale**
Increases in long-run average costs that occur as output increases.

FIGURE 22-6
Economies, constant economies, and diseconomies of scale shown with long-run average cost curve.
Long-run average cost curves will fall when there are economies of scale, as shown in panel (a). They will be constant (flat) when the firm is experiencing constant economies to scale, as shown in panel (b). They will rise when the firm is experiencing diseconomies of scale, as shown in panel (c).

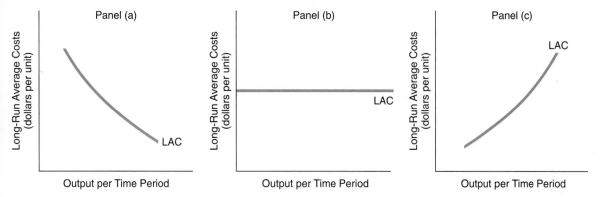

Specialization.   As a firm's scale of operation increases, the opportunities for specialization in the use of resource inputs also increase. This is sometimes called *increased division of tasks* or *operations*. Gains from such division of labor or increased specialization are well known. When we consider managerial staffs, we also find that larger enterprises may be able to put together more highly specialized staffs. Larger enterprises may have the ability to hire better managerial talent.

Dimensional Factor.   Large-scale firms often require proportionately less input per unit of output simply because certain inputs do not have to be physically doubled in order to double the output. Consider the cost of storage of oil. The cost of storage is basically related to the cost of steel that goes into building the storage container; however, the amount of steel required goes up less than in proportion to the volume (storage capacity) of the container (because the volume of a container increases more than proportionately with its circumference).

Improved Productive Equipment.   The larger the scale of the enterprise, the more the firm is able to take advantage of larger-volume (output capacity) types of machinery. Small-scale operations may not be able profitably to use large-volume machines that can be more efficient per unit of output. Also, smaller firms often cannot use technologically more advanced machinery because they are unable to spread out the high cost of such sophisticated equipment over a large output.

For any of these reasons, the firm may experience economies of scale, which means that equal percentage increases in output result in a decrease in average cost. Thus output can double, but total costs will less than double; hence average cost falls. Note that the factors listed for causing economies of scale are all *internal* to the firm; they do not depend on what other firms are doing or what is happening in the economy.

 **INTERNATIONAL EXAMPLE: The Beer Industry Goes International**

From 1960 to 1993 the value of world trade in beer increased almost fourfold while the value of world trade in general increased only a little more than threefold. World trade in beer has been increasing at an annual rate of almost 7 percent since the early 1960s.

Belgium, Canada, Germany, the Netherlands, and prebreakup Czechoslovakia exported beer at an increasing rate while France, Italy, Germany, the United States, and Great Britain were importing it. (Germany and the United States both import and export—variety is the spice of life.) Manufacturing beer involves economies of scale such that at higher production rates, unit costs fall. This explains not only the rise in exports of beer throughout the world but also the disappearance of many small breweries in the United States and elsewhere.

A countertrend is, however, occurring. Rather than taking advantage of scale economies in the home country, many beer producers are licensing their formulas to foreign countries. For example, Coors is brewed by Asahi in Japan and by Molson in Canada. Budweiser is brewed by Guinness in Ireland, Oriental in Korea, and Suntory in Japan. Heineken is brewed by Kirin in Japan and Whitehead in Great Britain. Presumably, the foreign brewers of these beers do not experience the same scale economies as the domestic brewers would. Why, then, does Coors license Asahi to brew its beer in Japan? The answer lies in the benefits of a foreign licensing arrangement. Coors brewed in Japan does not have to pay any tariffs. There are fewer transportation and distribution costs because beer is 90 percent water. Finally, because the shelf life of beer is normally no more than three or four months, saving the three weeks' shipping time increases shelf life in the foreign country.

For Critical Analysis: What additional costs might be incurred by licensing the foreign production of a beer? (Hint: Is a Coors brewed in Colorado the same as one brewed in Tokyo?) ●

WHY A FIRM MIGHT EXPERIENCE DISECONOMIES OF SCALE

One of the basic reasons that a firm can expect to run into diseconomies of scale is that there are limits to the efficient functioning of management. Moreover, as more workers are hired, a more than proportionate increase in managers and staff people may be needed, and this could cause increased costs per unit. This is so because larger levels of output imply successively larger *plant* size, which in turn implies successively larger *firm* size. Thus as the level of output increases, more people must be hired, and the firm gets bigger. However, as this happens, the support, supervisory, and administrative staff and the general paperwork of the firm all increase. As the layers of supervision grow, the costs of information and communication grow more than proportionately, hence the average per-unit cost will start to increase.

Some observers of corporate giants claim that many of them are experiencing some diseconomies of scale today. Witness the problems that General Motors and IBM have been having in the 1990s. Some say that the financial problems that they have experienced are at least partly a function of their size relative to their smaller, more flexible competitors, who can make decisions more quickly and then take advantage of changing market conditions more rapidly. This seems to be particularly true with IBM. It apparently adapted very slowly to the fact that the large mainframe computer business was declining as micro- and minicomputers became more and more powerful.

MINIMUM EFFICIENT SCALE

Economists and statisticians have obtained actual data of the relationship between changes in all inputs and changes in average cost. It turns out that for many industries the long-run average cost curve does not resemble that shown in panel (b) of Figure 22-5. Rather, it more closely resembles Figure 22-7. What you can observe there is a small portion of declining long-run average costs (economies of scale) and then a wide range of outputs

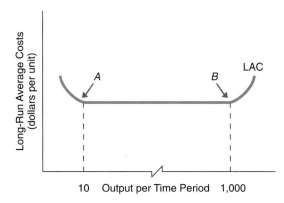

FIGURE 22-7
Minimum efficient scale.
This long-run average cost curve reaches a minimum point at *A*. After that point, long-run average costs remain horizontal, or constant, and then rise at some later rate of output. Point *A* is called the minimum efficient scale for the firm because at that point it reaches minimum costs. It is the lowest rate of output at which the average long-run costs are minimized.

▶ **Minimum efficient scale (MES)**
The lowest rate of output per unit time at which long-run average costs for a particular firm are at a minimum.

over which the firm experiences relatively constant economies of scale. At the output rate when economies of scale end and constant economies of scale start, the **minimum efficient scale (MES)** for the firm is encountered. It occurs at point *A*. (The point is, of course, approximate. The more smoothly the curve declines into its flat portion, the more approximate will be our estimate of the MES.) The minimum efficient scale will always be the lowest rate of output at which long-run average costs are minimized. In any industry with a long-run average cost curve similar to the one in Figure 22-7, larger firms will have no cost-saving advantage over smaller firms as long as the smaller firms have at least obtained the minimum efficient scale at point *A*.

Take a simple numerical example based on Figure 22-7. Assume that the minimum efficient scale is 10 units per day and the industry demand at the market price is 1,000 units per day. That means that 100 firms could exist at the MES. Point *A* is at 10 units per day. This is the minimum efficient scale. One thousand units per day can be produced at the MES, so 100 firms could each produce 10 units per day at the MES.

One of the uses of the minimum efficient scale is that it gives us a rough measure of the degree of competition in an industry. If the MES is small relative to industry demand, the degree of competition in that industry is likely to be high because there is room for many efficiently sized plants. Conversely, when the MES is large relative to industry demand, the degree of competition is likely to be small because there is room for a relatively small number of efficiently sized plants or firms. Looked at another way, if it takes a very large scale of plant to obtain minimum long-run average cost, the output of just a few of these very large firms can fully satisfy total market demand. This means that there isn't room for a large number of smaller plants if maximum efficiency is to be obtained in the industry.

 EXAMPLE: The Death of Small Airlines and the Minimum Efficient Scale of Operation

▶ **Hub-and-spoke system**
A transportation system in which there is an essential hub (a city) to and from which planes fly. These routes are called the spokes. Rather than a non-stop flight from say Tampa to Los Angeles, the flight may first go to the hub in Dallas, where the passenger changes planes to catch a flight to Los Angeles.

During the 1980s over 100 new airlines started in business in the United States. Now in the 1990s, there are about two dozen; the rest either went bankrupt or were bought out. The minimum efficient scale of operation for most airline routes requires a rather large airline company. About 95 percent of air traffic today is accounted for by the five largest domestic airlines. There are at least two reasons why the minimum efficient scale of operation of airlines is quite large. First and foremost, the **hub-and-spoke system** requires a large airline. This is the organization of an airline in which most traffic is funneled to and from various cities serviced by direct flights ("spokes") through large, now often overcrowded airports called hubs. These hubs are located in Denver, Atlanta, and New York, for example. Smaller airlines have not been able to offer enough flights to develop their own hub-and-spoke systems through which their own passengers from different originating points can be flown for connecting flights. The large airlines using the hub-and-spoke system are able to fly to many different locations at relatively low cost. An airline carrier needs at least 25 planes to establish one hub. Frequency of service is another reason why the minimum efficient scale of operation is so large. Competition in the airline industry is often based on frequency of service. Small carriers have been unable to offer the same frequency of service between two destinations as large carriers do. Business travelers typically prefer the convenience of many possible return flights and will therefore shun the small carrier.

For Critical Analysis: *How might the existence of frequent-flyer award points be a deterrent to the survival of small airlines?* ●

CONCEPTS IN BRIEF

- The long run is often called the planning horizon.
- The long-run average cost curve is the planning curve. It is found by drawing a line tangent to one point on a series of short-run average cost curves, each corresponding to a different plant size.
- The firm can experience economies of scale, diseconomies of scale, and constant economies of scale, all according to whether the long-run average cost curve slopes downward, slopes upward, or is horizontal (flat). Economies of scale refer to what happens to average cost when all factors of production are increased.
- We observe economies of scale for a number of reasons, among which are specialization, improved productive equipment, and the dimensional factor, because large-scale firms require proportionately less input per unit of output.
- The firm may experience diseconomies of scale primarily because of limits to the efficient functioning of management.
- The minimum efficient scale occurs at the lowest rate of output at which long-run average costs are minimized.

This 9-ton cocaine bust in Texas is part of the war on drugs. While the laws against drug dealers have been made more severe, the effect has not always been the one desired.

The FBI reported that in one recent month Los Angeles experienced 237 homicides: 196 persons were killed by handguns, including many by automatic and semiautomatic weapons; 19 were stabbed; and the remainder were beaten to death. To be sure, some of these were the result of domestic violence, but many were the result of settling scores, shootouts with police, "turf wars," and other activities by people involved in the drug trade.

TOUGHER DEALERS, TOUGHER LAWS
The politicians' response to increased drug dealing and drug-related violence has been to increase criminal sanctions. In 1970 the federal government passed the Comprehensive Drug Abuse, Prevention and Control Act (also known as the Controlled Substances Act). That act did not contain a rigid penalty system but rather established only upper bounds for the fines and prison terms to be imposed for offenses. In 1984 the act was amended in order to impose fixed penalties, particularly for dealers. For anyone caught with more than 1 kilogram of heroin, 50 grams of cocaine base, or 1,000 kilograms of marijuana, the applicable penalty was raised to imprisonment from 10 years to life plus a fine of $4 million. A variety of other prison penalties and fines were outlined in that amendment. Another amendment passed in 1988 included the death penalty for "drug kingpins." Such increased penalties have led to more rather than less violence. To understand why, we must reexamine the concept of marginal cost.

THE MARGINAL COST OF MURDER
Start out with the situation in which the penalty for drug dealing is five years in prison and the penalty for murder is 50 years in prison. A drug dealer who commits murder while engaged in a shootout with the police or while exterminating a stool pigeon is facing a potential marginal cost of 45 years more in prison. Some drug dealers, at least on the margin, will be dissuaded from engaging in murderous activities.

Now assume that the penalty for drug dealing is raised to 50 years in prison. The politicians who increased this penalty do so because they want to deter drug dealing. But in the process, the incentives facing drug dealers who decide to stay in the business have completely changed. Someone convicted of drug dealing will go to jail for 50 years, which means the end of a career in the drug trade and the end of freedom for life. What now is the marginal cost of committing a murder? It is probably zero. Even if a 50-year murder charge is tacked onto a 50-year drug dealing charge, the convicted drug dealer likely will not even see the beginning of the second sentence. Once the penalty for drug dealing is high enough, the marginal cost of other crimes committed in the course of dealing—extortion, assault, murder—becomes essentially zero.

INCREASING ONE MARGINAL COST DECREASES ANOTHER
The conclusion is that raising the penalties for drug dealing is equivalent to lowering the marginal cost of engaging in other crimes committed in the course of illegal drug business. More severe penalties for drug dealing result in more intimidation, violence, and lawlessness by drug dealers. It is not surprising that when police show up with an arrest warrant for a drug kingpin, the marginal cost to the dealer of killing a few of those arresting officers is virtually zero. Also, if there is a risk that a disgruntled customer or an envious competitor will "rat" on a drug dealer to the police, the best course for the drug dealer is homicide, for a murder rap means little to someone who already faces the prospect of life in jail. In fact, violence and intimidation become the only sensible ways for the dealer to conduct business. If he is caught for dealing, he loses everything; therefore, he is willing to do anything to avoid being caught.

FOR CRITICAL ANALYSIS

1. If increased penalties to drug kingpins leads to a reduction in the marginal cost of murder, does this necessarily argue in favor of reducing penalties to convicted drug kingpins? Why or why not?

2. If the law were changed so that penalties imposed for stealing $100 were the same as for stealing $1 million, what would you predict would happen, and why?

CHAPTER SUMMARY

1. It is important in economics to distinguish between accounting profits and economic profits. Accounting profits are equal to total revenues minus total explicit costs. Economic profits are equal to total revenues minus total opportunity costs of all factors of production.

2. The short run for the firm is defined as the period during which plant size cannot be altered. The long run is the period during which all factors of production can be varied.

3. Fixed costs are costs that cannot be altered in the short run. Fixed costs are associated with assets that the firm owns that cannot be profitably transferred to another use.

4. Variable costs are associated with input costs that vary as the rate of output varies. Wages are a good example of a variable cost.

5. There are definitional relationships between average, total, and marginal costs:

$$ATC = \frac{TC}{Q}$$

$$AVC = \frac{TVC}{Q}$$

$$AFC = \frac{TFC}{Q}$$

$$MC = \frac{\text{change in } TC}{\text{change in } Q}$$

6. When marginal costs are less than average costs, average costs are falling. When marginal costs are greater than average costs, average costs are rising. The marginal cost curve intersects the average variable cost curve and the average total cost curve at their minimum points.

7. When we hold constant all factors of production except one, an increase in that factor will lead to a change in total physical product. That is how we derive the total physical product curve. The marginal physical product curve is derived from looking at the change in total physical product.

8. After some output rate, firms enter the region of diminishing marginal returns, or diminishing marginal physical product. In other words, after some point, each increment of the variable input will yield a smaller and smaller increment in total output.

9. Given a constant wage rate, the marginal cost curve is the mirror image of the marginal physical product curve. Thus because of the law of diminishing marginal returns, marginal costs will eventually rise.

10. We derive the long-run average cost curve by connecting a smooth line that is just tangent to all of the short-run average cost curves. This long-run average cost curve is sometimes called the planning curve.

11. It is possible for a firm to experience increasing, constant, or decreasing economies of scale, in which case a proportionate increase in *all* inputs will lead, respectively, to decreasing, constant, or increasing average costs.

12. Firms may experience increasing economies of scale because of specialization, the dimensional factor, and the ability to purchase improved productive equipment. Firms may experience decreasing economies of scale because of the limitations of efficient management.

13. The long-run average cost curve will be downward-sloping, horizontal, or upward-sloping, depending on whether there are increasing, constant, or decreasing economies of scale.

14. Minimum efficient scale occurs at the lowest rate of output at which long-run average costs are minimized.

DISCUSSION OF PREVIEW POINTS

1. **How does the economist's definition of profit differ from the accountant's?**

   The accountant defines total profits as total revenues minus total costs; the economist defines total profits as total revenues minus total opportunity costs of all inputs used. In other words, the economist takes into account implicit as well as explicit costs; the economist's definition stresses that an opportunity cost exists for all inputs used in the production process. Specifically, the economist estimates the opportunity cost for invested capital, the owner's time, inventories on hand, and so on. Because the economist's definition of costs is more inclusive, accounting profits will almost always exceed economic profits; economic profits exist only when all the opportunity costs are taken into account.

2. **What distinguishes the long run from the short run?**

   The short run is defined as any time period when there is at least one factor of production that a firm cannot vary: in the long run, *all* factors of production can be varied by the firm. Because each industry is likely to be unique in its ability to vary all inputs, the long run differs from industry to industry. Presumably the long run is a lot shorter (in absolute time periods) for firms in the carpentry or plumbing industry than for firms in the automobile or steel industry. In most economic models, labor is usually assumed to be the variable input in the short run, whereas capital is considered to be fixed in the short run; this assumption is fairly descriptive of the real-world situation.

3. **How does the law of diminishing marginal returns account for an *eventually* increasing marginal cost curve for a firm in the short run?**

   By definition, the short run is a period during which the firm can change output only by varying one input; the other inputs are fixed in the short run. As a consequence, the firm can produce more and more only by using more and more of that one input, say, labor, other inputs being constant. *Eventually*, the law of diminishing returns comes into play (prior to this point, specialization benefits might increase the marginal

product of labor), and the marginal product of labor falls. That is, beyond the point of diminishing returns, extra laborers contribute less to total product than immediately preceding laborers do, per unit of time. In effect, this means that if output is to be increased by equal amounts (or equal "batches"), more and more labor time will be required due to its lower marginal product. Later units of output, which are physically identical to earlier units of output, embody more labor time. If wages are constant, later units, which require more worker-hours, have a higher marginal cost. We conclude that beyond the point of diminishing returns, the marginal cost of output rises for the firm in the short run. Prior to the point of diminishing returns, the marginal cost curve falls, due to rising marginal product of labor.

4. **Why is the short-run average total cost curve U-shaped?**

   Average total cost (ATC) equals the sum of average fixed costs (AFC) and average variable costs (AVC); that is, ATC = AFC + AVC. The AFC curve continuously falls because it is derived by dividing a constant number (total fixed costs) by larger and larger numbers (output levels). It falls rapidly at first, then slowly. The AVC curve falls during the early output stages because the benefits of specialization cause the marginal physical product of labor to rise and the marginal cost of output to fall; beyond the point of diminishing returns, the marginal physical product of labor falls, eventually forcing marginal cost to rise above AVC, and therefore AVC rises too. As we go from zero output to higher and higher output levels per unit of time, AFC and AVC both initially fall; therefore, ATC falls too. Beyond the point of diminishing marginal returns, AVC rises and outweighs the now slowly falling AFC curve; the net result is that somewhere beyond the point of diminishing marginal returns, the ATC curve rises. Because the ATC curve falls at low output levels and rises at higher output levels, we describe it as U-shaped. Of course, it doesn't look exactly like a *U*, but it is close enough.

PROBLEMS

(Answers to the odd-numbered problems appear at the back of the book.)

22-1. "Now that I have paid off my van, it won't cost me anything except for the running expenses, such as gas, oil, and tune-ups, when I actually go somewhere in it." What is wrong with that reasoning?

22-2. Examine this table.

UNITS OF LABOR (PER EIGHT-HOUR DAY)	MARGINAL PRODUCT OF LABOR (PER EIGHT-HOUR DAY)
1	2
2	4
3	6
.	.
.	.
.	.
12	20
13	10
14	5
15	3
16	2

a. Suppose that this firm wants to increase output over the short run. How much labor time is required to produce the first unit? The second and third? Do the fourth, fifth, and sixth units of output require more or less labor time than the earlier units?

b. Suppose that we have hired 11 laborers and now want to increase short-run output in batches of 20. To produce the first batch of 20 (beyond the eleventh laborer), how many labor hours are required? What will the next batch of 20 cost, in labor hours? Do additional batches of 20 cost more or less than earlier batches (beyond the eleventh laborer)?

c. What do parts (a) and (b) imply about the relationship between the marginal product of labor and labor time embodied in equal increments of output?

22-3. Refer to the table in Problem 22-2. Assume that wage rates equal $1 per eight-hour day.

a. By hiring the twelfth unit of labor, what was the cost to the firm of this first batch of 20?

b. What was the marginal cost of output in that range? (Hint: If 20 units cost $1, what did *one* unit cost?)

c. What will the next batch of 10 cost the firm?

d. What is the marginal cost of output over that range?

e. What is happening to the marginal cost of output?

f. How are the marginal product of labor and the marginal cost of output related?

22-4. Your school's basketball team had a foul-shooting average of .800 (80 out of 100) before last night's game, during which they shot 5 for 10 at the foul line.

a. What was their marginal performance last night?

b. What happened to the team's foul-shooting average?

c. Suppose that their foul shooting in the next game is 6 for 10. What is happening to their marginal performance?

d. Now what is the team average foul-shooting percentage?

22-5. Define long-run average total cost. In light of the fact that businesses are operated day to day in the short run, of what use is the concept of long-run average total cost to the entrepreneur?

22-6. A recent college graduate turns down a $20,000 per year job offer in order to open his own business. He borrows $150,000 to purchase equipment. Total sales during his first year were $250,000. Total labor costs for the first year were $160,000 and raw material costs were equal to $50,000. He pays $15,000 interest on the loan per year. Estimate the economic profit of this business for the first year.

22-7. Examine this table.

OUTPUT (UNITS)	AVERAGE FIXED COST	TOTAL COST
0	—	$200
5	$40	300
10	20	380
20	10	420
40	5	520

a. Find the average variable cost at each level of production.

b. What is the marginal cost of increasing output from 10 to 20 units? From 20 to 40 units?

c. Find the average total cost at each level of production.

22-8. You are given the following graph.
  a. At what output level is AVC at a minimum?
  b. At what output level is ATC at a minimum?
  c. At what output level is MC at a minimum?
  d. At what output level do the AVC and MC curves intersect?
  e. At what output level do the ATC and MC curves intersect?

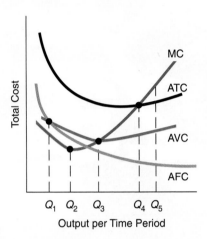

22-9. Fill in the missing values for marginal, average, and total product in the following table. Assume that capital and labor are the only two inputs in the production function and that capital is held fixed.

UNITS OF LABOR	TOTAL PRODUCT	MARGINAL PRODUCT	AVERAGE PRODUCT
6	120	N.A.	20
7	147	——	21
8	——	23	——
9	——	——	20

COMPUTER-ASSISTED INSTRUCTION
(Complete problem and answer on disk.)

How does the law of diminishing returns affect the marginal product of labor? When the marginal product of labor falls, why does the marginal cost of output rise? Specific calculations are required; such calculations reveal the answers to these important questions.

PERFECT COMPETITION

Every semester you go through the same ritual: choosing courses, registering for classes, and so on. Often a more painful part of the ritual awaits you—the purchase of your textbooks. Not only are they sometimes too heavy, but certainly most, if not all of them, seem outrageously expensive. But textbook publishing is a highly competitive industry. Further, the cost of production over the past decade has dropped as technology in the printing field has improved. Why, then, has the relative price of textbooks apparently not gone down? It will require the tools of your study of perfect competition to understand this issue.

After reading this chapter, you should be able to answer the following questions:

1. How much will a perfect competitor produce in the short run?
2. What is the perfectly competitive firm's short-run supply curve?
3. Can a perfectly competitive firm earn economic profits?
4. Why is the perfectly competitive market structure considered to be economically efficient?

INTRODUCTION

If you decided to open a desktop publishing business in any major city in America, you would face few obstacles. You would have to raise the money to buy or lease the equipment, but no one could stop you from renting a store, advertising, and attracting customers. You would immediately enter into competition with all of the other desktop publishing businesses in that city and in cities elsewhere that offer their services on a nationwide basis. Could you expect to get rich starting such a business? Probably not, for there is just too much competition to expect such an unexpected turn of events. Knowing that the desktop publishing industry is highly competitive tells you a lot about what kind of price you could set for your services. If you do not match competition in terms of price per constant-quality unit, you will consistently find yourself facing losses. That is the nature of one type of **market structure** called perfect competition. Perfect competition occurs when buyers and sellers assume, correctly, that they cannot affect the market price—it is simply given by the market forces of demand and supply.

▶ **Market structure**
Characteristics of a market, including the number of buyers and sellers, the degree to which products from different firms differ, and the ease of entry into or exit from the market.

CHARACTERISTICS OF A PERFECTLY COMPETITIVE MARKET STRUCTURE

In this chapter we are interested in studying how a firm acting within a perfectly competitive market structure makes decisions about how much to produce. In a situation of **perfect competition,** each firm is such a small part that it cannot significantly affect the price of the product in question. That means that each **perfectly competitive firm** in the industry is a **price taker**—the firm takes price as a given, something determined *outside* the individual firm.

This definition of a competitive firm is obviously idealized, for in one sense the individual firm *has* to set prices. How can we ever have a situation in which firms regard prices as set by forces outside their control? The answer is that even though every firm sets its own prices, a firm in a perfectly competitive situation will find that it will eventually have no customers at all if it sets its price above the competitive price. The best example is in agriculture. Although the individual farmer can set any price for a bushel of wheat, if that price doesn't coincide with the market price of a bushel of similar-quality wheat, no one will purchase the wheat at a higher price (nor would the farmer be inclined to reduce revenues by selling below the market price).

Let's examine the reasons why a firm in a perfectly competitive industry ends up being a price taker.

▶ **Perfect competition**
A market structure in which the decisions of individual buyers and sellers have no effect on market price.

▶ **Perfectly competitive firm**
A firm that is such a small part of the total industry that it cannot affect the price of the product it sells.

▶ **Price taker**
A competitive firm that must take the price of its product as given because the firm cannot influence its price.

1. **There must be a large number of buyers and sellers.** When this is the case, no one buyer or one seller has any influence on price.
2. **The product sold by the firms in the industry must be homogeneous.** The product sold by each firm in the industry must be a perfect substitute for the product sold by each other firm. Buyers must be able to choose from a large number of sellers of a product that the buyers believe to be the same.
3. **Any firm can enter or leave the industry without serious impediments.** Firms in a competitive industry cannot be hampered in their ability to get resources or relocate resources. They move labor and capital in pursuit of profit-making opportunities to whatever business venture gives them their highest expected rate of return on their investment.
4. **Buyers and sellers have good information that is symmetrically distributed to them.** Consumers have to be able to find out about lower prices charged by competing firms. Firms have to be able to find out about cost-saving innovations in order to lower production costs and prices, and they have to be able to learn about profitable opportunities in other industries.

⭐ **EXAMPLE: The Lemons Problem**

Asymmetric information about quality leads to what has been called the **lemons problem.**
A common example occurs with used cars. The potential buyer of a used car has relatively little information about the true quality of the car—its motor, transmission, brakes,
and so on. The only way the buyer can find out is to purchase the car and use it for a
time. In contrast, the seller usually has much greater information about the quality of the
car, for she or he has been using it for some time. The owner of the used car knows
whether or not it is a lemon. In situations like this, with asymmetric information between
buyer and seller, buyers typically tend to want to pay only a price that reflects the average quality of the used car in the market, not a price that reflects the higher value of a
truly good used car.

> ▶ **Lemons problem**
> The situation in which con-
> sumers, who do not know
> details about the quality of a
> product, are willing to pay no
> more than the price of a low-
> quality product, even if a
> higher-quality product at a
> higher price exists.

From the car seller's point of view, given that the price of used cars will tend to reflect average qualities, all of the owners of known lemons will want to put their cars up
for sale. The owners of high-quality used cars will be more reluctant to do so. The logical result of this adverse selection is a disproportionate number of "lemons" on the used
car market and consequently relatively fewer sales than would exist if information were
symmetric.

*For Critical Analysis: Obviously, it is possible to buy high-quality used cars today.
What are some of the techniques used in the marketplace to overcome the lemons problem that results from adverse selection in this market?* ●

THE DEMAND CURVE OF THE PERFECT COMPETITOR

When we discussed in Chapter 20 the existence and similarity of substitutes, we pointed
out that the more substitutes and the more similar they were to the commodity in question, the more demand was price-elastic. Here we assume for the perfectly competitive
firm that it is producing a homogeneous commodity that has perfect substitutes. That
means that if the individual firm raises its price one penny, it will lose all of its business.
This, then, is how we characterize the demand schedule for a perfectly competitive firm:
It is a horizontal line at the going market price determined by the forces of market supply and market demand, that is, where the market demand curve intersects the market supply curve. The single-firm demand curve in a perfectly competitive industry is completely
elastic at the going market price. Remember that with a perfectly elastic demand curve,
any increase in price leads to zero quantity demanded.

We show the market demand and supply curves in panel (a) of Figure 23-1. Their intersection occurs at the price of $5. The commodity in question is computer diskettes, and
assume for the purposes of this exposition that all diskettes are perfect substitutes for all
others. At the going market price of $5 apiece, a hypothetical individual demand curve
for a diskette producer who sells a very, very small part of total industry production is
shown in panel (b). At the market price, this firm can sell all the output it wants. At the
market price of $5 each, which is where the horizontal demand curve for the individual
producer lies, consumer demand for the diskettes of that one producer is perfectly elastic. This can be seen by noting that if the firm raises its price, consumers, who are assumed to know that this supplier is charging more than other producers, will buy elsewhere, and the producer in question will have no sales at all. Similarly, if the producer
lowers its price, everyone buys from that producer. Thus, the demand curve for that producer is perfectly elastic. We label the individual producer's demand curve *d*, whereas the
market demand curve is always labeled *D*.

FIGURE 23-1
The demand curve for a diskette producer.
At $5—where market demand, *D*, and market supply, *S*, intersect—the individual firm faces a horizontal demand curve, *d*. If it raises its price even one penny, it will sell no diskettes at all. The firm's demand curve is perfectly elastic. Notice the difference in the quantities of diskettes represented on the horizontal axis of panels (a) and (b).

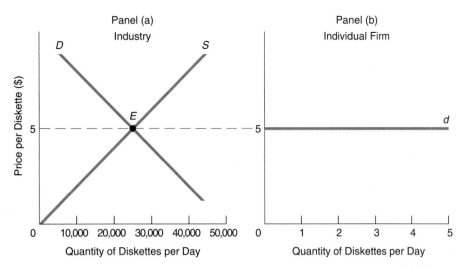

Panel (a)
Industry

Panel (b)
Individual Firm

HOW MUCH SHOULD THE PERFECT COMPETITOR PRODUCE?

As we have shown, a perfect competitor has to accept the price of the product as a given. If the firm raises its price, it sells nothing; if it lowers its price, it makes less money per unit sold than it otherwise could. The firm has one decision left: How much should it produce? We will apply our model of the firm to this question to come up with an answer. We'll use the profit-maximization model, which assumes that firms attempt to maximize their total profits—the positive difference between total revenues and total costs.

TOTAL REVENUES

▶ **Total revenues**
The price per unit times the total quantity sold.

Every firm has to consider its **total revenues.** Total revenues are defined as the quantity sold multiplied by the price. (They are the same as total receipts from the sale of output.) The perfect competitor must take the price as a given.

Look at Figure 23-2 on the next page. Much of the information in panel (a) comes from panel (a) of Figure 22-3, but we have added some essential columns for our analysis. Column 3 is the market price of $5 per diskette, which is also equal to average revenue (AR) because

$$AR = \frac{TR}{Q} = \frac{PQ}{Q} = P$$

If we assume that all units sell for the same price, it becomes apparent that another name for the demand curve is the average revenue curve (this is true regardless of the type of market structure under consideration).

Column 4 shows the total revenues, or TR, as equal to the market price, *P*, times the total output in sales per day, or *Q*. Thus TR = *PQ*. We are assuming that the market supply and demand schedules intersect at a price of $5 and that this price holds for all the firm's production. We are also assuming that because our diskette maker is a small part of the market, it can sell all that it produces at that price. Thus panel (b) of Figure 23-2 shows the total revenue curve as a straight line. For every unit of sales, total revenue is increased by $5.

Panel (a)

(1) TOTAL OUTPUT AND SALES PER DAY (Q)	(2) TOTAL COST (TC)[a]	(3) MARKET PRICE (P)	(4) TOTAL REVENUE (TR) (4) = (3) x (1)	(5) TOTAL PROFIT = TR − TC (5) = (4) − (2)	(6) AVERAGE TOTAL COST (ATC) (6) = (2) ÷ (1)[a]	(7) AVERAGE VARIABLE COST (AVC)[a]	(8) MARGINAL COST (MC) (8) = $\frac{\text{CHANGE IN (2)}^a}{\text{CHANGE IN (1)}}$	(9) MARGINAL REVENUE (MR) (9) = $\frac{\text{CHANGE IN (4)}}{\text{CHANGE IN (1)}}$
0	$10	$5	$ 0	−$10	—	—		
							$5	$5
1	15	5	5	− 10	$15.00	$5.00		
							3	5
2	18	5	10	− 8	9.00	4.00		
							2	5
3	20	5	15	− 5	6.67	3.33		
							1	5
4	21	5	20	− 1	5.25	2.75		
							2	5
5	23	5	25	2	4.60	2.60		
							3	5
6	26	5	30	4	4.33	2.67		
							4	5
7	30	5	35	5	4.28	2.86		
							5	5
8	35	5	40	5	4.38	3.12		
							6	5
9	41	5	45	4	4.56	3.44		
							7	5
10	48	5	50	2	4.80	3.80		
							8	5
11	56	5	55	− 1	5.09	4.18		

[a]From Figure 22-3.

FIGURE 23-2
Profit maximization.

Profit maximization occurs where marginal revenue equals marginal cost. Panel (a) indicates that this point occurs at a rate of sales of between seven and eight diskettes per day.

In panel (b) we find maximum profits where total revenues exceed total costs by the largest amount. This occurs at a rate of production and sales per day of seven or eight diskettes.

In panel (c) the marginal cost curve, MC, intersects the marginal revenue curve at a rate of output and sales of somewhere between seven and eight diskettes per day.

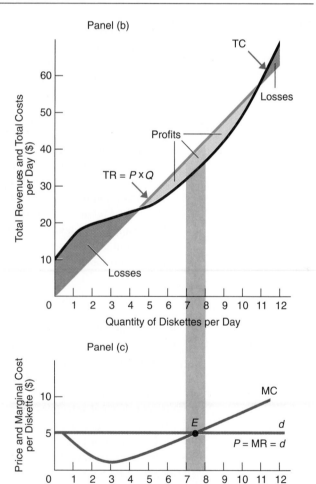

Panel (b)

Panel (c)

COMPARING TOTAL COSTS WITH TOTAL REVENUES

▶ **Total costs**
The sum of total fixed costs and total variable costs.

Total costs are given in column 2 of panel (a) of Figure 23-2 and plotted in panel (b). When the total cost curve is above the total revenue curve, the firm is experiencing losses. When it is below the total revenue curve, the firm is making profits. Remember that cost curves include a normal, or competitive, rate of return on capital as a cost of operations.

By comparing total costs with total revenues, we can figure out the number of diskettes the individual competitive firm should produce per day. Our analysis rests on the assumption that the firm will attempt to maximize total profits. In panel (a) of Figure 23-2 we see that total profits reach a maximum at a production rate of either seven or eight diskettes per day. We can see this graphically in panel (b) of the figure. The firm will maximize profits where the total revenue curve exceeds the total cost curve by the greatest amount. That occurs at a rate of output and sales of either seven or eight diskettes per day; this rate is called the **profit-maximizing rate of production.** (If output were continuously divisible or we were dealing with extremely large numbers of diskettes, we would get a unique profit-maximizing output.)

▶ **Profit-maximizing rate of production**
The rate of production that maximizes total profits, or the difference between total revenues and total costs; also, the rate of production at which marginal revenue equals marginal cost.

We can also find this profit-maximizing rate of production for the individual competitive firm by looking at marginal revenues and marginal costs.

USING MARGINAL ANALYSIS TO DETERMINE THE PROFIT-MAXIMIZING RATE OF PRODUCTION

It is possible—indeed, preferred—to use marginal analysis to determine the profit-maximizing rate of production. We end up with the same results derived in a different manner, one that focuses more on where decisions are really made—on the margin. Managers examine changes in costs and relate them to changes in revenues. In fact, all analysis is best put in the context of comparing changes in cost with changes in benefits, where change is occurring at the margin, whether it be with respect to how much more or less to produce, how many more workers to hire or fire, or how much more to study or not study.

▶ **Marginal revenue**
The change in total revenues resulting from a change in output (and sale) of one unit of the product in question.

Marginal revenue represents the increment in total revenues attributable to producing one additional unit of the product in question. Marginal revenue is also defined as the change in total revenues resulting from a one-unit change in output. Hence a more formal definition of marginal revenue is

$$\text{Marginal revenue} = \frac{\text{change in total revenues}}{\text{change in output}}$$

In a perfectly competitive market, the marginal revenue curve is exactly equivalent to the price line or the individual firm's demand curve because the firm can sell all of its output (production) at the market price. If price were not constant for all units sold—if the demand curve in panel (b) of Figure 23-1 were not horizontal—the price and marginal revenue would not be equal.

Thus in Figure 23-1 the demand curve, d, for the individual producer is at a price of $5—the price line is coincident with the demand curve. But so is the marginal revenue curve, for marginal revenue in this case also equals $5.

The marginal revenue curve for our competitive diskette producer is shown as a horizontal line at $5 in panel (c) of Figure 23-2. Notice again that the marginal revenue curve is equal to the price line, which is equal to the individual firm's demand, or average revenue, curve, d.

WHEN ARE PROFITS MAXIMIZED?

Now we add the marginal cost curve, MC, taken from column 8 in panel (a) of Figure 23-2. As shown in panel (c) of that figure, the marginal cost curve first falls and then starts to rise because of the law of diminishing returns, eventually intersecting the marginal revenue curve and then rising above it. Notice that the numbers for both the marginal cost schedule, column 8 in panel (a), and the marginal revenue schedule, column 9 in panel (a), are printed *between* the rows on which the quantities appear. This indicates that we are looking at a *change* between one rate of output and the next.

In panel (c) the marginal cost curve intersects the marginal revenue curve somewhere between seven and eight diskettes per day. The firm has an incentive to produce and sell until the amount of the additional revenue received from selling one more diskette just equals the additional costs incurred for producing and selling that diskette. This is how it maximizes profit. Whenever marginal cost is less than marginal revenue, the firm will always make more profit by increasing production.

Now consider the possibility of producing at an output rate of 10 diskettes per day. The marginal cost curve at that output rate is higher than the marginal revenue (or *d*) curve. The firm would be spending more to produce that additional output than it would be receiving in revenues; it would be foolish to continue producing at this rate.

But how much should it produce? It should produce at point *E*, where the marginal cost curve intersects the marginal revenue curve from below.[1] Because the firm knows that it can sell all the diskettes it wants at the going market price, marginal revenue from selling an additional diskette will always equal the market price. Consequently, the firm should continue production until the cost of increasing output by one more unit is just equal to the revenues obtainable from that extra unit. This is a fundamental rule in economics:

> **Profit maximization is always at the rate of output at which marginal revenue equals marginal cost.**

For a perfectly competitive firm, this is at the intersection of the demand schedule, *d*, and the marginal cost curve, MC. When MR exceeds MC, each additional unit of output adds more to total revenues than to total costs, causing losses to decrease or profits to increase. When MC is greater than MR, each unit produced adds more to total cost than to total revenues, causing profits to decrease or losses to increase. Therefore, profit maximization occurs when MC equals MR. In our particular example, our profit-maximizing, perfectly competitive diskette producer will produce at a rate of either seven or eight diskettes a day. (If we were dealing from a very large rate of output, we would come up with an exact profit-maximizing rate.)

CONCEPTS IN BRIEF

- Four fundamental characteristics of the market in perfect competition are (1) a large number of buyers and sellers, (2) a homogeneous product, (3) unrestrained exit from and entry into the industry by other firms, and (4) good information that is symmetrically distributed to both buyers and sellers.
- A perfectly competitive firm is a price taker. It has no control over price and consequently has to take price as a given, but it can sell all that it wants at the going market price.

---

[1] The marginal cost curve, MC, also cuts the marginal revenue curve, *d*, from above at an output rate of less than 1 in this example. This intersection should be ignored because it is irrelevant to the firm.

- The demand curve for a perfect competitor is a horizontal line at the going market price. The demand curve is also the perfect competitor's marginal revenue curve because marginal revenue is defined as the change in total revenue due to a one-unit change in output.
- Profit is maximized at the rate of output where the positive difference between total revenues and total costs is the greatest. This is the same level of output at which marginal revenue equals marginal cost. The perfectly competitive firm produces at an output rate at which marginal cost equals the price per unit of output, because MR = P.

SHORT-RUN PROFITS

To find what our individual, competitive diskette producer is making in terms of profits in the short run, we have to add the average total cost curve to panel (c) of Figure 23-2. We take the information from column 6 in panel (a) and add it to panel (c) to get Figure 23-3. Again the profit-maximizing rate of output is between seven and eight diskettes per day. If we have production and sales of seven diskettes per day, total revenues will be $35 a day. Total costs will be $30 a day, leaving a profit of $5 a day. If the rate of output in sales is eight diskettes per day, total revenues will be $40 and total costs will be $35, again leaving a profit of $5 a day. In Figure 23-3 the rectangle labeled "Profits" has a lower boundary that is determined by the intersection of the profit-maximizing quantity line represented by vertical dashes and the average total cost curve. Why? Because the ATC curve gives us the cost per unit, whereas the price ($5), represented by *d*, gives us the revenue per unit, or average revenue. The difference is profit per unit. So the height of the rectangular box representing profits equals profit per unit; the length equals the amount of units produced, and the product of the two quantities is in fact total profits. Note that

FIGURE 23-3
Measuring total profits.
Profits are represented by the shaded area. The height of the profit rectangle is given by the difference between average total costs and price ($5), where price is also equal to average revenues. This is found by the vertical difference between the ATC curve and the price, or average revenue, line *d*, at the profit-maximizing rate of output of between seven and eight diskettes per day.

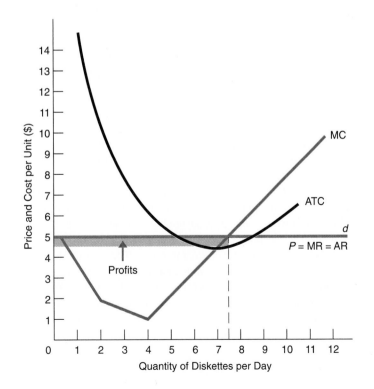

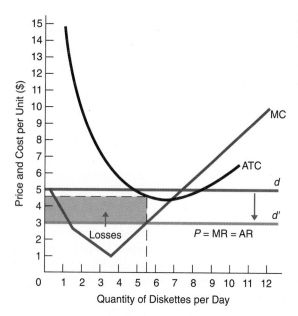

FIGURE 23-4
Minimization of short-run losses.
In cases in which average total costs exceed the average revenue, or price (and price is greater than or equal to average variable cost), profit maximization is equivalent to loss minimization. This again occurs where marginal cost equals marginal revenue. Losses are shown in the shaded area.

profits here are *economic profits* because a normal rate of return to investment is included in the average total cost curve, ATC.

It is certainly possible, also, for the competitive firm to make short-run losses. We give an example in Figure 23-4, where we show the firm's demand curve shifting from d to d'. The going market price has fallen from $5 to $3 per diskette because of changes in market supply or demand conditions (or both). The firm will always do the best it can by producing where marginal revenue equals marginal cost. We see in Figure 23-4 that the marginal revenue (d') curve is intersected (from below) by the marginal cost curve at an output rate of about 5½ diskettes per day. The firm is clearly not making profits because average total costs at that ouput rate are greater than the price of $3 per diskette. The losses are shown in the shaded area. By producing where marginal revenue equals marginal cost, however, the firm is minimizing its losses, that is, losses would be greater at any other output.

THE SHORT-RUN SHUTDOWN PRICE

In Figure 23-4 the firm is sustaining economic losses. Will it go out of business? In the long run it will, but surprisingly, in the short run the firm will not go out of business, for as long as the loss from staying in business is less than the loss from shutting down, the firm will continue to produce. A firm *goes out of business* when the owners sell it assets to someone else. A firm *shuts down* when it stops producing, but it still is in business.

Now how can we tell when the firm is sustaining economic losses in the short run and it is still worthwhile not to shut down? The firm must compare the cost of producing (while incurring losses) with the cost of closing down. The cost of staying in production in the short run is given by the total *variable* cost. Looking at the problem on a per-unit basis, as long as average variable cost (AVC) is covered by average revenues (price), the firm is better off continuing to produce. If average variable costs are exceeded even a little bit by the price of the product, staying in production produces some revenues in excess of variable costs that can be applied toward covering fixed costs.

A simple example will demonstrate this situation. The price of a product is $8, and average total costs equal $9 at an output of 100. In this example, average total costs are broken up into average variable costs of $7 and average fixed costs of $2. Total revenues, then, equal $8 × 100, or $800, and total costs equal $9 × 100, or $900. Total losses therefore equal $100. However, this does not mean that the firm will shut down. After all, if it does shut down, it still has fixed costs to pay. And in this case, because average fixed costs equal $2 at an output of 100, the fixed costs are $200. Thus the firm has losses of $100 if it continues to produce, but it has losses of $200 (the fixed costs) if it shuts down. The logic is fairly straightforward:

> As long as the price per unit sold exceeds the average *variable* cost per unit produced, the firm will be paying for at least part of the opportunity cost of the investment in the business, that is, part of its fixed costs.

CALCULATING THE SHORT-RUN BREAK-EVEN PRICE

Let's look at demand curve *d* in Figure 23-5. It just touches the minimum point of the average total cost curve, which, as you will remember, is exactly where the marginal cost curve intersects the average total cost curve. At that price, which is about $4.30, the firm will be making exactly zero short-run economic profits. Thus that particular price is called the **short-run break-even price,** and point *E* is therefore the short-run break-even price for a competitive firm. It is the point at which marginal revenue, marginal cost, and average total cost are all equal (that is, at which *P* = MC and *P* = ATC). The break-even price is the one that yields zero short-run economic profits or losses.

▶ **Short-run break-even price**
The price at which a firm's total revenues equal its total costs. At the break-even price, the firm is just making a normal rate of return on its capital investment. (It is covering its explicit and implicit costs.)

CALCULATING THE SHORT-RUN SHUTDOWN PRICE

To calculate the firm's shutdown price, we must introduce the average variable cost (AVC) to our graph. In Figure 23-5 we have plotted the AVC values from column 7 in panel (a) of Figure 23-2. For the moment, consider two possible demand curves, *d* and *d'*, which are also the firm's respective marginal revenue curves. Therefore, if demand is *d*, the firm

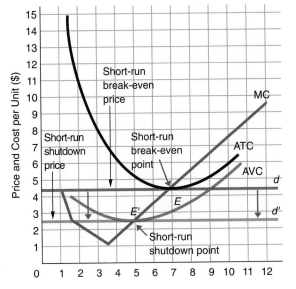

FIGURE 23-5
Short-run shutdown and break-even prices.
We can find the short-run break-even price and the short-run shutdown price by comparing price with average total costs and average variable costs. If the demand curve is *d*, profit maximization occurs at output *E*, where MC = marginal revenue (the *d* curve). Because the ATC curve includes all relevant opportunity costs, point *E* is the short-run break-even point, and zero economic profits are being made. The firm is earning a normal rate of return. If the demand curve falls to *d'*, profit maximization (loss minimization) occurs at the intersection of MC and MR (the *d'* curve), or *E'*. Below this price it does not pay the firm to continue in operation because its average variable costs are not covered by the price of the product.

will produce at *E*, where that curve intersects the marginal cost curve. If demand falls to *d'*, the firm will produce at *E'*. The special feature of the hypothetical demand curve, *d'*, is that it just touches the average variable cost curve at the latter's minimum point, which is also where the marginal cost curve intersects it. This price is the **short-run shutdown price.** Why? Below this price, the firm would be paying out more in variable costs than it is receiving in revenues from the sale of its product. Each unit it sold would add to its losses. Clearly, the way to avoid incurring these additional losses, if price falls below the shutdown point, is in fact to shut down operations. (Of course, if price falls below the short-run shutdown price, a firm still continues in business—as a nonproducer—in the short run because it is stuck with fixed costs and can't get out of the business even if it wants to.)

▶ **Short-run shutdown price**
The price that just covers average variable costs. It occurs just below the intersection of the marginal cost curve and the average variable cost curve.

The intersection of the price line, the marginal cost curve, and the average variable cost curve is labeled *E'*, the short-run shutdown price. It is valid only for the short run because, of course, in the long run the firm will not stay in business at a yield less than a normal rate of return and hence at least zero economic profits.

THE MEANING OF ZERO ECONOMIC PROFITS

The fact that we labeled point *E* in Figure 23-5 the break-even point may have disturbed you. At point *E*, price is just equal to average total cost. If this is the case, why would a firm continue to produce if it were making no profits whatsoever? If we again make the distinction between accounting profits and economic profits, then at that price the firm has zero economic profits but positive accounting profits. Recall that accounting profits are total revenues minus total explicit costs. What is ignored is the reward offered to investors—the opportunity cost of capital—plus all other implicit costs.

In economic analysis, the average total cost curve includes the full opportunity cost of capital. Indeed, the average total cost curve includes the opportunity cost of *all* factors of production used in the production process. At the short-run break-even price, economic profits are, by definition, zero. Accounting profits at that price are not, however, equal to zero; they are positive. Consider an example. A baseball bat manufacturer sells bats at some price. The owners of the firm have supplied all the funds in the business. They have borrowed no money from anyone else, and they explicitly pay the full opportunity cost to all factors of production, including any managerial labor that they themselves contribute to the business. Their salaries show up as a cost in the books and are equal to what they could have earned in the next-best alternative occupation. At the end of the year, the owners find that after they subtract all explicit costs from total revenues, they have earned $100,000. Let's say that their investment was $1 million. Thus the rate of return on that investment is 10 percent per year. We will assume that this turns out to be equal to the rate of return that, on average, all other baseball bat manufacturers make in the industry.

This $100,000, or 10 percent rate of return, is actually, then, a competitive, or normal, rate of return on invested capital in that industry or in other industries with similar risks. If the owners had made only $50,000, or 5 percent on their investment, they would have been able to make higher profits by leaving the industry. The 10 percent rate of return is the opportunity cost of capital. Accountants show it as a profit; economists call it a cost. We include that cost in the average total cost curve, similar to the one shown in Figure 23-5. At the short-run break-even price, average total cost, including this opportunity cost of capital, will just equal that price. The firm will be making zero economic profits but a 10 percent *accounting* rate of return.

Now we are ready to derive the firm's supply curve.

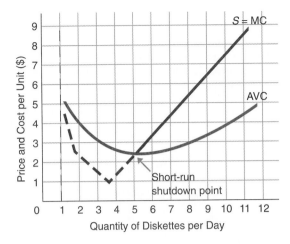

FIGURE 23-6
The individual firm's short-run supply curve.
The individual firm's supply curve is the portion of its marginal cost curve above the minimum point on the average variable cost curve.

THE PERFECT COMPETITOR'S SHORT-RUN SUPPLY CURVE

What does the supply curve for the individual firm look like? Actually, we have been looking at it all along. We know that when the price of diskettes is $5, the firm will supply seven or eight of them per day. If the price falls to $3, the firm will supply five or six diskettes per day. And if the price falls below $3, the firm will shut down in the short run. Hence in Figure 23-6 the firm's supply curve is the marginal cost curve above the short-run shutdown point. This is shown as the solid part of the marginal cost curve. The definition, then, of the individual firm's supply curve in a competitive industry is its marginal cost curve equal to and above the point of intersection with the average variable cost curve.

THE SHORT-RUN INDUSTRY SUPPLY CURVE

In Chapter 3, on demand and supply, we indicated that the market supply curve was the summation of individual supply curves. At the beginning of this chapter we drew a market supply curve in Figure 23-1. Now we want to derive more precisely a market, or industry, supply curve to reflect individual producer behavior in that industry. First we must ask, What is an industry? It is merely a collection of firms producing a particular product. Therefore, we have a way to figure out the total supply curve of any industry: We add the quantities that each firm will supply at every possible price. In other words, we sum the individual supply curves of all the competitive firms *horizontally.* The individual supply curves, as we just saw, are simply the marginal cost curves of each firm.

Consider doing this for a hypothetical world in which there are only two diskette producers in the industry, firm A and firm B. These two firms' marginal cost curves are given in panels (a) and (b) of Figure 23-7 on the next page. The marginal cost curves for the two separate firms are presented as MC_A in panel (a) and MC_B in panel (b). Those two marginal cost curves are drawn only for prices above the minimum average variable cost for each respective firm. Hence we are not including any of the marginal cost curves below minimum average variable cost. In panel (a) for firm A, at price P_1 the quantity supplied would be q_{A1}. At price P_2 the quantity supplied would be q_{A2}. In panel (b) we see the two different quantities corresponding to those two prices that would be supplied by firm B. Now for price P_1 we add horizontally the quantity of q_{A1} and q_{B1}. This gives us one point, F, for our short-run **industry supply curve,** S. We obtain the other point, G, by doing the same horizontal adding of quantities at P_2. When we connect points F and

▶ **Industry supply curve**
The locus of points showing the minimum prices at which given quantities will be forthcoming; also called the *market supply curve.*

FIGURE 23-7

Deriving the industry supply curve.

Marginal cost curves above average minimum variable cost are presented in panels (a) and (b) for firms A and B. We horizontally sum the two quantities supplied, q_{A1} and q_{B1} at price P_1. This gives us point F in panel (c). We do the same thing for the quantities at price P_2. This gives us point G. When we connect those points, we have the industry supply curve S, which is the horizontal summation of the firms' marginal cost curves above their respective average minimum costs.

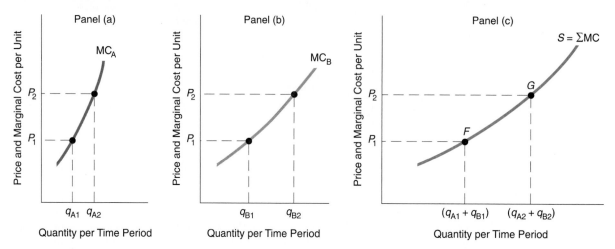

G, we obtain industry supply curve S, which is also marked ΣMC, indicating that it is the horizontal summation[2] of the marginal cost curves (above the respective minimum average variable cost of each firm). Because the law of diminishing returns makes marginal cost curves rise, the short-run supply curve of a perfectly competitive industry must be upward-sloping.

FACTORS THAT INFLUENCE THE INDUSTRY SUPPLY CURVE

As you have just seen, the industry supply curve is the horizontal summation of all of the individual firms' marginal cost curves above their respective minimum average variable cost points. This means that anything that affects the marginal cost curves of the firm will influence the industry supply curve. Therefore, the individual factors that will influence the supply function in a competitive industry can be summarized as the factors that cause the variable costs of production to change. These are factors that affect the individual marginal cost curves, such as changes in the individual firm's productivity, in factor costs (wages paid to labor, prices of raw materials, etc.), in taxes, and in anything else that would influence the individual firm's marginal cost curves.

All of these are nonprice determinants of supply. Because they affect the position of the marginal cost curve for the individual firm, they affect the position of the industry supply curve. A change in any of these will shift the market supply curve.

CONCEPTS IN BRIEF

- Short-run average profits or average losses are determined by comparing average total costs with price (average revenue) at the profit-maximizing rate of output. In the short run, the perfectly competitive firm can make economic profits or economic losses.

---

[2]The capital Greek sigma (Σ) is the symbol for summation.

- The competitive firm's short-run break-even output occurs at the minimum point on its average total cost curve, which is where the marginal cost curve intersects the average total cost curve.
- The competitive firm's short-run shutdown output is at the minimum point on its average variable cost curve, which is also where the marginal cost curve intersects the average variable cost curve. Shutdown will occur if price falls below average variable cost.
- The firm will continue production at a price that exceeds average variable costs even though the full opportunity cost of capital is not being met; at least some revenues are going toward paying fixed costs.
- At the short-run break-even price, the firm is making zero economic profits, which means that it is just making a normal rate of return in that industry.
- The firm's short-run supply curve is the portion of its marginal cost curve equal to or above minimum average variable costs.
- The industry short-run supply curve is a horizontal summation of the individual firms' marginal cost curves above their respective minimum average variable costs.

COMPETITIVE PRICE DETERMINATION

How is the market, or "going," price established in a competitive market? This price is established by the interaction of all the suppliers (firms) and all the demanders. The market demand schedule, D, in panel (a) of Figure 23-8 represents the demand schedule for the entire industry, and the supply schedule, S, represents the supply schedule for the entire industry. Price P_e is established by the forces of supply and demand at the intersection of D and the short-run industry supply curve, S. Even though each individual firm has no control or effect on the price of its product in a competitive industry, the interaction of *all* the producers and buyers determines the price at which the product will be sold. We say that the price P_e and the quantity Q_e in panel (a) of Figure 23-8 constitute the competitive solution to the pricing-quantity problem in that particular industry. It is the equilibrium where quantity demanded equals quantity supplied, and both suppliers and

FIGURE 23-8

Industry demand and supply curves and the individual firm demand curve.
The industry demand curve is represented by D in panel (a). The short-run industry supply curve is S and equal to ΣMC. The intersection of the demand and supply curves at E determines the equilibrium or market clearing price at P_e. The individual firm demand curve in panel (b) is set at the market clearing price determined in panel (a). If the producer has a marginal cost curve MC, this producer's individual profit-maximizing output level is at q_e. For AC_1 economic profits are zero, for AC_2 profits are negative, and for AC_3 profits are positive.

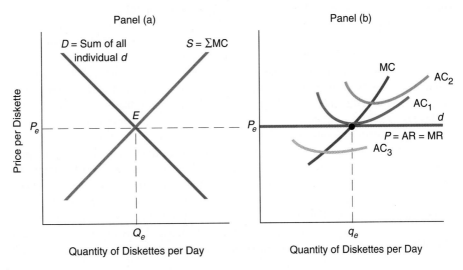

demanders are maximizing. The resulting individual firm demand curve, d, is shown in panel (b) of Figure 23-8 at the price P_e.

In a purely competitive industry, the individual producer takes price as a given and chooses the output level that maximizes profits. (This is also the equilibrium level of output from the producer's standpoint.) We see in panel (b) of Figure 23-8 that this is at q_e. If the producer's average costs are given by AC_1, q_e is also the short-run break-even point (see Figure 23-5); if its average costs are given by AC_2, at q_e, AC exceeds price (average revenue), and the firm is making losses. Alternatively, if average costs are given by AC_3, the firm will be making economic profits at q_e. In the former case we would expect, over time, that people will cease production (exit the industry), causing supply to shift inward, whereas in the latter case we would expect people to enter the industry to take advantage of the economic profits, thereby causing supply to shift outward. We now turn to these long-run considerations.

THE LONG-RUN INDUSTRY SITUATION: EXIT AND ENTRY

In the long run in a competitive situation, firms will be making zero economic profits. In the long run, we surmise that firms in perfect competition will tend to have average total cost curves that just touch the price (marginal revenue) curve, or individual demand curve d. How does this occur? It is through an adjustment process that depends on economic profits and losses.

EXIT AND ENTRY OF FIRMS

Go back and look at Figures 23-3 and 23-4. The existence of either profits or losses is a signal to owners of capital both within and outside the industry. If the industry is characterized by firms showing economic profits as represented in Figure 23-3, this will signal owners of capital elsewhere in the economy that they, too, should enter this industry. If, by contrast, there are firms in the industry like the ones suffering economic losses represented in Figure 23-4, this signals resource owners outside the industry to stay out. It also signals resource owners within the industry not to reinvest and if possible to leave the industry. It is in this sense that we say that profits direct resources to their highest-valued use. In the long run, capital and labor will flow into industries in which profitability is highest and will flow out of industries in which profitability is lowest.

The price system therefore allocates capital according to the relative expected rates of return on alternative investments. Entry restrictions will thereby hinder economic efficiency, and thus welfare, by not allowing resources to flow to their highest-valued use. Similarly, exit restrictions (such as plant closing laws) will act to trap resources (temporarily) in sectors in which their value is below that in alternative uses. Such laws will also inhibit the ability of firms to respond to changes in the domestic and international marketplace; yet to judge their desirability, we must weigh these factors against the costs to employees and local economies from such sudden economic disruptions.

Not every industry presents an immediate source of opportunity for every firm. In a brief period of time it is impossible for a firm that produces tractors to switch to the production of computers, even if there are very large profits to be made. Over the long run, however, we would expect to see such a change, whether or not the tractor producers want to change over to another product. In a market economy, investors supply firms in the more profitable industry with more investment funds, which they take from firms in less profitable industries. (Also, profits give existing firms internal investment funds for expansion.) Consequently, resources needed in the production of more profitable goods, such

▶ **Signals**
Compact ways of conveying to economic decision makers information needed to make decisions. A true signal not only conveys information but also provides the incentive to react appropriately. Economic profits and economic losses are such signals.

as labor, will be bid away from lower-valued opportunities. Investors and other suppliers of resources respond to market **signals** about their highest-valued opportunities.

Market adjustment to changes in demand will occur regardless of the wishes of the managers of firms in less profitable markets. They can either attempt to adjust their product line to respond to the new demands, be replaced by managers who are more responsive to new conditions, or see their firms go bankrupt as they find themselves unable to replace worn-out plants and equipment.

In addition, when we say that in a competitive long-run equilibrium situation firms will be making zero economic profits, we must realize that at a particular point in time it would be pure coincidence for a firm to be making *exactly* zero economic profits. Real-world information is not as precise as the curves we use to simplify our analysis. Things change all the time in a dynamic world, and firms, even in a very competitive situation, may for many reasons not be making exactly zero economic profits. We say that there is a *tendency* toward that equilibrium position, but firms are adjusting all the time to changes in their cost curves and in their (horizontal) *d* curves.

⭐ EXAMPLE: **The End of the Do-It-Yourself Era**

The Heath Company was founded a few years after the end of the World War II. It developed and sold do-it-yourself electronic radio kits. From the 1950s to the 1970s, Heath Kits were an American institution. Parents with soldering irons sat at kitchen tables, often showing their young sons and daughters how to put together a radio and later a stereo or television set. By the mid-1960s, Heath Kit had a dozen competitors. By the beginning of the 1990s, Heath Kit was again the sole producer in the do-it-yourself electronics market. In 1992 it too left this market. Its decision was based on the desire to concentrate on the more profitable market for home-improvement products and educational materials. Sales of do-it-yourself electronic kits had declined steadily since the beginning of the 1980s. Although some observers argued that reduced leisure time caused the decline, in reality it was competition from Sony, Hitachi, Panasonic, and other electronics companies that finally caused the do-it-yourself electronics era to come to an end. Integrated circuits, in which one small chip takes the place of numerous separate components, eventually sounded the death knell for the Heath Company's do-it-yourself division. Few people in the 1990s were willing to put together themselves a stereo or even a computer when the street prices of already-assembled units were so low.

For Critical Analysis: What happened to the demand curve facing Heath? ●

LONG-RUN INDUSTRY SUPPLY CURVES

In panel (a) of Figure 23-8 we drew the summation of all of the portions of the individual firm's marginal cost curve above each firm's respective minimum average variable costs as the upward-sloping supply curve of the entire industry. We should be aware, however, that a relatively steep upward-sloping supply curve may be appropriate only in the short run. After all, one of the prerequisites of a competitive industry is free entry.

▶ **Long-run industry supply curve**
A market supply curve showing the relationship between price and quantities forthcoming after firms have been allowed the time to enter into or exit from an industry, depending on whether there have been positive or negative economic profits.

Remember that our definition of the long run is a period of time in which adjustments can be made. The **long-run industry supply curve** is a supply curve showing the relationship between quantity supplied by the entire industry at different prices after firms have been allowed to either enter or leave the industry, depending on whether there have been positive or negative economic profits. Also, the long-run industry supply curve is drawn under the assumption that entry and exit have been completed.

There are three possible types of long-run industry supply curves, depending on whether input costs stay constant, increase, or decrease. What is at issue here is the effect on input prices of a change in the number of firms in the industry. In Chapter 22 we assumed

FIGURE 23-9

Constant-cost, increasing-cost, and decreasing-cost industries.

In panel (a) we show a situation in which the demand curve shifts from D to D'. Price increases from P_e to P'_e; however, in time the short-run supply curve shifts outward to S', and the equilibrium shifts from E' to E''. The market clearing price is again P_e. If we connect points such as E and E'', we come up with the long-run supply curve S_L. This is a constant-cost industry. In panel (b) costs are increasing for the industry, and therefore the long-run supply curve slopes upward and long-run prices rise from P_b to P'_b. In panel (c) costs are decreasing for the industry as it expands, and therefore the long-run supply curve slopes downward such that long-run prices decline from P_c to P'_c.

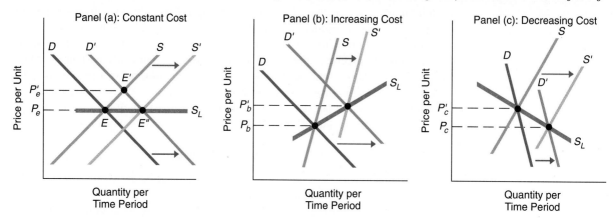

that input prices remained constant to the firm regardless of the firm's rate of output. When we look at the entire industry, that assumption may not be correct; for example, when all firms are expanding and new firms are entering, they may simultaneously bid up input prices.

Constant-Cost Industries.   In principle, there are small enough industries that use such a small percentage of the total supply of inputs necessary for their production that firms can enter the industry without bidding up input prices. In such a situation we are dealing with a **constant-cost industry.** Its long-run industry supply curve is therefore horizontal and is represented by S_L in panel (a) of Figure 23-9.

We can work through the case in which constant costs prevail. We start out in panel (a) with demand curve D and supply curve S. The equilibrium price is P_e. Market demand shifts rightward to D'. In the short run, the supply curve remains stable. The equilibrium price rises to P'_e. This generates positive economic profits for existing firms in the industry. Such economic profits induce capital to flow into the industry. The existing firms expand and/or new firms enter. The supply curve shifts outward to S'. The new intersection with the new demand curve is at E''. The new equilibrium price is again P_e. The long-run supply curve is obtained by connecting the intersections of the corresponding pairs of demand and supply curves, E and E''. Labeled S_L, it is horizontal; its slope is zero. In a constant-cost industry, long-run supply is perfectly elastic. Any shift in demand is eventually met by an equal shift in supply so that the long-run price is constant at P_e.

Retail trade is often given as an example of such an industry because output can be expanded or contracted without affecting input prices. Banking is another example.

Increasing-Cost Industries.   In an **increasing-cost industry,** expansion by existing firms and the addition of new firms cause the price of inputs specialized within that industry to be bid up. As costs of production rise, the ATC curve and the firms' MC curve shift upward, causing short-run supply curves (each firm's marginal cost curve) to shift

▶ **Constant-cost industry**
An industry whose total output can be increased without an increase in long-run per-unit costs; an industry whose long-run supply curve is horizontal.

▶ **Increasing-cost industry**
An industry in which an increase in industry output is accompanied by an increase in long-run per-unit costs, such that the long-run industry supply curve slopes upward.

upward. The result is a long-run industry supply curve that slopes upward, as represented by S_L in panel (b) of Figure 23-9. Examples are residential construction and coal mining—both use specialized inputs that cannot be obtained in ever increasing quantities without causing their prices to rise.

Decreasing-Cost Industries.   An expansion in the number of firms in an industry can lead to a reduction in input costs and a downward shift in the ATC and MC curves. When this occurs, the long-run industry supply curve will slope downward. An example is given in panel (c) of Figure 23-9. This is a **decreasing-cost industry.**

▶ **Decreasing-cost industry**
An industry in which an increase in output leads to a reduction in long-run per-unit costs, such that the long-run industry supply curve slopes downward.

LONG-RUN INDUSTRY RESPONSE TO INCREASING OR DECREASING DEMAND

One reason we attempt to develop a model of the behavior of the firm in different market structures is to predict what will happen when changes occur in the economy. Figure 23-9 allows us to predict what will happen to price in the long run in a perfectly competitive industry.

In the case of increasing demand, we must first determine whether we are dealing with a constant-, increasing-, or decreasing-cost industry. Having determined that, we have shown in Figure 23-9 what will happen to price as industry demand increases.

Our predictions can be made in a similar fashion if we are dealing with a perfectly competitive industry in which market demand is falling. In a constant-cost perfectly competitive industry, in the long-run, output will be reduced but price will remain constant at P_e, as in panel (a) of Figure 23-9. In an increasing-cost industry, a decline in demand will eventually lead to a reduction in output and a *reduction* in price because the industry is moving to the left and downward on an upward-sloping long-run supply curve.

Finally, in a decreasing-cost industry, a reduction in market demand will lead to a long-run reduction in output and an *increase* in prices because the industry moves to the left and upward along a downward-sloping long-run supply curve.

⭐ EXAMPLE: The Meaning of Competition in the Digital Age

Discussions of long-run industry responses to changes in demand conjure up the image of a well-defined group of firms selling similar products. But the digital electronics age makes both the definition of an industry and the concept of competition somewhat blurred. Consider the town of Glasgow, Kentucky. The Glasgow Electric Board installed a two-way monitoring system to help consumers conserve electricity. The same system is capable of delivering news information and video images. Now the Glasgow Electric Board offers cable TV in competition with the original cable company, which was forced to reduce rates. Because this digital system is already in place, Glasgow Electric Board will soon be offering telephone service to some of its customers.

Because of the digital revolution, four separate industries are slowly becoming one: consumer electronics, computers, communications, and entertainment. When everything is converted into a single stream of zeros and ones that can be decoded easily, text, images, video, sound, and information in general can then be offered by each of the four separate industries just mentioned. Why not offer all of those services at once? The Glasgow Electric Board has gone part of the way. Moreover, nationally, cable TV companies and consumer electronics producers are buying up music and movie producers. Software companies, such as Microsoft, are purchasing the rights to images, such as the world's great artworks, to offer them in digital electronic form.

For many years America has been losing out globally in the competitive consumer electronics field, particularly to the Japanese. The digital era, according to some observers, will give U.S. companies a new chance to compete in the international marketplace. Apple Computer and Hewlett-Packard have already started to leapfrog the Japanese in their presentation of digital home consumer products.

For Critical Analysis: *If entire movies can be sent digitally directly into people's homes, what industry or industries will be affected, and how?* ●

LONG-RUN EQUILIBRIUM

In the long run, the firm can change the scale of its plant, adjusting its plant size in such a way that it has no further incentive to change. It will do so until profits are maximized. Figure 23-10 shows the long-run equilibrium of the perfectly competitive firm. Given a price of P and a marginal cost curve, MC, the firm produces at output Q_e. Because profits must be zero in the long run, the firm's short-run average costs (SAC) must equal P at Q_e, which occurs at minimum SAC. In addition, because we are in long-run equilibrium, any economies of scale must be exhausted so that we are on the minimum point of the long-run average cost curve (LAC). In other words, the long-run equilibrium position is where "everything is equal," which is at point E in Figure 23-10. There, *price* equals *marginal revenue* equals *marginal cost* equals *average cost* (minimum, short-run, and long-run).

PERFECT COMPETITION AND MINIMUM AVERAGE TOTAL COST

Look again at Figure 23-10. In long-run equilibrium, the perfectly competitive firm finds itself producing at output rate Q_e. At that rate of output, the price is just equal to the minimum long-run average cost as well as the minimum short-run average cost. In this sense, perfect competition results in no "waste" in the production system. Goods and services are produced using the least costly combination of resources. This is an important attribute of a perfectly competitive long-run equilibrium, particularly when we wish to compare the market structure of perfect competition with other market structures that are less than perfectly competitive. We will examine these other market structures in later chapters.

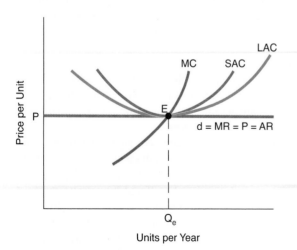

FIGURE 23-10
Long-run firm competitive equilibrium.
In the long run, the firm operates where price, marginal revenue, marginal cost, short-run minimum average cost, and long-run minimum average cost are all equal. This occurs at point *E*.

COMPETITIVE PRICING: MARGINAL COST PRICING

In a perfectly competitive industry, each firm produces where its marginal cost curve intersects its marginal revenue (*d*) curve from below. Thus perfectly competitive firms always sell their goods at a price that just equals marginal cost. This represents an optimal pricing situation because the price that consumers pay reflects the opportunity cost to society of producing the good. Recall that marginal cost is the amount that a firm must spend to purchase the additional resources needed to expand output by one unit. Given competitive markets, the amount paid for a resource will be the same in all of its alternative uses. Thus MC reflects relative resource input use; that is, if the MC of good 1 is twice the MC of good 2, one more unit of good 1 requires twice the resource input of one more unit of good 2. Because under perfect competition, price equals marginal cost, the consumer, in determining allocation of income on purchases on the basis of relative prices, is actually allocating income on the basis of relative resource input use.

▶ **Marginal cost pricing**
A system of pricing in which the price charged is equal to the opportunity cost to society of producing one more unit of the good or service in question. The opportunity cost is the marginal cost to society.

The competitive firm produces up to the point at which the market price just equals the marginal cost. Herein lies the element of the optimal nature of a competitive solution. It is called **marginal cost pricing.** The competitive firm sells its product at a price that just equals the cost to society—the opportunity cost—for that is what the marginal cost curve represents. (But note here that it is the self-interest of firm owners that causes price to equal social cost.) In other words, the marginal benefit to consumers, given by the price that they are willing to pay for the last unit of the good purchased, just equals the marginal cost to society of producing the last unit. If the marginal benefit exceeds the marginal cost ($P > $ MC), too little is being produced in that people value additional units more than the cost to society of producing them; if $P < $ MC, the opposite is true.

When an individual pays a price equal to the marginal cost of production, the cost to the user of that product is equal to the sacrifice or cost to society of producing that quantity of that good as opposed to more of some other good. (We are assuming that all marginal social costs are accounted for.) The competitive solution, then, is called *efficient,* in the economic sense of the word. Economic efficiency means that it is impossible to increase the output of any good without lowering the *value* of the total output produced in the economy. No juggling of resources, such as labor and capital, will result in an output that is higher in value than the value of all of the goods and services already being produced. In an efficient situation, it is impossible to make one person better off without making someone else worse off. All resources are used in the most advantageous way possible, and society therefore enjoys an efficient allocation of productive resources. All goods and services are sold at their opportunity cost, and marginal cost pricing prevails throughout.

▶ **Market failure**
A situation in which an unrestrained market operation leads to either too few or too many resources going to a specific economic activity.

Although perfect competition does offer many desirable results, situations arise when perfectly competitive markets cannot efficiently allocate resources. These situations are instances of **market failure.** Externalities and public goods are examples. For reasons discussed in later chapters, perfectly competitive markets cannot efficiently allocate resources in these situations, and alternative allocation mechanisms are called for. Finally, the rate of innovation by perfectly competitive firms may be socially suboptimal, and the distribution of income may differ from what our normative judgment indicates. In all cases, alternative market structures, or government intervention, *may* improve the economic outcome.

The fact that we use the model of perfect competition in an economic analysis does not mean that we should accept perfect competition as the only type of industry structure to be tolerated. Sometimes, however, the competitive model predicts surprisingly well, even in noncompetitive industries, and we may not wish to seek out alternative theories. Remember that the purpose of theory is not to provide an accurate description of the world but rather to help explain and predict.

CONCEPTS IN BRIEF

- The competitive price is determined by the intersection of the market demand curve and the market supply curve; the market supply curve is equal to the horizontal summation of the portions of the individual marginal cost curves above their respective minimum average variable costs.
- In the long run, competitive firms make zero economic profits because of entry and exit of firms into and out of the industry whenever there are industrywide economic profits or economic losses.
- Economic profits and losses are signals to resource owners.
- A constant-cost industry will have a horizontal long-run supply curve. An increasing-cost industry will have a rising long-run supply curve. A decreasing-cost industry will have a falling long-run supply curve.
- In the long run, a competitive firm produces where price, marginal revenue, marginal cost, short-run minimum average cost, and long-run minimum average cost are all equal.
- Competitive pricing is essentially marginal cost pricing, and therefore the competitive solution is called efficient because marginal cost represents the social opportunity cost of producing one more unit of the good; when consumers face a price equal to the full opportunity cost of the product they are buying, their purchasing decisions will lead to an efficient use of available resources.

SOLVING THE ASYMMETRY-OF-INFORMATION PROBLEM IN A COMPETITIVE INDUSTRY

At the beginning of this chapter we pointed out that one of the assumptions underlying a purely competitive model is the existence of symmetric information for both buyers and sellers. The absence of symmetric information leads to the adverse selection problem (lemons problem) that you read about with respect to the market for used cars. Let us now extend this discussion to the production of goods in a competitive marketplace. With perfect competition and good information, the price per constant-quality unit of goods tends toward uniformity. When quality is not known prior to the purchase of a good, however, two possibilities arise: (1) Firms that are producing low-quality products may try to fool customers into believing that they are high-quality products and worthy of high price, and (2) firms already producing high-quality products may have an incentive to start cutting quality costs while still charging a higher price. In that way they can make higher profits. Consumers cannot consistently be fooled, though, so if firms try either of these ploys, eventually consumers will simply assume that all products in a particular marketplace are of low quality (lemons), and that low-quality level is all they will be willing to pay for.

REPEAT SALES AND CUSTOMER REFERRALS

In most businesses, the customers come back for repeat purchases and old customers refer new customers. An ongoing firm selling high-quality products that decides to cheat its customers can only do so for only a short while. Soon old customers will not return, nor will they recommend the business to their friends. Repeat customers and referrals continue only as long as a firm selling high-quality products continues to provide high quality. For firms to be induced to continue this high-quality production, they must offer their goods at a price that supports that quality, known as the **quality-assuring price.** Firms calculate the quality-assuring price in the following way: The price has to be high enough to offer a stream of profits that is at least as great as the profits that could be earned in one period by cheating customers. The method of cheating is, of course, continuing to sell the product as if it were high-quality but cutting production costs and reducing quality.

> ▶ **Quality-assuring price**
> A price that is high enough to offer a stream of profits that is as great as or greater than the profits that could be made by cheating customers in one period by offering them a low-quality product at a relatively high price.

SPECIFIC INVESTMENTS BY HIGH-QUALITY-PRODUCT FIRMS

High-quality-product firms stay in business only if they are charging the quality-assuring price. This allows them high enough profits each period to prevent them from cheating on quality. But positive economic profits should attract entry into the high-quality end of the product marketplace. Entry would cause the market price of high-quality products to fall, and high-quality-product producers would be more tempted to cheat. We would end up back with only lemons.

> ▶ **Specific investments**
> Investments in a product that will lose their value rapidly if customers find out that a firm has cheated them; examples are logos, trademarks, and advertising.

Existing high-quality-product firms fight entry by making **specific investments** in the high-quality product line. These specific investments have a special characteristic: If the firm ever cheats by producing low-quality products, the value of those specific investments falls dramatically. If a firm invests in logos, trademarks, brand names, special signs, advertising, and the like, the value of such investments falls dramatically if customers find out that the firm has cheated. What good is all that advertising about a Lexus or a Mercedes if in fact those cars are no better than the lowest-priced Ford or Chevy? Firms that make these specific investments are in a way assuring customers that they will not be cheated. After all, why would a firm spend millions of dollars advertising high quality if the value of that advertising is going to go to zero in the period after its customers have been cheated?

Firms producing high-quality products consequently end up eliminating their positive economic profits by specific investment in advertising, logos, and trademarks. Any potential new entrant has to look at not only investing in making the product but also the specific investments in creating high-quality-product assurances for potential customers.

CONCEPTS IN BRIEF
- In a world of asymmetric information, firms producing low-quality products may try to fool customers by charging high prices or firms already producing high-quality products may try to cut quality while still charging a higher price.
- Even with asymmetric information, in a competitive marketplace, repeat customers and referrals will occur only as long as a firm selling high-quality products continues to provide high quality. Firms are induced to continue this high-quality production by being able to charge the quality-assuring price.
- Firms undertake specific investments in the form of logos, advertising, and trademarks. Their value falls dramatically if a firm ever cheats on its product's quality.

THE HIGH COST OF YOUR TEXTBOOK

Concepts Applied: Marginal cost, competition, asymmetric information, specific investment

The production costs of textbooks, corrected for inflation, have dropped as technology in printing and binding has improved. Nonetheless, the inflation-corrected price of textbooks has not dropped accordingly.

The price of computing memory and power has fallen dramatically in the past decade. Not surprisingly, because computers are a highly competitive market, the price of computers has also fallen. You can purchase a setup today for $1,000 that would have cost you $10,000 only a few years ago. The cost of producing textbooks has dropped, not by as much as computing power, but by quite a bit. From 1980 to 1994, estimated average four-color production costs per book dropped 60 percent (after correcting for inflation). Nonetheless, the average price of your economics textbook, even corrected for inflation, has not dropped. Does this mean that textbook publishing is not a competitive industry?

COMPETITION IN THE TEXTBOOK INDUSTRY

If the textbook industry were not competitive, we should be able to observe it in relatively high rates of return to investment. Such is not the case. The rate of return to textbook publishing has been about 8 percent per year for 30 years. There must be another explanation.

ASYMMETRIC INFORMATION WITH TEXTBOOKS

You do not decide on the textbook you are going to use for economics or any other class. Your professor normally makes that decision either individually or by committee within his or her department. In any course area, such as economics, there are numerous competing textbooks. Professors trying to decide on a textbook do not have the time or inclination to read 500 to 1,000 pages in each competing book to determine the quality. Each publisher (and author) has better information about the quality of the textbook being offered than most individual professors. There is asymmetric information. High-quality textbook producers need a way to signal to professors that their books are better than their competitors'.

SPECIFIC INVESTMENTS

Publishers signal professors that they have a high-quality book—modern, error-free, well researched—by making specific investments. In addition to some advertising, such as colorful brochures about new textbooks and new editions, over the years textbook publishers have chosen to increase the quantity of free supplements available with each book. To get an idea of the range of such specific investments, all you need do is look at the list at the beginning of this textbook. It includes 15 items for your instructor and 12 items for you. Most of these items are clearly book-specific. It is hard to use an instructor's manual or a study guide for one economics textbook when using another. The 27 free supplements with your textbook is a signal to your instructor that HarperCollins has made a large specific investment. The value of that specific investment would deteriorate rapidly if in fact HarperCollins (and the author) decided to "cheat" your professor (and you) by producing a lower-quality book, filled with errors, outdated theory, and factual misstatements. If this were done, your professor would discover it and never use the book again, and all that specific investment in the free supplements would have been wasted.

THE QUALITY-ASSURING PRICE GOES UP

As more and more specific investment is made in supplements, the quality-assuring price for new textbooks increases. After all, more supplements cost more money to produce. That means that there must have been higher economic profits available to pay for such specific investments. These higher economic profits could have come about through either relatively higher market prices or lower production costs. Judging from the unchanged relative price of textbooks, the declining production costs have made possible all those free supplements.

FOR CRITICAL ANALYSIS

1. Some publishers are trying to make *semispecific* investments by providing certain free supplements that can be used with all textbooks in a particular category, such as principles of economics books or American government texts. How does this affect our analysis?

2. Why doesn't one publisher come out with a generic textbook with few supplements that is sold at a significantly lower price than current textbooks?

CHAPTER SUMMARY

1. We define a competitive situation as one in which individual firms cannot affect the price of the product they produce. This is usually when the firm is very small relative to the entire industry. A firm in a perfectly competitive situation is called a price taker; it must take the price as a given.

2. The firm's total revenues will equal the price of the product times the quantity sold. Because the competitive firm can sell all it wants at the same price (the "going" price), total revenues equal the going price times the quantity the firm decides to sell.

3. The firm maximizes profits when marginal cost equals marginal revenue. The marginal revenue to the firm is represented by its own horizontal demand curve. This is because marginal revenue is defined as the change in total revenues due to a change in output and sales by one unit. But the competitive firm can sell all it wants at the same price; therefore, its marginal revenue will equal the price, which will equal its average revenue.

4. A perfectly competitive firm ends up in the long run making zero economic profits. However, it still makes a normal, or competitive, rate of return because that is the opportunity cost of capital. The competitive rate of return on investment is included in the costs as we have defined them for the firm.

5. The firm will always produce along its marginal cost curve unless the price falls below average variable costs; this would be the shutdown price. It occurs at the intersection of the average variable cost curve and the marginal cost curve. Below that price it is not profitable to stay in production because variable costs will not be completely covered by revenues.

6. The supply curve of the firm is exactly equal to its marginal cost curve above the shutdown price. The supply curve of the industry is equal to the horizontal summation of all the supply curves of the individual firms. This is a short-run industry supply curve, and it slopes upward.

7. The long-run supply curve will be upward-sloping, horizontal, or downward-sloping, depending on whether the industry is facing increasing, constant, or decreasing costs. The industry may have an upward-sloping long-run supply curve if it faces diseconomies of scale or increasing costs. The industry may have a downward-sloping long-run supply curve if it faces economies of scale or decreasing costs.

8. In a world of asymmetric information, firms producing low-quality products may try to fool customers by charging high prices or firms already producing high-quality products may try to cut quality while still charging a higher price.

9. Even with asymmetric information, in a competitive marketplace, repeat customers and referrals will occur only as long as a firm selling high-quality products continues to provide high quality. Firms are induced to continue this high-quality production by being able to charge the quality-assuring price.

10. Firms undertake specific investments in the form of logos, advertising, and trademarks. Their value falls dramatically if a firm ever cheats on its product's quality.

DISCUSSION OF PREVIEW POINTS

1. How much will a perfect competitor produce in the short run?

A perfect competitor will produce at the profit-maximizing rate of output; it will maximize the positive difference between total revenues and total costs. Another way of viewing this process is through analyzing marginal revenue (MR) and marginal cost (MC). The firm can maximize total profits by producing all outputs for which MR exceeds MC. Thus if MR > MC, the firm will produce the unit in question; if MR < MC, the firm will not produce the unit in question. If MC > MR, the extra cost of producing that unit is greater than the extra revenue that the firm can earn by selling it; producing a unit for which MC > MR leads to a reduction in total profits or an increase in total losses. In short, the perfect competitor will produce up to the output rate at which MR = MC; by doing so, it will have produced all units for which MR > MC, and it will be maximizing total profits.

2. What is the perfectly competitive firm's short-run supply curve?

A supply curve indicates the various quantities that will be offered, voluntarily, at different prices per unit of time, other things being constant. Under perfect competition, price (*P*) equals marginal revenue (MR), and because the profit-maximizing output occurs where *P* = MC, it follows that any price below MC will induce more output until MC is driven up to equal that price. Thus the marginal cost curve is the firm's short-run supply schedule. We qualify this to note that because the firm has a shutdown point at the minimum average variable cost point, the technical short-run supply curve is the firm's marginal cost curve *above* the minimum average variable cost point.

3. Can a perfectly competitive firm earn economic profits?

In the short run, yes; in the long run, no. Though it is possible for a perfectly competitive firm to earn profits in the short run, our assumption of free (unfettered but not costless) entry forces us to conclude that any positive economic (abnormal) profits will be bid away. This will happen because excess profits induce entry into the industry, which amounts to an increase in industry supply. Given demand, an increase in supply will cause market price to fall, thereby shifting the individual firm's demand curve downward. This process continues until economic profits equal zero; free entry allows new entrants to compete away economic profits.

4. Why is the perfectly competitive market structure considered economically efficient?

The perfectly competitive market structure is considered economically efficient for two reasons: In the long run economic profits are zero, and price equals marginal cost. We discuss each in turn. Profits are a signal; if economic profits are positive, the signal is that society wants *more* of this good; if economic profits are negative, this means that society wants *less* of this good; when economic profits are zero, just the "right" quantity of resources is being allocated to the production of a good. Also, the marginal cost of a good represents the social opportunity cost of producing one more unit of that good; the price of a good represents society's marginal valuation of that commodity. When price equals marginal cost, the value to society of the last unit produced (its price) is just offset by what society had to give up in order to get it (its marginal cost). Because under perfect competition, long-run economic profits equal zero and price equals marginal cost, an efficient allocation of resources exists.

PROBLEMS

(Answers to the odd-numbered problems appear at the back of the book.)

23-1. In the accompanying table we list cost figures for a hypothetical firm. We assume that the firm is selling in a perfectly competitive market. Fill in all of the columns that are left blank.

a. How low would the market price of its output have to go before the firm would shut down in the short run?

OUTPUT (UNITS)	FIXED COST	AVERAGE FIXED COST (AFC)	VARIABLE COST	AVERAGE VARIABLE COST (AVC)	TOTAL COST	AVERAGE TOTAL COST (ATC)	MARGINAL COST (MC)
1	$100	$___	$ 40	$___	$___	$___	$___
2	100	___	70	___	___	___	___
3	100	___	120	___	___	___	___
4	100	___	180	___	___	___	___
5	100	___	250	___	___	___	___
6	100	___	330	___	___	___	___

b. What is the price of its output at which the firm would just break even in the short run? (This is the same price below which the firm would go out of business in the long run.) What output would the firm produce at that price?

c. If the price of its output were $76, what rate of output would the firm produce, and how much profit would it earn?

23-2. Consider the accompanying graph. Then answer the questions.

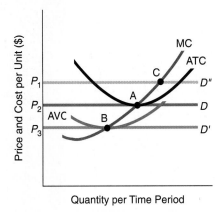

a. Which demand curve indicates that the firm is earning normal profits?

b. Which demand curve indicates that the firm is earning abnormal profits?

c. Which demand curve indicates that the firm is indifferent between shutting down and producing?

d. Which curve is the firm's supply curve?

e. Below which price will the firm shut down?

23-3. In a perfectly competitive market, what is the difference between the demand the industry faces and the demand an individual firm faces?

23-4. Why might a firm continue to produce in the short run, even though the going price is less than its average total cost?

23-5. A firm in a perfectly competitive industry has total revenue of $200,000 per year when producing 2,000 units of output per year.

a. Find the firm's average revenue.

b. Find the firm's marginal revenue.

c. Assuming that the firm is maximizing profits, what is the firm's marginal cost?

d. If the firm is at long-run equilibrium, what are its short-run average costs?

23-6. The accompanying graph is for firm J. Study it; then answer the questions.

a. How many units will firm J sell in order to maximize profits?

b. What is firm J's total profit from selling the amount of output in part (a)?

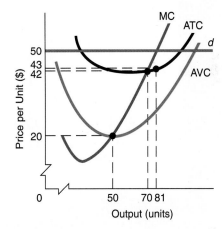

c. At what price will firm J shut down in the short run?

d. If the cost curves shown represent production at the optimal long-run plant size, at what price will firm J shut down in the long run?

23-7. You have a friend who earns $25,000 a year working for a collection agency. In a savings and loan account she has $200,000 that she inherited. She is earning 6 percent per year on that money. She quits her job and buys a car wash with the $200,000. At the end of one year, she shows you her tax return. It indicates that the car wash had a pretax profit of $40,000. "What do you think about that?" she remarks. What is your answer?

COMPUTER-ASSISTED INSTRUCTION
(Complete problem and answer on disk.)

Why do perfect competitors choose to produce at an output rate at which MR equals MC? What are the consequences for them if they fail to follow this rule?

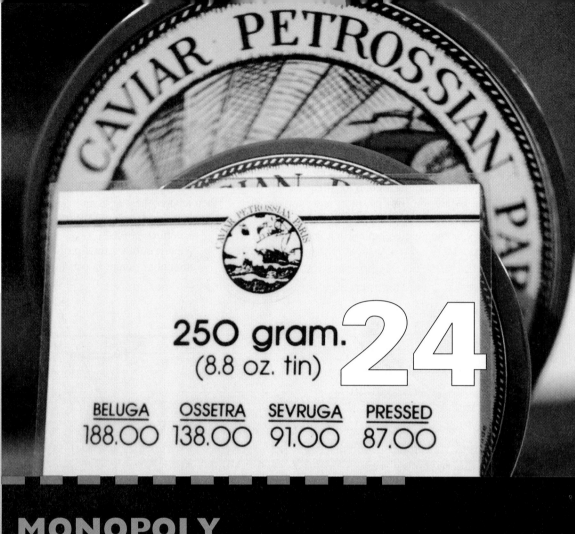

250 gram.
(8.8 oz. tin)

24

BELUGA | OSSETRA | SEVRUGA | PRESSED
188.00 | 138.00 | 91.00 | 87.00

MONOPOLY

For many, it is the food that smells funny and tastes too salty. But for others it is the food from heaven. It is called caviar. The most prized type of caviar has always come from the eggs of a sturgeon traditionally harvested in autumn close to the Volga River delta, along the Caspian Sea. Until the early 1990s, its price to the retail customer in America was roughly 10 times its price in the former Soviet Union. How is it possible to have a legal product with such a huge difference in price, a difference that cannot be accounted for by the cost of transportation? Typically such a situation can exist only if a firm has a way to keep out competitors. This is called a monopoly situation, which you will learn about in the pages that follow.

After reading this chapter, you should be able to answer the following questions:

1. For the monopolist, marginal revenue is less than selling price. Why?

2. What is the profit-maximizing rate of output for the monopolist?

3. What are some common misconceptions about monopolists?

4. What is the cost to society of monopoly?

INTRODUCTION

When you go to a national park and have lunch or dinner in one of the restaurants, the quality of the food for the price charged is usually poor. The same is often true at your college or university cafeteria. If you have ever been skiing and decided to eat lunch at the top of the mountain, the same is true. All three of these situations have something in common—there is no competition allowed. The company that sells food in the national park has been granted a monopoly by the National Park Service. The company that sells food in your school cafeteria has usually been granted an exclusive right to do so by your college or university. And the ski resort that offers you food on the top of the mountain does not allow anyone else to open a restaurant next to it. It is obvious that when you run a business that is the only one of its type in town, you can charge a higher price per constant-quality unit than when there is intense competition. This chapter is about situations in which competition is severely restricted. We call this situation *monopoly*.

DEFINITION OF A MONOPOLIST

The word *monopoly* probably brings to mind notions of a business that gouges the consumer, sells faulty products, gets rich, and other negative thoughts. But if we are to succeed in analyzing and predicting the behavior of noncompetitive firms, we will have to be more objective in our definition. Although most monopolies in the United States are relatively large, our definition will be equally applicable to small businesses: A **monopolist** is a *single supplier* of a good or service for which there is no close substitute.

▶ **Monopolist**
A single supplier that comprises its entire industry.

In a monopoly market structure, the firm (the monopolist) and the industry are one and the same. Occasionally there may be a problem in identifying an industry and therefore determining if a monopoly exists. For example, should we think of aluminum and steel as separate industries, or should we think of the industry in terms of basic metals? Our answer depends on the extent to which aluminum and steel can be substituted in the production of a wide range of products.

As we shall see in this chapter, a seller prefers to have a monopoly than to face competitors. In general, we think of monopoly prices as being higher than prices under perfect competition and of monopoly profits as being higher than profits under perfect competition (which are, in the long run, merely equivalent to a normal rate of return). How does a firm obtain a monopoly in an industry? Basically, there must be *barriers to entry* that enable firms to receive monopoly profits in the long run. Barriers to entry are restrictions on who can start a business or who can stay in a business.

BARRIERS TO ENTRY

For any amount of monopoly power to continue to exist in the long run, the market must be closed to entry in some way. Either legal means or certain aspects of the industry's technical or cost structure may prevent entry. We will discuss several of the barriers to entry that have allowed firms to reap monopoly profits in the long run (even if they are not pure monopolists in the technical sense).

OWNERSHIP OF RESOURCES WITHOUT CLOSE SUBSTITUTES

Preventing a newcomer from entering an industry is often difficult. Indeed, some economists contend that no monopoly acting without government support has been able to prevent entry into the industry unless that monopoly has had the control of some essential natural resource. Consider the possibility of one firm owning the entire supply of a raw material input that is essential to the production of a particular commodity. The exclusive ownership of such a vital resource input serves as a barrier to entry until an alternative source of the raw material input is found or an alternative technology not requiring the raw material in question is developed. A good example of control over a vital input is the Aluminum Company of America (Alcoa), a firm that prior to World War II controlled the world's bauxite, the essential raw material in the production of aluminum. Such a situation is rare, though, and is ordinarily temporary.

PROBLEMS IN RAISING ADEQUATE CAPITAL

Certain industries require a large initial capital investment. The firms already in the industry can, according to some economists, obtain monopoly profits in the long run because no competitors can raise the large amount of capital needed to enter the industry. This is called the "imperfect" capital market argument employed to explain long-run, relatively high rates of return in certain industries. These industries are generally ones in which large fixed costs must be incurred merely to start production. Their fixed costs are generally for expensive machines necessary to the production process.

ECONOMIES OF SCALE

Sometimes it is not profitable for more than one firm to exist in an industry. This is so if one firm would have to produce such a large quantity in order to realize lower unit costs that there would not be sufficient demand to warrant a second producer of the same product. Such a situation may arise because of a phenomenon we discussed in Chapter 22, economies of scale. When economies of scale exist, total costs increase less than proportionately to the increase in output. That is, proportional increases in output yield proportionately smaller increases in total costs, and per-unit costs drop. The advantage in economies of scale lies in the fact that larger firms (with larger output) have lower costs that enable them to charge lower prices, and that drives smaller firms out of business.

When economies of scale occur over a wide range of outputs, a **natural monopoly** may develop. The natural monopoly is the firm that first takes advantage of persistent declining long-run average costs as scale increases. The natural monopolist is able to underprice its competitors and eventually force all of them out of the market.

> ▶ **Natural monopoly**
> A monopoly that arises from the peculiar production characteristics in an industry. It usually arises when there are large economies of scale relative to the industry's demand, so one firm can produce at a lower average cost than can be achieved by multiple firms.

LEGAL OR GOVERNMENTAL RESTRICTIONS

Governments and legislatures can also erect barriers to entry. These include licenses, franchises, patents, tariffs, and specific regulations that tend to limit entry.

Licenses, Franchises, and Certificates of Convenience.

In many industries it is illegal to enter without a government license, or a "certificate of convenience and public necessity." For example, you could not form an electrical utility to compete with the electrical utility already operating in your area. You would first have to obtain a certificate of convenience and public necessity from the appropriate authority, which is usually the state's public utility commission. However, public utility commissions rarely, if ever, issue a certificate to a group of investors who want to compete directly in the same geographic area with an existing electrical utility; hence entry into the industry in a particular geographic area is prohibited, and long-run monopoly profits could conceivably be earned by the electrical utility already serving the area.

To enter interstate (and also many intrastate) markets for pipelines, trucking, television and radio broadcasting, and transmission of natural gas, to cite a few such industries, it is often necessary to obtain the equivalent of a certificate of convenience and public necessity. Because these franchises or licenses are restricted, long-run monopoly profits might be earned by the firms already in the industry.

⭐ EXAMPLE: **Monopoly Profits from Gambling**

In modern times, gambling has usually been illegal. What many people may not realize is that lotteries and other forms of legal gambling, such as roulette, cards, and dice, were widespread in the United States until about the 1820s. Another wave of legalized gambling started right after the Civil War and then declined in the early twentieth century. Nevada relegalized casinos in the 1930s; bingo halls and racetracks spread throughout the country. The big winner today, though, is the lottery, which started its comeback in 1964. Today 33 states have lotteries. Although more money is bet in casinos, 80 percent of all Americans now live in states that have lotteries. An amazing one-third of the adults who live in these 33 states buy tickets. The estimated profits to these states in 1993 is over $10 billion combined. The states are in effect reaping huge monopoly profits because it is illegal for anyone to compete with state lotteries. Just to make sure that the profits keep rolling in, states combined spend almost a half a billion dollars a year on advertising.

For Critical Analysis: What effect do you think legal state lotteries has had on horse racetrack attendance? On illegal numbers games? ●

Patents. A patent is issued to an inventor to provide protection from having the invention copied or stolen for a period of 17 years. Suppose that engineers working for Ford Motor Company discover a way to build an engine that requires 50 percent fewer parts and weighs 50 percent less than normal engines. If Ford is successful in obtaining a patent on this discovery, it can (in principle) prevent others from copying it. The patent holder has a monopoly. However, it is the patent holder's responsibility to defend the patent. That means that Ford—like other patent owners—must expend resources to prevent others from imitating its invention. If in fact the costs of enforcing a particular patent are greater than the benefits, the patent may not bestow any monopoly profits on its owner. The policing costs would be just too high.

⭐ EXAMPLE: **The Case of the Instant Camera**

Edwin H. Land invented instant photography in 1947. He founded Polaroid and held a monopoly in the instant photography market until 1976, the year Kodak entered the market. Polaroid believed that Kodak was infringing on many of its instant photograph patents. It went to court and sought $12 billion in damages. When the case was settled, Polaroid won, but not $12 billion. Kodak was forced to leave the business and to pay the Polaroid Corporation $925 million. The monopoly value of patents can be great indeed.

For Critical Analysis: What has happened since in the photography market to reduce the value of Polaroid's instant photography patents? ●

▶ **Tariffs**
Taxes on imported goods.

Tariffs. **Tariffs** are special taxes that are imposed on certain imported goods. Tariffs have the effect of making imports relatively more expensive than their domestic counterparts such that consumers switch to the relatively cheaper domestically made products. If the tariffs are high enough, imports become overpriced, and domestic producers gain *monopoly* advantage as the sole suppliers. Many countries have tried this protectionist strategy by using high tariffs to shut out foreign competitors and then develop their ·own domestic industries.

Regulations. During much of the twentieth century, government regulation of the American economy has increased, especially in the interest of safety and quality. For example, pharmaceutical quality-control regulations enforced by the Food and Drug Administration may require that each pharmaceutical company install a $2 million computerized testing machine that requires elaborate monitoring and maintenance. Presumably, this large fixed cost can be spread over a larger number of units of output by larger firms than by smaller firms, thereby putting the smaller firms at a competitive disadvantage. It will also deter entry to the extent that the scale of operation of a potential entrant must be sufficiently large to cover the fixed costs of the required equipment. We examine regulation in more detail in Chapter 26.

CONCEPTS IN BRIEF

- A monopolist is defined as a single seller of a product or a good for which there is no close substitute.
- To maintain a monopoly, there must be barriers to entry. Barriers to entry include ownership of resources without close substitutes; large capital requirements in order to enter the industry; economies of scale; legally required licenses, franchises, and certificates of convenience; patents; tariffs; and safety and quality regulations.

THE DEMAND CURVE A MONOPOLIST FACES

A *pure monopolist* is the sole supplier of *one* product, good, or service. A pure monopolist faces a demand curve that is the demand curve for the entire market for that good.

> The monopolist faces the industry demand curve because the monopolist is the entire industry.

SOME MODERN MONOPOLIES

Everyone is aware of at least some of the forms of pure monopoly that exist in our economy. When you turn on the light to read this text, you are probably purchasing the output of a local monopoly, the electrical power company in your area. There is only one company to which you can go to buy electric power. How did it get to be a monopoly? A government franchise gave it monopoly power.

When you mail a first-class letter at the post office, you are purchasing the services of a government monopoly. Although various groups have tested the legality of restricting first-class mail service to the U.S. Postal Service, for the moment first-class mail service is a government monopoly. There is a single seller of first-class mail service, and that is the government. (More and more alternatives exist for so-called urgent mail, though, such as Federal Express and faxing.)

INTERNATIONAL EXAMPLE: Diamonds Are Forever

Though it is true that diamonds are quite durable, many other materials found in nature are durable, too. The diamond industry, nonetheless, has effectively used an advertising campaign to remind us that "diamonds are forever." But the mere fact that diamonds are indestructible does not justify their extremely high price. Indeed, the actual world supply of diamonds is huge. By all rights diamonds should be cheap, but they are not because of a global **cartel** operated by De Beers, a South African company. De Beers has control over jewelry-quality diamonds, which constitute almost 90 percent of the $5 billion wholesale diamond market. De Beers does this by requiring big producers of rough diamonds to sell through De Beers' Central Selling Organization (CSO). The CSO regulates supply

▶ **Cartel**
An association of producers in an industry that agree to set common prices and output quotas to prevent competition.

by holding it back during slumps in the market for diamonds and releasing it during high demand periods. Producers of rough diamonds are enticed to stay in this cartel because De Beers guarantees a stable, higher price than would exist in a free market.

Every once in a while, pressure on the CSO results in a drop in diamond prices nonetheless. In 1982, for example, a worldwide recession caused individual diamond speculators to unload most of their stocks of diamonds. De Beers had to spend hundreds of millions of dollars to stabilize the price. In 1980 the wholesale price of investment grade D flawless (highest-quality) diamonds was about $55,000 per karat. By 1987 it had dropped to $15,000. In 1993 it was at about one-fourth of the 1980 price (corrected for inflation). But De Beers is still making huge monopoly profits through its CSO. The price of industrial-grade diamonds, which is not affected by CSO's price fixing, is only 1 percent of the price of jewelry-grade diamonds. The difference in production costs is certainly not 100 times. De Beers is still earning large monopoly returns for its international cartel.

For Critical Analysis: Most diamonds in the former Soviet Union are mined in Yakutia, an autonomous region in Siberia, Russia. This region is trying to assert its independence, in part by claiming more control over its diamond mines. How might this create a problem for the De Beers cartel? ●

PROFITS TO BE MADE FROM INCREASING PRODUCTION

How do firms benefit from changing production rates? What happens to price in each case? Let's first review the situation among perfect competitors.

MARGINAL REVENUE FOR THE PERFECT COMPETITOR

Recall that a competitive firm has a horizontal demand curve. That is because the competitive firm is such a small part of the market that it cannot influence the price of its product. It is a *price taker.* If the forces of supply and demand establish that the price per constant-quality pair of shoes is $50, the individual firm can sell all the pairs of shoes it wants to produce at $50 per pair. The average revenue is $50, the price is $50, and the marginal revenue is also $50.

Let us again define marginal revenue:

> Marginal revenue equals the change in total revenue due to a one-unit change in the quantity produced and sold.

In the case of a competitive industry, each time a firm changes production by one unit, total revenue changes by the going price, and price is always the same. Marginal revenue never changes; it always equals price, or average revenue. Average revenue was defined as total revenue divided by quantity demanded, or

$$\text{Average revenue} = \frac{\text{TR}}{Q} = \frac{PQ}{Q} = P$$

MARGINAL REVENUE FOR THE MONOPOLIST

What about a monopoly firm? Because a monopoly is the entire industry, the monopoly firm's demand curve is the market demand curve. The market demand curve slopes downward, just like the other demand curves that we have seen. Therefore, to sell more of a particular product given the industry demand curve, the monopoly firm must lower the

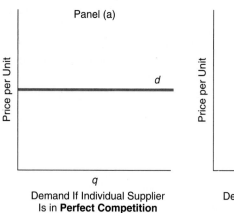
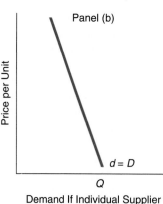

Demand If Individual Supplier
Is in **Perfect Competition**

Demand If Individual Supplier
Is the Only Supplier in a
Pure Monopoly

FIGURE 24-1
Demand curves for the perfect competitor and the monopolist.
The perfect competitor in panel (a) faces a horizontal demand curve d. The monopolist in panel (b) faces the entire industry demand curve, which slopes downward.

price. Thus the monopoly firm moves *down* the demand curve. If all buyers are to be charged the same price, the monopoly must lower the price on all units sold in order to sell more. It cannot just lower the price on the *last* unit sold in any given time period in order to sell a larger quantity.

Put yourself in the shoes of a monopoly ferryboat owner. You have a government-bestowed, legal franchise, and no one can compete with you. Your ferryboat goes between two islands. If you are charging $1 per crossing, a certain quantity of your services will be demanded. Let's say that you are ferrying 100 people a day each way at that price. If you decide that you would like to ferry more individuals, you must lower your price to all individuals—you must move *down* the existing demand curve for ferrying services. To calculate the marginal revenue of your change in price, you must first calculate the total revenues you received at $1 per passenger per crossing and then calculate the total revenues you would receive at, say, 90 cents per passenger per crossing.

It is sometimes useful to compare monopoly markets with perfectly competitive markets. The only way the monopolist can increase sales is by getting consumers to spend more of their incomes on the monopolist's product and less on all other products combined. Thus the monopolist is constrained by the entire market demand curve for its product. We see this in Figure 24-1, which compares the demand curves of the perfect competitor and the monopolist.

Here we see the fundamental difference between the monopolist and the competitor. The competitor doesn't have to worry about lowering price to sell more. In a purely competitive situation, the competitive firm accounts for such a small part of the market that it can sell its entire output, whatever that may be, at the same price. The monopolist cannot. The more the monopolist wants to sell, the lower the price it has to charge on the last unit (and on *all* units put on the market for sale). Obviously, the extra revenues the monopolist receives from selling one more unit are going to be smaller than the extra revenues received from selling the next-to-last unit. The monopolist has to lower the price on the last unit to sell it because it is facing a downward-sloping demand curve and the only way to move down the demand curve is to lower the price on all units.

THE MONOPOLIST'S MARGINAL REVENUE: LESS THAN PRICE

An essential point is that for the monopolist, marginal revenue is always less than price. To understand why, look at Figure 24-2, which shows a unit increase in sales due to a reduction in the price of a commodity from P_1 to P_2. After all, the only way that sales can

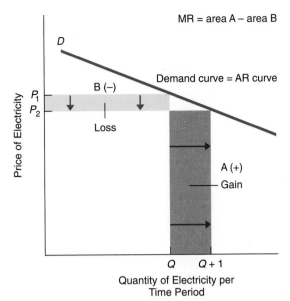

MR = area A – area B

D

Demand curve = AR curve

B (–)

P_1
P_2

Price of Electricity

Loss

A (+)

Gain

Q   Q + 1

Quantity of Electricity per
Time Period

FIGURE 24-2
Marginal revenue: always less than price.
The price received for the last unit sold is equal to P_2. The revenues received from selling this last unit are equal to P_2 times one unit, or the area of the vertical column. However, if a single price is being charged for all units, total revenues do not go up by the amount of the area represented by that column. The price had to be reduced on all the previous Q units that were being sold at price P_1. Thus we must subtract area B—the rectangle between P_1 and P_2 from the origin to Q—from area A in order to derive marginal revenue. Marginal revenue is therefore always less than price.

increase, given a downward-sloping demand curve, is for the price to fall. Price P_2 is the price received for the last unit. Thus price P_2 times the last unit sold represents what is received from the last unit sold. That would be equal to the vertical column (area A) showing the effects of a one-unit increase in sales. Area A is one unit wide by P_2 high.

But price times the last unit sold is *not* the addition to *total* revenues received from selling that last unit. Why? Because price had to be reduced on all previous units sold (Q) in order to sell the larger quantity Q + 1. The reduction in price is represented by the vertical distance from P_1 to P_2 on the vertical axis. We must therefore subtract area B from area A to come up with the *change* in total revenues due to a one-unit increase in sales. Clearly, the change in total revenues—that is, marginal revenue—must be less than price because marginal revenue is always the difference between areas A and B in Figure 24-2. For example, if current price is $8 and quantity demanded is 3, to increase quantity to 4 units, it is necessary to decrease price to $7, not just for the fourth unit but on all 3 previous units as well. Thus at a price of $7, marginal revenue is $7 − $3 = $4 because there is a $1 per unit reduction on 3 previous units. Hence marginal revenue, $4, is less than price, $7.

ELASTICITY AND MONOPOLY

The monopolist faces a downward-sloping demand curve (its average revenue curve). That means that it cannot charge just *any* price with no changes in sales (a common misconception) because, depending on the price charged, a different quantity will be demanded.

Earlier we defined a monopolist as the single seller of well-defined good or service with no *close* substitute. This does not mean, however, that the demand curve for a monopoly is vertical or exhibits zero price elasticity of demand. (Indeed, as we shall see, the profit-maximizing monopolist will never operate in a price range in which demand is inelastic.) After all, consumers have limited incomes and alternative wants. The downward slope of a monopolist's demand curve occurs because individuals compare the marginal satisfaction they will receive to the cost of the commodity to be purchased. Take the example of telephone service. Assume that there is absolutely no substitute whatsoever for telephone service. The market demand curve will still slope downward. At lower prices, people will add more phones and separate lines for different family members.

Furthermore, the demand curve for telephone service slopes down because there are at least several *imperfect* substitutes, such as letters, telegrams, in-person conversations, and CB and VHF-FM radios. Thus even though we defined a monopolist as a single seller of a commodity with no *close* substitute, we can talk about the range of *imperfect* substitutes. The more such imperfect substitutes there are, the more elastic will be the monopolist's demand curve, all other things held constant.

CONCEPTS IN BRIEF

- The monopolist must look at its marginal revenue curve, where marginal revenue is defined as the change in total revenues due to a one-unit change in quantity sold.
- For the perfect competitor, price equals marginal revenue equals average revenue. For the monopolist, price is always greater than marginal revenue. For the monopolist, marginal revenue is always less than price because of the negative slope of the demand curve.
- The price elasticity of demand for the monopolist depends on the number and similarity of substitutes. The more numerous and more similar the substitutes, the greater the price elasticity of demand of the monopolist's demand curve.

COSTS AND MONOPOLY PROFIT MAXIMIZATION

To find out the rate of output at which the perfect competitor would maximize profits, we had to add cost data. We will do the same thing now for the monopolist. We assume that profit maximization is the goal of the pure monopolist, just as for the perfect competitor. With the perfect competitor, however, we had only to decide on the profit-maximizing rate of output because price was given. The competitor is a price taker. For the pure monopolist we must seek a profit-maximizing *price-output combination* because the monopolist is a *price searcher.* We can determine this profit-maximizing price-output combination in either of two equivalent ways—by looking at total revenues and total costs or by looking at marginal revenues and marginal costs. We shall examine both approaches.

TOTAL REVENUES—TOTAL COSTS APPROACH

We show hypothetical demand (rate of output and price per unit), revenues, costs, and other data in panel (a) of Figure 24-3. In column 3 we see total revenues for our hypothetical monopolist, and in column 4 we see total costs. We can transfer these two columns to panel (b). The only difference between the total revenue and total cost diagram in panel (b) and the one we showed for a perfect competitor in Chapter 23 is that the total revenue line is no longer straight. Rather, it curves. For any given demand curve, in order to sell more, the monopolist must lower the price. The basic difference, therefore, between a monopolist and a perfect competitor has to do with the demand curve for the two types of firms. Thus, for clarity we assume that the costs for the perfect competitor and the pure monopolist are the same. Monopoly market power is derived from facing a downward-sloping demand curve.

FIGURE 24-3
Monopoly costs, revenues, and profits.

In panel (a) we give hypothetical demand (rate of output and price per unit), revenues, costs, and other relevant data. As shown in panel (b), the monopolist maximizes profits where the positive difference between TR and TC is greatest. This is at an output rate of between 9 and 10. Put another way, profit maximization occurs where marginal revenue equals marginal cost, as shown in panel (c). This is at an output rate of approximately 10. (The MC curve must cut the MR curve from below.)

Panel (a)

(1) OUTPUT (UNITS)	(2) PRICE PER UNIT	(3) TOTAL REVENUES (TR) (3) = (2) x (1)	(4) TOTAL COSTS (TC)	(5) TOTAL PROFIT (5) = (3) – (4)	(6) MARGINAL COST (MC)	(7) MARGINAL REVENUE (MR)
0	$8.00	$ 0	$10.00	-$10.00		
					$ 4.00	$7.80
1	7.80	7.80	14.00	-6.20		
					3.50	7.40
2	7.60	15.20	17.50	-2.30		
					3.25	7.00
3	7.40	22.20	20.75	1.45		
					3.05	6.60
4	7.20	28.80	23.80	5.00		
					2.90	6.20
5	7.00	35.00	26.70	8.30		
					2.80	5.80
6	6.80	40.80	29.50	11.30		
					2.75	5.40
7	6.60	46.20	32.25	13.95		
					2.85	5.00
8	6.40	51.20	35.10	16.10		
					3.20	4.60
9	6.20	55.80	38.30	17.50		
					4.00	4.20
10	6.00	60.00	42.30	17.70		
					6.00	3.80
11	5.80	63.80	48.30	15.50		
					9.00	3.40
12	5.60	67.20	57.30	9.90		
					13.00	3.00
13	5.40	70.20	70.30	-0.10		

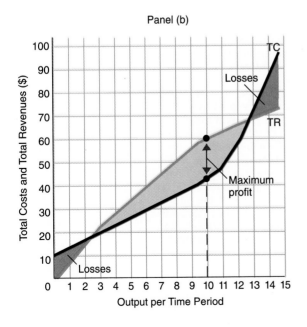

Panel (b)

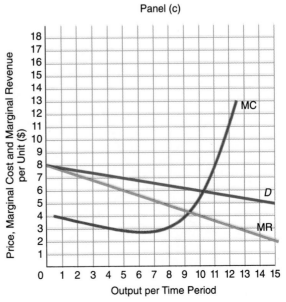

Panel (c)

Profit maximization involves maximizing the positive difference between total revenues and total costs. This occurs at an output rate of a little less than 10 units. We can also find this profit-maximizing rate of output by using the marginal revenue–marginal cost approach. The result will be the same.

MARGINAL REVENUE–MARGINAL COST APPROACH

Profit maximization will also occur where marginal revenue equals marginal cost. This is as true for a monopolist as it is for a perfect competitor (but the monopolist will charge a higher price). When we transfer marginal cost and marginal revenue information from columns 6 and 7 in panel (a) of Figure 24-3 to panel (c), we see that marginal revenue equals marginal cost at an output rate of a little less than 10 units. Profit maximization occurs at the same output as in panel (b).

Why Produce Where Marginal Revenue Equals Marginal Cost?   If the monopolist goes past the point where marginal revenue equals marginal cost (a little less than 10 units of output), marginal cost will exceed marginal revenue. That is, the incremental cost of producing any more units will exceed the incremental revenue. It just wouldn't be worthwhile, as was true also in perfect competition. But if the monopolist produces less than that, it is not making maximum profits. Look at output rate Q_1 in Figure 24-4. Here the monopolist's marginal revenue is at A, but marginal cost is at B. Marginal revenue exceeds marginal cost on the last unit sold; the profit for that *particular* unit, Q_1 is equal to the vertical difference between A and B, or the difference between marginal revenue and marginal cost. The monopolist would be foolish to stop at output rate Q_1 because if output is expanded, marginal revenue will still exceed marginal cost, and therefore total profits will rise. In fact, the profit-maximizing monopolist will continue to expand output and sales until marginal revenue equals marginal cost, which is at output rate Q_m. The monopolist won't produce at rate Q_2 because here, as we see, marginal costs are C and marginal revenues are F. The difference between C and F represents the reduction in total profits from producing that additional unit. Total profits will rise as the monopolist reduces its rate of output back toward Q_m.

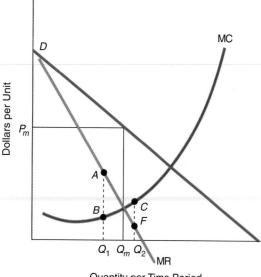

FIGURE 24-4
Maximizing profits.
The profit-maximizing production rate is Q_m, and the profit-maximizing price is P_m. The monopolist would be unwise to produce at the rate Q_1 because here marginal revenue would be Q_1A and marginal costs would be Q_1B. Marginal revenue exceeds marginal cost. The firm will keep producing until the point Q_m, where marginal revenue just equals marginal cost. It would be foolish to produce at the rate Q_2, for here marginal cost exceeds marginal revenue. It behooves the monopolist to cut production back to Q_m.

WHAT PRICE TO CHARGE FOR OUTPUT?

How does the monopolist set prices? We know the quantity is set at the point at which marginal revenue equals marginal cost. The monopolist then finds out how much can be charged—how much the market will bear—for that particular quantity, Q_m, in Figure 24-4. We know that the demand curve is defined as showing the *maximum* price for which a given quantity can be sold. That means that our monopolist knows that to sell Q_m, it can charge only P_m because that is the price at which that specific quantity, Q_m, is demanded. This price is found by drawing a vertical line from the quantity, Q_m, to the market demand curve. Where that line hits the market demand curve, the price is determined. We find that price by drawing a horizontal line from the demand curve over to the price axis; that gives us the profit-maximizing price, P_m.

In our detailed numerical example, at a profit-maximizing rate of output of a little less than 10 in Figure 24-3, the firm can charge a maximum price of almost $6 and still sell all the goods produced, all at the same price.

The basic procedure for finding the profit-maximizing short-run price-quantity combination for the monopolist is first to determine the profit-maximizing rate of output, by either the total revenue–total cost method or the marginal revenue–marginal cost method, and then to determine by use of the demand curve, D, the maximum price that can be charged to sell that output.

CALCULATING MONOPOLY PROFIT

We have talked about the monopolist's profit, but we have yet to indicate how much profit the monopolist makes. We have actually shown total profits in column 5 of panel (a) in Figure 24-3. We can also find total profits by adding an average total cost curve to panel (c) of that figure. We do that in Figure 24-5. When we add the average total cost curve, we find that the profit that a monopolist makes is equal to the shaded area. Given the

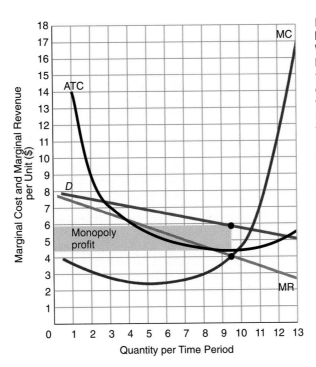

FIGURE 24-5
Monopoly profit.
We find monopoly profit by subtracting total costs from total revenues at an output rate of almost 10, which is the profit-maximizing rate of output for the monopolist. Monopoly profit is given by the shaded area. This diagram is similar to panel (c) of Figure 24-3, except that we have added the short-run average total cost curve (ATC).

demand curve and a uniform pricing system (i.e., all units sold at the same price), there is no way for a monopolist to make greater profits than those shown by the shaded area. The monopolist is maximizing profits where marginal cost equals marginal revenue. If the monopolist produces less than that, it will be forfeiting some profits. If the monopolist produces more than that, it will be forfeiting some profits.

The same is true of a perfect competitor. The competitor produces where marginal revenues equal marginal costs because it produces at the point where the marginal cost curve intersects the horizontal firm demand curve. The horizontal firm demand curve represents the marginal revenue curve for the pure competitor, for the same average revenues are obtained on all the units sold. Perfect competitors maximize profits at MR = MC, as do pure monopolists. But the perfect competitor makes no true economic profits in the long run; rather, all it makes is a normal, competitive rate of return.

NO GUARANTEE OF PROFITS

The term *monopoly* conjures up the notion of a greedy firm ripping off the public and making exorbitant profits. However, the mere existence of a monopoly does not guarantee high profits. Numerous monopolies have gone bankrupt. Figure 24-6 shows the monopolist's demand curve as *D* and the resultant marginal revenue curve as MR. It does not matter at what rate of output this particular monopolist operates; total costs cannot be covered. Look at the position of the average total cost curve. It lies everywhere above *D* (the average revenue curve). Thus there is no price-output combination that will allow the monopolist even to cover costs, much less earn profits. This monopolist will, in the short run, suffer economic losses as shown by the shaded area. The graph in Figure 24-6 depicts a situation for millions of typical monopolies that exist; they are called inventions. The owner of a patented invention or discovery has a pure legal monopoly, but the demand and cost curves may be such that production is not profitable. Every year at inventors' conventions one can see many inventions that have never been put into production because they were deemed "uneconomic" by potential producers and users.

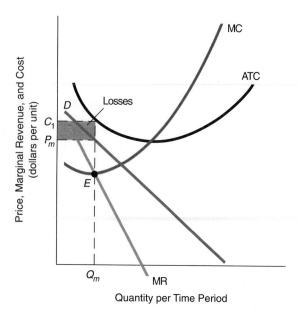

FIGURE 24-6

Monopolies: not always profitable.
Some monopolists face the situation shown here. The average total cost curve, ATC, is everywhere above the average revenue, or demand, curve, *D*. In the short run, the monopolist will produce where MC = MR at point *E*. Output Q_m will be sold at price P_m, but cost per unit is C_1. Losses are the shaded rectangle.

CONCEPTS IN BRIEF

- The basic difference between a monopolist and a perfect competitor is that a monopolist faces a downward-sloping demand curve, and therefore marginal revenue is less than price.
- The monopolist must choose the profit-maximizing price-output combination.
- It is found by choosing the output at which marginal revenue equals marginal cost and then charging the highest price possible as given by the demand curve for that particular output rate.
- Monopoly short-run profits are found by looking at average total costs compared to price per unit. This difference multiplied by quantity sold at that price determines monopoly profit.
- A monopolist does not necessarily earn a profit. If the average total cost curve lies entirely above the demand curve for a monopoly, production will not be profitable.

ON MAKING HIGHER PROFITS: PRICE DISCRIMINATION

In a perfectly competitive market, each buyer is charged the same price for every unit of the particular commodity (corrected for differential transportation charges). Because the product is homogeneous and we also assume full knowledge on the part of the buyers, a difference in price cannot exist. Any seller of the product who tried to charge a price higher than the going market price would find that no one would purchase it from that seller. In this chapter we have assumed until now that the monopolist charged all consumers the same price for all units. A monopolist, however, may be able to charge different people different prices or different unit prices for successive units sought by a given buyer. Either one or a combination of these strategies is called **price discrimination.** A firm will engage in price discrimination whenever feasible to increase profits. A price-discriminating firm is able to charge some customers, who want the product or service relatively very much, more than other customers, who do not want the product or service so much.

It must be made clear at the outset that charging different prices to different people or for different units that reflect differences in the cost of service to those particular people does not amount to price discrimination. This is **price differentiation:** differences in prices that reflect differences in marginal cost.

We can also say that a uniform price does not necessarily indicate an absence of price discrimination. Charging all customers the same price when production costs vary by customer is actually a case of price discrimination.

> ▶ **Price discrimination**
> Selling a given product at more than one price, with the price difference being unrelated to cost difference.

> ▶ **Price differentiation**
> Establishing different prices for similar products to reflect differences in marginal cost in providing those commodities to different groups of buyers.

NECESSARY CONDITIONS FOR PRICE DISCRIMINATION

There are four necessary conditions for the existence of price discrimination:

1. The firm must have some market power (that is, it must not be a price taker). It must face a downward-sloping demand curve.
2. The firm must be able to distinguish markets at a reasonable cost.
3. The buyers in the various markets must have different price elasticities of demand.
4. The firm must be able to prevent resale of the product or service.

For example, charging students a lower price than nonstudents for a movie can be done relatively easily. The cost of checking student IDs is apparently not significant. Also, it is fairly easy to make sure that students do not resell their tickets to nonstudents. Price discrimination for medical services is also easy. The resale value of a coronary bypass operation is zero.

 **INTERNATIONAL EXAMPLE: Price Discrimination with Japanese Computer Chips**

The Japanese have been accused of selling their semiconductors (computer chips) in U.S. markets at prices that are less than those charged domestically in Japan. We can analyze their activities as monopolistic price discrimination in a segmented market. In the Japanese domestic market, the producers are protected from outside competition by their government. In the U.S. market, they are not. Therefore, they face a relatively inelastic demand in Japan and a relatively elastic demand in the United States because of so much competition. Panel (a) of Figure 24-7 shows the relatively inelastic demand curve, D_J, that Japanese semiconductor producers face domestically. In the United States they face the relatively elastic demand curve D_{US}. For the sake of simplicity, marginal cost is assumed to be constant for Japanese semiconductor producers. At profit maximization, marginal revenue must equal marginal cost. Here we have common marginal costs, MC. There are two sets of marginal revenue curves, however—MR_J and MR_{US}. For profit maximization, $MR_J = MR_{US} = MC$. (In essence, it is as if the semiconductors sold in Japan and in the United States were two different goods having exactly the same marginal cost to produce.)

The market for semiconductors in Japan is given in panel (a) of Figure 24-7, and we see that marginal cost equals marginal revenue at quantity Q_J. The price at which this quantity can be sold is P_J. Buyers of Japanese semiconductors in the United States will

FIGURE 24-7
Price discrimination in semiconductors by the Japanese.
The Japanese semiconductor industry is protected from foreign competition and therefore faces a relatively inelastic demand curve, D_J, in panel (a). In the United States, as shown in panel (b), the industry faces competition such that its demand curve, D_{US}, is more elastic. Profit maximization occurs in each market where MC = MR. In Japan that is at Q_J, at which point semiconductors can be sold at a price of P_J. In the United States profit maximization occurs at Q_{US}, at which point semiconductors can be sold at a price of P_{US}. Prices charged in Japan for the same semiconductor are higher than prices charged in the United States.

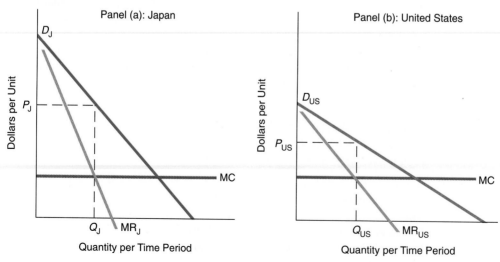

have more elastic demand because of the competition here and will end up paying only P_{US} for quantity Q_{US}. P_{US} is lower than P_J. The price-discriminating semiconductor industry in Japan sells the same product locally at higher prices, because of domestic protection against foreign competition, than it does internationally, where there is no protection for its output.

For Critical Analysis: *Would the Japanese engage in price discrimination if the Japanese domestic demand curve for semiconductors were identical to the U.S. demand curve for semiconductors?* ●

THE SOCIAL COST OF MONOPOLIES

Let's run a little experiment. We will start with a purely competitive industry with numerous firms, each one unable to affect the price of its product. The supply curve of the industry is equal to the horizontal sum of the marginal cost curves of the individual producers above their respective minimum average variable costs. In panel (a) of Figure 24-8 we show the market demand curve and the market supply curve in a perfectly competitive situation. The competitive price in equilibrium is equal to P_e, and the equilibrium quantity at that price is equal to Q_e. Each individual competitor faces a demand curve (not shown) that is coincident with the price line P_e. No individual supplier faces the market demand curve, D.

FIGURE 24-8
The effects of monopolizing an industry.
In panel (a) we show a competitive situation in which equilibrium is established at the intersection of D and S at point E. The equilibrium price would be P_e, and the equilibrium quantity would be Q_e. Each individual competitive producer faces a demand curve that is a horizontal line at the market clearing price, P_e. What happens if the industry is suddenly monopolized? We assume that the costs stay the same; the only thing that changes is that the monopolist now faces the entire downward-sloping demand curve. In panel (b) we draw the marginal revenue curve. Marginal cost is S because that is the horizontal summation of all the individual marginal cost curves. The monopolist therefore produces at Q_m and charges price P_m. P_m in panel (b) is higher than P_e in panel (a), and Q_m is less than Q_e. We see, then, that a monopolist charges a higher price and produces less than an industry in a competitive situation.

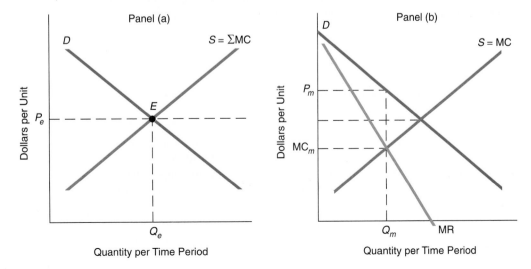

Now let's assume that a monopolist comes in and buys up every single competitor in the industry. In so doing, we'll assume that the monopolist does not affect any of the marginal cost curves or demand. We can therefore redraw D and S in panel (b) of Figure 24-8, exactly the same as in panel (a).

How does this monopolist decide how much to charge and how much to produce? If the monopolist is profit-maximizing, it is going to look at the marginal revenue curve and produce at the output where marginal revenue equals marginal cost. But what is the marginal cost curve in panel (b) of Figure 24-8? It is merely S because we said that S was equal to the horizontal summation of the portions of the individual marginal cost curves above each firm's respective minimum average variable cost. The monopolist therefore produces quantity Q_m and sells it at price P_m. Notice that Q_m is less than Q_e and P_m is greater than P_e. A monopolist therefore produces a smaller quantity and sells it at a higher price. This is the reason usually given when economists criticize monopolists. Monopolists raise the price and restrict production, compared to a competitive situation. For a monopolist's product, consumers are forced to pay a price that exceeds the marginal cost of production. Resources are misallocated in such a situation—too few resources are being used in the monopolist's industry, and too many are used elsewhere.

Notice from Figure 24-8 that by setting $MR = MC$, the monopolist produces at a rate of output where $P > MC$ (compare P_m to MC_m). The marginal cost of a commodity (MC) represents what society had to give up in order to obtain the last unit produced. Price, by contrast, represents what buyers are willing to pay to acquire that last unit. Thus the price of a good represents society's valuation of the last unit produced. The monopoly outcome of $P > MC$ means that the value to society of the last unit produced is greater than its cost (MC); hence not enough of the good is being produced. As we have pointed out before, these differences between monopoly and competition arise not because of differences in costs but rather because of differences in the demand curves the individual firms face. The monopolist has monopoly power because it faces a downward-sloping demand curve. The individual perfect competitor does not have any market power.

Before we leave the topic of the cost to society of monopolies, we must repeat that our analysis is based on a heroic assumption. That assumption is that the monopolization of the perfectly competitive industry does not change the cost structure. If monopolization results in higher marginal cost, the cost to society is even greater. Conversely, if monopolization results in cost savings, the cost, if any, to society is less than we infer from our analysis. Indeed, we could have presented a hypothetical example in which monopolization led to such a dramatic reduction in average cost that society actually benefited. Such a situation is a possibility in industries in which economies of scale exist for a very great range of outputs.

MONOPOLY RENT SEEKING

The existence of monopolies may give rise to additional costs in terms of resource misallocation. One involves the resources used by individuals in order to obtain and maintain monopoly.

There are potentially large profits to be captured when one obtains a monopoly. We would expect, therefore, that individuals will expend resources to capture such profits. Indeed, an army of lawyers, business executives, and expert witnesses crowd the halls of Congress and the courtrooms, attempting to obtain government-bestowed monopolies, trying to prevent competition when a monopoly already exists, and engaging in various other endeavors that allow them to control a source of monopoly profits. Put yourself in the place of a monopolist who has been given monopoly power through some act of Congress. Let's say that you are making monopoly profits—profits over and above what you would make in a competitive industry—of $1 million per year. Wouldn't you be willing to spend a quarter of that million dollars a year on a lobbying effort to make sure that Congress does not change the law to allow competition in your industry? Indeed, you might spend considerably more than that to protect your $1 million annual monopoly profit. From a use-of-resources point of view, the resources that you spend in protecting your monopoly do not yield any true social product.

Economist Gordon Tullock likened this activity to theft. A thief may steal $10,000 a year. This is a transfer from the victims to the thief. There are costs involved in theft, however. Thieves invest effort, time, and other resources. In addition, victims must invest resources to protect themselves from theft. From the viewpoint of society as a whole, both of these costs are wasted. Tullock argues that monopoly can be analyzed similarly. From a social point of view, monopolists waste various resources attempting to establish and maintain monopoly profits. Society ends up expending resources preventing monopolies or trying to break them up.

> **Monopoly rent seeking**
> The resources used in an attempt to create and maintain monopolies in order to earn monopoly profits.

In the economics profession, this additional cost of monopoly has been inelegantly labeled **monopoly rent seeking,** which is defined as the resources used in the attempt to establish and maintain monopolies in order to earn monopoly profits. The term *rent* as it is used here will be explained in more detail in Chapter 30. Briefly, it is not like the rent you pay on an apartment. Rather, it is an economic reward in excess of what is necessary to keep productive resources in a particular economic activity. So monopoly rent can be defined as the excess profit that a monopolist makes over and above what would be made in a perfectly competitive situation.

CONCEPTS IN BRIEF

- There are four necessary conditions for price discrimination: (1) The firm must have some market power, (2) the firm must be able to distinguish markets, (3) buyers in different markets must have different price elasticities of demand, and (4) resale of the product or service must be preventable.
- A monopolist can make higher profits if it can price-discriminate. Price discrimination requires that two or more identifiable classes of buyers exist whose price elasticities of demand for the product or service are different and that these two classes of buyers can be distinguished at little cost.
- Price differentiation should not be confused with price discrimination. The former occurs when there are differences in prices that reflect differences in marginal cost.
- Monopoly results in a lower quantity being sold because the price is higher than it would be in an ideal perfectly competitive industry in which the cost curves are essentially the same as the monopolist's.
- Monopoly creates a situation in which resources are spent to obtain and maintain monopoly status. These resources constitute what has been called monopoly rent seeking. From society's point of view, this is wasteful.

CONTINUED ➡

CAVIAR FOR THE PEOPLE
Concepts Applied: Monopoly, barriers to entry

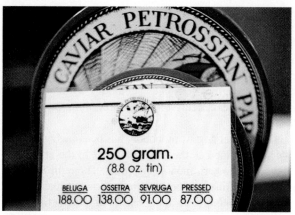

Before the demise of the Soviet Union, the supply of top-grade caviar from that part of the world was strictly controlled by the central government. Today there is much less control, more competition, and consequently lower prices to the consumer.

They say that caviar is an acquired taste. Certainly enough well-to-do people have acquired the taste for it to be selling at $400 per 14-ounce container in New York City in 1990. The relative price of fresh caviar from the former Soviet Union had stayed about the same for the previous 60 years. The only way that could have happened is for a monopoly to have been well protected, and that is indeed what had occurred.

BEFORE THE FALL OF COMMUNISM After the Bolshevik revolution in 1917, the entire process of harvesting, processing, packaging, and exporting Russian caviar was under the control of the Soviet Ministry of Fisheries. Actually, a small group of Western partners worked with a small group (formed a monopoly) from this ministry. The most important Western partner was the Paris-based Petrossian Company. So even though

some 2,000 tons of caviar were produced per year in the Soviet Union, only about 150 tons were available for export. Total American consumption was about 40 tons a year in the 1980s. During this time period, a kilogram of top-grade black caviar cost the equivalent of about $200 in Moscow. In New York City the same quantity of caviar went for about $2,000.

COMPETITION REARS ITS UGLY HEAD
Once the Soviet Union ceased to exist, it was virtually impossible for government officials to control all exports of caviar. Moreover, different former Soviet republics claimed jurisdiction over different parts of the Soviet fishing fleet. Kazakhstan took control of one fishery. Russia claimed another. And countless Caspian Sea fishermen set up their own export businesses. Numerous additional Western partners have been approached by Russians and others from the former Soviet Union who want to set up joint ventures. California Sunshine, out of San Francisco, started a business with a group of Russians who are now producing caviar not from the Caspian Sea but from eastern Russia. It is called Tsar Nicouli. In addition, many tourists from Russia and the other republics who go to France, Germany, and the United States bring tins of caviar with them. Some of them have actually ended up supplying small purveyors of caviar in these countries.

THE END RESULT The end result is, of course, lower prices. Export caviar prices dropped by 20 percent the first year after the Soviet breakup and have dropped consistently since then.

FOR CRITICAL ANALYSIS
1. Why was there no competition prior to the 1990s in the Russian caviar market?
2. What impediments are there to creating a monopoly in the caviar market today?

CHAPTER SUMMARY
1. We formally define a monopolist as a single supplier. A monopolist faces the entire industry demand curve because the monopolist *is* the industry. Pure monopolists are rare. In most cases a government franchise to operate permits them to remain pure monopolists.
2. A monopolist can usually remain a monopolist only if other firms are prevented from entering the industry and sharing in the monopoly profits. One bar-

rier to entry is government restrictions. Patents are another.

3. A monopoly could arise because of firm economies of scale, which are defined as a situation in which an increase in output leads to a more than proportionate decrease in average total costs. If this were the case, average total costs would be falling as production increased. The first company to produce a great deal and take advantage of firm economies of scale could conceivably lower price and drive everyone else out of the industry. This would be a natural monopolist.

4. Health and quality regulations can be a barrier to entry because the increased fixed costs put smaller firms at a competitive disadvantage.

5. The marginal revenue that a monopolist receives is defined in the same way as the marginal revenue that a competitor receives, with one difference: Because the monopolist faces the industry demand curve, it must lower price to increase sales, not only on the last unit sold but also on all the preceding units. The monopolist's marginal revenue is therefore equal to the price received on the last unit sold minus the reduction in price on all the previous units times the number of previous units sold.

6. The profit-maximizing price that the monopolist charges is the maximum price that it can get away with while still selling everything produced up to the point where marginal revenue equals marginal cost. We find this price by extending a vertical line from the intersection of the marginal revenue curve and the marginal cost curve up to the demand curve and then over to the vertical axis, which measures price.

7. Total profits are total revenues minus total costs. Total revenues are equal to the price of the product (the profit-maximizing price) times the quantity produced (the quantity found at the intersection of the marginal revenue and marginal cost curves). Total costs are equal to the quantity produced times average total costs. The difference between these total costs and total revenues is profits.

8. It can be shown that a competitive industry, if monopolized, will end up charging a higher price for its product but supplying a lower quantity of it. That is why monopolies are considered "bad" in an economic analysis. The monopolist will restrict production and increase price.

9. If a monopolist can effectively separate demanders into groups according to their demand elasticities, it can become a price-discriminating monopolist. (Resale between groups that were charged different prices must be prevented.) Price discrimination should not be confused with price differentiation, which occurs when differences in price reflect differences in marginal cost.

10. There are four necessary conditions for price discrimination to exist: (1) The firm must have market power, (2) the firm must be able to distinguish markets, (3) buyers in different markets must have different price elasticities of demand, and (4) the firm must be able to prevent resale of the product.

11. Monopoly involves costs to society because the higher price leads to a reduction in output and consumption of the monopolized good. Also, a monopolist will expend resources to obtain and maintain a monopoly situation. This is called rent seeking.

DISCUSSION OF PREVIEW POINTS

1. For the monopolist, marginal revenue is less than selling price. Why?

In the perfectly competitive model, the firm's selling price equals its marginal revenue (MR) because the firm can sell all it wants to sell at the going market price. This is not the case for the monopolist, which, as the sole supplier, faces the (downward-sloping) demand curve for the product. Thus the monopolist can sell more only by lowering price on all units sold per time period, assuming that it can't discriminate on price. Thus the monopolist's marginal revenue will equal price (which it gains from selling one more unit) *minus* the revenue that it loses from selling previously produced units at a lower price.

2. What is the profit-maximizing rate of output for the monopolist?

A monopolist will produce up to the point where marginal cost (MC) equals marginal revenue (MR). For example, if the output rate for the monopolist at which MR = MC is 80,000 units per week, and MR is falling while MC is rising, any output beyond 80,000 units will have MC > MR; to produce units beyond 80,000 units will lower total profits. To produce at a rate less than 80,000 units per week would mean that not all the outputs at which MR > MC will be produced; hence total profits would not be maximized. Total profits are maximized at the output rate where MR = MC because all outputs for which MR > MC will be produced.

3. What are some common misconceptions about monopolists?

Many people think that a monopolist charges the highest price possible. This is untrue; the monopolist tries to maximize *total profits,* not price. The monopolist produces where MR = MC and *then* charges the highest price consistent with that output rate. Note that a monopolist can't charge any price *and* sell any amount; it must choose a price and have the amount that it can sell be determined by the demand curve, or it must choose an output rate (where MR = MC) and have selling price determined by where that quantity intersects the demand curve. Another common misconception is that a monopolist must earn economic profits. This is not the case. To take an extreme example, if the monopolist's average cost curve lies above the demand curve, the monopolist will be suffering economic losses.

4. What is the cost to society of monopoly?

Because barriers to entry exist under monopoly, a monopolist could theoretically earn economic profits in the long run. Because profits are a signal that society wants more resources in that area, a misallocation of resources could exist; not enough resources flow to production of the monopolized commodity. Also, because the monopolist's selling price (P) exceeds its marginal revenue (MR) and the profit-maximizing output rate is where MR = MC (marginal cost), P > MR = MC, or simply P > MC (unlike under the perfectly competitive market structure, where P = MC). The marginal cost of the commodity reflects what society had to give up in order to get the last unit produced, and price is what buyers have to pay in order to get it. Because P > MC under monopoly, buyers must pay *more* to get this commodity than they must give up in order to get it; hence not enough of this commodity is produced. In short, under monopoly, price is higher and output is less than under perfect competition.

PROBLEMS

(Answers to the odd-numbered problems appear at the back of the book.)

24-1.   Use the graph below to answer the questions.

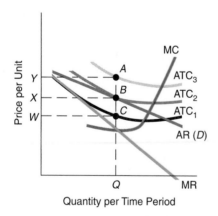

a. Suppose that a monopolist faces ATC_1. Define the rectangle that shows the monopolist's total costs at output rate Q. Also define the rectangle showing total revenue. Is the monopolist showing an economic loss, a break-even (normal profit), or an economic profit? What is the significance of the MC = MR output?

b. Suppose that the monopolist faces ATC_2. Define the rectangle that shows the monopolist's total costs. Also define the rectangle showing total revenue. Is the monopolist showing an economic loss, a break-even (normal profit), or an economic profit? What is the significance of the MC = MR output?

c. Suppose that the monopolist faces ATC_3. Define the rectangle that shows the monopolist's total costs. Also define the rectangle showing total revenue. Is the monopolist showing an economic loss, a break-even (normal profit), or an economic profit? What is the significance of the MC = MR output?

24-2.   Suppose that a monopolist faces the following demand schedule. Compute marginal revenue.

PRICE	QUANTITY DEMANDED	MARGINAL REVENUE
$1,000	1	$___
920	2	___
840	3	___
760	4	___
680	5	___
600	6	___
520	7	___
440	8	___
350	9	___
260	10	___

PRICE	QUANTITY DEMANDED	TOTAL REVENUE	MARGINAL REVENUE	TOTAL COST	MARGINAL COST	PROFIT OR LOSS
$20	0	$ ____	$ ____	$ 4	$ ____	$ ____
16	1	____	____	10	____	____
12	2	____	____	14	____	____
10	3	____	____	20	____	____
7	4	____	____	28	____	____
4	5	____	____	40	____	____
0	6	____	____	54	____	____

24-3. State the necessary conditions for price discrimination. Then discuss how they might apply to the medical services of a physician.

24-4. In the text we indicated that a monopolist will produce at the rate of output at which MR = MC and will then charge the highest price consistent with that output level. What conditions would exist if the monopolist charged a lower price? A higher price?

24-5. Summarize the relationship between price elasticity of demand and marginal revenue.

24-6. Explain why a monopolist will never set a price (and produce the corresponding output) at which the demand is price-inelastic.

24-7. Examine these revenue and cost figures for a monopoly firm in the table at the top of the page.
   a. Fill in the empty columns.
   b. At what rate(s) of output would the firm operate at a loss?
   c. At what rate(s) of output would the firm break even?
   d. At what rate(s) of output would the firm be maximizing its profits, and what would those profits be?

24-8. Answer the questions based on the accompanying graph for a monopolist.

a. If this firm is a profit maximizer, how much output will it produce?
b. At what price will the firm sell its output?
c. How much profit or loss will this firm realize?
d. ATC is at its minimum at what cost per unit?

24-9. Examine this information for a monopoly product.
   a. Calculate total revenue.
   b. Calculate marginal revenue.
   c. What is the maximum output that the producer of this product would ever produce?
   d. Why would this firm never produce more than the output amount in part (c)?

PRICE	QUANTITY
$10.0	1,000
8.0	2,000
6.0	3,000
4.0	4,000
2.0	5,000
.5	6,000

24-10. Suppose that a single-price monopolist and a comparable perfectly competitive industry experience a cost increase that causes average and marginal cost curves to shift upward by 10 percent. Will the resulting increase in market price be greater or less for the monopolist than for the perfectly competitive industry?

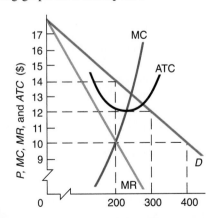

25

STRATEGIC COMPETITION AND OLIGOPOLY

The best of all possible worlds for powerful competitors is to join together and act as one big monopoly, known as a cartel. That is exactly what many major oil-producing countries did in 1960. The result was the Organization of Petroleum Exporting Countries (OPEC). World oil markets have not been the same since. The price of oil started its upward spiral in the 1970s. But something happened to oil prices' trip to the moon; in the 1980s they actually fell. What happened to the seemingly all-powerful OPEC cartel? At issue here is an understanding of the strategies taken by different participants in a particular market. This is all part of the topic of strategic competition.

After reading this chapter, you should be able to answer the following questions:

1. What are the characteristics of the monopolistically competitive market structure?

2. How does the monopolistic competitor determine the equilibrium price-output combination?

3. How does the monopolistically competitive market structure differ from that of perfect competition?

4. What are the characteristics of the oligopolistic market structure?

INTRODUCTION

When you decide to buy a car, your choices are many. You can buy from a domestic man-ufacturer or foreign one. Within each company there are numerous models, and within each model there are different colors, styles, and amenities. When you go to buy break-fast cereal, your choices are not quite as numerous, but they certainly do not seem very restrictive. As a consumer, you typically have lots of choices for whatever you want to buy. That means that normally you do not face a pure monopoly situation such as you do when you mail a first-class letter; nor, however, do you face a perfectly competitive situa-tion that, by assumption, involves a homogeneous product, such as wheat of a particu-lar grade. A combination of consumers' preferences for variety and competition among producers has led to similar but *differentiated* products in the marketplace. This situation has been described as *monopolistic competition,* the subject of the first part of this chap-ter. In the second part of the chapter we look at how firms that are neither perfect com-petitors nor pure monopolists make strategic decisions. Such decisions do not exist for pure monopolists, who do not have to worry about actual competitors. And clearly, per-fect competitors cannot make any strategic decisions, for they must take the market price as given. We call firms that have the ability to make strategic decisions *oligopolies,* which we will define more formally later in this chapter.

MONOPOLISTIC COMPETITION

In the 1920s and 1930s economists became increasingly aware that there were many in-dustries for which both the perfectly competitive model and the pure monopoly model did not apply and did not seem to yield very accurate predictions. Theoretical and empirical research was instituted to develop some sort of middle ground. Two separately developed models of **monopolistic competition** resulted. At Harvard, Edward Chamberlin published *The Theory of Monopolistic Competition* in 1933. The same year, Britain's Joan Robin-son published *The Economics of Imperfect Competition.* In this chapter we will outline the theory as presented by Chamberlin.

▶ **Monopolistic competition**
A market situation in which a large number of firms pro-duce similar but not identical products. There is relatively easy entry into the industry.

Chamberlin defined monopolistic competition as a market structure in which there was a relatively large number of producers offering similar but differentiated products. Mo-nopolistic competition therefore has the following features:

1. Significant numbers of sellers in a highly competitive market
2. Differentiated products
3. Sales promotion and advertising
4. Easy entry of new firms in the long run

NUMBER OF FIRMS

In a perfectly competitive situation, there is an extremely large number of firms; in pure monopoly, there is only one. In monopolistic competition, there is a large number of firms, but not as many as in perfect competition. This fact has several important implications for a monopolistically competitive industry.

1. **Small share of market.** With so many firms, each firm has a relatively small share of the total market. Thus it has only a very small amount of control over the market clear-ing price.
2. **Lack of collusion.** With so many firms, it is very difficult for all of them to get to-gether to collude—to cooperate in setting a pure monopoly price (and output). Price rigging in a monopolistically competitive industry is virtually impossible. Also, barri-ers to entry are minor, and the flow of new firms into the industry makes collusive

agreements less likely. The large number of firms makes the monitoring and detection of cheating very costly and extremely difficult. This difficulty is compounded by differentiated products and high rates of innovation; collusive agreements are easier for a homogeneous product than for heterogeneous ones.

3. **Independence.** Because there are so many firms, each one acts independently of the others. No firm attempts to take into account the reaction of all of its rival firms—that would be impossible with so many rivals. Rivals' reactions to output and price changes are largely ignored.

PRODUCT DIFFERENTIATION

Perhaps the most important feature of the monopolistically competitive market is **product differentiation.** We can say that each individual manufacturer of a product has an absolute monopoly over its own product, which is slightly differentiated from other similar products. This means that the firm has some control over the price it charges. Unlike the perfectly competitive firm, it faces a downward-sloping demand curve.

▶ **Product differentiation**
The distinguishing of products by brand name, color, minor attributes, and the like. Product differentiation occurs in other than perfectly competitive markets in which products are, in theory, homogeneous, such as wheat or corn.

Consider the abundance of brand names for such things as toothpaste, soap, gasoline, vitamins, and shampoo. Indeed, it appears that product differentiation characterizes most, if not all, American markets for consumer goods and services. We are not obliged to buy just one type of television set, just one type of jeans, or just one type of footwear. There are usually a number of similar but differentiated products from which to choose. One reason is that the greater a firm's success at product differentiation, the greater the firm's pricing (market) power.

Each separate differentiated product has numerous similar substitutes. This clearly has an impact on the price elasticity of demand for the individual firm. Recall from our discussion of price elasticity of demand that one determinant was the availability of substitutes. *The greater the number of substitutes available, other things being equal, the greater the price elasticity of demand.* If the consumer has a vast array of alternatives that are just about as good as the product under study, a relatively small increase in the price of that product will lead many consumers to switch to one of the many close substitutes. Thus the ability of a firm to raise the price above the price of *close* substitutes is very small. The result of this is that even though the demand curve slopes downward, it does so only slightly. In other words, it is relatively elastic or relatively flat compared to a monopolist's demand curve *at any given price.* In the extreme case, with perfect competition, the substitutes are perfect because we are dealing with only one particular undifferentiated product. In that case, the individual firm has a horizontal, or perfectly elastic, demand curve.

EASE OF ENTRY

For any current monopolistic competitor, potential competition is always lurking in the background. The easier—that is, the less costly—entry is, the more a current monopolistic competitor must worry about losing business.

A good example of a monopolistically competitive industry is the computer software industry. Many small firms provide different programs for many applications. The fixed capital costs required to enter this industry are small; all you need are skilled programmers. In addition, there are few legal restrictions. The firms in this industry also engage in extensive advertising in over 150 computer publications.

SALES PROMOTION AND ADVERTISING

Monopolistic competition differs from perfect competition in that no individual firm in a perfectly competitive market will advertise. A perfectly competitive firm, by definition, can sell all that it wants to sell at the going market price anyway. Why, then, would it ever spend even one penny on advertising? Furthermore, by definition, the perfect competitor is selling a product that is identical to the product that all other firms in the industry are selling. Any advertisement that induces consumers to buy more of that product will, in effect, be helping all the competitors, too. We would therefore not expect the perfect competitor to incur any advertising costs except for industry advertising, such as "buy more beef" or "drink more milk."

But because the monopolistic competitor has at least *some* monopoly power, advertising may result in increased profits. How much advertising should be undertaken? It should be carried to the point at which the additional revenue from one more dollar of advertising just equals that one dollar of marginal cost.

Shifting the Demand Curve

Shifting the Demand Curve The goal of advertising is to shift the demand curve to the right by influencing consumer tastes. Another goal may be to make the demand curve more inelastic by further differentiating the product so as to encourage "brand loyalty." In any event, advertising, it is hoped, will lead to a larger volume of business that more than covers the cost of advertising.

It is conceivable, however, that advertising is necessary just to keep the demand curve stable. Without advertising, the demand curve might shift inward to the left. This is presumably the case with so-called competitive advertising. For example, soap manufacturers may have to make large outlays in advertising just to keep the share of the market they now have. If they drop their advertising, they will lose ground to all the other companies that are engaged in extensive advertising.

Advertising of course, has other purposes. In particular, there is a large informational content to much advertising. A certain amount of advertising provides useful information that the consumer could gather only with considerable time and effort in the absence of advertising. Many ads presented by local retail firms through direct mail, radio, TV, and newspapers are of this type.

⭐ EXAMPLE: Coke's Effective Advertising Campaign

The Coca-Cola Company has used "The Real Thing" as its advertising motto for over 100 years. Coca-Cola continues to engage in extensive advertising. The biggest ad campaign it ever conducted occurred in the mid-1980s when it introduced New Coke. Management had determined in the early 1980s that it needed to compete more directly with Pepsi, which had a sweeter flavor than Coca-Cola. So it developed a new formula for the soft drink and dubbed it New Coke. Within 48 hours after its announcement of the new product, 80 percent of the American public was aware of Coca-Cola's formula change. (This is a higher percentage than those who were aware within 48 hours that an American had walked on the moon.) But heavy advertising of a new product does not guarantee success, as the Coca-Cola Company found out. Reaction to New Coke was at best lukewarm, at worst disastrous. Two months after its introduction, Coca-Cola was forced to bring back "Classic Coke." The Coca-Cola Company found out that over 100 years of advertising its brand name as "The Real Thing" was significant: Consumers truly did want the "real thing." How much did the New Coke fiasco cost the shareholders in Coca-Cola? One estimate is as high as $500 million dollars. That is the permanent reduction in the value of the company's shares that occurred after the introduction of New Coke.

For Critical Analysis: *The largest-selling American beer is Budweiser, produced by Anheuser-Busch. Anheuser-Busch has marketed many new brands of beer, such as Michelob, through the years. How has Anheuser-Busch's new-product strategy differed from the Coca-Cola Company's strategy when it introduced New Coke?* ●

CONCEPTS IN BRIEF

- Monopolistic competition is a market structure that lies between pure monopoly and perfect competition.
- A monopolistically competitive market structure has (1) a large number of sellers, (2) differentiated products, (3) advertising, and (4) easy entry of firms in the long run.
- Because of the large number of firms, each has a small share of the market, making collusion difficult; the firms are independent.
- The goal of advertising is to shift the demand curve outward to the right.

PRICE AND OUTPUT FOR THE MONOPOLISTIC COMPETITOR

Now that we are aware of the assumptions underlying the monopolistic competition model, we can analyze the price and output behavior of each firm in a monopolistically competitive industry. We assume in the analysis that follows that the desired product type and quality have been chosen. We further assume that the budget and the type of promotional activity have already been chosen and do not change.

THE INDIVIDUAL FIRM'S DEMAND AND COST CURVES

Because the individual firm is not a perfect competitor, its demand curve slopes downward, as is shown in all three panels of Figure 25-1. Hence it faces a marginal revenue curve that is also downward-sloping and below the demand curve. To find the profit-maximizing rate of output and the profit-maximizing price, we go to the output where the marginal cost curve intersects the marginal revenue curve from below. That gives us the profit-maximizing output rate. Then we draw a vertical line up to the demand curve. That gives us the price that can be charged to sell exactly that quantity produced. This is what we have done in Figure 25-1. In each panel, a marginal cost curve has been drawn in. It intersects the marginal revenue curve at E. The profit-maximizing rate of output is q_e, and the profit-maximizing price is P.

THE SHORT RUN: EQUILIBRIUM

In the short run, it is possible for a monopolistic competitor to make economic profits—profits over and above the normal rate of return or beyond what is necessary to keep that firm in that industry. In panel (a) of Figure 25-1 we show such a situation. The average total cost curve is drawn in below the demand curve d at the profit-maximizing rate of output q_e. Economic profits are shown by the shaded rectangle in that panel.

Losses in the short run are clearly also possible. They are presented in panel (b) of Figure 25-1. Here the average total cost curve lies everywhere above the individual firm's demand curve d. The losses are marked as the shaded rectangle.

Just as with any market structure or any firm, in the short run it is possible to observe either economic profits or economic losses. (In the long run such is not the case with monopolistic competition, however.) In either case the price does not equal marginal cost but rather is above it. Therefore, there is some misallocation of resources, a topic that we will discuss later in this chapter.

FIGURE 25-1

Short-run and long-run equilibrium with monopolistic competition.
In panel (a) the typical monopolistic competitor is shown making economic profits. If that were the situation, there would be entry into the industry, forcing the demand curve for the individual monopolistic competitor leftward. Eventually firms would find themselves in the situation depicted in panel (c), where zero economic profits are being made. In panel (b) the typical firm is in a monopolistically competitive industry making economic losses. If that were the case, firms would leave the industry. Each individual firm's demand curve would shift outward to the right. Eventually the industry's average firm would find itself in the situation depicted in panel (c).

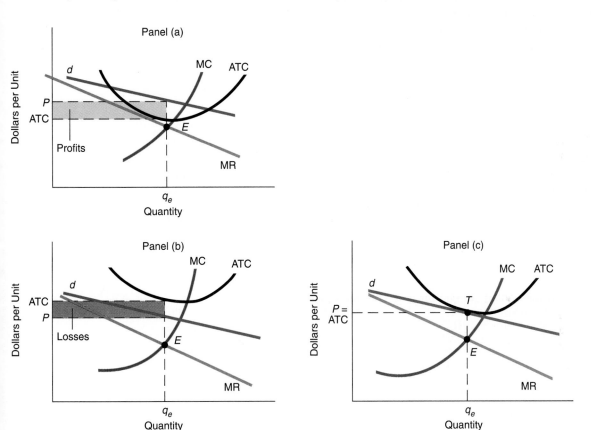

THE LONG RUN: ZERO ECONOMIC PROFITS

The long run is where the similarity between perfect competition and monopolistic competition becomes more obvious. In the long run, because so many firms produce substitutes for the product in question, any economic profits will disappear with competition. They will be reduced to zero either through entry by new firms seeing a chance to make a higher rate of return than elsewhere or by changes in product quality and advertising outlays by existing firms in the industry. (Profitable products will be imitated by other firms.) As for economic losses in the short run, they will disappear in the long run because the firms that suffer them will leave the industry. They will go into another business where the expected rate of return is at least normal. Panels (a) and (b) of Figure 25-1 therefore represent only short-run situations for a monopolistically competitive firm.

In the long run the average total cost curve will just touch the individual firm's demand curve *d* at the particular price that is profit-maximizing for that particular firm. This is shown in panel (c) of Figure 25-1.

A word of warning: This is an idealized, long-run equilibrium situation for each firm in the industry. It does not mean that even in the long run we will observe every single firm in a monopolistically competitive industry making *exactly* zero economic profits or *just* a normal rate of return. We live in a dynamic world. All we are saying is that if this model is correct, the rate of return will *tend toward* normal—economic profits will tend toward zero. Firms that can differentiate (the monopoly element in monopolistic competition) can maintain a profitable position in the industry.

COMPARING PERFECT COMPETITION WITH MONOPOLISTIC COMPETITION

If both the monopolistic competitor and the perfect competitor make zero economic profits in the long run, how are they different? The answer lies in the fact that the demand curve for the individual perfect competitor is horizontal—the perfect competitor's price elasticity of demand is infinite. Such is not the case for the individual monopolistic competitor. Its demand curve is less than perfectly elastic. This firm has some control over price; it has some market power. Price elasticity of demand is not infinite.

We see the two situations in Figure 25-2. Both panels show average total costs just touching the respective demand curves at the particular price at which the firm is selling

FIGURE 25-2

Comparison of the perfect competitor with the monopolistic competitor.
In panel (a) the perfectly competitive firm has zero economic profits in the long run. The price is set equal to marginal cost, and the price is P_1. The firm's demand curve is just tangent to the minimum point on its average total cost curve, which means that the firm is operating at an optimum rate of production. With the monopolistically competitive firm in panel (b), there are also zero economic profits in the long run. The price is greater than marginal cost; the monopolistically competitive firm does not find itself at the minimum point on its average total cost curve. It is operating at a rate of output to the left of the minimum point on the ATC curve.

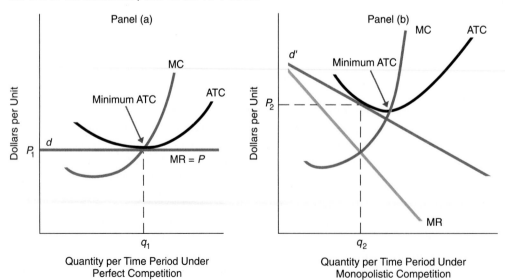

the product. Notice, however, that the perfect competitor's average total costs are at a minimum. This is not the case with the monopolistic competitor. The equilibrium rate of output is to the left of the minimum point on the average total cost curve where price is greater than marginal cost. The monopolistic competitor cannot expand output to the point of minimum costs without lowering price, and then marginal cost would exceed marginal revenue. A monopolistic competitor at profit maximization charges a price that exceeds marginal cost. In this respect it is similar to the monopolist.

It has consequently been argued that monopolistic competition involves waste because minimum average total costs are not achieved and price exceeds marginal cost. There are too many firms, each with excess capacity, producing too little output. According to critics of monopolistic competition, society's resources are being wasted.

Chamberlin had an answer to this criticism. He contended that the difference between the average cost of production for a monopolistically competitive firm in an open market and the minimum average total cost represented what he called the cost of producing "differentness." Chamberlin did not consider this difference in cost between perfect competition and monopolistic competition a waste. In fact, he argued that it is rational for consumers to have a taste for differentiation; consumers willingly accept the resultant increased production costs in return for choice and variety of output.

CONCEPTS IN BRIEF

- In the short run it is possible for monopolistically competitive firms to make economic profits or economic losses.
- In the long run monopolistically competitive firms will make zero economic profits—that is, they will make a normal rate of return.
- Because the monopolistic competitor faces a downward-sloping demand curve, it does not produce at the minimum point on its average total cost curve. Hence we say that a monopolistic competitor has higher average total costs per unit than a perfect competitor would have.
- Chamberlin argued that the difference between the average costs of production for a monopolistically competitive firm and the minimum average total cost at which a competitive firm would produce is the cost of producing "differentness."

OLIGOPOLY

There is another market structure that we have yet to discuss, and it is an important one indeed. It involves a situation in which there are several large firms that dominate an entire industry. They are not competitive in the sense that we have used the term; they are not even monopolistically competitive. And because there are several of them, a pure monopoly does not exist. We call such a situation an **oligopoly,** which consists of a small number of interdependent sellers. Each firm in the industry knows that other firms will react to its changes in prices, quantities, and qualities. An oligopoly market structure can exist for either a homogeneous or a differentiated product.

▶ **Oligopoly**
A market situation in which there are very few sellers. Each seller knows that the other sellers will react to its changes in prices and quantities.

CHARACTERISTICS OF OLIGOPOLY

Oligopoly is characterized by the small number of interdependent firms that constitute the entire market.

Small Number of Firms.   How many is "a small number of firms"? More than 2 but less than 100? The question is not easy to answer. Basically, though, oligopoly exists when a handful of firms dominate the industry enough to set prices. The top few firms in the industry account for an overwhelming percentage of total industry output.

Oligopolies usually involve three to five big companies dominating the industry. Between World War II and the 1970s, the U.S. automobile industry was dominated by three firms—General Motors, Chrysler, and Ford. Chewing-gum manufacturing and coin-operated amusement games are dominated by four large firms.

Interdependence.   All markets and all firms are, in a sense, interdependent. But when only a few large firms dominate an industry does the question of **strategic dependence** of one on the other's actions arise. The firms must recognize that they are interdependent. Any action on the part of one firm with respect to output, price, quality, or product differentiation will cause a reaction on the part of other firms. A model of such mutual interdependence is difficult to build, but examples are not hard to find in the real world. Oligopolists in the cigarette industry, for example, are constantly reacting to each other.

▶ **Strategic dependence**
A situation in which one firm's actions with respect to price changes may be strategically countered by one or more other firms in the industry. Such dependence can exist only when there are a limited number of major firms in an industry.

Recall that in the model of perfect competition, each firm ignores the reactions of other firms because each firm is able to sell all that it wants at the going market price. At the other extreme, the pure monopolist does not have to worry about the reaction of current rivals because there are none. In an oligopolistic market structure, the managers of firms are like generals in a war; *they must attempt to predict the reaction of rival firms*. It is a strategic game.

WHY OLIGOPOLY OCCURS

Why are some industries dominated by a few large firms? What causes an industry that might otherwise be competitive to tend toward oligopoly? We can provide some partial answers here.

Economies of Scale.   Perhaps the strongest reason that has been offered for the existence of oligopoly is economies of scale. Recall that economies of scale are defined as a production situation in which a doubling of output results in less than a doubling of total costs. When economies of scale truly exist, the firm's average total cost curve will slope downward as the firm produces more and more output. Average total cost can be reduced by continuing to expand the scale of operation. Smaller firms in such a situation will have a tendency to be inefficient. Their average total costs will be greater than those incurred by a large firm. Little by little, they will go out of business or be absorbed into the larger firm.

Barriers to Entry.   It is possible that certain barriers to entry have prevented more competition in oligopolistic industries. They include legal barriers, such as patents, and control and ownership over critical supplies. Indeed, we can find periods in the past when firms maintained market power because they were able not only to erect a barrier to entry but also to keep it in place year after year. In principle, the chemical, electronics, and aluminum industries have been at one time or another either monopolistic or oligopolistic because of the ownership of patents and the control of strategic inputs by specific firms.

Product Differentiation and Advertising.   Another important barrier to entry is product differentiation. Success at effective product differentiation may explain the existence of oligopoly in a number of industries, particularly in the short run. This is a barrier because new firms must meet the challenge of successfully differentiating their products from those already in the market. Advertising, too, has been an effective barrier to entry, particularly in oligopolistic industries. Potential new entrants face high entry costs, due to the necessity of waging a massive advertising campaign.

Oligopoly by Merger.   Another reason that oligopolistic market structures develop is that firms merge. A merger is the joining of two or more firms under a single ownership or control. The merged firm naturally becomes larger, enjoys greater economies of scale as output increases, and generally has a greater ability to control the market price for its product.

> **Horizontal merger**
> The joining of firms that are producing or selling a similar product.

There are two types of mergers—horizontal and vertical. A **horizontal merger** involves firms selling a similar product. If two shoe-manufacturing firms merge, that is a horizontal merger. If a group of firms, all producing steel, merge into one, that is also a horizontal merger. A **vertical merger** occurs when one firm merges with either a firm from which it purchases an input or a firm to which it sells its output. Vertical mergers occur, for example, when a coal-using electrical utility purchases a coal-mining firm or when a shoe manufacturer purchases retail shoe outlets. (Obviously, vertical mergers do not create oligopoly as we have defined it.)

> **Vertical merger**
> The joining of a firm with another to which it sells an output or from which it buys an input.

We have been talking about oligopoly in a theoretical manner until now. It is time to look at the actual picture of oligopolies in the United States.

MEASURING INDUSTRY CONCENTRATION

As we have stated, oligopoly is a situation in which a few interdependent firms control a large part of total output in an industry. This has been called *industry concentration.* Before we show the concentration statistics in the United States, let's determine how industry concentration can be measured.

> **Concentration ratio**
> The percentage of all sales contributed by the leading four or leading eight firms in an industry; sometimes called the *industry concentration ratio.*

Concentration Ratio.   The most popular way to compute industry concentration is to determine the percentage of total sales or production accounted for by the top four or top eight firms in an industry. This gives the four- or eight-firm **concentration ratio.** An example of an industry with 25 firms is given in Table 25-1. We can see in that table that the four largest firms account for almost 90 percent of total output in the hypothetical industry. That is an example of an oligopoly situation.

TABLE 25-1
Computing the four-firm concentration ratio.

ANNUAL SALES ($ MILLIONS)			
Firm 1	150		
Firm 2	100	$= 400$	Four-firm concentration ratio $= \dfrac{400}{450} = 88.9\%$
Firm 3	80		
Firm 4	70		
Firms 5–25	50		
Total	450		

INDUSTRY	PERCENTAGE OF VALUE OF TOTAL DOMESTIC SHIPMENTS ACCOUNTED FOR BY THE TOP FOUR FIRMS
Domestic motor vehicles	96
Electric bulbs	95
Household refrigerators and freezers	95
Cigarettes	90
Flat glass	85
Beer and ale	83
Greeting cards	82
Telephone and telegraph equipment	70
Tires and inner tubes	68
Newspapers	23

TABLE 25-2   Four-firm domestic concentration ratios for selected U.S. industries

Source: U.S. Bureau of the Census. *Concentration Ratios in Manufacturing,* Washington, D.C., 1986.

U.S. Concentration Ratios.   Table 25-2 shows the four-firm *domestic* concentration ratios for various industries. Is there any way that we can show or determine which industries to classify as oligopolistic? There is no definite answer. If we arbitrarily picked a four-firm concentration ratio of 60 percent, we could indicate that, in 1986, tires, beer, greeting cards, telephone and telegraph equipment, and domestic motor vehicles were oligopolistic. But we would always be dealing with an arbitrary definition.

The concept of an industry is necessarily arbitrary. As a consequence, concentration ratios rise as we narrow the definition of an industry and fall as we broaden it. Thus we must be certain that we are satisfied with the measurement of the industry under study before we jump to conclusions about whether the industry is too concentrated as evidenced by a high measured concentration ratio.

CONCEPTS IN BRIEF

- An oligopoly is a market situation in which there are a small number of interdependent sellers.
- Oligopoly occurs because of (1) economies of sale, (2) barriers to entry, (3) product differentiation and advertising, and (4) mergers.
- Horizontal mergers involve the joining of firms selling a similar product.
- Vertical mergers involve the merging of one firm either with the supplier of an input or with a firm to which it sells its output.
- Industry concentration can be measured by the percentage of total sales accounted for by the top four or top eight firms.

STRATEGIC BEHAVIOR AND GAME THEORY

At this point in this chapter we should be able to show oligopoly price and output determination in the way we showed it for perfect competition, pure monopoly, and monopolistic competition, but we cannot. Whenever there are relatively few firms competing in an industry, each can and does react to the price, quantity, quality, and product innovations that the others undertake. In other words, each oligopolist has a **reaction function.** Oligopolistic competitors are interdependent. Consequently, the decision makers in such firms must engage in strategic competition. And we must be able to model their strategic behavior if we wish to predict how prices and outputs are determined in oligopolistic market structures. In general, we can think of reactions of other firms to one firm's actions as part of a *game* that is played by all firms in the industry. Not surprisingly, economists have developed **game theory** models to describe firms' rational interactions.

▶ **Reaction function**
The manner in which one oligopolist reacts to a change in price (or output or quality) of another oligopolist.

▶ **Game theory**
A way of describing the various possible outcomes in any situation involving two or more interacting individuals when those individuals are aware of the interactive nature of their situation and plan accordingly. The plans made by these individuals are known as *game strategies*.

A SHORT HISTORY OF GAME THEORY

Game theory was invented by John von Neumann in 1937 and developed by Oskar Morgenstern in 1944. Together they published a book that was hailed by economists as a breakthrough in the study of imperfect markets, particularly oligopoly.[1] Because oligopolists must consider the reactions of their rivals, this pioneering book on game theory was considered applicable to these market structures.

Game theory is concerned with the general theory of conflict situations and may help the decision maker in selecting an optimum strategy. As such, game theory is considered a branch of decision theory. We will first consider some simple games and then discuss the famous prisoners' dilemma. This analysis will introduce the jargon and concepts of game theory and reveal the general flavor of the game-theory approach to decision making.

SOME BASIC NOTIONS ABOUT GAME THEORY

Games can be either cooperative or noncooperative. If firms get together to collude or form a cartel, that is considered a **cooperative game.** Whenever it is too costly for firms to negotiate such collusive agreements and too costly to enforce them, we are in a **noncooperative game** situation. Most strategic competition in the marketplace would be described as noncooperative game.

Games can be classified by whether the payoffs are negative, zero, or positive. A **zero-sum game** is one in which one player's losses are offset by another player's gains; at any time sum totals are zero. If you bet $50 on the outcome of a football game with a friend, that is a zero-sum game. If two retailers have an absolutely fixed total number of customers, the customers that one retailer wins over are exactly equal to the customers that the other retailer loses. A **negative-sum game** is one in which players as a group lose at the end of the game (although one perhaps by more than the other). A **positive-sum game** is one in which players as a group end up better off. Some economists describe all voluntary exchanges as positive-sum games. After an exchange, both the buyer and the seller are better off than they were prior to the exchange.

Strategies in Noncooperative Games. Players, such as decision makers in oligopolistic firms, have to devise a **strategy,** which is defined as a rule used to make a choice. The goal of the decision maker is of course to devise a strategy that is more successful than alternative strategies. Whenever a firm decision maker can come up with certain strategies that are generally successful no matter what actions competitors take, these are called **dominant strategies.** The dominant strategy always yields the unique best action for the decision maker no matter what action the other "players" undertake. Relatively few business decision makers over a long period of time have successfully devised dominant strategies. We know this by observation: Few firms in oligopolistic industries have maintained relatively high profits consistently over time.

⭐ EXAMPLE: The Prisoners' Dilemma

One real-world example of simple game theory involves what happens when two people, both involved in a bank robbery, are later caught. What should they do when questioned

---

▶ **Cooperative game**
A game in which the players explicitly collude to make themselves better off. As applied to firms, it involves companies colluding in order to make higher than competitive rates of return.

▶ **Noncooperative game**
A game in which the players neither negotiate nor collude in any way. As applied to firms in an industry, the common situation in which there are relatively few firms and each has some ability to change price.

▶ **Zero-sum game**
A game in which one player's losses are exactly offset by the other player's gains.

▶ **Negative-sum game**
A game in which players as a group are worse off at the end of the game.

▶ **Positive-sum game**
A game in which players as a group are better off at the end of the game.

▶ **Strategy**
Any rule that is used to make a choice, such as "Always pick heads." Any potential choice that can be made by players in a game.

▶ **Dominant strategies**
Strategies that always yield the highest benefit; regardless of what other players do, a dominant strategy will yield the most benefit for the player using it.

---

[1]John von Neumann and Oskar Morgenstern. *Theory of Games and Economic Behavior.* 3d ed. (New York: Wiley, 1964).

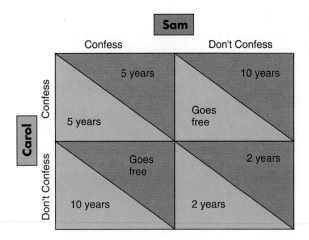

FIGURE 25-3
The prisoners' dilemma payoff matrix.

by police? The result has been called the **prisoners' dilemma.** The two suspects, Sam and Carol, are interrogated separately and confronted with alternative potential imprisonments. The interrogator indicates to Sam and Carol the following:

1. If both confess to the bank robbery, they will both go to jail for five years.
2. If neither confesses, they will each be given a sentence of two years on a lesser charge.
3. If one prisoner turns state's evidence and confesses, that prisoner goes free and the other one, who did not confess, will serve 10 years on bank robbery charges.

You can see the prisoners' alternatives in the **payoff matrix** in Figure 25-3. The two possibilities for each prisoner are "confess" and "don't confess." There are four possibilities:

1. Both confess.
2. Neither confesses.
3. Sam confesses (turns state's evidence) but Carol doesn't.
4. Carol confesses (turns state's evidence) but Sam doesn't.

In Figure 25-3 all of Sam's possible outcomes are shown on the upper half of each rectangle. All of Carol's possible outcomes are shown on the lower half.

By looking at the payoff matrix, you can see that if Carol confesses, Sam's best strategy is to confess also—he'll get only 5 years instead of 10. Conversely, if Sam confesses, Carol's best strategy is also to confess—she'll get 5 years instead of 10. Now let's say that Sam is being interrogated and Carol doesn't confess. Sam's best strategy is still to confess, because then he goes free instead of serving two years. Conversely, if Carol is being interrogated, her best strategy is still to confess even if Sam hasn't. She'll go free instead of serving 10 years. To confess is a dominant strategy for Sam. To confess is also a dominant strategy for Carol. The situation is exactly symmetrical. So this is the prisoners' dilemma. The prisoners know that both prisoners will be better off if neither confesses. Yet it is in each individual prisoner's interest to confess, even though the *collective* outcome of each prisoner's pursuing his or her own interest is inferior for both.

For Critical Analysis: Can you apply the prisoners' dilemma to the two firms in a two-firm industry that agree to split the market? (Hint: Think about the payoff to cheating on the market-splitting agreement.) ●

Can We Really Use Basic Game Theory?

Generals during wartime have to use a form of basic game theory, or they can just rely on intuition. To some extent the same thing can be said about decision makers in oligopolistic industries. Basic game

▶ **Prisoners' dilemma**
A famous strategic game in which two prisoners have a choice between confessing and not confessing to a crime. If neither confesses, they serve a minimum sentence. If both confess, they serve a maximum sentence. If one confesses and the other doesn't, the one who confesses goes free. The dominant strategy is always to confess.

▶ **Payoff matrix**
A matrix of outcomes, or consequences, of the strategies chosen by the players in a game.

theory models offer the promise of describing such behavior. Many economists believe that game-theoretical models are the only way we will ever be able to figure out such behavior. Other economists, however, find game theory a relatively frustrating method of analysis. It does not provide refutable predictions, such as the equilibrium analysis offered by supply and demand curves.

PRICE RIGIDITY AND THE KINKED DEMAND CURVE

Let's hypothesize that the decision makers in an oligopolistic firm assume that rivals will react in the following way: They will match all price decreases (in order not to be undersold) but not price increases (because they want to capture more business). There is no collusion. The implications of this reaction function are rigid prices and a kinked demand curve.

NATURE OF THE KINKED DEMAND CURVE

In Figure 25-4 we draw a kinked demand curve, which is implicit in the assumption that oligopolists match price decreases but not price increases. We start off at a given price of P_0 and assume that the quantity demanded at the price for this individual oligopolist is q_0. The starting price of P_0 is usually the stable market price. If the oligopolist assumes that rivals will not react, it faces demand curve $d_1 d_1$ with marginal revenue curve MR_1.

FIGURE 25-4
The kinked demand curve.
If the oligopolist firm assumes that rivals will not match price changes, it faces demand curve $d_1 d_1$ and marginal revenue curve MR_1. If it assumes that rivals will match price changes, it faces demand curve $d_2 d_2$ and marginal revenue curve MR_2. If the oligopolist believes that rivals will not react to price increases but will react to price decreases, at prices above P_0 it faces demand curve $d_1 d_1$ and at prices below P_0 it faces the other demand curve $d_2 d_2$. This demand curve will therefore have a kink, as is seen in panel (b) at price P_0. The marginal revenue curve will have a vertical break, as shown by the dashed line in panel (b).

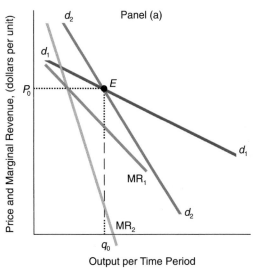

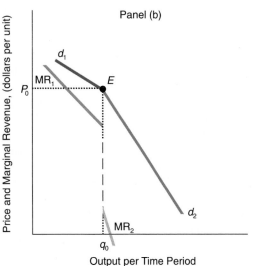

Conversely, if it assumes that rivals will react, it faces demand curve d_2d_2 with marginal revenue curve MR_2. More than likely, the oligopoly firm will assume that if it lowers price, rivals will react by matching that reduction to avoid losing their respective shares of the market. The oligopolist lowering price will not greatly increase its quantity demanded. So when it lowers its price, it believes that it will face demand curve d_2d_2. But if it increases price above P_0, rivals will probably not follow suit. Thus a higher price than P_0 will cause quantity demanded to decrease rapidly. The demand schedule to the left of and above point E will be relatively elastic, as represented by d_1d_1. At prices above P_0, the relevant demand curve is d_1d_1, whereas below price P_0, the relevant demand curve will be d_2d_2. Consequently, at point E there will be a *kink* in the resulting demand curve. This is shown in panel (b) of Figure 25-4, where the demand curve is labeled d_1d_2. The resulting marginal revenue curve is labeled MR_1MR_2. It has a discontinuous portion, or gap, represented by the dashed vertical lines in both panels.

PRICE RIGIDITY

The kinked demand curve analysis may help explain why price changes might be infrequent in an oligopolistic industry without collusion. Each oligopolist can see only harm in a price change: If price is increased, the oligopolist will lose many of its customers to rivals who do not raise their prices. That is to say, the oligopolist moves up from point E along demand curve d_1d_1 in panel (b) of Figure 25-4. However, if an oligopolist lowers its price, given that rivals will lower their prices too, its sales will not increase very much. Moving down from point E in panel (b) of Figure 25-4, we see that the demand curve is relatively inelastic. If the elasticity is less than 1, total revenues will fall rather than rise with the lowering of price. Given that the production of a larger output will increase total costs, the oligopolist's profits will fall. The lowering of price by the oligopolist might start a *price war* in which its rival firms will charge an even lower price.

The theoretical reason for price inflexibility under the kinked demand curve model has to do with the discontinuous portion of the marginal revenue curve shown in panel (b) of Figure 25-4, which we reproduce in Figure 25-5. Assume that marginal cost is represented by MC. The profit-maximizing rate of output is q_0, which can be sold at a price of P_0. Now assume that the marginal cost curve rises to MC'. What will happen to the profit-maximizing rate of output? Nothing. Both quantity and price will remain the same for this oligopolist.

Remember that the profit-maximizing rate of output is where marginal revenue equals marginal cost. The shift in the marginal cost curve to MC' does not change the profit-maximizing rate of output in Figure 25-5 because MC' still cuts the marginal revenue curve in the latter's discontinuous portion. Thus the equality between marginal revenue and marginal cost still holds at output rate q_0 even when the marginal cost curve shifts upward. What will happen when marginal costs fall to MC''? Nothing. This oligopolist will continue to produce at a rate of output q_0 and charge a price of P_0. Whenever the marginal cost curve cuts the discontinuous portion of the marginal revenue curve, fluctuations (within limits) in marginal cost will not affect output or price because the profit-maximizing condition $MR = MC$ will hold. The result is that even when firms in an oligopolistic industry such as this experience increases or decreases in costs, their prices do not change as long as MC cuts MR in the discontinuous portion. Hence prices are seen to be rigid in oligopolistic industries if oligopolists react the way we assume they do in this model.

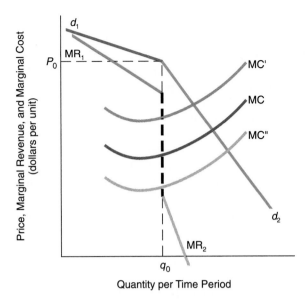

FIGURE 25-5
Changes in cost may not alter the profit-maximizing price and output.
As long as the marginal cost curve intersects the marginal revenue curve in the latter's discontinuous portion, the profit-maximizing price P_0 (and output q_0) will remain unchanged even with changes in MC. (However, the firm's rate of profit will change.)

CRITICISMS OF THE KINKED DEMAND CURVE

One of the criticisms directed against the kinked demand curve is that we have no idea how the existing price, P_0, came to be. If every oligopolistic firm faced a kinked demand curve, it would not pay for it to change prices. The problem is that the kinked demand curve does not show us how demand and supply originally determine the going price of an oligopolist's product.

As far as the evidence goes, it is not encouraging. Oligopoly prices do not appear to be as rigid, particularly in the upward direction, as the kinked demand curve theory implies. During the 1970s and early 1980s, when prices in the economy were rising overall, oligopolistic producers increased their prices frequently. Evidence of price changes during the Great Depression showed that oligopolies changed prices much more frequently than monopolies.

CONCEPTS IN BRIEF

- Each oligopolist has a reaction function because oligopolistic competitors are interdependent. They must therefore engage in strategic behavior. One way to model this behavior is to use game theory.
- Games can be either cooperative or noncooperative. A cartel is cooperative. When a cartel breaks down and its members start cheating, the industry becomes a noncooperative game. In a zero-sum game, one player's losses are exactly offset by another player's gains. In a negative-sum game, the players lose, perhaps one more than the other. In a positive-sum game, the players end up better off. ·
- Decision makers in oligopolistic firms must devise a strategy. A dominant strategy is one that is generally successful no matter what actions competitors take.
- The kinked demand curve oligopoly model predicts that major shifts in marginal cost will not cause any change in industry price.

STRATEGIC BEHAVIOR WITH IMPLICIT COLLUSION: A MODEL OF PRICE LEADERSHIP

What if oligopolists do not actually collude to raise prices and share markets but do so implicitly? There is no formal cartel arrangement and no formal meetings. Nonetheless, there is *tacit collusion.* This has been called the model of **price leadership.**

In this model, the basic assumption is that the dominant firm, usually the biggest, sets the price and allows other firms to sell all they can at that price. The dominant firm then sells the rest. The dominant firm always makes the first move in a price leadership model. By definition, price leadership requires one firm to be the leader. Because of laws against collusion, firms in an industry cannot communicate this directly. That is why it is often natural for the largest firm to become the price leader. In the automobile industry during the period of General Motors' dominance (until the 1980s), that company was traditionally the price leader. At various times in the breakfast food industry, Kellogg was the price leader. Some observers have argued that Harvard University was the price leader among Ivy League schools. In the banking industry, various dominant banks have been price leaders in announcing changes in the prime rate, the interest rate charged on loans offered to the best credit risks. One day a large New York–based bank, such as Chase Manhattan would announce an increase or decrease in its prime rate. Five or six hours later, all other banks would announce the same change in their prime rate.

▶ **Price leadership**
A practice in many oligopolistic industries in which the largest firm publishes its price list ahead of its competitors, who then match those announced prices. Also called *parallel pricing.*

PRICE WARS

Price leadership may not always work. If the price leader ends up much better off than the firms that follow, the followers may in fact not set prices according to those set by the dominant firm. The result may be a **price war.** The dominant firm lowers its prices a little bit, but the other firms lower theirs even more. Price wars have occurred in many industries. Supermarkets within a given locale often engage in price wars, especially during holiday periods. One may offer turkeys at so much per pound on Wednesday; competing stores cut their price on turkeys on Thursday; so the first store cuts its price even more on Friday. We see price wars virtually every year in the airline industry.

▶ **Price war**
A pricing campaign designed to drive competing firms out of a market by repeatedly cutting prices.

⭐ EXAMPLE: Airline Passengers Just Love Those Price Wars

The "Summer of '92" began on May 26, when Northwest Airlines announced that an adult and child traveling together would need only one ticket—effectively cutting air fares in half for appropriately sized families. The very next day, American Airlines, the industry leader with 20 percent of the domestic market, retaliated with half-price fares for *all* non-business travellers, and reduced its advance purchase requirement from 14 to seven days. Within hours, most other major carriers had followed American's lead—including Northwest. By week's end, the round-trip price of New York–Los Angeles flights had fallen to $200, while fares between Atlanta and Chicago dropped to only $130. (By way of comparison, the three-day, *one-way* rail journey between New York and Los Angeles cost $239.)

The response by vacation travellers was immediate and predictable. United Airlines reported that its reservations lines handled 45 percent more calls than usual after the low fares were announced. Within days, traffic on more popular routes was up 20 percent, and travel agents were leaving more callers on hold for longer periods than ever before—despite working overtime and hiring temporary help. Even hotels and rental car agencies reported a surge in business, as travellers flocked across the country in record numbers. By summer's end, the crush of air travellers had even stimulated a new business: emblazoned T-shirts selling briskly to flight attendants, ground crews, and flight officers. The message on the shirts? "I Survived the Summer of '92."

For Critical Analysis: What do you think causes airline companies to eventually raise their fares for awhile, only to subject themselves to another price war? ●

DETERRING ENTRY INTO AN INDUSTRY

Some economists believe that all decision making by existing firms in a stable industry involves some type of game playing. An important part of game playing does not have to do with how existing competitors might react to a decision by others. Rather, it has to do with how *potential* competitors might react. Strategic decision making requires that existing firms in an industry come up with strategies to deter entrance into that industry. One important way is, of course, to get a local, state, or federal government to restrict entry. Another way is to adopt certain pricing and investment strategies that may deter entry.

INCREASING ENTRY COSTS

▶ **Entry deterrence strategy**
Any strategy undertaken by firms in an industry, either individually or together, with the intent or effect of raising the cost of entry into the industry by a new firm.

One **entry deterrence strategy** is to raise the cost of entry by a new firm. The threat of a price war is one technique. To sustain a long price war, existing firms might invest in excess capacity so that they can expand output if necessary. When existing firms invest in excess capacity, they are signaling potential competitors that they will engage in a price war.

Another way that existing domestic firms can raise the entry cost of foreign firms is by getting the U.S. government to pass stringent environmental or health and safety standards. These typically raise costs more for foreign producers, often in developing countries, than for domestic producers.

LIMIT-PRICING STRATEGIES

▶ **Limit-pricing model**
A model that hypothesizes that a group of colluding sellers will set the highest common price that they believe they can charge without new firms seeking to enter that industry in search of relatively high profits.

If existing firms make it clear to potential competitors that the existing firms will not change their output rate after entry, this is a signal. It tells potential firms that the existing firm will simply lower its market price (moving down the firm demand curve) until it sells the same quantity as before the new entry came into the industry. The existing firms limit their price to be above competitive prices, but if there is a new entrant, the new limit price will be below the one at which the new firm can make a profit. This is called the **limit-pricing model.**

RAISING CUSTOMERS' SWITCHING COSTS

If an existing firm can make it more costly for customers to switch from its product or service to a competitor's, the existing firm can deter entry. There are a whole host of ways in which existing firms can raise customers' switching costs. Makers of computer equipment have in the past produced operating systems and software that would not run on competitors' computers. Any customer wanting to change from a Wang system to an IBM system, for example, faced a high switching cost. The same has been true for Xerox and Apple. This strategy is somewhat effective in the short run but usually not in the long run. Indeed, one of the reasons that the Wang computer company went bankrupt is that it did not make any equipment that could use IBM-compatible software. Apple and IBM are developing products that will use software made for either company's computers.

⭐ EXAMPLE: High Switching Costs in the University World

Colleges and universities are in competition with one another. One way to deter entry into this industry is to make switching across colleges and universities more costly. This is what many colleges and universities have done. Students who attempt to transfer from one school to another often find that many of the credits they earned are nontransferable. This means that courses must be repeated. If the cost of repeating courses is high enough, students will be deterred from switching universities. Typically, students who attempt to switch are not aware of this problem prior to the attempt. (But those who anticipate the problem can make sure that they take only courses that will be transferable to the university to which they want to switch.)

For Critical Analysis: Most switching in higher education occurs between community (two-year) colleges and four-year colleges and universities. What are some of the possible methods by which community colleges can reduce switching costs for their students who wish to transfer? ●

CONCEPTS IN BRIEF

- One type of strategic behavior involving implicit collusion is price leadership. The dominant firm is assumed to set the price and then allows other firms to sell all that they want to sell at that price. Whatever is left over is sold by the dominant firm. The dominant firm always makes the first move in a price leadership model. If the nondominant firms decide to compete, they may start a price war.
- One strategic decision may be to attempt to raise the cost of entry of new firms into an industry. The threat of a price war is one technique. Another is to lobby the federal government to pass stringent environmental or health and safety standards in an attempt to keep out foreign competition.
- If existing firms limit prices to a level above competitive prices before entry but are willing to reduce it, this is called a limit-pricing model.
- Another way to raise the cost to new firms is to make it more costly for customers to switch from one product or service to a competitor's.

COMPARING MARKET STRUCTURES

Now that we have looked at perfect competition, pure monopoly, monopolistic competition, and oligopoly, we are in a position to compare the attributes of these four different market structures. We do this in summary form in Table 25-3, in which we compare the number of sellers, their ability to set price, and whether product differentiation exists, and we give some examples of each of the four market structures.

TABLE 25-3   Comparing market structures.

MARKET STRUCTURE	NUMBER OF SELLERS	UNRESTRICTED ENTRY AND EXIT	ABILITY TO SET PRICE	LONG-RUN ECONOMIC PROFITS POSSIBLE	PRODUCT DIFFERENTIATION	NONPRICE COMPETITION	EXAMPLES
Perfect competition	Numerous	Yes	None	No	None	None	Agriculture
Monopolistic competition	Many	Yes	Some	Not for most firms	Considerable	Yes	Toothpaste, toilet paper, soap, retail trade
Oligopoly	Few	Partial	Some	Yes	Frequent	Yes	Cigarettes
Pure monopoly	One	No	Considerable	Yes	None (product is unique)	Yes	Electric company, local telephone company

COLLAPSING OIL PRICES: A CASE OF STRATEGIC BEHAVIOR?

Concepts Applied: Prisoners' dilemma, strategic behavior, cartels, price wars

Members of the international oil cartel are always faced with the possibility of cheating by increasing output. But cheating by one member may elicit an undesirable reaction by other members.

You will recall that the essential feature of the prisoners' dilemma is that the *joint* gains to the players are highest when they cooperate, but the *individual* gain to each of them is highest when he or she defects while the other cooperates. Yet if everyone defects, joint gains are at their lowest.

It is easy to see that the prisoners' dilemma is the basic problem faced by cartels: Jointly, the members have an incentive to cooperate (collude) to keep prices high, but individually each has an incentive to defect (cheat) by cutting prices while the others follow the rules. If each of the members follows its individual incentives and cuts prices, the cartel collapses, and all members lose. How can the members of the cartel try to avoid such collapse?

SOLVING THE PRISONERS' DILEMMA: THE STRATEGY OF TIT FOR TAT

One of the most important forms of strategic behavior used to deal with this problem is called "tit for tat." Under the terms of the tit-for-tat strategy, each cartel member begins by cooperating and continues to cooperate (by adhering to the cartel price) as long as the other members cooperate. But if anyone cheats on the cartel, the appropriate tit-for-tat response is to cut price and keep cutting price until the original cheater reverts to the higher price previously agreed on by the cartel members.

It appears that the tit-for-tat strategy closely resembles the strategy that has been used at times by Saudi Arabia, the largest oil-producing member of the Organization of Petroleum Exporting Countries (OPEC). As revealed both in its public pronouncements and in its behavior, Saudi Arabia has effectively said to other members of the OPEC cartel, "If you adhere to your agreed-on production limits, so shall we; but if you expand production beyond those limits, so shall we." And because Saudi Arabia is the largest oil producer within OPEC, such an output expansion would cause a calamitous decline in oil prices and lower prices for everyone in OPEC.

STRATEGIC MISTAKES CAN CAUSE PRICE WARS

Although tit for tat is widely regarded as perhaps the best strategic solution to the prisoners' dilemma, it does have one serious drawback: If someone makes a mistake, either in action or in perception, the tit-for-tat strategy can set off a ruinous price war. Suppose that Saudi Arabia thinks that a recent drop in crude oil prices was the result of an agreement-violating output expansion by fellow OPEC member Kuwait. Saudi Arabia's tit-for-tat response is to increase its own production, pushing prices down further, so as to punish Kuwait's apparent cheating. But Kuwait's tit-for-tat response to Saudi Arabia's (seemingly unprovoked) price cut is to expand production itself, thereby pushing prices down even further and touching off further retaliation by Saudi Arabia and perhaps other cartel members as well. Soon prices will be at competitive levels, much to the dismay of everyone (except, of course, consumers).

Perhaps the most important causes of mistakes are changes in demand or cost conditions that create the appearance that one or more cartel members are cheating. The early and mid-1980s were turbulent times for the oil industry. The overall inflation rate in the industrialized world had dropped from 13.5 percent per year to 1.9 percent, and important conservation measures were reducing worldwide energy consumption even as new sources of energy production were coming on line. All of these facts would tend to push oil prices down but need not have led to a collapse.

At the same time, however, Iraq and Iran were at war, and both depended on oil production to finance their defense expenditures. It was clear to OPEC members such as Saudi Arabia that there was downward pressure on oil prices; Iraq and Iran claimed that this downward pressure was not due to any cheating on their part, but OPEC members came to think otherwise. Eventually, Saudi Arabia responded, tit for tat, by hiking production, and prices collapsed: From 1985 to 1986, the price of crude oil plunged from $24.10 per barrel to $12.50. In retrospect it appears that at least some of the downward pressure was in fact due to cheating by Iraq and Iran, but the response by Saudi Arabia was probably excessive under the circumstances. Indeed, nearly a decade later, oil prices had yet to recover fully.

Even with the best of strategies, the prisoners' dilemma faced by members of cartels is a difficult problem to solve.

FOR CRITICAL ANALYSIS

1. How could the tit-for-tat strategy be modified to minimize the chances that a mistake might touch off a ruinous price war among cartel members?
2. Why would you expect a major producer such as Saudi Arabia to take the lead in enforcing the tit-for-tat strategy?

CHAPTER SUMMARY

1. Numerous market situations lie between the extremes of pure competition and pure monopoly. Monopolistic competition and oligopoly are two.

2. Monopolistic competition is a theory developed by Edward Chamberlin of Harvard University in 1933. It refers to a market situation composed of specific product groups in which the different companies involved have slight monopoly powers because each has a product slightly different from the others. Examples of product groups might include the toothpaste and soap industries. The monopolistic competitor ends up with zero economic profits because there is free entry into the industry. However, according to Chamberlin, the monopolistic competitor does not produce where price equals marginal costs and therefore does not produce at the minimum point on the average total cost curve.

3. Advertising occurs in industries in which the firms are not pure price takers. The basic goal of advertisers is to increase demand for their product.

4. In the short run, it is possible for a monopolistic competitor to make economic profits or economic losses. In the long run, monopolistic competitors make zero economic profits (that is, they make just the normal rate of return).

5. When we compare monopolistic competition with perfect competition, we find that the monopolistic competitor does not produce where average total costs are at a minimum, whereas the perfect competitor does.

6. Oligopoly is a market situation in which there are just a few firms. Each firm knows that its rivals will react to a change in price. Oligopolies are usually defined as industries in which the four-firm concentration ratio is relatively high.

7. Oligopolies are characterized by relatively high barriers to entry, interdependence, product differentiations, and growth through merger.

8. Each oligopolist has a reaction function because oligopolistic competitors are interdependent and must therefore engage in strategic behavior. One way to model this behavior is to use game theory.

9. Games can be either cooperative or noncooperative. A cartel is cooperative. When a cartel breaks down and its members start cheating, the industry becomes a noncooperative game. In a zero-sum game, one player's losses are exactly offset by another player's gains. In a negative-sum game, both players lose, perhaps one more than the other. In a positive-sum game, both players can end up better off.

10. The kinked demand curve oligopoly model indicates that prices will be relatively rigid unless demand or cost conditions change substantially.

11. Price leadership is strategic behavior that involves implicit collusion. The dominant firm is assumed to set the price and then allows other firms to sell all that they want to sell at that price. Whatever is left over is sold by the dominant firm. The dominant firm always makes the first move. If the nondominant firms decide to compete, they may start a price war.

12. One strategic decision may be to attempt to raise the cost of entry of new firms into an industry. The threat of a price war is one technique. Another is to lobby the federal government to pass stringent environmental or health and safety standards in an attempt to keep out foreign competition. A third is to make it more costly for customers to switch from one product or service to a competitor's.

DISCUSSION OF PREVIEW POINTS

1. What are the characteristics of the monopolistically competitive market structure?

The monopolistically competitive market structure lies between the extremes of monopoly and perfect competition, but closer to the latter. Under monopolistic competition there exists a large number of sellers, each with a small market share, acting independently of one another, producing a differentiated product. This product differentiation is advertised; advertising emphasizes product differences or, on occasion, "creates" differences.

2. How does the monopolistic competitor determine the equilibrium price-output combination?

The monopolistic competitor has some control over price; it faces a downward-sloping demand curve. The monopolistic competitor must lower price in order to increase sales; the marginal revenue curve for the monopolistic competitor is therefore downward-sloping. In equilibrium, the profit-maximizing rate of output will therefore be where the upward-sloping (increasing) marginal cost curve intersects the downward-sloping (decreasing) marginal revenue curve. The output rate being thus established, price is set at the corresponding market clearing level. Of course, any other output rate would lead to a reduction in total profits.

3. How does the monopolistically competitive market structure differ from that of perfect competition?

Like the perfect competitor, the monopolistic competitor acts independently of its competitors and is able to earn economic profits only in the short run; severe competition from entrants eliminates long-run economic profits under both market structures. Yet an important difference exists in the two models: The perfect competitor faces a perfectly elastic (horizontal) demand curve, whereas the monopolistic competitor faces a downward-sloping demand curve. Because economic profits must equal zero in the long run, the demand (average revenue) curve must be tangent to the average total cost (ATC) curve in both models. Under perfect competition, a horizontal (zero-sloped) demand curve can only be tangent to a U-shaped ATC curve at the latter's minimum point (where its slope is zero). Under monopolistic competition, the demand curve must be tangent to the firm's ATC somewhere to the *left* of the ATC's minimum point. Thus under perfect competition, long-run equilibrium will be at minimum ATC, whereas under monopolistic competition, long-run equilibrium will be at a higher ATC—and at a lower output rate.

4. What are the characteristics of the oligopolistic market structure?

Like the monopolistically competitive market structure, oligopoly lies between the extremes of perfect competition and monopoly. However, oligopoly is closer to being unique; under oligopoly a small number of firms dominate the market, and the firms cannot act independently. An oligopolist must take into account the reactions of its rivals when it sets policy; this interdependence makes the oligopoly model unique. It also makes the price-output decision a complex one for the oligopolists—and hence for economists who analyze this market structure. It is believed that oligopolies emerge because great economies of scale, in conjunction with a limited market demand, allow the few largest to drive out competitors. Also, oligopolies may arise because of barriers to entry and mergers.

PROBLEMS

(Answers to the odd-numbered problems appear at the back of the book.)

25-1. Suppose that you own a monopolistically competitive firm that sells automobile tune-ups at a price of $25 each. You are currently selling 100 per week. As the owner-operator, you initiate an ad campaign on a local AM radio station. You promise to smooth out any ill-running car at a price of $25. The result is that you end up tuning 140 cars per week. What is the "marginal revenue" of this ad campaign? What additional information do you need to determine whether your profits have risen?

PRICE	QUANTITY DEMANDED	TOTAL REVENUE	MARGINAL REVENUE	QUANTITY DEMANDED NO. OF FIRMS	TOTAL REVENUE NO. OF FIRMS	MARGINAL REVENUE NO. OF FIRMS	INDIVIDUAL FIRM QUANTITY SUPPLIED	LONG-RUN TOTAL COSTS	LONG-RUN MARGINAL COSTS
$20	5	$___	$___	___	___	___	1	$20	$___
18	10	___	___	___	___	___	2	30	___
16	15	___	___	___	___	___	3	36	___
14	20	___	___	___	___	___	4	44	___
12	25	___	___	___	___	___	5	60	___

25-2. In the graph we depict long-run equilibrium for a monopolistic competitor.

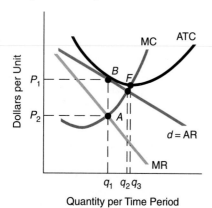

Quantity per Time Period

a. Which output rate represents equilibrium?
b. Which price represents equilibrium?
c. Which labeled point indicates that economic profits are zero?
d. Which labeled point indicates minimum ATC?
e. Is ATC at equilibrium above or at minimum ATC?
f. Is the equilibrium price greater than, less than, or equal to the marginal cost of producing the equilibrium output?

25-3. The table indicates some information for industry A.

	ANNUAL SALES ($ MILLIONS)
Firm 1	200
Firm 2	150
Firm 3	100
Firm 4	75
Firms 5–30	300

a. What is the four-firm concentration ratio for this industry?
b. Assume that industry A is the steel industry. What would happen to the concentration index if we redefined industry A as the rolled steel industry? As the metal industry?

25-4. Explain how, in the long run, any economic profits will be eliminated in a monopolistically competitive industry.

25-5. Explain why an oligopolist's demand curve might be kinked.

25-6. The table at the top of the page gives some cost and demand data for an oligopolistic industry. There are five firms. Assume that each one faces the same long-run total cost curve and that each firm knows that any change in price will be matched by all other firms in the industry.
a. Fill in the blanks.
b. What will the profit-maximizing rate of output be for each firm?
c. What price will be charged for this output?
d. What will the profits be for each of the five firms?

25-7. Suppose that you run a movie theater. At your price of $5 per person, you sell 5,000 tickets per week. Without changing your price, you initiate a $1,000-per-week advertising campaign. Assuming that all your nonadvertising costs are totally unrelated to the number of weekly viewers you have, how much additional revenue must you generate to justify continuation of the ad campaign? How many more customers would this require?

25-8. Study the accompanying graph for a firm in an oligopolistic industry.

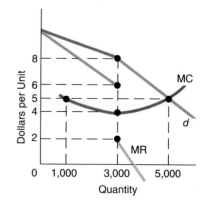

a. How much will this oligopolistic firm produce?

b. At what price will the firm sell this output?

c. How much can marginal cost vary without causing a change in price?

25-9. There are only two firms in an industry. They collude to share the market equally. They jointly set a monopoly price and split the quantity demanded at that price. Here are their options.

a. They continue to collude (no cheating) and make $10 million each in profits.

b. One firm cheats on the agreement but the other firm doesn't. The firm that cheats makes $12 million a year in profit, and the firm that doesn't cheat makes $7 million in profit.

c. They both cheat and each one makes $6 million a year in profit.

Construct a payoff matrix for these two firms. How does this situation relate to the prisoners' dilemma?

 COMPUTER-ASSISTED INSTRUCTION
(Complete problem and answer on disk.)

Given a table with relevant information, can you determine an industry's four-firm concentration ratio? Does this ratio overstate or understate the true concentration of that industry? Specific calculations reveal some interesting answers about the usefulness of concentration ratios.

26

REGULATION AND ANTITRUST POLICY

Question: What does the average American do about five hours a day, seven days a week? Answer: Watch television. A few decades ago, the choices that television viewers had were relatively limited: the Big Three networks (NBC, ABC, and CBS) plus a couple of local independent stations. Reception was not too good, either, in many parts of the country. Indeed, in some rural or mountainous areas, it was nonexistent. All that changed with the birth of cable TV. In most parts of the United States, there is only one cable TV company. Since 1986 the rates that cable TV companies charged have gone up about 65 percent. Were those rate increases necessary to cover costs? Or were they reflective of monopoly power being exercised, meaning that the Cable Reregulation Act of 1992 was justified? This issue is part of the broader topics of regulation and antitrust policy.

After reading this chapter, you should be able to answer the following questions:

1. What is a natural monopoly, and how does one arise?

2. If natural monopolies are required to price at marginal cost, what problem emerges?

3. What are some means of regulating a natural monopoly?

4. Why have economists been reevaluating the government's role as an economic regulator?

INTRODUCTION

It is hard to think of many true monopolies, offering products for which there are virtually no substitutes. The most common examples might be electrical power and local telephone service. Both are *natural monopolies,* a concept mentioned briefly in Chapter 25. A natural monopoly arises because of the cost structure of the industry. The natural monopolist is the firm that first takes advantage of persistent declining long-run average costs as scale increases. The natural monopoly is created when a firm is able to undercut its competitors' prices and eventually force all competitors out of the market. When such a situation occurs, government regulation is often used to attempt to protect the consumer from the undesirable effect of monopoly—prices higher than marginal cost—while at the same time allowing large, efficient size.

In this chapter we will look at government regulation of natural monopolies and of other industries deemed so important to the public interest that they must be overseen.

The second topic we will examine is antitrust legislation and theory. Antitrust legislation is a way of preventing monopolization in restraint of trade. Whereas regulation allows government to intervene directly into the decision-making processes of the regulated industries, antitrust legislation and enforcement seek to prevent monopolies from arising and hence seek to make regulation unnecessary.

HOW A NATURAL MONOPOLY CAN ARISE

Whenever a single firm has the ability to produce all of the industry's output at a lower per-unit cost than other firms attempting to produce less than total industry output, a natural monopoly arises. Local telephone service, natural gas, and electric utilities are examples. Long-run average costs of those firms typically fall as output increases. In a natural monopoly, economies of large-scale production dominate, creating a single-firm industry.

Technology is usually behind a natural monopoly. Consider local telephone service. Some years ago we would have written just "telephone service," including long distance. But today, with the advent of satellite communications, microwave relays, and fiber-optic systems, long-distance telephone service is no longer a natural monopoly. Indeed, since the forced breakup of AT&T, that firm as a long-distance carrier has numerous rivals. Technological change destroyed whatever natural monopoly there used to be in long-distance telephone service. Technology may cause monopolies by creating extensive economies of scale, but it may also destroy a natural monopoly.

In Figure 26-1 we have drawn a downward-sloping long-run average cost curve (LAC)

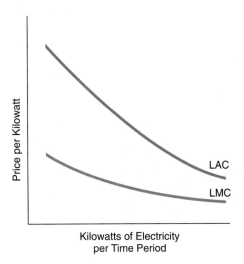

Price per Kilowatt

LAC
LMC

Kilowatts of Electricity per Time Period

FIGURE 26-1

The cost curves that might lead to a natural monopoly. The long-run marginal cost curve is below the long-run average cost curve when the average cost curve is falling. A natural monopoly might arise in this situation. The first firm to establish the low unit cost capacity would be able to take advantage of the lower average total cost curve. This firm would drive out all rivals by charging a lower price than the others could sustain at their higher average costs.

for electricity. When we explained the relationship between marginal costs and average costs, we pointed out that when average costs are falling, marginal costs are less than average costs, and when average costs are rising, marginal costs are greater than average costs. We can apply the same analysis to the long run. When long-run average costs are falling, the long-run marginal cost curve (LMC) is below the long-run average cost curve (LAC). In our example, long-run average costs are falling over such a large range of production rates (relative to demand) that we would expect only one firm to survive in such an industry. That firm would be the natural monopolist. It would be the first one to take advantage of the decreasing average costs; that is, it would construct the large-scale facilities first. As its average cost curve fell, it would lower prices and get an increasingly larger share of the market. Once that firm had driven all other firms out of the industry, it would set its price to maximize profits. Let's see what this price would be.

A monopolist (like any other firm) will set the output rate where marginal revenue is equal to marginal cost. We draw the market demand curve, D, and the revenue curve, MR, in panel (a) of Figure 26-2. The intersection of the marginal revenue curve and the marginal cost curve is at point A. The monopolist would therefore produce quantity Q_m and charge a price of P_m.

What do we know about a monopolist's solution to the price-quantity question? When compared to a competitive situation, we know that consumers end up paying more for the product, and consequently they purchase less of it than they would purchase under competition. The monopoly solution is economically inefficient from society's point of view; the price charged for the product is higher than the opportunity cost to society, and consequently there is a misallocation of resources. That is, the price does not reflect the true marginal cost of producing the good because the true social marginal cost is at the intersection A, not at price P_m.

REGULATING THE NATURAL MONOPOLIST

Assume that the government decides to make the natural monopolist produce as in a competitive situation, in which price equals marginal cost so that the value of the satisfaction that individuals receive from the marginal unit purchased is just equal to the marginal cost to society. Where is that competitive solution in panel (b) of Figure 26-2? It is at the intersection of the marginal cost curve and the demand curve, point B. Recall how we derived the competitive industry supply curve. We looked at all of the upward-sloping portions of actual and potential firms' marginal cost curves above their respective average variable costs. We then summed all of these portions of the firms' supply curves; that gave us the industry supply curve. We assume that the regulatory commission forces the natural monopolist to engage in marginal cost pricing and hence to produce at quantity Q_1 and to sell the product at price P_1. How large will the monopolist's profits be? Profits, of course, are the *positive* difference between total revenues and total costs. In this case, total revenues equal P_1 times Q_1, and total costs equal average costs times the number of units produced. At Q_1 average cost is equal to P_2. Average costs are higher than the price that the regulatory commission forces our natural monopolist to charge. Profits turn out to be losses and are equal to the shaded area in panel (b) of Figure 26-2. Thus regulation that forces a natural monopolist to produce and price as if it were in a competitive situation would also force that monopolist into negative profits, or losses. Obviously, the monopolist would rather go out of business than be subject to such regulation.

Regulators can't force a natural monopolist to engage in marginal cost pricing. Consequently, regulation of natural monopolies has often taken the form of allowing the regulated natural monopolist to set price where LAC intersects D in Figure 26-2 (b). This is called *average cost pricing*. Average cost includes what the regulators deem a "fair" rate of return on investment.

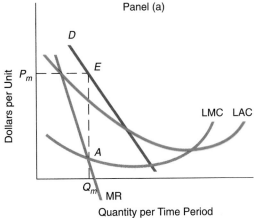

Panel (a)

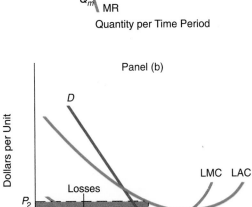

Panel (b)

FIGURE 26-2
Profit maximization and regulation through marginal cost pricing.
The profit-maximizing natural monopolist here would produce at the point in panel (a) where marginal costs equals marginal revenue—that is, at point A, which gives the quantity of production Q_m. The price charged would be P_m. If a regulatory commission attempted to regulate natural monopolies so that price equaled long-run marginal cost, the commission would make the monopolist set production at the point where the marginal cost curve intersects the demand schedule. This is shown in panel (b). The quantity produced would be Q_1, and the price would be P_1. However, average costs at Q_1 are equal to P_2. Losses would ensue, equal to the shaded area. It would be self-defeating for a regulatory commission to force a natural monopolist to produce at an output rate at which $MC = P$ without subsidizing some of its costs because losses would eventually drive the natural monopolist out of business.

 EXAMPLE: Is the Postal Service a Natural Monopoly?

For almost 200 years the U.S. Postal Service (USPS, formerly the U.S. Post Office) has had a legal monopoly, particularly in the delivery of first-class mail. When the President's Commission on Postal Organization looked at the U.S. Post Office in the 1970s, it accepted as "apparent" the existence of large economies of scale and the waste that would result from competition in postal services. It was saying, therefore, that the post office was a natural monopoly. When we think of a natural monopolist, we think of large fixed costs, such as those involved in the laying of power lines in a city grid. But labor costs account for 83 percent of the USPS budget; capital costs are low. It is hard to imagine such a labor-intensive industry exhibiting large economies of scale.

In any event, a natural monopolist by definition does not have to worry about competition because, presumably, no one else can produce at comparable average unit costs. In reality, it is its status as a legal monopoly, rather than as a natural monopoly, that has kept the U.S. Postal Service in business. Wherever competition has been allowed, the supposed natural monopolist, the USPS, has not fared well. Package delivery by the USPS, known as parcel post, is today only 18 percent of package delivery by United Parcel Service. (Remember, the USPS's legal monopoly is only over first-class mail.) Since 1973, when Fred Smith founded Federal Express, an overnight delivery service, an increasing number of people have turned to rapid services. The USPS's attempt at competing with private overnight delivery services, Express Mail, is not a major success. Only 12 percent of overnight mail is delivered by the USPS.

For Critical Analysis: In 1843 Postmaster General Charles Wickliff said he knew that most people thought the government's mail monopoly was "odious." He insisted, though, that it be preserved for the good of the country. What technological innovations have occurred in the past decade that have greatly reduced the demand for the U.S. Postal Service's first-class mail delivery services and thereby reduced the value of the government's mail monopoly? ●

CONCEPTS IN BRIEF

- A natural monopoly arises when the long-run average cost curve slopes downward over a large range of outputs in relation to industry demand.
- The first firm to take advantage of the declining long-run average cost curve can undercut the prices of all other sellers, forcing them out of business, thereby obtaining a natural monopoly.
- A natural monopolist allowed to maximize profit will set quantity where marginal revenue equals long-run marginal cost. Price is determined from the demand curve at that quantity.
- A natural monopolist that is forced to set price equal to long-run marginal cost will sustain losses.

REGULATION

The U.S. government began regulating social and economic activity early in the nation's history, but the amount of government regulation has increased in the twentieth century. There are three types of government regulation:

1. Regulation of natural monopolies
2. Regulation of inherently competitive industries
3. Regulation for public welfare across all industries, or so-called social regulation

For example, various state commissions regulate the rates and quality of service of electric power companies, which are natural monopolies. Trucking and interstate moving companies are inherently competitive industries but subject to government regulation. And federal and state governments impose occupational, health, and safety rules on a wide variety of employers.

OBJECTIVES OF ECONOMIC REGULATION

Economic regulation is typically intended to control the prices that regulated enterprises are allowed to charge. Various public utility commissions throughout the United States regulate the rates of electrical utility companies and telephone operating companies. This has usually been called rate regulation. The goal of rate regulation has, in principle, been the prevention of both monopoly profits and predatory competition.

Two traditional methods of rate regulation have involved cost-of-service regulation and rate-of-return regulation. A regulatory commission using **cost-of-service regulation** allows the regulated companies to charge only prices that reflect the actual average cost of providing the services to the customer. In a somewhat similar vein, regulatory commissions using the **rate-of-return regulation** method allow regulated companies to set prices that ensure a normal, or competitive, rate of return on the investment in the business. We mentioned these two types of regulation when discussing panel (b) of Figure 26-2. If the

▶ **Cost-of-service regulation**
Regulation based on allowing prices to reflect only the actual cost of production and no monopoly profits.

▶ **Rate-of-return regulation**
Regulation that seeks to keep the rate of return in the industry at a competitive level by not allowing excessive prices to be charged.

long-run average cost curve in that figure includes a competitive rate of return on investment, regulating the price at P_2 is an example of rate-of-return regulation.

A major problem with regulating monopolies concerns the quality of the service or product involved. Consider the many facets of telephone service: getting a dial tone, hearing other voices clearly, getting the operator to answer quickly, having out-of-order telephone lines repaired rapidly, putting through a long-distance call quickly and efficiently—the list goes on and on. But regulation of the telephone company usually deals with the prices charged for telephone service. Of course, regulators are concerned with the quality of service, but how can that be measured? Indeed, it cannot be measured very easily. Therefore, it is extremely difficult for any type of regulation to be successful in regulating the *price per constant-quality unit.* Certainly, it is possible to regulate the price per unit, but we don't really know that the quality remains unchanged when the price is not allowed to rise "enough." Thus if regulation doesn't allow prices to rise, quality of service may be lowered, thereby raising the price per constant-quality unit.

SOCIAL REGULATION

As mentioned, social regulation reflects concern for public welfare across all industries. In other words, regulation is focused on the impact of production on the environment and society, the working conditions under which goods and services are produced, and sometimes the physical attributes of goods. The aim is a better quality of life for all through a less polluted environment, better working conditions, and safer and better products. For example, the Food and Drug Administration (FDA) attempts to protect against impure and unsafe foods, drugs, cosmetics, and other potentially hazardous products; the Consumer Product Safety Commission (CPSC) specifies minimum standards for consumer products in an attempt to reduce "unreasonable" risks of injury; the Environmental Protection Agency (EPA) watches over the amount of pollutants released into the environment; the Occupational Safety and Health Administration (OSHA) attempts to protect workers against work-related injuries and illnesses; and the Equal Employment Opportunity Commission (EEOC) seeks to provide fair access to jobs.

Table 26-1 on the next page lists some major federal regulatory agencies and their areas of concern. Although most people agree with the idea behind such social regulation, many disagree on whether we have too much regulation—whether it costs us more than the benefits we receive. Some contend that the costs that firms incur in abiding by regulations run into the hundreds of billions of dollars per year. The result is higher production costs, which are then passed on to consumers. Also, the resources invested in complying with regulatory measures could have been invested in other uses. Furthermore, extensive regulation may have an anticompetitive effect because it may represent a relatively greater burden for smaller firms than for larger ones.

But the *potential* benefits of more social regulation are many. For example, the water we drink in some cities is known to be contaminated with cancer-causing chemicals; air pollution from emissions and toxic wastes from production processes cause many illnesses. Some contaminated areas have been cleaned up, but many other problem areas remain.

The benefits of social regulation may not be easy to measure and may accrue to society for a long time. Furthermore, it is difficult to put a dollar value on safe working conditions and a cleaner environment. In any case, the debate goes on. However, it should be pointed out that the controversy is generally not about whether we should have social regulation but about when and how it is being done and *whether* we take all of the costs and benefits into account. For example, is regulation best carried out by federal, state, or local authorities? Is a specific regulation economically justified through a complete cost-benefit analysis?

TABLE 26-1 **Some federal regulatory agencies.**

AGENCY	DATE FORMED	MAJOR REGULATORY FUNCTIONS
Product Markets		
Federal Communications Commission (FCC)	1954	Regulates broadcasting, telephone, and other communication services.
Labor Markets		
Equal Employment Opportunity Commission (EEOC)	1964	Investigates complaints of discrimination based on race, religion, sex, or age in hiring, promotion, firing, wages, testing, and all other conditions of employment.
Financial Markets		
Securities and Exchange Commission (SEC)	1934	Regulates all public securities markets to promote full disclosure.
Energy and Environment		
Environmental Protection Agency (EPA)	1970	Develops and enforces environmental standards for air, water, toxic waste, and noise.
Federal Energy Regulatory Commission	1977	Used to regulate well-head crude oil prices; to allocate wholesale and retail volume of crude oil; and to regulate importation of oil into the United States during energy emergencies.
Health and Safety		
Occupational Safety and Health Administration (OSHA)	1970	Regulates workplace safety and health conditions.

CREATIVE RESPONSE: RESULTS OF REGULATION

Regulated firms commonly try to avoid the effects of regulation whenever they can. In other words, the firms engage in **creative response,** which is a response to a regulation that conforms to the letter of the law but undermines its spirit. Take laws requiring pay-equity: The wages of women must be on a par with those paid to males who are performing the same tasks. Employers that pay the same wages to both males and females are clearly not in violation of the law. However, wages are only one component of total employee compensation. Another component is fringe benefits, such as on-the-job training. Because on-the-job training is difficult to observe from outside the firm, employers could offer less on-the-job training to women and still not be in technical violation of pay-equity laws. This unobservable difference means that males are able to acquire skills that could raise their future income even though current wages among males and females are equal, in compliance with the law.

▶ **Creative response**
Behavior on the part of a firm that allows it to comply with the letter of the law but not the spirit, significantly lessening the law's effects.

EXPLAINING REGULATORS' BEHAVIOR

Regulation has usually been defended by contending that government regulatory agencies are needed to correct market imperfections. We are dealing with a nonmarket situation because regulators are paid by the government and their decisions are not determined or constrained by the market. A number of theories have been put forward to describe the behavior of regulators. These theories can help us understand how regulation has often harmed consumers through higher prices and less choice and benefited producers through higher profits and fewer competitive forces. Two of the best-known theories of regulatory behavior are the *capture hypothesis* and the *share-the-gains, share-the-pains theory.*

THE CAPTURE HYPOTHESIS

▶ **Capture hypothesis**
A theory of regulatory behavior that predicts that the regulators will eventually be captured by the special interests of the industry being regulated.

It has been observed that with the passage of time, regulators often end up adopting the views of the regulated. According to the **capture hypothesis**,[1] no matter what the reason for a regulatory agency having been set up, it will eventually be captured by the special interests of the industry that is being regulated. Consider the reasons.

Who knows best about the industry that is being regulated? The people already in the industry. Who, then, will be asked to regulate the industry? Again, someone who has been in the industry. And people who used to be in the industry have allegiances and friendships with others in the industry.

Also consider that whenever regulatory hearings are held, the affected consumer groups will have much less information about the industry than the people already in the industry—the producers. Also, the cost to any one consumer to show up at a regulatory hearing to express concern about a change in the rate structure will certainly exceed any perceived benefit that that consumer could obtain from going to the rate-making hearing.

Because they have little incentive to do so, consumers and taxpayers will not be well organized, nor will they be greatly concerned with regulatory actions. But the special interests of the industry are going to be well organized and well defined. Political entrepreneurs within the regulatory agency see little payoff in supporting the views of consumers and taxpayers, anyway. After all, few consumers understand any benefits from regulatory agency actions. Moreover, how much could a consumer directly benefit someone who works in an agency? Regulators have the most incentive to support the position of a well-organized special-interest group within the industry that is being regulated.

"SHARE THE GAINS, SHARE THE PAINS"

▶ **Share-the-gains, share-the-pains theory**
A theory of regulatory behavior in which the regulators must take account of the demands of three groups: legislators, who established and who oversee the regulatory agency; members of the regulated industry; and consumers of the regulated industry's products or services.

A somewhat different view of regulators' behavior is given in the **share-the-gains, share-the-pains theory.**[2] This theory looks at the specific aims of the regulators. It posits that the regulator simply wants to continue in his or her job. To do so, a regulator must obtain the approval of both the legislators who established and oversee the regulatory agency and the industry that is being regulated. A third group that must be taken into account is, of course, the customers of the industry.

Under the capture hypothesis, only the special interests of the industry being regulated had to be taken into account by the regulators. The share-the-gains, share-the-pains model contends that such a position is too risky because customers who are really hurt by improper regulation will complain to legislators, who might fire the regulators. Thus each regulator has to attach some weight to these three separate groups. What happens if there is an abrupt increase in fuel costs for electrical utilities? The capture theory would predict that regulators would relatively quickly allow for a rate increase in order to maintain the profits of the industry. The share-the-gains, share-the-pains theory, however, would predict that there will be an adjustment in rates, but not as quickly or as completely as the capture theory would predict. The regulatory agency is not completely captured by the industry; it has to take account of legislators and consumers.

---

[1]See George Stigler, *The Citizen and the State: Essays on Regulation* (Chicago: University of Chicago Press, 1975).

[2]See Sam Peltzman, "Towards a More General Theory of Regulation," *Journal of Law and Economics,* 19 (1976), pp. 211–240.

⭐ EXAMPLE: **Regulation in a Milk Market**

An industry that has been heavily regulated for many years is the dairy industry. The 1937 Agricultural Adjustment Act (AAA) provided for federal control over the marketing of fluid milk (as opposed to milk used in the manufacture of cheese and for other purposes). Today the AAA still allows the producers of fluid milk sold fresh to the public to force marketing controls on dairies and bottlers. The federal government controls over 60 percent of today's milk markets, and states control the majority of the rest. The regulation of milk prices was justified by the 1962 Federal Milk Order Study Committee as "promoting orderly marketing conditions for farmers specializing in the production of fluid milk" by "equalizing the market power of buyers and sellers to obtain reasonable competition but not local monopoly resulting in undue price enhancement." The regulation of milk prices today has one continuing major effect: The market price of milk currently exceeds what it would be in the absence of regulation. One study estimated that regulation of the milk market has added about 24 percent to the cost of milk in the Northeast.

For Critical Analysis: *Which theory of regulatory behavior do you think describes what has happened in the regulated dairy industry? Explain.* ●

DEREGULATION AND REREGULATION

Regulation increased substantially during the 1970s. By the end of that decade there had been numerous proposals for **deregulation**—the removal of old regulations. Most of the proposals and actions of deregulation since then have been aimed at industries in which price competition and entry competition by new firms continued to be thwarted by the regulators. Some milestones in deregulation legislation are cited in Table 26-2.

> **Deregulation**
> The elimination or phasing out of regulations of economic activity.

Even prior to this spate of deregulatory acts by Congress, the Federal Communications Commission (FCC) had started in 1972 to deregulate the television broadcast industry. The result has been an increased number of channels, more direct satellite broadcasting, and more cable television transmissions. In 1975 the Securities and Exchange Commission (SEC) deregulated brokerage fees charged by brokers on the New York Stock Exchange.

Consider the Depository Institutions and Monetary Control Act of 1980. Prior to that act, the amount of interest paid depositors was severely limited by regulation. After the act was passed, depositors with small accounts were gradually allowed to receive market-determined interest rates. Consider the Motor Carriers Act of 1980. Prior to that act, the Interstate Commerce Commission (ICC) severely regulated interstate trucking rates and routes. After the act was passed, trucking companies were gradually allowed to determine their own routes and to determine the rates they charged companies and individuals who wanted to ship goods across state lines.

RESULTS OF DEREGULATION

Deregulation has had benefits and costs. In specific areas, the benefits have typically meant lower prices to consumers. This has occurred in the trucking industry, the airline industry, the long-distance telephone industry, and elsewhere. In the banking industry, one result of deregulation has been higher yields for small savers. Experience has generally shown that deregulation does lead to lower prices for most consumers, but not all. For example, in the airline industry, many individuals, particularly business travelers, often end up paying a relatively higher price for short trips on less heavily traveled routes than before deregulation. In general, customers in high-cost markets have had to pay more because under a deregulated industry structure, no cross subsidization can exist because of

TABLE 26-2 **Some milestones in deregulation legislation.**

LAW	YEAR	EFFECTS
Air Deregulation Act	1978	Eliminated the Civil Aeronautics Board; gave airlines control over fares charged and routes flown.
Natural Gas Policy Act	1978	Decontrolled interstate natural gas prices but allowed states to control such prices within their boundaries.
Depository Institutions and Monetary Control Act	1980	Deregulated interest rates offered on deposits; also allowed savings and loans and banks to expand the services they offered.
Motor Carriers Act	1980	Reduced control of the Interstate Commerce Commission (ICC) over interstate trucking rates and routes.
Staggers Rail Act	1980	Gave railroads more flexibility in setting rates and in dropping unprofitable routes.
Garn-St. Germain Depository Institutions Act	1982	Allowed banks and savings and loans to offer money market deposit accounts similar to those offered by securities dealers and mutual funds.
Bus Regulatory Reform Act	1982	Allowed inter-city bus lines to operate without applying for federal licenses in most circumstances.
Cable Communications Policy Act	1984	Deregulated 90 percent of cable TV rates by the end of 1986.

▶ **Cross subsidization**
The selling of a product or service in one market below cost, the losses being compensated by selling the same product or service in another market at above marginal cost.

competition. **Cross subsidization** occurs whenever price is below cost in one market and the losses are covered by the profits from another market within the same industry.

Not everyone in the previously regulated industries has benefited from deregulation, certainly not all firms already in the industry. Much more severe competition caused a number of bankruptcies in the airlines industries. In the banking industry, a combination of deregulation and perverse incentives having to do with federal deposit insurance have led to literally thousands of failures of savings and loan associations and commercial banks. Also, employees in deregulated industries have not fared as well as they would have without deregulation. This is certainly true for airline pilots, flight attendants, and baggage handlers.

SHORT-RUN VERSUS LONG-RUN EFFECTS OF DEREGULATION

The short-run effects of deregulation are not the same as the long-run effects. In the short run, a regulated industry that becomes deregulated may experience numerous temporary adjustments. One is the inevitable shakeout of higher-cost producers with the concomitant removal of excess monopoly profits. Another is the sometimes dramatic displacement of workers who have labored long and hard in the formerly regulated industry. The level of service for many consumers may fall; for example, after the deregulation of the telephone industry, some aspects of telephone service decreased in quality. When airlines were deregulated, service to some small cities was eliminated or became more expensive. The power of unions in the formerly regulated industry may decrease. And bankruptcies may cause disruptions, particularly in the local economy where the headquarters of the formerly regulated firm are located.

Proponents of deregulation, or at least of less regulation, contend that there are long-run, permanent benefits. These include lower prices that are closer to marginal cost. Furthermore, fewer monopoly profits are made in the deregulated industry. Such proponents argue that deregulation has had positive *net* benefits.

DEREGULATION AND CONTESTABLE MARKETS

A major argument in favor of deregulation is that when government-imposed barriers to entry are removed, competition will cause firms to enter markets that previously had only a few firms which had market power due to those entry barriers. Potential competitors will become actual competitors, and prices will fall toward a competitive level. Recently, this argument has been bolstered by a relatively new model of efficient firm behavior that predicts competitive prices in spite of a lack of a large number of firms. This model is called the **theory of contestable markets.** Under the theory of contestable markets, most of the outcomes predicted by the theory of perfect competition will occur in certain industries with relatively few firms. Specifically, where the theory of contestable markets is applicable, the few firms may still produce the output at which price equals marginal cost in both the short run and the long run. These firms will receive zero economic profits in the long run.

▶ **Theory of contestable markets**
A hypothesis concerning pricing behavior that holds that even though there are only a few firms in the industry, they are forced to price their products more or less competitively because of the ease of entry by outsiders. The key aspect of a contestable market is relatively costless entry into and exit from the industry.

Unconstrained and Relatively Costless Entry and Exit.   For a market to be perfectly contestable, firms must be able to enter and leave the industry easily. Freedom of entry and exit implies an absence of nonprice constraints and of unimportant fixed costs associated with a potential competitor's decision to enter a contestable market. Such an absence of unimportant fixed costs results if the firm need buy no specific durable inputs in order to enter, if it uses up all such inputs it does purchase, or if all of its specific durable inputs are salable upon exit without any losses beyond those normally incurred from depreciation. The important issue is whether or not a potential entrant can easily get his or her investment out at any time in the future.

The mathematical model of perfect contestability is complex, but the underlying logic is straightforward. As long as conditions for free entry prevail, any excess profits, or any inefficiencies on the part of incumbent firms, will serve as an inducement for potential entrants to enter. By entering, new firms can temporarily profit at no risk to themselves from the less than competitive situation in the industry. Once competitive conditions are again restored, they will leave the industry just as quickly.

Benefits of Contestable Markets.   Contestable markets have several desirable characteristics. One has to do with profits. Profits that exceed the opportunity cost of capital will not exist in the long run because of freedom of entry, just as in a perfectly competitive industry. The elimination of "excess" profits can occur even with only a couple of firms in an industry. The threat of entry will cause them to expand output to eliminate excess profit.

Also, firms that have cost curves that are higher than those of the most efficient firms will find that they cannot compete. These firms will be replaced by entrants whose cost curves are consistent with the most efficient technology. In other words, in contestable markets, there will be no cost inefficiencies in the long run.

⭐ EXAMPLE: Are the Airlines a True Contestable Market?

On the surface, the airline industry seems to be a good example of a contestable market. After all, there really do not seem to be many costs of entry or exit. Airplanes can be leased or purchased, but either way the investment is not a sunk cost. It may be easily sold or leased to another firm if the airline ceases operations. In the 12 years after deregulation in 1978, some 232 U.S. carriers (including commuter lines) entered the market. During that same time period, though, 171 of the new ones either merged or went out of business, as did 21 older airlines. The massive departure of new airlines from 1978 to

1990 might suggest that airlines are not a good example of a contestable market. A major reason is that to compete with the established carriers, a new entry has to put together a hub-and-spoke system, as described in Chapter 22, and hubs are expensive. Recently, though, new airlines have started. These are small airlines, such as Kiwi and others that do not try to compete with the major airlines on every route. Indeed, they usually only attempt to compete on less frequented routes such as from Newark airport to Fort Lauderdale airport (instead of from La Guardia or Kennedy to Miami International). These small airlines conform more to the contestable market theory because they are servicing only a limited number of routes. They do not have to invest in a hub system in a major city. Virtually all of them lease their planes as they need them.

For Critical Analysis: Will airline passengers necessarily pay higher prices if there are only a handful of major airlines? Why or why not? ●

CALLS FOR REREGULATION

▶ **Reregulation**
The reimposition of regulatory apparatus in an industry that has been deregulated. Reregulation may include new limits on price increases and on who may enter the industry.

The departure of so many start-up airlines caused many concerned industry participants to demand that Congress reregulate the industry. Talk of **reregulation** is now heard in a number of formerly heavily regulated industries. The most strident calls for reregulation are typically from heads of companies in formerly deregulated industries. For example, the head of USAir asked for reregulation of the airline industry as far back as 1987. His argument then was that the deregulated airline industry was offering customers worse and worse service. Though it is true that the rate of complaints per 10,000 passengers was relatively high in 1987, since then it has declined to an all time low of about one per 10,000 passengers.

Why would the heads of firms in previously regulated industries ask for reregulation? Some argue that the lives of managers in a regulated industry are much easier than in a deregulated industry. Prior to deregulation in the airline industry in 1978, there were no fare wars and no attempts to muscle in on other airlines' routes. Most airlines then were almost guaranteed profits, and virtually no new competitors could enter the industry.

A successful attempt at reregulation occurred in the cable industry. You will read about the Cable Reregulation Act of 1992 in the *Issues and Applications* section of this chapter.

CONCEPTS IN BRIEF

- Two types of regulation involve cost of service and rate of return.
- It is difficult to regulate the price per constant-quality unit because it is difficult to measure all dimensions of quality.
- The capture hypothesis indicates that regulatory agencies will eventually be captured by special interests of the industry. This is because consumers are a diffuse group who individually are not affected greatly by regulation, whereas industry groups are well focused and know that large amounts of potential profits are at stake and depend on the outcome of regulatory proceedings.
- In the share-the-gains, share-the-pains theory of regulation, regulators must take account of the interests of three groups: the industry, the legislators, and the consumers.
- The 1970s and 1980s were periods of deregulation during which formerly regulated industries became much more competitive. The short-run effects of deregulation in some industries were numerous bankruptcies and disrupted service. The long-run results in many deregulated industries included better service, more variety, and lower costs. **(Continued)**

● One argument in favor of deregulation involves the theory of contestable markets—if entry and exit are relatively costless, the number of firms in an industry is irrelevant in terms of determining whether consumers pay competitive prices.

● There have been calls for reregulation of previously deregulated industries. Often these requests are from industry managers who would prefer a less competitive industry (and hence an easier life).

ANTITRUST POLICY

It is the express aim of our government to foster competition in the economy. To this end, numerous attempts have been made to legislate against business practices that seemingly destroy the competitive nature of the system. This is the general idea behind antitrust legislation: If the courts can prevent collusion among sellers of a product, monopoly prices will not result; there will be no restriction of output if the members of an industry are not allowed to join together in restraint of trade. Remember that the competitive solution to the price-quantity problem is one in which the price of the item produced is equal to its social opportunity cost. Also, no *economic* profits are made in the long run.

THE SHERMAN ANTITRUST ACT OF 1890

The first antitrust law in the United States was passed during the period of the greatest merger movement in American history. A large number of firms were monopolizing and merging with other firms. When a number of firms merged, the resulting organizations were then called trusts. A copper trust, a steel-beam trust, an iron trust, a sugar trust, a coal trust, a paper-bag trust, and the most famous of all, the Standard Oil trust were formed. However, there was an increasing public outcry for legislation against these large trusts.

The Sherman Antitrust Act was passed in 1890. It was the first attempt by the federal government to control the growth of monopoly in the United States. The most important provisions of that act are as follows:

Section 1: Every contract, combination in the form of trust or otherwise, or conspiracy, in restraint of trade or commerce among the several states, or with foreign nations, is hereby declared to be illegal.

Section 2: Every person who shall monopolize, or attempt to monopolize, or combine or conspire with any other person or persons to monopolize any part of the trade or commerce . . . shall be guilty of a misdemeanor.[3]

Notice how vague this act really is. No definition is given for the terms *restraint of trade* or *monopolization*. Despite this vagueness, however, the act was used to prosecute the infamous Standard Oil trust of New Jersey. Standard Oil of New Jersey was charged with violations of Sections 1 and 2 of the Sherman Antitrust Act. This was in 1906, when Standard Oil controlled over 80 percent of the nation's oil-refining capacity. Among other things, Standard Oil was accused of both predatory price cutting to drive rivals out of business and obtaining preferential price treatment from the railroads for transporting Standard Oil products, thus allowing Standard to sell at lower prices.

Standard Oil was convicted in a district court. The company then appealed to the Supreme Court, which ruled that Standard's control of and power over the oil market created "a *prima facie* presumption of intent and purpose to maintain dominancy . . . not as a result from normal methods of industrial development, but by means of combination."

---

[3]This is now a felony.

Here the word *combination* meant taking over other businesses and obtaining preferential price treatment from railroads. The Supreme Court forced Standard Oil of New Jersey to break up into many smaller companies.

EXAMPLE: Price Fixing on College Campuses

For nearly 35 years, a number of private colleges and universities, mainly in the East, gathered together every year to review applications of students who had applied for financial aid. The goal of each review meeting was to make sure that each of the 10,000 students who had applied to more than one of the schools represented would be offered exactly the same financial aid package. The participating schools argued that these meetings were necessary to prevent schools from engaging in a biding war for talented students. (Participating universities have not been the only businesses to argue that price fixing is necessary to prevent ruinous competition.)

The Justice Department conducted an intensive analysis of several dozen colleges and universities that participated in these price-fixing activities. It also investigated the sharing of information about proposed tuition increases. In 1991 the Justice Department charged eight Ivy League universities and the Massachusetts Institute of Technology (MIT) with fixing the price of scholarship benefits. The Ivy Leagues—Brown, Columbia, Cornell, Dartmouth, Harvard, Princeton, Yale, and the University of Pennsylvania—consented to abandoning the practice without admitting guilt. MIT decided to defend against the charges. In 1992 Chief Judge Louis C. Bechtle, writing for the United States District Court, Eastern Division, stated that "the court had no choice but to respect 102 years of our nation's antitrust policy." He indicated that the member institutions held their biannual meetings "for the very purpose of eliminating economic competition for students." According to Assistant Attorney General Charles A. James, the district court's decision confirmed the Justice Department's contention that students and parents have "the right to compare prices among schools, just as they do in shopping for any service."

For Critical Analysis: The participating colleges and universities argued that they needed to fix the "price" of financial aid so that students would choose colleges and universities on the basis of academic quality alone. Could this argument apply to new cars? Explain. ●

THE CLAYTON ACT OF 1914

The Sherman Act was so vague that in 1914 a new law was passed to sharpen its antitrust provisions. This law was called the Clayton Act. It prohibited or limited a number of very specific business practice, which again were felt to be "unreasonable" attempts at restraining trade or commerce. Section 2 of that act made it illegal to "discriminate in price between different purchasers" except in cases in which the differences are due to actual differences in selling or transportation costs. Section 3 stated that producers cannot sell goods "on the condition, agreement or understanding that the . . . purchaser thereof shall not use or deal in the goods . . . of a competitor or competitors of the seller." And Section 7 provided that corporations cannot hold stock in another company if the effect "may be to substantially lessen competition."

The activities mentioned in the Clayton Act are not necessarily illegal. In the words of the law, they are illegal *only* when their effects "may be to substantially lessen competition or tend to create a monopoly." It takes the interpretation of the court to decide whether one of the activities mentioned actually has the effect of "substantially" lessening competition. But another provision in the Clayton Act applies to a **per se violation**—one that is *always* illegal. This activity is interlocking directorates. It is illegal per se for the same

▶ **Per se violation**
An activity that is specifically spelled out as a violation of the law, regardless of any other circumstances.

individual to serve on two or more boards of directors of corporations that are competitive and have capital surplus and undivided profits in excess of $11.3 million (or if competitve sales exceed $1.4 million per year). The existence of the interlock itself is enough to allow the government to prosecute.

THE FEDERAL TRADE COMMISSION ACT OF 1914 AND ITS 1938 AMENDMENT

The Federal Trade Commission Act was designed to stipulate acceptable competitive behavior. In particular, it was supposed to prevent cutthroat pricing—excessively aggressive competition, which would tend to eliminate too many competitors. One of the basic features of the act was the creation of the Federal Trade Commission (FTC), charged with the power to investigate unfair competitive practices. The FTC can do this on its own or at the request of firms that feel they have been wronged. It can issue cease and desist orders where "unfair methods of competition in commerce" are discovered. In 1938 the Wheeler-Lea Act amended the 1914 act. The amendment expressly prohibits "unfair or deceptive acts or practices in commerce." Pursuant to that act, the FTC engages in what it sees as a battle against false or misleading advertising, as well as the misrepresentation of goods and services for sale in the marketplace.

The significance of the Wheeler-Lea Act can be seen in its contrast to the original 1914 act. The original act was designed to protect competitors from each other. The Wheeler-Lea Act offered a very significant change in emphasis—to protect consumers. Indeed, we can view the Wheeler-Lea Act as part of a significant trend toward the protection of "ordinary people"—consumers and workers.

THE ROBINSON-PATMAN ACT OF 1936

In 1936, Section 2 of the Clayton Act was amended by the Robinson-Patman Act. The Robinson-Patman Act was aimed at preventing producers from driving out smaller competitors by means of selected discriminatory price cuts. The act has often been referred to as the "Chain Store Act" because it was meant to protect *independent* retailers and wholesalers from "unfair discrimination" by chain stores.

The act was the natural outgrowth of increasing competition that independents faced when chain stores and mass distributors started to develop after World War I. The essential provisions of the act are as follows:

1. It was made illegal to pay brokerage fees unless an independent broker was employed.
2. It was made illegal to offer concessions, such as discounts, free advertising, or promotional allowances, to one buyer of a firm's product if the firm did not offer the same concessions to all buyers of that product.
3. Other forms of discrimination, such as quantity discounts, were also made illegal whenever they "substantially" lessened competition.
4. It was made illegal to charge lower prices in one location than in another or to sell at "unreasonably low prices" if such marketing techniques were designed to "destroy competition or eliminate a competitor."

THE CELLER-KEFAUVER ACT OF 1950

In 1950, Section 7 of the Clayton Act was amended by the Celler-Kefauver Act. This act prohibits one firm from obtaining the physical assets of another firm whenever the effect of so doing would be to lessen competition. Prior to 1950, firms could evade Section 7 of the Clayton Act by buying the assets of a competing firm rather than by buying shares of stock in that firm.

EXEMPTIONS FROM ANTITRUST LAWS

Numerous laws exempt the following industries and business practices from antitrust legislation:

1. All labor unions
2. Public utilities—electric, gas, and telephone companies
3. Professional baseball
4. Cooperative activities among American exporters
5. Schools and hospitals
6. Public transit and water systems
7. Suppliers of military equipment
8. Joint publishing arrangement in a single city by two or more newspapers

ENFORCING ANTITRUST LAWS

Even if we accept the premise that monopolies should not be allowed, how can the government come up with a policy rule that will help determine which mergers should be stopped? How can the government decide which companies should be broken up into several companies? How can it know which business practices actually restrain trade? There have been numerous attempts by government officials and by interested academicians to derive specific policy rules. One of the most commonly mentioned rules states that the concentration ratio in a particular industry should not become too large. But does monopolization of the industry start when the four-firm concentration ratio becomes 50 percent, 60 percent, 70 percent, or 80 percent? Positive economic analysis cannot give us the answer.

A CHANGE IN MERGER RULES

In 1992 the Justice Department's and FTC's rules about mergers were changed quite dramatically. The new rules considerably narrow the range of mergers that the Justice Department would attempt to prevent. A number of mergers will no longer be considered candidates for intervention by the Justice Department. They include the following:

1. Conglomerate mergers (the merger of unrelated companies)
2. Customer-supplier mergers
3. Mergers between direct competitors that do not significantly affect competition

The Justice Department has come up with a different type of concentration index that will be used to determine when a merger of two competitors (horizontal mergers) will be deemed anticompetitive. Rather than the concentration ratio described in Chapter 25, they will use the **Herfindahl Index.** This index is obtained by squaring the market share of each supplier and adding them all together. An example is given in Table 26-3 on page 606.

The new merger guidelines of the Justice Department will allow any merger that leaves an industry with a Herfindahl Index of 1,000 or less, if between 1,000 and 1,800, the merger may be challenged. Any merger resulting in a Herfindahl Index greater than 1,800 will most likely be challenged. One problem that the Justice Department faces in using the Herfindahl Index is that it does not have accurate figures on the market shares of the most important companies in a particular industry.

▶ **Herfindahl Index**
An index of market concentration obtained by squaring the market share of each supplier and adding up these squared values.

TABLE 26-3 An alternative way of judging industrial concentration.

The traditional way to measure concentration has been to add the market shares of the four largest companies, A, B, C, and D. Their combined 50 percent market share would make this a fairly concentrated industry. If D and F wanted to merge, creating the industry's largest producer with 17 percent of the market, the merger would be suspect.

Under the 1992 guidelines, the Justice Department and FTC asserted that any merger that does not raise the Herfindahl Index above 1,000 is legal. Antitrusters would look at the makeup of the industry after the merger. Combining D's 10 percent and F's 7 percent and squaring them raises the index to 997, virtually ensuring legality.

Source: John E. Kwoka, using 1972 data from Economic Informations Systems, Inc. Reprinted by permission of McGraw-Hill from *Business Week,* May 17, 1982, p. 20.

COMPANY	MARKET SHARE METHOD (%)	HERFINDAHL INDEX (SHARE SQUARED)
A	16	256
B	13	169
C	11	121
D	10	100
E	8	64
F	7	49
G	6	36
H	5	25
I	4	16
24 others	20	21[a]
Total	100	857

[a]Estimated.

INDUSTRIAL SECTORS WITH THE HIGHEST HERFINDAHL INDEXES		. . . AND THE LOWEST	
Military tanks	5,823	Specialty dies and tools	11
Telephone and telegraph equipment	5,026	Concrete blocks	27
Sewing machines	4,047	Metal plating and polishing	31
Cellulosic synthetic fibers	3,189	Commercial lithography	32
Turbines	2,443	Ready-mix concrete	32

CONCEPTS IN BRIEF

● The first national antitrust law was the Sherman Antitrust Act, passed in 1890, which made illegal every contract and combination in the form of a trust in restraint of trade.

● The Clayton Act made price discrimination and interlocking directorates illegal.

● The Federal Trade Commission Act of 1914 established the Federal Trade Commission. The Wheeler-Lea Act of 1938 amended the 1914 act to prohibit "unfair or deceptive acts or practices in commerce."

● The Robinson-Patman Act of 1936 was aimed at preventing large producers from driving out small competitors by means of selective discriminatory price cuts.

● The Celler-Kefauver Act of 1950 amended Section 7 of the Clayton Act to prohibit firms from purchasing the physical assets of another firm if the effect would be to lessen competition.

IS THE REREGULATION OF CABLE TV JUSTIFIED?

Concepts Applied: Relative prices, monopoly, natural monopoly, competition

CNN is part of regular cable programming for all of the United States. Until the Cable TV Reregulation Act of 1992, cable operators were able to price their services without too much government interference.

P rior to the Cable TV Reregulation Act of 1992, *U.S. News and World Report* stated that "until Washington acts, consumers will continue to receive a monthly zapping from the cable industry."[4] The article pointed out that cable operators have a near 100 percent monopoly in cable-wired cities and that because of this monopoly and the deregulation of cable rates in 1986, cable TV bills have jumped at triple the rate of inflation. Was the Cable Communications Policy Act of 1984, which completely deregulated the prices charged by most cable companies, really that great a disaster for consumers?

REASONS BEHIND DEREGULATION
The cable TV deregulation act was based on "effective" competition from normal TV stations that transmitted to consumers using their own antennas. Under the act, any system in competition with an antenna alternative that could receive three stations was deregulated. That meant that about 90 percent of cable TV cities had no regulation after 1986. Furthermore, it meant that local and state regulatory bodies could no longer tell cable TV companies what prices to charge.

IS THERE REALLY "EFFECTIVE" COMPETITION?
Critics of cable TV deregulation argued that there is no comparison between an antenna offering three stations and a cable system offering 20, 30, or 40. Moreover, antennas are subject to much more reception interference than cable systems.

The relatively high rates of increase in fees for basic cable services plus these arguments convinced the Federal Communications Commission (FCC) to change its definition of effective competition. For about a year and a half prior to the Cable Reregulation Act of 1992, only cable systems that faced antenna competition of six or more broadcast channels were exempt from regulation. That dropped the percentage of deregulated cable companies to 70 percent.

COSTS PER CONSTANT-QUALITY UNIT CORRECTED FOR INFLATION
A cable system that offers 20 channels is not the same animal as one that offers 48. Between the time of deregulation at the end of 1986 and reregulation in the fall of 1992, the number of channels offered as part of basic cable service increased from 27 to 36. The relevant monthly figure is not how much basic service costs but how much each channel costs. That is how we correct for quality changes. That price increased from 43 cents in November 1986 to 55 cents in September 1992, a change of 27.9 percent. During that same time period, the average price of things consumers buy in general went up 28.6 percent. During that same time period the average price of medical care increased by more than 50 percent! It is not clear, then, that the inflation-corrected constant-quality-unit price of cable TV services increased at all under deregulation.

WHAT MIGHT HAPPEN UNDER REREGULATION OF CABLE TV?
In 1993, the FCC ordered a 10 to 15 percent cutback in cable rates. Subscribers were supposed to benefit to the tune of $1 billion. Critics of this type of reregulation of the cable industry believe that such reregulation will lead to a reduced number of channels made available to the TV-consuming

---

[4]February 3, 1992, p. 48.

public. They argue that if the price per constant-quality unit of cable television is kept at a below-market level, cable companies will respond by reducing the number of channels that could be made available. If, in contrast, the regulation of the price of cable TV coincides with what the market price would be in the absence of regulation, the number of channels offered to TV viewers will not be affected.

FOR CRITICAL ANALYSIS

1. Time Warner, which owns HBO and Cinemax, has expanded into cable franchising and is now the nation's

number 2 operator. How might consumers benefit from such cross-ownership? Alternatively, how might such cross-ownership serve to prevent entry into the cable industry?

2. Does evidence that average inflation-corrected prices per constant-quality unit in an industry have not risen guarantee that monopoly prices are not being charged? Why or why not?

CHAPTER SUMMARY

1. Regulation may be applied to a natural monopoly, which arises when, for example, the average total cost curve falls over a very large range of production rates. In such a situation, only one firm can survive. It will be the firm that can expand production and sales faster than the others to take advantage of the falling average total costs. If regulation seeks to force the natural monopolist to produce at the point where the marginal cost curve (supply curve in the competitive case) intersects the demand curve, the natural monopolist will incur losses because when average total costs are falling, marginal costs are below average total costs. The regulators are faced with a dilemma.

2. There are several ways of regulating monopolies, the most common ones being on a cost-of-service basis or a rate-of-return basis. Under cost-of-service regulation, the regulated monopolies are allowed to charge prices that reflect only reasonable costs. Under rate-of-return regulation, the regulated monopolies are allowed to set rates so as to make a competitive rate of return for the equity shareholders. Supposedly, no monopoly profits can therefore be earned.

3. The capture hypothesis predicts that because of the diffuse interests of consumers as compared to the well-focused interests of industry members, regulators will eventually be captured by those whom they regulate.

4. The share-the-gains, share-the-pains theory predicts that regulators must take account not only of the desires of members of the industry but also of the wishes of legislators and consumers.

5. The 1970s and 1980s were periods of deregulation during which formerly regulated industries became much more competitive. The short-run effects of deregulation in some industries were numerous bankruptcies and disrupted service. The long-run results in many deregulated industries included better service, more variety, and lower costs.

6. One argument in favor of deregulation involves the theory of contestable markets—if entry and exit are relatively costless, the number of firms in an industry is irrelevant in terms of determining whether consumers pay competitive prices.

7. There have been calls for reregulation of previously deregulated industries. Often these requests are from industry managers who would prefer a less competitive industry.

8. Antitrust legislation is designed to obviate the need for regulation. The major antitrust acts are the Sherman, Clayton, Robinson-Patman, and Celler-Kefauver acts.

DISCUSSION OF PREVIEW POINTS

1. **What is natural monopoly, and how does one arise?**
   A natural monopoly is a situation in which the long-run average cost curve falls persistently as output expands. Thus the natural monopolist is a firm that by

expanding is able to charge a price lower than its competitors can, thereby eliminating them. A natural monopolist arises due to tremendous economies of scale; expanding output causes ATC to fall.

2. If natural monopolies are required to price at marginal cost, what problem emerges?

We have noted in earlier chapters that efficiency requires that people pay the marginal cost for a good or a service. If regulators grant a firm monopoly privileges (recognizing it as a natural monopoly and regulating it to keep it in line) but force it to price at its marginal cost of production, a problem emerges. Because long-run ATC is persistently falling, it follows that long-run marginal cost must be below long-run ATC. Thus, forcing a firm to charge a price equal to marginal cost implies that average revenue = price = marginal cost < average total cost (in symbols, AR = P = MC < ATC). It follows that AR < ATC, and therefore the regulated natural monopolist would experience *negative* economic profits. In that case it would shut down unless subsidized. In short, forcing a regulated natural monopolist to price at marginal cost may be socially beneficial, but such a policy requires that the natural monopolist be subsidized to cover the resulting economic losses to the firm.

3. What are some means of regulating a natural monopoly?

Two important means of regulating a natural monopoly are cost of service and rate of return. Cost-of-service regulation aims at requiring a natural monopolist to price at levels that would result from a more competitive situation. In effect, the natural monopolist is required to charge the average cost of providing the service in question, thereby ensuring zero economic profits. The rate-of-return form of regulation in effect allows a natural monopolist to price at rates that permit it an *overall* "normal" rate-of-return. Because the natural monopolist will remain in operation only if it earns at least a normal return, this is a sensible idea.

4. Why have economists been reevaluating the government's role as an economic regulator?

Presumably regulation is an attempt to prevent monopoly abuses and to simulate a competitive market structure where one would not otherwise exist. Yet much academic research indicates that this is not the case; regulated industries apparently behave more like monopolies than the overall manufacturing sector does. Some analysts have claimed that the regulated firms sooner or later "capture" the regulatory agencies; before long, regulated industries have the protection and sanction of the regulatory bodies! Hence, many economists favor deregulation—at least of the older variety of regulation, as existed in the airlines, interstate transport, and communications industries. The consensus is less clear regarding regulation by the newer agencies such as the Environmental Protection Agency (EPA) and the Occupational Safety and Health Administration (OSHA).

PROBLEMS

(Answers to the odd-numbered problems appear at the back of the book.)

26-1. The accompanying graph depicts a situation for a natural monopolist.

a. If this monopolist were required to price at marginal cost, what would the quantity and price be?

b. What rectangle would indicate total economic losses if this monopolist were required to price at marginal cost?

26-2. "The elimination of all tariffs would dissipate more monopoly power than any other single government action." What do tariffs (taxes on imported goods only) have to do with monopoly power?

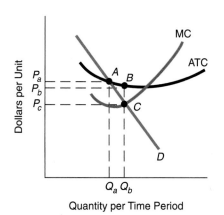

| | INDUSTRY A | | | INDUSTRY B | | | INDUSTRY C | |
| | | HERFINDAHL | | | HERFINDAHL | | | HERFINDAHL |
FIRM	SHARE (%)	INDEX	FIRM	SHARE (%)	INDEX	FIRM	SHARE (%)	INDEX
1	30	———	1	20	———	1	14	———
2	8	———	2	18	———	2	12	———
3	6	———	3	16	———	3	8	———
4	4	———	4	14	———	4	6	———
5	3	———	5	10	———	5	5	———
6	3	———	6	6	———	6	5	———
Others	46	30	Others	16	20	Others	50	40
Totals	———	———		———	———		———	———

26-3. Study the market shares for the six largest firms in three industries, A, B, and C in the table at the top of this page. Then answer the questions.

   a. Calculate the concentration ratio for each industry.

   b. Calculate the Herfindahl Index for each industry.

   c. If firm 5 in industry A merged with firm 3 in industry A, what would the new concentration ratio for industry A be? What would be A's new Herfindahl Index? Would the Justice Department be likely to allow this merger?

   d. Suppose that firms 5 and 6 in industry C both merged with firm 2 in industry C. What would the new concentration ratio for industry C be? What would be the new Herfindahl Index? Would the Justice Department be likely to allow this merger?

26-4. Would you expect to find more or less corruption of government officials in a regulatory agency that auctioned off "certificates of convenience" or in one that rationed them according to nonfinancial criteria? Why?

26-5. Why is the right of free entry insufficient to prevent sustained economic profits within a natural monopoly?

26-6. Suppose that you own the only natural mineral spring spa in your state. Why would we *not* expect to see the state government regulating the price you charge?

26-7. "Philosophically, I am vehemently opposed to government interference in the marketplace. As the owner of a liquor store, however, I can tell you that deregulation will be bad for the citizenry. You would not want a liquor store on every corner, would you?" Why would you predict that a liquor store owner would defend regulation of the liquor industry in this way?

26-8. The federal government brought an antitrust suit against IBM in 1982. Eventually the case was dismissed as being "without merit." In the 1990s, IBM has been laying off thousands of its workers. What has happened since the time IBM was being prosecuted as a monopoly and today, when it is suffering hard financial times?

COMPUTER-ASSISTED INSTRUCTION
(Complete problem and answer on disk.)

How do natural monopolies arise? This problem relates economies of scale and profit-maximizing behavior to the formation of natural monopolies.

27

PUBLIC CHOICE

America is indeed a country of wonders. Consider the farming sector. Two hundred years ago over 90 percent of the population was engaged in farming. By 1950 there were only 5 million farms, and by 1997 there will be fewer than 2 million. In the U.S. Department of Agriculture, the number of employees has nonetheless increased from about 84,000 in 1950 to close to 130,000 today. Just projecting these trends gives us a startling prediction: In the year 2001 the Department of Agriculture will employ more bureaucrats than there will be farmers. Why are there so many government "helpers" in the farm sector? The answer to this puzzle can be found by studying what is known as the theory of public choice, or how decisions are made in the public sector.

After reading this chapter, you should be able to answer the following questions:

1. What is the essence of the public-choice model?

2. Why is it that private choice can indicate intensity of wants but public choice cannot?

3. How can logrolling enable legislators to indicate the intensity of their wants?

4. When do distributional coalitions emerge?

INTRODUCTION

Every time you legally earn income and report it to the Internal Revenue Service, you owe taxes. With those taxes paid, millions of expenditures are made. Virtually all of what you have studied in this text until now has been a theory of decisions on how the money income you get to keep is spent and on how private businesses make decisions. What about the people in charge of billions upon billions of dollars collected each year for the government? That is the arena of the political marketplace. In this chapter you will learn the tools of analysis that will give you a better understanding of how political decisions are made.

THE THEORY OF PUBLIC CHOICE

Economists have developed the **theory of public choice,** which uses economic analysis to evaluate the operation of democratic governments. The theory views political decision making as occurring in a political marketplace that differs from the private marketplace chiefly in that people are not, in principle, allowed to vote directly with their dollars. The political marketplace has political entrepreneurs or suppliers, just like the private marketplace. There are also consumers—citizens. Fundamental to the theory of public choice is that all participants in the political marketplace—entrepreneurs (politicians), bureaucrats, and voters—follow the dictates of rational self-interest, just like private decision makers. That is, we assume self-interest in the political arena just as we assume it in the private arena.

▶ **Theory of public choice**
Hypotheses concerning political structures, the motives behind political actions, and their effect on economic policy.

WHAT THE THEORY PREDICTS

The theory of public choice results in numerous predictions. In a nutshell, it predicts that on average public officeholders will act in a way that maximizes their own well-being and not necessarily the well-being of the community. Public-choice theory also predicts the behavior of political parties. Political parties attempt to convince a sufficient number of voters to vote for their candidates so that they may have access to the "public trough." Consequently, each of the major political parties attempts to appear to satisfy the wishes of the largest number of potential voters. That means that ultimately candidates in most elections will appear to be similar by the time election day rolls around. This has been called the *principle of minimum differentiation.* Except for producers that produce for a "niche," producers try to make products and services that appeal to the widest variety of individuals. This is usually done by being minimally differentiated from the best-selling products or services.

WHY POLITICAL CANDIDATES MUST
APPEAR TO KNOW IT ALL

In the private marketplace, firms can and do specialize in the production of a single good. They do not have to produce products that are linked to each other in any way. This has been known as the *nonnecessity of activity tie-ins.* Presumably in an ideal political world, the same could be true for potential and actual political candidates—they could specialize in one area of knowledge. In the real world, such is not the case. All candidates must know—or at least give the appearance of knowing—something about every problem and economic and social activity that has existed, does exist, or could exist. Voters prefer such an arrangement because with their limited amount of political information, it is less costly to place one individual in charge of many activities rather than one individual in charge of each separate activity. The end result is that many issues are bundled together in the election process. The candidate who is elected either represents or misrepresents each individual voter on *all* decisions. In so doing, elected officials are given considerable leeway to violate the preferences of the people who elected them and at the same time to pursue their own self-interests (more personal wealth, more paid work for friends and relatives). If this were not the case, we would not have seen over $300 million spent on candidates seeking congressional seats in the 1992 elections.

THE POLITICAL PARTICIPANTS

When we think about economic activities in the private marketplace, it is often useful to focus on the behavior of three key groups of participants: consumers, employees, and owners. In the political marketplace, these three groups correspond to constituents, bureaucrats, and members of Congress. Consider the defense industry. The principal constituents (consumers of defense spending) are defense industry manufacturing companies such as Hughes Aircraft and McDonnell Douglas. The workers, managers, and shareholders of defense industry firms receive the benefits of defense spending programs in the form of wealth that is redistributed in their direction. Members of Congress in essence act as venture capitalists who provide the funding (via taxation) for defense spending programs and give overall direction to them. Bureaucrats in the Department of Defense provide technical support to Congress, for example, on program design and the cost and implementation of defense spending programs. To close the circle, workers, managers, and shareholders in defense industry firms provide an acceptable rate of return to members of Congress via campaign contributions and political support on nondefense issues. Much of this part of the circle involves lobbyists for the defense industry. The circle of participants for defense spending programs is shown in Figure 27-1.

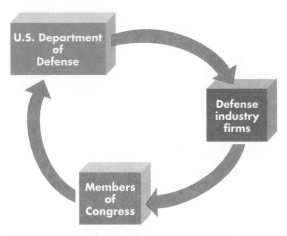

FIGURE 27-1
The circle of political participants for defense spending.

CONCEPTS IN BRIEF

- The theory of public choice uses economic analysis to evaluate the operation of democratic government; the theory assumes the self-interest of all political participants.
- Because political parties want to appear to satisfy the wishes of the largest number of potential voters, by the time elections occur, what their candidates say will differ very little. This is called the *principle of minimum differentiation*.
- Political candidates must appear to know all because voters prefer to put one individual in charge of many activities rather than an individual in charge of each separate activity.
- The circle of political participants includes constituents, bureaucrats, and appropriate members of Congress.

VOTING IN THE POLITICAL MARKETPLACE

We pointed out in Chapter 5 that there are distinct differences between dollar voting in the private marketplace and voting in the political marketplace. In particular, a political system is run by majority rule, whereas the market system is run by proportional rule. Winner takes all in a political system; that is not so in a private economic marketplace. A producer can sell to a very limited public in a marketplace and still survive. This is impossible in the political marketplace. Dollars can indicate intensity of want in a private marketplace, but because of the all-or-nothing nature of political voting, a vote cannot. In general, it is incorrect to assume that a political voting process will lead to the same decisions that a dollar-voting process will lead to in the marketplace.

In the real world, political competition is less than perfect because of the large-scale effort and financial resources required to organize political parties and activities. This is certainly true for presidential and gubernatorial offices, for which literally millions of voters must be reached. Even under the most ideal real-world situations, many groups that would like to compete for political office do not and will never have sufficient resources to reach a large number of voters.

THE MEDIAN VOTER

The theory of public choice assumes that voters are rational. This implies that all persons, politicians included, vote in accordance with their self-interest *as they perceive it*. Because most political decisions are made by majority rule, political decisions will in principle be made in accordance with the self-interest of the median voter. This is called the **median voter theorem.** If half the voters favor some government policy and half oppose it, the decision will be made in accordance with the desires of the voter who is exactly in the middle—the median voter. According to the median voter theorem, a political party will therefore promote programs that appeal to the median voter. Of course, the problem with the median voter theorem is that if there are two major parties, each attempting to appeal to the median voter, their programs will be virtually identical, and neither one will increase its share of the votes.

▶ **Median voter theorem**
The contention that political parties will pursue policies in accord with the wishes of the median voter.

The median voter theorem seems correctly to predict the reality of the principle of minimum differentiation among candidates from the two major parties, particularly for the office of president. Moreover, the median voter theorem seems to predict the outcome of political campaigning within the party primaries. The candidates take more extreme positions during the primaries because they are attempting to appeal to the median voter within their own parties. Once a candidate has been selected from each party, that candidate wants to appeal to the median voter in the entire United States, including independents.

When individuals are dissatisfied with a political outcome that satisfies the median voter, they sometimes do have a choice. They can "vote with their feet" by moving to a jurisdiction in which the median voter has tastes that correspond more with their own. This is not easy when considering moves between nations, but it can be done when considering the individual fifty states and the District of Columbia. People move from one state to another sometimes in response to a different political environment in the other state—different taxes, expenditures, public safety policies, drug regulation policies, and so on.

The problem with the median voter theorem is that it does not explain why small groups in society can obtain a disproportionate share of government benefits. If the median voter model predicted well, the farming sector, which represents only a few million farmers, would not be receiving literally tens of billions of dollars a year in government benefits. We must look elsewhere to explain public policy. We must look at the *concentration of benefits* and the *dispersion of cost* among voters.

DISTRIBUTIONAL COALITIONS

Even a cursory examination of the benefits of government programs shows that they are often concentrated in small groups of people—farmers, the defense industry, and so on. The cost of these programs is shared by all taxpayers. The way that small, concentrated groups in our democratic society succeed in transferring so much income to themselves from everybody else is through what is known as **distributional coalitions.** These coalitions are small groups that gain much individually at the expense of many individuals who lose much collectively, but little individually, from the special privileges granted members of the coalition. Most collective action—action designed to influence public officials—takes place in small homogeneous groups rather than large diverse groups. After all, individuals with a common interest will not voluntarily combine and act to further their common interest unless each individual has an incentive to participate in such collective action. Members of distributional coalitions have an incentive to act collectively to induce the median *legislator* to vote in a way that is not consistent with the interests of the median constituent.

▶ **Distributional coalitions**
Associations such as cartels, unions, and cooperatives that are formed to gain special government privileges in order to redistribute wealth by taking small amounts from each of many people and giving large amounts to each of only a few.

⭐ **EXAMPLE: Getting a Milking from the Milk Lobby**

One clear-cut, tightly knit, homogeneous small group of individuals is dairy farmers. Collectively they benefit very specifically from various handouts, rules, and regulations formulated by the federal government. One particular government "goody" that they get is milk **price supports.** These involve direct payments from the federal government to dairy farmers. An examination of how much dairy farmers benefit in one state, Florida, is illustrative. In a recent year Florida dairy farmers received $40.3 million in price support payments. Almost 100 percent went to 177 farmers. Each received an average payment in one year of $226,700. In the extreme, if the cost of these payments were borne solely by the residents of Florida, each resident in the state would pay $3.35. How much effort will the residents of Florida make—in other words, what is the value of the resources that they will spend—so as *not* to pay that $3.35 a year? At best they would pay $3.34. At worst they would pay nothing—why should they take the effort? The 177 Florida dairy farmers, however, each have a great incentive to ensure that their payments from the federal government continue. The residents of the state have no incentive to try to stop these payments. Nonetheless, a few years ago several consumer groups and producers of milk-based products pushed for a reduction in milk price supports. Dairy farmers acting via their marketing associations, such as the Associated Milk Producers and Mid-America Dairymen, responded with vigor. Those marketing associations lobbied intensively on behalf of price supports. Their political action committees (PACs) donated over $1 million to the reelection campaigns of more than two-thirds of the members of the House of Representatives. Even though 55 percent of all milk production takes place in just five states and even though the majority of all congressional districts have no significant milk production, dairy farmers preserved their price supports. Of the 21 urban and suburban members of Congress who received $5,000 or more from dairy PACs, 20 voted in accordance with the farmers' wishes.

▶ **Price supports**
Minimum prices set by the government. To be effective, price supports must be coupled with a mechanism to rid the market of surplus goods that arise whenever the support price is greater than the market clearing price.

For Critical Analysis: There is a lobbying group aimed at helping the general public. It is called Common Cause. How much success do you think Common Cause can have? ●

LOGROLLING

Sometimes even lobbying or well-placed campaign contributions are not sufficient to get the programs that distributional coalitions want. In such cases, **logrolling** has been an effective tool. This practice involves an exchange of votes among legislators: Representative A votes for a program that benefits representative B's constituents in return for B's

▶ **Logrolling**
The practice of exchanging political favors by elected representatives. Typically, one elected official agrees to vote for the policy of another official in exchange for the vote of the latter in favor of the former's desired policy.

vote on a program that benefits A's constituents. One official may want the continuation of an army base in his hometown while another may want a new dam to be built in her home state, and so it goes. You vote for my army base, and I'll vote for your dam.

One of the major benefits of logrolling is that it allows an elected representative to demonstrate his or her *intensity* of preference, which presumably reflects the intensity of preferences of the constituents. For example, if a representative knows that it is extremely important for his constituents to keep the army base in his hometown, he may be willing to vote for a larger number of pet projects of other representatives to make sure that his pet project is passed. The problem, of course, is that typically—and our example fits perfectly— elected representatives care about geographic representation. *We have a geographically based political system.* The legislator has an incentive to represent local interests when he or she acts in the national legislature (Congress). The broader national issues typically suffer. National legislation becomes the vehicle for local support. The result is what is often known as "pork barrel" legislation that benefits very specific local areas.

⭐ EXAMPLE: The Food Stamp Program

A classic example of logrolling as a device to facilitate the redistribution of wealth is found in government programs for "feeding the hungry."

No one enjoys watching others go hungry. Recognizing this, legislators from rural farming regions and lawmakers representing low-income urban areas have forged an effective alliance to promote subsidized food distribution to the poor. Urban legislators get cheap food for their constituents, and rural legislators get a convenient means of disposing of the surpluses generated by agricultural price supports. It may not be a marriage made in heaven, but it keeps this set of political bedfellows happy—and it does provide subsidized food for low-income individuals.

Federally subsidized domestic food distribution programs began during the Great Depression but remained modest in scope until the 1960s. The food stamp program, begun in 1939, and the national school lunch program, started in 1946, are currently the most important of these programs. Under the school lunch program, children are provided with subsidized or even free lunches while attending school. The food stamp program allows low-income individuals to obtain food stamps free in inverse proportion to their income; these stamps can then be used like money to purchase selected food items. Although both programs began on a modest level, the burgeoning food surpluses of the early 1960s prompted massive expansion of the programs. Low-income recipients of subsidized food have no doubt benefited from these programs; nevertheless, the chief objective of many program supporters has been higher incomes for farmers. Evidence of this can be found in the identity of the programs' supporters, the nature of the eligible commodities, and the fact that subsidized food programs are operated through the USDA, an agency designed to aid *farmers*.

Supporters of subsidized food distribution have been particularly successful in promoting and expanding the food stamp program. Indeed, according to the U.S. Senate Committee on Agriculture, the program "has been used in legislative strategy to entice urban legislators who might not otherwise support costly farm price support programs to do so in exchange for rural support for the Food Stamp Program." This process began with the Food Stamp Act of 1964, which laid the foundation for the present-day system. In 1968 the timing of food stamp legislation was tied to the legislative cycle of the farm bill—presumably to facilitate enforcement of logrolling deals made between rural and urban legislators. In 1970 federal expenditures on food stamps were doubled, then doubled again in 1971. By this time, legislating against hunger had become a favorite activity in

Congress, spurred by the rural-urban coalition of farm representatives and legislators from low-income districts. In 1973 spending on food stamps was hiked again, and items that could be purchased with food stamps were expanded to include seeds and garden plants, meals prepared for drug addicts and alcoholics in their treatment programs, and hunting and fishing equipment for households in remote areas of Alaska. In 1974 measures were introduced to provide food stamps on Indian reservations, to incorporate cost-of-living increases, and to prohibit the use of food stamps to purchase imported meats. In 1975 eligibility requirements were liberalized and appropriations for the food stamp program were increased. Attempts to curb the program in 1977 largely failed, and the program has continued to expand: From the beginning of 1989 to the beginning of 1993, an additional 7 million Americans received food stamps. The estimated number of participants in 1993 exceeds 27 million, or 10.5 percent of the entire U.S. population. Congress authorized $28 billion in food stamp program spending for the fiscal year ending September 30, 1993.

For Critical Analysis: During the aftermath of 1992's Hurricane Andrew in southern Florida, the federal government offered "emergency" food stamps to people living in the stricken area. Relatively soon, however, the emergency, no-questions-asked program was halted. What do you suppose happened? ●

CONCEPTS IN BRIEF

● Distributional coalitions, which are associations such as unions and farmers' cooperatives, are formed to gain special government privileges for their members. The members of these coalitions tend to gain a great deal individually, at the expense of the many, who lose much collectively but little individually.

● Logrolling is the exchange of votes among elected representatives, such as occurs when farm representatives agree to vote for food stamps for the poor in return for urban representatives' votes for farm subsidies.

THE ROLE OF BUREAUCRATS

▶ **Bureaucrats**
Nonelected government officials who are responsible for the day-to-day operation of government and the observance of its regulations and laws.

Programs require people to operate them. This is manifest in government today in the form of well-established bureaucracies, in which **bureaucrats** work. Bureaucracies can exert great influence on matters concerning themselves—the amount of funding granted them and the activities in which they engage. In the political marketplace, well-organized bureaucracies can even influence the expression of public demand itself. In many cases they organize the clientele (special-interest groups), coach that clientele on what is appropriate, and stick up for the "rights" of the clientele. Once again, farm programs are a good example.

GAUGING BUREAUCRATIC PERFORMANCE

It is tempting, but incorrect, to think of bureaucrats as mere technocrats—executors of orders and channels of information—in this process. For at least two reasons they have incentives to make government programs larger and more resistant to attack than we might otherwise expect. First, society has decided that in general, government should not be run on a profit-making basis. Measures of performance other than bottom-line profits must be devised. In the private market, successful firms typically expand to serve more customers; although this growth is often incidental to the underlying profitability, the two frequently go hand in hand. In parallel, performance in government is often measured by the number of clients served, and rewards are distributed accordingly. As a result, bureaucrats have an incentive to expand the size of their clientele—not because it is more profitable (beneficial) to society but because that is how *bureaucrats'* rewards are structured.

In general, performance measures that are not based on long-run profitability are less effective at gauging true performance. This makes it potentially easier for the government bureaucrat to *appear* to perform well, collect rewards for measured performance, and then leave for greener pastures. To avoid this, a much larger proportion of the rewards given bureaucrats are valuable only as long as they continue being bureaucrats—large staffs, expensive offices, generous pensions, and the like. Instead of getting large current salaries (which can be saved for a rainy day), they get rewards that disappear if their jobs disappear. Naturally, this increases the incentives of bureaucrats to make sure that their jobs don't disappear, as you will see in the *Issues and Applications* discussion at the end of this chapter.

RATIONAL IGNORANCE

At this point you may well be wondering, How do these guys get away with it? The answer lies in *rational ignorance* on the part of voters, ignorance that is carefully cultivated by the members of distributional coalitions.

For most issues there is little incentive for the individual voter to expend resources to determine how to vote. Moreover, the ordinary course of living provides most individuals with enough knowledge to decide whether they should invest in learning more about a given issue. For example, suppose that American voters were asked to decide if the sign marking the entrance to an obscure national park should be enlarged. Most voters would decide that the potential costs and benefits of this decision were negligible: The new sign is unlikely to be the size of the state of Rhode Island, and anybody who has even *heard* of the national park in question probably already has a pretty good idea of its location. Thus most voters would choose to remain rationally ignorant about the *exact* costs and benefits of enlarging the sign, implying that (1) many will choose not to vote at all and (2) those who do vote will simply flip a coin or cast their ballot based on some other, perhaps ideological, grounds.

Why Be Rationally Ignorant?   For most political decisions, majority rule prevails. Only a coalition of voters representing slightly more than 50 percent of those whose vote is needed. Whenever a vote is taken, the result is going to involve costs and benefits. Voters, then, must evaluate their share of the costs and benefits of any budgetary expenditure. Voters, however, are not perfectly informed. That is one of the crucial characteristics of the real world—information is a resource that is costly to obtain. Rational voters will, in fact, decide to remain at some level of ignorance about government programs because the benefits from obtaining more information may not be worth the cost, given each individual voter's extremely limited impact on the outcome of an election. For the same reason, voters will fail to inform themselves about taxes or other revenue sources to pay for proposed expenditures because they know that for any specific expenditure program, the cost to them individually will be small. At this point it might be useful to contrast this situation with what exists in the nonpolitical private market sector of the economy. In the private market sector, the individual chooses a mix of purchases and bears fully the direct and indirect consequences of this selection (ignoring for the moment the problem of externalities).

The Costs and Benefits of Voting.   Voters' incentives to remain rationally ignorant about most issues are compounded by other factors. First, even if the *total* costs or benefits of a political decision are large, the costs or benefits to any *individual* voter are likely to be small. We saw this earlier with price support payments for Florida dairy farmers. Even though these payments cost Floridians as a group roughly $40 million, the cost to any individual in the state is unlikely to be much more than about $3. Because individual benefits (to non–dairy farmers) are unlikely to be much different, most Floridians will not bother to find out whether or not it is in their interest to favor price supports for milk (and the tax costs are actually spread among all Americans).

Why Not Vote the Rascals Out?   Each time a legislator votes for a special-interest group at the expense of the general public (and this happens almost all the time), it would seem that voters have an incentive to "vote the rascal out." The problem is that even if the legislator's constituents as a group suffers substantial costs due to dairy price supports, the loss suffered by any individual constituent is quite small. In the case of dairy price supports, few nonfarmer constituents are likely to vote against the legislator just because he or she voted in favor of dairy price supports. A constituent's vote on a legislative candidate depends on the entire *package* of positions adopted by the legislator; for nonfarmers, the issue of price supports is a trivial component of that package. Moreover, campaign contributions from farmers enable the legislator to inform constituents of his or her supportive votes on other issues of more importance to nonfarmers—education, perhaps, or child care. This typically more than offsets any votes lost due to the legislator's support for farm subsidies. Thus the activities of distributional coalitions (special-interest groups) create a gap between the self-interest of the median *legislator* and the self-interest of the median *constituent*. For this reason, farm subsidies and other special-interest legislation that might not be enacted if all citizens voted on the issue may still be enacted when only legislators vote.

The Weight of One Person's Vote.   It is true that in most elections, the number of voters is so great that it is unlikely that the outcome will hinge on any one person's vote. In the last nine elections, an average of over 80 million people cast ballots for president. In the popular vote, the winning margins were 119,000 in 1960—the smallest—and 18 million in 1972—the largest. (Of course, the differences between the two parties in the electoral college are usually much greater—that's why we have the electoral college.) So even if a voter believes that the two presidential candidates take opposing stands on a particular issue, unless that voter is directly affected, he or she might not even bother to find out which candidate opposes and which candidate favors the program because the chance that this voter's single vote will affect the outcome is so small. Clearly, not everyone takes this information to heart. If everyone did, no one would come out to vote. Voting, particularly for presidential candidates, is often a consumption activity in which American citizens engage. Individuals also feel a sense of civic pride when they vote. Moreover, individuals who vote for the winning candidate are in less of a position to complain about what is happening and more likely to be accepting of the administration's policies. Although voter apathy may appear to be a problem, if measured by the percentage of registered voters who actually vote, low voter turnout may in fact be a sign that voters are happy with the system as it stands.

CONCEPTS IN BRIEF

- Voters may be rationally ignorant about many election issues because the cost of obtaining more information may outweigh the benefits of doing so. Distributional coalitions attempt to promote rational ignorance for their own benefit by hiding the true costs of the programs they favor.
- Bureaucrats often exert great influence on the course of policy because they are in charge of the day-to-day operation of current policy and provide much of the information needed to formulate future policy. Bureaucracies often organize their clientele, coach clients on what is appropriate, and stick up for their rights.

PUBLIC CHOICE AND YOU

Perhaps the most important information you can extract from this chapter is a better understanding of why many government programs seem to go against the grain of economic analysis. It is not sufficient for you to mount a campaign of economic education for politicians. They can learn microeconomic theory better than the best professor of economics and still end up voting for government programs that create inefficiencies and waste. So-called public servants, and particularly elected politicians, usually cannot survive if they are interested only in the "public good." In the case of politicians, if they don't "bring home the bacon" to their constituents, they will not get reelected. The theory of public choice tells you that one of the main jobs of an elected official is to get reelected. That job requires that he or she satisfy special-interest groups so that they will provide the contributions necessary to get that official reelected.

SO FEW FARMERS, SO MANY BUREAUCRATS

**Concepts Applied: Theory of public choice,
bureaucrats, distributional coalitions**

Agricultural activity in Iowa seems to be everywhere, yet farming actually occurs in only 16 percent of the 3,042 counties in the United States. Nonetheless, 94 percent of all counties have Department of Agriculture field offices.

Here is one of the great seeming paradoxes of the twentieth century: Farming occurs in 16 percent of the 3,042 counties in the United States. Nonetheless, the Department of Agriculture maintains 11,000 offices in 2,859 of these counties, or 94 percent. We must wonder what employees in the Agriculture Department in the 2,372 counties that do not have any farmers actually do. "Nice work if you can get it" is perhaps the best answer to that.

A FEW NUMBERS In Figure 27-2 you see the ratio of farmers to agricultural employees from 1950 to 1990 plus some estimates made to the year 2015 by economist David L. Littmann. Using the estimates in Figure 27-2, we come to the fateful prediction that in the year 2001 there will already be more bureaucrats in the Department of Agriculture than there are U.S. farmers.

WHY THERE ARE SO FEW FARMS AND FARMERS From Figure 27-3 on the next page you can see that the number of farms in the United States rose from 1.4 million in 1850 to a high of 6.8 million in 1935. Since then the number has declined fairly steadily to its present level of around 2.1 million. During this time the nature of the average farm has also changed sharply. Since 1960 alone, the size of the average farm has grown by almost 65 percent. Although the typical farm is still run by an individual owner-operator, the economic importance of such farms is shrinking rapidly. About 65 percent of all American farms have annual sales of less than $25,000. Together they count for only 6 percent of national farm output. In contrast, farms with sales in excess of $250,000 make up about 4 percent of all farms. They, however, account for about 50 percent of all U.S. farm output. Agriculture is rapidly becoming agribusiness. There are two major reasons why this is occurring.

INCREASED PRODUCTIVITY The first reason is increased productivity in the farming sector. Between 1935 and 1950 agricultural output per worker-hour doubled.

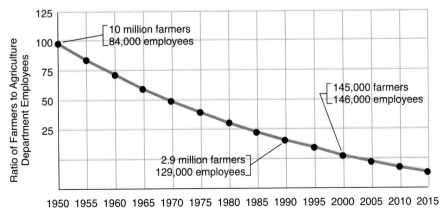

FIGURE 27-2

Farmers disappearing as bureaucrats increase.
The number of farmers in the United States has decreased steadily since 1950, yet the number of employees in the U.S. Department of Agriculture has steadily increased and may actually exceed the number of working farmers by the year 2001. (Figures for 1991–2015 are estimates.)

Source: USDA Economic Research Service.

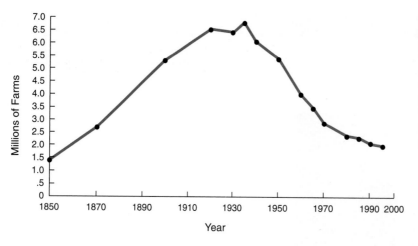

FIGURE 27-3
Farms in the United States, 1850–1995.
The number of farms in the United States rose from 1.4 million in 1850 to a high of 6.8 million in 1935. Today there are just over 2 million farms.

Source: U.S. Bureau of the Census.

Between 1950 and 1965 it more than doubled again. As you read this book it is doubling once more. A given amount of labor will now produce 10 times as much agricultural output as it did 60 years ago!

A LIMIT TO THE AMOUNT OF FOOD THAT PEOPLE CAN EAT   The second explanation has to do with the fact that there are limits to the amount of food that people can eat. As families get richer, they do not keep buying more and more food. The income elasticity of demand for food (see Chapter 20) is less than 1. As income rises, food expenditures become less important in each person's budget.

WHY SO MANY FARM BUREAUCRATS?

As farm productivity has reached higher and higher levels, the pressure for market prices to fall has increased. Enter the farm lobbies. They have attempted to slow the progress in the reduction of the existing levels of farm labor and capital. They have asked for and received large taxpayer subsidies. The estimate for 1993 alone is $22 billion, much of which has gone into subsidies that have kept farm prices up (and consumer spending on food about 14 percent higher than it would be otherwise).

Farmers are an odd lot. The majority of them take the extra profits they earn from the subsidy and plow it back into their farms. They continue to increase productivity. But then they produce even more, putting more downward pressure on farm prices. A vicious circle ensues in which well-to-do farmers pour in additional dollars lobbying for more federal government help. But along with federal government help come, of course, more bureaucrats.

IF IT IS SO OBVIOUS, WHY DOESN'T IT GO AWAY?   Anybody can read the meaning of Figure 27-2. The president, members of Congress, and even those wily bureaucrats working in Agriculture Department offices hundreds or even thousands of miles from the closest farm know the story. So why isn't something done? Why doesn't Congress eliminate, at a minimum, all of the wasted resources in the Department of Agriculture? Surely the federal government could subsidize the farming sector without such a large bureaucracy. The answer, of course, has to do with the theory of public choice. The bureaucrats in the Department of Agriculture have formed a coalition. They are part of an "iron triangle" that includes their own department, members of Congress who are involved in agricultural affairs, and agribusiness men and women. The members of this iron triangle have a clear-cut vested interest in preserving the status quo. You as a consumer of farm products have an interest also. But your interest is trivial compared to those in the iron triangle. If you spent time and effort to reduce the bloated bureaucracy in the Department of Agriculture, your tax liability might go down a few cents. Each employee in the Department of Agriculture is looking at the loss of a very well-paid job (per constant-quality unit of effort). Who do you think is going to spend more time on this issue?

FOR CRITICAL ANALYSIS

1. Where else in government do you think a similar analysis applies?
2. If you were working in an Agriculture Department field office in a county in which there are no farmers, how could you justify the field office's existence?

CHAPTER SUMMARY

1. Distributional coalitions, which are associations such as unions and farmers' cooperatives, are formed to gain special government privileges for their members. The members of these coalitions tend to gain a great deal individually, at the expense of the many, who lose much collectively but little individually. Distributional coalitions have played a major role in the growth of government in the twentieth century.

2. Logrolling is the exchange of votes among elected representatives, such as occurs when farm representatives agree to vote for food stamps for the poor in return for urban representatives' votes for farm subsidies.

3. Voters may be rationally ignorant about many election issues because the cost of obtaining more information may outweigh the benefits of doing so. Distributional coalitions attempt to promote rational ignorance for their own benefit by hiding the costs of the programs they favor.

4. Bureaucrats often exert great influence on the course of policy because they are in charge of the day-to-day operation of current policy and provide much of the information needed to formulate future policy. Bureaucracies often organize their clientele, coach clients on what is appropriate, and stick up for their rights.

5. Public-choice economics examines motives behind political entrepreneurs and the outcomes of political actions. Public-choice theory predicts that participants in the political marketplace, such as politicians, act so as to maximize their own self-interest rather than the public interest.

6. The political participants are constituents, bureaucrats, and members of Congress. They form a closed circle.

7. The median voter theorem states that political parties will pursue policies that maximize the situation of the median voter. When people are dissatisfied with the results, at least theoretically, they can "vote with their feet" by moving to a state with more attractive policies.

DISCUSSION OF PREVIEW POINTS

1. **What is the essence of the public-choice model?**

   The essence of the public-choice model is that politicians, bureaucrats, and voters will act so as to maximize *their own* self-interest (or economic well-being) rather than the community's. In other words, because such people are human, they are subject to the same motivations and drives as the rest of us. They will usually—but not always—make decisions in terms of what benefits them, not society as a whole. Such an assumption permits economists to apply economic maximization principles to voters, candidates, elected officials, and policymakers.

2. **Why is it that private choice can indicate intensity of wants but public choice cannot?**

   If Romano loves pasta, he can freely spend a high percentage of his income on it. The fact that he does spend a high percentage of his income on pasta and a zero percentage of his income on rice indicates the intensity of his wants. He can allocate his "dollar votes" in such a way as to reveal his preferences—and maximize his utility. In a "one-person, one-vote" situation, however, Romano has only *one* vote. He must choose among different candidates, each of whom offers a platform of many publicly provided goods. Romano's vote "buys" both the services he wants and the services he does not want.

3. **How can logrolling enable legislators to indicate the intensity of their wants?**

   Logrolling is a procedure whereby legislators can trade votes. If your legislator is in an oil-producing state, she presumably has an intense desire to vote for bills that promote the interests of the oil industry. Legislators, however, also have only one vote per bill. By trading her vote on issues that she (and her constituents) are not concerned with, she can induce other legislators to vote for the pro-oil bill. Such vote trading, in effect, gives her more than one vote on this bill—and no vote on other bills.

4. **When do distributional coalitions emerge?**

   Distributional coalitions emerge when it is possible for a small group to benefit (relatively) hugely at the expense of a large group that pays *individually* relatively small amounts. For example, assume that 10,000 honey producers value government price supports at $100 million; assume also that the cost of the program to the rest of society is about 1 cent per person in taxes and a 2 cent per pound higher price for honey. Honey producers will find it profitable to form a distributional coalition, which will contribute to a politician's campaign for election or reelection. Taxpayers and honey consumers will not find it beneficial to form a counterforce to that distributional coalition.

PROBLEMS

(Answers to the odd-numbered problems appear at the back of the book.)

27-1.   The existence of information and transaction costs has many implications in economics. What are some of these implications in the context of issues discussed in this chapter?

27-2.   Suppose that a government program that subsidizes a certain group in America ends up generating $200,000 per year in additional income to each member of the group. The average income in America for a family of four is less than $40,000 per year, and the official poverty line is much less than that. How could you explain the continued success of such a program? Under what circumstances might such a program be terminated?

27-3.   Much of the presidential debate between Clinton and Bush in 1992 seemed not to be a debate at all. Rather, they didn't seem to have many true fundamental differences, at least with respect to economic issues. How does the theory of public choice predict such a situation?

27-4.   Suppose that you see a distinct problem in our country that needs solving. You decide to run for office and learn everything you can about the problem so that you are an expert in how government can solve it. You don't know much else about other problems or issues. How successful might you be in your campaign to be a "niche" politician? Explain.

27-5.   A favorite presidential campaign theme in recent years has been to reduce the size, complexity, and bureaucratic nature of the federal government. Nonetheless, the size of the federal government, however measured, continues to increase. Use the theory of public choice to explain why.

27-6.   Civics textbooks often claim that voting is one of the most precious and important responsibilities of citizens living in a democracy. Yet if it is raining hard on election day, the percentage of eligible voters that actually votes usually falls. What does this tell you about the public's view of its voting responsibility?

27-7.   Term limits on congressional officeholders—senators and representatives—had been approved in 15 states by the end of 1992. Use the theory of public choice to explain how term limits might change the relationships between the participants in the political marketplace.

COMPUTER-ASSISTED INSTRUCTION
(Complete problem and answer on disk.)

Why have we had enormous food surpluses in the United States because our farmers are so efficient that they can produce more than we can eat? This problem requires the proper interpretation of graphs. It reveals that food surpluses are due not to efficiency but to government price supports above equilibrium.

PUBLIC CHOICE IN ACTION: FARM POLICY

Each year the federal government spends about $30,000 per farm on U.S. Department of Agriculture (USDA) programs. When the government speaks, farmers listen. But when the farmers speak, the government listens. Government agricultural programs exist almost exclusively to perform one function: to redistribute income from consumers and taxpayers to farmers. Farm programs provide a classic example of the theory of public choice in action.

AGRICULTURE IN THE UNITED STATES

There are about 2.1 million farms in the United States. Because of high farm productivity, the total output of the farm sector is staggering. Because the average farm produces an extremely small share of total U.S output, we have a situation about as close to perfect competition as we'll ever see: Each farmer must take the market price of the product as given, products are relatively homogeneous, and entry is fairly easy.

Historically, however, farmers as a group have been unwilling to take as given the unrestricted world market price of their products. They have argued that for a variety of reasons they deserve special treatment by the government. Farmers are said to be poor and to face much more uncertainty than other economic agents because they are subject to droughts and floods, infestations of insects, and crop-threatening diseases. Some protection from these uncertainties is warranted, perhaps in the form of government-guaranteed prices. Moreover, in the past 50 years a new concern has developed: The family farm, once a cornerstone of the American way of life, is disappearing. Hence it is argued that small farmers should be protected from the rigors of world competition. What are the facts?

FARM INCOME

A casual look at the income received by farmers seems to confirm that they do have lower than average incomes. At the beginning of the 1990s, for example, the median farm family earned about $24,000 per year from farm operations, well below the $30,000 earned by the median nonfarm family. Yet these figures ignore the fact that 95 percent of all farms are either hobby farms (sales of less than $20,000 per year) or family farms (annual sales of $20,000 to $200,000). Operators of both types of farms rely heavily on income from nonfarm activities (such as part-time jobs held by family members) to supplement their incomes. Family farm operators, for example, earn about as much from nonfarm activities as they do from farm operations, pushing their *total* incomes well above average. This is confirmed by looking at the assets of farmers compared to other individuals. In 1993 the average farm in the United States was worth about $420,000; after adjusting for debts, the net worth of the average farmer was well over $300,000, more than double the net worth of the average household in this country. In short, the average farmer is at least as well off financially as the average citizen.

THE WHIMS OF NATURE

Food production is heavily dependent on weather conditions. Though long-run weather patterns are fairly predictable, the weather in any given year is much more uncertain. Thus the incomes of farmers from one year to the next are subject to uncertainty. This uncertainty is compounded by the fact that the price elasticity of the demand for food is low—the demand for food is inelastic. Just as the low income elasticity of demand for food helps explain the long-run downward trend in the farm sector, the low price elasticity of demand for food is important for understanding the high variability of farmers' incomes in the short run.

Inelastic Demand for Food.   Consider the change in price that results from an increase in supply due to abnormally good weather. In Figure F-1 we show the supply curve shifting to the right from S to S', reflecting an increase in production due to good weather. Suppose first that the demand curve is relatively *elastic* (at point E), such as D. The good-weather equilibrium will be at point E', where the good-weather supply schedule, S', intersects the demand schedule, D. The normal-weather equilibrium was at point E, implying a price of P_e. The good-weather equilibrium occurs at E', implying a price of P_e', somewhat below P_e.

Suppose, alternatively, that the demand curve is relatively *inelastic* (at E). The normal-weather equilibrium is still at E, but the good-weather equilibrium occurs at E'', where the good-weather supply curve, S', intersects the inelastic demand curve, D'. The resulting good-weather price is P_e''—far below P_e'. Because the demand for food is in fact relatively inelastic, good weather produces an extremely large decrease in the price of farm products.

Consider now the effect of abnormally *bad* weather, such as a drought. Bad weather produces a sharp reduction in production—that is, a shift of the supply curve to the *left*. If the demand for food were elastic, the effect would be a fairly moderate rise in the price of food. However, because the demand for food is actually inelastic, bad weather produces an extraordinarily large increase in the price of farm products. These results suggest an important conclusion:

> **The more inelastic the demand for a good, the greater will be the impact on the price of the good when there is a change in supply.**

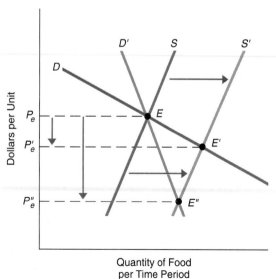

Dollars per Unit

P_e, P_e', P_e''

Quantity of Food per Time Period

FIGURE F-1
Consequences of relatively inelastic demand.
The quantity of food produced per time period is on the horizontal axis and the price per unit is on the vertical axis. Assume that the original supply curve is S—relatively inelastic supply in the short run at the current price. If the demand curve for farmers is D, a shift in the supply curve from S to S' due to good weather will lower the equilibrium price from P_e to P_e'. But if the demand curve is instead more inelastic at price P_e, such as D', when the supply curve shifts to S', the new equilibrium price falls to P_e''. This accounts for the large variability in incomes of farmers in different years when there is no government intervention.

Because the demand for food is relatively inelastic, we expect food prices to rise quite substantially when there is a drought. Conversely, when weather conditions are ideal, we expect food prices to be quite low. The inelastic demand for agricultural products has been an important reason why prices have fluctuated more from year to year in agriculture than they have in other industries.

CONCEPTS IN BRIEF

- On average, farmers are at least as well off financially as nonfarmers, although their incomes are inherently subject to higher than average uncertainty.
- Due to rapid technological progress, the number of farms in the United States has been declining steadily for 50 to 60 years, and their average size has been growing. Although small farms constitute a large proportion of the number of farms, together they produce only a small portion of farm output.
- Food has an income elasticity of demand that is much less than 1. There-fore, as income rises, the share of consumer spending going to food declines.
- When the demand for a good is inelastic, shifts in the supply of the good produce relatively large changes in the price of the good and in producers' incomes. Thus the inelastic demand for food, combined with the uncertainty of weather conditions, helps explain why food prices and farmers' incomes tend to fluctuate widely.

PRICE SUPPORTS

During the Great Depression the federal government swung into action to help farmers. In 1933 it established a system of price supports for many agricultural products. Today there are price supports for wheat, feed grains, cotton, tobacco, rice, peanuts, soybeans, sorghum, and dairy products. The nature of the supports was and remains quite simple: The government simply chooses a *support price* for an agricultural product and then acts to ensure that the price of the product never falls below the support level. Figure F-2 shows

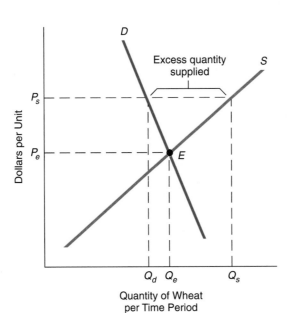

FIGURE F-2
Price supports.
Free market equilibrium occurs at E, with an equilibrium price of P_e and an equilibrium quantity of Q_e. When the government sets a support price at P_s, the quantity demanded is Q_d, and the quantity supplied is Q_s. The difference is the surplus, which the government buys. Note that farmers' total income is from consumers ($P_s \times Q_d$) plus taxpayers [$(Q_s - Q_d) \times P_s$].

the market demand and supply of wheat. Absent a price support program, competitive forces would yield an equilibrium price of P_e and an equilibrium quantity of Q_e. Clearly, if the government sets the support price at P_e or below, nothing will happen, because farmers can sell all they want at the market clearing price of P_e.

Typically, however, the government sets the support price *above* P_e, at P_s. At a support price of P_s, the quantity demanded is only Q_d, but the quantity supplied is Q_s. The difference between them is called the *excess quantity supplied* or *surplus*. As simple as this program seems, two questions arise: (1) How does the government decide on the level of the support price P_s? (2) How does it prevent market forces from pushing the actual price down to P_e?

SUSTAINING THE SUPPORT PRICE

If production exceeds the amount consumers want to buy at the support price, what happens to the surplus? Quite simply, the government must buy the surplus—the difference between Q_s and Q_d—if the price support program is to work. As a practical matter, the government acquires the quantity $Q_s - Q_d$ indirectly through a government agency called the **Commodity Credit Corporation (CCC).** The government either stores the surplus or sells it to foreign countries at a greatly reduced price (or gives it free of charge) under the Food for Peace program.

▶ **Commodity Credit Corporation (CCC)** A government agency that lends farmers an amount of money equal to the support price of crops, multiplied by the amount of the crop offered as collateral.

THE ECONOMICS AND POLITICS OF PRICE SUPPORTS

Traditionally, advocates of price supports have argued that it is a method to guarantee a decent income for low-income farmers. More recently, it has also been argued that the price support program helps keep small farmers in business, thus preventing agribusinesses from taking over all agricultural production. In fact, these political justifications make no economic sense.

Historically, the benefits of price support programs have been skewed toward the owners of very large farms. The benefits of the price support programs are proportional to output: Big farms with large incomes produce more output and therefore get more subsidies.

Price supports also fail to slow the move toward larger farms. Price support subsidies are made on a *per-bushel* basis, not on a *per-farm* basis. Thus the price support system provides no advantage to growing crops on small farms rather than large farms. If other factors make it more efficient to grow food on large farms, that is where it will be grown, whether there are price supports or not. Perhaps recognizing this, Congress has responded by imposing upper limits on the total cash payment that any given farmer can receive. These limits, however, are easily and routinely avoided by the owners of large farms, who, for example, "lease" portions of their land to numerous tenants, each of whom qualifies individually for the full allowable payment. Thus the limits have little practical impact.

There is one further point: *All* of the benefits derived from price support subsidies ultimately accrue to *landowners* on whose land price-supported crops can be grown. When price supports were announced and put into effect, the value of land rose to reflect the full value of the future price support subsidies. Thus the original landowners, rather than operators of farms, capture the benefit of the subsidies. Most of the benefit of the farm programs has been capitalized into the value of the farmland. So much for helping the poor and the landless.

> ### CONCEPTS IN BRIEF
> - With a price support system, the government sets a minimum price at which certain farm products can be sold. Any farmers who cannot sell at that price can "sell" their surplus to the government. Indeed, the only way a price support system can survive is for someone, such as the government, to buy up the excess quantity supplied at the support price.
> - Because price supports benefit farmers directly in proportion to the amount of farm goods they produce, owners of large farms receive the bulk of the payments. Also, because the payments are tied to output and not farms, price supports do not help keep small farmers in business in preference to large farmers.
> - The ultimate beneficiaries of price supports have been the owners of farmland, for the price of this land has risen whenever price supports have been increased.

ACREAGE RESTRICTIONS

The politicians who introduced price supports realized that farmers would respond to higher prices with higher production and that the government would be stuck with the resulting surpluses. So from the beginning, *acreage restrictions* were imposed on farmers who participated in the price support programs. Farmers agreeing to acreage restrictions, or *acreage allotment programs*, as they are called, consent to reduce the number of acres they plant. There are no direct payments to the farmers for abiding by their acreage allotments; the program is merely the implicit entry fee for farmers who wish to take advantage of the price supports.

When the government requires that land be removed from production, this causes a reduction in the supply of the crop. Nevertheless, if farmers are required to reduce the amount of land they use by, say, 20 percent, output at any given price will not fall by 20 percent because farmers will withdraw their *least* productive land from use. Moreover, they can be expected to figure out new ways of squeezing just a little more production from any given amount of land. They can still expand output by using other factors of production, such as fertilizer and machinery. To get any given level of output they will have to use more of these nonfixed inputs than they ordinarily would because they are not allowed to expand their usage of land. Thus the marginal cost of production must be higher than it would be in the absence of the acreage restriction.

The net effects of the acreage restrictions are thus twofold. First, crop surpluses are reduced but not eliminated. Second, the restrictions lead to an inefficient use of resources, not from the standpoint of the farmers, for they produce at the lowest possible cost given the acreage restriction, but from the standpoint of society. Because the most efficient means of production (more land) is not permitted, more expensive inputs must be used.

▶ **Target price**
A price set by the government for specific agricultural products. If the market clearing price is below the target price, a *deficiency payment*, equal to the difference between the market price and the target price, is given to farmers for each unit of the good they produce.

TARGET PRICES AND DEFICIENCY PAYMENTS

Starting in 1973, government policy toward agriculture added a new twist—the **target price.** Target prices differ from price supports in that the government guarantees that the farmer will *receive* at least the target price but permits the price *paid* by consumers to fluctuate depending on how much of the crop is produced. Instead of buying and storing commodities, the government simply sends a cash payment to farmers if the price paid by consumers is less than the target price. For example, if the target price for wheat is $4.50 per bushel and the price paid by consumers is $3.50, farmers receive **deficiency payments** equal to the $1 difference multiplied by the number of bushels they sell on the open market. A deficiency payment, then, is simply another way to pay a subsidy to farmers without having the government actually purchase and store their crops.

> ▶ **Deficiency payment**
> A direct subsidy paid to farmers equal to the amount of a crop they produce multiplied by the difference between the target price for that good and its market price.

TARGET PRICES VERSUS SUPPORT PRICES

In any comparison of target prices and support prices, farmers ultimately care only about the level of the price they receive for their crops because that is what determines the level of production and their profits. Politically, support prices offer the advantage (compared to target prices) of hiding the fact that farmers are being subsidized but have the disadvantage that the surpluses resulting from price supports can be embarrassing. Unless all of the surpluses caused by support prices are somehow distributed by the government (say, to other nations), consumption will be higher with target prices than with support prices because the price paid by consumers is lower. For society as a whole, target prices are generally a cheaper means of providing a given level of income to farmers than support prices because target prices involve no added storage costs or waste due to spoilage. Finally, both target prices and support prices cause losses in economic efficiency compared to the competitive equilibrium because both subsidy programs distort market prices.

CONCEPTS IN BRIEF

- Target prices are an attempt by the government to avoid the surpluses caused by price supports. The government sets a target price, which it guarantees that farmers will receive for their crops, but it allows the market price to adjust to clear the market. If the market price is less than the target price, farmers receive deficiency payments equal to the difference multiplied by the amount of the crop they produce.
- Target prices reduce surpluses, but they also make it more obvious that the government is making direct subsidy payments to farmers.

THE COST OF AGRICULTURAL PROGRAMS

During the late 1980s and early 1990s, government agricultural programs such as price supports and deficiency payments produced direct cash benefits to farmers worth about $25 billion per year. The combined cost to taxpayers and consumers of providing these benefits averaged about $31 billion per year. The difference—about $6 billion per year—is the efficiency loss, or waste, caused by these programs. Excepting only the Social Security system, government programs to subsidize farmers are the single largest, most expensive system of income transfers in the United States. Indeed, the cost of farm subsidies exceeds the *combined* cost of welfare payments (Aid to Families with Dependent Children) and unemployment insurance payments.

To put these numbers in some perspective, recall that there are about 2 million farmers in this country. Thus government agricultural programs produce direct cash benefits to the average farmer of $12,000 per year. Paying these subsidies costs each person in the United States about $125 per year. For the typical family of four, this amounts to $500 per year—$400 in higher taxes and $100 in higher food bills. The benefits, meanwhile, accrue somewhat differently. Approximately two-thirds of all farm aid goes to farms with annual sales in excess of $100,000, and payments to farms with sales in excess of $500,000 average nearly $40,000 per farm each year. Indeed, 15 percent of all federal farm pay-

FIGURE F-3
Subsidizing farmers around the world.
Although in the United States farmers receive 30 percent of their income through subsidies, farmers in other nations receive a much greater percentage.

Source: Organization for Economic Cooperation and Development, 1993.

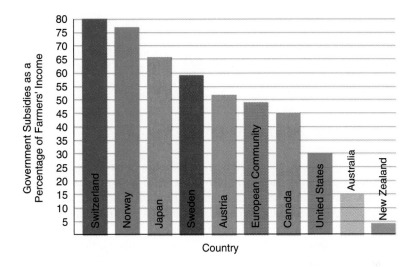

ments go to farmers with a net worth exceeding $1 million. It is little surprise that farm programs have received the reputation of being "welfare for the rich."

FARM POLICY IN AN OPEN ECONOMY

Though we do not yet live in "one world," the effects of living in an open economy are being felt increasingly in the farming sector. International trade is increasing, intensifying competitive pressures. Global competitive forces are affecting both American farmers and American farm policymakers in the federal government.

Some of America's most important trading partners subsidize their farmers much more than we do, as evidenced in Figure F-3. There you see transfers to farming producers expressed as a percentage of their annual income. In Japan it is 66 percent and in the European Community (EC) close to 50 percent. In the United States it comes to 30 percent. These are percentages of the average farmer's income in each country accounted for by government subsidies.

Three generations of farmers throughout most of the world have known nothing but protection against competition. The benefits of free world trade, however, are bringing pressure to bear on various governments, including that in the United States, to change.

🌐 INTERNATIONAL EXAMPLE: Farmers Go Cold Turkey in New Zealand

In the early 1980s, New Zealand's farmers enjoyed as much protection as those in the European Community. Today they receive only 4 percent of their income in subsidies. The demise of New Zealand's farm subsidy programs happened quickly and convincingly. The Labour party took power in 1984 and started the reform. At that time the country was in dire straits—high inflation, a huge external debt, and high unemployment. Dramatic steps had to be taken. Most farm price support programs and outright grants to farmers were reduced over a three-year period. Loans that used to be given to farmers at below-market interest rates were made at market rates.

Farmers felt the results immediately: Inflation-corrected net farm income fell by two-thirds from 1980 to 1986, and the elimination of the stream of future subsidies caused farmland prices to drop by more than 50 percent. The story, though, has a somewhat happy ending. Farmland values started to rise in 1988 and now exceed what they were 10 years earlier. There are now more farmers than there were at the beginning of the 1980s because hobby farmers have taken to the land (thanks to the fact that it became much cheaper than it was at its peak).

For Critical Analysis: Why is the value of farmland a function of future government farm programs? ●

REDUCING FARM SUBSIDIES BECAUSE OF GATT

As this book is being written, negotiations are continuing in the Uruguay Round of the General Agreement on Tariffs and Trade (GATT). GATT is an international association of more than 100 countries that has as its goal the promotion of freer world trade. During the Uruguay Round, the United States has proposed a 10-year phase-out of all agricultural tariffs and the elimination of agricultural exports subsidies over a five-year period. In addition, the United States wants a phase-out of any domestic farm support program that appears to distort world agricultural trade. The European Community has fought these proposals aggressively. When the EC finally agreed to accept them in modified form, French farmers protested throughout that country in 1992.

THE TREND IN WORLD FOOD PRICES

You can understand why French farmers and other farmers are fighting reductions in farm subsidy programs throughout the world. In Figure F-4 you see world food prices in inflation-corrected terms. The trend is definitely downward as you can see by the dotted line. Today world food prices in inflation-corrected terms are only 60 percent of what they were at the beginning of the twentieth century.

The zigzag line showing the actual changes in inflation-corrected world food prices do demonstrate that protection for farmers' incomes has actually made world food markets more unstable. During global shortages, consumers continue buying food as if there were just as much as before. During world food gluts, consumers don't buy any more than usual. This is because prices have stabilized through farming programs. Moreover, farmers do not respond to world crises either because they continue to get the same price thanks to government price stabilization.

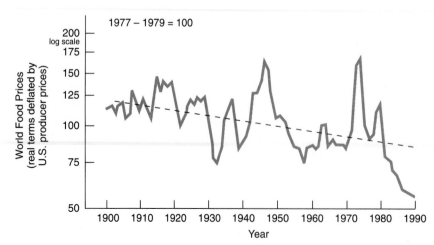

FIGURE F-4

The trend in world food prices.

World food prices, corrected for inflation, have been following a general downward trend throughout the twentieth century.

Source: Economist, December 12, 1992, p. F-8.

THE ESTIMATED BENEFITS OF UNDISTORTED AGRICULTURAL TRADE

In an open economy with undistorted agricultural trade, the industrially advanced economies would benefit to the tune of about $38 billion per year. The major beneficiaries would be Japan, the European Community, and the United States. These numbers alone suggest that there must be pressure to open up world agricultural markets and to reduce farm subsidies. The future is not so rosy, however.

Consider the theory of public choice outlined in Chapter 27. The cost of farming programs continues to be spread out among all consumers. Moreover, the cost per consumer in countries that become richer, all other things held constant, is falling. This is because food constitutes a declining share in the family budget as families get richer. Moreover, because of increases in farm productivity, the trend, as we saw in Figure F-4, is toward lower (inflation-corrected) prices for food. Hence, farmers can still maintain their relatively high subsidy levels while nonfarmers see food prices falling.

Perhaps more important, on the producer side, as the number of farmers decreases the benefits of farm programs are more highly concentrated. This means that lobbying efforts become more efficient to undertake. That is, as the number of farmers decreases, protection becomes relatively cheaper to obtain. Furthermore, the declining number of farmers and farms, particularly in the industrialized world, elicits a kind of sympathy. France is a particularly good example. Surveys continually show that the average French citizen believes that rural life would disappear without farm subsidies. And the French are apparently willing to continue paying those farm subsidies. Farm subsidies, though, in France and elsewhere, cannot stop the exodus from the farms. In France, for example, 3 percent of farmers and farmhands quit every year.

We can conclude that in spite of the pressures in an open economy to reduce farm subsidies throughout the world, they are not going to disappear overnight.

APPENDIX SUMMARY

1. The demand for agricultural products tends to rise more slowly than income rises because the income elasticity of demand for food is less than 1; that is, holding other relevant factors constant, a 1 percent increase in income causes less than a 1 percent rise in the demand for food.

2. Because farmers face an inelastic demand for their products, any shift in the supply curve will cause a relatively large change in the market clearing price of their products and thus a relatively large change in their incomes.

3. Price supports, started during the Great Depression, are minimum prices set by the government for food products. If the support price exceeds the market clearing price, there develops a surplus, which the government must take off the market if the program is to be effective. In a free market, a surplus cannot last.

4. Because price supports are tied to the volume of production, richer farmers receive the bulk of the subsidies that result from price supports. Also, because price supports are paid without regard to the size of farms, they generally do not help keep smaller farmers in business.

5. Acreage restrictions are an attempt to reduce surpluses by requiring farmers to stop cultivating part of their land in return for price support subsidies from the Commodity Credit Corporation. When they participate in acreage restriction programs, farmers put aside their least productive land and increase the use of nonland inputs on the remaining land in cultivation. These practices tend to offset the surplus-reducing intent of these programs.

6. Target prices avoid surpluses by making deficiency payments to farmers to make up for the difference between the government-established target price and the market clearing price.

7. Agriculture subsidies transfer about $25 billion a year from taxpayers and consumers to farmers and cause an efficiency loss of $6 billion a year.

8. Most other developed countries subsidize their farmers much more than the United States. There is international pressure to reduce subsidies both in America and elsewhere.

PROBLEMS

(Answers to the odd-numbered problems appear at the back of the book.)

F-1. Some people maintain that unless farmers are subsidized, many will leave the farms, a small number of farms will take over the industry (creating an oligopolistic market structure), and prices will rise correspondingly. In 1993 it was estimated that about 2.1 million farms were in existence in the United States and that 20 percent of these farms accounted for 75 percent of the value of total farm output.

    a. What is the number of farms accounting for this 75 percent of output?

    b. In light of this fact, is it likely that an oligopoly, defined as a market structure with only a few firms accounting for most production and sales, will arise in the agricultural industry in the United States?

F-2. Farmers are usually required to put aside some land to take part in government programs. The objective is for farm output to be reduced. How might this objective not be achieved?

F-3. Explain how the theory of public choice predicts the persistence of agricultural subsidies in the face of a declining farm population.

F-4. Assume that farmers are poor. What is the difference between a general income redistribution program that would give poor farmers income directly and a farming subsidy program that pays them so much per unit of farm product output?

F-5. Outline what would occur if Congress eliminated all farm subsidies tomorrow. How would these events change if Congress instead indicated that it would eliminate all farm programs in 20 years?

PRODUCTIVE FACTORS, POVERTY, AND THE ENVIRONMENT

7

RESOURCE DEMAND AND SUPPLY

If you work hard at college and even go on to graduate school, you can expect to make a pretty good living in the United States. You can hope eventually to earn between $35,000 and $75,000 per year (in today's dollars). How must you feel, then, when you read business publications that list the pay received by America's top chief executive officers in publicly held corporations? In recent years, the heads of such companies as Toys "Я" Us, Chrysler, Disney, Mattel, and General Dynamics have made in excess of $15 million a year. In 1992 alone, the head of Toys "Я" Us made over $64 million. Can these executives be worth so much? To understand why chief executive officers are so highly paid, you have to understand the general theory of resource demand and supply.

After reading this chapter, you should be able to answer the following questions:

1. In hiring labor, what general rule will be followed by employers who wish to maximize profits?

2. What is the profit-maximizing rate of employment for a perfectly competitive firm?

3. What is the profit-maximizing rate of employment for an imperfectly competitive firm?

4. How is an industry wage rate determined?

INTRODUCTION

When you look around, you see rich people and poor people and people in between. You find individuals who belong to labor unions and ones who do not. You find some people who are in favor of the government legislating higher minimum wages and others who disagree. You find instances within the same company in which women doing the same job as men may earn less. You will also find situations in which minorities earn significantly less than others. These are all issues and problems that occur in what we call the labor market. It is in the labor market that the demands for and supplies of different types of labor services interact. Sometimes that interaction brings about undesirable results—such as those just mentioned—and sometimes the market works slowly so that shortages and surpluses exist. At any rate, labor can be viewed as an input to a firm's production process.

A firm's demand for inputs can be studied in much the same manner as we studied the demand for output in different market situations. Again, various market situations will be examined. Our analysis will always end with the same commonsense conclusion: A firm will hire employees up to the point beyond which it isn't profitable to hire any more. It will hire employees to the point at which the marginal benefit of hiring a worker will just equal the marginal cost. Basically, in every profit-maximizing situation, it is most profitable to carry out an activity up to the point at which the marginal benefit equals the marginal cost. Remembering that guideline will help you in analyzing decision making at the firm level. We will start our analysis under the assumption that the market for input factors is perfectly competitive. We will further assume that the output market is perfectly competitive. This provides a benchmark against which to compare other situations in which labor markets or product markets are not perfectly competitive.

COMPETITION IN THE PRODUCT MARKET

Let's take as our example a compact disc (CD) manufacturing firm that is in competition with many companies selling the same kind of product. Assume that the laborers hired by our CD manufacturing firm do not need any special skills. This firm sells its product in a perfectly competitive market. A CD manufacturer also buys its variable input—labor—in a perfectly competitive market. A firm that hires labor under perfectly competitive conditions hires only a minuscule proportion of all the workers who are potentially available to the firm. By "potentially available" we mean all the workers in a given geographic area who possess the skills demanded by our perfect competitor. In such a market there is always enough slack to allow the individual firm to pick up extra workers without having to offer a higher wage. Thus the supply of labor to the firm is perfectly elastic, that is, a horizontal line at the going wage rate established by the forces of supply and demand in the entire labor market. The firm is a price taker in the labor market.

MARGINAL PHYSICAL PRODUCT

Look at panel (a) of Figure 28-1. In column 1 we show the number of worker-weeks that the firm can hire. In column 2 we show total physical product (TPP) per week, the total *physical* production that different quantities of the labor input (in combination with a fixed amount of other inputs) will generate in a week's time. In column 3 we show the additional output gained when a CD manufacturing company adds additional workers to its existing manufacturing facility. This column, the **marginal physical product (MPP) of labor,** represents the extra (additional) output attributed to employing additional units of the variable input factor. If this firm adds a seventh worker, the MPP is 118. The law of diminishing marginal returns predicts that additional units of a variable factor will, after some point, cause the MPP to decline, other things being held constant.

▶ **Marginal physical product (MPP) of labor**
The change in output resulting from the addition of one more worker. The MPP of the worker equals the change in total output accounted for by hiring the worker, holding all other factors of production constant.

FIGURE 28-1
Marginal revenue product.
In panel (a), column 4 shows marginal revenue product (MRP), which is the amount of additional revenue the firm receives for the sale of that additional output. Marginal revenue product is simply the amount of money the additional worker brings in—the combination of that worker's contribution to production and the revenue that that production will bring to the firm. For this perfectly competitive firm, marginal revenue is equal to the price of the product, or $6 per unit (net of all nonlabor variable costs). At $498 per week, the profit-maximizing employer will pay for only 12 worker-weeks, because then the marginal revenue product is just equal to the wage rate or weekly salary.

Panel (a)

(1)	(2)	(3)	(4)	(5)
LABOR INPUT (WORKER WEEKS)	TOTAL PHYSICAL PRODUCT (TPP) PER WEEK	MARGINAL PHYSICAL PRODUCT (MPP)	MARGINAL REVENUE (MR = P = $6 NET) x MPP = MARGINAL REVENUE PRODUCT ($ PER ADDITIONAL WORKER)	WAGE RATE ($ PER WEEK) ≡ MARGINAL FACTOR COST (MFC) ≡ CHANGE IN TOTAL COSTS CHANGE IN LABOR
6	882			
		118	708	498
7	1,000			
		111	666	498
8	1,111			
		104	624	498
9	1,215			
		97	582	498
10	1,312			
		90	540	498
11	1,402			
		83	498	498
12	1,485			
		76	456	498
13	1,561			

In panel (b) we find the number of workers the firm will want to hire by observing the wage rate that is established by the forces of supply and demand in the entire labor market. We show that this employer is hiring labor in a perfectly competitive labor market and therefore faces a horizontal supply curve represented by s at $498 per week. As in all other situations, we basically have a supply and demand model; in this example the demand curve is represented by MRP, and the supply curve is s. Equilibrium occurs at their intersection.

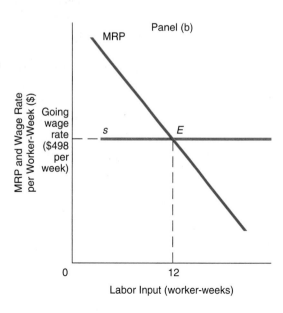

WHY THE DECLINE IN MPP?

We are assuming all other factors of production are held constant. So if our CD manufacturing firm wants to add one more worker to its production line, it has to crowd all the existing workers a little closer together because it does not increase its capital stock (the production-line equipment). Therefore, as we add more workers, each one has a smaller and smaller fraction of the available capital stock with which to work. If one worker uses one machine, adding another worker usually won't double the output because the machine can run only so fast and for so many hours per day. In other words, MPP declines because of the law of diminishing marginal returns.

MARGINAL REVENUE PRODUCT

We now need to translate the physical product that results from hiring an additional worker into a dollar value. This is done by multiplying the marginal physical product by the marginal revenue of the firm. Because our CD firm is selling its product in a perfectly competitive market, marginal revenue is equal to the price of the product. If the seventh worker's MPP is 118 and the marginal revenue is $6 per CD, the **marginal revenue product (MRP)** is $708 (118 × $6).[1] The MRP is shown in column 4 of panel (a) of Figure 28-1. *The marginal revenue product represents the worker's contribution to the firm's total revenues.*

When a firm operates in a competitive product market, the marginal physical product times the product price is also sometimes referred to as the *value of marginal product (VMP)*. Because price and marginal revenue are the same for a perfectly competitive firm, the VMP is also the MRP.

In column 5 of panel (a) of Figure 28-1 we show the wage rate, or *marginal factor cost,* of each worker. The marginal cost of workers is the extra cost incurred in employing that factor of production. We call that cost the **marginal factor cost (MFC).** Otherwise stated,

$$\text{Marginal factor cost} = \frac{\text{change in total cost}}{\text{change in amount of resource used}}$$

Because each worker is paid the same competitively determined wage of $498 per week, the MFC is the same for all workers. And because the firm is buying labor in a perfectly competitive labor market, the wage rate of $498 per week really represents the firm's supply curve of labor. That curve is horizontal because the firm can purchase all labor at the same wage rate, considering that it is a minuscule part of the entire labor-purchasing market. (Recall the definition of perfect competition.) We show this horizontal supply curve as *s* in panel (b) of Figure 28-1.

▶ **Marginal revenue product (MRP)**
The marginal physical product (MPP) times marginal revenue. The MRP gives the additional revenue obtained from a one-unit change in labor input.

▶ **Marginal factor cost (MFC)**
The cost of using an additional unit of an input. For example, if a firm can hire all the workers it wants at the going wage rate, the marginal factor cost of labor is the wage rate.

⭐ EXAMPLE: Superathletes' Marginal Revenue Product

At least once a year, some superathlete lands a multimillion-dollar contract, and the press is all agog over the seemingly astronomical salary. Before we can determine whether an athlete is overpaid, we must first establish the athlete's marginal revenue product. Economists have come up with several estimates of the MRP of athletic superstars. Wayne Gretzky, thought to be the best professional hockey player ever, was traded to the Los Angeles Kings a few years ago. The Edmonton Oilers, for whom Gretzky was playing previously, obtained $15 million (plus several first-round draft picks) in return for Gretzky. In effect, when we add in Gretzky's salary, we find out that the Los Angeles Kings paid

---

[1]The price of the product, $6, is net of all nonlabor variable costs. For example, the $6 price of CDs may reflect a $10 price at which the CDs sell in the market minus a $4 cost of raw materials.

about $6.5 million a year to have Gretzky play for them. What was his marginal revenue product? After the contract was announced, Los Angeles cable TV decided to expand its coverage from 37 to 60 games. Season ticket sales and attendance at home games experienced significant increases. Revenues from home-game sales doubled. It has been estimated that the Great Gretzky's first-year MRP was about $8 million.

In baseball, about 40 players each earn $3 million or more a year, and several earn $5 million or more a year. Are these "outrageous" salaries justified by the players' marginal revenue produce? According to economist Gerald W. Scully, the answer is a resounding yes. Although his data are from a number of years ago, the procedure he used to estimate players' marginal revenue product is still valid. He estimated that star hitters had a net MRP of over $3 million at a time when star players were getting about $500,000 per year. Further, he estimated that star pitchers' net MRP was about $4 million when the average star pitcher was only getting about $600,000 per year. A recalculation of the numbers today would certainly still show that high salaries for star players are justified by even higher marginal revenue products.

For Critical Analysis: How might you calculate the marginal revenue product of today's cinematic superstars? ●

GENERAL RULE FOR HIRING

Virtually every optimizing rule in economics involves comparing marginal benefits with marginal cost. The general rule, therefore, for the hiring decision of a firm is this:

> The firm hires workers up to the point at which the additional cost associated with hiring the last worker is equal to the additional revenue generated by that worker.

In a perfectly competitive situation, this is the point at which the wage rate just equals the marginal revenue product (MRP ≡ MPP times marginal revenue, which equals price in a perfectly competitive market). If the firm hired more workers, the additional wages would not be covered by additional increases in total revenue. If the firm hired fewer workers, it would be forfeiting the contributions that those workers could make to total profits.

Therefore, referring to columns 4 and 5 in panel (a) of Figure 28-1, we see that this firm would certainly employ the seventh worker, because the MRP is $708 while the MFC is only $498. The firm would continue to employ workers up to the point at which MFC = MRP because as workers are added, they contribute more to revenue than to cost.

THE MRP CURVE: DEMAND FOR LABOR

We can also use panel (b) of Figure 28-1 to find how many workers our firm should hire. First we draw a straight line across from the going wage rate, which is determined by demand and supply in the labor market. The straight line is labeled *s* to indicate that it is effectively the supply curve of labor for the *individual* firm purchasing labor in a perfectly competitive labor market. That firm can purchase all the labor it wants of equal quality at $498 per worker-week. This horizontal supply curve, *s*, intersects the marginal revenue product curve at 12 worker-weeks. At the intersection, *E*, the wage rate is equal to the marginal revenue product. This marginal revenue product curve is also a *factor* demand curve, assuming only one variable factor of production and perfect competition in both the factor and product markets. Equilibrium for the firm is obtained when the firm's demand curve for labor, which turns out to be its MRP curve, intersects the firm's supply curve for labor, which is the horizontal line at the going wage rate, *s*. The firm in our example would not hire the thirteenth worker, who will add only $456 to revenue but $498 to cost. If the price of labor should fall to, say, $456 per worker-week, it would become profitable for the firm to hire an additional worker; there is an increase in the quantity of labor demanded as the wage decreases.

DERIVED DEMAND

We have identified an individual firm's demand for labor curve as being its MRP curve. Under conditions of perfect competition in both product and labor markets, MRP is determined by multiplying MPP times the product's price. This suggests that the demand for labor is a **derived demand.** That is to say, our CD firm does not want to purchase the services of labor just for the services themselves. Factors of production are rented or purchased not because they give any intrinsic satisfaction to the firms' owners but because they can be used to manufacture output that is expected to be sold for profit.

> ▶ **Derived demand**
> Input factor demand derived from demand for the final product being produced.

We know that an increase in the market demand for a given product raises the product's price (all other things held constant), which in turn increases the marginal revenue product, or demand for the resource. Figure 28-2 illustrates the effective role played by increases in product demand in a perfectly competitive product market. The MRP curve shifts whenever there is a change in the price of the final product that the workers are making. If, for example, the market price of CDs goes down, the MRP curve will shift downward to the left from MRP_0 to MRP_1. We know that MRP = MPP × MR. If marginal revenue (here the output price) falls, so, too, does the demand for labor; at the same going wage rate, the firm will hire fewer workers. This is because at various levels of labor use, the marginal revenue product of labor falls so that at the initial equilibrium, the price of labor (here the MFC) becomes greater than MRP. Thus the firm would reduce the number of workers hired. Conversely, if the marginal revenue (output price) rises, the demand for labor will also rise, and the firm will want to hire more workers at each and every possible wage rate.

We just pointed out that MRP ≡ MPP × MR. Clearly, then, a change in marginal productivity, or in the marginal physical product of labor, will shift the MRP curve. If the

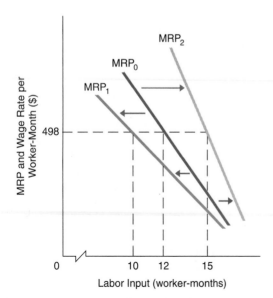

FIGURE 28-2
Demand for labor, a derived demand.
The demand for labor is derived from the demand for the final product being produced. Therefore, the marginal revenue product curve will shift whenever the price of the product changes. If we start with the marginal revenue product curve MRP at the going wage rate of $498 per week, 12 workers will be hired. If the price of CDs goes down, the value of marginal product curve will shift to MRP_1, and the number of workers hired will fall to 10. If the price of CDs goes up, the marginal revenue product curve will shift to MRP_2, and the number of workers hired will increase to 15.

marginal productivity of labor decreases, the MRP curve, or demand curve, for labor will shift inward to the left. Again, this is because at every quantity of labor used, the MRP will be lower. A lower quantity of labor will be demanded at every possible wage rate.

THE MARKET DEMAND FOR LABOR

The downward-sloping portion of each individual firm's marginal revenue product curve is also its demand curve for the one variable factor of production—in our example, labor. When we go to the entire market for a particular type of labor in a particular industry, we find that quantity of labor demanded will vary as the wage rate changes. Given that the market demand curve for labor is made up of the individual firm demand curve for labor, we can safely assume that the market demand curve for labor will look like D in panel (b) of Figure 28-3: It will slope downward. That market demand curve for labor in the CD industry shows the quantities of labor demanded by all of the firms in the industry at various wage rates.

It is important to note that the market demand curve for labor is not a simple horizontal summation of the labor demand curves of all individual firms. Remember that the demand for labor is a derived demand. Even if we hold labor productivity constant, the demand for labor still depends on both the wage rate and the price of the final output. Assume that we start at a wage rate of $20 per hour and employment level 10 in panel (a) of Figure 28-3. If we sum all such employment levels—point *a* in panel (a)—across firms, we get a market quantity demanded of 2,000—point A in panel (b)—at the wage rate of $20.

FIGURE 28-3
Derivation of the market demand curve for labor.
The market demand curve for labor is not simply the horizontal summation of each individual firm's demand curve for labor. If wage rates fall from $20 to $10, all firms will increase employment and therefore output, causing the price of the product to fall. This causes the marginal revenue product curve of each firm to shift inward, as from d_0 to d_1 in panel (a). The resulting market demand curve, D, in panel (b) is therefore less elastic than if output price remained constant.

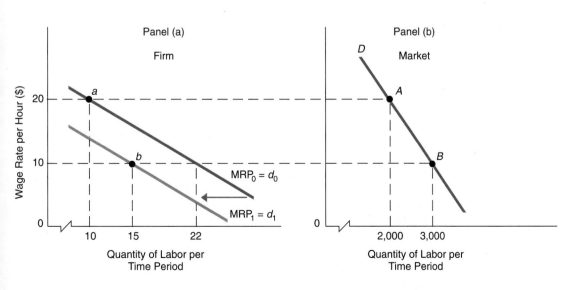

A decrease in the wage rate to $10 per hour induces individual firms' employment level to increase toward a quantity demanded of 22. As all firms simultaneously increase employment, however, there is a shift in the product supply curve such that output increases. Hence the price of the product must fall. The fall in the output price in turn causes a leftward shift of each firm's MRP curve (d_0) to MRP_1 (d_1) in panel (a). Thus each firm's employment of labor increases to 15 rather than to 22 at the wage rage of $10 per hour. A summation of all such employment levels gives us 3,000—point B—in panel (b).

CONCEPTS IN BRIEF

- The change in total output due to a one-unit change in one variable input, holding all other inputs constant, is called the marginal physical product (MPP).
- When we multiply marginal physical product times marginal revenue, we obtain the marginal revenue product (MRP).
- A firm will hire workers up to the point at which the additional cost of hiring one more worker is equal to the additional revenues generated. For the individual firm, therefore, its MRP of labor curve is also its demand for labor curve.
- The demand for labor is a derived demand, derived from the demand for final output. Therefore, if the price of final output changes, this will cause a shift in the MRP curve (which is also the firm's demand for labor curve).
- The market demand curve for labor slopes downward.

DETERMINANTS OF DEMAND ELASTICITY FOR INPUTS

Just as we were able to discuss the price elasticity of demand for different commodities in Chapter 20, we can discuss the price elasticity of demand for inputs. The price elasticity of demand for labor is defined in a manner similar to the price elasticity of demand for goods: the percentage change in quantity demanded divided by the percentage change in the price of labor. When the numerical value of this ratio is less than 1, it is inelastic; when it is 1, unit-elastic; and when it is greater than 1, elastic.

There are five principal determinants of the price elasticity of demand for an input. The price elasticity of demand for a variable input will be greater:

1. The greater the price elasticity of demand for the final product
2. The easier it is for a particular variable input to be substituted for by other inputs
3. The greater the price elasticity of supply of all other inputs
4. The larger the proportion of total costs accounted for by a particular variable input
5. The longer the time period being considered

FINAL PRODUCT ELASTICITY

The first determinant of factor demand elasticity is the elasticity of demand for the final product. We have seen that the demand for an input is a derived demand. Because it is derived from the demand for the final output, we would expect the elasticity of the derived demand to be correlated with the elasticity of the demand for the final product (all other things held constant).

Assume that the elasticity of demand for electricity is very low. If the wages of skilled workers in the electricity industry are forced up by a strong union, the companies will pass on at least part of the increase in costs to customers in the form of higher prices. Because the demand for electricity is inelastic, customers will not reduce by very much the quantity of electricity demanded. The electric companies will lay off very few workers. The low elasticity of demand for the final product leads to a low elasticity of demand for the factors of production, other things being held constant.

SUBSTITUTE FACTORS

The second determinant is fairly obvious. If one particular input can be substituted very easily for another, an increase in the price of one input will lead to much more extensive use of the other. For example, sleeping bag manufacturers can use either plastic or metal zippers on their bags. Both are equally useful and equally effective in doing the same job. They are also equally expensive and are used in equal proportions. If for some reason the price of plastic zippers rises by 20 percent, how many plastic zippers do you think a firm will use? Probably none; it will switch to metal zippers. Thus the demand for plastic zippers is highly elastic because of the availability of a close substitute. Conversely, thread is important for sewing the seams of the sleeping bags, and suppose that it cannot be easily replaced by anything else. We would expect the elasticity of demand for thread to be very low indeed. A rise in its price will not lead to a very large decrease in quantity demanded by the sleeping bag producer because few other inputs can be used as substitutes.

 EXAMPLE: Are Paralegals a Substitute for Lawyers?

The growth in paralegals—persons without law degrees employed to assist attorneys—has been dramatic. Whereas there were 83,000 paralegals in 1988, there will be 145,000 in the year 2000—an increase of 75 percent.

There are numerous restrictions on what paralegals are allowed to do. These restrictions have been imposed with the help of various bar associations throughout the country. The state bar associations (the governing bodies that regulate lawyers' professional behavior) have numerous rules that prohibit paralegals from engaging in the work that attorneys do. Many of these rules have been translated into state laws prohibiting paralegals from doing the work that attorneys do. Such rules and laws would seem to indicate that attorneys are trying to prevent paralegals from taking away work. This fact seems to suggest that attorneys believe that paralegals are substitutes for attorneys. Economist Robert M. Feinberg attempted to measure the degree to which paralegals really are substitutes for attorneys. He found that there was actually little substitution between paralegals and lawyers. In fact, his research results argue that rather than being substitutes, paralegals are more often complements to attorneys.

For Critical Analysis: If paralegals are complements to attorneys, would you expect an increasing supply of paralegals to have a negative effect on the salaries of attorneys? Explain. ●

SUPPLY ELASTICITY OF SUBSTITUTE FACTORS

The third determinant is the price elasticity of the supply of other inputs.[2] The greater the price elasticity of supply of other inputs, the greater the price elasticity of demand for the input under study. In other words, if firms in an industry can easily turn to a substitute input and obtain more of it by paying a very small increase in price, the reduction in the

---

[2]We assume the existence of technologically feasible substitutes and simply look at their price elasticities of supply.

quantity demanded of the input in question will be relatively great for any given increase in its price. Assume that aluminum and plastic are close substitutes for use in automobile headlight fixtures. If the supply elasticity of aluminum is very high—that is, if increasing quantities can be purchased without significantly affecting the price of aluminum—then whenever the price of plastic goes up, automobile manufacturers can easily switch to aluminum. This switch will be accomplished without a significant increase in the unit price of the input for making headlight fixtures because the supply elasticity of aluminum is assumed to be very high in this example. Thus, other things being constant, the price elasticity of demand for the plastic input by automobile manufacturers will be higher than it would have been with a low price elasticity of the supply for aluminum.

PROPORTION OF TOTAL INPUT COSTS

The fourth elasticity determinant is the proportion of total costs accounted for by the input under study. If a factor of production accounts for only a very small part of the total cost of the product, a change in its price will not affect total costs by much. Take the example of electricity as an input of manufacturing. On the average, the cost of electricity accounts for less than 1 percent of the total cost of manufactured goods. Let's assume that it accounts for exactly 1 percent. If the price of electricity now doubles, only 1 percent more will be added to total costs, and the amount of electricity demanded will not fall by very much. This may explain the relative amount of market power that a union has in raising wage rates. If the labor input constitutes a very small percentage of the total cost of producing a commodity, an increase in wages will not add very much to total cost. Presumably, in such situations unions would be able to get their members higher wage rates than they would in situations in which the labor input constituted a significantly greater percentage of total production costs.

TIME ALLOWED FOR ADJUSTMENT

The fifth determinant concerns the difference between the short run and the long run. The long run is usually defined as the time period during which business operators adjust to a change in their business environment. As pointed out previously, the more time there is for adjustment, the more elastic both the supply and the demand curves will be. This assertion holds for input demand curves as well. The longer the time allowed for adjustment to take place, the more responsive firms will be to a change in the price of a factor of production. Particularly in the long run, firms can reorganize their production process to minimize the use of a factor of production that has become more expensive relative to other factors of production.

Consider one implication of this fifth determinant of the price elasticity of demand of an input. A union could succeed in raising workers' wage rates—the price of the labor input—considerably above what they are without immediately experiencing a substantial cutback in employment. The short-run price elasticity of demand for labor might be relatively small. Once, however, time is allowed for adjustment, the union may find that the large increase in wage rates will result in significant cutbacks in employment—that is, in the quantity of the labor input demanded—because the firm will replace its old equipment with equipment that can be operated with less labor.

CONCEPTS IN BRIEF

- There are five determinants of the price elasticity of demand for inputs:

  1. The greater the price elasticity of demand for the final product, the greater the price elasticity of demand for the variable input.

2. The easier it is to substitute other inputs for the input under study, the more price-elastic that input's demand.
3. The greater the price elasticity of supply of substitutable inputs, the greater the price elasticity of demand for the variable input under study.
4. The larger the proportion of total costs accounted for by the variable input under study, the greater its price elasticity of demand.
5. The greater the time allowed for adjustment, the greater the price elasticity of demand for an input.

THE SUPPLY OF LABOR

Having developed the demand curve for labor (and all other variable inputs) in a particular industry, let's turn to the labor supply curve. By adding supply to the analysis, we can come up with the equilibrium wage rate that workers earn in an industry. We can think in terms of a supply curve for labor that slopes upward in a particular industry. At higher wage rates, more workers will want to enter that particular industry. The individual firm, however, does not face the entire *market* supply curve. Rather, in a perfectly competitive case, the individual firm is such a small part of the market that it can hire all the workers that it wants at the going wage rate. We say, therefore, that the industry faces an upward-sloping supply curve but that the individual *firm* faces a horizontal supply curve for labor. We show these two different supply curves of labor in Figure 28-4.

FIGURE 28-4
Two supply curves of labor.
An individual firm that represents a very small part of the total market faces a horizontal supply curve of labor at the going wage rate. This firm supply curve of labor is represented by *s* on the left side of the figure. The industry, by contrast, usually faces an upward-sloping supply curve, similar to the one labeled $S_{industry}$ on the right side of this figure.

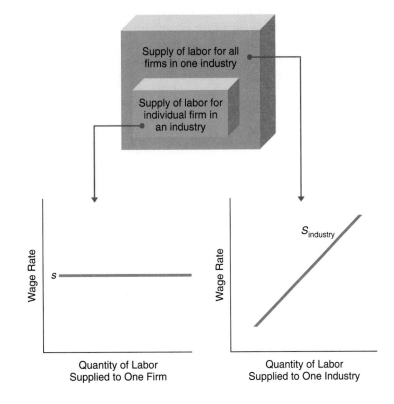

THE LABOR-LEISURE CHOICE AND THE
INDIVIDUAL LABOR SUPPLY CURVE

All work involves an opportunity cost—the highest-valued alternative nonwork choice. As such, analyzing the individual decision about how much to work is similar to analyzing the consumer's decision about how much to buy in the product market. In essence, the individual is choosing between leisure plus nonmarket activities versus the consumption of commodities that can be bought in the marketplace (because that's what one can do with the income earned from working). A decision to increase the consumption of purchased commodities is, of necessity, a decision to reduce the consumption of leisure and nonmarket activities.

To make a decision about the appropriate trade-off to be made, an individual must know the opportunity cost of leisure. That opportunity cost is represented by the wages that could have been earned (after taxes). Assume that the worker can make, after taxes, $8 an hour. A decision to work four hours less therefore represents a decision to refrain from consuming $32 of purchased commodities.

Consider, then, the effect of an increase in wages. The worker is given an incentive to work more because leisure has become more expensive. Therefore, the worker substitutes in favor of work and against leisure. This is called the *substitution effect* of an increase in wages. If only the substitution effect is looked at, any increase in wages will cause the worker to want to work longer hours.

But there is also an *income effect*, which operates in the opposite direction. A higher wage rate means that for any given number of hours worked, the worker has a greater income. With a greater income, the worker will tend to purchase more of most things, including leisure. Thus a wage increase has an income effect that causes the worker to want to reduce the number of hours worked in order to purchase more leisure. The income effect of an increase in wages, therefore, causes the worker to want to work less.

Generally, the substitution effect outweighs the income effect, so the individual labor supply curve slopes upward. That is to say, an increase in the wage rate tends to induce more hours worked, but eventually, at a high enough wage rate, the income effect may dominate so that after a certain wage rate, a further increase in the wage rate will cause a reduction in the number of hours worked. Look at Figure 28-5. This *backward-bending* supply curve of labor shows that up to wage rate W_1 the substitution effect overrides the

FIGURE 28-5

The individual's backward-bending labor supply curve.

As wages increase from zero up toward W_1, the higher the wage rate, the larger will be the quantity of labor supplied by the individual. The substitution effect overrides the income effect. After wage rate W_1, however, higher wage rates lead to a backward-bending labor supply curve such that a lower quantity of labor is supplied. After wage rate W_1, the income effect overrides the substitution effect. The maximum labor supplied by this person will be at wage rate W_1 and will equal q_1 hours.

income effect, and above wage rate W_1 the income effect overrides the substitution effect. (A backward-bending supply of labor curve is unlikely on a *national* scale because higher wage rates induce more individuals to join the labor force.)

The market supply curve of labor is simply the summation of the individual supply curves of labor. We do, however, assume that we are operating only in the range over which each individual's supply curve of labor slopes upward. That is why we show the industry supply curve sloping upward only, as is seen in the right-hand side of Figure 28-4.[3]

🌐 INTERNATIONAL EXAMPLE: The National Labor Supply Curve and Immigration

Our analysis thus far does not represent the national supply curve of labor. The reason is net inflows of new workers to the national labor market. A large and increasingly significant percentage of new entrants to the labor force are immigrants, mainly from Asia and Latin America. Whereas in the 1960s immigrants' share of total population growth was only 11 percent, in the 1980s it was almost 40 percent. From now until the year 2000 it is expected to exceed 40 percent. Asians will constitute 35 percent of that increase, and people from Mexico, Central America, and South America will constitute another 35 percent. A certain number of immigrants come to this country for political or family reasons, but the majority immigrate to the United States for economic reasons. Those who do compare the costs of moving with the benefits of moving. In effect, the immigration market is similar to the job market. Potential migrants implicitly receive offers from competing host countries as well as their home countries. They compare these offers and weigh them against the decision to migrate.

There are two types of immigration in the United States, legal and illegal. America welcomes about 1.5 million legal immigrants per year. The number of illegal immigrants is hard to estimate but is at least several million per year. When potential illegal immigrants do their cost-benefit calculation, they have to consider the risk of being caught and deported back to their home country. Apparently this cost does not loom very large in their calculations. Many who illegally enter the United States through Mexico engage in "border ritual": They get caught on numerous occasions and simply keep coming back to the United States until they make it through. The lure of higher salaries, better living conditions, and other aspects of life now and in the future is sufficient.

For Critical Analysis: Who benefits from increased immigration into the United States, and who loses? ●

WAGE RATE DETERMINATION

The demand curve for labor in the CD industry is D in Figure 28-6 on the next page, and the supply curve of labor is S. The equilibrium wage rate of $498 a week is established at the intersection of the two curves. The quantity of workers both supplied and demanded at that rate is Q_1. If for some reason the wage rate fell to $400 a week, in our hypothetical example, there would be an excess number of workers demanded at that wage rate. Conversely, if the wage rate rose to $600 a week, there would be an excess quantity of workers supplied at that wage rate.

We have just found the equilibrium wage rate for the entire CD industry. The individual firm must take that equilibrium wage rate as given in the competitive model used here

---

[3]Also, the labor supply in industry-specific geographic labor markets will slope upward because workers do not have homogeneous skills (noncompeting groups) and higher wages will attract workers from farther away.

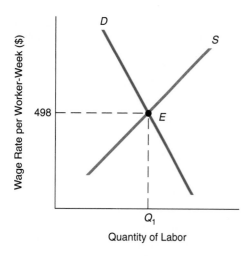

FIGURE 28-6

The equilibrium wage rate and the CD industry.

We take the industry demand curve for labor from the right side of Figure 28-4. We put in a hypothetical upward-sloping labor supply curve for the CD industry, S. The intersection is at point E, giving an equilibrium wage rate of $498 per week and an equilibrium quantity of labor demanded of Q_1. At a price above $498 per week there will be an excess quantity of workers supplied. At a price below $498 per week there will be an excess quantity of workers demanded.

because the individual firm is a very small part of the total demand for labor. Thus the individual firm purchasing labor in a perfectly competitive market can purchase all of the input it wants at the going market price.

⭐ EXAMPLE: The Effects of Minimum Wage Laws

Currently, there is a federal minimum wage of $4.25 an hour. Many states and cities have their own minimum wage laws also, which sometimes exceed this. What happens when the government passes a minimum wage law? The effects can be seen in Figure 28-7.

We start off in equilibrium with the equilibrium wage rate of W_e and the equilibrium quantity of labor demanded and supplied equal to Q_e. A minimum wage, W_m, higher than W_e, is imposed. At W_m the quantity demanded for labor is reduced to Q_D, and some workers now become unemployed. Note that the reduction in employment from Q_e to Q_D, or the distance from B to A, is less than the excess quantity of labor supplied at wage rate W_m. This excess quantity supplied is the distance between A and C, or the distance between Q_D and Q_S. The reason the reduction in employment is smaller than the excess supply of labor at the minimum wage is that the latter also includes a second component that consists of the additional workers who would like to work more hours at the new, higher

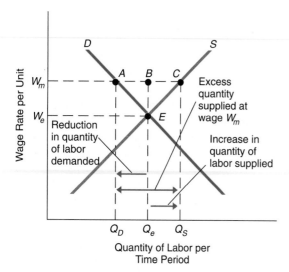

FIGURE 28-7

The effect of minimum wages.

The market clearing wage rate is W_e. The market clearing quantity of employment is Q_e, determined by the intersection of supply and demand at point E. A minimum wage equal to W_m is established. The quantity of labor demanded is reduced to Q_D; the reduction from employment from Q_e to Q_D is equal to the distance between B and A. That distance is smaller than the excess quantity of labor supplied at wage rate W_m. The distance between B and C is the increase in the quantity of labor supplied that results from the higher minimum wage rate.

minimum wage. Some workers may become unemployed as a result of the minimum wage, but others will move to sectors where minimum wage laws do not apply; wages will be pushed down in these uncovered sectors.

In the long run, some of the reduction in labor demanded will result from a reduction in the number of firms, and some will result from changes in the number of workers employed by each firm. Economists estimate a 10 percent increase in the real minimum wage decreases total employment by 1 to 2 percent.[4]

For Critical Analysis: What are some of the ways that employers can avoid paying minimum wages? ●

SHIFTS IN THE MARKET DEMAND AND SUPPLY OF LABOR

Just as we discussed shifts in the supply curve and the demand curve for various products in Chapter 3, we can discuss the effects of shifts in supply and demand in labor markets.

REASONS FOR LABOR DEMAND CURVE SHIFTS

Many factors can cause the demand curve for labor to shift. We have already discussed a number of them. Clearly, because the demand for labor or any other variable input is a derived demand, the labor demand curve will shift if there is a shift in the demand for the final product. There are two other important determinants of the position of the demand curve for labor: changes in labor's productivity and changes in the price of related factors of production (substitutes and complements).

Changes in Demand for Final Product. The demand for labor or any other variable input is derived from the demand for the final product. The marginal revenue product is equal to marginal physical product times marginal revenue. Therefore, any change in the price of the final product will change MRP. This happened when we derived the market demand for labor. The general rule of thumb is as follows:

> A change in the demand for the final product that labor (or any other variable input) is producing will shift the market demand curve for labor in the same direction.

Changes in Labor Productivity. The second part of the MRP equation is MPP, which relates to labor productivity. We can surmise, then, that, other things being equal,

> A change in labor productivity will shift the market labor demand curve in the same direction.

Labor productivity can increase because labor has more capital or land to work with, because of technological improvements, or because labor's quality has improved. Such considerations explain why the real standard of living of workers in the United States is higher than in most countries. American workers generally work with a larger capital stock, have more natural resources, are in better physical condition, and are better trained than workers in most countries. Hence the demand for labor in America is, other things held constant, greater. Conversely, labor is relatively scarcer in the United States than it

---

[4]Because we are referring to a long-run analysis here, the reduction in labor demanded would be demonstrated by an eventual shift inward to the left of the short-run demand curve, *D*, in Figure 28-7.

is in other countries. One result of relatively greater demand and relatively smaller supply is a relatively higher wage rate.

⭐ EXAMPLE: Does a College Education Increase Labor Productivity?

One way to increase labor productivity is to increase the skill level of workers. Potential workers can increase their skill level by going to college. It is almost a truism to state that more education leads to higher productivity and therefore higher wage rates. Indeed, college graduates enjoy a substantial wage premium over high school graduates. A recent estimate in 1993 is that a full-time worker with four years of college made $43,620. A high school graduate counterpart with four years of work experience earned only $27,110. The salary premium for going to college is around 60 percent. Some economists have pointed out, though, that this salary premium occurs not because college graduate salaries are being bid up but rather because high school graduates are doing poorly. One of the explanations for this is that a college degree is now becoming necessary for many jobs that never required one.

Some economists believe that a college degree is simply part of **labor market signaling.** Employers do not have much information about the future productivity of job applicants. Typically, the only way to find out is to observe someone working. Employers attempt to reduce the number of bad choices that they might make by using a job applicant's amount of higher education as a signal. According to the labor market signaling theory, even if higher education does not change productivity, it acts as an effective signal of greater individual abilities.

▶ **Labor market signaling** The process by which a potential worker's acquisition of credentials, such as a degree, is used by the employer to predict future productivity.

For Critical Analysis: Since 1969 the share of college graduates in the labor force has doubled and the share of high school dropouts has dropped in half. Nonetheless, some data show that living standards have advanced very little. Do these data support the labor market signaling theory? Why or why not? ●

Change in the Price of Related Factors. Labor is not the only resource used. Some resources are substitutes and some are complements. If we hold output constant, we have the following general rule:

> A change in the price of a substitute input will cause the demand for labor to change in the same direction. This is typically called the substitution effect.

Note, however, that if the cost of production falls sufficiently, the firm will find it more profitable to produce and sell a larger output. If this so-called *output effect* is great enough, it will override the substitution effect just mentioned, and the firm will end up employing not only more of the relatively cheaper variable input but also more labor. This is exactly what happened for many years in the American automobile industry. Auto companies employed more machinery (capital), but employment continued to increase in spite of rising wage rates. The reason? Markets were expanding and the marginal physical productivity of labor was rising faster than its wage rate.

With respect to complements, we are referring to inputs that must be used jointly. Assume now that capital and labor are complementary. In general, we predict the following:

> A change in the price of a complementary input will cause the demand for labor to change in the opposite direction.

If the cost of machines goes up but they must be used with labor, fewer machines will be purchased and therefore fewer workers will be used.

DETERMINANTS OF THE SUPPLY OF LABOR

There are a number of reasons why labor supply curves will shift in a particular industry. For example, if wage rates for factory workers in the CD industry remain constant while wages for factory workers in the computer industry go up dramatically, the supply curve of factory workers in the CD industry will shift inward to the left as these workers shift to the computer industry.

Changes in working conditions in an industry can also affect its labor supply curve. If employers in the CD industry discover a new production technique that makes working conditions much more pleasant, the supply curve of labor to the CD industry will shift outward to the right.

Job flexibility also determines the position of the labor supply curve. For example, in an industry in which workers are allowed more flexibility, such as the ability to work at home via computer, the workers are likely to work more hours. That is to say, their supply curve will shift outward to the right. Some industries in which firms offer *job sharing*, particularly to people raising families, have found that the supply curve of labor has shifted outward to the right.

SHIFTS IN DEMAND AND THE PROBLEM OF LABOR MARKET SHORTAGES

Labor markets do not adjust instantaneously. When there is an increase in demand, wage rates do not adjust right away. In Figure 28-8 we show the supply curve of computer programmers as S. The demand curve is D. The wage rate is W_1, and the equilibrium quantity of programmers is Q_1.

Suppose a big breakthrough has occurred in the computer industry, so that 50 percent more businesses want computers and hence more computer programmers. The demand curve shifts outward to D'. There would be no shortage if the wage rate increased to W_2 because at W_2 the new demand curve intersects the stable supply curve at E'. The equilibrium quantity of computer programmers would be Q_2.

But the wage rate may not rise immediately to its equilibrium rate. It moves gradually, and during this period of transition, shortages do indeed exist at lower than equilibrium

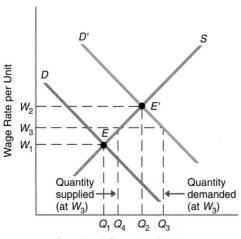

FIGURE 28-8
Adjustments to increases in demand for computer programmers.
We start at equilibrium at point E. When demand increases to D', the new market clearing equilibrium occurs at point E'. The wage rate would be W_2, and the quantity of computer programmers would be Q_2. However, because of lags in adjustment, the wage rate at first only rises to W_3. At that wage rate the quantity of computer programmers demanded will be Q_3, but the quantity of computer programmers supplied will be Q_4. Firms will experience a shortage of computer programmers at that wage rate.

wage rates. Take, for example, the wage rate W_3. Here the quantity demanded will be Q_3, but the quantity supplied will be only Q_4. The difference will be a shortage at wage rate W_3. Organizations wishing to hire computer programmers during this period will experience a shortage. They will not be able to hire all the computer programmers they want at the going wage rate. A shortage of this sort can take many years to be eliminated if the demand curve continues to shift to the right faster than the wage rate adjusts.

⭐ EXAMPLE: The Shifting Demand for Dentists

There was a time in this country when youngsters had to go to the dentist regularly to have their cavities filled. Later in life, as adults, those same persons had to have their fillings redone. Often they had to have inlays or crowns put on. A new generation of children is now on the scene. These are the children who have had fluoride in their drinking water as they grew up, have been taught how to "floss after every meal," brush more often, and eat less candy. The end result is a decreasing demand for the services of dentists. The demand curve for dentists has been shifting inward over time as preventive dentistry has become more widespread. As the demand for dentists has dropped, the demand for dental schools has, too. The changing demand for dentists has resulted in lower expected lifetime incomes and a reduction in the rate of applications to dental schools. In 1981 some 8,852 people applied to dental schools; in 1993, fewer than 5,000. Loyola University in Chicago closed its dental school recently because of this decreased demand.

For Critical Analysis: *What do you think has happened to the demand for orthodontic specialization over the past few decades, and why?* ●

CONCEPTS IN BRIEF

- The individual competitive firm faces a horizontal supply curve—it can buy all the labor it wants at the going market wage rate.
- The industry supply curve of labor slopes upward.
- Each individual faces a labor-leisure choice. An increase in wage rates has both a substitution effect, which causes the worker to work more, and an income effect, which causes the worker to work less. The individual may have a backward-bending labor supply curve, showing that initially the substitution effect overrides the income effect, and then, after a certain wage rate, the income effect overrides the substitution effect.
- By plotting on the same coordinate system an industrywide supply curve for labor and an industrywide demand curve for labor, we obtain the equilibrium wage rate in this industry.
- The labor demand curve can shift because (1) the demand for the final product shifts, (2) labor productivity changes, and (3) the price of a related (substitute or complementary) factor of production changes.
- The supply curve of labor will shift if there is a change in the alternative wage rate offered in other industries or in the nonmonetary aspects of the occupation in question.
- Abrupt changes in demand in a particular industry may lead to temporary shortages as wage rates move to the long-run equilibrium level.

MONOPOLY IN THE PRODUCT MARKET

So far we've considered only a perfectly competitive situation, both in selling the final product and in buying factors of production. We will continue our assumption that the firm purchases its factors of production in a perfectly competitive factor market. Now, however, we will assume that the firm sells its product in an *imperfectly* competitive output market. In other words, we are considering the output market structures of monopoly, oligopoly, and monopolistic competition. In all such cases, the firm, whether it be a monopolist, an oligopolist, or a monopolistic competitor, faces a downward-sloping demand curve for its product. Throughout the rest of this chapter we will simply refer to a monopoly output situation for ease of analysis. The analysis holds for all industry structures that are less than perfectly competitive. In any event, the fact that our firm now faces a downward-sloping demand curve for its product means that if it wants to sell more of its product (at a uniform price), it has to lower the price, *not only on the last unit but on all preceding units*. The *marginal revenue* received from selling an additional unit is continuously falling (and is less than price) as the firm attempts to sell more and more. This is certainly different from our earlier discussions in this chapter in which the firm could sell all that it wanted at a constant price. Why? Because the firm we discussed until now was a perfect competitor.

CONSTRUCTING THE MONOPOLIST'S INPUT DEMAND CURVE

In reconstructing our demand schedule for an input, we must account for the facts that (1) the marginal *physical* product falls because of the law of diminishing returns as more workers are added, and (2) the price (and marginal revenue) received for the product sold also falls as more is produced and sold. That is, for the monopolist we have to account for both the diminishing marginal physical product and the diminishing marginal revenue. Marginal revenue is always less than price for the monopolist. The marginal revenue curve is always below the downward-sloping demand curve.

Marginal revenue for the perfect competitor is equal to the price of the product, because all units can be sold at the going market price. In our CD example, we assumed that the perfect competitor could sell all it wanted at $6 per compact disc. A one-unit change in sales always led to a $6 change in total revenues. Hence marginal revenue was always equal to $6 for that perfect competitor.

The monopolist, however, cannot simply calculate marginal revenue by looking at the price of the product. To sell the additional output from an additional unit of input, the monopolist has to cut prices on all previous units of output. As output is increasing, then, marginal revenue is falling. The underlying concept is, of course, the same for both the perfect competitor and the monopolist. We are asking exactly the same question in both cases: When an additional worker is hired, what is the benefit? In either case, the benefit is obviously the change in total revenues due to the one-unit change in the variable input, labor. In our discussion of the perfect competitor, we were able simply to look at the marginal physical product and multiply it by the *constant* per-unit price of the product because the price of the product never changed (for the perfect competitor, $P = \text{MR}$).

The single monopolist (i.e., the entire industry) will always hire more workers than the single perfectly competitive firm. But the single monopolist ends up hiring fewer workers than all of the competitive firms added together. To see this, we must calculate the marginal revenue product for the monopolist. To make it simple, we will look at it as simply the change in total revenues due to a one-unit change in the labor input for a monopolist. This is what we do in panel (a) of Figure 28-9, which shows the change in total revenues. Column 6, headed "Marginal revenue product," gives the monopolistic firm a quantitative notion of how profitable additional workers and additional production actually are. The marginal revenue product curve for this monopolist has been plotted in panel (b) of the figure. To emphasize the steeper slope of the monopolist's MRP curve, MRP_m, the MRP curve for the perfect competitor in Figure 28-1, labeled MRP_c has been plotted on the same graph.

Why does the MRP_m curve represent the monopolist's input demand curve? Our profit-maximizing monopolist will continue to hire labor as long as additional profits result. Profits are made as long as the additional cost of more workers is outweighed by the

Panel (a)

(1) LABOR INPUT (WORKER-WEEKS)	(2) TOTAL PHYSICAL PRODUCT (TPP)	(3) MARGINAL PHYSICAL PRODUCT (MPP)	(4) PRICE OF PRODUCT (P)	(5) TOTAL REVENUE (TR) = (2) x (4)	(6) MARGINAL REVENUE PRODUCT (MRP$_m$) = $\frac{\text{CHANGE IN (5)}}{\text{CHANGE IN (1)}}$
7	1,000		$8.00	$ 8,000.00	
		111			$665.80
8	1,111		7.80	8,665.80	
		104			568.20
9	1,215		7.60	9,234.00	
		97			474.80
10	1,312		7.40	9,708.80	
		90			385.60
11	1,402		7.20	10,094.40	
		83			300.60
12	1,485		7.00	10,395.00	
		76			219.80
13	1,561		6.80	10,614.80	

FIGURE 28-9

A monopolist's marginal revenue product.
The monopolist hires just enough workers to make marginal revenue product equal to the going wage rate. If the going wage rate is $498 per week, the monopolist would want to hire somewhere between 9 and 10 worker-weeks. That is the profit-maximizing amount of labor. The MRP curve for the perfect competitor from Figure 28-1 is also plotted (MRP$_c$). The monopolist's MRP curve will always be less elastic than it would be if marginal revenue were constant.

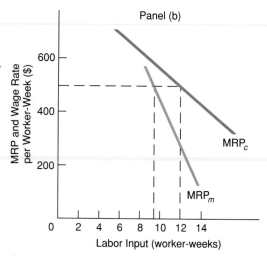

additional revenues made from selling the output of those workers. When the wage rate equals these additional revenues, the monopolist stops hiring. That is, it stops hiring when the wage rate is equal to the marginal revenue product because additional workers would add more to cost than to revenue.

WHY THE MONOPOLIST HIRES FEWER WORKERS

Because we have used the same numbers as in Figure 28-1, we can see that the monopolist hires fewer worker-weeks than the perfect competitor. That is to say, if we could magically change the CD industry in our example from one in which there is perfect competition in the output market to one in which there is monopoly in the output market, the amount of employment would fall. Why? Because the monopolist must take account of the declining product price that must be charged in order to sell a larger number of CDs. Remember that every firm hires up to the point at which marginal benefit equals marginal cost. The marginal benefit to the monopolist of hiring an additional worker is not simply the additional output times the price of the product. Rather, the monopolist faces a reduction in the price charged on all units sold in order to be able to sell more. So the monopolist ends up hiring fewer workers than all of the perfect competitors taken together, assuming that all other factors remain the same for the two hypothetical examples. But this should not come as a surprise. In considering product markets, by implication we saw that a monopolized CD industry would produce less output than a competitive one. Therefore, the monopolized CD industry would want fewer workers.

OTHER FACTORS OF PRODUCTION

The analysis in this chapter has been given in terms of the demand for the variable input labor. The same analysis holds for any other variable factor input. We could have talked about the demand for fertilizer or the demand for the services of tractors by a farmer instead of the demand for labor and reached the same conclusions. The entrepreneur will hire or buy any variable input up to the point at which its price equals the marginal revenue product.

A further question remains: How much of each variable factor should the firm use when all the variable factors are combined to produce the product? We can answer this question by looking at either the profit-maximizing side of the question or the cost-minimizing side.[5]

PROFIT MAXIMIZATION REVISITED

If a firm wants to maximize profits, how much of each factor should be hired (or bought)? As we just saw, the firm will never hire a factor of production unless the marginal benefit from hiring that factor is at least equal to the marginal cost. What is the marginal benefit? As we have pointed out several times, the marginal benefit is the change in total

---

[5]Many economic problems involving maximization of profit or other economic variables have *duals*, or precise restatements, in terms of *minimization* rather than maximization. The problem "How do we maximize our output, given fixed resources?" for example, is the dual of the problem "How do we minimize our cost, given fixed output?" Noneconomists sometimes confuse their discussions of economic issues by mistakenly believing that a problem and its dual are two problems rather than one. Asking, for example, "How can we maximize our profits while minimizing our costs?" makes about as much sense as asking, "How can we cross the street while getting to the other side?"

revenues due to a one-unit change in use of the variable input. What is the marginal cost? In the case of a firm buying in a competitive market, it is the price of the variable factor—the wage rate if we are referring to labor.

The profit-maximizing combination of resources for the firm will be where, in a perfectly competitive situation,

MRP of labor = price of labor (wage rate)
MRP of land = price of land (rental rate per unit)
MRP of capital = price of capital (cost per unit of service)

Alternatively, we can express this profit-maximizing rule as

$$\frac{\text{MRP of labor}}{\text{Price of labor}} = \frac{\text{MRP of land}}{\text{price of land}} = \frac{\text{MRP of capital}}{\text{price of capital}}$$

The marginal revenue product of each of a firm's resources must be exactly equal to its price. If the MRP of labor were $20 and its price were only $15, the firm would be underemploying labor.

COST MINIMIZATION

From the cost minimization point of view, how can the firm minimize its total costs for a given output? Assume that you are an entrepreneur attempting to minimize costs. Consider a hypothetical situation in which if you spend $1 more on labor, you would get 20 more units of output, but if you spend $1 more on machines, you would get only 10 more units of output. What would you want to do in such a situation? Most likely you would wish to hire more workers or sell off some of your machines, for you are not getting as much output per last dollar spent on machines as you are per last dollar spent on labor. You would want to employ factors of production so that the marginal products per last dollar spent on each are equal. Thus the least-cost, or cost minimization, rule will be as follows:

> To minimize total costs for a particular rate of production, the firm will hire factors of production up to the point at which the marginal physical product per last dollar spent on each factor of production is equalized.

That is,

$$\frac{\text{MPP of labor}}{\text{Price of labor}} = \frac{\text{MPP of capital}}{\text{price of capital (cost per unit of service)}} = \frac{\text{MPP of land}}{\text{price of land (rental rate per unit)}}$$

All we are saying here is that the profit-maximizing firm will always use *all* resources in such combinations that cost will be minimized for any given output rate. This is commonly called the *least-cost combination of resources*. There is an exact relationship between the profit-maximizing combination of resources and the least-cost combination of resources. In other words, either rule can be used to yield the same cost-minimizing rate of use of each variable resource.[6]

---

[6]This can be proved as follows: Profit maximization required that the price of every input must equal that input's marginal revenue product (the general case). Let i be the input. Then $P_i = \text{MRP}_i$. But MRP_i is equal to marginal revenue times marginal physical product of the input. Therefore, $P_i = \text{MR} \times \text{MPP}_i$. If we divide both sides by MPP_i, we get $P_i / \text{MPP}_i = \text{MR}$. If we take the reciprocal, we obtain $\text{MPP}_i / P_i = 1/\text{MR}$. That is another way of stating our cost minimization rule.

CONCEPTS IN BRIEF

- When a firm sells its output in a monopoly market, marginal revenue is less than price.
- Just as the MRP is the perfectly competitive firm's input demand curve, the MRP is also the monopolist's demand curve.
- For a less than perfectly competitive firm, the profit-maximizing combination of factors will occur where each factor is used up to the point where its MRP is equal to its unit price.
- To minimize total costs for a given output, the profit-maximizing firm will hire each factor of production up to the point where the marginal physical product per last dollar spent on each factor is equal to the marginal physical product per last dollar spent on each of the other factors of production.

CONTINUED ➞

IS $75 MILLION A YEAR TOO HIGH A SALARY?

Concepts Applied: marginal revenue product, demand for labor, supply of labor

Business executives are paid a variety of salaries. Many earn millions of dollars a year. Can such high salaries be justified?

In any society, the range of salaries that exists is usually quite large. When we look at the salaries of the highest-paid executives in America, we get the flavor of what people make at the upper end of the income scale. It is estimated today that about 700 executives in the United States earn more than $1 million, 100 earn more than $5 million, and 35 earn more than $30 million (see Table 28-1).

IS ANYONE WORTH $10,000 AN HOUR?

Let's take a really high-earning executive who will make $40 million this year. He likely works very hard—80 hours a week—and takes two weeks' vacation. That comes to 4,000 hours per year, meaning that the executive earning $40 million is getting paid $10,000 per hour. Is it possible that anybody's marginal revenue product is so high? The answer in some cases is yes. Consider the following not-so-hypothetical calculation from the Walt Disney Company. A couple of years ago, when its chief executive officer, Michael D. Eisner, actually did make $40 million, Disney had revenues of about $3.4 billion which works out to about $850,000 for each hour that Eisner worked. Let's assume that Eisner made only one important decision each month. If he is right, Disney sales would be 1 percent higher, and if he is wrong, Disney sales would be 1 percent lower. If Eisner made 12 correct decisions in the course of a year, Disney sales would rise by 12 percent, or approximately $456 million. If he

TABLE 28-1 **Fifteen highly paid chief executives.**

COMPANY	EXECUTIVE	1992 SALARY AND BONUS ($ THOUSANDS)	LONG-TERM COMPENSATION ($ THOUSANDS)	TOTAL PAY ($ THOUSANDS)
Abbott Labs	Duane L Burnham	1,444.0	5,468.8	6,912.9
Advanced Micro Devices	W. J. Sanders III	2,750.0	19,391.5	22,141.4
Bear Stearns	Alan C. Greenberg	15,832.0	0.0	15,832.0
Coca-Cola Company	Roberto C. Goizueta	3,201.0	12,016.7	15,217.7
Colgate-Palmolive	Reuben Mark	2,002.4	20,815.8	22,818.3
Disney (Walt)	Michael D. Eisner	7,459.0	197,500.0	204,959.0
General Dynamics	William A. Anders	2,300.0	21,166.0	23,466.0
General Electric	John F. Welch Jr.	3,500.0	14,470.0	17,970.0
HCA	Thomas F. Frist Jr.	1,068.0	125,934.4	127,002.4
Heinz (H. J.)	Anthony J. F. O'Reilly	1,046.2	35,600.2	36,646.4
Mattel	John W. Amerman	1,412.3	8,601.0	10,013.3
PepsiCo.	D. Wayne Calloway	2,293.1	8,843.8	11,136.8
Primerica	Sanford I. Weill	3,589.4	63,855.2	67,444.5
Toys "Я" Us	Charles Lazarus	7,025.2	57,205.7	64,230.9
U.S. Surgical	Leon C. Hirsch	1,694.6	59,018.7	60,713.3

Source: Wall Street Journal, April 21, 1993, pp. R14–R15. Note that many executives exercised their stock options in order to realize income in 1992 because of anticipated higher marginal tax rates that had been promised by Bill Clinton during his campaign.

made 12 incorrect decisions, sales would fall by $456 million. The potential total swing in sales is the sum of these, or $912 million. That is not the potential in profits, however, because of the various costs involved in generating those sales. If you assume the U.S. average of profits of 5 percent of sales, Eisner was personally responsible for 5 percent of $912 million, or $45.6 million. That comes out to $11,400 in potential profits per hour for the assumed 4,000 hours that Eisner worked. That was his potential marginal revenue product, and his pay was less than that.

WHAT HAPPENS WHEN COMPANIES DO POORLY?

During the recession of the early 1990s, the issue of executive pay came under fire. Companies that were doing poorly in terms of profits—some actually taking losses—continued to pay their chief executives (CEOs) millions of dollars. For example, during 1990 and 1991, the average return on an investment in Texas Instruments was a *negative* 6.4 percent. Nonetheless, during that same time period, Jerry R. Junkins, the CEO of Texas Instruments, earned over $2 million. Does that mean that executive pay should somehow be limited? Or does it mean, as some politicians argue, that executive pay over $1 million should not be a tax-deductible item for corporations? The answer, at least according to 1992 Nobel Prize–winning economist Gary Becker, is no. Becker has argued that the real problem is the difficulty in getting rid of company presidents who run their businesses poorly. He points out that CEOs control the appointments to most boards of directors. Therefore, they are protected against removal from office. Management puts forth a board of directors for the shareholders to elect. In 99 percent of the elections, that board of directors is voted in. Becker's solution is for corporations to adopt fixed-term appointments for CEOs similar to what we have for presidents, coaches, governors, and legislators. Short-term contracts for company CEOs would presumably reduce the number of situations in which these individuals get paid large salaries despite their companies' poor performances.

AMERICAN CEO PAY COMPARED TO THE REST OF THE WORLD

American companies reward their chief executive officers much more compared to those in other countries. Look at Figure 28-10. Here you see that the estimated pay for CEOs in companies with $250 million in sales was almost twice in the United States what it was in France, Switzerland, Italy, Canada, Britain, Japan, Germany, and Sweden.

What may be surprising is how little Japanese executives are paid given the great success that Japanese companies have had both domestically and in foreign markets, particularly in the United States.

FOR CRITICAL ANALYSIS

1. Is it conceivable that the skill level of multimillion-dollar salaried executives is no greater than the skill level of executives making $200,000 a year?
2. Does the amount that firm A is willing to pay an executive have any effect on the amount that firm B is willing to pay that executive? Does it have any effect on what firm B must pay the executive if firm B wished to hire that executive?

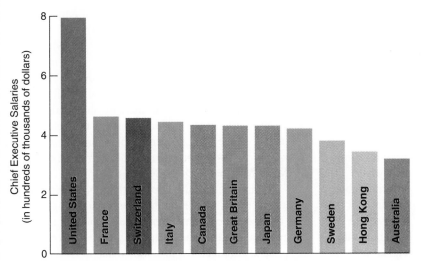

FIGURE 28-10
Comparing chief executive salaries across nations.
This bar chart shows the average remuneration of chief executives of companies that had $250,000 in sales in 1992. Remuneration includes cash, benefits, and other perquisites of the office of chief executive.
Source: The Economist, December 3, 1992.

CHAPTER SUMMARY

1. In a competitive situation in which the firm is a very small part of the entire product and labor market, the firm will want to hire workers up to the point at which the marginal revenue product just equals the going wage rate.

2. The marginal revenue product curve for the individual competitive firm is the input demand curve. The competitive firm hires up to the point at which the wage rate equals the MRP.

3. The summation of all the MRP curves does not equal the market demand curve for labor. The market demand curve for labor is less elastic than the sum of the MRP curves because as more workers are hired, output is increased and the price of the product must fall, lowering the MRP.

4. The demand for labor is derived from the demand for the product produced.

5. The elasticity of demand for an input is a function of several determinants, including the elasticity of demand for the final product and the elasticity of supply of other factors of production. Moreover, the price elasticity of demand for a variable input will usually be larger in the long run than it is in the short run because there is time for adjustment.

6. The firm buying labor in a perfectly competitive labor market faces a horizontal supply curve at the going wage rate. The industry supply curve of labor slopes upward.

7. The demand curve for labor will shift if (a) the demand for final product shifts, (b) the price of a substitute or a complementary factor of production changes, or (c) labor productivity changes.

8. The labor supply curve will shift if there is a change in the alternative wage rate offered in other industries or in the nonmonetary aspects of the occupation.

9. The MRP curve is also the monopolist's input demand curve. Because marginal revenue is less than the price of the product for a monopolist, the monopolist's input demand curve is usually steeper.

10. A firm minimizes total costs by equating the ratio of marginal physical product of labor divided by the price of labor with the ratio of marginal physical product of machines to the price of capital with all other such ratios for all the different factors of production. This is the mirror of profit maximization.

DISCUSSION OF PREVIEW POINTS

1. **In hiring labor, what general rule will be followed by employers who wish to maximize profits?**
   Employers who wish to maximize total profits will hire labor (or any other factor of production) up to the point at which the marginal cost of doing so equals the marginal benefit, MB. In that way, they will have used up all instances in which the marginal benefit of hiring labor exceeds the marginal cost, MC, of hiring labor. If MB > MC, they will hire more labor; if MB < MC, they will hire less; when MB = MC, they will be maximizing total profits.

2. **What is the profit-maximizing rate of employment for a perfectly competitive firm?**
   The perfectly competitive firm will accept prevailing wage rates; it can hire as much labor as it wishes at the going rate. It follows that the MC of hiring labor to the perfectly competitive firm is a constant that is equal to the prevailing wage rate; MC = W, where W is the market wage rate. The MB of hiring labor is the value of the marginal product of an additional unit of labor. The perfectly competitive firm will maximize total profits by hiring labor up to the point at which it drives the MRP down to equal the constant wage rate; MRP = W. This is also how the firm minimizes costs for a given output.

3. **What is the profit-maximizing rate of employment for an imperfectly competitive firm?**
   For an imperfectly competitive firm, P > MR. Thus in the short run the marginal benefit of hiring additional units of labor falls for two reasons: (a) The law of diminishing returns causes marginal physical product to diminish, and (b) to increase sales, price must fall—on previously produced units as well as the new one. Thus the MB of hiring labor equals the *marginal revenue* times the marginal physical product of labor; MB = MRP = MR × MPP.

   By assumption, the imperfectly competitive firm is a competitor in the input markets, so in hiring labor it (like the perfect competitor) faces a constant marginal cost equal to the going wage rate; MC = W for the imperfectly competitive firm too. What about the profit-maximizing rate of employment for the imperfectly competitive firm? It hires up to the point at which it drives down the marginal revenue product of labor (MRP = MR × MPP) until it equals the going wage rate; MRP = W is the equilibrium condition in this model.

4. How is an industry wage rate determined?

Wage rates are a price; they are the price of labor. As such, wage rates are determined like all prices, by the forces of supply and demand. The market, or industry, wage rate will be determined by the point of intersection of the industry supply of labor curve and the industry demand for labor curve. At the point of intersection, the quantity of labor supplied equals the quantity of labor demanded, and equilibrium exists; both buyers and sellers are able to realize their intentions.

PROBLEMS

(Answers to the odd-numbered problems appear at the back of the book.)

28-1. Assume that the product in the table is sold by a perfectly competitive firm for $2 per unit.
   a. Use the information in the table to derive a demand schedule for labor.
   b. What is the most that this firm would be willing to pay each worker if five workers were hired?
   c. If the going salary for this quality labor is $200 per week, how many workers will be hired?

QUANTITY OF LABOR	TOTAL PRODUCT PER WEEK	MPP	MRP
1	250	____	$____
2	450	____	____
3	600	____	____
4	700	____	____
5	750	____	____
6	750	____	____

28-2. The table below presents some production function data for a firm in which the only variable input is capital; the labor input is fixed. First fill in the other columns. What quantity of capital will the firm use if the price of capital is $90 per machine-week? If the price of capital is $300 per machine-week, what quantity of capital will the firm use? Explain.

QUANTITY OF CAPITAL (MACHINE-WEEKS)	TOTAL PRODUCT PER WEEK	MARGINAL PRODUCT OF CAPITAL PER WEEK	MARGINAL REVENUE (PRODUCT PRICE) PER UNIT	MARGINAL REVENUE PRODUCT PER WEEK
0	0	____	$10	$____
1	25	____	10	____
2	45	____	10	____
3	60	____	10	____
4	70	____	10	____
5	75	____	10	____

28-3. The accompanying graph indicates labor supply and demand in the construction industry.

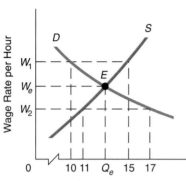

Quantity of Labor per Time Period
(millions of worker-hours)

a. When wage rates are W_1 per hour, how many worker-hours do workers intend to offer per unit?

b. How much do businesses intend to buy at this wage rate?

c. Which group can realize its intentions, and which can't?

d. What forces will be set in motion at wage rate W_1, given a free market for labor?

28-4. Using the graph in Problem 28-3, answer the following questions.

a. At wage rate W_2, how many worker-hours do workers intend to offer?

b. At W_2, how many worker-hours do businesses intend to purchase?

c. Which group can realize its intentions, and which can't?

d. What forces will be set in motion at W_2 if a free market for labor exists in this industry?

e. What will the equilibrium wage rate be?

28-5. The price elasticity of demand for the final output product directly affects the elasticity of demand for the input factor. Why?

28-6. Suppose that you are seeking to maximize output for a given outlay. If the marginal physical product of input x is 10 and that of input y is 20, and the prices of the two inputs are $3 and $7, respectively, how should you alter your input mix in order to increase output?

28-7. Suppose that you are a monopolist and labor is the only variable input you employ. You are currently producing 150 units of output and selling them for $20 apiece. You are considering the possibility of hiring an additional full-time employee. You estimate that daily output would increase to 160 units if you hired this additional person and that you would be able to sell all of those units at a price of $19 each. What is the MRP of labor (per worker-day)? Assuming that you take the price of labor as a given, what is the maximum daily wage that would make it in your interest to hire this additional employee?

28-8. When there is only one variable input, how does a monopoly seller's demand for that input differ from that of a perfectly competitive seller?

28-9. Assume that you have graduated from college. You decide to look for a job rather than go for further schooling. Indicate how the following criteria might affect the salary that you will receive and the type of job you may end up taking after you graduate.

a. You want to stay near your family, so you do not consider moving out of your immediate geographic area to find a job.

b. You look only for jobs that allow you to apply the knowledge and skills you have learned in your college major.

c. You now live in the city but decide that you will only work in a rural area.

COMPUTER-ASSISTED INSTRUCTION
(Complete problem and answer on disk.)

We explore the foundations of the demand for and the supply of labor, along the way demonstrating the consequences of the minimum wage.

29

UNIONS AND LABOR MARKET MONOPOLY POWER

In the past few years there have been riots in Los Angeles and other large cities, hurricanes in South Carolina and Florida, flooding in Arizona, and other disasters. All have one thing in common: major commercial and residential structures were destroyed. To help people get back on their feet, the federal government sent billions of dollars into these federally declared disaster areas to subsidize construction. Let's say that you decided to bid on some of those construction contracts. If you wanted to underprice other contractors' bids, you might lower your costs by hiring unemployed construction workers who are willing to work at relatively low wages. In fact, though, when you went to bid you might find that you just violated federal requirements for bidders on construction jobs that use any federal monies. To understand how you might be frustrated in your attempt to place low bids on federal construction contracts, you first need an understanding of various restrictions in the labor market.

After reading this chapter, you should be able to answer the following questions:

1. What are the major types of unions?

2. What do unions seek to maximize?

3. Do unions help workers?

4. What is a monopsonist, and how does one go about determining its profit-maximizing employment rate?

INTRODUCTION

"It's just not fair." That is certainly the way many people feel about the tremendous range of wages that are earned by various participants in the American economy. In a competitive labor market, however, it's not easy to make more than a competitive wage rate, given one's skills, talents, abilities, geographic location, health, and other considerations compared to the demand for those skills and abilities. Nonetheless, there are some workers who make more than the competitive wage rate, more than what we predicted in Chapter 28 when we looked at the demand for and supply of labor. The fact is that some workers make more than they would in a competitive labor market because they have obtained a type of monopoly power. These are members of effective **labor unions,** which are workers' organizations that seek to secure economic improvements for their members. In forming unions, a certain monopoly element enters into the supply of labor equation. That is to say, we can no longer talk about a perfectly competitive labor supply situation when active and effective unions bargain as a single entity with management. The entire supply of a particular group of workers is controlled by a single source. Later in the chapter we will examine the converse—a single employer who is the sole user of a particular group of workers.

▶ **Labor unions**
Worker organizations that usually seek to secure economic improvements for their members; they also seek to improve the safety, health, and other benefits of their members.

A SHORT HISTORY OF THE AMERICAN LABOR MOVEMENT

The American labor movement started with local **craft unions.** These were groups of workers in individual trades, such as shoemaking, printing, or baking. Initially, in the United States, laborers struggled for the right to band together to bargain as a unit. In the years between the Civil War and the Great Depression (1861–1930s), the Knights of Labor, an organized group of both skilled and unskilled workers, demanded an eight-hour workday, equal pay for women and men, and the replacement of free enterprise with the socialist system. In 1886 a dissident group from the Knights of Labor formed the American Federation of Labor (AFL) under the leadership of Samuel Gompers. Until World War I the government supported business's opposition to unions by offering the use of police personnel to break strikes. During World War I the image of the unions improved and membership increased to more than 5 million. But after the war the government decided to stop protecting labor's right to organize. Membership began to fall.

▶ **Craft unions**
Labor unions composed of workers who engage in a particular trade or skill, such as baking, carpentry, or plumbing.

Then came the Great Depression. Franklin Delano Roosevelt's National Industrial Recovery Act of 1933 gave labor the federal right to bargain collectively, but that act was declared unconstitutional. The 1935 National Labor Relations Act (NLRA), otherwise known as the Wagner Act, took its place. The NLRA guaranteed workers the right to start unions, to engage in **collective bargaining,** and to be members in any union that was started.

In 1938 the Congress of Industrial Organizations (CIO) was formed by John L. Lewis, the president of the United Mine Workers. Prior to the formation of the CIO, most labor organizations were craft unions. The CIO was composed of **industrial unions**—unions with membership from an entire industry such as steel or automobiles.

▶ **Collective bargaining**
Bargaining between the management of a company or of a group of companies and the management of a union or a group of unions for the purpose of setting a mutually agreeable contract on wages, fringe benefits, and working conditions for all employees in all the unions involved.

▶ **Industrial unions**
Labor unions that consist of workers from a particular industry, such as automobile manufacturing or steel manufacturing.

THE TAFT-HARTLEY ACT

The Taft-Hartley Act of 1947, otherwise called the Labor Management Relations Act, has been termed by some union people the "slave labor act." Among other things, it allows individual states to pass their own **right-to-work laws.** A right-to-work law makes it illegal for union membership to be a requirement for continued employment in any establishment.

▶ **Right-to-work laws**
Laws that make it illegal to require union membership as a condition of continuing employment in a particular firm.

▶ **Closed shop**
A business enterprise in which employees must belong to the union before they can be hired and must remain in the union after they are hired.

▶ **Union shop**
A business enterprise that allows the hiring of nonunion members, conditional on their joining the union by some specified date after employment begins.

▶ **Jurisdictional dispute**
A dispute involving two or more unions over which should have control of a particular jurisdiction, such as over a particular craft or skill or over a particular firm or industry.

▶ **Sympathy strike**
A strike by a union in sympathy with another union's strike or cause.

▶ **Secondary boycott**
A boycott of companies or products sold by companies that are dealing with a company being struck.

More specifically, the act makes a **closed shop** illegal; a closed shop requires union membership before employment can be obtained. A **union shop,** however, is legal; a union shop does not require membership as a prerequisite for employment, but it can, and usually does, require that workers join the union after a specified amount of time on the job. (Even a union shop is illegal in states with right-to-work laws.)

Jurisdictional disputes, sympathy strikes, and secondary boycotts are made illegal by this act as well. A **jurisdictional dispute** involves two or more unions fighting (and striking) over which should have control in a particular jurisdiction. For example, should a carpenter working for a steel manufacturer be part of the steelworkers' union or the carpenters' union? A **sympathy strike** occurs when one union strikes in sympathy with another union's cause or strike. For example, if the retail clerks' union in an area is striking grocery stores, teamsters may refuse to deliver products to those stores in sympathy with the retail clerks' demands for higher wages or better working conditions. A **secondary boycott** is the boycotting of a company that deals with a struck company. For example, if union workers strike a baking company, the boycotting of grocery stores that continue to sell that company's products is a secondary boycott. The secondary boycott brings pressure on third parties to force them to stop dealing with an employer who is being struck.

In general, the Taft-Hartley Act outlawed unfair labor practices of unions, such as make-work rules and forcing unwilling workers to join a particular union. Perhaps the most famous aspect of the Taft-Harley Act is its provision that the president can obtain a court injunction that will stop a strike for an 80-day cooling-off period if the strike is expected to imperil the nation's safety or health.

THE MERGING OF THE AFL AND THE CIO

Years after the CIO split from the AFL, the two merged in 1955 under the presidency of George Meany. Organized labor's failure to grow at a continuing rapid rate caused leaders in both associations to seek the merger. It was thought that a unified effort was needed to organize union firms. However, the AFL-CIO merger has not caused a resurgence of organized labor as a percentage of the total labor force.

THE LANDRUM-GRIFFIN ACT OF 1959

Internal union business procedures became more strictly regulated with the passage of the Landrum-Griffin Act (officially known as the Labor-Management Reporting and Disclosure Act), passed in 1959. The act regulates union elections. It requires that regularly scheduled elections of officers occur and that secret ballots be used. Ex-convicts are prohibited from holding union office. Moreover, union officials are made accountable for union property and funds. Any union officer who embezzles union funds violates a federal law. Certain other rights of union members were also laid out in the Landrum-Griffin Act. Workers have the right to attend and participate in union meetings for example, to nominate officers, and to vote in most union proceedings.

THE GROWTH IN PUBLIC-SECTOR UNIONS

Since 1965 the degree of unionization in the private sector has declined. There has been, nonetheless, growth in the unionization of public employees. The U.S. Department of Labor indicates that the number of government workers—federal, state, and local—in national unions and in employee associations rose from 3.9 million in 1968 to 8.5 million by 1993.

Many important issues arise when we consider the implications of strikes by public-sector unions. The disruption due to a strike by police personnel or fire fighters could be significant. The courts and legislators must grapple with this issue more and more often. In spite of the fact that several laws were passed at the federal, state, and local levels giving public employees more freedom to unionize, there are numerous restrictions against public-employee strikes. However, it should be noted that penalties imposed on unions that defy such laws against strikes are frequently ignored. Indeed, the right to strike is one of the most controversial issues in public-sector bargaining.

Even though many people believe that unions are important in the United States, the percentage of unionized workers is relatively small and falling. Look at Figure 29-1. Union membership is heading toward 14 percent of the labor force. Although this percentage is higher than it was prior to the Great Depression, it is far less than during unions' peak at one-quarter of the labor force in the 1960s. In effect, the use of nonunionized labor has become the norm rather than the exception in many industries. The shift from manufacturing—where unions have been strongest—to service-sector jobs has been one reason for this decline in the relative importance of unions. Persistent illegal immigration into this country has also weakened the power of unions. Much of the unskilled and typically nonunionized work in the United States is done by foreign-born workers, some of whom are "undocumented." The deregulation of certain industries has also led to a decline in unionism. More intense competition in formally regulated industries, such as the airlines,

FIGURE 29-1
Decline in union membership.
Numerically, union membership in the United States has increased dramatically since the 1930s, but as a percentage of the labor force, union membership peaked around 1960 and has been falling ever since. Most recently, the absolute number of union members has also diminished.

Sources: L. Davis et al., *American Economic Growth* (New York: Harper & Row, 1972), p. 220; U.S. Department of Labor, Bureau of Labor Statistics. 1993 data estimated.

has led to a movement towards nonunionized (cheaper) labor. Finally, increased labor force participation by women has led to a decline in union importance. Women have traditionally been less inclined to join unions than their male counterparts.

🌐 INTERNATIONAL EXAMPLE: The Strength of Unions in Western Europe and Japan

The most recent data for Sweden show that 82 percent of Swedish workers belong to unions. In England that number is over 35 percent. Though unionization rates differ substantially among European nations, they are much higher, on average, in Europe—48 percent—than they are in the United States, Canada, or Japan. Unionization in Canada is around 29 percent today; in Japan, around 24 percent.

The trend in deunionization in Japan has not been as dramatic in the United States, but it continues apace. In 1949 unionization was at 56 percent. Japanese unions differ from the typical American union in that virtually all Japanese unions are "enterprises," each of which represents the work force of a single company. As a result, the unions implicitly compete among themselves when bargaining for wage settlements. If they demand too much, their company's costs rise relative to competitors', thereby reducing their company's market share and thus the demand for their members' services. This may explain why wage demands on the part of Japanese unions have been more moderate than in the United States and in Europe.

For Critical Analysis: How do you think Europe's higher degree of unionization affects the mobility of workers, as compared to the United States? ●

CONCEPTS IN BRIEF

- The American labor movement started with local craft unions devoted to individual trades such as baking, shoemaking, and printing.
- The American Federation of Labor (AFL), composed of craft unions, was formed in 1886 under the leadership of Samuel Gompers. Membership increased until after World War I, at which time the government stopped protecting labor's right to organize.
- During the Great Depression, legislation was passed that allowed for collective bargaining. The National Labor Relations Act of 1935 guaranteed workers the right to start unions.
- The Congress of Industrial Organizations (CIO), composed of industrial unions, was formed during the Great Depression. John L. Lewis, president of the United Mine Workers, took it over in 1938.
- The Taft-Hartley Act of 1947 allowed individual states to pass their own right-to-work laws and declared closed shops and secondary boycotts, among other things, illegal. The Taft-Hartley Act allows for an 80-day court injunction against strikes that threaten national health or safety.
- In 1955 the AFL and CIO merged into one national organization, the AFL-CIO.
- Internal union business procedures became more uniformly regulated with the passage of the Landrum-Griffin Act (Labor-Management Reporting and Disclosure Act) in 1959.

UNIONS AND COLLECTIVE BARGAINING CONTRACTS

Unions can be regarded as setters of minimum wages. Through collective bargaining, unions establish minimum wages below which no individual worker can offer his or her services. Each year collective bargaining contracts covering wages as well as working conditions and fringe benefits for about 8 million workers are negotiated. Union negotiators act as agents for all members of the bargaining unit. They bargain with management about the provisions of a labor contract. Once union representatives believe that they have an acceptable collective contract, they will submit it to a vote of the union members. Once approved by the members, the contract sets forth maximum workdays, wage rates, working conditions, fringe benefits, and other matters, usually for the next two or three years. Typically, collective bargaining contracts between management and the union apply also to nonunion members who are employed by the firm or the industry.

STRIKE: THE ULTIMATE BARGAINING TOOL

Whenever union-management negotiations break down, union negotiators may turn to their ultimate bargaining tool, the threat or the reality of a strike. The first recorded strike occurred shortly after the Revolutionary War, when Philadelphia printers walked out in 1786 over a demand for a weekly minimum wage of $6. Strikes make headlines, but in only 4 percent of all labor-management disputes does a strike occur before the contract is signed. In the other 96 percent of cases, contracts are signed without much public fanfare.

The purpose of a strike is to impose costs on recalcitrant management to force its acceptance of the union's proposed contract terms. Strikes disrupt production and interfere with a company's or industry's ability to sell goods and services. The strike works both ways, though. Workers draw no wages while on strike (they may be partly compensated out of union strike funds). Striking union workers may also be eligible to draw state unemployment benefits.

The impact of a strike is closely related to the ability of striking unions to prevent nonstriking (and perhaps nonunion) employees from continuing to work for the targeted company or industry. Therefore, steps are usually taken to prevent others from working for the employer. **Strikebreakers** can effectively destroy whatever bargaining power rests behind a strike. Numerous methods have been used to prevent strikebreakers from breaking strikes. Violence has been known to erupt, almost always in connection with attempts to prevent strikebreaking.

▶ **Strikebreakers**
Temporary or permanent workers hired by a company to replace union members who are striking.

⭐ EXAMPLE: Automation and the Telephone Workers' Union

The threat of a strike is most powerful when workers in an industry are absolutely critical. That used to be the way it was with telephone workers. In past years, if telephone company employees went on strike, the long-distance telephone network practically closed down. Today about 95 percent of all long-distance calls are made without the aid of an operator. That proportion will increase even more as American Telephone and Telegraph (AT&T) replaces 6,000 operators with computerized voice-recognition systems. Not surprisingly, when collective bargaining talks started to falter between AT&T and unions representing 125,000 workers in early 1992, AT&T was not too worried. AT&T flatly stated that if a strike occurred, it would replace workers with current, former, and retired managers. When the talks started, almost 100,000 nonmanagement jobs had already been eliminated. Automation had been taking its toll since 1984. Automation and the reduction in workers at AT&T was fostered, at least in part, by fierce increased competition from firms such as MCI and Sprint. AT&T presumably felt that it could not give in to union demands for pay increases, pension benefits, and job security and still remain competitive. In the end, there was no strike.

For Critical Analysis: Would you predict that in any given year there would be a high percentage of collective bargaining negotiations that result in actual strikes? Why? (Hint: How disruptive and costly is a strike to both company and workers?) ●

WHAT ARE UNION GOALS?

We have already pointed out that one of the goals of unions is to set minimum wages. In many situations, any wage rate set higher than a competitive market clearing wage rate will reduce total employment in that market. This can be seen in Figure 29-2. We have a competitive market for labor. The market demand curve is D and the market supply curve is S. The market clearing wage rate will be W_e; the equilibrium quantity of labor will be Q_e. If the union establishes by collective bargaining a minimum wage rate that exceeds W_e, an excess quantity of labor will be supplied (assuming no change in the labor demand schedule). If the minimum wage established by union collective bargaining is W_u, the quantity supplied would be Q_S; the quantity demanded would be Q_D. The difference is the excess quantity supplied, or surplus. Hence the following point becomes clear:

> **One of the major roles of a union that establishes a wage rate above the market clearing wage rate is to ration available jobs among the excess number of workers who wish to work in unionized industries.**

Note also that the surplus of labor is equivalent to a shortage of jobs at wage rates above equilibrium.

The union may use a system of seniority, a lengthening of the apprenticeship period to discourage potential members from joining, and other such rationing methods. This has the effect of shifting the supply of labor curve to the left in order to support the higher wage, W_u.

There is a trade-off here that any union's leadership must face: Higher wages inevitably mean a reduction in total employment, as more persons are seeking a smaller number of positions. (Moreover, at higher wages, more workers will seek to enter the industry, thereby adding to the surplus that occurs because of the union contract.) Faced with higher wages, management may replace part of the work force with machinery.

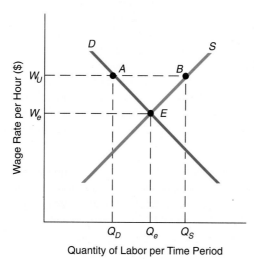

FIGURE 29-2
Unions must ration jobs.
If the union succeeds in obtaining wage rate W_u, the quantity of labor demanded will be Q_D, but the quantity of labor supplied will be Q_S. The union must ration a limited number of jobs to a greater number of workers; the surplus of labor is equivalent to a shortage of jobs at that wage rate.

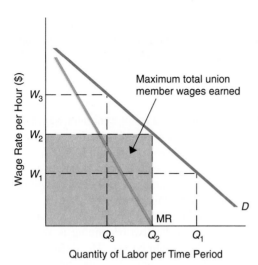

FIGURE 29-3
What do unions maximize?
Assume that the union wants to employ all its Q_1 members. It will attempt to get wage rate W_1. If the union wants to maximize total wage receipts, it will do so at wage rate W_2, where the elasticity of the demand for labor is equal to 1. (The shaded area represents these maximum total wages that the union would earn at W_2.) If the union wants to maximize the wage rate for a given number of workers, say, Q_3, it will set the wage rate at W_3.

TYPES OF UNION BEHAVIOR

If we view unions as monopoly sellers of a service, we can identify three different wage and employment strategies: ensuring employment for all members of the union, maximizing wage rates for all workers, and maximizing wage rates for some workers.

Employing All Members in the Union. Assume that the union has Q_1 workers. If it faces a labor demand curve such as D in Figure 29-3, the only way it can "sell" all of those workers' services is to accept a wage rate of W_1. This is similar to any other demand curve. The demand curve tells the maximum price that can be charged to sell any particular quantity of a good or service. Here the service happens to be labor.

Maximizing Member Income. If the union is interested in maximizing the gross income of its members, it will want a smaller membership than Q_1, namely Q_2 workers, all employed and paid a wage rate of W_2. The aggregate income to all members of the union is represented by the wages of only the ones who work. Total wages earned by union members are maximized where the price elasticity of demand is numerically equal to 1. That also happens to occur where marginal revenue equals zero. In Figure 29-3 marginal revenue equals zero at a quantity of labor Q_2. So we know that if the union obtains a wage rate equal to W_2, and therefore Q_2 of workers are demanded, the total revenues to the union membership will be maximized. In other words, $Q_2 \times W_2$ (the shaded area) will be greater than any other combination of wage rates and quantities of union workers demanded. It is, for example, greater than $Q_1 \times W_1$. Note that in this situation, if the union started out with Q_1 members, there would be $Q_1 - Q_2$ members out of *union* work at the wage rate W_2. (Those out of union work either remain unemployed or go to other industries, which has an effect on wages in nonunion industries due to the increase in supply of nonunion workers there.)

Maximizing Wage Rates for Certain Workers. Assume that the union wants to maximize the wage rates for some of its workers—perhaps those with the most seniority. If it wanted to keep a quantity of Q_3 workers employed, it would seek to obtain a wage rate of W_3. This would require deciding which workers should be unemployed and which workers should work and for how long each week or each year they should be employed.

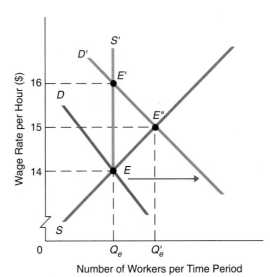

FIGURE 29-4
Restricting supply over time.
When the union was formed, it didn't affect wage rates or employment, which remained at $14 and Q_e (the wage rate equilibrium quantity). However, as demand increased—that is, as the demand schedule shifted outward to D' from D—the union restricted membership to its original level of Q_e. The new supply curve is SS', which intersects D' at E', or at a wage rate of $16. Without the union, equilibrium would be at E'' with a wage rate of $15 and employment of Q'_e.

LIMITING ENTRY OVER TIME

One way to raise wage rates without specifically setting wages is for unions to limit the size of their membership to the size of their employed work force when the union was first organized. No workers are put out of work at the time the union is formed. Over time as the demand for labor in the industry increases, there is no net increase in union membership, so larger wage increases are obtained than would otherwise be the case. We see this in Figure 29-4. Union members freeze entry into their union, thereby obtaining a wage rate of $16 per hour instead of allowing a wage rate of $15 per hour with no restriction on labor supply.

ALTERING THE DEMAND FOR UNION LABOR

Another way in which unions can increase wages is to shift the demand curve for labor outward to the right. This approach compares favorably with the supply restriction approach because it increases both wage rates and employment level. The demand for union labor can be increased by increasing worker productivity, increasing the demand for union-made goods, and decreasing the demand for non-union-made goods.

Increasing Worker Productivity.   Supporters of unions have argued that unions provide a good system of industrial jurisprudence. The presence of unions may induce workers to feel that they are working in fair and just circumstances. If so, they work harder, increasing labor productivity. Productivity is also increased when unions resolve differences and reduce conflicts between workers and management, thereby providing a smoother administrative environment.

Increasing Demand for Union-made Goods.   Because the demand for labor is a derived demand, a rise in the demand for products produced by union labor will increase the demand for union labor itself. One way in which unions attempt to increase the demand for union labor–produced products is by advertising "Look for the union label."

Decreasing the Demand for Non-union-made Goods.   When the demand for goods that are competing with (or are substitutes for) union-made goods is reduced, consumers shift to union-made goods, increasing the demand. A good example is when various unions campaign against imports; restrictions on imported cars are supported by the United Auto Workers as strongly as the Textile Workers Unions support restrictions on imported textile goods. The result is greater demand for goods "made in the USA," which in turn presumably increases the demand for American union (and nonunion) labor.

HAVE UNIONS RAISED WAGES?

We have seen that unions are able to raise the wages of their members if they are successful at limiting the supply of labor in a particular industry. They are also able to raise wages above what wages would otherwise be to the extent that they can shift the demand for union labor outward to the right. This can be done using the methods we have just discussed, including collective bargaining agreements that require specified workers for any given job—for example, by requiring a pilot, a copilot, and an engineer in the cockpit of a jet airplane even if an engineer is not needed on short flights. Economists have done extensive research to determine the actual increase in union wages relative to nonunion wages. They have found that in certain industries, such as construction, and in certain occupations, such as commercial airline pilot, the union wage differential can be 50 percent or more. That is to say, unions have been able in some industries and occupations to raise wage rates 50 percent or more above what they would be in the absence of unions.

In addition, the union wage differential appears to increase during recessions. This is because unions often, through collective bargaining, have longer-term contracts than nonunion workers so that they do not have to renegotiate wage rates, even when overall demand in the economy falls.

On average, unions appear to be able to raise the wage rates of their members relative to nonunion members by 10 to 20 percent. Note, though, that when unions increase wages beyond what productivity increases would permit, some union members will be laid off. A redistribution of income from low- to high-seniority union workers is not equivalent to higher wages for *all* union members.

CAN UNIONS INCREASE PRODUCTIVITY?

A traditional view of union behavior is that unions decrease productivity by shifting the demand curve for union labor outward through excessive staffing and make-work requirements. For example, some economists have traditionally felt that unions tend to bargain for excessive use of workers, as when requiring an engineer on all flights. This is called **featherbedding.** Many painters' unions, for example, resisted the use of paint sprayers and required that their members use only brushes. They even specified the maximum width of the brush. Moreover, whenever a union strikes, productivity drops, and this reduction in productivity in one sector of the economy can spill over into other sectors.

▶ **Featherbedding**
Any practice that forces employers to use more labor than they would otherwise or to use existing labor in an inefficient manner.

This traditional view against unions has recently been countered by a view that unions can actually increase productivity. The new labor economists contend that unions act as a collective voice for their members. In the absence of a collective voice, any dissatisfied worker either simply remains at a job and works in a disgruntled manner or quits. But unions, as a collective voice, can listen to worker grievances on an individual basis and then apply pressure on the employer to change working conditions and the like. The individual worker does not run the risk of being singled out by the employer and harassed. Also, the individual worker doesn't have to spend time trying to convince the employer that some change in the working arrangement should be made. Given that unions provide this collective voice, worker turnover in unionized industries should be less, and this should contribute to productivity. Indeed, there is strong evidence that worker turnover is reduced when unions are present. Of course, this evidence may also be consistent with the fact that wage rates are so attractive to union members that they will not quit unless working conditions become truly intolerable.

A MODERN THEORY OF LABOR UNIONS

It should by now be clear that there are two opposing views about unions. One portrays them as monopolies whose main effect is to raise the wage rate of high-seniority members at the expense of low-seniority members. The other contends that they can increase labor productivity through a variety of means. Harvard economists Richard B. Freeman and James L. Medoff argue that the truth is somewhere in between.[1] They examine many aspects of union theory and try to answer "which face of unions is quantitatively more important." They come up with the following conclusions:

1. Unionism probably raises social efficiency, thereby contradicting the traditional monopoly interpretation of what unions do. Even though unionism reduces employment in the unionized sector, it does permit labor to develop and implement workplace practices that are more valuable to workers. In some settings, unionism is associated with increased productivity.
2. Unions appear to reduce wage inequality.
3. Unions seem to reduce profits.
4. Internally, unions provide a political voice for all workers, and unions have been effective in promoting general social legislation.
5. Unions tend to increase the stability of the work force by providing services, such as arbitration proceedings and grievance procedures.

Freeman and Medoff take a positive view of unionism. But their critics point out that they may have overlooked the fact that many of the benefits that unions provide do not require that unions engage in restrictive labor practices, such as the closed shop. Unions could still do positive things for workers without restricting the labor market.

CONCEPTS IN BRIEF

- When unions raise wage rates above market clearing prices, they face the problem of rationing a restricted number of jobs to a more than willing supply of workers.
- Unions may pursue one of three goals: (1) to employ all members in the union, (2) to maximize total wages for the union's workers, or (3) to maximize wages for certain workers.
- Unions can increase the wage rate of members by engaging in practices that shift the union labor supply curve inward or shift the demand curve for union labor outward (or both).
- Unions are able to increase relative wages of union members, particularly during recessions. On average, unions appear to raise wage rates for their members relative to nonunion workers by 10 to 20 percent.   **(Continued)**

---

[1]Richard B. Freeman and James L. Medoff, *What Do Unions Do?* (New York: Basic Books, 1984).

● Some economists believe that unions can increase productivity by acting as a collective voice for their members, thereby freeing members from the task of convincing their employers that some change in working arrangements should be made. Unions may reduce turnover, thus improving productivity.

MONOPSONY: A BUYER'S MONOPOLY

Let's assume that a firm is a perfect competitor in the product market. The firm cannot alter the price of the product it sells, and it faces a horizontal demand curve for its product. We also assume that the firm is the only buyer of a particular input. Although this situation may not occur often, it is useful to consider. Let's think in terms of a company town, like those dominated by textile mills or in the mining industry. One company not only hires the workers but also owns the businesses in the community, owns the apartments that workers live in, and hires the clerks, waiters, and all other personnel. This buyer of labor is called a **monopsonist,** the single buyer.

▷ **Monopsonist**
A single buyer.

A monopsonist faces an *upward-sloping supply curve* for labor. The market supply curve has also been shown to slope upward. In general, firms do not usually face the market supply curve; most firms can hire all the workers they want at the going wage rate and thus usually face a fairly horizontal supply curve for each factor of production.

What does an upward-sloping supply curve mean to monopsonists in terms of the costs of hiring extra workers? It means that if they want to hire more workers, they have to offer higher wages. Our monopsonist firm cannot hire all the labor it wants at the going wage rate. If it wants to hire more workers, it has to raise wage rates. It also has to raise the wage rates of all its current workers (assuming a non-wage-discriminating monopsonist). It therefore has to take account of these increased costs when deciding how many more workers to hire.

 EXAMPLE: Monopsony in College Sports

How many times have you read stories about colleges and universities violating National Collegiate Athletic Association (NCAA) rules? If you keep up with the sports press, these stories about alleged violations occur every year. About 600 four-year colleges and universities belong to the NCAA, which controls over 20 sports. In effect, the NCAA operates an intercollegiate cartel that is dominated by universities that operate big-time athletic programs. It operates as a cartel with monopsony power in four ways:

1. It regulates the number of student athletes that universities can recruit.
2. It often fixes the prices that the university charges for tickets to important intercollegiate sporting events.
3. It sets the prices—the wages—and the conditions under which the universities can recruit these student athletes.
4. It enforces its regulations and rules with sanctions and penalties.

The NCAA rules and regulations expressly prohibit bidding for college athletes in an overt manner. Rather, the NCAA requires that all athletes be paid the same for tuition, fees, room, board, and books. Moreover, the NCAA limits the number of athletic scholarships that can be given by a particular university. These rules are ostensibly to prevent the richest universities from "hiring" the best student athletes.

Not surprisingly, from the very beginning of the NCAA, individual universities and colleges have attempted to cheat on the rules in order to attract better athletes. The original agreement among the colleges was to pay no wages. Almost immediately after this agreement was put into effect, colleges switched to offering athletic scholarships, jobs, free room and board, travel expenses, and other enticements. It was not unusual for athletes to be paid $10 an hour to rake leaves when the going wage rate for such work was only $5 an hour. Finally, the NCAA had to agree to permit wages up to a certain amount per year.

If all universities had to offer exactly the same money wages and fringe benefits, the academically less distinguished colleges in metropolitan areas (with a large potential number of ticket-buying fans) would have the most inducement to engage in violation of the NCAA agreements (to compensate for the lower market value of their degrees). They would figure out all sorts of techniques to get the best student athletes. Indeed, such schools have in fact cheated more than other universities and colleges, and their violations have been detected and punished with a greater relative frequency than those of other colleges and universities.

For Critical Analysis: College and university administrators argue that the NCAA rules are necessary to "keep business out of higher education." To what extent can we consider college athletics to be related to academics? ●

MARGINAL FACTOR COST

The monopsonist faces an upward-sloping supply curve of the input in question because as the only buyer, it faces the entire market supply curve. Each time the monopsonist buyer of labor, for example, wishes to hire more workers, it must raise wage rates. Thus the marginal cost of another unit of labor is rising. In fact, the marginal cost of increasing its work force will always be greater than the wage rate. This is because in the situation in which the monopsonist pays the same wage rate to everyone in order to obtain another unit of labor, the higher wage rate has to be offered not only to the last worker but also to all its other workers. We call the additional cost to the monopsonist of hiring one more worker the marginal factor cost (MFC).

The marginal factor cost for the last worker is therefore his or her wages plus the increase in the wages of all other existing workers. As we pointed out in Chapter 28, marginal factor cost is equal to the change in total variable cost due to a one-unit change in the one variable factor of production, in this case, labor. In Chapter 28, marginal factor cost was simply the competitive wage rate because the employer could hire all workers at the same wage rate.

DERIVATION OF A MARGINAL FACTOR
COST CURVE

Panel (a) of Figure 29-5 on the next page shows the quantity of labor purchased, the wage rate per hour, the total cost of the quantity of labor purchased per hour, and the marginal factor cost per hour for the additional labor bought.

We translate the columns from panel (a) to the graph in panel (b) of the figure. We show the supply curve as *S*, which is taken from columns 1 and 2. (Note that this is the same as the *average* factor cost curve; hence you can view Figure 29-5 as showing the relationship between average factor cost and marginal factor cost.) The marginal factor cost curve (MFC) is taken from columns 1 and 4. The MFC curve must be above the supply curve whenever the supply curve is upward sloping. If the supply curve is upward sloping, the firm must pay a higher wage rate in order to attract a larger supply of labor. This higher wage rate must be paid to all workers; thus the increase in total costs due to an increase in the labor input will exceed the wage rate. Note that in a perfectly competitive input market, the supply curve is horizontal and the marginal factor cost curve is identical to the supply curve.

Panel (a)

(1) QUANTITY OF LABOR SUPPLIED TO MANAGEMENT	(2) REQUIRED HOURLY WAGE RATE	(3) TOTAL WAGE BILL (3) = (1) x (2)	(4) MARGINAL FACTOR COST (MFC) = CHANGE IN (3) / CHANGE IN (1)
0	—	—	
			$1.00
1	$1.00	$1.00	
			3.00
2	2.00	4.00	
			3.20
3	2.40	7.20	
			4.00
4	2.80	11.20	
			6.80
5	3.60	18.00	
			7.20
6	4.20	25.20	

FIGURE 29-5
Derivation of a marginal factor cost curve.
The supply curve, S, in panel (b) is taken from columns 1 and 2 of panel (a). The marginal factor cost curve (MFC) is taken from column 4. It is the increase in the total wage bill resulting from a one-unit increase in labor input.

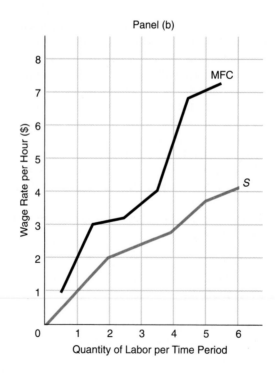

Panel (b)

EMPLOYMENT AND WAGES UNDER MONOPSONY

To determine the number of workers that a monopsonist desires to hire, we compare the marginal benefit to the marginal cost of each hiring decision. The marginal cost is the marginal factor cost curve, and the marginal benefit is the marginal revenue product curve. In Figure 29-6 we assume perfect competition in the output market and monopsony in the input market. A monopsonist finds its profit-maximizing quantity of labor demanded at E, where the marginal revenue product is just equal to the marginal factor cost.

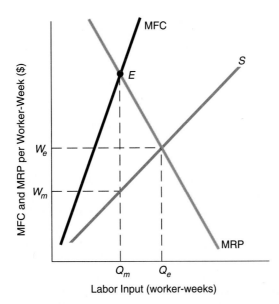

FIGURE 29-6
Marginal factor cost (MFC) curve for a monopsonist.
The monopsonist firm looks at a marginal cost curve, MFC, that slopes upward and is above its labor supply curve, S. The marginal benefit of hiring additional workers is given by the firm's MRP curve. The intersection of MFC with MRP, at point E, determines the number of workers hired. The firm hires Q_m workers but has to pay them only W_m in order to attract them. Compare this with the competitive solution, in which the wage rate would have to be W_e and the quantity of labor would be Q_e.

How much is the firm going to pay these workers? In a nonmonopsonistic situation it would face a given wage rate in the labor market, but because it is a monopsonist, it faces the entire supply curve, S. It therefore sets the wage rate so that it will get exactly the quantity, Q_m, supplied to it by its "captive" labor force. We find that wage rate is W_m. There is no reason to pay the workers any more than W_m because at that wage rate the firm can get exactly the quantity it demands. The actual quantity demanded is established at the intersection of the marginal factor cost curve and the demand curve for labor—that is, at the point at which the marginal revenue from expanding employment just equals the marginal cost of doing so.

Notice that the profit-maximizing wage rate paid to workers (W_m) is lower than the marginal revenue product. That is to say that workers are paid a wage that is less than their contribution to the monopsonist's revenues. This is sometimes referred to as **monopsonistic exploitation** of labor. The monopsonist is able to do this because each individual worker has little power in bargaining for a higher wage. The organization of workers into a union, though, creates a monopoly supplier of labor, which gives the union some power to bargain for higher wages.

▶ **Monopsonistic exploitation**
Exploitation due to monopsony power. It leads to a price for the variable input that is less than its marginal revenue product. Monopsonistic exploitation is the difference between marginal revenue product and the wage rate.

⭐ EXAMPLE: Monopsony in Professional Sports

A real-world example of monopsony can be found in professional sports, such as the National Basketball Association (NBA). Athletes who wish to play basketball at the highest level of competition would have nowhere else to go but the NBA. Rookies are typically drafted by teams and signed to multiyear contracts without the players themselves having the opportunity to choose for which team they will play. A rookie could be traded or released without the opportunity to bargain independently with another team. This is a case in which teams have monopsony power over players, who are paid salaries well below their contribution to the team's revenues (the MRP). For example, Lawrence Kahn and Peter Sherer of the University of Illinois have estimated that a popular star such as Wilt Chamberlain could have earned about $2.9 million (in 1993 dollars) in the 1972–1973 season if he had been able to sell his services to the highest bidder. Instead, he was paid the equivalent of $1.6 million.

A similar study was done by economist Gerald W. Scully. He found that star hitters in baseball averaged less than $500,000 a year in the 1968–1969 season while their marginal revenue product was over $3 million a year, thus contributing to a $2.5 million amount of monopsonistic exploitation per star hitter. For star pitchers, the average salary was $600,000 versus net marginal revenue product of $4 million, for a monopsonistic exploitation of $3.4 million per year per star pitcher.

For Critical Analysis: How might players fight monopsonistic exploitation in professional sports? ●

What happens when a monopsonist meets a monopolist? This is the situation called **bilateral monopoly,** defined as a market structure in which a single buyer faces a single seller. An example is a state education employer facing a single teachers' union in the labor market. Another example is a professional players' union facing an organized group of team owners. To analyze bilateral monopoly, we must look at the interaction of both sides, buyer and seller. The price outcome is indeterminate. All we can tell for sure is that on the seller's side marginal costs will equal marginal revenue and marginal revenue will be less than price because the seller is a monopolist. On the buyer's side marginal factor cost will be greater than the wage rate because the buyer is a monopsonist. The MFC will, as always, equal marginal revenue product. But marginal revenue product will be less than what exists in a competitive industry.

▶ **Bilateral monopoly**
A market structure consisting of a monopolist and a monopsonist.

SUMMARIZING MONOPOLY AND MONOPSONY SITUATIONS

We have studied the pricing of labor in various situations, including perfect competition in both the output and input markets and monopoly in both the output and input markets. In Table 29-1 we present a summary of the various conditions under which output will be produced and a variable input, such as labor, will be demanded. Figure 29-7 shows Table 29-1 graphically.

TABLE 29-1   A summary of monopsony and monopoly situations.
Optimal input employment. (The subscript *c* stands for perfect competition; the subscript *m* stands for monopoly.)

		OUTPUT MARKET STRUCTURE	
		PERFECT COMPETITION	MONOPOLY
INPUT MARKET STRUCTURE	PERFECT COMPETITION	(a) $MC = MR = P$ $W = MFC = MRP_c$	(b) $MC = MR(< P)$ $W = MFC = MRP_m(< MRP_c)$
	MONOPSONY	(c) $MC = MR = P$ $W < MFC = MRP_c$	(d) $MC = MR(< P)$ $W < MFC = MRP_m(< MRP_c)$

FIGURE 29-7
Summary of pricing and employment under various market conditions.

The panels in this diagram correspond to the sections marked (a), (b), (c), and (d) in Table 29-1. In panel (a) the firm operates in perfect competition in both input and output markets. It purchases labor up to the point where the going rate W_e is equal to MRP_c. It hires quantity Q_e of labor. In panel (b) the firm is a perfect competitor in the input market but has a monopoly in the output market. It purchases labor up to the point where W_e is equal to MRP_m. It hires a smaller quantity of labor, Q_m, than in panel (a). In panel (c) the firm is a monopsonist in the input market and a perfect competitor in the output market. It hires labor up to the point where $MFC = MRP_c$. It will hire quantity Q_1 and pay wage rate W_c. Panel (d) shows bilateral monopoly. The firm hires labor up to the point where $MFC = MRP_m$, which is quantity Q_2.

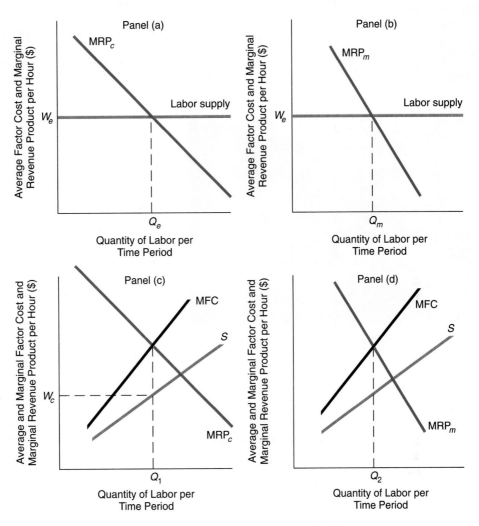

CONCEPTS IN BRIEF

● A monopsonist is a single buyer. The monopsonist faces an upward-sloping supply curve of labor.

● Because the monopsonist faces an upward-sloping supply curve of labor, the marginal factor cost of increasing the labor input by one unit is greater than the wage rate. Thus the marginal factor cost curve always lies above the supply curve.

● A monopsonist will hire workers up to the point at which marginal factor cost equals marginal revenue product. Then the monopsonist will find what minimal wage is necessary to attract that number of workers. This is taken from the supply curve.

GOVERNMENT'S HELPING HAND TO CONSTRUCTION UNIONS
Concepts Applied: Union power, relative wages, labor market restrictions

Contractors must pay workers "prevailing wages" on any construction job that is federally paid for or federally subsidized. Prevailing wages usually mean the highest union wage in a wide surrounding geographic area.

After major riots broke out in Los Angeles in 1992, vast sums of federal money came rolling in to subsidize reconstruction of the downtown area that was affected. Virtually all of the employees of the businesses that were burned out became unemployed in south-central Los Angeles. Most outsiders assumed that many of the workers who lost their jobs after the riot could easily find new ones in the construction industry. After all, there is a certain percentage of construction jobs that do not require a lot of specialized training. Therefore, workers with nonconstruction backgrounds could easily switch. You would think that contractors from either out of the city or even within the city could hire low-wage, lower-skilled workers from the area. The reality is that virtually none of the people who worked in rebuilding Los Angeles after the riots was from the area in which the riots occurred. Moreover, virtually none of those who helped rebuild the area working in the construction industry was African American or Hispanic. The reason has to do with a law passed in 1931 called the Davis-Bacon Act.

THE DAVIS-BACON ACT The Davis-Bacon Act of 1931 specifies that the secretary of labor can establish minimum "prevailing wages" that contractors must pay workers when engaging in any construction that is paid for or subsidized with federal funds. The term *prevailing*

wages has been determined to mean union rates for similar work in local areas or even areas that are not contiguous with the counties in which the government construction work is actually being done. On many occasions, prevailing rates for St. Louis, Missouri, have been determined by looking at union wages in Chicago and rates in Indiana have been determined by looking at union wages in Illinois.

WHY THE DAVIS-BACON ACT WAS PASSED Congressman Robert Bacon of New York was primarily responsible for the Davis-Bacon Act. Back in 1927 a contractor from the South had won a bid to build a large veterans' hospital in New York. Instead of using laborers from New York, the contractor brought in several thousand southern construction workers who were willing to work for less than New Yorkers would. The contractor paid his southern workers wages that were considerably below the wages that prevailed in Congressman Bacon's district. Bacon's act was therefore designed to prevent workers from coming into an area and taking jobs away from workers accustomed to higher prevailing wages, namely, union workers.

IS RACIAL DISCRIMINATION A FACTOR TOO? Little known, but equally important, were the racial undertones in the congressional discussions surrounding the passage of the Davis-Bacon Act. During the House discussion, Representative Miles Allgood of Alabama expressed his regret for sending cheap labor from his state. He explicitly apologized and decried the Alabama contractor's use of African-American labor that competed with nonminority labor in New York City.

THE CONTINUING RACIAL BIAS OF THE DAVIS-BACON ACT The Davis-Bacon Act has for many years effectively barred minority workers from federally subsidized construction projects. In 1932, for example, only 30 of 4,100 employees on the Boulder Dam project were African American. Currently, the Davis-Bacon Act has effectively shut out inner-city federal construction projects from the very people who live in the inner cities. Many of these workers are not yet trained and therefore cannot command premium construction wages. Consequently, because of the Davis-Bacon Act, low-income housing is being built by $25-an-hour carpenters and $20-

an-hour day laborers. Indeed, until 1992 the Davis-Bacon Act barred unemployed public-housing tenants from being hired to rehabilitate their own buildings.

EFFECT ON UNION WAGES The Department of Labor Wage Determination Division has typically looked at union wages in order to determine the so-called prevailing wages that can be applied to federally financed construction projects. We can be sure that the unions are fully aware of this. In their bargaining sessions with employers, negotiators for construction unions become more and more set on increasing negotiated rates. In a normal situation, an increase in wage rates (when there is no inflation) will lead to a decrease in employment, but this is not the case for all federally assisted construction projects. The government requires that the contractors hire workers at the prevailing minimum. Therefore, the government will foot whatever increase in the bill is due to increased union wages.

Federal projects account for almost 30 percent of all construction work in the United States. That means that almost 30 percent of all construction projects have the Davis-Bacon minimum applied to them. Obviously, construction union negotiators realize that there are many federal projects for which they can get the high wage rates that they establish in negotiation. As can be expected, with construction rates rising rather rapidly, the number of jobs available in private construction at the union rate has declined. Union members are taking more nonunion jobs these days in order to offset the decrease in employment opportunities at the high rate.

FOR CRITICAL ANALYSIS

1. When Senator Don Nickles attempted to suspend the Davis-Bacon Act in Los Angeles County for the four months after the Los Angeles riots, he lost, 63 to 36 in the Senate. If the Davis-Bacon Act is so onerous, why would the Senate not vote to rescind it, at least temporarily? (Hint: Think of what you learned in the theory of public choice.)

2. How might the Davis-Bacon Act actually end up reducing union employment in the long run?

CHAPTER SUMMARY

1. The American labor movement started with local craft unions but was very small until the twentieth century. Important organizations in the history of labor in the United States are the Knights of Labor, the American Federation of Labor, and the Congress of Industrial Organizations.

2. The Great Depression facilitated passage of the National Industrial Recovery Act. This act established the right of labor to bargain collectively. It was later supplanted by the Wagner Act, which is called labor's Magna Carta.

3. Unions, on average, raise union wage rates relative to nonunion wage rates by 10 to 20 percent. The union wage differential increases during recessions because of the longer-term nature of union collective bargaining contracts.

4. Because unions act as a collective voice for individual employees, they may increase productivity by reducing the time that employees spend trying to alter unproductive working arrangements. Unions may also increase productivity by reducing turnover.

5. Monopsony is a situation in which there is only one buyer of a particular input. The single buyer faces an upward-sloping supply curve and must therefore pay higher wage rates to get more workers to work. The single buyer faces a marginal factor cost curve that is upward-sloping and above the supply curve. The buyer hires workers up to the point at which the marginal revenue product equals the marginal factor cost. Then the labor buyer will find out how low a wage rate can be paid to get that many workers.

6. When a single buyer faces a single seller, a situation of bilateral monopsony exists.

DISCUSSION OF PREVIEW POINTS

1. What are the major types of unions?

The earliest, and one of the most important forms today, is the craft union, which is an organization of skilled laborers. Another major form of collective labor is the industrial union, in which all (or most) laborers in an industry, such as the steelworkers or mineworkers, unite. Since 1965, public-sector unions, which are organizations of public employees such as fire fighters, have grown dramatically, while membership in non-public-employee unions has leveled off or even fallen.

2. What do unions seek to maximize?

Unions do not have unlimited power; in the United States the rules that have evolved declare that unions can set wage rates *or* the number of laborers who will be employed, but not both. Consequently, a trade-off exists for union leaders: If they maximize wages, some members will become unemployed; if they maximize employment, wages will be relatively low. Union leaders often decide to maximize wages for a given number of workers—presumably the higher-seniority workers. Each union reaches its own decision as to how to resolve the trade-off.

3. Do unions help workers?

If unions are to be considered effective, they must increase real wage rates *above* productivity increases; after all, market forces will increase real wage rates at the rate of productivity change. Yet if real wage rates are increased more rapidly than the rate of productivity increases, unions will create unemployment; hence some laborers will be helped (those who retain their jobs at above-productivity wage levels), and some will be hurt (those who become unemployed). The evidence is that unions are neither a necessary nor sufficient condition for high real wages. Wages in the United States were relatively high before the U.S. labor movement. Moreover, labor's overall share of national income has not changed significantly since the 1930s, although *union* labor's share may have increased relative to nonunion labor's share.

4. What is a monopsonist, and how does one go about determining its profit-maximizing employment rate?

A monopsonist is a single buyer. A monopsonist hires labor up to the point at which the marginal benefit of doing so equals the marginal cost of doing so. The marginal benefit of hiring labor is labor's marginal revenue product: MB = MRP of labor. The marginal cost of hiring labor must reflect the fact that the monopsonist faces the industry labor supply schedule; hence the monopsonist must increase wage rates in order to hire more labor. Of course, it must increase wage rates for all the labor that it hires, not just the marginal laborer. Thus the MC of hiring labor for a monopsonist (the marginal factor cost, MFC) will be greater than the wage rate. Because the profit-maximizing employment rate is generally where MB = MC, the monopsonist will hire labor up to the point where MRP = MFC. It then pays the lowest wage rate required to attract that quantity of labor. This wage rate will be below the MRP of labor.

PROBLEMS

(Answers to the odd-numbered problems appear at the back of the book.)

29-1. The accompanying graph indicates a monopsonistic firm that is also a perfect competitor in the product market.
    a. Which curve is the monopsonistic firm's demand for labor curve?
    b. Which is the supply of labor curve?

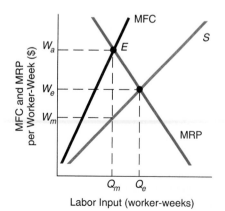

Labor Input (worker-weeks)

    c. How many laborers will this firm voluntarily hire?
    d. Given the profit-maximizing employment rate, what is the lowest wage rate that this firm can offer to get this quantity of labor?

29-2. Does a perfectly competitive firm have to worry about the impact of its own demand for labor on the going wage rate?

29-3. Give examples of perfectly competitive sellers having monopsony power in the input market.

29-4. Suppose that you operate a firm that sells its output in a perfectly competitive market. However, you are the only employer in your island economy. You are currently employing 10 full-time employees at a wage rate of $50 per person per day, and you are producing 100 units of output per day. Labor is your only variable input. The market price of your output is $8 per unit. You estimate that daily output would rise to 108 units per day if you increased your work force to 11 people. To attract the eleventh worker, you would have to pay a wage rate of $52. Should you expand your work force?

29-5. Imagine yourself managing a plant that is a monopsony buyer of its sole input and is also the monopoly seller of its output. You are currently employing 30 people, producing 20 units of output per day, and selling them for $100 apiece. Your current wage rate is $60 per day. You estimate that you would have to raise your wage scale to $61 per day in order to attract one more person to your firm. The 31 employees would be able to produce 21 units of output per day, which you would be able to sell at $99.50 apiece. Should you hire the thirty-first employee?

29-6. If a union, in its collective bargaining, sets a wage rate that maximizes total union members' income, will all union members be employed? Explain your answer.

29-7. Why will a union never want to bargain collectively for a wage rate that would exist with perfect competition in the labor market?

29-8. "The states that have right-to-work laws deprive workers from enjoying the full benefits of unions." Comment.

29-9. The marginal factor cost curve faced by a firm buying an input in a perfectly competitive market is identically equal to its supply curve for that input. Why is this not true for a monopsonist? Explain your answer.

COMPUTER-ASSISTED INSTRUCTION
(Complete problem and answer on disk.)

How does the behavior of monopsonists differ from the behavior of competitive purchasers of labor? What are the consequences of these differences?

RENT, INTEREST, AND PROFITS

In the credit card business, competition reigns. The largest supplier of consumer installment credit is Citibank, which has only 4 percent of the market. The next three largest firms each have only about 1 percent. With so much competition, you would think that the rate of interest charged on credit cards would change to reflect changing interest rates in the economy. But at the beginning of the 1990s, interest rates in general had fallen to record lows throughout the economy. Nonetheless, the rates that many credit card companies continued to charge remained above 18 percent per year. How can this be in such a competitive industry? Would a Senate proposal to cap credit card interest rates solve the problem? You will understand this issue more clearly once you have read about rent, interest, and profits.

After reading this chapter, you should be able to answer the following questions:

1. What is rent?
2. What is interest?
3. What is the economic function of interest rates?
4. What is the economic function of profits?

INTRODUCTION

Although it is probably true that most of us think about how much we get paid, at some time in our lives we have more than just labor services to offer to the economy. Compensation for labor services does make up 75 percent of national income. But what about the other 25 percent? It consists of compensation to the owners of the other factors of production that you read about in Part 1: land, capital, and entrepreneurship. Somebody owns the real estate downtown for which the monthly commercial rents are higher for one square foot than you might pay to rent a whole apartment. Land, obviously, is a factor of production, and it has a market clearing price. Businesses also have to use capital. Compensation for that capital is interest, and it, too, has a market clearing level. Finally, some of you may have entrepreneurial ability that you offer to the marketplace. Your compensation is called profit. In this chapter you also will learn about the sources and functions of profit.

RENT

The term *rent* has a specific meaning in economic analysis. Economists originally used the term to designate payment for the *use of land* to distinguish it from payment for the *use of capital equipment*. What was thought to be important about land was that its supply is completely inelastic. Hence the supply curve for land is a vertical line; no matter what the prevailing market price for land, the quantity supplied will remain the same. The term **economic rent** has been associated with payment for the use of land, for land seems to be the best example of a resource that is in fixed supply. When, no matter what the price, the *quantity* and *quality* of a resource will remain at current levels, we speak of **pure economic rent.** We define pure economic rent as the price paid for land (or any other productive factor) that has a completely inelastic supply.

▶ **Economic rent**
A payment for the use of any resource over and above its opportunity cost.

▶ **Pure economic rent**
The payment for the use of any resource that has a completely inelastic supply.

DETERMINING LAND RENT

The concept of economic rent is associated with the British economist David Ricardo (1772–1823). He looked at two plots of land on which grain was growing, one of which happened to be more fertile than the other. The owners of these two plots sold the grain that came from their land, but the one who owned the more fertile land grew more grain and therefore made more profits. According to Ricardo, the owner of the fertile land was receiving economic rents that were due not to the landowner's hard work or ingenuity but rather to an accident of nature. Here is how he analyzed economic rent for land. Ricardo assumed that the quantity of land in a country is *fixed*. Graphically, then, in terms of supply and demand, we draw the supply curve of land vertically (zero price elasticity). In Figure 30-1 the supply curve of land is represented by S. If the demand curve is D, it intersects the supply curve, S, at price P_1. The entire amount of revenues obtained, $P_1 \times Q_1$, is labeled "Economic rent." If the demand for land increased to D', the equilibrium price would rise to P_2. Additions to economic rent are labeled "More economic rent." Notice that the quantity of land remains insensitive to the change in price; its supply is inelastic.

🌐 INTERNATIONAL EXAMPLE: Economic Rents and OPEC

We can apply Ricardo's analysis of economic rent to the production of oil. After all, it was nature, not people, who put so much accessible oil under the ground in the Middle East countries. Half a century ago the various nations of the Middle East were extremely poor. They had rented their land to Western (mainly American) oil companies. Those oil companies risked their capital in search of oil in the region. When the tenants (oil companies) struck oil, the value of the landlords' property increased dramatically. But the

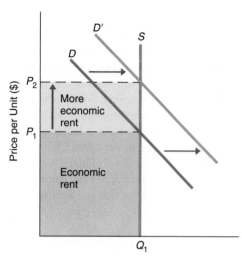

FIGURE 30-1
Pure economic rent.
If indeed the supply curve of land were completely price-inelastic in the long run, it would be depicted by S. At the quantity in existence, Q_1, any and all revenues are pure economic rent. If demand is D, the price will be P_1; if demand is D', price will rise to P_2. Economic rent would be $P_1 \times Q_1$ and $P_2 \times Q_1$, respectively.

tenants were still paying the same low price for the land. In the 1950s every rich oil discovery in the Middle East meant a more dissatisfied landlord. The landlord knew that the tenant was making a profit that greatly exceeded what was necessary to keep it producing oil. In the eyes of the landlords, tenants were receiving large economic rents.

The oil-producing countries, wanting, quite understandably, to keep more of the economic rents for themselves, sought to raise the taxes on their tenants to ever higher levels. The Organization of Petroleum Exporting Countries (OPEC), established in 1960, thus began as a body intended to keep some of the economic rents in the Middle East. Much of its discussion, however, was couched more in terms of "getting back at the foreigners" who were "exploiting" these countries than in terms of economic sovereignty and nation building.

For Critical Analysis: Would oil exploration, production, and marketing companies from the United States and elsewhere have invested so much in the Middle East in the 1940s and 1950s had they known that they would not be able to keep all the economic rents they hoped to receive? ●

ALLOCATING RESOURCES
It may appear that rents have no allocative function in the sense that they aren't really necessary for the supply of something to exist. Rents, though, help us decide to which use land will be allocated—for example, how much land should go into corn, wheat, or barley.

ECONOMIC RENTS FOR OTHER FACTORS OF PRODUCTION
So far we have limited our discussion to the pure economic rent obtainable from a fixed supply of land. The analysis, however, is equally applicable to any other factor of production that is fixed in supply. Let's consider the economic rents accruing to individuals who possess scarce natural talents. Remember that economic rent is defined as any payment over and above what is necessary to maintain a factor of production in its current activity (in other words, economic rent is any payment in excess of a factor of production's opportunity cost). Natural talents that human beings possess are more significant in

some occupations than in others. They seem to be particularly important in athletics, acting, music, and other entertainment endeavors. In some cases economic rents can explain a great part of the difference between the extraordinary earnings of highly successful musicians, for example, and the average musician. At least part of the wages of "superstars" consists of economic rents. They would be willing to work just about as hard as they do now for less pay. The question then becomes, Why do they get paid so much if they are willing to work for less? The answer, you will soon see, is that economic rent may seem like a surplus; nevertheless, it still serves a rationing, or allocative, function.

★ EXAMPLE: Giving the Fans a Fair Deal

A number of popular entertainers, particularly rock stars, have sometimes decided to "give their fans a fair deal" by charging a below–market clearing price for a concert performance. Such performers have based their concert pricing practices on egalitarian ideals, believing that ticket prices for performances are often too high. Consider an example of a performer insisting that all tickets be sold at the same price, $15. The performer wishes to give only five concerts a year, in concert halls with exactly 20,000 seats. Hence 20,000 tickets are available at a price of $15, meaning that 100,000 individuals per year will be allowed to see this particular performer. This is represented by point *A* in Figure 30-2.

By assumption, this performer is still receiving economic rents because we are assuming that the supply curve of concerts is vertical at 100,000 seats per year. At a price per ticket of $15, however, the annual quantity of seats demanded will be 150,000, represented by point *B*. The difference between points *A* and *B* is the excess quantity of tickets demanded at the below–market clearing price of $15 a seat. The *additional* economic rent that could be earned by this performer by charging the clearing price of $25 per seat in this graph would serve as the rationing device that would make the quantity demanded equal to the quantity supplied.

In such situations, which are fairly common, part of the economic rent that could have been earned is dissipated—it is captured, for example, by radio station owners in the form of promotional gains when they are allowed to give away a certain number of tickets on the air (even if they have to pay $15 per ticket) because the tickets are worth $25. Ticket holders who resell tickets at higher prices ("scalpers") also capture part of the rents. Conceivably, at 100,000 seats per year, this performer could charge the market clearing price of $25 per ticket and give away to charity the portion of the economic rents ($10 per ticket)

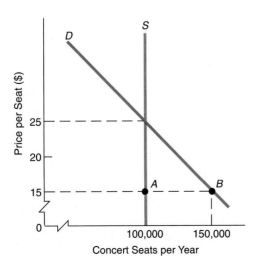

FIGURE 30-2
The allocative function of rent.
If the performer agrees to give five concerts a year "at any price" and there are 20,000 seats in each concert hall, the supply curve of concerts, *S*, is vertical at 100,000 seats per year. The demand curve is given by *D*. The performer wants a price of only $15 to be charged. At that price, the quantity of seats demanded per year is 150,000. The excess quantity demanded is equal to the horizontal distance between points *A* and *B*, or 50,000 seats per year.

that would be dissipated. In such a manner, the performer could make sure that the recipients of the rents are worthy in his or her own esteem.

For Critical Analysis: *If the market clearing price of concert tickets is $25 apiece, how are the available 100,000 concert seats per year for this performer rationed to the 150,000 fans who are willing to pay $15 per seat?* ●

⭐ EXAMPLE: **Economic Rents and Past Presidents**

Virtually every past United States president in recent times has made it known that he plans to write at least one book "telling all" about his term in the White House. That means that every ex-president has indicated that he is going to write a book, "no matter what." Nixon, Carter, Reagan, and Bush all received million dollar plus advances. Ronald Reagan, for example, received $6 milion in advances for two books

Quite a few other well-known individuals have also periodically indicated that they were willing to write an autobiography. When Marlon Brando announced his intention to do so, Random House paid him an estimated $4 million. When "Stormin' Norman" Schwarzkopf, the general who masterminded the 1991 Persian Gulf War, so indicated, he garnered a $5 million advance to write a book about the military operation.

All of these individuals, in addition to making such huge advances on their books, are also able to command, at least for a while, $20,000 to $60,000 per speaking engagement. Some of them even obtain huge fees if they agree to lend their faces or names to an advertising campaign for an important consumer product.

Given that these individuals indicated their willingness to write or speak or to appear in public, a certain percentage of what they receive must be considered economic rents. This is clearly money over and above what would be necessary to get those individuals to complete the tasks they are asked to do.

For Critical Analysis: *How might the quality of a book by an ex-president differ according to the size of the advance?* ●

ECONOMIC RENTS AND TRANSFER EARNINGS

You will recall that pure economic rent was defined as payment for a fixed resource over and above what is necessary to keep the resource in supply at its current level. Many rock stars, as mentioned earlier, would be willing to continue to work in the entertainment industry for less pay. Say that a rock star currently earning $2 million a year could use his or her talent as a music teacher earning $40,000 a year. The job as a music teacher could be thought of as the next-best alternative for the rock star. This means that the individual must earn at least $40,000 per year as a rock star in order to transfer, or supply, his or her talents to the entertainment industry. The $40,000 per year represents this rock star's **transfer earnings**—what could have been earned in the next-best alternative employment. Hence transfer earnings are a measure of the opportunity cost of a resource. (Recall that opportunity cost is defined as the highest-valued alternative use of a resource.)

▶ **Transfer earnings**
The portion of total earnings equal to what the factor of production could earn in its next-best alternative use; a measure of the opportunity cost of a resource.

Economic rent, by contrast, is the part of total earnings in excess of the transfer earnings. Economic rent for the rock star is the $1.96 million per year—the excess over and above what is necessary to keep the individual in the entertainment profession.

Notice that the proportion of total earnings that is composed of economic rent depends on the elasticity of supply of the resource. *The more inelastic the supply, the greater the proportion of total earnings made up of economic rents.* Refer again to Figure 30-1. When

FIGURE 30-3

Economic rent versus transfer earnings.
The resource supply curve, S, in panel (a) is perfectly elastic: All income that the resource earns is transfer earnings, which are an exact measure of the opportunity cost
of a resource. However, if supply slopes upward, like S' in panel (b), part of the resource's income will be transfer earnings and part will be economic rent. The area under the supply curve indicates transfer earnings, and the area above the supply curve
measures economic rent. An increase in price from P_1 to P_2 for a resource will increase
both its transfer earnings and its economic rent.

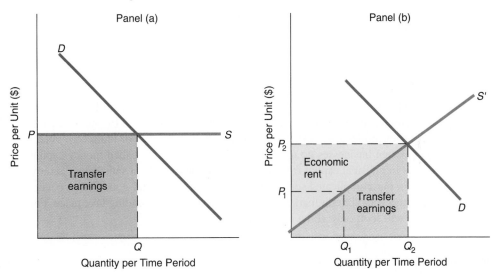

the supply of a resource is completely inelastic, whatever the price might be, the quantity
supplied will remain the same because the resource has no alternative use. In this case the
earnings of the resource are made up entirely of economic rent. At the other extreme,
when the supply of a resource is completely elastic, all of the resource earnings are transfer earnings. An example might be the supply of physicians to a medical school. If physicians could either teach at the university or go into private practice and earn a roughly
equivalent amount of money (assuming that the physician has no personal preference for
either line of work), the supply of physicians to the medical school is perfectly elastic because medical schools hire only a small proportion of the total number of physicians. This
situation is depicted in panel (a) of Figure 30-3.

The intermediate situation is when the supply curve is upward-sloping—a rise in the
price of the resource increases the quantity supplied of the resource. This case is presented
in panel (b) of Figure 30-3. As the resource price increases from P_1 to P_2, the quantity
supplied increases from Q_1 to Q_2. However, because some units of the resource would be
willing to supply their services at a price that is below P_2, they are receiving economic
rent. Generally, economic rent is represented by the area above the supply curve up to the
market price. Transfer earnings are depicted by the area below the supply curve.

CONCEPTS IN BRIEF

- Pure economic rent is defined as any payment for a factor of production
  that is completely inelastic in supply.

(Continued)

- Economic rent is a payment for a resource over and above what is necessary to keep that resource in existence at its current level in the long run.
- Economic rent serves an allocative function by guiding available supply to the most efficient use.
- As the supply of a resource becomes more and more inelastic, a greater proportion of the resource's earnings is comprised of economic rent and a smaller and smaller proportion is comprised of transfer earnings.
- Transfer earnings represent the opportunity cost of a resource earning economic rents.

INTEREST

The term **interest** is used to mean two different things: (1) the price paid by debtors to creditors for the use of loanable funds and (2) the market return earned by (nonfinancial) capital as a factor of production. Owners of capital, whether directly or indirectly, obtain interest income. Often businesses go to credit markets to obtain so-called money capital in order to invest in physical capital from which they hope to make a satisfactory return. In other words, in our complicated society, the production of capital goods often occurs because of the existence of credit markets in which borrowing and lending take place. For the moment, we will look only at the credit market.

▶ **Interest**
The payment for current rather than future command over resources; the cost of obtaining credit. Also, the return paid to owners of capital.

INTEREST AND CREDIT

When you obtain credit, you actually obtain money to have command over resources today. We can say, then, that interest is the payment for current rather than future command over resources. Thus interest is the payment for obtaining credit. If you borrow $100 from me, you have command over $100 worth of goods and services today. I no longer have that command. You promise to pay me back $100 plus interest at some future date. The interest that you pay is usually expressed as a percentage of the total loan calculated on an annual basis. Thus if at the end of one year you pay me back $110, the annual interest is $10 ÷ $100, or 10 percent. When you go out into the marketplace to obtain credit, you will find that the interest rate charged differs greatly. A loan to buy a house (a mortgage) may cost you 7 to 10 percent annual interest. An installment loan to buy an automobile may cost you 9 to 14 percent annual interest. The federal government, when it wishes to obtain credit (issues U.S. Treasury securities), may have to pay only 3 to 8 percent annual interest. Variations in the rate of annual interest that must be paid for credit depend on the following factors.

1. **Length of loan.** In some (but not all) cases, the longer the loan will be outstanding, other things being equal, the greater will be the interest rate charged.
2. **Risk.** The greater the risk of nonrepayment of the loan, other things being equal, the greater the interest rate charged. Risk is assessed on the basis of the creditworthiness of the borrower and whether the borrower provides collateral for the loan. Collateral consists of any asset that will automatically become the property of the lender should the borrower fail to comply with the loan agreement.
3. **Handling charges.** It takes resources to set up a loan. Papers have to be filled out and filed, credit references have to be checked, collateral has to be examined, and so on. The larger the amount of the loan, the smaller the handling (or administrative) charges as a percentage of the total loan. Therefore, we would predict that, other things being equal, the larger the loan, the lower the interest rate.

WHAT DETERMINES INTEREST RATES?

The overall level of interest rates can be described as the price paid for loanable funds. As with all commodities, price is determined by the interaction of supply and demand. Let's first look at the supply of loanable funds and then at the demand for them.

The Supply of Loanable Funds.

The supply of loanable funds (credit available) depends on individuals' willingness to save.[1] When you save, you exchange rights to current consumption for rights to future consumption. The more current consumption you give up, the more valuable is a marginal unit of present consumption in comparison with future consumption.

Recall from our discussion of diminishing marginal utility that the more of something you have, the less you value an additional unit. Conversely, the less of something you have, the more you value an additional unit. Thus when you give up current consumption of a good—that is, have less of it—you value an additional unit more. The more you save today, the more utility you attach to your last unit of today's consumption. So to be induced to save more—to consume less—you have to be offered a bigger and bigger reward to match the marginal utility of current consumption you will give up by saving. Because of this, if society wants to induce people to save more, it must offer a higher rate of interest. Hence we expect that the supply curve of loanable funds will slope upward. At higher rates of interest, savers will be willing to offer more current consumption to borrowers, other things being constant.[2] When the income of individuals increases or when there is a change in individual preferences toward more saving, the supply curve of loanable funds will shift outward to the right, and vice versa.

The Demand for Loanable Funds.

There are three major sources of the demand for loanable funds:

1. Households that want loanable funds for the purchase of services and nondurable goods, as well as consumer durables such as automobiles and homes
2. Businesses that want loanable funds to make investments
3. Governments that want loanable funds, usually to cover deficits—the excess of government spending over tax revenues

We will ignore the government's demand for loanable funds and consider only consumers and businesses.

Loans are taken out both by consumers and by businesses. It is useful for us to separate the motives underlying the demand for loans by these two groups of individuals. We will therefore treat consumption loans and investment loans separately. In the discussion that follows, we will assume that there is no inflation; that is, that there is no persistent increase in the overall level of prices.

Consumer Demand for Loanable Funds.

In general, consumers demand loanable funds because they tend to prefer earlier consumption to later consumption. That is to say, people subjectively value goods obtained immediately more than the same goods of the

---

[1] Actually, the supply of loanable funds also depends on business and government saving and on the behavior of the monetary authorities and the banking system. For simplicity of discussion, we ignore these components here.

[2] A complete discussion would include the income effect: At higher interest rates, households receive a higher yield on savings, permitting them to save less to achieve any given target.

same quality obtained later on. Consider that sometimes an individual household's present income falls below the average income level expected over a lifetime. Individuals may go to the credit market to borrow whenever they perceive a temporary dip in their current income—assuming that they expect their income to go back to normal later on. Furthermore, by borrowing they can spread out purchases more evenly during their lifetimes. In so doing, they're able to increase their lifetime total utility.

Consumers' demand for loanable funds will be inversely related to the cost of borrowing—the rate of interest. Why? For the same reason that all demand curves slope downward: A higher rate of interest means a higher cost of borrowing, and a higher cost of borrowing must be weighed against alternative uses of limited income. At higher costs of borrowing, consumers will forgo current consumption.

Business Demand for Loanable Funds.   Businesses demand loanable funds to make investments that they believe will increase productivity or profit. Whenever a business believes that by making an investment, it can increase revenues (net of other costs) by more than the cost of capital, it will make the investment. Businesses compare the interest rate they must pay in the loanable funds market with the interest rate they think they can earn by investing. This comparison helps them decide whether to invest.

In any event, we hypothesize that the demand curve for loanable funds by firms for investment purposes will be negatively sloped. At higher interest rates, fewer investment projects will make economic sense to businesses because the cost of capital (loanable funds) will exceed the net revenues derivable from the capital investment. Conversely, at lower rates of interest, more investment projects will be undertaken because the cost of capital will be less than the expected rate of return on the capital investment.

THE EQUILIBRIUM RATE OF INTEREST

When we add together the demand for loanable funds by households and businesses (and government in more complex models), we obtain a demand curve for loanable funds, as given in Figure 30-4. The supply curve is S. The equilibrium rate of interest is i_e.

REAL VERSUS NOMINAL INTEREST RATES

We have been assuming that there is no inflation. In a world of inflation—a persistent rise in an average of all prices—the **nominal rate of interest** will be higher than it would be in a world with no inflation. Basically, nominal, or market, rates of interest eventually rise to take account of the anticipated rate of inflation. If, for example, there is no inflation and no inflation is expected, the nominal rate of interest might be 5 percent for home mortgages. If the rate of inflation goes to 10 percent a year and stays there, everybody will anticipate that inflation rate. The nominal rate of interest will rise to about 15 percent to take account of the anticipated rate of inflation. If the interest rate did not rise to 15 percent, the interest earned at 5 percent would be worth less in the future because inflation would have eroded its purchasing power. We can therefore say that the nominal, or market, rate of interest is approximately equal to the real rate of interest plus the anticipated rate of inflation, or

$$i_n = i_r + \text{anticipated rate of inflation}$$

where i_n equals the nominal rate of interest and i_r equals the real rate of interest. In short, you can expect to see high nominal rates of interest in periods of high or rising inflation rates. The **real rate of interest** may not necessarily be high, though. We must first cor-

▷ **Nominal rate of interest**
The market rate of interest expressed in terms of dollars.

▷ **Real rate of interest**
The rate of interest obtained by subtracting the anticipated rate of inflation from the nominal rate of interest.

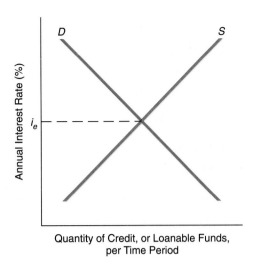

FIGURE 30-4
The supply and demand of loanable funds.
We draw *D* as the demand curve for all loanable funds by households and businesses (and governments). It slopes downward. *S* is the supply curve of credit, or loanable funds. It slopes upward. The intersection of *S* and *D* gives the equilibrium rate of interest at i_e.

rect the nominal rate of interest for the anticipated rate of inflation before determining whether the real interest rate is in fact higher than normal.

THE ALLOCATIVE ROLE OF INTEREST

Back in Chapter 6 we talked about the price system and the role that prices play in the allocation of resources. Interest is a price that allocates loanable funds (credit) to consumers and to businesses. Within the business sector, interest allocates loanable funds to different firms and therefore to different investment projects. Investment, or capital, projects with rates of return higher than the market rate of interest in the credit market will be undertaken, given an unrestricted market for loanable funds. For example, if the expected rate of return on the purchase of a new factory in some industry is 15 percent and loanable funds can be acquired for 11 percent, the investment project may take place. If, however, that same project had an expected rate of return of only 9 percent, it would not be undertaken. In sum, the interest rate allocates loanable funds to industries whose investments yield the highest returns—where resources will be the most productive.

It is important to realize that the interest rate performs the function of allocating money capital (loanable funds) and that this ultimately allocates real physical capital to various firms for investment projects. Often noneconomists view the movement of loanable funds (credit) simply as something abstractly "financial" rather than an important part of the real world of machines and factories.

INTERNATIONAL EXAMPLE: *Riba* (Interest) Rates in Islam

According to some interpretations of Islamic law, any interest is un-Islamic. In Pakistan the federal Shari'ah court, the highest Islamic lawmaking body, declared in 1992 that all interest—*riba*—was illegal. The Islamic court immediately wanted the government of Pakistan to amend all financial laws to eliminate positive interest. It went so far as to argue that any law not so altered would be held "repugnant to the injunctions of Islam" and would cease to have effect. Even before the court's decision, the government had appointed a commission to eliminate *riba* from the economy. How can any borrowing take place in an economy without creditors' being paid a reward? Clearly, something has to give in Pakistan. The finance minister there noted that "although *riba* is totally prohibited in Islam, unfortunately there is no universally acceptable definition of *riba* in the Muslim world according to which existing financial practices can be tested on the basis of Islamic law." Perhaps all that this means is that creditors will come up with different forms of interest to charge debtors. One common way to avoid the prohibition against charging interest is for the lender (banks, other institutions, or a private party) to enter into a partnership with a borrower and charge a periodic payment in exchange for a lump sum used to buy an asset, such as a car. In this matter an implied interest rate can be calculated.

The Islamic prohibition against *riba* follows a long tradition. One of the earliest writers in economics, Aristotle, considered money sterile. The "breeding" of money for money was unnatural and to be hated. During the Roman Republic, no interest charges were permitted. In the Middle Ages, the Catholic church had very specific rules against lending money at interest (usury). Such pursuit of wealth was considered "unnatural" and sinful because humility and charity were considered the greatest virtues that could be obtained.

For Critical Analysis: *Why do you think organized religions have tended to view lending at interest in such a negative light?* ●

INTEREST RATES AND PRESENT VALUE

Businesses make investments in which they often incur large costs today but don't make any profits until some time in the future. Somehow they have to be able to compare their investment cost today with a stream of future profits. How can they relate present cost to future benefits?

Interest rates are used to link the present with the future. After all, if you have to pay $110 at the end of the year when you borrow $100, that 10 percent interest rate gives you a measure of the premium on the earlier availability of goods and services. If you want to have things today, you have to pay the 10 percent interest rate in order to have current purchasing power.

The question could be put this way: What is the present value (the value today) of $110 that you could receive one year from now? That depends on the market rate of interest, or the rate of interest that you could earn in some appropriate savings institution, such as in a savings account. To make the arithmetic simple, let's assume that the rate of interest is 10 percent. Now you can figure out the **present value** of $110 to be received one year from now. You figure it out by asking the question, How much money must I put aside today at the market interest rate of 10 percent to receive $110 one year from now? Mathematically we represent this equation as

$$(1 + .1)PV_1 = \$110$$

▶ **Present value**
The value of a future amount expressed in today's dollars; the most that someone would pay today to receive a certain sum at some point in the future.

where PV_1 is the sum that you must set aside now.

Let's solve this simple equation to obtain PV_1:

$$PV_1 = \frac{\$110}{1.1} = \$100$$

That is to say, $100 will accumulate to $110 at the end of one year with a market rate of interest of 10 percent. Thus the present value of $110 one year from now, using a rate of interest of 10 percent, is $100. The formula for present value of any sums to be received one year from now thus becomes

$$PV_1 = \frac{FV_1}{(1 + i)}$$

where

PV_1 = present value of a sum one year hence
FV_1 = future sum of money paid or received one year hence
i = market rate of interest

Present Values for More Distant Periods.   The present-value formula for figuring out today's worth of dollars to be received at a future date can now easily be seen.
How much would have to be put in the same savings account today to have $110 two
years from now if the account pays a rate of 10 percent per year compounded annually?

After one year the sum that would have to be set aside, which we will call PV_2, would
have grown to $PV_2 \times 1.1$. This amount during the second year would increase to $PV_2 \times 1.1$
$\times 1.1$, or $PV_2 \times (1.1)^2$. To find the PV_2 that would grow to $110 over two years, let

$$PV_2 \times (1.1)^2 = \$110$$

and solve for PV_2:

$$PV_2 = \frac{\$110}{(1.1)^2} = \$90.91$$

Thus the present value of $110 to be paid or received two years hence, discounted at an
interest rate of 10 percent per year compounded annually, is equal to $90.91. In other
words, $90.91 put into a savings account yielding 10 percent per year compounded in-
terest would accumulate to $110 in two years.

▶ **Discounting**
The method by which the
present value of a future sum
or a future stream of sums is
obtained.

The General Formula for Discounting.   The general formula for **discounting**
becomes

$$PV_t = \frac{FV_t}{(1 + i)^t}$$

where t refers to the number of periods in the future the money is to be paid or received.

▶ **Rate of discount**
The rate of interest used to
discount future sums back to
present value.

Table 30-1 gives the present value of $1 to be received in future years for various in-
terest rates. The interest rate used to derive the present value is called the **rate of
discount.**

TABLE 30-1   Present values of a future dollar.
This table shows how much a dollar received at
the end of a certain number of years in the future
is worth today. For example, at 5 percent a year, a
dollar to be received 20 years in the future is
worth 37.7 cents; if received in 50 years, it isn't
even worth a dime today. To find out how much
$10,000 would be worth a certain number of years
from now, just multiply the figures in the table by
10,000. For example, $10,000 received at the end
of 10 years discounted at a 5 percent rate of interest would have a present value of $6,140.

| | COMPOUNDED ANNUAL INTEREST RATE | | | | |
YEAR	3%	5%	8%	10%	20%
1	.971	.952	.926	.909	.833
2	.943	.907	.857	.826	.694
3	.915	.864	.794	.751	.578
4	.889	.823	.735	.683	.482
5	.863	.784	.681	.620	.402
6	.838	.746	.630	.564	.335
7	.813	.711	.583	.513	.279
8	.789	.677	.540	.466	.233
9	.766	.645	.500	.424	.194
10	.744	.614	.463	.385	.162
15	.642	.481	.315	.239	.0649
20	.554	.377	.215	.148	.0261
25	.478	.295	.146	.0923	.0105
30	.412	.231	.0994	.0573	.00421
40	.307	.142	.0460	.0221	.000680
50	.228	.087	.0213	.00852	.000109

CONCEPTS IN BRIEF

- Interest is the price paid for the use of capital. It is also the cost of obtaining credit.
- In the credit market, the rate of interest paid depends on the length of the loan, the risk, and the handling charges, among other things.
- The interest rate is determined by the intersection of the supply curve of credit, or loanable funds, and the demand curve for credit, or loanable funds.
- The major sources for the demand for loanable funds are households, businesses, and governments.
- Nominal, or market, interest rates include a factor to take account of the anticipated rate of inflation. Therefore, during periods of high anticipated inflation, nominal, or market, interest rates will be relatively high.
- Payments received or costs incurred in the future are worth less than those received or incurred today. The present value of any future sum is lower the farther it occurs in the future and the greater the discount rate used.

PROFITS

In Chapter 2 we identified entrepreneurship, or entrepreneurial talent, as the fourth factor of production. Profit is the reward that this factor earns. You may recall that entrepreneurship involves engaging in the risk of starting new businesses. In a sense, then, nothing can be produced without an input of entrepreneurial skills.

Until now we have been able to talk about the demand and supply of labor, land, and capital. We can't talk as easily about the demand and supply of entrepreneurship. For one thing, we have no way to quantify entrepreneurship. What measure should we use? We do know that entrepreneurship exists. We cannot, however, easily present a supply and demand analysis to show the market clearing price per unit of entrepreneurship. We must use a different approach, focusing on the reward for entrepreneurship—profit. First we will determine what profit is *not*. Then we will examine the sources of true, or economic, profit. Finally, we will look at the functions of profits in a market system.

DISTINGUISHING BETWEEN ECONOMIC PROFITS AND BUSINESS, OR ACCOUNTING, PROFITS

In our discussion of rent, we had to make a distinction between the common notions of rent and the economist's concept of economic rent. We must do the same thing when we refer to profit. We always have to distinguish between **economic profit** and **accounting profit.** The accountant calculates profit for a business as the difference between total explicit revenues and total explicit costs. Consider an extreme example. You are given a large farm as part of your inheritance. All of the land, fertilizer, seed, machinery, and tools are fully paid for. You take over the farm and work on it diligently with half a dozen workers. At the end of the year you sell the output for $1 million. Your accountant then subtracts your actual ("explicit") expenses.

The difference is called profit, but it is not economic profit. Why? Because no accounting was taken of the *implicit* costs of using the land, seed, tools, and machinery. The only explicit cost considered was the workers' wages. But, as long as the land could be rented out, the seed could be sold, and the tools and machinery could be leased, there was

▶ **Economic profit**
The difference between total revenues and the opportunity cost of all factors of production.

▶ **Accounting profit**
The difference between total revenues and total explicit costs.

an opportunity cost of using them. To derive the economic profits that you might have earned last year from the farm, you must subtract from total revenues the full opportunity cost of all factors of production used (which will include both implicit and explicit costs).

In summary, then, accounting profit is used mainly to define taxable income and, as such, may include returns to both owner's labor and capital. Economic profit, by contrast, represents a return over and above the opportunity cost of all resources (including a normal return on the owner's entrepreneurial abilities).

When viewed in this light, it is possible for economic profits to be negative, even if accounting profits are positive. Turning to our farming example again, what if the opportunity cost of using all of the resources turned out to be $1.1 million? The economic profits would have been –$100,000. You would have suffered economic losses.

In sum, the businessperson's accounting definition and the economist's economic definition of profits usually do not coincide. Economic profits are a residual. They are whatever remains after all economic, or opportunity, costs have been taken into account.

EXPLANATIONS OF ECONOMIC PROFIT

Alternative explanations of profit are numerous. Let us examine a few of them: exploitation, restrictions on entry, innovation, and reward for bearing uninsurable risks.

Exploitation.   German political philosopher Karl Marx (1818–1883) argued that the source of profits was *exploitation*, defined in quite different terms from our normal use of the word. As he used the word, businesspeople exploited (made use of) workers by paying them precisely what their labor was worth.

▶ **Labor theory of value**
A theory that the value of all commodities is equal to the value of the labor used in producing them.

Marx based his argument on the **labor theory of value,** a theory initially accepted by all the classical economists, which stated that the value underlying the true worth of all goods was the amount of labor required to produce them. This amount included direct labor—the actual amount of work expended by a laborer of average skill—and indirect labor—the value of the *tools* used in producing the commodity.

Marx put forward his exploitation thesis by asking, If the total value of any commodity is measured by the direct and indirect labor needed to produce it, what can the value of labor itself be? He answered that it must be *subsistence*—the amount of goods and services needed to enable a worker and dependent family to keep body and soul together. In other words, this is what it costs for society to maintain one worker. Therefore, a worker earning subsistence was earning a "fair wage" because the labor power provided by the worker was priced in a fashion similar to that of all other commodities.

Marx was only restating (albeit in a potent and political fashion) what the classical economists in his day believed: Owners of businesses earned profit because they could legitimately claim anything left over after all costs of production had been paid. What Marx added was a remarkable twist, however. Even though the source of profit was "exploitation," in that workers produced goods of much higher value than the price of their subsistence, by the rules of the game of capitalism itself, exploitation created a perfectly fair wage. When workers "sold their labor power," as Marx put it, if they earned subsistence, they received the full value of the service they provided. This argument led to Marx's conclusion that a complete revolutionary change in the capitalist system, rather than mere reform, was in the best interests of the working class. (It should be noted that Marx did appear to recognize that entrepreneurial talent was a legitimate factor of production that was entitled to receive a return.)

Restrictions on Entry.   We pointed out in Chapter 24 that monopoly profits—a special form of economic profits—are possible when there are barriers to entry, and these profits are often called monopoly rents by economists. Entry restrictions exist in many industries, including taxicabs, cable television franchises, and prescription drugs and eyeglasses. Basically, monopoly profits are built into the value of the business that owns the particular right to have the monopoly.

Innovation.   A number of economists have maintained that economic profits are created by innovation, which is defined as the creation of a new organizational strategy, a new marketing strategy, or a new product. This source of economic profit was popularized by Harvard economics professor Joseph Schumpeter.[3] The innovator creates new economic profit opportunities through innovation. The successful innovator obtains a temporary monopoly position, garnering temporary economic profits. When other firms catch up, those temporary economic profits disappear.

REWARD FOR BEARING UNINSURABLE RISKS

There are risks in life, including those involved in any business venture. Many of these risks can be insured, however. You can insure against the risk of losing your house to fire, flood, hurricane, or earthquake. You can do the same if you own a business. You can insure against the risk of theft, also. Insurance companies are willing to sell you such insurance because they can relatively accurately predict what percentage of a class of insured assets will suffer losses each year. They charge each insured person or business enough to pay for those fully anticipated losses and to make a normal rate of return.

But there are risks that cannot be insured. If you and a group of your friends get together and pool your resources to start a new business, no amount of statistical calculations can accurately predict whether your business will still be running a year from now or 10 years from now. Consequently, you can't, when you start your business, buy insurance against losing money, bad management, miscalculations about the size of the market, aggressive competition by big corporations, and the like. Entrepreneurs therefore incur uninsurable risks. According to a theory of profits advanced by economist Frank H. Knight (1885–1973), this is the origin of economic profits.

THE FUNCTION OF ECONOMIC PROFIT

In a market economy, the expectation of profits induces firms to discover new products, new production techniques and new marketing techniques—literally all the new ways to make higher profits. Profits in this sense spur innovation and investment.

Profits also cause resources to move from lower-valued to higher-valued uses. Prices and sales are dictated by the consumer. If the demand curve is close to the origin, there will be few sales and few profits, if any. The lack of profits therefore means that there is insufficient demand to cover the opportunity cost of production. In the quest for higher profits, businesses will take resources out of areas in which either accounting losses or

---

[3]Joseph Schumpeter, *Capitalism, Socialism, and Democracy* (New York: Harper & Row, 1942).

lower than normal rates of return are being made and put them into areas in which there is an expectation of higher profits. The profit reward is an inducement for an industry to expand when demand and supply conditions warrant it. Conversely, the existence of economic losses indicates that resources in the particular industry are not as valued as highly as they might be elsewhere. These resources therefore move out of that industry, or at least no further resources are invested in it. Therefore, resources follow the businessperson's quest for higher profits. Profits allocate resources, just as wages and interest do.

INCOME SHARES IN THE UNITED STATES

We have discussed the four factors of production and their payments. It is interesting to see what percentage of national income is accounted for by these various factor payments. We cannot, however, obtain data on exactly the same categories that we have been discussing. Table 30-2 shows five different categories for which data are available: wages and salaries, proprietors' income, corporate profits, interest, and rent.

Wages and salaries correspond to factor payments to labor. However, part of those labor payments are also included in what is called proprietors' income. Economically, this represents the opportunity cost of capital, owners' labor, and some element of economic profit. The columns headed "Corporate Profits" and "Interest" do not correspond at all well to the terms *profit* and *interest* as used in this chapter. Finally, the column headed "Rent" includes more than pure economic rent.

Nonetheless, it is instructive to see what has happened to the relative shares of national income since 1900. We see that wages and salaries account for about three-fourths of national income today. In 1900 they accounted for only 55 percent. We might jump to the conclusion that labor income has grown in importance in our economy, but if we look at the summation of wages and salaries plus proprietors' income, that figure changed very little in nine decades. Because some labor payments are included in what is called proprietors' income, we can simply state that throughout the twentieth century, income from labor has been the single most important source of national income in the economy.

TABLE 30-2 **Relative income shares over time.**

Source: Irving Kravis, "Income Distribution: Functional Share," *International Encyclopedia of Social Sciences* (New York: Macmillan, 1968), vol. 7, p. 134; U.S. Department of Commerce; U.S. Bureau of Labor Statistics.

	(1) WAGES AND SALARIES (%)	(2) PROPRIETORS' INCOME (%)	(3) CORPORATE PROFITS (%)	(4) INTEREST (%)	(5) RENT (%)
1900–1909	55.0	23.7	6.8	5.5	9.0
1910–1919	53.6	23.8	9.1	5.4	8.1
1920–1929	60.0	17.5	7.8	6.2	7.7
1930–1939	67.5	14.8	4.0	8.7	5.0
1940–1948	64.6	17.2	11.9	3.1	3.3
1949–1954	67.3	13.9	12.5	2.9	3.4
1955–1963	69.9	11.9	11.2	4.0	3.0
1964–1968	71.6	9.6	12.1	3.5	3.2
1969–1977	76.7	7.9	8.0	5.1	2.3
1976–1980	74.9	6.2	8.5	8.5	1.9
1981–1991	73.7	6.8	8.4	9.9	1.2

CONCEPTS IN BRIEF

- Profit is pay for entrepreneurial talent, the fourth factor of production.
- It is necessary to distinguish between accounting profits and economic profits. Accounting profits are measured by the difference between total revenues and all explicit costs. Economic profits are measured by the difference between total revenues and the total of all opportunity costs of all factors of production.
- Marx's theory of profits involved exploitation of laborers by capitalists. Other theories of why profits exist include restriction on entry, innovation, and payment to entrepreneurs for taking uninsurable risks.
- The function of profits in a market economy is to allocate scarce resources. Resources will flow to wherever profits are highest.

SHOULD WE CAP CREDIT CARD INTEREST RATES?

Concepts Applied: Interest rate, cost of credit, risk, rate of return

Individuals who are denied credit through normal means must turn to alternate sources of borrowing, such as pawnshops.

If you are like some college students, you have at least one credit card. When you purchase anything using that credit card, you normally do not have to pay interest if

FIGURE 30-5
Capping interest rates.
If the demand and supply curves for credit card debt are S and D, respectively, the equilibrium rate of interest is 18 percent per year. If the government caps the interest at 12 percent, there will be an excess quantity demanded, shown as the difference between Q_D and Q_S. Credit card debt-issuing institutions will devise ways to restrict the amount of credit card debt sold.

you pay off the monthly balance by a certain date. In effect you have received an interest-free loan. (Some low-cost credit cards do charge interest from the day of purchase until payment is received, with no grace period.) If, however, you keep a balance outstanding, you have to pay a rate of interest that is often 14 or 18 percent per year. In this period of low inflation and low interest rates for mortgages and other bank loans, such high interest rates seem odd, particularly given that there are at least 5,000 credit card issuers in the United States. A few years ago the U.S. Senate introduced a bill that set the maximum interest rate for credit cards at 4 percentage points above what the Internal Revenue Service charges for overdue taxes. Today, this would mean a credit card interest rate of about 12 percent. What would happen if this legislation passed?

THE EFFECTS OF CAPPING CREDIT CARD INTEREST RATES
If the market clearing rate of interest is above 12 percent, the Senate bill (or one in any state) that caps credit card interest rates at 12 percent would have a relatively straightforward effect. In Figure 30-5 you see the supply and demand curves for credit card debt. The equilibrium rate of interest is 18 percent, but the legal maximum is 12 percent. As with all price controls, at 12 percent there would be an excess quantity demanded of credit card debt equal to the difference between Q_D and Q_S. How is this situation resolved?

The first thing that would happen is that the lenders of money would seek ways to get around the legal interest rate limit. Many companies would start imposing a service charge on small amounts of borrowed money. Some might start charging a fee for opening an account. There are numerous methods of skirting the law. Insofar as these methods are not fully effective, lenders will eventually find that at the rate of 12 percent, their profits aren't as high as before.

If we assume that the equilibrium was at 18 percent before the legislation, a credit cap of 12 percent means that the less efficient firms in the business of lending now earn less than the normal, or competitive, rate of return. Their costs are now high relative to the revenues made from lending money elsewhere. These companies, and some of the others too, would attempt to find ways to cut their costs. One way to do this is to eliminate some of the bad (potential and actual) accounts, the ones that are less likely to pay what is owed. But how do companies decide which are the bad accounts when people apply for credit cards? They look at past behavior and at future earnings possibilities. Which people do you think will be denied credit at 12 percent?

THE POOR LOSE OUT AGAIN   Obviously, the people who have the worst credit ratings are the ones denied credit at 12 percent. People with records of unstable employment, welfare recipients, easily identifiable minority groups, students, and some of the elderly fall into this category. The fact is that this list includes just about every group of people that the legislation was originally supposed to help.

WHO BENEFITS?   Surprise! The people who benefit from required lower interest rates on consumer credit are the ones who are the most creditworthy. They are the ones with the most income, the best jobs, and the highest probability of being able to pay their bills. These are the people who gain, and the poor are once again left out.

THE EVIDENCE   We do have evidence that credit card restrictions effectively reduce the size of the market. In 1978 the Supreme Court held that interstate loans made by nationally chartered banks are governed by the interest rate ceiling of the banks' home state. South Dakota, in 1979, abolished interest rate controls on consumer credit. New York's Citibank moved its credit card operations to South Dakota. It then became a nationwide credit card operation almost overnight. From 1979 to 1984 one-third of the states repealed their interest rate ceilings and another third relaxed them. During this time period the number of active U.S. Visa and MasterCard accounts increased by over 40 percent. The bulk of these new accounts went to recent college graduates and lower-income families. Today more than half of American households with incomes of $10,000 to $20,000 have credit cards. Prior to 1978 virtually none did.

During the high-growth period in U.S. consumer credit, the 1980s, economist Christopher Demuth estimated that banks in states that had no interest rate controls increased their Visa card business almost 30 percent faster than the national average. They did this by marketing new accounts among students and blue-collar workers who had no credit history.

THOSE HIGH CREDIT CARD INTEREST RATES MAY NOT BE SO HIGH   In any event, those high credit card interest rates may not actually be so

high. Every credit card holder gets a grace period during which no interest need be paid. Indeed, about half the users of credit cards typically pay off their full amount each month and thus pay no interest. When you take account of the one-month free period on the average credit card and then calculate the average time period during which credit balances are actually paid off, the effective interest rate paid is usually several points below the stated rate.

In addition, you have to correct the interest charged for risk factors. Credit card purchases are a type of unsecured loan. If the credit card user defaults, the issuer of the credit card has nothing to repossess. It is costly, therefore, for credit card issuers to collect when high-risk households default. And because of adverse selection (see Chapter 21), it is mainly higher-risk households that do use credit cards for consumer installment credit. These households will usually opt for credit card debt at 18 percent because this rate is attractive when compared with the alternative avenues of credit available. Thus the relatively high interest rate on credit cards is consistent with the riskiness of the households that tend to use credit card debt as a form of consumer finance.

THE LONG-RUN EFFECTS OF CREDIT CARD INTEREST RATE CAPS   What happens when the interest rate on credit cards is capped is relatively straightforward. Individuals who had opted to use credit cards for consumer credit at relatively high interest rates will be slowly frozen out of that marketplace. They will have to go to alternatives. One alternative is a local finance company that charges an even higher interest rate.

Other alternatives are pawnshops and loan sharks. Yet another alternative, and one that is growing fast, is obtaining consumer durable goods from "rent-to-own" companies. In a rent-to-own transaction, you rent a TV or a VCR, for example, with an option to buy, in which part of your payment counts toward the purchase price. A refrigerator with a cash price of $350 may be offered for $16.99 a week to rent. At the end of 69 weeks, the consumer owns it. The total price paid is $1,172. Thus, whether it be through pawnshops, loan sharks, or rent-to-own deals, borrowers who do not qualify for normal credit end up paying a much higher price for credit.

FOR CRITICAL ANALYSIS

1. What would happen if the maximum interest rate on credit cards were set above the market clearing rate?
2. "The consumer credit market is one in which the information imbalance between supplier and purchaser is so great that some degree of government intervention is always economically justified." Do you agree or disagree with this statement? Why?

CHAPTER SUMMARY

1. Resources that have a fixed supply are paid what is called economic rent. We therefore define economic rent as the payment over and above what is necessary to keep a resource of constant quality and quantity in supply at its current level.

2. Resource owners (including labor owners) of factors with inelastic supply earn economic rent because competition among potential users of those resources bids up the price offered.

3. Interest can be defined as the payment for command over resources today rather than in the future. Interest is typically seen as the payment for credit, but it can also be considered the payment for the use of capital. Interest charged depends on length of loan, risk, and handling charges.

4. The equilibrium rate of interest is determined by the intersection of the demand for credit, or loanable funds, and the supply of credit, or loanable funds.

5. The nominal rate of interest includes a factor that takes account of the anticipated rate of inflation. In periods of high anticipated inflation, nominal, or market, interest rates will be high. Real interest rates may not actually be higher, however, because they are defined as the nominal rate of interest minus the anticipated rate of inflation.

6. The present value of any sum in the future is less than that same sum today. Present value decreases as the sum is paid or obtained further and further in the future and as the rate of discount increases.

7. Karl Marx believed that profit was created by the exploitation of the working class by the capitalist class. Frank Knight believed that profit was a payment to entrepreneurs for undertaking risks that are uninsurable. Other reasons why profit exists include restrictions on entry and reward for innovation.

DISCUSSION OF PREVIEW POINTS

1. What is rent?

Rent is payment for the use of land. Economists have long played with the notion that land is completely inelastic in supply, although this is a debatable issue and depends on various definitions. Modern economists now refer to a payment to any factor of production that is in completely inelastic supply as pure economic rent. For instance, from society's point of view, the total supply of land is fixed. Also, athletes and entertainers presumably earn pure economic rents: Beyond some "normal" income, the opportunity cost to superstars for performing is zero; hence "abnormal" income is not necessary to induce them to perform. Note that we usually discuss positively sloped supply schedules indicating that higher relative prices are necessary to induce increased quantity supplied. This is not the case with pure economic rents.

2. What is interest?

On the most obvious level, interest is a payment for the use of money. On another level, interest can be considered payment for obtaining credit; by borrowing, people (consumers or businesses) obtain command over resources now rather than in the future. Those who wish to make purchases now instead of later are allowed to do so even if they do not currently earn purchasing power. They do so by borrowing, and interest is the price they must pay for the privilege of making expenditures now instead of later.

3. What is the economic function of interest rates?

Interest rates are the price of credit, and like all prices, interest rates play an allocative role. That is, interest is a rationing device. We have said that interest is the price of credit; this credit is allocated to the households and businesses that are willing to pay the highest price (interest rate). Such is the rationing function of credit. On a more fundamental level, we can see that something other than scarce loanable funds is allocated. After all, businesses don't borrow money simply for the privilege of paying interest! The key to understanding what *physical* resources are being allocated is to follow the money: On what do businesses spend this borrowed money? The answer is for the most part, capital goods. Thus the interest rate plays the crucial role of allocating scarce capital goods; the firms that are willing to pay the highest interest rates will be the ones that will be able to purchase the most scarce capital goods. Presumably, the most profitable firms will be able to pay the highest interest rates (and be most acceptable to lenders) and will therefore receive disproportionately greater quantities of new capital. Interest rates help bring about this capital rationing scheme in a market economy.

4. What is the economic function of profits?

Profit is the return on entrepreneurial talent or the price paid to risk takers. Profits also play a rationing role in society. Profits (in conjunction with interest rates) perform the all-important function of deciding which industries (and which firms within an industry) expand and which are forced to contract. Profitable firms can reinvest profits (and offer to pay higher interest rates), while unprofitable firms are forced to contract or go bankrupt. In short, businesses' quests for profits assure that scarce resources flow from less profitable to more profitable uses; profits help society decide which firms are to expand and which are to contract.

PROBLEMS

(Answers to the odd-numbered problems appear at the back of the book.)

30-1. "All revenues obtained by the Italian government from Renaissance art museums are pure economic rent." Is this statement true or false, and why?

30-2. Some people argue that the extraordinary earnings of entertainment and sports superstars are not pure economic rents at all but merely the cost of ensuring that a steady stream of would-be stars and starlets continues to flow into the sports and entertainment fields. How would the argument go?

30-3. "If employers paid marginal revenue product (MRP) to each of their inputs, there would be no profits left over." Is this statement true or false, and why?

30-4. The accompanying graph shows the supply and demand for land. The vertical axis is the price per year received by landowners for permitting the land to be used by farmers.

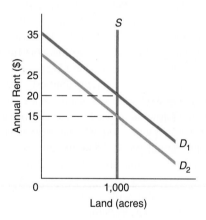

a. Assume that the demand curve for land is D_1. How much economic rent is received by landowners?

b. Now assume that the demand curve for land falls to D_2. How much economic rent is received now?

30-5. The graph below shows the demand and supply for loanable funds.

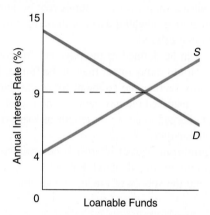

a. What is the equilibrium interest rate?

b. If the supply of loanable funds decreases, what would happen to the equilibrium interest rate?

c. If anticipated inflation is 4 percent for the year, what is the real equilibrium interest rate?

30-6. Make a list of risks that you might face in your life that you believe are insurable. Now make a list of risks that you believe are uninsurable. What is the general distinction between these lists?

30-7. Why do you think that the interest rate you have to pay on an automobile loan is greater than what you have to pay for a loan on a house? Why is the interest rate charged for a loan to purchase a used car usually more than for a loan to purchase a new car?

30-8. At the beginning of the 1980s virtually all interest rates were much higher than they are in the 1990s. What do you think the major difference is between these two periods that might have caused interest rates to fall so dramatically?

30-9. Assume that everybody has perfect information about all events in the future. What would you expect to happen to economic profits in such a world?

COMPUTER-ASSISTED INSTRUCTION

(Complete problem and answer on disk.)

We explore the many implications of the fact that differently dated goods are fundamentally different commodities.

31

INCOME, POVERTY, AND HEALTH CARE

"The following scales shall apply: If it is a male from 20 to 60 years of age, the equivalent is 50 shekels of silver, but . . . if it is female, the equivalent is 30 shekels." This quote is from Leviticus 27:1–4. Presumably, society in the time of Moses valued women at 60 percent of the going rate for men. In the job market today, a few thousand years later, the situation is only slightly improved. Women who work full time year round earn about 72 cents for every dollar that men make. Is the income differential between males and females a result of gender discrimination? This issue is part of the broader issue of the distribution of income, which you will read about in the pages that follow.

After reading this chapter, you should be able to answer the following questions:

1. What is a Lorenz curve, and what does it measure?

2. What has been happening to the distribution of income in the United States?

3. What is the difference between income and wealth?

4. Why do people earn different incomes?

INTRODUCTION

Everyone knows that there are a lot of rich people around, and everyone knows there are a lot of poor people, too. Why do some people earn more income than others? Why is the **distribution of income** the way it is? Economists have devised various theories to explain this distribution. We will present some of these theories in this chapter. We will also present some of the more obvious institutional reasons why income is not distributed equally in the United States as well as what can be done about health care.

▶ **Distribution of income**
The way income is allocated among the population.

INCOME

Income provides each of us with the means of either consuming or saving. Income can be derived from a payment for labor services or a payment for ownership of one of the other factors of production besides labor—land, capital, and entrepreneurship. In addition, individuals obtain spendable income from gifts and transfers to them from the government. (Some individuals also obtain income by stealing, but we will not treat this matter here.) Right now let us examine how money income is distributed across classes of income earners within the United States.

MEASURING INCOME DISTRIBUTION: THE LORENZ CURVE

We can represent the distribution of money income graphically with what is called the **Lorenz curve,** named after a U.S.-born statistician, Max Otto Lorenz, who proposed it in 1905. The Lorenz curve shows what portion of total money income is accounted for by different proportions of the nation's families. Look at Figure 31-1. On the horizontal axis we measure the *cumulative* percentage of families, lowest-income families first. Starting at the left corner, there are zero families; at the right corner, we have 100 percent of families; and in the middle, we have 50 percent of families. The vertical axis represents the cumulative percentage of money income. The 45-degree line represents perfect equality: 50 percent of the families obtain 50 percent of total income, 60 percent of the families obtain 60 percent of total income, and so on. Of course, in no real-world situation is there such perfect equality of income; no actual Lorenz curve would be a straight line. Rather,

▶ **Lorenz curve**
A geometric representation of the distribution of income. A Lorenz curve that is perfectly straight represents perfect income equality. The more bowed a Lorenz curve, the more unequally income is distributed.

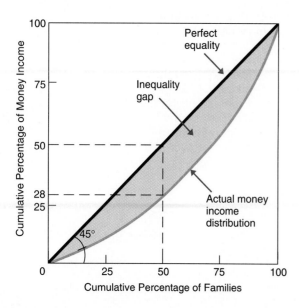

FIGURE 31-1
The Lorenz curve.
The horizontal axis measures the cumulative percentage of families from 0 to 100 percent. The vertical axis measures the cumulative percentage of money income from 0 to 100. A straight line at a 45-degree angle cuts the box in half and represents a line of perfect income equality, in which 25 percent of the families get 25 percent of the money income, 50 percent get 50 percent, and so on. The Lorenz curve, showing actual money income distribution, is not a straight line but rather a curved line as shown. The difference between perfect money income equality and the Lorenz curve is the inequality gap.

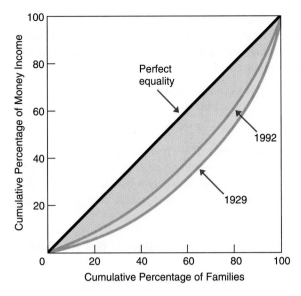

FIGURE 31-2
Lorenz curves of income distribution, 1929 and 1992.
Notice that since 1929 the Lorenz curve has moved slightly inward toward the straight line of perfect income equality.

Source: U.S. Department of Commerce.

it would be some curved line, like the one labeled "Actual money income distribution" in Figure 31-1. For example, the bottom 50 percent of families in the United States receive about 28 percent of total money income.

In Figure 31-2 we again show the actual money income distribution Lorenz curve, and we also compare it to the distribution of money income in 1929. Since that year the Lorenz curve has become less bowed; that is, it has moved closer to the line of perfect equality.

Criticisms of the Lorenz Curve.   In recent years economists have placed less and less emphasis on the shape of the Lorenz curve as an indication of the degree of income inequality in a country. There are five basic reasons why the Lorenz curve has been criticized:

1. The Lorenz curve is typically presented in terms of the distribution of *money* income only. It does not include **income in kind,** such as government-provided food stamps, education, or housing aid, and goods or services produced and consumed in the home or on the farm.
2. The Lorenz curve does not account for differences in the size of families or the number of wage earners they contain.
3. It does not account for age differences. Even if all families in the United States had exactly the same *lifetime* incomes, chances are that young families would have lower incomes, middle-aged families would have relatively high incomes, and retired families would have low incomes. Because the Lorenz curve is drawn at a moment in time, it could never tell us anything about the inequality of *lifetime* income.
4. The Lorenz curve ordinarily reflects money income *before* taxes.
5. It does not measure unreported income from the underground economy, a substantial source of income for some individuals.

▶ **Income in kind**
Income that is received in the form of actual goods and services, such as housing or medical care. To be contrasted with money income, which is simply income in dollars, or general purchasing power, that can be used to buy *any* goods and services.

▶ **Gini coefficient of inequality**
A numerical representation of the degree of income inequality in a nation; defined as the ratio of the area between the diagonal line and the actual Lorenz curve to the triangular area under that diagonal line.

MEASURING INCOME INEQUALITY: THE GINI COEFFICIENT

One measure of the degree of income inequality is the **Gini coefficient of inequality,** devised by the Italian statistician Corrado Gini (1884–1965). A diagram showing a Lorenz curve, such as the one in Figure 31-1, can also demonstrate the concept of the Gini coefficient. We compare the area between the straight 45-degree line and the Lorenz curve of actual income distribution with the entire area under the diagonal—that is, to the triangle that represents half of the box in Figure 31-1. In other words,

$$\text{Gini coefficient of inequality} = \frac{\text{area between diagonal line and Lorenz curve of actual money income distribution}}{\text{triangular area under diagonal line}}$$

The Gini coefficient will range from zero to unity. If we had perfect equality, the Gini coefficient would obviously be zero because there would be no area between the diagonal line, or curve of absolute equality, and the curve of actual distribution of income. The greater that area becomes, however, the greater the Gini coefficient becomes and hence the measure of inequality.

 INTERNATIONAL EXAMPLE: Income Inequality in the Rest of the World

One way to measure income inequality is by using the Gini coefficient. In Table 31-1 you see international comparisons of the Gini coefficient ranked from lowest to highest. Sweden is at the top of the list with the Gini coefficient of .291; France is at the bottom with .399. The coefficient for the United States is relatively high, indicating somewhat more income inequality here than in certain other countries.

	NATION	GINI COEFFICIENT
Most equal	Sweden	.291
	Norway	.309
	United Kingdom	.333
	Canada	.339
	United States	.374
	Spain	.381
Least equal	France	.399

TABLE 31-1 International comparisons of the Gini coefficient.

Source: United Nations.

In the United States, the Gini coefficient as it is commonly calculated does not include nonmoney income or income from the underground economy. Moreover, it does not take account of age as the determining factor in income differences. These criticisms apply to the international comparisons given in Table 31-1. In particular, the underground economy is much more prevalent in the United Kingdom, Spain, and France than it is in the United States, thus making those data more suspect.

For Critical Analysis: Why do you think the underground economy is more important in the countries just mentioned than in the United States? ●

INCOME DISTRIBUTION IN THE UNITED STATES

We could talk about the percentage of income earners within specific income classes—those earning between $20,001 and $30,000 per year, those earning between $30,001 and $40,000 per year, and so on. The problem with this type of analysis is that we are a growing economy. Income, with some exceptions, is going up all the time. If we wish to make comparisons of the relative share of total income going to different income classes, we cannot look at specific amounts of money income. We talk about a distribution of income over five groups. Then we can talk about how much the bottom fifth (or quintile) makes

TABLE 31-2
Percentage share of money income for families before direct taxes.

Source: U.S. Bureau of the Census

INCOME GROUP	1991[a]	1973[a]	1960[a]	1947[a]
Lowest fifth	4.2	5.5	4.8	5.1
Second fifth	10.7	11.9	12.2	11.8
Third fifth	16.9	17.5	17.8	16.7
Fourth fifth	24.2	24.0	24.0	23.2
Highest fifth	44.2	41.1	41.3	43.3

[a]May not sum to 100 percent due to rounding.

compared with the top fifth, and so on. In Table 31-2 we see the percentage share of income for families before direct taxes. The table groups families according to whether they are in the lowest 20 percent of the income distribution, the second lowest 20 percent, and so on. We see that in 1991 the lowest 20 percent had a combined money income of 4.2 percent of the total money income of the entire population. This is a little less than the lowest 20 percent had at the end of World War II. Accordingly, the conclusion has been drawn that there have been only slight changes in the distribution of money income. Indeed, considering that the definition of money income used by the U.S. Bureau of the Census includes only wage and salary income, income from self-employment, interest and dividends, and such government transfer payments as Social Security and unemployment compensation, we have to agree that the distribution of money income has not changed. *Money* income, however, understates *total* income for individuals who receive in-kind transfers from the government in the form of food stamps, public housing, free education, and so on.

⭐ EXAMPLE: Mobility Among Income Groups

During the 1992 presidential debates, a major issue was what happened to the "poor" versus the "rich" during the preceding 12 years. The Democrats argued that the rich got richer at the expense of the poor. The Republicans argued that we all got richer. Neither the Republicans nor the Democrats, however, focused on a crucial fact: No matter what happened to the rich versus the poor, during any recent 12-year period, the "rich" are not the same people, nor are the "poor." There is tremendous mobility among the arbitrary five groupings of households based on income that we just discussed.

   Both the U.S. Treasury's Office of Tax Analysis and the Urban Institute have discovered through tracking more than 14,000 individuals during a fairly long time period that in the 1980s, between 10 and 20 percent of the members of each income quintile moved to a higher group each year. Similarly, between 10 and 20 percent moved down each year. In 1979, for example, among individuals whose incomes were in the bottom 20 percent, 10 years later 86 percent were in a higher income bracket. That means that only about 14 percent of those considered the "poor" in America stayed at the bottom during that 10-year period. In contrast, about an equal percentage actually rose from the bottom quintile to the top quintile during that decade. Overall, during the 1980s turnover was never less than 33 percent. The fact is that as people grow older, they get more experience and training and move out of lower income brackets.

For Critical Analysis: Under what circumstances would you be concerned about the "rich getting richer"? ●

THE DISTRIBUTION OF WEALTH

We have been referring to the distribution of income in the United States. We must realize that income can be viewed as a return on wealth, both human and nonhuman.

FIGURE 31-3
The distribution of wealth in the United States.
In panel (a) you see what assets are owned by the richest 1 percent of the population, the next 9 percent, and the remaining 90 percent. Securities include stocks and bonds. Bank accounts include both checking and savings accounts. Net worth is the difference between what is owned and what is owed. In panel (b) you see what happened to total wealth distribution from 1983 to 1989.

Source: Federal Reserve Survey, Board of Governors of the Federal Reserve.

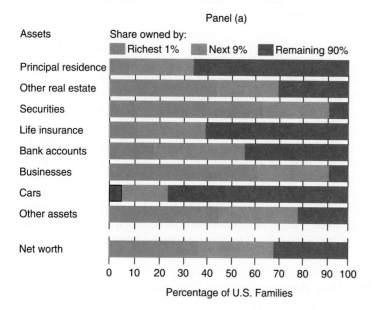

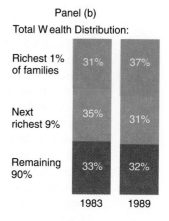

The discussion of the distribution of income in the United States is not the same thing as a discussion of the distribution of wealth. A complete concept of wealth would include tangible objects, such as buildings, machinery, land, cars, and houses—nonhuman wealth—as well as people who have skills, knowledge, initiative, talents, and so on—human wealth. The total of human and nonhuman wealth in the United States gives us our nation's capital stock. (Note that the terms *wealth* and *capital* are often used only with reference to nonhuman wealth.) The capital stock consists of anything that can generate utility to individuals in the future. A fresh ripe tomato is not part of our capital stock. It has to be eaten before it turns rotten, and once it has been eaten, it can no longer generate satisfaction.

In panel (a) of Figure 31-3 you see the share of the value of assets owned by families in each part of the wealth spectrum. In panel (b) you see the share of total net worth of American families in 1983 and 1989, the latest year for which the Federal Reserve Survey was taken. The conclusion you might draw from these figures is that the top 1 percent had a greater net worth than the bottom 90 percent of U.S. households. At the beginning of this decade, 834,000 households owned about $5.7 trillion of net worth, which was more than the $4.8 trillion of net worth that the remaining 84 million households owned. The whole story, though, is a bit more complicated.

Survey Inaccuracies. The Federal Reserve Survey included only 3,143 households out of an estimated 85 million. According to the Federal Reserve, the error in estimating the wealth of the top 1 percent could be $600 billion in either direction, or a margin of error of $1.2 trillion, or 20 percent. The same is true of the estimates of the lowest 90 percent of income-earning households.

Other Assets Missing.   The Federal Reserve's data did not take account of two major components of household wealth. The first is the value of workers' claims on private pension plans. Economist Lawrence B. Lindsey estimated that these account for about $4 trillion if you include military pensions. Merely adding the value of all of these pensions would have increased household wealth by almost a quarter, the majority of which would have gone to the middle class.

Furthermore, Social Security wealth is left out of these data and out of many other reports. This wealth consists of claims by individuals on the Social Security System. It is estimated to be close to $6 trillion. Taken together, both private and military pension plans plus Social Security wealth add another $10 trillion to household wealth.

 INTERNATIONAL EXAMPLE: Are We Really So Bad Off?

Much of the discussion in the 1990s of both income and wealth points to the same conclusions: Only the rich have been doing well; the average working family either has not made any increases in real income in the past 20 years or has lost ground. Though there are no hard and fast rules on how to compare well-being between two time periods, some data seem to show that even if household income in the United States has not grown much (or not at all) in the past two decades, households are generally better off. Just look at the statistics in Table 31-3.

Part of the reason for the dramatic increase in percentage of households owning major appliances is the drop in their relative price. A 21-inch black-and-white television set in 1951 cost almost $2,000 in today's dollars. A 21-inch color TV with remote control today runs not too much more than $200. In effect, the electronics revolution and the microchip have made a wide variety of appliances available even to members of the lowest quintile of households in the United States.

Many comparisons are made between this country and Japan. In particular, Japan has had a much higher rate of economic growth than the United States. Its rapid rise in income per capita could indicate that the Japanese are better off than Americans. The data do not bear this out. Table 31-4 on the next page provides some data about the quality of life in the United States and in Japan. The average worker in Japan lives in approximately half the housing space as his or her counterpart in America (and pays twice as much). Fewer than half the houses in Japan have flushing toilets, and only about 10 percent have central heating. Not surprisingly, when surveyed, not even 1 percent of the people in Japan classify themselves as upper class. Almost 90 percent classify themselves as middle class.

For Critical Analysis: Do the data on quality of life comparisons between Japan and the United States necessarily tell the whole story? What other aspects of life are important in comparing the quality of life? ●

	PERCENTAGE OF FAMILIES OWNING AT LEAST ONE		
APPLIANCE	1951	1971	1991
Telephone answering machine	0	0	42
Cable TV service	0	7	53
Automobile	60	83	87
Computer	0	0	26
Microwave oven	0	0	86
Television set	23	94	98
Telephone	62	91	93
VCR	0	0	79

TABLE 31-3 Appliance ownership in the United States.

Source: Fortune, October 21, 1991, p. 55.

	JAPAN	UNITED STATES
Television sets per 100 people	26.6	82.9
Hospital beds per 1,000 people	5.8	13.3
Size of average residence	881 sq. ft.	1,645 sq. ft.
Percentage of homes with central heating	10.3%	85.0%
Percentage of homes with flushing toilets	45.4%	99.8%

TABLE 31-4
Comparing Japan with the United States: some selected statistics.

Source: Business Week, September 9, 1992, p. 128.

CONCEPTS IN BRIEF

- The Lorenz curve graphically represents the distribution of income. If it is a straight line, there is perfect equality of income. The more it is bowed, the more inequality of income exists.
- The degree of income inequality can be measured by the Gini coefficient of inequality.
- The Gini coefficient ranges from zero to 1. For perfect equality, the Gini coefficient would be zero because there would be no area between the diagonal line, or curve of absolute equality, and the curve of actual distribution of income.
- The distribution of wealth is not the same as the distribution of income. Wealth includes assets such as houses, stocks, and bonds. Although the apparent distribution of wealth seems to be more concentrated at the top, the data used are not very accurate nor do most summary statistics take account of workers' claims on private and public pensions.

DETERMINANTS OF INCOME DIFFERENCES

We know that there are income differences—that is not in dispute. A more important question is why these differences in income occur. For if we know why income differences occur, then perhaps we can change public policy, particularly with respect to helping those in the lowest income classes climb the income ladder. What is more, if we know the reasons for income differences, we can ascertain whether any of these determinants have changed over time. We will look at four income difference determinants: age, marginal productivity, inheritance, and discrimination.

AGE

Age turns out to be a determinant of income because with age comes, usually, more education, more training, and more experience. It is not surprising that within every class of income earners, there seem to be regular cycles of earning behavior. Most individuals earn more when they are middle-aged than when they are younger or older. We call this the **age-earnings cycle.**

The Age-Earnings Cycle.   Every occupation has its own age-earnings cycle, and every individual will probably experience some variation from the average. Nonetheless, we can characterize the typical age-earnings cycle graphically in Figure 31-4. Here we see that at age 18 income is relatively low. Income gradually rises until it peaks about age 45 to 50. Then it falls until retirement, when it becomes zero (that is, currently earned income becomes zero, although retirement payments may then commence). The reason for such a regular cycle in earnings is fairly straightforward.

▶ **Age-earnings cycle**
The regular earnings profile of an individual throughout his or her lifetime. The age-earnings cycle usually starts with a low income, builds gradually to a peak at around age 45 to 50, and then gradually curves down until it approaches zero at retirement age.

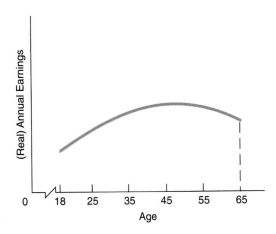

FIGURE 31-4
Typical age-earnings profile.
Within every class of income earners there is usually a typical age-earnings profile. Earnings are lowest when starting work at age 18, reach their peak around age 45–50, and then taper off until retirement around age 65, when they become zero for most people. The rise in earnings up to age 45–50 is usually due to increased experience, longer working hours, and better training and schooling. (We abstract from economywide productivity changes that would shift the entire curve upward.)

When individuals start working at a young age, they typically have no work-related experience. Their ability to produce is less than that of more seasoned workers—that is, their productivity is lower. As they become older, they obtain more training and accumulate more experience. Their productivity rises, and they are therefore paid more. They also generally start to work longer hours. At the age of 45 to 50, the productivity of individual workers usually peaks. So, too, do the number of hours per week that are worked. After this peak in the age-earnings cycle, the detrimental effects of aging—decreases in stamina, strength, reaction time, and the like—usually outweigh any increases in training or experience. Also, hours worked usually start to fall for older people. Finally, as a person reaches retirement age, his or her productivity and hours worked diminish rather drastically.

Note that general increases in overall productivity for the entire work force will result in an upward shift in the typical age-earnings profile given in Figure 31-4. Thus even at the end of the age-earnings cycle, when just about to retire, the worker would not receive a really low wage compared with the starting wage 45 years earlier. The wage would be higher due to factors that contribute to rising real wages for everyone, regardless of the stage in the age-earnings cycle.

Now we have some idea why specific individuals earn different incomes at different times in their lives, but we have yet to explain why different people are paid different amounts of money for their labor. One way to explain this is to recall the marginal productivity theory developed in Chapter 28.

MARGINAL PRODUCTIVITY

When trying to determine how many workers a firm would hire, we had to construct a marginal revenue product curve. We found that as more workers were hired, the marginal revenue product fell due to diminishing marginal returns. If the forces of demand and supply established a certain wage rate, workers would be hired until their marginal physical product times marginal revenue was equal to the going wage rate. Then the hiring would stop. This analysis suggests what workers can expect to be paid in the labor market: They can each expect to be paid their marginal revenue product (assuming that there are low-cost information flows and that the labor and product markets are competitive).

In a competitive situation, with mobility of labor resources (at least on the margin), workers who are being paid less than their marginal revenue product will be bid away to better employment opportunities. Either they will seek better employment themselves, or other employers will offer them a slightly higher wage rate. This process will continue until each worker is being paid his or her marginal revenue product.

You may balk at the suggestion that people are paid their marginal revenue product because you may personally know individuals whose MRP is more or less than what they are being paid. Such a situation may, in fact, exist because we do not live in a world of perfect information or in a world with perfectly competitive input and output markets. Employers cannot always seek out the most productive employees available. It takes resources to research the past records of potential employees, their training, their education, and their abilities.

Determinants of Marginal Productivity.

If we accept marginal revenue product theory, we have a way to find out how people can earn higher incomes. If they can increase the value of their marginal physical product, they can expect to be paid more. Some of the determinants of marginal physical product are talent, education, experience, and training. Most of these are means by which marginal physical product can be increased. Let's examine them in greater detail.

Talent. This factor is the easiest to explain but impossible to acquire if you don't have it. Innate abilities and attributes can be very strong, if not overwhelming, determinants of a person's potential productivity. Strength, coordination, and mental alertness are facets of nonacquired human capital and thus have some bearing on the ability to earn income. Someone who is extremely tall has a better chance of being a basketball player than someone who is short. A person born with a superior talent for abstract thinking has a better chance of making a relatively higher income as a mathematician or a physicist than someone who is not born with that talent.

Experience. Additional experience at particular tasks is another way to increase productivity. Experience can be linked to the well-known *learning curve* that applies when the same task is done over and over. The worker repeating a task becomes more efficient: The worker can do the same task in less time or in the same amount of time but better. Take an example of a person going to work on an automobile assembly line. At first she is able to fasten only three bolts every two minutes. Then the worker becomes more adept and can fasten four bolts in the same time plus insert a rubber guard on the bumper. After a few more weeks, another task can be added. Experience allows this individual to improve her productivity. The more effectively people learn to do something, the quicker they can do it and the more efficient they are. Hence we would expect experience to lead to higher rates of productivity. And we would expect people with more experience to be paid more than those with less experience. More experience, however, does not guarantee a higher wage rate. The *demand* for a person's services must also exist. Spending a long time to become a first-rate archer in modern society would probably add very little to a person's income. Experience has value only if the output is demanded by society.

Training. Training is similar to experience but is more formal. Much of a person's increased productivity is due to on-the-job training. Many companies have training programs for new workers. On-the-job training is perhaps responsible for as much of an increase in productivity as is formal education beyond grade school.

Investment in Human Capital.

Investment in human capital is just like investment in any other thing. If you invest in yourself by going to college, rather than going to work after high school and earning more current income, you will presumably be re-warded in the future with a higher income or a more interesting job (or both). This is ex-actly the motivation that underlies the decision of many college-bound students to obtain a formal higher education. Undoubtedly there would be students going to school even if the rate of return on formal education were zero or negative. But we do expect that the higher the rate of return on investing in ourselves, the more such investment there will be. U.S. Labor Department data demonstrate conclusively that, on average, high school grad-uates make more than grade school graduates and college graduates make more than high school graduates. The estimated annual income of a full-time worker with four years of college in 1995 is about $50,000. That person's high school counterpart is estimated to earn only $30,000, which gives a "college premium" of more than 60 percent. Generally, the rate of return on investment in human capital is on a par with the rate of return on investment in other areas.

To figure out the rate of return on an investment in a college education, we first have to figure out the mrginal costs of going to school. The main cost is not what you have to pay for books, fees, and tuition but rather the income you forgo. *The main cost of edu-cation is the income forgone, or the opportunity cost of not working.* In addition, the di-rect expenses of college must be paid for. Not all students forgo all income during their college years. Many work part time. Taking account of those who work part time and those who are supported by state tuition grants and other scholarships, the average rate of return on going to college is somewhere between 8 and 12 percent. This is not a bad rate. Of course, this type of computation does leave out all the consumption benefits you get from attending college. Also omitted from the calculations is the change in personality after going to college. You undoubtedly come out a different person. Most people who go through college feel that they have improved themselves both culturally and intellectually in addition to having increased their potential marginal revenue product so that they can make more income. How do we measure the benefit from expanding our horizons and our desire to experience different things in life? This is not easy to measure, and such non-money benefits from investing in human capital are not included in normal calculations.

INHERITANCE

It is not unusual to inherit cash, jewelry, stocks, bonds, homes, or other real estate. Yet only about 10 percent of income inequality in the United States can be traced to differences in wealth that was inherited. We should not be surprised that this is the case, because only about one-sixth of all income in the United States comes from rent and interest on prop-erty that is owned. If for some reason the government confiscated all property that had been inherited, there would be very little measured change in the distribution of income in the United States.

DISCRIMINATION

Economic discrimination occurs whenever minority or female workers who have the same training, experience, abilities, and education as white male workers are given lower wages, less chance for promotion, or unequal occupational access to the labor market. It is pos-sible—and indeed quite obvious—that discrimination affects the distribution of income. Certain groups in our society are not paid wages at rates comparable to those received by other groups, even when we correct for productivity. There still are differences in income between whites and nonwhites and between men and women. For example, the median income for black families is about 60 percent that of white families. The median wage rate of women is about 70 percent that of men. Some people argue that all of these dif-ferences are due to discrimination against nonwhites and against women. We cannot simply accept *any* differences in income as due to discrimination, though. What we need to do is discover why differences in income between groups exist and then determine if factors other than discrimination in the labor market can explain them. The unexplained part of income differences can rightfully be considered the result of discrimination.

Access to Education.

African Americans and other minorities have faced discrimination in the acquisition of human capital. The amount and quality of schooling offered black Americans has generally been inferior to that offered whites. Even if minorities attend school as long as whites, their scholastic achievement can be lower because they are typically allotted fewer school resources than their white counterparts. Nonwhite urban individuals are more likely to live in lower-income areas, which have fewer resources to allocate to education due to the lower tax base. One study showed that nonwhite urban males receive between 23 and 27 percent less income than white urban males because of lower-quality education. This would mean that even if employment discrimination were substantially reduced, we would still expect to see a difference between white and nonwhite income because of the low quality of schooling received by the nonwhites and the resulting lower level of productivity. We say, therefore, that among other things, African Americans and certain other minority groups, such as Hispanics, suffer from too small an investment in human capital. Even when this difference in human capital is taken into account, however, there still appears to be an income differential that cannot be explained. The unexplained income differential between whites and blacks is often attributed to discrimination in the labor market. Because no better explanation is offered, we will stick with the notion that discrimination in the labor market does indeed exist.

The Doctrine of Comparable Worth.

Discrimination against women can occur because of barriers to entry in higher-paying occupations and because of discrimination in the acquisition of human capital, just as has occurred for African Americans. Discrimination against women in the labor market is perhaps best exemplified by the distribution of highest-paying and lowest-paying occupations. The lowest-paying jobs are dominated by females, both white and nonwhite. For example, the proportion of women in secretarial, clerical, janitorial, and food service jobs ranges from 70 percent (food service) to 97 percent (secretarial). Proponents of the **comparable-worth doctrine** feel that female secretaries, janitors, and food service workers should be making salaries comparable to those of male truck drivers or construction workers, assuming that the levels of skill and responsibility in these jobs are comparable. They also believe that a comparable-worth policy would benefit the economy overall. They contend that adjusting the wages of workers in female-dominated jobs upward would create a move toward more efficient and less discriminatory labor markets.

▶ **Comparable-worth doctrine**
The belief that women should receive the same wages as men if the levels of skill and responsibility in their jobs are equal or equivalent.

⭐ EXAMPLE: The Persistent Inequality in Income Between the Races

Figure 31-5 shows what happened to median family income for white and black Americans during the Johnson, Nixon, Ford, Carter, Reagan, and Bush administrations. All of these administrations made concerted government efforts to reduce the wage gap between the two races. In spite of these efforts, the absolute wage gap continued to increase. The relative difference remained between 60 and 70 percent.

For Critical Analysis: Why does the income gap appear to be widening but really isn't? ●

FIGURE 31-5
Median family income in the United States, 1964–1992.
Both Democratic and Republican administrations have made attempts at narrowing the
gap between median family incomes for whites and blacks in the United States. According to this figure, no policy has been particularly successful.
Source: U.S. Bureau of the Census.

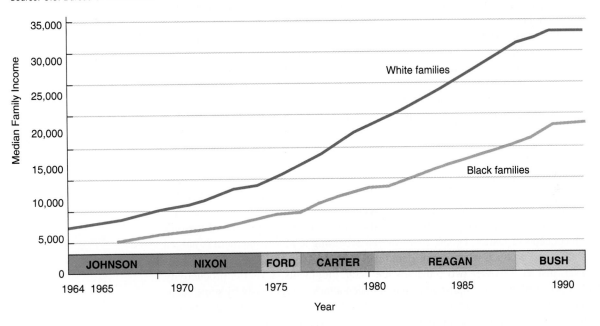

THEORIES OF DESIRED INCOME DISTRIBUTION

We have talked about the factors affecting the distribution of income, but we have not yet
mentioned the normative issue of how income *ought* to be distributed. This, of course, requires a value judgment. We are talking about the problem of economic justice. We can
never completely resolve this problem because there are always going to be conflicting
values. It is impossible to give all people what each thinks is just. Nonethess, three particular normative standards for the distribution of income have been popular with social
philosophers, economists, and politicians. These normative standards are income distribution based on need, equality, and productivity.

NEED

"To each according to his or her needs." So goes the distributive principle of pure communism, associated most often with Karl Marx. Although this principle, or standard, of
income distribution certainly has little to do with how income is distributed in this country (except for private and public charitable transfers), it does apply roughly to the way
income is distributed within a family unit and also to the way income is distributed within
a geographic area during wartime or other periods of emergency. There is little doubt that
this distribution standard has a great appeal to many individuals. However, its implementation poses a number of extremely thorny problems. The most difficult problem, perhaps,
is the establishment of an unbiased objective operational mechanism for measuring "need."
In general, the only way we can determine need is by using subjective judgment. It is very
difficult for us to establish just what is a necessity for each individual.

EQUALITY

The egalitarian principle of income distribution can be simply stated as "To each exactly the same." In other words, everyone would have exactly the same amount of income. This criterion of distribution has been debated as far back as biblical times. Similar to the need criterion, the equality criterion has problems.

If there were an equal distribution of income, the incentive of rewards would be eliminated. What would motivate people to develop and apply their skills and capacities to the most productive uses? What incentive would there be for individuals to use economic resources efficiently? Who would take the risky, hazardous, or unpleasant jobs? Who would be willing to work overtime without additional pay? If we used the equality principle in the distribution of income, this nation would probably suffer a decline in economic living standards. However, this does not necessarily mean that the equality criterion should be eliminated—the benefits from equalizing income might still outweigh the costs.

PRODUCTIVITY

The productivity standard for the distribution of income can be stated simply as "To each according to what he or she produces." This is also called the *contributive* standard because it is based on the principle of rewarding according to the contribution to society's total output. It is also sometimes referred to as the *merit* standard and is one of the oldest-known concepts of justice. People are rewarded according to merit, and merit is judged by one's ability to produce what is considered useful by society.

However, just as the other two standards are value judgments, so is the productivity standard. It is rooted in the capitalist ethic and has been attacked vigorously by some economists and philosophers, including Karl Marx, who, as we pointed out, felt that people should be rewarded according to need and not according to productivity.

We measure a person's productive contribution in a capitalist system by the market value of that person's output. We have already referred to this as the marginal revenue product theory of wage determination.

Do not immediately jump to the conclusion that in a world of income distribution determined by productivity, society will necessarily allow the aged, the infirm, and the disabled to die of starvation because they are unproductive. In the United States today the productivity standard is mixed with the need standard so that the aged, the disabled, the involuntarily unemployed, the very young, and other unproductive (in the market sense of the word) members of the economy are provided for through private and public transfers.

CONCEPTS IN BRIEF

- Most people follow an age-earnings cycle in which they earn relatively small incomes when they first start working, increase their incomes until about age 45 to 50, then slowly experience a decrease in their real incomes as they approach retirement.
- If we accept the marginal revenue product theory of wages, workers can expect to be paid their marginal revenue product. However, full adjustment is never obtained, so some workers may be paid more or less than their MRP.
- Marginal physical productivity depends on talent, education, experience, and training.
- Going to school and receiving on-the-job training can be considered an investment in human capital. The main cost of education is the opportunity cost of not working.

- Discrimination is most easily observed in various groups' access to high-paying jobs and to quality education. Minorities and women are disproportionately underrepresented in high-paying jobs. Also, minorities sometimes do not receive access to higher education of the same quality offered to majority-group members.
- Proponents of the comparable-worth doctrine contend that disparate jobs can be compared by examining efforts, skill, and educational training and that wages should therefore be paid on the basis of this comparable worth.
- There are at least three normative standards for income distribution: income distribution based on need, equality, and productivity.

POVERTY AND ATTEMPTS TO ELIMINATE IT

Throughout the history of the world, mass poverty has been accepted as inevitable. However, this nation and others, particularly in the Western world, have sustained enough economic growth in the past several hundred years so that *mass* poverty can no longer be said to be a problem for these fortunate countries. As a matter of fact, the residual of poverty in the United States appears bizarre, an anomaly. How can there still be so much poverty in a nation of so much abundance? Having talked about the determinants of the distribution of income, we now have at least some ideas of why some people are destined to remain low-income earners throughout their lives.

There are methods of transferring income from the relatively well-to-do to the relatively poor, and as a nation we have been using them for a long time. Today we have a vast array of welfare programs set up for the purpose of redistributing income. However, we know that these programs have not been entirely successful. Are there alternatives to our current welfare system? Is there a better method of helping the poor? Before we answer these questions, let's look at the concept of poverty in more detail and at the characteristics of the poor.

We see in Figure 31-6 on the next page that the number of individuals classified as poor fell rather steadily from 1959 to 1969. For a few years the number of poor leveled off until the recession of 1981–1982. The number then fell only to rise again during the recession of the early 1990s.

DEFINING POVERTY

The threshold income level, which is used to determine who falls into the poverty category, was originally based on the cost of a nutritionally adequate food plan designed by the U.S. Department of Agriculture for emergency or temporary use. The threshold was determined by multiplying the food plan cost by 3 on the assumption that food expenses comprise approximately one-third of a poor family's income. Annual revisions of the threshold level were based only on price changes in the food budget. In 1969 a federal interagency committee looked at the calculations of the threshold and decided to set new standards, with adjustments made on the basis of changes in the Consumer Price Index. For example, in 1993 the official poverty level for an urban family of four was $14,343. It has gone up to reflect whatever inflation has occurred since then.

ABSOLUTE POVERTY

Because the low-income threshold is an absolute measure, we know that if it never changes in real terms, we will reduce poverty even if we do nothing. How can that be? The reasoning is straightforward. Real incomes in the United States have been growing at a

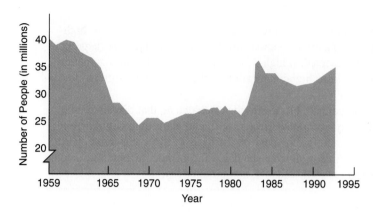

FIGURE 31-6
The official number of poor in the United States.
The number of individuals classified as poor fell steadily from 1959 through 1969. From 1970 to 1981 the number stayed about the same. It then increased during the 1981–1982 recession, dropped off for a while, and rose again during the early 1990s.
Source: U.S. Department of Labor.

compounded annual rate of almost 2 percent per capita for at least the past century and at about 2.5 percent since World War II. If we define the poverty line at a specific real level, more and more individuals will make incomes that exceed that poverty line. Thus in absolute terms we will eliminate poverty (assuming continued per capita growth and no change in income distribution).

RELATIVE POVERTY

Be careful with this analysis, however. Poverty has generally been defined in relative terms; that is, it is defined in terms of the income levels of individuals or families relative to the rest of the population. As long as the distribution of income is not perfectly equal, there will always be some people who make less income than others, even if their relatively low income is high by historical standards. Thus in a relative sense the problem of poverty will always exist, although it can be reduced. In any given year, for example, the absolute poverty level *officially* decided on by the U.S. government is far above the average income in many countries in the world.

TRANSFER PAYMENTS AS INCOME

The official poverty level is based on pretax income, including cash but not in-kind subsidies—food stamps, housing vouchers, and the like. If we correct poverty levels for such benefits, the percentage of the population that is below the poverty line drops dramatically, as can be seen in Figure 31-7. Some economists argue that the way the official poverty level is calculated makes no sense in a nation that redistributed over $696.7 billion in cash and noncash transfers in 1993.

ATTACKS ON POVERTY: MAJOR INCOME MAINTENANCE PROGRAMS

There are a variety of income maintenance programs designed to help the poor. We examine a few of them here.

Social Security.   For the retired, the unemployed, and the disabled, social insurance programs provide income payments in prescribed situations. The best known is Social Security, which includes what has been called old-age, survivors', and disability insurance (OASDI). This is essentially a program of compulsory saving financed from compulsory payroll taxes levied on both employers and employees. Workers pay for Social Security while working and receive the benefits after retirement. The benefit payments are usually

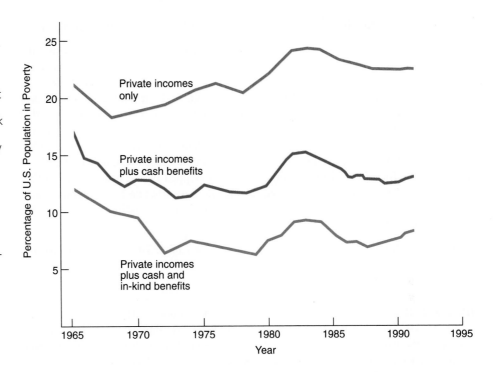

FIGURE 31-7

Three measures of poverty.

The percentage of the U.S. population living in poverty depends on what we include in the definition of income. If we look at private money income only, the share of poverty in the early 1990s was well above 20 percent. If we add cash benefits paid to individuals by the government, the 1990s' poverty level represents something less than 13 percent of the U.S. population. Finally, if we take account of cash, in-kind benefits, and the underreporting of income, the share of the U.S. population in poverty was estimated to be about 8 percent in 1993.

Source: U.S. Congress, Office of the Budget.

made to people who have reached retirement age. When the insured worker dies, benefits accrue to the survivors, including widows and children. Special benefits provide for disabled workers. Over 90 percent of all employed persons in the United States are covered by OASDI. Social Security was originally designed as a social insurance program that workers paid for themselves and under which they received benefits that varied with the size of past contributions. Today it is simply an intergenerational income transfer that is only vaguely related to past earnings. It transfers income from Americans who work—the young through the middle aged—to those who do not work—older retired persons.

In 1993 more than 37 million people were receiving OASDI checks averaging about $673 a month. Benefit payments from OASDI redistribute income to some degree. However, benefit payments are not based on the recipients' need. Participants' contributions give them the right to benefits even if they would be financially secure without them. Social Security is not really an insurance program because people are not guaranteed that the benefits they receive will be in line with the contributions they have made. It is not a personal savings account. The benefits are legislated by Congress. In the future, Congress may not be as sympathetic toward older people as it is today. It could (and probably will have to) legislate for lower real levels of benefits instead of higher ones.

Supplemental Security Income (SSI) and Aid to Families with Dependent Children (AFDC).

Many people who are poor but do not qualify for Social Security benefits are assisted through other programs. Starting in 1974, the federally financed and administered Supplemental Security Income (SSI) program was instituted. The purpose of SSI is to establish a nationwide minimum income for the aged, the blind, and the disabled.

Aid to Families with Dependent Children (AFDC) is a state-administered program, financed in part by federal grants. This program provides aid to families in which dependent children do not have the financial support of the father because of desertion, disability, or death. (Some critics argue that AFDC provides an incentive for fathers to desert their families because that may be the only way for a family to receive such payments.)

⭐ EXAMPLE: Saving for College and AFDC Don't Go Together

One of the most important methods that people can use to rise out of poverty and the welfare system is a higher education. But most higher education requires more income than a potential student can obtain in grants, scholarships, and part-time work while going to college. Consequently, many potential college entrants, particularly poor ones, have to save while they are in high school. Sandra Rosado did just that while working part time in a community center in New Haven, Connecticut. She was able to save almost $5,000 for college expenses. When state officials discovered her savings in 1992, they told her mother to spend the money if she wanted the family to remain eligible for AFDC. Federal authorities then stepped in and ordered the mother to repay $9,342 in benefits she received during the period when her daughter maintained a savings account. Under federal law, AFDC is not available to families that have assets over $1,000.

For Critical Analysis: What alternatives do recipients of AFDC benefits have to saving money for higher education? ●

Food Stamps.   Food stamps are government-issued coupons that can be used to purchase food. The food stamp program was started in 1964, seemingly, in retrospect, mainly to shore up the nation's agricultural sector by increasing demand for food through retail channels. In 1962 some 367,000 Americans were receiving food stamps. In 1993 the estimate is over 26 million recipients. The annual cost has jumped from $860,000 to more than $29 billion. In 1993 about one in every 10 citizens (including children) were using food stamps. The food stamp program has become a major part of the welfare system in the United States. The program has also become a method of promoting better nutrition among the poor.

SHORTCOMINGS OF INCOME MAINTENANCE PROGRAMS

Current programs attempt to correct income inequalities by transferring income to the poor to help them obtain basic essentials of life. However, they do not correct for inequality of *opportunities*. Moreover, the manner in which aid is currently delivered to those who need it generates undesirable behavioral responses such as reductions in work effort and changes in family structure.

Reduction in Work Effort.   Provision of aid to the needy sometimes induces recipients to reduce their work efforts as a result of the easier-to-obtain income provided by welfare. The fact that the level of benefits is inversely related to income from other sources creates an even more powerful disincentive effect. That is, the more a recipient earns, the fewer other benefits are received. In the AFDC program, a $1 increase in income earned by the recipient family reduces the benefits by $1—a 100 percent marginal tax rate. Many economists have argued that such high marginal tax rates reduce incentives to work; recipients feel that it is not worth their while to work because an additional dollar earned reduces their income by the same amount. This may be reflected in the fact that only 5 percent of AFDC recipients work. What's more, taxes have to be levied to finance welfare payments. The taxes also have some disincentive effects on the work effort of higher-income individuals. Taxes reduce take-home pay and thus reduce the reward for hard work by higher-income individuals. This may encourage some to reduce their work or, in the case of older workers, to retire earlier.

Changes in Family Structure. Welfare payments are inversely related to the income of the family. Because the father's income is usually the highest in a family, the inclusion of his income may be enough to disqualify a family even though it is barely subsisting. This may force the father to move out, creating single-parent families headed by women. This group constitutes a growing portion of today's poor.

 INTERNATIONAL EXAMPLE: U.S. Poverty Programs Compared to Those in Other Countries

According to economist Anthony M. Smeedin, the United States poverty rates are at least twice as high as those in Canada, Australia, Sweden, Germany, the Netherlands, France, and Great Britain. He argues that we choose to tolerate more poverty than other developed countries do. During the 1980s, social programs in the countries just mentioned eliminated about 75 percent of their poverty. In the United States, welfare programs eliminated only about a third of this country's poverty. In the mid-1980s these other countries had poverty rates of about 22.5 percent. After social programs were included, the figure fell to about 6 percent. According to a study, these countries spend more money and target programs better than we do. For example, because the largest single poverty group consists of elderly women living alone, Canada and Australia combine a special widow's benefit with all other welfare benefits. The other countries studied have a form of national child allowance that is independent of work effort and is simply given to parents on behalf of the children. In Canada such allowances are obtained through income tax credits; in France they are obtained via a direct transfer system. In addition, these countries allow parental leave for several months with pay, guarantee child support by the father, and provide high minimum benefits for the permanently disabled.

For Critical Analysis: Is it possible to take antipoverty programs from other countries and apply them in the United States? What are some differences between the United States and the countries mentioned? ●

THE CHANGING FACE OF THE POOR

Minorities (especially African Americans), the elderly, and women are the main groups traditionally identified with poverty. These groups, broadly defined, accounted for more of the incidence of poverty 30 years ago. But the composition of the poor in the United States today is quite different. For instance, even though black Americans as a group continue to earn less than whites, the income gap has been narrowed somewhat for certain subgroups within the black community. In the early 1960s, African-American two-parent families had incomes that were only 64 percent that of Caucasian two-parent families. Today this figure has risen to 79 percent. Also, in the early 1960s, African-American men earned only 61 percent as much as white men. Today they earn 74 percent as much. This reduction in racial income inequality is due partly to efforts at reducing discrimination as well as to government redistribution policies.

The nation's young adults are now relatively poorer than young people used to be. Part of this is due to an increase in their unemployment. The unemployment rate among youths has increased even more dramatically among African Americans. For black Americans aged 16 to 24, the unemployment rate was 13.4 in 1960; in 1993 the estimate is 38.7

percent. Furthermore, young people in the 1980s and 1990s are earning less relative to older workers than they did 30 years earlier.

In the 1960s the poverty rate among the elderly was at least double the rate for younger people. Today the elderly, taken as a group, have less poverty than the average for the rest of the population. Part of the reason for this is rising Social Security benefits. Also, many of the elderly own their own homes with the mortgages already paid off. Therefore, they are receiving income in kind from their owned stock of housing. Some of the elderly, nonetheless, have fallen through the cracks—particularly widows of men with low incomes and the single elderly who are not working. About 25 percent of the single elderly are estimated to be living in poverty.

The income gap between men and women has narrowed somewhat as more women become established in better professions and as small-business owners. This is in sharp contrast with the past, when most women had low-paying jobs. However, when women head up single-parent families, the statistics are much grimmer. The number of these households is increasing, and their average income is falling. For example, in the early 1960s the per capita income of white mother-only families was about 67 percent of that of two-parent families. Today it is only about 55 percent. African-American mother-only families had income that was 61 percent of that of two-parent families in the 1960s; it has now fallen to 47 percent.

Also, in the 1980s and 1990s there arose a new awareness of the plight of the homeless. Surveys show that about two-thirds of the homeless have serious personal problems that contribute to their homelessness. For example, recent studies show that over one-third are alcoholics and about a quarter are either drug abusers or former felons. Families are becoming a growing part of the homeless. About 20 percent of the homeless are families who are housed in temporary shelters throughout the country. Most of them are young single women with children. As a charitable response to the plight of the homeless, many shelters have sprung up around the nation that provide for short-term emergency needs. For the homeless to be truly helped, however, they need the transitional services offered by these shelters plus rehabilitative help, classes in parenting, and assistance in obtaining disability benefits. The problem of the homeless will be with us for years to come.

NO APPARENT REDUCTION IN POVERTY RATES

In spite of the numerous programs in existence and the hundreds of billions of dollars transferred to the poor, the officially defined rate of poverty in the United States has shown no long-run tendency to decline. It reached its low of around 11 percent in 1973, peaked at over 15 percent in 1983, fell steadily to 13.1 percent in 1990, and then rose again to over 14 percent in 1993. Why, with all of the billions transferred to the poor, is there still so much poverty in the United States?

 INTERNATIONAL EXAMPLE: Poverty Pays in Ireland

Every system of redistribution of income to the poor involves a different set of incentives. Implicitly, these incentives can be translated into different marginal tax rates depending on income and the amount of food stamps, housing services, cash transfers, and other benefits given to individuals or households depending on their incomes. In 1991 the *Wall Street Journal* reported that the Irish tax and welfare system actually made it more beneficial to earn a low income than a high income. A worker earning 3,000 Irish pounds (approximately $5,000) ends up having more disposable income than one paid 12,000 Irish pounds (about $20,000). If both workers are married men with four children, each living in government housing, the higher income earner ends up with 137 pounds a week. The lower income earner ends up with 138 pounds per week.

For Critical Analysis: *Is there any way to eliminate the disincentive effect that welfare systems have on work effort?* ●

CONCEPTS IN BRIEF

- If poverty is defined in absolute terms, economic growth eventually decreases the number of officially defined poor. If poverty is defined relatively, however, we will never eliminate it.
- In the 1960s the poverty rate among the elderly was double that of younger people. The poverty rate among the elderly has now fallen below the average rate for the rest of the nation.
- New poverty is most identified with single-parent families, minority young people, and the single elderly.
- Major attacks on poverty have been social insurance programs in the form of Social Security, Supplemental Security Income, Aid to Families with Dependent Children, and food stamps.

HEALTH CARE

It may seem strange to be reading about health care in a chapter on the distribution of income and poverty. Yet health care is in fact intimately related to those two topics. For example, sometimes people become poor because they do not have adequate health insurance (or have none at all), fall ill, and deplete all of their wealth on care. Moreover, sometimes individuals remain in certain jobs simply because their employer's health care package seems so good that they are afraid to change jobs and risk not being covered by health care insurance in the process.

It is hard to think of health care as an important topic when you are young and healthy. But consider what might happen when you are no longer covered by your parents' health insurance or by a relatively cheap policy that may be offered at your school. The yearly health insurance fee at most colleges and universities is no more than a few hundred dollars per year. The day you graduate and can no longer purchase that cheap health insurance (or have your parents cover you), you might be faced with a tenfold increase in health insurance costs. A 23-year-old female nonsmoker not covered by an employer's group health insurance might have to pay $3,500 a year in New York City. Clearly there is an incentive for college graduates to find jobs with companies that offer group health insurance that costs much less.

AMERICA'S HEALTH CARE CRISIS

Spending for health care in this country is rapidly approaching $850 billion per year. Expressed as a percentage of total income created in our economy during one year, health care expenditures are estimated to account for 14 percent in 1993. You can see from

YEAR	PERCENTAGE OF TOTAL NATIONAL INCOME
1965	6.0
1970	8.0
1975	8.5
1980	8.8
1985	11.0
1990	13.0
1993	14.0

TABLE 31-5
Percentage of total national income spent on health care in the United States.

Source: U.S. Department of Commerce.

Table 31-5 that in 1965 about 6 percent of annual income was spent on health care, but that percentage has been growing steadily since then. Per capita spending on health care is greater in the United States than anywhere else in the world today. Table 31-6 shows the percentage by which the United States exceeds other countries' per capita health care spending. In 1993, U.S. spending on health care was estimated at around $2,800 per person. According to Table 31-6, Netherlands and Luxembourg spend about half that; Japan, Denmark, Italy, and the United Kingdom spend even less.

Why Have Health Care Costs Risen So Much? There are numerous explanations for why health care costs have risen so much. At least one has to do with changing demographics: The U.S. population is getting older.

The Age–Health Care Expenditure Equation. The top 5 percent of health care users incur over 50 percent of all health costs. The bottom 70 percent of health care users account for only 10 percent of health care expenditures. Not surprisingly, the elderly make up most of the top users of health care services. Nursing home expenditures are made primarily by people older than 70. The use of hospitals is also dominated by the aged.

COUNTRY	PERCENTAGE BY WHICH U.S. EXPENDITURES ARE HIGHER
Canada	43
Switzerland	59
Sweden	62
France	86
Germany	88
Norway	89
Netherlands	97
Luxembourg	100
Austria	114
Finland	115
Australia	119
Japan	132
Belgium	134
Denmark	140
Italy	151
New Zealand	170
United Kingdom	172
Ireland	253
Spain	294

TABLE 31-6 **U.S. spending on health care compared to that in other developed countries.**

Source: Organization for Economic Cooperation and Development. Data are for 1992.

The U.S. population is aging steadily. More than 12 percent of the current 256 million Americans are over 65. It is estimated that by the year 2035, senior citizens will comprise about 22 percent of our population. This aging population stimulates the demand for health care. The elderly consume more than four times the per capita health care services that the rest of the population uses. In short, whatever the demand for health care services is today, it is likely to be considerably higher in the future as the U.S. population ages.

New Technologies.   Another reason that health care costs have risen so dramatically is high technology. A CT (computerized tomography) scanner costs around $1 million. An MRI (magnetic resonance imaging) scanner can cost over $2 million. A PET (positron emission tomography) scanner costs around $4 million. All of these machines became available in the 1990s and are desired throughout the country. Typical fees for procedures using them range from $300 to $500 for a CT scan to as high as $2,000 for a PET scan. The development of new technologies that help physicians and hospitals prolong human life is an ongoing process in an ever advancing industry. New procedures at even higher prices can be expected in the future.

Third-Party Financing.   Currently, government spending on health care constitutes over 40 percent of total health care spending (of which the *federal* government pays about 70 percent). Private insurance accounts for a little over 30 percent of payments for health care. The remainder—about 25 percent—is paid directly by individuals. Medicare and Medicaid are the main sources of hospital and other medical benefits to 33 million Americans, most of whom are over 65. Medicaid—the joint state-federal program—provides long-term health care, particularly for people living in nursing homes. Medicare, Medicaid, and private insurance companies are considered **third parties** in the medical care equation. Caregivers and patients are the two primary parties. When third parties step in to pay for medical care, the quantity demanded for those services increases. For example, when Medicare and Medicaid went into effect in the 1960s, the volume of federal government–reimbursed medical services increased by more than 65 percent.

> **Third parties**
> Outsiders involved in a transaction between two parties; for example, in the relationship between caregivers and patients, fees may be paid by third parties (insurance companies, government).

The availability of third-party payments for costly medical care has generated increases in the availability of hospital beds. Between 1974 and 1993 the number of hospital beds increased by 50 percent. Present occupancy rates are only around 65 percent.

Physicians and Hospitals.   Third-party payments have dominated health care for many decades. Normally when you buy something, you pay for it directly. With health care, you are buying the services of physicians and hospitals, but a third party ends up paying, usually an insurance company or the government. Such third-party payments have allowed physicians to dominate the health care decision-making process for several decades because the people receiving the services—the patients—have not had to worry about the expense. Consequently, payment for physician services rose more rapidly than for other health care category payments in the past decade. Physicians are typically reimbursed on the basis of medical procedures. Most physicians have no financial stake in trying to keep hospital costs down. Indeed, many have an incentive to raise costs. To protect themselves against malpractice lawsuits, they often prescribe excessive testing or elaborate procedures. They are also often paid more by insurance companies if they are involved in more medical procedures per patient.

Such actions are most evident with terminally ill patients. A physician may order a CT scan and other costly procedures for a terminally ill patient. The physician knows that Medicare or some other type of insurance will pay. Then the physician can charge a fee for analyzing the CT scan. It is not surprising that 30 percent of Medicare expenditures are for Americans who are in the last year of their lives.

IS NATIONAL HEALTH INSURANCE THE ANSWER?

Proponents of a national health care system believe that the current system relies too heavily on private insurers. They argue in favor of a Canadian-style system. In Canada the government sets the fees that are paid to each doctor for seeing a patient and prohibits private practice. The Canadian government also imposes a cap on the incomes that any doctor can receive in a given year (about U.S. $400,000). The Canadian federal government provides a specified amount of funding to hospitals, leaving it to them to decide how to allocate the funds. If we were to follow the Canadian model, the average American would receive fewer health services than at present. Hospital stays would be longer, but there would be fewer tests and procedures. Today there is no discernible difference in infant mortality or life expectancy between the United States and Canada. If we switched to using the Canadian health care system model, we would hence not expect to see any change in those two statistics.

There are many political forces aligned against a national health care system. The American Medical Association (AMA) has every incentive to fight it intensively. The United States has a significantly higher ratio of specialists to general practitioners than Canada. In this country, surgeons and other specialists order a large number of all medical procedures. They also experience a lower average workload compared to their counterparts in Canada.

Alternatives to a national health care policy involve some type of national health insurance, perhaps offered only to people who qualify on the basis of low annual income. A number of politicians have offered variations on such a program. The 30 million Americans who currently have no health insurance would certainly benefit. The share of annual national income that goes to health care expenditures would rise, however. Also, the federal budget deficit might increase by another $30 billion to $50 billion (or more) per year to pay for the program. Other analysts do not anticipate that a national health care program would increase the federal government budget deficit. They point out that now that the Cold War is over, federal government expenditures on defense will decrease. The reduction in defense spending could, they contend, easily be reallocated to health care.

EXAMPLE: Government Payment for Medical Services and Gamman's Law

Economist Milton Friedman has proposed what he calls Gamman's law, named after a British physician. His line of reasoning is that a bureaucratic system will always experience increases in expenditures that are matched by a fall in the value of production (output). Friedman looked at health costs before and after Medicare and the number of hospital beds per 1,000 citizens before and after Medicare. He found that the cost of medical care per resident of the United States (adjusted for inflation) rose at the rate of 5 percent per year from 1929 to 1940 while the number of occupied beds increased at only 2.4 percent per year. But from 1946 to the present, hospital costs per occupied bed multiplied seven times. The cost to patients per day (adjusted for inflation) increased 26 times. He argued that the federal government's assumption of financial responsibility for hospital medical care for the elderly and the poor through Medicare and Medicaid provided additional funds that were quickly taken by the medical care industry. Since 1965, when Medicare was instituted, personnel per occupied bed more than tripled. From 1965 to present the cost per patient-day increased more than eight times.

For Critical Analysis: Is it possible that technological advances accounted for the dramatic increase in costs per patient-day since Medicare was instituted in 1965? ●

CONCEPTS IN BRIEF

● America is facing a health care crisis because it is spending an increasing share of national income on health care, yet millions of Americans have no health insurance. The price of medical care has been rising steadily.

● Health care costs have risen because (1) our population has been getting older and the elderly use more health care services; (2) new technologies and medicine cost more; and (3) third-party financing—private and government-sponsored health insurance—reduces the incentive for individuals to reduce their spending on health care services.

● National health insurance has been proposed as an answer to our current problems, but it does little to alter the reasons why health care costs continue to rise.

CONTINUED ⟶

THE PERSISTENT GENDER GAP IN PAY

Concepts Applied: Income differences, discrimination, marginal revenue product, human capital

Although in many instances males and females perform exactly the same tasks, they sometimes are paid different wages.

Income differences exist in this country and elsewhere. They always have and to some extent they always will. Income differences because of gender, similar to other income differences, continue to persist in spite of legislation intended to eliminate them.

In 1972 the United States Congress passed the Equal Pay Act, which was an attempt to remove income differences due to gender. It stipulated that males and females should receive equal pay for equal work. Nonetheless, throughout the 1970s the median earnings of females working full time remained at slightly less than 60 percent of the earnings of males. This chronic gender gap was thought to be a result of discrimination against women in the labor market. But Figure 31-8 shows what has happened since 1980: Women's pay has risen to about 75 percent of men's in a little more than a decade. Professor June O'Neill predicts that women's pay will reach 80 percent of men's by the year 2000.

DOES THE REDUCTION IN THE GENDER GAP MEAN LESS DISCRIMINATION?
If the gender gap in income remained constant for two decades, does the current relatively rapid reduction in that gap mean that there is less discrimination against women? Some economists do not think so. They point out that there are several reasons why the pay gap between men and women is shrinking, none of which have to do with less discrimination against women.

FIGURE 31-8

Women's pay relative to men's.
There has been steady progress since 1980 in terms of women's pay relative to men's. For every dollar a man made on average in 1980, a woman on average made 60 cents. By 1993, for every dollar the average man made, the average woman made 75 cents.
Source: U.S. Department of Labor, Bureau of Labor Statistics.

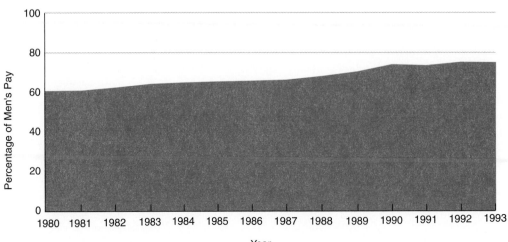

INCREASED PARTICIPATION Whereas from the 1950s through the 1970s only 30 percent of married women with young children were part of the labor force, today more than 60 percent of these women hold jobs. (On average they work 10 percent fewer hours a week than their male counterparts, so the reported income gap is overstated in terms of hourly pay.)

AN INCREASING NUMBER OF PROFESSIONALS Since the late 1970s women have been entering professions at a higher rate than ever before in the history of this country. Today 40 percent of law, medical, business, architecture, and journalism students are females. Even engineering is experiencing a rapid growth in the percentage of women students. In the medical profession, for example, women now constitute about 25 percent of the medical student body, compared to less than 1 percent three decades ago.

EUROPE'S EXPERIENCE Throughout most of Europe (except in Sweden and Norway) the pay gap between men and women is about the same as in the United States. This seems something of an anomaly because the United States had laws protecting the right to equal access to jobs and equal pay well before Sweden and Nor-

way. Economists Lawrence Kahn and Francine Blau examined the problem and came up with one conclusion: Most differences in pay in all countries is a function not of legislation but rather of the training and experience of each worker. Consequently, only to the extent that the skill and training level of females tends to match that of males will pay differences disappear, according to these two economists.

DISCRIMINATION: NOT AN INTENT BUT A RESULT Some theorists argue that the reality of women's need to leave the labor market to have children guarantees discrimination against women in the labor market, at least in result. If female workers are expected to leave their careers and jobs sooner because of family responsibilities, a firm may give preference in hiring to male workers or may pay female workers less.

FOR CRITICAL ANALYSIS

1. Will mandatory unpaid leave for parents when children are born or sick help reduce the pay differential between men and women?
2. Would mandatory or subsidized child care facilities reduce the pay gap between men and women?

CHAPTER SUMMARY

1. We can represent the distribution of income graphically with a Lorenz curve. The extent to which the line is bowed from a straight line shows how unequal the distribution of income is.

2. The distribution of pretax money income in the United States has remained fairly constant since World War II. The lowest fifth of income earners still receive only about 5 percent of total pretax money income, while the top fifth of income earners receive about 40 percent.

3. The distribution of wealth is not the same as the distribution of income. Wealth includes assets such as houses, stocks, and bonds. Though the apparent distribution of wealth seems to be more concentrated at the top, the data used are not very accurate, nor do most summary statistics take account of workers' claims on private and public pensions.

4. Most individuals face a particular age-earnings cycle. Earnings are lowest when starting out to work at age 18 to 24. They gradually rise and peak at about age 45 to 50, then fall until retirement age. They go

up usually because of increased experience, increased training, and longer working hours.

5. The marginal productivity theory of the distribution of income indicates that workers can expect to be paid their marginal revenue product. The marginal physical product is determined largely by talent, education, experience, and training.

6. Discrimination is usually defined as a situation in which a certain group is paid a lower wage than other groups for the same work. It also exists in hiring and promotions.

7. One way to invest in your own human capital is to go to college. The investment usually pays off; the rate of return is somewhere between 8 and 12 percent.

8. A definition of poverty made in relative terms means that there will always be poor in our society because the distribution of income will never be exactly equal.

9. The major income maintenance programs are Social Security (OASDI), Aid to Families with Dependent Children (AFDC), and Supplemental Security Income (SSI).

10. America is facing a health care crisis because it is spending an increasing share of national income on health care, yet millions of citizens have no health insurance. The price of medical care has been rising steadily. Costs have risen because (a) our population has been getting older and the elderly use more health care services, (b) new technologies and medicine cost more, and (c) third-party financing (health insurance) lessens the incentive to reduce spending on health care services.

11. National health insurance has been proposed as a solution, but it would do little to stem rising costs.

DISCUSSION OF PREVIEW POINTS

1. **What is a Lorenz curve, and what does it measure?**
    A Lorenz curve indicates the portion of total money income accounted for by given proportions of a nation's families. It is a measure of income inequality that can be found by plotting the cumulative percentage of money income on the *y* axis and the percentage of families on the *x* axis. Two major problems with using the Lorenz curve to measure income equality are that it typically does not take into account income in kind, such as food stamps and housing aid, and that it does not account for differences in family size (and effort) or age. Adjustments for these would undoubtedly reduce the degree of measured income inequality in the United States.

2. **What has been happening to the distribution of income in the United States?**
    Since World War II the distribution of *money* income has not changed significantly, but the distribution of *total* income—which includes in-kind government transfers—has changed a great deal. Since the 1960s, *total* income inequality has been reduced significantly. The fact that more (total) income equality has been achieved in the United States in recent years is of tremendous importance, yet few people seem to be aware of this fact.

3. **What is the difference between income and wealth?**
    Income is a *flow* concept and as such is measured per unit of time; we usually state that a person's income is X dollars *per year*. Wealth is a *stock* concept; as such it is measured at a given point in time. We usually say that a person's wealth is $200,000 or $1 million. If people save out of a given income, it is possible for their wealth to be rising while their income is constant. Technically, a person's wealth may be defined as the value of his or her assets (human and nonhuman) minus his or her liabilities (wealth being equivalent to net worth) at some point in time.

4. **Why do people earn different incomes?**
    The major theory to account for income differentials in market economies is the marginal productivity theory. This theory says that laborers (as well as other resources) tend to be paid the value of their marginal revenue product. Laborers who are paid less than their MRP will go to other employers who will gladly pay them more (it will be profitable for them to do so); laborers who are being paid more than their MRP may well lose their jobs (at least in the private sector). Thus productivity differences due to age, talent (intelligence, aptitudes, coordination), experience, and training can account for income differences. Of course, imperfect markets can potentially lead to income differences, at a given productivity, due to exploitation and discrimination. Income differences can also be accounted for by differences in nonhuman wealth—individuals can earn income on their property holdings.

PROBLEMS

(Answers to the odd-numbered problems appear at the back of the book.)

31-1.   It is often observed that blacks, on average, earn less than whites. What are some possible reasons for these differences?

31-2.   The accompanying graph shows Lorenz curves for two countries.
   a. Which line indicates perfect equality of income?
   b. Which line indicates the most income inequality?

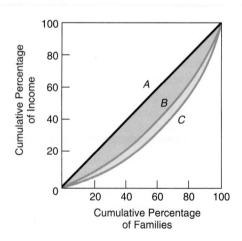

c. One country's "income inequality" is described by line *B*. Suppose that this country's income is to be adjusted for age and other variables such that income on the *y* axis reflects *lifetime* income instead of income in a given year. Would the new, adjusted Lorenz curve move inward toward *A* or outward toward *C*?

31-3. What are the three well-known normative standards of income distribution?

31-4. The graphs in the next column show the Lorenz curves for two countries, A and B. The percentages indicate the area of each triangle.

  a. Find the Gini coefficient for country A.

  b. Find the Gini coefficient for country B.

  c. Which country is more likely to be an aristocracy where most of the people are peasants?

  d. If the income distribution were perfectly equitable, what would the Gini coefficient be?

  e. How would a progressive tax (properly applied) change each of these curves and their Gini coefficients?

31-5. How might a program that truly made every household's income equal affect economy efficiency?

31-6. "Universal access" to health insurance has been a rallying cry for some people who wish to reform our current system. Under universal access, anyone who applies for insurance must be given it at the same rate that everybody else is paying. What might be some of the problems with such a system? (Hint: Would individuals want to join health insurance plans immediately or wait until they are sick with some long-term illness?)

31-7. Outline the incentives underlying Gamman's law. (Hints: What incentives do hospitals face when

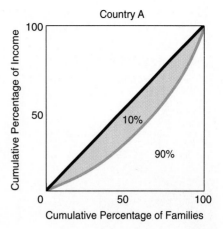

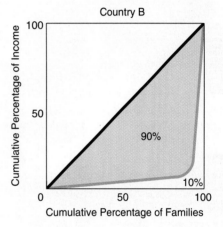

the federal and state governments pay for patients' health care? What incentives do government bureaucrats who work in the health care area face? What incentives do patients face when the government pays for their health care?)

COMPUTER-ASSISTED INSTRUCTION
(Complete problem and answer on disk.)

Many people believe that in the United States there is too much income inequality; that is, the rich earn too much and the poor earn too little. This problem shows that the normal method of measuring income inequality is biased; it overstates true income inequality.

ENVIRONMENTAL ECONOMICS

If you have ever been to San Francisco's Pier 39, you have probably seen a sea lion or two, even hundreds. If you have ever been to the locks that connect Lake Washington in Seattle with the Puget Sound, you have seen even more sea lions. Sea lions were once almost extinct. Today there are close to 200,000 of them, thanks in part to strong wildlife conservation laws that have been vigorously enforced. But not everybody is happy with the proliferation of the sea lion. How could anyone be against this playful, colorful sea mammal? To understand this issue, you must study the topic of environmental economics.

After reading this chapter, you should be able to answer the following questions:

1. What is a negative externality?

2. How can poorly defined property rights create negative externalities?

3. If property rights are poorly defined, *must* negative externalities arise?

4. What is the optimal quantity of pollution?

INTRODUCTION

Some surveys show that as many as 94 percent of all college students are willing to pay more for environmentally sound products. The American public in general appears to be willing to pay more to keep the environment "in good shape." Clearly, the environment is important to all of us. How did we get to a point at which there is so much concern about the environment? Why is there so much pollution? Why don't we use alternative forms of energy that seemingly do not pollute, such as solar energy? Why does the United States, with only 5 percent of the world's population, account for some 25 percent of world resource consumption each year? These are important questions, and they deserve answers. The goal of this chapter is to help you find those answers.

As you might expect, after having read the previous chapters in this textbook, the economic way of thinking about the environment has a lot to do with costs. But of course your view of how to clean up the environment has a lot to do with costs also. Are you willing to give up driving your car in order to have a cleaner environment? Or would you pay $4 for a gallon of gas to help clean up the environment? In a phrase, how much of your current standard of living are you willing to give up to help the environment? The economic way of looking at ecological issues is often viewed as anti-environmental. But this is not so. Economists want to help citizens and policymakers opt for informed policies that have the maximum *net* benefits (benefits minus costs) possible. As you will see, every decision in favor of "the environment" involves a trade-off.

PRIVATE VERSUS SOCIAL COSTS

Human actions often create unwanted side effects—the destruction of our environment is one. Human actions generate pollutants that go into the air and the water. The question that is often asked is, Why can individuals and businesses continue to create pollution without necessarily paying directly for the negative consequences?

Until now we've been dealing with situations in which the costs of an individual's actions are borne directly by the individual. When a business has to pay wages to workers, it knows exactly what its labor costs are. When it has to buy materials or build a plant, it knows quite well what these will cost. An individual who has to pay for car repairs or a theater ticket knows exactly what the cost will be. These costs are what we term **private costs.** Private costs are borne solely by the individuals who incur them. They are *internal* in the sense that the firm or household must explicitly take account of them.

What about a situation in which a business dumps the waste products from its production process into a nearby river or in which an individual litters a public park or beach? Obviously, a cost is involved in these actions. When the firm pollutes the water, people downstream suffer the consequences. They may not want to swim in or drink the polluted water. They may also be unable to catch as many fish as before because of the pollution. In the case of littering, the people who come along after our litterer has cluttered the park or the beach are the ones who bear the costs. The cost of these actions is borne by people other than those who commit the actions. The creator of the cost is not the sole bearer. The costs are not internalized by the individual or firm; they are external. When we add *external* costs to *internal*, or private, costs, we get **social costs.** Pollution problems—indeed, all problems pertaining to the environment—may be viewed as situations in which social costs exceed private costs. Because some economic participants don't pay the full social costs of their actions but rather only the smaller private costs, their actions are socially "unacceptable." In such situations in which there is a divergence between social and private costs, we therefore see "too much" steel production, automobile driving, and beach littering, to pick only a few of the many examples that exist.

▶ **Private costs**
Costs borne solely by the individuals who incur them. Also called *internal costs*.

▶ **Social costs**
Costs borne by society whenever a resource use occurs. Social costs can be measured by adding internal costs to external costs.

THE COSTS OF POLLUTED AIR

Why is the air in cities so polluted from automobile exhaust fumes? When automobile drivers step into their cars, they bear only the private costs of driving. That is, they must pay for the gas, maintenance, depreciation, and insurance on their automobiles. However, they cause an additional cost, that of air pollution, which they are not forced to take account of when they make the decision to drive. Air pollution is a cost because it causes harm to individuals—burning eyes, respiratory ailments, dirtier clothes, cars, and buildings. The air pollution created by automobile exhaust is a cost that individual operators of automobiles do not yet bear directly. The social cost of driving includes all the private costs plus at least the cost of air pollution, which society bears. Decisions made only on the basis of private costs lead to too much automobile driving or, alternatively, to too little money spent on the reduction of automobile pollution for a given amount of driving. Clean air is a scarce resource offered to automobile drivers free of charge. They will use more of it than they would if they had to pay the full social costs.

 INTERNATIONAL EXAMPLE: Paying for the Lack of Incentives in Eastern Europe

From the end of World War II until the beginning of the 1990s, the countries in Eastern Europe to a large extent were governed by the politico-economic systems of socialism and communism. In those systems, few individual policymakers had an incentive to keep the environment clean. Most property was owned by the state. In principle, the state—government bureaucrats—could look at the benefits of pollution abatement for the entire country and act accordingly. But the theory of public choice (Chapter 27) tells us that we can better predict bureaucratic behavior using a model of individual self-interest. That is to say, bureaucrats in Eastern Europe under communism had an incentive to ignore the pollution emitted from factories, for example. Bureaucrats were rewarded for output, not for preserving the environment. The end result was decades of ecological damage. Consider what happened in the following countries:

Bulgaria
- Farmland soils destroyed by metallic pollution
- Black Sea polluted by oil and sewage

Former Czechoslovakia
- 50 percent of the forests damaged or dying
- Over half of the rivers heavily polluted
- Almost half of sewage untreated

Former East Germany
- In many areas a majority of children suffer respiratory diseases
- Groundwater polluted by open uranium waste dumps
- City air pollution 40 times higher than in West Germany

Hungary
- 50 percent of the population breathe air with pollution levels exceeding maximum safety limits
- Arsenic contaminates drinking water in southern half of country

Poland
- Almost all rivers polluted
- In some areas 40 percent of children suffer pollution-related illnesses

Romania

● Black Sea ports poisoned by toxic waste
● Heart disease and infant mortality high because of high pollution levels

Though all of these countries are now "cleaning up their act," the process is expensive. That's why many observers are worried that too many resources spent on pollution clean-up will reduce the rate of economic growth.

For Critical Analysis: Is there necessarily a trade-off between pollution clean-up and the rate of economic growth? ●

EXTERNALITIES

▶ **Externality**
A situation in which a private cost or benefit diverges from a social cost or benefit; a situation in which the costs or benefits of an action are not fully borne by the two parties engaged in exchange or by an individual engaging in a scarce-resource-using activity.

When a private cost differs from a social cost, we term the situation a problem of **externality** because individual decision makers are not paying (internalizing) all the costs. Rather, some of these costs remain external to the decision-making process. Remember that the full cost of using a scarce resource is borne one way or another by all who live in the society. That is, society must pay the full opportunity cost of any activity that uses scarce resources. The individual decision maker is the firm or the customer, and external costs and benefits will not enter into that individual's or firm's decision-making processes.

We might want to view the problem as it is presented in Figure 32-1. Here we have the market demand curve, D, for the product X and the supply curve, S, for product X. The supply curve, S, includes only internal, or private, costs. The intersection of the demand and supply curves as drawn will be at price P_e and quantity Q_e (at E). However, we will assume that the production of good X involves externalities that the private firms did not take into account. Those externalities could be air pollution, water pollution, scenery destruction, or anything of that nature.

We know that the social costs of producing X exceed the private costs. We show this by drawing curve S'. It is above the original supply curve, S, because it includes the full social costs of producing the product. If firms could be made to bear these costs, the price would be P_1, and the quantity Q_1 (at E'). The inclusion of external costs in the decision-making process leads to a higher-priced product and a decline in quantity produced. We

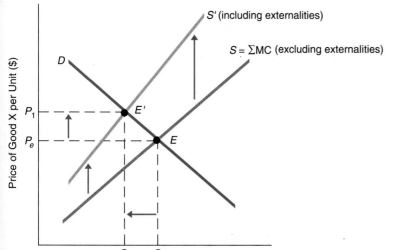

FIGURE 32-1
Reckoning with full social costs.
The supply curve, S, is equal to the horizontal summation (Σ) of the individual marginal cost curves above the respective minimum average variable costs of all the firms producing good X. These individual marginal cost curves include only internal, or private, costs. If the external costs were included and added to the private costs, we would have social costs. The supply curve would shift upward to S'. In the uncorrected situation the equilibrium price would be P_e and the equilibrium quantity would be Q_e. In the corrected situation the equilibrium price would rise to P_1 and the equilibrium quantity would fall to Q_1.

can say, therefore, that in an unrestricted situation in which social costs are not being fully borne by the creators of those costs, the quantity produced is "excessive," and the price is too low because it does not reflect all costs.

CORRECTING FOR EXTERNALITIES

We can see here an easy method for reducing pollution and environmental degradation. Somehow the signals in the economy must be changed so that decision makers will take into account *all* the costs of their actions. In the case of automobile pollution, we might want to devise some method whereby motorists are taxed according to the amount of pollution they cause. In the case of a firm, we might want to devise a system whereby businesses are taxed according to the amount of pollution for which they are responsible. In this manner they would have an incentive to install pollution abatement equipment.

THE POLLUTERS' CHOICE

Facing an additional cost of polluting, firms will be induced to (1) install pollution abatement equipment or otherwise change production techniques so as to reduce the amount of pollution, (2) reduce pollution-causing activity, or (3) simply pay the price to pollute. The relative costs and benefits of each option for each polluter will determine which one or combination will be chosen. Allowing the choice is the efficient way to decide who pollutes and who doesn't. In principle, each polluter faces the full social cost of its actions and makes a production decision accordingly.

IS A UNIFORM TAX APPROPRIATE?

It may not be appropriate to levy a *uniform* tax according to physical quantities of pollution. After all, we're talking about social costs. Such costs are not necessarily the same everywhere in the United States for the same action.

Essentially, we must establish the amount of the *economic damages* rather than the amount of the physical pollution. A polluting electrical plant in New York City will cause much more damage than the same plant in Remote, Montana. There are already innumerable demands on the air in New York City, so the pollution from smokestacks will not be cleansed away naturally. Millions of people will breathe the polluted air and thereby incur the costs of sore throats, sickness, emphysema, and even early death. Buildings will become dirtier faster because of the pollution, as will cars and clothes. A given quantity of pollution will cause more harm in concentrated urban environments than it will in less dense rural environments. If we were to establish some form of taxation to align private costs with social costs and to force people to internalize externalities, we would somehow have to come up with a measure of *economic* costs instead of *physical* quantities. But the tax, in any event, would fall on the private sector and modify private-sector economic agents' behavior. Therefore, because the economic cost for the same physical quantity of pollution would be different in different locations according to population density, the natural formation of mountains and rivers, and so forth, so-called optimal taxes on pollution would vary from location to location. (Nonetheless, a uniform tax might make sense when administrative costs, particularly the cost of ascertaining the actual economic costs, are relatively high.)

CONCEPTS IN BRIEF

- Private costs are explicit costs that are borne directly by consumers and producers when they engage in any resource-using activity.

- Social costs are private costs plus any other costs that are external to the decision maker. For example, the social costs of driving include all the private costs plus any pollution and congestion caused.
- When private costs differ from social costs, externalities exist, because individual decision makers are not internalizing all the costs that society is bearing.
- When social costs exceed private costs, environmental problems may ensue, such as excessive pollution of air and water. These are problems of externalities.

POLLUTION

The term *pollution* is used quite loosely and can refer to a variety of by-products of any activity. Industrial pollution involves mainly air and water but can also include noise and such concepts as aesthetic pollution, as when a landscape is altered in a negative way. For the most part, we will be analyzing the most common forms, air and water pollution.

When asked how much pollution there should be in the economy, many people will respond, "None." But if we ask those same people how much starvation or deprivation of consumer products should exist in the economy, many will again say, "None." Growing and distributing food or producing consumer products creates pollution, however. In effect, therefore, there is no correct answer to how much pollution should be in an economy because when we ask how much pollution there *should* be, we are entering the realm of normative economics. We are asking people to express values. There is no way to disprove somebody's value system scientifically. One way we can approach a discussion of the "correct" amount of pollution would be to set up the same type of marginal analysis we used in our discussion of a firm's employment and output decisions. That is to say, we should pursue measures to reduce pollution only up to the point at which the marginal benefit from further reduction equals the marginal cost of further reduction.

Look at Figure 32-2. On the horizontal axis we show the degree of cleanliness of the air. A vertical line is drawn at 100 percent cleanliness—the air cannot become any cleaner.

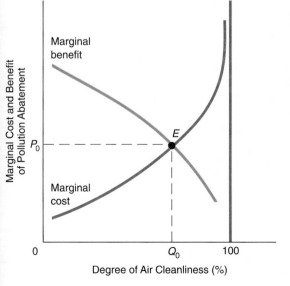

FIGURE 32-2
The optimal quantity of air pollution.
As we attempt to get a greater degree of air cleanliness, the marginal cost rises until even the slightest attempt at increasing air cleanliness leads to a very high marginal cost, as can be seen at the upper right of the graph. Conversely, the marginal benefit curve slopes downward: The more pure air we have, the less we value an additional unit of pure air. Marginal cost and marginal benefit intersect at point E. The optimal degree of air cleanliness is something less than 100 percent at Q_0. The price that we should pay for the last unit of air clean-up is no greater than P_0, for that is where marginal cost equals marginal benefit.

Consider the benefits of obtaining a greater degree of air cleanliness. These benefits are represented by the marginal benefit curve, which slopes downward because of the law of diminishing marginal utility.

When the air is very dirty, the marginal benefit from air that is a little cleaner appears to be relatively high, as shown on the vertical axis. As the air becomes cleaner and cleaner, however, the marginal benefit of a little bit more air cleanliness falls.

Consider the marginal cost of pollution abatement—that is, the marginal cost of obtaining cleaner air. In the 1960s automobiles had no pollution abatement devices. Eliminating only 20 percent of the pollutants emitted by internal-combustion engines entailed a relatively small cost per unit of pollution removed. The cost of eliminating the next 20 percent certainly rose, though. Finally, as we now get to the upper limits of removal of pollutants from the emissions of internal-combustion engines, we find that the elimination of one more percentage point of the amount of pollutants becomes astronomically expensive. To go from 97 percent cleanliness to 98 percent cleanliness involves a marginal cost that is many times greater than going from 10 percent cleanliness to 11 percent cleanliness.

It is realistic, therefore, to draw the marginal cost of pollution abatement as an upward-sloping curve, as shown in Figure 32-2. (The marginal cost curve slopes up because of the law of diminishing returns.)

THE OPTIMAL QUANTITY OF POLLUTION

The **optimal quantity of pollution** is defined as the level of pollution at which the marginal benefit equals the marginal cost of obtaining clean air. This occurs at the intersection of the marginal benefit curve and the marginal cost curve in Figure 32-2, at point E, which is analytically exactly the same as for every other economic activity. If we increased pollution control by one more unit greater than Q_0, the marginal cost of that small increase in the degree of air cleanliness would be greater than the marginal benefit to society.

As is usually the case in economic analysis, the optimal quantity of just about anything occurs when marginal cost equals marginal benefit. That is, the optimal quantity of pollution occurs at the point at which the marginal cost of reducing (or abating) pollution is just equal to the marginal benefit of doing so. The marginal cost of pollution abatement rises as more and more abatement is achieved (as the environment becomes cleaner and cleaner, the *extra* cost of cleansing rises). The state of technology is such that early units of pollution abatement are easily achieved (at low cost), but attaining higher and higher levels of environmental quality becomes progressively more difficult (as the extra cost rises to prohibitive levels). At the same time, the marginal benefits of a cleaner and cleaner environment fall; the marginal benefit of pollution abatement declines as a cleaner and cleaner environment moves from human to nonhuman life-support requirements, to recreation, to beauty, to a perfectly pure environment. The point at which the increasing marginal cost curve of pollution abatement intersects the decreasing marginal benefit curve of pollution abatement defines the (theoretical) optimal quantity of pollution.

Recognizing that the optimal quantity of pollution is not zero becomes easier when we realize that it takes scarce resources to reduce pollution. It follows that a trade-off exists between producing a cleaner environment and producing other goods and services. In that sense nature's ability to cleanse itself is a resource that can be analyzed like any other resource, and a cleaner environment must take its place with other societal wants.

▶ **Optimal quantity of pollution**
The level of pollution for which the marginal benefit of one additional unit of clean air just equals the marginal cost of that additional unit of clean air.

⭐ EXAMPLE: The High Cost of Pollution Clean-up

When the supertanker *Exxon Valdez* struck Bligh Reef in the pristine frigid waters of Prince William Sound in Alaska on March 24, 1989, it caused one of the worst oil spills in North American history—about 11 million gallons gushed into the sea. Within four weeks the slick had grown to 1,600 square miles and threatened wildlife living hundreds of miles to the southwest of the accident site. By the end of the summer of 1989, the Exxon Corporation had already spent $1 billion on clean-up efforts. One of the species that was most affected by the oil spill was the sea otter; 357 oiled sea otters were captured and treated at a cost of $18.3 million. One-third of these died. Of the 222 survivors, almost 200 were returned to the wild; the remainder were moved to aquariums. The International Wildlife Research Foundation described the rescue effort as "the most expensive program to rehabilitate oiled marine animals ever sponsored by a private company or a government agency." If you do the arithmetic, each saved sea otter cost $51,260. This cost includes 13 fishing boats, a helicopter, and the salaries needed to pay 320 staff members at four treatment centers. Veterinarians were on duty 24 hours a day in an emergency ward. Although those who worked on the otter project in Alaska claim that $51,260 per recovered otter was "worth the money," others argue that because otters are so abundant throughout the area (there are many, many thousands), the optimal amount of "pollution clean-up" with respect to saving otters was grossly exceeded.

For Critical Analysis: *How would you determine the optimal quantity of species recovery after a human-caused or natural disaster occurs?* ●

⭐ EXAMPLE: Regulating Hazardous Waste: Superfund

In 1980, Congress passed the Comprehensive Environmental Response, Compensation, and Liability Act (CERCLA), commonly known as Superfund. The basic purpose of Superfund, which was amended in 1986 by the Superfund Amendments and Reauthorization Act, is to regulate the clean-up of leaking hazardous waste disposal sites. A special federal fund was created for that purpose. Superfund provides that when a release or a threatened release from a site occurs, the Environmental Protection Agency (EPA), an independent federal agency, can clean up the site and recover the cost of the clean-up from (1) the person who generated the wastes disposed of at the site, (2) the person who transported the wastes to the site, (3) the person who owned or operated the site at the time of the disposal, or (4) the current owner or operator. Liability is usually assessed on all who might have been responsible—for example, a person who generated only a fraction of the hazardous waste disposed of at the site may nevertheless be liable for all of the clean-up costs.

After 12 years, only 84 of the 1,245 designated sites on Superfund's high-priority list have been cleaned up. The cost was $11.1 billion. Critics of the Superfund program point out that only one-tenth of the money spent by insurance companies to settle Superfund claims is used to clean up hazardous materials. According to the Rand Corporation in Santa Monica, California, the remaining 90 percent goes to legal fees and related costs. Other critics point out that the potential benefits of such expensive toxic waste clean-ups are not worth the cost. The EPA believes that 1,000 cancer cases result each year from exposure to hazardous waste sites. Through Superfund it is allocating $1.75 billion for clean-up. That comes out to $1.75 million per predicted cancer case, under the assumption, of course, that a significant number of the hazardous waste sites are actually cleaned up. Compare the costs and benefits of the National Cancer Institute's 1993 budget for breast cancer research of $133 million, when there are an estimated 176,000 breast cancer cases diagnosed each year, or $755 per diagnosed case.

New EPA studies suggest that other environmental problems pose a greater risk than hazardous wastes. For example, indoor air pollution may cause more cancer deaths per year than those caused by uncleaned Superfund sites.

For Critical Analysis: *If you were advising the EPA about how much it should spend on each designated hazardous waste disposal site, what would you recommend?* ●

CONCEPTS IN BRIEF

- The marginal cost of cleaning up the environment rises as we get closer to 100 percent cleanliness. Indeed, it rises at an increasing rate.
- The marginal benefit of environmental cleanliness falls as we have more of it.
- The optimal quantity of pollution is the quantity at which the marginal cost of clean-up equals the marginal benefit of clean-up.
- Pollution abatement is a trade-off. We trade off goods and services for cleaner air and water; and vice versa.

COMMON PROPERTY

In most cases, you do not have **private property rights** to the air surrounding you, nor does anyone else. Air is a **common property** resource. Therein lies the crux of the problem. When no one owns a particular resource, people do not have any incentive (conscience aside) to consider their particular misuse of that resource. If one person decides not to pollute the air, there normally will be no significant effect on the total level of pollution. If one person decides not to pollute the ocean, there will still be approximately the same amount of ocean pollution—provided, of course, that the individual was previously responsible for only a small part of the total amount of ocean pollution.

Basically we have pollution where we have poorly defined private property rights, as in air and common bodies of water. We do not, for example, have a visual pollution problem in people's attics. That is their own property, which they choose to keep as clean as they want—given their preferences for cleanliness as weighed against the costs of keeping the attic neat and tidy.

Where private property rights exist, individuals have legal recourse to any damages sustained through the misuse of their property. When private property rights are well defined, the use of property—that is, the use of resources—will generally involve contracting between the owners of those resources. If you own land, you might contract with another person who wants to use your land for raising cows. The contract would most likely be written in the form of a lease agreement.

> ▶ **Private property rights**
> Exclusive rights of ownership that allow the use, transfer, and exchange of property.
>
> ▶ **Common property**
> Property that is owned by everyone and therefore by no one. Air and water are examples of common property resources.

⭐ EXAMPLE: Fish as Common Property

An individual who fishes for a living will fish until the marginal benefit equals the marginal cost. That individual considers only his or her actual private costs when computing marginal costs. These include the opportunity cost of investing in equipment, depreciation, and supplies, as well as the individual's opportunity cost of time. What the private fisher does not take into account is the potential cost to society if common property fishing grounds are overfished. The result has been called by some people the "tragedy of the commons." The tragedy occurs because of the overuse of the common property resource. In the case of fish there is strong evidence that the tragedy of the commons has occurred. For example, haddock have virtually disappeared from New England's coastal waters. Fishers in this area report average catches of 50 percent of what they were 10 years ago. These same individuals report that there are virtually no more large flounder or cod. Two researchers with the National Marine Fisheries Service have estimated that overfishing in the New England area may be as high as 70 percent. Biologist Stephen Murawski and economist Steven Edwards believe that if the fishing effort were reduced in that area by 70 percent, the fishing stock size would increase by at least four times. They argue that there should be a high-priced fishing fee to reduce the quantity of fishing effort in that area.

For Critical Analysis: Assume that it is obvious to everyone who studies the numbers that Murawski and Edwards are correct. Why don't individuals who fish for a living voluntarily opt for a system that would increase the size of the fish stock in New England? ●

VOLUNTARY AGREEMENTS AND TRANSACTION COSTS

Is it possible for externalities to be internalized via voluntary agreement? Take a simple example. You live in a house with a nice view of a lake. The family living below you plants a tree. The tree grows so tall that it eventually starts to cut off your view. In most cities, no one has property rights to views; therefore, you cannot usually go to court to obtain relief. You do have the option of contracting with your neighbor, however.

Voluntary Agreements: Contracting.
You have the option of paying your neighbors (contracting) to cut back the tree. You could start out with an offer of a small amount and keep going up until your neighbors agree or until you reach your limit. Your limit will equal the value you place on having an unobstructed view of the lake. Your neighbors will be willing if the payment is at least equal to the reduction in their intrinsic property value due to a stunted tree. Your offering the payment makes your neighbors aware of the social cost of their actions. The social cost here is equal to the care of the tree plus the cost suffered by you from an impeded view of the lake.

In essence, then, your offering your neighbors money indicates to them that there is an opportunity cost to their actions. If they don't comply, they forfeit the money that you are offering them. The point here is that *opportunity cost always exists with whoever has property rights.* Therefore, we would expect under some circumstances that voluntary contracting will occur to internalize externalities.[1] The question is, When will voluntary agreements occur?

Transaction Costs.
One major condition for the outcome just outlined is that the **transaction costs**—all costs associated with making and enforcing agreements—must be low relative to the expected benefits of reaching an agreement. If we expand our example to a much larger one such as air pollution, the transaction costs of numerous homeowners trying to reach agreements with the individuals and companies that create the pollution are relatively high. Consequently, we don't expect voluntary contracting to be an effective way to internalize the externality of air pollution.

▶ **Transaction costs**
All costs associated with making, reaching, and enforcing agreements.

CHANGING PROPERTY RIGHTS

In considering the problem of property rights, we can approach it by assuming that initially in a society, many property rights and many resources are not defined. But this situation does not cause a problem so long as no one cares to use the resources for which there are no property rights or as long as enough of these resources are available that people can have as much as they want at a zero price. Only when and if a use is found for a resource or the supply of a resource is inadequate at a zero price does a problem develop. The problem requires that something be done about deciding property rights. If not, the resource will be wasted and possibly even destroyed. Property rights can be assigned to individuals

---

[1]This analysis is known as the *Coase theorem*, named after its originator, Ronald Coase, who demonstrated that negative or positive externalities do not necessarily require government intervention in situations in which property rights are defined and enforceable transaction costs are relatively low.

who will then assert control; or they may be assigned to government, which can maintain and preserve the resource, charge for its use, or implement some other rationing device. What we have seen with common property such as air and water is that governments have indeed attempted to take over the control of those resources so that they cannot be wasted or destroyed.

Another way of viewing the pollution problem is to argue that property rights are "sacred" and that there are property rights in every resource that exists. We can then say that each individual does not have the right to act on anything that is not his or her property. Hence no individual has the right to pollute because that amounts to using property that the individual does not specifically own.

Clearly, we must fill the gap between private costs and true social costs in situations in which we have to make up somehow for the fact that property rights are not well defined or assigned. There are three ways to fill this gap: taxation, subsidization, and regulation. Government is involved in all three. Unfortunately, government does not have perfect information and may not pick the appropriate tax, subsidy, or type of regulation. We also have to consider cases in which taxes are hard to enforce or subsidies are difficult to give out to "worthy" recipients. In such cases, outright prohibition of the polluting activity may be the optimal solution to a particular pollution problem. For example, if it is difficult to monitor the level of a particular type of pollution that even in small quantities can cause environmental damage, outright prohibition of such pollution may be the only alternative.

ARE THERE ALTERNATIVES TO POLLUTION-CAUSING RESOURCE USE?

Some people cannot understand why, if pollution is bad, we continue to use pollution-causing resources such as coal and oil to generate electricity. Why don't we forgo the use of such polluting resources and opt for one that apparently is pollution free, such as solar energy? Contrary to some people's beliefs, there is no nationwide or worldwide conspiracy to prevent us from shifting to solar power. The plain fact is that the cost of generating solar power in most circumstances is relatively much higher than generating that same power through conventional means. We do not yet have the technology that allows us the luxury of driving solar-powered cars. Moreover, with current technology, the solar panels necessary to generate the electricity for the average town would cover massive sections of the countryside, and the manufacturing of those solar panels would itself generate pollution.

THE MARKET FOR POLLUTION RIGHTS AND THE CLEAN AIR ACT

For many years various levels of government have charged individuals and companies for the right to pollute. For a fee in many municipalities, you can dispose of garbage in the city dump. In essence, then, governments have created pollution rights. After one of the first federal clean air acts was passed in 1963, the EPA formalized this policy by approving an **offset policy** that required a company wishing to build a plant in an already polluted area to work out a corresponding reduction in pollution at some existing plant. Such a "workout" usually involved the buying and selling of so-called pollution rights. This concept was actually put into law in 1990 when Congress passed an amendment to the Clean Air Act of 1970. The 1990 amendment included an important new Title IV, which allows for a market-based approach for controlling the emissions of sulfur dioxide from electrical power plants and other emitting sources. (Sulfur dioxide is a chemical that is thought to be the primary cause of acid rain. Such rain may harm forests, lakes, and other natural resources, particularly in the northeastern United States and Canada.) Each sulfur-emitting source is allowed to emit a fixed number of tons of sulfur dioxide each year. For

▶ **Offset policy**
A policy requiring one company wishing to build a plant that would pollute to work out an offsetting reduction in pollution at some other plant in a specific geographic area.

TABLE 32-1
Estimated trading value of various pollution permits.
This table shows the estimated trading value of credits that allow emissions of various pollutants. (Trading of credits is currently permitted only for sulfur dioxide.)

Sources: McIlvaine Co.; *Business Week*, July 13, 1992, p. 134F.

POLLUTANT	TRADING VALUE (PER TON)
Sulfur dioxide	$400
Manganese	25 million
Mercury	250 million
Nickel	250 million
Cadmium	250 million
Beryllium	250 million
Arsenic	2.5 billion
Chromium	2.5 billion

example, a generating unit in the Midwest might be allowed to emit 2.6 million tons of sulfur dioxide each year. Once the sulfur dioxide emission allowances are assigned to each pollution-generating facility, the allowances can be traded among companies rather than used for emissions. Also, allowances can be traded between years using a concept called *emission banking*, in which allowances can be kept as a reserve for future use.

Proponents of this system point out that rather than using mandatory pollution abatement technology or abandoning production completely, polluting firms have the flexibility to reduce pollution any way they want—using alternative fuels, using alternative time schedules, and so on. In the meantime, firms can either sell or buy emission allowances in the open market. Table 32-1 shows the estimated trading value of credits allowing emission of various pollutants. Tradable sulfur dioxide pollution permits have already started public trading on the Chicago Board of Trade. It is interesting to note that groups interested in reducing the total amount of pollution can purchase tradable pollution permits from the Chicago Board of Trade and never resell them. This drives the price of tradable permits up, thereby providing an incentive to firms to reduce pollution more than they otherwise would.

 EXAMPLE: **The Tennessee Valley Authority Buys Pollution Credits**

The first publicly disclosed deal involving the sale and purchase of pollution credits occurred between two electric utilities hundreds of miles apart. Specifically, Wisconsin Power and Light found out that it would emit fewer pollutants than allowed under the Clean Air Act of 1990. In May 1992 it therefore sold to the Tennessee Valley Authority (TVA) the rights to 10,000 tons of sulfur dioxide emissions. It also sold to Pittsburgh's Duquesne Light the right to emit 25 tons of sulfur dioxide. The price of the TVA deal was not disclosed, but the *New York Times* estimated that $2.5 to $3 million changed hands. Less than a year later, the formal process of selling pollution rights, often called "smog futures," took place on the Chicago Board of Trade on March 30, 1993. A total of 150,010 air pollution allowances granted by the Environmental Protection Agency were auctioned off. The government obtained about $21 million from successful bidders. The right to emit one ton of sulfur dioxide sold for between $122 and $450. Included among the successful bidders were, obviously, electric utilities, but also public interest groups, brokerage firms, and private investors.

For Critical Analysis: *How can private individuals now reduce the amount of pollution emitted by electrical utilities?* ●

CONCEPTS IN BRIEF
- A common property resource is one that no one owns—or, otherwise stated, that everyone owns. **(Continued)**

- Common property exists when property rights are indefinite or nonexistent.
- When no property rights exist, pollution occurs because no one individual or firm has a sufficient economic incentive to care for the common property in question, be it air, water, or scenery.
- Private costs will not equal social costs when common property is at issue, unless only a few individuals are involved and they are able to contract among themselves.
- Alternatives to pollution-causing resource use exist. Consider solar energy. We do not use solar energy because it is too expensive relative to conventional alternatives and the creation of solar panels itself would generate pollution.
- Pursuant to Title IV of the 1990 amendments to the Clean Air Act of 1970, there are tradable pollution permits for sulfur dioxide. These permits are traded on the Chicago Board of Trade.

RECYCLING AND PRECYCLING

As part of the overall ecology movement, there has been a major push to save scarce resources via recycling. **Recycling** involves reusing paper products, plastics, glass, and metals rather than putting them into solid waste dumps. Many cities have instituted mandatory recycling programs.

▶ **Recycling**
The reuse of raw materials derived from manufactured products.

The benefits of recycling are straightforward. Fewer *natural* resources are used. But currently some economists argue that recycling does not necessarily save *total* resources. For example, recycling paper products may not necessarily save trees, according to A. Clark Wiseman, an economist for Resources for the Future in Washington, D.C. He argues that an increase in paper recycling will eventually lead to a reduction in the demand for virgin paper and thus for trees. Because most trees are planted specifically to produce paper, a reduction in the demand for trees will mean that certain land now used to grow trees will be put to other uses. The end result may be smaller rather than larger forests. Nevertheless, every ton of recycled paper saves 17 trees and 3 cubic yards of landfill space.

RECYCLING'S INVISIBLE COSTS

The recycling of paper can also pollute. Used paper has ink on it that has to be removed during the recycling process. According the National Wildlife Federation, the product of 100 tons of deinked (bleached) fiber generates 40 tons of sludge. This sludge has to be disposed of, usually in a landfill. A lot of recycled paper companies, however, are beginning to produce unbleached paper. In general, recycling does create waste that has to be disposed of.

There is also an issue involved in the use of resources. Recycling requires human effort. The labor resources involved in recycling are often many times more costly than the potential savings in scarce resources not used. That means that net resource use, counting all resources, may sometimes be greater with recycling than without it.

LANDFILLS

One of the arguments in favor of recycling is to avoid a solid waste "crisis." Some people believe that we are running out of solid waste dump sites in the United States. This is perhaps true in and near major cities, and indeed the most populated areas of the country might ultimately benefit from recycling programs. In the rest of the United States, however, the data do not seem to indicate that we are running out of solid waste landfill sites. Throughout the United States, the disposal price per ton of city garbage has actually fallen. These prices, of course, vary for the 180 million tons of trash generated each year. In San Jose, California, it costs $10 a ton to dump, whereas in Morris County, New Jersey, it costs $131 a ton.

Currently, municipalities burn about 16 percent of their solid waste and recycle a few percentage points more. The amount of solid waste dumped in landfills estimated for 1995 is 125 million tons. By the year 2000 it is expected to drop to 100 million tons even as the total trash output rises above 200 million tons. In all likelihood, partly because of recycling efforts, the cost of solid waste disposal will continue to drop as the supply curve of solid waste disposal shifts out faster than the demand curve. Thus in some instances the use of recycling in order to reduce solid waste disposal ends up costing society more resources because simply throwing waste into a landfill may be less costly.

SHOULD WE SAVE SCARCE RESOURCES?

Periodically, the call for recycling focuses on the necessity of saving scarce resources because "we are running out." There is little evidence to back up this claim because virtually every natural resource has fallen in price (corrected for inflation) over the past several decades. In 1980 economist Julian Simon made a $1,000 bet with well-known environmentalist Paul Erlich. Simon bet $200 per resource that any five natural resources that Erlich picked would decline in price (corrected for inflation) by the end of the 1980s. Simon won. (When Simon asked Erlich to renew the bet for $20,000 for the 1990s, Erlich declined.) During the 1980s the price of virtually every natural resource fell (corrected for inflation), and so did the price of every agricultural commodity. The same was true for every forest product. Though few people remember the dire predictions in the 1970s, many noneconomists throughout the world argued at that time that the world's oil reserves were vanishing. If this were true, the pretax, inflation-corrected price of gasoline would not be the same today as it was in the late 1940s (which it is).

In spite of predictions in the early 1980s by World Watch Institute president Lester Brown, real food prices did not rise. Indeed, the real price of food fell by more than 30 percent for the major agricultural commodities during the 1980s. A casual knowledge of supply and demand tells you that, considering that demand for food did not decrease, supply must have increased faster than demand.

With respect to the forests, at least in the United States and Western Europe, there are more forests today than there were 100 years ago. In this country the major problems of deforestation seem to be on land owned by the United States Forest Service for which private timber companies are paid almost $1 billion a year in subsidies to cut down trees.

IS "PRECYCLING" THE ANSWER?

One way to avoid so much waste is to "precycle." This new term is usually used to mean making products in such a way that they are not overpackaged or can be refilled. Detergent companies, for example, have found it advantageous for themselves, the consumer, and the environment to package and sell more concentrated forms of detergent. The packages are smaller, the use of resources in packaging is less, and waste requiring disposal is less than with older formulations of detergent. Concentrated juices also represent a form of precycling. In short, any approach to packaging products in a more concentrated and less wasteful form can be considered precycling and may help the environment.

INTERNATIONAL EXAMPLE: **The Trade-offs Between Energy and Birds**

In an attempt to find clean and cheaper alternatives to electricity-generating facilities now in use, a number of countries have turned to wind farms. One of those is Spain. Sevillana de Electricidad S.A., with the help of the European Community, started building Europe's biggest wind farm in 1992. By 1993 there were over 200 wind turbines, one-tenth of the planned 2,000. They are all located on a scrub-covered hillside in Tarifa, Spain. So far so good, but not so good for storks and kestrels, migratory birds that make a round-trip flight between Europe and Africa every year. The scrub-covered hills around Tarifa are where the birds normally stop to rest during their long migration. Bird experts in Europe are certain that 2,000 wind turbines in this area will disrupt these birds' migration to the point at which they might become extinct.

Trade-offs exist, then, and it is not clear what the correct answer is. The people who live around Tarifa believe that there is enough wind to generate electricity for 100,000 people. But at what cost?

For Critical Analysis: What type of legislation would have to be passed to force electric companies throughout Europe (or in the United States, for that matter) to take acount of any negative effects on migratory birds? ●

CONCEPTS IN BRIEF

- Recycling involves reusing paper, glass, and other materials rather than putting them into solid waste dumps. Recycling does have a cost both in the resources used for recycling and in the pollution created during recycling, such as the sludge from deinking paper for reuse.
- Landfills are an alternative to recycling. Expansion of these solid waste disposal sites is outpacing demand increases.
- Resources may not be getting scarcer. The inflation-corrected price of most resources has been falling for decades. The real price of food, for example, fell by more than 30 percent during the 1980s.

MORE SEA LIONS AND FEWER FISH
Concept Applied: Trade-offs

There is no one simple way to "help the earth." Many policy decisions to help one aspect of the environment involve trade-offs.

The locks between Lake Washington and the Puget Sound in Seattle were built in 1915. Sea lions were unknown there until 1984. Now, between December and April, you can spot at least 60 sea lions at a time at these locks. Why are they there only during these months? Because that is the time during which steelhead trout migrate across the fish ladder upstream for spawning. The sea lions love to eat steelhead trout and have big appetites. Area steelhead fishers would like to shoot the sea lions but cannot because the federal Marine Mammal Protection Act of 1972 protects them. This act makes it illegal to harass, harm, or kill most sea mammals in United States waters.

TRADE-OFFS
The trade-off here between protecting sea lions and promoting the migration of steelhead trout is straightforward. The more sea lions are protected, the more steelhead trout they will eat, and the fewer fish there will be for sports fishers and commercial fishers such as the Muckleshoot tribe. Currently, sea lions eat about 60 percent of the steelhead run each year. Washington wildlife managers have tried to truck the sea lions back to the Channel Islands off the coast of California. They succeeded in trucking them, but it took the sea lions only a month to get back to the Seattle locks.

OTHER TRADE-OFFS INVOLVED IN SPECIES PRESERVATION
Wildlife managers throughout the United States are discovering that species preservation often involves a trade-off between two different species: in favor of the one that is regulated and against the natural food supply of that protected species. In Canada there is a hunting ban on harp seals. The result has been the almost total elimination of cod. Bison and grizzly bears are protected. They overgraze sanctuaries. Mountain goats are protected, and at Olympic National Park in Washington State they are eating and destroying rare and endangered plants. (These goats were originally brought into the Olympic Mountains in the 1920s by local hunters who did not want to travel all the way to Alaska to hunt them.)

Another protected animal, the white-tailed deer, is proliferating throughout the United States. These animals are threatening almost 70 species of rare plants, according to the National Parks Association. Wild horses have been protected since 1971. Their numbers have grown to the point where there is not enough vegetation to support them. Rabbits in Nevada are dying due to overgrazed land.

THE ECONOMICS OF SPECIES PRESERVATION
Unfortunately for people who wish to preserve species, there are often trade-offs, as we have just seen, between preserving one species at the expense of another. As with all environmental problems, there is no one right answer. Economists using economic analysis are not antienvironmental simply because they point out the costs of different programs compared to the benefits. Even the most hardened economist is not against species preservation. That is not the issue. Rather, the problem is determining the optimal amount of species preservation. Today we are living with .2 percent of all of the species that have ever existed since the earth began. What percentage of the existing species should be preserved, and how much are we willing to pay for this preservation? Once we have decided how much we are willing to pay for species preservation, then we should choose methods that have maximum effectiveness per dollar spent.

FOR CRITICAL ANALYSIS
1. How might you place a value on the cost of the extinction of one or more species?
2. If you could obtain all the relevant data, how, as a policymaker, would you determine the optimal amount of species protection?

CHAPTER SUMMARY

1. In some situations there are social costs that do not equal private costs. That is, there are costs to society that exceed the cost to the individual. These costs may include air and water pollution, for which private individuals do not have to pay. Society, however, does bear the costs of these externalities. Few individuals or firms voluntarily consider social costs.

2. One way to analyze the problem of pollution is to look at it as an externality situation. Individual decision makers do not take account of the negative externalities they impose on the rest of society, In such a situation they produce "too much" pollution and "too many" polluting goods.

3. It might be possible to ameliorate the situation by imposing a tax on polluters. The tax, however, should be dependent on the extent of the economic damages created rather than on the physical quantity of pollution. This tax will therefore be different for the same level of physical pollution in different parts of the country because the economic damage differs, depending on location, population density, and other factors.

4. The optimal quantity of pollution is the quantity at which the marginal cost of clean-up equals the marginal benefit of clean-up. Pollution abatement is a trade-off. We trade off goods and services for cleaner air and water, and vice versa.

5. Another way of looking at the externality problem is to realize that it involves the lack of definite property rights. We are talking about common property resources such as air and water. No one owns them, and therefore no one takes account of the long-run pernicious effects of excessive pollution.

6. There are alternatives to pollution-causing resource use, for example, solar energy. We do not use solar energy because it is too expensive relative to conventional alternatives and the creation of solar panels itself would generate pollution.

7. Title IV of the 1990 amendments to the Clean Air Act of 1970 created tradable pollution permits for sulfur dioxide. These permits are traded on the Chicago Board of Trade.

8. Recycling involves reusing paper, glass, and other materials rather than putting them into solid waste dumps. Recycling does have a cost both in the resources used for recycling and in the pollution created during recycling. Landfills are an alternative to recycling. These solid waste disposal sites are being expanded faster than the demand for them.

9. Resources may not be getting scarcer. The inflation-corrected price of most resources has been falling for decades.

DISCUSSION OF PREVIEW POINTS

1. What is a negative externality?

A negative externality exists if the social costs exceed the private costs of some activity; if third parties outside a two-party transaction are adversely (negatively) affected, negative externalities are said to exist. Pollution is an example of a negative externality; for example, transactions between automobile producers and users impose costs (pollution) on third parties (people who neither produce nor consume the autos).

2. How can poorly defined property rights create negative externalities?

Nature's ability to cleanse itself can be considered a scarce resource, and as such, it behooves society to use this resource efficiently. However, if everyone owns these resources, in effect, *no one* owns them. Consequently, people will use these resources (as dumping grounds for consumer and producer waste) as though they were free. Of course, excessive use of these resources eventually impairs nature's ability to

cleanse itself; enter the concept of pollution (a collection of unwanted matter). Now the marginal cost to *private* polluters is still zero (or nearly zero), whereas the cost to society of using this (now scarce) resource is positive. In short, third parties are adversely affected when pollution results from the production and consumption of goods that lead to waste, which creates pollution.

3. If property rights are poorly defined, *must* negative externalities arise?

No. If contracting costs are small, and enforcement is relatively easy, voluntary contracts will arise and the full opportunity costs of actions will be accounted for. That is, when transaction costs are small, private and social costs will converge, as the parties affected contract with the parties creating the additional costs, and externalities will disappear. What is interesting is that regardless of how property rights are assigned, resources will be allocated in the same way. Of course, the specific assignment of property rights does affect the distribution of wealth, even though resource allocation is independent of the specific property right assignment; what is important for efficient resource allocation is that *someone* have property rights. It should be noted that, unfortunately, the main externalities, such as air and water pollution, are very complex, contracting costs are very high, and enforcement is difficult. As a consequence, free market solutions are not likely to emerge—indeed, they have not.

4. What is the optimal amount of pollution?

It is obvious that the optimal quantity of pollution is not zero. At 100 percent cleanliness, the marginal cost

of pollution abatement would greatly exceed the marginal benefit. We would have too much pollution abatement; we would be using resources in a socially suboptimal manner. That means that the resources being used in pollution abatement would have a higher value elsewhere in society.

We live in a world of scarce resources. If the value we receive from spending one more dollar on cleaning up the environment is less than the value we would receive by spending that dollar on something else—such as cancer research—we are not allocating our resources efficiently if we still choose to spend that dollar on pollution abatement.

PROBLEMS

(Answers to the odd-numbered problems appear at the back of the book.)

32-1. Construct a typical supply and demand graph. Show the initial equilibrium price and quantity. Assume that the good causes negative externalities to third parties (persons not involved in the transactions). Revise the graph to compensate for that fact. How does the revised situation compare with the original?

32-2. Construct a second supply and demand graph for any product. Show the equilibrium price and quantity. Assuming that the good generates external benefits, modify the diagram to allow for them. Show the new equilibrium price and quantity. How does the revised situation compare with the original?

32-3. Suppose that polluters are to be charged by governmental agencies for the privilege of polluting.
   a. How should the price be set?
   b. Which firms will treat waste, and which will pay to pollute?
   c. Is it possible that some firms will be forced to close down because they now have to pay to pollute? Why might this result be good?
   d. If producers are charged to pollute, they will pass this cost on to buyers in the form of higher prices. Why might this be good?

32-4. Why has the free market not developed contractual arrangements to eliminate excess air pollution in major U.S. cities?

32-5. What is the problem with common property resources?

32-6. The accompanying graph shows external costs arising from the production of good Y.

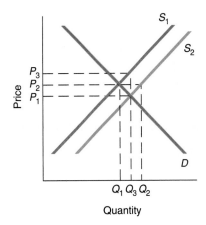

   a. Which curve includes only the private costs of producing good Y?
   b. Which supply curve includes the external costs of producing good Y?
   c. How much of good Y is produced and at what price?
   d. Who bears the cost of producing the amount of good Y in part (c)?
   e. If external costs are included, how much of good Y should be produced, and at what price should it be sold?

32-7.   The table shows the costs and benefits of removing air pollution.

ANNUAL UNITS OF POLLUTION	ANNUAL AIR POLLUTION DAMAGE	ANNUAL TOTAL COSTS OF AIR POLLUTION REDUCTION
0	0	410
1	30	260
2	70	160
3	150	80
4	270	20
5	430	0

a. Find the marginal benefits of pollution reduction.
b. Find the marginal costs of pollution reduction.
c. Assume that society is currently allowing 5 units of air pollution per year. If pollution is reduced to 3 units, what is the net gain or loss to society?
d. Suppose that all air pollution is eliminated. What would be the net gain or loss to society?
e. If air pollution were regulated efficiently, how many units of air pollution would be allowed each year?

32-8.   Examine this marginal cost and marginal benefit schedule for air cleanliness:

QUANTITY (%)	MARGINAL BENEFIT	MARGINAL COST
0	$50,000	$ 5,000
20	45,000	10,000
40	35,000	15,000
60	25,000	25,000
80	10,000	40,000
100	0	∞

a. Graph the marginal benefit and marginal cost curves.
b. What is the optimal degree of air cleanliness?
c. How much will the optimal amount of air cleanliness cost?
d. What is the optimal amount of air pollution?
e. Would we want a level of zero pollution? Why or why not?

32-9.   Explain why it is possible to have too little pollution. What might government do to cause private individuals and businesses to generate too little pollution?

COMPUTER-ASSISTED INSTRUCTION
(Complete problem and answer on disk.)

Environmental problems almost always involve externalities. You are asked to examine some of them in this exercise.

part

8

GLOBAL ECONOMICS

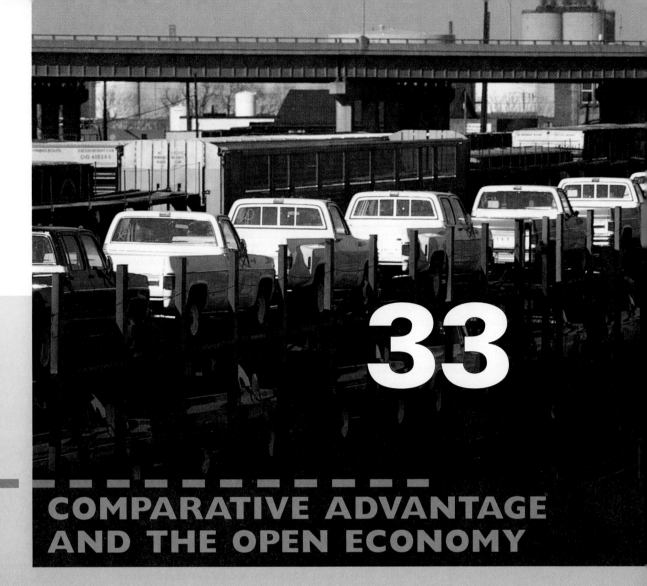

33

COMPARATIVE ADVANTAGE AND THE OPEN ECONOMY

Every time you buy something not made in America, you know that certain American workers might get hurt. For example, if you buy a Japanese car instead of an American one, that means less demand for American automobile workers. If you buy clothes produced with foreign-made textiles, that means less demand for American textile workers. If you buy foreign-made glassware, that creates less demand for American workers in that industry. But it is possible to save American jobs in specific industries. Restrictions can and have been put on the quantity of certain imports into the United States. The important question is not whether American jobs can be saved but rather at what price? To be able to address this issue, you must first understand how the open economy works.

After reading this chapter, you should be able to answer the following questions:

1. How is an import demand curve derived?

2. How is an export supply curve derived?

3. How is international equilibrium for a commodity established?

4. What are some arguments against free trade?

INTRODUCTION

A few years ago the Boeing Company in Seattle, Washington, announced that it would build a 777, a plane larger than its 218-passenger 767 and smaller than its 419-passenger 747. Boeing seems like the archtypical American manufacturing company that has been highly successful in a globally competitive market. One of Boeing's successes has been its ability to sell its product in other countries. Fully 49 percent of the 7,171 delivered planes it has built since 1916 have been sold to foreign governments or companies. But the model 777 will not be built 100 percent by Americans. International suppliers will provide rudders, elevators, outboard flaps, wing-tip assemblies, main landing gears, engines, nose landing gears, and nose landing-gear doors. Japanese suppliers, in particular, will provide cargo doors, fuselage panels, the center wing section, main landing-gear doors, and passenger doors. The complicated Boeing 777 is a jigsaw puzzle in which the pieces come from all over the world.

And how about an American car? The Ford Crown Victoria has shock absorbers from Japan; front-wheel spindles from England; electronic engine controls from Spain; electronic antilock brake system controls from Germany; and seats, windshields, instrument panels, and fuel tanks from Mexico.

If you buy an American-made IBM computer, you will find that many of its parts are made abroad. If you drink American-brand orange juice, such as Minute Maid (owned by Coca-Cola) or Tropicana (owned by Beatrice Foods), you will find in tiny print on the frozen orange juice that it is made from concentrate not only from the United States but also from Brazil and Mexico.

International trade affects you whether you know it or not. It is almost impossible to tell these days how much it affects you because it is so widespread. We are truly entering an age of global economy. Learning about international trade is simply learning about everyday life.

THE SIZE OF INTERNATIONAL TRADE

An examination of panel (a) of Figure 33-1 reveals that among the industrialized nations of the world, the United States ranks low in terms of the percentage of its national output (GDP) devoted to imports. Panel (b) indicates that international trade as a part of the American economy has almost tripled since 1955. This is a reflection of a dramatic increase in international trade globally. Today the international trade sector still represents a relatively small part of the total American consumer market. Global competition, though, is an important engine driving the American economy. Competition from abroad forces American manufacturers to improve efficiency and the quality of their products faster than they might otherwise. The same is true elsewhere. Competition from American producers forces other countries to improve their efficiency and quality. We export more than just American-made goods. We also export a certain way of doing things. When the first McDonald's opened up in Moscow and in the People's Republic of China, they were not just exposing Russians and Chinese to Quarter Pounders. Those business ventures were also exposing them to a way of being treated as consumers. Whether or not you believe that fast-food restaurants are going to add to the well-being of the Russians or the Chinese, if domestic businesses attempt to imitate the rapid and pleasant service given to McDonald's customers, their way of doing business will improve, and customers will perhaps become better off.

International trade is a two-way street. It involves imports and exports, and there is a direct relationship between the two.

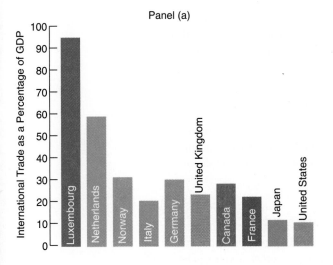

Panel (a)

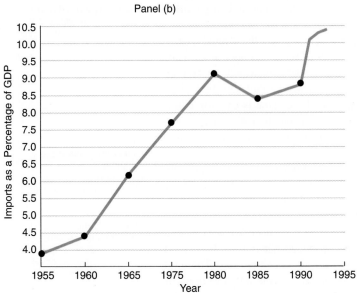

Panel (b)

FIGURE 33-1

Imports as a percentage of GDP.

Panel (a) shows international trade represented by imports as a percentage of the gross domestic product of various countries. The United States is low at around 10.4 percent, compared to other industrialized nations. Panel (b) shows that the United States' proportion of imports has increased since 1955.

Source: International Monetary Fund.

THE RELATIONSHIP BETWEEN IMPORTS AND EXPORTS

Figure 33-1 shows imports as a percentage of GDP. But imports are only half the story. The rest of the world doesn't send goods to the United States out of goodwill. The basic proposition in understanding all of international trade is this:

In the long run, imports are paid for by exports.

We have to modify this rule by adding that, in the short run, imports can also be paid for by the sale (or export) of real and financial assets, such as land, stocks, and bonds, or through an extension of credit from other countries.

The reason that imports are ultimately paid for by exports is that foreigners want something in exchange for the goods that are shipped to the United States. For the most part, they want goods made in the United States. From this truism comes a remarkable corollary:

Any restriction of imports ultimately reduces exports.

This is a shocking revelation to many people who want to restrict foreign competition to protect domestic jobs. Although it is possible to protect certain U.S. jobs by restricting foreign competition, it is virtually impossible to make *everyone* better off by imposing import restrictions. Why? Because ultimately such restrictions lead to a reduction in employment in the export industries of the nation.

COMPARATIVE AND ABSOLUTE ADVANTAGE

The reason there are gains from trade lies in one of the most fundamental principles of economics: A nation gains by doing what it can do best *relative to other nations*. The United States benefits by specializing in endeavors in which it has a **comparative advantage.**

To demonstrate this concept, let's take the example of France and the United States. In Table 33-1 we show the comparative costs of production of wine and beer in terms of worker-days. This is a simple two-country, two-commodity world in which we assume that labor is the only factor of production. As you can see from the table, in the United States it takes one worker-day to produce 1 liter of wine and the same is true for 1 liter of beer. In France it takes one worker-day for 1 liter of wine but two worker-days for 1 liter of beer. In this sense, Americans appear as good at producing wine as the French. And they have an **absolute advantage** in producing beer.

Trade will still take place, however, which may seem paradoxical. How can trade take place if we can produce both goods at least as cheaply as the French can? Why don't we just produce both ourselves? To understand why, let's assume first that there are no trade and no specialization and that the work force in each country consists of 200 workers. These 200 workers are divided equally in the production of wine and beer. We see in Table 33-2 that 100 liters of wine and 100 liters of beer are produced per day in the United States. In France, 100 liters of wine and 50 liters of beer are produced per day. The total daily world production in our two-country world is 200 liters of wine and 150 liters of beer.

Now the countries specialize. What can France produce more cheaply? Look at the comparative costs of production expressed in worker-days in Table 33-1. What is the cost of producing 1 liter more of wine? One worker-day. What is the cost of producing 1 liter more of beer? Two worker-days. We can say, then, that in France the opportunity cost of producing wine is less than that of producing beer. France will specialize in the activity that has the lower opportunity cost. In other words, France will specialize in its comparative advantage, which is the production of wine.

According to Table 33-3, after specialization, the United States produces 200 liters of beer and France produces 200 liters of wine. Notice that the total world production per

▶ **Comparative advantage**
The ability to produce at lower cost compared to other producers, whether they are countries, firms, or individuals.

▶ **Absolute advantage**
The ability to produce more output from given inputs of resources than others can. For example, America may have an absolute advantage in the production of agricultural goods in the sense that, per unit of labor, we can produce more bushels of wheat than any other country.

PRODUCT	UNITED STATES (WORKER-DAYS)	FRANCE (WORKER-DAYS)
Wine (1 liter)	1	1
Beer (1 liter)	1	2

TABLE 33-1 Comparative costs of production.

TABLE 33-2 Daily world output before specialization.
It is assumed that 200 workers are available in each country.

| PRODUCT | UNITED STATES | | FRANCE | | WORLD OUTPUT (LITERS) |
	WORKERS	OUTPUT (LITERS)	WORKERS	OUTPUT (LITERS)	
Wine	100	100	100	100	200
Beer	100	100	100	50	150

day has gone up from 200 liters of wine and 150 liters of beer to 200 liters of wine and 200 liters of beer per day. This was done without any increased use of resources. The gain, 50 "free" liters of beer, results from a more efficient allocation of resources worldwide. World output is greater when countries specialize in their comparative advantage and then engage in foreign trade. Another way of looking at this is to consider the choice between two ways of producing a good. Obviously, each country would choose the less costly production process. One way of "producing" a good is to import it, so that if in fact the imported good is cheaper than the domestically produced good, we will "produce" it by importing it. Not everybody, of course, is better off when free trade occurs. In our example, U.S. wine makers and French beer makers are worse off because those two industries domestically have disappeared.

TABLE 33-3 Daily world output after specialization.
It is assumed that 200 workers are available in each country.

| PRODUCT | UNITED STATES | | FRANCE | | WORLD OUTPUT (LITERS) |
	WORKERS	OUTPUT (LITERS)	WORKERS	OUTPUT (LITERS)	
Wine	—	—	200	200	200
Beer	200	200	—	—	200

Some people are worried that the United States (or any country, for that matter) might someday "run out of exports" because of overaggressive foreign competition. The analysis of comparative advantage tells us the contrary. No matter how much other countries compete for our business, the United States (or any other country) will always have a comparative advantage in something that it can export. In 10 or 20 years, that something may not be what we export today, but it will be exportable nonetheless because we will have a comparative advantage in producing it.

INTRA-INDUSTRY INTERNATIONAL TRADE

The foregoing analysis seems to rely on the differences among countries, particularly in their natural resource bases. Also, the examples typically given to demonstrate comparative advantage involve goods in different industries. In reality, however, much of world trade is **intra-industry trade.** For example, in the United States over 60 percent of world trade is intra-industry; in France it exceeds 80 percent. Intra-industry trade involves Americans exporting automobiles to Europe while at the same time importing automobiles. It involves Americans buying Fords, Chryslers, and Chevrolets as well as BMWs, Peugeots, and Mercedeses. The Germans and French also buy Fords, Chryslers, and Chevrolets as well as Peugeots, BMWs, and Mercedeses.

The traditional international trade theory of comparative advantage doesn't seem to explain how intra-industry trade could be so prevalent. To understand why it is, we must understand the microeconomic concepts of economies of scale and differentiated products.

▶ **Intra-industry trade**
International trade involving goods in the same industry, such as automobiles.

ECONOMIES OF SCALE AND DIFFERENTIATED PRODUCTS

Consumers have widely varying tastes. The consumers of automobiles, for example, have numerous preferences. They are not satisfied with a homogeneous product but rather prefer *differentiated products*. Let's say that it is profitable for the United States to produce 20 different models of automobiles. Another country, Germany, can also produce these 20 different models. If the United States decides, however, to specialize in the production of only 10 models, leaving Germany to specialize in the production of the other 10, the firms in each country will be able to expand their scale of operations and benefit from greater division of labor and the use of faster and more specialized machinery, which will lead to *economies of scale*. The result is often lower unit costs in each country. Consumers, though, do not have to sacrifice variety, thanks to international trade. The 10 models that are made abroad can be imported to the United States, and the 10 models made domestically can be exported so that consumers in both countries can choose from a total of 20 models. The result will be the exchange of similar, *but not identical*, automobiles back and forth.

CONCEPTS IN BRIEF

- Countries can be better off materially if they specialize in producing goods for which they have a comparative advantage.
- It is important to distinguish between absolute and comparative advantage; the former refers to the ability to produce a unit of output with fewer physical units of input; the latter refers to producing output that has the lowest opportunity cost for a nation.
- Different nations will always have different comparative advantages because of differing opportunity costs due to different resource mixes.
- Much international trade involves like goods; this is called intra-industry trade. It occurs because of investment in specialized resources that create a cost advantage in the production of a particular type of product within an industry.

DEMAND AND SUPPLY OF IMPORTS AND EXPORTS

Let's explore the mechanism that establishes the level of trade between two nations. We will assume that the world consists of only the two nations under study. Therefore, we are considering total world trade in our analysis. First we will need to develop a demand schedule for imports and a supply schedule for exports. In the examples that follow, transportation costs are ignored, merely to keep things simple.

IMPORTS

We will try to calculate graphically how many liters of wine Americans will wish to import every year. We do this by deriving the **excess demand schedule** for wine. Panel (a) of Figure 33-2 shows the usual supply and demand curves for wine in the United States. We draw parallel price lines starting at the equilibrium price and going down. At the equilibrium price of $2 per constant-quality liter of wine, there is no excess demand or excess supply for U.S. wine. In panel (b) we again show that at the price of $2, *excess* quantity demanded is zero. If $2 were the world price of wine, there would be no net imports of wine. (In our two-country model we're assuming that the world is comprised of France

▶ **Excess demand schedule** The difference between the quantities of goods supplied domestically and the quantities demanded at prices below the domestic equilibrium price.

FIGURE 33-2
Derivation of an import demand schedule for the United States.
In panel (a) we show the U.S. domestic supply (S) and demand (D) schedules for wine. The equilibrium price is $2 per liter. At $2 per liter there will be no excess quantity of wine demanded. Therefore, the quantity of imports demanded will be zero. At a price of $1 per liter, however, there will be an excess quantity of wine demanded. The excess quantity demanded is represented by the distance AB. We transfer AB to panel (b) to show the excess quantity of wine demanded at a price of $1. The curve D* is the excess demand curve for wine—in other words, it is the U.S. demand for imports of French wine. If the world price were $1 per liter, we would demand quantity Q_1 of imported wine. The excess demand curve for wine slopes downward, starting at the domestic equilibrium price of wine—in this case, $2 per liter.

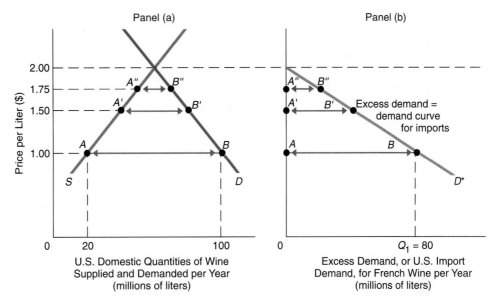

and the United States). In other words, at $2 per liter, no wine trade would take place between these two countries.

But what about prices lower than $2 per liter? At a price of $1 there is an excess quantity demanded for wine in the United States. This is represented in panel (a) by the quantity (horizontal distance) between the domestic supply curve and the domestic demand curve at that price. We take that distance AB, and transfer it, at that price level, to panel (b), where we draw the excess quantity demanded for wine at a price of $1 (the amount of wine represented by AB). AB is the same in both graphs. If we would continue doing this for all the prices below $2, we would come up with an *excess demand schedule for wine*, which is the same thing as the demand schedule for imports. We import wine because at prices below $2, U.S. wine producers are unwilling to supply the total quantity demanded by American consumers at those lower prices. Whatever the world price is, we can find out how much the United States will import. If the world price is established at $1, for example, we will bring in imports equal to Q_1. As we would expect, the excess demand schedule for imports slopes downward, like the regular demand schedule. The lower the world price of wine, the more imports we will buy.

EXPORTS

What about the possibility of the United States exporting wine? Europeans are, in fact, starting to drink more American wines. The situation is depicted graphically in Figure 33-3,

FIGURE 33-3

Derivation of an export supply schedule for the United States.
The domestic demand and supply of wine are shown in panel (a). At an equilibrium
price of $2, no excess quantity of domestic wine is demanded, nor is an excess quan-
tity supplied. In panel (b) we show the excess supply of wine curve. At prices higher
than $2, an excess quantity of wine is supplied. The excess quantity supplied is repre-
sented by the three distances FG, $F'G'$, and $F''G''$. We transfer these distances from
panel (a) to panel (b) to derive the amount of excess quantity supplied that can be used
for export purposes. In this manner we derive the supply schedule of exports, S^*. It
slopes upward, like most supply curves. If the world price of wine were $3, we would
export quantity Q_2 to other countries.

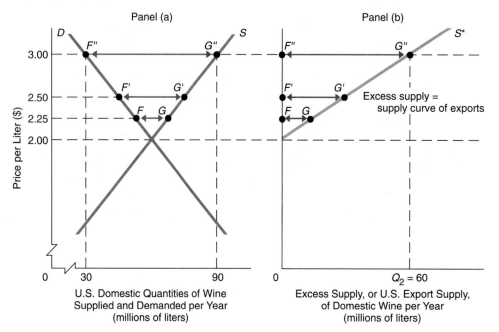

Panel (a)

Panel (b)

U.S. Domestic Quantities of Wine
Supplied and Demanded per Year
(millions of liters)

Excess Supply, or U.S. Export Supply,
of Domestic Wine per Year
(millions of liters)

where we derive the **excess supply schedule.** Let's look at prices above $2 per liter. At
a price of $3, the excess quantity supplied of wine is equal to the amount represented in
panel (a) by the distance between the demand curve and the supply curve ($F''G''$). The excess supply curve is shown in panel (b). The supply curve of exports slopes upward, like
most supply curves. At a price of $2, there are no net exports from the United States. At
any price above $2, however, there will be exports. The amount of these exports is rep-
resented by the length of the three arrows. Thus if the world price rises above $2, the
United States will become a net exporter of wine. The higher the world price, the more
wine we will export. The lower the world price, the less wine we will export. Below a
price of $2, we will start importing. The **zero trade price,** then, is $2. At a world price
of $2, we will not engage in world trade in wine. (Note that the world price is established
by the interaction of total world demand and world supply.)

▶ **Excess supply schedule**
The difference between the
quantities of a product supplied domestically and the
quantities demanded at
prices above domestic equilibrium prices.

▶ **Zero trade price**
The price of an excess demand and supply schedule
at which there is no foreign
trade in a good; the price at
which the domestic demand
and supply schedules intersect.

THE QUANTITY OF TRADE IN A FOREIGN COUNTRY

We can draw the graph in Figure 33-4 for France, our trading partner, in a similar manner. We must establish a common set of measurements for the price of wine. Let's do this

FIGURE 33-4
Derivation of excess demand and supply of wine for France.
Panel (a) shows France's domestic demand and supply curves for wine. The domestic equilibrium price of wine in France, at an exchange rate of 5 francs to the dollar, translates into $1 per liter. At $1 per liter France will have neither an excess quantity of wine demanded nor an excess quantity supplied. At higher prices it will have an excess quantity supplied—that is, it will *export* wine. At lower prices it will have an excess quantity demanded—it will *import* wine. We have drawn France's excess supply (*S**) and excess demand (*D**) curves in panel (b).

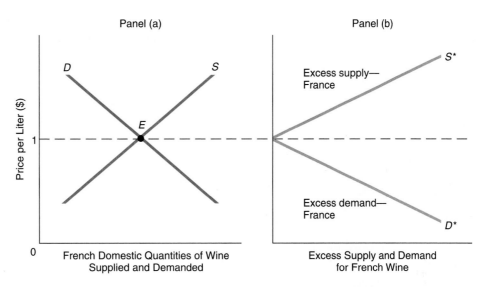

Panel (a)

Panel (b)

French Domestic Quantities of Wine
Supplied and Demanded

Excess Supply and Demand
for French Wine

in terms of dollars and liters, and let's say that the exchange rate is 5 francs to the dollar. (We will examine the foreign exchange market in Chapter 34.) We place the excess demand schedule for imports and excess supply schedule for exports on the same graph. Figure 33-4 shows a standard supply and demand schedule for French wine in terms of dollars per liter. The equilibrium price of French wine is established at $1 per liter. At a world price of $1 per liter, the French will neither import nor export wine. At prices below $1, the French will import wine; at prices above $1, they will export wine. We see in panel (b) of Figure 33-4 that the excess supply schedule of French wine slopes upward, starting at $1 per liter. The French excess demand schedule for imports of wine slopes downward, starting at $1 per liter.

INTERNATIONAL EQUILIBRIUM

We can see the quantity of international trade that will be transacted by putting the French and the American export and import schedules on one graph. The zero trade price for wine in America was established at $2 per liter, whereas in France it was established at $1 per liter. We see in Figure 33-5 on the next page that the excess supply schedule of exports in France intersects the excess demand schedule for imports in the United States at point *E*, with an equilibrium world price of wine of $1.50 per liter and an equilibrium quantity of trade of 10 million liters per year. Here we see how much trade takes place and under what terms. The amount is determined by the excess demand and supply schedules in each country and the point at which they intersect. If the tables were turned and America's equilibrium price were below France's equilibrium price, Americans would be exporting wine and the French would be importing it.

In this example, the free trade international equilibrium price will not fall below $1 per liter, nor will it rise above $2 per liter. Moreover, you should realize that the equilibrium price in this example turns out to be $1.50 because of the particular linear way in which the curves are drawn. If we were to treat the example differently, we might come out with a somewhat different equilibrium price—though it would still lie between $1 and $2 per liter, given the domestic equilibrium price for each country in our example.

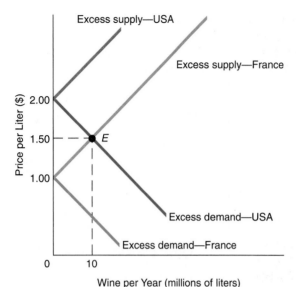

FIGURE 33-5
International equilibrium.
We plot excess demand and supply curves for both France and the United States. France's excess supply curve intersects the U.S. excess demand curve at point *E*, which establishes an equilibrium world price of wine (when the world is *only* the United States and France). That world price is $1.50, which will be the price of wine everywhere. America will import 10 million liters of wine at that price, and France will export 10 million liters of wine.

CONCEPTS IN BRIEF

- International trade represents a small part of the GDP of the United States but a large part of the GDP of many countries, such as Belgium and the Netherlands.
- To derive the domestic demand curve for imports, we construct an excess demand schedule showing the difference between domestic demand and domestic supply at prices below the domestic equilibrium price.
- The demand curve for imports slopes downward.
- We derive the excess supply schedule by looking at the difference between domestic demand and domestic supply at prices above the equilibrium price. This supply schedule of exports slopes upward.
- In a two-country world, international trade equilibrium occurs where one country's excess demand schedule intersects the other's excess supply schedule; the quantity of imports demanded equals the quantity of exports supplied.

ARGUMENTS AGAINST FREE TRADE

There are numerous arguments against free trade. They mainly point out the costs of trade; they do not consider the benefits or the possible alternatives for reducing the costs of free trade while still reaping benefits.

THE INFANT INDUSTRY ARGUMENT

A nation may feel that if a particular industry were allowed to develop domestically, it could eventually become efficient enough to compete effectively in the world market. Therefore, if some restrictions were placed on imports, domestic producers would be given the time needed to develop their efficiency to the point where they would be able to compete in the domestic market without any restrictions on imports. In graphic terminology, we would expect that if the protected industry truly does experience improvements in pro-

▶ **Infant industry argument**
The contention that tariffs should be imposed to protect from import competition an industry that is trying to get started. Presumably, after the industry becomes technologically efficient, the tariff can be lifted.

duction techniques or technological breakthroughs toward greater efficiency in the future, the supply curve will shift outward to the right so that the domestic industry can produce larger quantities of each and every price. This **infant industry argument** has some merit in the short run and has been used to protect a number of industries in their infancy around the world. Such a policy can be abused, however. Often the protective import-restricting arrangements remain even after the infant has matured. If other countries can still produce more cheaply, the people who benefit from this type of situation are obviously the stockholders (and specialized factors of production that will earn economic rents) in the industry that is still being protected from world competition. The people who lose out are the consumers, who must pay a price higher than the world price for the product in question. In any event, it is very difficult to know beforehand which industries will eventually survive. In other words, we cannot predict very well the specific infant industries that should be protected. Note that when we talk about which industry "should be" protected, we are in the realm of normative economics. We are making a value judgment, a statement of what *ought to be*.

COUNTERING FOREIGN SUBSIDIES AND DUMPING

Another strong argument against unrestricted foreign trade has to do with countering other nations' subsidies to their own producers. When a foreign government subsidizes its producers, our producers claim that they cannot compete fairly with these subsidized foreigners. To the extent that such subsidies fluctuate, it can be argued that unrestricted free trade will seriously disrupt domestic producers. They will not know when foreign governments are going to subsidize their own producers and when they are not. Our competing industries will be expanding and contracting too frequently.

▶ **Dumping**
Selling a good or a service abroad at a price below its cost of production or below the price charged in the home market.

The phenomenon called **dumping** is also used as an argument against unrestricted trade. Dumping occurs when a producer sells its products abroad at a price below its cost of production or below the price that is charged in the home market. Although cries of dumping against foreign producers are often heard, they typically occur only when the foreign nation is in the throes of a serious recession. The foreign producer does not want to slow down its production at home. Because it anticipates an end to the recession and doesn't want to hold large inventories, it dumps its products abroad at prices below its costs. This does, in fact, disrupt international trade. It also creates instability in domestic production and therefore may impair commercial well-being at home.

⭐ EXAMPLE: Competition or Dumping?

In the steel business, either you can sell high-quality steel at a relatively competitive price and make profits, or you can take advantage of the 1974 antidumping law to make sure that foreign producers cannot compete in your market. A few years ago the least efficient U.S. steelmakers filed 84 antidumping complaints against 21 foreign countries. Their complaints took up 2 million pages. The International Trade Commission accepted 72 of the 84 complaints for review. If the steel industry is like others, 97 percent of these complaints are likely to be upheld. The U.S. steelmakers took a year and a half to formulate their cases, but foreign companies that were accused of dumping had only 45 days to file their response. A typical foreign company was Belgium's Sidmar Steel, which had to hire 15 employees to compile data for 20,000 transactions with 1,000 different customers over a six-month period to satisfy our government's request for data. The average cost for these foreign firms of defending an antidumping case is $500,000 to $1 million.

Other countries are not standing idly by. The United States was the target of more antidumping actions in the 1980s than any other country except Japan. Indeed, United States steel producers faced antidumping complaints in Mexico during the same year that they were complaining about Mexico dumping here.

For Critical Analysis: *Under what circumstances would a foreign producer want repeatedly to sell its product to Americans at a lower cost than it sells it domestically? (Hint: How does the price elasticity of demand enter into this argument?)* ●

PROTECTING AMERICAN JOBS

Perhaps the argument used most often against free trade is that unrestrained competition from other countries will eliminate American jobs because other countries have lower-cost labor than we do. (Less restrictive environmental standards in other countries might also lower their costs relative to ours.) This is a compelling argument, particularly for politicians from areas that might be threatened by foreign competition. For example, a representative from an area with shoe factories would certainly be upset about the possibility of constituents losing their jobs because of competition from lower-priced shoe manufacturers in Brazil and Italy. But of course this argument against free trade is equally applicable to trade between the states.

You will read more about attempts at protecting American jobs in the *Issues and Applications* section at the end of this chapter.

PROTECTING THE NATION'S ECONOMIC SECURITY

Prior to the end of the Cold War, from the 1950s through the 1980s, supporters of protectionism in the form of high tariffs and low quotas on foreign products could in some instances claim that national security was at issue. Lobbyists for a particular industry might have convinced Congress to pass protective legislation because that industry was producing vital parts for the military. Now that the Cold War is (more or less) over, industries are lining up for government protection against foreign competition by contending that their survival is vital to the nation's *economic* security. Oil companies and the makers of computer chip housings are trying to convince the federal government that their industries are crucial to the U.S. economy and are consequently entitled to protection on national economic security grounds. Commercial aircraft producers are advancing the same argument.

The problem with such arguments, however, is that there is no definition of "national economic security." Moreover, even if there were a definition, there is no objective way to measure when national economic security is being threatened simply because of aggressive foreign competition.

CONCEPTS IN BRIEF

● The infant industry argument against free trade contends that new industries should be protected against world competition so that they can become technologically efficient in the long run.

● Unrestricted foreign trade may allow foreign governments to subsidize exports or foreign producers to engage in dumping—selling products in other countries below their cost of production. To the extent that foreign export subsidies and dumping create more instability in domestic production, they may impair our well-being.

● A recent argument in favor of protectionism and against free trade involves protecting national economic security. However, it is difficult to define what this means and why or how it should be protected.

WAYS TO RESTRICT FOREIGN TRADE

There are many ways in which international trade can be stopped or at least stifled. These include quotas and taxes (the latter are usually called *tariffs* when applied to internationally traded items). Let's talk first about quotas.

QUOTAS

▶ **Quota system**
A government-imposed restriction on the quantity of a specific good that another country is allowed to sell in the United States. In other words, quotas are restrictions on imports. These restrictions are usually applied to a specific country or countries.

In the **quota system,** countries are restricted to a certain amount of trade. An import quota specifies the maximum amount of a commodity that may be imported during a specified period of time. For example, the government might not allow more than 50 million barrels of foreign crude oil to enter the United States in a particular year. In the extreme case, quotas are zero. This is obviously true for illegal drugs, but it is sometimes true for certain food items.

⭐ **EXAMPLE: Higher-priced Peanut Butter, Thanks to Quotas**

When the peanut crop fell short in 1991, peanut processors petitioned the president to reduce the allowable imports of foreign peanuts into the country. The administration decided to allow only 100 million pounds. As a consequence, the price of peanut butter went up from $3 to $4 a jar. For a nation that consumes about 1.5 billion pounds of peanuts a year, that is quite a jolt. You can see why the price of peanut butter went up by looking at Figure 33-6. The world price of peanuts is established by the world supply and the world demand. Because the United States is a small part of the total world market for peanuts, it can purchase all of the peanuts it wants at the world price. Its supply curve without any restrictions is a horizontal line at price P_W. Its excess demand curve, or import demand curve, is shown as D^*. In the absence of any restrictions it will import quantity Q_I of peanuts per year. If an import quota is imposed at Q_Q, the price will rise to P_Q. The higher price of peanuts benefits domestic peanut producers, who sell their peanuts at price P_Q rather than P_W. Processors have to pay more for peanuts, though, so consumers end up paying more for peanut butter.

For Critical Analysis: *Is it possible to argue that import quotas benefit consumers?* ●

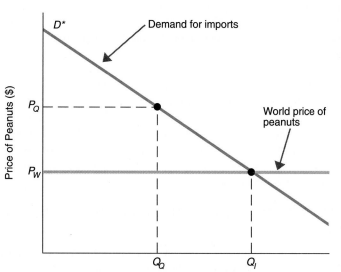

FIGURE 33-6
The effect of peanut quotas.
If the demand curve for imports is shown as D^*, with no quotas, peanut producers pay P_W and import Q_I. If a quota is instituted by the government at Q_Q, the price rises to P_Q. Peanut processors pay a higher price, and so peanut butter becomes more expensive.

Quantity of Peanut Imports per Year

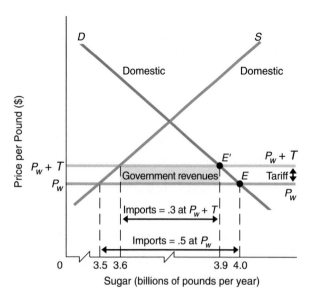

FIGURE 33-7
An import tariff.
Equilibrium is established at *E*, where the quantity demanded is 4 billion pounds per year. The quantity supplied domestically is 3.5 billion pounds. The difference is imports, or 500 million pounds per year. Now the government puts a tariff, *T*, on every pound of sugar that enters the United States from abroad. Americans must now pay $P_W + T$. This shifts the effective horizontal world supply curve up to the higher line, $P_W + T$. At this price the domestic quantity demanded is at *E'*, or 3.9 billion pounds per year. The domestic quantity supplied increases to 3.6 billion pounds per year. Imports fall from 500 million to 300 million pounds per year. The government collects taxes equal to *T* times the new quantity of imports, 300 million pounds.

TARIFFS

We can use our graphic analysis to analyze the effect of a **tariff,** a tax imposed by one country only on goods imported from other countries. The nature of a protective tariff is such that no similar tax is applied to identical goods produced domestically. A U.S.-imposed tariff on an import raises the price of a product, both foreign and domestic, to United States residents. Let's assume that the tariff is 10 percent of the price of sugar entering this country. In Figure 33-7 we show the domestic supply and demand schedules for sugar, with the world price of P_W. Now we add a tariff. The tariff, *T*, is equal to the difference between the world price, P_W, and the horizontal line above it, $P_W + T$. Domestic demanders of sugar must now pay the world price plus the tariff. They cannot get sugar any cheaper because everyone must pay the tariff. On domestically produced and sold sugar there is no import tariff. That means that the U.S. Treasury does not collect taxes on domestically produced sugar; the producers get to keep all of the revenues. They are able to charge the world price plus the tariff, $P_W + T$, because no consumers have the possibility of obtaining sugar at the world price, P_W. Now that the price goes up to $P_W + T$, we move up the domestic supply curve and find that domestic producers are willing to increase their output of sugar from 3.5 billion to 3.6 billion pounds per year. But consumers will demand a lower quantity at the higher price. They will reduce the quantity demanded from 4 billion to 3.9 billion pounds per year. We see, then, that the level of imports will decrease from 500 million to 300 million pounds per year. This decrease in imports is similar to the one we discussed with a quota system; however, the big difference is that with the quota system, no government revenues (taxes) are collected. With the tariff system, the government keeps the tariff, *T*, times the quantity of imports (300 million pounds per year). These revenues can be used to reduce other taxes, to increase government expenditures, or to reduce federal government budget deficits.

▶ **Tariff**
A tax on imported goods.

INTERNATIONAL EXAMPLE: **A Case History of Tariffs: Rubber Thread Imports**

A major supplier of rubber thread in the world is Malaysia, the country that produces most of the world's latex, which accounts for 50 percent of the cost of producing rubber thread. As of 1992 there were total tariffs of 29 percent on rubber thread imports. A large portion of these tariffs was passed on to consumers of socks, underwear, and bungee cords—products that use lots of rubber thread. Apparently not content with a 29 percent tariff, two small Falls River, Massachusetts, companies—Globe Manufacturing and North American Rubber Thread—petitioned the U.S. International Trade Commission to add another 25 percent tariff. Their argument was that they needed to be able to charge higher prices for rubber thread in order to buy new equipment. They argued that if they could not charge a higher price, they would have to lay off workers. The total number of workers in the two plants was 150. Left out of these two companies' arguments were the secondary effects of an increase in rubber thread tariffs. Total employment in the companies that use rubber thread in the United States exceeds 3,000 workers. An increase in the price of rubber thread within the United States can easily put those workers' jobs at risk because of foreign competition. Manufacturers of underwear and socks outside the United States that can obtain rubber thread imports at world prices already pose serious competition to their American counterparts. An increase in tariffs on rubber thread would make such world competition even more formidable.

For Critical Analysis: If the number of workers involved in thread making in the United States is only 150, compared to the potential of 3,000 who are involved in making products that use rubber thread, why might the two companies requesting higher tariffs on rubber thread nonetheless succeed in obtaining them? (Hint: Review Chapter 27.) ●

Tariffs in the United States.
In Figure 33-8 on the next page we see that tariffs on all imported goods have varied widely. The highest tariff rates in the twentieth century occurred with the passage of the Smoot-Hawley Tariff in 1930. Some economists contend that this tariff actually worsened the impact of the Great Depression of the 1930s.

Current Tariff Laws.
The Trade Expansion Act of 1962 gave the president the authority to reduce tariffs by up to 50 percent. Subsequently, tariffs were reduced by about 35 percent. In 1974 the Trade Reform Act allowed the president to reduce tariffs further. In 1984 the Trade and Tariff Act resulted in the lowest tariff rates ever. All such trade agreement obligations of the United States are carried out under the auspices of the **General Agreement on Tariffs and Trade (GATT),** which was signed in 1947. Member nations of GATT account for more than 85 percent of world trade. As you can see in Figure 33-8 there have been a number of "rounds" of negotiations to reduce tariffs since the early 1960s. The latest round, which started in 1987, was called the Uruguay Round because that is where the meetings were held.

▶ **General Agreement on Tariffs and Trade (GATT)**
An international agreement established in 1947 to further world trade by reducing barriers and tariffs.

REGIONAL TRADE AGREEMENTS
Throughout the world the proponents of freer trade are succeeding in getting legislation passed to reduce tariff barriers. The most important of these for Americans are the U.S.-Canadian Free Trade Agreement and the North American Free Trade Agreement (NAFTA).

THE U.S.-CANADIAN FREE TRADE AGREEMENT
On January 1, 1989, an historic free trade agreement (FTA) between the United States and Canada took effect. All goods traded between the two countries are supposed to be duty-free—not subject to taxes—but not all products were included in the agreement. The goal, nonetheless, was to eliminate the high tariffs on **bilateral trade** in furniture, textiles, appliances, petrochemicals, plastics, and many metal, paper, and fish products. The

▶ **Bilateral trade**
Trade between two countries only.

FIGURE 33-8

Tariff rates in the United States since 1820.

Tariff rates in the United States have bounced around like a football; indeed, in Congress tariffs are a political football. Import-competing industries prefer high tariffs. In the twentieth century the highest tariff we have had was the Smoot-Hawley Tariff of 1930, which was almost as high as the "tariff of abominations" in 1828.

Source: U.S. Department of Commerce.

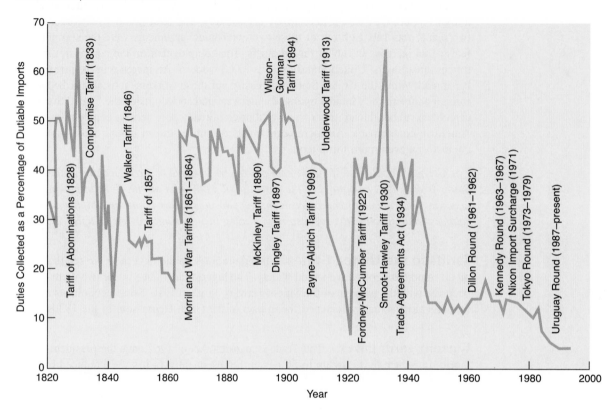

U.S.-Canada FTA provided precedent-setting provisions for services, foreign investment, and energy. With respect to services, such as computer repair, a U.S. company can start up a business in Canada with Canadian treatment under their tax laws, antitrust laws, and business regulations and also have access to local distribution systems. That means that U.S. service businesses will not be denied access or unfairly taxed in Canada any longer. The same consideration is now given to Canadian service businesses in the United States.

The U.S.-Canada FTA guarantees that both countries have access to each other's petroleum, gas, coal, and electricity at prices paid by nationals under comparable commercial circumstances. In other words, attempts to raise export prices of these products above domestic prices are prohibited. During any period of energy "shortage," the FTA requires that available supplies be shared "equitably" (whatever that may be interpreted to mean) between consumers in the two countries.

Some critics of the U.S.-Canada pact point out that it is inconsistent with Adam Smith's version of free trade because it is only bilateral. Others also point out that the U.S.-Canada FTA is not consistent with the GATT. The GATT is committed to the principle of nondiscriminatory, *multilateral*, and *universal* free trade. The U.S.-Canada pact is none of these, for it is regional, preferential, and discriminatory against countries not a party to it. Some economists object to bilateral trade agreements on principle. They point out that whereas completely open trade increases the total value of output by allowing specialization, opening only one border in a world riddled with restrictions might actually reduce efficiency by diverting "natural" trade flows.

THE NORTH AMERICAN FREE TRADE AGREEMENT

Mexico saw the benefits of the U.S.-Canada FTA. Consequently, Mexican President Carlos Salinas de Gortari asked President Bush in early 1990 for a U.S.-Mexico free trade agreement. This idea was extended to what is now known as the North American Free Trade Agreement, or NAFTA. This is a proposed North American free trade zone that would include Canada, the United States, and Mexico. This area would have a total output similar to that of the European Community (EC). There has been much more controversy over NAFTA than over the U.S.-Canada FTA. Canada and the United States are similar in many respects, but Mexico is much less developed and therefore its workers earn less than do workers to the north; the average industrial wage in Mexico is less than $1 an hour compared to over $10 an hour in the United States. Similarly, many fringe benefits that are taken for granted north of the Rio Grande are unknown in Mexico. Such benefits add $4 an hour to the average U.S. industrial wage in this country but almost nothing to the average Mexican industrial wage. There is a fear, therefore, that NAFTA will cause thousands of U.S. (and Canadian) jobs to be "exported." The industries hardest hit in this country would be apparel, footwear, steel, agriculture, and some furniture. Citrus growers, for example, particularly in California and Florida, currently rely on trade barriers to keep lower-priced competing Mexican fruit out of the U.S. market.

But a number of industries would benefit from NAFTA in spite of Mexico's low wages. Banking would be one, for American banks could profit if allowed to assist the expanding Mexican banking industry. The machinery industry in the United States would obtain new orders if Mexico modernizes its factories. Also, the Mexican cattle industry requires lots of grain, and farmers in the midwestern United States would probably supply it.

There are also environmental concerns that cannot be overlooked. Though Mexican environmental regulations may be just as strict as those in the United States, the country's relative high poverty rates make it difficult, if not impossible, to enforce such stringent environmental regulations. Nuevo Laredo, across the Rio Grande from Laredo, Texas, dumps an estimated 25 million gallons of raw sewage into the river each day.

Critics of NAFTA believe that Mexico would have the most to gain and the United States the least. Proponents say that if such an agreement is not passed, consumers in all three countries will be denied the choice of purchasing lower-cost imported items.

CONCEPTS IN BRIEF

- One means of restricting foreign trade is a quota system, as the United States has instituted for sugar. Beneficiaries of such quotas are the importers who get the quota rights and the domestic producers of the restricted good.
- Another means of restricting imports is a tariff, which is a tax on imports only. An import tariff benefits import-competing industries and harms consumers in general by raising prices.
- The main international institution created to improve trade among nations is the General Agreement on Tariffs and Trade (GATT). The latest round of trade talks under GATT started in 1987 in Uruguay.
- Numerous regional trade agreements are being put into place. Americans signed the U.S.-Canadian Free Trade Agreement, which took effect on January 1, 1989. There is an effort in support of the North American Free Trade Agreement (NAFTA), involving Canada, the United States, and Mexico.
- Some Americans and Canadians are against freer trade with Mexico because they are worried that Mexico's low wage rates might include the "export" of jobs to Mexico.

The U.S. automobile industry has effectively reduced competition from abroad by supporting government-imposed, "voluntary" import quotas from Japan. Nationwide, though, any reduction in imports leads to a reduction in exports because imports are ultimately paid for by exports.

An easy way to earn points as a political campaigner, virtually at any level and for any office, is to talk about foreigners taking away American jobs. During the 1992 presidential primaries, the majority of contenders could not say enough about how the Japanese and other foreigners were stealing American jobs and taking food off American tables. The discussion approached a fever pitch when the campaigners were in Detroit, Michigan, home of the U.S. automobile industry. After all, a few decades earlier, imported cars were a negligible part of the total car market. Today they account for 30 percent. One way that jobs in the automobile industry have been "saved" is by the imposition of a so-called voluntary import restraint system. This "voluntary" quota system has prohibited Japan from sending to the United States as many cars as its manufacturers would otherwise have shipped. Before we look at how this quota program affects American jobs, consider something that we said earlier about the relationship between exports and imports.

PAYING FOR IMPORTS *We always pay for imports with exports.* In the short run, we can sell off assets or borrow from abroad if we happen to import more goods and services than we export. But we have only a finite amount of assets to sell, and foreigners do not want to wait forever before we pay our bills. Ultimately, our accounts can be settled only if we provide (export) goods and services to the trading partner from whom we *pur-*

chase (import) goods and services. Thus any decrease in imports leads to a decrease in exports and hence job opportunities in the export industries. So when quotas of any type enhance job opportunities in import-competing industries, they also cost us jobs in export industries.

Just as important, import restrictions impose costs on American consumers as a whole. By reducing competition from abroad, import restrictions push up the prices of foreign goods and enable American producers to hike up their own prices. The best-documented example of this is in fact the "voluntary restrictions" on Japanese imports.

THE START OF IMPORT RESTRICTIONS ON THE JAPANESE Due in part to the enhanced quality of imported cars, sales of domestically produced automobiles fell from 9 million units in 1978 to an average of 6 million units per year between 1980 and 1982. Profits of U.S. carmakers plummeted as well, turning into substantial losses for some of them. American automakers and autoworkers unions demanded protection from import competition. They were joined in their cries by politicians from auto-producing states. The result was a "voluntary" agreement entered into by Japanese car companies (the most important competitors of U.S. firms), which restricted U.S. sale of Japanese cars to 1.68 million units per year. This agreement—which amounted to a quota, even though it never officially bore that name—began in April 1981 and has continued into the 1990s in various forms.

THE COST OF SAVING AMERICAN AUTOMOBILE JOBS Robert W. Crandall, an economist with the Brookings Institution, has estimated how much this voluntary trade restriction has cost American consumers in terms of higher car prices. According to his estimates, the reduced supply of Japanese cars pushed their prices up by $1,000 apiece. The higher price of Japanese imports in turn enabled domestic producers to hike their prices an average of $400 a car. The total tab in 1983 alone was $4.3 billion—and it shows few signs of shrinking in the 1990s. Crandall also estimated the number of jobs in auto-related industries that were saved by the voluntary import restrictions: about 26,000. Dividing $4.3 billion by 26,000 jobs yields a cost to consumers of more than $160,000 *per year* for every job saved in the auto industry. American consumers could have saved nearly

$2 billion on their car purchases in 1983 if, instead of implicitly agreeing to import restrictions, they had simply given $100,000 to every autoworker whose job was to be preserved by the voluntary import restraints.

SAVING JOBS IN OTHER INDUSTRIES   The numbers for the auto industry are no fluke. The same sort of calculations have been made for other industries. Tariffs in the apparel industry, for example, were increased between 1977 and 1981, saving the jobs of about 116,000 U.S. apparel workers—at a cost of $45,000 per job each year. The producers of citizens band (CB) radios also managed to get tariffs raised between 1978 and 1981. About 600 workers in the industry kept their jobs as a result, but at an annual cost to consumers of over $85,000 per job. The cost of protectionism has been even higher in other industries. Every job preserved in the glassware industry due to trade restrictions costs $200,000 each and every year. In the maritime industry, the yearly cost of trade protections is $270,000 per job. In the steel industry, the cost of preserving a job has been estimated at an astounding $750,000 per year. If free trade were permitted, each worker losing a job could be given a cash payment of even half that amount each year and the consumer would still save a lot of money.

SOME JOBS SAVED IN THE SHORT RUN BUT NOT FOREVER   In principle, trade restrictions are imposed to help specific industries and increase employment in those industries. Ironically, the long-run effects may be just the opposite. GATT researchers in Switzerland have examined employment in three industries that have been heavily protected throughout the world—textiles, clothing, and iron and steel. Between 1973 and 1984, despite stringent trade protections for these industries, employment in them actually declined, in some cases dramatically. In textiles, for example, employment fell 22 percent in the United States and 46 percent in the European Community. The clothing industry saw employment losses ranging from 18 percent in America to 56 percent in Sweden. Employment declines in the iron and steel industry ranged anywhere from 10 percent in Canada to 54 percent in the United States. In short, GATT researchers found that restrictions on free trade were no guarantee against job losses, even in the industries supposedly being protected.

The evidence seems clear: The cost of protecting jobs in the short run is enormous. And in the long run, it appears that jobs *cannot* be protected, especially if we consider all aspects of protectionism. Free trade is a tough platform on which to run for office. But it looks as if it is the one that will yield the most general benefits if implemented—though that does not, of course, mean that politicians will embrace it.

FOR CRITICAL ANALYSIS

1. If it is so obvious that protecting American jobs is too expensive per job saved, why does this nation (and others) continue to impose import restrictions to protect jobs?
2. Mark Twain was rumored to have said that the free traders win all the arguments but the protectionists win all the votes. Why do you think he might have been right?

CHAPTER SUMMARY

1. We can draw an excess demand schedule for foreign goods by looking at the difference between the quantities demanded and the quantities supplied domestically at prices below our domestic equilibrium price.

2. We find the excess supply schedule of domestic goods by looking at the difference between quantities supplied and demanded at prices above our domestic equilibrium price. The excess supply schedule is our supply schedule of exports.

3. The world equilibrium price and quantity traded are established at the point where one country's excess demand schedule intersects another country's excess supply schedule. As long as the zero trade prices of two countries are different, there will be trade (in the absence of restrictions).

4. It is important to distinguish between absolute and comparative advantage. A person or country that can do everything "better" (with higher labor productivity) than every other person or country has an absolute advantage in everything. Nevertheless, trade will still be advantageous if people will specialize in the things that they do relatively best. They will exploit their respective comparative advantage. Comparative advantage follows from different relative efficiencies and from the fixed nature of our resources at any point in time.

5. Along with the gains, there are costs from trade. Certain industries and their employees may be hurt if trade is opened up. There are numerous arguments, therefore, against free trade. A recent argument in favor of

protectionism and against free trade involves protecting national economic security. However, it is difficult to define what this means and why or how it should be protected.

6. An import quota restricts the quantity of imports coming into the country. It therefore raises the price. Consumers always lose.

7. An import tariff raises the price of internationally produced goods. It therefore allows domestic producers to raise their own prices. The result is a higher price to consumers, a lower quantity of imports, and a lower volume of international trade.

8. The main international institution created to improve trade among nations is the General Agreement on Tariffs and Trade (GATT). The latest round of trade talks under GATT started in 1987 in Uruguay.

9. Numerous regional trade agreements are being put into place. Americans signed the U.S.-Canadian Free Trade Agreement, which took affect on January 1, 1989. The North American Free Trade Agreement (NAFTA), linking Canada, the United States, and Mexico, is under discussion. Some Americans and Canadians are against freer trade with Mexico because they are worried that Mexico's low wage rates would lure away domestic jobs.

DISCUSSION OF PREVIEW POINTS

1. How is an import demand curve derived?

An import demand curve can be derived from the domestic demand for the commodity in question. In effect, the import demand curve for some commodity is the domestic quantity demanded for the commodity in question minus the domestic quantity supplied—at all prices below equilibrium. Thus at relatively low prices (below equilibrium) domestic suppliers will produce less than domestic buyers want to purchase (quantity demanded will exceed quantity supplied at all prices below domestic equilibrium). This excess demand for the commodity in question can be met by importing from abroad; the locus of all points, which shows the excess quantity demanded at all prices below equilibrium, defines the domestic import demand curve for the commodity in question.

2. How is an export supply curve derived?

An export supply curve can be derived from the domestic supply curve of the commodity in question. In effect, the export supply curve for some commodity is the domestic quantity supplied of the commodity minus the domestic quantity demanded at all prices above the domestic equilibrium price. At relatively high prices (above domestic equilibrium) the domestic quantity supplied of this commodity will exceed the domestic quantity demanded. That is, a surplus will exist at all prices above equilibrium. If foreigners are willing to buy this domestically produced commodity at prices above equilibrium, the excess supply can be exported to them. Thus the domestic export supply curve is defined as the difference between domestic quantity supplied and quantity demanded at all prices above domestic equilibrium.

3. How is international equilibrium for a commodity established?

Consider a two-country world, each country with the capability of producing VCRs. Country A has an import demand curve and an export supply curve, and so does country B. Assuming that each country has different supply and demand conditions (and that each, therefore, has a different domestic equilibrium price level for VCRs), we can define the international equilibrium position. International equilibrium will occur where one country's excess supply curve intersects the other country's excess demand curve—at a price somewhere between both countries' domestic equilibrium prices. At that intersection point, one country's exports will be equated with the other country's imports of VCRs; hence international equilibrium will be established for that good.

4. What are some arguments against free trade?

The infant industry argument maintains that new industries developing domestically need protection from foreign competitors until they are mature enough themselves to compete with foreigners, at which time protection will be removed. One problem with this argument is that it is difficult to tell when maturity has been reached, and domestic industries will fight against weaning. Moreover, this argument is hardly one that most U.S. industries can presently use. It is also alleged (and is true to a large extent) that free trade leads to instability for specific domestic industries as comparative advantage changes in a dynamic world. Nations that have traditionally held a comparative advantage in the production of some goods occasionally lose that advantage (while gaining others).

Regional hardships are a result, and protection of domestic jobs is demanded. Yet if carried to its logical conclusion, this argument leads to restriction of trade between states, then between the cities and towns within states, and finally between families! Some insecurity is a price that nations must pay for higher average and total incomes; nothing is free in this world.

PROBLEMS

(Answers to the odd-numbered problems appear at the back of the book.)

33-1. Examine the hypothetical table of worker-hours required to produce caviar and wheat in the United States and in Russia.

PRODUCT	UNITED STATES	RUSSIA
Caviar (oz)	6 worker-hours	9 worker-hours
Wheat (bu)	3 worker-hours	6 worker-hours

  a. What is the opportunity cost to the United States of producing one ounce of caviar per time period? What is the opportunity cost to the United States of producing one bushel of wheat?
  b. What is the opportunity cost to Russia of producing one ounce of caviar per time period? What is the opportunity cost to Russia of producing one bushel of wheat?
  c. The United States has a comparative advantage in what? Russia has a comparative advantage in what?

33-2. Study the hypothetical table of worker-hours required to produce coffee and beans in Colombia and Turkey.

PRODUCT	COLOMBIA	TURKEY
Coffee (lb)	2 worker-hours	1 worker-hour
Beans (lb)	6 worker-hours	2 worker-hours

  a. What is the opportunity cost to Colombia of producing one pound of coffee? One pound of beans?
  b. What is the opportunity cost to Turkey of producing one pound of coffee? One pound of beans?
  c. Colombia has a comparative advantage in what? Turkey has a comparative advantage in what?

33-3. Consider the international equilibrium situation for wine in the accompanying graph.

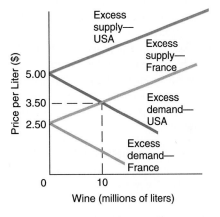

  a. What is the equilibrium price per liter of wine in the United States?
  b. What is the equilibrium price per liter of wine in France?
  c. What is the international equilibrium price per liter?
  d. Why won't $3 be the international equilibrium price?
  e. Why won't $4 be the international equilibrium price?

33-4. Examine the hypothetical table of worker-hours required to produce cheese and cloth in two countries, A and B.

PRODUCT	COUNTRY A	COUNTRY B
Cheese (lb)	$\frac{2}{3}$ worker-hours	2 worker-hours
Cloth (yd)	$\frac{1}{2}$ worker-hours	1 worker-hour

  a. What is the opportunity cost to country A of producing one pound of cheese? One yard of cloth?
  b. What is the opportunity cost to country B of producing one pound of cheese? One yard of cloth?
  c. Country A has a comparative advantage in what?
  d. Country B has a comparative advantage in what?

33-5. The use of tariffs and quotas to restrict imports results in higher prices and is successful in reducing imports. In what way is using a tariff different from using a quota?

33-6. Two countries, Austral Land and Boreal Land, have the following production opportunities shown in the graphs.

   a. Who has an absolute advantage in corn? In oranges?

   b. Who has a comparative advantage in corn? In oranges?

   c. Should Boreal Land export at all? If so, which good should it export?

   d. What is Austral Land's opportunity cost of oranges in terms of corn? What is Boreal Land's opportunity cost of corn in terms of oranges?

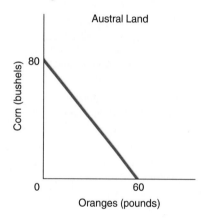

Austral Land

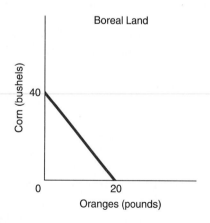

Boreal Land

33-7. The accompanying graph gives the supply and demand for grapes. *S* and *D* are the United States supply and demand curves, respectively. Assume that the price of grapes is 50 cents per pound.

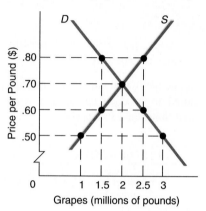

   a. How many pounds are produced domestically? How many pounds are imported?

   b. Suppose that the United States imposes a 10-cent-per-pound tariff. How many pounds would now be produced domestically? How many pounds would be imported? What are the U.S. government's revenues?

   c. Suppose now that the government imposes a 20-cent-per-pound tariff. What price can domestic growers now receive for their grapes? How many pounds will domestic growers produce? How many pounds will be imported? What are government revenues?

33-8. If free trade is so obviously beneficial, why are there so many restrictions on international trade? (Hint: Review the theory presented in Chapter 27.)

33-9. Explain why an increase in taxes on imports (tariffs) will reduce exports.

33-10. Assume that a country with whom the United States is trading imposes restrictions on U.S.-made imports into that country. Will the United States be better off by simultaneously imposing restrictions on the other country's imports into the United States? Why or why not?

COMPUTER-ASSISTED INSTRUCTION
(Complete problem and answer on disk.)

We show that the combination of specialization and exchange is the next best thing to a free lunch.

BILLETES		COMPRA	VENTA
▦ DOLAR U.S.A.	I		
▣ DOLAR CANAD.	I		
▮ FRANCO FRANCES	I		
▧ LIBRA ESTERLINA	I		
✚ FRANCO SUIZO			
▮ FRANCOS BELGAS			
▬ MARCO ALEMAN	I		
▮ LIRAS ITALIANAS	100		

34

EXCHANGE RATES AND THE BALANCE OF PAYMENTS

The 1990s so far has been a period of relatively high rates of unemployment, particularly compared to those during the second half of the 1980s. Some economists argue that we could reduce unemployment by getting rid of our huge annual foreign trade deficits. Others argue that in so doing we could stop being a debtor nation with respect to the rest of the world. Are trade deficits really bad, and is the United States truly the world's biggest debtor nation? To understand this issue better, you need to know about foreign exchange rates and the balance of payments mechanism.

After reading this chapter, you should be able to answer the following questions:

1. What is the difference between the balance of trade and the balance of payments?

2. What is a foreign exchange rate?

3. What is a floating exchange rate system?

4. What is a fixed exchange rate system?

INTRODUCTION

"The dollar weakened today." "The dollar is clearly overvalued." "The dollar is under attack." "Members of the Group of Seven agreed to prevent the dollar from rising." If you are confused by such newspaper headlines, join the crowd. Surprisingly, though, if you regard the dollar, the pound, the deutsche mark, the yen, and the franc as assets that are subject to the laws of supply and demand, the world of international finance can be quickly demystified. Perhaps the first step is to examine the meaning of the numerous terms used with respect to America's international financial transactions during any one-year period.

THE BALANCE OF PAYMENTS IN INTERNATIONAL CAPITAL MOVEMENTS

Governments typically keep track of each year's economic activities by calculating the gross domestic product—the total of expenditures on all newly produced final domestic goods and services—and its components. In the world of international trade, a summary information system has also been developed. It relates to the balance of trade and the balance of payments. The **balance of trade** refers specifically to exports and imports of *goods and services* as discussed in Chapter 33. When international trade is in balance, the value of exports equals the value of imports.

> ▶ **Balance of trade**
> The value of goods and services bought and sold in the world market.

The **balance of payments** is a more general concept that expresses the total of all economic transactions between two nations, usually for a period of one year. Each country's balance of payments summarizes information about that country's exports, imports, earnings by domestic residents on assets located abroad, earnings on domestic assets owned by foreign residents, international capital movements, and official transactions by central banks and governments. In essence, then, the balance of payments is a record of all the transactions between households, firms, and government of one country and the rest of the world. Any transaction that leads to a *payment* by a country's residents (or government) is a deficit item, identified by a negative sign (−) when we examine the actual numbers that might be in Table 34-1. Any transaction that leads to a *receipt* by a country's residents (or government) is a surplus item and is identified by a plus sign (+) when actual numbers are considered. Table 34-1 gives a listing of the surplus and deficit items on international accounts.

> ▶ **Balance of payments**
> A summary record of a country's economic transactions with foreign residents and governments over a year.

ACCOUNTING IDENTITIES

Accounting identities—definitions of equivalent values—exist for financial institutions and other businesses. We begin with simple accounting identities that must hold for families and then go on to describe international accounting identities.

> ▶ **Accounting identities**
> Statements that certain numerical measurements are equal by accepted definition (for example, "assets equal liabilities plus stockholders' equity").

SURPLUS ITEMS (+)	DEFICIT ITEMS (−)
Exports of merchandise	Imports of merchandise
Private and governmental gifts from foreigners	Private and governmental gifts to foreigners
Foreign use of domestic-owned transportation	Use of foreign-owned transportation
Foreign tourist expenditures domestically	Tourism expenditures abroad
Foreign military spending domestically	Military spending abroad
Interest and dividend receipts from foreigners	Interest and dividends paid to foreigners
Sales of domestic assets to foreigners	Purchases of foreign assets
Deposits in domestic depository institutions made by foreigners	Deposits made in foreign depository institutions
Sales of gold to foreigners	Purchases of gold from foreigners
Sales of domestic currency to foreigners	Purchases of foreign currency

TABLE 34-1 Surplus (+) and deficit (−) items on the international accounts.

If a family unit is spending more than its current income, such a situation necessarily implies that the family unit must be doing one of the following:

1. Drawing down its wealth. The family must reduce its money holdings, or it must sell stocks, bonds, or other assets.
2. Borrowing.
3. Receiving gifts from friends or relatives.
4. Receiving public transfers from a government, which obtained the funds by taxing others. (A transfer is a payment, in money or in goods or services, made without receiving goods or services in return.)

In effect, we can use this information to derive an identity; if a family unit is currently spending more than it is earning, it must draw on previously acquired wealth, borrow, or receive either private or public aid. Similarly, an identity exists for a family unit that is currently spending less than it is earning: It must increase its wealth by increasing its money holdings or by lending and acquiring other financial assets, or it must pay taxes or bestow gifts on others. When we consider businesses and governments, each unit in each group faces its own identities or constraints; for example, net lending by households must equal net borrowing by businesses and governments.

Even though our individual family unit's accounts must balance, in the sense that the identity discussed previously must hold, sometimes the item that brings about the balance cannot continue indefinitely. *If family expenditures exceed family income and this situation is financed by borrowing, the household may be considered to be in disequilibrium because such a situation cannot continue indefinitely.* If such a deficit is financed by drawing on previously accumulated assets, the family may also be in disequilibrium because it cannot continue indefinitely to draw on its wealth; eventually, it will become impossible for that family to continue such a lifestyle. (Of course, if the family members are retired, they may well be in equilibrium by drawing on previously acquired assets to finance current deficits; this example illustrates that it is necessary to understand circumstances fully before pronouncing an economic unit in disequilibrium.)

Individual households, businesses, and governments, as well as the entire group of households, businesses, and governments, must eventually reach equilibrium. Certain economic adjustment mechanisms have evolved to ensure equilibrium. Deficit households must eventually increase their incomes or decrease their expenditures: they will find that they have to pay higher interest rates if they wish to borrow to finance their deficits. Eventually their credit sources will dry up, and they will be forced into equilibrium. Businesses, on occasion, must lower costs and/or prices—or go bankrupt—to reach equilibrium.

When nations trade or interact, certain identities or constraints also must hold. Nations buy goods from people in other nations; they also lend to and present gifts to people in other nations. If a nation interacts with others, an accounting identity ensures a balance (but not an equilibrium, as will soon become clear). Let's look at the three categories of balance of payments transactions: current account transactions, capital account transactions, and official reserve account transactions.

CURRENT ACCOUNT TRANSACTIONS

During any designated period, all payments and gifts that are related to the purchase or sale of both goods and services constitute the current account in international trade. The three major types of current account transactions are the exchange of merchandise goods, the exchange of services, and unilateral transfers.

Merchandise Trade Transactions.

The largest portion of any nation's balance of payments current account is typically the importing and exporting of merchandise goods. During 1993, for example, as can be seen in lines 1 and 2 of Table 34-2, the United States exported $446.51 billion of merchandise and imported $562.78 billion. As we pointed out, the balance of trade is defined as the difference between the value of merchandise exports and the value of merchandise imports. For 1993 the United States had a balance of trade deficit because the value of its merchandise imports exceeded the value of its merchandise exports. This deficit amounted to $116.27 billion (line 3).

Service Exports and Imports.

The balance of (merchandise) trade has to do with tangible items—you can feel them, touch them, and see them. Service export and imports have to do with invisible or intangible items that are bought and sold, such as shipping, insurance, tourist expenditures, and banking services. Also, income earned by foreigners on U.S investments and income earned by Americans on foreign investments are part of service imports and exports. As can be seen in lines 4 and 5 of Table 34-2, in 1993 service exports were $314.01 billion and service imports were $254.43 billion. Thus the balance of services was about $59.58 billion in 1993 (line 6). Exports constitute receipts or inflows into the United States and are positive. Imports constitute payments abroad or outflows of money and therefore are negative.

When we combine the balance of trade with the balance of services, we obtain a balance on goods and services equal to $-89.00 billion in 1993 (line 7).

Unilateral Transfers.

Americans give gifts to relatives and others abroad. The federal government grants gifts to foreign nations. Foreigners give gifts to Americans, and some foreign governments have granted money to the U.S. government. In the current ac-

---

TABLE 34-2   1993 U.S. balance of payments account (estimated, in billions of dollars).

Sources: U.S. Department of Commerce, Bureau of Economic Analysis; U.S. Department of the Treasury.

CURRENT ACCOUNT		
(1) Exports of goods	$+446.51	
(2) Imports of goods	−562.78	
(3) Balance of trade		$−116.27
(4) Exports of services	+314.01	
(5) Imports of services	−254.43	
(6) Balance of services		+59.58
(7) Balance on goods and services [(3) + (6)]		−56.69
(8) Net unilateral transfers	−32.31	
(9) Balance on current account		−89.00
CAPITAL ACCOUNT		
(10) U.S. capital going abroad	−48.27	
(11) Foreign capital coming into the United States	+135.11[a]	
(12) Balance on capital account [(10) + (11)]		+86.84
(13) Balance on current account plus balance on capital account [(9) + (12)]		−2.16
(14) Official transactions		+2.16
(15) Total (balance)		$00.00

[a]Includes a $47 billion statistical discrepancy, probably unaccounted capital inflows, many of which relate to the illegal drug trade.

count we see that net unilateral transfers—the total amount of gifts given by Americans minus the total amount received by Americans from abroad—came to $-32.31 billion in 1993 (line 8). The fact that there is a minus sign before the number for unilateral transfers means that Americans gave more to foreigners than foreigners gave to Americans.

Balancing the Current Account.

The balance on current account tracks the value of a country's exports of goods and services (including military receipts plus income on investments abroad) and transfer payments (private and government) relative to the value of that country's import of goods and services (including military payments) and transfer payments (private and government). In 1993, it was a *negative* $89 billion.

If exports exceed imports, a current account surplus is said to exist; if imports exceed exports, a current account deficit (a negative number) is said to exist. A current account deficit means that we are importing more than we are exporting. Such a deficit must be paid for by the export of money or money equivalent, which means a capital account surplus.

CAPITAL ACCOUNT TRANSACTIONS

In world markets it is possible to buy and sell not only goods and services but also real and financial assets. This is what the capital accounts are concerned with in international transactions. Capital account transactions occur because of foreign investments—either foreigners investing in the United States or Americans investing in other countries. The purchase of shares of stock on the London stock market by an American causes an outflow of funds. The building of a Japanese automobile factory in the United States causes an inflow of funds. Anytime foreigners buy U.S. government securities, that is an inflow of funds. Anytime Americans buy foreign government securities, there is an outflow of funds. Loans to and from foreigners cause outflows and inflows.

Line 10 of Table 34-2 indicates that in 1993 the value of private and government capital going out of the United States was $-48.27 billion, and line 11 shows that the value of private and government capital coming into the United States (including a statistical discrepancy) was $135.11 billion. U.S. capital going abroad constitutes payments or outflows and is therefore negative. Foreign capital coming into the United States constitutes receipts or inflows and is therefore positive. Thus there was a positive net capital movement of $86.84 billion into the United States (line 12). This could also be called the balance on capital account.

There is a relationship between the current account and the capital account, assuming no interventions by the central banks of nations. The current account and the capital account must sum to zero. Stated differently, the current account deficit equals the capital account surplus, or the increase in purchases of domestic assets by foreigners. Any nation experiencing a current account deficit, such as the United States, must also be running a capital account surplus.

EXAMPLE: Is the United States' Current Account Deficit a Serious Problem?

Examination of the current account for the United States shows that the current account has been in deficit consistently since 1981. Many observers contend that this represents a crisis in America's ability to compete globally. Look at Figure 34-1 on the next page.

Remember, though, that if the current account balance were zero in the United States, the capital account could not be positive. Look at the upper line in Figure 34-1. The capital account has been in surplus since 1982. In fact, it is approximately the mirror image of the current account deficit. Some observers contend that the current account deficit does not show that America is weak but rather that America is strong. Why? Because this

FIGURE 34-1

The relationship between the current account and the capital account.
To some extent the capital account is the mirror image of the current account. We can see this during the years 1970 to the beginning of the 1990s. When the current account was in surplus, the capital account was in deficit. When the current account was in deficit, the capital account was in surplus. Indeed, virtually the only time foreigners can invest in America is when the current account is in deficit.

Sources: International Monetary Fund, Balance of Payments Statistics Yearbook, various issues; U.S. Government Printing Office *Economic Indicators*.

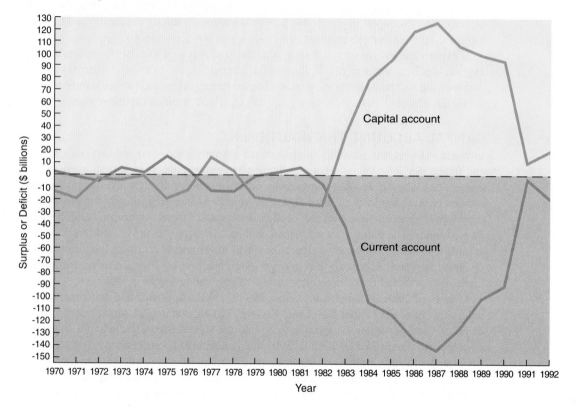

surplus in the U.S. capital account indicates that some foreigners, such as the Germans and the Japanese, still find it more attractive to invest in the United States than in their own countries. This may be an indication of U.S. strength. Capital flows from other countries have created productive investment in the United States and enabled investment to be higher than the amount that Americans have been willing to finance.

For Critical Analysis: Assume that the current account is equal to zero (neither surplus nor deficit). Assume also that the capital account is equal to zero (neither surplus nor deficit). Is it still possible for foreigners to invest in the United States? (Hint: With a current account and capital account both equal to zero, can Americans still be investing in the rest of the world?) ●

OFFICIAL RESERVE ACCOUNT TRANSACTIONS

The third type of balance of payments transaction concerns official reserve assets, which consist of the following:

1. Foreign currencies
2. Gold

▶ **Special drawing rights (SDRs)**
Reserve assets created by the International Monetary Fund that countries can use to settle international payments.

3. **Special drawing rights (SDRs),** which are reserve assets that the International Monetary Fund created to be used by countries to settle international payment obligations
4. The reserve position in the International Monetary Fund
5. Any financial asset held by an official agency, such as the U.S. Treasury Department

To consider how official reserve account transactions occur, look again at Table 34-2. The surplus in our capital account was +$86.84 billion. But the deficit in our current account was $-89.00 billion, so we had a net deficit on the combined accounts (line 13) of $-2.16 billion. In other words, the United States obtained less in foreign money in all its international transactions than it used. How is this deficiency made up? By our central bank drawing down its existing balances of foreign monies, or the +$2.16 billion in official transactions shown on line 14 in Table 34-2, which shows this reduction in foreign currencies. You might ask why there is a plus sign on line 14. The answer is because this represents a *supply* (an inflow) of foreign exchange into our international transactions.

The balance (line 15) in Table 34-2 is zero, as it must be with double-entry bookkeeping. Our balance of payments deficit is measured by the official transactions figure on line 14. (This does not mean we are in equilibrium, though.)

WHAT AFFECTS THE BALANCE OF PAYMENTS?

A major factor affecting our balance of payments is our rate of inflation relative to the rate of inflation of our trading partners. Assume that the rate of inflation in the United States and in France is equal. Suppose that all of a sudden, our inflation rate increases. That means that the French will find that American products are becoming more expensive, and we will export fewer of them to France. Americans will find French products relatively cheaper, and we will import more. The converse will occur if our rate of inflation suddenly falls relative to that of France. All other things held constant, whenever our rate of inflation exceeds that of our trading partners, we expect to see a worsening of our balance of trade and payments. Conversely, when our rate of inflation is less than that of our trading partners, other things being constant, we expect to see an improvement in our balance of trade and payments.

Another important factor that sometimes influences our balance of payments is our relative political stability. Political instability causes *capital flight:* Owners of capital in countries anticipating or experiencing political instability will often move assets to countries that are politically stable, such as the United States. Hence our balance of payments is likely to improve whenever political instability looms in other nations in the world.

CONCEPTS IN BRIEF

- The balance of payments reflects the value of all transactions in international trade, including goods, services, financial assets, and gifts.
- The merchandise trade balance gives us the difference between exports and imports of tangible items. Merchandise trade transactions are represented by exports and imports of tangible items.
- Service exports and imports relate to the trade of intangible items, such as shipping, insurance, and tourist expenditures. They include income earned by foreigners on U.S. investments and income earned by Americans on foreign investments. **(Continued)**

- Unilateral transfers involve international private gifts and federal government grants or gifts to foreign nations.
- When we add the balance of trade plus the balance of services and take account of net unilateral transfers, we come up with the balance on current account, which is a summary statistic taking into account the three transactions that form the current account transactions.
- There are also capital account transactions that relate to the buying and selling of financial and real assets. Foreign capital is always entering the United States, and American capital is always flowing abroad. The difference is called the balance on capital account.
- Another type of balance of payments transaction concerns the official reserve assets of individual countries, or what is often simply called official transactions. By standard accounting convention, official transactions are exactly equal to but opposite in sign to the balance of payments of the United States.
- Our balance of trade can be affected by our relative rate of inflation and political instability elsewhere compared to the stability that exists in the United States.

DETERMINING FOREIGN EXCHANGE RATES

When you buy foreign products, such as French wine, you have dollars with which to pay the French winemaker. The French winemaker, however, cannot pay workers in dollars. The workers are French, they live in France, and they need francs to buy goods and services in that country. There must therefore be some way of exchanging dollars for the francs that the winemaker will accept. That exchange occurs in a **foreign exchange market,** which in this case specializes in exchanging francs and dollars. (When you obtain foreign currencies at a bank or an airport currency exchange, you are participating in the foreign exchange market.)

▶ **Foreign exchange market**
The market for buying and selling foreign currencies.

The particular exchange rate between francs and dollars that would prevail depends on the current demand for and supply of francs and dollars. In a sense, then, our analysis of the exchange rate between dollars and francs will be familiar, for we have used supply and demand throughout this book. If it costs you 20 cents to buy one franc, that is the **foreign exchange rate** determined by the current demand for and supply of francs in the foreign exchange market. The French person going to the foreign exchange market would need five francs to buy one dollar. (Our numbers are of course hypothetical.)

▶ **Foreign exchange rate**
The price of foreign currency in terms of domestic currency. For example, if the foreign exchange rate for francs is 20 cents, it takes 20 cents to buy one franc. An alternative way of stating the exchange rate is that the value of the dollar is 5 francs. It takes 5 francs to buy one dollar.

We will continue our example in which the only two countries in the world are France and the United States. Now let's consider what determines the demand for and supply of foreign currency in the foreign exchange market.

DEMAND FOR AND SUPPLY OF FOREIGN CURRENCY

You wish to buy some French Bordeaux wine. To do so, you must have French francs. You go to the foreign exchange market (or your American bank). Your desire to buy the French wine therefore causes you to offer (supply) dollars to the foreign exchange market. Your demand for French francs is equivalent to your supply of American dollars to the foreign exchange market. Indeed:

> Every U.S. transaction concerning the importation of foreign goods constitutes a supply of dollars and a demand for some foreign currency, and vice versa for export transactions.

In this case it constitutes a demand for French francs.

In our example we will assume that only two goods are being traded—French wine and American jeans. Thus the American demand for French wine creates a supply of dollars and a demand for francs in the foreign exchange market. Similarly, the French demand for American jeans creates a supply of francs and a demand for dollars in the foreign exchange market. In the situation of **freely floating** (or **flexible**) **exchange rates,** the supply of and demand for dollars and francs in the foreign exchange market will determine the equilibrium foreign exchange rate. The equilibrium exchange rate will tell us how many francs a dollar can be exchanged for—that is, the dollar price of francs—or how many dollars (or fractions of a dollar) a franc can be exchanged for—the franc price of dollars.

▶ **Freely floating (or flexible) exchange rates**
Exchange rates that are allowed to fluctuate in the open market in response to changes in supply and demand. Sometimes called *flexible exchange rates* or *floating exchange rates.*

THE EQUILIBRIUM FOREIGN EXCHANGE RATE

To determine the equilibrium foreign exchange rate, we have to find out what determines the demand for and supply of foreign exchange. We will ignore for the moment any speculative aspect of buying foreign exchange; that is, we assume that there are no individuals who wish to buy francs simply because they think that their price will go up in the future.

The idea of an exchange rate is not different from the idea of paying a certain price for something you want to buy. If you like coffee, you know you have to pay about 75 cents a cup. If the price went up to $2.50, you would probably buy fewer cups. If the price went down to 5 cents, you might buy more. In other words, the demand curve for cups of coffee, expressed in terms of dollars, slopes downward following the law of demand. The demand curve for francs slopes downward also, and we will see why.

Demand Schedule for French Francs. Let's think more closely about the demand schedule for francs. Let's say that it costs you 20 cents to purchase one franc; that is the exchange rate between dollars and francs. If tomorrow you had to pay 25 cents for the same franc, the exchange rate would have changed. Looking at such an increase with respect to the franc, we would say that there has been an **appreciation** in the value of the franc in the foreign exchange market. But this increase in the value of the franc means that there has been a **depreciation** in the value of the dollar in the foreign exchange market. The dollar used to buy five francs; tomorrow, the dollar will be able to buy only four francs at a price of 25 cents per franc. If the dollar price of francs rises, you will probably demand fewer francs. Why? The answer lies in looking at the reason you demand francs in the first place.

▶ **Appreciation**
An increase in the value of a currency in terms of other currencies.

▶ **Depreciation**
A decrease in the value of a currency in terms of foreign currencies.

You demand francs in order to buy French wine. Your demand curve for French wine, we will assume, follows the law of demand and therefore slopes downward. If it costs you more American dollars to buy the same quantity of French wine, presumably you will not buy the same quantity; your quantity demanded will be less. We say that your demand for French francs is *derived* from your demand for French wine. In panel (a) of Figure 34-2 on the next page we present the hypothetical demand schedule for French wine in the United States by a representative wine drinker. In panel (b) we show graphically the American demand curve for French wine in terms of American dollars taken from panel (a).

FIGURE 34-2

Deriving the demand for French francs.

In panel (a) we show the demand schedule for French wine in the United States, expressed in terms of dollars per liter. In panel (b) we show the demand curve, *D*, which slopes downward. In panel (c) we show the number of francs required to purchase up to 4 liters of wine. If the price per liter of wine in France is 20 francs, we can now find the quantity of francs needed to pay for the various quantities demanded. In panel (d) we see the derived demand for francs in the United States in order to purchase the various quantities of wine given in panel (a). The resultant demand curve, *D'*, is shown in panel (e). It is the American derived demand for francs.

Panel (a)

DEMAND SCHEDULE FOR FRENCH WINE IN THE UNITED STATES PER WEEK

PRICE PER LITER ($)	QUANTITY DEMANDED (LITERS)
10	1
8	2
6	3
4	4

Panel (c)

QUANTITY DEMANDED	FRANCS REQUIRED TO PURCHASE QUANTITY DEMANDED (AT *P* = 20 FRANCS/LITER)
1	20
2	40
3	60
4	80

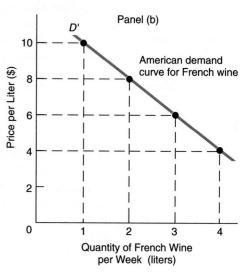

Panel (b)

Panel (d)

DERIVED DEMAND SCHEDULE FOR FRANCS IN THE UNITED STATES WITH WHICH TO PAY FOR IMPORTS OF WINE

PRICE OF ONE FRANC ($)	QUANTITY OF FRANCS DEMANDED PER WEEK
.50	20
.40	40
.30	60
.20	80

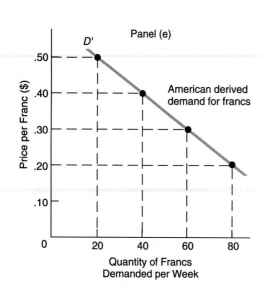

Panel (e)

Let us assume that the price per liter of French wine in France is 20 francs. Given that price, we can find the number of francs required to purchase up to 4 liters of French wine. That information is given in panel (c) of Figure 34-2. If one liter requires 20 francs, 4 liters require 80 francs. Now we have enough information to determine the derived demand curve for French francs. If one franc costs 20 cents, a bottle of wine would cost $4 (20 francs per bottle ÷ 5 francs per dollar = $4 per bottle). At $4 per bottle, the typical representative American wine drinker would, we see from panel (a) of Figure 34-2, demand 4 liters. From panel (c) we see that 80 francs would be demanded to buy the 4 liters of wine. We show this quantity demanded in panel (d). In panel (e) we draw the derived demand curve for francs. Now consider what happens if the price of francs goes up to 30 cents. A bottle of French wine costing 20 francs in France would now cost $6 in the United States. From panel (a) we see that at $6 per liter, 3 liters will be imported from France into the United States by our representative domestic wine drinker. From panel (c) we see that 3 liters would require 60 francs to be purchased; thus in panels (d) and (e) we see that at a price of one franc per 30 cents, the quantity demanded will be 60 francs. We continue similar calculations all the way up to a price of 50 cents per franc. At that price a bottle of French wine costing 20 francs in France would cost $10 in the United States, and our representative wine drinker would import only one bottle.

Downward-sloping Derived Demand.   As can be expected, as the price of francs falls, the quantity demanded will rise. The only difference here from the standard demand analysis developed in Chapter 3 and used throughout this text is that the demand for francs is derived from the demand for a final product, French wine in our example.

Supply of French Francs.   The supply of French francs is a derived supply in that it is derived from a French person's demand for American jeans. We could go through an example similar to the one for wine to come up with a supply schedule of French francs in France. It slopes upward. Obviously, the French want dollars in order to purchase American goods. In principle, the French will be willing to supply more francs when the dollar price of francs goes up because they can then buy more American goods with the same quantity of francs; that is, the franc would be worth more in exchange for American goods than when the dollar price for francs was lower. Let's take an example. A pair of jeans in the United States costs $10. If the exchange rate is 25 cents for one franc, the French have to come up with 40 francs (= $10 at 25 cents per franc) to buy one pair of jeans. If, however, the exchange rate goes up to 50 cents for one franc, the French must come up with only 20 francs (= $10 at 50 cents per franc) to buy a pair of American jeans. At a lower price (in francs) of American jeans, they will demand a larger quantity. In other words, as the price of French francs goes up in terms of dollars, the quantity of American jeans demanded will go up, and hence the quantity of French francs supplied will go up. Therefore, the supply schedule of foreign currency (francs) will slope upward.[1]

---

[1]Actually, the supply schedule of foreign currency will be upward-sloping if we assume that the demand for American imported jeans on the part of the French is price-elastic. If the demand schedule for jeans is price-inelastic, the supply schedule will be negatively sloped. In the case of unit elasticity of demand, the supply schedule for francs will be a vertical line. Throughout the rest of this chapter we will assume that demand is price-elastic. Remember that the price elasticity of demand tells us whether or not total expenditures by jeans purchasers in France will rise or fall when the French franc drops in value. In the long run, of course, it is quite realistic to think that the price elasticity of demand for imports is numerically greater than 1 anyway.

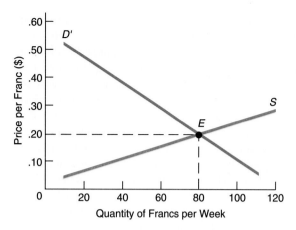

FIGURE 34-3
The equilibrium exchange rate for two individuals.
The derived demand curve for French francs is taken from panel (e) of Figure 34-2. The derived supply curve, *S*, results from the representative French purchaser of American jeans, who supplies francs to the foreign exchange market when demanding U.S. dollars in order to buy American jeans. *D'* and *S* intersect at *E*. The equilibrium exchange rate is 20 cents per franc. The equilibrium quantity of francs in the foreign exchange market will be 80 per week.

We could easily work through a detailed numerical example to show that the supply curve of French francs slopes upward. Rather than do that, we will simply draw it as upward-sloping in Figure 34-3. In our hypothetical example, assuming that there is only one wine drinker in America and one demander of jeans in France, the equilibrium exchange rate will be set at 20 cents per franc, or 5 francs to one dollar. Let us now look at the aggregate demand and supply of French francs. We take all demanders of French wine and all demanders of American jeans and put their demands and supplies of francs together into one diagram. Thus we are showing an aggregate version of the demand for and supply of French francs. The horizontal axis in Figure 34-4 represents a quantity of foreign exchange—the number of francs per year. The vertical axis represents the exchange rate—the price of foreign currency (francs) expressed in dollars (per franc). Thus at the foreign currency price of 25 cents per franc, you know that it will cost you 25 cents to buy one franc. At the foreign currency price of 20 cents per franc, you know that it will cost you 20 cents to buy one franc. The equilibrium is again established at 20 cents for one franc. This equilibrium is not established because Americans like to buy francs or because the French like to buy dollars. Rather, the equilibrium exchange rate depends on how many pairs of jeans the French want and how much French wine the Americans want (given their respective incomes, their tastes, and the relative price of wine and jeans).[2]

A Shift in Demand.

Assume that a successful advertising campaign by American wine importers has caused the American demand (curve) for French wine to double. Americans demand twice as much wine at all prices. Their demand curve for French wine has shifted outward and to the right.

The increased demand for French wine can be translated into an increased demand for francs. All Americans clamoring for bottles of French wine will supply more dollars to the foreign exchange market while demanding more French francs to pay for the wine. Figure 34-5 presents a new demand schedule, *D'*, for French francs; this demand schedule is to the right of and outward from the original demand schedule. If the French do not change their desire for jeans, the supply schedule for French francs will remain stable. A new equilibrium will be established at a higher exchange rate. In our particular example,

---

[2]Remember that we are dealing with a two-country world in which we are considering only the exchange of American jeans and French wine. In the real world more than just goods and services are exchanged among countries. Some Americans buy French financial assets; some French buy American financial assets. We are ignoring such transactions for the moment.

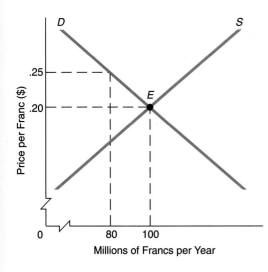

FIGURE 34-4
The aggregate demand and supply of French francs.
The aggregate supply curve of French francs results from the total French demand for American jeans. The demand curve, *D*, slopes downward like most demand curves, and the supply curve, *S*, slopes upward. The foreign exchange price, or the U.S. dollar price of francs, is given on the vertical axis. The number of francs, in millions, is represented on the horizontal axis. If the foreign exchange rate is 25 cents—that is, if it takes 25 cents to buy one franc—Americans will demand 80 million francs. The equilibrium exchange rate is at the intersection of *D* and *S*. The equilibrium exchange rate is 20 cents. At this point, 100 million French francs are both demanded and supplied each year.

the new equilibrium is established at an exchange rate of 30 cents per franc. It now takes 30 cents to buy one French franc, whereas it took 20 cents before. This is translated as an increase in the price of French wine to Americans and as a decrease in the price of American jeans to the French. (Otherwise stated, there has been a decline in the foreign exchange value of the dollar.)

A Shift in Supply.   We just assumed that Americans' preference for French wine had shifted. Because the demand for French francs is a derived demand by Americans for French wine, it has caused a shift in the demand curve for francs. Alternatively, assume that the supply curve of French francs shifts outward to the right. This may occur for many reasons, the most probable one being a relative rise in the French price level. For example, if the price of all French-made clothes went up 100 percent in francs, American jeans would become relatively cheaper. That would mean that French people would want to buy more American jeans. But remember that when they want to buy more American jeans,

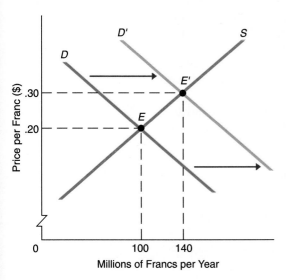

FIGURE 34-5
A shift in the demand schedule.
The demand schedule for French wine shifts to the right, causing the derived demand schedule for francs to shift to the right also. We have shown this as a shift from *D* to *D'*. We have assumed that the French supply schedule of francs has remained stable—that is, French demand for jeans has remained constant. The old equilibrium foreign exchange rate was 20 cents. The new equilibrium exchange rate will be *E'*; it will now cost 30 cents to buy one franc. The higher price of francs will be translated into a higher U.S. dollar price for French wine and a lower French franc price for jeans.

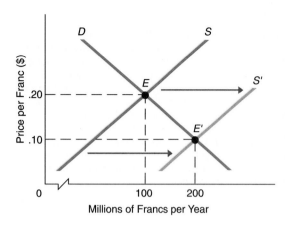

FIGURE 34-6
A shift in the supply of French francs.
There has been a shift in the supply curve of French francs. The new equilibrium will occur at *E'*. Ten cents, rather than 20 cents, will now buy one franc. After the exchange rate adjustment, the amount of francs demanded and supplied will increase to 200 million per year.

they supply more francs to the foreign exchange market. Thus we see in Figure 34-6 that the supply curve of French francs moves from *S* to *S'*. In the absence of restrictions—that is, in a system of floating exchange rates—the new equilibrium exchange rate will be one franc equals 10 cents, or $1 equals 10 francs. The quantity of francs demanded and supplied will increase from 100 million per year to 200 million per year. We say, then, that in a flexible (or floating) international exchange rate system, shifts in the demand and supply of foreign currencies will cause changes in the equilibrium foreign exchange rates. Those rates will remain in effect until supply or demand shifts.

PURCHASING POWER PARITY

Different countries have different rates of inflation. These different inflation rates are an important factor in determining floating exchange rates. Indeed, one theory of the determination of exchange rates is called **purchasing power parity (PPP),** which exists between any two currencies whenever changes in the exchange rate exactly reflect relative changes in price levels in the two countries. More specifically, over the long run, the average value of exchange rates depends on their purchasing power parity because in that way the relative prices in the two countries will stay the same (measured in a common currency). For example, if the U.S. price level rises by 10 percent but the French price level by only 5 percent, the PPP value of the French franc should appreciate by approximately 5 percent. Changes in the relative values of the two currencies compensates exactly for differences in national inflation rates. If indeed the actual exchange rate equals the PPP rate, the competitive positions of firms in the two countries will remain unchanged. American firms, even though domestically facing a higher inflation rate, will still be able to sell their output to France just as before because the exchange rate will have adjusted to offset the effect of higher U.S. prices.

The PPP theory seems to work well in the long run when the differences in inflation rates between two countries are relatively large. When such inflation rate differences are not big, other, market-oriented forces enter and often obscure the picture.

▶ **Purchasing power parity (PPP)**
The relationship of two currencies when changes in the exchange rate exactly reflect relative changes in the price levels in the two countries.

 INTERNATIONAL EXAMPLE: Big MacCurrency

Any weekday you can find the price of foreign currencies by looking in the *Wall Street Journal*, the *New York Times*, or other newspapers. Once a year, *The Economist* publishes its version of foreign exchange prices. *The Economist*'s Big Mac Index for 1993 is reproduced in Table 34-3. It provides a rough guide to whether the official exchange rate

TABLE 34-3 The real test: hamburger prices.

Sources: McDonald's; *The Economist,* April 17, 1993, p. 79.

COUNTRY	PRICE[a] IN LOCAL CURRENCY	PRICES IN DOLLARS	ACTUAL EXCHANGE RATE APRIL 1993	IMPLIED PPP[b] OF THE DOLLAR	% OVER (+) OR UNDER (−) VALUATION VS. THE DOLLAR[c]
Australia	A$2.45	1.76	1.39	1.07	−23
Belgium	BFr109	3.36	32.45	47.81	+47
Britain	£1.79	2.79	1.56[d]	1.27[d]	+23
Canada	C$2.76	2.19	1.26	1.21	−4
Denmark	DKr25.75	4.25	6.06	11.29	+86
France	FFr18.50	3.46	5.34	8.11	+52
Germany	Dm4.60	2.91	1.58	2.02	+28
Hong Kong	HK$9.00	1.16	7.73	3.95	−49
Hungary	Forint157	1.78	88.18	68.86	−22
Ireland	I£1.48	2.29	1.54[d]	1.54[d]	0
Italy	Lire4,500	2.95	1,523	1,974	+30
Japan	¥391	3.45	113	171	+51
Russia	Rouble780	1.14	686[e]	342	−50
South Korea	Won2,300	2.89	796	1,009	+27
Spain	Ptas325	2.85	114	143	+25
Sweden	SKr25.50	3.43	7.43	11.18	+50
United States[f]	$2.28	2.28	—	—	—

[a]Prices may vary locally. [b]Purchasing-power parity in local currency: local price divided by dollar price. [c]Against dollar. [d]Dollars per pound. [e]Market rate. [f]New York, Chicago, San Francisco and Atlanta.

undervalues or overvalues a currency. The index itself is based on purchasing power parity (PPP). The basket of goods and services that *The Economist* publishes contains but a single item: a Big Mac hamburger from McDonald's. *The Economist*'s writers gorge themselves on Big Macs around the globe to come up with the Big Mac Index.

For Critical Analysis: Would it be possible to come up with an alternative to the Big Mac Index? What are the attributes of the good that would make it as valid as a Big Mac? ●

MARKET DETERMINANTS OF EXCHANGE RATES

The foreign exchange market is affected by many other changes in market variables in addition to changes in relative price levels, including these:

1. **Changes in real interest rates.** If the United States' interest rate, corrected for people's expectations of inflation, abruptly increases relative to the rest of the world, international investors elsewhere will increase their demand for dollar-denominated assets, thereby increasing the demand for dollars in foreign exchange markets. An increased demand for dollars in foreign exchange markets, other things held constant, will cause the dollar to appreciate and other currencies to depreciate.
2. **Changes in productivity.** Whenever one country's productivity increases relative to another's, the former country will become more competitive in world markets. The demand for its exports will increase, and so, too, will the demand for its currency.
3. **Changes in product preferences.** If Germany's citizens suddenly develop a taste for American-made automobiles, this will increase the derived demand for American dollars in foreign exchange markets.
4. **Perceptions of economic stability.** As already mentioned, if the United States looks economically and politically more stable relative to other countries, more foreigners will want to put their savings into U.S. assets than in their own domestic assets. This will increase the demand for dollars.

CONCEPTS IN BRIEF

- The foreign exchange rate is the rate at which one country's currency can be exchanged for another's.
- The demand for foreign exchange is a derived demand; it is derived from the demand for foreign goods and services (and financial assets).
- The supply of foreign exchange is derived from foreigners' demands for our goods and services.
- In general, the demand curve of foreign exchange slopes downward and the supply curve of foreign exchange slopes upward. The equilibrium foreign exchange rate occurs at the intersection of the demand and supply curves for a currency.
- A shift in the demand for foreign goods will result in a shift in the demand for foreign exchange. The equilibrium foreign exchange rate will change.
- A shift in the supply of foreign currency will also cause a change in the equilibrium exchange rate.
- Purchasing power parity occurs when changes in the exchange rate for two currencies reflect only changes in the relative rates of inflation in those two countries.
- Changes in relative real interest rates, productivity, product preferences, and perceptions of relative economic stability affect foreign exchange rates.

FIXED EXCHANGE RATES

We have just described the workings of a freely floating, or flexible, exchange rate system in international finance. Now we consider a situation in which central banks intervene to prevent foreign exchange rates from changing. This is a system of **fixed exchange rates.** As with most systems in which the price of a particular good or service is fixed, the only way that it can remain so is for the government to intervene.

▶ **Fixed exchange rates** Foreign exchange rates held constant by means of central bank purchases and sales of domestic and foreign currency.

Let's take our two-country example again. Suppose that the price of jeans has gone up. Suppose, in fact, that there is a general rise in the price of everything made in the United States including jeans. The French will now buy fewer jeans than before. They supply fewer francs to the foreign exchange market and demand fewer dollars at the fixed exchange rate. But Americans continue to demand French wines. In fact, they will demand more, because at the fixed exchange rate, the relative price of French wines has fallen. Americans will now supply more dollars to the foreign exchange market and demand more francs. As in Figure 34-7, the demand curve for francs will shift to D'. (We assume that the supply curve does not shift.)

In the absence of any intervention by central banks, the exchange rate will change. The price of French francs in terms of dollars will go from 20 cents per franc to 25 cents. That is, the value of a dollar in terms of francs will go down. The dollar will suffer a depreciation in its value relative to the franc, and the franc will experience an appreciation in its value in terms of the dollar. But suppose that the U.S. government is committed to maintaining a *fixed* price of dollars in the foreign exchange market. When the French take their excess dollars and throw them onto the foreign exchange markets, the U.S. Federal Reserve will be forced to go into the foreign exchange market and buy up those excess dollars. The Federal Reserve has to have foreign currency (or gold) to buy up the excess dollars. That is, it has to have a reserve of francs or gold in its foreign exchange reserves to buy the dollars that the French want to sell. It must supply 25 million francs per year to

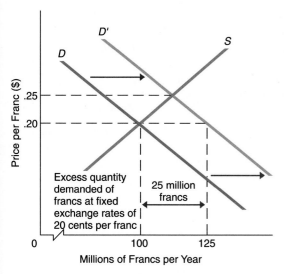

FIGURE 34-7
Supporting the value of the dollar in the foreign exchange market.
There is inflation in the United States, and all prices go up. We assume that prices remain constant in France, so French goods become relatively cheaper. The demand schedule for French goods shifts to the right, as does the derived demand schedule for French francs, from D to D'. Without exchange rate controls, the exchange rate would rise to 25 cents. The U.S. government maintains the price of a dollar at 5 francs—it keeps the price at 20 cents per franc. But at that exchange rate there is an excess quantity demanded of 25 million francs per year at the fixed exchange rate. The U.S. government must step in and supply 25 million francs from its foreign exchange reserves annually in order to support the dollar in the foreign exchange market.

American buyers of French wine or to French exporters of wine to keep the exchange rate fixed, as seen in Figure 34-7.

To make this process clear, let's review it step by step.

1. Prices in the United States go up.
2. French wine becomes a better deal for Americans at the fixed exchange rate; American jeans become a worse deal for French buyers at the fixed exchange rate.
3. Therefore, Americans buy more wine and the French buy fewer American jeans.
4. At the fixed exchange rate, the value of American imports (French wine) exceeds the value of American exports (American jeans).
5. The dollars that Americans spend abroad are only partly compensated by the French purchase of American jeans.
6. The French end up with excess dollars that are not put back into circulation in the United States because the French have not bought as much from us as we have bought from them at the fixed exchange rate.
7. The Federal Reserve buys up those excess dollars with French francs in the foreign exchange market to support the price of the dollar.

Thus we can see that, other things being equal, the only way for the Fed to maintain the fixed exchange rate when there is downward pressure on the price of the dollar in foreign exchange markets is to purchase excess dollars in the foreign exchange market with francs (or gold) that the Fed has in its reserves.

CURRENCY CRISES

▶ **Currency crisis**
A situation in the international money market that occurs when a country no longer has the resources (foreign exchange, gold, credit, and so on) to support the price of its currency. A currency crisis brings forced devaluation under a fixed exchange rate system.

The only way for the United States and other countries to support the price of the dollar is to buy up excess dollars with foreign reserves—in this case, with French francs (or gold). But the United States might eventually run out of francs (or gold). It would no longer be able to stabilize the price of the dollar, and a **currency crisis** would ensue. A currency crisis occurs when a country can no longer support the price of its currency in foreign exchange markets under a fixed exchange rate system. Many such crises have occurred in the past several decades when countries have attempted to maintain a fixed exchange rate that was in disequilibrium.

DEVALUATION AND REVALUATION

One alternative to a currency crisis or to continuing to try to support a fixed exchange rate is to devalue unilaterally. **Devaluation** is equivalent to depreciation except that it occurs under a fixed exchange rate regime. The country officially lowers the price of its currency in foreign exchange markets, a *deliberate* public action by the government following a fixed exchange rate policy. The opposite of devaluation is **revaluation.** This occurs when, under a fixed exchange rate regime, there is pressure on a country's currency to rise in value in foreign exchange markets. Unilaterally, that country can declare that the value of its currency in foreign exchange markets is higher than it has been in the past. Revaluation is the equivalent of appreciation except that it occurs under a fixed exchange rate regime and is mandated by the government.

▶ **Devaluation**
An official unilateral decrease in a currency's fixed exchange rate.

▶ **Revaluation**
An official unilateral increase in a currency's fixed exchange rate.

THE DIRTY FLOAT AND MANAGED EXCHANGE RATES

The United States went off a fixed exchange rate system in 1973, but it has nonetheless tried to keep certain elements of that system in play. We have occasionally engaged in what is called a **dirty float,** or management of flexible exchange rates. The management of flexible exchange rates has usually come about through international policy cooperation. For example, the Group of Five (G-5) nations—France, Germany, Japan, the United Kingdom, and the United States—and the Group of Seven (G-7) nations—the G-5 nations plus Canada and Italy—have for sometime shared information on their policy objectives and procedures. They do this through regular meetings between economic policy secretaries, ministers, and staff members. One of their principle objective has been to "smooth out" foreign exchange rates. Initially, the G-5 attempted to push the value of the dollar downward to help correct U.S. trade deficits and reduce Japanese foreign trade surpluses. What the five nations agreed to do was supply dollars in foreign exchange markets. This increased supply would reduce the dollar's value.

▶ **Dirty float**
A system between flexible and fixed exchange rates in which central banks occasionally enter foreign exchange markets to influence rates.

Is it possible for these groups to "manage" foreign exchange rates? Some economists do not think so. For example, economists Michael Bordo and Anna Schwartz studied the actions of the foreign exchange intervention actions coordinated by the Federal Reserve and the United States Treasury for the second half of the 1980s. Besides showing that such interventions were sporadic and variable, Bordo and Schwartz came to an even more compelling conclusion: Exchange rate interventions were trivial relative to the total trading of foreign exchange on a daily basis. For example, in April 1989 total foreign exchange trading amounted to $129 billion per day, yet the American central bank purchased only $100 million in deutsche marks and yen during that entire month (and did so on a single day). For all of 1989, Fed purchases of marks and yen were only $17.7 billion, or the equivalent of less than 14 percent of the amount of an average *day's* trading in April of that year. Their conclusion is that neither the American government nor the governments of the other G-7 nations can influence exchange rates in the long run.

THE GOLD STANDARD AND THE INTERNATIONAL MONETARY FUND

The current system of more or less freely floating exchange rates is a recent development. We have had, in the past, periods of a gold standard, fixed exchange rates under the International Monetary Fund, and variants of these two.

THE GOLD STANDARD

▶ **Gold standard**
An international monetary system in which nations fix their exchange rates in terms of gold. Thus all currencies are fixed in terms of each other. Any balance of payments problems could be made up by shipments of gold.

Until the 1930s many nations were on a pure **gold standard.** The values of their currencies were tied directly to gold.[3] Nations operating under this gold standard agreed to redeem their currencies for a fixed amount of gold at the request of any holder of that currency. Although gold was not necessarily the means of exchange for world trade, it was the unit to which all currencies under the gold standard were pegged. And because all currencies in the system were linked to gold, exchange rates between those currencies were fixed. Indeed, the gold standard has been offered as the prototype of a fixed exchange rate system. The heyday of the gold standard was from about 1870 to 1914. Britain had been on such a standard as far back as the 1820s.

There turns out to be a relationship between the balance of payments and changes in domestic money supplies throughout the world. Under a gold standard, the international financial market reaches equilibrium through the effect of gold flows on each country's money supply. When a nation suffered a deficit in its balance of payments, more gold would flow out than in. Because the domestic money supply was based on gold, an outflow of gold to foreigners caused an automatic reduction in the domestic money supply. This caused several things to happen. Interest rates rose, thereby attracting foreign capital and improving the balance of payments. At the same time, the reduction in the money supply was equivalent to a restrictive monetary policy, which caused national output and prices to fall. Imports were discouraged and exports were encouraged, thereby again improving the balance of payments.

Two problems that plagued the gold standard were that no nation had control of its domestic monetary policy and that the world's commerce was at the mercy of gold discoveries.

BRETTON WOODS AND THE INTERNATIONAL MONETARY FUND

▶ **International Monetary Fund (IMF)**
An institution set up to manage the international monetary system, established in 1945 under the Bretton Woods Agreement Act, which established fixed exchange rates for the world's currencies.

In 1944, as World War II was ending, representatives from the world's capitalist countries met in Bretton Woods, New Hampshire, to create a new international payments system to replace the gold standard, which had collapsed during the 1930s. The Bretton Woods Agreement Act was signed on July 31, 1945, by President Harry Truman. It created a new permanent institution, the **International Monetary Fund (IMF),** to administer the agreement and to lend to member countries in balance of payments deficit. The arrangements thus provided are now called the old IMF system, or the Bretton Woods system.

Each member nation was assigned a contribution quota determined by its international trade volume and national income. Twenty-five percent of the quota was contributed in gold or U.S. dollars and 75 percent in its own currency. At the time the IMF therefore consisted of a pool of gold, dollars, and other major currencies.

▶ **Par value**
The legally established value of the monetary unit of one country in terms of that of another.

Member governments were then obligated to intervene to maintain the values of their currencies in foreign exchange markets within 1 percent of the declared **par value.** The United States, which owned most of the world's gold stock, was similarly obligated to maintain gold prices within a 1 percent margin of the official rate of $35 an ounce. Except for a transitional arrangement permitting a one-time adjustment of up to 10 percent in par value, members could alter exchange rates thereafter only with the approval of the

---

[3]This is a simplification. Most nations were on a *specie metal standard* using gold, silver, copper, and other precious metals as money. Nations operating under this standard agreed to redeem their currencies for a fixed exchange rate.

IMF. The agreement stated that such approval would be given only if the country's balance of payments was in *fundamental disequilibrium*, a term that has never been officially defined.

Special Drawing Rights.

In 1967 the IMF created a new type of international money, *special drawing rights (SDRs)*. SDRs are exchanged only between monetary authorities (central banks). Their existence temporarily changed the IMF into a world central bank. The IMF creates SDRs the same way that the Federal Reserve can create dollars. The IMF allocates SDRs to member nations in accordance with their quotas. Currently, the SDR's value is determined by making one SDR equal to a bundle of currencies. In reality, the SDR rises or falls in terms of the dollar.

End of the Old IMF.

On August 15, 1971, President Richard Nixon suspended the convertibility of the dollar into gold. On December 18, 1971, we officially devalued the dollar against the currencies of 14 major industrial currencies. Finally, on March 16, 1973, the finance ministers of the European Economic Community announced that they would let their currencies float against the dollar, something Japan had already begun doing with its yen. Since 1973 the United States and most other trading countries have had either freely floating exchange rates or managed ("dirty") floating exchange rates.

PROBLEMS IN INTERNATIONAL TRADE AND THE J CURVE

Floating exchange rates do not guarantee immediate changes in international trade accounts that will correct balance of payments deficits in any country. In principle, if a country is experiencing a balance of trade deficit, there should be a depreciation of that country's currency and an improvement in its balance of payments. This happens, but only slowly. Indeed, even after the dollar depreciated dramatically in 1986, for example, America's net export position continued to deteriorate. How could this be? The explanation comes from the phenomenon called the **J curve.**

▶ **J curve**
A graph portraying the situation following a depreciation in a country's currency. At first the country's foreign trade deficit worsens, but soon its foreign trade position improves. The graph of net exports over time resembles the letter J.

The J Curve.

Figure 34-8 shows a J curve. Net exports (exports minus imports) are measured on the vertical axis; time is on the horizontal axis. According to the J curve, if

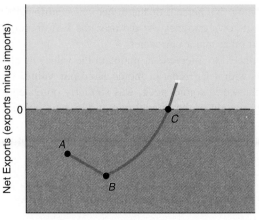

FIGURE 34-8
The J curve.
On the vertical axis we measure net exports. On the horizontal axis we measure time. The country is at point *A*, with a foreign trade deficit. Its currency depreciates. Initially, net exports become more negative—the trade deficit worsens—and we move to point *B*. In the long run, the foreign trade deficit disappears, and we move to point *C*, where net exports are zero. The resulting curve resembles a J.

we start at point *A*, we have to go down to point *B* with a worsening of the foreign trade deficit until we start to move back up to balance at point *C*. Point *C* is the situation in the long run. All previous points on the J curve are representative of foreign trade deficits in the short run that occurred just after depreciation of a country's currency.

The explanation of the J curve phenomenon has to do with the price elasticity of the demand for imports in the short run. As it turns out, import demand price elasticity is relatively low—imports are not immediately very responsive to a change in price. That means that as the dollar depreciates, the increased relative price of imports does not cause Americans to cut back very much on their consumption of imported goods. Let's say that the price of imports increases by 20 percent but the quantity demanded falls by only 10 percent. Total expenditures on imports will go up, not down. The foreign trade deficit will initially increase. In the long run, however, demand elasticities are higher. Thus the currency depreciation ultimately brings about the requisite rise in net exports.

CONCEPTS IN BRIEF

- A system of fixed exchange rates is one in which the government intervenes to set the value of each nation's currency in terms of another nation's currency.
- In any fixed exchange rate system, currency crises will occur when a country is no longer able to support the value of its currency in the foreign exchange market.
- In a fixed exchange rate system, devaluation occurs when the government officially reduces the value of its currency in foreign exchange terms. Revaluation is the opposite. Both are deliberate acts that are announced by the government.
- A dirty float occurs in a flexible exchange rate system whenever central banks intervene to influence exchange rates.
- The International Monetary Fund was developed after World War II as an institution to maintain fixed exchange rates in the world. Since 1973, however, fixed exchange rates have disappeared in most major trading countries.
- Whenever there is depreciation in a country's currency, the graph of its net exports takes the form of a J, and this is called the J curve phenomenon. Because the price elasticity of demand of imports is low in the short run, a depreciation in the dollar, which increases the relative price of imports, does not cause Americans to cut back immediately on the consumption of imported goods, thereby temporarily worsening the trade deficit.

CONTINUED ➡

WOULD ENDING OUR TRADE DEFICIT BE A CURE-ALL?

Concepts Applied: Trade deficit, exports, imports, rate of saving

With floating exchange rates, the value of a nation's currency typically changes to reflect balance of payments deficits and surpluses. A significant change in the foreign-currency value of a nation's money may have serious effects on import and export industries.

By definition, the U.S. balance of payments is always in balance. But how it gets there is, of course, another matter. During the 1980s and 1990s the United States has persistently bought more goods and services from the rest of the world than it has sold. These trade deficits have created anxiety among politicians and ordinary citizens alike. The two major problems associated with large U.S. trade deficits are high unemployment and a very large foreign (external) debt.

DO TRADE DEFICITS CREATE UNEMPLOYMENT?

A common argument is that high trade deficits costs Americans jobs. This argument has problems, however. Flows of funds between nations as payment for trade simply veil the fact that, ultimately, Americans pay for imports with exports, either today or in the future. Even if the United States could shut off all trade today, doing so would end its own export business in the long run, costing whatever jobs might be gained in the short run.

Economist Paul Krugman has pointed out that even short-run increases in employment from reduced trade deficits are unlikely. Suppose that at prevailing unemployment rates between 5 and 7 percent, the U.S. Congress decided to impose quotas that effectively shut out all trade from other nations. Naturally, this would produce an immediate trade surplus—though it might be short-lived if other nations responded by shutting out U.S. exports. The issue is, would eliminating the trade deficit create a lot more jobs in the short run? The answer is probably not. Most economists believe that the natural rate of unemployment in the United States is *at least* 5 percent, probably somewhat higher. If quotas shut out international trade, where would the workers come from to make up the difference? A likely result of such a drastic effort to remove the trade deficit, Krugman argues, would be higher inflation. Furthermore, if we prohibited all foreign trade, we would be moving to a less desirable position relative to our production possibilities curve (see Chapter 2).

TRADE DEFICITS EQUAL INCREASED INDEBTEDNESS

This does not mean that continued U.S. trade deficits are costless. To buy more goods from foreigners than U.S. citizens sell to others abroad year after year requires that U.S. citizens somehow come up with the cash to make up the difference. They do this by borrowing abroad. For this reason the United States became a net debtor to other nations. As a result, American residents must make (net) interest payments to citizens of other nations who lend to them; that is, they transfer some of their income abroad. This is the primary cost of high trade deficits.

There are at least three causes of increase in U.S. indebtedness.

LOW NATIONAL SAVINGS RATE The national savings rate in the United States is low relative to other nations. A reflection of this low savings rate is that Americans consume relatively more of their incomes than foreigners do, which places foreigners in a position to lend to Americans, who can then buy more foreign goods.

Some observers blame households and firms for the low national savings rate, arguing that they use too much debt. This is a questionable point, however. Although the *level* of firm and household debt issued in the United States has increased in recent years, the debt of private Americans, measured relative to output produced in the United States, is not much greater than in earlier years.

For example, the ratio of American private debt to national output is lower in this country than in Germany and Japan.

THE TWIN-DEFICIT PROBLEM If the American private sector is not so easily blamed for the high trade deficit and the growing U.S. indebtedness to other nations, that potentially leaves the U.S. government as the main culprit. Indeed, many economists believe that the blame lies at the federal government's doorstep. A key reason that the total national saving rate of the United States is so low is that the federal government continually runs budget deficits; by so doing, it effectively captures a lot of funds that would have gone into national saving. This in turn leads to the trade deficit: Lacking accumulated savings to invest at home, households and firms borrow from foreigners and purchase goods from abroad. This relationship between the federal budget deficit and the trade deficit is commonly called the *twin-deficit problem.*

MEASUREMENT PROBLEMS Not all economists agree that the federal government is completely to blame for the high American trade deficits. In fact, some econ-

omists believe that U.S. trade deficits aren't really as high as official figures indicate. For one thing, U.S. exports to other countries are understated because (1) exporters have a strong incentive to underreport sales because their taxable income is thereby reduced, and (2) export licenses are required (and in some cases outright bans exist) on sales of "sensitive" national-security-related machinery—hence nonreporting, underreporting, and smuggling result. In contrast, import data are collected directly by a single governmental agency, which collects revenues from tariffs. Consequently, U.S. import data are reliable, but U.S. export data are understated. Indeed, using 1987 data, St. Louis Federal Reserve economist Mack Ott estimated that the U.S. trade deficit may be overstated by between 10 and 15 percent annually. This revelation may not solve the problem, but it indicates that the scope of the problem may not be as great as some people have feared.

FOR CRITICAL ANALYSIS
1. Why should the United States worry that it is the world's largest debtor nation?
2. Who benefits from America's large trade deficit?

- -

CHAPTER SUMMARY

1. The balance of trade is defined as the value of goods bought and sold in the world market, usually during the period of one year. The balance of payments is a more inclusive concept that includes the value of all transactions in the world market.

2. Americans purchase financial assets in other countries, and foreigners purchase American financial assets, such as stocks or bonds. The buying and selling of foreign financial assets has the same effect on the balance of payments as the buying and selling of goods and services.

3. Our balance of trade and payments can be affected by our relative rate of inflation and by political instability elsewhere compared to the stability that exists in the United States.

4. The theory of purchasing power parity (PPP) holds that exchange rate changes exactly reflect changes in the relative price levels of two different countries over the long run.

5. Market determinants of exchange rates are changes in real interest rates (interest rates corrected for inflation), changes in productivity, changes in product preferences, and perceptions of economic stability.

6. To transact business internationally, it is necessary to convert domestic currencies into other currencies. This is done via a foreign exchange market. If we were trading with France only, French producers would want to be paid in francs because they must pay their workers in francs. American producers would want to be paid in dollars because American workers are paid in dollars.

7. An American's desire for French wine is expressed in terms of a supply of dollars, which is in turn a demand for French francs in the foreign exchange market. The opposite situation arises when the French wish to buy American jeans. Their demand for jeans creates a demand for American dollars and a supply of French francs. We put the demand and supply schedules together to find the equilibrium foreign exchange rate. The demand schedule for foreign exchange is a derived demand—it is derived from the Americans' demand for foreign products.

8. With no government intervention, a market clearing equilibrium foreign exchange rate will emerge. After a shift in demand or supply, the exchange rate will change so that it will again clear the market.

9. If Americans increase their demand for French wine, the demand curve for French wine shifts to the right. The derived demand for francs also shifts to the right. The supply schedule of francs, however, remains stable because the French demand for American jeans has remained constant. The shifted demand schedule intersects the stable supply schedule at a higher price (the foreign exchange rate increases). This is an appreciation of the value of French francs (a depreciation of the value of the dollar against the franc).

10. A fixed exchange rate system requires government intervention to keep the price of its currency stable. Government intervention involves selling foreign currencies (or gold) to prop up the price of the domestic currency in the foreign exchange market when a country is running a payments deficit.

11. In a managed exchange rate system (a "dirty float"), central banks occasionally intervene in foreign exchange markets to influence exchange rates.

12. Under a gold standard, movement of gold across countries changes domestic money supplies, causing price levels to change and to correct balance of payments imbalances.

13. In 1945 the International Monetary Fund (IMF) was created to maintain fixed exchange rates throughout the world. This system was abandoned in 1973.

14. The J-curve phenomenon occurs when a country's currency depreciates but its foreign trade deficit continues to worsen and only after time improves. The graph of net exports resembles a J.

DISCUSSION OF PREVIEW POINTS

1. What is the difference between the balance of trade and the balance of payments?

The balance of trade is defined as the difference between the value of exports and the value of imports. If the value of exports exceeds the value of imports, a trade surplus exists; if the value of exports is less than the value of imports, a trade deficit exists; if export and import values are equal, we refer to this situation as a trade balance. The balance of payments is more general and takes into account the value of *all* international transactions. Thus the balance of payments identifies not only goods and services transactions among nations but also investments (financial and nonfinancial) and gifts (private and public). When the value of all these transactions is such that one nation is sending more to other nations than it is receiving in return, a balance of payments deficit exists. A payments surplus and payments balance are self-explanatory.

2. What is a foreign exchange rate?

We know that nations trade with each other; they buy and sell goods, make and receive financial and nonfinancial investments, and give and receive gifts. However, nations have different currencies. People who sell to, invest in, or receive gifts from the United States ultimately want their own currency so that they can use the money domestically. Similarly, U.S. residents who sell in, invest in, or receive gifts from people in other countries ultimately want U.S. dollars to spend in the United States. Because most people ultimately want to end up with their own currencies, foreign exchange markets have evolved to enable people to sell one currency for other currencies. A foreign exchange rate, then, is the rate at which one country's currency can be exchanged for another's. For example, the exchange rate between England and the United States might dictate that one pound sterling is equivalent to $1.50; alternately stated, the U.S. dollar is worth .667 pound sterling.

3. What is a floating exchange rate system?

A floating exchange rate system is an international monetary system in which foreign exchange rates are allowed to adjust to reflect changes in the supply of and demand for international currencies. Say that the United States and England are in payments balance at the exchange rate of one pound sterling to U.S. $1.50. The U.S. demand for sterling is derived from private and government desires to buy British goods, to invest in England, or to send gifts to the British people and is *inversely* related to the number of dollars it takes to buy one pound. Conversely, the supply of sterling is derived from England's private and governmental desires to buy U.S. goods and services, to invest in the United States, and to send gifts to U.S. residents. The supply of sterling is *directly* related to the number of dollars one pound is worth. The intersection of the supply and demand curves for sterling determines the market foreign exchange rate of dollars per pound. In a system of floating exchange rates, shifts in the supply or demand curves will lead to changes in the foreign exchange rates between nations.

4. **What is a fixed exchange rate system?**

Under a fixed exchange rate international monetary system, nations agree to fix, or "peg," their currency units among themselves. For instance, the United States and England might officially agree to peg their exchange rates at one pound sterling to U.S. $1.50. Each nation is pledged not to allow its currency to depreciate (fall in value relative to other currencies) below some permissible percentage of the agreed fixed exchange rate. Suppose that we start from a payments balance position at the agreed exchange rate (one pound sterling equals $1.50) and U.S. residents now increase their demand for British goods (other things being constant). This would cause the U.S. dollar to depreciate; the equilibrium value of the pound might rise to $1.60. But if the United States is committed to not allowing the dollar to depreciate by more than 1 percent (here the value of the dollar must not be allowed to fall lower than $1.515 per pound), it must intervene in the foreign exchange market. It can do so by using its reserves of pounds sterling or gold to buy U.S. dollars to support the dollar. This decision could potentially lead to a U.S. payments deficit for prolonged periods unless supply and demand conditions again change toward a market equilibrium of one pound equals $1.50. This system, like all systems that peg prices at non–market clearing levels, potentially lead to periods of prolonged shortages or surpluses of currencies and to prolonged payments imbalances.

PROBLEMS

(Answers to the odd-numbered problems appear at the back of the book.)

34-1.   In the graph, what can be said about the shift from D to D_1?

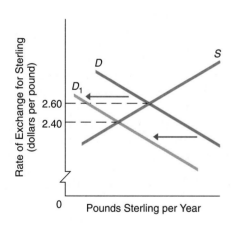

a. It could be caused by Britons demanding fewer U.S. products.
b. It is a result of increased U.S. demand for British goods.
c. It causes an appreciation of the dollar relative to the pound.
d. It causes an appreciation of the pound relative to the dollar.

34-2.   If the rate of exchange between the pound and the dollar is $1.45 for one pound, and the United States then experiences severe inflation, we would expect the exchange rate (under a flexible rate system) to shift. What would be the new rate?
a. More than $1.45 for one pound
b. Less than $1.45 for one pound
c. More than one pound for $1.45
d. None of the above

34-3.   The dollar, the pound sterling, and the deutsche mark are the currency units of the United States, England, and Germany, respectively. Suppose that these nations decide to go on a gold standard and define the value of their currencies in terms of gold as follows: $35 = 1 ounce of gold; 10 pounds sterling = 1 ounce of gold, and 100 marks = 1 ounce of gold. What would the exchange rate be between the dollar and the pound? Between the dollar and the mark? Between the mark and the pound?

34-4.   Examine the following hypothetical data for U.S. international transactions, in billions of dollars.

Exports: goods, 165.8; services, 130.5
Imports: goods, −250.7; services, −99.3
Net unilateral transfers: −20.0

a. What is the balance of trade?
b. What is the balance on goods and services?
c. What is the balance on current account?

34-5.   Maintenance of a fixed exchange rate system requires government intervention to keep exchange rates stable. What is the policy implication of this fact? (Hint: Think in terms of the money supply.)

34-6. Suppose that we have the following demand schedule for German beer in the United States per week:

PRICE PER CASE	QUANTITY DEMANDED (CASES)
$40	2
32	4
24	6
16	8
8	10

  a. If the price is 30 deutsche marks per case, how many marks are required to purchase each quantity demanded?
  b. Now derive the demand schedule for marks per week in the United States to pay for German beer.
  c. At a price of 80 cents per mark, how many cases of beer would be imported from Germany per week?

34-7. The accompanying graph shows the supply of and demand for pounds sterling.

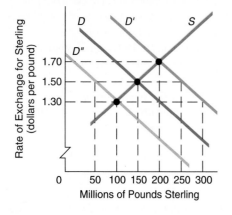

  a. Assuming that the demand for sterling is represented by *D*, what is the dollar price of pounds? What is the equilibrium quantity?
  b. Suppose that there is general inflation in the United States. Which demand curve could represent this situation? If exchange rates are allowed to float freely, what would be the new dollar price of one pound sterling? What would be the equilibrium quantity?
  c. Suppose that the inflation in part (b) occurs and the United States has the dollar price of one pound sterling fixed at $1.50. How would the Federal Reserve be able to accomplish this?
  d. Now suppose that instead of inflation, there was general deflation in the United States. Which demand curve could represent this situation? How could the United States maintain a fixed price of $1.50 per pound sterling in this situation?

34-8. Which of the following will cause the yen to appreciate? Explain.
  a. U.S. real incomes increase relative to Japanese real incomes.
  b. It is expected that in the future the yen will depreciate relative to the dollar.
  c. The U.S. inflation rate rises relative to the Japanese inflation rate.
  d. The after-tax, risk-adjusted real interest rate in the United States rises relative to that in Japan.
  e. U.S. tastes change in favor of Japanese-made goods.

COMPUTER-ASSISTED INSTRUCTION
(Complete problem and answer on disk.)

Suppose that the United States and France have formed a two-country gold standard, and a balance of payments equilibrium exists. What happens if tastes change so that U.S. residents now prefer French goods more than they did previously, other things being constant? This problem shows how balance of payments equilibrium is restored under a gold standard, a specific fixed exchange rate system.

35

DEVELOPMENT ECONOMICS

Throughout the world's history, disease has devastated populations and economies. In the fourteenth century an acute infectious disease caused by the bacillus *Pasteurella pestis* swept through Europe during a four-year period (1347–1351), reducing the population of the Continent by about 35 percent. That plague set back severely the prospects for economic development. In modern times we are not used to thinking of plagues or other diseases as being so virulent that they affect the development of nations. Does modern medicine guarantee that a plague as devastating as that of the Middle Ages will never again affect the world's economies? Some people are no longer certain that the answer is yes. To understand this issue and its impact on the world, you will need to know something about development economics.

After reading this chapter, you should be able to answer the following questions:

1. What is a developing country?

2. Must developing countries develop by industrializing?

3. Can developing countries create their own capital stock?

4. Does a lack of protected property rights hinder a developing country's development?

INTRODUCTION

Most Americans cannot even begin to understand the reality of poverty in the world to-day. At least one-half, if not two-thirds, of the world's population lives at subsistence level, with just enough to eat for survival. The official poverty level in the United States exceeds the average income in at least half the world. That is not to say that we should ignore problems at home with the poor and homeless simply because they are living better than many people elsewhere in the world. Rather, it is necessary for Americans to keep their perspective on what are considered problems for this country relative to what are considered problems elsewhere.

WHAT IS DEVELOPMENT ECONOMICS?

It is hard to imagine, but at one time the United States was a developing country. Now we are considered a developed country. All countries that we classify as developed started out like much of today's Third World. How did developed countries travel the path out of extreme poverty to relative riches? That is the essential issue of development economics. It is the study of why some countries develop and others do not. Further, it is the study of changes in policies that might help developing countries get richer. Certainly, it is not good enough simply to say that people in different countries are different and therefore that is why some countries are rich and some countries are poor. Economists do not deny that different cultures create different work ethics, but they are unwilling to accept such a pat and fatalistic answer.

Look at the world map in the front of the book. About four-fifths of the countries you see on that map are considered relatively poor. The goal of students of development economics is to help the more than 4 billion people today with low living standards join the billion or so who have relatively high living standards.

INDUSTRIALLY ADVANCED ECONOMIES

Any system of defining poor countries and rich countries, developing countries and developed countries is, of course, arbitrary. Nonetheless, it is instructive to examine some figures on the difference between **industrially advanced countries (IACs)** and so-called developing countries. There are 19 IACs. (Excluded from this classification are countries whose economies are based on a single resource, such as oil, but whose industrial development in other fields is minimal.) The latest data available on the IACs (1992) show an estimated per capita income of $14,850, an annual growth rate of about 2.2 percent, and a population growth of about 0.6 percent. At the other end of the scale, the more than 100 developing countries have a per capita income of $700, an annual growth rate of almost 3 percent, and a population growth rate of 2 percent per year, more than three times that of the IACs.

▶ **Industrially advanced countries (IACs)**
Canada, Japan, the United States, and the countries of Western Europe, all of which have market economies based on a large skilled labor force and a large technically advanced stock of capital goods.

To be sure, we must be careful about accepting such data at face value. There is a tremendous disparity in incomes among the developing countries, and the data are notoriously inaccurate. Nonetheless, it is certain that a tremendous gap exists between average incomes in the IACs and in the developing countries.

NEWLY INDUSTRIALIZED ECONOMIES

Not all developing countries are stuck in abject poverty. The developing countries vary greatly in their ability to experience economic growth, but one group of recently industrialized economies has achieved annual growth rates two and three times that of the United States. These newly industrialized economies are the so-called Four Tigers—Singapore,

Hong Kong, Taiwan, and South Korea—all on the Pacific Rim. From 1960 to 1990 per capita income in these economies grew over fivefold.

During the same period, a number of sub-Saharan African nations experienced a *fall* in real per capita income. For many parts of the world, the income gap between rich and poor has increased rather than decreased over the past several decades.

CONCEPTS IN BRIEF

- Any definition of developing countries or industrialized advanced countries (IACs) is arbitrary. Nonetheless, we have identified 19 IACs and over 100 developing countries.
- The IACs have per capita incomes that are roughly 20 times the per capita incomes in the developing nations. Population in developing nations is growing more than three times as fast as in the IACs.
- Four newly industrialized nations on the Pacific Rim—Singapore, Taiwan, South Korea, and Hong Kong—have increased their real per capita incomes more than fivefold since 1960.
- The gap between the IACs and most of the developing countries either remained stable or widened in the past decade or two.

SOCIOECONOMIC FACTORS OF DEVELOPMENT

A country can have a very high economic growth rate, but many of the basic needs of its citizens remain unmet. Economic development means more than simply economic growth. It means creating an environment in which citizens can expect long lives, adequate food, and the ability to understand better the world around them because they are literate.

Just looking at per capita income levels does not provide the full picture of the difference between the developing countries and the rest of the world. Table 35-1 shows some interesting socioeconomic indicators of development, including life expectancy, infant mortality (death rate), literacy, and per capita daily caloric supply. People living in the United States and Australia, for example, have a life expectancy that is nearly 60 percent

TABLE 35-1 **Socioeconomic indicators of development for selected countries.**
Developing countries suffer from relatively low life expectancy, high infant mortality, low levels of literacy, and low levels of per capita daily caloric supply.

COUNTRY	LIFE EXPECTANCY AT BIRTH, 1991	INFANT MORTALITY PER 1,000 LIVE BIRTHS	LITERACY (%)	PER CAPITA DAILY CALORIC SUPPLY
United States	76	10	99[a]	3,702
Japan	79	4	99	2,700
Australia	75	10	98	3,810
Israel	74	13	88	3,140
Italy	73	12	94	3,004
China	68	31	32	2,620
Mexico	64	52	81	2,580
Pakistan	59	110	27	2,220
India	54	94	44	2,121
Mozambique	50	135	29	1,642
Bangladesh	48	107	34	1,840
Afghanistan	38	172	7	1,690

[a] True functional literacy is much lower in the United States and perhaps in other countries also.

Source: United Nations, *World Development Report,* 1993.

greater than that in Bangladesh. The infant mortality rate is 10.7 times greater in Bangladesh than in the United States. Literacy rates and dietary adequacy are also dramatically higher in developed countries.

When we look at the amount of world output accounted for by developed countries, the inequality between the haves and the have-nots is even more striking. The industrialized market economies have less than 17 percent of world population but generate almost 65 percent of total world output. The United States, with about 5 percent of the world's population, generates about one-fourth of total world output.

POPULATION PROBLEMS

Population growth in developing countries is more than three times that in advanced industrial countries. The slowest-growing nations are the United Kingdom, Germany, Belgium, Switzerland, Denmark, Austria, Sweden, Japan, and New Zealand. The fastest-growing nations have been in Africa—Kenya, Zimbabwe, Ivory Coast, Uganda, Nigeria, Zambia, and Guinea. Other fast-growing countries are in Latin America. There seems to be a relationship between high population growth rates and low per capita income.

Typically, we measure improvement in economic well-being by the rate of growth of national income each year, corrected for inflation. Sub-Saharan Africa, for example, has experienced a 2 to 3 percent growth in domestic output each year. But that does not mean that the population in that region is better off. Why? Because its population is growing faster than domestic output. We therefore have to look at the per-person rate of annual growth in domestic product. When this is done for sub-Saharan Africa, for example, real standards of living fell over the past decade. Figure 35-1 shows that recent years have not been good years for many developing nations. These nations have actually experienced declines in per capita domestic product.

Is Population Growth the Cause of Poverty?   Often we hear that excessive population growth is the cause of poverty among nations. Consider the global picture. That there are about 5.5 billion people in the world sounds phenomenal, but in reality, if we put all these human beings into the state of Texas, each person would have about 1,500 square feet. A family of four could have 6,000 square feet—which is about the size of a typical middle-class American home, with yards in front and back.

On an international basis there is little relationship between poverty and population density. For example, Ethiopia has the same number of people per square mile as the United States. But Ethiopia's average per capita income is only about $300 per year. Japan

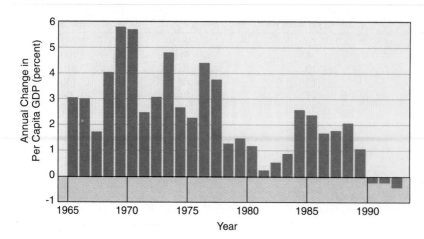

FIGURE 35-1
Income in developing nations, 1965–1992.
This graph shows the average annual percentage change in per capita gross domestic product in developing countries, adjusted for inflation. In recent years per capita GDP has actually been declining.
Source: World Bank.

has a higher per capita income than many Western European nations, yet it has more people per square mile than India, one of the poorest nations. Rapid population growth does not necessarily create poverty either. Consider the example of Malaysia, which grew from a sparsely populated country of villages in the 1890s to a nation of cities in the 1930s. During this period its population increased from 1.5 million to 6 million, but its standard of living also increased, by about 140 percent. Indeed, historically, the largest increases in Western living standards took place during periods when the Western population was growing faster than it is in today's Third World.

Developing Countries and Population Control. One of the most troublesome problems facing developing countries in their quest for higher per capita standards of living is typically high population growth rates. It is certainly no secret that a developing country might have a better chance at raising its citizens' per capita standard of living if there were fewer mouths to feed. Indeed, many students of economic development believe that the major problem in the developing countries is excess population growth. A typical international development conference will be divided into two groups: (1) representatives from developing countries who want development and (2) representatives from developed nations who want family planning (birth control) to be instituted as a prerequisite for the development of these countries.

Ironically, generosity on the part of the developed countries has contributed to high population growth rates in developing countries. Specifically, aid and transfer of knowledge about health, nutrition, and sanitation have reduced death rates in numerous developing countries. It is arithmetically impossible to avoid an increase in population growth if death rates are reduced without a concomitant reduction in birthrates. Some proponents of increased Western aid to developing countries are quick to point out that excess population growth was caused by Western aid to begin with and therefore the results of excess population growth should be coped with by the developed countries.

Recent research on population and economic development has revealed that social and economic modernization has been accompanied by what might be called a fertility revolution—the spread of deliberate family-size limitation within marriage and a decline in childbearing. Modernization reduces infant mortality, which in turn reduces the incentive for couples to have many children to make sure that enough will survive to satisfy each couple's demand. Also, modernization lowers the demand for children for a variety of reasons, not the least being that couples in more developed countries do not need to rely on their children to take care of them in old age.

LITERACY AND POVERTY

Another important socioeconomic datum that seems to correlate with poverty and the lack of economic development is a low literacy rate. There appears to be a vicious cycle with respect to literacy and poverty. Individuals in any nation can rarely hope to break out of poverty if they remain illiterate. Yet extremely poor families rarely choose to sacrifice household production (usually through farming or at-home artisanal labor) to allow their school-aged children to attend school. Thus in truly poor countries, even if education is offered by the government, poor families choose not to send their children to school. Entire families remain illiterate and often unable to achieve living standards above subsistence.

🌐 **INTERNATIONAL EXAMPLE: Nutrition and Well-being in England over Time**

One of the indicators of well-being shown in Table 35-1 is per capita daily caloric supply. As it turns out, we can measure the effects of low calorie intake on human well-being for thousands of years back. Archaeologists do this by examining the bones discovered in burial sites throughout the world. They can reconstruct average body height. Body height is dependent on not only the average number of calories consumed per day but also the nutritional quality of those calories. And there is a direct correlation between income per capita and nutritional intake. Data from England tend to confirm these relationships. Average heights increased slightly from around A.D. 400 to 900; then they dropped steadily until the middle of the 1700s. Not surprisingly, this was a time of economic stagnation throughout Europe. But in the 1700s, discoveries in both industry and agriculture started England and the rest of Europe toward continual economic development. Although average heights of people in England have not grown consistently since the mid-1700s, on average they have. Interestingly, though, today they are still below what they were estimated to be in A.D. 850 to 900.

For Critical Analysis: *Is minimal economic development a cause of poor nutrition? Or is it possible that poor nutrition prevents economic development?* ●

CONCEPTS IN BRIEF

● Important socioeconomic indicators of development include life expectancy, infant mortality, literacy rates, and per capita daily caloric supply.
● Some people believe that population growth is the cause of poverty in developing nations, but there are many counter examples that tend to dispute this notion. Nonetheless, developing countries might have a better chance at raising their citizens' per capita standard of living if population grew at a slower rate.
● As countries develop, we see the spread of deliberate family-size limitations within marriage and a decline in childbearing.
● Literacy is highly correlated with economic development. Literacy and poverty are locked in a vicious cycle.

ECONOMIC DEVELOPMENT: INDUSTRY VERSUS AGRICULTURE

One of the most widely discussed theories of development concerns the need for balanced growth, with industry and agriculture given equal importance. One characteristic of many developed countries is their high degree of industrialization, although there are clearly exceptions—Hong Kong, for example. In general, nations with relatively high standards of living are more industrialized than countries with low standards of living. Some analysts have taken this to mean that industrialization can be equated with economic development. The policy prescription is then obvious: Less developed nations in which a large percentage of the total resources are devoted to agricultural pursuits should attempt to obtain more balanced growth by industrializing.

Although the theory is fairly acceptable at first glance, it leads to some absurd results. We find in many developing countries with steel factories and automobile plants that the people are actually worse off because of this attempted industrialization. The reason is not hard to find. Most developing countries currently cannot profitably produce steel or automobiles because they lack the necessary domestic human and physical capital. They can engage in such industrial activities only with heavy government subsidization of the industry itself. Import restrictions abound, preventing the purchase of foreign, mostly cheaper substitutes for the industrial products that the country itself produces. Also, in general, the existence of subsidies leads to a misallocation of resources and a lower economic welfare for the country as a whole. The owners in the subsidized industry and the workers with skills specific to that industry may be better off, but the consumer ends up paying a higher total cost for the domestically made goods, and the total output of the nation remains less than it could be if the resources were reallocated *away from* the subsidized industries.

The fact is that in less developed countries there is a bias toward large, obvious investments. Adam Smith noted this more than two centuries ago in his *Wealth of Nations*:

> The proud minister of an ostentatious court may frequently take pleasure in executing a work of splendour and magnificence, such as a great highway. . . . But to execute a great number of little works [that] have nothing to recommend them but their extreme utility is a business which appears in every respect too mean and paltry to merit the attention of so great a magistrate.

INTERNATIONAL EXAMPLE: **Industrialized Poverty**

Amazingly, some of the poorest countries in the world today have some of the highest rates of industrialization. Industry's share of gross output is greater in sub-Saharan Africa than in Denmark. Industry's share of gross output in Zimbabwe, Botswana, and Trinidad and Tobago is greater than in Japan. Industry's share of gross output in Zaire is greater than in the United States. Industry's share of gross output in Argentina is greater than in every country in the European Community.

Agriculture represents a relatively low share of gross output in some of the nation's poorest countries. For example, agriculture represents a greater share of national output in Denmark than it does in Trinidad and Tobago. The same is true in Spain relative to Botswana and in Portugal relative to Gabon. It is clear that industrialization does not necessarily lead to high standards of living.

For Critical Analysis: If industry represents a large share of gross output in extremely poor countries, what does this tell you about the rate of return on investment in industry in those countries? ●

THE STAGES OF DEVELOPMENT: AGRICULTURE TO INDUSTRY TO SERVICES

If we analyze the development of modern rich nations, we find that they went through three stages. First, there is the agricultural stage, when most of the population is involved in agriculture. Then there is the manufacturing stage, when much of the population becomes involved in the industrialized sector of the economy. And finally there is a shift toward services. That is exactly what happened in the United States: The so-called tertiary, or service, sector of the economy continues to grow, whereas the manufacturing sector (and its share of employment) is declining in relative importance.

However, it is important to understand the need for early specialization in a nation's comparative advantage. We have continuously referred to the doctrine of comparative advantage, and it is even more appropriate for the developing countries of the world. If trading is allowed among nations, a nation is normally best off if it produces what it has a comparative advantage at producing and imports the rest (see Chapter 33). This means that many developing countries should continue to specialize in agricultural production or in labor-intensive manufactured goods.

HOW SUBSIDIZED AGRICULTURE AFFECTS DEVELOPING NATIONS

Modern Western countries have continually subsidized their own agricultural sectors to allow them to compete more easily with the developing countries in this area. If we lived in a world of no subsidization, we would probably see less food being produced in the highly developed Western world (except for the United States, Canada, and Australia) and much more being produced in the developing countries of the rest of the world. They would trade food for manufactured goods. It would seem, then, that one of the most detrimental aspects of our economic policy for the developing countries has been the continued subsidization of the American farmer. The United States, of course, is not alone; Germany, France, and England do exactly the same thing.

Even with this situation, however, a policy of using higher taxes on imported goods or domestic manufacturing subsidies in order to increase industrialization in the developing countries may do more harm than good. Industrialization is generally beneficial only if it comes about naturally, when the market conditions are such that the countries' entrepreneurs freely decide to build factories instead of increasing farm output because it is profitable to do so.

CONCEPTS IN BRIEF

- A balanced-growth theory predicts that industry and agriculture must grow together in order for a nation to experience growth.
- For many developing countries, balanced growth requires subsidization of manufacturing firms.
- Historically, there are three stages of economic development: (1) the agricultural stage, (2) the manufacturing stage, and (3) the service-sector stage, when a large part of the work force is employed in providing services.

NATURAL RESOURCES AND ECONOMIC DEVELOPMENT

One theory of development states that for a country to develop, it must have a large natural resource base. The theory continues to assert that much of the world is running out of natural resources, thereby limiting economic growth and development. We must point out that only the narrowest definition of a natural resource could lead to such an opinion. In broader terms, a natural resource is something scarce occurring in nature that we can use for our own purposes. Natural resources therefore include knowledge of the use of something. The natural resources that we could define several hundred years ago did not, for example, include hydroelectric power—no one knew that such a natural resource existed or, indeed, how to make it exist.

In any event, it is difficult to find a strong correlation between the natural resources of a nation and its stage of development. Japan has virtually no crude oil and must import most of the natural resources that it uses as inputs for its industrial production. Brazil has huge amounts of natural resources, including fertile soil and abundant minerals, yet Brazil has a much lower per capita income than Japan. Only when we include the human element of natural resources can we say that natural resources determine economic development.

Natural resources by themselves are not particularly useful for economic development. They must be transformed into something usable for either investment or consumption. This leads us to another aspect of development, the trade-off between investment and consumption. The normal way this subject is analyzed is by dealing with investment simply as capital accumulation.

CAPITAL ACCUMULATION

It is often asserted that a necessary prerequisite for economic development is a large capital stock—machines and other durable goods that can be used to aid in the production of consumption goods and more capital goods in the future. It is true that industrially advanced countries indeed have larger capital stocks per capita than developing countries. It is also true that the larger the capital stock for any given population, the higher the possible rate of economic growth (assuming that the population makes good use of the capital goods). This is basically one of the foundations for many of the foreign aid programs in which the United States and other countries have engaged. We and other nations have attempted to give developing countries capital so that they, too, might grow. However, the amount of capital that we have actually given to other nations is quite small: a steel mill here, a factory there.

DOMESTIC CAPITAL FORMATION

How does a developing nation accumulate capital? The answer is that it must save and invest those accumulated savings profitably. Saving, of course, means not consuming. Resources must be released from consumer goods' production in order to be used for investment.

Saving and the Poor.

It is often stated that people in developing countries cannot save because they are barely subsisting. This is not actually true. Many anthropological studies—of villages in India, for example—have revealed that saving is in fact going on, but it takes forms that we don't recognize in our money economy. In some places, saving may even involve storing dried onions that can later be traded for other goods. Some researchers speculate that much saving in developing countries takes the form of rearing children who then feel a moral obligation to support their parents during the latter's retirement. In any event, saving does take place even in the most poverty-stricken areas. In general, there is no pronounced relationship between the *percentage* of income saved and the level of income (over the long run).

Basically, then, saving is a method by which individuals can realize an optimal consumption stream throughout their expected lifetimes. The word *optimal* here does not mean adequate or necessary or decent; it means most desirable from the *individual's* point of view (given that individual's resources).

Evidence of Saving in Developing Countries.

Savings in developing countries do not necessarily flow into what we might consider productive capital formation projects. We do see the results of literally centuries of saving in the form of religious monuments, such as cathedrals and government monuments. Indeed, one major problem in developing nations is that much of the saving that occurs does not get channeled into productive capital formation. This is also true of much of the foreign aid that has been sent to developing nations. These nations need more factories and a better infrastructure—roads and communications—rather than more government monuments and fancy stadiums built exclusively for merrymaking and sport.

PROPERTY RIGHTS AND ECONOMIC DEVELOPMENT

If you were in a country in which bank accounts and businesses were periodically expropriated by the government, how willing would you be to leave your money in a savings account or to invest in a business? Certainly you would be less willing than if such things never occurred. Periodic expropriation of private property rarely occurs in developed countries. It *has* occurred in numerous developing countries, however. For example, private property was once nationalized in Chile and still is in Cuba. In some cases, former owners are compensated, but rarely for the full value of the property taken over by the state.

Empirically we have seen that, other things being equal, the more certain private property rights are, the more private capital accumulation there will be. People are more willing to invest their savings in endeavors that will increase their wealth in future years. They have property rights in their wealth that are sanctioned and enforced by the government. In fact, some economic historians have attempted to show that it was the development of well-defined private property rights that allowed Western Europe to increase its growth rate after many centuries of stagnation. The degree of certainty with which one can reap the gains from investing also determines the extent to which business people in *other* countries will invest capital in developing countries. The threat of nationalization that hangs over some Latin American nations may scare away foreign investment that would allow these nations to become more developed.

Are People the Most Important Element in Economic Development?

When economic development is discussed, natural resources, capital accumulation, and reduced population growth are almost always mentioned as important factors. But we have to remember that lack of one or more of these factors does not necessarily put a less developed country into the trap of underdevelopment or into the **vicious cycle of poverty.** Presumably, developing nations are poor because they can't save and invest, but they can't save and invest because they are poor.

▶ **Vicious cycle of poverty**
A theory that low per capita incomes are an obstacle to realizing the necessary amount of saving and investment that is required to achieve acceptable rates of economic growth.

Nevertheless, we would do well to remember that every developed country today was at one time an underdeveloped country. In 1800 Hong Kong was a barren rock; 100 years later it was a substantial port. What is now the United States was once completely underdeveloped; today it is a dynamic, sophisticated economic superpower. Clearly we must look to factors beyond poverty to determine the various routes to development. Paramount among these other factors are the following three:

1. **Trade with the outside world.** To the extent that any country reduces its trade barriers, it will normally grow faster. Unfortunately, developing countries attempt to protect domestic industries by raising high tariff walls, thereby cutting back on imports. As we learned in Chapter 33, because imports are paid by export sales, exports are reduced accordingly.
2. **Human attitudes and aptitudes.** Some people argue that specific cultures foster thriftiness, productivity, and the quest for a better material life. Others are not so certain. They claim that it is best to look at the *incentive* structure in any economy to determine how fast that economy will grow and develop. For example, developing countries often have very high marginal tax rates that discourage work and saving as well as investment. Also, many developing countries have legal systems that do not protect private property rights (or forbid them altogether). In such systems, entrepreneurship may be stifled, thus reducing the rate of economic growth and development.
3. **Political institutions.** This factor is related to the human factor. Some political institutions foster rapid development; others do not. To the extent that the body politic encourages free entry into any industry and does not subsidize losing industries, there will be more economic development. Typically, in countries in which government-owned businesses account for a small percentage of GDP, all other things held constant, there will be more economic development. In political systems that support and enforce price controls, there will be less incentive for entrepreneurs to enter businesses for which the goods produced are in relatively scarce supply.

In a sentence, economic development depends more on individuals who are able to perceive opportunities and then take advantage of those opportunities than it does on capital or natural resources.[1] Remember that entrepreneurship was listed at the beginning of your text as one of the four factors of production. It is entrepreneurs who are willing to take risks and who will in fact take advantage of economic opportunities when they arise. But risk taking will not occur if the risk takers cannot expect a reward. The political institutions must be such that risk takers are rewarded. That requires well-established property rights, lack of the threat of expropriation of profits, and no fear of government nationalization of businesses.

DEVELOPMENT AND MODERN ECONOMIC GROWTH THEORY

▶ **Modern economic growth (MEG)**
The theory of economic growth in which growth is characterized by increases in per capita output accompanied by increases in population and driven by the application of science to the problems of economic production.

Economists have found it useful to develop the concept of **modern economic growth (MEG).** A country experiencing modern economic growth is characterized by a sustained increase in per capita output, most often accompanied by an increase in population and usually by structural changes in government and industry. Modern economic growth is driven by the application of science to the problems of economic production and to the material satisfaction of wants. Thus the driving forces of modern economic growth are scientific advancement and its application to production. Such forces ensure sustained economic growth and increases in per capita income and provide for permanent change. They also generate further scientific advances.

The countries experiencing modern economic growth undergo continual shifts in their leading economic sectors. The nature of an economy can change from agricultural to industrial; after a nation has industrialized, it can change from a manufacturing economy to a high-tech electronics or an information economy. Such structural changes can be brought about through changes in tastes, in comparative advantage (see Chapter 33), or in technology itself.

DEVELOPING COUNTRIES

Students of modern economic growth theory stress that the conditions for economic growth for developing countries differ from those of developed countries. The mere existence of advanced economies changes the environment of modern economic growth for newcomers—less advanced countries that are beginning to experience modern economic growth. For that reason alone, MEG is likely to take a different path for latecomers from that taken by early starters. As is usually the case in economics, a trade-off exists; there are advantages and disadvantages to being a late starter.

Latecomers have an advantage in that they can borrow technologies from economically advanced nations without having to allocate resources to the costly and time-consuming trial-and-error process of developing their own technologies from scratch. However, the ability to borrow technology and use it fruitfully depends on minimal levels of scientific and technological sophistication—a precondition often lacking in latecomers.

The major disadvantage of being a latecomer is that such a status creates tremendous tensions within the country. Two types of tensions emerge. The first results from an impatience to narrow the huge gap in real incomes between latecomer nations and advanced nations. The later a country enters the growth arena, the larger the real income gap—and the greater the tension. The second source of tension derives from the fact that preconditions for attaining modern economic growth (entrepreneurial experience, developed

---

[1]The member nations of OPEC might be considered exceptions to this generalization.

financial and nonfinancial markets, a skilled and disciplined labor force, and so on) are less likely to exist in latecomer nations. Indeed, the more backward the country, the greater the tensions arising from the lack of preconditions for attaining modern economic growth.

Impatience and the existence of different preconditions for attaining sustained growth have led different nations to use different paths and strategies for growth. For example, advanced nations first experienced agricultural advances, which freed labor to help in their industrialization process. Latecomers have often chosen to *start* with industrialization and to postpone the technological development of agriculture. Many former communist countries, such as the republics of the former Soviet Union, tried the "industry before agriculture" model—at great cost and with little success.

Another result of impatience and tension is a greater willingness to accept radical ideas, dictatorial regimes, and tremendous governmental control over the economy. Thus impatience with closing the income gap and a lack of preconditions for modern economic growth have led leaders of developing nations to take radical steps in the economic, political, and social spheres.

FOREIGN AID

Many nations, including the United States, extend assistance to developing countries. A number of reasons are given to justify this assistance, which can be in the form of grants, low-interest loans, food, military supplies, or technical expertise. Although the humanitarian argument in support of foreign aid is often given, certainly security and economics enter into the discussion. During the Cold War, the United States gave foreign aid to developing countries in order to support noncommunist regimes or to prevent communist takeovers. The United States also extends foreign aid to help develop foreign markets for the output of U.S. firms. This is particularly true when foreign aid is tied to the purchase of American products. Tied foreign aid requires that the recipient spend all or part of the sum extended as foreign aid on U.S.-produced goods.

The major landmark in the history of foreign aid from the United States was the Marshall Plan. Proposed by Secretary of State George Marshall in an address at Harvard University in June, 1948, the plan established the European Recovery Program, which granted over $10 billion ($60 billion in 1993 dollars) in foreign assistance to Europe following World War II. Many observers contend that the Marshall Plan was instrumental in allowing Europe's productive capacity to grow dramatically during the late 1940s and early 1950s.

The United States gives relatively little aid to developing countries on a per capita basis today, and this amount is shrinking in inflation-corrected terms because of the U.S. federal government deficit. Most foreign aid goes to two countries, Israel and Egypt. Japan now gives a greater absolute amount of foreign aid than the United States.

THE SITUATION IN THE DEVELOPING COUNTRIES

The developing countries in the world today cannot be compared to those war-torn European countries at the end of World War II. The modernization of developing countries is a much more complicated task than the restoration of postwar Europe. In many cases, foreign aid to Europe simply helped those countries rebuild an existing and well-functioning capital base. It is one thing merely to replace locomotives and repair tracks in an existing railroad system and quite another to build a railroad system in a country that has none. Perhaps more important is potentially misdirected aid to developing countries. Remember that post–World War II Europe had the human capital of an experienced industrial work force. Today's developing countries do not, so we cannot expect that foreign aid given to them will have the same result as the aid given to Europe for its restoration after the war. There are many barriers to economic growth in developing countries, including a lack of technical skills and capacities, poorly organized markets, political and social elites unreceptive to change, and non-growth-oriented foreign trade policies.

🌐 INTERNATIONAL EXAMPLE: Unexpected Results of Foreign Aid

Between 1956 and 1993 the developed world transferred about $2 trillion (in today's dollars) to the developing world. Consider Tanzania. Between 1970 and 1988, for example, this African country received $8.6 billion, four times that country's 1988 gross domestic product. This is the equivalent of someone giving the United States around $20 trillion. During the same period, the Sudan was given $9.6 billion, an amount equal to one year's output. Zaire, Togo, Zambia, Mozambique, and Niger each received around $6 billion during the same period. What happened to these billions of dollars? All of these countries are still extremely poor. From 1970 to 1988, in spite of foreign aid, Tanzania's annual gross output actually fell. Critics of foreign aid point out that much of the money went into new government centers, showy airports, and grand conference halls. Some of it also went into government officials' Swiss bank accounts. According to economist George Ayittey, Zaire's Mobutu Sese Seko is now worth $10 billion, and Zambia's Kenneth Kaunda is worth $6 billion.

There is also a question of how much aid goes to the importation of arms. Figure 35-2 shows that many poor countries do in fact spend huge sums on armaments. According to *The Economist*, between 1984 and 1987, some 22 poor countries with a combined population of 1.8 billion people spent more on their armies than they invested in health and education. Currently, African nations spend $12 billion per year to import arms to maintain their militaries.

For Critical Analysis: Some developing countries that have received foreign aid contend that they have not spent that aid on arms but rather used other parts of their budget to build up their military. Why is this a weak argument? ●

FIGURE 35-2
Countries that import the most arms.
This figure shows the purchase of arms by various countries in the period 1980–1988.

Source: United Nations Arms Control and Disarmament Agency.

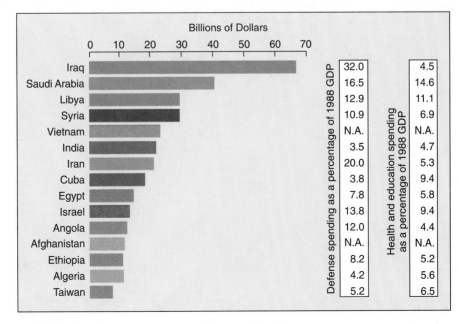

	Billions of Dollars	Defense spending as a percentage of 1988 GDP	Health and education spending as a percentage of 1988 GDP
Iraq		32.0	4.5
Saudi Arabia		16.5	14.6
Libya		12.9	11.1
Syria		10.9	6.9
Vietnam		N.A.	N.A.
India		3.5	4.7
Iran		20.0	5.3
Cuba		3.8	9.4
Egypt		7.8	5.8
Israel		13.8	9.4
Angola		12.0	4.4
Afghanistan		N.A.	N.A.
Ethiopia		8.2	5.2
Algeria		4.2	5.6
Taiwan		5.2	6.5

CONCEPTS IN BRIEF

- Some policymakers believe that a large capital stock is a prerequisite for economic growth and development. They therefore suggest that developing countries need more capital.
- The human element, however, is vital; the labor force must be capable of using any capital that the developing country acquires. This requires training and education.
- Saving is a prerequisite for capital formation.
- Saving goes on even in poor developing countries, although not necessarily in the same form as in rich developed countries.
- Saving and individual capital accumulation will be greater, the more certain individuals are about the safety of their wealth.
- Modern economic growth (MEG) theory hypothesizes that growth is driven by the application of science to the problems of economic production. Latecomers to economic growth are often able to borrow technology from economically advanced nations.
- Latecomers to economic growth, however, experience tension due to the large income gap between them and the developed nations.
- Critics of foreign aid point out that foreign aid will not increase the rate of economic growth unless a well-functioning capital base and infrastructure are in place.

WILL AIDS AFFECT ECONOMIC DEVELOPMENT?

Concepts Applied: Long run versus short run, supply of labor, real wages

Economic development can be fragile even when a country such as Mexico is already in an advanced stage. It is possible that a worldwide plague of something such as AIDS might have an impact on developing countries.

For over a decade, we have known about acquired immune deficiency syndrome, or AIDS. This disease attacks the immune system. Virtually everyone who has the disease eventually dies. To date, no one has discovered a cure for AIDS, and all of the drugs used to treat it simply delay the onset of symptoms. It is widely believed that a virus causes AIDS. Approximately 20 million inhabitants of this planet are known to harbor the human immunodeficiency virus, or HIV. In certain African cities, 50 percent of the inhabitants are infected with HIV. AIDS is in fact a worldwide epidemic. What will happen to development in many poor countries today if a cure for AIDS is not found?

A COMPARISON WITH THE PLAGUE

As mentioned in the beginning of this chapter, a bacterial plague, known as the Black Death, swept through Europe in the middle of the fourteenth century. In a period of four to five years, 25 to 50 percent of the entire European population was wiped out. Outbreaks of plague continued to occur until the early fifteenth century.

EFFECT OF REDUCTION IN POPULATION Figure 35-3 presents the labor supply and demand curves for fourteenth- and fifteenth-century Europe. The labor demand curve over this period was assumed to be relatively stable. The labor supply curve, however, shifted inward be-cause of the plague. Consequently, equilibrium real wage rates were predicted to have risen after the plague.

Rising real wages led to some obvious changes: agriculture shifted from more labor-intensive activities, such as crop cultivation, to less labor-intensive activities, such as sheep farming.

Land and capital did not change in supply because of the plague. Consequently, it was the poorest farming land that laid fallow after the plague. (This actually contributed to the reforestation of Europe.)

AFRICA REACTS TO AIDS   Much of what is happening in certain parts of Africa today is similar to what happened in Europe after the plague. In areas where AIDS and other diseases are reducing population growth, we can predict that there will be a shift from more labor-intensive to less labor-intensive crops. Consequently, we should see a reduction in cotton and tobacco farming and an increase in root crop farming.

FIGURE 35-3
Effects of the plague on labor supply and real wages.
If the demand for labor was D_L and the supply curve was S_1, the real (inflation-corrected) wage rate was W_1. The labor supply decreased due to the plague, so that the supply curve shifted to S_2. The real wage rate increased to W_2.

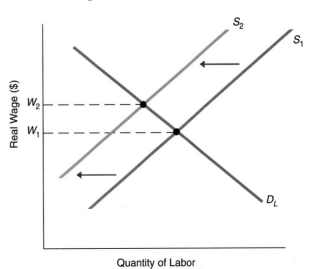

There is also an immediate impact on development in certain African nations that has to do with high and rising public health costs.

WHAT THE FUTURE HOLDS It is possible that the AIDS epidemic will reach an equilibrium that is not disastrous on a worldwide scale. It is equally possible, according to economist Ken Goldin, that in the long run AIDS may destroy centuries of population growth and economic development. Particularly today in a global economy, if one part of the world, such as Africa, is largely affected by AIDS, there will be repercussions in the rest of the world, including the United States. In other words, developed countries may not escape the economic impact of the long-run effects of AIDS if a cure is not found. Results of a recent study by the economic consulting firm of DRI/McGraw-Hill puts the problem in prospective. That company's researchers estimate that by the year 2000, AIDS-related medical expenses and lost productivity across the world might cost as much as $500 billion a year, or the equivalent of losing an economy the size of Mexico's. Africa and the Middle East might see

their gross domestic product depressed by more than 4 percent. Asia, except Japan, could lose as much as 3 percent.

Perhaps such grim statistics are too pessimistic, though. Past predictions of the number of AIDS cases in the United States have consistently turned out to be too large, due in part to massive educational campaigns and increased awareness of how to avoid AIDS. It is possible that predictions for the rest of the world could turn out to be too high if similar educational campaigns work as well. Finally, some researchers hold out hope that within the next decade a vaccine or a cure will be discovered.

FOR CRITICAL ANALYSIS
1. Does the analysis of the effect of AIDS on the labor market depend on which age group is most affected by the disease?
2. Economic historians contend that the Black Death led to a reversal of environmental degradation in Western Europe. Why might this have been true?

CHAPTER SUMMARY

1. The 19 industrially advanced countries (IACs)—the United States, Japan, Canada, and the countries of Western Europe—have market economies based on a large skilled labor force and a large technically advanced stock of capital goods.

2. Developing countries have the following traits in common: Their life expectancies are less than in the developed countries, their infant mortality rates are higher, they have lower levels of literacy, and their per capita daily caloric supply is lower than in most developed countries.

3. One of the major characteristics of developing countries is a high rate of population growth. However, high population growth does not necessarily prevent or retard economic development.

4. Some authorities contend that balanced development of industry and agriculture is necessary for growth in the developing countries. There are, however, exceptions to this rule; Hong Kong is one.

5. Industrialization in many developing countries has involved subsidization of manufacturing. Such subsidization leads to a misallocation of resources and

to a lower per capita standard of living for the population even though such a country may become more highly industrialized.

6. Capital accumulation is an important determinant of economic development. However, massive transfers of capital to developing countries do not guarantee economic development. Appropriately trained personnel must be available to use the capital given to these countries.

7. Domestic capital formation requires saving—nonconsumption of current income. Even the poorest countries' citizens do some saving. In fact, there is no pronounced relationship between percentage of income saved and level of income.

8. Saving in the developing countries may take on different forms than in more developed countries. For example, having children is a form of saving if those children feel an obligation to support their parents during retirement.

9. The more certain private property rights are, the more private capital accumulation there will be, other things being equal.

10. Modern economic growth (MEG) theory hypothesizes that growth is driven by the application of science to the problems of economic production. Latecomers to economic growth are often able to borrow technology from economically advanced nations. However, latecomers experience tension due to the large income gap between them and the developed nations.

DISCUSSION OF PREVIEW POINTS

1. What is a developing country?

Developing countries are arbitrarily defined as those with very low per capita incomes. Relative to developed countries, people in developing countries have lower incomes, life expectancies, literacy rates, and daily caloric intake and higher infant mortality rates.

2. Must developing countries develop by industrializing?

Proponents of the balanced-growth theory point out that the industrially advanced countries (IACs) are highly industrialized and the developing countries are mostly agrarian. They feel that balanced growth requires that the developing countries expand the manufacturing sector; laborers and other resources should be reallocated to promote industrialization. It is often suggested that the developing countries restrict imports of nonagricultural goods to help industrialization. It is alleged that these nations must industrialize even if their comparative advantage lies in the production of agricultural goods because they can't compete with the subsidized agricultural sectors of the IACs. Yet it is easy to oversell the pro-industrialization balanced-growth approach. Numerous examples of gross inefficiency can be cited when the developing countries attempted to develop steel and automobile industries. Moreover, when the developing countries restrict the imports of manufactured goods, they lower living standards and promote inefficiency. It would seem that the time to develop the industrial sector would be when it is profitable for businesses to do so.

3. Can developing countries create their own capital stock?

It is often asserted that (a) a large capital stock is necessary for economic development, (b) the developing countries are too poor to save sufficient amounts to develop domestic capital formation, and (c) the IACs should therefore give capital to the developing countries. Experts disagree about the validity of each contention. The question under discussion here deals with proposition (b). A good deal of evidence exists to support the notion that the developing countries do save—although in forms that are not easily observed or cannot be readily converted into capital. Even people with extremely low incomes are forced by economic circumstances to provide for future consumption; they often store dried or cured food. On a nationwide scale, much evidence of capital formation exists: cathedrals, pyramids, great walls, fortresses, government buildings, and so on. Of course, the problem is to get savings into forms that can be used to produce goods or services.

4. Does a lack of protected property rights hinder a developing country's development?

Yes. When individuals fear that their property rights will not be protected, they invest in ways that reflect this risk. Thus people in politically and economically unstable countries prefer to accumulate diamonds, gold, silver, and currency in foreign banks rather than invest in factories, equipment, and savings in domestic bank accounts. Similarly, a nation that expropriates property or nationalizes industry discourages investment by foreign businesses. Many developing countries could be aided to a great extent by attracting foreign investment—but foreign investors will require property right guarantees.

PROBLEMS

(Answers to the odd-numbered problems appear at the back of the book.)

35-1. List five developing countries and five industrially advanced countries.

35-2. What problems are associated with advancements in medicine and health that are made available to developing countries?

35-3. Outline a typical pattern of economic development.

35-4. Suppose that you are shown the following data for two countries, known only as country X and country Z:

	GDP	POPULATION
X	$ 81 billion	9 million
Z	135 billion	90 million

a. From this information, which country would you expect to be classified as a developing country? Why?

b. Now suppose that you were also given the following data:

	LIFE EXPECTANCY AT BIRTH	INFANT MORTALITY PER 1,000 LIVE BIRTHS	LITERACY (%)
X	70	15	60
Z	58	50	70

Are these figures consistent with your answer to part (a)?

c. Should we expect the developing country identified in part (a) to have a much greater population density than the other country?

35-5. Would unrestricted labor immigration end up helping or hurting developing countries? Explain.

35-6. Many countries in Africa have extremely large potential stocks of natural resources. Nonetheless, those natural resources often remain unexploited. Give reasons why this situation continues to exist.

35-7. Sketch a scenario in which population growth causes an increase in income per capita.

COMPUTER-ASSISTED INSTRUCTION
(Complete problem and answer on disk.)

This chapter brings the tutorial full circle; it applies the principles of scientific thinking to questions of economic development, illustrating once again such concepts as observational equivalence, the fallacy of composition, tautologies, and correlation versus causation.

answers to odd-numbered problems

CHAPTER 1

1-1A. There are, of course, a very large number of possible factors that might affect the probability of death. Perhaps the most common would be age, occupation, diet, and current health. Thus one model would show that the older someone is, the greater is the probability of dying within the next five years; another would show that the riskier the occupation, other things being equal, the greater the probability of dying within five years; and so forth.

1-3A. a. We should observe younger drivers to be more frequently involved in traffic accidents than older persons.
    b. Slower monetary expansion should be associated with less inflation.
    c. Professional basketball players receiving smaller salaries should be observed to have done less well in their high school studies.
    d. Employees being promoted rapidly should have lower rates of absenteeism than those being promoted more slowly.

1-5A. The decreasing relative attractiveness of mail communication has no doubt decreased students' demand for writing skills. Whether or not the influence has been a significant one is a subject for empirical research. As for the direction of causation, it may well be running both ways. Cheaper nonwritten forms of communication may decrease the demand for writing skills. Lower levels of writing skills probably further increase the demand for audio and video communications media.

1-7A. a. Normative, involving a value judgment about what should be
    b. Positive, for it is a statement of what has actually occurred
    c. Positive, for it is a statement of what actually is
    d. Normative, involving a value judgment about what should be

CHAPTER 2

2-1A. The law of increasing costs does seem to hold because of the principle that some resources may be more suited to one productive use than to another. In moving from butter to guns, the economy will first transfer those resources most easily sacrificed by the butter sector, holding on to the very specialized (to butter) factors until the last. Thus different factor intensities will lead to increasing relative costs.

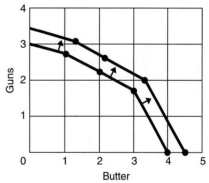

Production Possibilities Curve
for Guns and Butter
(and after 10 percent growth)

2-3A. a. Neither, because each can produce the same total number of jackets per time period (2 jackets per hour)
    b. Neither, because each has the same cost of producing ties ($\frac{2}{3}$ of a jacket per tie)
    c. No, because with equal costs of production, there are no gains from specialization
    d. Output will be the same as if they did not specialize (16 jackets per day and 24 ties per day)

2-5A. a. Only the extra expense of lunch in a restaurant, above what lunch at home would have cost, is part of the cost of going to the game.

b. This is part of the cost of going to the game because you would not have incurred it if you had watched the game on TV at home.

c. This is part of the cost of going to the game because you would not have incurred it if you had watched the game on TV at home.

2-7A. For most people, air is probably not an economic good because most of us would not pay simply to have a larger volume of the air we are currently breathing. But for almost everyone, *clean* air is an economic good because most of us would be willing to give something up to have clearner air.

APPENDIX A

A-1A.

y	x
12	4
9	3
6	2
3	1
0	0
−3	−1
−6	−2
−9	−3
−12	−4

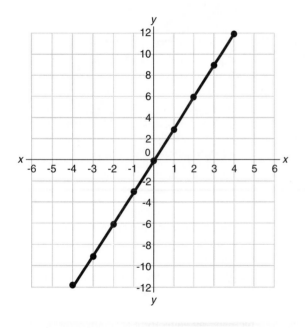

CHAPTER 3

3-1A. The equilibrium price is $30. The quantity supplied and demanded is about 10.5 million skateboards per year.

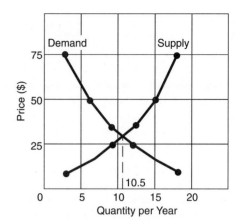

3-3A. a. The demand curve for vitamin C will shift outward to the right because the product has taken on a desirable new quality.

b. The demand curve for stenographic services will shift inward to the left because the substitute good, the tape recorder, is now a lower-cost alternative (change in the price of a substitute).

c. The demand curve for beer will shift outward to the right because the price of a complementary good—pretzels—has decreased. Is it any wonder that tavern owners often give pretzels away? (Change in the price of a complement.)

3-5A. As the diagram indicates, demand doesn't change, supply decreases, the equilibrium price of oranges rises, and the equilibrium quantity falls.

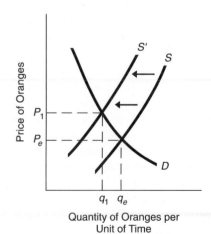

3-7A. This person has learned well the definition of a surplus but has overlooked one point. The "surpluses" that result from the above-equilibrium minimum prices don't go begging; the excess quantities supplied are in effect purchased by the Department of Agriculture. In that sense, they are not surpluses at all. When one includes the quantity that is demanded by the Department of Agriculture, along with the quantities being purchased by private purchasers at the support price, the quantity demanded will equal the quantity supplied, and there will be an equilibrium of sorts.

3-9A. As the diagram illustrates, rain consumers are not willing to pay a positive price to have nature's bounty increased. Thus the equilibrium quantity is 200 inches per year (the amount supplied freely by nature), and the equilibrium price is zero (the amount that consumers will pay for an additional unit, given that nature is already producing 200 inches per year).

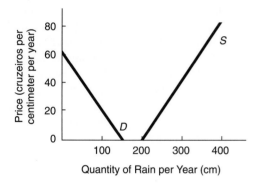
Quantity of Rain per Year (cm)

CHAPTER 4

4-1A. a. The demand curve will shift to the right (increase).
 b. The supply curve will shift to the right (increase).
 c. Because the price floor, or minimum price, is below the equilibrium price of 50 cents, there will be no effect on price or quantity.
 d. Because the price floor is now greater than the equilibrium price, there will be a surplus at the new price of 75 cents.
 e. Assuming that grapefruits are a substitute for oranges, the demand curve for oranges will shift to the right (increase).
 f. Assuming that oranges are a normal good, the demand curve will shift to the left (decrease).

4-3A. The equilibrium price is $40 per calculator, and the equilibrium quantity is zero calculators per year. This is so because at a price of $40, the quantity demanded—zero—is equal to the quantity supplied—also zero. None will be produced or bought because the highest price that any consumer is willing to pay for even a single calculator ($30) is below the lowest price at which any producer is willing to produce even one calculator ($50).

4-5A. a. $100 - .02Q_d = .06Q_s$ (at equilibrium, $Q_d = Q_s$)

 $100 = .08Q$, leading to $Q = 1,250$ pounds

 b. $P = .06(1,250) = 75$ cents per pound
 c. Because 80 cents is above the equilibrium price of 75 cents, there will be a surplus.
 d. The quantity supplied is as follows:

$$Q_s = \frac{80}{.06} = 1,333 \text{ pounds}$$

 The quantity demanded would be

$$Q_d = \frac{100 - P}{.02} = \frac{100 - 80}{.02} = 1,000 \text{ pounds}$$

 The surplus would be equal to $Q_s - Q_d$, or 333 pounds of cantaloupes.

4-7A. As shown in the diagram, if the equilibrium price of oranges is 10 cents, a price floor of 15 cents will result in a surplus equal to $Q_s - Q_d$. A price floor of 5 cents per orange will have no effect, however, because it is below the equilibrium price and thus does not prevent suppliers and demanders from doing what they want to do—produce and consume Q_e oranges at 10 cents each.

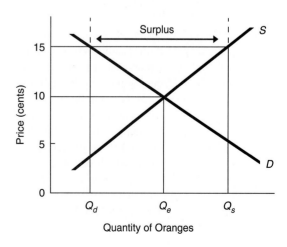
Quantity of Oranges

CHAPTER 5

5-1A. The marginal tax rate on the first $3,000 of taxable income is zero percent, because no taxes are imposed until $5,000 is earned. The marginal rate on $10,000 is 20 percent, as it is on $100,000 and all other amounts above the $5,000 level, because for each additional dollar earned after $5,000, 20 cents will be taxed away. The average tax rate, which is the tax amount divided by the pretax income, is zero for $3,000, 10 percent for $10,000, and 19 percent for $100,000. The average tax rate will *approach* a maximum of 20 percent as income increases. It cannot reach *exactly* 20 percent because of the untaxed $5,000 at the beginning. Such is the nature of a *degressive* tax system.

5-3A. Mr. Smith pays nothing on his first $1,500 of income, 14 percent on the $500 of earnings between $1,500 and $2,000 ($70), and 20 percent on the $500 that he earns above $2,000 ($100). Thus Mr. Smith has a total tax bill of $170 on an income of $2,500; his average tax rate is 6.8 percent, and his marginal tax rate is 20 percent.

5-5A. Among the ideas that have been proposed is that a good tax system should meet the requirements of equity, efficiency, and ease of administration. Equity means that each person should pay a "fair share." The efficiency requirement is that the tax system should minimize interferences with economic decisions. Ease of administration means that the tax system should not be excessively costly to administer and that it should be understandable to the taxpayer. Even though the U.S. tax system was not designed through a master plan, these ideas have had their influence on the American system.

5-7A. There are both public good and private good aspects to police protection. When an officer patrols the neighborhood in a police car, criminals are deterred from burglarizing every home in the neighborhood; this is a public good aspect of police protection because the protection afforded one person is simultaneously afforded all of the neighbors. But when an officer spends time arresting the person who broke into Mr. Smith's home, that is time the officer cannot spend arresting the person who broke into Ms. Jones's home; this is the private good aspect of police protection, for when these services are provided Mr. Smith, Ms. Jones is excluded from simultaneously using those services.

5-9A. a. If you give and everyone else does also, you account for 1 percent. If you are the only one who gives, you account for 100 percent. If you give nothing, you account for 0 percent, regardless of what others give.

b. In principle, your contribution matters whatever the level of participation. But as a practical matter, if participation is near 100 percent, the absence of your contribution may have little practical effect.

c. There is no free ride. If you do not make your contribution, total contributions will be lower, and the quality of the services provided will be lower.

5-11A. Strictly speaking, probably all the items except national defense should go into the column labeled "Private Goods," either because residents *could* be excluded from consuming them or because one person's consumption reduces the amount available for other individuals. As a practical matter, however, there are several goods on the list (public television, elementary education, and the museum) for which full exclusion generally does not take place and/or consumption by one person reduces the amount that other persons can consume by only a small amount.

CHAPTER 6

6-1A. On the supply side, all of the industries responsible for automobile inputs would have to be considered. This would include steel (and coke and coal), glass, tires (and rubber), plastics, railroads (and thus steel again), aluminum (and electricity), and manufacturers of stereos, hubcaps, and air conditioners, to name a few. On the demand side, you would have to take into account industries involving complements (such as oil, gasoline, concrete, and asphalt) and substitutes (including bicycles, motorcycles, buses, and walking shoes). Moreover, resource allocation decisions regarding labor and the other inputs, complements, and substitutes for these goods must also be made.

6-3A. a. Profit equals total revenue minus total cost. Because revenue is fixed (at $172), if the firm wishes to maximize profit, this is equivalent to minimizing costs. To find total costs, simply multiply the price of each input by the amount of the input that must be used for each technique.

Costs of A = ($10)(7) + ($2)(6) + ($15)(2) + ($8)(1) = $120
Costs of B = ($10)(4) + ($2)(7) + ($15)(6) + ($8)(3) = $168
Costs of C = ($10)(1) + ($2)(18) + ($15)(3) + ($8)(2) = $107

Because C has the lowest costs, it yields the highest profits, and thus it will be used.
b. Profit equals $172 − $107 = $65.
c. Each technique's costs rise by the increase in the price of labor multiplied by the amount of labor used by that technique. Because technique A uses the least amount of labor, its costs rise the least, and it actually becomes the lowest-cost technique at $132. (The new cost of B is $182, and the new cost of C is $143.) Hence technique A will be used, resulting in profits of $172 − $132 = $40.

6-5A. a. In the market system, the techniques that yield the highest (positive) profits will be used.
b. Profit equals total revenue minus total cost. Because revenue from 100 units is fixed (at $100), if the firm wishes to maximize profit, this is equivalent to minimizing costs. To find total costs, simply multiply the price of each input by the amount of the input that must be used for each technique.

Cost of A = ($10)(6) + ($8)(5) = $100
Cost of B = ($10)(5) + ($8)(6) = $98
Cost of C = ($10)(4) + ($8)(7) = $96

Because technique C has the lowest costs, it also yields the highest profits ($100 − $96 = $4).
c. Following the same methods yields these costs: A = $98, B = $100, and C = $102. Technique A will be used because it is the most profitable.
d. The profits from using technique A to produce 100 units of X are $100 − $98 = $2.

CHAPTER 7
7-1A. Although your boss gave you a raise of $1,200 ($30,000 × .04), you are not $1,200 better off after taxes. You are now in the 28 percent mar-

ginal tax bracket. You must pay .28 × $1,200 in additional taxes, or $336. That leaves you with an additional $864 in take-home pay. That is how much better off you are because of the raise.

7-3A. a. 5 percent
b. One month
c. 5 percent
d. 10 percent
e. In this example, the unemployment rate doubled, but it is not obvious that the economy has gotten "sicker" or that workers are worse off.

7-5A. a. The nominal rate of interest is composed of the real rate of interest plus the anticipated rate of inflation. If the current rate of inflation is zero and people anticipate that there will continue to be no inflation, the real rate of interest equals the nominal rate of interest—in this example, 12 percent.
b. If the nominal rate of interest stays at 12 percent while the rate of inflation goes to 13 percent, and if that rate is anticipated to last, the real rate of interest drops to a *negative* 1 percent! Lending money at 12 percent would not normally be advisable in such a situation.

7-7A. a. 10, 9, 8, 7, 6, 5, 4, 3
b. 8.0, 8.3, 9.4, 10.9, 12.0, 13.8, 16.0

CHAPTER 8
8-1A. a. GDP = $950; NDP = $900; NI = $875
b. GDP = $825
c. The value of depreciation exceeding gross private investment implies that the total capital stock of the country is declining. This would likely decrease future productivity because capital is a productive resource.

8-3A. a. Coal; $2
b. $3. Auto manufacturers took something worth $5 and transformed it into an auto that they sold for $8.
c. $9 because intermediate goods are *not* counted.
d. $9, resulting from adding the value added at each stage. Note that in this economy, which produces only autos, the earnings and the income approaches both yield a GDP estimate of $9.

8-5A. a. It falls.
b. It is unchanged because illegal transactions are not measured anyway.
c. It rises.

8-7A. a. Nominal GDP for 1987 = ($4)(10) + ($12)(20) + ($6)(5) + ($25)(10) = $560. Nominal GDP for 1994 = ($8)(12) + ($36)(15) + ($10)(15) + ($30)(12) = $1,146.

b. Real GDP for 1987 = $560. Real GDP for 1994 = ($4)(12) + ($12)(15) + ($6)(15) + ($25)(12) = $618.

CHAPTER 9

9-1A. At P_1 the quantity of AS exceeds the quantity of AD; therefore, a surplus of real national income (output) exists. At that price level, suppliers are willing to produce more than buyers want to purchase; in this surplus situation, producers find their inventories rising involuntarily, and they find it profitable to reduce prices and output. At P_2 the quantity of AD exceeds the quantity of AS, and a shortage exists. At that price level, buyers want more than producers are willing to produce, and buyers, competing for goods and services, will bid the price level upward. A higher price level induces an increase in the quantity of AS and a decrease in the quantity of AD. Only at P_e does the quantity of AS equal the quantity of AD; at P_e equilibrium exists.

9-3A. The long-run aggregate supply curve is vertical at the point representing the maximum potential output possible. Prices can vary but output cannot. In the short run, some increase in the level of output is possible with prices rising. This is possible because of the existence of some excess capacity, as well as flexibility in the nature and intensity of work. Therefore, the positively sloped portion of the aggregate supply curve constitutes the short-run aggregate supply curve.

9-5A. a. P increases.

b. Q decreases.

CHAPTER 10

10-1A.

DISPOSABLE INCOME	CONSUMPTION	SAVING
$ 500	$510	$−10
600	600	0
700	690	10
800	780	20
900	870	30
1,000	960	40

a.

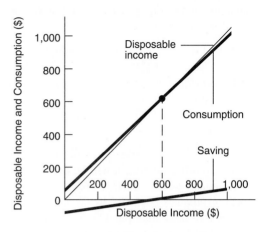

b. The marginal propensity to consume is .9; the marginal propensity to save is .1.

c.

DISPOSABLE INCOME	AVERAGE PROPENSITY TO CONSUME	AVERAGE PROPENSITY TO SAVE
$ 500	1.0200	−.0200
600	1.0000	0
700	.9857	.0142
800	.9750	.0250
900	.9667	.0333
1,000	.9600	.0400

10-3A. a. At $100, the APC is 80 percent (80 ÷ 100 = 80 percent); at $200, it is 77.5 percent (155 ÷ 200 = 77.5 percent).

b. It falls.

c. The MPC is 75 percent from $0 to $100 [(80 − 5) ÷ (100 − 0) = 75 percent]; from $100 to $200, it is also 75 percent [(155 − 80) ÷ (200 − 100) = 75 ÷ 100 = 75 percent].

d. It remains constant.

e. The APC is always falling and approaches the MPC, or 75 percent.

f. $C = 5 + .75Y$.

g. Because the y intercept is positive, the MPC is less than the APC, and the APC therefore falls.

10-5A. Stock: a, c; Flow: b, d, e, f, g

10-7A. They are restricted by cost of capital (interest rates).

10-9A. a. $C = 55$, 125, and 195, respectively.
        b. $S = -5$, 25, and 55, respectively.
        c. The APC = 1.10, .83, and .78, respectively.

10-11A. a. Savings must equal $150 billion.
        b. MPS = .2.
        c. APC = .769.

CHAPTER 11

11-1A.

REAL NATIONAL INCOME	CONSUMPTION EXPENDITURES	SAVING	INVESTMENT	APC	APS	MPC	MPS
$1,000	$1,100	$-100	$100	1.1	-.1	.9	.1
2,000	2,000	0	100	1.0	.0	.9	.1
3,000	2,900	100	100	.967	.033	.9	.1
4,000	3,800	200	100	.950	.050	.9	.1
5,000	4,700	300	100	.940	.060	.9	.1
6,000	5,600	400	100	.933	.067	.9	.1

a.

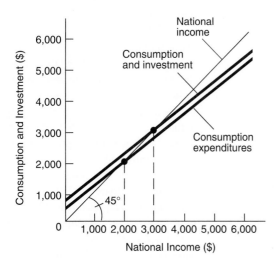

b.

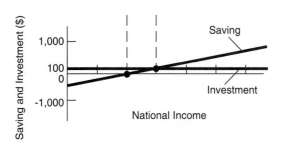

c. The multiplier effect from the inclusion of investment is to raise equilibrium national income by $1,000 over the equilibrium level it would otherwise have reached.

d. The value of the multiplier is 10.

e. The equilibrium level of national income without investment is $2,000; with investment, it is $3,000.

f. Equilibrium income will rise by $1,000.

g. Equilibrium income will again rise by $1,000 to $4,000.

11-3A. Aggregate supply $\equiv Y = C + I \equiv$ aggregate demand

$$Y = (30 + \tfrac{3}{4}Y) + 25$$
$$Y = 55 + \tfrac{3}{4}Y$$
$$Y - \tfrac{3}{4}Y = 55$$
$$\tfrac{1}{4}Y = 55$$
$$Y = \$220$$

11-5A. Aggregate supply $\equiv Y = C + I$ in equilibrium; therefore,

$$Y = (35 + \tfrac{3}{4}Y) + 25$$
$$Y = \$240$$

11-7A. When planned expenditures rise (in the short run), prices rise. Through interest rate, wealth, and foreign trade effects, the $C + I$ curve shifts downward, partially offsetting the initial rise.

11-9A. a. Multiplier = 10.
        b. Multiplier = 3.33.
        c. Multiplier = 6.67.
        d. Multiplier = 2.86.

CHAPTER 12

12-1A. Discretionary fiscal policy is policy in which the levels of G and T change as a result of a deliberate decision by the government. *Example:* A change in the structure of tax rates, a change in government expenditures not associated with a change in government revenues.

Automatic stabilizers cause the level of *G* or *T* to change as a result of endogenous changes in a variable such as income, other than changes due to deliberate decisions of the government. *Example:* Government revenues increasing from taxes during an economic expansion.

12-3A. Consumers must not regard current budget deficits as equivalent to higher future taxes and current budget surpluses as equivalent to lower future taxes. For example, if consumers regard a $1 million deficit as imposing an equivalent amount of new taxes on them in the future, they will increase current saving so as to be in a position to pay the higher future taxes. As a result, current consumption will decline, and at least some and possibly all of the stabilizing effect of the deficit will be wiped out.

CHAPTER 13

13-1A. The federal budget deficit is the difference between federal spending and federal taxes—in this case, $300 billion.

13-3A. Ultimately, all government debt must be repaid by means of taxation. (The government cannot forever "repay" its debt by issuing more debt because ultimately the public debt would exceed the wealth of the entire nation!) Thus when the government adds to the debt, it is simultaneously adding to future taxes that must be equivalent in present value to the added debt.

13-5A. Some say that the true burden of government is the real value of the resources it uses. Changing the way the books are kept leaves this burden unchanged. Moreover, neither current nor future taxes would be affected by this accounting change, so no one's tax liability would be altered. In brief, the change will have no real consequences. The net public debt equals the gross public debt *minus* the portion held by government agencies (what the government owes to itself). The gross public debt is simply the sum of all past (and current) federal budget deficits, so that the net public debt equals the sum of these past and current deficits minus what the federal government owes to itself.

CHAPTER 14

14-1A. a. The painting by Renoir would have the greatest advantage as a store of value, for works of art have generally appreciated over time. As a medium of exchange or a unit of accounting, it would be deficient because of its high and sometimes variable value and the limited market for its exchange.

b. A 90-day U.S. Treasury bill also has a good store of value; it is guaranteed by the government and it will pay some interest. Of course, to the extent that the money to be returned for the matured bill is an imperfect store of value, so will be the bill. A 90-day bill will not vary much in value over its life because the redemption date is not far off and there is a ready market for its exchange; thus it is a serviceable medium of exchange and unit of accounting. But the large denominations in which these bills are issued detract from the latter functions.

c. It is important to distinguish between the balances in a time account and the account itself. The account is a relationship between depositor and bank. The money in the account will have the attributes of money, qualified by the increased return that interest pays, the "notice" risk of withdrawal, and the solvency of the savings and loan association in Reno.

d. There are significant transaction costs in exchanging one share of IBM stock, and its value can be volatile in the short run, making it an imperfect medium of exchange and unit of accounting. Its qualities as a store of value depend on the health of the company and the economy in which it operates.

e. A $50 Federal Reserve note is cash, and its qualities will correspond accordingly. Of course, its denomination is a multiple of the common unit of our account, which is $1.

f. A MasterCard, like the savings account, indicates the existence of a relationship. Its transferability is severely limited, and its value depends on the terms of the credit agreement. (There is probably an illegal market for MasterCards, in which they assume an independent value for exchange, although they probably lack most of the advantages of a store of value or unit of accounting.)

g. Because it is negotiable, a checkable account could be a useful medium of exchange, as long as its size does not restrict the available market too strongly. The only limits on its qualities as a store of value are the reliability of the bank and the value of the money into which it can be converted. Because the value is determined by the size of an anticipated transaction, there is no real independent unit of accounting to be measured by the checkable account.

h. Assuming that the pass is for the lifetime of the Dodgers and not for an owner who could not trade the pass, the ticket would be like many other nonmoney goods. Its money qualities would depend on the market available for its exchange and the value taken on by the good in the market. The fortunes of the Dodgers, the Los Angeles consumers' taste for baseball, and other demand determinants would affect the three monetary qualities of a lifetime pass.

14-3A. M2 consists of the values of M1 plus overnight repurchase agreements (REPOs), overnight Eurodollars, money market mutual funds, savings deposits, and small-denomination time deposits.

14-5A. a. V
b. A
c. P
d. E

14-7A. If there are n goods, the number of exchange rates will be $n(n-1)/2$. In this case, $n = 10$, so the number of exchange rates will be $10(10-1)/2 = 90/2 = 45$.

14-9A. The *number* of payments and the *value* of the payments are two different concepts. Specifically, the value of the payments must equal the average size of the payments, multiplied by the number of payments. Consider this example: A family of four buys a secondhand Rolls-Royce for $99,900, using a wire transfer to pay for it. To celebrate their purchase, the family goes out and has lunch, each family member using cash to pay for their own lunch. Each person's lunch costs $25, for a total of $100. There are five transactions (one car plus four lunches), so cash accounts for $4/5 = 80$ percent of the *number* of transactions. Yet there is $100,000 worth of transactions, so the wire transfer accounts for $99,000/$100,000 = 99.9$ percent of the *value* of the transactions.

CHAPTER 15

15-1A. a.   MULTIPLE DEPOSIT CREATION

ROUND	DEPOSITS	RESERVES	LOANS
Bank 1	$1,000,000	$ 250,000	$ 750,000
Bank 2	750,000	187,500	562,500
Bank 3	562,500	140,625	421,875
Bank 4	421,875	105,469	316,406
Bank 5	316,406	79,102	237,304
All other banks	949,219	237,304	711,915
Totals	4,000,000	1,000,000	3,000,000

The deposit multiplier is 4.

b.   MULTIPLE DEPOSIT CREATION

ROUND	DEPOSITS	RESERVES	LOANS
Bank 1	$ 1,000,000	$ 50,000	$ 950,000
Bank 2	950,000	47,500	902,500
Bank 3	902,500	45,125	857,375
Bank 4	857,375	42,869	814,506
Bank 5	814,506	40,725	773,781
All other banks	15,475,619	773,781	14,701,838
Totals	20,000,000	1,000,000	19,000,000

The deposit multiplier is 20.

15-3A. a. No change.
b. The money supply decreases by $50,000.
c. The money supply rises by $100,000.
d. This is a little tricky. If the Fed had been "keeping track" of currency, the $1,000 currency buried in Smith's backyard is accounted for; therefore, the money supply will rise by $9,000 because the Fed did not have to "create" the $1,000 already in existence.
e. The money supply will decrease by $9,000; see (d).

15-5A. a.

ASSETS		LIABILITIES	
Total reserves	+$1,000,000	Demand deposits	+$1,000,000
Required reserves ($50,000) + excess reserves ($950,000)			
Total	+$1,000,000	Total	+$1,000,000

b. Bank 1 can increase its lending by $950,000.

15-7A. a. The bank's excess reserves have decreased by $2,550,000.
 b. The money supply has decreased by $3 million.
 c. The money supply can decrease by as much as $20 million.

15-9A. a. The maximum money multiplier will be $1/r$ where r = reserve ratio. In this case, $r = .05$, so the multiplier is $1/.05 = 20$.
 b. Deposits will rise by an amount equal to the multiplier times the initial change in reserves. In this case, the rise will be equal to $1 million $\times 20 = \$20$ million.

CHAPTER 16

16-1A. By its purchase of $1 billion in bonds, the Fed increased excess reserves by $1 billion. This ultimately caused a $3 billion increase in the money supply after full multiple expansion. The 1 percent drop in the interest rate, from 10 to 9 percent, caused investment to rise by $25 billion, from $200 billion to $225 billion. An investment multiplier of 3 indicates that equilibrium national income rose by $75 billion to $2,075 trillion.

16-3A.

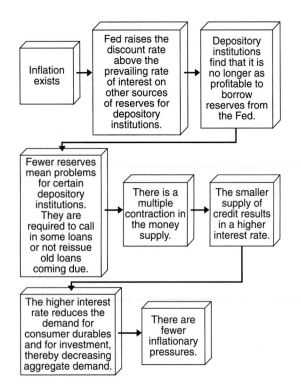

16-5A. A change in monetary policy leads to a change in interest rates, which leads to a change in investment. This, then, through the multiplier process, leads to a change in income.

CHAPTER 17

17-1A. a. 10 percent
 b. A rise in the expected rate of inflation will cause the curve to shift upward by the amount of the rise.
 c. Because the systematic policies that attempt to exploit the seeming trade-off will be incorporated into workers' and firms' expectations. As a result, the expected inflation rate will move in lockstep with the actual rate (excepting random errors), so that the unemployment rate will not change when the inflation rate changes.

17-3A. The existence of contracts, menu costs, and efficiency wages will increase the amount of discretion available to policymakers because all of these will tend to slow the adjustment of wages to changes in expectations.

17-5A. A rise in the duration of unemployment will tend to raise the average unemployment rate because each unemployed person will be counted as unemployed more times over any given time period.

17-7A. Yes. It is precisely the fact both employers and workers incorrectly perceive a change in nominal demand as a change in real demand that generates the negatively sloping Phillips curve.

CHAPTER 18

18-1A. a. 18, 14.4, 12, and 10.28 years, respectively (in each case, 72 was divided by the annual growth rate)
 b. 12.52 years

18-3A. Point B is associated with the highest feasible growth rate. Capital goods implicitly represent future consumption, and point B has the highest feasible ratio of capital goods to current consumption (and thus the highest ratio of future consumption to current consumption).

18-5A. At a growth rate of 3 percent per year, real income doubles every 24 years. So over this 120-year span, real income doubled five times (120/24 = 5), which is to say it grew by a factor of $2^5 = 32$. Thus median family income in 1873 was approximately $36,000/32 = $1,125, measured in terms of 1993 dollars.

CHAPTER 19

19-1A. For you, the marginal utility of the fifth pound of oranges is equal to the marginal utility of the third ear of corn. Apparently, your sister's tastes differ from yours—for her, the marginal utilities are not equal. For her, corn's marginal utility is too low, while that of oranges is too high—that's why she wants you to get rid of some of the corn (raising its marginal utility). She would have you do this until marginal utilities, for her, were equal. If you follow her suggestions, you will end up with a market basket that maximizes *her* utility subject to the constraint of *your* income. Is it any wonder that shopping from someone else's list is a frustrating task?

19-3A. Her marginal utility is 100 at $1, 200 at 50 cents, and 50 at $2. To calculate marginal utility per dollar, divide marginal utility by price per unit.

19-5A. Optimum satisfaction is reached when marginal utilities per dollar of both goods are equal. This occurs at 102 units of A and 11 units of B. (Marginal utility per dollar is 1.77.)

19-7A. Either your income or the relative price of eggs and bacon must have changed. Without more information, you can't make any judgments about whether you are better or worse off.

19-9A. a. 20
b. 10
c. With consumption of the third unit of *X*

APPENDIX E

E-1A. The problem here is that such preferences are inconsistent (*intransitive* is the word that economists use). If this consumer's tastes really are this way, then when confronted with a choice among A, B, and C, she will be horribly confused because A is preferred to B, which is preferred to C, which is preferred to A, which is preferred to B, which is preferred to C, and so on forever. Economists generally assume that preferences are consistent (or *transitive*): If A is preferred to B and B is preferred to C, then A is preferred to C. Regardless of what people may *say* about their preferences, the assumption of transitivity seems to do quite well in predicting what people actually do.

E-3A.

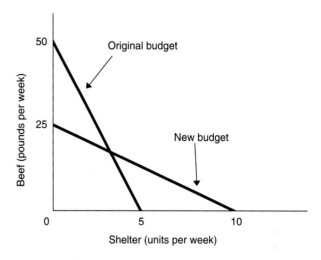

With an income of $100 and the original prices, you could have consumed *either* 50 pounds of beef *or* 5 units of shelter *or* any linear combination shown by the budget line labeled "Original." With the same income but the new prices, you can now consume 25 pounds of beef or 10 units of shelter or any linear combination shown by line labeled "New budget." Without information about your preferences, there is no way to tell whether you are better off or worse off. Draw a few indifference curves on the diagram. You will find that if you are a "shelter lover" (your indifference curves are relatively steep), the decline in the relative price of shelter will tend to make you better off. Conversely, if you are a "beef lover" (your indifference curves are relatively flat), the rise in the relative price of beef will make you worse off.

E-5A. The first burrito is substituted at a rate of 10 yogurts per burrito; the second burrito is substituted at a rate of 4:1; the third at a rate of 3:1; and the fourth at a rate of 2:1.

E-7A. a. This person is simply indifferent between going or staying, an attitude that is perfectly consistent with our assumptions about consumer preferences.
b. This statement denies the law of substitution and so is inconsistent with our assumptions about preferences.
c. If we interpret "if I had my way" to mean "if I had an unlimited budget," then this

statement simply says that there is nonsatiation for these goods for this consumer—which is perfectly consistent with our assumptions about preferences.

CHAPTER 20

20-1A. a.

QUANTITY DEMANDED PER WEEK (OUNCES)	PRICE PER OUNCE	ELASTICITY
1,000	$ 5	
800	10	$\frac{1}{3}$, or .33
600	15	$\frac{5}{7}$, or .714
400	20	$\frac{7}{5}$, or 1.4
200	25	$\frac{9}{3}$, or 3

b. There are several ways to explain why elasticity is greater at higher prices on a linear curve. At higher prices, a given price change will result in a smaller percentage price change. The smaller resulting denominator of the elasticity ratio leads to a larger overall ratio. Similarly, as prices rise, quantities fall, thereby implying greater percentage quantity changes for a given absolute quantity change, and a larger numerator. Alternatively, the sizes of total revenue changes first increase and then decrease as price is lowered throughout a linear demand curve, thus implying declining elasticity.

20-3A. Using the midpoint elasticity equation, the income elasticity of demand for VCRs is .6666 ÷ .2857 = 2.33. It is income-elastic, and it is presumably a luxury good.

20-5A. The problem is with the denominator, percentage change in P. Because the initial price was zero, any increase in price is of infinite percentage. However, if we take the average elasticity over a segment, there will be no problem. P will become the average of $P_1(=0)$ and $P_2(=10)$, or $(P_1 + P_2)/2 = 5$.

20-7A. a. $E_p = \dfrac{50}{(475 + 525)/2} \div \dfrac{.02}{(.15 + .17)/2} = .8$

b. Demand is price-inelastic.

c. $E_s = \dfrac{75}{(525 + 600)/2} \div \dfrac{.02}{(.15 + .17)/2}$
$= 1.067$

d. Supply is price-elastic (but only slightly so).

20-9A. In each case, the "before" is before the development of an acceptable substitute for the good in question, and the "after" is after the development of that substitute. For example, between 1840 and 1880, the railroad emerged as a good substitute for canal transportation. In general, the better the substitutes for a good, the greater the price elasticity of demand for that good. Thus in each case we would expect the price elasticity of demand to be higher after the emergence of the substitute.

CHAPTER 21

21-1A. Taxation of corporate dividend income can be thought of as a tax on the corporate form of organization. Increasing the amount of dividends exempt from taxes thus amounts to reducing taxes on dividends and hence reducing the tax on the corporate form of organization. As a result, more firms would choose to incorporate, and fewer would choose to be proprietorships or partnerships. Similarly, the number of limited partnerships and S corporations would decline because both are, in part, means of avoiding the current double taxation of corporate dividends.

21-3A. For simplicity, assume that potential lenders care only about the expected value of their lending decisions. If $10,000 is lent to a risk-free borrower at 10 percent interest, the borrower is certain to have ($10,000)(1 + .10) = $11,000 one year from now. If a loan is made to the risky firm, the borrower has a 20 percent chance of ending up with nothing and an 80 percent chance of repayment in full. Hence the amount the borrower expects to end up with is $E = (.20)(0) + (.80)($10,000)(1 + R)$, where R is the rate of interest charged to the risky firm. We seek the value of R that makes E equal to $11,000 because that will make the lender equally well off whether lending to the risk-free borrower or to the risky borrower. Thus we solve $11,000 = 0 + ($8,000)(1 + R)$ so that at a rate of interest $R = 37.5$ percent, the risky firm will be able to borrow the $10,000.

CHAPTER 22

22-1A. The opportunity cost of continuing to possess the van is being ignored. For example, if the van could be sold without much problem for $10,000 and you could earn 10 percent per year by investing that $10,000 in something else, the opportunity cost of keeping the van is $1,000 per year.

22-3A. a.-$1
b. 5 cents
c. $1
d. 10 cents
e. It is rising.
f. When the marginal product of labor is rising, the marginal cost of output falls; when the marginal product of labor is falling, the marginal cost of output rises.

22-5A. The long-run average costs represent the points that give the least unit cost of producing any given rate of output. The concept is important when one must decide which scale of operations to adopt. Such a decision usually takes the form of deciding what size "plant" to construct.

22-7A. a.

OUTPUT	AVC
0	$ 0
5	20
10	18
20	11
40	8

b. The marginal cost is $40 when increasing output from 10 to 20 units and $100 when increasing from 20 to 40.

c.

OUTPUT	ATC
0	$ 0
5	60
10	38
20	21
40	13

22-9A.

UNITS OF LABOR	TOTAL PRODUCT	MARGINAL PRODUCT	AVERAGE PRODUCT
6	120	Unknown	20
7	147	27	21
8	170	23	21.25
9	180	10	20

CHAPTER 23

23-1A.

OUTPUT (UNITS)	FIXED COST	AVERAGE FIXED COST (AFC)	VARIABLE COST	AVERAGE VARIABLE COST (AVC)	TOTAL COST	AVERAGE TOTAL COST (ATC)	MARGINAL COST (MC)
1	$100	100	$ 40	40	$140	$140	$40
2	100	50	70	35	170	85	30
3	100	33.33	120	40	220	73.33	50
4	100	25	180	45	280	70	60
5	100	20	250	50	350	70	70
6	100	16.67	330	55	430	71.67	80

a. The price would have to drop below $35 before the firm would shut down in the short run.

b. $70 is the short-run break-even point for the firm. The output at this price would be 5 units per period.

c. At a price of $76, the firm would produce 5 units and earn a profit of $30 ($6 per unit over 5 units).

23-3A. The industry demand curve is negatively sloped; it is relevant insofar as its interaction with the industry supply curve (ΣMC) determines the product price. The demand facing the individual firm, however, is infinitely elastic (horizontal) at the current market price.

23-5A. a. $100
        b. $100
        c. $100
        d. $100

23-7A. For simplicity, assume that your friend computed her "profit" the way many small businesses do: She ignored the opportunity cost of her time and her money. Instead of operating the car wash, she could have earned $25,000 at the collection agency plus $12,000 ($200,000 × 6 percent) on her savings. Thus the opportunity cost to her of operating the car wash was $37,000. Subtracting this amount from the $40,000 yields $3,000, which is her actual profit, over and above opportunity costs.

CHAPTER 24

24-1A. a. The rectangle that shows total costs under ATC_1 is $0WCQ$. Total revenue is shown by $0XBQ$. This monopolist is in an economic profit situation. MC = MR is the output at which profit—the difference between total cost and total revenue—is maximized.

        b. With ATC_2, the rectangle showing total costs is $0XBQ$. The same rectangle, $0XBQ$, gives total revenue. This monopolist is breaking even. MC = MR shows the only quantity that does not cause losses.

        c. Under ATC_3, total costs are represented by rectangle $0YAQ$, total revenue by $0XBQ$. Here the monopolist is operating at an economic loss, which is minimized by producing where MC = MR.

24-3A. The four are: (1) market power; (2) ability to separate markets at a reasonable cost; (3) differing price elasticities of demand; and, (4) ability to prevent resale.

24-5A. If E_p is numerically greater than 1 (elastic), marginal revenue is positive; a decrease in price will result in more total revenues. If E_P is numerically equal to 1 (unit-elastic), marginal revenue is 0; a change in price will not affect total revenues at all. If E_P is numerically less than 1 (inelastic), marginal revenue is negative; a decrease in price will result in less total revenues.

24-7A. a.

PRICE	QUANTITY DEMANDED	TOTAL REVENUE	MARGINAL REVENUE	TOTAL COST	MARGINAL COST	PROFIT OR LOSS
$20	0	$ 0	—	$ 4	—	$−4
16	1	16	$16	10	$ 6	6
12	2	24	8	14	4	10
10	3	30	6	20	6	10
7	4	28	−2	28	8	0
4	5	20	−8	40	12	−20
0	6	0	−20	54	14	−54

        b. The firm would operate at a loss if it produced 0, 5, or 6 units.

        c. The firm would break even at a rate of output of 4 units.

        d. The firm would maximize its profits by producing either 2 or 3 units. At either of those two outputs, it would be earning a profit of $10.

24-9A. a. TR = $10,000, $16,000, $18,000, $16,000, $10,000, $3,000

        b. MR = $6,000, $2,000, −$2,000, −$6,000, −$7,000

        c. 3,000 units

        d. A profit-maximizing firm always sets MR = MC, and at any output level greater than 3,000, MR is negative. Naturally, MC can never be negative, thus ensuring that output levels where MR is negative are impossible for a profit-maximizing firm.

CHAPTER 25

25-1A. The marginal revenue of this ad campaign is $1,000. There was an addition of 40 cars per week at $25 per car. To determine whether profits have risen, we would have to know how much additional cost was incurred in the tuning of these cars, as well as the cost of the advertisement itself.

25-3A.   a. Approximately 64 percent ($525 million ÷ $825 million).

b. The ratio would rise as the industry is more narrowly defined and fall as it is more broadly defined. Because an "industry" is arbitrarily defined, concentration ratios may be misleading.

25-5A.   The kink arises from the assumptions of the model. It is assumed that if any one firm raises its price, none of the others will follow. Consequently, a maverick firm's price increase will result in a drastic decrease in its total revenue. Conversely, the model assumes that any price decrease will be matched by all rivals. For this reason, the quantity demanded will probably not increase enough to cover increased costs. And profit will probably be less. Under these assumptions, it is in no individual firm's interest to "rock the boat."

25-7A.   The advertising campaign must increase weekly ticket revenues by at least $1,000 per week or it will be discontinued. This will require an additional 200 movie viewers each week.

25-9A.   The payoff matrix looks like this:

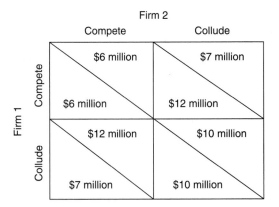

Firm 2

This situation parallels that of the prisoners' dilemma in that it is in the firms' *collective* in-

terest to collude but in their *individual* interests to compete. If the possibility for collusion is a one-time-only arrangement, we have exactly the circumstances of the classic prisoners' dilemma, in which the dominant strategy is to compete, resulting in profits of $6 million for each firm. (This sounds good until you remember that each is *losing* $4 million relative to the joint maximum possible with collusion!) If this is a repeating game and if each firm can observe the behavior of its rival, it may be possible for the firms to overcome their dilemma and reach the joint maximum—for example, by employing the "tit for tat" strategy discussed in the text.

CHAPTER 26

26-1A.   a. Quantity produced would be Q_b, and price would be P_c.

b. Losses would equal the rectangle $P_b BCP_c$.

26-3A.   a. The concentration ratios for industries A, B, and C are 48, 68, and 40, respectively.

b. The respective Herfindahl Indexes are 1,064, 1,332, and 530.

c. The new concentration ratio would be 51 and the new Herfindahl Index would be 1,100. Justice Department guidelines permit mergers that leave the affected industry with a Herfindahl Index of 1,000 or less. Because this merger would result in an index in excess of 1,000, the Justice Department might challenge it.

d. The new concentration ratio would be 50, and the new Herfindahl Index would be 820. The Justice Department would likely permit this merger because it leaves the Herfindahl Index below 1,000.

26-5A.   By definition, a natural monopolist's costs are lower than those of potential entrants. Hence although other firms may be free to enter, they are unlikely to do so. The natural monopolist can thus earn economic profits equal to the difference between its costs and its potential rivals' costs.

26-7A.   Liquor store owners do not like to compete any more than anyone else does. Nevertheless, simply telling the truth about this distaste is unlikely to garner them much political support in favor of restricting entry into their industry. What the liquor store owners seek is an argument that what is good for them is also good for you, and many people probably find the idea of a liquor store next door distasteful.

CHAPTER 27

27-1A. The existence of these costs implies the notion of rational ignorance, so that individuals choose not to be informed about certain issues because the cost of being informed is high relative to any benefit forthcoming from the state of the issue. This also contributes to the growth of special-interest groups because individuals have no strong economic incentive to act against them.

27-3A. Winning an election requires policies that please the median voter, located in the middle of the political spectrum. Hence the candidates have a tendency to converge in the middle, advocating policies that differ little from those of their competitors.

27-5A. Legislators find themselves in a situation much like a prisoners' dilemma (see Chapter 25): They have a collective incentive to act in the best interests of society as a whole but individual incentives to act in the interests of their own constituents or other narrow special interests. The favors handed out by legislators could, in principle, come in the form of either lower taxes or higher spending. As a practical matter, it is usually easier to disguise higher spending as something socially beneficial for which the recipient is uniquely qualified. Hence spending (and thus the size of the government) tends to increase. (Clearly there is some limit to this process, for the government cannot be larger than the economy as a whole. Nevertheless, the limit does not appear to be in sight.)

27-7A. Term limits appear likely to have conflicting implications for the behavior of legislators and other participants in the political marketplace. Term limits make it more costly for special interests to capture a vote because the person in charge of that vote changes identity more often. Nevertheless, term limits also reduce the incentives of legislators to do what they promise to do because they cannot reap the rewards for faithful performance. Whether term limits will improve the performance of the political marketplace remains an open question.

APPENDIX F

F-1A. a. 20 percent of 2.1 million is 420,000 farms.

b. Oligopoly seems highly unlikely in this industry in the foreseeable future—there are simply too many firms.

F-3A. One of the trickiest things about handing out subsidies is that everybody wants to receive them but not everyone can receive them (at least not after netting out the taxes used to pay for them). Farmers are uniquely positioned to be the recipients of subsidies because of the natural limiting factor— farmland—that constrains their numbers.

F-5A. The demand for farmland would fall, resulting in lower prices for such land and a diversion of some of it to other uses, possibly including residential neighborhoods or national parks. The demand for other farm resources—including the labor of farmers—would also fall, inducing some of these resources to move into alternative occupations as well. The price of food would fall, reducing malnutrition but also possibly increasing obesity. Imports of some crops (such as sugar) would rise sharply, while production of goods that use foodstuffs as inputs would also rise. These (and many other) effects would be greatly dampened today if the change in policy were not to take place until 20 years from now—partly because the present value of distant events is small and partly because Congress would have plenty of opportunities over 20 years to reverse itself.

CHAPTER 28

28-1A.

QUANTITY OF LABOR	TOTAL PRODUCT PER WEEK	MPP	MRP
1	250	250	$500
2	450	200	400
3	600	150	300
4	700	100	200
5	750	50	100
6	750	0	0

a. Demand schedule for labor:

WEEKLY WAGE	LABORERS DEMANDED PER WEEK
$500	1
400	2
300	3
200	4
100	5

b. $100 each

c. Four

28-3A. a. 15 million worker-hours per time period

b. 10 million per time period

c. Buyers can get all the labor they want at W_1; laborers can't sell all they want to sell at W_1.

d. Because a surplus of labor exists, the unemployed will offer to work for less, and industry wage rates will fall toward W_e.

28-5A. Suppose that the demand for the output product is highly elastic. Even a relatively small increase in the price of the input factor, which correspondingly raises the price of the output product, will cause a large decrease in the quantity of output demanded and therefore in the employment of the input.

28-7A. The MRP of labor is $40 per worker-day ($3,040 less $3,000, divided by a change in labor input of one worker-day). The maximum wage that would still make it worthwhile to hire this additional employee would be $39.99 per day. If the going market wage is above that figure, you will not expand output.

28-9A. Imposing limitations such as these implicitly reduces the ability of employers to compete for your services. Thus you can expect to receive a lower wage and to work in a less desirable job.

CHAPTER 29

29-1A. a. MRP

b. S

c. Q_m

d. W_m

29-3A. Some examples would be Coors beer in Golden, Colorado; Bethlehem Steel in Bethlehem, Pennsylvania; Winnebago Corporation in Forest City, Iowa; and many coal-mining companies in towns in West Virginia. As long as your example is one of a dominant employer (dominant in its local labor market, that is) selling its product(s) in fairly competitive markets, you are correct.

29-5A. No, you should not. The MRP when you employ 31 people is $89.50 ($99.50 in revenue from selling the twenty-first unit, less $10 forgone in selling the first 20 units for 50 cents less than originally). The MFC is $91 ($61 to attract the thirty-first employee to your firm, plus the additional $1 per day to each of the original 20 employees). Because MFC exceeds MRP, you should not expand output.

29-7A. Because the union acts in the interests of its members and the competitive wage is lower than the highest wage the union can obtain for its members.

29-9A. The monopsonist's decisions about how much to purchase influence the price of the good it is buying. As a result, the marginal factor cost curve facing a monopsonist lies above the average factor cost curve (which is the supply curve of the industry producing the good being purchased by the monopsonist).

CHAPTER 30

30-1A. The statement is false. Although there may be a substantial portion of rent in the revenues from these museums, we would have to assume that the museums are absolutely costless to keep in their current use in order to make the statement that *all* revenues are economic rent. The most obvious expenses of keeping the museums operating are the costs of maintenance: cleaning, lighting, and other overhead costs. But these may be minor compared to the opportunity cost involved in keeping the museum *as a museum.* The buildings might make ideal government office buildings. They may be on land that would be extremely valuable if sold on the private real estate market. If there are any such alternative uses, the value of these uses must be subtracted from the current revenues in order to arrive at the true level of pure economic rent. Forgoing these alternative opportunities is as much a cost of operating the museum as the monthly utility bill.

30-3A. The statement is false. Because a firm utilizes an input only to the point that the input's MRP is equal to its price, and marginal product is declining, it follows that all the intramarginal (up-to-the-marginal) units are producing more value than they are being paid. This differential is used to compensate for other factor inputs. The residual, if any, would be profits.

30-5A. a. 9 percent

b. The equilibrium interest rate will increase.

c. 5 percent

30-7A. In each case, the asset that qualifies the borrower for a lower interest rate is better collateral (or security) for the lender and thus reduces both the chances of default and the lender's losses in the event that default does occur.

30-9A. They would be reduced but not necessarily elim- inated (because, for example, economic profits due to entry restrictions might still persist).

CHAPTER 31

31-1A. Whites might invest more in human capital; blacks might receive less and lower-quality edu- cation and/or training; blacks in the work force may, on average, be younger; discrimination may exist; and so on.

31-3A. Need, equality, and productivity.

31-5A. Such a program would drastically reduce effi- ciency. It would eliminate individuals' incentives to maximize the economic value of resources because they would receive no reward for doing so. It would also eliminate their incentive to min- imize production costs because there would be no penalty for failing to do so.

31-7A. When governments pay for health care, hospitals have reduced incentives to operate efficiently because they are less likely to be penalized for being inefficient. Bureaucrats are less likely to provide the services that patients want at the low- est cost because the rewards from doing so are diminished when the government (rather than the patient) pays for the services. Finally, because the patient is not directly footing the bill, the patient has less incentive to choose wisely (that is, in a manner that equates the true marginal benefits and costs) when choosing health care.

CHAPTER 32

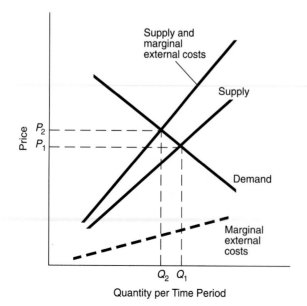

31-1A. When the external costs are added to the supply curve (which is itself the sum of marginal costs of the industry), the total (private plus public) marginal costs of production are above the pri- vate supply schedule. At quantity Q_1, marginal costs to society are greater than the value attached to the marginal unit. The demand curve is below the social supply curve. To bring marginal cost and marginal benefit back into line, thus pro- moting an economically efficient allocation of re- sources, quantity would have to be reduced to Q_2 and price raised to P_2.

32-3A. a. The price of polluting should be set ac- cording to the marginal economic damage imposed by polluters; this means that sim- ilar quantities of pollution will cost pol- luters different prices in different parts of the country; pollution will be more costly in New York City than in a small town in the Midwest.

b. Firms that find it cheaper to treat will do so; firms that find it cheaper to pay to pollute will pollute.

c. Yes, some firms will be forced to shut down due to increased costs; this is efficient, as the true costs to society of their operations were not paid by them and their customers; they were able to remain in business only by im- posing costs on third parties.

d. This might be good because now the peo- ple who are using the resources will be forced to pay for them instead of imposing costs on others. Those who are *not* using these products were, in effect, subsidizing lower prices to those who were. This new solution seems more fair and is certainly ef- ficient.

32-5A. Everyone owns them and nobody owns them. Consequently, there is no incentive for any user to be concerned with the future value of the re- source in question. This is perhaps most clearly observable in the behavior of fishing boat own- ers. The goal of each boat owner is to harvest fish as long as marginal private cost is less than the going price of such fish. The opportunity cost of depleting the stock of fish does not affect the de- cisions of the proprietor. In light of the nonown- ership of the fish, any single boat operator would be foolish to behave otherwise.

32-7A.

ANNUAL UNITS OF POLLUTION	a. MARGINAL BENEFITS	b. MARGINAL COSTS
0	—	—
1	30	150
2	40	100
3	80	80
4	120	60
5	160	20

   c. The net gain is $(430 - 150) - 80 = 200$.
   d. The net gain is $430 - 410 = 20$.
   e. The optimal level is between 2 and 3 units, or where MB = MC.

32-9A. The economically efficient amount of pollution occurs at a level at which the marginal costs of reducing it further would just exceed any benefits from that reduction. If pollution is reduced below this point, we would be better off with more pollution. The government might directly require firms or individuals to generate too little pollution (for example, through inappropriate environmental regulations), or it might establish pollution fees, fines, or taxes that overstate the damages done by the pollution and thus induce firms or individuals to reduce pollution too much.

CHAPTER 33

33-1A. a. The opportunity cost to the United States of producing one ounce of caviar is two bushels of wheat. The six hours that were needed to make the caviar could have been used to grow two bushels. The opportunity cost of producing one bushel of wheat is $\frac{1}{2}$ ounce of caviar.

   b. The opportunity cost to Russia of producing one ounce of caviar is $1\frac{1}{2}$ bushels of wheat. The opportunity cost of producing a bushel of wheat in Russia is $\frac{2}{3}$ ounce of caviar.

   c. The United States has a comparative advantage in wheat because it has a lower opportunity cost in terms of caviar. Russia has a comparative advantage in caviar. Less wheat is forgone to produce an ounce of caviar in Russia.

33-3A. a. $5
   b. $2.50
   c. $3.50
   d. At $3 per liter, the quantity demanded by the

United States exceeds the quantity of French wine supplied; hence a shortage will exist, and the dollar price will fall.

   e. At $4 per liter, the quantity of French wine supplied exceeds the U.S. quantity demanded; hence a surplus exists, and the dollar price of French wine will fall.

33-5A. Tariffs yield government revenues; quotas do not.

33-7A. a. 1 million pounds are produced and 2 million pounds are imported.

   b. With a 10-cent tariff, 1.5 million pounds would be produced and 1 million pounds would be imported. Government revenues would amount to ($2.5 million − $1.5 million) × $.10 = $100,000.

   c. With a 20-cent tariff, domestic growers can receive 70 cents per pound. They will produce 2 million pounds, and no grapes will be imported, in which case government revenues are zero.

33-9A. Consider trade between the United States and Canada. The United States purchases timber from Canada, and Canada purchases computers from the United States. Ultimately, the Canadians pay for U.S.-made computers with the timber that they sell here. If the United States imposes a tax on Canadian timber and thus reduces the amount of timber that the Canadians are able to sell to the United States, the necessary result is that the Canadians will be able to buy fewer American computers. American exports of computers will decline as a result of the reduction in American imports of timber.

CHAPTER 34

34-1A. The answer is (c). A declining dollar price of the pound implies an increasing pound price of the dollar—appreciation of the dollar. (a) is incorrect because an increase in demand for U.S. products would affect the supply of pounds and the demand for dollars, whereas here we are dealing with the demand for pounds. (b) explains a phenomenon that would have just the opposite result as that shown in the graph: An increased U.S. demand for British goods would lead to an increase in the demand for the pound, not a decrease as shown. (d) is incorrect because the pound depreciates.

34-3A. One pound equals $3.50; $1 equals .2857 pounds. One mark equals 35 cents; $1 equals 2.857 marks.

One mark equals .1 pound; one pound equals 10 marks.

34-5A. To maintain the exchange rate, domestic policy variables such as the money supply are also affected. Suppose that the government plans an expansive monetary policy to encourage output growth. A balance of payments deficit leads the government to buy up dollars, which in turn leads to a contraction in the domestic money supply. Therefore, in order to maintain the expansionary monetary policy, the government would have to expand the money supply in larger magnitudes than it would without the balance of payments deficits with a fixed exchange rate system.

34-7A. a. The dollar price of pounds is $1.50. The equilibrium quantity is 150 million.
b. Curve D' describes this situation. The new dollar price of pounds would be $1.70, and the equilibrium quantity would be 200 million.
c. At a price of $1.50 per pound, 250 million pounds sterling would be demanded and only 150 million would be supplied, so the Fed would have to supply an extra 100 million to American buyers of British goods or British exporters.
d. Curve D'' describes this situation. 150 million pounds sterling would be supplied at a price of $1.50, but only 50 million pounds would be demanded. Therefore, the Fed would have to buy up 100 million pounds sterling.

CHAPTER 35

35-1A. The following countries may be considered developing countries: Burkina Faso, Bangladesh, Afghanistan, India, and China. There are many others. The following are considered more developed countries: the United States, Canada, Australia, Germany, and France. There are many others.

35-3A. Initially, there is an agricultural stage where most of the population is involved in agriculture. Many developing countries are still in this stage. Then comes the manufacturing stage. Industry dominates the economy, and gains from the division of labor lead to rapid increases in output. In the final stage, the service sector becomes prominent in the economy. The United States and other advanced countries are in this stage.

35-5A. Economic development depends greatly on individuals who are able to perceive and take advantage of opportunities. Immigrants who possessed attributes such as these started America on the road to greatness. In general, voluntary exchange is mutually beneficial. If the potential immigrants are willing and able to offer their services at prices (wages) that existing residents are willing to pay and to purchase the goods and services offered for sale by existing residents, their arrival is likely to benefit existing residents as well as themselves.

35-7A. It is important to remember that all resources are owned by human beings and that in general there is an optimal (wealth-maximizing) mix of land, labor, and capital. So even though population growth (relative to growth in capital or land) would be expected to lower wages, it would also be expected to raise the earnings of capital and land. On balance, if the population growth moved the country closer to the optimal mix of land, labor, and capital, the added income accruing to the owners of land and capital would more than offset the reduced earnings of labor, producing an overall rise in per capita income.

Glossary

Absolute advantage   The ability to produce a good or service at an "absolutely" lower cost, usually measured in units of labor or resource input required to produce one unit of the good.

Accounting identities   Statements that certain numerical measurements are equal by accepted definition (for example, "assets equal liabilities plus stockholders' equity").

Accounting profit   The difference between total revenues and total explicit costs.

Action time lag   The time required between recognizing an economic problem and putting policy into effect. The action time lag is short for monetary policy but quite long for fiscal policy, which requires congressional approval.

Adverse selection   A problem created by asymmetric information prior to a transaction. Individuals who are the most undesirable from the other party's point of view end up being the ones who are most likely to want to engage in a particular financial transaction, such as borrowing.

Age-earnings cycle   The regular earnings profile of an individual throughout his or her lifetime. The age-earnings cycle usually starts with a low income, builds gradually to a peak at around age 45 to 50, and then gradually curves down until it approaches zero at retirement age.

Aggregate demand   The sum of all planned expenditures for the entire economy.

Aggregate demand curve   A curve showing planned purchase rates for all goods and services in the economy at various price levels.

Aggregate demand shock
Any shock that causes the aggregate demand curve to shift inward or outward.

Aggregate supply   The sum of all planned production for the entire economy.

Aggregate supply shock
Any shock that causes the aggregate supply curve to shift inward or outward.

Aggregates   Total amounts or quantities; aggregate demand, for example, is total planned expenditures throughout a nation.

Anticipated inflation   The inflation rate that we believe will occur; when it does, we are in a situation of fully anticipated inflation.

Antitrust legislation   Laws that restrict the formation of monopolies and regulate certain anticompetitive business practices.

Appreciation   An increase in the value of a currency in terms of other currencies.

Asset demand   Holding money as a store of value instead of other assets such as certificates of deposits, corporate bonds, and stocks.

Assets   Amounts owned; all items to which a business or household holds legal claim.

Asymmetric information   Information possessed by one side of a transaction only. The side that has relatively more information will be at an advantage.

Automatic, or built-in, stabilizers   Special provisions of the tax law that cause changes in the economy without the action of Congress and the president. Examples are the progressive income tax system and unemployment compensation.

Autonomous consumption
The part of consumption that is independent of (does not depend on) the level of disposable income. Changes in autonomous consumption shift the consumption function.

Average fixed costs   Total fixed costs divided by the number of units produced.

Average propensity to consume (APC)   Consumption divided by disposable income; for any given level of income, the proportion of total disposable income that is consumed.

Average propensity to save (APS)   Saving divided by disposable income; the proportion of total disposable income that is saved.

Average tax rate   The total tax payment divided by total income. It is the proportion of total income paid in taxes.

Average total costs   Total costs divided by the number of units produced; sometimes called *average per-unit total costs*.

Average variable costs   Total variable costs divided by the number of units produced.

Balance of payments   A summary record of a country's economic transactions with foreign residents and governments over a year.

Balance of trade The value of merchandise bought and sold in the world market.

Balance sheet A statement of the assets and liabilities of any business entity, including financial institutions and the Federal Reserve System. Assets are what is owned; liabilities are what is owed.

Bank runs Attempts by many of a bank's depositors to convert checkable and time deposits into currency out of fear for the bank's solvency.

Bargaining The process of making counteroffers to a person's offer to sell a good or service at a particular price.

Barter The direct exchange of goods and services for other goods and services without the use of money.

Base year The year that is chosen as the point of reference for comparison of prices in other years.

Bilateral monopoly A market structure consisting of a monopolist and a monopsonist.

Bilateral trade Trade between two countries only.

Black market A market in which goods are traded at prices above their legal maximum prices.

Bond A legal claim against a firm usually entitling the owner of the bond to receive a fixed annual coupon payment, plus a lump-sum payment at the bond's maturity date; bonds are issued in return for funds lent to the firm.

Budget constraint All of the possible combinations of goods that can be purchased (at fixed prices) with a specific budget.

Bureaucrats Nonelected government officials who are responsible for the day-to-day operation of government and the observance of its regulations and laws.

Business fluctuations The ups and downs in overall business activity, as evidenced by changes in national income, employment, and the price level.

Capital All manufactured resources, including buildings, equipment, machines, and improvements to land that is used for production.

Capital consumption allowance Another name for depreciation, the amount that businesses would have to save in order to take care of the deterioration of machines and other equipment.

Capital gain The positive difference between the purchase price and the sale price of an asset. If a share of stock is bought for $5 and then sold for $15, the capital gain is $10.

Capital goods Producer goods; nonconsumable goods that firms use to make other goods.

Capital loss The negative difference between the purchase price and the sale price of an asset.

Capitalism An economic system in which individuals own productive resources; these individuals can use the resources in whatever manner they choose, subject to common protective legal restrictions.

Capture hypothesis A theory of regulatory behavior that predicts that the regulators will eventually be captured by the special interests of the industry being regulated.

Cartel An association of producers in an industry that agree to set common prices and output quotas to prevent competition.

Central bank A banker's bank, usually an official institution that also serves as a country's treasury's bank. Central banks normally regulate commercial banks.

Certificate of deposit (CD) A time deposit with a fixed maturity date offered by banks and other financial institutions.

Ceteris paribus [KAY-ter-us PEAR-re-bus] **assumption** The assumption that nothing changes except the factors being studied.

Checkable deposits Any deposits in a thrift institution or a commercial bank on which a check may be written.

Closed shop A business enterprise in which employees must belong to the union before they can be hired and must remain in the union after they are hired.

Collateral An asset pledged as security for the payment of a loan.

Collective bargaining Bargaining between the management of a company or of a group of companies and the management of a union or a group of unions for the purpose of setting a mutually agreeable contract on wages, fringe benefits, and working conditions for all employees in all the unions involved.

Collective decision making How voters, politicians, and other interested parties act and how these actions influence nonmarket decisions.

Command socialism An economic system in which there is virtually no private property and the state owns virtually all the factors of production. Decisions about what and how much, by whom, and for whom are decided by command from a central authority.

Command system A system in which the government controls the factors of production and makes all decisions about their use and about the distribution of income.

Commodity Credit Corporation (CCC) A government agency that lends farmers an amount of money equal to the support price of crops, multiplied by the amount of the crop offered as collateral.

Common property Property that is owned by everyone and therefore by no one. Air and water are examples of common property resources.

Communism In its purest form, an economic system in which the state has disappeared and in which individuals contribute to the economy according to their productivity and are given income according to their needs.

Comparable-worth doctrine The belief that women should receive the same wages as men if the levels of skill and responsibility in their jobs are equal or equivalent.

Comparative advantage The ability to produce at lower cost compared to other producers, whether they are countries, firms, or individuals.

Complements Two goods are complements if both are used together for consumption or enjoyment—for example, coffee and cream. The more you buy of one, the more you buy of the other. For complements, a change in the price of one causes an opposite shift in the demand for the other.

Concentration ratio The percentage of all sales contributed by the leading four or leading eight firms in an industry; sometimes called the *industry concentration ratio*.

Constant dollars Dollars expressed in terms of real purchasing power using a particular year as the base or standard of comparison, in contrast to current dollars.

Constant economies of scale No change in long-run average costs when output increases.

Constant-cost industry An industry whose total output can be increased without an increase in long-run per-unit costs; an industry whose long-run supply curve is horizontal.

Consumer optimum A choice of a set of goods and services that maximizes the level of satisfaction for each consumer, subject to limited income.

Consumer Price Index (CPI) A statistical measure of a weighted average of prices of a specified set of goods and services purchased by wage earners in urban areas.

Consumption Spending on new goods and services out of a household's current income. Whatever is not consumed is saved. Consumption includes such things as buying food and going to a concert.

Consumption function The relationship between amount consumed and disposable income. A consumption function tells us how much people plan to consume at various levels of disposable income.

Consumption goods Goods bought by households to use up, such as food, clothing, and movies.

Consumption tax A tax system in which taxes are paid only on the income that individuals actually spend, not on what they earn. What is not spent would be untaxed saving.

Contraction A business fluctuation during which the pace of national economic activity is slowing down.

Contractionary gap Gap that exists whenever the equilibrium level of real national output is less than the full-employment level; the negative difference between total desired expenditures and the full-employment level of real national income.

Cooperative game A game in which the players explicitly collude to make themselves better off. As applied to firms, it involves companies colluding in order to make higher than competitive rates of return.

Corporate raiders People or firms that specialize in seeking out corporations that are potential targets for takeovers.

Corporation A legal entity that may conduct business in its own name just as an individual does; the owners of a corporation, called shareholders, own shares of the firm's assets and profits and enjoy the protection of limited liability.

Cost-of-living adjustments (COLAs) Clauses in contracts that allow for increases in specified nominal values to take account of changes in the cost of living or the Consumer Price Index.

Cost-of-service regulation Regulation based on allowing prices to reflect only the actual cost of production and no monopoly profits.

Craft unions Labor unions composed of workers who engage in a particular trade or skill, such as baking, carpentry, or plumbing.

Creative response Behavior on the part of a firm that allows it to comply with the letter of the law but not the spirit, significantly lessening the law's effects.

Cross elasticity of demand (E_{xy})
The percentage change in the quantity demanded of one good (holding its price constant) divided by the percentage change in the price of a related good.

Cross subsidization The selling of a product or service in one market below cost, the losses being compensated by selling the same product or service in another market at above marginal cost.

Cross-sectional data Empirical observations about one or more variables gathered at a particular point in time.

Crowding-out effect The tendency of expansionary fiscal policy to cause a decrease in planned investment or planned consumption in the private sector; this decrease normally results from the rise in interest rates.

Crude quantity theory of money
The belief that changes in the money supply lead to proportional changes in the price level.

Currency crisis A situation in the international money market that occurs when a country no longer has the resources (foreign exchange, gold, credit, and so on) to support the price of its currency. A currency crisis brings forced devaluation under a fixed exchange rate system.

Cyclical unemployment
Unemployment resulting from business recessions that occur when aggregate (total) demand is insufficient to create full employment.

Debt monetization The process by which deficit financing induces the Federal Reserve simultaneously to purchase government securities. That open market operation monetizes part of the public debt.

Decreasing-cost industry An industry in which an increase in output leads to a reduction in long-run per-unit costs, such that the long-run industry supply curve slopes downward.

Deficiency payment A direct subsidy paid to farmers equal to the amount of a crop they produce multiplied by the difference between the target price for that good and its market price.

Deflation The situation in which the average of all prices of goods and services in an economy is falling.

Demand A schedule of how much of a good or service people will purchase at each different possible price during a specified time period, other things being constant.

Demand curve A graphic representation of the demand schedule. A negatively sloped line showing the inverse relationship between the price and the quantity demanded.

Demerit good A good that has been deemed socially undesirable via the political process. Heroin is an example.

Dependent variable A variable whose value changes according to changes in the value of one or more independent variables.

Deposit expansion multiplier
The reciprocal of the required reserve ratio, assuming no leakages into currency and no excess reserves. It is equal to 1 ÷ required reserve ratio.

Depository institutions Financial institutions that accept deposits from savers and lend those deposits out at interest.

Depreciation Reduction in the value of capital goods over a one-year period due to physical wear and tear and also to obsolescence; also

called *capital consumption allowance*.

Depreciation A decrease in the value of a currency in terms of foreign currencies.

Depression An extremely severe recession.

Deregulation The elimination or phasing out of regulations of economic activity.

Derived demand Input factor demand derived from demand for the final product being produced.

Devaluation An official unilateral decrease in a currency's fixed exchange rate.

Diminishing marginal utility
The principle that as more of any good or service is consumed, its extra benefit declines. Otherwise stated, there are smaller and smaller increases in total utility from the consumption of a good or service as more is consumed during a given time period.

Direct expenditure offsets
Actions on the part of the private sector in spending money income that offset government fiscal policy actions. Any increase in government spending in an area that competes with the private sector will have some direct expenditure offset.

Direct relationship A relationship between two variables that is positive, meaning that an increase in one is associated with an increase in the other and a decrease in one is associated with a decrease in the other.

Dirty float A system between flexible and fixed exchange rates in which central banks occasionally enter foreign exchange markets to influence rates.

Discount rate The interest rate that the Federal Reserve charges for reserves that it lends to depository institutions. It is sometimes referred to as the rediscount rate or, in Canada and England, as the bank rate.

Discounting   The method by which the present value of a future sum or a future stream of sums is obtained.

Discouraged workers   Individuals who have stopped looking for a job because they are convinced that they will not find a suitable one. Typically, they become convinced after unsuccessfully searching for a job.

Diseconomies of scale   Increases in long-run average costs that occur as output increases.

Disposable personal income (DPI)   Personal income after personal income taxes have been paid.

Dissaving   Negative saving; a situation in which spending exceeds income. Dissaving can occur when a household is able to borrow or use up existing owned assets.

Distribution of income   The way income is allocated among the population.

Distributional coalitions   Associations such as cartels, unions, and cooperatives that are formed to gain special government privileges in order to redistribute wealth by taking small amounts from each of many people and giving large amounts to each of only a few.

Dividends   Portion of a corporation's profits paid to its owners (shareholders).

Division of labor   The segregation of a resource into different specific tasks; for example, one automobile worker puts on bumpers, another doors, and so on.

Dominant strategies   Strategies that always yield the highest benefit; regardless of what other players do, a dominant strategy will yield the most benefit for the player using it.

Dumping   Selling a good or a service abroad at a price below its cost of production or below the price charged in the home market.

Durable consumer goods   Goods used by consumers that have a life span of more than three years, that is, goods that endure and can give utility over a long period of time.

Economic goods   Any goods or services that are scarce.

Economic growth   Increases in per capita real GDP measured by its rate of change.

Economic profit   The difference between total revenues and the opportunity cost of all factors of production.

Economic rent   A payment for the use of any resource over and above its opportunity cost.

Economic system   The institutional means through which resources are used to satisfy human wants.

Economics   The study of people's behavior as they make choices to satisfy their wants.

Economies of scale   Decreases in long-run average costs resulting from increases in output.

Effect time lag   The time that elapses between the onset of policy and the results of that policy.

Efficiency   The situation in which a given output is produced at minimum cost. Alternatively, the case in which a given level of inputs is used to produce the maximum output possible.

Efficiency wage theory   The hypothesis that the productivity of workers depends on the level of the real wage rate.

Effluent fee   A charge to a polluter that gives the right to discharge into the air or water a certain amount of pollution. Also called a *pollution tax.*

Elastic demand   A demand relationship in which a given percentage change in price will result in a larger percentage change in quantity demanded. Total revenues and price are inversely related in the elastic portion of the demand curve.

Empirical   Relying on real-world data in evaluating the usefulness of a model.

Endowments   The various resources in an economy, including both physical resources and such human resources as ingenuity and management skills.

Entitlements   Guaranteed benefits under a government program such as Social Security or unemployment compensation.

Entrepreneurship   The factor of production involving human resources that perform the functions of raising capital, organizing, managing, assembling other factors of production, and making basic business policy decisions. The entrepreneur is a risk taker.

Entry deterrence strategy   Any strategy undertaken by firms in an industry, either individually or together, with the intent or effect of raising the cost of entry into the industry by a new firm.

Equation of exchange   The number of monetary units times the number of times each unit is spent on final goods and services is identical to the price level times output (or nominal national income).

Equilibrium   A situation when quantity supplied equals quantity demanded at a particular price.

Eurodollar deposits   Deposits denominated in U.S. dollars but held in banks outside the United States, often in overseas branches of U.S. banks.

Excess demand schedule   The difference between the quantities of goods supplied domestically and the quantities demanded at prices below the domestic equilibrium price.

Excess reserves   The difference between legal reserves and required reserves.

Excess supply schedule   The difference between the quantities of a product supplied domestically and the quantities demanded at prices above domestic equilibrium prices.

Exclusion principle   The principle that no one can be excluded from the benefits of a public good, even if that person hasn't paid for it.

Expansion   A business fluctuation in which overall business activity is rising at a more rapid rate than previously or at a more rapid rate than the overall historical trend for the nation.

Expansionary gap   Gap that exists whenever the equilibrium level of real national income exceeds the full-employment level of real national income; the positive difference between total desired spending and the full-employment level of real national income.

Expenditure approach   A way of computing national income by adding up the dollar value at current market prices of all final goods and services.

Explicit costs   Costs that business managers must take account of because they must be paid; examples are wages, taxes, and rent.

Externality   A situation in which a private cost or benefit diverges from a social cost or benefit; a situation in which the costs or benefits of an action are not fully borne by the two parties engaged in exchange or by an individual engaging in a scarce-resource-using activity.

Featherbedding   Any practice that forces employers to use more labor than they would otherwise or to use existing labor in an inefficient manner.

Federal Deposit Insurance Corporation (FDIC)   A government agency that insures the deposits held in member banks; all members of the Fed and other banks that qualify can join.

Federal funds market   A private market (made up mostly of banks) in which banks can borrow reserves from other banks that want to lend them. Federal funds are usually lent for overnight use.

Federal public, or national, debt   The total value of all outstanding federal government securities.

Fiduciary monetary system   A system in which currency is issued by the government, and its value is based uniquely on the public's faith that the currency represents command over goods and services.

Final goods and services   Goods and services that are at their final stage of production and will not be transformed into yet other goods or services. For example, wheat is not a final good because it is used to make bread, which is a final good.

Financial capital   Money used to purchase capital goods such as buildings and equipment.

Financial intermediaries   Institutions that transfer funds between ultimate lenders (savers) and ultimate borrowers.

Financial intermediation   The process by which financial institutions accept savings from households and lend the savings to businesses, households, and government.

Firm   A business organization that employs resources to produce goods or services for profit. A firm normally owns and operates at least one plant in order to produce.

Fiscal policy   The discretionary changing of government expenditures and/or taxes in order to achieve national economic goals, such as high employment with price stability.

Fixed costs   Costs that do not vary with output. Fixed costs include such things as rent on a building and the cost of machinery. These costs are fixed for a certain period of time; in the long run they are variable.

Fixed exchange rates   Foreign exchange rates held constant by means of central bank purchases and sales of domestic and foreign currency.

Fixed investment   Purchases by businesses of newly produced producer durables, or capital goods, such as production machinery and office equipment.

Flow   Any activity that occurs over time. For example, income is a flow that occurs per week, per month, or per year. Consumption is also a flow, as is production.

Forced saving   Nonconsumption forced by the government through such techniques as requiring payments into a pension plan.

Foreign exchange market   The market for buying and selling foreign currencies.

Foreign exchange rate   The rate of exchange between one country's currency and another country's currency. When the foreign exchange rate for the dollar falls, a dollar purchases less of other currencies.

45-degree reference line The line along which planned real expenditures equal real national income per year; a line that bisects the total planned expenditures/real national income quadrant.

Fractional reserve banking system A system of banking in which member banks keep only a fraction of their deposits in reserve.

Freely floating (or flexible) exchange rates Exchange rates that are allowed to fluctuate in the open market in response to changes in supply and demand. Sometimes called *flexible exchange rates* or *floating exchange rates.*

Free-rider problem A problem associated with public goods when individuals presume that others will pay for the public goods so that, individually, they can escape paying for their portion without causing a reduction in production.

Frictional unemployment Unemployment associated with costly job market information. Because workers do not know about all job vacancies that may be suitable, they must search for appropriate job offers. This takes time, and so they remain temporarily ("frictionally") unemployed.

Full employment The amount of employment that would exist year in and year out if everybody in the economy fully anticipated any inflation or deflation that was occurring.

Game theory A way of describing the various possible outcomes in any situation involving two or more interacting individuals when those individuals are aware of the interactive nature of their situation and plan accordingly. The plans made by

these individuals are known as *game strategies.*

GDP deflator A price index measuring the changes in prices of *all* goods and services produced by the economy.

General Agreement on Tariffs and Trade (GATT) An international agreement established in 1947 to further world trade by reducing barriers and tariffs.

Gini coefficient of inequality A numerical representation of the degree of income inequality in a nation; defined as the ratio of the area between the diagonal line and the actual Lorenz curve to the triangular area under that diagonal line.

Gold standard An international monetary system in which nations fix their exchange rates in terms of gold. Thus all currencies are fixed in terms of each other. Any balance of payments problems could be made up by shipments of gold.

Golden parachute A guarantee to the existing managers of a firm that if they are ousted as a result of a takeover, they will receive large severance payments.

Goods Any things from which individuals derive satisfaction or happiness and are thus valued.

Government, or political, goods Goods (and services) provided by the public sector; they can be either private or public goods.

Greenmail Payment by a target firm of a substantial premium for shares held by a corporate raider in return for the raider's agreement to cease attempts at a takeover.

Gresham's law Bad money drives out good money; whenever currency that is depreciated, mutilated, or debased is circulated at a fixed rate along with money of higher value,

the latter—good money—will disappear from circulation, with only the bad remaining.

Gross domestic income (GDI) The sum of all income paid to the four factors of production, i.e., the sum of wages, interest, rent, and profits.

Gross domestic product (GDP) The total market value of all final goods and services produced by factors of production located within a nation's borders.

Gross private domestic investment The creation of capital goods, such as factories and machines, that can yield production and hence consumption in the future. Also included in this definition are changes in business inventories and repairs made to machines or buildings.

Gross public debt All federal government debt irrespective of who owns it.

Herfindahl Index An index of market concentration obtained by squaring the market share of each supplier and adding up these squared values.

Horizontal merger The joining of firms that are producing or selling a similar product.

Hostile takeover Purchase of a firm that is opposed by the target firm's current management, sometimes because it appears likely that the managers will lose their jobs if the takeover is successful.

Hub-and-spoke system A transportation system in which there is an essential hub (a city) to and from which planes fly. These routes are called the spokes. Rather than a nonstop flight from say Tampa to Los Angeles, the flight may first go to the hub in Dallas, where the passenger changes planes to catch a flight to Los Angeles.

Human capital The endowment of abilities to produce that exists in each human being. It can be increased through formal education, on-the-job training, and improved health and psychological well-being.

Hyperinflation Extremely rapid rise of the average of all prices in an economy.

Implicit costs Costs that business managers do not necessarily calculate, such as the opportunity cost of factors of production that are owned; examples are owner-provided capital and owner-provided labor.

Import quota A physical supply restriction on imports of a particular good, such as sugar. Foreign exporters are unable to sell in the United States more than the quantity specified in the import quota.

Incentive structure The motivational rewards and costs that individuals face in any given situation. Each economic system has its own incentive structure. The incentive structure is different under a system of private property than under a system of government-owned property, for example.

Incentive-compatible contract A loan contract under which a significant amount of the borrower's assets are at risk, providing an incentive for the borrower to look after the lender's interests.

Income approach A way of measuring national income by adding up all components of national income, including wages, interest, rent, and profits.

Income elasticity of demand (E_i) The percentage change in quantity demanded for any good, holding its price constant, divided by the percentage change in income; the responsiveness of the quantity demanded to changes in income, holding the good's relative price constant.

Income in kind Income that is received in the form of actual goods and services, such as housing or medical care. To be contrasted with money income, which is simply income in dollars, or general purchasing power, that can be used to buy *any* goods and services.

Income velocity of money The number of times per year a dollar is spent on final goods and services; equal to GDP divided by the money supply.

Income-consumption curve The set of optimum consumption points that would occur if income were increased, nominal and relative prices remaining constant.

Increasing-cost industry An industry in which an increase in industry output is accompanied by an increase in long-run per-unit costs, such that the long-run industry supply curve slopes upward.

Independent variable A variable whose value is determined independently of, or outside, the equation under study.

Indifference curve A curve composed of a set of consumption alternatives, each of which yields the same total amount of satisfaction.

Indirect business taxes All business taxes except the tax on corporate profits. Indirect business taxes include sales and business property taxes.

Industrial unions Labor unions that consist of workers from a particular industry, such as automobile manufacturing or steel manufacturing.

Industrially advanced countries (IACs) Canada, Japan, the United States, and the countries of Western Europe, all of which have market economies based on a large skilled labor force and a large technically advanced stock of capital goods.

Industry supply curve The locus of points showing the minimum prices at which given quantities will be forthcoming; also called the *market supply curve.*

Inefficient point Any point that does not lie on the production possibilities curve (and is below it), at which resources are being used inefficiently.

Inelastic demand A demand relationship in which a given change in price will result in a less than proportionate change in the quantity demanded. Total revenue and price are directly related in the inelastic region of the demand curve.

Infant industry argument The contention that tariffs should be imposed to protect from import competition an industry that is trying to get started. Presumably, after the industry becomes technologically efficient, the tariff can be lifted.

Inferior goods Goods for which demand falls as income rises.

Inflation The situation in which the average of all prices of goods and services in an economy is rising.

Inside information Information about what is happening in a corporation that is not available to the general public.

Interest The payment for current rather than future command over resources; the cost of obtaining credit. Also, the return paid to owners of capital.

Interest rate effect The effect on desired spending caused by a change in the price level, said effect that works through resulting changes in the rate of interest. An indirect effect on desired demand due to a change in the price level.

Intermediate goods Goods used up entirely in the production of final goods.

International Monetary Fund (IMF) An institution set up to manage the international monetary system, established in 1945 under the Bretton Woods Agreement Act, which established fixed exchange rates for the world's currencies.

Intra-industry trade International trade involving goods in the same industry, such as automobiles.

Inventory investment Changes in the stocks of finished goods and goods in process, as well as changes in the raw materials that businesses keep on hand. Whenever inventories are decreasing, inventory investment is negative; whenever they are increasing, inventory investment is positive.

Inverse relationship A relationship that is negative, meaning that an increase in one variable is associated with a decrease in the other and a decrease in one variable is associated with an increase in the other.

Investment Any use of today's resources to expand tomorrow's production or consumption.

Investment The spending by businesses on things such as machines and buildings, which can be used to produce goods and services in the future. The investment part of total income is the portion that will be used in the process of producing goods in the future.

J curve A graph portraying the situation following a depreciation in

a country's currency. At first the country's foreign trade deficit worsens, but soon its foreign trade position improves. The graph of net exports over time resembles the letter J.

Job leaver An individual in the labor force who voluntarily quits.

Job loser An individual in the labor force who was employed and whose employment was involuntarily terminated or who was laid off.

Job offer curve The curve showing over time the highest-paying job offers obtainable by a job searcher. As the duration of unemployment increases, the expected wage offers also increase.

Junk bonds Risky bonds offering high coupon yields, sometimes issued by corporate raiders to finance takeovers.

Jurisdictional dispute A dispute involving two or more unions over which should have control of a particular jurisdiction, such as over a particular craft or skill or over a particular firm or industry.

Keynesian short-run aggregate supply curve The horizontal portion of the aggregate supply curve in which there is unemployment and unused capacity in the economy.

Labor Productive contributions of humans who work, involving both mental and physical activities.

Labor force Individuals aged 16 years or older who either have jobs or are looking and available for jobs; the number of employed plus the number of unemployed.

Labor force participation rate The percentage of noninstitutionalized working-age individuals who are employed or seeking employment.

Labor market signaling The process by which a potential worker's acquisition of credentials, such as a degree, is used by the employer to predict future productivity.

Labor productivity Total domestic output (GDP) divided by the number of workers (output per worker).

Labor theory of value A theory that the value of all commodities is equal to the value of the labor used in producing them.

Labor unions Worker organizations that usually seek to secure economic improvements for their members; they also seek to improve the safety, health, and other benefits of their members.

Laffer curve A graphical representation of the relationship between tax rates and total tax revenues raised by taxation.

Land The natural resources that are available from nature. Land as a resource includes location, original fertility and mineral deposits, topography, climate, water, and vegetation.

Law of demand There is a negative, or inverse, relationship between the price of any good or service and the quantity demanded, holding other factors constant.

Law of diminishing (marginal) returns The observation that after some point, successive equal-sized increases in a variable factor of production, such as labor, added to fixed factors of production, will result in smaller increases in output.

Law of increasing relative costs The observation that the opportunity cost of additional units of a good generally increases as society attempts to produce more of that good. This causes the bowed-out shape of the production possibilities curve.

Least-cost combination   The level of input use that produces a given level of output at minimum cost.

Legal reserves   Reserves that depository institutions are allowed by law to claim as reserves—for example, deposits held at district Federal Reserve banks and vault cash.

Lemons problem   The situation in which consumers, who do not know details about the quality of a product, are willing to pay no more than the price of a low-quality product, even if a higher-quality product at a higher price exists.

Liabilities   Amounts owed; the legal claims against a business or household by nonowners.

Limited liability   A legal concept whereby the responsibility, or liability, of the owners of a corporation is limited to the value of the shares in the firm that they own.

Limited partnership   A firm in which some partners, called limited partners, are granted limited liability; at least one general partner, responsible for managing the partnership, must accept unlimited liability.

Limit-pricing model   A model that hypothesizes that a group of colluding sellers will set the highest common price that they believe they can charge without new firms seeking to enter that industry in search of relatively high profits.

Liquidity   The degree to which an asset can be acquired or disposed of without much danger of any intervening loss in *nominal* value and with small transaction costs. Money is the most liquid asset.

Liquidity approach   A method of measuring the money supply by looking at money as a temporary store of value.

Logrolling   The practice of exchanging political favors by elected representatives. Typically, one elected official agrees to vote for the policy of another official in exchange for the vote of the latter in favor of the former's desired policy.

Long run   The time period in which all factors of production can be varied.

Long-run aggregate supply curve   A vertical line representing real output of goods and services based on full information and after full adjustment has occurred.

Long-run average cost curve (LAC)   The locus of points representing the minimum unit cost of producing any given rate of output, given current technology and resource prices.

Long-run industry supply curve   A market supply curve showing the relationship between price and quantities forthcoming after firms have been allowed the time to enter into or exit from an industry, depending on whether there have been positive or negative economic profits.

Lorenz curve   A geometric representation of the distribution of income. A Lorenz curve that is perfectly straight represents perfect income equality. The more bowed a Lorenz curve, the more unequally income is distributed.

Lump-sum tax   A tax that does not depend on income or the circumstances of the taxpayer. An example is a $1,000 tax that every family must pay, irrespective of its economic situation.

M1   The total value of currency plus checkable deposits (demand deposits in commercial banks and other checking-type accounts in thrift institutions), as well as traveler's checks not issued by banks.

M2   M1 plus (1) savings and small-denomination time deposits at all depository institutions, (2) overnight repurchase agreements at commercial banks, (3) overnight Eurodollars held by U.S. residents other than banks at Caribbean branches of member banks, (4) balances in money market mutual funds, and (5) money market deposit accounts (MMDAs).

Macroeconomics   The study of the behavior of the economy as a whole, including such economy-wide phenomena as changes in unemployment, the price level, and national income.

Majority rule   A collective decision-making system in which group decisions are made on the basis of 50.1 percent of the vote. In other words, whatever more than 50 percent of the population votes for, the entire population has to take.

Marginal cost pricing   A system of pricing in which the price charged is equal to the opportunity cost to society of producing one more unit of the good or service in question. The opportunity cost is the marginal cost to society.

Marginal costs   The change in total costs due to a one-unit change of production rate.

Marginal factor cost (MFC)   The cost of using an additional unit of an input. For example, if a firm can hire all the workers it wants at the going wage rate, the marginal factor cost of labor is the wage rate.

Marginal physical product   The physical output that is due to the addition of one more unit of a variable factor of production; the change in total product occurring when a variable input is increased and all other inputs are held constant.

Marginal physical product (MPP) of labor The change in output resulting from the addition of one more worker. The MPP of the worker equals the change in total output accounted for by hiring the worker, holding all other factors of production constant.

Marginal propensity to consume (MPC) The ratio of the change in consumption to the change in disposable income. A marginal propensity to consume of .8 tells us that an additional $100 in take-home pay will lead to an additional $80 consumed.

Marginal propensity to save (MPS) The ratio of the change in saving to the change in disposable income. A marginal propensity to save of .2 indicates that out of an additional $100 in take-home pay, $20 will be saved. Whatever is not saved is consumed. The marginal propensity to save plus the marginal propensity to consume must always equal 1, by definition.

Marginal revenue The change in total revenues resulting from a change in output (and sale) of one unit of the product in question.

Marginal revenue product (MRP) The marginal physical product (MPP) times marginal revenue. The MRP gives the additional revenue obtained from a one-unit change in a variable input.

Marginal tax rate The change in the tax payment divided by the change in income, or the percentage of additional dollars that must be paid in taxes. The marginal tax rate is applied to the highest tax bracket of taxable income reached.

Marginal utility The change in total utility due to a one-unit change in the quantity of a good consumed.

Market An abstract concept concerning all of the arrangements that individuals have for exchanging with one another. Thus we can speak of the labor market, the automobile market, and the credit market.

Market clearing, or equilibrium, price The price that clears the market, at which quantity demanded equals quantity supplied; the price where the demand curve intersects the supply curve.

Market demand The demand of all consumers in the marketplace for a particular good or service. The summing at each price of the quantity demanded by each individual.

Market failure A situation in which the operation of supply and demand fails to produce a solution that truly reflects all of the costs and benefits that go into producing and consuming a good or service.

Market structure Characteristics of a market, including the number of buyers and sellers, the degree to which products from different firms differ, and the ease of entry into or exit from the market.

Market system A system in which individuals own the factors of production and decide individually how to use them; a system with decentralized economic decision making.

Median voter theorem The contention that political parties will pursue policies in accord with the wishes of the median voter.

Medium of exchange Any asset that sellers will accept as payment.

Menu cost theory A hypothesis that it is costly for firms to change prices in response to demand changes because of the cost of negotiating contracts, printing price lists, and so on.

Merit good A good that has been deemed socially desirable via the political process. Museums are an example.

Microeconomics The study of decision making undertaken by individuals (or households) and by firms.

Minimum efficient scale (MES) The lowest rate of output per unit time at which long-run average costs for a particular firm are at a minimum.

Mixed economy An economic system in which decisions about how resources should be used are made partly by the private sector and partly by the government, or the public sector.

Models, or theories Simplified representations of the real world used as the basis for predictions or explanations.

Modern economic growth (MEG) The theory of economic growth in which growth is characterized by increases in per capita output accompanied by increases in population and driven by the application of science to the problems of economic production.

Monetarists Macroeconomists who believe that inflation is always caused by excessive monetary growth and that changes in the money supply directly affect aggregate demand.

Monetary and fiscal policy coordination Cooperation between central bank authorities (the Fed) and the U.S. Treasury and Congress to attain specific national policy goals, such as reduced inflation or less unemployment.

Monetary rule A monetary policy that incorporates a rule specifying the annual rate of growth of some monetary aggregate.

Money   Any medium that is universally accepted in an economy both by sellers of goods and services as payment for those goods and services and by creditors as payment for debts.

Money illusion   Reacting to changes in money prices rather than relative prices. If a worker whose wages double when the price level also doubles thinks he or she is better off, the worker is suffering from money illusion.

Money market deposit accounts (MMDAs)   Accounts issued by banks yielding a market rate of interest with a minimum balance requirement and a limit on transactions. They have no minimum maturity.

Money market mutual funds   Funds of investment companies that obtain funds from the public that are held in common and used to acquire short-maturity credit instruments, such as certificates of deposit and securities sold by the U.S. government.

Money, or deposit, multiplier process   The process by which an injection of new money into the banking system leads to a multiple expansion in the total money supply.

Money price   The price that we observe today, expressed in today's dollars. Also called the *absolute, nominal,* or *current price.*

Money supply   The amount of money in circulation. There are numerous ways of defining the money supply.

Monopolist   A single supplier that comprises its entire industry.

Monopolistic competition   A market situation in which a large number of firms produce similar but not identical products. There is relatively easy entry into the industry.

Monopoly   A firm that has great control over the price of a good. In the extreme case, a monopoly is the only seller of a good or service.

Monopoly rent seeking   The resources used in an attempt to create and maintain monopolies in order to earn monopoly profits.

Monopsonist   A single buyer.

Monopsonistic exploitation   Exploitation due to monopsony power. It leads to a price for the variable input that is less than its marginal revenue product. Monopsonistic exploitation is the difference between marginal revenue product and the wage rate.

Moral hazard   A situation in which, after a transaction has taken place, one of the parties to the transaction has an incentive to engage in behavior that will be undesirable from the other party's point of view.

Multiplier   The ratio of the change in the equilibrium level of real national income to the change in autonomous expenditures; the number by which a change in autonomous investment or autonomous consumption, for example, is multiplied to get the change in the equilibrium level of real national income.

National income accounting   A measurement system used to estimate national income and its components. This is one approach to measuring an economy's aggregate performance.

National income (NI)   The total of all factor payments to resource owners. It can be obtained by subtracting indirect business taxes from NDP.

Natural monopoly   A monopoly that arises from the peculiar production characteristics in an industry. It usually arises when there are large economies of scale relative to the industry's demand, so one firm can produce at a lower average cost than can be achieved by multiple firms.

Natural rate of unemployment   That rate of measured unemployment that is estimated to prevail in long-run macroeconomic equilibrium with no money illusion, when employees and employers both correctly anticipate the rate of inflation.

Near monies   Assets that are almost money. They have a high degree of liquidity; they can be easily converted into money without loss in value. Time deposits and short-term U.S. government securities are examples.

Negative-sum game   A game in which players as a group are worse off at the end of the game.

Net domestic product (NDP)   GDP minus depreciation.

Net investment   Gross private domestic investment minus an estimate of the wear and tear on the existing capital stock. Net investment therefore measures the change in capital stock over a one-year period.

Net public debt   Gross public debt minus all government interagency borrowing.

Net worth   The difference between assets and liabilities.

New classical model   A modern version of the classical model in which wages and prices are flexible and there is pure competition in all markets. Furthermore, the rational expectations hypothesis is assumed to be working.

New entrant   An individual who has never held a full-time job lasting two weeks or longer but is now in the labor force.

New Keynesian economics Economic models based on the idea that "demand creates its own supply" as a result of various possible government fiscal and monetary coordination failures.

Nominal rate of interest The market rate of interest expressed in terms of dollars.

Nominal values The values of variables such as GDP and investment expressed in current dollars, also called *money values;* measurement in terms of the actual market prices at which goods are sold.

Noncooperative game A game in which the players neither negotiate nor collude in any way. As applied to firms in an industry, the common situation in which there are relatively few firms and each has some ability to change price.

Nondurable consumer goods Goods used by consumers that are used up within three years.

Nonincome expense items The total of indirect business taxes and depreciation.

Nonprice rationing devices All methods used to ration scarce goods that are price-controlled. Whenever the price system is not allowed to work, nonprice rationing devices will evolve to ration the affected goods and services.

Normal goods Goods for which demand rises as income rises. Most goods that we deal with are normal.

Normal rate of return (NROR) The amount that must be paid to an investor to induce investment in a business; also known as the *opportunity cost of capital.*

Normative economics Analysis involving value judgments about economic policies; relates to whether things are good or bad. A statement of *what ought to be.*

Number line A line that can be divided into segments of equal length, each associated with a number.

Offset policy A policy requiring one company wishing to build a plant that would pollute to work out an offsetting reduction in pollution at some other plant in a specific geographic area.

Oligopoly A market situation in which there are very few sellers. Each seller knows that the other sellers will react to its changes in prices and quantities.

Open market operations The buying and selling of existing U.S. government securities (such as bonds) in the open private market by the Federal Reserve System.

Open-economy effect The effect on desired spending caused by a change in the price level, said effect that works through resulting changes in the relative price of imports and exports and in their relative quantities demanded.

Opportunity cost The highest-valued, next-best alternative that must be sacrificed to attain something or to satisfy a want.

Opportunity cost of capital The normal rate of return. Economists consider this a cost of production, and it is included in our cost examples.

Optimal quantity of pollution The level of pollution for which the marginal benefit of one additional unit of clean air just equals the marginal cost of that additional unit of clean air.

Origin The intersection of the *y* axis and the *x* axis in a graph.

Par value The legally established value of the monetary unit of one country in terms of that of another.

Partnership A business owned by two or more co-owners, or partners,

who share the responsibilities and the profits of the firm and are individually liable for all of the debts of the partnership.

Payoff matrix A matrix of outcomes, or consequences, of the strategies chosen by the players in a game.

Per se violation An activity that is specifically spelled out as a violation of the law, regardless of any other circumstances.

Perfect competition A market structure in which the decisions of individual buyers and sellers have no effect on market price.

Perfectly competitive firm A firm that is such a small part of the total industry that it cannot affect the price of the product it sells.

Perfectly elastic demand A demand that has the characteristic that even the slightest increase in price will lead to zero quantity demanded.

Perfectly elastic supply A supply characterized by a reduction in quantity supplied to zero when there is the slightest decrease in price.

Perfectly inelastic demand A demand that exhibits zero responsiveness to price changes; no matter what the price is, the quantity demanded remains the same.

Perfectly inelastic supply A supply for which quantity supplied remains constant, no matter what happens to price.

Personal income (PI) The amount of income that households actually receive before they pay personal income taxes.

Phillips curve A curve showing the relationship between unemployment and changes in wages or prices. It was long thought to reflect a trade-off between unemployment and inflation.

Planning curve   The long-run average cost curve.

Planning horizon   The long run, during which all inputs are variable.

Plant size   The physical size of the factories that a firm owns and operates to produce its output. Plant size can be defined by square footage, maximum physical capacity, and other physical measures.

Poison pill   In general, any maneuver by the management of a target firm that makes the firm either unattractive to a potential raider or prohibitively expensive.

Policy irrelevance proposition The new classical conclusion that policy actions have no real effects in the short run if the policy actions were anticipated and none in the long run even if the policy actions were unanticipated.

Positive economics   Analysis that is strictly limited to making either purely descriptive statements or scientific predictions; for example, "If A, then B." A statement of *what is*.

Positive-sum game   A game in which players as a group are better off at the end of the game.

Posted-offer pricing   A pricing technique in which retail firms post a specific offer and do not entertain the possibility of accepting a lower offer, nor do they attempt to raise prices above those posted either. This is a practice of posting prices before demand is actually known.

Precautionary demand   Holding money to meet unplanned expenditures and emergencies.

Present value   The value of a future amount expressed in today's dollars; the most that someone would pay today to receive a certain sum at some point in the future.

Price ceiling   A legal maximum price that can be charged for a particular good or service.

Price controls   Government-mandated minimum or maximum prices that can be charged for goods and services.

Price differentiation   Establishing different prices for similar products to reflect differences in marginal cost in providing those commodities to different groups of buyers.

Price discrimination   Selling a given product at more than one price, with the price difference being unrelated to cost difference.

Price elasticity of demand (E_p) The responsiveness of the quantity demanded of a commodity to changes in its price. The price elasticity of demand is defined as the percentage change in quantity demanded divided by the percentage change in price.

Price elasticity of supply (E_s) The responsiveness of the quantity supplied of a commodity to a change in its price; the percentage change in quantity supplied divided by the percentage change in price.

Price floor   A legal minimum price below which a good or service cannot be sold. Legal minimum wages are an example.

Price index   The cost of today's market basket of goods expressed as a percentage of the cost of the same market basket during a base year.

Price inertia   A tendency for the level of prices to resist change with the passage of time.

Price leadership   A practice in many oligopolistic industries in which the largest firm publishes its price list ahead of its competitors, who then match those announced prices. Also called *parallel pricing*.

Price supports   Minimum prices set by the government. To be effective, price supports must be coupled with a mechanism to rid the market of surplus goods that arise whenever the support price is greater than the market clearing price.

Price system   An economic system in which (relative) prices are constantly changing to reflect changes in supply and demand for different commodities. The prices of those commodities are signals to everyone within the system about what is relatively scarce and what is relatively abundant.

Price taker   A competitive firm that must take the price of its product as given because the firm cannot influence its price.

Price war   A pricing campaign designed to drive competing firms out of a market by repeatedly cutting prices.

Price-consumption curve   The set of consumer optimum combinations of two goods that the consumer would choose as the relative price of the goods changes, while money income remains constant.

Principal-agent problem   The conflict of interest that occurs when agents—managers of firms—pursue their own objectives to the detriment of the goals of the firms' principals, or owners.

Principle of rival consumption Individuals are rivals in consuming private goods because one person's consumption reduces the amount available for others to consume.

Principle of substitution   The principle that consumers and producers shift away from goods and resources that become relatively higher priced in favor of goods and resources that are now relatively lower priced.

Prisoners' dilemma A famous strategic game in which two prisoners have a choice between confessing and not confessing to a crime. If neither confesses, they serve a minimum sentence. If both confess, they serve a maximum sentence. If one confesses and the other doesn't, the one who confesses goes free. The dominant strategy is always to confess.

Private costs Costs borne solely by the individuals who incur them. Also called *internal costs.*

Private goods Goods that can be consumed by only one individual at a time. Private goods are subject to the principle of rival consumption.

Private property rights Exclusive rights of ownership that allow the use, transfer, and exchange of property.

Privatization The sale or transfer of state-owned property and businesses to the private sector, in part or in whole.

Producer durables, or capital goods Durable goods having an expected service life of more than three years that are used by businesses to produce other goods and services.

Producer Price Index (PPI) A statistical measure of a weighted average of prices of commodities that firms purchase from other firms.

Product differentiation The distinguishing of products by brand name, color, minor attributes, and the like. Product differentiation occurs in other than perfectly competitive markets in which products are, in theory, homogeneous, such as wheat or corn.

Production Any transformation of materials that makes them more valuable. The use of resources that transforms any good or service into a different good or service.

Production function The relationship between inputs and output. A production function is a technological, not an economic, relationship.

Production possibilities curve (PPC) A curve representing all possible combinations of total output that could be produced assuming (1) a fixed amount of productive resources of a given quality and (2) the efficient use of those resources.

Profit-maximizing rate of production The rate of production that maximizes total profits, or the difference between total revenues and total costs; also, the rate of production at which marginal revenue equals marginal cost.

Progressive taxation A tax system in which as income increases, a higher percentage of the additional income is taxed. The marginal tax rate exceeds the average tax rate as income rises.

Property rights The rights of an owner to use and to exchange property.

Proportional rule A decision-making system in which actions are based on the proportion of the "votes" cast and are in proportion to them. In a market system, if 10 percent of the dollar votes are cast for blue cars, 10 percent of the output will be blue cars.

Proportional taxation A tax system in which as the individual's income goes up, the tax bill goes up in exactly the same proportion. Also called a *flat-rate tax.*

Proprietorship A business owned by one individual who makes the business decisions, receives all of the profits, and is legally responsible for all the debts of the firm.

Public goods Goods to which the principle of rival consumption does not apply; they can be jointly consumed by many individuals simultaneously at no additional cost and with no reduction in the quality or quantity of the good.

Purchasing power The value of your money income in buying goods and services. If your money income stays the same but the price of one good that you are buying goes up, your effective purchasing power falls.

Purchasing power parity (PPP) The relationship of two currencies when changes in the exchange rate exactly reflect relative changes in the price levels in the two countries.

Pure economic rent The payment for the use of any resource that has a completely inelastic supply.

Quality-assuring price A price that is high enough to offer a stream of profits that is as great as or greater than the profits that could be made by cheating customers in one period by offering them a low-quality product at a relatively high price.

Quota system A government-imposed restriction on the quantity of a specific good that another country is allowed to sell in the United States. In other words, quotas are restrictions on imports. These restrictions are usually applied to a specific country or countries.

Random walk theory The theory that successive prices are independent of each other in security markets. Because there are no predictable trends in prices, today's prices cannot be used to predict future prices.

Rate of discount The rate of interest used to discount future sums back to present value.

Rate-of-return regulation Regulation that seeks to keep the rate of return in the industry at a competitive level by not allowing excessive prices to be charged.

Rational contracting theory A set of hypotheses that deals with the nominal wage that workers and firms would choose to set in a contractual agreement. The main requirement of this theory is that the chosen wage must be consistent with the rational behavior of workers and firms, that is, one based on their rational expectations of what economic conditions will be during the wage contract period.

Rational expectations hypothesis A theory stating that people combine the effects of past policy changes on important economic variables with their own judgment about the future effects of current and future policy changes.

Rationality assumption The assumption that people do not intentionally make decisions that would leave them worse off.

Reaction function The manner in which one oligopolist reacts to a change in price (or output or quality) of another oligopolist.

Real business cycle theory An extension and modification of the theories of the new classical economists of the 1970s and 1980s, in which money is neutral and only real, supply-side factors matter in influencing labor employment and real output.

Real rate of interest The nominal rate of interest minus the anticipated rate of inflation.

Real values Measurement of economic values after adjustments have been made for changes in the average of prices between years.

Real-balance effect The change in the real value of money balances when the price level changes, all other things held constant. Also called the *wealth effect.*

Real-income effect The change in people's purchasing power that occurs when, other things being constant, the price of one good that they purchase changes. When that price goes up, real income, or purchasing power, falls, and when that price goes down, real income, or purchasing power, increases.

Recession A period of time during which the rate of growth of business activity is consistently less than its long-term trend, or is negative.

Recognition time lag The time required to gather information about the current state of the economy.

Recycling The reuse of raw materials derived from manufactured products.

Reentrant An individual who used to work full time but left the labor force and has now reentered it looking for a job.

Regressive taxation A tax system in which as more dollars are earned, the percentage of tax paid on them falls. The marginal tax rate is less than the average tax rate as income rises.

Reinvestment Profits (or depreciation reserves) used to purchase new capital equipment.

Relative price The price of a commodity expressed in terms of another commodity or the (weighted) average price of all other commodities.

Rent control The placement of price ceilings on rents in particular municipalities.

Repricing, or menu, cost of inflation The cost associated with recalculating prices and printing new price lists when there is inflation.

Repurchase agreement (REPO, or RP) An agreement made by a bank to sell Treasury or federal agency securities to its customers, coupled with an agreement to repurchase them at a price that includes accumulated interest.

Required reserve ratio The percentage of total deposits that the Fed requires depository institutions to hold in the form of vault cash or on deposit with the Fed.

Required reserves The value of reserves that a depository institution must hold in the form of vault cash or on deposit with the Fed.

Reregulation The reimposition of regulatory apparatus in an industry that has been deregulated. Reregulation may include new limits on price increases and on who may enter the industry.

Reservation wage The lowest wage that an unemployed worker will accept in a job offer.

Reservation wage curve A downward-sloping curve showing the relationship between the reservation wage and the duration of unemployment.

Reserves In the U.S. Federal Reserve System, deposits held by district Federal Reserve banks for depository institutions, plus depository institutions' vault cash.

Resource allocation The assignment of resources to specific uses by determining what will be produced, how it will be produced, and for whom it will be produced.

Resources Inputs used to produce goods and services. (Also called *factors of production.)*

Resource-using government expenditures Expenditures by the government that involve the use of land, labor, capital, or entrepreneurship; to be contrasted with pure transfers, in which the government taxes one group and pays some of those taxes to another without demanding any concurrent services in return.

Retained earnings Earnings that a corporation saves, or retains, for investment in other productive activities; earnings that are not distributed to stockholders.

Revaluation An official unilateral increase in a currency's fixed exchange rate.

Ricardian equivalence theorem The proposition that an increase in the government budget deficit has no effect on aggregate demand.

Right-to-work laws Laws that make it illegal to require union membership as a condition of continuing employment in a particular firm.

Rule of 72 A simple rule that allows you to find the approximate time it takes any quantity to double, given its annual growth rate. To find doubling time, divide the annual percentage rate of growth (times 100) into 72.

S corporation A type of corporation in which the owners are largely exempt from the double taxation of corporate income.

Saving The act of not consuming all of one's current income. Whatever is not consumed out of spendable income is, by definition, saved. *Saving* is an action measured over time (a flow), whereas *savings* are

an accumulation resulting from the act of saving in the past (a stock).

Savings deposits Interest-earning funds that can be withdrawn at any time without payment of a penalty.

Say's law A dictum of J.B. Say that supply creates its own demand; producing goods and services generates the means and the willingness to purchase other goods and services.

Scarcity A situation in which the ingredients for producing the things that people desire are insufficient to satisfy all wants.

Scatter diagram A graph showing the points that represent observations of the dependent and independent variables. These points are scattered throughout the *x-y* quadrant.

Seasonal unemployment Unemployment resulting from the seasonal pattern of work in specific industries, usually due to seasonal fluctuations in demand or to changing weather conditions, rendering certain work difficult, if not impossible, as in the agriculture, construction, and tourist industries.

Secondary boycott A boycott of companies or products sold by companies that are dealing with a company being struck.

Separation of ownership and control A situation that exists in corporations in which the owners— shareholders—are not the people who control the operation of the corporation—the managers. The goals of these two groups often are different.

Services Things purchased by consumers that do not have physical

characteristics. Examples of services are actions provided by doctors, lawyers, dentists, repair personnel, housecleaners, educators, retailers, and wholesalers.

Share of stock A legal claim to a share of a corporation's future profits; if it is *common stock,* it incorporates certain voting rights regarding major policy decisions of the corporation; if it is *preferred stock,* its owners are accorded preferential treatment in the payment of dividends.

Share-the-gains, share-the-pains theory A theory of regulatory behavior in which the regulators must take account of the demands of three groups: legislators, who established and who oversee the regulatory agency; members of the regulated industry; and consumers of the regulated industry's products or services.

Short run The time period when some inputs, such as plant size, cannot be changed.

Shortage A situation in which quantity demanded is greater than quantity supplied at a price below the market clearing price.

Short-run aggregate supply curve The relationship between aggregate supply and the price level in the short run; normally positively sloped.

Short-run break-even price The price at which a firm's total revenues equal its total costs. At the break-even price, the firm is just making a normal rate of return on its capital investment. (It is covering its explicit and implicit costs.)

Short-run shutdown price The price that just covers average variable costs. It occurs just below the intersection of the marginal cost curve and the average variable cost curve.

Signals Compact ways of conveying to economic decision makers information needed to make decisions. A true signal not only conveys information but also provides the incentive to react appropriately. Economic profits and economic losses are such signals.

Slope The change in the *y* value divided by the corresponding change in the *x* value of a curve; the "incline" of the curve.

Social costs Costs borne by society whenever a resource use occurs. Social costs can be measured by adding internal costs to external costs.

Socialism An economic system in which the state owns the major share of productive resources except labor. Socialism also usually involves the redistribution of income.

Special drawing rights (SDRs) Reserve assets created by the International Monetary Fund that countries can use to settle international payments.

Specialization The division of productive activities among persons and regions so that no one individual or one area is totally self-sufficient. An individual may specialize, for example, in law or medicine. A nation may specialize in the production of coffee, computers, or cameras.

Specific investments Investments in a product that will lose their value rapidly if customers find out that a firm has cheated them; examples are logos, trademarks, and advertising.

Spillover, or externality A situation in which a benefit or a cost associated with an economic activity affects third parties.

Standard of deferred payment A property of an asset that makes it desirable for use as a means of settling debts maturing in the future; an essential property of money.

Stock The quantity of something, measured at a given point in time—for example, an inventory of goods or a bank account. Stocks are defined independently of time, although they are assessed at a point in time.

Store of value The ability of an item to hold value over time; a necessary property of money.

Strategic dependence A situation in which one firm's actions with respect to price changes may be strategically countered by one or more other firms in the industry. Such dependence can exist only when there are a limited number of major firms in an industry.

Strategy Any rule that is used to make a choice, such as "Always pick heads." Any potential choice that can be made by players in a game.

Strikebreakers Temporary or permanent workers hired by a company to replace union members who are striking.

Structural unemployment Unemployment resulting from fundamental changes in the structure of the economy. Structural unemployment occurs, for example, when the demand for a product falls drastically so that workers specializing in the production of that product find themselves out of work.

Subsidy A negative tax; a payment to a producer from the government, usually in the form of a cash grant.

Substitutes Two goods are substitutes when either one can be used for consumption—for example, coffee and tea. The more you buy of one, the less you buy of the other. For substitutes, the change in the price of one causes a shift in demand for the other in the same direction as the price change.

Substitution effect The tendency of people to substitute in favor of cheaper commodities and against more expensive commodities.

Substitution options Those alternatives that exist for any given activity for use of income or time. Virtually every aspect of one's life has a substitution option.

Supply A schedule showing the relationship between price and quantity supplied, other things being equal, for a specified period of time.

Supply curve The graphic representation of the supply schedule; a line (curve) showing the supply schedule, which generally slopes upward (has a positive slope).

Supply-side economics Attempts at creating incentives for individuals and firms to increase productivity, thereby causing the aggregate supply curve to shift out.

Surplus A situation in which quantity supplied is greater than quantity demanded at a price above the market clearing price.

Sympathy strike A strike by a union in sympathy with another union's strike or cause.

Target price A price set by the government for specific agricultural products. If the market clearing price is below the target price, a *deficiency payment,* equal to the difference between the market price and the target price, is given to farmers for each unit of the good they produce.

Tariff A tax on imported goods.

Tax bracket A specified interval of income to which a specific and unique marginal tax rate is applied.

Tax incidence The distribution of tax burdens among various groups in society.

Technological unemployment Unemployment caused by technological changes that reduce labor demands for specific tasks.

Technology Society's pool of applied knowledge concerning how goods and services can be produced.

Terms of exchange The terms under which trading takes place. Usually the terms of exchange are equal to the price at which a good is traded.

The Fed The Federal Reserve System; the central bank of the United States.

Theory of contestable markets A hypothesis concerning pricing behavior that holds that even though there are only a few firms in the industry, they are forced to price their products more or less competively because of the ease of entry by outsiders. The key aspect of a contestable market is relatively costless entry into and exit from the industry.

Theory of public choice The study of collective decision making.

Third parties Outsiders involved in a transaction between two parties; for example, in the relationship between caregivers and patients, fees may be paid by third parties (insurance companies, government).

Thrift institutions Financial institutions that receive most of their funds from the savings of the public; they include credit unions, mutual savings banks, and savings and loan associations.

Time cost The value of the time necessary to complete an activity, including search costs, waiting time, transportation time, and time actually engaging in the activity.

Time deposit A deposit in a financial institution that requires a notice of intent to withdraw or must be left for an agreed period. Withdrawal of funds prior to the end of the agreed period results in a penalty.

Time-series data Empirical observations about the value of one or more economic variables taken at different periods over time.

Total costs The sum of total fixed costs and total variable costs.

Total income The yearly amount earned by the nation's resources (factors of production). Total income therefore includes wages, rent, interest payments, and profits that are received, respectively, by workers, landowners, capital owners, and entrepreneurs.

Total revenues The price per unit times the total quantity sold.

Transaction costs All of the costs associated with exchanging, including the informational costs of finding out price and quality, service record, and durability of a product, plus the cost of contracting and enforcing that contract.

Transactions accounts Checking account balances in commercial banks and other types of financial institutions, such as credit unions and mutual savings banks; any accounts in financial institutions on which you can easily write checks without many restrictions.

Transactions approach A method of measuring the money supply by looking at money as a medium of exchange.

Transactions demand Holding money as a medium of exchange to make payments. The level varies directly with nominal national income.

Transfer earnings The portion of total earnings equal to what the factor of production could earn in its next-best alternative use; a measure of the opportunity cost of a resource.

Transfer payments Money payments made by governments to individuals for which no services or goods are concurrently rendered. Examples are welfare, Social Security, and unemployment insurance benefits.

Transfers in kind Payments that are in the form of actual goods and services, such as food stamps, low-cost public housing, and medical care, and for which no goods or services are rendered concurrently.

Traveler's checks Financial instruments purchased from a bank or a nonbanking organization and signed during purchase that can be used as cash upon a second signature by the purchaser.

Unanticipated inflation Inflation at a rate that comes as a surprise; unanticipated inflation can be either higher or lower than the rate anticipated.

Underground economy The part of the economy that does not pay taxes and so is not directly measured by government statisticians. Also called the *subterranean* or *unreported economy.*

Unemployment The total number of adults (aged 16 years or older) who are willing and able to work and who are actively looking for work but have not found a job.

Union shop A business enterprise that allows the hiring of nonunion members, conditional on their joining the union by some specified date after employment begins.

Unit elasticity of demand A demand relationship in which the quantity demanded changes exactly in proportion to the change in price. Total revenue is invariant to price changes in the unit-elastic portion of the demand curve.

Unit of accounting A measure by which prices are expressed; the common denominator of the price system; a central property of money.

Universal banking The right of commercial banks to offer a complete line of banking-related services. Under such a system, banks can underwrite securities.

Unlimited liability A legal concept whereby the personal assets of the owner of a firm may be used to pay off the firm's debts.

Util A representative unit by which utility is measured.

Utility The want-satisfying power of a good or service.

Utility analysis The analysis of consumer decision making based on utility maximization.

Value added The dollar value of an industry's sales minus the value of intermediate goods (for example, raw materials and parts) used in production.

Value-added tax (VAT) A tax assessed on the value added by a firm. The value added by a firm is the value of the products that firm sells minus the value of the materials (goods) that it bought and used to produce those products. The tax is usually imposed as a percentage of this difference. It is heavily used in Europe.

Variable costs Costs that vary with the rate of production. They include wages paid to workers and purchases of materials.

Vertical merger The joining of a firm with another to which it sells an output or from which it buys an input.

Vicious cycle of poverty A theory that low per capita incomes are an obstacle to realizing the necessary amount of saving and investment that is required to achieve acceptable rates of economic growth.

Voluntary exchange An act of trading, done on a voluntary basis, in which both parties to the trade are subjectively better off after the exchange.

Wants What people would buy if their incomes were unlimited.

Wealth The stock of assets owned by a person, household, firm or nation. For a household, wealth can consist of a house, cars, computers, bank accounts, and cash.

Welfare state A society in which the government is responsible for providing "cradle to grave" social services for all citizens, including prenatal care, daycare, health care, schooling, and retirement.

White knight A buyer of a firm that is willing to execute a "friendly" takeover, typically one that retains the management of the acquired firm.

x axis The horizontal axis in a graph.

y axis The vertical axis in a graph.

Zero trade price The price of an excess demand and supply schedule at which there is no foreign trade in a good; the price at which the domestic demand and supply schedules intersect.

Zero-sum game A game in which one player's losses are exactly offset by the other player's gains.

index

Our National Income Accounts Since 1929*
(for selected years)

In this table we see historical data for the various components of nominal GDP. These are given in the first four columns. We then show the rest of the national income accounts going from GDP to NDP to NI to PI to DPI.

	The Sum of These Expenditures				Equals	Less	Equals	Plus	Less	Equals	Less			Plus	Equals	Less	Equals
Year	Personal Consumption Expenditures	Gross Private Domestic Investment	Government Purchases of Goods and Services	Net Exports	Gross Domestic Product	Depreciation	Net Domestic Product	Net U.S. Income Earned Abroad	Indirect Business Taxes	National Income	Undistributed Corporate Profits	Social Security Taxes	Corporate Income Taxes	Transfer Payments (Includes Government and Business)	Personal Income	Personal Income Tax and Nontax Payments	Disposable Personal Income
1929	77.3	16.7	8.9	0.3	103.2	9.9	93.2	0.8	9.3	84.7	2.4	0.3	1.4	3.7	84.3	2.6	81.7
1933	45.8	1.6	8.3	0.1	55.7	7.6	48.1	0.3	9.0	39.4	-4.0	0.3	0.5	3.7	46.3	1.4	44.9
1940	71.0	13.4	14.2	1.4	100.1	9.4	90.7	0.4	11.5	79.6	2.0	2.4	2.8	5.1	77.6	2.6	75.0
1944	108.2	7.7	97.1	-2.2	210.9	12.0	198.9	0.5	16.8	182.6	6.7	5.2	12.9	6.7	164.5	18.9	145.6
1950	192.1	55.1	38.8	0.7	286.7·	23.6	263.1	1.5	24.6	239.8	8.2	7.4	17.9	21.8	228.1	20.6	207.5
1955	257.9	69.7	75.3	0.4	403.3	34.4	368.9	2.6	35.2	336.3	14.8	12.0	22.0	26.7	314.2	35.4	278.8
1960	332.4	78.7	99.8	2.4	513.4	56.3	467.1	3.2	44.6	425.7	14.5	21.9	22.7	42.6	409.2	48.7	360.5
1965	444.6	118.0	136.3	3.9	702.7	57.3	645.4	5.4	63.9	586.9	31.9	31.6	30.9	60.4	552.9	61.9	591.0
1970	646.5	150.3	212.7	1.2	1010.7	888.8	921.9	6.4	94.8	833.5	19.3	62.2	34.4	113.4	831.0	109.0	722.0
1975	1024.9	226.0	321.4	13.6	1585.9	165.2	1420.7	13.3	148.7	1285.3	40.8	118.5	50.9	232.2	1307.3	156.4	1150.9
1980	1748.1	467.6	507.1	-14.7	2708.0	311.9	2396.1	34.1	232.0	2198.2	33.9	216.5	84.8	402.4	2265.4	312.4	1952.9
1982	2059.2	503.4	607.6	-20.6	3149.6	399.1	2750.5	30.2	258.1	2522.5	18.4	269.6	63.1	519.5	2690.9	371.4	2319.6
1985	2667.4	714.5	772.3	-115.6	4038.7	454.5	3584.2	14.9	330.7	3268.4	91.8	353.8	96.5	653.5	3379.8	436.8	2943.0
1987	3052.2	749.3	881.5	-143.1	4539.9	502.2	4037.7	4.6	350.0	3692.3	86.5	400.7	127.1	724.0	3802.0	512.5	3289.5
1990	3742.6	802.6	1042.9	-74.4	5513.8	594.8	4919.0	10.7	470.1	4459.6	49.9	501.7	135.3	907.1	4679.8	621.0	4058.8
1993[a]	4237.1	836.4	1118.2	-33.1	6158.8	621.7	5537.1	5.1	567.4	4974.8	90.1	588.7	148.7	1089.4	5236.7	656.4	4580.3

*Note: All figures in billions of dollars. Some rows may not add up due to rounding errors.
[a]Estimated 1993 first quarter annualized.

MICROECONOMIC PRINCIPLES

Opportunity Cost

In economics, cost is always a foregone opportunity

Law of Demand

When the price of a good goes up, people buy less of it, *other things being equal.*

Supply

At higher prices a larger quantity will generally be supplied than at lower prices, *all other things held constant.*

Or stated otherwise:

At lower prices, a smaller quantity will generally be supplied than at higher prices, *all other things held constant.*

Movement along, Versus Shift in, a Curve

If the relative price changes, we *move along* a curve—there is a change in quantity demanded and/or supplied. If something else changes, we *shift* a curve—there is a change in demand and/or supply.

Income Elasticity of Demand

$$\text{Income elasticity of demand} = \frac{\text{percentage change in the amount of good purchased}}{\text{percentage change in income}}$$

Profits

$$\text{Accounting profits} = \text{total revenues} - \text{total costs}$$

$$\text{Economic profits} = \text{total revenues} - \begin{array}{l}\text{total opportunity} \\ \text{cost of all} \\ \text{inputs used}\end{array}$$

Elasticity of Demand

$$E_p = \frac{\text{percentage change in quantity demanded}}{\text{percentage change in price}}$$

Law of Diminishing Returns

As successive equal increases in a variable factor of production, such as labor, are added to other fixed factors of production, such as capital, there will be a point beyond which the extra, or marginal, product that can be attributed to each additional unit of the variable factor of production will decline.

Elasticity of Supply

$$E_s = \frac{\text{percentage change in quantity supplied}}{\text{percentage change in price}}$$

Monopsony and Monopoly

		OUTPUT MARKET STRUCTURE	
		PERFECT COMPETITION	**MONOPOLY**
INPUT MARKET STRUCTURE	**PERFECT COMPETITION**	$MC = MR = P$ $W = MFC = MRP_c$	$MC = MR(<P)$ $W = MFC = MRP_m(<MRP_c)$
	MONOPSONY	$MC = MR = P$ $W < MFC = MRP_c$	$MC = MR(<P)$ $W < MFC = MRP_m(<MRP_c)$